The New York Times

BOOK OF
BASEBALL HISTORY

The New York Times

BOOK OF
BASEBALL HISTORY

Major League Highlights

From the Pages of The New York Times

Foreword by Red Smith

An Arno Press Book

QUADRANGLE / THE NEW YORK TIMES BOOK CO.

New York • 1975

Edited by Gene Brown.

Library of Congress Cataloging in Publication Data
Main entry under title:

The New York times book of baseball history.

    "An Arno Press book."
    Includes index.
    1. Baseball—History. I. New York times.
II. Title.
GV862.5.N48   1975   796,357'64'0973   74,25205
ISBN 0-8129-0550-4

    The editors express special thanks to The Associated Press and United Press International for permission to include in this book a number of dispatches originally distributed by those news services.

    Note: Wherever possible material in this book is reproduced exactly as it appeared in The New York Times, though by necessity sometimes in a different typographical configuration. But in the interest of legibility, some of the original type has been reset, and because of the poor quality or unavailability of some photographs, some illustrative material included here did not appear originally in The New York Times.

Contents

Foreword

Late in a game they were losing to the Chicago Cubs by one run, the St. Louis Cardinals got Pepper Martin to third base and Ernie Orsatti to second. Burgess Whitehead grounded to Bill Jurges, the shortstop, who fumbled briefly, then threw home to cut off the tying run. The ball and Martin reached the plate in the same instant, and squeamish spectators averted their eyes.

Moments later the catcher, Ken O'Dea, scrambled to his feet, retrieved the loose ball and threw to Lon Warneke, the pitcher, who had sprinted in to cover the plate. Some time passed before Warneke realized that what hit him from behind just then was Orsatti, barreling in with the winning run.

That night the Chicago newspaperman, Warren Brown, boarded a train to accompany the Cubs on an Eastern trip. In those days baseball teams traveled in old-style Pullmans with open berths. The cars reserved for the club were dark, all curtains drawn. Brown made no effort to keep his voice down.

"What's the matter, boys? Afraid Pepper Martin's on the train? Better be good, or the Gas House Gang will get you."

That probably was the origin of the tribal name by which the St. Louis team came to be known in 1934 as it went storming through September with a rush that devoured the New York Giants' eight-game lead and won the National League pennant on the last day of the season.

That was the year Bill Terry, manager of the Giants, brought down on his head the wrath of every Brooklyn fan from Greenpoint to Coney. "Is Brooklyn still in the league?" he asked before the season opened, not without justice, for the Dodgers of those days had gifts better suited to vaudeville than to baseball. Many times during the summer Terry was reminded of his springtime flippancy, and in the season's final series his chickens came home to roost.

By the next to the last day, the Cardinals had forged into a tie with the Giants. With a capacity crowd in the Polo Grounds screaming taunts that afternoon, the Dodgers' redoubtable Van Lingle Mungo pitched a 5-1 victory over Terry's team while the Cardinals won their game to take the lead. The next day the Dodgers poured it on again while out in St. Louis Dizzy Dean was pitching a shutout.

Earlier that summer Dean had strolled into the Brooklyn clubhouse before a game and sat nodding sagely while Casey Stengel, the manager, led a discussion on how to pitch to each man in the St. Louis lineup.

"You got us tabbed pretty good," he said as the meeting ended. "Now just to make it all fair and square, here's how I'm gonna pitch to you guys." He went through the Brooklyn batting order, man by man.

He went out and proceeded to pitch exactly as promised. They didn't get a run off him.

The Cardinals' last appearance in Brooklyn that year was a double-header wedged into the schedule to make up two games that had been rained out earlier in September. In the first game the Dodgers went eight and two-thirds innings without a hit off Dizzy. Then they got three, but no runs. In the second game they went nine innings without a hit or run off Dizzy's kid brother, Paul.

"Why didn't you tell me you were gonna pitch a no-hitter?" Dizzy demanded. "I'da throwed one, too."

The Dean brothers, Pepper Martin, Joe Medwick, Leo Durocher, Frank Frisch, the manager—these were the leaders of the Gas House Gang: colorful, combative, and unforgettable. Wherever they went there was excitement, as John Drebinger made clear to Times readers in his report of the final game of the World Series of 1934. (Going, Going, Gone, Page 81.)

That was the game when Joe Medwick provoked the Detroit public to a demonstration of rage unprecedented in World Series competition and never repeated in postseason play until the pennant playoff of 1973 when bottle-throwing sportsmen in Shea Stadium took target practice on the head of Pete Rose, Cincinnati's admirable outfielder.

The customers in Shea were angry at Rose for swapping punches with Bud Harrelson, shortstop for the New York Mets. The unrest in Detroit had two causes—indignation over a bit of unnecessary roughness on Medwick's part and the frustration of watching Dizzy and his accomplices humiliate the Tigers in the deciding game, 11-0. Medwick is in the Hall of Fame now, the only inmate of the pantheon who could boast that it took no mere umpire but the commissioner of baseball himself to run him out of a ball game.

The New York Times Book of Baseball History is not going to crowd Edward Gibbon's Decline and Fall off the library shelves or threaten Thomas Babington Macauley's standing among historians. If it captures and preserves for readers some of the flavor and fun of a game that has had a place in our culture for more than a century, then it will have accomplished what the editors hoped for it.

It is contemporary history, recorded by eyewitnesses as it was made, although not all the witnesses are identified by name. Few, if any, by-lines appeared in newspapers during baseball's early days, which may have been just as well. Take the account of Fred Merkle's classic boner that cost the Giants the pennant in 1908. Merkle was a lean and fit 195 pounds standing six-feet-one, a trained athlete. Had the story beginning, "Censurable stupidity on the part of player Merkle" borne the author's name, there might have been an opening on the Times sports staff the next morning.

Identified or not, there was a Times man present when Merkle neglected to step on second base and when the Chicago Black Sox threw the 1919 World Series. The Times took note of the glory that was Cobb and the grandeur that was Ruth, of the rise and fall of the Yankees, the passing of Joe DiMaggio, Mickey Mantle, and Willie Mays.

Speaking of Babe Ruth, there is one story in the book that manages in a few short paragraphs to reflect the man's stature in the game, to underscore the quality of Hank Aaron's accomplishment forty years later, and to illustrate the fallibility of all men—including Times reporters.

Concerning Ruth's 700th home run, the story mentions that only two other players in history had hit more than 300, giving us a measure of how far the Babe towered over other players and reminding us of how unapproachable were the heights that Aaron would scale. The headline warns us of the perils of prophecy: "Ruth's Record of 700 Home Runs Likely to Stand for All Time in Major Leagues."

Jane Austen wrote about baseball. And a history buff named Harold Peterson has followed the game's roots back to the lost village of Jadum in Tripolitania where Norsemen, who colonized North Africa 3,000 to 6,000 years before Christ, played a kind of ball they called om el mahag. Wherever baseball has been transplanted, as in Latin America and Japan, it has attained enormous popularity. Yet it remains, in essence, an American sport, a part of our childhood that we have not had to put behind us.

Some years ago an Englishwoman married to an American stationed in London accompanied her husband to the United States to visit his parents in Seattle. When business took him back to England she remained behind to go through the naturalization process, which required some six or eight weeks. Finding herself with time on her hands, she took to attending Pacific Coast League ball games. By the time she went home, she was a fan.

A year later she was in the United States again. "You know," she told an American friend, "I was made a citizen last summer, but when I went back to London I never mentioned that to my friends. It wasn't that I was ashamed of it, but somehow, living there where I've always lived, it seemed strange and rather incomplete, unfinished."

She paused to sip a martini, not very dry and not very cold. When she spoke again her voice had a new ring in it.

"Today," she said, "I was in Yankee Stadium and I saw Joe DiMaggio hit a home run and now—now I am an American!"

Red Smith

PART I

Baseball Catches On

1870-1919

Ty Cobb sliding.
Courtesy Wide World Photos.

THE NATIONAL GAME

Close of the First Decade of Ball-Playing

Brief Review of the Past Season —The Play of Professionals and Amateurs—The Championship Question.

There is no outdoor sport in which all classes of our people can so fully participate, or one which has so few objectionable surroundings, as the national game of baseball; and no season in the brief history of the game has more conclusively shown the fact of its great popularity with our people than the season which has just closed. Baseball started on its voyage of life in 1860, for its existence prior to that year may be said to have amounted only to a series of trial trips, as it were, preparatory for its great trip around the civilized world. In 1860, what we now term "amateur" playing was then in its glory. In that year the Excelsior Club of Brooklyn—ranking second to none in social standing at any time—then occupied the highest position in the country as the leading exemplars of the beauties of the game; and during that year the Excelsior Club did more to establish baseball on a permanent and reputable footing than had before been attempted by any other organization, the veteran Knickerbocker Club of this City—the social equals of the Excelsiors—having been more limited in their sphere of operations. The advent of CREIGHTON—the ball-player *par excellence* of the period—during that memorable year, with the accompanying brilliant career of the Excelsior nine, would have been promptly followed by the strenuous efforts of rival organizations during ensuing seasons but for the inauguration of the great rebellion in 1861, which, of course, materially interfered with the progress of baseball; indeed, in effect it put it back several years, and it was not until 1864 that the game began to recover its lost ground. In that year, however, the great struggle for the honors of the championship was commenced, all prior contests for the title having been merely nominal battles for something which had only a questionable existence; for up to 1864 the circle of the baseball arena did not extend far beyond the place of its christening, if not of its birth, viz.: New York. In 1864, the system of professional ball-playing began to openly manifest itself, for though previously in existence to some extent, it had not been prominently brought into public notice. With his new system came the real struggle for the championship title. Since then professional baseball playing has been officially recognized as a legitimate occupation; and no doubt the distinction of classes which now exists will prevail as long as the game is known. Unfortunately, certain evils have followed in the train of professional ball-playing, which, if not checked in their progress, will ultimately so damage the reputation of the fraternity as to materially interfere with the future welfare of the game.

A REVIEW OF THE SEASON

The brilliant success of the noted Red Stocking nine of the Cincinnati Club in 1869 was the incentive to the establishment of rival nines not only in New York, Philadelphia and other leading cities, but especially in Chicago, where the most strenuous exertions were made to organize a nine which should grasp the palm of superiority from the victorious Cincinnati Club. In the East, too, the desire to regain the laurels of 1869, which had been so creditably won from the older clubs by the comparatively new nine of the Western club, led to more than ordinary efforts to strengthen the nines of the Eastern organizations so as to recover their lost prestige.

The appended statistics are from the scores of games in which these professional clubs have played with each other:

Clubs	Games lost	Games won	Average
Cincinnati, "Red Stockings"	6	14	14
Chicago, "White Stockings"	7	13.2	14
Athletic, "Blue Stockings"	3	15.16	16
Union, "Haymakers"	10	14.16	7
Forest City, Cleveland	10	11.13	4
Forest City, Rockford	10	13.0	6
Minni, "Green Stockings"	10	11.19	13
Atlantic, "Old Champions"	15	11.10	7

A.G. Spalding

The estimate of the fewest games lost is the fairest test of skill, and in this respect the two Western clubs take the lead. In the averages of runs made by opponents, on which an estimate of fielding is generally made, shows that the opposing nines on the Cincinnati Club have made the smallest average, the Athletics being second and the Chicago third.

THE CHAMPIONSHIP

At present the Mutual Club hold the nominal title of the champion club of the United States; but, in reality, there is no champion club this season, and consequently, all the more interest will be imparted to the campaign of 1871, in which season the questions involved in championship disputes will be permanently disposed of. The Chicago Club claim the championship, but on what grounds we do not exactly see.

PROFESSIONALISM IN BASEBALL

There is no doubt that professional baseball playing is an established institution, but in order for it to be permanent some changes are necessary in its management, for the general impression from the past season in regard to the conduct of professional clubs, has been that it has been characterized by too much of the hippodrome principle, and that professionals have played too much into the hands of regular gamblers. Be this as it may, there is no questioning the fact that at present some professional players and their clubs are in bad odor with the public. In regard to amateur organizations the success of the Star Club, of Brooklyn; the Harvards, of Boston; the Experts and Intrepids, of Philadelphia; the Pastimes, of Baltimore, and the Amateurs, of Chicago, not to number a dozen other first-class amateur clubs, shows pretty conclusively that the amateur interest is still strong in the land.

The brilliant success, pecuniary and otherwise, attendant upon the Red Stocking nine in 1869 has had the effect of innoculating a number of capitalists with quite a fever for organizing professional nines. This year Chicago, Cleveland, Fort Wayne and Riverside added professional men to the list of existing organizations of that class, and now there is a prospect of an addition to the list from Boston, Indianapolis and Brooklyn. To offset this increase of professionalism, we have to record the disbandment of the noted Cincinnati "Red Stocking" nine, and the return of the Club to the old amateur basis. The fact is, the fraternity of Cincinnati, and especially the class who have had to put their hands deep in their pockets in order to insure the success of the professional experiment, have begun to realize the fact that the credit and renown attached to the success of the professional nine of the Club does not inure to the credit of the Club as a Western organization, from the fact that the players who have won the laurels are experts who belong to the East. Not fancying this style of things any longer, they now propose to organize a nine on the footing of employing only amateur talent and home players at that. In this the Club do wisely, for despite the victories obtained by the three professional nines of Cincinnati, Chicago and Cleveland, this season, the career of the Rockford nine, in reality, is the most creditable of all the Western organizations, inasmuch as their success has been obtained at the hands of bona fide Western players. This example the Cincinnati Club propose to follow in 1871, in which year they will endeavor to bear off the palm of supremacy in the amateur arena, as they did in 1869 in the professional circle.

THE CONVENTION

The year of baseball for 1871 will close with the annual Convention of the National Association, which takes place at the Grand Central Hotel on Wednesday next at 11 A.M. At this meeting delegates from all the States containing baseball associations will gather, the principal business being a revision of the laws of the game.

November 27, 1870

BASEBALL

A MEETING OF THE MANAGERS OF THE PROFESSIONAL NINES—THE PHILADELPHIA CLUB EXCLUDED FROM THE CHAMPIONSHIP CONTESTS—NEW RULES.

A meeting of the managers of all the professional baseball organizations in the country, excepting the Philadelphia Club, was held at the Grand Central Hotel on Wednesday, Feb. 2, at 2 o'clock. The first action was the passage of a resolution preventing two clubs from any one city entering for the championship. As the Athletics were represented at the meeting, and took part in its action, the Philadelphias were, as a consequence, shut out from entering their nine for the whip pennant. The next action was the passage of a resolution preventing any two clubs from playing in a city in which neither of them belongs. This was done for the purpose of "heading off" two or three clubs and preventing their going to Philadelphia during the Exhibition and playing a series of games. This will be a sore disappointment to those clubs, and will doubtless result in the disbanding of more than one of them before the season is half over. The amending of the rules was taken up, and several important changes were made. Among others, a rule allowing the base-runner to run on a foul fly catch, after he has touched his base, the same as on a fair fly-catch, was adopted. Another of the new rules allows a base-runner to return to his base after a foul ball has been hit, without running the risk of being put out, and still another virtually allows the batsman refuses to strike at it, warn the striker, but shall not be allowed to call a strike until still another fair ball has been pitched.

The following clubs entered for the championship: Athletic, Mutual, New-Haven, Hartford, Boston, Chicago, St.Louis, Louisville, and Cincinnati. The association will be known as the National League of Professional Baseball Clubs, and has nothing whatever to do with the old National Association. The officers are M.G. Buckley, of the Hartford Club, President, and N.E. Young, of Washington, Secretary. The League will be governed by a board of five Directors. Those chosen for the current year are from the Hartford, Louisville, Boston, Mutual, and St.Louis Clubs. This board will sit annually as a Board of Appeals to decide all disputed points and their decisions will be final. A most wholesome regulation of this League is one to the effect that when a player has been suspended he must wait until the end of the season, or until December, when the Directors meet before his appeal can be heard. Thus, if a player is expelled from a club, he cannot join another nine and continue in the field, as under the old system. The League will hold its next meeting in March of next year.

February 7, 1876

A NEW BASEBALL LEAGUE.

Organization of Eight Clubs Was Formed in Chicago Yesterday— New York Is Represented.

CHICAGO, Sept. 17.—A new baseball league, whose circuit will include cities in both the National and Western Leagues and which will be known as the American Association of Baseball Clubs, was formed here today at a meeting of baseball men and lovers of the National game.

The circuit, as decided on today, will include the following cities: St. Louis, Milwaukee, Detroit, and Chicago in the West, and Baltimore, New York, Philadelphia, and Washington in the East.

Those present at the meeting were the following: Chris Von Der Ahe, George Shafer, and Al Spinks, representing St. Louis, and a reputed agent of a brewing company of that city, which is supposed to be intered in the new league; H.D. Quinn, formerly of the American Association Club, and Alderman Havenor, representing Milwaukee; A.C. Anson and his son-in-law, W.H. Clough, representing Chicago; Assemblyman Beckley, representing New York; Frank Hough, sporting editor of The Philadelphia Enquirer,representing Philadelphia; M. Scanlan, representing Washington.The names of the representative of Detroit and Baltimore were not given out.

Tom Loftus of the Grand Rapids team of the Western League was in consultation with the new league representatives during the day, but was not present at the meeting.

"Ted" Sullivan, the veteran baseball manager, was also present at the meeting.

A.C. Anson was offered the Presidency of the new league, but he refused to accept, and H.D. Quinn of Milwaukee was elected Temporary President. Other temporary officers were elected as follows: Vice President—M.D.Scanlan; Treasurer—George Shaefer; Secretary—frank Hough; Directors—Chris Von Der Ahe, M.D. Scanlan, Frank Beckley, and C.S. Havenor.

The platform of the new league was announced as follows: "Honest competition, no syndicate baseball, no reserve rule, to respect all contracts, and popular prices."

The surprise of the conference was the avowal of the promoters to invade Western League territory. All of the gentlemen present disclaimed any intention of going to war with the minor league, but they strongly intimated that it was war to the finish with the National organization.

By abolishing the reserve ule the new league thinks it will get a hold on the best baseball talent in the country, and by catering to the public with lower prices, is certain to get the masses. The promoters also argue that the evils engenderedby forcing syndicate ball upon the public are too patent to be overlooked.

September 18, 1899

BALTIMORE IN THE LEAGUE.

American Baseball League Now Complete with Eight Clubs.

BALTIMORE, Nov. 13.—After a series of conferences among the promoters of the American Baseball League and a number of local capitalists and sports, it was decided today that Baltimore will be included in the eight-club circuit of the new association. McGraw and Robinson of last season's St. Louis team, it was announced, own the Baltimore franchise, and say they will go ahead at once to secure grounds and players for the coming season. The circuit as planned at present is as follows: Philadelphia, Baltimore, Washington, and Buffalo in the East, and Cleveland, Detroit, Chicago, and Milwaukee in the West.

President "Ban" Johnson of the American League, Charley Comiskey of Chicago, and Charles Somers of Cleveland, with the others who had been in Baltimore since Monday afternoon, left tonight for Chicago. Before leaving President Johnson said that a meeting of the American League will be held in Chicago on Nov. 20. The details of the new circuit will be arranged at that time and other matters necessary of adjustment will be considered. Among the more important of these will be a new agreement with the National League.

November 14, 1900

NATIONAL BASEBALL AGREEMENT

Minor League Organizations Will Discuss Provisions of Proposed Uniformity of Rules To-day—Professional Interests in the Game Throughout the Country to be Protected.

An important meeting of minor league baseball representatives will take place today at the Victoria Hotel, Broadway and Twenty-seventh Street, at which the new National agreement, adopted by the National League and American League delegates at Buffalo, last week, will be discussed in detail. This meeting has been called by President P.T. Powers of the National Association of Minor Baseball Leagues, an organization which embraces all the professional baseball associations in this country, with the exception of the two big leagues.

Ever since the baseball war between the major organizations was amicably settled by the signing of the Cincinnati peace pact last January, most of the those who have interests in baseball clubs throughout the United States and part of Canada have been urging the adoption of a new National agreement for the protection of every person, club owners as well as players, connected with the game.

President Johnson of the American League was opposed to the arranging of a measure of such importance as a National agreement until the clubs in the National as well as the American League could be certain that there would be no friction in the workings of the peace agreement.

The case of George Davis and the New York National League Club, which was allowed to play Davis on its team for a short time, while the Chicago American League Club, to which he was assigned at the Cincinnati conference, strenuously objected, having been adjusted at a meeting of the National League club owners, left the way clear for the American League President to take definite action on the National measure.

The Presidents of the major leagues, with two representatives from each organization, were in conference recently in Buffalo, and the outcome of the conference was the adoption of a lengthy document embracing, seemingly, every point of importance for the absolute government of professional baseball. One of its articles created a National commission for the purpose of enforcing the terms and provisions of the agreement. The members of this body were named as August Herrmann of Cincinnati, Chairman; President Johnson of the American League, and President Pulliam of the National League.

The most important objects of the new agreement are as follows:

(1) Perpetuation of baseball as the National pastime of America by surrounding it with such safeguards as will warrant absolute public confidence in its integrity and methods, and by maintaining a high standard of skill and sportsmanship in its players.

(2 Protection of the property rights of those engaged in baseball as a business without sacrificing the spirit of competition in the conduct of the clubs.

(3) Promotion of the welfare of ball players as a class by developing and perfecting them in their profession, and enabling them to secure adequate compensation for expertness.

(4) Adoption of a uniform code of rules for playing baseball.

The agreement is to be indissoluble except by the unanimous vote of the parties to it. Each party to the agreement retains the right to conduct its affairs and govern its players according to its constitution and by-laws, but there shall be no conflict between such constitution and by-laws and the objects and terms of the agreement. Should the measure be adopted by the National Association of Minor Leagues, these minor organizations will have absolute control of their own affairs.

Under the terms of the agreement the major Leagues shall adopt all rules governing the game of baseball. Neither major League circuit shall be changed without the consent of a majority of the clubs of each major League, and the circuit of each League is to consist of the following cities:

National League—Boston, New York, Brooklyn, Philadelphia, Pittsburg, Chicago, St. Louis, and Cincinnati. American League—Boston, New York, Philadelphia, Washington, Cleveland, Detroit, Chicago, and St. Louis.

Contracts with players must be respected under the penalties specified. The right and title of a major league club to its players shall be absolute, and can only be terminated by release or failure to reserve under the terms of the agreement by the club to which a player has been under contract.

The practice of "farming" is prohibited. All right or claim of a major league club to a player shall cease when such player becomes a member of a minor league club, and no arrangement between the clubs for the loan or return of a player shall be binding between the parties to it or recognized by other clubs.

The right of a minor league club to its players shall be absolute, except that from Aug. 15 to Oct. 15 of each year major leagues shall have the privilege of selecting players from National association clubs for the following season upon payment of $750 for each player so selected from clubs in Class A leagues; $500 for each player so selected from clubs in Class B leagues; $300 for each player so selected from clubs in Class C leagues, and $200 for each player so selected from clubs of a lower class.

A major league club may at any time purchase the release of a player from a minor league club, to take effect forthwith or at a specified date, provided such purchase is recorded with the Secretary of the commission for promulgation within five days of the date of the transaction.

Many of the articles in the agreement are designed to protect the interests of the players, one of which gives a player suspended for a period of longer than ten days the right to appeal to the commission. The leagues are strictly enjoined to enforce the provision in the constitution against open betting on baseball grounds, and club officials are obliged to cause the arrest and prosecution of those who may engage in such practice.

No game or a series of games are to be played for a stake between clubs of any league according to the agreement, and neither clubs nor players shall accept or agree to accept a sum of money or present of great value as an inducement or reward for winning or trying to win a game.

Articles of the agreement which do not find favor with the minor league representatives are the drafting clause and the method of paying for players drafted. Under the terms of the agreement the major leagues have two months in which to draft players, while the old rule gave them only one month.

At the meeting this afternoon there will be present representatives of the Eastern League, New York State League, Southern League, American Association, Central League, Connecticut League, and New England League. President Powers says that there is a good deal of work to be done, but he expects that the labors of the delegates will be concluded late this evening.

August 30, 1903

McGinnity Pitched Two Winning Games for New York Against Philadelphia.

Pitching two winning games of baseball on the same afternoon is an unusual feat, but "Joe" McGinnity of the New York National League Club has accomplished it three times this season. A few weeks ago he won both games of a double-header on the Boston grounds, and duplicated the trick against the Brooklyn team on the Polo Grounds six days later. Yesterday afternoon he again scored a double win, the Philadelphia players being the victims. The actual time of both contests was three hours and three minutes, and at the end McGinnity showed no sign of fatigue—in fact, he seemed fresh enough to tackle the visitors for a third contest if that were necessary.

Gloomy weather kept many of the local "rooters" from the grounds during the afternoon, but there were over 3,000 of the more enthusiastic patrons on hand. They went away well pleased with the excellent exhibitions which the local team gave during both games. In the earlier contest neither side made a misplay, and this was remarkable considering the wretched condition of the field from the recent heavy rains.

McGinnity began by giving Thomas a base on balls, and Gleason's sacrifice sent the runner to second. Bresnahan caught Wolverton's fly, and Titus was hit with a pitched ball, but Barry hit to McGann, who tossed the ball to McGinnity as the latter ran to first base. Frazer failed to locate the plate, and Browne walked to first; Bresnahan drove the ball safely between short and third, and both men advanced a base each on McGann's neat sacrifice. Mertes was fielded out at first base, but Browne scored on the play, and Babb foul flied to Wolverton. In the second inning the first two of the visiting side were disposed of quickly on a fly and an out at first base, and the third, Zimmer, struck out. In New York's half of this inning Lauder drove a liner over short and Dunn was hit with a pitched ball. Warner bunted safely, filling the bases. Then McGinnity singled, scoring Lauder. Browne did the same for Dunn with a single to left. Bresnahan struck out and Thomas caught McGann's fly, but Warner scored on the return of the ball, and Mertes sent one straight into Hulswitt's hands, retiring the side. After this both pitchers were very effective, and there was no further scoring until the Philadelphians went in for their ninth turn at bat. Titus doubled to centre and Barry struck out, as did Douglass. Hulswitt's drive to left field got past Mertes, who fell in his attempt to stop it, and Titus scored the only tally made for Philadelphia, as Zimmer ended the game, being thrown out, Lauder to McGann.

Thomas got a base on balls for a starter in the second game, but neither side scored until the third inning, when Titus, with a fine drive past Bresnahan for two bases, scored Gleason and Wolverton. These were the only runs the visitors got in this game, and the home team tallied once in the following inning, and took the lead in the fifth with two more. They scored again in the sixth, and swamped the visitors by tallying five times in the seventh.

During the fourth inning Hulswitt objected very vigorously to a decision made by Umpire Hurst, who called Bresnahan safe in a steal to second. While the argument was going on Bresnahan stole to third, and scored on Duggleby's wild throw. Hulswitt was put out of the game and ordered off the field, his position being played by Hallman during the remainder of the game. The scores:

NEW YORK.	R	1B	PO	A	E	PHILADELPHIA.	R	1B	PO	A	E
Browne, rf.	1	1	1	0	0	Thomas, cf.	0	1	3	0	0
Bresnahan, cf	0	1	6	0	0	Gleason, 2b.	0	1	1	1	0
McGann, 1b.	0	0	9	1	0	Wilv'rton, 3b	0	1	1	1	0
Mertes, lf.	0	1	2	1	0	Titus, rf.	1	1	0	0	0
Babb, ss.	0	2	2	3	0	Barry, lf.	0	0	1	0	0
Lauder, 3b.	1	1	0	3	0	Douglass, 1b.	0	0	11	0	0
Dunn, 2b.	1	1	1	3	0	Hulswitt, ss.	0	1	1	3	0
Werner, c.	1	1	4	0	0	Zimmer, c.	0	0	4	1	0
McGinnity, p.	0	1	2	1	0	Frazer, p.	0	0	2	6	0
Totals	4	9	27	12	0	Totals	1	5	24	12	0

New York	1	3	0	0	0	0	0	0	x	—4
Philadelphia	0	0	0	0	0	0	0	0	1	—1

Earned runs—New York, 2; Philadelphia, 1. Two-base hits—Titus, Hulswitt. Left on bases—New York, 10; Philadelphia, 7. Sacrifice hits—Bresnahan, McGann, Lauder, Gleason. Stolen bases—Bresnahan. Double plays—Mertes, Babb, and McGann. First base on balls—Off McGinnity, 3; off Frazer, 4. Hit by pitched ball—By McGinnity, 1; by Frazer, 1. Struck out—by McGinnity, 4; by Fraser, 4. Time—1:30. Umpire—Messrs. Hurst and Moran.

SECOND GAME.

NEW YORK.	R	1B	PO	A	E	PHILADELPHIA.	R	1B	PO	A	E
Browne, rf.	1	1	1	0	0	Thomas, cf.	0	0	1	0	0
Bres'h'n, cf.	3	4	1	0	0	Gleason, 2b.	1	0	3	1	0
McGann, 1b.	0	0	8	0	0	Wolv'ton, 3b	1	1	3	3	0
Mertes, lf.	0	0	3	0	0	Titus, rf.	0	1	3	0	0
Babb, ss.	0	0	3	3	0	Barry, lf.	0	1	0	0	0
Lauder, 3b.	1	2	0	0	0	Douglass, 1b.	0	0	8	1	1
Dunn, 2b.	1	0	0	3	1	Hulswitt, ss.	0	1	3	0	1
Warner c.	2	1	11	1	0	Hallman, ss.	0	0	0	1	2
McGinnity, p	1	3	0	3	0	Dooin, c.	0	0	2	4	1
						Duggleby, p.	0	2	1	2	1
Total	9	11	27	10	1	Total	2	6	24	12	6

New York	0	0	0	1	2	1	5	0	..	—9
Philadelphia	0	0	2	0	0	0	0	0	0	—2

Left on bases—New York, 5; Philadelphia, 6. Two-base hits—Bresnahan, 2; Titus. Sacrifice hits—McGann, Dunn, Douglass. Stolen bases—Bresnahan, McGann. Double plays—Duggleby and Gleason. First base on balls—Off McGinnity, 1; off Duggleby, 4. First base on errors—New York, 4; Philadelphia, 1. Struck out—By McGinnity, 9. Wild pitch—Duggleby. Time—One hour and thirty-three minutes. Umpires—Messrs. Moran and Hurst. Attendance—3,496.

September 1, 1903

BOSTON'S CHAMPION TEAM.

Pittsburg Unable to Score in the Deciding Game of the Championship Baseball Series.

BOSTON, Oct. 13.—The Boston Americans shut out the Pittsburg Nationals to-day and won the world's baseball championship, to the almost frenzied delight of 7,000 enthusiasts. While the attendance at all the previous games of the series has been larger than to-day, the demonstration which followed Dineen's striking out of "Hans" Wagner in the ninth equaled any college football game.

Phillippi, who was such an enigma to the Bostons in the first few games, essayed to pitch for the visitors for the sixth time. He was not only batted hard, but he saw his rival, Dineen, carry off the honors by holding the Nationals down to four scattered hits, which, backed by perfect fielding, prevented a single Pittsburg man getting further than third base. Dineen struck out seven men, and his support by Criger contributed materially to the success of the game. The latter's bluff throw to second in the fourth inning, followed by a quick snap of the ball to Collins, catching Leach off the bag, was the best piece of work in the game.

Other features were mainly contributed by the visitors, and Boston's score would undoubtedly have been larger but for the great running catches of Beaumont and Clarke, Wagner's work at short, and Leach's at third base. For the home team, Parent's hauling down of a liner from Clarke's bat roused the greatest enthusiasm. The score:

BOSTON.	R	1B	PO	A	E	PITTSBURG.	R	1B	PO	A	E
D'herty, lf.	0	0	3	0	0	B'mont, cf.	0	0	5	0	0
Collins, 3b.	0	1	0	2	0	Clarke, lf.	0	1	3	0	0
Stahl, cf.	0	0	2	0	0	Leach, 3b.	0	0	0	3	0
Freeman, rf.	1	1	2	0	0	Wagner, ss.	0	1	3	0	1
Parent, ss.	1	0	1	1	0	Br'nsf'd, 1b.	0	0	7	1	1
Lach'ce, 1b.	1	1	11	0	0	Ritchey, 2b.	0	0	2	1	0
Ferris, 2b.	0	2	0	3	0	Sebring, rf.	0	1	1	1	0
Criger, c.	0	2	8	3	0	Phelps, c.	0	0	3	0	1
Dineen, p.	0	1	0	3	0	Phillippi, p.	0	1	0	2	0
Total	3	8	27	12	0	Total	0	4	24	8	3

Boston	0	0	0	2	0	1	0	0	..	—3
Pittsburg	0	0	0	0	0	0	0	0	0	—0

Earned runs—Boston, 2. Three-base hits—Freeman, Lachance, and Sebring. Sacrifice hits—Lachance. Stolen base—Wagner. Double play—Criger and Lachance. First base on balls—Off Dineen, 2. Struck out—By Dineen, 7; by Phillippi, 2. Time of game—One hour and thirty-five minutes. Umpires—Messrs. O'Day and Connolly. Attendance—7,455.

October 14, 1903

Pitcher Young Shuts Out Philadelphia Without a Hit or Run.

WASHINGTON WINS FIRST GAME

Easy Victories for New York and Brooklyn Nationals—Comiskey's Team Advancing in Race.

Pitcher "Cy" Young of the Boston American League team performed the record-breaking feat yesterday, so far as the major leagues are concerned, of not allowing the Philadelphia Athletics to make a run, a safe hit, or a man to reach first base. The latter pinned their faith to Waddell, who on Tuesday had the Bostons so much at his mercy that they could secure but one hit, but in yesterday's contest the celebrated pitcher was batted rather freely. Another notable incident of the games yesterday was the victory of the Washington team over the Greater New Yorks. It was the Washington's fourteenth effort of the season to win, and they outplayed their opponents at all points. Chicago's success over St. Louis places Comiskey's team third in the championship race and quite close to the Greater New Yorks.

Three games were played in the National League, the New Yorks having no difficulty to beat Boston, Brooklyn had a walkover at Cincinnati, while at Philadelphia the local team, after a sharp contest, shut out St. Louis by a score of 3 to 0.

May 6, 1904

MATHEWSON PITCHES BEST GAME OF YEAR

Shuts Chicago Out Without a Hit or a Run.

NEW YORK SCORES ONCE

Mathewson's Great Pitching Prevents Chicago from Making Run or Hit.

Special to The New York Times.

CHICAGO, Ill., June 13.—Christopher Mathewson, the New York pitcher, did wonders with the ball to-day. Not only did he break the winning streak of the Chicagos short off, but he stopped Selee's breezy players to a standstill. Neither run, nor hit, nor base on balls did Mathewson allow Chicago in the full nine innings, and if his support had been perfect he would have tied "Cy" Young's record of not permitting an opponent to reach first base. Mathewson had to do it to win, because all the "Giants" could make off Brown was one run, and that in the ninth inning.

Chicago's recent successes, combined with the possibility of an injunction row,

attracted a big weekly crowd in spite of the weather, which promised to stop the game before it had gone far. Nothing happened either of an aquatic or fistic kind, and the spectators were obliged to see their idols made to look like animated automata of putty, so completely did Mathewson have them faded.

Just twenty-eight men, one more than the necessary three per inning, faced the champions' pitcher during the game. Two of them reached first base because of blunders by Dahlen and Gilbert on easy chances, and one of them passed on to second, while the other was doubled up off first after a pretty catch by Browne. Only once did the Chicagos even make a noise like a base hit, and that was when Evers hit a line drive straight into Donlin's waiting hands in the fifth inning.

The score:

CHICAGO.	R	1B	PO	A	E	NEW YORK.	R	1B	PO	A	E
Slagle, cf.	0	0	3	0	0	Donlin, cf.	0	1	3	0	0
Schulte, lf.	0	0	1	0	0	Browne, rf.	0	1	1	1	0
Maloney, rf.	0	0	5	0	0	McGann,1b.	1	1	14	0	0
Chance, 1b.	0	0	8	0	0	Mertes, lf.	0	1	3	0	0
Tinker, ss.	0	0	3	4	1	Dahlen, ss.	0	1	2	3	1
Evers, 2b.	0	0	2	2	0	Devlin, 3b.	0	0	0	1	0
Casey, 2b.	0	0	1	2	0	Gilbert, 2b.	0	0	1	5	1
Kling, c.	0	0	4	2	1	Bow'man,c.0	0	3	0	0
Brown, p.	0	0	0	0	0	M'th'son, p.0	0	0	4	0
Total....	0	0	27	10	3	Total....	1	5	27	14	2

Chicago ....0 0 0 0 0 0 0 0 0—0
New York ....0 0 0 0 0 0 0 0 1—1

First base by errors—Chicago, 2; New York, 2. Left on bases—Chicago, 1; New York, 4. Stolen bases—Schulte, Dahlen. Double plays—Browne and McGann, 2; by Matthewson, 2. Struck out—By Brown, 3; by Matthewson, 2. Bases on balls—Off Brown, 2. Balk—Brown. Time of game—One hour and twenty-five minutes. Umpires—Messrs. Bausewine and Emslie. Attendance—9,066.

June 4, 1905

GIANTS CHAMPIONS, THE SCORE, 2-0

Mathewson's Superb Work Ends the Inter-League Series.

CROWD GOES WILD WITH JOY

McGraw's Men Besieged in Their Clubhouse by 10,000 Cheering Admirers.

Two neatly dressed, ruddy faced, athletic looking young men, grinning broadly; one a giant in contrast to the squatiness of the other, walked along the veranda of the clubhouse at the Polo Grounds about 5 o'clock yesterday afternoon. Below them was a sea of 10,000 faces, wildly emitting a thunderous eruption of enthusiasm. The two young men

looked down upon the reverberating ocean of humanity for a moment, and then walked to a point directly in front of the plaza, where they were in view of all. The ten thousand throats bellowed forth a tribute that would have almost drowned a broadside of twelve-inch guns.

The two smiling athletes stopped, one of them drew forth a long sheet of yellow paper rolled under his arm. As the crowd pushed and fought and cheered he unwrapped an impromptu banner and let it flutter on the breeze. The multitude pressed forward like a wave to read this inscription:

> THE GIANTS,
> WORLD'S CHAMPIONS, 1905.

Geological records show that Vesuvius disturbs the earth and that seismic demonstrations are felt by the greater number. But if that doctrine had been promulgated in the vicinity of the Polo Grounds yesterday, as Christie Mathewson and Roger Bresnahan of the New York Baseball Club unfurled their victorious banner, it would have been minimized. For, as volcanoes assert themselves upon the earth's surface surely must that deafening, reverberating roar have lifted Manhattan's soil from its base.

The Giants, the most intelligent, the quickest, strongest, and grittiest combination of baseball players that have ever represented this city in any league, demonstrated beyond opportunity for quibble or claim their paramount superiority over anything extant in diamond life of to-day by winning the fourth and deciding game of the world's championship series by the score of 2 to 0.

The victory meant an honor which has not hitherto fallen to the lot of New York through any other team, and by the victory of yesterday the Giants may hold up their heads in the athletic world as being the one collection of peerless ball tossers.

The crowd, in the neighborhood of 27,000 people, saw the battle, and a battle it was, to cheer the baseball heart and satisfy the innermost cravings of the rooter's mind. It was a fight of slow stages, but at no time during the contest were the Giants in danger, and at all times were they masters. It settled the question so often propounded whether the National or the American League offers the better brand of baseball. The championship decree of yesterday, to be accepted as final, lays at rest all doubt and demonstrates the transcendent superiority of the National brand and the indisputable invulnerability of the Giants.

And be it recorded right here that New York possesses the pitching marvel of the century. Christie Mathewson, the giant slabman, who made the world's championship possible for New York, may be legitimately designated as the premier pitching wonder of all baseball records. The diamond has known its Clarkson, its Keefe, and its Caruthers. Their records radiate. But to Mathewson belongs the palm, for his almost superhuman accomplishment during the series which closed yesterday will stand as a mark for all pitchers of the future.

Mathewson's Great Record.

Figures show best just what Mathewson accomplished. In the three victories over which he presided he twirled twenty-seven innings. During that series he allowed not a single run; not an Athletic even reached third base. He was touched for only a total of fifteen hits, and by men who are reckoned as the American League's strongest batters; he allowed only one pass to first, hit only a single batsman, and struck out sixteen men. The record is a classic. Baseball New York appreciates this work. That fact was amply demonstrated yesterday, when it gave Mathewson a marvelous vocal panegyric and placed upon his modest brow a hollowed wreath that evoked only a half-suppressed smile and bow.

The game yesterday was one of giants—clean, fast, and decisive. Both teams were keyed to the point of desperation, for to the Giants it meant rosy conquest and to the Athletics a saving clause which would offer them yet a chance to redeem themselves. But the Giants were not to be repulsed. They went at the ball in the first inning with a we-never-can-lose expression of dogged determination, and there was not a minute during play in which that spirit didn't manifest itself. Philadelphia tried its best, but, strive as hard as it did, it was only a shadow reflecting the masterful Mathewson's will. He bestrode the field like a mighty Colossus, and the Athletics peeped about the diamond like pigmies who struggled gallantly for their lives, but in vain.

Bender, the much feared brave from the Carlisle reservation, sought to repeat his scalping bee of Tuesday, but the Spartan McGraw laconically expressed the situation when at the beginning of the game he remarked good-naturedly to the Athletics' pitcher:

"It will be off the warpath for you to-day, Chief." The stolid, phlegmatic copper-colored man only smiled grimly.

"It's uncertain," he replied, "but I did it once, and I'm going to do my best to do it again."

Analyzed to the statistical point the twirling feature of the game shows little advantage to either side, but when weighed in parts Mathewson had by far the advantage. Five hits were all that the Giants could register off Bender, while the Athletics rang up for a total of six against Mathewson. Mathewson fanned only three to Bender's five, but the Indian gave three passes. Mathewson proved a surprise to his admirers by poorly fielding his position. He made two errors, but they luckily resulted in nothing harmful in the net result.

Giants Get $1,141 Each.

The Giants were well rewarded for their hard work in defeating the Athletics, for by the week's labor each man to-day has a check in his wallet for $1,141.41. That is the share of each of the eighteen Giants for the series. The figures given out officially yesterday show the receipts of the first four games, from which the players derive their profit, to have been $50,730.50. The share for which the two teams struggled amounted to $27,394. Seventy-five per cent. of that amount was divided among the Giants. The remainder went in equal shares to the Athletics.

The crowd which saw yesterday's game was immense, exceeding by a small margin that of Tuesday. All the stands were filled, while men and women stood in a line ten deep back of the ropes from the right to the left field bleachers. Men hung on the fence and sat on the grandstand roof, and some peered at the game through glasses from distant poles and housetops. The crowd was there to cheer its idols, and every move was followed by a roar.

The New York management had a band on the field to enliven things until play began, and it was kept busy as the players walked to the field and started practice. As McGraw appeared on the diamond, coming from the clubhouse, he was met with a volley of applause and was obliged to lift his hat in response.

"Clinch it to-day, Mac," yelled the crowd. "Nothing but the championship will suit us now."

"That's what you'll get," he responded smilingly.

While McGraw was walking across the field the Athletics appeared from the clubhouse with Bender in the lead.

"Back to the tepee for yours," hooted a rooter. "Giants grab heap much wampum," yelled another, giving an imitation Indian yell. Bender looked at his foes in stolid silence, but smiled widely as the running fire of comments continued. James J. Corbett, with an eye for all public opportunities, walked into the field with the Giants and helped the players to warm up. He was subjected to a good deal of bantering. Just before play was called Corbett and Bresnahan posed with an Irish flag between them and were snapped by a photographer. Mathewson was the last to arrive on the scene and got a magnificent reception. He was applauded for a full minute and the crowd yelled for him to doff his cap. Instead of doing so, however, he walked over to McGinnity, the conqueror of yesterday, and ostentatiously removed Joe's headgear. McGinnity returned the compliment.

"Shake 'em up, Matty. Go after 'em," screamed the bleachers. Mathewson waved his arm as though he would do his utmost. As McGraw went to the plate to bat out in practice the band began to play:

> We'll all get stone blind,
> Johnnie go fill up the bowl

The crowd cheered, and a half dozen men went through the grandstand offering to bet 100 to 75 that the Giants would win the game. There were no takers.

Couldn't Rattle Bender.

Time and again Bender was yelled at, for the crowd wanted to rattle him, but its noise might as well have been directed at a steamboat, for he was impassive and cool at all stages. In one inning he gave two bases on balls in succession and the crowd jumped to its feet in glee. Bender was thunderously informed that at that particular stage he was booked for the soap factory, but stuck grimly to his task. At another time two bunts were made in succession. Again the crowd rose in its might and expressed itself as of the opinion that the chief would surely go to the happy hunting grounds, but he refused to die and stood gamely and quietly to the end.

Danny McGann was again a target for the Bender brand of curves, and added to his strike-out performance of Tuesday, when he slashed the air in a way that was distressing. The first time up yesterday McGann, with his strike-out record fresh in the minds of the fans, was cautioned to be wary and smash the ball to the earth's ends.

"Look out, Danny, the Heap-Much-Kill-'em-Giants man'll get you. Lace it out of the lot."

McGann's face bespoke ill for the future of the ball, but, much to the chagrin of the rooters, he was called out on strikes. As McGann walked toward the home bench the crowd raised a hiss of protest at Sheridan. McGraw, Dahlen, Bresnahan, and Clark had heart-to-heart talks with the indicator, but they were shooed away.

As the game proceeded the crowd saw that it was to be a magnificent pitching struggle, and both twirlers were cheered. After the fourth, when Bender had acquitted himself by retiring the Giants in one, two, three order, he was heartily applauded.

"You're the real thing: kangaroo out of the American and come to us next season," howled one fan. Bender lifted his cap in acknowledgment.

Philadelphia had men on bases in the first, second, third, fifth, and sixth innings, but couldn't get one past the second sack. In the fifth inning they came close to pushing a man to third, but Mathewson, evidently intent upon keeping his record intact, interfered. Powers had made a two-base hit to left. Bender, the next man up, lined one to Mathewson. There were two out, and by the ordinary rules of baseball the batter should have been retired. Powers started off for third, however, and Mathewson, seeing him approaching the bag, took the insult to heart. He threw quickly to Devlin, who touched the runner before he could put his spikes upon the bag.

New York made its runs in the fifth and eighth. In the fifth inning Mertes got a pass and Dahlen followed suit by passing four bad ones. With two on bases the crowd, keen for an opportunity to root, stood up and roared for Devlin to drive in a run.

"Show 'em the way to the clubhouse, Arthur," shouted Clark, who stood upon the coaching line. Devlin, however, had his orders and bunted. He sacrificed the runners to third and second, respectively and as the men chased down the line the crowd nearly yelled itself hoarse.

Besieged by the Rooters.

"Come on, Gilbert, you can do it!" roared the stands. Then came a volley of taunts to Bender, who viewed the situation with absolute imperturbability and wound up his pitching arm for New York's second baseman. But Gilbert was equal to the occasion, for he caught one of Bender's twists on the end of his bat and sent the sphere to deep left. Hartzel got under the base and caught it, but Mertes on third raced home with the first tally of the game. Then the crowd went wild and cheered everything and everybody.

In the eighth the Giants rolled up another. After Gilbert had flied to Lord, Mathewson went to the bat amid a storm of yells. He passed four bad ones, and walked. Bresnahan put an extra coat of dust upon his hands as he stalked to the plate and carefully inspected the business end of his bat. The crowd yelled for him to "Swat it off the earth!"

"Put it in a balloon, Roger, and send it away for good!" screamed the fans. Roger did the next best thing by driving the ball on a straight line to the left field bleachers. Ordinarily it would have counted for a home run, but under the ground rules he was allowed only two bases. Even Matty was enamored of the coup, for as he trotted around to third he paused, under the ground rule allowance, and clapped his hands with satisfaction. Browne, the next up, did his best to imitate Bresnahan, and swung viciously at one of Bender's curves. It went like a shot straight for the Indian. Bender grabbed at the leather, and it struck his right hand, caroming off to Murphy, who retired Browne. Matty, however, jumped across the rubber and registered a second tally.

The Giants also came within an ace of scoring in the sixth. Mathewson went out to Lord on a high fly, to be followed by Bresnahan who bunted safely along the third-base line. The crowd wanted blood in this round, and told as much to Browne, who followed.

"Once more, boys," yelled McGraw, who was standing on the coaching line. "Let's get at the Indian here and fix 'em."

Browne was equal to the occasion and put one exactly where Roger had sent it. Donlin walked to the plate with the air of a man capable of great things.

"I'm sorry, old Pitch-Em-Heap," he remarked to Bender jokingly, "but here's where you go back to the reservation."

"Is that so?" answered Bender sarcastically. "Your conclusion, Mr. Donlin, is right in this immediate vicinity." Donlin went out to Lord, and McGann, who followed, cut off three slices of air, and walked away a heart-broken man.

* * * * *

The score:

PHILADELPHIA.	R	1B	PO	A	E	NEW YORK.	R	1B	PO	A	E
Hartsel, lf.	0	2	4	1	0	Bresn'h'n, c.	0	2	5	2	0
Lord, cf.	0	0	3	0	0	Browne, rf.	0	1	0	0	0
Davis, 1b.	0	1	10	0	0	Donlin, cf.	0	0	1	0	0
L. Cross, 3b.	0	0	1	1	0	M'Gann, 1b.	0	0	12	1	0
Seybold, rf.	0	1	0	0	0	Mertes, lf.	1	1	1	0	0
Murphy, 2b.	0	0	0	0	0	Dahlen, ss.	0	0	3	4	0
M. Cross, ss.	0	1	1	5	0	Devlin, 3b.	0	0	1	4	0
Powers, c.	0	1	5	1	0	Gilbert, 2b.	0	1	3	6	0
Bender, p.	0	0	0	5	0	M'th'son, p.	1	0	1	3	1
Total	0	6	24	13	0	Total	2	5	27	20	1

Philadelphia	0	0	0	0	0	0	0	0	0	—0
New York	0	0	0	0	1	0	0	1	..	—2

First base on errors—Philadelphia, 1. Bases on balls—Off Bender, 3. Struck out—By Mathewson, 4; by Bender, 4. Left on bases—New York, 4; Philadelphia, 6. Two-base hits—Powers, Bresnahan. Sacrifice hits—Devlin, Mathewson. Double plays—Dahlen, Gilbert, and McGann; Hartsel, M. Cross, and L. Cross. Umpires—Messrs. Sheridan and O'Day. Time of game—One hour and twenty-eight minutes. Attendance—24,187.

October 15, 1905

NO HITS FOR YANKEES OFF VETERAN YOUNG

Veteran Boston Pitcher's Remarkable Performance in Hilltop Game.

MAKES THREE HITS HIMSELF

Famous Twirler Also Leads His Team at Bat and Brings In Several Runs with His Big Stick.

AMERICAN LEAGUE.

Results of Yesterday's Games.

Boston, 8; New York, 0.
Philadelphia, 3; Washington, 1.
Cleveland, 2; St. Louis, 1.
Chicago, 2; Detroit, 1.

Where They Play To-day.

Boston at New York.
Washington at Philadelphia.
Cleveland at St. Louis.
Detroit at Chicago.

Standing of the Clubs.

	W.	L.	P.C.		W.	L.	P.C.
St. Louis	38	26	.593	Phila'phia	31	31	.500
Cleveland	37	26	.587	New York	29	37	.439
Chicago	36	28	.562	Boston	26	36	.419
Detroit	34	29	.540	Washington	22	40	.355

Did you hear about what old Young did up at the American League Park yesterday? He didn't exactly beggar description, but he came mighty nigh it. He beggared the Elberfeld aggregation so far as runs were concerned, and he made hitless Yankees out of the whole outfit, and he smashed out singles thisaway and thataway, and he scored people that he liked, and he scored people that we don't know whether he cares much about or not, and he was the jolly old plot of the piece, and there wasn't an inning that you could lose track of him.

Even aside from his pitching proclivities, this gay old blade was the life of the party. He galloped around the bases like he was out for the Swift Stakes, and an observant clocker whose occupation at the track is o'er now that they're insisting that somebody pay some attention to the law, gave it out honest and official when he said to the stand generally:

"They must have gave that old skate the electric battery; watch um sail past them bags—why, he's fast as a ghost, I tell you."

The score, which is an entirely immaterial consideration, was 8. That's all, just 8. There were several reasons for this. To wit:

Pitcher Manning.
Pitcher Newton.
Pitcher Lake.

If the gentle reader will imagine quotation marks before and after the word pitcher in each of the foregoing instances he won't go wrong. Manning was so wild his reformation was despaired of after an inning and a half. He started out by assaulting Thoney so that Thoney had to be out of the game after the first inning. Sullivan filed to Keeler, and, after the pain-crazed Thoney had got himself out between bases and sought the restful bench, Manning passes McConnell. Gessler, and Laporte one dozen bad balls in succession, which we beg to submit is going some. Unglaub's hit scores McConnell.

There's another run for Boston in the second inning, consequent upon the senile Mr. Young's hit to centre, and hits by Cravath—who succeeded Thoney—and Sullivan and a long fly to Stahl by McConnell. Newton is pitching the last part of the second inning, the entire third, and the first half of the fourth—playing and tossing, more like a boat than a gent on the American League payroll.

And Boston goes right on, getting in runs whether it needs them or not, and now and then there is a long, low ominous growl, and it sure is the voice of the slugger, and we hear him exclaim, "Let's score a few more just to sew up the game."

The good old man Young had his eye and his hand on the ball yesterday. In the third inning he pounded one over to

right and faraway, and on this substantial encouragement Unglaub and Wagner scored. And again, by one of those curious quick repetitions of history that sometimes happen on the ball field. Uncle Cy does exactly the same thing in the ninth. That is, his slam is to left, in this instance, but he scores the same two men, Unglaub and Wagner.

Lake finished the session for the Yanks, and had the bad taste to question some of Silk O'Loughlin's decisions. Not only the bad taste but the bad judgment. Nothing in this for you at all, Jose, amigo. Besides, it's too hot. Silk looks around at the Yankee bench to see if there are any more pitchers available. No more. Oh, very well, pitch the game out, you fiery Lake.

W. W. AULICK.

With malice toward Young—

BOSTON.	R	H	PO	A	E	NEW YORK.	R	H	PO	A	E
Thoney, lf.	0	0	0	0	0	Niles, 2b.	0	0	3	6	0
Cravath, lf.	0	1	4	0	0	Keeler, rf.	0	0	2	1	1
Sullivan, cf.	1	1	0	0	0	Mor'ty, 1b.	0	0	10	1	1
McC'nell, 2b.	2	2	4	0	0	H'phill, cf.	0	0	0	0	0
Gessler, rf.	0	1	2	0	0	Ball, ss.	0	0	3	3	0
Laporte, 3b.	0	2	2	2	0	Stahl, lf.	0	0	2	1	0
Ungl'b, 1b.	2	2	13	0	0	Conroy, 3b.	0	0	1	0	
Wagner, ss.	2	1	0	3	0	Blair, c.	0	0	7	2	0
Criger, c.	0	0	3	2	0	Manning, p.	0	0	0	2	0
Young, p.	1	3	0	1	0	Newton, p.	0	0	0	1	1
						Lake, p.	0	0	0	0	0
Total	8	13	27	12	0	Total	0	0	27	18	3

Boston .... 1 1 2 1 0 1 0 0 2—8
New York .... 0 0 0 0 0 0 0 0 0—0

Hits—Off Manning, 3 in one and two-thirds innings; off Newton, 8 in two-thirds of an inning; off Lake, 7 in five and two-thirds innings. Sacrifice hits—McConnell, (2.) Criger, (2.) Stolen base—McConnell. Double play—Stahl and Blair. Left on bases—Boston, 11. First base on balls—Off Manning, 3; off Newton, 1; off Lake, 1; off Young, 1. First base on errors—Boston, 2. Hit by pitcher—By Manning, 1; by Newton, 1. Struck out—By Manning, 1; by Newton, 1; by Lake, 4; by Young, 2. Time of game—Two hours. Umpire—Mr. O'Loughlin.

YOUNG'S FAMOUS CAREER.

Most Remarkable Pitcher in Point of Excellent Service in Baseball.

The performance of Denton T. (Cy) Young yesterday at the American League Park in shutting out the Yankees without a hit stamps him as the most remarkable pitcher in the history of major league baseball. Not only is he the oldest pitcher in National or American League ranks, but he is the only player in the history of the National pastime who has shut out an opposing team without a hit on three different occasions. In addition, he shares with John M. Ward the unique distinction of pitching a no-hit game with no player reaching first base. Ward performed the feat for Providence against Buffalo in 1880, while Young established his record on May 15, 1904, against the Philadelphia Athletics while pitching for Boston. Yesterday only one New York player reached first base—Niles, on a base on balls.

"Cy" Young pitched his first no-hit game for Cleveland against Cincinnati in 1897. This was in the National League. His next shut-out game was against the Philadelphia Athletics in 1904, and his third yesterday.

In addition to his remarkable record for no-hit games Young holds the record for effective pitching in the major league, pitching fifty-four innings without a run in 1904.

The last shut-out game in the American League was on Sept. 27, 1905, when Dineen did the trick for Boston against Chicago. In the National League, Pfeffer for Boston against Cincinnati, and Maddox for Pittsburg against Brooklyn performed the "shut-out" feat last year.

Young was born at Gilmore, Ohio, March 29, 1867, stands 6 feet in height, and weighs 210 pounds. Canton, Ohio, was where "Cy" made his first appearance, and the Cleveland Club took him in charge that year, 1890, making eighteen years' active pitching in the major league. He remained with Cleveland until that club was transferred to St. Louis, where he remained one year and then went to Boston the first year of the American League. Young is the most remarkable ball player the game has yet produced when good work for a long period is considered.

July 1, 1908

Neither Hit Nor Run for Suburbas.

A double-header was on yesterday's card for the St. Louis and Brooklyn clubs, but rain interfered, and the first game was called with the score 2 to 0 in favor of the visitors. The second contest was postponed owing to rain.

Lush pitched a no-hit game for St. Louis. In the third inning, with two out and the bases filled on two hits and a base on balls, Jordan muffed Murray's high fly. Lush and Shaw scoring for the visitors.

The score:

ST. LOUIS.	A	B	R	H	PO	A	BROOKLYN.	A	B	R	H	PO	A
Shaw, cf.	3	1	1	2	0		Pattee, 2b.	0	0	0	0	3	
Byrne, ss.	2	0	0	1		Hummel, lf.	3	0	0	1	0	
Murray, rf.	3	0	0	1	0		Lumley, rf.	3	0	0	1	0	
K'tchy, 1b.	3	0	0	8	0		Jordan, 1b.	3	0	0	2	1	0
Deleh'ty, lf.	2	0	0	1	0		Lewis, ss.	2	0	0	0	4	
Hostet.r, 3b.	2	0	0	3		Bergen, c.	1	0	0	5	1	
Bliss, c.	2	0	0	3	1		Sh'han, 3b.	2	0	0	0	1	
Gilbert, 2b.	2	0	1	0		Maloney, cf.	1	0	0	2	0	
Lush, p.	2	1	1	0	2		Bell, p.	1	0	0	0	1	
Total	21	2	3	18	8		Total	16	0	0	18	10	

Error—Jordan.

St. Louis .... 0 0 2 0 0 0—2
Brooklyn .... 0 0 0 0 0 0—0

Sacrifice hit—Bell. Stolen bases—Pattee, 2. Left on bases—St. Louis, 2; Brooklyn, 4. First base on balls—Off Bell, 1; off Lush, 5. First base on error—St. Louis, 1. Struck out—By Bell, 2; by Lush, 3. Time of game—Fifty-eight minutes. Umpire—Mr. Klem.

August 7, 1908

JOSEPH JEROME McGINNITY
"IRONMAN"
DISTINGUISHED AS THE PITCHER WHO HURLED TWO GAMES ON ONE DAY THE MOST TIMES. DID THIS ON FIVE OCCASIONS. WON BOTH GAMES THREE TIMES. PLAYED WITH BALTIMORE, BROOKLYN AND NEW YORK TEAMS IN N.L. AND BALTIMORE IN A.L. GAINED MORE THAN 200 VICTORIES DURING CAREER. RECORDED 20 OR MORE VICTORIES SEVEN TIMES. IN TWO SUCCESSIVE SEASONS WON AT LEAST 30 GAMES.

PITCHER JOHNSON AGAIN DOWNS YANKS

Washingtonian Prevents New Yorks Scoring in Three Straight Games.

DETROIT NOW FAR IN LEAD

American League Champions Trim Browns in Two Games and Chicago Loses Twice to Cleveland.

AMERICAN LEAGUE.

Scores of Yesterday's Games.

MORNING GAMES.

Detroit, 4; St. Louis, 3.
Boston, 6; Philadelphia, 1.
Cleveland, 6; Chicago, 0.

AFTERNOON GAMES.

Washington, 4; New York, 0.
Washington, 9; New York, 3.
Boston, 3; Philadelphia, 2.
Cleveland, 5; Chicago, 2.
Detroit, 9; St. Louis, 3.

Where They Play To-day.

New York at Philadelphia.
Boston at Washington.
St. Louis at Cleveland.
Chicago at Detroit.

Standing of the Clubs.

	W.	L.	P.C.		W.	L.	P.C.
Detroit	73	51	.589	Phila'phia	61	63	.492
Chicago	71	55	.564	Boston	61	65	.484
St. Louis	70	55	.567	Washington	54	67	.446
Cleveland	69	58	.543	New York	40	85	.320

We are grievously disappointed in this man Johnson of Washington. He and his team had four games to play with the champion (sic) Yankees. Johnson pitched the first game and shut us out. Johnson pitched the second game and shut us out. Johnson pitched the third game, and shut us out. Did Johnson pitch the fourth game and shut us out? He did not. Oh, you quitter!

Most pitchers would have gone on and taken a chance after this demonstration of comparative strength. But did Johnson? No, Sir. He weakened. He passed up the fourth game, refusing to sit in as slabsman, and another Washingtonian, named Youse, according to Umpire Evans, and spelled Hughes, according to the card, pitched the final of yesterday's double-header, and beat the local wonders even worse than is customary. Oh, rare Pitcher Johnson! Why did you not preserve your record intact? Oh, thou of little faith!

Johnson won the first game of the holiday by a score of 4 to shut-out, and 10,000 souls chanted his service. Washington's runs came this way: Third inning—Johnson is hit by a pitched ball and walked. Chesbro's a good-natured person ordinarily, but something's got to be done to keep this Johnson from continuous performance. Pickering is safe on Laperte's fumble, though later he is out trying to make third. Ganley is safe on Conroy's fumble, and two score when Unglaub doubles. Then, in the seventh, Street doubles and scores on Johnson's single to centre. Whose single? Oh, you know. And Delehanty's single scores Johnson. (Can't help it if the composing room does run out of upper case "J's.")

We could write a sensational tale about any second-story chapter, but one inning, the sixth, will suffice. Hogg had started in to pitch, but they didn't root very much for Hogg and he died after five innings and four runs had been recorded. Then along comes the dilatory Doyle, and the groan that went up from the would-be early home-goers was deeper than the disgust over the ninth inning from Philadelphia.

When Mr. Doyle sets out to pitch he takes the heel of his shoe and scrapes determinedly at the inoffensive earth, like a plow making a furrow, or a dime-novel reading boy after a Capt. Kidd treasure in the backyard. Then he stares condemningly at the batter for thirty seconds and forms his arms into a maltese cross. And after he has fixed his little cap straight he is ready to pitch. Not all of the vicissitudes of that sixth inning spoiled his schedule. To be brutally photographic, here it is, or was—Hughes made first on Hemphill's muff. Pickering was safe on Conroy's bad throw. Ganley flied out. Unglaub singled to left, scoring Hughes. Delehanty walked. Clymer doubled, scoring Pickering and Unglaub. Freeman went out on a squeeze play and Delehanty scored, and, if you will believe it, while Doyle was pawing up the earth and fixing his little cap and arranging his arm, Clymer stole home, right out in public, and we don't believe Doyle knows it yet. Count those runs up and see if they don't make five.

After that Mr. Billiard obliged, and the Washingtons didn't score any more. The Yanks went exactly thirty-three innings in the series with the Senators before they counted, and the three runs they got toward the finish seemed only a part of the great big joke of getaway day. And the funniest part of the afternoon was a managerial envoy coming around and confiding the importantly true tidings that Cree and Warhop of Williamsport and Quinn of Richmond are joiners to-morrow and that it'll be all off with the other fellows from now on. Amen.

W. W. AULICK.

The last sad writes—

WASHINGTON.

	AB	R	H	PO	A
Picker'g, cf.	4	0	0	1	0
Ganley, lf.	5	1	0	3	0
Unglaub, 3b.	5	0	4	1	5
Deleh'ty, 2b.	5	0	2	3	4
Clymer, rf.	4	0	0	1	0
Freem'n, 1b.	3	0	0	12	0
McBride, ss.	4	0	1	1	3
Street, c.	4	1	1	5	0
Johnson, p.	2	2	1	0	2
Total	36	4	9	27	14

NEW YORK

	AB	R	H	PO	A
Conroy, 3b.	4	0	0	2	2
McIlv'n, rf.	4	0	1	0	0
Laporte, 2b.	4	0	0	1	3
H'phill, cf.	4	0	0	2	0
Mor'ty, 1b.	2	0	0	10	1
O'Rourke, lf.	3	0	0	4	0
Ball, ss.	3	0	0	3	3
Kleinow, c.	3	0	0	5	3
Chesbro, p.	3	0	0	0	2
Total	30	0	2	27	11

Errors—Freeman, Conroy, Laporte, Ball, (2,) Kleinow.

Washington ....0 0 2 0 0 0 2 0 0—4
New York ....0 0 0 0 0 0 0 0 0—0

Two-base hits—Unglaub, Street. Three-base hit—Delehanty. Sacrifice hit—Johnson. Stolen bases—Ganley, Ball. Left on bases—Washington, 9; New York, 3. First base on balls—Off Chesbro, 2. Hit by pitcher—By Chesbro, 2; by Johnson, 1. Struck out—By Chesbro, 4; by Johnson 5. Time of game—One hour and forty minutes. Umpire—Mr. Evans.

SECOND GAME.

WASHINGTON.

	AB	R	H	PO	A
Picker'g, cf.	5	2	0	0	1
Ganley, lf.	5	1	0	3	0
Unglaub, 3b.	5	3	8	1	1
Deleh'ty, 2b.	4	1	2	3	2
Clymer, rf.	5	1	3	0	1
Freem'n, 1b.	0	1	0	7	0
McBride, ss.	3	0	1	2	5
Street, c.	3	0	0	6	2
Warner, c.	1	0	1	4	0
Hughes, p.	4	1	0	0	0
Total	36	9	11	26	12

NEW YORK.

	AB	R	H	PO	A
Conroy, 3b.	4	0	1	6	0
McIlv'n, rf.	3	0	0	1	0
Laporte, 2b.	4	0	2	3	2
H'phill, cf.	3	1	1	3	0
O'Rourke, lf.	3	1	1	1	0
Mor'ty, 1b.	4	0	0	7	1
Ball, ss.	4	0	1	1	6
Kleinow, c.	1	0	0	2	1
Blair, c.	2	1	2	2	1
Hogg, p.	1	0	0	0	2
Doyle, p.	0	0	0	0	0
Billiard, p.	2	0	1	0	1
Total	31	3	9	27	15

*Conroy out; hit by batted ball.

Errors—Ganley, Conroy, McIlveen, Laporte, Hemphill, Ball.

Washington ....1 0 0 3 5 0 0 0—9
New York ....0 0 0 0 0 0 2 0 1—3

Two-base hits—Unglaub, Laporte. Home run—Blair. Hits—Off Hogg, 6 in 5 innings; off Doyle, 2 in 1 inning; off Billiard, 8 in 3 innings. Sacrifice hits—Pickering, Freeman, (2,) McBride, Hughes, McIlveen. Stolen bases—Clymer, O'Rourke. Left on bases—Washington, 11; New York, 5. First base on balls— Off Hughes, 4; off Hogg, 3; off Doyle, 2; off Billiard, 1. First base on errors—Washington, 5. Struck out—By Hughes, 7; by Hogg, 1; by Billiard, 2. Time of game—One hour and fifty-five minutes. Umpire—Mr. Evans.

September 8, 1908

NO HIT GAME FOR SMITH.

Chicago Pitcher Was Invincible and Shut Out Philadelphia, 1—0.

CHICAGO, Sept. 20.—Smith pitched a no-hit game against Philadelphia here to-day, Chicago winning, 1—0. Plank was also in fine form, allowing the locals but four hits, which were scattered. Isbell opened the last inning with a line drive between first and second, which Murphy went after, but nobody covered first base and the runner was safe. He went to second on a passed ball, and a wild pitch sent him to third base. Davis walked. Plank endeavored to pass Parent, but the shortstop stepped across the plate and lined the ball down to Murphy, who tried to catch Isbell at the plate, but the throw was late.

Score:

CHICAGO.

	AB	R	H	PO	A
Hahn, rf.	4	0	1	1	0
Jones, cf.	4	0	0	3	0
Isbell, 1b.	3	1	2	15	0
And'son, lf.	4	0	0	3	0
Davis, 2b.	3	0	0	2	3
Parent, ss.	4	0	0	1	2
Sullivan, c.	3	0	1	2	1
Tan'hill, 3b.	3	0	0	0	5
Smith, p.	3	0	0	0	4
Total	31	1	4	27	14

PHILADELPHIA

	AB	R	H	PO	A
Nichols, ss.	4	0	0	1	3
Oldring, lf.	4	0	0	3	0
Murphy, 1b.	3	0	0	12	0
Coombs, cf.	3	0	0	1	0
Seybold, rf.	3	0	0	1	0
Manu'h, 1b.	3	0	0	1	2
Barr, 2b.	3	0	0	2	2
Lapp, c.	3	0	0	5	1
Plank, p.	3	0	0	0	1
Total	29	0	0	25	10

Errors—Isbell, Manusch, Barr.

*One out when winning run was scored.

Chicago ....0 0 0 0 0 0 0 0 1—1
Philadelphia ....0 0 0 0 0 0 0 0 0—0

Stolen base—Davis. Double play—Murphy, (unassisted.) Left on bases—Chicago, 7; Philadelphia, 2. First base on balls—Off Smith, 1; off Plank, 1. Hit by pitcher—By Plank, 1. Struck out—By Plank, 5; by Smith, 2. Passed ball—Lapp. Wild pitch—Plank. Time of game—One hour and thirty minutes. Umpires—Messrs. Egan and O'Loughlin.

September 21, 1908

BLUNDER COSTS GIANTS VICTORY

Merkle Rushes Off Base Line Before Winning Run Is Scored, and Is Declared Out.

CONFUSION ON BALL FIELD

Chance Asserts That McCormick's Run Does Not Count— Crowd Breaks Up Game.

UMPIRE DECLARES IT A TIE

Singular Occurrence on Polo Grounds Reported to President Pulliam, Who Will Decide Case.

Censurable stupidity on the part of player Merkle in yesterday's game at the Polo Grounds between the Giants and Chicagos placed the New York team's chances of winning the pennant in jeopardy. His unusual conduct in the final inning of a great game perhaps deprived New York of a victory that would have been unquestionable had he not committed a breach in baseball play that resulted in Umpire O'Day declaring the game a tie.

With the score tied in the ninth inning at 1 to 1 and the New York's having a runner, McCormick, on third base waiting for an opportunity to score and Merkle on first base looking for a similar chance, Bridwell hit into centre field. It was a fair hit ball and would have been sufficient to win the game had Merkle gone on his way down the base path while McCormick was scoring the winning run. But instead of Merkle going to second to make sure that McCormick had reached home with the run necessary to a victory, Merkle ran toward the clubhouse, evidently thinking that his share in the game was ended when Bridwell hit the ball into safe territory.

Manager Chance of the Chicago Club quickly grasped the situation and directed that the ball be thrown to second base, which would force out Merkle, who had not reached that corner.

Manager Chance, who plays first base for the Chicago club, ran to second base and the ball was thrown there, but, immediately Pitcher McGinnity interfered in the play and a scramble of players ensued, in which, it is said, McGinnity obtained the ball and threw it into the crowd before Manager Chance could complete a force play on Merkle, who was far away from the base line. Merkle said that he had touched second base, and the Chicago players were equally positive that he had not done so.

Manager Chance then appealed to Umpire O'Day, who was head umpire of the game, for a decision in the matter. The crowd, thinking that the Giants had won the game, swarmed upon the playing field in such a confusion that none of the "fans" seemed able to grasp the situation, but finally their attitude toward Umpire O'Day became so offensive that the police ran into the crowd and protected the umpire, while arguments were being hurled pro and con on the point in question by Manager Chance and McGraw and the umpire.

Umpire O'Day finally decided that the run did not count, and that inasmuch as the spectators had gained such large numbers on the field that the game could not be resumed O'Day declared the game a tie. Although both Umpires O'Day and Emslie, it is claimed, say that they did not see the play at second base, Umpire O'Day's action in declaring that McCormick's run did not count was based upon the presumption or fact that a force play was made on Merkle at second base. The rule covering such a point is as follows:

One run shall be scored every time a base runner, after having legally touched the first three bases, shall legally touch the home base before three men are put out, provided, however, that if he reach home on or during a play in which the third man be forced out or be put out before reaching first base a run shall not count. A force-out can be made only when a base runner legally loses the right to the base he occupies and is thereby obliged to advance as the result of a fair hit ball not caught on the fly.

The singular ending of the game aroused intense interest throughout the city, and everywhere it was the chief topic of discussion. Early in the evening a report was widely circulated that President Pulliam had decided the game was a tie and must be played again. When this rumor reached Mr. Pulliam he authorized the following statement:

"I made no decision in the matter at all and I will not do so until the matter is presented to me in proper form. The statement on the 'ticker' that I had decided the game a tie is entirely unauthorized."

But according to Umpire O'Day the game is a tie and will remain so until either the National League or the National Commission decides the matter. Last night Umpire O'Day made an official report of the dispute to President Pulliam. Manager Chance declared that the game was a tie, and the management of the Giants has recorded the game as a 2 to 1 victory.

The result of this game may prove to be the deciding factor in the championship race, and inasmuch as it is a serious matter to be dealt with President Pulliam may ask the league to act upon the question or go still further and place it in the hands of the National Commission—the supreme court of baseball.

In any event there will be no doubleheader this afternoon, and it may be several days before the problem will be decided. The official reporter of the league in New York credits the Giants with a victory, but, of course, this is subject to any action President Pulliam or the league may take in the matter.

President Murphy of the Chicago Club last night entered formal claim to yesterday's Chicago-New York game in behalf of Chicago. President Murphy bases his claim on the ground that Merkle of the New York team, who was at first when the ball was hit safely to centre by Bridwell in the ninth inning, had failed to continue to second when his team mate scored the winning run from third. President Murphy entered his claim in a letter to President Harry C. Pulliam of the National League, wherein Mr. Murphy cites in support of his contention the decision rendered in the game at Pittsburg, Sept. 4, between Pittsburg and Chicago, in which precisely the same contingency, he asserts, arose. The Chicago club protested the game, but the protest was not allowed, because the single umpire who officiated declared that he had not seen the play. In yesterday's game the omission of Merkle to continue to second, Mr. Murphy declares, was noted by Umpire O'Day.

CLASSY AND THRILLING BALL.

Third Battle of Leading Teams Produces Sensational Sport.

Well, anyway, it was a classy baseball game from the time in the first inning when Roger Bresnahan makes an entrance, accompanied by a dresser, who does him and undoes him in his natty mattress and knee pads, till the end of the ninth, when Bridwell singles safely to centre, bringing in what looks like the winning run.

And, from a spectacular point of view, that mix-up at the finish was just the appropriate sensation to a bang-up, all-a-quiver game. They all know they have seen a mighty snappy game of ball; that New York has brought over one more run than the enemy, whether the run counts or not; that McGinnity in holding on to the ball after the ninth-inning run, has done so with the idea that it belongs to the home team, and that good Master O'Day has said, as he exits: "I didn't see the play on second—the run doesn't count."

Up to the climactic ninth it was the toss of a coin who would win. For here is our best-beloved Mathewson pitching as only champions pitch, striking out the power and the glory of the Cubs, numbering among his slain Schulte in the first, Pfeister in the third, Steinfeldt in the fourth, Pfeister in the fifth, Hayden and Schulte in the sixth, Hayden in the eighth, and Evers and Schulte in the ninth—these last in one-two order. Proper pitching, and for this and other things we embrace him.

But then, Pfeister is pitching good ball, too. Not so good as the Matty article, for this isn't to be expected, or desired, even. Pfeister doesn't strike anybody out, and Pfeister gives an occasional base on balls, and once he hits a batter, but aside from these irregularities Pfeister must be accounted in the king row of Wednesday matinée pitchers. The gentleman who feels the weight of the delivery, and thereafter takes his base, is the plodsome McCormick. It is in the second inning, and Pfeister whirls up a curve that doesn't break right. In fact, it breaks directly in McCormick's tummy, and Pfeister is forced to figure that the joke's on him. After the heroic Dr. Creamer has emptied half a hydrant on the prostrate McCormick the latter walks wanly to first, but he has to wait to walk home till the ninth inning.

Meantime, the game has progressed swiftly, remarkable for excellent plays by a number of us on either side, and remarkable also for the in-and-out work of Evers at second for Chicago.

It is in the fifth that the Cubs, or one of them, find the solitary run that represents the day's work. Hofman has been thrown out at first by Bridwell, and then the admirable Tinker takes his bat in his hand and faces Matty with determination writ large on his expressive features. Mr. Tinker drives the ball away out to right centre for what would be a two-bagger if you or I had made it, gentle reader—and this is no disparagement of the Tinker, for he is well seeming in our sight. As the ball approaches Master Donlin this good man attempts to field it with his foot. It's a home run all right, when you get down to scoring, but if this Donlin boy was our boy we'd have sent him to bed without his supper, and ye mind that, Mike.

We found the stick all right in the sixth, and tied the score. Herzog—and, by the way, he led the batting list yesterday in the absence of Tenney; that is, the playing absence, for Fred was among those present in the stand—Herzog, then, belts boldly to Steinfeldt, and it's a hit all right, but the throw that Steinfeldt makes to first is particularly distressing, and Herzy goes on to second. Bresnahan yields up a sacrifice bunt. Donlin hits over second base; Herzog scores, and 18,000 people go out of their minds.

It is at this stage of the game that reputable prophets speak confidently of ten innings, mayhap eleven, or so many thereof as may be pulled off before day becomes night. But darkness never stops this Wednesday game at the Polo Grounds. It goes the limit without interference by the dimming skies. We fancy ourselves mightily in the ninth, after Devlin has made a clean single to centre. To be sure, Seymour has just gone out at first on a throw by Evers, but we have a chance. Devlin is on first, and the start is splendid. But here is McCormick, with a drive over to Evers, who throws out Devlin at second, and we're not very far advanced—and two are down and out. Merkle, who failed us the day before in an emergency is at bat, and we pray of him that he mend his ways. If he will only single we will ignore any errors he may make in the rest of his natural life.

On this condition, Merkle singles. McCormick advances to third, and everybody in the inclosure slaps everybody else and nobody minds. Perfect ladies are screaming like a batch of Coney barkers on the Mardi Gras occasion, and the elderly banker behind us is beating our hat to a pulp with his gold-handled cane. And nobody minds. Aided by these indications of the popular sentiment, Master Bridwell hits safely to centre, McCormick trots home, the reporter boys prepare to make an asterisk under the box score of the game with the line—"Two out when winning run was scored"—the merry villagers flock on the field to worship the hollow where the Mathewson feet have pressed, and all of a sudden there is a doings around second base. McGinnity, walking off the field with the ball, as is the custom by some member of the winning team, is held up by Tinker and Evers, who insist that the run does not count, as Merkle has not touched second. And then begins the argument which will keep us in talk for the rest of the season, and then some. Certainly the Cubs have furnished us sport.

W. W. AULICK.

Bewildering biography of a grizzly—

CHICAGO.						NEW YORK.					
	AB	R	H	PO	A		AB	R	H	PO	A
Hayden, rf.	4	0	0	1	0	Herzog, 2b.	3	1	1	1	1
Total..	30	1	5	27	15	Bres'h'n, c.	3	0	0	10	0
Schulte, lf.	4	0	0	1	0	Donlin, rf.	4	0	1	2	0
Chance, 1b.	3	0	0	11	1	Seymour,cf.	4	0	1	1	0
St'nf'dt, 2b.	2	0	0	1	0	Devlin, 3b.	4	0	2	0	2
Hofman, cf.	3	0	1	0	0	McC'm'k,lf.	3	0	0	1	0
Tinker, ss.	3	1	1	2	4	Merkle, 1b.	3	0	1	10	0
Kling, c.	3	0	1	0	1	B'dwell, ss.	4	0	1	2	3
Pfeister, p.	3	0	0	1	0	M'th's'n, p.	3	0	0	0	2
Total..	20	1	5	27	13	Total..	31	1	7	27	9

Errors—Steinfeldt, Tinker. (2.)

Chicago .... 0 0 0 0 1 0 0 0 0—1
New York .... 0 0 0 0 0 1 0 0 0—1

Home run—Tinker. Sacrifice hits—Steinfeldt, Bresnahan. Double plays—Tinker and Chance, (2;) Evers and Chance; Mathewson, Bridwell, and Merkle. Left on bases—New York, 7; Chicago, 2. First base on balls—Off Pfeister, 2. First base on errors—New York, 1. Hit by pitcher—By Pfeister, 1. Struck out—By Pfeister, none; by Mathewson, 9. Time of game—One hour and thirty minutes. Umpires—Messrs. O'Day and Emslie.

September 24, 1908

Cleveland

Wins Remarkable Game

CLEVELAND, Oct. 2.—Cleveland defeated Chicago to-day in the most remarkable game of the year in the big leagues by the score of 1 to 0. Joss, pitching for Cleveland, not only shut Chicago out without a hit, but he did not allow one of his opponents to reach first base, although the visitors used three pinch hitters in the ninth inning. Joss was aided by some remarkable support from Manager Lajoie, who made several phenomenal pickups. On the other hand, Walsh, the Chicago man, pitched a sensational game, striking out fifteen men in eight innings. He struck out Goode four times and Lajoie and Clarke twice each, and these three were Cleveland's best batters. Cleveland was able to bat but four balls past the infield, and only five of the locals reached first base. Cleveland scored its only run in the third. Birmingham led with a single. Walsh caught him napping off first, but Isbell's throw to second hit the runner in the head, and he went to third. He scored when Walsh and Schreck became crossed in their signals, and a ball went to the grand stand. With Joss at bat in the eighth, Schreck had a finger broken, which will keep him out of the game for the rest of the season. Score:

REULBACH A DOUBLE VICTOR.

Chicago Pitcher Beats Brooklyn in Both Games at Washington Park.

Every one of the twelve thousand persons who witnessed the two games played yesterday between the Chicago and Brooklyn teams was impressed with the clean-cut work of the world's champions. Manager-Captain Chance selected Reulbach to pitch the first game, with Kling behind the bat. That he made no mistake in his choice was fully proved by the 5 to 0 shut-out scored by Reulbach, and Chance sent the same battery back to work out the second game.

Reulbach did not seem to be a bit tired. He played his position so effectively in the second that a 3 to 0 shut-out was the result. Superb baseball in every detail was played by the visitors, and the only one to make a misplay was Reulbach in the second contest. He received errorless support by all his clubmates. The scores:

CHICAGO.						BROOKLYN.					
	AB	R	H	PO	A		AB	R	H	PO	A
Hayden, rf.	4	0	0	2	2	Cat'son, lf.	4	0	0	4	0
Evers, 2b.	5	1	2	4	0	Lumley, rf.	4	0	0	2	0
Schulte, lf.	4	0	1	0	Hum'll, 2b.	4	0	2	1	1
Chance, 1b.	4	0	0	8	0	Jordan, 1b.	4	0	0	8	0
St'nf'dt, 3b.	4	1	2	1	1	Burch, cf.	4	0	0	3	0
Hofman, cf.	4	0	0	1	0	McMil'n,ss.	3	0	1	1	4
Tinker, ss.	4	1	1	2	3	Sh'han, 3b.	3	0	1	0	2
Kling, c.	4	2	3	9	1	Dunn, c.	3	0	0	1	3
R'lbach, p.	3	0	1	0	Wilhelm, p.	3	0	1	0	6
Total..	36	5	10	27	11	Total..	31	0	5	27	11

Errors—Hummel, McMillan. (2.)

Chicago .... 0 0 0 0 1 0 1 2 1—5
Brooklyn .... 0 0 0 0 0 0 0 0 0—0

Two-base hits—Kling, Evers. Sacrifice hits—Hayden, Schulte, Reulbach. Stolen bases—Steinfeldt, Kling, (2.) Left on bases—Chicago, 7; Brooklyn, 5. First base on errors—Chicago, 1. Struck out—By Wilhelm, 8; by Reulbach, 7. Passed ball—Dunn. Time of game—One hour and forty minutes. Umpires—Messrs. Owens and Emslie.

SECOND GAME.

CHICAGO.						BROOKLYN.					
	AB	R	H	PO	A		AB	R	H	PO	A
Hayden, rf.	4	1	1	2	0	Cat'son, lf.	4	0	1	5	0
Evers, 2b.	4	0	1	1	1	Lumley, rf.	4	0	2	2	0
Schulte, lf.	3	0	0	1	0	H'mell, 2b.	4	0	0	1	0
Chance, 1b.	4	0	0	9	0	Jordan, 1b.	2	0	0	4	1
St'nf'dt, 3b.	4	0	1	0	0	Burch, cf.	4	0	0	2	0
H'fman, cf.	3	0	0	1	0	McM'lan,ss.	3	0	0	2	2
Tinker, ss.	4	0	0	3	0	Sh'han, 3b.	3	0	0	1	2
Kling, c.	3	1	2	6	1	Dunn, c.	2	0	0	3	3
R'lbach, p.	1	1	0	0	2	Past'rs, p.	2	0	0	1	4
						*Pattee	1	0	0	0	0
Total..	28	3	5	27	10	Total..	29	0	3	27	12

*Batted for Pasterius in the ninth inning.
Errors—Reulbach, McMillan, Dunn.

Chicago .... 0 0 1 0 0 0 0 2 0—3
Brooklyn .... 0 0 0 0 0 0 0 0 0—0

Left on bases—Chicago, 2; Brooklyn, 3. Sacrifice hits—Lumley, Reulbach. Stolen bases—Schulte. First base on balls—Off Pasterius, 3; off Reulbach, 1. Struck out—By Reulbach, 4; by Pasterius, 2. Wild pitch—Pasterius, Reulbach. Double plays—Reulbach, Tinker, and Chance; McMillan, Hummel, and Jordan. Time of game—One hour and twelve minutes. Umpires—Messrs. Emslie and Owens.

September 27, 1908

CLEVELAND.						CHICAGO					
	AB	R	H	PO	A		AB	R	H	PO	A
Goode, rf.	4	0	0	1	0	Hahn, rf.	3	0	0	1	0
Bradley, 3b.	4	0	0	0	1	Jones, cf.	3	0	0	1	0
H'ch'n, lf.	3	0	0	3	0	Isbell, 1b.	3	0	0	7	1
Lajoie, 2b.	3	0	1	2	8	D'gh'ty, lf.	3	0	0	0	0
Stovall, 1b.	3	0	0	16	0	Davis, 2b.	3	0	0	1	0
Clarke, c.	3	0	0	4	1	Parent, ss.	3	0	0	0	3
Birm'm,cf.	3	1	2	0	0	Schreck, c.	2	0	0	12	1
Perring, ss.	2	0	1	1	3	Tan'hill,2b.	2	0	0	0	1
Joss, p.	3	0	0	0	5	Walsh, p.	2	0	0	1	1
						Shaw, c.	0	0	0	2	0
						*White	1	0	0	0	0
						†Donohue	1	0	0	0	0
						‡Anderson	1	0	0	0	0
Total..	29	1	4	27	16	Total..	27	0	0	24	8

Error—Isbell.
*Batted for Shaw in ninth inning.
†Batted for Tannehill in ninth inning.
‡Batted for Walsh in ninth inning.
Cleveland .... 0 0 1 0 0 0 0 0 .—1
Chicago .... 0 0 0 0 0 0 0 0 0—0
Stolen bases—Birmingham, 2; Lajoie, Perring. First base on balls—Walsh, 1. Left on bases—Cleveland, 4; Chicago, 0. Struck out—Joss, 3; Walsh, 15. Wild pitch—Walsh, 1. Time of game—One hour and forty minutes. Umpires—Messrs. Connolly and O'Loughlin.

October 3, 1908

THE CUBS WIN THE PENNANT

Hit Mathewson for Four Runs in Third Inning of Decisive Game and Beat the Giants.

GIANTS SCORE TWO RUNS

"Three-Fingered" Brown, Chicago's Star Twirler, Has Home Team at His Mercy.

40,000 SEE GREAT CONTEST

Probably as Many More Shut Out Wall Street Left Outside—One Would-Be Spectator Killed by a Fall.

A rather bulky person, with a persistent and annoying habit of twisting his arms and legs into cabalistic designs and then shooting a ball with terrific speed and snakelike twist toward a man sixty feet away took the National League championship pennant away from the Giants at the Polo Grounds yesterday and gave it to the Chicago team in a deciding game the like of which, for spectacular setting, had never been witnessed in the history of baseball.

This pitcher, who wrung the hearts of near a hundred thousand New York fans, was referred to with an approach to familiarity, as "Three Fingered" Brown. Against him was placed the idol of New York baseball lovers, Mathewson, called sometimes "Matty," and again "Big Six," originator of the "fade away." And if it was grievous to the vast multitude who rose and yelled greetings to this "fade away" inventor, to see "Three Fingered" fan out the faithful and tried Giants it was more than grievous to behold Matty himself fade gradually until he disappeared from the box and the gangling, left-handed Wiltse taking his place to lead the forlorn hope.

The close race for the pennant carried the deciding game of yesterday beyond the length of the season because of the decision making a tie of a game which would have been won from the Chicago team by the New Yorks but for the error of judgment of First Baseman Merkle, who destroyed a run by failing to run to second base on another player's safe hit. New Yorkers felt that their team was entitled to the pennant and had won it, but they were game enough to view with keen sporting spirit the contest which resulted yesterday and confident enough to believe that they would win up to the minute the last out was made.

There is no record of a sporting event that stirred New York as did the game of yesterday. No crowd so big ever was moved to a field of contest as was moved yesterday. Perhaps never in the history of a great city, since the days of Rome. and its arena contests, has a people been pitched to such a key of excitement as was New York "fandom" yesterday.

Stormed Gates at Daybreak

The break of day found men and boys waiting at the gates of the Polo Grounds to

Champions of the Past.

Year.	Champions.	Won.	Lost.	P.C.
1876..	Chicago	52	14	.788
1877..	Boston	31	17	.645
1878..	Boston	41	19	.707
1879..	Providence	55	23	.705
1880..	Chicago	67	17	.798
1881..	Chicago	55	28	.657
1882..	Chicago	55	29	.655
1883..	Boston	63	35	.643
1884..	Providence	84	28	.750
1885..	Chicago	87	25	.776
1886..	Chicago	90	34	.725
1887..	Detroit	79	45	.637
1888..	New York	84	47	.641
1889..	New York	83	43	.639
1890..	Brooklyn	86	43	.667
1891..	Boston	87	51	.630
1892..	Boston	102	48	.680
1893..	Boston	86	44	.662
1894..	Baltimore	89	39	.695
1895..	Baltimore	87	43	.669
1896..	Baltimore	90	39	.698
1897..	Boston	93	39	.705
1898..	Boston	102	47	.685
1899..	Brooklyn	101	47	.682
1900..	Brooklyn	82	54	.603
1901..	Pittsburg	90	49	.647
1902..	Pittsburg	103	36	.745
1903..	Pittsburg	91	49	.650
1904..	New York	106	47	.693
1905..	New York	105	48	.686
1906..	Chicago	116	36	.763
1907..	Chicago	107	45	.704
1908..	Chicago	99	55	.643

secure admission hours afterward. The early morning started the flow of humanity northward through the main avenues of travel which the tight little island affords.

At 10 o'clock there were 2,000 people gathered at the gates, and in another half an hour more than 5,000, with streets beginning to bulk with human freight and streets blacken with hurrying men, women, and children.

Thousands piled upon thousands in a fearful tangle in the howwlo below Coogan's Bluff, and the rusty structure of the elevated railroad tracks. The police were swept aside like corks before a torrent, and the horses of the mounted men were pushed and jammed against the high walls surrounding the grounds.

At 12:45 o'clock, more than two hours before the appointed time for the start of the game, the last inch of standing and sitting room in the grounds had been filled, and between 35,000 and 40,000 people were in view of the field where the battle was fought out. Thousands of people congested in he aisles of the grandstand and flocking into spaces around the bleachers, suddenly burst through the bonds that kept them from the field, and a great rush was made across the grounds for places on the sward beyond the whitewash lines of the diamond.

Outside the grounds as many more would-be spectators fought or begged for admission. An hour of desperate effort, which was futile, turned he wits of hundreds to planning methods of forcing an entrance. The great 15-foot fence back of the grandstand, topped with two strands of barbed wire, was scaled by scores of men and boys. These showed an agility that was remarkable, and a daring in jumping within the grounds that one might look for, perhaps, in life convicts endeavoring to break jail. The fence at the north end of the field was also hurdled, and several hundred people got in there without paying.

So greatly was the capacity of the grounds taxed that finally the high-pitched roof of the grandstand was reached by hundreds. Toward the sky the crowd seemed to pile, and over the highest fringe of fans reared the 155th Street viaduct and Coogan's Bluff, higher yet and dense with men, women, and children.

Man Killed Trying to See Game

The elevated trains dumped thousands at the 155th Street station after it was im-

possible for them to get anywhere near the grounds. These flocked upon the tracks, seeking points of vantage, daring even the third rail. One man was killed by falling from the structure, which was the only fatality of the day. His vacant place was quickly filled.

When the crowd on the elevated structure got beyond control of the railroad employes a special detachment of police was sent to dislodge it. Those who had clambered to the tops of trains were quickly disposed of by having the trains moved away from the neighborhood, carrying the fans, wildly gesticulating and screaming protests.

With the first wild outbursts of applause inside the grounds as the spectators greeted their favorite players when they came on the field the mobs outside made even more desperate attempts to get within view of the field. Black specks could be seen climbing the thin edge of a giant sign reared high above the roof of the elevated station, and within a few minutes the top of the sign was black lined with men and boys, many of whom would have gone to certain death had the frail structure toppled. Even on the tops of signal posts of the elevated structure some of them as high as a hundred feet from the ground— said a man for each post.

Starting with only 150 policemen, under Inspector Thompson, the department did not show up well in the face of the crushing demand on it, and it was a wonder that many people were not crushed to death or trampled under foot. The universal good nature of the great throng made more to do with averting a catastrophe than did the police with clubs and horses. Reinforcements were sent for, and throughout the afternoon men were rushed to the grounds from almost every precinct in the city. Chief inspector Cortwright and Gen. Bingham both reported for duty to prepare for the outrush of the multitude at the end of the game and its orderly dispersal.

Conservative estimates put the number of persons who either witnessed the game or tried to witness it at 80,000. Other estimates went as high as 100,000 and this latter estimate may have been a good one, for there was no keeping tabs on the hundreds and thousands who rode to the grounds and turned around and rode right back without trying to reach the gates.

40,000 See Game Begun

At last 3 o'clock came. The weather was ideal for the sport. The sunshone brightly, and the shadows of the fielders were cast black and sharp cut upon the rich, velvety spread of greensward. The multitude in grandstand and on bleachers rose for one big, comforting stretch before the passing of the first ball over the plate. Then an umpire tossed a disk of white toward the pitcher's box. The ball sent up a little puff of clay dust, and Matty, the idol, baywreathed in the hearts of the thousands of New Yorkers who love the game he has played so well for them, picked up the ball and hunched himself.

One long, deafening roar from 40,000 throats went up to cheer him on to victors, and the game was on.

Sheckard picked up a bat, and, rubbing his shoes into the clay, made a firm foothold for himself. He drew back the stick, and it was easy to see that it was easy to see and understand that in Sheckard's mind and heart and soul had sprung the determination to hit that ball so hard it would never again see the field. But Matty, who was as limber and strong and clear of head as ever in his life, or will be again, sent the ball whizzing into Bresnahan's hands, and air. Sheckard smote it not.

Whiff! Whiff! Whiff! went Mr. Sheckard's bat, and as he retired from further endeavor the multitude arose again and proclaimed Matty their little idol of baseball worship with wild screams of "The Fade Away! Matty! You're giving us the pennant!"

Evers and Schulte followed and suffered a like fate, the "fade away" ball with its sudden drop toward the shanks of each batsman fooling them. The Chicagos were retired, and as Matty walked in from the box the people went crazy with excitement. The din was ear-

splitting, horns and megaphones punctuating the wild cries of exultant fans, while at regular intervals the tooting of a trumpeter split the

Then as the Chicago team went to the field the trumpeter played "Taps" over it as a last rite for the militant dead and the crowd understood and laughed a great, big, hearty laugh of delight.

The enthusiasm over the early and fatal work of the "fade" was as nothing to the enthusiasm which followed when the Giants began by sending men to the bases.Tenneygot to first by being hit by a pitched ball and Herzog sent him to second by waiting for four bad ones from Pfeister. Bresnahan struck out and Herzog was run down between first and second. But there was Mike Donlin at the bat, and if there was a human being who held a tight hold on the hearts of the fans, next to Matty, it was that same Mike.

And Mike found the ball and sent it red hot, along the first base line past Chance for a two-bagger, bringing in Tenney with the first run. The multitude was seeing the game through rose-colored spectacles now, and in its mind's eye the pennant was already done up in camphor, to float next season over New York's home grounds.

But Capt. Chance gave pause, and after pondering somewhat waved a gloved paw in the air, and "Three Fingered" Brown got in the game and Mr. Pfeister disappeared. In short order the tide turned. The way "Three Fingered" contorted his bulky person and shot the ball over the plate during the subsequent innings was awful. There was a quick subsidence of exultation. There were half-hearted toots of defiance and shrill cries from hopeful small boys, and a woman or two piped words of cheer, but the Titanic yawps of the leather-lunged 40,000 faithful had ceased.

Tinker's Slashing Three-bagger

The third inning almost brought sobs from the crowd. One Tinker of the busy Chicago crew got next to Matty's celebrated "fadeaway," and with a sharp crack the ball shot toward the sky. Smaller and smaller grew that ball, and faster and faster it sailed high above Cy Seymour's head, and all the while Mr. Tinker's stout legs were twinkling as he shot around the bases like a drab streak. When the multitude regained consciousness they beheld Mr. Tinker sitting placidly on third base.

Then Kling reached down and found and annihilated another "fade," bringing in the industrious Mr. Tinker. Thereupon "Three-Fingered" Brown took the bat and sacrificed Kling to second. Matty evidently began to see things in a blur, for he gave the next man his base on balls and let Schulte drive out a cracking hit, which brought in Kling. Evers, who meanwhile had got to first on balls, moved around to third on the hit and scored, with Schulte, when Chance drove out a hot double to right field.

Matty, from being the bay-wreathed pet of a sport-loving people had now become just a somewhat perplexed and hard-working baseball pitcher. The inning ended with the Chicago team having four runs to the Giants' one.

There had been at first some inclination on the part of the Chicago team to be disagreeable and "kick." Hofman was ordered out of the game for barking and snapping at Umpire Johnstone, but thereafter the game settled down to hard, grinding work. The plays were swift and clean, and the work of the Chicago team frequently showed head of that of the home team.

Hopes Dashed in the Seventh

Until the seventh inning things looked good and black for the Giants, and then came the one big chance to win the game and the pennant. "Three-fingered" Brown had been burning holes in the air over the plate with such success that he began to take things a bit easier. He would stop occasionally, pick up a bit of sand, and finger it in a nonchalant manner, as if to convey the idea to the 40,000 and their ball players that it was just a simple problem for him.

But the seventh inning saw the Giants

open up with fine promise and the heart came back to the crowd. Devlin singled to centre and the old yell with trimmings broke forth. McCormick followed with another clean hit, and " Three-fingered " got rattled and gave Bridwell his base on balls. Capt. Chance went to his pitcher of bulk and varied convulsions and addressed him earnestly for a few minutes. The bases were filled, and Matty was due to take the bat. But McGraw decided to replace him with Doyle, who stepped to the plate to see what he could do.

" If you knock a home run you'll be made the Governor of this State!" yelled an excited fan through a megaphone.

Instead Mr. Doyle produced nothing more than a pop foul of such insignificant nature that Kling had only to hold out his hands and let the ball drop into them. So disappointed was the crowd that a shower of empty bottles, cushions, and bundles of paper was sent toward Kling as he caught Doyle out.

Tenney by a sacrifice brought in Devlin and the score was two for the Giants against four for the "Cubs." It never changed. The big chance had been and was lost. The "Three-fingered" one was once more steady on his pins, while Matty was replaced at the start of the eighth by Wiltse.

There was no hope for the Giants after that promising but unproductive seventh, and the last half of the ninth brought a quick finish to a great game. The first three men up went out in order, and with the last play the mighty throng of fans poured forth across the field and started for home to fight all over again a wordy baseball contest. The game had been cleanly fought and was lost because New York's opponents were better ball players and "Three-fingered" Brown had once again sent down to defeat Matty, the pride of Manhattan and inventor of the " fade away."

* * * * *

The score:

CHICAGO.						NEW YORK.					
	AB	R.	H	PO	A		AB	R.	H	PO	A
Sheck'd, lf.	4	0	0	4	0	Tenney, 1b.	2	1	1	9	0
Evers, 2b.	3	1	1	0	3	Herzog, 2b.	3	0	0	1	2
Schulte, rf.	4	1	1	4	0	Bres'h'n, c.	4	0	1	10	2
Chance, 1b.	4	0	3	13	0	Donlin, rf.	4	0	1	0	0
St'nf'dt, 3b.	4	0	1	0	3	Seym'r, cf.	3	0	2	9	0
Hofm'n, cf.	0	0	0	0	0	Devlin, 3b.	4	1	1	2	0
Howard, cf.	4	0	0	1	0	McC'm'k,lf.	6	1	3	1	1
Tinker, ss.	4	1	1	4	4	B'dwell, ss.	3	0	0	0	1
Kling, c.	3	1	1	4	1	M'th'son, p.	2	0	0	0	3
Pfeister, p.	0	0	0	0	0	*Doyle	1	0	0	0	0
Brown, p.	2	0	0	0	1	Wiltse, p.	0	0	0	0	0
Total	32	4	8	27	12	Total	30	2	5	27	9

Error—Tenney.
*Batted for Mathewson in seventh inning.
Chicago ....0 0 4 0 0 0 0 0 0—4
New York ....1 0 0 0 0 1 0 0 0—2
Two-base hits—Donlin, Schulte, Chance, Evers. Three-base hit—Tinker. Hits—Off Pfeister, 1 in two-thirds of an inning; off Brown, 4 in eight and one-third innings; off Mathewson, 7 in seven innings; off Wiltse, 1 in two innings. Sacrifice hits—Tenney, Brown. Double plays—Kling and Chance, McCormick and Bresnahan. Left on bases—Chicago, 3; New York, 6. First base on balls—Off Pfeister, 2; off Brown, 1; off Mathewson, 2. First base on error—Chicago, 1. Hit by pitcher—By Pfeister, 1. Struck out—By Mathewson, 7; by Wiltse, 2; by Pfeister, 1; by Brown, 1. Time of game—One hour and forty minutes. Umpires—Messrs. Johnstone and Klem.

October 9, 1908

30,000 SEE GIANTS LOSE TO SUPERBAS

Lumley Starts to Break Up Game with His Bat in Thirteenth Inning.

RALLY FOLLOWS HIS DRIVE

Pitcher Ames, Who Had Been Invincible, Then Weakens, and Brooklyn Quickly Scores Three Runs.

Manager Lumley, who is also right fielder for the Brooklyn team, called the Superbas and took his stand at the home plate yesterday afternoon at the Polo Grounds. The Giants in their new white suits were watching him closely, because they were watching everything at that stage of the game. The 30,000 people in the grand stand and the bleachers and upon Coogan's Bluff did not pay particular attention to him. It was the first half of the thirteenth inning, and the score stood nothing to nothing. Brooklyn's Sebring had been put out.

"Ah!"—a long, low, expiratory, ever-increasing cry of surprise, joy, and disgust started in the bleachers, rose through the grand stand, went on up the rocks to the Coogan reserved stands, and came billowing back to the diamond. For Manager Lumley had lifted the ball with a sharp crack over second base, over the centre fielder's head, and against the fence in front of the eastern bleachers. And while the outfielders were chasing it Manager Lumley was racing around the bases. He stopped at the third. And still the crowd was sighing and wailing and yelling and stamping on the boards.

Ames Meets His Waterloo.

That was the beginning of the way the Brooklyn Superbas won the first game of the season from the renowned Giants. For this three-base hit seemed to stagger the Giants a little; it put a fierce flow of life into the Brooklyn team. Capt. Tenney talked with Pitcher Ames. Ames pitched balls far away from Batter Jordan, who walked to the first base. Lennox knocked a ball to centre field, which brought in Lumley. Bergen put a ball into right field, which brought in Jordan. Burch bunted toward third base, and Devlin would not pick up the ball, thinking it would go foul. It did not go foul, and Lennox ran home. This made three for Brooklyn. The Giants had one inning to catch up. The crowd in the grand stand, in the bleachers, on Coogan's Bluff even, howled out their commands:

"Put in the Indian!"
"Give us Meyers. He can hit a ball."
"Oh, for Donlin now!"

But the Indian did not get to the bat early enough. Donlin was far away on the vaudeville stage. Two Giants knocked long flies, which were easily caught, and then, after a man or two of theirs got on the bases, another was easily put out at first by Brooklyn Pitcher Wilhelm.

Three to nothing, and in favor of Brooklyn! And this the first game of the season, too! The crowd poured down on the field. The Giants ran out. Brooklyn supporters stopped awhile to yell. The Giant supporters were vehement in their comments as they went out of the Polo Grounds.

Poor Start for Giants.

Where was McGraw that he didn't put in the Indian sooner? He was away with

a hand cut, having undergone a slight operation. Why hadn't Mathewson been used some? He, too, had suffered an accident to his hand. Well, it was a fearful beginning, the Giant men growled. But there will be a big crowd there to-day.

The 30,000 people began to get into the Polo Grounds about noon, though the game was not to be called until 4 o'clock. In the morning the skies had been a little dark, so that fears had been felt that maybe it would rain again yesterday, thus spoiling a good beginning day as it had done Wednesday. But the sun remained out almost all afternoon, darkened only for a moment or two by a stray cloud.

The grass was green. The diamond with more than two inches of recent rain soaked into it looked solid; the drainage had done good work, and the sun had done better. The crowd spread around through the grand stand and then upon the old bleachers. They then advanced upon the new bleachers back of centre field. Spreading through and away from both ends of the grand stand the crowd almost touched far out beyond centre field, making almost a complete circle of wild, tense beings. They were hungry for baseball; their appetite had been whetted for six months by news about this and that Giant and Superba; now they wanted to see them get down to business.

First Straw Hat of Season.

At 1:58 o'clock a lone man in a straw hat walked into the northern bleachers. He was greeted with vociferous enthusiasm. The young army of photographers, who had been taking the pictures of ball players, rushed to get the man with the straw hat.

At 2 o'clock a few Brooklyn players in gray drifted through the gate. Five minutes later the Giants, all diked out in cream white new suits, came trailing through the big gate. The players did not march around the diamond, according to the old custom on opening days. They all got upon the diamond in some way and began to limber up. The crowd had two hours in which to watch them gambol.

The Indian catcher Meyers seemed to be the most popular Giant present, though he is a new man. His two home runs last week have boosted him high in notoriety. "Hello, Chief," a thousand called. "Get in the game and lift 'em over the fence."

In the grandstand behind the catcher's box was a crank who wanted to be noticed. He arose and began to say things against the Giants. He was noticed. Some 500 people around him threw everything at him they could lay their hands on. Moreover, throughout the game they pelted him whenever they were dissatisfied with the progress of the game.

The various significant gongs having sounded and the gray and white players having exercised themselves in the classic way, the gong rang for the beginning of the game. The crowd had been held in suspense a long time; it was at a high pitch. The Giants trotted out on the field. The crowd cheered. Umpire Johnstone buckled on his chest protector, swept off the home plate with his toy whiskbroom, and put on his mask.

Mr. Croker Tosses Out the Ball.

Richard Croker, in a box just behind the catcher's stand, acting for Mayor McClellan, threw the new ball out into the field. Left Fielder Burch took the bat for the visitors from across the bridge. Ames prepared to do his best. Catcher Schlei, and not the Indian, took the position behind the bat.

Ames got both hands behind his head. He screwed up his face. He blew upon the ball. He surveyed the batter fixedly, as if to hypnotise him at long range. He may have spat upon the ball. He worked it around in his mit. He seemed suddenly to have a convulsion. The ball was in Schlei's hand with a hard " paff."

"Str-rike." bellowed Johnstone. The crowd bellowed back at him.

And so the game began at 4 o'clock, ending long after 6 o'clock. A man was hit by a foul ball, but was not hurt badly. The 30,000 spectators saw nothing but big round zeros rise on the huge black bulletin board across the field for twelve innings. They saw their admiration for Brooklyn rising steadily. The game went on with little spectacular incident until the thirteenth, and then came the cataclysm.

Which will be good for the gate receipts to-day.

HOW GAME WAS PLAYED.

Wonderful Exhibition of Pitching

The game produced one of the most hotly contested pitchers' battles ever witnessed on the local diamond. For thirteen innings Wilhelm for Brooklyn and Ames for New York battled for supremacy, but the former won out. It was a brilliant exhibition of pitching, especially for sc early in the season. Whether it is that the pitchers are unusually well advanced this year or whether the players are below their batting form, does not detract from the exhibition. Ames pitched a no-hit game up to the tenth inning, and had his teammates given him good batting support, the New York pitcher might have earned a new laurel. While Ames was doing great things for the Giants, Wilhelm suffered little by comparison, as he pitched a great game for the team on the other side of the bridge.

To Lumley largely belongs the credit of victory. He smashed out a three-bagger, which robbed Ames of his nerve. The next man, Jordan, was purposely walked, and this proved Ames's undoing, as three singles followed in succession, and the damage was past repair. The fielding was very clean, several beautiful stops punctuating the contest, and the returns were in the main swift and true.

A mighty roar greeted the downfall of Burch, the first Brooklyn man to face Ames. He received but three balls, and fanned the air each time he essayed to smite the leather. Clever pickups by Fletcher at second were responsible for the dismissal of both Alperman and Hummell. It was a joyous greeting for Ames as he returned to the players' bench. Herzog led the Giants' batting list. His was a weak effort, and Alperman threw him out at first. Jordan did not require any assistance to dispose of Fletcher, and Murray retired the side when he died at first on Wilhelm's easy toss to Jordan.

Sebring was no trouble for Ames and Tenney, but Lumley put up the first kick when Umpire Cusack called him out at first. It was a close decision, but Bridwell's throw beat the runner. Jordan tried in vain to locate the ball.

Tenney opened the Giants' second inning, but died in an effort to reach the initial bag after propelling the sphere to Alperman. O'Hara's patience was rewarded with a base on balls, and he showed his appreciation of the kindness by stealing second. Devlin also walked, and New York's chances began to take a roseate hue. Bridwell forced Devlin at second and O'Hara went on to third. The Giants' shortstop made a desperate effort to steal second, but failed in his attempt. The game passed on through the following innings until the eighth, when the first hit came.

Then O'Hara went out, Alperman to Jordan. Devlin received his base by courtesy of Wilhelm, and the latter purposely added another base on balls when Bridwell came to bat. Two men on bases and one down looked good to the fans. Schlei made a clean single to Sebring in centre field. Devlin started for home, but the throw to Bergen was true and Devlin was nailed at the plate. Ames dissipated any lingering hope when he died at first.

The extra innings session began when Bridwell disposed of Burch on a smart return to Tenney. Alperman then spoiled Ames's no-hit record by driving the ball to left field for two bases. He was advanced to third on Hummel's out, Fletcher to Tenney, but Sebring was unable to send him over the plate. A faint hope fanned the breasts of the faithful in the second half of the inning. Tenney was an easy out for Wilhelm and Jordan. O'Hara walked, as did Devlin. Bridwell's out advanced O'Hara and Devlin each a base, but Schlei could not produce the necessary hit. The next two innings were nonproductive and the game passed into the thirteenth.

This was unlucky for the Giants, and when the smoke of the battle cleared away, the Brooklynites had secured a safe lead and clinched the game. Ames and Tenney were responsible for Sebring's dismissal. Lumley smashed out a three-bagger, and Tenney held a heart-to-heart conference with Ames. The result was Leon sent Jordan to first on balls. A long single by Lennox scored Lumley, and the local fans discerned the handwriting on the wall. A heavy pall hung over the field, which was intensified when Bergen added another single. Murray fielded the ball, and made a good throw to the plate, but Schlei let it pass through his legs, and Jordan added the second run. Wilhelm fouled to Tenney, Burch bunted down the third-base line. Devlin let the ball roll, thinking it would go foul, but it rolled safe, and Lennox crossed the plate. Alperman closed the inning by striking out. The Giants were powerless in their half. The score:

BROOKLYN.	AB	R	H	PO	A
Burch, lf.	6	0	1	5	0
Alp'man, 2b.	6	0	2	2	10
Hum'l, ss	5	0	0	3	3
Sebring, cf.	3	0	0	3	1
Lumley, rf.	5	1	1	1	0
Jordan, 1b.	4	1	1	19	0
Lennox, 3b.	4	1	1	1	2
Bergen, c.	5	0	1	5	2
Wilheim,	5	0	0	0	4
Total	45	3	7	39	22

NEW YORK.	AB	R	H	PO	A
Herzog, lf.	6	0	1	0	0
Fletcher, 2b.	5	0	0	0	7
*McC'mick	1	0	0	0	0
Murray, rf.	5	0	0	0	1
Tenney, 1b.	5	0	0	24	1
O'Hara, cf.	3	0	0	0	0
Devlin, 3b.	2	0	0	0	0
B'dwell, ss.	4	0	0	4	7
Schlei, c.	4	0	1	10	1
Ames, p.	4	0	0	1	9
†J. Myers	1	0	1	0	0
Total	40	0	3	39	26

*Batted for Fletcher in the thirteenth inning.
†Batted for Ames in the thirteenth inning.
Errors—Lennox, Fletcher, Schlei.

Brooklyn	0	0	0	0	0	0	0	0	0	0	0	0	3	—3
New York	0	0	0	0	0	0	0	0	0	0	0	0	0	—0

Two-base hits—Alperman, (2.) Jordan. Three-base hit—Lumley. Stolen bases—O'Hara, Burch. Left on bases—Brooklyn, 5; New York, 8. First base on errors—Brooklyn, 1; New York, 1. Double play—Fletcher, Bridwell, and Tenney. Struck out—By Ames, 10; by Wilhelm, 4. Bases on balls—Off Wilhelm, 7; off Ames, 2. Umpires—Messrs. Johnstone and Cusack. Time of game—Two hours and twenty minutes.

April 16, 1909

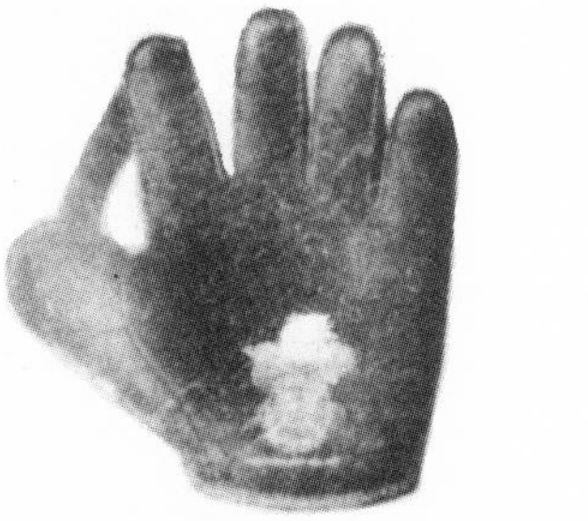

Ball Makes Triple Play Unassisted.

CLEVELAND, Ohio, July 19.—Cleveland and Boston broke even to-day in the first double-header of the year here, Cleveland winning the first, 6 to 1, and Boston the second, 3 to 2. Ball's playing was a decided feature. He made an unassisted triple play in the second inning, and when he came to bat in the same inning he hit for a home run to deep centre. He had six more put outs than either the first baseman or the catcher. Scores:

FIRST GAME.

CLEVELAND.	AB	R	H	PO	A
Flick, rf.	4	2	1	0	[illegible]
Stovall, 1b.	3	0	1	6	2
Easterly, c.	4	1	1	6	[illegible]
H'hman, lf.	3	1	2	1	0
Perring, 2b.	3	0	0	3	3
B'r'ham, cf.	4	0	2	2	0
Bradley, 3b.	4	1	1	0	0
Ball, ss.	4	1	2	9	2
Young, p.	3	0	0	0	2
Total	[illegible]	6	10	27	[illegible]

BOSTON.	AB	R	H	PO	A
Niles, lf.	4	0	1	1	[illegible]
Lord, 3b.	4	0	0	1	0
Speaker, cf.	3	0	0	1	1
Gessler, rf.	4	0	1	0	2
Wagner, ss.	4	0	1	2	5
Stahl, 1b.	4	1	3	9	0
McCon'l, 2b.	2	0	0	4	4
Donohue, c.	3	0	1	5	2
Chech, p.	1	0	0	0	0
Collins, p.	2	0	1	1	2
*Welter	1	0	0	0	0
†Gardner	1	0	0	0	0
Total	[illegible]	1	6	24	16

*Batted for Donohue in ninth inning.
†Batted for Collins in ninth inning.
Errors—Stovall, Ball, Gessler, (2.) Stahl.

Cleveland	1	1	2	0	0	0	0	2	..	—6
Boston	0	0	0	0	0	0	1	0	0	—1

Two-base hit—Ball. Home run—Ball. Sacrifice hits—Perring, McConnell. Sacrifice fly—Hinchman. Stolen bases—Hinchman, McConnell. Double play—Collins and Stahl. Triple play—Ball. (unassisted.) Hits—Off Chech, 6 in three innings; off Collins, 4 in five innings. First base on balls—Off Young, 1; off Chech, 1. Hit by pitched balls—By Young, 1, (Speaker;) by Chech, 1, (Flick.) Struck out—By Young, 2; by Chech, 1; by Collins, 2. Passed ball—Donohue. First base on errors—Cleveland, 3; Boston, 1. Left on bases—Cleveland, 5; Boston, 8. Time of game—One hour and forty-one minutes. Umpires—Messrs. Kerin and Sheridan.

July 20, 1909

Cleveland and St. Louis Divide Double Header, Closing the Season.

ST. LOUIS, Mo., Oct. 9.—Cleveland and St. Louis divided a double-header today, the locals winning the first 5 to 4, and the visitors taking the second 3 to 0. Lajoie got eight hits in eight times at bat. Today's games closed the local season. Scores:

FIRST GAME

ST. LOUIS	AB	R	H	PO	A
Tru'd'e 2b.	5	0	0	1	3
Cor'den, 3b.	5	2	3	1	1
Stone, lf.	5	0	2	1	0
Griggs, 1b.	5	1	0	13	1
Wallace, ss.	3	0	1	3	6
North'n, cf.	4	0	0	2	0
H'rtzell, rf.	3	2	1	1	0
Stephens, c	3	0	2	4	4
Nelson, p.	3	0	1	1	6
Total	36	5	10	27	21

CLEVELAND	AB	R	H	PO	A
Bronkie, 3b	3	1	1	1	1
Graney, lf.	4	1	1	4	0
Jackson, cf.	4	1	2	1	0
Lajole, 2b.	4	1	4	4	1
East'ly, rf.	4	0	0	1	0
Stovall, 1b.	4	0	2	7	0
Smith, c.	4	0	0	4	1
P'k'p'h, ss.	4	0	0	2	6
Brand'g, p.	4	0	0	0	1
Total	35	4	10	24	10

None out when winning run was scored.
Errors—Truesdale, Wallace, Bronkie.

St. Louis	1	1	1	0	0	1	0	0	1	—5
Cleveland	3	1	0	0	0	0	0	0	0	—4

SECOND GAME

CLEVELAND	AB	R	H	PO	A
Bir'h'm, 3b.	4	1	2	1	5
Graney, lf.	5	2	0	1	0
Jackson, cf.	4	0	2	1	0
Lajole, 2b.	4	0	4	0	4
East'ly, rf.	4	0	0	2	0
Hn'h'st, 1b.	3	0	1	18	0
McGuire, c.	3	0	0	2	1
P'k'p'h, ss.	4	0	1	2	4
Falk'b'g, p.	3	0	0	0	5
Total	34	3	10	27	19

ST. LOUIS	AB	R	H	PO	A
Tr'dale, 2b.	4	0	0	2	0
Cor'den, 3b	4	0	2	3	1
Stone, lf.	4	0	1	0	0
Griggs, 1b.	4	0	0	10	0
Wallace, ss.	3	0	1	1	4
North'n, cf.	3	0	0	2	0
H'rtzell, rf.	3	0	1	2	0
O'Con'er, c.	0	0	0	1	0
Malloy, p.	3	0	0	0	5
Killifer, c.	3	0	0	6	2
Total	31	0	5	27	12

Eroors—Truesdale, Corriden, Malloy, Graney, (2).

Cleveland	1	0	2	0	0	0	0	0	0	—3
St. Louis	0	0	0	0	0	0	0	0	0	—0

Two-base hits—Jackson, Corriden, Griggs, Graney, Stephens. Three-base hits—Lajoie, Griggs. Sacrifice hit—Stephens. Stolen bases—Bronkie, Stovall, Griggs. Wild pitch—Blanding. Bases on balls—Off Nelson, 1; off Blanding, 4. struck out—By Nelson, 4; by Blanding, 4. Left on bases—St. Louis, 12; Cleveland, 5. Time of game—One hour and forty-two minutes. Umpire—Mr. Evans.

Two-base hits—Birmingham, Corriden. Sacrifice hit—Lajoie. Double plays—Malloy, Truesdale, and Griggs; Lajoie, Peckinpaugh, and Hohnhorst. Passed balls—McGuire, Killifer. Stolen base—Stone. Hit by pitched ball—By Malloy (McGUIRE.(Wild pitch—Malloy. Bases on balls—Off Malloy, 4. Struck out—By Malloy, 6; by Falkenberg, 1. Left on bases—St. Louis, 4; Cleveland, 10. Time of game—One hour and sixteen minutes. Umpire—Mr. Evans.

October 10, 1910

Lajole Leads Cobb In Batting.

CLEVELAND, Ohio, Oct. 9.—By making eight hits in eight times at bat in St. Louis to-day, Napoleon Lajoie of the Cleveland team pulled ahead of Tyrus Cobb of Detroit in the race for the batting championship of the American League. According to the unofficial figures, Lajoie's average now is 386.8 and Cobb's 383.4.

October 10, 1910

Hans Wagner, the hard hitting shortstop of the Pittsburg team, doesn't like to have photographers snapping at him during a ball game. Like many ball players he has superstition in plenty and believes that a photograph taken while handling his favorite bat might have a disastrous effect on his great batting average. When the above photograph was taken Wagner heard the click of the shutter and jumping to his feet, threw his bat at the camera. It didn't connect, and consequently this remarkable picture of the mighty Teuton, fondling the old bat which has made him a terror in baseball, was made possible.

Last year was the thirteenth season that Wagner's batting average has been more than .300. He started to break the fences in 1897, when he finished with a mark of .343. Each year since his mark has been high, and in 1900 he had his greatest year, making 201 hits during the season for an average of .380. In 1908, he again made 201 hits, and had an average of .354. Last year Wagner finished the season with a mark of .320.

May 7, 1911

Hans Wagner

Copyright American Press Association.

Walsh Pitches No Hit Game

CHICAGO, Aug. 27.—Ed. Walsh pitched the first no-hit, no-run game of his career to-day against Boston. It was the second game of this kind this season in the American League. Chicago won, 5 to 0. Only one of the visitors reached first base. Engle getting a base on balls. The locals fielded well behind Walsh, who struck out eight batsmen. Wood of Boston is the only other man who has pitched a hitless and runless game in this league this season. The locals bunched hits off Collins, and with the assistance of an error and a wild pitch scored five runs. Early in the game Henriksen and Speaker collided when running for Tannehill's long fly. Speaker retired from the game and Henriksen was taken to a hospital suffering severe pains in the shoulders, ribs, and legs.

The score:

CHICAGO.						BOSTON.					
	AB	R	H	PO	A		AB	R	H	PO	A
M'Intyre, rf.	5	1	1	3	0	Hen'ks'n, rf.	4	0	0	0	0
Lord, 3b	3	0	1	0	3	Riggert, rf.	3	0	0	1	0
Callah'n, lf.	4	1	1	0	0	Speaker, cf.	1	0	0	0	0
Bodie, cf.	4	1	2	1	0	Will'ms,1b.	2	0	0	6	0
M'Con'l,2b.	4	0	1	0	5	Engle, 1b. &					
T'n'hill, ss.	4	1	2	0	8	cf.	2	0	0	4	1
Mullen, 1b.	3	0	0	17	0	Lewis, lf.	3	0	0	3	0
Block, c.	4	0	2	6	3	G'dner, 3b.	3	0	0	1	5
Walsh, p.	4	1	1	0	2	Car'gan, c.	3	0	0	4	0
						Wagner, 2b.	3	0	0	1	0
Total.	35	5	11	27	15	Yerkes, ss.	3	0	0	4	3
						Collins, p.	2	0	0	0	1
						*N'nam'ker.	1	0	0	0	0
						Total.	27	0	0	24	10

*Batted for Collins in the ninth inning. Errors—Williams, Engle.

Chicago .... 3 0 0 0 0 0 1 1 .—5
Boston .... 0 0 0 0 0 0 0 0 0—0

Two-base hits—McConnell, Lord, Tannehill. Three-base hits—McIntyre, Tannehill. Sacrifice hits—Lord, Mullen. Left on bases—Chicago, 8; Boston, 1. First base on balls—Off Walsh, 1. Struck out—By Walsh, 8; by Collins, 1. Wild pitch—Collins. Time of game—One hour and fifty minutes. Umpires—Messrs. Evans and Mullen.

August 28, 1911

COBB'S GREAT RECORD

Detroit Player Leads in Hitting, Run-Getting, and Base-Running.

The official batting averages of the American League were announced last night by President Ban Johnson, and they differ only slightly from unofficial averages of the players already announced. Ty Cobb, the Detroit slugger, of course tops the list with an average of .420, which is only two points short of equaling the league record of .422 made by Lajoie when he was a member of the Philadelphia club in 1901. Second to Cobb is Joe Jackson of Cleveland, who has an average of .408. Birdie Cree is the highest Yankee in the list, and ranks ninth among the batsmen, with an average of .348.

The world's champion Athletics have seven men in the select .300 class, Collins leading with .365. The others are Lapp, .353; "Home Run" Baker, .334; Murphy, .329; McInnes, .321; Coombs, .319, and Lord, .310. Baker, the hero of the World's Series, leads the home-run hitters with a total of nine circuit smashes, while Cobb is close behind him with eight. Jackson of Cleveland had seven home runs, and Ping Bodie of the White Sox, who came into the league heralded as a sensation, had four home runs all season, one of which was made on the Hilltop last Summer.

The Athletics lead the league in club batting, with an average of .299, with Detroit second with .291. The Yankees ranked fifth in team batting, with an average of .270.

Cobb of Detroit also led the league in run-getting, scoring 147 times, and also made the largest number of hits, 248. Of these, 47 were two-base hits and 24 were three-base drives. Cobb is the leader in stolen bases, with a total of 83, and Milan of Washington is second, with 58. Cree of the Yankees is third, with 48 stolen bases.

Other members of the New York team in the .300 class of batters are Chase, .315; Brockett, .308; Wolter, .304, and Dolan, .304.

November 6, 1911

TWENTY GREATEST PLAYS

Baseball Men Make Their Selection of Most Notable Achievements.

Bill Dahlen—Lejeune's throw home, which hit a fan in the left field bleachers.

Christy Mathewson—Frank Baker's home run off Rube Marquard.

Rube Marquard—Frank Baker's home run off Christy Mathewson.

Dee Scanlon—Myself, Bill Bergen, and George Bell pulling off a triple steal.

Clarke Griffith—Jack Chesbro's wild pitch, which cost New York a pennant.

Connie Mack—Ames's throw in the final game of the 1911 world's series. The ball bounded off Barry's head and four runs scored.

Joe Cantillon—John Anderson's slide as he stole second with the bases full.

John McGraw—Merkle's dash for the clubhouse while Johnny Evers was tagging second base on that late September day in 1908.

Bill Finneran—Sherwood Magee's strikeout when he made a hit off the umpire.

Fielder Jones—When the ball hit Dave Altizer's head and was caught, giving Dave an assist and a putout.

Larry Doyle—That fake force play by Barry and Collins while Baker caught a high fly and doubled Barry at first base.

Andy Coakley—That safe hit I made back rear the close of the 1905 season.

Silk O'Loughlin—The assist by the Philadelphia policeman, who prevented Sam Crawford from catching a fly ball in that memorable seventeen-inning game in 1905.

Bill Donovan—Charley Schmidt's passed ball in the first game of the Detroit-Chicago series of 1907, which cost the Tigers the game.

Bill Klem—Larry Doyle's failure to touch the plate in the fifth world's series game. Nobody else saw it.

Tim Hurst—Kid Elberfeld's attempt to score from second through the pitcher's box.

Ty Cobb—These eight hits that Larry Lajoie grabbed in one afternoon just at the close of the 1910 season.

Frank Chance—Larry McLean trying to make a clean steal of third base against Johnny Kling in his prime.

Hugh Duffy—Germany Schaefer's steal of first base from second against the White Sox at Washington last July when ten Chicago players were on fair ground at the time of the putout.

Jimmy Callahan—Nick Altrock's discovery of the only thing that Ty Cobb cannot hit—a base on balls.

December 31, 1911

DETROIT TEAM OUT ON STRIKE

Won't Play Until Cobb, Who Beat Defenseless Cripple at Game, Is Reinstated.

NEW MOVE IN BASEBALL

Entire Squad Walks Off Field, Leaving Jennings to Utilize Amateur Nine.

DISAFFECTION MAY SPREAD

Effort to Get Stars of Other Clubs to Join Revolt Against President Johnson.

Special to The New York Times.

PHILADELPHIA, May 18.—Nineteen baseball players, comprising the regular team of the Detroit Tigers, three-time champions of the American League, made baseball history at Shibe Park this afternoon by going on strike and refusing to play the Athletics, following the refusal of B. B. Johnson, President of the league, to lift the suspension against Tyrus Raymond Cobb, the Detroit's star outfielder, who, last Wednesday, climbed into the grand stand during the game with the New York Highlanders and mauled a spectator who had said things reflecting upon the player.

Just as if they were freight handlers, New England millworkers, striking longshoremen, or belonging to any of the disaffected class of craftsmen who have wage troubles, the athletes paraded off the field just before the hour for calling play—literally a walk-out.

"Hughey" Jennings, manager of the Tigers, recruited a team on the field, played the Athletics with these "misfits" and thus avoided the imposition of a $1,000 fine, as prescribed by the rules of the league. The score was: Athletics, 24; Detroit, 2.

As the regular Detroit players left the field, the Saturday half-holiday crowd of more than 15,000 spectators, arose and cheered. A few hissed, but their hisses were drowned in the roar of cheers and handclapping. The spectators had an inkling of conditions, and when the players started from the field, the occupants of the stands knew what had taken place.

Jennings, with the venerable "Deacon" Jim McGuire, former Cleveland manager, but now a Tiger scout, and the cotton-topped "Joe" Sugden, who at some time or other has played on nearly every team in either league, alone remained on the field. Jennings had said that his sympathies were with his players, but he had promised President Navin of the Detroit Club that he would have nine men on the field to meet the Athletics, and he made good this promise.

Veteran Catchers at Work.

McGuire and Sugden, both veteran catchers, were mustered into service first, although it had been years since they were active on the diamond. Through the stands was carried the rumor that Jennings wanted volunteers. By the dozens, amateurs, semi-professionals, and college athletes left their seats and swarmed around the Detroit bench trying to look like real ball players.

Jennings sorted over the bunch and picked out six likely-looking young men. They were hustled into the dressing rooms under the grandstand and told to jump into the Detroit traveling uniforms. They put on a broad grin with their suits, for Jennings announced that each would receive $30 for his services for the afternoon.

Out on the field trotted the "misfits." In their uniforms they looked to the average fan like the regular Detroit team. Sugden picked up a glove and ran down to first base like a colt. "Deacon" McGuire strapped on a breast protector, shoved his left hand into a catcher's mitt and took his stand to receive the delivery of "Al" Travers, manager and formerly the star pitcher of St. Joseph's College team.

McGarvey and McGarr, old Georgetown College stars, went to left field and second base respectively. "Billy" Maig, a former lightweight pugilist, got a job. He was recommended by "Bill" Burns, one of the "rebels," who a short time ago pitched for the Phillies. Maig cast anchor off third base. "Joe" Harrigan, who has a reputation in Southwark, was sent out to plug up the gap at shortstop. E. Ward, who played right, and "Billy" Feinhauser, whom Jennings sent to centre field, nobody knew, but they played, just the same.

Players in the Grandstand.

Although it was not generally known by the crowd, the striking Detroit players witnessed the game from the stand. They had left the grounds and boarded taxicabs, but instead of going to the hotel, they returned by a round-about way, and, buying tickets, entered as spectators. They were scattered all through the stand. Jim Delehanty was in the lower stand.

"Yes, the boys are all here," he said as the game was about to begin, "but they are scattered around. This is great. I wouldn't have missed it for a minute."

Owen Bush, in another part of the upper pavilion, voiced the same sentiment. "It's a circus," he declared. "I'm glad I came."

Connie Mack, manager and part owner of the Champion Athletics, took advantage of the remarkable line-up and put in several of his substitutes, including Magert and Strunk. Jack Coombs faced the patched-up aggregation and Lapp took his delivery.

What the final outcome of the controversy will be no person seems willing to-night to predict. The players are forecasting that it means an upheaval in organized baseball, and the final triumph of the players over the officers of the League. The Detroit players spent most of the morning sending telegrams to their friends on other American League teams asking them to take similar action and walk out unless Cobb was reinstated immediately and kept reinstated until after a hearing.

It is known that such telegrams were sent to Joe Wood, pitcher for the Boston Red Sox, and Harry Lord, Captain of the Chicago White Sox, which finished a series in Boston yesterday afternoon. Lord and Wood were requested to act as leaders in obtaining an expression of sympathy in such a movement among players of their respective teams. Dispatches from Boston to-night said that neither Lord nor Wood would discuss the action they would take.

Answers from other players, however, were received to-night, and the Detroit players made no secret of their belief that a splendid nucleus had been lined up to make the walk-out a real revolt. They refused to give the names of the players of the other clubs who have agreed to join them.

The players expressed the best feeling toward the owners of the Detroit Club, but were outspoken in their criticism of Mr. Johnson. They said that if the matter is not settled they may go on a "barnstorming trip."

"Besides the money to be made on a barnstorming trip," said one of the players, "there is the new United States League, which we have reason to believe will open its doors to us."

Everything around the Aldine Hotel, where the Detroit players are putting up, sizzled all morning. Manager Jennings awakened to find a telegram from President Johnson awaiting

him. The telegram told Jennings in so many words that Johnson was the boss and in charge of the situation. The message read:

Cobb's suspension stands until the matter is fully investigated. If the teams refuse to play that is a matter for the club owners to make good on. The umpire would have put the man off the stand. Cobb had no right to attack him.

Immediately after receiving the message Jennings called a meeting of his players. It was an executive session, and although Jennings's sympathy is with the men, he used all his arguments to persuade them to play this afternoon.

Statement from Hugh Jennings.

Immediately upon their refusal Jennings took a taxi cab to call on numerous old friends to assist him in getting together a team. Before he left the Aldine Jennings issued this statement regarding his personal attitude:

The boys are determined, and in order to protect the Detroit club owners I am going scouting around for players in order to play a team on the field this afternoon. Failure to do so means that a fine of $5,000 will be imposed in addition to the forfeiture of the game. Its a good lesson for the club owners. They must realize that the players must be protected from insult.

Asked if he had made a report of the

New York incident to Mr. Johnson, Mr. Jennings said that he had, and that he had also told him that Cobb was justified, and that he knew several New York men who would make affidavits that the language of the spectator was insulting.

Cobb, after reading President Johnson's statement, made this comment:

"Johnson has always believed himself to be infallible. He suspends a man first and investigates afterward. It should be the reverse."

"I know from my own experiences as a ball player that one gets little sympathy from the grand stand and far less from the bleachers, and some of the things a big league player is forced to listen to make one's blood boil in resentment," was Connie Mack's reply to a request for his views. "Yet I think they can adopt more telling methods than by going into the spectator's reservations and dealing out summary punishment."

Players in Secret Meeting.

The members of the team held a secret meeting at the Aldine Hotel to-night, but outside of the announcement that they will stick to the agreement they signed to support Cobb and refrain from playing ball until he is reinstated, they revealed no move in their plans.

Tyrus Raymond Cobb

Moriarty, the third baseman, said they were marking time until Frank Navin, the owner of the club, arrives from Detroit. He left there last evening and is due some time to-morrow. Manager Jennings is also awaiting not only the arrival of Mr. Navin, but President Johnson as well. A message that he was coming here was received by Jennings to-night.

None of the players would attempt to define his status as the result of the failure to play. Baseball experts said it might be possible for Jennings to suspend the entire team. Such action has been taken by managers when players failed to report or did not keep in condition to play. In the case of suspension by a manager, the player has generally been brought before the National Commission and blacklisted as far as organized baseball goes.

Cobb has received enough letters and telegrams from fans of the country to fill a waste paper basket. Each letter carrier brought scores of missives to the hotel, while there was a steady procession of telegraph messenger boys. At least ten letters from New Yorkers, who assert they were seated within ten feet of the man who was hit, were received. Each writer declared he was willing to appear before President Johnson or the National Commission and relate the words which passed from the fan and the phrases used by the player in remonstrating with him.

"I treasure those letters, and these men may be of some help to me if Johnson gives me a hearing, which is all that I ask," said Cobb to-night.

Cobb said that he was not sorry for his action at the Highlanders' park. He asserted that he was pleased that his teammates had supported him, but that he did not wish to have their positions endangered. "I do not believe that they will be," he continued.

The outfielder was asked what effect the strike would have on organized baseball, and if the players could not only be suspended, but dropped from the league for their action.

"I do not think that Mr. Johnson or the National Commission would bowl out an entire club," was the reply. "League Presidents and managers have to listen to players some time, and this is a good chance.

"Players are subjected to abuse each afternoon. I do not object to being 'kidded' or 'ragged,' but I do not want to be cursed at. The fans appreciate a strong opponent, and I play the game to win. If I made a good play — one that knocks the hopes of the home team — I have sometimes grinned at the fans, but I have never cursed or lost my temper.

"I stood the raking of that man in New York until I could stand no more. There was only one thing to do, and that was to teach him a lesson. Players are not ruffians, and the majority of the spectators at ball games realize it. But there are some who think they can curse and denounce any player in the most insulting terms. I will not stand such language or action.

Lawyers conversant with the legal complications involved by organized baseball are completely at sea over the standing of the members of the scrub team which played to-day. They cannot be members of the Detroit team, as Detroit has a right to carry only a certain number of men on the pay roll, and the club is up to the requisite number now. Some lawyers argue that a team may play a man for five days before signing him, and therefore Detroit may play the scrubs for five days and then get a new set of substitutes, still keeping the franchise.

The consensus of opinion here is that there will be an immediate meeting of the Directors of the American League, and the matter will be taken out of the hands of President Johnson and will be settled by the Directors. If this action is taken it is believed the present difficulty will be smoothed over and the old Detroit players will be back in the game, including Cobb.

May 19, 1912

DETROIT PLAYERS FINED

Each One of Cobb's Sympathizers Must Pay $100 for Striking.

Special to The New York Times.

PHILADELPHIA, Penn., May 21.—All that superfluous language and the forty-eight hour vacation taken by the eighteen members of the Detroit team who endeavored to persuade fandom that they and not Ban Johnson were running the American League will cost each of them $100 in cash. This is the punishment meted out to the "strikers" to-day by President Johnson and the eight owners of the American League Clubs or their representatives. The "strikers" will have to pay $50 each for every day they were loyal to Ty Cobb. Cobb still is under suspension for his attack upon Claude Lueker, the New York fan, whom he attacked in the grand stand, during the game last Wednesday, between the Tigers and the Yankees.

Mr. Johnson left this afternoon for New York to gather evidence of the attack. Before going he intimated that he would be lenient with Cobb. President Navin of the Detroit team, will be unable to keep his promise to the eighteen strikers that the club will pay all fines. When the fines were imposed it was expressly declared that they must be paid by the individual players and not by the club. Navin said he felt no uneasiness over this ruling as he knew the players were with him and that they would stand by him to the end.

Another action, the direct outcome of the baseball strike, was a change in the rules by which the individual clubs hereafter will be held responsible for the action of the fans attending the games. The clubs must take some action to prevent the abuse of players by fans, but it is left to the clubs as to the best method to bring about this result. It is likely that the majority of the clubs will hire special officers who will be stationed in the stands and bleachers during the game and who will have the authority to eject any noisy or abusive fan. Warning posters will be displayed at all American League Parks calling upon the spectators at games to be orderly.

Cobb, who was under suspension at the inauguration of the strike, will not have to pay a fine just yet, but he may be given a little extra fine for appearing on the field in uniform while he was under suspension. "Wild Bill" Donovan, who is ill, also escapes a fine, as does Manager Jennings.

May 22, 1912

EDWARD ARTHUR WALSH
"BIG ED"
OUTSTANDING RIGHTHANDED PITCHER OF
CHICAGO A.L. FROM 1904 THROUGH 1916
WON 40 GAMES IN 1908 AND WON TWO
GAMES IN THE 1906 WORLD SERIES. TWICE
PITCHED AND WON TWO GAMES IN ONE
DAY, ALLOWING ONLY ONE RUN IN
DOUBLEHEADER AGAINST BOSTON ON
SEPT. 29, 1908. FINISHED BIG LEAGUE PITCHING
CAREER WITH BOSTON N.L. IN 1917.

MARQUARD DRIVEN FROM BOX BY CUBS

Giants' Great Pitcher Defeated After Winning Nineteen Successive Games.

THE SCORE:

Chicago ....0 2 0 2 0 2 0 1 .—7
New York...0 0 1 0 1 0 0 0 0—2

CHICAGO.

	AB.	R.	H.	PO.	A.	E.
Sheckard, lf	4	0	0	1	0	0
Shulte, rf	4	0	1	1	1	0
Tinker, ss	4	0	0	3	3	0
Zimmerman, 3b	3	1	1	2	1	0
Leach, cf	3	1	1	1	0	0
Saier, 1b	4	3	3	7	0	0
Evers, 2b	2	0	1	1	4	0
Archer, c	3	0	1	11	2	0
Lavender, p	4	0	1	0	2	0
Total	31	7	10	27	13	0

NEW YORK.

	AB.	R.	H.	PO.	A.	E.
Snodgrass, lf	2	1	1	0	0	2
Becker, rf	4	0	2	1	0	0
Merkle, 1b	4	0	1	7	1	0
Murray, rf	4	0	1	0	0	0
Herzog, 3b	3	0	0	1	3	0
Meyers, c	3	0	0	7	1	0
Wilson, c	1	0	0	1	0	0
Fletcher, ss	3	0	0	2	2	0
Groh, 2b	3	0	0	3	3	1
Marquard, p	2	0	0	0	1	0
*Devore	1	0	0	0	0	0
Tesreau, p	0	0	0	1	0	0
	30	2	5	24	11	3

*Batted for Marquard in the seventh inning.

Two-base hit—Saier. Three-base hit—Evers. Hits—Off Marquard, 8 in 6 innings; off Tesreau, 2 in 2 innings. Sacrifice hits—Evers, 2. Sacrifice fly—Archer. Double play—Groh to Merkle. Left on bases—Chicago, 6; New York, 5. First base on balls—Off Lavender, 2; off Marquard, 3. Hit by pitcher—By Lavender, (Fletcher, Snodgrass.) Struck out—By Marquard, 5; by Lavender, 7; by Tesreau, 1. Wild pitch—Marquard. Time of game —Two hours and five minutes. Umpires—Messrs. Klem and Bush.

Special to The New York Times.

CHICAGO, Ill., July 8.—Rube Marquard's winning streak was smashed by the Cubs this afternoon, after the great southpaw had annexed nineteen successive victories. The score was 7 to 2, and the Chicago win was due to the timely hitting of the locals, together with their knack of taking advantage of every slip of the visitors.

Rube pitched better ball than the score indicates, although the Cubs scored six of their tallies during the six innings that he was on the mound. The Giants had an off day in the field, booting the pellet around four times, and in addition pulling a "bonehead" play which paved the way for the first Cub counter.

While the home boys were touching up the offerings of the eleven-thousand-dollar pitcher, the New Yorkers were having considerable difficulty in locating the slants served by Jimmy Lavender, who before the Giants had scored their first run had pitched thirty-six consecutive innings of shutout ball. Lavender yielded only five hits, but had trouble finding the pan in the early frames. But he steadied down every time a couple of Giants were on the runways, being assisted by some wonderful support. The Cubs played errorless ball, and in the pinches came through with the marvelous efforts which were needed to check the visitors.

In the third inning Schulte cut down Merkle at the plate with a perfect throw when Fred tried to count on Murray's long single. Archer and Tinker broke up an attempted double steal by Becker and Merkle in the fifth inning by clever headwork and accurate throwing which nipped Merkle at the plate again.

The Cubs were the first to score, getting two runs in the second inning, when Zimmerman and Leach singled at the start. Saier then hit to Groh, who would have started an easy double play by tossing to Fletcher, but Hank tried to touch Leach as he ran past him and then hurl to Merkle. Tommy upset the dope by turning back toward first, and the move surprised Groh so much that he clung to the ball until too late to get Zimmerman, who had moved around from second on the play. This stupid move on the part of Groh yelled in glee at the filled the sacks, with none out, but Marquard promptly fanned the three following batters, although a wild pitch while the third man was at the bat allowed another run to cross.

Lavender walked the first man up in the first two frames, and in the second inning also hit a man after one was down, but in both instances pitched himself out of danger. He started the third by hitting Snodgrass. Becker came through with a single, sending Fred to third. Merkle then hit a hard grounder through the box, which Lavender knocked down after a hard try, and succeeded in running down Snodgrass. This play was a life-saver, as Murray came through with a hit to right, and Becker scored.

The Cubs' two runs in the fourth were made without a hit. A pass, two errors, and two sacrifices were all that was necessary.

Devore batted for Marquard in the seventh, and the crowd yelled in glee at the announcement, for it meant that the Cubs had driven the southpaw from the slab.

Josh fanned, but Snodgrass, Becker, and Merkle singled in succession, the first named counting. At this juncture the Becker-Merkle attempted double steal was queered, and Schulte made a good catch off Murray's bat.

The Giants failed to hit safely in any round except in the ones in which they counted. In the last four innings Lavender retired the side in order and fanned five.

The Cubs got their final runs off Marquard in the sixth on Saier's single, Evers's triple, and Lavender's Texas Leaguer, which Snodgrass kicked against the bleachers and then threw over Meyers's head.

Tesreau succeeded Marquard in the seventh and Wilson displaced Meyers, but the Cubs nicked this new battery for their seventh run on Saier's double, a sacrifice, and a single.

July 9, 1912

JOSEPH B. TINKER

FAMOUS AS A MEMBER OF ONE OF BASEBALL'S GREATEST DOUBLE PLAY COMBINATIONS-FROM TINKER TO EVERS TO CHANCE. A BIG LEAGUER FROM 1902 THROUGH 1916 WITH THE CHICAGO CUBS AND CINCINNATI REDS AND THE CHICAGO FEDS. MANAGER CINCINNATI 1913 AND CHICAGO N.L. 1916. SHORTSTOP ON CUBS' TEAM THAT WON PENNANTS IN 1906,'07 '08 AND 1910.

SOX CHAMPIONS ON MUFFED FLY

Snodgrass Drops Easy Ball, Costing Teammates $29,514, Boston Winning, 3-2.

GIANTS EXPLODE IN TENTH

Bostonians, Angry at Sox Management, Start Boycott, Keeping Crowd Down to 17,000.

LUCK WITH SOX—FULLERTON

Boston Outguessed and Outgeneraled, He Declares—McGraw Blames Nobody—$490,833 Receipts.

Special to The New York Times.

BOSTON, Mass., Oct. 16.—Write in the pages of world's series baseball history the name of Snodgrass. Write it large and black. Not as a hero; truly not. Put him rather with Merkle, who was in such a hurry that he gave away a National League championship. Snodgrass was in such a hurry that he gave away a world championship. It was because of Snodgrass's generous muff of an easy fly in the tenth inning that the decisive game in the world's series went to the Boston Red Sox this afternoon by a score of 3 to 2, instead of to the New York Giants by a score of 2 to 1.

It is the tenth inning of the eighth game of the series. The score of games is 3 to 3, and the score of this contest is 1 to 1. Mathewson, the veteran, has given the lie to his own announcement that he could never again pitch in such a contest by holding the Red Sox enemy at bay for nine innings in decisive fashion. One run has been made off him, but that has been through the fortunate hit of a youngster who has never faced him before. The regular members of the Boston team have been helpless in the face of his speed and his elusive fadeaway. They have been outfought, outgeneraled, outspeeded, and their only hope is that Wood, who has gone in fresh only two innings before, will hold out until the veteran shall give way to the strain.

Murray Breaks the Tie.

And who is this that comes to the bat for the Giants? 'Tis "Red" Murray—once the hitless. And what does he do? He pierces the mark of one of the smokiest of Wood's shoots and puts the ball far over the head of Speaker into the left field stands. It is a home run hit, but ground rules limit it to two bases. Yet what is the difference? Merkle also sees through the smoke, and the ball

which Wood has sent so speedily toward him is returned so fast that Wood can hardly see it as it goes toward centre field. So Murray is in with the run that unties the score, and it only remains for Mathewson to hold himself for one more inning and New York has a world championship and the Giant players the lion's share of the big purse hung up for the players, a difference of $29,514.

Is Mathewson apprehensive as he walks to the box? He is not. All the confidence that was his when the blood of youth ran strong in his supple muscles is his now. Even though the mountainous Engle faces him—this Engle who brought in the two runs of the Red Sox on Monday—he shows not a quiver, and he is right. All that Engle can do with the elusive drop served up is to hoist it high between centre and right fields. Snodgrass and Murray are both within reach of it, with time to spare. Snodgrass yells, "I've got it," and sets himself to take it with ease, as he has taken hundreds of the sort. Murray stops, waiting for the play that will enable him to line the ball joyfully to the infield just to show that his formidable right wing is still in working order.

When the Fly Ball Falls.

While the ball is soaring its leisurely way let us pause for a moment to think what hangs upon that fly.

It is not the 2,000 Giant rooters who are gayly waving their blue and white flags and yelling exultantly over the certain downfall of the foe. It is not the 15,000 Boston fans who have groaned and sat silent, as though at a funeral. A President is forgetting the bitter assaults that have been made upon him. A former President is being eased of his pain by his interest in it. A campaign which may mean a change in the whole structure of the Nation's Government has been put into the background. What happens will be flashed by telegraph the length and breadth of the land, and thereby carried over and under the sea, and millions will be uplifted or downcast.

And now the ball settles. It is full and fair in the pouch of the padded glove of Snodgrass. But he is too eager to toss it to Murray and it dribbles to the ground. Before Snodgrass can hurl the ball to second Engle is perching there.

Mathewson stands in the box, stunned for a moment, then swings his gloved hand in a gesture that is eloquent of his wrath. He has lost none of his courage and determination, but it can be seen as he faces Hooper that there is just a bit of uncertainty in his bearing. Proof comes that he has lost some of his cunning, for Hooper hits the ball so hard that Snodgrass has to sprint and reach to pull down his liner. For Yerkes he cannot put them over at all, and two Red Sox are on the bases.

Three Giants Let It Drop.

And now that something which upsets a ball team—which McGraw has called an explosion—becomes evident. Speaker pops up a high foul near first base, and Merkle, Meyers, and Mathewson converge on it with none collected enough to say which shall take it, and it drops among them. The three who have made the muss walk to the box arguing, Mathewson saying things which he emphasizes with angry gestures.

Now the Boston throng calls for the blood of the veteran—and gets it.

His control is gone, and Speaker, saved by a blunder, hammers the ball hard to right field, and Engle is over the plate. Lewis stands still while four bad ones pass him, and then Gardner steps up and puts all his weight against the ball,

THE OFFICIAL SCORE.

BOSTON.	AB.	R.	H.	TB.	SO.	BB.	SH.	SB.	LB.	TC.	PO.	A.	E.
Hooper, rf.	5	0	0	0	0	0	0	0	0	3	3	0	0
Yerkes, 2b	4	1	1	1	1	1	0	0	0	3	0	3	0
Speaker, cf.	4	0	2	2	1	1	0	0	2	3	2	0	1
Lewis, lf.	4	0	0	0	1	1	0	0	2	1	1	0	0
Gardner, 3b	3	0	1	2	0	1	1	0	0	7	1	4	2
Stahl, 1b	4	1	2	3	1	0	0	0	2	16	15	0	1
Wagner, ss.	3	0	1	1	0	1	0	0	2	9	3	5	1
Cady, c.	4	0	0	0	0	0	0	0	0	8	5	3	0
Bedient, p.	2	0	0	0	0	0	0	0	0	1	0	1	0
Wood, p.	0	0	0	0	0	0	0	0	0	2	0	2	0
*Henriksen	1	0	1	2	0	0	0	0	1	0	0	0	0
†Engle	1	1	0	0	0	0	0	0	0	0	0	0	0
Total	35	3	8	11	4	5	1	0	9	53	30	18	5

NEW YORK.	AB.	R.	H.	TB.	SO.	BB.	SH.	SB.	LB.	TC.	PO.	A.	E.
Devore, rf.	3	1	1	1	0	2	0	1	2	5	3	1	0
Doyle, 2b	5	0	0	0	0	0	0	0	0	7	1	5	1
Snodgrass, cf.	4	0	1	1	0	1	0	0	2	5	4	1	1
Murray, lf.	5	1	2	4	0	0	0	0	1	3	3	0	0
Merkle, 1b	5	0	1	1	1	0	0	0	1	10	10	0	0
Herzog, 3b	5	0	2	3	1	0	0	0	2	3	2	1	0
Meyers, c.	3	0	0	0	0	1	1	0	2	5	4	1	0
Fletcher, ss.	3	0	1	1	1	0	0	0	1	5	2	3	0
Shafer, ss.	0	0	0	0	0	0	0	0	0	0	0	0	0
Mathewson	4	0	1	1	1	0	0	0	0	3	0	3	0
‡McCormick	1	0	0	0	0	0	0	0	0	0	0	0	0
Total	38	2	9	12	4	4	1	1	11	46	§29	15	2

Boston	0	0	0	0	0	0	1	0	0	2—3
New York	0	0	1	0	0	0	0	0	0	1—2

Two-base hits—Gardner, Stahl, Henriksen, Murray, (2,) Herzog. First base on errors—Boston, 1; New York, 1. Struck out—By Bedient, 2; by Wood, 2; by Mathewson, 4. Bases on balls—Off Bedient, 3; off Wood, 1; off Mathewson, 5. Hits—Off Bedient, 6 in 7 innings, (at bat, 26;) off Wood, 3 in 3 innings, (at bat, 12.) Sacrifice fly—Gardner. Left on bases—Boston, 9; New York, 11.

Umpire in chief, Mr. O'Loughlin; umpire on bases, Mr. Rigler; left field umpire, Mr. Klem; right field umpire, Mr. Evans.

Time of game—Two hours and thirty-seven minutes.

and it goes far out to Devore, too far for him to stop Yerkes with the winning run, even though his throw comes true as a bullet.

Too bad! Too bad! The world championship belongs in New York and Boston is perfectly aware of it. Here as well as there admiration is ungrudging for a team that could come from behind, win two decisive victories on its gameness, and deserve to win a third, and sympathy is widespread for a gallant pitcher and his gallant mates, who were cheated of their triumph by a bit of bravado. After the game the Red Sox rooters gave hearty cheers "for the best player on the giants' team—Snodgrass."

Most of all the sympathy is due to Mathewson. Three times he has given prodigally of his waning vigor to bring the world championship to New York, and three times he has deserved victory, but has had it denied because his team has failed to play its real game behind him. What it meant to him to pitch the game to-day he only knows.

As he sat in the corridor of his hotel this morning it could be seen that he had little left to give. The skin was drawn tightly over the bone on his jaw and chin, and in his hollowed cheeks the furrows that have been graven by hard campaigns of recent years were startling in their depth. As he warmed up his gauntness was evident, and the Boston fans gloated over the thought that he could not long stand the rush of their sluggers.

Yet up to that disastrous tenth he was "Big Six" at his best. His fast ball shot with a thud into the glove of Meyers, his drop shot down in front of the batters and his fadeaway had the best of them, breaking their backs. Now and again he seemed in trouble, and the Boston rooters yelled that he was going, but no sign of a crack appeared, and only eight safe hits were made off him in the ten periods.

It was in the first inning that he showed what he meant to do. Yerkes, second up, fanned on a fadeaway. Speaker got to second on an error by Doyle, but Lewis went out on three pitched balls. With two on bases in the second and one out, he made Cady pop up, and Bedient sent a grounder to Doyle. In the third he sent the Red Sox to the field with three pitched balls.

So he went along to the seventh, holding the game as he wished, and it was only in this round that two hits were bunched on him. That luck had some part here cannot be denied. Stahl got on with a pop up, which first eluded the rush of Murray, Snodgrass, and Doyle. Wagner walked, but it seemed as though nothing would come of it when "Big Six" with two out had fooled Henriksen, who was batting for Bedient, twice on strikes and had started a fadeaway over the plate. Henriksen had never faced him before and was not at all familiar with the fadeaway, but his bat happened to connect with the ball as he made a wide swing, and the sphere shot over third base for a double, bringing in Stahl. The ball was rapidly curving over the foul line, and six inches more of this deflection would have made the hit vain.

In the eighth and ninth the Sox hit him hard, but could not place the ball out of reach of the Giant fielders. In the fatal tenth the whole Boston side should have been put out on flies and none should have reached first base.

Yet credit must not be denied to young Bedient. When he went to the box Gardner, Stahl, and Cady were as solicitous for his welfare as though he were an only child with the croup. After each ball in the early innings, Gardner walked in and told him pleasant things and soothed him, and on frequent occasions the others added their attentions. It was made evident before the game had gone very far, however, that others on the Red Sox team were in far greater need of an anchor than he.

Whatever nervousness he might have had at first, it was not long before both his feet were firmly planted on the ground and he refused to let them be lifted. He was dangerously wild at times, but in the pinches he was as cool as the east wind that wafted its chilling way across the field. At first he was exceedingly deliberate in his work, but as the game went on he took things calmly and pitched almost as fast as Mathewson. His departure from the box after the seventh inning was a matter of batting strategy, not of necessity.

The one run scored against him in the third inning had in it elements of luck and misfortune. He let Devore walk to first, but a double play would have been possible had not Gardner, too intent on watching him, fumbled Doyle's swift grounder. Murray's drive to left centre which scored Devore was just missed by Speaker, his fingers touching the ball. In the fourth Bedient showed his class. With Herzog on third and only one out he forced Fletcher, who had made a safe hit the first time up, and Mathewson to send up high flies.

Wood, who went to the box in the eighth, gave promise at first showing the form of the first two games he won. In the ninth, however, the Giants showed that they could find his smoke ball, and in the tenth they made it plainly evident that he could not last long. Murray's drive was one of the hardest hits of the series, and Merkle's fairly sizzled. Meyers sent one of the same sort to the box, and it was simply good fortune that Wood's bare hand found itself in the way. He gave plain indication of distress and was legally out of the game, Engle having batted for him in the last half of the tenth.

At the bat, in the field and in the baserunning the Giants excelled. They got nine hits off Bedient and Wood to eight off Mathewson, in the error column they showed up two to five and in the baserunning they were fast, while the Sox at times were slow and blundering.

In the error-making Gardner was the worst offender. He made a bad mess of a slow tap by Meyers in the second, the ball being right in his hand. He was equally bad on an attempted double-steal in the same inning when he muffed a perfect throw by Wagner to cut down the Indian. He contributed another on Doyle's drive in the third when he missed the double play.

After that he settled down and was in the game whenever opportunity offered. Wagner also was an offender, dropping a fine throw by Cady to head off a steal by Snodgrass. Stahl contributed the fifth Red Sox bungle in the seventh, when he badly misjudged a high foul and let it get away from him.

On the Giants' side Doyle erred in the first inning, when he muffed a perfect throw by Devore to catch Speaker, who was trying to stretch a long single. The other was made by Snodgrass. Nothing more need be said. He will miss the $1,283 it cost him.

Mixed in with the errors were some fine plays. The best of all was the catch of Hooper of a high drive from Doyle's bat, which was going for a home run into the bleachers back of right field. He picked it out of the air with a jump and almost fell over the low fence.

Fletcher made a startling play in the second. On a hard hit by Stahl with Wagner on first, Doyle threw wildly to the shortstop on the bag. Fletcher dived forward and retrieved the ball, jamming his foot on the bag just before Gardner rushed into it. On the base paths the worst exhibition was that of Yerkes. He was on third when Speaker started a steal from first. Meyers whipped the ball to Mathewson, and he shot it to Herzog, and Yerkes was nipped by feet.

A peculiar piece of hard luck for the Giants resulted from a protest that had been made by Manager McGraw. In Saturday's game Lewis scored one of the Red Sox runs because of a triple he drove into a blind alley off the left field bleachers. McGraw insisted that thereafter such a hit should be good for only two bases, and the rule was made. Herzog, in the fourth with nobody out, drove a vicious ball into this same alley, and was waved back to second after easily getting to the third sack. He did not get home, as he probably would have except for McGraw's protest. With his run scored the series would have been won by the Giants in the ninth, for there would have been no fatal tenth inning.

The setting for the most stirring finish of a world championship in the history of baseball was not calculated to be inspiring. Little would one have thought that such an event was taking place in one of the best baseball cities in the country. There was an atmosphere of dreariness about the affair. The ramshackle structures of the Boston field, the rusty grass interspersed with dry patches did not look good to one who had been used to the glories of the Brush Stadium. The sun shone brightly, but the east wind was chilly.

The Royal Rooters were not there. Offended by the neglect to recognize their unwavering loyalty by providing seats for them the day before they boycotted the game and their influence was shown by the fact that thousands of others did the same thing.

Then, too, there was a general feeling among the Boston rooters that the series had been lost by the routs of Monday and Tuesday. One could scarcely find one this morning who believed that the Red Sox could stop the rush of the Giants. Mixed with this was some worse feeling. There had been many rumors afloat of trouble among the Red Sox. It was said that Wood on the train coming from New York on Monday had accused O'Brien of deliberately giving his game to the Giants, and that they had engaged in a fight which accounted for the inability of Wood to win his third victory. According to a local newspaper report charges were widely made among fans that the management of the Boston's had deliberately sent O'Brien in to be slaughtered for the purpose of swelling their income from the series. At all such things the persons responsible for baseball here scoffed, but they had their effect in keeping down the attendance.

Of the 17,000 odd who were present, however, many were loyal to the team and were quite willing to show it when the occasion arose. The management of the club helped them to make noise by distributing thousands of rattles, which, when beaten together or on the backs of seats, set up a chorus like that of giant crickets. At times this noise was weird in the extreme.

When the game was over there was no Royal Rooters' band to lead a zigzag procession and no delirious outburst. Hundreds of fans, however, made a rush on the Red Sox bench, where they cooped the players in almost suffocating confinement and insisted on cheering them again and again, not even forgetting Snodgrass of the Giants.

Here the only really violent incident of the hard-fought series occurred. After the game was finished Manager McGraw ran over to the Red Sox bench to shake hands with Manager Stahl and congratulate him on his victory and sportsmanship. A Boston fan, rushing from behind, ran into him and almost tipped him into the bench pit. McGraw turned and in saving himself half pushed, half struck the man. There was a bit of excitement for a moment, but good feeling was running too high for anything serious to happen, and the Giants' manager was able to pay his courtesies and escape.

Boston has shown no great jubilation to-night over the victory. What it wanted was proof of the superiority of the Red Sox, not a championship handed to them as a gift. Fans admit that the Sox were played to a standstill and that no large honor accrues to them. Beyond the cheering at the grounds there has been no demonstration in the city.

Mayor Fitzgerald, however, is determined that the team shall have some recognition. After the game he went to the clubhouse and congratulated Manager Stahl and President McAleer and suggested that a big dinner be given to the team. This was declined because the men were anxious to get away and take up other affairs. There will be instead a parade to-morrow morning from the ball park to Faneuil Hall and addresses there at noon.

October 17, 1912

Washington Senators

Federal Ball League Formed

INDIANAPOLIS, Ind., March 8.—John T. Powers of Chicago was elected President of the Federal League of Baseball Clubs here late this afternoon. The organization was incorporated under the laws of Indiana earlier in the day. Other officers are: M.R. Bramley, Cleveland, Vice President; James A. Ross, Indianapolis, Secretary, and John A. George, Indianapolis, Treasurer. The Board of Managers is composed of: William T. McCullough, Pittsburgh; Michael Kinney, St. Louis; Charles X. Zimmerman, Cleveland; John A. Spinney, Cincinnati; James A. Ross, John A. George, and John S. Powell, Indianapolis, and Charles L. Sherlock, Chicago. Each club will be required to post a forfeit of $5,000 before the opening of the season, which is scheduled to take place between May 10 and May 15. It was announced that the Indianapolis club would be incorporated Tuesday with a capital of $100,000.

JOHNSON'S GREAT PITCHING RECORD

Figures Prove Latest Performance the Best in Recent Years.

A sigh of regret echoed the length and breadth of the baseball world on Thursday last when word was flashed that Walter Johnson's second notable effort of the season to hang up a world's record of consecutive pitching victories had been broken just at a time when it seemed that the king of pitchers was destined to achieve success. Bill Carrigan's hit, that barely went over the Washington infield, brought to a close one of the greatest pitching performances of baseball history, at the same time showing Johnson greater in defeat than in victory. But Walter Johnson needs no records of consecutive victories to establish beyond doubt his title as the greatest pitcher of modern days, undoubtedly the greatest the game has produced.

Last year Johnson hung up a record of sixteen consecutive wins, a mark also made last year by Joe Wood, and now standing as the best performance since the American League branched out as a major organization. In the National League Rube Marquard's 1912 performance of nineteen straight stands as the mark for aspiring moundsmen to shoot at. But neither the memorable run of the New York southpaw nor the performances of Wood and Johnson a year ago show any such figures as were compiled by Johnson in his recent run of victories. He fell two games short of his 1912 mark, but in achievement he far excelled his previous run.

That the best pitched game of ball shown in either major league this season was the one which could not carry Johnson along on his winning streak is an example of the irony of fate in toying with ball tossers. No such pitching performance as Johnson showed last Thursday was shown by the Senatorial marvel while he was compiling his run of victories, yet he went down to defeat with it, and his chance of establishing a new mark for consecutive wins is gone, for the present year at least. Johnson will undoubtedly close the year

with the best pitching record, counted by games won and lost, in either league, and he will carry the distinction of two successive runs of victories—eleven the first time and fourteen the second—which in themselves constitute a record in later day baseball. But the time is too short for Johnson or any other pitcher to hang up a new mark during 1913.

Every run of victories has its share of luck for the player or team most interested, and there is no denying that Johnson did not escape. Against Cleveland on Aug. 8 the Naps had Washington 3 to 2 when the Senators went to bat in the ninth inning. Johnson was taken out of the game when it came his turn to bat, and Alva Williams was sent in as a pinch hitter. Williams delivered the hit and Germany Schaefer was put in as runner for Williams, ultimately scoring the run which tied up the game. It was won in the same inning when Moeller followed Williams over the plate.

But luck was the exception, and not the rule, while the Washington speed marvel was adding up one victory after another. Hard luck, or misfortune, was a bit more prominent than the so-called luck of baseball. In two months of play, over which Johnson's great winning streak extended, his two finest efforts in pitching went for nothing. On July 25 he pitched eleven and one-third innings of a game that went fifteen innings against St. Louis, holding the Browns to a single run, and striking out sixteen batsmen in that time. He went into the game with Washington one run behind, and even this high-class performance was not sufficient to bring him a victory. The game was called with the teams deadlocked, 8 to 8. On Aug. 28, when Johnson turned in the best pitching performance of the year, allowing three hits and fanning ten men in eleven innings, he suffered a shutout and saw his winning streak broken.

A close analysis of the figures shows just how wonderful Johnson was in that winning streak. On June 25 Walter was knocked out of the box by the Athletics in four innings, during which time a double, three singles, and a home run by Frank Baker put the coming champions on the road to an easy victory. Two days later Johnson came back at the same team, the hardest hitting club in either league, held them to three hits, and scored a shutout victory, 2 to 0. That was the start of his long run which culminated on Thursday last in the eleven-inning defeat by the Red Sox. Between these two defeats there was one pitching classic after another.

In some of the games Johnson did not have to go the full route, being taken out when the game was safely packed away by the Senators. Including his tie game against St. Louis and his defeat by Boston last Thursday, as both are part of Johnson's wonderful work since he began his now-broken winning streak, the Washington star figured in 127 1-3 innings, just a shade more than fourteen nine-inning games. In that time Johnson allowed only eighteen runs, an average of less than 1 1-3 runs to each nine-inning game. He was reached for eighty-two hits, an average of less than six hits per game, and as Johnson is a heady pitcher, who does not go after strike-outs unless pressed, the hit record of his opponents is more

March 9, 1913

to be marveled at than would ordinarily be the case.

Johnson gave sixteen bases on balls in fourteen full games, showing that the wonderful speed is not the only asset of his great success. He struck out seventy-eight batsmen, less than six to each game.

The record is all the more remarkable in view of the fact that the batting ability of Johnson's own team, which really plays a prominent part in every pitcher's winning or losing, is not of high ranking. Every team in the National League and four of the eight teams in the American League rank above the Senators in batting strength, only the Browns, Yankees and White Sox being lower in team batting than Griffith's team. This was a handicap that Johnson had to battle against in game after game, requiring pitching that was next to the shutout brand. He had to go fifteen innings to beat Ray Collins, 1 to 0, on July 3, and in eight of the sixteen games tabulated below the Senators scored two runs or less while Johnson was in the box. In some of these games Johnson did not work the full nine innings, but was called upon to work with the score close. Six of the fourteen games which Johnson won were decided by a single run over the regulation nine-inning period or longer, and another was a 1 to 1 tie for nine innings, with Washington getting four runs in the tenth.

On Aug. 2 Johnson celebrated his sixth anniversary as a major leaguer, and each succeeding year sees him add more glory to himself and his team. Three years ago the baseball world suspected that Johnson carried more natural ability than any other pitcher in the game. To-day every baseball fan is certain that the Washington speed marvel stands first among the pitchers. Such pitching as he has shown during the present season, considered from the standpoint of effectiveness alone, and with no consideration of consecutive victories, far excels the work of any other pitcher of recent years. The dim past may carry some records that in black figures look better than what Johnson has done this season, but few present-day fans will believe that the pitching equal of the Washington star ever graced the diamond.

Following are the pitching records of Johnson since he began his winning streak on June 27, including his eleven-inning defeat at Boston during the last week. The scores given are not the full scores of games in every instance, simply showing the number of runs scored by Washington while Johnson occupied the box. The other columns, in order, show the runs scored off Johnson, the number of innings he pitched, with the bases on balls and strike-outs in each game. The figures:

Washington.

Date. Runs.	Runs.	Inn. ings.	Hits.	BB.	Strike- outs.
June 27—2 Phila.	0	9	3	1	6
June 30—1 Boston	1	4	4	4	4
July 3—1 Boston	0	15	15	1	4
July 9—7 Detroit	6	2	1	1	
July 13—5 Cleveland ..	4	9	10	0	6
July 17—2 St. Louis..	1	1	0	0	0
July 18—5 St. Louis..	1	4	0	0	3
July 21—2 Chicago ...	1	9	4	2	5
July 23—2 St. Louis..	1	11½	7	3	16
Aug. 2—3 Detroit	2	9	9	1	4
Aug. 6—6 Detroit	0	4	1	0	3
Aug. 8—4 Cleveland ..	3	9	7	3	5
Aug. 15—1 Detroit	2	7	6	1	6
Aug. 19—5 Cleveland ..	1	10	7	1	8
Aug. 24—2 Chicago ...	1	9	6	0	6
Aug. 28—0 Boston	1	11	3	0	10
56	18	127½	82	16	78

August 31, 1913

BASEBALL SALARIES REACH TOP MARK

Federal League's Promise of $75,000 to Cobb for 5 Years' Play Is Banner Offer.

The high-water mark in the frenzied finance of baseball was reached with the Federal League's big offer to "Ty" Cobb of $15,000 a year for five years. Cobb last year was the highest salaried outfielder in the game, receiving $12,000 from Detroit. He has assured President Navin of the Tigers that he will sign a contract for next year, stating in a recent communication that he was satisfied with the terms of last year's contract.

Cobb has always been a bone of contention on the Detroit team, and on more than one occasion has sulked and had to be humored before he would consent to come back into the fold. As he is in baseball for the money, as he has stated often before, it would not be surprising if Cobb used the Federal League offer as a means to obtain more money from the Tigers. But it isn't supposed that he will take the Federal's offer seriously.

The recent activity of the outlaw league in threatening to invade the territory of the major league clubs has given an artificial impetus to the salaries of baseball players. Experienced baseball men say that the high salaries which are now being offered are absurd, in contrast to the profits made in baseball, and that when the reaction comes the result will be the loss of a great deal of money by club owners. The only baseball clubs which really make money from season to season are those which are in the first three positions in the pennant race. A losing team does not draw crowds in its home city or on the road.

During the past few years club owners have been trying to outdo each other in paying abnormal prices for baseball players. Since the days when Boston gave $10,000 to Chicago for catcher Mike Kelly, the price of players has soared until it now reaches a stage when Cobb is promised $75,000 for five years' service on the diamond. During the Brotherhood trouble and during the American League raid, the value of baseball players jumped considerably, and the price has been going up ever since. At the time of the Brotherhood war, the National League had a monthly salary limit of $2,000 a month. There is no salary limit in the major leagues now, and in the International League, the leading minor organization, the salary limit is $6,000, $4,000 more than the salary limit of the National League in 1888.

Club owners nowadays have become so reckless that they take a gambler's chance in purchasing players. Sometimes the player is worth what is paid for him, but oftentimes he fails to come up to the value that is placed upon him. In the case of "Rube" Marquard, for whom New York paid $11,000, the pitcher was carried by the club for a few seasons before he showed any real merit. In the case of "Lefty" Russell, for whom Connie Mack paid $12,000, the pitcher failed to measure up to major league calibre and was shipped back to the minors. Larry Chappelle, for whom the White Sox paid $18,000, has not yet shown anything like that value.

Joe Tinker is the latest example of the uncertainty of baseball deals. Tinker was sold by Cincinnati to Brooklyn for $25,000, the largest amount ever involved in the purchase of a single player. Tinker refused to abide by the transaction and jumped to the Federal League, whereby the Brooklyn Club is running a chance of losing $15,000 on the transaction. At best the deal will probably involve much litigation and trouble before final settlement of the Tinker matter is made. Tinker's reported arrangement with the Federal League is another example of the frenzied condition of baseball finance. He has been promised $30,000 for three years, and $15,000 of this is already supposed to be in a Chicago bank in Tinker's name, and that he is now drawing the interest on this deposit. Otto Knabe is also supposed to have received $7,000 of his three years' guarantee. Minor Brown also says that he has received part of his St. Louis Federal League salary in advance. If this state of affairs is true, it is contrary to the business principles of baseball, and the leveler heads of the game predict that it is sure to result in a financial smash.

Last year, Cobb refused to sign a contract unless Detroit gave him $15,000 a year salary. President Navin replied to Cobb's demands by showing him that, although he was one of the greatest drawing cards of the game, the amount of money taken in by the Detroit Club would not warrant paying any one man such a large amount. So Cobb finally consented to take $12,000. There are several players who receive almost as much as that. Mathewson of the Giants and Wagner of the Pirates have been $10,000 men for several seasons, and they have been worth it. Walter Johnson is said to receive $10,000 from Washington.

Last year, when Detroit was having trouble signing Cobb, Clarke Griffith of Washington startled the baseball world by saying that the Washington Club would be willing to buy Cobb from Detroit for $100,000. This offer, however, was not taken seriously by any one, but Griffith pointed out that Cobb would bring back much of this money in the advertising the club would receive. Connie Mack says that Eddie Collins is worth $100,000 to the Athletics. Pittsburgh paid $22,500 for Pitcher Marty O'Toole, but the Pirate twirler has not shown that he was worth the price as a player. Pittsburgh, however, did not lose much by the investment, because O'Toole has been a big attraction everywhere Pittsburgh plays. There is no sport in the world which gets the publicity that baseball receives, and clubowners are quick to see this, and know that any deal which involves a large amount of money will get countryside attention. This is the principle on which the Federal League has been working, and they have made known only the deals which involve large purchase prices or large salaries. They say nothing of their attempts to sign players to make up the rank and file of the eight clubs.

January 18, 1914

Ty Cobb Versus Walter Johnson

Walter Johnson has faced Cobb in the capacity of pitcher just 133 times, and of that many times at bat the champion batsman of the American League has been sent back to the bench 109 times hitless, the gentleman from Georgia failing to swat the ball in his usual consistent and blithesome manner when facing the consistent Mr. Johnson. So Walter Johnson has the honor of being about the only hurler to hold the fiery Cobb, the champion batsman of the Tigers and the world, in subjugation. In the 133 times that Cobb faced the Washington star he made 31 base hits, 9 runs; just 6 of the hits were better than singles, consisting of three doubles and three triples. These figures give Cobb a batting average for the eight seasons he has maintained a calling acquaintance with Mr. Johnson of .233.

May 30, 1915

Detroit Beats Cleveland

DETROIT, Oct. 3.—Detroit, playing its last game of the season, defeated Cleveland 6 to 5, and established an American League record. The Tigers won 100 games this year, something no club in the league, which finished in second place, had previously accomplished. Cobb also set a base stealing record. His theft of second base in the second inning gave him an unofficial total of ninety-seven stolen sacks. The Tigers won the game in the eighth when Burns scored on Dubuc's sacrifice fly. Score:

DETROIT.						CLEVELAND.					
	AB	R	H	PO	A		AB	R	H	PO	A
Bush, ss.	5	2	2	2	2	Wille, lf.	4	1	2	2	0
Vitt, 3b.	4	0	1	2	1	Ch'an, ss.	4	1	2	3	7
Cobb, cf.	3	0	2	1	1	Roth, cf.	5	0	1	1	0
Veach, lf.	4	0	0	0	0	Smith, rf.	5	1	1	2	0
C'ford, rf.	4	0	0	1	0	Kirke, 1b.	5	0	2	14	0
Burns, 1b.	4	2	3	12	0	H'bare, 3b.	4	0	1	0	2
Young, 2b.	4	0	1	2	4	Trner, 2b.	4	0	0	0	3
McKee, c.	4	1	3	7	1	O'Neil c.	3	2	2	2	3
C'leskie, p.	2	1	1	0	5	Klepfer, p.	3	0	1	0	2
†Moriarity	1	0	0	0	0	*W'gans	1	0	0	0	0
James, p.	0	0	0	0	2	Jones, p.	0	0	0	0	2
Dubuc, p.	0	0	0	0	0						
Total	35	6	13	27	17	Total	38	5	12	24	18

*Batted for Klepfer in the eighth inning.
†Batted for Coveleskie in the sixth inning.
Errors—Roth, Smith, Kirke, Veach.

Detroit ....1 3 1 0 0 0 0 1 ..—6
Cleveland ....0 0 0 1 2 1 0 1 0—5

Three-base hit—Smith. Stolen bases—Bush, Cobb, O'Neil. Earned runs—Cleveland, 4; Detroit, 2. Sacrifice fly—Dubuc. Double plays—Turner, Chapman and Kirke; Cobb, Bush and McKee. Left on bases—Cleveland, 9; Detroit, 7. Bases on balls—Off Klepfer, 1; off Coveleskie, 3. First base on errors—Detroit, 1. Hits—Off Coveleskie, 10 in 6 innings; off Hames, 2 in 2 innings; off Dubuc, 0 in 1 inning; off Klepfer, 11 in 7 innings; off Jones, 2 in 1 inning. Struck out—By Klepfer, 2; by Coveleskie, 4; by James, 1. Umpires—Messrs. Wallace and Evans. Time of game—One hour and forty-five minutes.

October 4, 1915

LONG BASEBALL WAR IS SETTLED

Federal League Passes Out of Existence—Contract Jumpers Reinstated.

BEST PLAYERS TO BE SOLD

Major Leagues Agree to Reimburse Ward Interests in Brooklyn—New Owners for Cubs and Browns.

CINCINNATI, Dec. 22.—The most disastrous war that the baseball game has ever experienced came to a close here tonight when a treaty of peace between the Federal League and both parties to the national baseball agreement, known as Organized Baseball, was signed. The war has lasted about two years.

Two major league clubs will change hands as the result of the bringing about of peace and two new faces will be seen among major league club owners in the future. Charles H. Weeghman, who has been President of the Chicago Federal League Club, will purchase the controlling interest in the Chicago National League team from Charles P. Taft of Cincinnati. Philip Ball and his associates, who were connected with the St. Louis Federal League team, gain control of the St. Louis American League Club from Robert Hedges, John E. Bruce, and others, who have long been connected with major league circles.

Contract Jumpers Reinstated.

The agreement gives immunity to all men who have jumped their contracts from both the major and minor leagues of Organized Baseball, as well as all other Federal League players. All of them have been reinstated or made eligible to Organized Baseball.

That there will be a wild scramble for some of the best Federal League players was clearly indicated by a provision in the treaty that the Federal League, as a league, and which, in so far as actual baseball playing is concerned, ceases to exist, will assume all of the contracts of Federal League players.

In this connection rumors flew thick and fast here tonight regarding the future status of a number of Federal League players. One of these, despite the lack of confirmation, was that Benny Kauff of the Brooklyn Federal League team would be seen next season in a Giant uniform.

Semi-officially it became known that several former Federal players will be seen in the New York American League club.

The agreement does not go into the distribution of any players, and it was announced that the bars have been thrown down, and that inasmuch as all are eligible, those who are for sale will probably go to the highest bidder. The Federal League clubs in Chicago and St. Louis are excepted, inasmuch as Weeghman and Ball will be permitted to keep what players they desire of the Federal League clubs in these cities.

Major Leagues to Pay Wards $400,000.

The announcement concerning the reimbursement of the Ward interests in the Brooklyn Federal League Club was short. It was:

"The Ward interests will be reimbursed, both major leagues assuming this responsibility."

There was no announcement of any figures in respect to this, but it is unofficially, though authoritatively, stated it will be $400,000, payable at the rate of $20,000 a year.

These five principal conditions took little time of the meeting, which extended over two days. The chief stumbling block in the way of a quick decision to have peace was the International League. Two propositions were concerned. One was that the Buffalo Federal League club wanted to be consolidated with the Buffalo International League club, but the International League would not agree to this.

Dunn Claims Baltimore Territory.

The other was relative to the Baltimore Federal League Park. Jack Dunn of the Richmond, Va., team has for some time, according to President E. G. Barrow of the International League, been considered as having the legitimate right to an International League franchise in Baltimore when peace was declared. Dunn appeared here today and demanded this right, and, it was reported, made an offer for the Federal League grounds. The Federal League made a counter proposition, but the difference in the two figures was so wide that no agreement was reached.

However, in order not to delay the signing of the treaty of peace, it was mutually agreed by all of the conferees at today's session that a committee be appointed with full power to act in settling both of these questions relative to the International League.

Following the appointing of this committee the conferees made quick work of the remainder of the business, and shortly before 6 o'clock tonight they announced that all of the provisions of the treaty of peace had been agreed to; that the lawyers were then drawing up the document and putting it into legal form and that it would be signed as soon as this was completed.

Those who signed the agreement were August Herrmann, Chairman of the National Commission; President John K. Tener of the National League, President B. B. Johnson of the American League, President James A. Gilmore of the Federal League, President Charles Weeghman of the Chicago Federal League Club, Harry N. Sinclair of the Newark Federal League Club, Secretary J. H. Farrell of the National Association, President Edward G. Barrow of the International League, and President Thomas Chivington of the American Association.

Anti-Trust Suit to be Withdrawn.

When asked what disposition would be made of the suit of the Federal League against organized baseball charging violation of the anti-trust law, now pending before Judge Landis in Chicago, President Tener of the National League, acting as spokesman, said: "The suit will be withdrawn."

Mr. Weeghman, who will become the new owner of the Chicago Cubs, intended to leave tonight for Texas to make the final transfer, as Mr. Taft is on a hunting trip there. He changed his mind at the last moment, however, and will see Mr. Taft on Jan. 4 on his return to this city.

The meeting of the committee to take up the International League question will be held here in conjunction with the annual meeting of the National Commission on Jan. 3 next.

It was announced late tonight that all suits pertaining to baseball pending in any court would be withdrawn in the next day or two.

When asked tonight as to the future status of Roger Bresnahan, Charles H. Weeghman, who will purchase the Cubs, said:

"I don't know what disposition will be made of Bresnahan. Tinker, of course, will be our manager, and that

Five Principal Conditions In Baseball Peace Terms

Chicago Nationals and St. Louis Americans to be sold to Federal League club owners.

Reinstatement of all players who have jumped their contracts.

Federal League players, excepting those of Chicago and St. Louis clubs, to be sold to highest bidders.

Federal League club owners to assume all contracts of their players.

National and American Leagues to reimburse Ward interests.

is as far as I have taken up the question of players."

The National Commission issued a statement tonight praising the attitude that was taken during the entire negotiations by President Gilmore of the Federal League.

"He has played the game with the cards on the table, and has been fair in every respect," said the statement.

Philip Ball, who gains control of the St. Louis Americans, stated tonight that Fielder Jones would be the new manager of the team. Inasmuch as Branch Rickey's contract as manager of the St. Louis Americans expired last season, nothing definite was officially announced about him, but rumors had it he would retire from the league.

A majority of those who attended the meeting here tonight departed for their homes tonight, following the adjournment of the conference.

December 23, 1915

RESERVE CLAUSE A BOON.

How Baseball's Saving Agreement Has Stood the Test of Time.

The reserve rule in a baseball player's contract—a provision which empowers a club to hold the services of a player for the ensuing year—has more than any one thing been the foundation of the success of the National League. About the time the league was organized, contract jumping and desertion of players was one of the evils which had wrecked the old National Association.

Colonel A. G. Mills, the league's third President, with other baseball men, realized that some iron-clad rule was necessary to hold a player to the team which had him under contract. Colonel Mills wrote a circular letter which was signed by Al Spalding, calling the players' attention to the evil. The letter of Colonel Mills was the first move toward the reserve clause. The campaign for reform grew until Colonel Mills drew up the first national agreement, which provided that each club should "reserve eleven players" at a salary of not less than $1,000 for the ensuing year, players released from reservation being ineligible to contract with any other club within twenty days of their release.

This first document was called the Tripartite Agreement, being an amalgamation of common interest between the National League, the American Association, and the Northwestern League. The agreement put a stop to the widespread evil of contract jumping. It placed baseball on a firm footing.

War has been waged at different times on the reserve rule, both by outlaw organizations and by the courts, but it still stands as the bulwark of baseball. The National League has fought for it steadfastly through thick and thin, and came out victorious with this rule in the recent war with the Federal League.

February 6, 1916

HUGHES
ALLOWS NOT A HIT

Holds Pirates Utterly Helpless While Braves Score Twice.

BOSTON, June 16.—Hughes pitched a no-hit, no-run game against Pittsburgh today, the Braves winning, 2 to 0. The Boston twirler had great control, passing only two men and striking out seven. Wagner fanned twice, the second time ending the game. Most of the time the visitors hit the ball into the air, Wilhoit making several fine running catches.

Maranville scored the first run when he walked and took second on a single by Snodgrass. Wilhoit popped to Kantlehner and the latter threw into centre field trying to double Maranville, the latter scoring. Maranville was passed in the eighth after two were out, took third on Snodgrass's third hit, and scored on a double steal. The score:

BOSTON.	AB	R	H	PO	A	PITTSBURGH.	AB	R	H	PO	A
M'ville,ss	1	2	0	4	1	Carey,cf	4	0	0		
Snodgr's,cf	4	0	3	0	0	Johnston,1b	4	0	0		
Wilhoit,rf	4	0	0	0	0	Wagner,ss	4	0	0		
Magee,lf	3	0	1	2	0	H'chman,rf	4	0	0		
Konetchy,1b	3	0	1	5	0	Schults,3b	3	0	0		
Smith,3b	3	0	0	0	0	Barney,lf	3	0	0		
Egan,2b	3	0	1	1	1	Viox,2b	3	0	0		
Tragresser,c	0	0	0	0	0	Schmidt,c	3	0	0		
Gowdy,c	3	0	1	9	0	K'tlehner,p	3	0	0		
Hughes,p	3	0	1	1		Harmon,p	0	0	0		
						aCostello	1	0	0		
Total	27	2	7	27	3	Total	28	0	0	26	15

a-Batted for Kantlehner in the eighth inning.

Errors—Smith, Kantlehner.

Boston ....1 0 0 0 0 0 0 1—2
Pittsburgh ....0 0 0 0 0 0 0 0—0

Two-base hit—Gowdy. Stolen bases—Wagner, Maranville, Snodgrass. Left on bases—Pittsburgh, 8; Boston, 4. First base on errors—Pittsburgh, 1. Bases on balls—Off Kantlehner, 2; off Harmon, 1; off Hughes, 2. Hits and earned runs—Off Kantlehner, 6 hits and no runs in seven innings; off Harmon, 1 run and one hit in one inning. Struck out—By Kantlehner, 5; by Harmon, 2; by Hughes, 7. Time of game—One hour and thirty minutes. Umpires—Messrs. Klem and Emslie.

June 17, 1916

INDIANS
WEAR NUMBERS

Players Carry Them on Sleeves for First Time In Baseball History.

CLEVELAND, Ohio, June 26.—Cleveland American League players wore numbers on the sleeves of their uniforms in today's game with Chicago for the first time in the history of baseball so far as is known. The numbers corresponded to similar numbers set opposite the players' names on the score cards, so that all fans in the stands might easily identify the members of the home club.

June 27, 1916

BRAVES END FLARE OF GIANTS' METEOR

McGraw's Men Win First Game, the Twenty-sixth Straight, and Then Fall.

BOSTON BATS ARE VICIOUS

Multitude of 38,000 Sadly Watches Visitors Pile Up Five Runs in Seventh and Win 8 to 3.

The Giants lost a game, not an unusual happening in the routine of baseball, but it filled with grief 38,000 spectators at the Polo Grounds yesterday. From every quarter of the big city hero worshippers flocked to the baseball park firm in the belief that the machine built up by John McGraw would remain invincible. The belief grew to conviction after the first game of the doubleheader with Boston, in which the Braves were shut out and the twenty-sixth straight victory perched on the home team's banner by the score of 4 to 0. Then came a shock great as the fall of Troy, when the heavy hitters from the Hub came back in the second with a terrific bombardment which buried the Giants under an avalanche of eight runs, to three collected by the home contingent.

It was hard for the immense crowd to realize that an end had come to the remarkable winning streak, which has gained more renown for the local team than would be achieved by the winning of a brace of pennants. Every club in the National League had been met and conquered in the forced march of the Giants on an almost hopeless chase for the coveted pennant before the disaster came with crushing force. All major league straight victory marks had fallen by the wayside, and the only record left to shoot at was that of the Corsican team of twenty-seven victories, made in the four-club Texas League in 1902.

Another victory would have tied that, and under vastly more trying conditions than those that prevailed away down in Texas. But the breaks that have been with the New Yorkers in this unparalleled run went against them, and the chance to finish the season with the string unbroken faded away under the influence of the lusty bats of the boisterous Braves.

It took the best efforts of George Tyler, one of the most formidable left handed pitchers in the National League, to subdue the bold warriors who make Coogan's Bluff their stamping ground. Yet, capable as was his work on the mound, it is doubtful whether he would have succeeded where so many others had failed if it had not been for the almost superhuman efforts of the diminutive Maranville, probably the most alert shortstop in captivity.

Maranville Nips Off Runs

This energetic little parcel of humanity jumped all around the edge of the diamond with the celerity of a grasshopper and on nearly every leap he was instrumental in cutting off runs and nipping desperate rallies in the bud. Formidable as were the numerals arrayed against them, they were by no means overwhelming when matched against the sturdy batters who faced Tyler. But whenver the vigorous stickwork threatened runs in any liberal quantity little Maranville pounced on the ball and by a marvelous catch or lightning fielding rendered the efforts futile.

Even before the scoreboard was disfigured by any hostile runs the sinister influence of the active shortstop made itself felt. A well-planned double steal in the second inning, when two were out, was shut off when he cut the throw to catch McCarty racing to second, but kept in position to nail Holke by a well-directed heave as he made his dash for the plate. Again, in the fourth he ran almost to left field to catch a fly by Fletcher that would have brought one run in and left only one out. His crowning achievement came in the fifth, when the Giants had Tyler up in the air, and, though they tallied twice and tied the score at that time, there is no knowing how many more runs would have crossed the plate but for one of the smartest double plays seen this season, in which Maranville was the chief factor.

Slim Sallee was the pitcher sacrificed in the game which terminated the record run. Three others followed in the forlorn hope of redeeming the situation, and Tesreau was almost as badly treated by the Braves, who were making runs while the making was good. The slender lad might well have been called Sad Sallee as he left the mound in the fatal seventh, when three runs had been scored with none out, so crestfallen did he appear with the consciousness that he had failed to sustain the winning streak. In attenuation it may be recalled that he has been ill nearly all the time the Giants have been compiling their long list of victories. He was scarcely keyed up to the same pitch as the other twirlers, and gave way under the terrific onslaught of the fighting Braves. An error by Fletcher also helped in his defeat, as the Braves first conceived the idea that they at last had a chance to perform the almost impossible after his bad throw had given Maranville a life in the fourth, with two runs resulting.

Braves Ruthless with Bats.

It was in the seventh that the real whaling commenced, however, the hitting being of a character seldom seen in these days of pitching effectiveness. Sufficient to say that the cluster of five tallies which put the seal on the hopes of the Giants included two home runs, most remarkable of all being the fact that they were made in succession. That inning is the real story of the collapse of McGraw's mighty organization, and it was the pesky Konetchy, who twice during the series has robbed the Giant pitchers of a no-hit game, that began the attack.

FIRST GAME.

NEW YORK. (N.)						BOSTON. (N.)					
	Ab	R	H	Po	A		Ab	R	H	Po	A
Burns,lf	4	1	1	2	0	Snodgr's,cf	4	0	0	3	2
Herzog,2b	4	1	2	3	5	Mar'ville,ss	3	0	0	2	7
Roberts'n,rf	3	0	0	1	0	Fitzp'k,rt	3	0	0	2	0
Zim'man,3b	3	0	0	0	5	Konetchy,1b	3	0	1	10	1
Fletcher,ss	4	1	2	0	5	Smith,3b	3	0	0	2	2
Kauff,cf	3	1	2	1	0	Magee,lf	3	0	0	3	1
Holke,1b	2	0	1	15	0	Egan,2b	3	0	0	0	0
McCarty,c	3	0	1	3	0	Gowdy,c	2	0	0	3	0
Benton,p	3	0	0	2	2	Rudolph,p	2	0	0	0	3
						aBlackburn	1	0	0	0	0
Total....	29	4	9	27	17	Total....	27	0	1	24	16

a-Batted for Rudolph in ninth inning.

Boston............0 0 0 0 0 0 0 0 0—0
New York..........0 0 0 0 0 0 2 2 .—4

Three-base hits—Burns, Fletcher. Stolen bases—Kauff, (2) Holke. Sacrifice hit—Robertson. Sacrifice fly—Zimmerman. Double plays—Fletcher, Herzog, and Holke; Benton, Herzog, and Holke. Left on bases—New York, 4; Boston, 1. First base on errors—New York, 1; Boston, 1. Bases on balls—Off Benton, 1; off Rudolph, 1. Earned runs—Off Rudolph, 2. Struck out—By Benton, 5; by Rudolph, 2. Time of game—One hour and twenty-seven minutes. Umpires—Messrs. Rigler and Byron.

SECOND GAME.

BOSTON. (N.)						NEW YORK. (N.)					
	Ab	R	H	Po	A		Ab	R	H	Po	A
Snodg's,cf	3	0	2	1	0	Burns,lf	5	0	1	2	0
Chappelle,rf	2	0	2	1	0	Herzog,2b	4	0	0	3	4
F'patrick,rf	3	0	0	0	0	R'tson,rf	4	0	1	1	0
Collins,cf	2	0	0	0	0	Zim'man,3b	4	0	0	1	1
Konetchy,1b	4	2	2	8	2	Fletcher,ss	4	0	2	1	2
J. Smith,3b	4	1	1	2	2	Kauff,cf	4	0	0	1	0
Magee,lf	3	1	2	0	0	Holke,1b	4	1	1	11	1
Egan,2b	4	1	2	1	1	McCarty,c	3	2	0	6	2
Blackburn,c	4	2	1	8	2	Sallee,p	2	0	0	0	1
Tyler,p	3	0	1	1	3	Tesreau,p	0	0	0	0	0
						Anderson,p	0	0	0	0	2
Total...	35	8	13	27	11	aLobert	1	0	0	0	0
						G. Smith,p	0	0	0	1	0
						bKocher	1	0	0	0	0
						Total....	36	3	8	27	14

a-Batted for Anderson in seventh inning.
b-Batted for G. Smith in ninth inning.
Errors—J. Smith, Egan, Tyler, Fletcher, (2.)

Boston............0 0 0 2 0 0 5 0 1—8
New York..........0 0 0 0 2 0 1 0 0—3

Two-base hits—Konetchy, Robertson, Fletcher, McCarty. Three-base hit—McCarty. Home runs—J. Smith, Magee. Sacrifice hits—Maranville, (2.) Tyler. Double plays—Sallee, Herzog, and Holke; Maranville and Konetchy; Holke, Fletcher, and Holke. Left on bases—Boston, 4; New York, 7. First base on errors—New York, 2; Boston, 2. Bases on balls—Off G. Smith, 1; off Tyler, 1. Hits and earned runs—Off Sallee, 7 hits and 3 runs in six innings, none out in seventh; off Tesreau, 4 hits and 2 runs, (only four men faced him;) off Anderson, no hits and no runs in one inning; off G. Smith, 2 hits and no runs in two innings; off Tyler, no runs. Struck out—By Sallee, 3; by G. Smith, 1; by Tyler, 6. Wild pitches—Tyler, 1; Tesreau, 1. Passed ball—Blackburn. Time of game Two hours and eighteen minutes. Umpires—Messrs. Byron and Rigler.

He fired the ambition of the visiting batsmen by singling to centre and was followed to the plate by Smith. This same Smith was the perpetrator of the first home run, and it was committed with malice aforethought. He fouled about half a dozen times, one of these going so nearly safe and into the crowd that the mighty throng was seized with cold shivers. The premonition of danger was fulfilled a few seconds later when he caught the ball squarely and it sailed far over Burns's head to find a resting place among the occupants of the left field bleachers. Needless to say Konetchy and the instigator of the home run strolled home at their leisure. Had McGraw realized that the visitors had solved Sallee's slants the defeat might have been less decisive, but it is scarcely in the book for one home run to follow another. Magee, the next up, it is true, used to have a reputation as a home run hitter, and Smith had revived the feeling. His eye was on the spot where Smith's pellet lay buried and the very first ball that the unfortunate Sallee served to him was met with a mighty smash, for an even longer journey than the one that had preceded it. The curfew bell rang loudly for Sallee then, and Tesreau came in to take his share of the furious attack.

Tesreau Fails to Stem Tide.

Egan singled to left, and when Blackborn bunted he managed to reach first safely, as the bag was not covered. This put Egan on second and Tesreau speeded up the progress of both runners with a wild pitch. Tyler's little tap enabled Egan to score and Chapple entering the game to bat for Snodgrass, banged one to left so that Blackburn could keep up the procession of runs.

That ended Big Jeff's short but eventful career, two more runs having come in with no casualties to the batters. Anderson was more successful, as Maranville sacrificed, Collins, batting for Fitzpatrick, fanned, and the pitcher threw out Konetchy, who came up for his second turn at the feast.

October 1, 1916

BABE RUTH LED HIS LEAGUE.

Red Sox Twirler Gave Fewest Earned Runs in American Circuit.

Babe Ruth of the Boston Red Sox led the American League pitchers last season, according to the official averages, which were made public by President Ban Johnson yesterday. The pitchers are rated on the same basis as the National League twirlers, not on the games won and lost, but on the number of earned runs per game. Ruth allowed only 1.75 runs per game and he took part in forty-four games. Eddie Cicotte of Chicago was second, allowing 1.78 runs per game. Walter Johnson of Washington was third. He allowed 1.89 runs per game.

Davenport of St. Louis was the hardest worked pitcher, taking part in fifty-nine games. Reb Russell of Chicago was next, with fifty-six, and Bob Shawkey of the Yankees pitched in fifty-three games. Walter Johnson, however, pitched the greatest number of innings, 371. He also led the league in strikeouts, with 228 to his credit. Myers of the Athletics was the most liberal of the twirlers, and gave 168 bases on balls. Joe Bush of the Athletics was the wildest, with fifteen wild heaves. Dauss of Detroit did the most damage to his opponents by hitting sixteen players.

Nick Cullop led the Yankee pitchers, permitting 2.05 earned runs per game. He stood ninth among the league pitchers. Shawkey was eleventh, and he took part in more games than any other of Donovan's boxmen. Mogridge was rated twelfth in the list.

December 10, 1916

NO HITS, NO RUNS FOR NINE INNINGS

Reds Nose Out Cubs in Tenth by 1 to 0 When Kopf and Jim Thorpe Get Singles.

CHICAGO, May 2.—Probably a world's record was established here today in a ten-inning game between Cincinnati and Chicago. Neither club registered a hit or run in nine full innings. Cincinnati won in the tenth, 1 to 0.

For the nine innings Vaughn, assisted by remarkable defense by the Chicago infield, did not permit a Cincinnati player to reach second base, and in doing this feat only slightly surpassed his pitching opponent. Toney, who allowed only one Chicago runner to reach second, Vaughn struck out ten Cincinnati

batsmen while three were being fanned by Toney.

The game was won in the tenth inning after one out. Kopf singled, advanced to third when Williams dropped Chase's fly, and scored when Thorpe hit a slow bounder to Vaughn.

The Cincinnati outfielders several times saved the game for Toney, Chase on one occasion backing into the left field to take Merkle's fly.

The score:

CINCINNATI. (N.)						CHICAGO. (N.)					
	Ab	R	H	Po	A		Ab	R	H	Po	A
Groh,3b	4	0	0	2	2	Zeider,ss	4	0	0	1	0
Getz,2b	4	0	0	2	1	Wolter,rf	4	0	0	0	0
Ko.f,ss	4	1	1	1	4	Doyle,2b	4	0	0	5	4
Neale,cf	4	0	1	0	0	Merkle,1b	4	0	0	7	1
Chase,1b	4	0	0	12	0	Williams,cf	2	0	0	2	0
Thorpe,rf	4	0	1	1	0	Mann,lf	3	0	0	0	0
Shean,2b	3	0	0	3	2	Wilson,c	3	0	1	4	1
Cueto,lf	3	0	0	3	0	Deal,3b	3	0	0	1	0
Huhn,c	3	0	0	3	0	Vaughn,p	3	0	0	0	3
Toney,p	3	0	0	0	1						
Total....	30	1	2	30	10	Total....	30	0	0	30	9

Errors—Zeider, Williams.

Cincinnati..........0 0 0 0 0 0 0 0 0 1—1
Chicago.............0 0 0 0 0 0 0 0 0 0—0

Stolen base—Chase. Double plays—Doyle, Merkle, and Zeider; Vaughn, Doyle, and Merkle. Left on bases—Chicago, 2; Cincinnati, 2. First base on errors—Toney, 2; Vaughn, 2. Bases on balls—Off Vaughn, none in 10; off Toney, none in 10. Struck out—By Vaughn, 10; Toney, 3. Time of game—One hour, 50 minutes. Umpires—Orth and Rigler.

May 3, 1917

SHORE JOINS RANKS OF NO-HIT PITCHERS

Red Sox Whitewash Senators Twice — Ruth Strikes Umpire Owens.

BOSTON, June 23.—A no-hit, no-run, no-man-reached-first base pitching performance by Ernest Shore, Boston twirler; an assault upon Umpire Owens by Babe Ruth, another Boston pitcher, in which the umpire was struck behind the ear, and the defeat of Walter Johnson by Dutch Leonard, were incidents of the world champions' double victory over Washington today. The scores were 4 to 0 and 5 to 0.

Shore's entry into the select list of pitchers who have shown perfect performances was made possible by Ruth's banishment from the first game. Ruth had pitched only to Ray Morgan, and Umpire Owens had given the latter his base on balls. Ruth argued the decision, the umpire ordered him off the field, and the Boston pitcher then struck at Owens. Other players intervened, and Ruth left the field.

Shore was called in with Morgan on first base, but a moment later the latter was thrown out attempting to steal second. Thereafter the Boston pitcher and his fielders turned back every Washington batsman. Ayers, who pitched for Washington, was hit hard.

In the second game Leonard held Washington to four hits, while the world champions cracked out hits in bunches off Johnson, and, with errors, won easily. The scores:

FIRST GAME.

BOSTON. (A.)	Ab	R	H	Po	A	WASHINGTON. (A.)	Ab	R	H	Po	A
Hooper,rf	4	0	1	0	0	Morgan,2b	2	0	0	4	2
Barry,2b	4	0	0	2	1	Foster,3b	3	0	0	1	3
Hoblitzell,1b	4	0	0	12	2	Leonard,3b	0	0	0	0	1
Gardner,3b	4	1	1	2	1	Milan,cf	3	0	0	1	0
Lewis,lf	4	0	3	2	0	Rice,rf	3	0	0	3	0
Walker,cf	3	1	1	4	0	Gharrity,1b	3	0	0	0	0
Scott,ss	3	0	0	1	5	Judge,1b	3	0	0	11	1
Thomas,c	0	0	0	0	0	Jamieson,lf	3	0	0	0	0
Agnew,c	3	1	3	2	1	Shanks,ss	3	0	0	1	0
Ruth,p	0	0	0	0	0	Henry,c	3	0	0	1	0
Shore,p	2	1	0	2	6	Ayres,p	2	0	0	2	8
						aMenosky	1	0	0	0	0
Total	31	4	9	27	16	Total	26	0	0	24	17

a Batted for Ayres in ninth.
Errors—Foster, (2,) Rice.

Boston ....0 1 0 0 0 0 3 0.—4
Washington ....0 0 0 0 0 0 0 0 0—0

Two-base hits—Walker, Shore, Scott. Double plays—Ayres, Foster, and Judge; Ayres and Judge. Left on bases—Boston, 6. First base on errors—Boston, 8. Base on balls—Off Ruth, 1. Hits and earned runs—Off Shore, no hits, no runs in no inning, (none out in first;) Shore, none and none in 9; Ayres, 9 and 4 in 8. Struck out—By Shore, 2. Time—1 hour 40 minutes. Umpires—Owen, McCormick, and Dineen.

SECOND GAME.

BOSTON. (A.)	Ab	R	H	Po	A	X SECOND BOX WASHINGTON. (A.)	Ab	R	H	Po	A
Hooper,rf	4	0	0	1	1						
Barry,2b	3	1	2	1	3	Morgan,2b	5	0	1	1	5
Hoblitzell,1b	3	1	0	11	1	J. Leonard,3b	2	0	0	1	0
Gardner,3b	3	0	1	2	3	Milan,cf	3	0	2	4	0
Lewis,lf	4	1	1	3	0	Rice,rf	4	0	1	3	0
Walker,cf	3	0	0	1	0	Gharrity,1b	4	0	0	8	0
Scott,ss	4	1	2	0	2	Shanks,ss	4	0	0	1	6
Thomas,c	4	1	3	7	0	Ainsmith,c	4	0	0	6	1
H. Leonard,p	3	0	0	1	2	Johnson,p	3	0	0	1	3
						aHenry	0	0	0	0	0
Total	31	5	9	27	12	Jamieson,lf	3	0	0	0	0
						Total	31	0	4	24	11

a Batted for Jamieson in ninth.
Errors—Milan, Shanks.

Boston ....0 0 2 0 0 0 2 1.—5
Washington ....0 0 0 0 0 0 0 0 0—0

Two-base hit—Scott. Sacrifice hit—Walker. Double plays—Shanks, Morgan, and Gharrity. Left on bases—Boston, 7; Washington, 10. First base on errors—Boston, 1. Bases on balls—Off Johnson, 2; Leonard, 5. Earned runs—Off Johnson, 4 runs in 8 innings; Leonard, 0 in 9. Hit by pitcher—By Johnson, (Barry, Hoblitzell.) Struck out—By Leonard, 7; Johnson, 5. Wild pitch—Leonard. Time—1 hour 58 minutes. Umpires — McCormick, Dineen, and Owens.

ALEXANDER BREAKS PITCHERS' RECORDS

Has Hurled in Greatest Number of Few-Hit and No-Run Games Since 1893.

During the season just ended, Grover Cleveland Alexander, the great pitcher of the Phillies, equaled the phenomenal record which up to that time was held only by Christy Mathewson, the former Giant idol, in winning thirty games for three successive years. Alex the Great is the only twirler baseball has produced who has been able to equal this mark.

A year ago Alexander showed that he ranked with the greatest in the game when he established a newer record by winning sixteen of his 1916 victories by the shut-out route. This is one of the truly wonderful feats of major league pitching. Alexander has completed his seventh year as a major league twirler, and he is not through yet by any means. Before he lays aside his uniform it will not be surprising if he is hailed as Alexander the Greatest, instead of just the Great.

EDWARD S. PLANK
"GETTYSBURG EDDIE"
ONE OF GREATEST LEFTHANDED PITCHERS OF MAJOR LEAGUES. NEVER PITCHED FOR A MINOR LEAGUE TEAM, GOING FROM GETTYSBURG COLLEGE TO THE PHILADELPHIA A.L. TEAM WITH WHICH HE SERVED FROM 1901 THROUGH 1914. MEMBER OF ST. LOUIS F.L. IN 1915 AND ST. LOUIS A.L. IN 1916-17. ONE OF FEW PITCHERS TO WIN MORE THAN 300 GAMES IN BIG LEAGUES. IN EIGHT OF 17 SEASONS, WON 20 OR MORE GAMES.

Old Cy Young, Ed Walsh, and Bill Dineen displayed great work in the box year after year, but none of the game's great pitchers have been able to win thirty victories three years in succession but Matty and Alexander. Toward the end of the season it was doubtful whether Alex would equal Matty's record, as the Quakers' winning streak was snapped and their pennant chances spoiled in the last Giant series in New York.

Then everybody was asking. "Will Alex equal Matty's great record?" During the final series with the Giants in Philadelphia Alexander had won 29 games and lost 13. The day before the season closed Alex pitched against the Giants and won his thirtieth victory. In 1915, with a pennant-winning club behind him, Alexander won 31 games and lost 10, and in 1916 he won 33 games and lost 12.

"Not only is Alexander great because of his pitching work," says Pat Moran, leader of the Phillies, "but he's an invaluable member of the team because of his splendid character. He is the easiest star pitcher to handle I have ever known. He is willing to work out of turn, no matter what the weather, no matter if he is feeling fit or not. He is always ready for the call of duty. He is a model athlete and one of the cleanest, manliest fellows I have ever known."

HOLDS TIGERS HITLESS.

Leonard Rules with Iron Arm and Red Sox Win by 5 to 0.

DETROIT, June 3.—Holding Detroit hitless, Leonard pitched Boston to a 5 to 0 victory here this afternoon. Only one Detroiter reached first base, the result of the only base on balls Leonard issued.

Boston hit Dauss freely, bunching the blows with bases on balls and errors. Ruth, sent to centre field to replace Strunk, duplicated his home run of yesterday by again placing he ball in the right field bleachers.

The score:

BOSTON. (A.)	Ab	R	H	Po	A	DETROIT. (A.)	Ab	R	H	Po	A
Hooper,rf	4	1	1	4	0	Bush,ss	4	0	0	2	3
Shean,2b	4	0	0	2	1	Young,2b	3	0	0	4	1
Ruth,cf	5	1	1	3	0	Veach,lf	2	0	0	0	0
Whiteman,lf	4	0	1	1	0	Hellman,rf	3	0	0	0	0
McInnis,1b	3	1	1	7	0	Dyer,1b	3	0	0	8	2
Thomas,3b	3	1	1	1	2	Walker,cf	3	0	0	3	1
Scott,ss	4	1	2	3	4	Vitt,3b	3	0	0	2	2
Schang,c	4	0	1	6	0	Yelle,c	3	0	0	7	1
Leonard,p	4	0	0	0	1	Dauss,p	1	0	0	0	1
						Cunn'ham,p	0	0	0	1	1
Total	35	5	8	27	8	aSpencer	1	0	0	0	0
						bCobb	1	0	0	0	0
						Total	27	0	0	27	12

a Batted for Dauss in sixth.
b Batted for Cunningham in ninth.
Errors—Young, (2.)

Boston ....1 0 0 1 1 2 0 0 0—5
Detroit ....0 0 0 0 0 0 0 0 0—0

Two-base hit—Whiteman. Three-base hit—Hooper. Home run—Ruth. Stolen bases—Whiteman, Hooper, McInnis. Sacrifice hit—Thomas. Double play—Yelle and Vitt. Left on bases—Boston, 7; Detroit, 1. First base on errors—Boston, 2. Bases on balls—Off Leonard, 1; Dauss, 2; Cunningham, 1. Hits—Off Dauss, 8 in 6 innings; Cunningham, 0 in 3. Struck out—By Dauss, 5; Cunningham, 2; Leonard, 4. Wild pitch—Dauss. Losing pitcher—Dauss.

BASEBALL SEASON WILL CLOSE SEPT. 1

National League Votes Against Continuing Pastime with Men Not in Draft.

There will be no major league baseball after Sept. 1, the date set by Secretary of War Baker for the ball players within the draft age to get into essential work. This was decided yesterday at a special meeting of the National League in this city. Some of the club owners were in favor of continuing play after that date with clubs made up of players under and above the draft age, but the majority ruled that major league baseball of this inferior type would injure the game more than it would help it.

The National League was to have met here today, but when August Herrmann, Chairman of the National Commission, called a meeting of that body at Cleveland for today he also called a meeting of the National League club owners. President Tener, a member of the National Commission, has refused to meet with the commission because of the American League's refusal to abide by the decision of that body in the Scott-Perry case. Most of the National League club owners were ready to abandon today's meeting of the National League and attend the joint meeting of the two leagues in Cleveland.

With the leagues and the club owners at loggerheads, the baseball season is very likely to end in a bad muddle, and the whole structure of the national pastime may have to be reconstructed after the war.

There was not a full representation of the National League at the meeting here, but a majority of the clubs were represented. After the league had passed a resolution deciding that no championship games would be played after Labor Day, Barney Dreyfuss was appointed a committee of one to attend the meeting with the American League in Cleveland. He is vested with full power to act in regard to any readjustment of the schedule.

There is sure to be a clash between the leagues over the world's series. The American League—that is, President B. B. Johnson—wants to end the season on Aug. 20 and play the series before Sept. 1, the time set by Secretary Baker. Chairman August Herrmann of the National Commission believes that the clubs should play right up to Sept. 1 before awarding the pennant, and then play the world's series. He takes this attitude on the assumption that the players on the two winning clubs will have another time extension until the big series is finished. It is not known that Mr. Herrmann has any grounds for believing that Provost General Crowder will grant this extra time to the world's series contestants.

The National League club owners are strongly opposed to closing the leagues by Aug. 20 because they want all the clubs to play out their schedules up to Sept. 2 and get the benefit of the receipts up to that date. It is believed that Dreyfuss at Cleveland will strongly oppose any attempt of the American League to start the world's series on Aug. 20. It is not unlikely that, if the American League insists on starting the series on Aug. 20, some arrangement may be made whereby all the clubs will share in the world's series money. Under a new arrangement, adopted last Winter, the first four clubs in each league will share in the receipts, but it may be necessary to declare every club owner in on the division in order to keep peace in the baseball family.

RUTH WALLOPS OUT HIS 28TH HOME RUN

Terrific Crash Over the Polo Grounds Stands Sets New World's Record.

YANKS SPLIT WITH RED SOX

Lose the First by 4 to 0, but Take the Second Game, 2 to 1, After 13 Innings.

A new world's batting record was made up at the Polo Grounds yesterday, when Babe Ruth, Boston's superlative slugger, boosted his twenty-eighth home run of the season high over the right field grand stand into Manhattan Field, which adjoins the Brush Stadium. This smashes the thirty-five-year-old record made by Ed Williamson of Chicago, who was credited with twenty-seven homers in 1884.

Ruth's glorious smash yesterday was the longest drive ever made at the Polo Grounds. It came in the ninth inning of the second game of a double-header with the Yankees and tied the score at 1 to 1. Bob Shawkey was doing the pitching and he heaved over a slow curve, hoping to fool Ruth as he has done before.

Ruth stood firmly on his sturdy legs like the Colossus of Rhodes, and, taking a mighty swing at the second ball pitched to him, catapulted the pill for a new altitude and distance record. Several seasons ago Joe Jackson hit a home run over the top of the right field stand but the ball landed on the roof. Ruth's bang yesterday cleared the stand by many yards and went over into the weeds in the next lot.

The Boston mauler not long ago made his twenty-sixth home run at the Polo Grounds, smashing the modern home run record made by Buck Freeman. Then it was discovered in the dusty archives of the game that Williamson had made twenty-seven in one season. Ruth's mark now surpasses all home run achievements, ancient or modern. Ruth got a great reception from the crowd of 5,000 or more fans, and throughout the afternoon he was hailed with cheers every time he came up to bat.

Yanks Need Thirteen Innings to Win.

Ruth's homer tied the score, and it wasn't until the thirteenth inning of this second game that the Yanks finally won out by 2 to 1. In the thirteenth, with two out, Wallie Pipp pasted a triple against the front of the bleachers in right field and trotted home with the winning run when Del Pratt boomed a high sacrifice fly out to Ruth in left field.

This belated victory gave the Yanks an even break on the day's pastime, for Boston shut out Huggins's men in the first game by a score of 4 to 0. Waite Hoyt, the Brooklyn schoolboy, pitched for the Red Sox in the second and Bob Shawkey officiated for the Yanks. Hoyt gave a remarkable performance of his pitching skill, and from the fourth inning to the thirteenth he did not allow a hit and not a Yankee runner reached first base. In these nine hitless innings the youngster was at the top of his form and pitched with the coolness and skill of a veteran.

Shawkey came through the seething fray with flying colors after one of the hardest battles he ever entered. There were times when the Red Sox had victory within their grasp, only to be baffled at the last moment by Shawkey's wonderful generalship. The menace of Ruth's mighty bat was always a shadow in Shawkey's path. In the sixth inning Ruth shot out a mighty blow to right centre field for three bases. It looked like a home run, but Ruth in his anxiety to break the record cut second base by a few feet and was declared out by the watchful umpire Tommy Connolly.

Again in the twelfth inning, Ruth brought the crowd to its feet by thumping a tremendous slam to deep right centre which for a moment looked as if it were going to clear the centre field bleachers. Young Chick Fewster then covered himself with glory by romping back at top speed to snare the ball just as it was getting away.

Stuffy McInnis to the Fore.

This second game bristled with brilliant fielding, the star of the defensive work being Stuffy McInnis, the Boston first baseman. There were times yesterday when he covered the territory around first base with all the brilliancy of Hal Chase in his hey-day. There was one play which fans will not soon forget. It came in the tenth inning when Duffy Lewis slammed a red hot grounder to short. Scott speared it with his usual skill and made a low, wide throw to first. McInnis reached out as if he were made of India rubber and pinched the ball between his thumb and index finger. There the ball stuck and Lewis was out. The crowd gave McInnis a howling reception when he walked to the bench after that inning.

The Yankees played a listless game in the first affair, and although Sam Jones was so wild that he gave nine bases on balls, the Yanks couldn't harvest a single run. Twice—in the third and in the fourth—they had the bases full and failed to produce a tally. No less than fourteen of the Yanks were left stranded and opportunities to score came so fast that they couldn't keep track of them.

Jack Quinn was also inclined to be wild, and his few passes were costly. Bases on balls figured in both innings in which the Red Sox got their runs. Joe Wilhoit, who used to be with the Giants and before that with the Boston Braves, played in right field in place of Harry Hooper. Wilhoit set the Western League afire in Wichita by batting over .300 and he has come back to the majors to try his hand again. He nailed the first ball that Quinn pitched to left for a Texas Leaguer, but didn't do much after that.

Jack Quinn Tames Ruth in First.

All eyes were on Babe Ruth in this first game but he failed to do anything. Quinn walked him purposely in the first inning and when the home-run king came to bat in the third inning, Quinn struck him out. There was much commotion in the fifth when Babe fanned again. On his fourth trip to the plate Ruth skied to Fewster.

Joe Wilhoit welcomed Quinn in the first inning of the opening game with a Texas Leaguer to left. He sailed along on Vitt's sacrifice and Bill Lamar hoisted one to Fewster. Quinn walked Ruth intentionally and Schang got a pass, filling the bases. McInnis streaked a single to the right field wall, and Wilhoit and Ruth scrambled over the plate. McInnis and Schang then tried to launch a double steal and Schang died in the attempt.

Pipp and Lewis got aboard on singles in the second inning with one out but Fewster and Ruel both died at the hands of Scott. Scotty made a great catch of Ruel's foul over near the boxes back of third. In the third Jones was as wild as a Fiji but the Yanks couldn't take advantage of it. With one out, Vick ambled and went to second on a wild pitch. Peck also got a pass and Baker skied to Wilhoit. Pipp got a pass and the bases were loaded up with dead head passengers. It was up to Del Pratt to clean the corners, but the very nicest that Del could produce was a foul fly to Vitt.

The Red Sox grabbed another brace of tallies in the fourth. McInnis walked and Shannon was safe on Peck's fumble, while Scotty pushed them along with a sacrifice. After Jones fanned, Wilhoit cracked a single to right centre and encouraged McInnis and Shannon over the platter.

Yanks Crowd Bases, Then Quit.

In the Yankees' half of this same inning Jones was still wild, and again the three corners were profusely decorated with New York citizens. Peckinpaugh had a chance to do something for his country, but fell down on the job. With two out in this stanza, Ruel singled and Quinn got a pass. Vick also got a free ticket, and there they were, three of them all ready and willing to race home. Peckinpaugh lofted a foul or two into the stand and then struck out, to the mournful chorus of 5,000 moans.

Peckinpaugh opened the ninth with a single to left and Baker soaked a liner to Shannon, who made a great catch. Shannon tried to double Peck off first and threw the ball into the grand stand. Peck, instead of com-

Five Leading Batsmen of the Major Leagues

American League.

Player.	G.	AB.	R.	H.	P.C.
Cobb	121	485	88	184	.379
Jackson	136	511	79	179	.350
Veach	135	519	82	180	.347
Sisler	129	499	91	170	.341
Jacobson	117	439	68	143	.326

National League.

Player.	G.	AB.	R.	H.	P.C.
Roush	129	490	69	158	.322
Hornsby	135	499	63	158	.317
Stock	133	483	55	149	.309
Myers	131	501	58	154	.307
Groh	120	440	79	135	.307

ing back to touch first, went right on to third but the ball was out of play and Peck had to come back to first. Pipp rocketed to Wilhoit and Jones tossed Pratt out at first and the lifeless affair was ended.

The Yanks showed a little more gumption early in the second game and culled a run in the second inning off Hoyt. Pipp beat out an infield tap between first and second and raced to third on Pratt's single to left, Del going to second on the throw to catch Pipp. Duff Lewis knocked a single to centre, scoring Pipp, while Pratt scooted to third. Fewster was thrown out by Vitt and Ruel hammered a hot liner to McInnis, who tossed to Vitt, and Pratt was doubled before he could get back to third.

The Red Sox nicked Shawkey for three hits in the fifth, but could not get a run. After Peck tossed McNally out at first, McNeil singled to right. Scott singled to left, McNeil halting at second. Hoyt banged a single to centre and filled the bases. Gilhooley cracked a hot grounder to Pipp, who soaked the ball home, forcing McNeil. Oscar Vitt skied to Vick and Shawkey was saved from an embarrassing situation.

The scores:

FIRST GAME.

BOSTON. (A.)	Ab	R	H	Po	A	NEW YORK. (A.)	Ab	R	H	Po	A
Wilhoit.rf	5	1	2	4	0	Vick.rf	3	0	1	1	0
Vitt.3b	4	0	0	1	3	Peck'p'gh.ss	4	0	1	3	3
Lamar.cf	4	0	1	0	0	Baker.3b	3	0	0	0	2
Ruth.lf	3	1	0	0	0	Pipp.1b	3	0	1	11	3
Schang.c	3	0	1	3	0	Lewis.lf	4	0	1	2	0
McInnis.1b	3	1	1	13	0	Pratt.2b	3	0	0	1	3
Shannon.2b	4	1	0	2	4	Fewster.cf	3	0	0	3	0
Scott.ss	3	0	0	2	1	Ruel.c	3	0	1	6	2
Jones.p	3	0	1	1	5	Quinn.p	2	0	0	0	4
						Thormahlen.p	0	0	0	0	0
Total	32	4	6	27	31	a[illegible]	0	0	0	0	0
						Total	32	0	5	27	14

Errors—McInnis, Shannon, Peckinpaugh Pratt.

a Batted for Quinn in eighth.

Boston .... 2 0 0 2 0 0 0 0 0—4
New York ..... 0 0 0 0 0 0 0 0 0—0

Stolen base—Fewster, Schang. Sacrifice hit—Scott. Left on bases—New York, 11; Boston, 6. First base on errors—New York, 0; Boston, 2. Bases on balls—Off Quinn, 4; Jones, 9. Hits—Off Quinn, 6 in 8 innings; Thormahlen, 0 in 1. Struck out—By Quinn, 3; Thormahlen, 1; Jones, 3. Wild pitch—Jones. Losing pitcher—Quinn.

SECOND GAME.

NEW YORK. (A.)	Ab	R	H	Po	A	BOSTON. (A.)	Ab	R	H	Po	A
Vick.rf	5	0	0	3	0	Gilhooley.rf	6	0	2	2	1
Peck'p'gh.ss	5	0	1	2	7	Vitt.3b	6	0	1	2	3
Baker.3b	5	0	0	2	1	Lamar.cf	6	0	2	1	0
Pipp.1b	5	2	2	14	2	Ruth.lf	4	1	2	2	1
Pratt.2b	5	0	1	4	5	McInnis.1b	5	0	0	19	2
Lewis.lf	4	0	1	2	0	McNally.2b	5	0	1	1	3
Fewster.cf	4	0	0	5	2	McNeill.c	4	0	2	5	1
Ruel.c	4	0	0	6	2	Scott.ss	5	0	1	2	5
Shawkey.p	4	0	0	1	1	Hoyt.p	5	0	1	1	4
						Schang.c	3	0	1	1	0
Total	41	2	5	39	20	Total	49	1	13	*37	18

a Batted for McNeil in eleventh.

*Winning run scored with one out.

Error—Fewster.

New York..... 0 1 0 0 0 0 0 0 0 0 0 0 1—2
Boston .... 0 0 0 0 0 0 0 0 1 0 0 0 0—1

Two-base hit—Pratt. Three-base hit—Schang. Home run—Ruth. Stolen bases—Gilhooley, Ruth, Scott. Sacrifice fly—Pratt. Double play—McInnis and Vitt. Left on bases—New York, 2; Boston, 13. Bases on balls—Off Shawkey, 4; Hoyt, 6. Struck out—By Shawkey, 4; Hoyt, 3. Wild pitch—Shawkey.

FREAK PITCHING IS DOOMED IN MAJORS

American League Comes Out for Reform in Deliveries—National Favors Plan.

CHICAGO, Oct. 30.—President Ban Johnson of the American League tonight requested August Herrmann, Chairman of the National Commission, and John A. Heydler, President of the National League, to call a joint meeting of the Rules Committee of the two Leagues to take action in regard to the abolition of the "spitball," the "shineball," and other freak pitching deliveries. President Johnson said these deliveries should be legislated out of the major leagues. He also has several suggestions to make on the scoring rules.

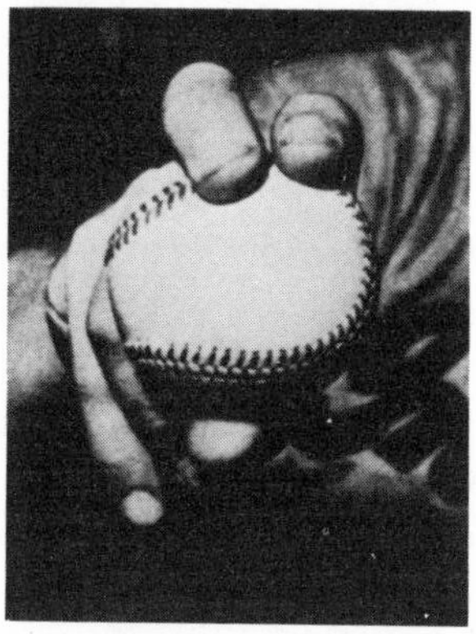

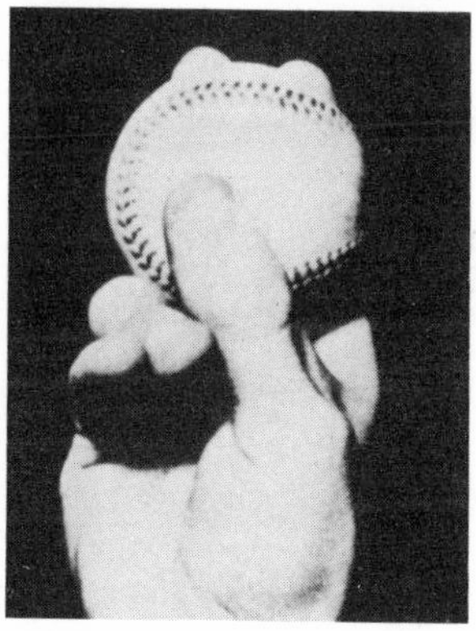

This action by the President of the American League, who will be backed up by his club owners, foreshadows the end of the spitball, a delivery which has been used with marked success by many major league boxmen during the past twenty years. At various times in the last few seasons reports have spread that the major leagues would take action against the delivery, but not until now has any official action been directed at this and other of the so-called freak deliveries.

That the National League will prove a willing ally in Johnson's effort to curb the practice of using foreign substances on the ball or in any way changing the surface condition of the sphere goes withing saying. President John Heydler has been against such pitching for some time. Barney Dreyfuss, owner of the Pittsburgh club, has been a strong opponent of freak pitching for some time, and only a few weeks ago he announced that he will bring the matter to the attention of the National League at its coming meeting in December. Other club owners are known to hold similar views.

Ban May Be Delayed.

If the majors vote to place a ban on the spitball they will not be original in their action, as the American Association went on record a year ago against the use of the delivery. During the past season umpires in the big minor league of the Middle West were instructed to see that the pitchers made no attempt to put saliva on the ball, and as a result numerous spitball pitchers, ineffective with this delivery curbed, were sent to other leagues.

Just what procedure the major leagues will follow in putting an end to the use of the spitball is problematical. It is expected that the ban will not become effective immediately after its passage. Such a move would drive from the majors several boxmen who rely almost entirely on the delivery, either in actual use or as a threat, to retain their places in the big leagues. The argument has been advanced that these pitchers should have time to perfect themselves in another style of delivery, and it would not be surprising if the rule makers should decide to make the ban effective one or two seasons after passage.

A rule forbidding the pitcher to raise the ball above his shoulder before delivering it to the batsman or to wet his fingers with saliva should put an end to the spitball. The other deliveries can be stopped by enforcing a rule that neither the pitcher nor any other player shall rub the ball against any part of his uniform or roughen the outside surface of the ball. These are the methods employed in doctoring the ball for the deliveries other than the spitter. By giving umpires broad powers in enforcing these rules and adding a fine for violation the freak deliveries would soon go.

Stricklett the Pioneer.

The spitball discovery has been variously claimed, but it is generally agreed that Elmer Stricklett, a pitcher who flourished about twenty years ago, developed the delivery until it attracted wide attention. Old timers contend that they got peculiar breaks in pitching by wetting the ball, but none specialized in this peculiar delivery up to the time of Stricklett. Jack Chesbro and Ed. Walsh, outstanding stars of the pitching ranks between the seasons of 1901 and 1910, were perhaps the most successful of the spitballers. Many boxmen have used the delivery in recent years, but none attained the success of either Chesbro or Walsh. In recent seasons every major league club has carried a pitcher or two who depended upon the spitball for success.

The shine ball and other freak deliveries have been of more recent origin. Russell Ford started a craze with the emery ball which finally resulted in the delivery being legislated out of the game. Eddie Cicotte and Hod Eller are supposed to be shine ball experts, but the methods used in doctoring this particular ball never has been clearly explained.

Many prominent pitchers of both the National and American League will be affected by a rule that would bar the use of the so-called freak deliveries.

October 31, 1919

PART II

Going, Going, Gone

1920-1935

YANKS BUY BABE RUTH FOR $125,000

Highest Purchase Price in Baseball History Paid for Game's Greatest Slugger.

WILL GET NEW CONTRACT

Miller Huggins Is Now in California to Sign Home-Run King at Large Salary.

SLATED FOR RIGHT FIELD

Acquisition of Noted Batsman Gives New York Club the Hard-Hitting Outfielder Long Desired.

Babe Ruth of the Boston Red Sox, baseball's super-slugger, was purchased by the Yankees yesterday for the largest cash sum ever paid for a player. The New York Club paid Harry Frazee of Boston $125,000 for the sensational batsman who last season caused such a furore in the national game by batting out twenty-nine home runs, a new record in long-distance clouting.

Colonel Ruppert, President of the Yanks, said that he had taken over Ruth's Boston contract, which has two years more to run. This contract calls for a salary of $10,000 a year. Ruth recently announced that he would refuse to play for $10,000 next season, although the Boston Club has received no request for a raise in salary.

Manager Miller Huggins is now in Los Angeles negotiating with Ruth. It is believed that the Yankee manager will offer him a new contract which will be satisfactory to the Colossus of the bat.

President Ruppert said yesterday that Ruth would probably play right field for the Yankees. He played in left field for the Red Sox last season, and had the highest fielding average among the outfielders, making only two errors during the season. While he is on the Pacific Coast Manager Huggins will also endeavor to sign Duffy Lewis, who will be one of Ruth's companions in the outfield at the Polo Grounds next season.

Home Run Record in Danger.

The acquisition of Ruth strengthens the Yankee club in its weakest department. With the added hitting power of Ruth, Bob Shawkey, one of the Yankee pitchers, said yesterday the New York club should be a pennant winner next season. For several seasons the Yankees have been experimenting with outfielders, but never have been able to land a consistent hitter. The short right field wall at the Polo Grounds should prove an easy target for Ruth next season and, playing seventy-seven games at home, it would not be surprising if Ruth surpassed his home-run record of twenty-nine circuit clouts next Summer.

Ruth was such a sensation last season that he supplanted the great Ty Cobb as baseball's greatest attraction, and in obtaining the services of Ruth for next

season the New York club made a ten-strike which will be received with the greatest enthusiasm by Manhattan baseball fans.

Ruth's crowning batting accomplishment came at the Polo Grounds last Fall when he hammered one of the longest hits ever seen in Harlem over the right field grandstand for his twenty-eighth home run, smashing the home record of twenty-seven, made by Ed Williamson way back in 1884. The more modern home-run record, up to last season, had been held by Buck Freeman, who made twenty-five home runs when a member of the Washington club in 1899. The next best home-run hitter of modern times is Gavvy Cravath, now manager of the Phillies, who made twenty-four home runs a few seasons ago.

Ruth's home-run drives were distributed all over the circuit, and he is the one player known to the game who hit a home run on every park on the circuit in the same season.

Specializes in Long Hits.

Ruth's batting feats last season will stand for many years to come, unless he betters the record himself with the aid of the short right field under Coogan's Bluff. The record he made last season was a masterpiece of slugging. He went up to the bat 432 times in 130 games and produced 139 hits. Of these hits 75 were for extra bases. Not only did he make 29 home runs, but he also made 34 two-baggers and 12 three-baggers. Ruth's batting average for extra base hits was .657, a mark which probably will not be approached for many years to come.

Ruth scored the greatest number of runs in the American League last season, crossing the plate 103 times. Cobb scored only 97 runs last year. Ruth was so dangerous that the American League pitchers were generous with their passes and the superlative hitter walked 101 times, many of these passes being intentional. Ruth also struck out more than any other batsman in the league, fanning 58 times. He also made three sacrifice hits and he stole seven bases.

Ruth is a native of Baltimore and is 26 years old, just in his prime as a baseball player. He was discovered by Jack Dunn, owner of the Baltimore Club, while playing with the baseball team of Mount St. Joseph's, a school which Ruth attended in that city, in 1913. In 1914 Ruth played with the Baltimore team and up to that time little attention had been paid to his batting. It was as a pitcher that he attracted attention in Baltimore. Boston bought Ruth along with Ernie Shore and some other players in 1914. The price paid for Ruth was said to have been $2,700.

Holds World's Series Record

Ruth was a big success in the major league from the start. In 1916, when the Red Sox won the pennant, he led the American League pitchers in effectiveness and in the world's series of 1916 and 1918, Ruth hung up a new world's series pitching record for shut out innings. He pitched twenty-eight consecutive scoreless innings, which beat the record of twenty-seven scoreless innings made in world's series games by Christy Mathewson of the Giants.

For the past few seasons Ruth's ambition has been to play regularly. While he was doing only pitching duty with Boston he was a sensational pinch hitter and when he played regularly in the outfield last season he blossomed forth as the most sensational batsman the game has ever known. He was also a great success as a fielder and last season he made only two errors and had 230 putouts. He also had twenty-six assists, more than any outfielder in the American League. This was because of his phenomenal throwing arm. His fielding average last season was .992. Ruth didn't do much pitching last season. He pitched thirteen games and won eight and lost five.

Manager Huggins is expected back in New York at the end of next week with Ruth's contract in his inside pocket. It is believed that the New York Club will not try to hold Ruth to the Boston contract which he has decided is unsatisfactory.

The new contract which the Yankees have offered Ruth is said to be almost double the Boston figure of $10,000 a year. While he is out on the coast interviewing Ruth, Huggins is also getting into line, not only Duffy Lewis, but also Bob Meusel, the sensational young slugger of the Pacific Coast League, who is regarded by baseball scouts as the minor league find of the year.

The Perfect Hitter.

Ruth's principle of batting is much the same as the principle of the golfer. He comes back slowly, keeps his eye on the ball and follows through. His very position at the bat is intimidating to the pitcher. He places his feet in perfect position. He simply cannot step away from the pitch if he wants to. He can step only one way—in. The weight of Ruth's body when he bats is on his left leg. The forward leg is bent slightly at the knee. As he stands facing the pitcher more of his hips and back are seen by the pitcher than his chest or side. When he starts to swing his back is half turned toward the pitcher. He goes as far back as he can reach, never for an instant taking his eye off the ball as it leaves the pitcher's hand.

The greatest power in his terrific swing comes when the bat is directly in front of his body, just half way in the swing. He hits the ball with terrific impact and there is no player in the game whose swing is such a masterpiece of batting technique.

Largest Sums on Record for Purchase of Ball Players	
Babe Ruth, Boston to Yankees	$125,000
Tris Speaker, Boston to Cleveland	*50,000
Eddie Collins, Athletics to Chicago	50,000
Carl Mays, Boston to Yankees	*40,000
Art Nehf, Boston to Giants	*40,000
Frank Baker, Athletics to Yankees	37,500
Joe Jackson, Cleveland to Chicago	*31,500
Benny Kauff, Feds to Giants	30,000
Lee Magee, Feds to Yankees	22,500
Strunk, Schang, and Bush, Athletics to Boston	*60,000
Alexander and Killefer, Phillies to Chicago	*55,000
*And players.	

January 6, 1920

LONG TIE IN HUB SETS NEW RECORD

Robins and Braves Battle for Twenty-Six Innings, Two More Than Big League Mark.

CORRAL ONLY RUN APIECE

Oeschger and Cadore Go Entire Distance in the Box Without Sign of Weakening.

DARKNESS PUTS END TO IT

McCormick Calls Halt After Figures That Had Stood for Fourteen Years Had Faded Away.

BOSTON, May 1.—The Robins and the Braves celebrated May Day in this ordinarily peaceful city by staging a prolonged, heart-breaking struggle for twenty-six innings at Braves Field and bombing to bits all major league records for duration of hostilities. When darkness drew its mantle over the scene, forbidding further battling, both teams were still on their feet, interlocked in a death clutch and each praying for just one more inning in which to get in the knockout blow.

As far as results in the chase for the pennant go the game was without effect, for the final score was 1 to 1. In the matter of thrills, however, the oldest living man can remember nothing like it, nor can he find anything in his granddad's diary worthy of comparison. Heart disease was the mildest complaint that grasped the spectators as they watched inning after inning slip away and the row of ciphers on the scoreboard began to slide over the fence and reach out into the Fenway. Nervous prostration threatened to engulf the stands as the twentieth inning passed away in the scoreless routine and the word was passed from the knowing fans to those of inferior baseball erudition that the National League record was twenty-two innings, the Robins having beaten the Pirates by 6 to 5 in a game of that length played in Brooklyn on August 22, 1917.

The twenty-second inning passed in the history-making clash, and then the twenty-third, with a total result of four more ciphers on the scoreboard and a new National League record for duration. The less hardy of the fans began to show signs of the strain by moving restlessly in their seats and babbling about perpetual motion and eternity. But the warriors down there on the field had no thoughts of records and no eyes for the fans, whose very presence they seemed to have forgotten. With a gameness that makes pebbles seem like chewing gum by comparison, they bent apparently unflagging energies on that one great object—to "beat these guys."

Rooting for a New Record.

Now the old-timers in the stands began to whisper to each other with tense faces that the big-league record was twenty-four innings, established in an American League game in the Hub on Sept. 1, 1906, on which occasion the Athletics downed the Red Sox by a tally of 4 to 1. The Robins and the Braves didn't care. They didn't know it. They simply w---- along in their sublime ignorance and tied this record, then smashed it, and by way of emphasis, tacked on a twenty-sixth session.

At this stage of the proceedings Umpire McCormick yawned twice and observed that it was nearly bedtime. He didn't seem particularly thrilled by what was going on. To him and his brother arbiter, Hart, it was merely an infernally long day's work.

McCormick remembered that he had an appointment pretty soon with a succulent beefsteak. He wondered if it wasn't getting dark. He held out one hand as a test and decided that in the gloaming it resembled a Virginia ham. He knew it wasn't a Virginia ham and became convinced that it was too dark to play ball. Thereupon he called the game, to the satisfaction of himself and Mr. Hart and the chagrin of everybody else concerned.

Some Great Fielding Bits.

The fielding on both sides was brilliant in the crises. Olson saved Brooklyn in the ninth, when, with the bases filled and one out, he stopped Pick's grounder, tagged Powell on the base line and then threw out the batter.

In the seventeenth inning one of the most remarkable double plays ever seen in Boston retired Brooklyn. The bases were filled and one was out when Elliott grounded to Oeschger. Wheat was forced at the plate, but Gowdy's throw to Holke was low and was fumbled. Konetchy tried to score from second and Gowdy received Holke's throw to one side and threw himself blindly across the plate to meet Konetchy's spikes with bare fist.

Joe Oeschger and Leon Cadore were the real outstanding heroes among a score of heroes in the monumental affray of this afternoon. The two twirlers went the entire distance, pitching each practically the equivalent of three full games in this one contest, and, mirabile dictu, instead of showing any sign of weakening under the prolonged strain, each of them appeared to grow stronger. In the final six innings neither artist allowed even the shadow of a safe bingle.

The Braves' twirler had rather the better of the duel in some respects. Fewer hits were made from his delivery than from that of Cadore. Oeschger practically twirled three three-hit games in a row, while Cadore pitched three five-hit games in the afternoon's warfare. In only one inning, the seventeenth, did Oeschger allow two safe blows, and Cadore let the local batters group hits only in the sixth and ninth.

At the receiving end of the batteries, O'Neill gave way to Gowdy for the Braves before hostilities were concluded, and Elliott took Krueger's place behind the bat for Brooklyn.

Starts Without Fireworks.

There was no indication in the early stages of the combat that anything startling was brewing. The Robins got one lone single in the first, second and fourth innings, and the Braves got lone hits in the second, third and fourth, but without tangible results in the score column.

In the fifth Robbie's men got their valuable tally. Krueger was walked by Oeschger, who offended in this way very seldom this afternoon. Krueger went down to second while Oeschger was fielding Cadore's little pat and getting his man at first. Ivy Olson played a most important rôle at this juncture by slashing a line drive over Maranville's head for a single, on which Krueger completed his journey and weighed in at the home plate. Olson went to second on a wild pitch but was left there as Oeschger tightened up and fanned Neis and Johnston lined to Mann in left field.

The Braves tied up the score in the succeeding inning, jamming over the final run of a game which was destined to go on for twenty scoreless innings thereafter, tying the existing record in this respect.

In the sixth session Cadore fielded Mann's bounder and threw him out at first. Cruise came along with a mighty drive to the scoreboard which netted three bases. Holke popped up a short fly to left which Wheat ran in and caught. Boeckel delivered the goods in the form of a single to centre upon which Cruise tallied. When Maranville followed with a double to centre it looked a bit dubious for Mr. Cadore and his pals. Boeckel was caught at the plate, however, in the effort to score on the Rabbit's blow, Hood, Cadore and Krueger participating in the putout.

After this session, save for the Braves' flash in the ninth and the Robins' effort in the seventeenth, the two twirlers were entire masters of the situation.

The score:

BROOKLYN (N.)	Ab	R	B	H	Po	A		BOSTON (N.)	Ab	R	B	H	Po	A
Olson,ss	10	0	1	6	9		Powell,cf	7	0	1	8	0	
Neis,rf	10	0	1	9	0		Pick,2b	11	0	0	5	10	
Johnston,3b	10	0	2	3	1		Mann,lf	10	0	2	6	0	
Wheat,lf	9	0	2	3	0		Cruise,rf	9	1	1	4	0	
Myers,cf	2	0	1	2	0		Holke,1b	10	0	2	32	1	
Hood,cf	6	0	1	3	1		Boeckel,3b	11	0	3	1	7	
Konetc'y,1b	9	0	1	30	1		Maran'le,ss	10	0	3	1	9	
Ward,ss	10	0	0	5	3		O'Neil,c	3	0	0	4	2	
Krueger,c	2	1	0	4	3		aChristen'y	1	0	1	0	0	
Elliott,c	7	0	0	1	3		Gowdy,c	6	0	1	6	1	
Cadore,p	10	0	0	1	13		Oeschger,p	8	0	1	1	10	
Total	85	1	9	78	34		Total	85	1	15	78	42	

a Batted for O'Neil in ninth inning.

Errors—Pick (2), Olson, Krueger.

Brooklyn .... 0 0 0 0 1 0 0 0 0 0 0 0 0 0 0 0 0 0 0 0 0 0 0 0 0 0—1
Boston .... 0 0 0 0 0 0 1 0 0 0 0 0 0 0 0 0 0 0 0 0 0 0 0 0 0 0—1
Called darkness.

Two-base hits—Maranville, Oeschger. Three-base hit—Cruise. Stolen base—Myers. Sacrifice hits—Hood, Oeschger, Powell, O'Neil, Holke, Cruise. Double play—Olson and Konetchy. Bases on balls—Off Cadore 5, Oeschger 3. Struck out—By Cadore 8, Oeschger 4. Wild pitch—Oeschger. Umpires—Messrs. McCormack and Hart.

May 2, 1920

CHARLES A. (KID) NICHOLS
RIGHT HANDED PITCHER WHO WON 30 OR MORE GAMES FOR SEVEN CONSECUTIVE YEARS (1891-97) AND WON AT LEAST 20 GAMES FOR TEN CONSECUTIVE SEASONS (1890-99) WITH BOSTON N.L. ALSO PITCHED FOR ST. LOUIS AND PHILADELPHIA N.L. ONE OF FEW PITCHERS TO WIN MORE THAN 300 GAMES, HIS MAJOR LEAGUE RECORD BEING 360 VICTORIES, 202 DEFEATS.

Major League Baseballs Not Changed One Iota, Says Shibe

PHILADELPHIA, June 5.—The big increase in home runs this season is not due to any change in the ball, according to Thomas Shibe, a member of the firm that manufactures all the baseballs used in the major leagues, and Vice President of the Philadelphia American League Club. "The baseball used this year," said Mr. Shibe, " is the same as used last year and several seasons before that. The specifications this year called for the same yarn, the same cork centre, the same size and weight of rubber and the same horsehide. It has not been changed one iota and no effort has been made to turn out a livelier ball."

Mr. Shibe said his theory was that the abolition of all freak deliveries was the cause of the hard hitting. " With all freak deliveries dead," he said, " and the spitter almost dead, the batsmen are able to hit the ball more solidly."

June 6, 1920

KLEM IS ATTACKED BY PITCHER LUQUE

Red Twirler Accuses Umpire of Abusive Language—Cards Win Twice, 5-0 and 4-3.

CINCINNATI, June 26.—St. Louis went to second place in the National League race today by winning both games of a double header from the champions, 5 to 0 and 4 to 3. Both teams played perfect ball in the field, but the hitting of the visitors was much more effective than that of the Reds. Ruether was pounded hard in the first game, while Haines pitched almost perfectly, allowing only three hits. In the second game, long drives by the Cardinals gave them the victory.

In the eighth inning of the second game, Pitcher Luque of the Reds attacked Umpire Klem and dealt him several hard blows about the head. The assault took place while Luque was in the box with no one on base, and the pitcher claims that it was due to vicious language used by the official. Luque and Catcher Allen of the Reds both made affidavit that Klem had used such language.

If the claims are proved, the club will bring charges against Klem. Luque was put out of the game and Eller finished it. Previous to this incident, a shower of pop bottles had fallen around Klem, when he called Fournier safe at the plate in the sixth inning. Wingo was put out of the game at this time for abusive language.

The scores:

FIRST GAME.

ST. LOUIS (N.)	Ab	R	H	Po	A	CINCINNATI (N.)	Ab	R	H	Po	A
Janvrin,lf	4	1	1	4	0	Rath,2b	4	0	2	2	
Schultz, rf	4	0	1	3	0	Groh,3b	4	0	1	2	2
Stock,3b	5	2	3	0	1	Roush,1b	3	0	1	11	0
Hornsby,2b	4	0	0	1	3	Duncan,lf	3	0	0	1	0
Fournier,1b	4	1	2	10	1	Kopf,ss	3	0	1	1	0
McHenry,cf	4	1	1	2	0	Neale,rf	3	0	0	3	0
Lavan,ss	3	0	1	3	6	See,cf	2	0	0	5	0
Dilhoefer,c	4	0	2	4	1	Wingo,c	3	0	0	2	2
Haines,p	3	0	0	0	3	Ruether,p	3	0	1	0	1
Total	35	5	11	27	15	Total	28	0	3	27	8

St. Louis .... 2 0 0 0 0 0 3 0 0—5
Cincinnati .... 0 0 0 0 0 0 0 0 0—0

Two-base hits—Kopf, Janvrin, Stock, McHenry. Three-base hits—Fournier, Dilhoefer. Sacrifice hits—Schultz, Haines. Left on bases—St. Louis, 7; Cincinnati, 3. Base on balls—Off Ruether 2, Haines 1. Hit by pitcher—By Haines 1. Struck out—By Ruether 1, Haines 1. Umpires—Klem and Emslie.

SECOND GAME.

ST. LOUIS (N.)	Ab	R	H	Po	A	CINCINNATI (N.)	Ab	R	H	Po	A
Shotten,lf	3	1	0	2	0	Rath,2b	3	0	1	1	4
Heathcote,cf	3	0	1	6	0	Groh,3b	1	1	0	0	2
Stock,3b	4	0	2	0	1	Roush,1b	3	0	0	13	1
Hornsby,2b	4	0	1	4	3	Duncan,lf	4	0	2	0	0
Fournier,1b	4	1	1	15	0	Kopf,ss	4	1	1	3	4
Schultz,rf	3	1	1	3	0	Neale,rf	4	0	1	0	0
Lavan,ss	4	0	1	2	2	See,cf	3	0	1	1	0
Clemons,c	4	1	1	3	2	aCrane	1	0	0	0	0
Doak,p	3	0	1	0	2	Wingo,c	2	0	4	4	
Sherdel,p	1	0	0	0	2	Allen,c	1	1	0	5	0
						Luque,p	2	0	0	2	3
Total	33	4	9	27	18	Eller,p	1	0	0	0	1
						Total	29	3	6	27	19

a Batted for See in ninth.

St. Louis .... 1 0 0 2 0 1 0 0 0—4
Cincinnati .... 0 0 0 2 0 0 1 0 0—3

Two-base hit—Lavan. Three-base hits—Heathcote, Fournier, Clemons. Stolen bases—Heathcote, Schultz. Sacrifice hits—Rath, Groh. Double plays—Stock, Hornsby and Fournier. Left on bases—St. Louis 5, Cincinnati 6. Bases on balls—Off Luque 5, Doak 5. Hits—Off Luque 8 in 7 2-3 innings, Eller 1 in 1 1-3 innings; Doak 6 in 6, Sherdel 0 in 3. Struck out—By Luque 3, Eller 2, Doak 2. Wild pitch—Luque. Winning pitcher—Doak. Losing pitcher—Luque. Umpires—Messrs. Klem and Emslie. Time of game—Two hours ten minutes.

June 27, 1920

NO-HIT GAME FOR JOHNSON IN BOSTON

Senators' Pitcher Twirls First Hitless Battle of His Career, Beating Red Sox, 1 to 0.

BOSTON, July 1.—Walter Johnson of Washington pitched the first no-hit, no-run game of his big league career of fourteen years today, defeating Boston, 1 to 0. Hooper, on Harris's error of an easy chance in the seventh, was the only Boston player to reach first. Johnson fanned ten men.

Harper pitched well for Boston. In the seventh Rice singled through the box and was forced by Roth, McInnis to Scott. Shanks singled through the box to centre, putting Roth on third, Shanks moving up to second on the throw to third. Shannon fanned. Harris bounced the ball off Harper's glove and Scott could not get it soon enough to prevent Roth from scoring. Shanks tried to score, but was out at the plate, Scott to Walters.

After two pinch hitters had fanned in the last of the ninth Hooper bounded the ball over first base, but Judge made a remarkable stop with his gloved hand and threw to Johnson, who covered first, for the final out. The Washington players overwhelmed Johnson with congratulations.

The score:

WASHINGTON (A.)	Ab	R	H	Po	A	BOSTON (A.)	Ab	R	H	Po	A
Judge,1b	4	0	1	2	1	Hooper,rf	4	0	1	0	
Milan,lf	4	0	0	3	0	McNally,2b	3	0	0	1	3
Rice,cf	3	0	1	3	0	Menosky,lf	3	0	0	2	0
Roth,rf	4	1	0	0	0	Schang,cf	3	0	0	0	1
Shanks,3b	4	0	3	1	1	McInnis,1b	3	0	0	10	1
Shannon,ss	3	0	0	1	0	Foster,3b	3	0	0	2	4
Harris,2b	2	0	1	0	2	Scott,ss	3	0	0	4	3
Picinich,c	3	0	1	14	0	Walters,c	2	0	0	7	3
Johnson,p	2	0	0	3	0	Harper,p	2	0	0	0	1
						aKarr	1	0	0	0	0
Total	29	1	7	27	4	bEibel	1	0	0	0	0
						Total	23	0	0	27	16

a Batted for Walters in ninth.
b Batted for Harper in ninth.
Errors—Harris, Harper.

Washington .... 0 0 0 0 0 0 1 0 0—1
Boston .... 0 0 0 0 0 0 0 0 0—0

Stolen base—Rice. Double play—Walters and McNally. Left on bases—Washington 4, Boston 1. Bases on balls—Off Harper 1. Hit by pitcher—By Harper 2 (Rice and Harris). Struck out—By Johnson 10, by Harper 7. Umpires—Messrs. Chill and Moriarty. Time of game—One hour and forty-six minutes.

July 2, 1920

Washington Senators

RAY CHAPMAN DIES; MAYS EXONERATED

Widow Takes Body of Ball Player, Killed by Pitched Ball, Back to Cleveland.

HUNDREDS WEEP AT BIER

Pitcher Who Threw Ball Unnerved by Accident — Other Teams Would Bar Him.

MIDNIGHT OPERATION FAILS

Player's Brain Crushed by Force of Blow — District Attorney Says Accident Was Unavoidable.

The body of Ray Chapman, the Cleveland shortstop, who died early yesterday in St. Lawrence Hospital after being hit in the head by a pitched ball thrown by Carl Mays at the Polo Grounds Monday afternoon, was taken to his home in Cleveland last night. A group of baseball fans stood with bared heads at the Grand Central Terminal as the body was taken through the gates to the train. The ball player's widow, who went with the body, was accompanied by her brother, Daniel Daly of Cleveland; Miss Jane McMahon, a friend; Tris Speaker, manager of the ball club, and Joe Wood, one of the players.

Chapman's death has cast a tragic spell over the baseball fans of the city, and everywhere the accident was the topic of conversation. Chapman was a true sportsman, a skillful player, and one of the most popular men in the major leagues. And this was to have been his last season in professional baseball.

Carl Mays, the New York pitcher, who threw the ball which felled Chapman on Monday, voluntarily went before Assistant District Attorney Joyce and was exonerated of all blame.

The game which was to have been played between Cleveland and New York was put over until Thursday and the players of both clubs joined in mourning.

Cleveland Suppresses Bitterness.

Although there is some bitterness against Mays among some of the Cleveland players, Manager Tris Speaker of the Cleveland Club, in a telephone conversation with Colonel T. L. Huston, part owner of the New York Club, said he and his clubmates would do everything in their power to suppress this feeling.

"It is the duty of all of us," said Speaker, "of all the players, not only for the good of the game, but also out of respect to the poor fellow who was killed, to suppress all bitter feeling. We will do all in our power to avoid aggravating the unfortunate impression in any way."

Chapman died at 4:40 o'clock yesterday morning following an operation performed by Dr. T. M. Merrigan, surgical director of the institution. He was unconscious after he arrived at the hospital.

The operation began at 12:29 o'clock and was completed at 1:44. The blow had caused a depressed fracture in Chapman's head three and a half inches long. Dr. Merrigan removed a piece of skull about an inch and a half square and found the brain had been so severely jarred that blood clots had formed. The shock of the blow had lacerated the brain not only on the left side of the head where the ball struck but also on the right side where the shock of the blow had forced the brain against the skull, Dr. Merrigan said.

Teammates Wait in Hospital.

For a time following the operation Chapman breathed easier and his pulse improved. His teammates who had been waiting anxiously in the hospital were relieved. They went back to their hotel with the hope that the dawn would bring encouraging news. They were notified, instead, of Chapman's death.

This news spread rapidly. Among Chapman's clubmates and among their rivals for the American League pennant alike it caused universal grief. With all the players Chapman was popular. To many of them he had confided his hopes and plans. If Cleveland got into the World's Series this season he would retire from baseball and enter business in Cleveland. He wanted to be with the wife whom he had married only a year ago, and to whom he gave his last conscious thoughts. As the injured ballplayer was being taken from the clubhouse at the ball park on his way to the hospital he tried to speak to Percy Smallwood, trainer of the Cleveland Club. Before the game the player had placed in the trainer's custody his diamond ring, a gift from his wife. Several times the stricken man tried to say "Ring." But he could not speak. He pointed to his finger. Smallwood then understood and gave him his wife's gift.

Mrs. Chapman had been notified of the accident shortly after it occurred and before it was believed to be so serious.

Wife Is Told of Death.

In response to this message Mrs. Chapman arrived here at 10 A. M., to be at her husband's bedside. She was met at the train by Father Connors, a Philadelphia friend of the ballplayer, who had come to New York immediately on hearing of the accident. Father Connors accompanied Mrs. Chapman to a hotel. There he told her of her husband's death. She fainted.

Chapman's body was removed in the afternoon to the undertaking establishment of James F. McGowan, 153d Street and Amsterdam Avenue. There is was viewed by hundreds of baseball fans, many of whom had gone to the Polo Grounds expecting to see a game. The players of both the New York and Cleveland teams also viewed the body there. Several completely lost control of their emotions, and at one time there was not a dry eye among the scores of men who thronged the room about the bier.

Mays is greatly shocked over the accident. He said he had tried to be unusually careful this season to avoid just such an accident. Mays said that Chic Fewster was his close friend, and when the Yankee player was seriously injured in the same way last Spring, the horror of the accident made a deep impression on him. Mays believed that one of the reasons for his failure to pitch successfully earlier in the season was due to the fact that he pitched the ball too far away from the batsman because he was wary of repeating the Fewster accident.

Thought Ball Hit Bat.

Mays said he threw a high, fast ball at a time when Chapman was crouched over the plate. He thought the ball hit the handle of Chapman's bat, for he fielded the ball and tossed it to first base. It wasn't until after that, when he saw Umpire Connelly calling to the stands for a physician, that he realized he had hit Chapman in the head.

"Chapman was one of the gamest players and one of the hardest men to pitch to in the league," said Mays. "I always dreaded pitching to him because of his crouching position at the bat."

The pitcher first learned of Chapman's death through a telephone message from a newspaper. He immediately communicated with the District Attorney's office, and visited Assistant District Attorney Joyce of the Homicide Bureau at 1 o'clock.

"It is the most regrettable incident of my baseball career," he said, "and I would give anything if I could undo what has happened. Chapman was a game, splendid fellow." After hearing Mays's version of the accident, the Assistant District Attorney exonerated Mays from all blame, and as far as the office is concerned the case is closed.

Manager Tris Speaker stayed in his room at his hotel and received no callers.

Huggins Version of Accident.

Manager Miller Huggins of the Yankees believes Chapman's left foot may have caught in the ground in some manner which prevented him from stepping out of the ball's way. Manager Huggins explained that batsmen usually had one foot loose and free at just such moments and Chapman had got out of the way of the same kind of pitched balls before. The fact that he did not move his feet made Manager Huggins believe his spikes might have caught when he tried to duck.

Ray Caldwell, one of the Cleveland pitchers, and a former member of the Yankees, said that, as it looked to him from the Cleveland bench, Chapman ducked his head right into the path of the ball. He said that if he had stood up straight and not attempted to duck, the ball probably would have hit him on the shoulder.

The fatality is expected to have a depressing effect on the Cleveland and New York players. It is feared that it may impair Mays's effectiveness as a pitcher, although he said it would do him no good to brood over something which seemed unavoidable. The Cleveland players are so badly affected by the loss of one of their star players that their chances of winning this year's pennant have received a severe setback. Manager Speaker has no seasoned player to put in the vacant position, and grief among the players over Chapman's death is sure to affect their playing for some time to come.

Flags Ordered at Half-Mast.

When Colonel Huston of the New York Club was asked about the reported action of the Boston and Detroit players to have Mays barred from organized baseball, he said the New York Club viewed the fatality purely as an accident, and did not care to express an opinion on any action which the players mentioned might anticipate. If these players, however, do send a petition to the league asking for the removal of Mays, the New York Club will then take action.

President Heydler of the National League yesterday ordered all flags at National League parks at half-mast for a week. Similar action is expected by President Johnson of the American League.

Raymond Chapman was born in McHenry, Ky., Jan. 15, 1891. He had been a member of the Cleveland American League team since Aug. 30, 1912, and was considered one of the best shortstops in the game.

Chapman played his first professional baseball in 1909 with Mount Vernon, Ill. In 1910 he went to Springfield, Ill., and from there to Davenport, Iowa, in the Three I League.

Cleveland first obtained Chapman from Davenport in 1911 and sold him to Toledo in the American Association on option. He was recalled to Cleveland in 1912 and had played in more than 1,000 games in an Indian uniform. Chapman was one of the fastest men in baseball. On Sept. 27, 1917, Tim Murnane Day at Boston, he won a loving cup for the fastest time in circling the bases, doing it in fourteen seconds. In 1917 he broke all major league sacrifice hit records with a total of sixty-seven and also led the American League in sacrifices in the following two years.

August 18, 1920

EIGHT WHITE SOX PLAYERS ARE INDICTED ON CHARGE OF FIXING 1919 WORLD SERIES; CICOTTE GOT $10,000 AND JACKSON $5,000

COMISKEY SUSPENDS THEM

Promises to Run Them Out of Baseball if Found Guilty

TWO OF PLAYERS CONFESS

Cicotte and Jackson Tell of Their Work in Throwing Games to Cincinnati.

BOTH ARE HELD IN CUSTODY

Prosecutor Says More Players Will Be Indicted and Gamblers Brought to Task.

Special to The New York Times

CHICAGO, Sept. 28.—Seven star players of the Chicago White Sox and one former player were indicted late this afternoon, charged with complicity in a conspiracy with gamblers to "fix" the 1919 world's series. The indictments were based on evidence obtained for the Cook County Grand Jury by Charles A Comiskey, owner of the White Sox, and after confessions by two of the players told how the world's championship was thrown to Cincinnati and how they had received money or were "double-crossed" by the gamblers.

The eight players indicted are:
EDDIE CICOTTE, star pitcher.
"SHOELESS JOE" JACKSON, left fielder and heavy hitter.
OSCAR "HAP" FELSCH, centre fielder.
CHARLES "SWEDE" RISBERG, short-stop.
GEORGE "BUCK" WEAVER, third baseman.
ARNOLD GANDIL, former first baseman.
CLAUDE WILLIAMS, pitcher.
FRED McMULLIN, utility player.

The specific charge against the eight players is "conspiracy to commit an illegal act," which is punishable by five years' imprisonment or a fine up to $10,000, but this charge may be changed when the full indictments are drawn by the Grand Jury.

No sooner had the news of the indictments become public than Comiskey suspended the seven players, wrecking the team he had given years to build up and almost certainly forfeiting his chances to beat out Cleveland for the American League pennant.

Would Run Them Out of Baseball

His letter notifying the players of their suspension follows:

Chicago, Sept. 26
To Charles Risberg, Fred McMullin, Joe Jackson, Oscar Felsch, George Weaver, C.P. Williams and Eddie Cicotte:

You and each of you are hereby notified of your indefinite suspension as a member of the Chicago American League Baseball Club.

Your suspension is brought about by information which has just come to me directly involving you and each of you in the baseball scandal resulting from the world's series of 1919.

If you are innocent of any wrongdoing you and each of you will be reinstated; if you are guilty you will be retired from organized baseball for the rest of your lives if Ican accomplish it.

Until there is a finality to this investigation it is due to the public that Itake this action, even though it costs Chicago the pennant.
CHICAGO AMERICAN BASEBALL CLUB.
By CHARLES A COMISKEY

Officials of the Grand Jury lifted the curtain on the proceedings and declared that Cicotte and Jackson made open confessions, Cicotte admitting receiving $10,000 and throwing two games, and Jackson admitting receiving $5,000 of $20,000 promised him by the gamblers and telling of his efforts to defeat his own team.

Cicotte Breaks Down and Weeps

Cicotte's confession came after he and Alfred S. Austrian, counsel for the White Sox management, had conferred with Judge Charles A. McDonald in the latter's chambers.

Toward the end of this conference they were joined by Assistant State Attorney Hartley Repiogle. A few moments later he and Cicotte proceeded to the Grand Jury room.

There the great baseball pitcher broke down and wept.

"My God! think of my children," he cried. Cicotte has two small children.

"I never did anything I regretted so much in my life," he continued. "I would give anything in the world if Icould undo my acts in the last world's series. I've played a crooked game and Ihave lost, and Iam here to tell the whole truth.

"I've lived a thousand years in the last year."

Describing how two games were thrown to Cincinnati, Cicotte, according to court officials, said:

"In the first game at Cincinnati Iwas knocked out of the box. I wasn't putting a thing on the ball. You could have read the trade mark on it when I lobbed the ball up to the plate.

"In the fourth game, played at Chicago, which I also lost, I deliberately intercepted a throw from the outfield to the plate which might have cut off a run. I muffed the ball on purpose.

"At another time in the same game I purposely made a wild throw. All the runs scored against me were due to my own deliberate errors. I did not try to win."

Cicotte, it was learned late tonight confessed first to Comiskey, "He went to the latter's office early in the morning."

"I don't know what you'll think of me," he said, "but Igot to tell you how I double-crossed you. Mr. Comiskey, I did double-cross you. I'm a crook, and I got $10,000 for being a crook."

"Don't tell it to me," replied Comiskey," tell it to the Judge."

Cicotte told it to the Judge in tears and shame, slowly, haltingly, hanging his head, now and then pausing to wipe his streaming eyes.

"Risberg and Gandil and McMullin were at me for a week before the world's series started," he said. "They wanted me to go crooked. I didn't know — Ineeded the money. I had the wife and the kids. The wife and kids don't know this. I don't know what they'll think.

Says He Needed It to Pay Mortgage

"I bought a farm. There was a $4,000 mortgage on it. There isn't any mortgage on it now. I paid it off with the crooked money.

"The eight of us (the eight under indictment) got together in my room three or four days before the games started. Gandil was the master of ceremonies. We talked about throwing the series. Decided we could get away with it. We agreed to do it.

"I was thinking of the wife and kids and how I needed the money. I told them Ihad to have the cash in advance. I didn't want any checks. I didnt want any promise, as I wanted the money in bills. I wanted it before I pitched a ball.

"We all talked quite a while about it, I and the seven others. Yes, all of us decided to do our best to throw the games to Cincinnati.

"When Gandil and McMullin took us all, one by one, away from the others, and we talked 'turkey,' they asked me my price. I told them $10,000. And I told them that $10,000 was to be paid in advance.

" 'Cash in advance,' I said. 'Cash in advance, and nothing else.'

"It was Gandil I was talking to. He wanted to give me some money and the rest after the games were played and lost. But it didn't go with me.

" ' I said cash.' I reminded him. 'Cash in advance, and not C.O.D. If you can't trust me. I can't trust you. Pay or I play ball.'

Well, the arguments went on for days — the arguments for 'some now and some later.' But I stood pat. I wanted the $10,000 and got it. "And how I wih that I didn't.

"The day before I went to Cincinnati I put it up to them squarely for the last time, that there would be nothing doing unless I had the money.

"That night I found the money under my pillow. There was $10,000, I counted it. I don't know who put it there but it was there. It was my price. I had sold out 'Commy', I had sold out the other boys, sold them for $10,000 to pay off a mortgage on a farm, and for the wife and kids.

"If I had reasoned what that meant to me, the taking of that dirty crooked money-the hours of mental torture, the days and nights of living with an unclean mind; the weeks and months of going along with six of the seven crooked players and holding a guilty secret, and of going along with the boys who had stayed straight and clean and honest — boys who had nothing to trouble them — say it was hell.

"I got the $10,000 cash in advance, that's all."

Jackson Only "Tapped" Ball

Cicotte after his testimony was taken from the courtroom by a back door, and shortly afterward Austrian appeared with Joe Jackson. There was another conference in the chambers of Judge McDonald and a meeting with Assistant State Attorney Repiogle, and then Jackson ran the gantlet of newspaper cameramen to the Grand Jury room.

Jackson hung his head and covered his face with his hands. Repiogle tried to keep the cameramen away. They refused and there was a volley of flashes. Jackson cursed newspapermen, gamblers and baseball and fled to the security of the jury room.

His story, it was learned, was a confirmation of Cicotte's. It was the story of a low "feeling out" of the cupidity of players by Gandil, McMullin and Risberg.

Joe Jackson, in his confession, said he went into the deal through the influence of Gandil and Risberg. He was promised $20,000 and got $5,000, which was handed to him in Cincinnati by "Lefty" Williams. When he threatened to talk about it, Williams, Gandil and Risberg said, "You poor simp, go ahead and squawk. Where do you get off if you do? We'll all say you're a liar, and every honest baseball player in the world will say you're a liar. You're out of luck. Some of the boys were promised a lot more than you, and got a lot less."

"And that's why I went down and told Judge McDonald and told the Grand Jury what I knew about the frame-up," said Jackson tonight. And I'm giving you a tip. A lot of these sporting writers who have been roasting me have been talking about the third game of the World's Series being square. Let me tell you something. The eight of us did our best to kick it and little Dick Kerr won the game by his pitching. And because he won it these gamblers 'double-crossed' us for 'double-crossing' them.

"They've hung it on me. They ruined me when I went to the shipyards. But I don't care what happens now. I guess I'm through with baseball. I wasn't wise enough, like Chick, to beat them to it. But some of them will sweat before the show is over.

"Who gave me the money." Lefty Williams slipped it to me the night before I left for Cincinnati and told me I'd get the other $15,000 after I delivered the goods. I took Lefty's word for it. Now Risberg threatens to bump me off if I squak. That's why I had all the bailiffs with me when I left the Grand Jury room this afternoon.

"I'm not under arrest yet and I've got the idea that after what I told them old Joe Jackson isn't going to jail. But I'm not going to get far from my protectors until this blows over. Swede is a hard guy."

Jackson testified, according to the officials, that throughout the series he either struck out or hit easy balls when hits would mean runs.

Jackson also testified, it is said, that Claude Williams received $10,000.

Jackson Comes Out Smiling

Jackson was before the Grand Jury nearly two hours, and he came out walking erect and smiling.

"I got a big load off my chest," he told a friend who accosted him. "I'm feeling better."

"Don't ask Joe any questions," Repiogle cautioned the newspaper men.

"He's gone through beautifully and we don't want him bothered."

Joe intimated he was "willing to tell the world now, if they'll let me."

The crowd outside the Criminal Court buildings cheered and jeered as he rode off in the custody of bailiffs.

Cicotte is also in the custody of officers from the State Attorney's office.

"We are taking no chances on anything," was the only explanation Mr. Repiogle offered of this.

Mrs. Henrietta Kelley, owner of an apartment house on Grand Boulevard, with whom many of the players and their families lived, gave testimony in the morning which Mr. Repiogle declared was "extremely important."

Mrs. Kelley herself denied that she had given any important evidence.

President Heydler Testifies

President Heydler of the National League also was a witness. No hint of the nature of his testimony could be obtained from the prosecutors. Mr. Repiogle dismissed questioners with his stock statement, "It is of great importance."

Mr. Austrian, attorney for the White Sox, said:

"Mr. Comiskey and myself, as his counsel, have been working on this for a year. We have spent a great deal of Mr. Comiskey's money to ferret it out. It is because of our investigation the lid has been blown off this scandal."

"Mr. Heydler is also testifying," he said: "Mr. McGraw will appear also—of their own volition, of course."

The significance of Heydler's testimony appeared when it was announced that two National League players would be summoned by the Grand Jury, Olsen, shortstop, of Brooklyn, and Rawlings, second baseman, of Philadelphia. Each is said to have won $2,000 on the first two games of the 1919 world's series.

The announcement of the calling of these players was followed by the intimation from the State Attorney's office that the investigation would soon reach far beyond Bill Maharg, former pugilist; Bill Burns, a retired ball player now interested in the oil industry of Texas, and Abe Attell who so far have been named in the investigation as connected with 'the gamblers' end.

The Grand Jury recessed for the day with the conclusion of Jackson's testimony, but there was promise of more fireworks tomorrow.

"It'll be hotter, and there'll be more of it," Mr. Repiogle promised. He declined to say whether immunity had been promised Jackson and Cicotte or whether it would be promised any others.

Two witnesses, Dr. Raymond B. Prettyman, a friend of Buck Weaver and John J. McGraw, manager of the New York Giants, who appeared to testify today, were told they could not be heard until tomorrow.

Claude "Lefty" Williams, the man who handed Joe Jackson $5,000 will be the central figure in the baseball investigation tomorrow.

Williams will be asked who handed him the money. He also may be asked as to his career in the Coast League, and he may be asked as to his knowledge of a scandal regarding fixed games after Salt Lake City entered the league.

Williams was questioned tonight as to his part in the conspiracy, but was non-committal.

Comiskey Commends Court

Mr. Comiskey tonight made the following statement:

"The consideration which the Grand Jury gave to this case should be greatly appreciated by the general public. Charles A. McDonald, Chief Justice, and the foreman of the Grand Jury, Harry Brigham, and his associates, who so diligently strived to save and make America's great game the clean sport which it is, are to be commended in no uncertain terms by all sport followers, in spite of what happened today.

"Thank God it did happen. Forty-four years of baseball endeavor have convinced me more than ever that it is a wonderful game and a game worth keeping clean.

"I would rather close my ball park than send nine men on the field with one of them holding a dishonest thought toward clean baseball-the game which John McGraw and I went around the world with to show to the people on the other side.

"We are far from through yet. We have the nucleus of another championship team with the remainder of the old world's championship team."

He named the veterans, Eddie and John Collins, Ray Schalk, Urban Faber, Dick Kerr, Eddie Murphy, Nemo Leibold and Amos Strunk and declared that, with the addition of Hodge, Falk, Jordan and McClellan. "I guess we can go along and win the championship yet."

Buck Weaver, when seen just after receiving notice of his suspension, declared he never received any of the money said to have been distributed and denied all knowledge of the deal to throw games in the world's series.

He said his own record, in the series of 1919, in which he batted .333 and made only four errors out of thirty chances, ought to exonerate him.

"Any man who bats .333 is bound to make trouble for the other team in a ball game," he said. "The best team cannot win a world's championship without getting the breaks."

How Chicago Lost Championship

CHICAGO, Sept. 28 (Associated Press). —Last year's world series records show that in the first inning of the first game Cicotte started by hitting Rath, the first Cincinnati batter, in the back. Daubert followed with a single over second base that sent Rath to third, and he scored when Groh flied to Jackson, Rath beating Jackson's throw to the plate.

Chicago tied this run in the next inning, Kopf putting Jackson on second with a wild throw. Feisch sacrificed him to third and Gandil dropped a little fly safely in centre, scoring Jackson.

The end of Cicotte's pitching and the runs that ultimately won the game were scored by Cincinnati in the fourth inning. All the damage was done with two out. With Kopf on first, Neale and Wingo singled and Reuther, the hard-hitting Cincinnati pitcher, drove a three-base hit to the centre field bleachers. Rath doubled and Daubert singled, the combination resulting in five runs.

Wilkinson took Cicotte's place after Daubert's single and Groh flied to Feisch. The final score of this game was 9 to 1.

The fourth game, played at Chicago, was won by the Reds by a score of 2 to 0, Ring pitching for Cincinnati, holding the American League champions to three hits. Both Cincinnati runs were made in the fifth inning, when two of Cincinnati's hits were bunched with a wild throw to first by Cicotte and a bad throw to the plate by Jackson, which the pitcher intercepted and muffed. The play of this inning was sent over the Associated Press as follows:

"Rousch was out, Schalk to Gandil, the ball rolling half way to the pitcher's box. Duncan was safe when Cicotte threw his drive to first, the ball going to the stand and Duncan reaching second. Kopf singled to left and Duncan stopped at third, but scored when Jackson threw wild to the plate. Kopf reached second.—Correction: The official scorer gives Cicotte the error for muffling Jackson's throw. Neale sent one over Jackson's head and Kopf scored. Neale reached second. It was a two-base hit. Wingo, out, Ed. Collins to Gandil, Neale going to third. Ring drove a vicious grounder that Ed Collins got and threw him out at first. Two runs. Two hits. Two errors."

The rest of the game was played sharply and, so far as the records show cleanly. Cicotte pitched through the nine innings.

Cicotte Won the Sixth Game

Cicotte's next appearance in the series was in the sixth game, when Cincinnati had four victories to its credit against one defeat, Richard Kerr, the diminutive left-handed pitcher, having shut out the National League champions in the third game. The veteran twirler, who today confessed the big gambling deal, went through nine innings and held his opponents to seven hits. Chicago won the game 4 to 1, hitting Sallee hard in the first five innings. Jackson and Feisch each got two hits and between them drove in all of Chicago's runs.

Billy Manarg, Philadelphia prize fighter, who last night, in Philadelphia, issued a statement connecting Cicotte with the gambling deal and charging Abe Attell, former fighter, headed the gambling clique asserted that the Sox were "double-crossed" by Attell and never received $100,000 which had been promised them. It was late in the series before they found this out, Maharg asserted, as Attell kept postponing the day of settlement, saying he needed the money to bet.

Besides the two defeats registered against Cicotte in the series, three others were chalked up against Claude Williams. The latter, a "side arm" left-hander, was wild in the second and fifth games, which went to the Reds 4 to 2 and 5 to 9. In the eighth and last game of the series he was found for four solid hits in the first inning, and that game and the title of world champions went to Cincinnati, 10 to 5. Williams's lack of control was generally recorded as the cause of his defeats, the record of the second game saying:

"While Cincinnati obtained only four hits, these came at opportune times when they had been preceded by bases on balls off Williams."

The fifth game of the series was a shut out triumph for Hod Eller, the big "shine ball" expert of the Cincinnati pitching staff. Only three hits were two successive innings. All told, Eller had nine strikeouts that day.

Four of Cincinnati's five runs were grouped in the sixth inning. Eller doubled, Rath scored him with a single and moved to second on Daubert's "bunt perfectly laid," as the report of the game said. Williams walked. Groh. Rousch drove a three-base hit to Feisch's territory, scoring two runners and himself tallied after Duncan flied to Jackson.

In Custody, but Not Arrested

Both Cicotte and Jackson were closeted with the Grand Jury for a considerable time today, and later court officials reported that they told their stories in substantial detail. As they left the room they were taken in custody by detectives of the State's Attorney's office. Their detention was not in the nature of an arrest, and it was announced that they would be released later.

Cicotte, who earlier in the day had vehemently denied any part in the alleged plot, as described by Maharg at Philadelphia yesterday, admitted on the stand, officials of the courts said that the Philadelphian's story was substantially correct.

The court officials also quoted Cicotte as saying that the players had believed that "Chick" Gandil who, he said, was interested in the dealings with the gamblers had "double-crossed" them, and that Maharg's story was the first intimation they had had that Attell had "held out" on the $100,000 which had been promised them.

The investigation by the Grand Jury will continue until all phases of baseball gambling have been bared, it was said by officials. The investigation started two weeks ago following reports that a game played here Aug. 31 by the Cubs and the Philadelphia Nationals was "fixed" and the inquiry into last year's world series came up only as an incident to the other inquiry

Assistant State's Attorney Hartley Repiogle, in charge of the case, said tonight that indictments to be drawn up tomorrow on today's true bills may contain several counts. The true bills themselves specified but one alleged offense, "conspiracy to commit an illegal act." The penalty provided upon conviction on this count would be one to five years in the penitentiary, and a fine of not more than $10,000.

"This is just the beginning" Mr. Repiogle said tonight. "We will have more indictments within a few days and before we get through we will have purged organized baseball of everything that is crooked and dishonest.

"We are going after the gamblers now. There will be indictments within a few days against men in Philadelphia, Indianapolis, St. Louis, Des Moines, Pittsburgh, Cincinnati and other cities. More baseball players also will be indicted. We've got the goods on these men and we are going the limit."

Harry Grabiner, Secretary of the White Sox, announced that the club would play out the schedule to the end if it had to "employ Chinamen" to fill the vacancies in the team.

September 29, 1920

SMITH THE HERO AS INDIANS WIN FROM ROBINS, 8-1

Outfielder Smashes Home Run in First Inning with the Bases Filled.

GRIMES BATTED FROM BOX

Retires in the Fourth Under a Fusillade of Hits, Including Homer by Bagby.

WAMBY MAKES TRIPLE PLAY

Cleveland Second Baseman Performs Rare Feat for First Time in History of Series.

Special to The New York Times.

CLEVELAND, Oct. 10.—The unromantic name of Smith is on everybody's lips in Cleveland tonight, for Elmer Smith, the right fielder of Speaker's Indians, accomplished something in the

fifth world's series clash this afternoon that is the life ambition of every big league ball player. Elmer crashed a home run over the right field fence with the bases full in the first inning and sent the Indians on their merry way to a 8 to 1 victory over Brooklyn. Fate tried to conceal this lucky boy by naming him Smith, but with that tremendous slap Elmer shoved his commonplace identity up alongside the famous Smiths of history, which include Captain John, the Smith Brothers, and the Village Smithy.

This home-run punch which shoved over four runs in a cluster is the first of its kind that has ever been made in a world's series game. Cleveland now has won three games to Brooklyn's two, and an overjoyed city this evening has about come to the conclusion that the championship streamer will float over the proud fifth city of the U. S. A.

While the delirious crowd of more than 25,000 was still rejoicing over Smith's sumptuous smash, Bill Wambsgans broke into the celebration to steal some of Smithy's thunder by accomplishing the first unassisted triple play that has ever whisked a world's series populace up to the heights of happiness.

Cleveland's Joy Complete.

The crowd was already husky-voiced and nerve-wrecked with wild excitement when Wamby started to make baseball history. It seemed as if everything that could happen to make Cleveland's joy complete had happened.

Along in the fifth inning, when Bagby, with a commanding lead behind him, was taking it easy, Kilduff and Otto Miller both made singles and were perched on second and first. Clarence Mitchell, who had long since succeeded

the badly wrecked Burleigh Grimes on the pitching mound, was at bat, and for the first time during the afternoon it looked as if the slipping Robins were going to accomplish something.

Uncle Robbie had evidently wigwagged a sign from the bench for a hit and run play, which means that the runners were expected to gallop just as soon as Mitchell swung his bat.

Mitchell connected solidly and jammed a tearing liner over second base. Wamby was quite a distance from second, but he leaped over toward the cushion and with a mighty jump speared the ball with one hand. Kilduff was on his way to third base and Miller was almost within reach of second.

Three Out on One Play.

Wamby's noodle began to operate faster than it ever did before. He hopped over to second and touched the bag, retiring Kilduff, who was far down the alley toward third base. Then Wamby turned and saw Otto Miller standing there like a wooden Indian. Otto was evidently so surprised that he was glued to the ground, and Wamby just waltzed over and touched him for the third out.

The crowd forgot it was hoarse of voice and close to nervous exhaustion and gave Wamby just as great a reception as it had given Elmer Smith.

Those two-record-breaking feats were not all that happened in today's game to make Cleveland feel proud of its baseball club and itself. Not by a long shot! Along in the fourth inning when Grimes was still trying to pitch, Jim Bagby, the Indians' big, slow, lazy boxman, became suddenly inspired and with two fellow Indians on the bases he soaked a home run into the new bleachers which protrude far out into right centrefield.

No World's Series pitcher has ever received such a humiliating cudgeling as Grimes did this afternoon, for the simple reason that no other pitcher has

Official Score of Fifth World's Series Game

CLEVELAND (A. L.)

	AB.	R.	H.	TB.	2B.	3B.	HR.	BB.	SO.	SH.	SB.	PO.	A.	E.
Jamieson, lf......	4	1	2	1	0	0	0	0	0	0	0	2	1	0
Graney, lf......	1	0	0	0	0	0	0	0	1	0	0	0	0	0
Wambsgans, 2b..	5	1	1	1	0	0	0	0	0	0	0	7	2	0
Speaker, cf......	3	2	1	1	0	0	0	1	0	0	0	1	0	0
E. Smith, rf......	4	1	3	8	0	1	1	0	0	0	0	1	0	0
Gardner, 3b......	4	0	1	1	0	0	0	0	0	0	0	2	2	1
W. Johnston, 1b..	3	1	2	2	0	0	0	0	1	0	9	1	0
Sewell, ss......	3	0	0	0	0	0	0	1	0	0	0	2	4	0
O'Neill, c......	2	1	0	0	0	0	0	2	0	0	0	3	1	1
Thomas, c......	0	0	0	0	0	0	0	0	0	0	0	1	0	0
Bagby, p......	4	1	2	5	0	0	1	0	0	0	0	0	2	0
Total	33	8	12	19	0	1	2	4	1	1	0	27	13	2

BROOKLYN (N. L.)

	AB.	R.	H.	TB.	2B.	3B.	HR.	BB.	SO.	SH.	SB.	PO.	A.	E.
Olson, ss........	4	0	2	2	0	0	0	0	0	0	0	3	5	0
Sheehan, 3b......	3	0	1	1	0	0	0	0	1	0	1	1	1
Griffith, rf......	4	0	0	0	0	0	0	0	1	0	0	0	0	0
Wheat, lf......	4	1	2	2	0	0	0	0	1	0	0	3	0	0
Myers, cf......	4	0	2	2	0	0	0	0	0	0	0	0	0	0
Konetchy, 1b....	4	0	2	4	0	1	0	0	1	0	0	9	2	0
Kilduff, 2b......	4	0	1	1	0	0	0	0	0	0	0	5	6	0
Miller, c......	2	0	2	2	0	0	0	0	0	0	0	0	1	0
Krueger, c......	2	0	1	1	0	0	0	0	0	0	0	2	1	0
Grimes, p........	1	0	0	0	0	0	0	0	0	0	0	0	1	0
Mitchell, p........	2	0	0	0	0	0	0	0	0	0	0	1	0	0
Total	34	1	13	15	0	1	0	0	3	1	0	24	17	1

SCORE BY INNINGS.

Cleveland .... 4 0 0 3 1 0 0 0 ..—8
Brooklyn .... 0 0 0 0 0 0 0 0 1—1

Triple play—Wambsgans, unassisted. Double plays—Olson, Kilduff and Konetchy; Jamieson and O'Neill; Gardner, Wambsgans and W. Johnston; W. Johnston, Sewell and W. Johnston. Left on bases—Brooklyn, 7; Cleveland, 6. Bases on balls—Off Grimes, 1; Mitchell, 3. Struck out—By Bagby, 3; Mitchell, 1. Hits—Off Grimes, 9 in 3 1-3 innings, 3 in 4 2-3. Wild pitch—Bagby. Passed ball—Miller. Losing pitcher—Grimes. Umpires—Klem (N. L.), at plate; Connolly (A. L.), first base; O'Day (N. L.), second base; Dinneen (A. L.), third base. Time of game—One hour and forty-nine minutes.

ever been kept in the box so long after he had started to slip. Uncle Robbie kept him on the mound for three and two-third innings and in that time he was badly plastered for nine hits, including two home runs and a triple.

Grimes Badly Battered.

With half a dozen able-bodied pitchers basking in the warm sun, Grimes was kept in the game until he was so badly battered that the game became a joke. Instead of being enormously wealthy in pitchers as Robbie was supposed to be, he became a pauper as far as pitching talent is concerned. When the Indians had the score 7 to 0 Grimes limped out of the game and Clarence Mitchell, who had been faithfully warming up ever since he hit Cleveland, went out to the box and one more run was the best that the Indians could do off him.

That first inning is one which will ever linger in baseball memory. The Sunday crowd jammed every inch of the park and was even more enthusiastic than the throng at the opening game here. Strong-lunged young men went through the grandstands with megaphones and implored the fans to give the

Indians their vocal and moral encouragement as they had at the opening game. "We want to make it four straight," they yelled, "and fly the world's championship silk from our flagpole."

The memory of Grimes's great pitching still lingered in the minds of the spectators, but the Cleveland Club on its own meadow is a far different kind of ball club from that which the residents of Flatbush saw last week. The Indians were on their toes and ran back and forth to their positions in the field like a college baseball nine.

Indians Revel in Applause.

The roar of the faithful followers was like a tonic and Speaker's men reveled in the wonderful reception they received. The thing that was uppermost in their minds was to show the home folks how they appreciated the loyalty. The best way they could show it was to win and they showed 'em. It didn't matter that it was a one-sided ball game and that the Brooklyn Club, minus good pitching, looked woefully weak and with the absence of the injured

Jimmy Johnston at third base was inclined to be panicky. The only thing that mattered was that Cleveland was winning the ball game and the more runs the Indians could make the more fun there was in it for the Cleveland fans.

Jamieson was the first Indian to face Burleigh Grimes in the opening inning. He pounded a roller down through Koney which was too warm for the Dodger first baseman to handle. Wamby poked another single off Grimes and Jamieson went to second. The crowd chanted a flattering chorus of cheers to Speaker when he came to the bat. The wee bit of a tap which bounded off Tris's bat dropped in the infield and Grimes ran over to pick up the Indian manager's bunt and throw him out at first. Grimes slipped as he was about to pick up the ball and he was reclining on his back when he made a useless throw to first. It was a hit, and the bases were loaded with no one out.

The National Boiler Works laboring overtime never made the racket that was now taking place in the ball park. The noise waves flowed up in gushes and echoed all over the city of Cleveland, finally rumbling far out on Lake Erie.

Then Comes Mr. Smith.

Elmer Smith is at the bat. You'll find Smiths here, there and everywhere, so there was nothing about the name to arouse enthusiasm. Elmer took a fond look at the high screen on top of the right field fence and Grimes began to pitch to him. The three Indians on the bases jumped up and down on their toes impatiently.

Elmer took two healthy swings at the ball and missed, and the next one was wide and he let it waft by.

Grimes looked around the bases and saw that he was entirely surrounded by Indians. He was ambushed by the Redskins. He felt that danger lurked in this Smith boy at the bat.

When Grimes hurled the next ball over, Smith took a mighty blow at the ball and it rose like a bird, went so far up in the air that it looked like a quinine pill.

Jamieson, Wamby and Speaker all took one good look at that rapidly rising ball, then they bent their heads, dug their spikes into the dirt and started to run. Grimes was knocked dizzy. As he looked about him he could see nothing but Indians chasing themselves around in a circle.

Smith, who just a few seconds before was just plain Elmer Smith, had become Home Run Smith before he had trotted as far as second base. When he had reached third, he was Hero Smith, and by the time he had crossed the plate he was a candidate for a bronze statue in City Square along with General Moses Cleveland, who founded this town, and Tom L. Johnson, who decorates the park just opposite old General Mose.

Speaker Waits at Plate.

Manager Speaker, still a young man, yet gray and bald from baseball worries, was waiting at the plate when Smith touched the platter. Around Smith's neck went Tris's arm and he was the first to pat him on the back. Grimes stood out in the pitcher's box stupefied. The other Brooklyn players walked about in a daze and waited for the noise riot to subside.

Grimes was still pitching when the game was resumed. The Cleveland players wondered just what had to be done to a Brooklyn pitcher before he is taken out of the game. However, Grimes became a little better, and the side was retired after Burleigh had been aided by a double play.

Big Ed Konetchy walloped a triple to left centre field in the Brooklyn second, with one gone, but when Kilduff hoisted a fly to Jamieson and Koney tried to score after the catch Jamieson chucked him out at the plate with a perfect throw.

This was the first of a series of three double plays which, with Wamby's matchless triple killing, furnished a defense for Bagby's loose pitching that would have prevented any pitcher from losing, no matter how badly he was flinging. The Dodgers got ten hits off Bagby in eight innings and couldn't put over a single run. Peerless defensive work saved him.

Robins Waste Hits.

Brooklyn's most wasteful inning was the third, when Miller singled and Grimes hit into a double play. Olson and Sheehan, who was playing by special dispensation at third in place of the injured Jimmy Johnston, both singled. Griffith hoisted a foul to Gardner, ending the inning. There were three smacking singles without a runner getting beyond second base.

Smith got a tremendous cheer when he came to the bat in the third inning. There were two down at the time, and he jarred a terrific triple to left centre. The smash went to seed because Kilduff tossed Gardner out at first for the final out of the inning.

The next citizen to be hailed as a hero is lazy James Bagby. No pitcher was ever before pounded for thirteen hits in a world's series and emerge a hero. Jim Bagby, big Sergeant Jim, did it. He pitched what was really a bad game of ball, but when it was over he was proud of it.

Doc Johnston opened the fourth inning when he bounded a hit off Grimes's leg. Yes, Grimes is still pitching for Brooklyn. Clarence Mitchell is warming up out in left field. He warmed up all day yesterday and started warming up early today.

Anyway, Doc got his hit off Grimes's leg. He went to second on a passed ball and to third as Sheehan was retiring Sewell at first. Grimes walked O'Neill purposely to get Bagby, and that is just where Jim, the barge, has the laugh on Grimes. Bagby slammed a long drive to right centre that dropped just inside the fence that is built around the new centre field bleachers. Johnston and O'Neill both romped home ahead of Jim amid scenes of wild, barbarous disorder.

Grimes Still on Mound.

When the riot was quelled, Grimes was still pitching for Brooklyn. Does this fellow Grimes stand so strongly with Uncle Robbie that he is never taken out of a game, no time, no place, no how?

Jamieson spanked a roller down to first base, and although three Brooklyn fielders, Grimes, Koney and Kilduff, tried to retire the runner at first, Jamieson was too swift and got a hit for himself out of the confusion.

It suddenly dawned upon Manager Robinson that the Indians were hitting Grimes, so he took him out and Mitchell went to the box.

Sheehan was naturally nervous in his first big game, and in the fifth, when Speaker hit a roller to him, Sheehan threw the ball right over Konetchy's head, and Speaker went to second. "Home Run" Smith got a single and Speaker went to third. Gardner cracked a single to centre and Speaker crossed the plate with the Indians' last run.

Brooklyn's run came in the ninth inning when many of the jubilant Cleveland spectators were hurrying toward the gates. They were already shouting Cleveland victory to the world and the scoring of the lone tally commanded absolutely no attention at all.

Bagby fanned Griffith as a starter, and then, as he listlessly chucked the ball over, Wheat singled to right. Jim was still listless when he threw the ball at Myers, who slapped a single to centre which sent Wheat to second. Konetchy hit a mean hopper down through Doc Johnston, the ball bounding out into the field as Wheat scampered home and saved the Dodgers from a shutout. Brooklyn's stock has taken an awful drop.

October 11, 1920

BASEBALL PEACE DECLARED; LANDIS NAMED DICTATOR

Chicago Jurist Is Appointed a One-Man Court of Last Resort for Major Leagues.

CLUB OWNERS COMPROMISE

Adjust Points of Difference in Three - Hour Conference — Expect Minors to Concur.

LANDIS RETAINS OLD POST

Stays on Bench While Accepting $42,500 Salary in New Position —A Seven-Year Arrangement.

Special to The New York Times.

CHICAGO, Nov. 12.—With Judge Kenesaw Mountain Landis of the United States District Court as arbitrator, a one-man court of last resort, peace will obtain in professional baseball for at least seven years, while the eminent jurist will also continue to strike terror into the hearts of criminals by retaining his position as a Federal Judge.

Sixteen club owners of the National and American Leagues reached this happy solution of their difficulties after a three-hour conference at the Congress Hotel today. They then adjourned, to wait upon Judge Landis in a body and present their proposition to him. After only a few minutes' talk with the major league magnates, the Judge accepted the highest responsibility that can be conferred by the promoters of the national sport, and in his acceptance made it plain that he was undertaking the task as a public trust, having in mind the millions of fans of all ages who are interested in baseball.

By this action the former three-man National Commission was permanently discarded, and the supreme authority over baseball was centralized in the hands of one man. Up to date this statement applies only to the major leagues, but it is expected the minors will join with the big fellows in submitting all their future disputes, which they cannot decide within their own ranks, to the decision of Judge Landis. The committee of six named at the Kansas City meeting of the minor leagues to confer with a committee of three each from the National and American Leagues will function only in the matter of drafting a new agreement and a set of rules to govern future relations. That committee has no voice in the selection of the proposed Board of Control, which has now been concentrated into a membership of one man, the unanimous choice of sixteen club owners.

Expect Minors to Concur.

If the minors fail to approve the action of the majors they will be permitted to handle their own affairs in any way they may choose, but it is not expected they will fail to concur.

The joint committee now will have only to prepare the rules and regulations of their combined business affairs. The interpretation and enforcement of those rules and regulations will be vested in a one-man commission.

In their conference with Judge Landis the major leaguers quickly sensed the fact that he was unwilling to leave his position on the bench despite his great interest in the game which he had characterized several years ago as a national institution. The club owners had made their financial argument so strong that they thought it would be unanswerable, but Judge Landis made it plain that his hesitancy was due solely to his great reluctance to quit the bench. They then suggested the plan which was accepted whereby the jurist could continue to interpret the criminal laws of the land and at the same time keep crooks out of baseball.

The Salary Arrangement.

When this point was reached Judge Landis proposed that the salary offered him by the baseball magnates be reduced by the amount of his salary as District Court Justice, so that instead of receiving $50,000 a year as the Supreme Court of baseball, he would get $42,500.

In accepting the responsibility Judge Landis gave out a formal statement, in which he emphasized his reasons in the following words:

"The opportunities for real service to baseball are limitless. It is a matter to which I have devoted nearly forty years on the question of policy. All I have to say is this: The only thing in anybody's mind now, is to make baseball what the millions of fans throughout the United States want it to be."

This climax to nearly a month of "crucial" days is believed to mark the beginning of a new era in professional baseball. For the first time in the history of the sport, its promoters have sought and obtained a supreme ruler who has not had, and never expects to have, any interest in the pastime other than that which is born in every red-blooded American. They have selected in Judge Landis a man in whom the men of all branches of sport, as well as business, have such great confidence that if one of his important decisions were ever questioned by a club owner, player or fan, the questioner would be in bad favor with the public and the burden of proof would rest with him. Hitherto, when a club owner has emitted a yell about a verdict of the National Commission, he has been sure of the sympathy of at least the fans of his own town. Now he will not get even that.

Resolutions Adopted.

The formality of reaching this settlement of their differences occupied the magnates several hours, during which they aired their varying views without the aid of league Presidents or other intermediaries. The magnates selected as their Chairman President Baker of the Philadelphia Nationals, who was obliged to leave to catch a train for the East before the conclusion was reached. His successor in the Chair was President Veick of the Chicago Cubs. After reaching an understanding informally, the meeting became formal enough to pass the following resolutions:

"That the Chairman of the Board of Control shall be elected by a majority vote of the clubs composing the American and National Leagues.

"That his successor be elected in the same manner and that this shall be incorporated in the new national agreement.

"That upon all questions of an interleague nature or in any matter coming up at a joint meeting of the two major leagues, the roll be called and, after voting by clubs of each league, if there be a division, then the American League shall cast one vote and the National League one vote. Should these two votes be at variance, then the Commissioner shall cast the deciding vote and there shall be no appeal therefrom.

"Further, that the Commissioner shall preside at all joint meetings."

A Compromise Measure.

The foregoing means that the club owners reached a compromise on the chief point of difference which has kept them apart for weeks. That was the controversy over the right to vote by clubs or by leagues. The National League contention that, in the selection of a governing body, the majority vote of the sixteen clubs should decide, was conceded by the American League. In all other matters it was conceded by the National League that interleague disputes should be decided by a vote of the leagues, each having an equal voice, but that, if no agreement could be reached in this way, the commission should have the right to decide without appeal.

In disposing of the question of associate members of the commission to act with Judge Landis, no final action was taken at this meeting, but it was provided that the President of the American League should appear before the commissioner as a special pleader in cases involving the American League and that the President of the National League should be empowered to act in a similar capacity in cases involving the veteran circuit. And it was further understood that these men should appear only in cases in which their respective leagues of clubs were concerned.

It was also stipulated that, if the minor leagues decide to operate with the majors in the new arrangement, they shall appoint a special pleader to appear before the commission in all cases in which a minor league or a minor club-owner may be involved.

Lasker Plan Approved.

President Herrmann of the Cincinnati Club introduced a resolution which was seconded by President Dunn of the Cleveland Club indorsing the Lasker plan without specifically mentioning its author.

Details of the new agreement for the control and perpetuation of baseball will be worked out by a draft committee to be composed of twelve members equally divided between the majors and minors. The minors already have named their six. The National League had nominated a committee of four consisting of Herrmann, Ebbets, Dreyfuss and Ruppert, but this will be reduced to three and it is likely that President Heydler of the National League will be included on it. Likewise it is believed the committee of three to be appointed by the American League will include President Johnson of that circuit and Clark Griffith of the Washington Club, who is generally credited with having been the most efficacious factor in bringing about peace between the warring factions.

Statement of Owners.

CHICAGO, Nov. 12.—The following statement was issued by the sixteen club owners after today's meeting:

"At the joint meeting of the sixteen club owners of the major leagues held at the Congress Hotel today, Judge Kenesaw Mountain Landis was unanimously elected as the head of organized baseball for a term of seven years. The clubs of the American and National Leagues were represented by club owners and club Presidents. All of the differences existing between members of the American and National Leagues were adjusted in such a manner that the decision was agreeable to all.

"The following men were in the meeting room:

"American League—Cleveland, James C. Dunn; Chicago, Charles A. Comiskey, Harry Grabiner; Boston, Harry Frazee; New York, Jacob Ruppert; Philadelphia, Theodore Shibe, Connie Mack; St. Louis, Phil D. C. Ball, Robert Quinn; Detroit, Frank C. Navin; Washington, Clark Griffith.

"National League—Boston, George W. Grant; Brooklyn, Charles H. Ebbets; Chicago, William L. Veeck, A. D. Lasker; Cincinnati, Garry Herrmann; New York, Charles Stoneham, John McGraw; Philadelphia, William F. Baker, Charles Roch; St. Louis, Sam Breadon; Pittsburgh, Barney Dreyfuss."

The following resolution was introduced by Garry Herrmann of the Cincinnati Club and seconded by James C. Dunn of the Cleveland Club and unanimously adopted:

"Resolved, That the meeting endorse the principles of ethical control of baseball proposed in the plan submitted to all professional league clubs by four major league club owners in October last, and instruct the Drafting Committee that the spirit contained therein be embodied in the new national agreement.

"That the unreviewable control of all ethical matters be invested in the Chairman of the Control Board."

"A Peace That Will Last."

"We've made a real peace—one that will last," was the comment of President Veeck of the Chicago National League Club as the meeting broke up. "The full details of the reorganization have not been settled, of course, but we expect to issue a formal statement soon telling all about it. It's enough to say now that the war is over and every one of us is mighty glad of it."

Chicago will be headquarters for the baseball commissioners, and offices will be opened here immediately.

If second and third members are chosen for the commission, it is virtually certain, according to the club owners, that Judge Charles A. MacDonald of Chicago will be one of them, although no vote was taken today. Judge MacDonald indirectly brought on the baseball war, for he started the baseball scandal investigation which brought about the proposals for reorganization of control of baseball.

Judge Landis was hearing a case in which $15,000 bribery in connection with an income tax was charged when the committee of magnates filed into the courtroom, hats in their hands. The Judge sharply banged his gavel and ordered them to make less noise. When informed of their mission he had them escorted to his chambers, where they were kept in waiting for forty-five minutes before the Judge would listen to the offer which increased his annual salary from $7,500 a year to $50,000.

While the magnates waited the Judge conducted the bribery trial in his usual vigorous fashion and gave vent to some scathing remarks about the men who falsify their income tax returns. Waiting on the Judge were Charles Comiskey, President of the Chicago American League club; William Veeck, President of the Chicago Nationals; Jacob Ruppert of the New York Americans, Clark Griffith of Washington, Charles Ebbets of Brooklyn, Garry Herrmann of Cincinnati, Barney Dreyfus of Pittsburgh and John Breedon of the St. Louis Nationals. Later they were joined by Connie Mack of the Philadelphia Americans, Robert Quinn and James Dunn of Cleveland.

Why Judge Landis Accepted.

After the meeting Judge Landis took Clark Griffith, a personal friend, over to a window.

"Grif," he said, "I'm going to tell you just why I took this job. See those kids down there on the street? See that airplane propeller on the wall? Well, that explains my acceptance.

"You see that propeller was on the plane in which my son, Major Reed Landis, flew while overseas. Reed and I went to one of the world's series games at Brooklyn. Outside the gate was a bunch of little kids playing around. Reed turned to me and said: 'Dad, wouldn't it be a shame to have the game of these little kids broken up? Wouldn't it be awful to take baseball away from them?' Well, while you gentlemen were talking to me, I looked up at this propeller and thought of Reed. Then I thought of his remark in Brooklyn. Grif, we've got to keep baseball on a high standard for the sake of the youngsters—that's why I took the job, because I want to help."

Johnson Says He's Satisfied.

President B. B. Johnson of the American League, leader of the opponents of the Lasker plan, received his first information concerning the meeting from The Associated Press and expressed pleasure at the action taken.

"I am for Judge Landis and I think these club owners have acted wisely," he said. "Baseball will be placed on the highest possible standard now, and there will be no more fights. I am well satisfied with everything that took place today."

President John Heydler of the National League made the following statement to The Associated Press:

"I am very happy over this solution of the baseball problem. It is an upward step for baseball, and forever eliminates politics from the national game. One of the chief worries of a League President is to vote fairly in the National Commission, and I am glad to be relieved of that responsibility."

HAD HARDING'S GOOD WISHES.

Lasker Says President-Elect Hoped for Peace in Baseball.

CHICAGO, Nov. 12.—A. D. Lasker, originator of the Lasker plan of baseball control, tonight let it become known that he had given up a trip to the South with President-elect Harding to attend today's baseball meeting and that Senator Harding had requested him to remain at the meeting here rather than join him in the trip.

"Senator Harding called me by telephone a few days ago to ask me to join him, but when I told him of the meeting scheduled for today, he said to me by all means to stay here. He said he was very much interested in baseball and hoped everything would be settled peacefully."

LANDIS A NATIONAL FIGURE.

Has Sat in Many Famous Cases—A Close Student of Baseball.

CHICAGO, Nov. 12.—Judge Landis is a national figure for the important cases he has passed upon, and his wit and sarcasm—sometimes humorous and sometimes caustic—which he directs at prisoners and counsel from his bench have made him famous.

Baseball has always been one of his hobbies. In the little town of Logansport, Ind., where he was reared, the Judge played on amateur and semi-professional teams. His brilliant playing brought him many offers to turn professional, but he always declined, saying he played merely for love of the game.

In 1914 Judge Landis presided in the legal battle which resulted from the greatest baseball war in history—the fight of the Federal League against the National and American Leagues. The Judge never rendered a decision in this case, however, for it was settled out of court while he was still forming his official opinion. While studying the case the Judge spent many hours looking into baseball history, examining the national agreement and other documents giving information concerning baseball. The knowledge acquired during this period made him a legal authority on the administration of the game's affairs.

Judge Landis attends many major league games here every year and seldom misses a world's series. At the annual ball classic, he generally may be found in a box back of third base, his old, black slouch hat pulled down over his eyes and a long black cape falling from his shoulders. He never talks during a game, but studies every play closely and enjoys analyzing the strategy used by the opposing players. One of his hobbies at a game is to try to guess the next play.

Judge Landis was born in Millville, Ohio, Nov. 20, 1866, and was named for Kenesaw Mountain, near Atlanta, Ga., where his father was wounded in the civil war. He first became nationally prominent when he fined the Standard Oil Company $29,240,000, after forcing John D. Rockefeller to come here to testify. His decision was reversed by the Appellate Court, however.

During the World War Judge Landis presided at the famous I. W. W. trial, sentencing Big Bill Haywood, Secretary-Treasurer of the organization, and ninety-two other members to prison. Shortly afterward an explosion in the Federal Building killed several persons, but the Judge was uninjured. He also sentenced Congressman Victor Berger to prison for alleged obstruction of the nation's war preparations.

Judge Landis drew Congressional attention shortly after the war. He found that most of the lawyers appearing before him who were wearing wrist watches had not been in the service.

"Have all these wrist-watch lawyers file a statement what branch of the service they were in," he ordered his clerk.

Senator Thomas of Colorado in an address in the Senate said Judge Landis should be impeached for his order. The Judge's only comment was: "Doesn't it beat the devil what some Senators will do to pass the time away?"

HOME RUN EPIDEMIC HITS MAJOR LEAGUES

Spring Slugging Puts Records in Danger — Yanks Lead American, Phils National.

An epidemic of home run hitting has broken out in both major leagues and if the average maintained to date continues through the season some new records in circuit drives will be established. In the 1920 campaign the American League set up the remarkable total of 370 circuit drives, while clubs of the other major organization hit a total of 261. Both figures were so far beyond the normal totals for home runs that they occasioned considerable comment. The 1920 figures, however, seem destined for decisive eclipse in the campaign now under way.

A livelier ball is the only answer that fits the case. It is true that the restrictions which were imposed on pitchers, starting with the opening of the 1920 pennant races and still in force, have made hitting easier, but even this does not explain the great advance in home run hitting. The fact that many players who seldom hit for the circuit have branched out as long distance sluggers is not explained satisfactorily by changes in pitching rules. They are no stronger physically than before, yet their drives are carrying far beyond the former limits.

The firm which manufactures the baseballs used in the two leagues makes the statement that it is following exactly the same procedure as in the years when the hitting did not attract as much attention. The same amount of cork and wool is used in each ball, but the manufacturers admit that they are getting a better grade of Australian wool. This may be the answer. At any rate the ball is livelier than in the past and home runs are blooming where they never bloomed before.

Home-run hitting in the National League has increased this year to a greater extent than in the American League. With about one-fifth of the playing scheduled completed, the clubs of the Heydler circuit have batted more than one-third of their 1920 total in circuit drives. The Brooklyn team already has made 14 homers, as against 28 during the pennant-winning campaign last year. The Cardinals are within one homer of reaching one-half of their 1920 total, having 15 to date, as against 32 last season.

Pirates and Giants High.

The Pirates and Giants are closing in on the mark which will equal half of their grist in 1920. Pittsburgh made 16 last year and has 6 to date, while the Giants got 46 a year ago and now have 17. At their present clip, the Phillies should reach the century mark, the Braves should double their last year's total and the Reds should collect several more than in 1920. The Cubs alone in the National League are falling behind their pace of last season.

In the American League six of the eight clubs have been hitting homers at a rate which should carry them beyond their 1920 marks. The White Sox have taken a big slump, but this can be answered by the passing of Jackson and Felsch, their leading long-distance hitters. The Mackmen have not been getting home runs as frequently as during the preceding season, but the six other clubs are doing much better. Even the Yankees, who set a record far above the best previous mark, are likely to improve on their 1920 total of 115.

Taking the individual records, the improvement in figures also is quite marked. Ty Cobb hit twice for the circuit last season and he has made five homers this Spring. Wrightstone of the Phillies, with six to date, has doubled his 1920 total; Max Carey has three

now, as against one all last season; Earl Smith of the Giants can show four, as against solitary homer in 1920, while Sam Rice and Jacques Fournier already have equaled their last year's totals. Babe Ruth, the Meusel brothers and Cy Williams are hitting homers more frequently than last year, and George Kelly needs only three more to reach his 1920 total. These players are mentioned because all have three or more to date. Many players on this year's home-run list did not make one all last year.

As might be expected, the Yankees are showing the way in hitting for the circuit. The Hugmen have hit 25 homers to date, of which number Ruth has poled 12. Babe has equaled the Cleveland total, and has more to his credit than any of the six other American League clubs. Four National League teams also have failed to hit as many circuit drives as Ruth alone has made.

Phillies Lead National.

In the National League the Phillies are showing the way with 21, and the Giants are second with 17. The Cardinals with 15 and the Robins with 14 also have done better than any American League club, with the exception of the Yankees. The White Sox trail all other clubs, having only four to their credit.

Three players in the American League and four in the National have hit five or more home runs to date. Ruth is in front with twelve, and Kelly is next in line with eight. Wrightstone and Emil Meusel of the Phillies have six apiece, while Ty Cobb, Bob Meusel and Jacques Fournier have five each. Players who have hit four homers are Earl Smith of the Giants, Cy Williams of the Phillies, Austin McHenry of the Cardinals, Elmer Smith of Cleveland and Harry Heilman of Detroit. In the appended list are forty-eight National and thirty-nine American Leaguers who have made one or more home runs this season. Following is the complete list of home runs made in the major leagues to date:

AMERICAN LEAGUE.

New York 25—Ruth 12, Meusel 5, Pipp 2, Roth 2, Schang 2, Ward, Peckinpaugh.
Cleveland 12—Smith 4, Speaker 2, Gardner 2, Uhle, O'Neill, Sewell, Stephenson.
Detroit 11—Cobb 5, Heilman 4, Veach 2.
St. Louis 11—Sisler 3, Williams 3, Tobin 2, Severeid, Wetzel, Gerber.
Washington 9—Rice 3, Shanks 3, Gharrity 2, Judge.
Philadelphia 8—Dugan 2, Perkins 2, C. Walker 2, Dykes, Griffin.
Boston 5—Pratt 2, Menosky, Jones, Ruel.
Chicago 4—Falk 2, Hooper, Mostil.
Total—85.

NATIONAL LEAGUE.

Philadelphia 21—Meusel 6, Wrightstone 6, Williams 4, Meadows 2, Bruggy, R. Miller, Lebourveau.
New York 17—Kelly 8, Smith 4, Walker 2, Young, Burns, Snyder.
St. Louis 15—Fournier 5, McHenry 4, Schultz 2, Hornsby 2, Mann, Shotton.
Brooklyn 14—Wheat 3, Griffith 3, Neis 3, Konetchy 2, Johnston, Krueger, Miller.
Boston 6—Cruise 2, Powell 2, Fillingim, McQuillan, Nicholson, Southworth, O'Neil.
Chicago 6—Terry, Sullivan, Twombley, Grimes, Flack, O'Farrell.
Pittsburgh 6—Carey 3, Tierney 2, Whitted.
Cincinnati—Hargrave, Duncan, Bee, Fonseca, Wingo, Bressler.
Total—94.

May 24, 1921

FANS MAY KEEP BASEBALLS.

Pittsburgh Official Rules That Police Are Not to Interfere.

PITTSBURGH, July 9.—Fans who attend games at the National baseball park here may keep balls knocked into the stands without fear of being molested by policemen, according to an order issued yesterday by Robert J. Alderdice, Director of Public Safety. Director Alderdice made the ruling following threatened damage suits against policemen who placed three fans under arrest for refusing to throw balls back onto the diamond.

Policemen placed in the park are there to preserve order and to protect the public, the director said. Hereafter, any action taken against fans for refusing to give up balls must be taken by park employes, Mr. Alderdice said.

July 10, 1921

BASEBALL LEADERS WON'T LET WHITE SOX RETURN TO THE GAME

Judge Landis, Ban Johnson and Comiskey Not Moved by Jury Verdict.

HOLD CROOKEDNESS SHOWN

And the Decision in Court Was Only Technical Under State Law.

"BUCK" WEAVER MAY SUE

But the Other Accused Men Are Not Likely to Attempt Reinstatement.

Special to The New York Times.

CHICAGO, Aug. 3.—The rulers of organized baseball promptly declared today that the acquitted White Sox players would not be reinstated despite the verdict of the jury last night.

Charles A. Comiskey, the White Sox owner; Judge Landis, who is official arbitrator, and Ban Johnson, President of the American League, issued separate statements, each of which contributed its bit toward destroying any hopes the players may have had for reinstatement.

"Cicotte confessed to me that he had been 'crooked,'" said Mr. Comiskey, "and implicated seven other players. Until they all are able to explain this to my satisfaction none of them will play with the Sox."

Judge Landis gave out this statement:

"Regardless of the verdict of juries, no player that throws a ball game; no player that undertakes or promises to throw a ball game; no player that sits in a conference with a bunch of crooked players and gamblers where the ways and means of throwing games are planned and discussed and does not promptly tell his club about it, will ever play professional baseball.

"Of course, I don't know that any of these men will apply for reinstatement, but if they do, the above are at least a few of the rules that will be enforced. Just keep in mind that, regardless of the verdict of juries, baseball is entirely competent to protect itself against crooks, both inside and outside the game."

President Johnson said:

"The trial of the indicted players and gamblers which closed yesterday uncovered the greatest crime it was possible to commit in baseball. The fact that the men were freed by a Cook County jury does not alter the conditions one iota or minimize the magnitude of such offenses."

"The energetic prosecution of the State clearly indicates that crimes of this character will not be permitted to go unchallenged."

Speculation as to whether there will

be any further prosecution of the indicted players' was definitely disposed of by the State's Attorney, Robert E. Crowe.

"As far as I am concerned the case is closed," said Mr. Crowe. "There are several other indictments against the men, but the one under which they were tried contained virtually all the charges. We shall quash the remaining indictments."

Despite the statements of Judge Landis, Comiskey and Johnson, not all of the "Black Sox" have abandoned hope for reinstatement.

"I am entirely innocent and the jury has proved that," said Risberg. "I leave my future in the hands of organized baseball."

"I never had anything to do with the so-called conspiracy," said Happy Felsch. "The jury has cleared my name."

"If it had not been for those two liars, Bill Burns and Billy Maharg, I would not have been mixed up in this," said "Chick" Gandil. "Anyway, it's all over now."

Eddie Cicotte refused to discuss the case.

"I talked once on this, never again," he said. "All I want is to get back to Detroit."

Joe Jackson, former outfielder, said he was through with baseball. He and Claude Williams are said to have prospered with a Chicago poolroom, and it is not thought likely either will make much effort to get back on the diamond. It is said that "Buck" Weaver will probably bring suit to recover payments that stopped when he was suspended.

There were rumors of suits on "injuries to reputations," but attorneys for the defense did not confirm these.

"My clients, so far as I have been informed, will not seek any redress," said Benedict Short, who defended Cicotte, Williams and Jackson. "The jury has cleared them, and I believe they will be content to let it go at that."

Thomas D. Nash and Michael J. Ahern, attorneys for Weaver, Felsch and Risberg, also seemed inclined to "let well enough alone," so far as damage suits were concerned. But Mr. Ahern said that Weaver had a legitimate claim in connection with his contract.

Mr. Comiskey was undisturbed by reports concerning civil action.

"We are prepared for any of these men who want to 'go to law' with us," said the Old Roman. "They have all been paid every nickel they had coming."

August 4, 1921

A major league record which had endured for years was broken yesterday, and Walter Johnson now takes a place in baseball's Hall of Fame where Cy Young had held forth. In a stretch of twenty-two seasons of pitching in the majors, Cy registered a total of 2,290 strike-outs. Johnson, now in his seventeenth consecutive year with the Washington club, has been steadily approaching this mark, and he needed only three to equal Young's record when he went into the box yesterday morning at Philadelphia against the Mackmen. At the Polo Grounds last week Johnson retired seven Yankees on strikes, thereby running his total up to 2,287. Six Mackmen fell before Walter's speed yesterday morning, so the Washington Siege Gun now has to his credit three more strike-outs than Young recorded over a considerably longer period. It is probable, too, that Johnson will see many more batsmen carry their bats back to the bench before he passes out of major league baseball.

September 6, 1921

RUTH'S 59TH HOMER FEATURE OF FINALE

Yankees End League Season With Ninth-Inning Victory Over Red Sox, 7 to 6.

The Yankees, champions of the American League and also of a portion of New York City, played their final scheduled league ball game of the season yesterday afternoon at the Polo Grounds, and, with a view to keeping their highly-prized escutcheon as free from stains as possible, pried the victory from the nerveless fingers of Hugh Duffy's Red Sox in the ninth inning. The score was 7 to 6.

With the chief issue, the race for the flag, decided, the transit routes didn't break down under their burden of humanity bound for the Brush Stadium. Still, there was one important matter to be decided, and that was largely what drew 12,000 persons to what was expected to prove an anti-climactic affair. The question was: How many home runs would be officially credited to George Herman Ruth for the season of 1921? The right answer proved to be fifty-nine.

In the third inning, with two of his little pals stamping nervously on the sacks, the Babe extricated them from their predicament by slashing a gigantic looping hoist to the upper stand opposite right field. It was a mighty slam, and mighty was the vocal outburst that greeted it.

The score and the eleventh-hour finish make it evident that it was a pretty good game to watch. It was all of that in the later stages. It started out, however, to be a landslide, and people don't, as a rule, go to see landslides. They are more inclined to depart hurriedly in the opposite direction.

Collins in Erratic Mood.

With Bob Shawkey at the helm, the Yankees piled up a lead of five runs to none in the first three innings. Then Rip Collins was summoned to the box to shuffle the cards for the visitors, and they almost broke Rip's bank. In a two-inning display of wildness and weakness on the part of Collins the parties from Massachusetts tied the score. Then Bill Piercy took the pitching post and the visitors squeezed a tally over on Piercy in the eighth through his own peccadilloes. This one-run lead vanished in the latter half of the ninth before the steaming heat of two doubles, with a pass and a force play interspersed. Peck's bat being the weapon which drove in the tying and winning runs.

One of those trances which are likely to affect poetic natures during the harvest moon cut the Red Sox down in the first inning when they had a promising chance to score. Leibold opened with a hit to deep short and beat Peck's throw to Pipp. Shawkey walked Pittenger, depositing Leibold on second. Pratt popped to Ward and McInnis raised one to Peck. For some reason not set forth in the text books Leibold chose to gallop to third on Stuffy's hoist, and was doubled up at second by Peck's toss to Ward.

Once again in the second stanza the Boston crew threatened, filling the sacks with one down on passes to Collins and Chaplin and Scott's single to centre. However, Fullerton hit into a double slaughter, Peck to Ward to Pipp.

In their portion of the second the Yankees landed three solid thumps in a row after two batters had been mowed down and took forcible possession of a pair of runs. Ward shot a single to right and skipped to the far turn on McNally's double to the same region. Devormer planted a two-base blow in left and both of his galloping comrades crossed the scoring tablet. Pratt threw out Shawkey for the third casualty.

Ruth Takes a Swing.

Elmer Miller started the home half of the third with a one-bagger to left. He paused at second on Peckinpaugh's one-base thrust to right centre. Thereupon appeared, staggering toward the plate under the weight of his bat, the emaciated form of the invalid Babe

Ruth. The Babe was out there merely because his physician had recommended gentle exercise. He swung feebly and the ball, merely from force of habit, swished into the upper layer of the right field stand. The crippled Ruth was much annoyed over the incident because it made it incumbent upon him to jog around the base paths in the dust raised by the feet of Miller and Peck.

In the fourth inning Bob Shawkey, who held the guests to a brace of useless singles in three chukkers, yielded his position on the mound to Rip Collins, the idea being that Rip needed the practice far more than did Bob. Collins got a lot of practice, too, for it took him a long time to retire the Red Sox in the fourth, and even longer in the fifth. Indeed, he never did get them retired in the fifth, Bill Piercy finally achieving the feat.

In the fourth McInnis flied to left at the outset and the Babe, who hadn't lost any flies and, consequently, wasn't looking for any, allowed the sphere to trickle through between his thumb and his forefinger. Collins belted a single to left, McInnis stopping at the midway. On Bush's out, Peck to Pipp, both runners advanced. While Ward was tossing out Scott, McInnis scored and Collins took third. Then Rip's jungle blood assumed the ascendant and he became wilder than any tiger of your acquaintance. He walked Chaplin, Fullerton and Leibold in rapid sequence, forcing his grandfather, John Shano Collins, over the plate. Pittenger fouled to Pipp.

Red Sox Tie It Up.

In the fifth, Pratt tripled to left to open the session and tallied on McInnis's two-base poke to right centre. Ruth made a stunning catch, with a run and a jump for Collins's fly. Then Bush tripled to left and McInnis ended his homeward journey. Scott singled to centre and Bush reported at the plate. That closed the career of Rip Collins for the time being, and Piercy took a fling at it. He managed to retire the Red Sox without further scoring, but the soft berth of the Yankees in the afternoon's pastime had been replaced by a 5 to 5 tie.

The Red Sox assumed a one-lead run in the eighth. After McNally had attended to Fullerton's bounder and tossed him out, Leibold drew a pass, but was forced by Pittenger, Fewster to Peck. Pratt was walked. Piercy threw away to Pipp after fielding McInnis's tap and

Pittenger managed to scramble all the way to the disk. Pipp absorbed Collins's foul for the third out.

The story of that ninth-inning finale runs something like this: Devormer bashed the ball through short and scampered to second on the blow. Baker batted for Piercy and drew four wide ones. Miller forced Baker at second. Scott to Pratt, Devormer scrambling to the last corner on the play. Peck slammed the sphere to the right field wall for a double so extensive that Miller was enabled to follow Devormer across the plate.

The score:

NEW YORK (A.)						BOSTON (A.)					
	Ab	R	H	Po	A		Ab	R	H	Po	A
Miller,cf	5	2	1	1	0	Leibold,cf	3	0	1	3	0
Peck'p'gh,ss	4	1	2	2	8	Neitzke,lf	0	0	0	0	0
Ruth,lf	4	1	2	1	0	Pittenger,3b	4	1	0	0	4
Meusel,rf	4	0	0	0	0	Pratt,2b	4	1	2	1	2
Pipp,1b	4	0	0	16	0	McInnis,1b	5	2	1	11	0
Ward,2b	2	1	1	3	2	J. Collins,rf	4	1	1	4	0
Fewster,2b	1	0	0	1	3	Bush,lf,cf	5	1	2	0	0
McNally,3b	4	1	2	0	0	Scott,ss	5	0	2	0	6
Devormer,c	4	1	2	8	0	Chaplin,c	2	0	0	5	0
Shawkey,p	1	0	0	0	1	Fullerton,p	3	0	0	1	0
W. Collins,p	1	0	0	0	0						
Piercy,p	1	0	0	0	1	Total	35	6	9	*25	13
aBaker	0	0	0	0	0						
bHawks	0	0	0	0	0						
Total	35	7	10	27	16						

* One out when winning run was scored.
a Batted for Piercy in ninth.
b Ran for Baker in ninth.
Errors—Ruth, Pipp, Ward.

New York .... 0 2 3 0 0 0 0 0 2—7
Boston .... 0 0 0 2 3 0 0 1 0—6

Two-base hits—McNally (2), Devormer (2), McInnis, Peckinpaugh. Three-base hits—Pratt, Bush. Home run—Ruth. Stolen base—Ruth, Pittenger. Double plays—Peckinpaugh, Ward and Pipp; Peckinpaugh and Ward. Left on bases—New York 6, Boston 10. Bases on balls—Off Shawkey 3, W. Collins 2, Piercy 3, Fullerton 3. Hits—Off Shawkey 2 in 3 innings, W. Collins 5 in 1 1-3, Piercy 2 in 4 2-3. Struck out—By Shawkey 1, W. Collins 1, Fullerton 4. Winning pitcher—Piercy. Losing pitcher—Fullerton. Umpires—Wilson, Chill and Connolly. Time of game—1:49.

October 3, 1921

Boston Red Sox

ROBERTSON PITCHES PERFECT BALL GAME

Only 27 Tigers Face White Sox Rookie, Who Allows Neither a Hit Nor a Run.

FIVE OTHERS TURNED TRICK

Bradley, Richmond, Ward, Young and Joss Performed Stunt—Chicago Beats Detroit by 2-0.

Special to The New York Times.

DETROIT, April 30.—Charley Robertson, a rookie pitcher with the Chicago White Sox, carved a niche in sport's hall of fame for himself here this afternoon when he twirled a perfect game against the Detroit Tigers. He pitched a no-hit and no-run game and not a Detroit player reached first base, but twenty-seven men facing him. This is not the first time that the feat has been performed in major league baseball, but it is the first time since Addie Joss, then pitching for Cleveland, performed the stunt in a game against the White Sox on Oct. 2, 1908. The White Sox today won by a score of 2 to 0.

Robertson was obtained from the Minneapolis Club of the American Association and today's was the second victory of the year that he has turned in for Kid Gleason's clan. Last year he had a pitching average of .531 while with the Millers.

In turning in the feat Robertson was accorded fine support by his teammates. He fanned six batters as a part of his share in the afternoon's work. McClellan and Collins were particularly brilliant afield. They retired six Tigers at first base and Collins also retired four

others on flies. Only six balls were driven into the outfield and these were corralled by Hooper and Mostil.

Pillette, who pitched for the Tigers, was effective in all but the second inning, when the White Sox scored their two runs. He allowed the Chicagoans but seven hits. These, however, proved ample.

In the long history of major league baseball since 1875 but five other perfectly pitched games in which no batter reached first base safely have been turned in.

The first of these was pitched by G. W. Bradley of St. Louis against Hartford in the old National League on July 15, 1876. On June 12, 1880, J. L. Richmond, pitching for Worcester, turned the trick against Cleveland in the National League, and in the same year on June 17 John M. Ward, later manager of the Giants, while pitching for Providence, defeated the Buffalo National League Club in like fashion.

Then followed a stretch of twenty-four years before another hurler was able to duplicate these performances. It was the pitcher of pitchers, Denton T. (Cy.) Young who performed the feat. He was pitching for the Boston Red Sox of the American League against the Philadelphia Athletics, and the game was played on May 5, 1904.

Thus but two other pitchers besides Charles Robertson have been able to contribute such an excellent piece of work to baseball history under modern rules—Joss and Young. When Bradley, Richmond and Ward succeeded in pitching perfect games the old rules were in force.

The score of the White Sox-Tigers game follows:

CHICAGO (A.)						DETROIT (A.)					
	Ab	R	H	Po	A		Ab	R	H	Po	A
Mulligan,ss	4	0	1	0	0	Blue,1b	3	0	0	11	3
McClellan,3b	3	0	1	1	3	Cutshaw,2b	3	0	0	2	3
Collins,2b	3	0	1	4	3	Cobb,cf	3	0	0	1	0
Hooper,rf	3	1	0	3	0	Veach,lf	3	0	0	2	0
Mostil,lf	3	0	1	1	0	Heilmann,rf	3	0	0	1	0
Strunk,cf	3	0	0	0	0	Jones,3b	3	0	0	1	5
Sheely,1b	4	0	2	9	0	Rigney,ss	2	0	0	2	1
Schalk,c	4	0	1	7	1	Manion,c	3	0	0	7	1
Robertson,p	4	0	0	0	1	Pillette,p	2	0	0	0	3
						aClark	1	0	0	0	0
Total	32	2	7	27	8	bBassler	1	0	0	0	0
						Total	27	0	0	27	16

a Batted for Rigney in ninth.
b Batted for Pillette in ninth.
Error—Blue.

Chicago .... 0 2 0 0 0 0 0 0 0—2
Detroit .... 0 0 0 0 0 0 0 0 0—0

Two-base hits—Mulligan, Sheely. Sacrifices—McClellan, Collins, Strunk. Left on bases—Chicago 8, Detroit 0. Bases on balls—Off Pillette 2. Struck out—By Pillette 5, Robertson 6. Umpires—Nallin and Evans. Time of game—1:56.

May 1, 1922

RUTH IN ROW WITH UMPIRE AND FAN AT POLO GROUNDS

Following Dispute Over Decision Babe Throws Dirt in the Official's Face.

CHASES ROOTER IN STAND

Attempts to Attack Spectator —Banished From Game, May Be Fined or Suspended.

HOME-RUN KING NOT SORRY

Says He Merely Resented Insulting Remarks—Ban Johnson Must Decide Case of Yanks' Star.

Babe Ruth today faces another indefinite suspension from baseball. At the Polo Grounds yesterday, only six days after he had been restored to good standing by Judge K. M. Landis, Baseball Commissioner, following more than a five weeks' suspension, the home-run slugger threw a handful of dust into the face of Umpire Hildebrand and was put out of the game. Incensed by the jeers of the crowd. Ruth then climbed into the stand and tried to punish a fan he said had made insulting remarks.

It was in the third inning of the game with the Washington Senators, which the Yankees won by a score of 6 and 4. With one man out, Ruth singled to centre. When Sam Rice of the Senators fumbled the ball slightly Ruth tried to stretch his hit into a two-bagger. He slid into second base in a cloud of dust and Umpire Hildebrand called him out.

This decision sent the home-run slugger into a rage. He leaped to his feet with the quickness of a cat and he brought up with him a handful of dirt, which he threw in the direction of the umpire. From the grandstand it seemed that the dust spattered over Hildebrand's face and neck. Some of it seeped down inside his collar and the rest fell on his arm and on the front of his plaid uniform.

Hildebrand at once waved Ruth out of the game, and the Babe walked back to the Yankee bench. Every step of the journey was a signal to the crowd to jeer and hoot. To this demonstration Ruth made the retort courteous. He lifted his cap in courtly manner, a satirical gesture that had only the effect of increasing the volume of jeers and hisses.

Climbs Into Grand Stand.

A minute later Ruth was not so gracious and smiling. Back of the Yankee bench sat two Pullman conductors. One of them shouted something at Ruth which the Babe did not like. In a flash he vaulted to the roof of the dugout, clambered through a box filled with people and started up the aisle in the direction of his tormentor.

As Ruth approached the fan receded. He climbed back over the tops of the seats, put several rows between him and the Babe and from this point of safety listened to a series of scathing remarks from the irate player. Several neutral bystanders pushed Ruth away gently, and some of the crowd—those further away—yelled, "Hit the big stiff!" When nobody followed the advice Ruth climbed back on the field, disappeared inside the bench for an instant and then walked across the field to the clubhouse.

On this second march he was again booed, but some of the crowd cheered and applauded. To these friends Ruth lifted his cap.

At the Hotel Ansonia, where Ruth has an apartment, the homerun hitter gave his version of the affair last night. He said he wasn't a bit sorry for his action in invading the grandstand.

"They can boo and hoot me all they want," said Ruth. "That doesn't matter to me. But when a fan calls insulting names from the grandstand and becomes abusive I don't intend to stand for it. This fellow today, whoever he was, called me a 'low-down bum' and other names that got me mad, and when I went after him he ran.

"Furthermore, I didn't throw any dust in Hildebrand's face. It didn't go into his face, only on his sleeve. I don't know what they will do to me for this. Maybe I'll be fined or suspended for kicking on the decision, but I don't see why I should get any punishment at all. I would go into the stand again if I had to."

May Get Off With Fine.

The Pullman conductor whose remarks started the trouble refused to give his name. Shortly after the incident was over he was requested by the Yankee authorities to leave the park, and he did so.

Baseball men last night were agreed that Ruth would be punished in some way, but there were many who believed that a heavy fine would be the extent of the action by Ban Johnson, President of the American League. One high official, who refused to permit his name to be used, said that probably Ruth would only be fined, and this because of his attack on the umpire.

If baseball precedent, however, is followed, Ruth will draw an indefinite suspension. The nearest parallel to his case is that of Ty Cobb, now manager of the Detroit Tigers, who climbed into the stand after a fan during a game at the Yankees' old Hilltop grounds in 1911. Cobb, then at the peak of his career, was set down indefinitely by President Johnson, and the Detroit team promptly went on its celebrated "sympathy strike," refusing to play until its star player was reinstated. The strike was overcome and Cobb stayed out for ten days before Johnson lifted the ban. Ruth's case is complicated by the fact that he also threw dust in the umpire's face and had been put out of the game before he made his sortie into the grand stand. In any event, however, it is not considered likely that he will be out for more than ten days, if that long. It was pointed out by baseball men last night that under the terms of an American League agreement made in Chicago in February, 1920, any indefinite suspension must be lifted at the end of ten days or else be subject to action by a board of review.

This rule was passed as a result of the Carl Mays case, when the pitcher was indefinitely barred by Ban Johnson. If Ruth is not reinstated before ten days his case will go before the Board of Review, the members of which are Colonel Jacob Ruppert, one of the two owners of the Yankees, and Clark Griffith, President of the Washington Club. If this board cannot agree, the case goes to a Federal Judge in Chicago for settlement.

Landis Has No Jurisdiction.

Judge Landis, Commissioner of Baseball, has no jurisdiction in the case. The decision is up to President Johnson, who will receive confidential reports from Umpire Hildebrand, the recipient of the handful of dust, and from Um-

pire Dick Nallin, who was in charge of yesterday's game. The umpires' testimony was wired to American League headquarters last night, and a decision may be expected today.

Colonel Jacob Ruppert, President of the club, was out of town yesterday and did not know of the latest outbreak of Ruth's until he was told by a NEW YORK TIMES reporter last night.

"Probably Ruth acted in the heat of the moment," the Colonel said, "but even so he deserves to be punished for what he did. It's very unfortunate, coming so soon after Ruth's reinstatement. As I said, I was not at the game, and therefore can't speak as an eyewitness."

Huston and Huggins Silent.

The same reticence was shown by Colonel T. L. Huston, Ruppert's partner, and by Manager Miller Huggins. "I have nothing to say," Huston told reporters. Huggins referred questioners to the owners of the club.

Another Yankee official declared that he does not look for a suspension. "Cobb was set down because he thrashed the fan severely," this official said. "Ty didn't stop at merely 'bawling' the other fellow out, as Ruth did. There have been several cases in both the American and National Leagues where players have gone up to a fan and castigated him verbally, and the custom has been to reprimand the offender or, at most, to fine him."

Other baseball observers, however, recalled that Ban Johnson has been unusually strict in upholding his umpires this year. Shortly after the beginning of the season he barred Miller Huggins indefinitely for merely talking roughly to an umpire, and the suspension lasted several days. Ruth's prominence and the fact that last Fall he defied Judge Landis and baseball law by going on a barnstorming trip are regarded as factors that may influence Johnson to make the punishment as stiff as possible.

Only once before in his major league career did Ruth have serious trouble with an umpire. Back in 1919 he struck Brick Owens when the umpire called a strike on him during a game at Fenway Park, Boston. The Babe then was a member of the Boston Red Sox. He was suspended indefinitely by Ban Johnson and not reinstated until five days had passed.

Already thirty-eight days behind his home run record, Ruth would be hit hard by any additional lay off. Ten days more out of the game would mean that he would have missed more than a quarter of the season, and in that case to tie his last year's record of fifty-nine home runs would be nearly impossible. Kenneth Williams of the Browns has twelve homers to the Babe's one, and if again suspended Ruth might lose his home run crown.

Two Homers for Meusel.

In fact, right now Ruth is two homers behind Bob Meusel, who was one of his partners on the ill-fated barnstorming trip last Fall which resulted in Judge Landis's five-week sentence. Meusel was very much in the limelight yesterday. He started the game even with the Bambino in the matter of four-baggers and he ended two ahead, both drives coming after Ruth had been banished from the field.

The Yankees won by only two runs, 6 to 4, and as late as the first half of the sixth inning they were tied with the hustling Senators, who hit Waite Hoyt with a certain amount of éclat and tied the score after the Yanks had taken a 4—1 lead.

In the same inning the Hugmen scored another run, and that won the game. But, for safety's sake, Bob Meusel came to the plate in the eighth inning, espying a spot in the corner of the left field bleachers, pumped a low line drive right against the bull's-eye. Bob's previous homer was made in the fourth inning. He started the inning by taking hold of one of Tom Phillips's curves and depositing it clear on the other side of the high fence at the rear of the left field bleachers. It was considerable of a blow, and it was extremely timely, coming on the heels, so to speak, of Ruth's incursion into the stand and excursion from the park.

Two home runs helped the Senators to keep in the running. With one out in the first frame Sam Rice, who delivered a circuit drive on Wednesday, sent a hard drive spinning between Witt and Ruth. The ball rolled to the fence while Rice was skimming around the bases.

In the same inning the home lads scored twice on Witt's walk, Ward's bunt, which he beat out; Ruth's sacrifice and Baker's neat single to centre. They picked up a couple more in the fourth on Meusel's homer, a walk to Scott and Hoyt's surprising double against the right field grandstand.

Judge Hits for Circuit.

This made the game appear safe, but the Senators had one punch left, which they delivered in the sixth. As a starter Harris was hit by a pitched ball, and Ward fumbled Rice's splash to second base. Then came the second Washington home run, Judge driving the ball into a box in the upper right field tier. The score was tied, but Pipp and Scott untied it in the same inning. After Meusel had flied out, Pipp drove to right for one base, and Scott immediately followed with a whistling double down the third-base line. Pipp came all the way from first with a run. In the eighth, Meusel's second home run made it 6 to 4, where it stood to the end. Brillheart, a new left-hander, pitched for the Senators after the seventh, when Milan batted for Phillips.

Chick Fewster almost got himself put out of the game in the seventh. He was called out at the plate by Nallin, and Chick was so enraged that he kicked dust all over the umpire's nice new shine. After kicking with both feet and mouth, Chick was led out to centre field, and the game went on.

The score:

NEW YORK (A.)						WASHINGTON (A.)					
	Ab	R	H	Po	A		Ab	R	H	Po	A
Witt,cf	2	1	0	2	0	Harris,2b	4	1	1	2	5
Fewster,lf	1	0	1	1	0	Rice,cf	4	2	1	5	1
Ward,2b	3	1	1	2	1	Judge,1b	4	1	2	8	0
Ruth,lf	1	0	1	0	0	Brower,rf	4	0	0	0	0
Miller,cf	2	0	0	2	0	Goslin,lf	4	0	1	2	0
Baker,3b	4	0	2	2	3	Shanks,3b	3	0	0	2	0
Meusel,rf	4	2	2	1	0	Gharrity,c	4	0	1	3	0
Pipp,1b	4	1	1	15	0	P'paugh,ss	4	0	0	2	3
Scott,ss	4	0	1	2	6	Phillips,p	2	0	0	0	1
Schang,c	4	0	1	2	0	aMilan	1	0	0	0	0
Hoyt,p	3	0	1	0	0	Brillheart,p	0	0	0	0	0
						bSmith	1	0	0	0	0
Total..30		6	11	27	14	Total....35		4	6	24	10

aBatted for Phillips in seventh.
bBatted for Brillheart in ninth.
Errors—Ward, Baker.

New York ....2 0 0 2 0 1 0 1..—6
Washington ....1 0 0 0 0 3 0 0 0—4

Two-base hits—Hoyt, Scott. Home runs—Rice, Meusel (2), Judge. Stolen base—Fewster. Sacrifice—Ruth. Double plays—Phillips, Harris and Judge; Harris, Peck and Judge. Left on bases—New York 5, Washington 7. Bases on balls—Off Hoyt 1, Phillips 3. Struck out—By Hoyt 2, Phillips 1, Brillheart 1. Hits—Off Phillips 8 in 6 innings, Brillheart 3 in 2. Hit by pitcher—By Phillips (Scott), Hoyt (Harris and Shanks). Losing pitcher—Phillips. Umpires —Nallin, Hildebrand and Evans. Time of game—1:45.

'SORRY TO HEAR THAT,' IS JOHNSON'S COMMENT

League President Unable to State What Action Will Be Taken in Ruth Case.

Special to The New York Times.

CHICAGO, May 25.—"I am sorry to hear that," was the comment of Ban Johnson, American League President, tonight when informed that Ruth had kicked over the traces in today's Yankee-Senator game at the Polo Grounds in New York.

Johnson was unable to say what action he would take in the matter. He will be guided by what Umpires Nallin and Hildebrand have to say in their telegraphic reports of the affair. The reports will not be received by the American League chief until tomorrow morning.

May 26, 1922

HORNSBY RETAINS BATTING LAURELS

Finishes Season With .401, the Highest National League Mark Since 1899.

CHICAGO, Oct. 1.—Rogers Hornsby of the St. Louis Cardinals today batted himself into the Hall of Fame, among the select .400 hitters, the first man in the National League to accomplish the feat since 1899 when Ed Delehanty of the Philadelphia club won the batting honors with an average of .408. Hornsby's mark for the season is .401. This is the third consecutive year the St. Louis star has won the batting championship of the senior major league.

Hornsby's name will be recorded alongside of those of R. Barnes, Chicago, who hit .403 in 1876; Cap A. C. Anson, Chicago, .407 in 1879, and who in 1877 made a mark of .421; J. Stenzel, Pittsburgh, .409 in 1893; Hughey Duffy, Boston, .438 in 1894; Jess Burkett, Cleveland, who won the championship in 1895 and 1896 with marks of .423 and .410; Willie Keeler, Brooklyn, .432 in 1897, and Ed Delehanty, the last of the .400 hitters until the present day.

Hornsby's average was .397 last season. The year previous he topped the league with .370. On his first appearance at the plate today he smashed one of Kaufmann's offerings for a single. The crowd cheered and applauded the new champion. He repeated his performance on his next trip to the plate. Silence fell over the crowd when he smashed out his third drive. It was a hot grounder to Kelleher, who made a great stop. Kelleher recovered and set himself for the throw but the peg was wild, and the officials scored it an error. The throw if perfect would have beaten the St. Louis star by a step. On his fourth time up Fred Fussell, a southpaw, was on the mound and Hornsby cracked a single to right, his third hit of the day. On his last appearance at the plate he flied to Hollocher in deep short.

October 2, 1922

American League Batting Title Is Won by Sisler; Cobb Second

Johnson Overrules Official Scorer Here to Give Detroit Manager His Third Mark of .400 or Better—St. Louis Takes First Honors in Club Averages.

The leading batter of the year in the American League, according to the official records released for publication today, was George H. Sisler, star first baseman of the St. Louis Browns, who hung up the remarkable average of .419, the second successive year in which this player has reached the .400 mark.

However, the greatest surprise in the records was contained in the average credited to Ty Cobb of Detroit, whose mark has been changed by Ban Johnson from its original .398 to .401, thereby entitling the veteran to join Jesse Burkett in the very select circle which can boast of three .400 marks or better in its big-league career. The records reveal for the first time that President Johnson officially overrode the decision of the scorer in New York on one play and changed an official error into an official hit.

In the game with the Yanks here on May 15 Cobb hit a grounder to Scott, who fumbled and was credited with an error by the official scorer. The unofficial box score gave Cobb a single, and it was this one play which made the difference between .398 and .401. At the end of the season, while reviewing the records to see if Cobb had been unjustly deprived of a .400 average, Johnson came upon this discrepancy, and now he has ruled in favor of the Detroit manager.

Every team had its home run hero, Kenneth R. Williams of the Browns being the leader with 39, 20 less than the mark set by Ruth in 1921. C. W. Walker of Philadelphia was second with 37, while Babe Ruth in 110 games cracked out 35 circuit smashes. Several other "fly ball hitters" made home-run records that would have won them much attention in former years.

The advance guard of a new army of extra-base sluggers appeared, and it was largely through the efforts of these new men that the greatly improved pitching made so little impress on the season averages. No less than sixteen men in their first or second year are found among the .300 hitters.

St. Louis ousted Detroit from its favorite position as batting leader. The Browns' record is .313, as compared with .316 for the Tigers in 1921, while Boston, low club this season with .263, is 11 points below the Athletics' mark of .274 last year.

There was a slight increase in the use of the sacrifice to advance runners, 1,582, as compared with 1,551 last year, but there were 12 fewer bases stolen, the figures being 681, against 693. Cleveland worked opposing hurlers for 554 bases on balls, Detroit had 530, the champion New York team 497, Chicago 482 and St. Louis 473 passes.

December 4, 1922

74,200 SEE YANKEES OPEN NEW STADIUM; RUTH HITS HOME RUN

Record Baseball Crowd Cheers as Slugger's Drive Beats Red Sox, 4 to 1.

25,000 ARE TURNED AWAY

Gates to $2,500,000 Arena Are Closed Half an Hour Before Start of Game.

MANY NOTABLES ATTEND

Governor Smith Throws Out First Ball—Shawkey, in Great Form, Allows Only Three Hits.

Governors, generals, colonels, politicians and baseball officials gathered together solemnly yesterday to dedicate the biggest stadium in baseball, but it was a ball player who did the real dedicating. In the third inning, with two team mates on the base lines, Babe Ruth smashed a savage home run into the right field bleachers, and that was the real baptism of the new Yankee Stadium. That also won the game for the Yankees, and all the ceremony which had gone before was only a trifling preliminary.

The greatest crowd that ever saw a baseball game sat and stood in this biggest of all baseball stadia. Inside the grounds, by official count, were 74,200 people. Outside the park, flattened against doors that had long since closed, were 25,000 more fans, who finally turned around and went home, convinced that baseball parks are not nearly as large as they should be.

The dream of a 100,000 crowd at a baseball game could easily have been realized yesterday if the Yankee Colonels had only piled more concrete on concrete, more steel on steel, and thus provided the necessary space for the overflow. In the face of this tremendous outpouring all baseball attendance records went down with a dull thud. Back in 1916, at a world's series game in Boston, some 42,000 were present, and wise men marveled. But there were that many people in the Yankee Stadium by 2 o'clock yesterday, and when the gates were finally closed to all but ticket holders at 3 o'clock the Boston record had been exceeded by more than 30,000.

Shawkey Pitches Fine Game.

It was an opening game without a flaw. The Yankees easily defeated the Boston Red Sox, 4 to 1. Bob Shawkey, war veteran and oldest Yankee player in point of service, pitched the finest game of his career, letting the Boston batters down with three scattered hits. The Yankees raised their American League championship emblem to the top of the flagpole—the chief feature of an opening-day program that

went off perfectly. Governor "Al" Smith, throwing out the first ball of the season, tossed it straight into Wally Schang's glove, thus setting another record. The weather was favorable and the big crowd was handled flawlessly.

Only one more thing was in demand, and Babe Ruth supplied that. The big slugger is a keen student of the dramatic, in addition to being the greatest home run hitter. He was playing a new rôle yesterday—not the accustomed one of a renowned slugger, but that of a penitent, trying to "come back" after a poor season and a poorer world's series. Before the game he said that he would give a year of his life if he could hit a home run in his first game in the new stadium. The Babe was on trial, and he knew it better than anybody else.

He could hardly have picked a better time and place for the drive that he hammered into the bleachers in the third inning. The Yankees had just broken a scoreless tie by pushing Shawkey over the plate with one run. Witt was on third base, Dugan on first, when Ruth appeared at the plate to face Howard Ehmke, the Boston pitcher. Ruth worked the count to two and two, and then Ehmke tried to fool him with one of those slow balls that the Giants used successfully in the last world's series.

The ball came in slowly, but it went out quite rapidly, rising on a line and then dipping suddenly from the force behind it. It struck well inside the foul line, eight or ten rows above the low railing in front of the bleachers, and as Ruth circled the bases he received probably the greatest ovation of his career. The biggest crowd in baseball history rose to its feet and let loose the biggest shout in baseball history. Ruth, jogging over the home plate, grinned broadly, lifted his cap at arm's length and waved it at the multitude.

Home Run Settles Outcome.

That homer was useful as well as dramatic and decorative. It drove three runs across the plate, and those runs, as later events proved, were the margin by which the Yankees won. All the New York scoring was in that one inning, and the Red Sox, although they touched Shawkey for one run in the seventh, could not close the gap.

But the game, after all, was only an incident of a busy afternoon. The stadium was the thing. For the Yankee owners it was the realization of a dream long cherished. For the fans it was something which they had never seen before in baseball. It cost about $2,500,000 to build, and eleven months were spent in the construction work. It is the most costly stadium in baseball, as well as the biggest.

First impressions—and also last impressions—are of the vastness of the arena. The stadium is big. It towers high in the air, three tiers piled one on the other. It is a skyscraper among baseball parks. Seen from the vantage point of the nearby subway structure, the mere height of the grandstand is tremendous. Baseball fans who sat in the last row of the steeply sloping third tier may well boast that they broke all altitude records short of those attained in an airplane.

Once inside the grounds, the sweep of the big stand strikes the eye most forcibly. It throws its arms far out to each side, the grandstand ending away over where the bleachers begin. In the centre of the vast pile of steel and concrete was the green spread of grass and diamond, and fewer ball fields are greener than that on which the teams played yesterday.

The Yankees' new home, besides being beautiful and majestic, is practical. It was emptied yesterday of its 74,000 in quicker time than the Polo Grounds ever was. Double ramps from top to bottom carried the stream of people steadily and rapidly to the lower exits,

which are many and well situated. Fans from the bleachers and far ends of the grand stand poured out onto the field and were swept through gates in left field. The grandstand crowd passed through exits opening on both Doughty Avenue and 157th Street, which lies along the south side of the stadium.

Throng Handled Without Confusion.

The record-breaking throng was handled with almost no confusion at all. Transportation facilities were strained before the game because of the big flow of people from downtown points, but the subway, elevated and surface lines handled the heavy traffic without a break after the game. There was little congestion in the 161st Street station of the Lexington Avenue subway, much of the crowd walking to nearby elevated and surface lines.

The fans were slow in coming to the stadium. When the gates were thrown open at noon only about 500 persons were in line before the ticket windows. But by 1 o'clock the guardians of law and order in front of the main entrance began finding their hands full. The supply of 50,000 unreserved grand stand and bleacher seats began dwindling rapidly, and by 2 o'clock the huge grand stand was beginning to bulge at the sides. Ten minutes later the gates to the main stand were ordered closed, and patrons who arrived more than an hour before game time were greeted with the "Standing Room Only" sign and the gentle announcement that bleacher seats only were available. When 3 o'clock came around even the bleachers were packed solidly with humanity, and after that there was nothing to do but close the gates and padlock them.

Inspector Thomas Riley, in charge of police arrangements outside the grounds, estimated that 25,000 fans were turned away, and officials of the club agreed with this estimate.

Kenesaw M. Landis, High Commissioner of Baseball, travelled to the scene in democratic style. He disembarked from an Interborough train shortly before 2 and was caught up in the swirl before the main entrance, being rescued finally by the police and escorted inside the stadium.

Preceding him by an hour was the Seventh Regiment Band, which arrived at 1 o'clock and immediately launched on a musical program. Just about the same time the Yankees and Red Sox deployed on the scene, the champions looking neat and natty in new home uniforms of white. The Bostonians were a symphony in red—red sweaters, red-peaked caps, red striped stockings. At their head was Frank Chance, Peerless Leader of the old-time Cubs, returned now to lead the Red Sox out of the baseball wilderness.

Governor Greeted Warmly.

Then at 3 o'clock the spotlight shifted from the players to the celebrities of opening day. Governor Smith moved down to his box, accompanied by Mrs. Smith, and got a rousing greeting. Judge Landis in gray overcoat, doffing his wide brimmed hat in greeting, came on to the field and immediately strode out to centre field, where the American League flag was waiting. The Seventh Regiment Band assembled near the Yankee bench on the third base line, and John Philip Sousa, in bandmaster's uniform, took his baton in hand and moved to the head of the musicians. The two teams clustered into platoon formation and the parade began.

Once out at the flagpole, the old traditional ritual of opening day began. While the band played "The Star-Spangled Banner," the Stars and Stripes were pulled slowly to the peak of the flagpole. After it fluttered the red, white and blue American League pennant, and as the last note of the national anthem died away and the halyards were made fast, the big crowd let loose a roar that floated across the Harlem and far beyond.

That wasn't the end of it, by any means. Back to the home plate came the band and the players and the notables. In the front line of march were the Yankee Colonels, Ruppert and Huston, side by side and beaming broadly; Judge Landis, Mrs. Smith, the Governor and Harry Frazee, the Boston club owner. It was noticed for the first time that Mayor Hylan was absent, and club officials explained that the city's chief executive was unable to attend because of illness. Byron Bancroft Johnson, President of the American League, was also missing because of a sudden attack of influenza.

Major Gen. Robert Lee Bullard, commander of the Department of the East, and his staff took part in the exercises, and other prominent military men present were Major Gen. Frank T. Hines, Director of the Veterans' Bureau; Major Gen. F. W. Sladen, Superintendent of West Point; Major Gen. William Weigle of Governors Island and Major Charles D. Daley and Captain M. B. Ridgway of West Point. State Commander Callan represented the American Legion and Captain Robret Woodside the Veterans of Foreign Wars.

Governor Smith and Judge Landis were escorted to their boxes along the third base side, and the photographers then got in their deadly work. Mr. Smith was snapped throwing an imaginary first ball. Judge Landis had to take off his hat and have his white locks photographed. Somebody stepped up and presented a big floral horseshoe to the Yankee club, and Colonel Ruppert and Managers Huggins and Chance were lined up for a picture in front of this. Charles A. Stoneham, President of the Giants, was taken in friendly converse with the Yankee owners.

Babe Ruth Receives Gift.

Then the teams converged around the plate again, and Babe Ruth was presented with a case containing a big bat—a delicate hint to the slugger, possibly. After Babe had blushingly mumbled his thanks, Governor Smith stood up in his box, took a shiny white ball between thumb and first finger and threw it carefully at Wally Schang.

New here was the first deviation from a decent and proper opening day program. Tradition demands that the thrower miss the objective by several feet. But the Governor, unwinding the official arm, hit Schang's glove as well as Bob Shawkey ever did. Old-time baseball men considered it a distinct social error.

After that there was nothing to do but to play the game. Frank Chance walked out on the coaching line. The Yankees scattered briskly to their positions, Everett Scott going to shortstop as a signal to the world that the record of 986 consecutive games would not be broken yet. Umpire Tommy Connolly, dean of the American League staff, who unexpectedly appeared to take charge of the game, mumbled something to the effect that the contest might begin, and Shawkey, twirling his red sleeved arms, pitched "Ball One" to the first batter, Chick Fewster, who used to play with the Yankees. The season was started.

As events turned out, the game was an easy one for the Yankees. After the third inning they were never seriously extended, that one concentrated burst of gunfire being the undoing of the long and lanky Ehmke, who was

pitching the game for Frank Chance. In all his career Shawkey never pitched a finer game. Although slightly shy on control, the sailor worked carefully and shrewdly, and kept the three Boston hits sparsely scattered throughout the nine innings..

Burns Gets First Hit.

The first hit off him—in fact, the first hit in the new stadium—came from the bat of first baseman George Burns in the second inning, but Burns was cut down trying to steal and the rally died down. In the sixth Ehmke singled to centre with none out, and that was the second hit. In the seventh, after Burns walked, Norman McMillan, traded by the Yanks last Winter, prodded a triple to right centre, and that was the third hit. It was the only one which did any damage, for Burns scampered home from first with the sole Boston run of the game.

The Yanks' big third inning started with Ward's single to left, the first Yankee hit. Scott bunted him to second, but Ward was nipped at third on Shawkey's grounder straight at Ehmke. Shawkey moved up to second while Ward was being run down. Witt coaxed a pass out of Ehmke, and Shawkey came in from second when Dugan dropped a single in short centre. Witt trotted to third, and the stage was set for Ruth's blast into the right-field bleachers.

In the fourth the Yanks got after Ehmke again, but lost a run because of bad work on the bases. To start the inning Bob Meusel got a two-bagger out of a Texas League fly to short left, Fewster barely getting his glove under the ball. But Schang bunted to Ehmke and Meusel was nailed by a shade at third base. Ward then fanned, but Scott rammed a hard hit double between Collins and Skinner. Schang tried to come all the way from first on the drive and was out for his pains, a fast relay from Collins to Burns to Devormer slaying the catcher at the plate.

Ruth got his first walk in the fifth, and the crowd joined in a chorus of boos and jeers that smacked of the good old days of 1921. The Yanks went out in order in the sixth, and Shawkey's single was the only incident in the seventh, which was Ehmke's last inning. Menosky batted for him, and Fullerton finished up for Chance's team. He walked Ruth again in the eighth and was heartily hooted by the assembled citizenry.

Shawkey's only sign of weakening came in the seventh, when he passed Burns and McMillan tripled. There was still only one out, but Sailor Bob fanned the veteran Shanks and Dugan made a

clever play on DeVormer's hard grounder for the third out. Fine support helped Shawkey again in the eighth. Fewster was hit with none out, but Scott got in front of Collins's ground ball and started a fast double play through Ward and Pipp. This was the last time the Red Sox showed signs of life.

Ruth Makes Error.

Everything wasn't milk and honey for Ruth. To start the fifth he muffed Harris's high fly to short right, juggling the ball twice and then letting it hit the turf. This faux pas placed Harris on second, and Shawkey passed McMillan after fanning Burns. With runners on second and first and only one out the Yankee veteran settled down, outwitted Shanks on a third strike and made DeVormer roll gently to Pipp.

The Yankees looked like a new team on their own ball field. They hustled every minute, kept their heads up and struck hard when the time came to strike. Aaron Ward played one of the best games of his life at second base, and his stop of Ehmke's fast grounder behind second in the third inning was by all odds the finest fielding play of the game.

Everett Scott, who sprained his ankle last week, was not the fastest athlete on the field, but he showed little effects from the injury. He handled five chances deftly at shortstop and wasted no time in getting around the bases when he doubled to right centre in the fourth. It was Scott's 987th consecutive game; only thirteen more and he will be up to the 1,000 mark.

The score:

NEW YORK (A.)	Ab	R	H	Po	A		BOSTON (A.)	Ab	R	H	Po	A
Witt,cf	3	1	1	3	0		Fewster,ss	3	0	0	2	6
Dugan,3b	4	1	1	1	1		Collins,rf	4	0	0	2	1
Ruth,rf	2	1	1	3	0		Skinner,cf	4	0	0	0	0
Pipp,1b	4	0	1	10	0		Harris,lf	4	0	0	0	0
Meusel,lf	4	0	1	0	0		Burns,1b	3	1	1	8	2
Schang,c	4	0	0	4	2		McMillan,2b	2	0	1	2	0
Ward,2b	3	0	1	3	5		Shanks,3b	3	0	0	3	0
Scott,ss	2	0	1	1	4		Devormer,c	3	0	0	6	2
Shawkey,p	3	1	1	0	0		Ehmke,p	2	0	1	0	4
							aMenosky	1	0	0	0	0
Total....	28	4	7	27	12		Fullerton,p	0	0	0	0	0
							Total....	29	1	3	24	15

aBatted for Ehmke in eighth.

New York.............. 0 0 4 0 0 0 0 0—4
Boston .... 0 0 0 0 0 0 1 0 0—1

Two-base Hits—Meusel, Scott. Three-base hit—McMillan. Home run—Ruth. Sacrifice—Scott. Double play—Scott, Ward and Pipp. Left on bases—New York 5, Boston 4. Bases on balls—Off Shawkey 2, Ehmke 3, Fullerton 1. Struck out—By Shawkey 5, Ehmke 4, Fullerton 1. Hits—Off Ehmke 7 in 7 innings, Fullerton none in 1. Hit by pitcher—By Shawkey (Fewster). Losing pitcher—Ehmke. Umpires—Connolly, Evans and Holmes. Time of game—2:05.

April 19, 1923

W. JOHNSON PITCHES SHORT NO-HIT GAME

Veteran Washington Star Beats the Browns, 2 to 0, in Seven Innings.

SIXTH SHUT-OUT OF SEASON

Brings Total for His Career to 107 —Issued Two Passes—Second Game Postponed.

WASHINGTON, Aug. 25.—Holding the St. Louis Browns hitless, Walter Johnson today pitched Washington to a 2-to-0 victory in the first game of a scheduled double-header which was halted by rain after seven innings. The

second game was called off on account of wet grounds. It was Johnson's sixth scoreless game of the season and the 107th shutout victory of his career. The veteran speed-ball star gave two bases on balls.

Davis forced in the first local run by issuing a base on balls with the bases filled in the third. The other tally was due to McNeely's single and a triple by Goslin in the seventh.

The score:

WASHINGTON (A.)	Ab	R	H	Po	A		ST. LOUIS (A.)	Ab	R	H	Po	A
McNeely,cf	3	1	1	4	0		Tobin,rf	3	0	0	1	0
Harris,2b	2	0	0	0	3		Rob'tson,3b	2	0	0	2	1
Rice,rf	4	0	1	2	0		Sisler,1b	3	0	0	3	1
Goslin,lf	3	0	1	1	0		Williams,lf	2	0	0	3	1
Judge,1b	3	0	2	8	0		McManus,2b	3	0	0	4	2
Bluege,3b	3	0	2	0	2		Jacobson,cf	2	0	0	1	0
Ruel,c	3	0	1	2	0		Severeid,c	2	0	0	5	0
Peckinp'h,ss	3	0	2	2	2		Gerber,ss	2	0	0	2	1
Johnson,p	2	1	1	0	0		Davis,p	2	0	0	0	0
Total....	26	2	9	21	5		Total....	21	0	0	21	6

Errors—Washington 0, St. Louis 1 (Davis).

Washington .... 0 0 1 0 0 0 1—2
St. Louis .... 0 0 0 0 0 0 0—0

Two-base hits—Judge 2. Three-base hit—Goslin. Sacrifices—Harris 2, Johnson. Left on base—St. Louis 2, Washington 9. Bases on balls—Off Johnson 2, Davis 3. Struck out—By Johnson 2, Davis 2. Passed ball—Severeid. Umpires—Nallin, Holmes and Evans. Time of game—1:25.

August 26, 1924

ROBINS BEATEN, 17-3; BOTTOMLEY IS STAR

Cards' Infielder Sets Record, Driving In 12 Runs on 6 Hits in Row, 2 of Them Homers.

LOSERS USE FIVE HURLERS

Ehrhardt, Hollingsworth, Decatur, Wilson and Roberts Fail— Sherdel Is Winner.

James Bottomley of the St. Louis Cardinals did some record batting at Ebbets Field yesterday afternoon that was entirely unappreciated by a crowd of about 8,000 spectators who had assembled for the sole purpose of seeing the Robins win a ball game and not Mr. Bottomley crack records by knocking baseballs all out of shape. As may be expected, this lack of appreciation toward Mr. Bottomley was due to the fact that the Robins did not win.

Instead, they took a terrific drubbing by a count of 17 to 3, and at a late hour last night accountants still were brushing up a few details in the official box score. It is safe to say no Brooklynite will ever look at the job when it's done, for the matter is one to be forgotten as swiftly as possible. With the Reds splitting a pair of games with the Giants, the opportunity was at hand for the Robins to edge half a game closer to the top. Instead, the day saw them advance half a game to the rear, and now they are one and a half games away from the top.

It was a terrific offensive that struck the Robins in which Bottomley easily was the leading offender. All this young man did was to drive out six consecutive hits, which included two homers in succession, a double and three singles for a total of thirteen bases. More destructive than this, however, was the fact that he batted in twelve runs for the Cardinals, smashing all known records for this sort of thing in a single game. The best previous mark was eleven set by Wilbert Robinson, who sat as an unwilling onlooker to the deed yesterday. Robbie performed his feat away back in 1892 for the Baltimore Orioles in a game against, incidentally, the St. Louis National League club. Bottomley's work also effaced the modern mark of eight kept since 1907, in which six players are listed as joint holders, including George Kelly, who made the mark this year, and Travis Jackson, who did it a year ago.

Five Robin Hurlers Battered.

In addition to this, Bottomley crossed the plate with still another run, so that, in all, he accounted directly or indirectly for thirteen of the Cardinals' seventeen runs. Five Robin pitchers fell in this amazing exhibition of effective swatting, and Bottomley smacked them all, which is probably another record.

Rube Ehrhardt was the first to fall, going out after four hits had scored four runs before a man had been retired. This, incidentally, finished his little winning streak which he painstakingly had built up to five. The Rube was followed, in order of appearance, by Hollingsworth, Decatur, Wilson and Roberts. Bottomley made his two homers off Decatur, one in the fourth with the bases full and the other in the sixth with one on.

The spectators had barely settled back in their seats before the Cards' scoring began. Ehrhardt drew the distinction of starting the thing himself by walking Blades, the first man to face him. Douthit then got an infield hit to short and Hornsby beat out a bunt, filling the bases. Bottomley then inserted his first blow of the afternoon, a single, scoring Blades and Douthit, and Hornsby and Bottomley counted when Hafey tripled.

That finished Ehrhardt, and Hollingsworth came in to see what he could do about it. He retired the next three batters. But two walks and a double by the troublesome Mr. Bottomley accounted for another tally in the second.

Bottomley Clears Bags.

The fourth, however, was the real heartbreaker for the Robins, for up to then they still appeared to have a fighting chance, having picked up a run in the second on a pass to Fournier and hits by Brown and De Berry. Sherdel started the Cards' drive in this frame with a double, Blades walked and Decatur relieved Hollingsworth. Douthit sacrificed Blades and Sherdel to second and third, respectively, whereupon Decatur passed Hornsby, filling the bases. The unsuspecting Decatur did not know that Bottomley, next up, had selected this day for a record. The St. Louis first baseman hit the ball over the right field fence, clearing the bases.

In the sixth Douthit walked and Bottomley again lifted the ball over the right field fence. A single by Hafey, a triple by Gonzales and Cooney's single accounted for two more runs.

In the seventh, with Wilson pitching and men on second and third, Bottomley singled, scoring both. Bottomley took a rest in the eighth while the Cards scored a run on Sherdel's single and Mueller's triple, but he came back for a final shot in the ninth, with Roberts pitching. Hornsby tripled and Bottomley sent him home with his sixth straight hit of the day, a single. He

had no chance at Wilbert Robinson's consecutive mark of seven hits, set in 1892, as he did not come a seventh time to bat.

As for the Robins, they were helpless before Lefty Sherdel. After their run in the second, they didn't get another until the eighth, when hits by Taylor and High and an out scored a tally. Rehm, working the ninth inning, presented the Robins with another tally by issuing three passes and adding a wild pitch to boot.

The score:

ST. LOUIS (N.)	Ab	R	H	Po	A	BROOKLYN (N.)	Ab	R	H	Po	A
Mueller,rf	3	3	2	4	0	High,2b	4	0	2	4	0
Douthit,cf	3	3	1	2	0	Mitchell,ss	4	0	1	1	4
Hornsby,2b	4	2	2	2	2	Wheat,lf	4	0	0	3	0
Blades,3b	0	1	0	1	0	Fournier,1b	2	1	0	5	1
Bottomley,1b	6	3	6	5	0	Loftus,1b	1	0	1	2	0
Smith,rf	0	0	0	0	0	Brown,cf	4	0	1	3	0
Hafey,cf	6	1	2	3	1	Stock,3b	3	1	1	1	1
Gonzales,c	4	1	1	2	0	Griffith,rf	2	0	0	2	0
Clemons,c	2	0	0	1	0	De Berry,c	3	0	1	4	0
Toporcer,2b	1	0	0	0	0	Ehrhardt,p	0	0	0	0	0
Cooney,ss	4	0	1	0	0	Hollgsw'h,p	1	0	0	0	0
Thevenow,ss	5	0	0	6	4	Decatur,p	0	0	1	1	
Sherdel,p	4	3	3	1	0	aJohnston	1	0	1	0	0
Rehm,p	0	0	0	0	0	Wilson,p	0	0	0	0	1
						bTaylor	1	1	1	0	0
Total	42	17	18	27	7	Roberts,p	0	0	0	0	1
						cHargreaves	1	0	0	0	0
						Total	31	3	9	27	9

Errors—St. Louis 0, Brooklyn 1 (Fournier).

a Batted for Decatur in sixth.
b Batted for Wilson in eighth.
c Batted for Roberts in ninth.

St. Louis .... 4 1 0 4 0 4 2 1 1—17
Brooklyn .... 0 1 0 0 0 0 0 1 1—3

Two-base hits—Bottomley, Sherdel. Three-base hits—Mueller, Hornsby, Hafey, Gonzales. Home runs—Bottomley (2). Stolen bases—Douthit, Cooney. Sacrifices—Douthit (2), Hornsby. Double plays—Thevenow and Hornsby; Thevenow, Hornsby and Bottomley; Mueller (unassisted). Left on bases—St. Louis 7, Brooklyn 6. Bases on balls—Off Ehrhardt 1, Hollingsworth 2, Decatur 2, Sherdel 2, Rehm 3. Struck out—By Hollingsworth 2, Wilson 1, Sherdel 1. Hits—Off Ehrhardt 4 in 0 innings (none out in first), Hollingsworth 2 in 3 (none out in fourth), Decatur 5 in 2, Wilson 4 in 2, Roberts 2 in 1, Sherdel 8 in 8, Rehm 1 in 1. Wild pitches—Decatur 1, Rehm 1. Passed ball—Clemons. Winning pitcher—Sherdel. Losing pitcher—Ehrhardt. Umpires—Klem and Wilson.

Time of game—1:55.

September 17, 1924

TWO NEW RECORDS MADE BY HORNSBY

St. Louis Star Leads League in Batting Fifth Year in Row With Mark of .42351.

ST. LOUIS, Sept. 29.—Rogers Hornsby, Cardinal second baseman, today took a

place beside the greatest hitters in baseball history. In the season just closed Hornsby established two new records, one in batting average and the other in leading his league for the fifth consecutive season.

Hornsby finished with 227 hits in 142 games, making a season average of .42351, 4 points above George Sisler's mark of two years ago. Sisler had an approximate .420 average which had tied Tyrus Cobb's record set in 1911, the high mark of modern baseball.

The previous consecutive year batting record was held by Honus Wagner, who led his league four successive years.

Hornsby failed in his effort to lead the league in runs scored. He tallied only once in the double-header yesterday and thus raised his total to 121, which ties Frankie Frisch of the New York Giants.

Between games yesterday the Cardinal slugger was presented with a silver bat and ball, known as the Dick Richards trophy, for leading his team in batting.

September 30, 1924

47

COBB TIES RECORD WITH 3 HOME RUNS

Leads Tigers to 14-8 Victory Over Browns, Also Getting 2 Singles and a Double.

BREAKS TOTAL BASE MARK

Surpasses Modern Major League Record of 13 by 3—Sisler Hits Safely in 20th Game.

ST. LOUIS, May 5.—Tying the modern major league record, the veteran Ty Cobb, playing manager of the Detroit Tigers, poled out three home runs in to-day's game against the St. Louis Browns, which the Tigers won by a score of 14 to 8. In all Cobb made six hits, getting two singles and a double in addition to his three circuit drives.

Cobb made the first of his homers in the first inning off Bush. Van Gilder was the victim of his second in the second inning, while the third drive was made off Gaston in the eighth.

George Sisler, manager of the Browns, hit safely in his twentieth consecutive game.

Cobb in smashing out six hits collected a total of sixteen bases, a new world's record for modern major league baseball. The previous record for modern baseball was held by Eddie Gharrity, Washington catcher, who ran his total of bases for one game to thirteen, in June, 1919.

The old record, made before the advent of the American League, was held jointly by Bobby Lowe of the Boston Nationals, who in 1894 collected four homers and a single, and Ed Delehanty of the Philadelphia Nationals duplicated the stunt in 1896. Each of these players had a total of seventeen bases.

The only other major league players who have made three home runs in a single game in the twentieth century are George Kelly of the Giants, Ken Williams of the Browns, Cy Williams of the Phillies and Walter Henline of the Phillies.

The score:

DETROIT (A.)	Ab	R	H	Po	A		ST. LOUIS (A.)	Ab	R	H	Po	A
Blue,1b	5	3	2	8	1		Robe'son,3b	4	1	1	2	2
O'Rourke,2b	5	3	3	4	2		Bennett,rf	6	1	1	3	0
Cobb,cf	6	4	6	5	0		Sisler,1b	5	1	2	11	1
Heilmann,rf	3	1	2	1	0		Williams,lf	5	2	4	2	0
Manush,lf	4	2	1	2	1		McManus,2b	3	1	0	0	1
Rigney,ss	2	0	0	0	2		Jacobson,cf	4	2	2	1	0
Tavener,ss	1	0	0	3	3		Gerber,ss	5	0	3	4	5
Jones,3b	4	1	1	1	3		Dixon,c	1	0	0	2	1
Woodall,c	2	0	2	0	0		Rego,c	1	0	0	0	0
Leonard,p	3	0	1	0	0		Bush,p	0	0	0	1	1
Holloway,p	0	0	0	0	0		VanGilder,p	1	0	0	0	0
Wells,p	2	0	1	1	1		Gian',p	0	0	0	0	2
aWingo	0	0	0	0	0		Stauffer,p	0	0	0	0	0
							Gaston,p	1	0	1	0	0
Total	37	14	17	27	13		Springer,p	1	0	0	0	1
							bEvans	1	0	0	0	0
							cRice	0	0	0	0	0
							dTobin	1	0	0	0	0
							eSevereld	1	0	0	0	0
							Total	39	8	16	27	16

Errors—Detroit 1 (Cobb); St. Louis 1 (McManus).

a Batted for Rigney in sixth.
b Batted for Giard in fourth.
c Batted for Dixon in fifth.
d Batted for Stauffer in fifth.
e Batted for Springer in ninth.

Detroit ....3 5 1 1 0 1 0 2 1—14
St. Louis ....4 0 0 0 4 0 0 0 0—8

Two-base hits—O'Rourke (3), Robertson, Blue, Cobb, Heilmann, Wells, Jones, Gerber. Three-base hit—Blue. Home runs—Cobb (3). Jacobson, Manush. Stolen base—Gerber. Sacrifices—Heilmann, Manush, McManus, O'Rourke. Double plays—Bush, Gerber and Sisler; Robertson, Rego and Sisler. Left on bases—Detroit 9, St. Louis 12. Bases on balls—Off Leonard 2, Holloway 1, Wells 4, Bush 2, Vangilder 1, Gaston 3, Stauffer 1, Giard 1, Springer 2. Struck out—By Leonard 1, Wells 1, Bush 1, Stauffer 1. Hits—Off Leonard 10 in 4 1-3 innings, Vangilder 4 in 2-3, Holloway 0 in 0, Giard 1 in 1-3, Wells 4 in 4 2-3, Stauffer 0 in 1, Bush 5 in 1 2-3, Gaston 6 in 3, Springer 1 in 1. Wild pitch—Holloway. Winning pitcher—Leonard. Losing pitcher—Bush. Umpires—Evans and Hildebrand and Rowland. Time of game—2:44.

BABE'S TYING BLOW HELPS YANKEES WIN

Convalescent Slugger's Two-Bagger in Eighth Starts Senators' Downfall by 8 to 5.

BOB MEUSEL GETS 2 HOMERS

Second Drive Brings Combs and Witt in-Right After the Bambino's Big Bang.

RADICAL SHIFT BY HUGGINS

Gehrig Supplants Pipp, Shanks Has Ward's Place and Bengough Does the Catching.

By JAMES R. HARRISON.

He may be a trifle peaked and pallid, but the Babe still packs a terrific wallop. He may still be a pale and interesting invalid, but the Washington Senators found him a healthy and able-bodied citizen in the eighth inning yesterday, when his ringing two-bagger to right centre drove in the tying run at the Stadium.

The ball soared over Joe Harris's head and rolled to the right field bleachers on the short bound. With a little sharper trajectory toward the bleachers the pill would have drifted into the sun seats for a home run. As it was, Bob Meusel followed with a four-base gem to left centre—his second homer of the game—and the three resultant tallies gave the Yanks an 8-5 victory over the Senators.

Day by day the Babe is getting better and better. In four official times at bat he gathered two hits. He was hit by a pitched ball the first time, fanned the second, singled the third, grounded out the fourth and doubled the fifth.

After slapping the two-bagger in the eighth George retired to let Whitey Witt scamper for him. Whitey was one of the advance guard which preceded Meusel to the plate.

Miller Huggins took his favorite line-up and shook it to pieces. Wally Pipp, after more than ten years as regular first baseman, was benched in favor of Lou Gehrig, the former Columbia University fence-wrecker. Aaron Ward, another old standby, surrendered second base to Howard Shanks. Steve O'Neill and Wally Schang perched themselves comfortably on the bench while Benny Bengough donned the mask and protector.

Only Three Regulars on Hand.

The most radical shakeup of the Yankee line-up in many years left only three regulars of last season in the batting order—Dugan, Ruth and Meusel. Gehrig made two singles and a double in his first three trips to the front. Shanks's single played a prominent rôle in the first run, and Bengough covered himself with glory and perspiration by socking three clean singles in four times at bat. And still they say that little Bennah can't hit.

The Yanks were a run in arrears when Veach, hitting for Wanninger, pried loose the eighth with a single to right. Ernie Johnson ran for him. Dugan sacrificed and Combs got a walk.

Along came Ruth. The outfielders went back to the edge of the greensward. Babe looked over Allan Russell's assortment carefully and finally picked out one he liked. He took an old-time lunge at it and whipped a fly to right centre. Despite the fleetest footwork of Messrs. Rice and Joe Harris, the ball landed in the great open spaces and reached the bleachers in a couple of bounces. Johnson scored, Combs legged it to third and the Bambino trudged along to second.

Meusel followed with a thunderous clout to left centre. Combs and Witt were over in a jiffy. The ball landed on the running track and bounced to the fence, Meusel coming over the plate without the formality of a slide. It was California Bob's fourteenth homer of the season.

Shocker Retires in Fifth.

Urban Shocker lasted only five innings under the Senatorial gunfire. In the second frame Bluege singled and Peck doubled to right for one run. The Yanks feasted on George Mogridge in the same inning. Gehrig, Shanks, Bengough and Shocker singled in succession for two runs, and after Wanninger's out Dugan drove in Bengough with a hit to left.

Three to one, but the Senators tied it in the third when Stan Harris singled and Joseph Ignatius Judge tickled a homer into the right field bleachers.

Meusel's first homer, a smack into the bleachers in right centre, sent the Yanks out in front again in the same inning, by which time Russell had taken the burden off Mogridge's shoulders. But in the fifth the Senators came even again on Ruel's single, Russell's sacrifice and Rice's base hit. When Bucky Harris singled, Shocker receded in favor of Ferguson, who showed unexpected prowess by fanning Judge and Goslin.

Off Ferguson the Nationals counted what looked like the triumphant tally in the sixth. Joe Harris pried it open with a single and Bluege did the sacrificial stuff successfully. On Peckinpaugh's single to left centre Harris trekked homeward.

Ferguson tolerated no runs and only two hits thereafter and kept away from trouble while his playmates assassinated Mr. Russell in the eighth. This was only as it should be.

The score:

NEW YORK (A.)	Ab	R	H	Po	A		WASHINGTON (A.)	Ab	R	H	Po	A
Wan'ger,ss	4	0	1	2	5		Rice,cf	5	0	2	0	0
aVeach	1	0	1	0	0		S.Harris,2b	5	1	2	1	2
E.John'n,ss	0	1	0	0	0		Judge,1b	4	1	1	12	0
Dugan,3b	2	0	2	1	1		Goslin,lf	4	0	2	0	0
Combs,cf	4	1	0	3	1		J.Harris,rf	4	1	1	2	0
Ruth,rf	4	0	2	2	0		Bluege,3b	3	1	1	1	1
bWitt	0	1	0	0	0		Peck'p'gh,ss	4	0	3	1	1
Paschal,rf	0	0	0	1	0		Ruel,c	4	1	2	5	1
Meusel,lf	5	2	2	2	0		Mogridge,p	0	0	0	0	1
Gehrig,1b	5	1	3	8	1		cLiebold	1	0	0	0	0
Shanks,2b	4	1	1	2	2		Russell,p	1	0	0	0	4
Bengough,c	4	1	3	5	0		dRuether	1	0	0	0	0
Shocker,p	2	0	0	1	2		Total	36	5	12	24	11
Ferguson,p	2	0	0	1	2							
Total	37	8	16	27	12							

Errors—None.

a Batted for Wanninger in eighth.
b Ran for Ruth in eighth.
c Batted for Mogridge in third.
d Batted for Russell in ninth.

New York...........0 3 1 0 0 0 0 4 .—8
Washington ....0 1 2 0 1 1 0 0 0—5

Two-base hits—Peckinpaugh, Gehrig, Ruth. Three-base hits—Peckinpaugh. Home runs—Judge, Meusel (2). Sacrifices—Russell, Bluege, Dugan (2). Left on bases—New York 11, Washington 6. Bases on balls—Off Russell 1, by Mogridge 1, by Russell 4, by Shocker 1, by Ferguson 3. Struck out—By Mogridge 1, Russell 4, Shocker 1, Ferguson 3. Hits—Off Mogridge 6 in 2 innings, Russell 10 in 6, Shocker 8 in 4 1-3, Ferguson 4 in 4 2-3. Hit by pitcher—By Mogridge (Ruth). Winning pitcher—Ferguson. Losing pitcher—Russell. Umpires—Hildebrand, Connolly and Evans. Time of game—2:00.

13 RUNS IN EIGHTH WIN FOR ATHLETICS

Mackmen Stage Most Spectacular Rally Ever Seen in Philadelphia to Beat Indians, 17-15.

UMPIRE OWENS IS INJURED

Taken to Hospital After Collision With Player—Hauser Retires for the Season.

Special to The New York Times.

PHILADELPHIA, June 15.—When the eighth inning dawned on the Athletics in their game with the Cleveland Indians here today it also dawned on the Mackmen that they were eleven runs behind the Indians and that if they were to win the game they would have to do some hard and fast hitting. They determined to take the game then and there and they did. They scored thirteen runs in the eighth and beat their rivals, 17 to 15.

The rally was by far the greatest ever seen in this city and has few equals in the annals of baseball. Once the Ath-

letics got started it seemed that they never would stop and before it was over the Indians also were very much of the same opinion.

This is how, in the eighth inning, the Athletics scored their thirteen runs: Galloway walked. Glass flied to Lee and Bishop walked. Dykes lined the ball to the scoreboard for three bases scoring Galloway and Bishop. Lamar then singled over second scoring Dykes. Speaker yanked W. Miller and Speece went into pitch, but Simmons bounced a hit over Knode's head and Lamar went to third. Welch singled to right, scoring Lamar and putting Simmons on third. Berry singled to left and scored Simmons and that finished Speece.

Yowell went to the hill. Poole walked, filling the bases. Galloway singled to left centre, scoring Welch and Berry and putting Poole on third. Hale went to bat for Glass and Uhle, the Cleveland ace, came in from the bullpen to replace Yowell. Hale drove a single that hopped over J. Sewell's head, scoring Poole and putting Galloway on third. Hale stole second. Bishop singled over second, scoring Galloway and Hale. Dykes forced Bishop, J. Sewell to Spurgeon.

French ran for Dykes. Lamar walked. Simmons hammered the ball on to the roof of the left field grandstand for a home run that scored Dykes, Lamar and himself and gave the Athletics a two-run lead. Welch then flied to Lee.

In the second inning of the game, Spurgeon of Cleveland crashed into Umpire Owens at the plate and the latter was so painfully hurt that he had to be taken to the hospital. There, however, it was reported that he had suffered only a sprain in his back and would be able to report for duty within a day or so.

Connie Mack announced today that Joe Hauser, veteran first baseman, would be retired for the rest of the season. He was hurt in a pre-season game and has not been in the best of condition since. It also was announced that Ed Andrews, a pitcher, had been released.

The score:

PHILADELPHIA (A.)	Ab	R	H	Po	A	CLEVELAND (A.)	Ab	R	H	Po	A
Bishop,2b	4	1	2	1	2	Jamieson,lf	6	2	5	2	0
Dykes,3b	6	2	2	1	2	McNulty,rf	1	0	0	1	0
aFrench	0	1	0	0	0	Lee,rf	4	1	2	5	0
Lamar,lf	5	3	4	2	1	Speaker,cf	6	1	2	1	0
Simmons,cf	6	2	3	5	0	J.Sewell,ss	6	1	4	2	5
E.Miller,rf	2	0	0	0	0	Myatt,c	6	2	2	2	0
Welch,rf	3	1	1	0	0	Spurgeon,2b	6	2	2	3	2
Perkins,c	2	0	0	6	1	Lutzke,3b	4	2	2	1	1
Berry,c	2	1	2	2	0	Knode,1b	5	0	4	6	1
Cochrane,c	0	0	0	0	0	cL.Sewell	1	0	0	0	0
Poole,1b	4	3	2	6	0	J.Miller,p	5	0	1	2	0
Galloway,ss	3	2	2	1	0	Speece,p	0	0	0	0	0
Rommel,p	0	0	0	0	0	Yowell,p	0	0	0	0	0
Baumg'er,p	0	0	0	0	0	Uhle,p	0	0	0	0	0
bFox	1	0	0	0	0						
Heimach,p	0	0	0	0	0						
Stokes,p	0	0	0	0	2						
Glass,p	1	0	0	0	0						
Hale,3b	1	1	1	0	0						
Walberg,p	0	0	0	0	0						
Total	40	17	19	27	8	Total	50	15	24	24	10

Errors—Philadelphia 2 (Berry, Galloway); Cleveland 0.

a Ran for Dykes in eighth.
b Batted for Baumgartner in second.
c Batted for Knode in ninth.

| Philadelphia | 0 | 1 | 1 | 0 | 0 | 1 | 1 | 13 | .—17 |
| Cleveland | 0 | 4 | 2 | 2 | 4 | 2 | 1 | 0 | 0—15 |

Two-base hits—Lee, Poole, Dykes, Jamieson, Speaker, Lamar. Three-base hits—Lee, Poole, Dykes. Home runs—J. Sewell, Myatt, Simmons. Stolen bases—Jamieson (2), Spurgeon, Myatt, Lutzke, Hale. Sacrifices—Glass. Double plays—Sewell and Knode, Sewell, Spurgeon and Knode. Left on bases—Cleveland 11, Philadelphia 9. Bases on balls—Off J. Miller 6, Yowell 1, Uhle 1, Rommel 1, Stokes 1. Struck out—By W. Miller 2, Baumgartner 1, Stokes 3, Glass 1, Walberg 2. Hits—Off J. Miller 12 in 7 1-3 innings, Speece 2 in 0 (pitched to three batters), Yowell 1 in 0 (pitched to two batters), Rommel 3 in 1, Uhle 3 in 2-3, Baumgartner 2 in 2-3, Heimach 6 in 1 1-3, Stokes 5 in 1 2-3, Glass 7 in 3, Walberg 1 in 1. Hit by pitcher—By J. Miller (Welch). Wild pitches—Rommel, Stokes. Winning pitcher—Glass. Losing pitcher—Uhle. Umpires—Owens, Dineen and Rowland. Time of game—3:00.

June 16, 1925

MAGNATES APPROVE THE 'RABBIT BALL'

National League Owners Decide Against Changes, but Suggest Help to Pitchers.

TEST SHOWS NO ALTERATION

Prof. Fales of Columbia Finds Sphere Same as in 1914—Cut for World Series Players.

The "rabbit ball" will not be caged. The so-called lively sphere, which has been responsible for the home run epidemic, according to many followers of the game, will remain the official horsehide in the National League. This action was taken yesterday at the regular midsummer meeting of the club owners of the National League, held in the offices of John A. Heydler, President of the league, 8 West Fortieth Street. During the four-hour discussion, which started at 11 o'clock yesterday morning, two reports were read on the "rabbit ball," one by Professor Harold A. Fales of the chemistry division at Columbia University, and the other by Julian A. Curtis, President of the A. G. Spalding Company which supplies baseballs for the National League.

It was the testimony of Professor Fales which had much to do with the decision made by the magnates. The professor experimented with balls used in 1914, 1923 and 1925 and after making many tests concluded that to all intents and purposes, there is only a slight difference in the spheres in use during the last eleven years. It was apparent,

the professor reported, that the recent rules restricting the pitcher, the larger number of new balls put into play in each game and the smoother, tighter surface of the ball and the closer "undercut" stitching of the seam, all have conspired in favor of freer and longer hitting.

So convincing was Professor Fales' report that the magnates authorized President Heydler to confer with Ban Johnson, President of the American League, as to the advisability of the umpire bringing a bag of resin to each game and placing it behind the pitcher's box for the pitcher's use in drying his perspiring hands and enabling him to get a better grip on the ball, which now is being done in the Southern Association. The magnates also seemed agreed when the meeting adjourned that the tighter, thinner and all but seamless cover had more to do with the freer hitting and home runs than has any difference in the make and manufacture or the materials placed in the ball.

Elasticity the Same.

The summary of Professor Fales's report follows:

"The 1925 ball is larger in size, weighs more, and gives the pitcher much less control in that the seam of the ball is much smoother and the thread of same almost completely countersunk so as to be flush with the leather of the seam. The elasticity of the ball for small heights of fall, namely 13.5 feet, is practically the same."

Just to show the increased use of new balls, it was announced that a few years ago twelve dozen balls were used on an average weekly at the Polo Grounds and that now the total is ninety dozen a week.

Mr. Curtis, in his talk to the magnates, said:

"Gentlemen, I give you my word of honor that there has been absolutely no change in the manufacture of the ball in recent years. Since 1919 we have used a little better material in the way of wool yarn, otherwise the ball is exactly the same. It is the same weight, the same size and has the same resiliency."

Mr. Curtis said his belief that the increase in home runs was due to the fact that the players nowadays are taking a toe hold and swinging and not

choking their bats as they did in the old days in an effort to place their hits. The fame and fortune acquired by Babe Ruth as a home-run hitter had a lot to do with starting the epidemic, Mr. Curtis said.

It also was said that no action was taken on the suggestion of Barney Dreyfuss of the Pittsburgh club to limit the drives over short fences and into short left and right field stands to two base hits instead of allowing them to go as home runs. It was said that the size of the ball parks did not enter into the discussion.

Out for World Series Teams.

The league unanimously ratified the advisory council's amendment to the world series rules which provides for including fourth-place teams as participants in the players' share of the world series receipts. Such distribution calls for a reduction of the players' share from 75 to 70 per cent of the players' pool. The new rule would give the players finishing second and third exactly the same proportion as they have received heretofore, the 5 per cent. taken from the world series teams going to the fourth place teams. Figures from the last five world series showed that under the new plan of distribution a single winning player's share would be reduced approximately $250, and the losing player's share would be reduced approximately $250.

Resolutions of regret were passed on the deaths of four prominent baseball men. They were Charles H. Ebbets, President of the Brooklyn club; Edward McKeever, Vice President of the Brooklyn club; Sam Crane, baseball writer, and John Montgomery Ward.

Those attending the meeting, in addition to President Heydler, were: Charles A. Stoneham, President of the New York club; Wilbert Robinson, President of the Brooklyn club; Judge Emil Fuchs, President of the Boston club; Barney Dreyfuss, President of the Pittsburgh club; L. C. Widrig of the Cincinnati club; Sam Breadon, President of the St. Louis club, and William A. Veeck of the Chicago club. William A. Baker of the Philadelphia club was unable to attend.

July 16, 1925

SENATORS CONQUER PIRATES BY 4 TO 3 IN GAME OF THRILLS

President Coolidge and Crowd of 38,000 See Series Battle in Wintry Setting.

CRISIS COMES IN SEVENTH

Pittsburgh Leading by 3 to 2 When Stirring Washington Rally Wins Third Contest.

RICE'S CATCH SENSATIONAL

Nabs Smith's Drive, Saving Senators' Series Lead — Contemplated Protest Dropped.

By HARRY CROSS.

Special to The New York Times.

WASHINGTON, Oct. 10.—The Washington ball culb, game and confident, came from behind this afternoon and beat Pittsburgh in the third game of the world's series under adverse weather conditions, which were trying for both players and spectators. The score was 4 to 3 and the victory gave the Senators the edge in the series. They have won two games to the Pirates' one and Bucky Harris and his men are now favorites to take the Autumn classic, because tomorrow Walter Johnson, refreshed after his notable victory in the first game in Pittsburgh, is coming back to do his best to tame the Pirates' batsmen.

After it was all over the Pirates contemplated a protest on the ground that Sam Rice did not catch Earl Smith's drive in the eighth inning, but this was abandoned. Had Rice not caught the ball the blow would have been a home run and tied the score. Pittsburgh adherents were under the impression that he had knocked the ball into the lap of a bleacherite who returned it to Rice.

Chilled by a cutting northwest wind, a crowd of 38,000, which included President Coolidge, who, like a real fan, stayed to the end, Washington and Pittsburgh not only fought each other, but also fought the cold and the wind. Fans swarmed to the game late and there was much confusion at the turnstiles at the last moment. Many did not get into the park until after the game started.

Once inside, they saw a topsy-turvy ball game. It was shot up to the world's series standard, but it was exciting and produced what every baseball fan likes to experience—the element of uncertainty. No one knew at what moment the whistling wind would carry a ball out of the reach of the outfielders and change the result.

Senators Prove Smarter.

The Senators won today's game because they were smarter than the dangerous Pirates. The turn of the battle came in the seventh inning when Pittsburgh was leading 3 to 2 after half a dozen innings of uncertain, erratic baseball. In this momentous seventh, Harris called his pitcher, Alex Ferguson, out of the game and sent Nemo Leibold to bat in his place. Ever a cagey, little left-hander who seldom fails to worry a pitcher, Leibold proved himself smarter than Ray Kremer, who shouldered the pitching responsibility for McKechnie. Patiently little Nemo waited until Kremer spun over four balls and the batsman walked.

There was much activity on the Senators' bench and Stanley Harris sent up McNeely to run for Leibold. The Senators' manager wanted speed and was concentrating all his efforts on this inning. Sam Rice drove Barnhart, the Pirates' flying Dutchman, to the leftfield foul line to pull down his high fly. Then came a play which was an important factor in the outcome of the game. Stanley Harris at the bat spun an inconsequential roller along the third base line which was covered with reverse English. Earl Smith, the Pirate catcher, followed the ball, waiting for it to roll into foul territory. Smith was too impatient and picked up the ball close to the foul line, heaved it to first but too late to cut down the Senators manager. McNeely went to second on the play.

Goslin Fools the Pirates.

Then came Goose Goslin. In the previous inning Goslin had hammered the ball into the right centre field temporary stand for a home run, the sphere hopping into the steerage spectators on the first bound. The Pirate outfielders spread out for Goslin and after driving a long foul into the stands, the Goose completely outguessed the whole Pirate outfit by laying a perfect bunt down along the third-base line on the second pitch.

Traynor, rated as one of the wisest third basemen, was taken completely by surprise, so was Kremer and so was Smith. Goslin galloped to first and was safe and the bases were filled.

At the bat now, was Joe Judge, a competent, efficient batsman, with runners tarrying on the bases. Judge found that he was having some trouble with the service of Kremer. He did not fail. He lifted a sacrifice fly to Max Carey in centre, and after the catch, McNeely romped home with the tying run. The score was 3 to 3.

It is one of those unusual strokes of fate that the next man at the bat should be J. Harris. It is unusual because Joe comes from Coulterville, which is not far from Pittsburgh, and he is a native Pennsylvanian. And it had to be a Pennsylvanian who was ordained by fate to turn the tide of battle against the Pirates today.

Joe smashed a seething single along the ground to left field and over the plate dashed Stanley Harris with the run which won the game.

Thats baseball for you. Though no one can tell in whose hands rests the balance of victory, Joe Harris did his part for his club today and Manager Harris did his part. Both of them did it well.

Then came another peculiar play in a peculiar game. Buddy Myer, the infant rookie, who has willingly and anxiously

Walter Johnson, Senators.

assumed the large job of filling in for the wounded Bluege, snapped a mean ball in front of the plate and as he was bounding toward first base he accidentally kicked the ball and was out for interfering with a batted ball. The inning was over.

Senators' Defense Stands Test.

The rally halted, but the Senators were in front and all that they had to do from that time on was to tighten up their defense and keep the ambitious Freebooters away from the plate.

One who did not see the game can even imagine the extremes to which Washington went in their defense in the last two innings. It was an exhibition of nerve and wonderful spirit—yes, winning spirit.

After Ferguson had retired in that seventh for a pinch hitter, Harris sent Fred Marberry, Washington's big, lazy moundsman, who possesses in his powerful right arm more speed than he has ever been called upon to display. Marberry came in after a long period of warming up. He was equal to the occasion and his slow, indifferent attitude in such a trying situation had a disturbing effect on the Pirates.

Glenn Wright and George Grantham, both hitters of note, blinked as the ball flashed past their eyes, and they both struck out. Irritable Earl Smith, who had been trying his best to disturb the even disposition of the Washington players all afternoon, was at the bat. A dangerous hitter is this Smith.

He looked over Marberry's pitching with an arrogant sneer. Crouched at the plate, Earl is not an easy batsman to pitch to. He worried Marberry. Then Smith caught hold of one amidships. His left-handed swing was deadly and true, and the ball went soaring far and straight into right field.

Rice Makes Startling Catch.

Sam Rice, who was shifted over to right field after the seventh, took one look at the ball, turned around and raced toward the bleachers. On and on he ran, straight for the fence which separated the right centre field terrace from the bleachers.

At the barrier Rice halted. He could go no further. He turned about quickly, saw the ball on its rampant flight into the bleachers, raised his gloved hand on high and the ball stuck in the leather.

It was all so sudden and sensational that not even the friendly Washington crowd of fans would believe it. Umpire Charley Rigler, officiating at second base, was the nearest official to the point of the catch. His eye is true and he has had years of experience in watching close plays on the diamond.

Rigler saw the catch better than any one could in the grand stand. He had a far better view of it than Manager McKechnie or any of the Pirates. With a gesture of his right hand he waved Smith out and Rice came in with the ball in his hand.

In all the future years that world's series will be played, in all the games that have been played under high nervous tension in the past, one will never see a more thrilling catch than that grand grab by Sam Rice. The Pittsburgh players protested. They wouldn't and couldn't believe that it was humanly possible for any fielder to make such a catch.

To pull a ball out of the azure, with one's back turned to it, as Rice's was, is not so much skill as it is baseball intuition.

All Washington, and, in fact, American League fans from the Atlantic to the Pacific, who followed this afternoon's battle before the scoreboard or

Official Score of Third Game of World's Series

WASHINGTON SENATORS.

	AB	R	H	TB	2B	3B	HR	BB	SO	SH	SB	PO	A	E
Rice, cf, rf	5	1	2	2	0	0	0	0	0	0	0	2	0	0
S. Harris, 2b	3	1	1	1	0	0	0	0	0	1	0	2	1	0
Goslin, lf	4	1	2	5	0	0	1	0	1	0	0	3	0	0
Judge, 1b	3	0	1	2	1	0	0	0	0	1	0	8	0	0
J. Harris, rf	4	0	2	2	0	0	0	0	1	0	0	1	0	0
McNeely, cf	0	1	0	0	0	0	0	0	0	0	0	1	0	0
Myer, 3b	3	0	0	0	0	0	0	1	1	0	0	0	1	0
Peckinpaugh, ss	4	0	1	1	0	0	0	0	0	0	0	2	3	1
Ruel, c	3	0	1	1	0	0	0	1	0	0	0	8	2	0
Ferguson, p	2	0	0	0	0	0	0	0	2	0	0	0	0	0
aLeibold	0	0	0	0	0	0	0	1	0	0	0	0	0	0
Marberry, p	0	0	0	0	0	0	0	0	1	0	0	0	0	0
Total	31	4	10	14	1	0	1	3	5	3	0	27	7	1

a Batted for Ferguson in the seventh.

PITTSBURGH PIRATES.

	AB	R	H	TB	2B	3B	HR	BB	SO	SH	SB	PO	A	E
Moore, 2b	3	0	1	1	0	0	0	2	1	0	0	2	2	0
Carey, cf	4	0	2	3	1	0	0	1	0	0	0	3	0	1
Cuyler, rf	4	1	1	1	0	0	0	0	0	0	0	1	0	0
Barnhart, lf	5	0	1	1	0	0	0	0	0	0	0	2	0	0
Traynor, 3b	4	1	1	3	0	1	0	1	0	0	0	1	3	0
Wright, ss	3	1	0	0	0	0	0	0	1	1	0	1	2	1
Grantham, 1b	4	0	0	0	0	0	0	2	0	0	0	8	1	0
Smith, c	3	0	1	1	0	0	0	1	0	0	0	5	2	0
Kremer, p	3	0	1	1	0	0	0	0	2	0	0	0	0	0
bBigbee	1	0	0	0	0	0	0	0	0	0	0	0	0	0
Total	34	3	8	11	2	1	0	4	7	1	0*28		11	2

b Batted for Kremer in the ninth.
*Myer out, hit by batted ball.

SCORE BY INNINGS.

Washington .... 0 0 1 0 0 0 1 2 0 .—4
Pittsburgh .... 0 1 0 1 0 1 0 0 0—3

Double plays—Peckinpaugh, Harris and Judge; Moore and Grantham. Left on bases—Washington 9, Pittsburgh 11. Bases on balls—Off Ferguson 4, Kremer 3. Struck out—By Ferguson 5, Kremer 5, Marberry 2. Hits—Off Ferguson 6 in 7 innings, Kremer 10 in 8, Marberry 2 in 2. Hit by pitcher—By Ferguson (Carey), by Marberry (Cuyler). Passed ball—Smith. Winning pitcher—Ferguson. Umpires—McCormick (N. L.) at plate, Moriarty (A. L.) at first base, Rigler (N. L.) at second base, Owens (A. L.) at third base. Time of game—2:10.

on the radio, raise their hats to Samuel Rice tonight. He just saved the game for Washington; that's all he did.

Then Pirates Come to Bat.

But the drama was not finished yet. The Pirates had one more turn at the bat in the ninth. It was plainly up to Fred Marberry, and although he gave the Washington populace a feeling which was akin to heart failure he measured up to his job and came through with flying colors.

Picture, if you can, the scenario and the conditions at the Griffith Stadium. Washington is leading, 4 to 3, but there is a deep feeling that these Pirates may at any time break loose and raise havoc as the Sea Hawks of the story books are supposed to do.

There was not as much confidence in that roaring, cheering crowd of Washington fans as there was hope. They were heart and soul with Marberry. They sighed or suffered with every ball he pitched.

McKechnie, now reaching at extreme measures, sent Carson Bigbee up in the ninth to bat in place of Kremer. Bigbee hoisted a ball to McNeely in centre, who fooled the strong wind and crushed it safely in his hands. Eddie Moore was more successful. He hasn't done much in this series, but he blossomed forth

at this moment with a lob to left centre which went for a single. Max Carey crashed a single to right and Moore slid safely into third.

Kiki Cuyler, a hero in Pittsburgh, was at the bat and Marberry inadvertently banged him in the back with a wild pitch. Kiki went to first, where the Pirates' trainer came out and rubbed his left arm to extract the immediate pain.

The crowd shivered. They did not know at the moment whether they were shivering from the cold or from nervousness and extreme doubt about what was going to happen. They were nervous, far more nervous than Marberry.

Muddy Ruel went out and spoke soft words in Marberry's ear. The Flying Dutchman, Barnhart, was at the bat, and don't forget, he is a dangerous hitter. Marberry spun the ball as he has never spun it before. Here was the moment when he had to deliver and he knew it.

A hit at this time would mean victory for the Pirates, for two Pirate runners could romp home on a single. Marberry was there. Barnhart lifted a high fly to the infield, and it smashed into the outstretched mitt of Muddy Ruel. Two out!

The worst was not over yet. Harold Traynor, called Pie, is at the bat. If Marberry was worried, he did not show it. In fact, that is one thing about this Washington club which has been significant. They are not disturbed in a crisis as the Pirates are apt to be.

Marberry started out as if he was about to blow up. He couldn't find the plate, or if he could he was not throwing the ball where Traynor could hit it. Three times Marberry shot the ball and Barry McCormick, the umpire behind the plate, called three balls. With the count three and nothing on him it almost a certainty that Traynor would at least get his base on balls and force over the tying run.

Then Marberry Delivers.

Then Marberry buckled up and started to pitch. The next two which flashed over were strikes and with the count two strikes and three balls, Traynor swung his mighty bat and the ball sailed into the wind between centre and right. McNeeley raced over and with encouraging words from the veteran Sam Rice ringing in his ears he grabbed the ball and grabbed it so hard that it would have been impossible to get it away from him with a set of burglar tools. The game was over, Washington rejoiced, rejoiced with far more enthusiasm and sincerity than Pittsburgh enthused when the Pirates won the second game.

It would be entirely wrong to suppose that those last few innings constituted this whole game. They did not. There was plenty of excitement before that, excitement which was the sort that made the spectators forget about cold wintry blasts.

The Pirates struck the first telling blow in the second inning when Traynor slammed a triple to right and came over with the first run on Wright's sacrifice fly to Goslin. The advantage of the Pirates was short lived. Rice opened the third with a single to centre which fairly burned the grass as it streaked through second base. Manager Harris laid down a sacrifice and after Goslin lofted a long fly to Cuyler in right, Rice raced to third after the catch. Joe Judge, peerless and matchless in a pinch, cudgled a two-bagger to right along the foul line and Rice came over with a tying run.

Pittsburgh edged to the front again in the fourth. Cuyler hit a liner to centre and while Rice was on one knee trapping the ball, the fleet irrepressible Cuyler fairly leaped his way to second and turned a single into a double with all the skill of a magician. Barnhart followed this up with a single to left and Cuyler skipped home.

Roger Peckinpaugh faltered a moment in the first half of the sixth and aided the Pirates in gathering another run. After Traynor flied out to Rice, Wright was safe when Peckinpaugh picked up his grounder and made a wild heave to first. Then Granham fanned, and Smith's single to right pushed Wright around to third.

Kremer tapped a harmless-looking hopper toward second, but Stanley Harris was so anxious to get it that he fell and Wright crossed the plate.

The Washington fans picked up courage in the Washington section of the same inning. Goslin was up and the populace implored him to larrup the ball over the hills and far away.

The Wild Goose swung mightily and the ball went to right-center, took one bound and hopped into the bleachers for a home run. If the fans of this town had entertained any doubt that Washington was not coming along with a rush, that doubt was dispelled after Goslin's drive had brought them up within a run of the Pirates.

It was after this drive that the Senators came into the seventh, chock full of confidence and fight in their eyes to hammer out a victory.

Although the bottom fell out of the ticket market today because of the cold weather, Washington fans will crowd to the ball park tomorrow, because they admire a club which can fight themselves out of a difficult jamb, as Harris and his lads did today. Win or lose, Washington is going to fight the Pirates to the bitter end.

There is a frost here tonight but it rests on the Pirates. The Senators are not thinking about the weather. They are warm in the enthusiasm that tomorrow Walter Johnson is going back at the Corsair's crew to sink their lawless craft if such a thing is within the reason of world's series competition.

October 11, 1925

VOTE HORNSBY BEST IN NATIONAL LEAGUE

Baseball Writers Pick Cardinal Star for Most Valuable Player Award.

KIKI CUYLER IS SECOND

George Kelly Third and Wright of Pirates Fourth—Vance Drops to Fifth Place.

By JAMES R. HARRISON.

Polling seventy-three votes out of a possible eighty, Rogers Hornsby, St. Louis manager and second baseman, has been voted the most valuable player in the National League for the season of 1925. Announcement to this effect was made yesterday by James M. Gould, President of the Baseball Writers' Association of America, under whose direction the contest was held.

Hornsby will receive a bronze medal and a cash prize award of $1,000, both of which will be presented to him some time during the 1926 season.

Second man in the voting was Pittsburgh's sensational young outfielder, Hazen (Kiki) Cuyler, whose two-bagger with the bases full broke up the last game of the World's Series. In third place came Long George Kelly, the Giants' jack-of-all-trades, and the fourth choice was Glenn Wright, shortstop of the world's champion Pirates. Dazzy Vance, last year's winner, was fifth. The Robin star did not score a single first place, but he had one second and one third.

Wheat Out of First Ten.

The only Giant besides Kelly among the first ten was Frank Frisch, who ranked ninth with thirteen votes. Frisch was third last year. The shifting tides of baseball fortune are seen in the makeup of the first ten stars as compared with the leaders of 1924. Zack Wheat, fourth, and Ross Young, fifth in last season's standing, are missing entirely, as are Rabbit Maranville and Jack Fournier. Glenn Wright, Dave Bancroft, Jim Bottomley and Pie Traynor are the men who have joined the charmed circle.

Hornsby polled one vote less than Vance did last year when the Dazzler rang up a total of 74. Rogers won three firsts, three seconds and two thirds. No committeeman ranked the great St. Louisan below third place. Cuyler, with two firsts and one second, compiled 61 points, and Kelly, getting one first and two seconds, scored 52 points.

Hornsby's selection was a foregone conclusion. Although Vance had another great year, he was overshadowed by the wonderful batting feats of Hornsby, whose mark of .403 was the culmination of a six-year batting record that has never been equaled in the major leagues. For three years the marvelous Rogers has hit .400 or better, and he has led his league in batting six straight seasons. His general average for that period is .397, 1 point better than Ty Cobb's mark in his six best years.

In addition to his hitting, Hornsby's fielding skill, smartness, steadiness and excellent deportment on and off the field weighed heavily in his favor.

Infielders Rule the Roost.

Infielders were much in favor with the committee. Seven of the first ten players were infielders. The champion Pirates landed three of the ten places, the Cardinals and Giants two each, and Brooklyn, Cincinnati and Boston one apiece. Philadelphia and Chicago drew blanks.

The committee was composed of one baseball writer in each league city. First place counted 10 points, second 9, third 8, and so forth. It would have been possible for eighty players to re-

ceive votes, but only twenty-one were honored.

Following were the committeemen: Burt Whitman, Boston; Thomas Meany, Brooklyn; Tom Swope, Cincinnati; James Crusinberry, Chicago; F. O. Grauley, Philadelphia; Charles J. Doyle, Pittsburgh; Frank Graham, New York, and Martin Haley, St. Louis.

Here is the vote for the first ten:

Hornsby	9	9	8	10	9	10	8	10—73
Cuyler	4	6	10	8	6	8	10	9—61
Kelly	5	7	9	9	10	0	6	6—52
Wright	8	10	6	0	2	5	9	3—43
Vance	1	8	6	7	7	9	3	7—42
Bancroft	10	3	7	1	8	0	4	8—41
Bottomley	6	4	5	2	0	7	0	4—28
Traynor	7	1	4	6	0	2	7	0—27
Frisch	0	0	3	5	0	3	2	0—13
Roush	3	0	0	3	0	1	5	—12

Players below the first ten were as follows:

Player—Club.	Votes.
Carey Pittsburgh	11
Meusel, New York	6
Luque, Cincinnati	5
Grimm, Chicago	5
Wheat, Brooklyn	4
Donohue, Cincinnati	4
Hargrave, Cincinnati	4
Harper, Philadelphia	3
Sand, Philadelphia	3
Gautreau, Boston	2
Aldridge, Pittsburgh	1

December 7, 1925

Washington Senators

SPORT NEWS SERVICE ARRANGED BY WRC

PLAY-BY-PLAY descriptions of all games to be played out of town by the Washington American League champions will be broadcast this season by WRC.

The out-of-town season will begin April 21 when the Senators make their début at Greater Shibe Park, Philadelphia, against the Mackmen. Beginning with the Philadelphia series, WRC will be on the air continuously during every game played on both the Eastern and Western trips. Plans for broadcasting the opening games of the season in Washington, April 13, are under consideration.

In addition to the play-by-play descriptions of games played by the Washington team, bulletins from other major league games will be announced between innings throughout the season.

Complete scores in all leagues will be announced every evening by WRC. The latter information will be included in a sports résumé that will contain late news from all the sporting world, including golf, tennis, rowing and the important turf races of the season.

April 4, 1926

JOHNSON TRIUMPHS IN 15 INNINGS, 1-0

Washington Veteran Shuts Out Athletics to Start His 19th Season.

VICE PRESIDENT ATTENDS

Dawes Among 25,000 Who Brave Chilly Weather—S. Harris Scores Lone Run.

WASHINGTON, April 13 (P).—Washington and Philadelphia opened the baseball season in gala style here today, battling fifteen innings before the champion Senators won, 1 to 0. The game was a brilliant duel between pitching veterans, Walter Johnson for the Senators, beginning his twentieth season, and Ed Rommel for the Athletics.

More than 25,000 fans braved the chilly weather and saw Vice President Dawes toss out the first ball. A floral piece was presented to Manager Bucky Harris, and Johnson received a loving cup.

Manager Harris crossed the plate with the winning run after he had singled, Goslin doubled and Joe Harris singled. Twice the Senators had filled the bags with two out only to fall before Rommel's pitching. The Senators went hitless during the first four innings.

Twelve of the Athletics went down by the strike-out route, Johnson's curves and fast ones appearing as effective as ever. Rommel struck out one man and walked five, while Johnson passed three.

The veteran Peckinpaugh sat on the bench and watched his substitute, Buddy Myer, play at short. The youngster handled four chances and muffed one.

The box score:

WASHINGTON (A)							PHILADELPHIA (A)						
	ab.	r.	h.	po.	a.	e.		ab.	r.	h.	po.	a.	e.
Rice, cf	7	0	2	4	0	0	Bishop, 2b	5	0	1	5	5	0
S.Harris, 2b	5	1	1	3	4	0	Lamar, lf	6	0	2	3	0	0
Goslin, lf	5	0	1	5	0	0	French, lf	5	0	1	3	0	0
J. Harris, rf	7	0	2	5	0	0	Simmons, cf	6	0	1	2	0	0
Judge, 1b	3	0	2	14	1	0	Hauser, 1b	4	0	0	23	0	0
Bluege, 3b	5	0	1	1	3	0	Cochrane, c	6	0	2	3	0	0
Myer, ss	5	0	0	1	2	1	Dykes, 3b	6	0	1	2	2	0
Ruel, c	4	0	0	11	6	0	Galloway, ss	5	0	0	2	4	0
Severeid, c	1	0	0	1	0	0	Rommel, p	6	0	0	1	7	0
Johnson, p	6	0	0	0	3	0							
aTobin	1	0	0	0	0	0	Total	49	0	6	*43	23	0
Total	49	1	9	45	12	1							

*One out when winning run was scored.
aBatted for Ruel in twelfth.

Washington ....0 0 0 0 0 0 0 0 0 0 0 0 0 0 1—1
Philadelphia ....0 0 0 0 0 0 0 0 0 0 0 0 0 0 0—0

Two-base hits—French, Goslin. Stolen base—Rice. Sacrifices—Judge, French (2), Goslin. Galloway. Double play—S. Harris, Meyer and Judge. Left on bases—Philadelphia 10, Washington 13. Bases on balls—Off Rommel 5, Johnson 3. Struck out—By Rommel 1, Johnson 12. Hit by pitcher—By Rommel 1 (Myer). Umpires—Connolly, Nallin and Geisel.

Time of game—2:33

RUTH HITS 3 HOMERS AND YANKS WIN, 10-5; SERIES EVEN AGAIN

Babe Breaks Six Records Hitting Two Balls Out of Park, One Into Distant Bleachers.

EVEN ST. LOUIS CHEERS HIM

40,000 See Yankees Get 14 Hits Off Five Pitchers—Hoyt Gives 14, Too, but Survives.

VICTORY CLINCHED IN FIFTH

Five Bases on Balls and a Double Net 4 Runs—Pennock vs. Sherdel Today—Sixth Game Here.

By JAMES R. HARRISON.
Special to The New York Times.
ST. LOUIS, Oct. 6.—Contrary to reports, the king is not dead. Long live the king, for today he hit three home runs and smashed six world's series records as completely as his fellow-Yankees smashed the Cardinals, to tie the world's series at two victories apiece.

After all, there is only one Ruth. He is alone and unique. Tonight he is securely perched on the throne again, and the crown does not rest uneasy on this royal head. For to his record of fifty-nine homers in one season he added today the achievement of three home runs in one world's series game.

Behind his bulky, swaggering figure, the Yankees marched to an overwhelming victory, 10 to 5. When they were going down for the third and almost the last time, Ruth tossed them the rope of three homers. He took personal charge of the world's series and made the game his greatest single triumph. He led the charge of a faltering battalion and turned the tide of battle so much that tonight most of the neutral critics were conceding the championship to the Yankees.

Yanks Find Batting Eye.

Hearing the old familiar ring of Ruth's big bat, the Yankees came out of their coma, made ten runs and fourteen hits and bore the Cardinals to earth with a rugged, slashing attack.

Besides setting world's series records that may stand for all time, George Herman Ruth hit a baseball where only two other men had hit it—into the centrefield bleachers of Sportsmans Park. It is 430 feet to the bleacher fence. The wall is about twenty feet high. Back of it stretches a deep bank of seats, and almost squarely in the middle of this bank

Ruth crashed the third homer that made all the history.

It was not one of his longest drives but it was by all odds his best, for it automatically wiped four marks off the record book. It was, as noted above, the first time anybody had hit that many homers in a series game. It made Ruth's number of homers for all series games seven, beating by one the former record of "Goose" Goslin. It made his total bases in one game twelve, three more than Harry Hopper in 1915. His extra bases on long hits amounted to nine. Again three better than any other man had ever done.

Besides those four marks, which were shattered by the one heroic blow, Ruth broke two more. He scored four runs, the most which any player has scored in a world's series game, beating a record of three set by Mike Donlin in 1905, which has been equalled often. Ruth also raised his own record of eighteen extra bases achieved in world series games to a grand total of twenty-seven.

Ruth's first contribution to the gayety of more than 40,000 fans today came in the first inning, when Flint Rhem, the first of five Cardinal pitchers, decided that a fast ball, adroitly served, would fool the king. Ruth swung under the ball and raised it high in the air. The pellet floated out to right field, hugging the foul line and blown by the wind toward foul territory.

Over the Fence It Goes.

At the last moment, with the ball veering closer and closer to the chalk line of extinction, it disappeared over the stand and fell to the broad avenue below—not two feet from the foul line.

In the third, when Ruth came up next, young Mr. Rhem had changed his mind and decided that a fellow who could hit that far might be slightly deceived by a pitch of slower pace. So he tossed up a dew-drop slow ball between the waist and shoulder and on the inside corner.

Ruth must have been expecting it, for he leaned back, swung from the floor and, with perfect timing, drove a long, high and hard poke over the bleacher roof in deep right-centre.

In both cases he swung at the first ball. Two pitches and two home runs. Two pitches and the game was practicaly over, with the Yanks inspired and rejuvenated and crowding to the plate to hit with old-time vim.

Two pitches and, who knows, the series was practically over. With his star left-hander, Pennock, thoroughly rested and ready to pitch tomorrow, Miller Huggins has the upper hand once more, with the Yanks finally awake and out of their batting slump.

After the third inning, the Cardinal pitchers treated Mr. Ruth with great aloofness and attempted no familiarities but one. That one was disastrous. In the sixth inning, Herman Bell, a young right-hander, was pitching. Combs opened with a single too deep for Thevenow and Koenig fanned and Bell was so pleased with this conquest that he attempted conclusions with Ruth, which was equivalent to tampering with a stick of dynamite.

When the count was finally three and two Mr. Bell did a foolish thing. He drew back his arm and cut loose with a fast ball straight through the middle. When Ruth is hitting as he was today, there is not a pitcher in the world who can afford this gamble. Even a schoolboy pitcher knows better than that.

Ruth waded into the fast ball and put all his shoulders and back behind the 52-ounce bat that has brought more ruin than any other in baseball. He caught the ball as flush as an expert marksman. It was a terrific blow and there was no doubt where it was going. Douthit ran back as far as he could, and having no scaling irons or ladder, stood helplessly while the ball shot over the wall and landed in the laps of the St. Louis rooters. It was still going with unabated speed when it arrived. It struck with force and bounced up, and then there came the finest ovation that St. Louis has ever given a visiting athlete.

Babe Gets Ovation.

Three home runs in one world's series game! Only seven men in modern baseball have hit three in any ordinary game. Even the hardened partisans of St. Louis had to admit the grandeur of the feat. In Boston or New York or several other cities they would have torn the grandstand down and given Babe the pieces, but for St. Louis it was a gigantic tribute that poured out from more than 40,000 throats.

The folks in the grandstand were inclined to be a bit conservative. A few bitter-enders committed the lèse-majesté of booing the king, but out in the bleachers it was all tumult and uproar. The boys in the sun seats in left, where Ruth was stationed, got to their feet as if one man. They waved papers and programs and Cardinal banners and tossed a few ancient straw hats out on the field.

There have been few more gallant figures than Ruth leading the charge of the Yanks today. It had been a dark hour for the New York gladiators. Before the game, it was reported, Ban Johnson, President of the American League, went to the Yankee dressing room to give the players the sort of talk that a football coach delivers to his men before the big game. There was a general conviction that the Cards were the better team and would win, an opinion that was not changed until the slumbering menace in Babe Ruth's bat awoke and made a new team of the Yanks.

There have been few figures as gallant as Ruth as he strode from the bench to receive the thrice-repeated homage of an enemy crowd—his portly frame swaggering ever so slightly, his face alight with the fire of determination.

If the Babe was going down, he would go down fighting. There was only one man who could jar the Yanks out of their depressing slump. It is still a one-man team and the happy fortune today was that that one man found his batting eye and blazed the trail for his dejected colleagues.

A Lively Ball Game.

With the greatest home-run hitter of them all hitting three homers, it was, naturally enough, a lively occasion. The game was long and one-sided, but it was a good one—a great game, indeed, with attacks and counterattacks, a seesawing score. Twenty-eight hits on both sides and sensation following sensation, even to the almost disastrous collision of two Cardinal outfielders.

The paid attendance was 38,825, more than 1,000 above yesterday's first St. Louis game. This number of people paid $165,190 at the gate, bringing the total receipts of the series up to $730,001, a new record.

The previous record for receipts in four games was $723,104, made in 1923. The record for players' share, also made in that year, was $368,783.

With the playing of the fourth game, the players ceased to share in the receipts. However, the players' pool totaled $372,300, a world's series record, surpassing by more than $4,000 the record set in 1923. Of this total the world's series players will share in only 70 per cent., as the remaining 30 per cent. goes to the second, third and fourth place teams in the pennant races of the two leagues.

On this basis the world's series players will divide $260,510. Each club has twenty-five eligible players, which means that each player for the winning team will receive about $5,254 and each player for the losing team will get $4,168. Both these sums are records in world's series.

The series is sure to go back to New York, and that means a Saturday game

at the Stadium, with the two club owners cutting heavily into the net proceeds. With Pennock at hand, refreshed by a four-day rest, and the New York war clubs again playing the music of the solid wallop, the Yanks are favorites here to win, when last night they were poor second-money choices.

It was, until today, a lifeless world's series. Three games had been played, and in none of them was there a great play or a thrilling rally, or hardly an event that the baseball field had not seen dozens of times before.

The Series Awakes.

But today the series awoke and put on its best show. And there was sparkling fielding and the heavy ring of busy bats and enough mistakes to keep the fans on edge from start to finish.

The Cardinals opened brusquely on Waite Hoyt, but fell behind until the fourth. Then four hits and three runs put them one to the good, and raised the grave suspicion that Mr. Hoyt would take an early trip to the clubhouse. But to gain those three runs

in the fourth Hornsby had to take out Rhem. Arthur Reinhart, his left-handed successor, threw the game away in the fifth by setting another world's series record, and giving five bases on balls. Four, as a matter of fact, were charged to Reinhart and the fifth to Herman Bell. With only one hit, the Yanks scored four runs, and in the sixth Ruth struck another home run blow and the game was over.

With all this friendly assistance Hoyt was able to stagger through, although he did not pitch a good game. He struck out eight, but was so much in trouble that Urban Shocker pitched almost a complete game in the bull pen, where he was joined later by Shawkey and Pennock, as the Cardinals made their constant threats.

Once Rhem had passed out, Hornsby was at sea and called on four more pitchers in vain. Reinhart, Bell, a young southpaw named William Hallahan and the right-hander, Vic Keen, strayed forth from the bench at odd moments, with Keen showing in the ninth the only flash of ability.

There was one other record tied during the sunny afternoon. Between and among them the five Cardinal pitchers issued ten bases on balls.

In the fourth the exultant fans were

Times Wide World Photos.
Ruth and Hornsby Before Tuesday's Game in St. Louis.

frightened speechless as Chick Hafey and Taylor Douthit, two of the outfield guard, crashed together in pursuit of a fly and were knocked groggy. Lazzeri was on first base with one out, when Joe Dugan looped a fly to left centre. Douthit rushed over from centre and Hafey dashed in from left. Eyes glued on the ball, they saw nothing else in the world. Players of more experience would have avoided the crash. Either of them could have caught the ball, but as Douthit touched it he bumped into Hafey, and the ball flew to the ground. Both players were stretched out apparently unconscious.

They were so badly dazed that neither could get up and chase the ball. Bell rushed out from third and retrieved it, but by that time Lazzeri was almost at the plate.

Doctor Rushes Out.

Douthit, as he rushed in, rammed his elbow against Hafey's chest and stomach, and the left fielder was the worse hurt of the two. He went down on his side and lay still. Players of both teams ran out. On their heels came the St. Louis trainer and the club doctor. For a moment it looked like a stretcher case, with the Cardinals out two good ball players, but smelling salts, a dash of cold water and frenzied towel-swinging did the trick and brought them both to normal.

Douthit did one of the gamest things of the series only a minute later. With Dugan on second, Severeid sliced a pretty single to dead centre. Although only sixty seconds before he had been reclining on his back, Douthit sprinted in and tore loose a wonderful throw which nailed Joe fast at the plate.

It was one of four great throws to-day. In the second Lazzeri hit against the left field bleachers, but was out at third on Thevenow's fine relay of the ball from Douthit. In the fourth Douthit tried to score from second on a single, but was cut down by Ruth's marvelous line fling straight into Severeid's glove.

Again in the sixth, Meusel singled to right and tried a smart manoeuvre by rounding first base slowly and then suddenly putting on a burst of speed, hoping that Southworth would be taken in by the trick. Billy, however, was wideawake. He erased the big city slicker at second with a throw true and straight.

There was still another interval

... medical talents of the club trainer were needed to resuscitate an athlete. In the fourth, Bob Meusel suddenly stopped the game and walked into the diamond to complain of a dizzy spell and failing eyesight. The fans were not surprised to hear it, for they believed that by that time the Cardinals had knocked all the Yanks dizzy. Expert first-aid ministrations by Trainer Woods restored Robert, and there were no more complaints during the afternoon.

Rhem, in the first inning, struck out Combs and Koenig, but after this gay beginning, he tossed the celebrated fast ball to Mr. Ruth who stowed it away on the outside of the park. Meusel walked and Gehrig singled to right. The Cards had trouble getting hold of the ball and Meusel, smartly, kept on running from first to the plate. That he didn't make it was no fault of the strategy, for a better slide would have landed him safe and sound.

For the Cardinals. Douthit outran a tap to deep short, and Southworth sent him to third with a single through second. Hornsby emulated Ruth to some degree by dashing a rugged hit to right, scoring Douhit and moving Southworth to second.

Cardinals Hitting Fiercely.

The Cardinal hitting was fierce, and Hornsby wisely ordered Bottomley to keep the attack going instead of bunting. Bottomley, however flied to Ruth and Lester Bell did likewise to Combs. Hoyt got out of a very bad hole by fanning Hafey.

Lazzeri's two bagger to left opened the second. Tony thought the ball was going into the stand, and loafed down to first. So was a second late in arriving at third, where Bell did a nice job of touching. Followed Severeid's single, on which Lazzeri could have scored. It was one of three or more runs tossed away by the opulent Yanks.

The second Ruthian product enlivened the third inning. The score was now: Ruth 2, St. Louis 1. The Yanks showed more signs of life in the fourth, when Lazzeri walked and scored during the Hafey-Douthit head-on collision, which also allowed Dugan to reach second. On Severeid's single Joe was tagged out at home, Joe's speed being less than his earnest intentions.

The fourth was almost the end for Waite Hoyt. Up to this time he had done excellent work. Although his curve was nothing to boast about, he had nice control and an effective change of pace, working the corners with low fast balls that were called strikes but were hard to hit.

Koenig charged out to left to make a rattling good catch of L. Bell's fly. Hafey singled and then the Yankee shortstop made up for his good work by fumbling O'Farrell's grounder, an error which nearly cost the game, giving the Cards three unearned runs.

It was a bad break of luck for Hoyt. Thevenow whipped a two-bagger an inch inside first base and Hafey scored while O'Farrell paused at second. Hornsby had no confidence in Rhem and yanked him for Pinch Hitter Toporcer. It was a move that Rogers lived to regret, for Rhem certainly would have done better than the miscellaneous collection of talent which followed him.

Toporcer didn't deliver much at that, though his sacrifice fly to Combs scored O'Farrell with the tying run. Combs' throw was fast, but badly aimed.

Douthit's Two-Bagger.

Here. Douthit sent a rollicking two-bagger out to the bleacher wall in right centre and put his team a run ahead, while the local enthusiasts went crazy with joy. Sportsman's Park was a madhouse for two or three minutes, and the purple-faced rooters went into another spasm when Southworth singled to left. Douthit went for home and Ruth stopped him dead. The vocal storm subsided somewhat.

Back came the Yanks in the fifth to have the game presented to them on a

Official Score of Fourth Game of World's Series

NEW YORK YANKEES.

	AB	R	H	TB	2B	3B	HR	BB	SO	SH	SB	PO	A	E
Combs, cf	5	2	2	3	1	0	0	1	1	0	0	4	0	0
Koenig, ss	6	1	1	2	1	0	0	0	3	0	0	1	3	1
Ruth, lf	3	4	3	12	0	0	3	2	0	0	0	1	1	0
Meusel, rf	2	1	1	1	0	0	0	3	0	0	0	1	0	0
Gehrig, 1b	3	0	2	3	1	0	0	1	1	0	8	0	0	
Lazzeri, 2b	3	1	1	2	1	0	0	1	0	1	0	1	3	0
Dugan, 3b	4	0	1	2	1	0	0	1	0	0	0	1	2	0
Severeid, c	4	1	3	3	0	0	0	1	0	0	0	10	0	0
Hoyt, p	4	0	0	0	0	0	0	0	1	1	0	0	0	0
Total	34	10	14	23	5	0	3	10	6	3	0	27	9	1

ST. LOUIS CARDINALS.

	AB	R	H	TB	2B	3B	HR	BB	SO	SH	SB	PO	A	E
Douthit, cf	5	1	2	3	1	0	0	0	0	0	0	2	2	0
Southworth, rf	5	0	3	3	0	0	0	0	0	0	1	2	0	
Hornsby, 2b	5	1	2	2	0	0	0	2	0	1	3	4	0	
Bottomley, 1b	4	0	1	1	0	0	0	1	0	0	6	1	0	
L. Bell, 3b	4	0	1	1	0	0	0	0	1	0	3	0	0	
Hafey, lf	5	1	1	1	0	0	0	2	0	0	2	0	0	
O'Farrell, c	4	1	2	2	0	0	0	0	0	8	1	0		
Thevenow, ss	4	1	2	3	1	0	0	1	0	3	2	0		
Rhem, p	1	0	0	0	0	0	0	1	0	0	1	0		
aToporcer	0	0	0	0	0	0	0	1	1	0	0	0		
Reinhart, p	0	0	0	0	0	0	0	0	0	0	0	0		
H. Bell, p	0	0	0	0	0	0	0	0	0	0	0	0		
bFlowers	1	0	0	0	0	0	0	1	0	0	0	0		
Hallahan, p	0	0	0	0	0	0	0	0	0	1	0	0		
Holm	1	0	0	0	0	0	0	1	0	0	0	0		
Keen, p	0	0	0	0	0	0	0	0	0	1	0			
Total	39	5	14	16	2	0	1	8	2	1	27	14	0	

a Batted for Rhem in the fourth.
b Batted for H. Bell in the sixth.
c Batted for Hallahan in the eighth.

SCORE BY INNINGS.

New York	1 0 1 1 4 2 1 0 0—	10
St. Louis	1 0 0 3 0 0 0 0 1—	5

Left on bases—New York 10, St. Louis 10. Bases on balls—Off Rhem 2, Reinhart 4, H. Bell 1, Hallahan 3, Hoyt 1. Struck out—By Rhem 4, H. Bell 1, Hallahan 1, Hoyt 8. Hits—Off Rhem 7 in 4 innings, Reinhart 1 in none (pitched to five men in fifth inning), H. Bell 4 in 2, Hallahan 2 in 2, Keen none in 1. Balk—H. Bell. Losing pitcher—Reinhart. Umpires—Klem (N. L.) at plate, Dinneen (A. L.) at first base, O'Day (N. L.) at second base, Hildebrand (A. L.) at third base. Time of game—2:39.

silver platter. Reinhart, a stalwart left-hander with a tricky service like Sherdel's, was nervous and wild. Altogether he gave the most pathetic spectacle of many a world's series. He walked Combs without getting over even one strike, and the Yanks got a break when Koenig popped a fluky double down the right-field line, the ball landing in the one exact spot where no fielder could reach it.

Hornsby slipped when he picked up the ball, and Combs was fast enough to score. With Ruth at bat, Reinhart went on an ascension and neglected to take his parachute with him.

True, he favored Mr. Ruth with a strike, but the other four were balls. Another walk to Meusel filled up the bases and Reinhart went from bad to worse by chucking two bad ones to Gehrig.

Here was the point where Hornsby should have acted. He had Herman Bell warmed up, and it was no secret that Reinhart was now in the clouds. The left-hander steadied a little, but when the count was two and two he walked Gehrig, forcing Koenig in and sending New York ahead.

Bell took up the assignment with the bases still full and no one out, and no one thinking of getting out. Lazzeri's fly to Southworth scored Ruth, while Meusel occupied third after the catch. Dugan's grounder spouted up in the air and during his subsequent demise at the hands of O'Farrell, Meusel raced home with the fourth run.

In the sixth came Combs's single and the third of the Ruth home-run series. The score was now 9 to 4. The Cards in their half of the inning made attempts at reprisals. O'Farrell and Thevenow singled, but Flowers, a hitter for H. Bell fanned. Douthit and Southworth were powerless.

A single by Severeid, Hoyt's sacrifice, and Combs's two-bagger inside third put the Yanks into double figures in the seventh. Protected by his big lead, Hoyt went along in able style now. When O'Farrell led off with a single in the eighth, there was a flutter in the New York bull pen, but it was all a mistake. Hoyt struck out Thevenow and also Holm, who batted for Hallahan. Douthit flied to centre.

Wee Willie Sherdel will come back for the Cards tomorrow and the Cards need that victory very much, for it will be their last home game. Tomorrow night the procession wends back to New York.

October 7, 1926

BOY REGAINS HEALTH AS RUTH HITS HOMERS

John D. Sylvester, Son of National City Bank Executive, Now on Road to Recovery.

Special to The New York Times.

ESSEX FALLS, N. J., Oct. 7.—John Dale Sylvester, 11 years old, to whom physicians allotted thirty minutes of life when he was stricken with blood poisoning last week, was pronounced well on the road to recovery this afternoon, after he had contentedly listened to the radio returns of the Yankees' defeat of the Cardinals. His father, Horace Sylvester Jr., Vice President of the National City Bank, and the physicians are convinced that John owes his life to messages of encouragement which the boy received Wednesday from Babe Ruth and other world series players. They had learned of his plight and of his request for autographed baseballs from his father.

The physicians say that the boy's return to health began when he learned the news of Ruth's three homers in the fourth game of the series. His fever began to abate at once, and the favorable course was hastened today after he had listened to the radio returns, clutching the autographed baseballs which he received by air mail on Wednesday night.

John's intense interest in the world series and in home runs especially, were explained to his family today when his chums told of the boys ability on the sand lots. He had modestly refrained from mentioning the fact that he has a reputation as a home run hitter and a skilful third baseman.

His recovery had reached the point tonight where he was already making plans for a return to the diamond, and he promised one caller that he would soon bring his team to a neighboring town for a game.

The boy's father sent letters to the managers of both teams today thanking them for their assistance in helping his boy to recover.

October 8, 1926

GIANTS GET HORNSBY; TRADE BIG SURPRISE

Record Baseball Deal Sends Frisch and Ring to Cardinals for Famous Batsman.

ST. LOUIS REFUSES TERMS

Demand by Manager of World's Champions of $150,000 for Three Years Brings Break.

By JAMES R. HARRISON.

In the biggest deal of modern baseball history, Rogers Hornsby, greatest batsman of the game, and manager of the world's champion St. Louis Cardinals, was traded to the Giants last night for Frank Frisch and Pitcher Jimmy Ring.

The transaction, completed over the long-distance telephone between St. Louis and New York at 7:30 last night, involves players valued at more than half a million dollars and brings to this city the second of the two outstanding figures of the sport—Babe Ruth, king of the long distance hitters, and Hornsby, six-time batting champion of the National League.

Although President Charles A. Stoneham of the Giants declared that no money was paid to the Cardinals, baseball men were unanimous in insisting that the New York club must have handed over at least $100,000, in addition to its star second baseman and a veteran pitcher who is almost at the end of his career.

Hornsby, it was pointed out, is worth much more than $300,000 at present baseball prices. Several years ago John McGraw, manager of the Giants, offered $250,000 and five players for him. Not long afterward the Brooklyn club raised this figure to a straight $275,000.

Value Increased Steadily.

Since that time Hornsby's value has increased greatly. He went on to win his sixth successive hitting championship of the league, was universally recognized as the finest right-handed batter of them all and climaxed his career last season by leading the Cardinals to the first pennant ever won by a modern St. Louis team and later to the world's championship.

At the very peak of his career, when his money value was close to the $350,-000 mark, Hornsby is traded for Frank Frisch, who might bring $250,000 in the open market, and for a pitcher of slight value.

There is a difference here of about $100,000 that baseball experts wanted explained to them last night. They considered it unbelievable that President Breadon of the Cardinals would have traded the popular hero of St. Louis for Frisch and Ring alone.

On the other hand, the Giants would gladly turn over Frisch and Ring and $100,000, for in Hornsby they have the long-sought metropolitan rival for Babe Ruth. That they would pay Hornsby $50,000 a year for three years was likewise taken for granted; his box office value in the biggest baseball city is tremendous.

Moreover, Hornsby now looms up as the next manager of the Giants, to take the reins when John McGraw finally decides to lay them down, as he has threatened to do for the past year.

It was President Breadon of the Cardinals who suggested this trade involving $600,000 worth of ball players. Breadon and Hornsby had a conference in St. Louis yesterday on salary matters; they disagreed hopelessly, and Breadon then did the next best thing by offering him to the Giants.

Deal Closed in Few Minutes.

Shortly after the meeting with Hornsby, Breadon called President Stoneham of the Giants on the phone. According to Stoneham, the St. Louis club owner broached the trade of

Year. Club.	G.	AB.	R.	H.	SB.	P.C.
1914—(a)Dallas	..	..	..	..	..	...
1914—(b)Hugo	....	..	..	..	..	...
1914—Dennison	113	393	47	91	19	.232
1915—(c)Dennison	119	429	75	119	24	.277
1915—St. Louis	18	57	5	14	..	.246
1916—St. Louis	139	495	63	155	17	.313
1917—St. Louis	145	523	36	171	17	.327
1918—St. Louis	115	416	51	117	8	.281
1919—St. Louis	138	512	68	163	17	.318
1920—(d)St. Louis	149	589	96	218	12	.370
1921—St. Louis	154	592	131	235	13	.397
1922—St. Louis	154	623	141	250	17	.401
1923—St. Louis	107	424	89	163	3	.384
1924—(e)St. Louis	143	536	121	227	5	.424
1925—(f)St. Louis	138	504	133	203	5	.403
1926—St. Louis	134	528	96	167	3	.316

World's Series Record.

	G.	AB.	R.	H.	SB.	P.C.
1926—St. Louis	7	28	2	7	1	.250

Complete Major League Totals.

Years.	Games.	A.B.	R.	Hits.	SB.	P.C.
12	1,534	5,799	1,080	2,063	117	.359

a On trial, released April 29.
b Released July 2—Hugo to Dennison.
c Sold Aug. 20 to St. Louis, reported sales price $500.
d Started six-year National League batting championship string.
e Set modern major league batting mark of .4235.
f Appointed St. Louis manager June 1, 1925. Won National League Most Valuable Player Award.

Hornsby for Frisch and Ring. It was immediately accepted; a few minutes of telephone conversation and the big deal was put through.

President Stoneham denied that the trade had been previously arranged.

"In an off-hand way," he said, "we had talked with Breadon about trading Hornsby, but the negotiations did not get very far. We were not very hopeful, and when Breadon called us tonight I was as much surprised as any one."

According to another story, however, Breadon had agreed that if he could not make Hornsby accept a one-year contract at $50,000 a year, he would trade his manager and star batsman to the Giants after yesterday's conference. President Stoneham, this account said, was waiting here for the long-distance call.

John McGraw, who pulled the strings of this momentous trade, was mysteriously in the background last night and it could not be learned whether or not he was present when the telephone bell rang.

The rival second basemen greeted the news with a marked lack of enthusiasm. Hornsby was quoted in St. Louis as saying that "it doesn't look right that I should be traded from a club that I just managed to a world's championship."

At his home in this city Frisch, the Fordham Flash, born and brought up in New York, seemed stunned by the tidings.

"It's pretty hot out there, but I suppose I'll play," he said in a listless tone.

Among other things, this is the first time in baseball history that a manager has been traded within a year of his having won the world's championship. From that angle alone the trade was enough to set the baseball tongues wagging.

McGraw's Ambition Gratified.

The acquisition of Hornsby gratifies an ambition long cherished by John McGraw. For many years he has cast a covetous eye at the man whom McGraw himself called "the greatest right-handed hitter of all time." Fabulous offers were in vain. The Cardinals would have traded Hornsby for Frisch and other players several years ago, but McGraw declared that he

would not give up Frisch for Hornsby under any circumstances.

The next move came last week at the meetings of the major leagues, when the split between Hornsby and Breadon loomed up as very serious. It was known that McGraw again was talking trade with the Cardinals; the trail became so hot that he canceled a reservation on the Twentieth Century Limited to travel with Breadon to Chicago on another train.

It was in a compartment on this train, the story goes, that the deal was completed which was announced last night—conditional, of course, on Breadon's failing to sign Hornsby to a one-year contract instead of the three-year agreement that Rogers demanded.

Two years ago Hornsby signed a three-year contract at $30,000 a season. When he was made manager in the middle of the 1925 season, his contract as a player went on and Rogers received nothing extra for being manager. However, as soon as the Cardinals had won the world's series, Hornsby announced that he wanted his present contract torn up and a new document drawn up calling for $150,000 for three years.

The dispute between Breadon and Hornsby involved only the question of one year or three. President Breadon considered the latter risk too great.

One of his arguments was that Hornsby as a player had been far below his usual level this year. Rogers batted only .316, almost 100 points under his customary figure; both his batting and fielding suffered from the strain of piloting a team through the thick of a pennant battle.

Breadon and his popular manager also had sharp disagreements on other matters. Hornsby insisted on the complete retirement from the club of Vice President Branch Rickey, Rogers's predecessor as manager. Although Hornsby owned 15 per cent. of the club, Breadon stuck to Rickey, his chief adviser.

McGraw-Frisch Also Split.

There was also a rupture between McGraw and Frisch, who suddenly left the team last August in St. Louis and came home. Frisch was angered by McGraw's biting remarks and by the manager's intention to switch him to third base.

The trouble was smoothed over, but Frisch, after being ill for some time, was fined $500 when he returned to uniform. It was a foregone conclusion then that this season would be his last as a Giant.

Not since the sale of Ruth to the Yankees in 1920 has there been a baseball trade which might be compared with the trading of a world's championship manager and possibly the flashiest second baseman of any day.

Last year was Hornsby's eleventh full season with the Cardinals. He played minor league ball at Dallas and Dennison, Texas, in 1914 and was sold to St. Louis on Aug. 20, 1915, for the munificent sum of $500. For five years alternating among shortstop, third base and second, he finally drifted to the latter position.

At the same time his tremendous hitting began to attract attention. His first big year was 1920, when he batted .370. After reaching .397 the next year, he went over the .400 mark in 1922, 1924 and 1925.

His .424 in 1924 established a new modern major league batting mark. In 1922 he hit forty-two homers, still the National League record. His batting feats eclipsed even those of Delehanty and Honus Wagner. Last year he was voted the most valuable player in his league.

Frisch, a baseball and football star at Fordham, joined the Giants in 1919 after the Yanks had bid unsuccessfully

for him. He became a full-fledged regular in 1921, hit .341 that year and .348 in 1923, his greatest season.

Frisch was probably the best of all world's series players and holds a record in having hit .300 or better in four series. His spectacular fielding and dazzling speed made him a popular favorite, but he was below form in both 1925 and 1926, hitting only .314 last season.

Ring was a star for the Reds in the world's series of 1919. In 1921 he was traded to the Phillies and last Winter to the Giants for Dean, Bentley and cash. He pitched only five full games for McGraw and had a record of 11 won and ten lost.

December 21, 1926

NEUN'S TRIPLE PLAY CHECKS INDIAN RALLY

Feat, Second in Two Days, Comes in Ninth to Clinch Detroit Victory, 1 to 0.

DETROIT, May 31 (AP).—The breaks of a tight game favored Johnny Neun, Detroit first baseman, in the game with the Indians here today and he executed one of the rarest of baseball plays—an unassisted triple play.

His lightning action also won the game for the Tigers, 1 to 0, by retiring the three Cleveland runners in the ninth inning who threatened to tally after the Indians had been held scoreless for eight innings.

Myatt batted for Buckeye in the Cleveland half of the ninth and drew the second pass issued by Collins. Jamieson bunted toward first and beat it out, putting Myatt on second. Summa lined to Neun, who took the ball standing still, ran over and tagged Jamieson between first and second and continued to second base, landing there before Myatt could return.

The box score:

CLEVELAND (A.).	ab.	r.	h.	po.	a.	e.		DETROIT (A.).	ab.	r.	h.	po.	a.	e.
Jamieson, lf.	3	0	1	1	0	0		Warner, 3b.	4	1	1	1	1	0
Summa, rf.	4	0	1	1	0	0		Gehringer, 2b.	3	0	0	1	3	0
Fonseca, 2b.	3	0	0	3	5	0		Manush, cf.	3	0	1	1	0	0
Burns, 1b.	3	0	0	10	0	0		Fothergill, lf.	3	0	1	2	0	0
J. Sewell, ss.	3	0	0	3	2	0		Heilmann, rf.	3	0	0	0	0	0
L. Sewell, c.	3	0	1	0	3	1		Neun, 1b.	3	0	1	18	0	0
Nels, cf.	3	0	1	3	0	0		Tavener, ss.	3	0	1	3	1	2
Hodapp, 3b.	3	0	0	3	3	0		Woodall, c.	2	0	0	2	1	0
Buckeye, p.	2	0	0	0	2	0		Collins, p.	2	0	1	0	9	0
aMyatt	0	0	0	0	0	0								
Total	27	0	4	24	15	1		Total	26	1	6	27	17	0

aBatted for Buckeye in ninth.

Cleveland .... 0 0 0 0 0 0 0 0 0—0
Detroit .... 1 0 0 0 0 0 0 0 0—1

Three-base hit—L. Sewell. Double plays—Hodapp, Fonseca and Burns; J. Sewell, Fonseca and Burns; Collins, Gehringer, Fonseca and Burns; Collins, Gehringer and Neun. Triple play—Neun (unassisted). Left on bases—Cleveland 2, Detroit 3. Bases on balls—Off Buckeye 3, Collins 2. Struck out—By Collins 1. Umpires—Evans, Hildebrand and McGowan. Time of game—1:34.

June 1, 1927

LACK OF BASEBALLS HELPED PAUL WANER

Used Corncobs Instead in Kid Days and Developed Perfect Timing Ability.

IS NATURAL .300 HITTER

Pirate Star Never Under That Mark in Five Years—Comes From a Baseball Family.

If the Pirates get into the world's series with the Yankees the fans will have a chance to watch one of baseball's most sensational young players parading in the same territory as that famous home-run maker Babe Ruth, and there are those followers of the national pastime who predict that Paul Waner will outshine the illustrious Babe. The fans also will see, if Barney Dreyfuss's boys get into the classic in the final sprint in the next few days, the rather unusual sight of two brothers playing in the outfield on one team. For Paul Waner is flanked in centre field by no less a player than Lloyd Waner, his younger but hardly less brilliant brother.

The story of the sudden rise of the Waner brothers is very interesting, and the climax of their present scintillating performances in the National League pennant race has not yet been reached. In the last official batting averages Paul Waner is leading the National League and Brother Lloyd is running only a few jumps back, being separated from his brother by only the bulky form of Rogers Hornsby of the Giants, the runner-up to Paul. There also is a chance that Lloyd will pass Hornsby, and for the first time make it possible for brothers to be the leader and runner-up in a major league batting race.

Paul Waner was the first of this fast-fielding, hard-hitting pair to break into the big leagues. Paul made his bow last year and Lloyd did not come to the Pirates until this season. Paul started his active professional baseball career with the San Francisco club of the Pacific Coast League in 1923, and for three years was a sensation in that circuit, both as a fielder and as a batter, so much so, in fact, that the Pirate scouts paid a handsome sum for his release, along with Hal Rhyne, and made him a member of the Pirates' 1926 outfit.

Paul played in 144 games last season, becoming a regular from the start and making good with such a vengeance that he soon stood out as the greatest find of the season. He wound up the year with a batting average of .336, which is more than fair for a first-year man.

Never Batted Under .300.

As a matter of fact, to bat at less than a .300 pace would be strange for Paul. He started with San Francisco in 1923 and compiled an average of .369, came back the following season with .356 and then rolled up the best he ever has enjoyed, .401. That distinguished mark attracted the eyes of the major league scouts, who soon camped upon his trail with tempting offers. Paul has been hitting a pace of better than .375 in the National League for some weeks.

Paul, and Lloyd as well, was born with baseball in their blood, for their father had been a player back in the days of Cap Anson and his Chicago White Stockings. He could have been one of Cap's players, but refused the offer that Anson made

for his services, for he then was a star in the old Three-Eye League. Baseball did not pay so well in those days, and the elder Waner decided that, as a family man, he ought to look into the future. So he moved to Oklahoma City, purchased a farm just outside of the city, and it was on this farm that Paul, and then Lloyd, got their first baseball lessons.

The baseball fever never entirely died out of the elder Waner, and when his boys grew big enough to be initiated into the fundamentals of the game Papa Waner went out instructing them. In 1905 Papa Waner organized a team that consisted of members of the Waner and Beaver families, Mrs. Waner having been one of the Beaver clan. Paul wasn't a member of that team, however, because Paul was only 3 years old at the time. But he still remembers that team, the first he ever saw in action.

Baseball having been in his blood, it was no wonder that he demanded his chance to learn the game, and under the tutelage of his father became an apt pupil. However, baseball with baseballs did not furnish all of the early education that made Paul Waner the batter that he is, according to his own version of it. As a matter of fact, that keen batting eye, that perfect timing that has made many a manager sit up in admiration, came from the very lack of baseballs.

Used Corncob for Ball.

Out on that particular farm there were times when baseballs weren't always available and when this sad state of affairs threatened to keep Paul idle from his favorite pastime of swinging a bat at something he would collect whatever kids there were about, boys from adjoining farms and from his own immediate family, and down in the old pasture these boys would gather to play base-

ball without baseballs, substituting instead of the leather sphere the homely corncob.

"There is nothing in the world that will take a freakish spin, a sudden hop, a wide, sweeping curve like a corncob," says Paul. "The kids used to toss these cobs up as hard as they could. They would get hold of a short cob between the index finger and the thumb and let go. Whiz, it would come screaming up, and, believe me I mean it, they would scream. There were more curves in those corncob games than I have ever seen in a baseball game.

"Well, I used to bat against those corncobs just as the other boys did, only I became obsessed with the idea of mastering the hitting of them. I really believe that this constant practice at hitting at those strange curves of the corncob did more than anything else to build up my batting. In the first place, it made my eyes keen. You had to keep your eye peeled on the cob that came swishing up, because if it hit you in the eye it might blind you and if it hit you any place on the head it would hurt and probably leave a bad cut.

"So I had to keep my eye on the cob all the time. That is the secret of batting in baseball. You have to keep that ball in your eye from the minute it leaves the pitcher's hand until you hit it with your bat or it misses your bat. When you have that ability, to keep your eye on the ball down as sort of second nature and have learned to swing at just the right time you can hit. So corncob baseball did a lot for me, after all."

Times Wide World Photo.

Paul Waner, Brilliant Batting Star of the Pirates.

September 25, 1927

RUTH CRASHES 60TH TO SET NEW RECORD

Babe Makes It a Real Field Day by Accounting for All Runs in 4-2 Victory

1921 MARK OF 59 BEATEN

Fans Go Wild as Ruth Pounds Ball Into Stands With One On, Breaking 2-2 Tie

CONNECTS LAST TIME UP

Zachary's Offering Converted Into Epochal Smash, Which Old Fan Catches—Senators Then Subside

Babe Ruth scaled the hitherto unattained heights yesterday. Home run 60, a terrific smash off the southpaw pitching of Zachary, nestled in the Babe's favorite spot in the right field bleachers, and before the roar had ceased it was found that this drive not only had made home run record history but also was the winning margin in a 4 to 2 victory over the Senators. This also was the Yanks' 109th triumph of the season. Their last league game of the year will be played today.

When the Babe stepped to the plate in that momentous eighth inning the score was deadlocked. Koenig was on third base, the result of a triple, one man was out and all was tense. It was the Babe's fourth trip to the plate during the afternoon, a base on balls and two singles resulting on his other visits plateward.

The first Zachary offering was a fast one, which sailed over for a called strike. The next was high. The Babe took a vicious swing at the third pitched ball and the bat connected with a crash that was audible in all parts of the stand. It was not necessary to follow the course of the ball. The boys in the bleachers indicated the route of the record homer. It dropped about half way to the top. No. 60 was some homer, a fitting wallop to top the Babe's record of 58 in 1921.

While the crowd cheered and the Yankee players roared their greetings the Babe made his triumphant, almost regal tour of the paths. He jogged around slowly, touched each bag firmly and carefully and when he imbedded his spikes in the rubber disk to record officially Homer 60 hats were tossed into the air, papers were torn up and tossed liberally and the spirit of celebration permeated the place.

The Babe's stroll out to his position was the signal for a handkerchief salute in which all the bleacherites, to the last man, participated. Jovial Babe entered into the carnival spirit and punctuated his Ringly strides with a succession of snappy military salutes.

Ruth 4, Senators 2

Ruth's homer was a fitting climax to a game which will go down as the Babe's personal triumph. The Yanks scored four runs, the Babe personally crossing the plate three times and bringing in Koenig for the fourth. So this is one time where it would be fair, although not original, to record Yankee victory 109 as Ruth 4, Senators 2.

There was not much else to the game. The 10,000 persons who came to the Stadium were there for no other purpose than to see the Babe make home run history. After each of Babe's visits to the plate the expectant crowd would relax and wait for his next effort. They saw him open with a base on balls, follow with two singles and then clout the epoch-making circuit smash.

The only unhappy individual within the Stadium was Zachary. He realized he was going down in the records as the historical home run victim, in other words the goat. Zachary was one of the most interested spectators of the home run fight. He tossed his glove to the ground, muttered to himself, turned to his mates for consolation and got everything but that. There is no denying that Zachary was putting everything he had on the ball. No pitcher likes to have recorded after his name the fact that he was Ruth's victim on his sixtieth homer.

The ball that the Babe drove, according to word from official sources, was a pitch that was fast, low and on the inside. The Babe puffed away from the plate, then stepped into the ball, and wham! According to Umpire Bill Dinneen at the plate and Catcher Muddy Ruel the ball traveled on a line and landed a foot inside fair territory about half way to the top of the bleachers. But when the ball reached the bleacher barrier it was about ten feet fair and curving rapidly to the right.

Fan Rushes to Babe With Ball

The ball which became Homer 60 was caught by Joe Forner of 1937 First Avenue, Manhatta . He is about 40 years old and has been following baseball for thirty-five, according to his own admission. He was far from modest and as soon as the game was over rushed to the dressing room to let the Babe know who had the ball.

For three innings both sides were blanked. The Senators broke through in the fourth for two runs.

The Yanks came back with one run in their half of the fourth. Ruth opened with a long single to right and moved to third on Gehrig's single to centre. Gehrig took second on the throw to third. Meusel drove deep to Goslin, Ruth scoring and Gehrig taking third after the catch.

With two out in the sixth Ruth singled to right. Gehrig's hit was so fast that it went right through Gillis for a single, Ruth holding second. The Babe tied the score on Meusel's single to centre. Lazzeri was an easy third out.

The box score:

WASHINGTON (A)	ab	r	h	po	a	e
Rice, rf	3	0	1	2	0	0
Harris, 2b	3	0	0	3	4	0
Genzel, cf	4	0	1	1	0	0
Gostin, lf	4	1	1	5	0	0
Judge, 1b	4	0	0	5	0	0
Ruel, c	2	1	1	2	0	0
Riuege, 3b	3	0	1	1	4	0
Gillis, ss	4	0	0	2	1	0
Zachary, p	2	0	0	0	1	0
aJohnson	1	0	0	0	0	0
Total	30	2	5	24	10	0

NEW YORK (A.)	ab	r	h	po	a	e
Combs, cf	4	0	0	3	0	0
Koenig, ss	4	1	1	3	5	0
Ruth, rf	3	3	3	4	0	0
Gehrig, 1b	4	0	2	10	0	1
Meusel, lf	9	0	1	3	0	0
Lazzeri, 2b	3	0	0	2	2	0
Dugan, 3b	3	0	1	1	1	0
Benguogh, c	8	0	1	1	2	0
Piperas, p	2	0	0	0	2	0
Pennock, p	1	0	0	0	1	0
Total	30	4	0	25	13	1

a Batted for Zachary in nineth.

Washington .... 0 0 0 2 0 0 0 0 0 -2
New York .... 0 0 0 1 0 1 0 2 -4

Two-base hit—Rice, Tree-base hit—Koenig. Home run—Ruth. Stolen bases—Ruel. Bluerge, Rice. Sacrifices—Meusert. Double plays—Harris and Bruege. Gillis, Harris and Judge. Left on bases—New York 4, Washington 7. Bases on balls—Off Pipgras 4, Pennock, 1, Zachary 1. Struck out—By Zachary 1. Hits—Off Pipgras 4 in 6 innings. Pennock 1 in 3. Hit by pitcher—By Pipgras (Rice). Winning pitcher—Pennock. Umpires—Dinneen, Connolly and Owens. Time of game—1:38.

October 1, 1927

YANKEES WIN TWICE AND PASS ATHLETICS

Record Throng Sees Hugmen Put Pace-Setters to Rout, 5-0 and 7-3.

VICTORS 1½ GAMES AHEAD

Pipgras Masters Mackmen in 1st Game—Yanks, Blanked Till 6th, Fall on Quinn.

MEUSEL DECIDES 2D FRAY

Hits Homer Off Rommel With the Bases Filled in 8th, Breaking 3-3 Deadlock.

By RICHARDS VIDMER.

The Yanks are looking up again. But not at the Athletics.

Before the largest crowd that ever saw a baseball game in the United States, Asia, Africa, Australia or other parts, the champions of the world rose in their wrath and battered their way into the American League leadership again at the Yankee Stadium yesterday.

Twice they beat the Athletics, who came into Ruppert's ramparts with a half-game lead over the Yanks. Twice the Yankees turned them back convincingly, and when the twin bill ended gray shadows were creeping across the field and five hours of baseball had ended. The Yanks were leading the pack once more with a margin of a game and a half over their only rivals.

A crowd of 85,265 cheered and chortled while George Pipgras shut out the Athletics in the first game, 5 to 0.

The same multitude stayed to be thrown into a state of hysteria in the second game, while the lead swayed back and forth until finally Bob Meusel broke a tie in the eighth inning by the most emphatic means known to science. He hit a home run with the bases filled. The Yankees won, 7 to 3.

Fans Go Wild With Delight.

When Homer smote his bloomin' lyre he didn't make any more music than Meusel did when he smote that mighty homer. From the grand stands and the bleachers, from the boxes and the runways came a scream of delight from the frenzied thousands. Hats were hurled onto the field—old straw hats, new felt hats, derbies and caps. Torn and tattered score cards fell in flakes and covered the diamond like dust. Pandemonium reigned and a hoarse shout couldn't be heard more than a foot away.

Until just a few moments before, Rube Walberg, the Athletics' famous southpaw, had held the Yanks to one meagre hit over the span of six innings. In the seventh the Yanks had come from behind to tie the score. And then in the eighth Meusel's clout broke the tie, broke the tense silence and probably broke the Athletics' hearts.

The Athletics ought to be convinced by now that they can't beat the Yankees. Not very often. anyway. Up to the present the Yanks have won fifteen games from the A's and the Philadelphians have taken only five from the Yanks There are still two more games to be played, one on Tuesday and the last on Wednesday, but the sluggin' Huggins crew is flying high again. The Yanks had a taste of second place and they don't like it. They'll be hard to catch from here on.

Quinn Meets Waterloo.

Old Jack Quinn, who was pitching for the Yankees when they played in the Highlands and Pipgras played with dolls, was knocked out of the box by an uprising that broke a scoreless tie in the sixth inning of the first game.

Combs, Koenig and Gehrig all hit safely to start that rally, which netted three runs, and Lazzeri put the finishing touches on it with a single. He also put a finish to Quinn's working day with the same blow. Eddie Rommel, who also served for part of the second game, relieved him, and in turn was relieved by Oswald Orwoll.

The Yanks made three hits off Orwoll in the eighth, adding two runs to their total. The Athletics made, in all, only nine off Pipgras, who spread them out where they would do the least harm.

Fred Heimach faced the Athletics in the second game and made a one-run lead stand up for him until the sixth, when Simmons hit a home run with a man on and drove the A's to the front.

Yanks Finally Reach Walberg.

But the thundering Yanks, who hadn't thundered against Walberg for six sessions, making only one hit, came back in the seventh to tie the score, Walberg's wildness filling the bases and then forcing in the tying run. Then in the eighth they smashed their way to the fore once more with Rommel in the box again.

Back in the lead, the Yanks should be hard to catch from now on.

The pitching was all that could be desired, Pipgras and Heimach holding the mackmen scoreless in fourteen consecutive innings, and though the Yankees made only six hits in the second game off Walberg and Rommel, they had the habit of getting them in bunches, and that's when they do the most damage.

The fielding was fine, even though a couple of errors developed around the keystone sack in the second game, but most heartening of all was the dash and fire with which the Yankees played. They emerged from their recent lethargy. They had speed, they had brains, and their eyes were wide open to opportunity at all times.

For five innings the first game was as void of runs as the grand stands were of empty seats. The Yanks made only three hits off the ancient deceptions of Jack Quinn in that span, and only because Pipgras was just as puzzling to the Athletics did the game stay on an even keel.

The A's hit safely in every inning except the third, and they even went so far as to make two in the fifth, but Pipgras bore down with his iron arm when men were on bases and each attack was turned back as it threatened.

But in the sixth, after Pipgras had held off the Athletics for one more frame, the slugging Hugmen broke out with the sort of thunder that made them feared from Boston to St. Louis and earned them the title of the ball busters from the Bronx.

Combs led off with a singing single to centre. Koenig sunk another in the same sector. Gehrig doubled, scoring Combs with the first run, which proved to be the only necessary tally of the contest. However, the Yanks weren't taking any chances on what might happen later. With sails set they kept on sailing.

Box Score of First Game.

PHILADELPHIA (A).

	AB.	R.	H.	PO.	A.	E.
Bishop, 2b	4	0	1	1	3	1
Haas, c. f.	4	0	2	3	0	0
Cochrane, c.	3	0	0	5	2	0
Simmons, l. f.	3	0	1	1	0	0
Foxx, 1b.	4	0	1	10	0	0
Miller, r. f.	4	0	0	2	0	0
Dykes, 3b	4	0	2	1	2	0
Boley, s. s.	3	0	0	1	2	0
aE. Collins	1	0	1	0	0	0
Quinn, p.	2	0	1	0	2	0
Rommel, p.	0	0	0	0	0	0
bFrench	1	0	0	0	0	0
Orwoll, p.	1	0	0	0	0	0
Total	34	0	9	24	11	1

NEW YORK (A).

	AB.	R.	H.	PO.	A.	E.
Combs, c. f.	4	1	2	2	0	0
Koenig, s. s.	4	1	2	2	1	0
Gehrig, 1b.	3	2	2	7	2	0
Ruth, r. f.	3	1	1	1	0	0
Meusel, l. f.	2	0	0	1	0	0
Lazzeri, 2b.	4	0	3	4	2	0
Durocher, 2b.	0	0	0	0	0	0
cPaschal	1	0	0	0	0	0
Robertson, 3b.	2	0	0	2	1	0
Dugan, 3b.	0	0	0	0	0	0
Bengough, c.	4	0	1	7	2	0
Pipgras, p.	4	0	2	1	0	0
Total	31	5	11	27	10	0

a Batted for Boley in ninth.
b Batted for Rommel in eighth.
c Batted for Robertson in eighth.

Philadelphia ...0 0 0 0 0 0 0 0 0—0
New York.....0 0 0 0 0 3 0 2 ..—5

Runs batted in—eGehrig, Meusel, Lazzeri 2.
Two-base hits—Dykes, Gehrig. Ruth, Lazzeri. Three-base hits—Simmons, Gehrig. Sacrifices—Gehrig, Robertson, Meusel 2. Left on bases—Philadelphia 9, New York 7. Bases on balls—Off Pipgras 2, Quinn 1. Struck out—By Pipgras 7, Quinn 2. Rommel 2. Hits—Off Quinn 7 in 5 1-3 innings, Rommel 0 in 1 2-3, Orwoll 4 in 1. Losing pitcher—Quinn. Umpires—McGowan at the plate, Owens at first base, Nallin at second base, Dineen at third base. Time of game—2:08.

Meusel's Fly Scores Koenig.

Ruth was purposely passed, filling the bases, and then Meusel drove Miller back to the running track for his long fly, which scored Koenig and moved Gehrig to third. Still moving along in the right direction. Lazzeri whipped a single to right that sent Gehrig plodding home. It also sent Quinn through the shadows of the dugout. The old man had gone too far.

Rommel replaced him and not only ended the outburst, but held the Yankees hitless and helpless through the seventh. But he gave way to a pinch hitter in the first half of the eighth. Orwoll faced the Yanks in the last half and they broke out in another barrage.

Gehrig drove a ball far over Haas's head in deep centre field and tore around the bases like a wild bull in full flight. He was stopped at third by the upraised hand of Arthur Fletcher, coaching there, but Bishop dropped Haas's throw to the infield and the same hand waved the galloping Gehrig on again and he scored. It was a triple, but it might have been a home run if he had kept running.

Ruth drove a double to right, and after Meusel had sacrificed the Babe to third, Lazzeri came through with his third straight hit and sent Ruth home with the second run of the inning and the fifth and last of the game.

Though Quinn passed out, Rommel passed in and out, and Orwoll finally finished. Pipgras kept along his even way, allowing a hit here and another there, but keeping them so widely scattered that they did no material harm. Only in the eighth was he in any real danger and in that crisis, with the bases filled, two

Box Score of Second Game.

PHILADELPHIA (A).

	AB.	R.	H.	PO.	A.	E.
Bishop, 2b.	4	1	0	1	2	0
Haas, c. f.	5	1	1	1	0	0
Cochrane, c.	4	0	2	7	0	0
Perkins, c.	0	0	0	0	0	0
aE. Collins	1	0	0	0	0	0
Simmons, l. f.	4	1	2	3	0	0
Foxx, 1b	4	0	0	8	0	0
Miller, r. f.	4	0	1	2	0	0
Dykes, 3b.	2	0	1	0	0	0
Boley, ss.	4	0	1	2	3	0
Walberg, p.	3	0	0	0	2	0
Rommel, p.	1	0	0	0	0	0
Total	36	3	8	24	7	0

NEW YORK (A).

	AB.	R.	H.	PO.	A.	E.
Combs, c. f.	3	1	1	5	0	0
Koenig, s. s.	4	1	1	1	7	1
Gehrig, 1b.	4	1	1	12	0	0
Ruth, r. f.	3	2	0	1	0	0
Meusel, l. f.	4	2	2	1	0	0
Durocher, 2b.	0	0	0	0	1	0
Dugan, 3b.	2	0	0	0	0	0
bPaschal	1	0	1	0	0	0
Hoyt, p.	1	0	0	0	1	0
Bengough, c.	2	0	0	4	0	0
cGazella, 3b.	2	0	0	0	0	0
Heimach, p.	2	0	0	0	2	0
Moore, p.	0	0	0	0	0	0
dP. Collins	0	0	0	0	2	0
Total	30	7	6	27	14	2

a Batted for Perkins in ninth.
b Batted for Dugan in seventh.
c Batted for Bengough in seventh.
d Batted for Moore in seventh.

Philadelphia ...0 0 0 0 0 2 1 0 0—3
New York.....1 0 0 1 0 0 4 1 ..—7

Runs batted in—Simmons 3, Koenig, Paschal, Collins, Meusel 4.
Two-base hit—Gehrig. Three-base hit—Combs. Home runs—Simmons, Meusel. Stolen base—Paschal. Sacrifice—Dykes. Left on bases—Philadelphia 9, New York 4. Bases on balls—Off Heimach 2, Walberg 4, Rommel 1. Struck out—By Heimach 3, Moore 1, Hoyt 1, Walberg 6. Hits—Off Heimach 7 in 6 2-3 innings, Moore 0 in 1-3, Hoyt 1 in 2, Walberg 3 in 6 2-3, Rommel 3 in 1 1-3. Winning pitcher—Hoyt. Losing pitcher—Rommel. Umpires—Owens at plate, Nallin at first base, Dineen at second base, McGowan at third base. Time of game—2:15.

out and the Yanks three runs ahead, he fanned Jimmy Foxx in the pinch.

Pipgras Extricates Himself.

He started the inning by striking out French, who was sent in to pinch hit for Rommel, but couldn't obey orders. Bishop singled, but was forced at second by Haas, so there were two out and no indication of danger. Then suddenly with no warning, Pipgras lost control. Up to that point he had not passed a man, but he walked two in succession, Cochrane and Simmons.

Here was the sort of situation from which heroes emerge. The bases were filled, two were out, the Athletics were three runs behind and the youthful Jimmy Foxx faced the opportunity of a life time. A home run would send his team out in front. But the responsibility was too much for a 19-year-old kid.

Jimmy didn't hit a home run. He didn't even hit a triple, a double, or a single. He didn't hit anything, as a matter of fact, he struck out.

And that was the last chance the Athletics had, for the next time they came to bat a home run with the bases filled would not have done them any good. They were five runs behind, instead of three. Anyway, they did not even get the bases filled.

Pipgras was the master all the way in that first game. The A's never had a chance of winning because they never made a run.

Combs Starts With Triple.

Combs battered a triple to left, starting off for the Yanks in the

Crowd in Right and Centre Field Bleachers at Yankee Stadium Yesterday.

Mayor James J. Walker (Left) and John E. McGeehan, District Attorney of the Bronx.

Times Wide World Photos.

Miller Huggins, Yankee Manager (Left), Exchanging Greetings With Connie Mack, Manager of Athletics.

second game, and scored on Koenig's infield out. But that was the last hit the Yanks made off Walberg until the seventh inning. In fact, the next seventeen batsmen were retired in order. Still, that run seemed quite sufficient until the sixth, for the Athletics were doing no more damage to Heimach.

Haas beat out an infield single in the first and Dykes and Boley each hit safely in the fifth, but otherwise the A's were as harmless and practically as helpless as canaries in a cage. It seemed as though Heimach was going to keep them that way, but Cochrane was called safe on a hit to Dugan to start the sixth.

though it looked as though he was out. Then Simmons hit his homer. It wasn't a mighty clout. It wasn't even a screaming liner. It was just a high fly that fell barely over the screen in right field, but it served the purpose, which was to put the Athletics ahead. Cochrane scored in front of Simmons and the Yanks found themselves trailing by one run instead of leading by the same margin.

That was bad enough in view of Walberg's pitching, but when the A's made another run in the seventh it was worse. With one out, Bishop walked. Haas grounded to Koenig, who started what he confidently expected to be a double play, but it wasn't. Lazzeri dropped the throw at second and instead of getting two out, the Yanks didn't get any.

Cochrane forced Haas at second, but Bishop moved to third, from where he scored when Simmons singled to centre. This man Simmons was getting to be a pest. Already he had driven in three runs.

The Yanks were two runs in arrears when Walberg weakened in the Seventh. Koenig, the first man up, walked and was forced at second by Ruth, but Meusel singled to short. Lazzeri popped to Boley for the second out and hope wasn't what might be called high. But Paschal batted for Dugan and singled to right, scoring Ruth, and the Yanks needed only one run to tie.

At that crucial point Walberg had a lapse of memory. He couldn't for the life of him remember where the plate had been. Gazella batted for Bengough and walked, filling the bases. Collins batted for Moore, who had taken Heimach's place in box, and Collins also walked, forcing in the run that tied the score.

With all this walking going on, Connie Mack decided that Walberg might just as well join the procession. He did—in the direction of the clubhouse. Rommell appeared on the scene for the second time and quelled the uprising. But only temporarily. Hoyt having halted the Athletics in their half of the eighth, the Yanks came in for their turn with the score still 6-1, 3—3.

Koenig singled to centre. Gehrig doubled to centre. Ruth was purposely passed and the bases were filled, the score tied and none out. Then up stepped Bob Meusel. He drove the ball into the left field stands for a home run. That ended all argument, at least for the day. But the Athletics will be back, still striving and struggling tomorrow.

September 10, 1928

BASEBALL PROVIDED TWO GREAT RACES

Most Thrilling Season in Major Leagues Since 1908—Athletics a Power Again.

YANKEES RULED SUPREME

Routing Cards, They Won Second World Series in Row in Four Straight Games.

By JOHN DREBINGER.

A pair of thrilling pennant races, the like of which had not been seen running concurrently in the two major leagues in twenty years; banner attendances, which included an all-time record crowd for a single day, and a dramatic world series that witnessed a team score a four-game sweep for the second year in succession, combined to make the baseball season of 1928 one of those red-letter campaigns similar to 1905, 1908 and 1914, which doubtless will be remembered as long as the game is played.

It was back in 1908 that the Tigers, Indians and White Sox carried their American League race right down to the final day, while the Cubs and Giants had to battle still an extra day to break their deadlock. In 1928 history almost repeated itself.

A review of the season past is largely a story of the fortunes of the the Yanks—the wonder team of 1927 and an even more amazing outfit in 1928. As the Spring training season got under way ominous reports sifted north that the championship team of the year before possibly had passed its peak and soon would follow the trail of all great teams. It lost numerous exhibition games to minor league clubs.

Once the championship campaign started, however, the Yanks again hit their stride. Before midseason they once more had spreadeagled the field, and on July 1 they held a lead of thirteen and a half games over the Athletics, who were the next best in the league.

Yanks Struck a Slump.

Then came August and the Yanks began to lose, and misfortune struck them simultaneously. The arm of Wilcy Moore, their effective relief hurler of 1927, went bad. Herb Pennock, southpaw ace, suffered a similar ailment, and Tony Lazzeri, crack second baseman, contracted trouble in his right shoulder that impaired his playing.

Meanwhile the Athletics continued to win. Mack, making a heroic effort to win his first pennant since 1914, had added Tris Speaker and Ty Cobb at the outset of the race, but now he benched both veterans and made frequent shifts among his youngsters with satisfactory results.

By the end of August the Yanks' lead had been whittled to less than three games; on Sept. 7 the teams were tied, and on Sept. 8, though the Yanks beat the Senators, the A's won twice from the Red Sox and Mack was on top in the American League for the first time in fourteen years.

But his joy was short lived. On the following day the Yanks and A's met in a double-header at the Stadium and 85,265 persons, the greatest crowd ever to turn out in baseball on a single afternoon, saw the Yanks crush the Mackmen twice. They

Photo by Freudy
MILLER HUGGINS,
Who Again Led the Yankees to the World's Championship.

broke even in the two remaining games of the series, and then the two headed West with the Yanks again in front.

Yanks Won Flag on Sept. 28.

From then it was a grueling tussle, but the Yanks never again relinquished the lead. They clinched the race on Sept. 28 and finished two and a half games in front on Sept. 30.

The National League race furnished an equally thrilling race, though fought along entirely different lines. It was one of those free-for-all battles in which five or six teams at various times threatened to break through and win.

During the early stages the Reds, Giants, Cards and Robins furnished most of the contention. The Cards went into the lead on June 16, but though they remained there to the end they never were able to shake off the remainder of the field. By August the Reds and Robins faded, leaving the fight to the Cards, Giants and Cubs.

Near the end of August the Giants received a stunning blow in losing eight games in a row, only to rally and make a tremendous bid for the pennant in the closing month. On Sept. 26, after the Cubs had been put out of the race by the Robins, only a half game separated the Giants from the Cards.

But a disastrous series with the Cubs wrecked the Giant hopes, and on Sept. 29 the Cards clinched their second pennant in three years. The Giants finished two games behind and the Cubs two behind the Giants.

Yanks Supreme in World Series.

What happened in the world series scarcely needs repeating. It saw the Yanks, crippled and bruised, the shortenders in the betting, and with Earl Combs added to the hospital list on the eve of the classic, rise to their greatest heights. They won four straight, repeating what they had done to the Pirates in 1927. The receipts were $777,290, and the climax came in the final game, when Babe Ruth smashed three homers out of Sportsman Park in St. Louis.

The year was surprisingly free from spectacular events off the field of play, although a trade by the Giants which sent Hornsby to the Braves in exchange for Hogan, a first-year catcher, and Welsh created consternation at the time. Hornsby subsequently became manager of the Braves, but at the close of the season was sold to the Cubs.

December 30, 1928

CARDS VICTORS, 28-6, SET SCORING MARK

Eclipse Modern Record for Runs in One Game by 1 in Second of Twin Bill With Phils.

END SLUMP OF 11 IN ROW

Two 10-Run Drives in First and Fifth Feature Nightcap After St Louis Loses Opener, 10-6.

PHILADELPHIA, July 6 (Æ).—The Cardinals' losing streak was broken today. After dropping the first game of a double-header to the Phillies, 10—6, the Missourians turned about and crushed the Shottonmen under an avalanche of twenty-eight hits that chased a like amount of runs over the plate, thus defeating the Phillies, 28 to 6. The Cards had lost eleven games in a row.

Willoughby, Miller, Roy and Green, who worked in that order in the second game, failed to stop the Cardinals at any time.

Two of the big blows in this game were home-run blasts with the bases loaded. The first was by Jim Bottomley and the second by Chick Hafey. In the first game Bottomley hit two homers to make his record nineteen. Klein of the Phillies hit his twenty-first homer of the season in the first game, and Hafey's blow was his twenty-first circuit drive.

Wildness on the part of the Phil pitchers started the 1928 champions off with ten runs in the first inning, and the Westerners had another big round, the fifth, which saw ten more tallies tabulated on the scoring sheet.

While the Cardinals were doing all this to the Phil pitchers, Frankhouse was coasting through to an easy victory in spite of being hit for seventeen safeties that included a home run by Denny Sothern.

The box scores:

FIRST GAME.

ST. LOUIS (N)	ab.	r.	h.	po.	a.	e.		PHILADELPHIA (N)	ab.	r.	h.	po.	a.	e.
Douthit, cf.	5	0	1	5	0	0		Sothern, cf.	6	1	1	1	0	0
High, 3b.	5	2	4	1	0	0		O'Doul, lf.	4	3	3	2	0	0
Seiph, 2b.	1	0	0	0	0	0		Thomps'n, 2b	4	0	1	1	3	0
Frisch, 2b.	4	0	1	2	0	0		Hurst, 1b.	4	1	2	12	3	0
Bottomley, 1b	5	2	3	5	0	0		Whitney, 3b.	4	2	3	2	1	0
Hafey, lf.	5	1	1	2	0	0		Klein, rf.	5	2	2	1	0	0
Roettger, rf.	3	1	1	3	0	0		Thevenow, ss	3	0	1	5	5	0
Holm, rf.	1	0	0	0	0	0		Lerian, c.	2	0	1	5	0	0
Smith, c.	2	0	1	2	0	0		Benge, p.	1	0	0	0	1	0
Jennard, c.	1	0	0	3	0	0		Elliott, p.	1	0	0	0	1	0
Gelbert, ss.	4	0	3	1	5	0		cDavis	0	0	0	0	0	0
Sherdel, p.	5	0	6	0	1	0		dCollins	0	1	0	0	0	0
Johnson, p.	0	0	0	0	0	0								
aDelker	0	0	0	0	0	0								
bOrsatti	1	0	0	0	0	0								
Total	49	6	15	24	9	0		Total	36	10	15	27	14	0

a Ran for Smith in sixth.
b Batted for Roettger in seventh.
c Batted for Benge in seventh.
d Ran for Davis in seventh.

St. Louis ....0 0 0 4 0 0 2 0 0—6
Philadelphia ....0 0 0 2 4 1 3 0 .—10

Runs batted in—Bottomley 4, Gelbert 2, Whitney 2, Klein 2, Thevenow 1, Hurst 2, O'Doul 1, Thompson 1. Two-base hits—High, Lerian, O'Doul, Klein, Hurst. Home runs—Bottomley 2, Whitney, Klein. Sacrifices—Thompson, Thevenow. Hits—Off Benge 12 in 7 innings, Elliott 3 in 2, Sherdel 15 in 6 1-3, Johnson 0 in 1 2-3. Struck out—By Benge 2, Sherdel 4, Johnson 1, Elliott 1. Bases on balls—Off Benge 1, Sherdel 6, Johnson 1. Left on bases—St. Louis 8, Philadelphia 11. Double play—Hurst, Thevenow and Hurst. Wild pitch—Sherdel. Winning pitcher—Benge. Losing pitcher—Sherdel. Umpires—Rigler, Reardon and Hart. Time of game—2:20.

SECOND GAME.

ST. LOUIS (N)	ab.	r.	h.	po.	a.	e.		PHILADELPHIA (N)	ab.	r.	h.	po.	a.	e.
Douthit, cf.	4	5	4	5	2	0		Sothern, cf.	5	2	2	3	1	1
Seiph, 2b.	3	1	2	1	3	0		O'Doul, lf.	3	2	2	2	0	0
Delker,	3	2	1	3	1	0		Klein, rf.	5	0	2	2	0	0
High, 3b.	5	4	2	0	5	0		Hurst, 1b.	5	0	2	10	1	0
Bottomley, 1b	5	4	4	12	0	0		Whitney, 3b.	5	0	1	2	3	1
Hafey, lf.	7	4	5	6	0	0		Thompson, 2b	5	1	4	3	4	0
Holm, rf.	6	2	1	0	1	0		Thevenow, ss.	5	0	1	3	4	0
Wilson, c.	6	2	2	3	1	0		Davis, c.	4	0	1	3	1	0
Gelbert, ss.	6	3	2	0	3	4		Susce, c.	2	1	1	1	0	0
Frkhouse, p.	7	2	4	0	2	0		Willoughby, p.	0	0	0	0	0	0
								Miller, p.	0	0	0	0	0	0
								Roy, p.	2	0	0	0	0	0
								Green, p.	1	0	1	0	2	0
Total	55	28	28	27	16	0		Total	41	6	17	27	15	2

St. Louis ....10 1 0 2 10 0 0 5 0—28
Philadelphia .....2 1 0 1 0 0 0 1 1—6

Runs batted in—High 2, Bottomley 6, Hafey 5, Frankhouse 2, Thompson 2, Douthit 2, Wilson 3, Sothern 1, Seiph 1, Hurst 1, Holm 1, O'Doul 1, Thevenow 1. Two-base hits—Gelbert 2, Hafey 2, Green, Susce, Thevenow. Three-base hits—Seiph. Home runs — Sothern, Bottomley, Holm. Sacrifices—Holm, O'Doul. Hits—Off Willoughby 3 in 0 innings (none out in first), Miller 0 in 0 (walked only 2 batters to face him), Roy 13 in 4 1-3, Green 12 in 4 2-3. Struck out—By Green 1, Frankhouse 2. Base on balls—Off Willoughby 3, Frankhouse 3, Miller 2, Roy 1, Green 3. Hit by pitcher—By Green (High). Left on bases—St. Louis 11, Philadelphia 12. Double plays—Thevenow and Hurst; High, Seiph and Bottomley; Gelbert, Delker and Bottomley. Losing pitcher — Willoughby. Umpires — Reardon, Hart and Rigler. Time of game—2:28.

SCORING RECORD SURPASSED.

28 Runs by Cardinals Eclipse the Mark by Indians.

The Cardinals established a new modern major league record for most runs by a club in one game in the 28-to-6 victory over the Phillies yesterday, eclipsing by one run the total of 27 runs scored by the Indians against the Red Sox in a first game on July 7, 1923.

The Reds scored 26 runs against the Braves on June 4, 1916, and the Cubs recorded as many against the Phillies on Aug. 25, 1922. Prior to 1900, the Cubs won a 36-to-7 count against Louisville on June 29, 1897. The record for most runs by both clubs in one game is 49, made in the game between the Cubs and Phillies in 1922.

Before the organization of the National League the Mutuals of New York made 38 runs against Chicago in the National Association in 1874.

July 7, 1929

ALEXANDER EQUALS MATHEWSON'S FEAT

Beats Robins for Cards, 5-2, Tying League Record of 372 Games Won.

EXHIBITS PERFECT CONTROL

St. Louis Reaches Morrison for Four Runs in First Inning and Clinches Game.

By ROSCOE McGOWEN.

Special to The New York Times.

ST. LOUIS, Aug. 1.—By beating the Robins today, 5 to 2, Grover Cleveland Alexander, veteran right-hander of the Cardinals, equaled a record held by Christy Mathewson in the National League.

Alexander pitched himself into his 372d winning box score of the many years he has been a headliner in the National League. The veteran pitched a typical Alexander game, his greatest asset, control, being in evidence from start to finish. No bases on balls, no wild pitches or hit batters marred his performance. Alexander has been in the National League since 1911.

A first inning assault on Johnny Morrison gave Alex a four-run lead to work on and Jim Bottomley's twenty-third home run of the season added the fifth run in the eighth.

Del Bissonette bounced a home run off the right field pavilion roof in the fifth to give the Robins their first run and Bressler's double in the seventh followed by an infield out and Jake Flowers's sacrifice fly to Douthit made up the Brooklyn total.

Air-tight support kept him out of trouble several times, notably in each of the first three innings when three double plays, in all of which Frankie Frisch figured prominently, cleared the bases and stopped the Robins.

The fast time of the game was particularly fitting, as the contest was delayed in getting underway by the ceremonial greetings accorded to the Robin fliers, Jackson and O'Brine, who briefly occupied a special box near the Cardinal dugout.

Morrison was not threatened much after the first inning. In the fourth and sixth innings, Herman singled and Hendrick followed with a double, but the first time Herman was held at third and the next time thrown out at the plate on a fast relay, Roettger, Bottomley and Wilson.

Bissonette hit a long triple almost against the centre field wall in the ninth after two were out, but Frisch went far into right to nab Flowers's pop fly to end the game.

BROOKLYN (N.)	ab.	r.	h.	po.	a.	e.		ST. LOUIS (N.)	ab.	r.	h.	po.	a.	e.
Frederick, cf.	4	0	1	5	0	0		Douthit, cf.	4	0	1	4	1	0
Moore, ss.	1	0	0	0	0	0		High, 3b.	2	1	0	1	0	0
Bancroft, ss.	3	0	0	0	4	0		Frisch, 2b.	4	0	0	3	5	0
Herman, rf.	4	0	2	3	0	0		Bottomley.1b	4	2	2	11	1	0
Hendrick,3b.	4	0	3	0	1	0		Orsatti, lf.	3	1	1	3	0	0
Bressler, lf.	4	1	1	3	0	0		Roettger, rf.	4	1	3	3	0	0
Bissonette.1b	4	1	2	7	0	0		Gelbert, ss.	4	0	1	1	3	0
Flowers, 2b.	3	0	0	5	2	0		Wilson, c.	3	0	1	1	1	0
Henline, c.	3	0	2	1	1	0		Alexander, p.	3	0	0	0	1	0
Morrison, p.	3	0	0	0	0	0								
Total	33	2	11	24	8	0		Total	31	5	9	27	11	0

Brooklyn ....0 0 0 0 1 0 1 0 0—2
St. Louis ....4 0 0 0 0 0 0 1 .—5

Runs batted in—Roettger 2, Gelbert 2, Bissonette 1, Flowers 1, Bottomley 1. Two-base hits—Bottomley, Hendrick 2, Douthit, Wilson, Bressler. Three-base Hit—Bissonette. Home runs—Bissonette, Bottomley. Sacrifices—High, Flowers. Stolen base—Gelbert. Double plays—Frisch, Gelbert and Bottomley; Gelbert, Frisch and Bottomley; Frisch and Bottomley. Left on bases—St. Louis 5, Brooklyn 5. Umpires—Rigler, Jorda and Hart. Time of game—1:26.

August 2, 1929

63

ATHLETICS' 10 RUNS IN 7TH DEFEAT CUBS IN 4TH SERIES GAME

Trailing, 8-0, Mackmen Unleash Attack That Beats McCarthy's Men, 10-8, Before 30,000.

15 MEN BAT IN ONE INNING

Four Pitchers, Root, Nehf, Blake and Malone, Used Before Athletics Are Retired.

DYKES'S DOUBLE DECIDES

Simmons, Foxx and Dykes Each Get Two Hits in One Frame—Philadelphians Need One More Game.

By JOHN DREBINGER.

Special to The New York Times.

PHILADELPHIA, Pa., Oct. 12.—Somebody dropped a toy hammer on a stick of dynamite today and touched off an explosion that shook to its heels a continent that Christopher Columbus had discovered 437 years ago to the day.

It happened in the seventh inning of the fourth game of the world's series at a time when more than 30,000 spectators sat in the packed stands of Shibe Park steeped in despair. For all one knows, they may have been the same 30,000 who jammed these game stands the day before, for the number of paid admissions, 29,921, was exactly the same.

The receipts, $140,815, also were the same, making the total for the four games $718,679 and the total paid attendance 160,709. But the feelings of the crowd—all but those of the 500 loyal rooters of Chicago—were infinitely worse.

For the Athletics, beaten in the third game yesterday, were trailing, 8 to 0, and if there is anything at all that can appear certain in this most curious of all possible worlds it was that the Cubs would win this game and square the series at two all.

Chicago Rooters Stunned.

Then started the seventh and it brought in its wake a typhoon, tornado and hurricane, a rush of blood to the head of the spectators and the complete collapse of the 500 loyal rooters from Chicago as a surging Mack attack swept on and flattened all before it to roll up a total of ten runs for the inning.

And so to the Athletics went the fourth game of the series by a score of 10 to 8, and the hopes of the shattered Cub forces tonight are hanging on something slightly thinner than a thread. For the Athletics are now leading in this world's series by a margin of three victories to one, and

they need only one more game to conclude the struggle and win for themselves the lion's share of the spoils.

Never in all world series history was there such an inning. Records, large and small, collapsed in wholesale lots, while a crowd, held speechless for hours, howled itself into a perfect delirium and smashed a few more records.

Root Appeared Out for Revenge.

For six innings the bulky, stolid Charlie Root, whom the fates had treated rather unkindly in the first game in Chicago, appeared riding on his way to a merited revenge. Over the period he had held the mightiest of Mack sluggers in a grip of iron, allowing only three scattered hits and mowing them down as though they were men of straw.

And while Charlie was doing this the Cubs, at last thoroughly aroused, cuffed and battered four of Connie Mack's prized hurlers to all sectors of the field. They hammered Jack Quinn, who brought his forty-odd years and his famed spitball into the fray with high hopes only to carry both out badly shattered. They pulverized Rube Walberg and smashed Ed Rommel.

Charlie Grimm hit a homer, Rogers Hornsby hit a single and a triple. Kiki Cuyler hit three singles in a row, and the 500 loyal rooters from Chicago split their 500 throats. The Philadelphians tried hard to ignore them, but it is difficult to ignore 500 loyal rooters from Chicago.

It was warm and sunny, but the great crowd sulked and sat in silence as Al Simmons stepped to the plate to open the Athletic half of the seventh. Two and three-fifths seconds later the storm broke.

Simmons Collects Homer.

Simmons crashed a home-run on top of the roof of the left-field pavilion. It was Al's second circuit clout of the series and the crowd gave him a liberal hand, though the applause was still lacking in enthusiasm.

"Well," they said, "that at least saves us from a shutout."

But the rumbling continued and increased in volume. Jimmy Foxx singled to right. Bing Miller singled to centre and Jimmy Dykes singled to left. The Dykes' hit scored Foxx and when Joe Boley singled to centre Miller raced over the plate.

There was a momentary pause as the veteran George Burns, coming up in the role of pinch hitter, popped to Shortstop English but when Max Bishop laced a single to centre Dykes counted, the Athletics had four runs over and the Cub lead had been cut squarely in half.

By now the crowd had set up a terrifying din. The Cubs began to squirm uneasily and there was much activity on the Chicago bench as Manager Joe McCarthy waved frantically to four or five pitchers warming up furiously in the bull pen. Root was taken out of the box and Arthur Nehf, veteran lefthander, took his place.

There were two on the bases and only one out as George William Haas, called mule for short, stepped to the plate. A moment later there was a roar that almost shook the famed Liberty Bell off its pedestal six miles away.

Haas hit a long high fly to deep centre. The squat Hack Wilson, Cub centrefielder, wheeled about and ran at top speed, his short, stubby legs leaving nothing but a blur as they carried him over the ground. He got under the ball in time to make the catch, but as it came down it crossed the glaring sun. Hack lost sight of it. The ball almost struck him as it landed at his feet, and as it rolled away Boley and Bishop scampered wildly over the plate and Haas, too, completed the circuit for a home run.

The hit had scored three runs and

the Athletics were now only one run behind. A sinking feeling must have gripped the Cubs, and as for the five hundred loyal rooters from Chicago, they had passed out long ago. But the assault was not ended yet. Its fury seemed to gain momentum with each succeeding minute.

Cochrane walked and Manager McCarthy unceremoniously yanked Nehf, a world's series hero of another day, and called on Sheriff Blake to stem the surging Mack attack. He stemmed it like a man sticking his head in an electric fan.

Simmons up for 2d Time.

Simmons, up for the second time, singled to left. Foxx singled to centre for his second hit of the inning and Cochrane crossed the plate.

That tied the score at 8-all and the turmoil in the stands was now quite indescribable. A great gathering of staid Philadelphians had suddenly gone completely out of their minds.

McCarthy, fairly beside himself, waved again to his rapidly fading forces in the Chicago bull pen and called on Pat Malone to succeed Blake.

Pat's first effort resulted in Miller getting a crack in the ribs with the ball, and that filled the bases. Then came the concluding stroke.

Dykes, who, it will be remembered, had singled the first time up in this inning, sent a low, hard liner screaming to the left corner of the playing field. Riggs Stephenson, Cub left fielder, chased it desperately, got both hands on the ball, but failed to hold it and, as it bounded away for a two-base hit, Simmons and Foxx scored the two runs that finally put the Mackmen in front.

That was all. It was enough. Malone struck out Boley. He also fanned Burns, who was still in the game as a pinch-hitter, and the crowd fell back in its seats exhausted. No attempts were made to revive the 500 Chicagoans.

All Sorts of Records Toppled.

All sorts of records had been

Official Box Score of the Fourth World's Series Game

CHICAGO CUBS.

	AB.	R.	H.	TB.	2B.	3B.	HR.	BB.	SO.	SH.	SB.	PO.	A.	E.
McMillan, 3b	4	0	0	0	0	0	1	2	0	0	0	1	3	0
English, ss	4	0	0	0	0	0	1	1	0	0	2	1	0
Hornsby, 2b	5	2	2	4	0	1	0	0	1	0	0	1	1	0
Wilson, c	3	1	2	2	0	0	0	1	0	0	0	3	0	1
Cuyler, rf	4	2	3	3	0	0	0	1	0	0	0	0	0	1
Stephenson, lf	4	1	1	1	0	0	0	0	0	0	2	1	0
Grimm, 1b	4	2	2	5	0	0	1	0	0	0	0	7	0	0
Taylor, c	3	0	0	0	0	0	0	1	1	0	8	1	0
Root, p	3	0	0	0	0	0	0	0	1	0	0	0	0	0
Nehf, p	0	0	0	0	0	0	0	0	0	0	0	0	0	0
Blake, p	0	0	0	0	0	0	0	0	0	0	0	0	0	0
Malone, p	0	0	0	0	0	0	0	0	0	0	0	0	0	0
aHartnett	1	0	0	0	0	0	0	0	1	0	0	0	0
Carlson, p	0	0	0	0	0	0	0	0	0	0	0	0	1	0
Total	35	8	10	15	0	1	1	3	8	1	0	24	8	2

PHILADELPHIA ATHLETICS.

	AB.	R.	H.	TB.	2B.	3B.	HR.	BB.	SO.	SH.	SB.	PO.	A.	E.
Bishop, 2b	5	1	2	2	0	0	0	0	0	0	2	3	0
Haas, cf	4	1	1	4	0	0	1	0	1	0	2	0	0
Cochrane, c	4	1	2	3	1	0	0	1	0	0	0	9	0	0
Simmons, lf	5	2	2	5	0	0	1	0	2	0	0	2	0	0
Foxx, 1b	4	2	2	2	0	0	0	0	0	0	0	10	0	0
Miller, rf	3	1	2	2	0	0	0	0	0	0	0	3	0	1
Dykes, 3b	4	1	3	4	1	0	0	0	0	0	0	2	0
Boley, ss	3	1	1	1	0	0	0	0	1	1	0	1	5	0
Quinn, p	2	0	0	0	0	0	0	0	2	0	0	0	0
Walberg, p	0	0	0	0	0	0	0	0	0	0	0	0	1
Rommel, p	0	0	0	0	0	0	0	0	0	0	0	0	0
bBurns	2	0	0	0	0	0	0	0	1	0	0	0	0
Grove, p	0	0	0	0	0	0	0	0	0	0	0	0	0
Total	36	10	15	23	2	0	2	1	6	2	0	27	10	2

a Batted for Malone in the eighth.
b Batted for Rommel in the seventh.

SCORE BY INNINGS.

Chicago .... 0 0 0 2 0 5 1 0 0—8
Philadelphia .... 0 0 0 0 0 0 10 0 x—10

Runs batted in—Cuyler 2, Stephenson 1, Grimm 2, Taylor 1, Bishop 1, Haas 3, Simmons 1, Foxx 1, Dykes 3, Boley 1.

Left on bases—Chicago 4, Philadelphia 6. Bases on balls—Off Quinn 2, Rommel 1, Nehf 1. Struck out—By Quinn 2, Walberg 2, Grove 4, Root 3, Malone 2, Carlson 1. Earned runs—Off Quinn 5, Rommel 1, Root 6, Nehf 2, Blake 2. Hits—Off Quinn, 7 in 5 innings (none out in sixth); Walberg, 1 in 1; Rommel, 2 in 1; Grove, 0 in 2; Root, 9 in 6 1-3; Nehf, 1 in 0 (pitched to two batters); Blake, 2 in 0 (pitched to two batters); Malone, 1 in 2-3; Carlson, 2 in 1. Double plays—Dykes, Bishop and Foxx. Hit by pitcher—By Malone (Miller). Winning pitcher—Rommel. Losing pitcher—Blake. Umpires—Van Graflan (A. L.) at plate, Klem (N. L.) at first base, Dinneen (A. L.) at second base, Moran (N. L.) at third base. Time of game—2:12.

broken as the game collapsed on top of the heads of the stunned Cubs. By scoring ten tallies the Athletics surpassed by two the record for most runs scored in a single inning by a team in a world series game, which was set by the Giants against the Yankees on Oct. 7, 1921.

In that same game and inning the Giants had totaled eight runs, which stood as the record until today, when the Athletics pummeled the four luckless Chicago pitchers for ten in that one tumultuous round.

Again, in that same inning eight years ago, the late Ross Young hit safely twice to stand as the only player ever to perform this feat in world series play. Today Simmons, Foxx and Dykes equaled that achievement.

And there was still another record equaled, for after this tempestuous hitting orgy had put the Athletics two runs ahead Connie Mack still had an ace in the hole with which to protect that margin. He trotted out Lefty Grove to pitch the eighth and ninth innings.

Grove Retires Bewildered Cubs.

Lefty Bob, his smoke ball fairly burning down the trail, retired the bewildered Cubs in order in both innings, fanning four of them. And when he fanned the fourth it brought the Cubs' total of strike-outs for the game up to eight and for the series, forty-four.

Underwood and Underwood.
Jimmy Dykes.

Underwood & Underwood.
Mule Haas.
Their Batting Helped Athletics Win Fourth Game.

This enabled the Cubs to tie the rather unenviable record set by the Giants in the series of 1911 in six games and tied by the Yankees in eight games in 1921. The Cubs, it will be noted, have equaled that mark in four.

Up to the moment that that cataclysm descended upon their unsuspecting heads, the Cubs had appeared almost certain winners of this game. Mack had chosen old John Quinn as his pitcher, and though old John skirted safely through the first three innings he plunged into difficulties in the fourth.

Cuyler singled in this round and raced all the way to third when Right Fielder Miller allowed the ball to get away from him. Stephenson's pop fly held the fleet Kiki glued to third, but Grimm walloped the ball over the right-field barrier for a homer and the Cubs were two runs in front.

Quinn's Downfall Comes in Sixth.

Quinn regained his composure in the fifth, but his years and also the Cubs got to him in the sixth and he went down in a heap. Hornsby, who previously had struck out for the seventh time in the series, slashed a single to centre. Wilson and Cuyler also singled, the latter's hit scoring the Rajah. Came another single by Stephenson to drive in Wilson and old John was carted tenderly off the playing field.

Rube Walberg, left-handed ace of

Left to Right—Rogers Hornsby, Hack Wilson, Al Simmons and Jimmy Foxx.
Heavy Hitters of the World's Series Teams, as They Appeared at Shibe Park.

Times Wide World Photo.

65

the Mack staff, replaced him and added to the confusion. He fielded a tap by Grimm and hurled it wildly past first. It was scored as a hit for Grimm, an error for Walberg and accounted for two more runs, as both Cuyler and Stephenson tallied on the misplay, while Grimm pulled up at third. A moment later Grimm came in with the fifth Chicago run for the round on a sacrifice fly by Zach Taylor to Haas in centre.

Although Walberg succeeded in ending the inning well enough by fanning the next two batters, Mack chose to withdraw him, and when the Cubs came up for the seventh they found the right-handed Ed Rommel opposing them.

Hornsby Triples in Seventh.

This did not seem to displease them at all. With one out, Hornsby tripled to left centre and, after Wilson had walked, Cuyler banged a single to right to score the Rajah. It was Kiki's third straight hit and the entire Cub machine was now clicking perfectly.

Root, in the meantime, was pitching superbly and never did he appear greater than in the fifth when Miller beat out an infield hit and Wilson, in some inexplicable manner, muffed a pop fly that fell squarely in his hands in centre.

But a piece of Mack strategy went wrong here and helped the Cubs. Maybe it was the now alert Cub team which caught the sign. In any event Miller and Dykes dashed for second and third as Root wound up to pitch to Boley. It was a hit-and-run play, but there was no hit, as Root pitched wide of the plate and as catcher Taylor whipped the ball to third Miller was thrown out at the post by yards.

Then Wilson redeemed himself by making a spectacular catch of a mighty wallop to right centre by Boley and another Mack rally had been effectually blocked.

In the sixth Root effaced the leaders of the Mack batting order in less time than it takes to tell it. The Cub machine was now moving along magnificently and in all its glistening splendor. Twenty minutes later it lay strewn all over the field, a jangled mass of junk.

Whether McCarthy will be able to patch the broken pieces together is a matter that all Philadelphia is convinced cannot be done. To win the series the Cubs must take three in a row. One more game, the fifth, will be played here on Monday, there being no game tomorrow, and if the Cubs do manage to win that one the series will have to move back to Chicago for completion. But Philadelphia is confident Chicago will not see its Cubs in action again this year.

October 13, 1929

WILSON, CUBS' STAR, LED THE SLUGGERS

His Average of .723 Was Best in the National League, Official Figures Show.

DROVE IN THE MOST RUNS

Total of 190 Created New Record— Klein of Phillies Hit for Most Total Bases, 445.

Hack Wilson, powerful hitter of the Chicago Cubs, was the National League's leading slugger for the season of 1930, the official averages announced yesterday show. His percentage of .723 was the best compiled during the year. In addition, he had the largest total of runs batted in, 190, establishing a new record. He broke his own mark of 159, made in 1929.

Wilson drew the most bases on balls, 105, and also struck out more often than any other player. He was called out on strikes 84 times.

Chuck Klein of the Phillies not only gained the most total bases on his hits, 445, but also shattered Wilson's old record of runs batted in, the young outfielder driving 170 tallies across the plate.

The Cubs had the best club slugging percentage, .481, the most bases on balls, 588, the most strike-outs, 635, and the most hit batsmen, 37. The St. Louis Cardinals set a new record in runs batted in, driving across 942, which surpassed the mark of 933 made by the Cubs in 1929.

December 30, 1930

GROVE IS BEATEN AFTER 16 IN A ROW

Coffman of Browns Victor in Duel, 1-0—Athletics Suffer First Shut-Out of Year.

LOSERS HELD TO 3 HITS

Hoyt Pitches Brilliantly in Nightcap to Blank St. Louis, 10-0, With Four Safeties.

ST. LOUIS, Aug. 23 (AP).—Robert Moses Grove will have to be content with being a joint holder of the American League record for consecutive pitching victories for the present at least, instead of owning the record outright.

Already a joint holder of the record of sixteen straight games, established in 1912 by Smoky Joe Wood of the

Terry Topped National League In Batting With Average of .401

New York Star Tied Record for Most Hits With 254, Official Figures Show—Hack Wilson's 56 Homers New Mark—Giants' .319 Average Set Modern Record.

Bill Terry, crack first baseman of the New York Giants, captured the National League batting championship for the 1930 season with a mark of .401, according to the official averages released today.

Terry also made the most safe hits, 254, tying the National League record, made by Lefty O'Doul, new Brooklyn outfielder, while playing with Philadelphia in 1929. Terry also collected the most one-base hits, 177.

The runner-up to Terry for the hitting crown was Babe Herman, slugging outfielder of the Brooklyn Robins, who finished with an average of .393. Chuck Klein, young Philadelphia outfielder, was third on the list with .386.

Terry's achievement brought the batting championship to the local club for the first time since 1915, when Larry Doyle finished first in the National League with the comparatively low mark of .320.

Klein was credited with 158 runs, the highest number, and drove out the most two-base hits, 59, creating new league records in both these departments, and also gained the most bases on his hits with a total of 445.

The former record for runs scored was 156, made by Rogers Hornsby while playing with Chicago in 1929. Edward J. Delehanty, Philadelphia outfielder, set the former two-base-hit record of 56 way back in 1899.

Adam Comorosky of Pittsburgh pounded out the most triples, 23, while Hack Wilson, in clouting 56 home runs, set a league record. Klein set the previous record with 43 in 1929. Kiki Cuyler of Chicago led in stolen bases for the third season in a row, totaling 37.

A total of seventy-one players batted .300 or better, and six men took part in every game played by their respective clubs, including Klein and Tommy Thevenow, Philadelphia; Cuyler and Woody English, Chicago; Terry, New York, and Taylor Douthit, St. Louis.

Club batting honors were captured by the Giants with the mark of .319, a new modern record. The former mark, .309, was made by Pittsburgh in 1928 and tied by Philadelphia in 1929.

December 26, 1930

Boston Red Sox and equaled the same year by Walter Johnson of the Washington Senators, Grove attempted to better it today at the expense of the St. Louis Browns, but ran up against a three-hit pitching performance by Dick Coffman, who shut out the Athletics, 1 to 0, in the first game of a double-header. The Athletics won the nightcap, 10 to 0, behind Waite Hoyt's airtight hurling.

Grove, as usual, was good today, but Coffman was a little better. The Browns touched the southpaw fireball artist for seven hits, compared to the three allowed by Coffman. Grove fanned six, two more than Coffman. The only base on balls was issued by Coffman. Grove made a wild pitch.

The Browns put over the only run in the third inning on a single by Schulte and a double, which Moore misjudged, by Melillo after two were out.

Grove's record for the season now is twenty-five triumphs, against only three defeats.

Hoyt limited the Browns to four hits in the second game, while the Athletics were pounding Stewart, Stiles and Kimsey for seventeen. Coffman, in blanking the Mackmen, became the first American League pitcher of the year to accomplish the feat.

The box scores:

FIRST GAME.

PHILADELPHIA (A.)	ab.	r.	h.	po.	a.	e.		ST. LOUIS (A.)	ab.	r.	h.	po.	a.	e.
Bishop, 2b.	4	0	0	3	1	0		Schulte, cf.	4	1	3	2	0	0
Cramer, cf.	4	0	0	2	0	0		Melillo, 2b.	4	0	2	1	4	0
Cochrane, c.	4	0	1	8	0	0		Goslin, lf.	4	0	0	2	0	0
Moore, lf.	3	0	1	0	0	0		Kress, 3b.	4	0	0	2	2	0
Foxx, 1b.	3	0	1	6	1	0		Bettencourt, rf	3	0	1	1	0	0
Miller, rf.	2	0	0	2	0	0		Burns, 1b.	3	0	0	11	3	0
McNair, 2b.	3	0	0	0	2	0		Bengough, c.	3	0	1	4	0	0
Williams, ss.	3	0	0	2	0	0		Levey, ss.	3	0	0	1	2	0
Grove, p.	3	0	0	1	1	0		Coffman, p.	3	0	0	3	2	0
Total	30	0	3	24	5	0		Total	30	1	7	27	13	0

Philadelphia .... 0 0 0 0 0 0 0 0 0—0
St. Louis .... 0 0 1 0 0 0 0 0 .—1

Run batted in—Melillo.
Two-base hit—Melillo. Sacrifices—Moore, Coffman. Left on bases—Philadelphia 5, St. Louis 6. Base on balls—Off Coffman 1. Struck out—By Grove 6, Coffman 4. Wild pitch—Grove. Umpires—Van Graflan, Guthrie and Dinneen. Time of game—1.25.

SECOND GAME.

PHILADELPHIA (A.)	ab.	r.	h.	po.	a.	e.		ST. LOUIS (A.)	ab.	r.	h.	po.	a.	e.
Bishop, 2b.	6	1	1	1	4	0		Schulte, cf.	3	0	1	5	0	0
Cramer, cf.	5	1	3	5	0	0		Melillo, 2b.	4	0	0	1	1	0
Heving, c.	5	1	1	2	0	0		Goslin, lf.	3	0	1	3	0	0
Moore, lf.	5	0	3	0	0	0		Kress, 3b.	4	0	1	2	1	0
Foxx, 1b.	5	2	2	9	0	0		Bettencourt, rf	4	0	2	0	0	0
Miller, rf.	5	2	3	1	0	0		Burns, 1b.	3	0	0	3	0	0
Dykes, 3b.	4	1	3	0	3	0		Ferrell, c.	3	0	0	10	1	0
Williams, ss.	5	2	2	1	0	0		Levey, ss.	3	0	0	1	1	0
Hoyt, p.	4	0	0	0	3	0		Stewart, p.	2	0	1	0	0	0
								Stiles, p.	0	0	0	0	0	0
								Kimsey, p.	0	0	0	0	0	0
Total	44	10	17	27	10	0		aGrimes	1	0	0	0	0	0
								Total	30	0	4	27	4	0

aBatted for Stiles in eighth.
Philadelphia .... 0 0 0 0 2 1 4 0 3—10
St. Louis .... 0 0 0 0 0 0 0 0 0— 0

Runs batted in—Hoyt 2, Cramer, Dykes 4, Heving 2, Miller.
Two-base hits—Schulte, Hoyt, Goslin, Williams, Miller 2, Heving. Double play—Williams, Bishop and Foxx. Left on bases—Philadelphia 9, St. Louis 5. Bases on balls—Off Hoyt 2, Stewart 3. Struck out—By Hoyt 2, Stewart 5, Stiles 3, Kimsey 2. Hits—Off Stewart 9 in 6 innings (none out in seventh), Stiles 3 in 2, Kimsey 5 in 1. Losing pitcher—Stewart. Umpires—Guthrie, Dinneen and Van Graflan. Time of game—2.00.

August 24, 1931

Gehrig Ties All-Time Record With Four Straight Home Runs

EQUALS TWO MARKS IN 20 TO 13 VICTORY

Lou Ties Record of Four Circuit Drives in One Game as the Athletics Are Beaten.

DUPLICATES LOWE'S FEAT

He Connects in First Four Times at Bat and Nearly Makes Fifth in Ninth.

RUTH PRODUCES HIS 15TH

Total Base Marks Fall, With 50 for Yanks, 77 for Both Clubs—Victors Tie Team Homer Record.

By WILLIAM E. BRANDT.

Special to THE NEW YORK TIMES.

PHILADELPHIA, June 3.—Henry Louis Gehrig's name today took rank in baseball's archives along with Bobby Lowe and Ed Delehanty, the only other sluggers who, in more than half a century of recorded diamond battles, ever hit four home runs in one major league game.

Largely because of Gehrig's quartet of tremendous smashes the Yankees outstripped the Athletics in a run-making marathon, winning, 20 to 13, after twice losing the lead because of determined rallies by the American League champions.

Homers by Combs, Lazzeri and Ruth, the latter the Babe's fifteenth of the season, enabled the Yankees to tie the all-time record of seven homers by one club in one game, performed three times before 1900, by Detroit, New York and Pittsburgh, of the old National League, and once in modern times, by the Athletics on June 3, 1921.

Yankees Set Team Mark.

The Yanks, with their twenty-three hits, also set a new modern club-batting record for total bases, with fifty, which eclipsed the previous modern major league mark of forty-six, and the American League's best total of forty-four. This achievement fell short by only five bases of the all-time record, set by Cincinnati in 1923. Both clubs' total of seventy-seven bases also set an American League mark.

Gehrig in his first four times at bat hammered the ball outside the playing area. In the first and fifth innings he sailed balls into the stands in left centre. In the fourth and seventh he fired over the right-field wall.

Saltzgaver was on base when Lou connected in the first inning, but the other three came with the bases empty. His fifth-inning homer, which made him the first man in baseball

history ever to hit three homers in one game for the fourth time, came after Combs and Ruth had reached Earnshaw for drives over the right-field wall.

Lazzeri Clears Bases.

Lazzeri's drive into the left-field stands in the ninth, the last Yankee homer, came with the bases filled. In Philadelphia's half of the ninth Jimmy Foxx, the major league leader, sent his nineteenth homer of the year shooting into the left-field stands.

Cochrane had driven the ball over the right-field wall in the first inning, but the collective homer total, nine, fell one short of the major league record for both teams in a game.

The outcome of the game evened the series, two to two, but the crowd of 5,000 seemed to concentrate on encouraging Gehrig to hit a fifth homer and thus surpass a brilliant record in baseball's books.

Lou had two chances. He grounded out in the eighth, but in the ninth he pointed a terrific drive which Simmons captured only a few steps from the furthest corner of the park. A little variance to either side of its actual line of flight would have sent the ball over the fence or into the stands.

As it was, Lou's four homers tied the all-time record of Lowe in hitting for the circuit in four successive times at bat in 1894. Only three of Delehanty's were in successive times at bat. Both Lowe and Delehanty had a single in the same game with their four homers, so that Gehrig fell one short of tying their record for total bases.

Gehrig's four made his season's total eleven, six of which have been hit against Philadelphia, four off Earnshaw and two off Mahaffey.

The defeat of the Mackmen, coupled with the Indians' double victory, dropped the Athletics to fifth place, Cleveland supplanting them in fourth.

Lazzeri's homer with the bases filled was his fifth hit of the game. He and Gehrig each drove in six runs.

The box score:

NEW YORK (A.)	ab.r.h.po.a.e.	PHILADELPHIA (A.)	ab.r.h.po.a.e.
Combs, cf	5 2 3 3 0 0	Bishop, 2b	4 2 2 3 2 0
Saltzg'er, 2b	4 1 1 3 2 0	Cramer, cf	5 1 1 1 0 0
Ruth, lf	5 2 2 3 0 1	aRoettger	1 0 0 0 0 0
Hoag, lf	0 1 0 1 0 0	Miller, lf	0 0 0 0 0 0
Gehrig, 1b	6 4 4 7 0 1	Cochrane, c	5 1 1 1 0 2 0
Dickey, c	5 3 2 4 0 0	bWilliams	1 0 0 0 0 0
Lazzeri, 2b	6 3 5 0 1 0	Sim'ns, lf,cf	4 2 2 3 0 0
Crosetti, ss	6 1 2 0 5 2	Foxx, 1b	3 3 2 3 0 0
Allen, p	2 0 0 1 0 1	Coleman, rf	6 2 2 2 1 0
Rhodes, p	1 0 1 0 0 0	McNair, ss	5 1 3 1 2 0
Brown, p	1 0 0 0 1 0	Dykes, 3b	4 1 1 0 1 0
Gomez, p	1 1 1 0 0 0	rFoss	1 0 1 0 0 0
		Earnshaw, p	2 0 0 0 2 1
Total	46 20 23 27 9 5	cPoss	1 0 1 0 0 0
		Walberg, p	0 0 0 0 0 0
		Krause, p	0 0 0 0 0 0
		dMadjeski	1 0 0 0 0 0
		Rommel, p	0 0 0 0 1 0
		Total	42 13 13 27 11 1

aBatted for Cramer in eighth.
bBatted for Cochrane in ninth.
cBatted for Earnshaw in fifth.
dBatted for Krause in eighth.

New York . . . . 2 0 0 2 3 2 3 2 6—20
Philadelphia . . . . 0 0 0 6 0 2 0 2 1—13

Runs batted in—Gehrig 6, Combs, Ruth, Corsetti 2, Saltzgaver, Lazzeri 6, Chapman, Dickey, Cochrane 2, Cramer 3, Coleman 2, Foxx, McNair 2. Two-base hits—Lazzeri, McNair, Ruth, Coleman. Three-base hits—Bishop, Cramer, Chapman, Lazzeri, Foxx. Home runs—Gehrig 4, Cochrane, Combs, Ruth, Lazzeri, Foxx. Stolen base—Lazzeri. Sacrifices—Bishop, Saltzgaver. Double plays—Cochrane and McNair; Bishop and Foxx; Coleman and Cochrane. Left on bases—New York 6, Philadelphia 11. Bases on balls—Off Allen 5, Rhodes 2, Brown 1, Earnshaw 2, Walberg 1, Rommel 3. Struck out—By Allen 1, Gomez 1, Earnshaw 3, Walberg 1. Hits—Off Allen 7 in 3 2-3 innings, Rhodes 1 in 1 1-3, Brown 3 in 2, Gomez 2 in 2, Earnshaw 8 in 5, Mahaffey 4 in 1 (none out in seventh), Walberg 2 in 1, Krausse 4 in 1, Rommel 3 in 1. Wild pitch—Rhodes. Winning pitcher—Brown. Losing pitcher—Mahaffey. Umpires—Geisel, McGowan and Van Graflan. Time of game—2:55.

June 4, 1932

New York Times

Lou Gehrig

FOXX HITS NO. 58, BUT MACKMEN BOW

Senators Win, 2-1, Despite His Perfect Day at Bat—Take Season's Series, 12-10.

CROWDER EXCELS ON MOUND

Scores 26th Triumph and 15th in Row to Lead League in Pitching Victories.

WASHINGTON, Sept. 25 (P).—Jimmy Foxx blasted his fifty-eighth home run of the season in a perfect day at bat, but the Athletics by 2 to 1 today in closing their 1932 rivalry.

Foxx made a homer and two singles in three times at bat.

General Alvin Crowder of the Senators took the league lead in games won, chalking up his twenty-sixth of

the year and fifteenth straight. Except for Foxx, only two Athletics got as far as second and none to third off his delivery.

The victory gave the third-place Washington team a lead of two games over the Mackmen for the season, the Senators winning 12 and losing 10 to their second-place opponents.

Cain, the Philadelphia pitcher, got into trouble right off the start, but a double play, McNair to Foxx, saved him and resulted in the Senators being held to one run on four singles in the first inning.

The box score:

PHILADELPHIA (A.)	ab.r.h.po.a.e.	WASHINGTON (A.)	ab.r.h.po.a.e.
Williams, 2b	3 0 1 1 1 0	Rice, lf	3 1 1 3 0 0
Haas, cf	4 0 0 2 0 0	Kerr, 2b	3 0 0 2 6 0
Madjeski, c	4 0 0 6 1 0	Reynolds, rf	4 1 1 0 0 0
Simmons, lf	4 0 1 4 0 0	Cronin, ss	4 0 2 4 1 1
Foxx, 1b	3 1 3 6 0 0	Kuhel, 1b	3 0 1 10 0 0
McNair, ss	4 0 0 2 2 1	West, cf	3 0 1 4 0 0
Miller, rf	4 0 0 1 0 0	Bluege, 3b	3 0 0 2 0 0
Dykes, 3b	3 0 0 2 1 0	Spencer, c	3 0 1 2 0 0
Cain, p	3 0 1 0 1 0	Crowder, p	3 0 0 0 5 0
Total	33 1 6 24 6 1	Total	29 2 7 27 12 1

Philadelphia . . . . 0 0 0 0 0 0 0 0 1—1
Washington . . . . 1 0 0 0 0 0 0 1 .—2

Runs batted in—Kuhel, Cronin, Foxx. Two-base hits—Cronin. Home run—Foxx. Sacrifice—Kerr. Double plays—McNair and Foxx; Cronin, Kerr and Kuhel; Madjeski and Williams. Left on bases—Philadelphia 6, Washington 4. Bases on balls—Off Cain 2, Crowder 1. Struck out—By Cain 4, Crowder 1. Umpires—McGowan, Van Graflan and Nallin. Time of game—1:17.

September 26, 1932

YANKEES BEAT CUBS FOR 3D IN ROW, 7-5, AS 51,000 LOOK ON

Ruth and Gehrig, Each With 2 Homers, Set Pace as New York Nears Series Title.

BABE'S FIRST TALLIES 3

His Second Brings Wild Acclaim —Hartnett and Cuyler Also Deliver Circuit Drives.

PENNOCK STARS ON MOUND

Veteran Relieves Pipgras in Ninth and Halts Chicago Rally—Governor Roosevelt in Crowd.

By JOHN DREBINGER.

CHICAGO, Oct. 1.—Four home runs, two by the master hitter of them all, Babe Ruth, and the other pair by his almost equally proficient colleague, Columbia Lou Gehrig, advanced the New York Yankees to within one game of their third World's Series sweep today.

The American League champions once again overpowered the Cubs to win their third straight game of the current classic which, for the first time, went on display in this city.

Those four blows made the final score 7 to 5. They crushed not only the National League standard-bearers, but a gathering of 51,000 which jammed Wrigley Field to the limits of its capacity and packed two wooden temporary bleachers outside the park. Included in the gathering was Governor Roosevelt of New York, the Democratic Presidential candidate.

It was by far the most turbulent and bitterly fought engagement of the series thus far. The Cubs, inspired by a show of civic enthusiasm, battled fiercely and courageously.

They even struck back with a couple of lusty homers on their own account, one by Kiki Cuyler, the other by Gabby Hartnett.

Wallop Retires Pipgras.

Hartnett's wallop came in the ninth inning and brought about the retirement of George Pipgras, the first Yankee pitcher to appear in the series who had also taken part in the clean-sweep triumphs of 1927 and 1928.

But this move merely provided a setting that added still further to the glamour of the Yankee triumph. For it brought on the scene one of the greatest world's series pitchers of all time, the talented Herbie Pennock, who started pitching in these classics

back in 1914. In that long interval he had recorded five personal triumphs without a single defeat. Consequently he did not mean to let this game slip from his fingers even though credit for the victory still would remain with Pipgras.

In short, the famous Squire of Kennett Square sharply halted the belated Cub rally, fairly smothering the desperate bid of the Chicagoans with consummate ease and skill.

With a Cub lurking on the base paths poised to dart for the plate, Pennock fanned a pinch-hitter and retired the next two on soft, infield taps, one of which he fielded himself. The other was snared by Gehrig for the final put-out.

Chance to Add to Record.

Thus, with three victories tucked away against no defeats, the Yankees, now skillfully piloted by Joe McCarthy, who bossed these same Cubs only two years ago, have advanced to a point where they need only one more game to clinch the world's championship. In addition they have a chance to add still further to their remarkable world's series record. They have now competed in eleven straight series encounters without suffering a single reversal.

Both the game and all its trimmings provided a much livelier spectacle than either of the two previous encounters. In sharp contrast to the rather matter-of-fact manner in which New York had accepted the first two battles, the crowd today was as keyed up as the players, if not more so.

It was a warm day, clear and sunny, though rather windy. There was a gay, holiday spirit in the air that never forsook the gathering, for Chicago puts a great deal more fervor in its baseball than does New York. It seemed as though the fans of this mid-Western metropolis simply would not believe how severely and decisively their champions had been manhandled by the mighty Yankees in the first two games in the East.

Ruth's Drive Awes Throng.

They roared their approval of every good play made by the Cubs. They playfully tossed bright yellow lemons at Babe Ruth and booed him thoroughly as the great man carried on a pantomime act while standing at the plate.

Then they sat back, awed and spellbound, as the Babe, casting aside his buffoonery, smashed one of the longest home runs ever seen at Wrigley Field.

It was an amazing demonstration by baseball's outstanding figures, who a few weeks ago was ill and confined to his bed. It confounded the crowd, which in paid attendance numbered 49,986 and which had contributed $211,912 in receipts.

The Cubs took the field with their hopes resting upon the stout right arm of Charlie Root, but Charlie was unequal to the task. He failed to survive five rounds, retiring immediately after Ruth and Gehrig had blasted their second two homers. These came in succession in the fifth like a flash of lightning and a clap of thunder.

Both were held fairly well in restraint in the latter rounds by Pat Malone and the left-handed Jakie May. But aside from providing the crowd with a chance to give vent to

Box Score of Third Game of World's Series.

CHICAGO CUBS.

	ab.	r.	h.	tb.	2b.	3b.	hr.	bb.	so.	sh.	sb.	po.	a.	e.
Herman, 2b	4	1	0	0	0	0	0	1	0	0	0	1	2	1
English, 3b	4	0	0	0	0	0	1	0	0	0	0	3	0	
Cuyler, rf	4	1	3	7	1	0	1	0	0	0	0	1	0	0
Stephenson, lf	4	0	1	1	0	0	0	0	0	0	0	1	0	0
J. Moore, cf	3	0	0	0	0	0	0	1	0	0	0	3	0	0
Grimm, 1b	4	0	1	2	1	0	0	0	0	0	0	8	0	0
Hartnett, c	4	1	1	4	0	0	1	0	0	0	0	10	1	1
Jurges, ss	4	1	3	4	1	0	0	0	0	0	1	3	3	2
Root, p	2	0	0	0	0	0	0	0	1	0	0	0	0	0
Malone, p	0	0	0	0	0	0	0	0	0	0	0	0	0	0
May, p	0	0	0	0	0	0	0	0	0	0	0	0	0	0
Tinning, p	0	0	0	0	0	0	0	0	0	0	0	0	0	0
aGudat	1	0	0	0	0	0	0	0	0	0	0	0	0	0
bKoenig	0	0	0	0	0	0	0	0	0	0	0	0	0	0
cHemsley	1	0	0	0	0	0	0	0	0	1	0	0	0	0
Total	35	5	9	18	3	0	2	3	2	0	1	27	9	4

NEW YORK YANKEES.

	ab.	r.	h.	tb.	2b.	3b.	hr.	bb.	so.	sh.	sb.	po.	a.	e.
Combs, cf	5	1	0	0	0	0	0	0	2	0	0	1	0	0
Sewell, 3b	2	1	0	0	0	0	0	2	0	0	0	2	2	0
Ruth, lf	4	2	2	8	0	0	2	1	1	0	0	2	0	0
Gehrig, 1b	5	2	2	8	0	0	2	0	0	0	0	13	1	0
Lazzeri, 2b	4	1	0	0	0	0	0	1	1	0	0	3	4	1
Dickey, c	4	0	1	1	0	0	0	1	0	0	0	2	1	0
Chapman, rf	4	0	2	3	1	0	0	1	1	0	0	0	0	0
Crosetti, ss	4	0	1	1	0	0	0	1	0	0	0	4	4	0
Pipgras, p	5	0	0	0	0	0	0	0	5	0	0	0	0	0
Pennock, p	0	0	0	0	0	0	0	0	0	0	0	0	1	0
Total	37	7	8	21	1	0	4	7	10	0	0	27	13	1

a Batted for Malone in seventh.
b Batted for Tinning in ninth.
c Batted for Koenig in ninth.

SCORE BY INNINGS.

New York	3	0	1	0	2	0	0	0	1—7
Chicago	1	0	2	1	0	0	0	0	1—5

Runs batted in—New York: Ruth 4, Gehrig 2, Chapman 1. Chicago: Cuyler 2, Grimm 1, Hartnett 1.

Left on bases—New York 11, Chicago 6. Double plays—Sewell, Lazzeri and Gehrig; Herman, Jurges and Grimm. Hits—Off Root 6 in 4 1-3 innings, Malone 1 in 2 2-3, May 1 in 1 1-3, Tinning 0 in 2-3, Pipgras 9 in 8 (none out in ninth), Pennock 0 in 1. Struck out—By Root 4, Malone 4, May 1, Tinning 1, Pipgras 1, Pennock 1. Bases on balls—Off Root 3, Malone 4, Pipgras 3. Hit by pitcher—By May (Sewell). Winning pitcher—Pipgras. Losing pitcher—Root. Umpires—Van Graflan (A. L.) at the plate; Magerkurth (N. L.) at first base; Dinneen (A. L.) at second base; Klem (N. L.) at third base. Time of game—2:11.

boos, the earlier damage these two had inflicted proved far sufficient to carry the day.

Ruth and Gehrig simply dominated the scene from start to finish, and they began their performance early. When the two marched to the plate during the batting rehearsal they at once thrilled the crowd by uncorking a series of tremendous drives into the temporary wooden stands.

Almost Clears Bleachers.

The Babe's very first practice shot almost cleared the top of the wooden structure, and he followed it with several more prodigious drives. Gehrig produced some more, and each time the ball soared into those densely packed stands the crowd gasped. The spectacle certainly could not have been very heartening to the Cubs.

And when the battle proper began, both kept right on firing. The Babe's two homers were his first of the cur-

rent series, but they sent his all-time world's series record for home runs to fifteen. For Gehrig, his two gave him a total of three for the series and an all-time record of seven.

Fittingly enough, the Babe was the first to touch off the explosion and his opening smash sent the Yanks away to a three-run lead in the very first inning. In fact, the crowd had scarcely recovered its composure after a tumultuous reception it had accorded a tumultuous reception when it was forced to suffer its first annoyance.

There was a sharp wind blowing across the playing field toward the right-field bleachers that threatened to raise havoc with the players, and it did very shortly.

Jurges Makes Wild Throw.

Eager and tense, the crowd watched Root pitch to Earle Combs, the first Yankee batter. It at once roared approbation as Combs sent a drive squarely into the hands of young Billy Jurges who was again playing shortstop for the Cubs in place of the injured Mark Koenig.

But the next moment the throng voiced its dismay as Jurges unfurled a throw that sailed high over Manager Charlie Grimm's head at first and into the Yankee dugout.

Root was plainly flustered as Combs, under the prevailing ground rule, was allowed to advance to second base. Root strove to steady himself, but he passed Joey Sewell and faced Ruth. Cheers and jeers mingled as the great Yankee batter made his first official appearance at the plate in Chicago's portion of the setting.

Root pitched cautiously, fearful of what would happen if he allowed the Babe to shoot one high in the air with that brisk breeze behind it. His first two offerings went wide of the plate. Then he put one over, and away the ball went. It was a lofty shot that soared on and on until it dropped deep in the temporary stands. Thus, the Cubs, who had planned to fight so desperately for this game, already were three runs to the bad.

Cubs Fight Courageously.

But desperately they fought, nevertheless, and in the lower half of the same inning they gave their cohorts the chance to do some wholehearted cheering by getting one of these tallies back.

The wind, which had annoyed Root so much, also seemed to trouble Pipgras. He passed Herman, whereupon the crowd set up a roar as though the series already had been won. Woody English was retired on a fly to Ruth, who was performing in left field today in order to avoid the glare of the sun.

But Kiki Cuyler, who might have been the hero of this struggle had Ruth and Gehrig been playing elsewhere, lifted a two-bagger over Ben Chapman's head in right against the wire screening in front of the bleachers, and Herman scored amid tumultuous cheering.

But two innings later Gehrig, after an uneventful first inning, stepped into the picture. Leaning heavily into Root's pitch, he sent another mighty shot soaring into the right-field bleachers. That made the score 4 to 1.

At this point, however, the Cubs staged their most gallant fight of the day. With one out in the lower half of the third, Cuyler again produced a jubilant uproar by shooting a homer into the right-field stands, and this at once inspired his comrades to redouble their efforts against Pipgras. Stephenson slashed a single to right, and though he was forced by Johnny Moore Manager Grimm lined a drive to right that Chapman did not play any too well. The ball shot past the Alabama arrow for a two-bagger and Moore scored all the way from first.

That left the Cubs only one run in arrears, and in the fourth they drew even amid the most violent vocal demonstration of the afternoon. Jurges, eager to make amends for his earlier miscue, slapped a low liner to left, and the crowd howled with glee as Ruth failed in a heroic attempt to make a shoe-string catch of the ball. Jurges gained two bases on the hit.

Ruth Doffs His Cap.

Good naturedly, the Babe doffed his cap in acknowledgment to the adverse plaudits of the fans and the play went on. Tony Lazzeri made a spectacular catch of Herman's high, twisting pop-fly back of second base. But the next moment Tony booted English's grounder and Jurges raced over the plate with the tally that tied the score at 4-all.

But it seems decidedly unhealthy for any one to taunt the great man Ruth too much and very soon the crowd was to learn its lesson. A single lemon rolled out to the plate as Ruth came up in the fifth and in no mistaken motions the Babe notified the crowd that the nature of his retaliation would be a wallop right out the confines of the park.

Root pitched two balls and two

strikes, while Ruth signaled with his fingers after each pitch to let the spectators know exactly how the situation stood. Then the mightiest blow of all fell.

It was a tremendous smash that bore straight down the centre of the field in an enormous arc, came down alongside the flagpole and disappeared behind the corner formed by the scoreboard and the end of the right-field bleachers.

It was Ruth's fifteenth home run in world's series competition and easily one of his most gorgeous. The crowd, suddenly unmindful of everything save that it had just witnessed an epic feat, hailed the Babe with a salvo of applause.

Root, badly shaken, now faced Gehrig and his feelings well can be imagined. The crowd was still too much excited over the Ruth incident to realize what was happening when Columbia Lou lifted an enormous fly high in the air. As it sailed on the wings of the lake breeze the ball just cleared the high flagpole and dropped in the temporary stand.

Grimm, the player-manager of the Cubs, called time. Consolingly he invited Root to retire to the turbulent confines of the clubhouse and ordered Pat Malone to the mound.

Pat filled the bases with three passes but he escaped the inning without further trouble. From then on the game, like its two predecessors, passed on to its very obvious conclusion with the exception of a final flurry in the ninth.

May Takes Up Mound Duties.

Two very fine plays by Grimm and Moore rescued Malone from possible trouble in the sixth. He also went well through the seventh despite a second misplay by Jurges and a single by Crosetti, then he faded out for a pinch-hitter. Jakie May, lone lefthander of the Chicago pitching staff, came to the mound to pitch the eighth.

Jakie got by that inning exceedingly well, closing out by inducing Ruth to slap into a double play. But in the ninth Jakie found that trouble can be found at either end of the Yankee batting order.

The lake breeze had now developed into a young gale and it seemed as though the Yanks strategically had decided upon capitalizing on it to the full. Gehrig, Lazzeri and Chapman successively touched off three sky-rocket infield flies that in their descent veered in all directions.

Woody English caught the first one right in the centre of the diamond after bumping into three of his comrades. But Gabby Hartnett, the ambitious Cub catcher, insisted on going after the second one and dropped it.

Then Herman muffed Dickey's and the Yankees had two aboard, one of which scored immediately on Chapman's double to left, a low drive for which the Cubs seemingly were totally unprepared. That blow removed May, and Bud Tinning, an apprentice right-hander, collected the last two outs that finally checked the Yanks.

Hartnett's Drive Stirs Crowd.

The score was now 7 to 4, and, as Pipgras had done some really fine pitching from the fifth through the eighth, the crowd appeared definitely wilted. But it seems to be a simple matter to revive a Chicago crowd, and when Hartnett, first Cub up in the ninth, walloped a homer over the left-field wall into the temporary bleachers there was again a mighty roar.

The applause doubled in volume when Jurges whistled a single into left, and Manager McCarthy decided to withdraw Pipgras, for he had still another trump card up his sleeve. It was Herbie Pennock, and the veteran southpaw's finishing strokes to the combat produced another masterpiece.

Hemsley, batting for Tinning, struck out on three tantalizing slow balls. Herman topped one into the dirt in front of the plate which Pennock himself fielded, and Gehrig smothered English's grounder. That also smothered the Cubs.

Johnny Allen is scheduled to pitch tomorrow for the Yankees. His opponent will be Guy Bush. The weather forecast is fair and warmer.

October 2, 1932

Pick of Leagues to Meet in World's Fair Feature.

CHICAGO, May 18 (AP).—The baseball fans' dream—a game between the pick of American and National League talent—will be sponsored July 6 by The Chicago Tribune as a World's Fair feature. It became possible through the cooperation of the sixteen club owners.

The fans of the country will select the teams by vote to help settle arguments over the relative merits of the players in the two leagues for the first time in the history of the game.

The newspaper will underwrite the expense of staging the game. The profits will be turned over to the Association of Professional Baseball Players of America, baseball's charity organization.

May 19, 1933

GIANTS WIN TWICE, 1ST IN 18 INNINGS

Beat Cards in Both Contests by 1-0 to Extend League Lead to 5½ Games.

HUBBELL IRON-MAN HERO

Allows Only Six Hits and Issues No Passes in Four-Hour Opening Struggle.

By JOHN DREBINGER.

Pitching of a superman variety that dazzled a crowd of 50,000 and

bewildered the Cardinals gave the Giants two throbbing victories at the Polo Grounds yesterday over a stretch of six hours.

Carl Hubbell, master lefthander of Bill Terry's amazing hurling corps, blazed the trail by firing away for eighteen scoreless innings to win the opening game from the Cards, 1 to 0. A single by Hughie Critz broke up this four-hour struggle in the last half of the eighteenth.

Then the broad-shouldered Roy Parmelee strode to the mound and through semi-darkness and finally a drizzling rain, blanked the St. Louisans in a nine-inning nightcap, 1 to 0. A homer in the fourth inning by Johnny Vergez decided this battle.

Win the Series, 3—2.

The two triumphs gave the Giants the series with the Cards, three out of five, and enabled them to conclude their home stand against the West with a record of eleven victories against five defeats. It also lengthened their margin over the second-place Cardinals to five and a half games.

The opener was a titanic pitching duel in which Hubbell gave one of the most astounding exhibitions of endurance and mound skill seen in many years as he survived the combined efforts of the elongated Tex Carleton and the veteran Jess Haines.

Carleton, who stepped the first sixteen innings for the Cards, gave no mean performance himself. As he had beaten the Giants in the opening game of the series on Thursday, it was not his turn to pitch. Yet he requested that he start, despite only two days of rest, and for sixteen rounds kept the straining Terrymen away from the plate.

But it was Hubbell who commanded the centre of the stage. The tall, somber left-hander rose to his greatest heights, surpassing even his brilliant no-hit classic of 1928. He pitched perfect ball in twelve of the eighteen innings yesterday, with not a man reaching first base.

Fans Twelve of Cards.

He allowed six hits, never more than one to an inning. Two of the blows were doubles, the others were infield singles. He fanned twelve and gave no bases on balls. As

69

the Giants played errorless ball behind him, only the hitters reached first base.

Five of the hitters advanced as far as second and only one reached third. It was an exhibition that held the packed arena spellbound throughout the four hours.

Carleton, allowing eight hits in his sixteen innings, was only slightly less brilliant. He issued seven passes, four of them intentional, but really was only crowded twice.

The first Giant threat did not appear until the eleventh, when O'Doul walked and took second on Terry's sacrifice. Ott was passed intentionally, but Vergez also drew four wide ones and the bases were filled with only one out.

Threat Fails to Materialize.

Carleton, however, refused to break ground any further. Moore hit into a forced play at the plate and Mancuso ended the threat by also grounding out.

With two out in the fifteenth, Terry drove a tremendous triple to left centre. But Carleton again purposely passed Ott and retired Vergez on a foul.

With Carleton retiring for a pinch-hitter in the seventeenth, the 39-year-old Haines took up the pitching in the lower half for the Cards and safely skirted by that round, though the Giants got two on base.

But in the eighteenth the veteran ran into difficulty. Moore walked, Mancuso sacrificed, and Jackson, batting for Ryan, was purposely passed. Hubbell forced Jackson, but Moore landed on third and a moment later was over the plate when Critz rifled a single to right centre.

Dean Hurls After Day's Rest.

So desperate was Manager Street after this reversal that he called on his other star right-hander, Dizzy Dean, to start the second game, despite the fact that the Dizzy one had blanked the Giants on Friday and therefore had only a single day's rest.

He drew Parmelee for his opponent and in the gloaming the two embarked on another scoreless battle which was interrupted in the fourth when Verges shot his homer into the upper left tier.

That margin Parmelee preserved right through to the end, which was reached in almost total darkness, with Parmelee allowing only four hits and striking out thirteen, tying the season's record.

The box scores:

FIRST GAME.

ST. LOUIS (N.)

	ab.	r.	h.	po.	a.	e.
Martin, 3b	7	0	0	3	6	0
Frisch, 2b	7	0	0	7	5	0
Orsatti, cf	7	0	1	0	0	0
Collins, 1b	7	0	2	15	5	0
Medwick, lf	7	0	1	7	0	0
Allen, rf	6	0	0	4	0	0
Wilson, c	6	0	2	11	1	0
Durocher, ss	3	0	0	3	4	1
aHornsby	1	0	0	0	0	0
Slade, ss	1	0	0	1	2	0
Carleton, p	4	0	0	2	3	0
bO'Farrell	1	0	0	0	0	0
Haines, p	0	0	0	0	2	0
Total	57	0	6	*33	28	1

NEW YORK (N.)

	ab.	r.	h.	po.	a.	e.
Critz, 2b	9	0	3	4	12	0
O'Doul, lf	4	0	1	0	0	0
cJames	0	0	0	0	0	0
Davis, cf	2	0	0	2	0	0
Terry, 1b	6	0	2	26	1	0
Ott, rf	6	0	0	2	0	0
Vergez, 3b	5	0	0	3	1	0
Moore, cf.lf	7	1	0	3	0	0
Mancuso, c	7	0	1	13	1	0
Ryan, ss	6	0	2	0	5	0
dJackson	0	0	0	0	0	0
Hubbell, p	7	0	1	1	7	0
Total	59	1	10	54	27	0

*Two out when winning run scored.
aBatted for Durocher in eleventh.
bBatted for Carleton in seventeenth.
cRan for O'Doul in eleventh.
dBatted for Ryan in eighteenth.

St. Louis.....0 0 0 0 0 0 0 0 0 0 0 0 0 0 0 0 0 0—0
New York.....0 0 0 0 0 0 0 0 0 0 0 0 0 0 0 0 0 1—1

Run batted in—Critz.

Two-base hits—Orsatti, Collins. Three-base hit—Terry. Sacrifices—Carleton, Hubbell, Terry, Davis, Mancuso, Slade. Double play—Ryan, Critz and Terry. Left on bases—New York 19, St. Louis 5. Bases on balls—Off Carleton 7, Haines 3. Struck out—By Hubbell 12, Carleton 7, Haines 1. Hits—Off Carleton 8 in 16 innings, Haines 2 in 1 2-3. Losing pitcher—Haines. Umpires—Klem, Pfirman and Barr. Time of game—4:03.

SECOND GAME.

ST. LOUIS (N).

	ab.	r.	h.	po.	a.	e.
Martin, 3b	4	0	0	0	1	0
Frisch, 2b	4	0	1	4	3	0
Orsatti, cf	4	0	1	4	0	0
Collins, 1b	3	0	0	7	0	0
Medwick, lf	3	0	0	1	0	0
Watkins, rf	3	0	0	1	0	0
O'Farrell, c	2	0	0	5	0	0
aCrawford	1	0	1	0	0	0
Wilson, c	0	0	0	1	0	0
Durocher, ss	2	0	0	0	2	0
bCrabtree	1	0	0	0	0	0
Slade, ss	0	0	0	1	0	0
Dean, p	2	0	0	0	2	0
cHornsby	1	0	1	0	0	0
dAllen	0	0	0	0	0	0
Total	30	0	4	24	8	0

NEW YORK (N).

	ab.	r.	h.	po.	a.	e.
Critz, 2b	4	0	1	2	2	0
O'Doul, lf	3	0	0	0	0	0
Terry, 1b	4	0	0	4	0	0
Ott, rf	4	0	1	1	0	0
Vergez, 3b	3	1	1	1	2	1
Moore, cf	3	0	0	0	0	0
Mancuso, c	3	0	1	15	2	0
Ryan, ss	0	0	0	1	0	0
Jackson, ss	2	0	1	3	0	0
Parmelee, p	3	0	0	0	0	0
Total	29	1	5	27	6	1

aBatted for O'Farrell in eighth.
bBatted for Durocher in eighth.
cBatted for Dean in ninth.
dRan for Hornsby in ninth.

St. Louis.................0 0 0 0 0 0 0 0 0—0
New York.................0 0 0 1 0 0 0 0 ..—1

Run batted in—Vergez.

Two-base hit—Mancuso. Home run—Verges. Left on bases—New York 6, St. Louis 3. Bases on balls—Off Dean 2. Struck out—By Parmelee 13, Dean 6. Umpires—Pfirman, Barr and Klem. Time of game—1:25.

July 3, 1933

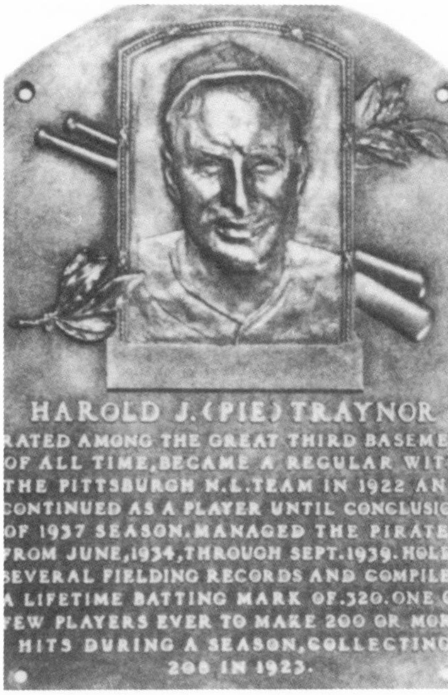
HAROLD J. (PIE) TRAYNOR
RATED AMONG THE GREAT THIRD BASEMEN OF ALL TIME, BECAME A REGULAR WITH THE PITTSBURGH N.L. TEAM IN 1922 AND CONTINUED AS A PLAYER UNTIL CONCLUSION OF 1937 SEASON. MANAGED THE PIRATES FROM JUNE, 1934, THROUGH SEPT. 1939. HOLDS SEVERAL FIELDING RECORDS AND COMPILED A LIFETIME BATTING MARK OF .320. ONE OF FEW PLAYERS EVER TO MAKE 200 OR MORE HITS DURING A SEASON, COLLECTING 208 IN 1923.

AMERICAN LEAGUE BEATS RIVALS, 4-2

49,000 See Ruth's Homer Yield Two Runs as Nationals Are Toppled.

LONG HIT COMES IN THIRD

Frisch Also Gets Circuit Smash —Gomez, Crowder, Grove Baffle Losers.

By JOHN DREBINGER.
Special to THE NEW YORK TIMES.

CHICAGO, July 6.—The National League is still trying to catch up with Babe Ruth, but apparently with no more success than in recent world's series conflicts.

Today, in the presence of a capacity throng of 49,000 in Comiskey Park, the great man of baseball fittingly whaled a home run into the right-field pavilion that gave the American League's all-star cast the necessary margin to bring down the pick of the National League in the "game of the century."

That smash, propelled off Willie Hallahan, star left-handed pitcher of the Cardinals, and with a runner on base, gave the team piloted by the venerable Connie Mack the victory by a score of 4 to 2. There was nothing the equally sagacious John J. McGraw could do about it.

McGraw, coming out of retirement for this singular event, the first of its kind in the history of the two major leagues, threw practically all his available manpower into the fray.

Stage Mild Uprising.

But there seemed to be no way whatever of effacing the effect of that Ruthian wallop, even though the National Leaguers later staged a mild uprising of their own with Frankie Frisch, the erstwhile Fordham flash, banging a homer into the stands.

Mack and McGraw, matching wits for the first time since their last world series clash in 1913, each sent three hurlers to the mound, but to Mack went the honors because the greater power was to be found in the mighty bludgeons of the American Leaguers.

Mack's selections were Vernon Gomez, ace left-hander of the Yankees; Alvin Crowder, star right-hander of the Senators, and finally his own master southpaw, Lefty Bob Grove. Each went three innings, and only off Crowder were the National League forces able to make any headway. They scored both their tallies off the Washington flinger.

Hallahan, Lon Warneke, brilliant right-hander of the Cubs, and Carl Hubbell, foremost left-hander of the National League, did the pitching for McGraw. Though the battle plan had been that this trio, too, should work three rounds apiece, the plan bogged down when Hallahan sagged in the third.

It was in this round that Ruth belted his homer. Before the round had ended the tall Warneke had to be rushed to Hallahan's assistance. It seems that when the Babe smacks one, the whole park rocks and few survive.

Hallahan Not Effective.

Hallahan, who unfortunately had pitched a full nine-inning game for the Cardinals only the day before yesterday, was obviously not quite himself as he squared off with Gomez. The latter, incidentally, also had had only a single day's rest after pitching a trying game against the Senators on the Fourth, but the willowy Yankee left-hander apparently is made of a little sterner stuff.

Hallahan's troubles began in the second when, with one out, he passed Dykes and Cronin. He seemed out of his difficulties when he retired Rick Ferrell and had only Gomez to face, but the gallant Castillian, known for his eccentricities, here did a very odd thing.

Admittedly one of the weakest hitters in all baseball, in this "game of the century" with the greatest clouters assembled, he struck the first damaging blow. He rifled a single to centre and Dykes tallied.

In the third, Hallahan's misfortunes engulfed him in less than a jiffy. He passed Gehringer and tried to whip one past Ruth. But the Babe drove it on a low line, just inside the right field foul pole and into the lower pavilion. The crowd, sweltering in the heat of a broiling sun, roared in acclamation.

Warneke Goes to Rescue.

Hallahan then pitched four more wide ones to Lou Gehrig, who also was waving his bat menacingly, and the tall, angular Warneke came rushing on the scene. He checked the American Leaguers for a time, but in the sixth dropped a run himself when Cronin singled, Ferrell sacrificed and Earl Averill, batting for Crowder, also singled.

Only for a brief moment did Gomez appear in trouble. That was at the start of the second when Chick Hafey and Bill Terry opened fire with a pair of one-base wallops. But Berger slapped into a double play and Bartell struck out. Gomez then swept through the third without allowing a man to reach first.

Crowder did equally well through the fourth and fifth, but in the sixth Warneke did a surprising thing. He banged a long hit down the right field foul line which the aging Ruth did not play any too well. Before the ball was retrieved, Warneke had converted the smash into a triple.

Pepper Martin's out sent the Chicago pitcher hustling over the plate with the Heydler circuit's first run and a moment later Frisch slashed a drive into the lower right pavilion for the circuit.

Crowder Halts Attack.

Though Chuck Klein followed with a single, Crowder clamped down the lid and the high spot of the National League's attack had passed.

With the seventh, baseball's two greatest southpaws, Grove and Hubbell, took the mound. Both blanked the opposition, though the McGraw legions did threaten Grove twice.

Terry opened the seventh with his second single of the day and Pie Traynor, pinch-hitting for Bartell, doubled to right centre, between Simmons and Ruth. But Grove fanned Gabby Hartnett, retired Woody English on a fly and the back of that rally was broken.

In the eighth Frisch, flashing as of yore, drove a single to right. There was a cry of keen expectancy from the National League supporters in the crowd as Hafey sent a

Associated Press Photo.

Frank Frisch.

soaring fly heading in the direction of the right-field pavilion. But the Babe caught this one just as he was about to back into the wall, and the last National League threat faded.

Three Mack Stars Idle.

With the exception of Hal Schumacher, who was held in reserve in case Hubbell ran into difficulties, McGraw used all his available players. But the finish saw Mack with still a lot of punch up his sleeve which he never had to use. Jimmy Foxx, Tony Lazzeri and Bill Dickey did not get into the fray at all.

The official attendance was 49,200, which was not a record for Comiskey Park, but on this occasion no standing room was permitted, by order of Commissioner Landis. The receipts totaled $51,000, which will be turned over to the National Association of Professional Baseball Players, which takes care of retired ball players in need.

During the early preliminaries the great crowd could not have found itself more occupied had a nine-ringed circus been in progress. Never before had baseball put on a show with all its greatest luminaries on the stage at the same time.

Box Score of Chicago Game

NATIONAL LEAGUE.

	AB	R	H	TB	2b	3b	hr	bb	so	sh	sb	po	a	e
Martin, St. L., 3b.....	4	0	0	0	0	0	0	0	1	0	0	0	3	0
Frisch, St. L., 2b.....	4	1	2	5	0	0	1	0	0	0	0	5	3	0
Klein, Phila., rf......	4	0	1	1	0	0	0	0	0	0	0	3	0	0
P. Waner, Pitt., rf....	0	0	0	0	0	0	0	0	0	0	0	0	0	C
Hafey, Cincin., lf.....	4	0	1	1	0	0	0	0	0	0	0	0	0	0
Terry, N. Y., 1b......	4	0	2	2	0	0	0	0	0	0	0	7	2	0
Berger, Boston, cf....	4	0	0	0	0	0	0	0	0	0	0	4	0	0
Bartell, Phila., ss...	2	0	0	0	0	0	0	1	0	0	0	3	0	
a Traynor, Pitt.......	1	0	1	2	1	0	0	0	0	0	0	0	0	0
Hubbell, N. Y., p....	0	0	0	0	0	0	0	0	0	0	0	0	0	0
b Cuccinello, Bklyn...	1	0	0	0	0	0	0	0	1	0	0	0	0	0
J. Wilson St. L., c...	1	0	0	0	0	0	0	0	0	0	0	2	0	0
c O'Doul, N. Y.......	1	0	0	0	0	0	0	0	0	0	0	0	0	0
Hartnett, Chi., c.....	1	0	0	0	0	0	0	0	1	0	0	2	0	0
Hallahan, St. L., p...	1	0	0	0	0	0	0	0	0	0	0	1	0	0
Warneke, Chi., p.....	1	1	1	3	0	1	0	0	0	0	0	0	0	0
English, Chi., ss.....	1	0	0	0	0	0	0	0	0	0	0	0	0	0
Total 34	2	8	14	1	1	1	0	4	0	0	24	11	0	

AMERICAN LEAGUE.

	AB	R	H	TB	2b	3b	hr	bb	so	sh	sb	po	a	e
Chapman, N. Y., lf.,rf.	5	0	1	1	0	0	0	0	1	0	0	1	0	0
Gehringer, Detr., 2b..	3	1	0	0	0	0	0	2	0	0	1	1	3	0
Ruth, N. Y., rf......	4	1	2	5	0	0	1	0	2	0	0	1	0	0
West, St. L., cf......	0	0	0	0	0	0	0	0	0	0	0	0	0	0
Gehrig, N. Y., 1b....	2	0	0	0	0	0	0	2	1	0	0	12	0	1
Simmons, Chi., cf., lf.	4	0	1	1	0	0	0	0	0	0	0	4	0	0
Dykes, Chi., 3b.....	3	1	2	2	0	0	0	1	0	0	0	2	4	0
Cronin, Wash., ss.....	3	1	1	1	0	0	0	1	0	0	0	2	4	0
R. Ferrell, Boston, c..	3	0	0	0	0	0	0	0	1	0	0	4	0	0
Gomez, N. Y., p......	1	0	1	1	0	0	0	0	0	0	0	0	0	0
Crowder, Wash., p....	1	0	0	0	0	0	0	0	0	0	0	0	0	0
d Averill, Cleve......	1	0	1	1	0	0	0	0	0	0	0	0	0	0
Grove, Phila., p......	1	0	0	0	0	0	0	0	0	0	0	0	0	0
Total 31	4	9	12	0	0	1	6	4	1	1	27	11	1	

a Batted for Bartell in seventh. b Batted for Hubbell in ninth. c Batted for Wilson in sixth. d Batted for Crowder in sixth.

SCORE BY INNINGS.

National League.............	0	0	0	0	0	2	0	0	0—2	
American League.............	0	1	2	0	0	1	0	0	.—4	

Runs batted in—American League: Ruth 2, Gomez, Averill. National League: Martin, Frisch.

Left on bases—American League 10, National League 5. Double plays—Bartell, Frisch and Terry; Dykes and Gehrig. Hits—Off Hallahan 2 in 2 (none out in third), Warneke 6 in 4, Hubbell 1 in 2, Gomez 2 in 3, Crowder 3 in 3, Grove 3 in 3. Struck out—By Hallahan 1, Warneke 2, Hubbell 1, Gomez 1, Grove 3. Bases on balls—Off Hallahan 5, Hubbell 1. Winning pitcher, Gomez; losing pitcher, Hallahan. Umpires—Dinneen (A. L.) at the plate, Klem (N. L.) at first, McGowan (A. L.) at second, Rigler (N. L.) at third, for the first four and one-half innings; Klem (N. L.) at the plate, McGowan (A. L.) at first, Rigler (N. L.) at second, Dinneen (A. L.) at third, for remainder of game. Time of game—2:05.

Ruth, of course, was the chief magnet of the autograph seekers. But there was plenty of attention bestowed upon the other great performers such as Terry, Klein, Foxx, Simmons and Cronin.

One of the warmest receptions of the day was tendered to Lefty Grove when the crowd's attention was called to the fact that the famous Mack southpaw was warming up in the bull pen.

But the greatest ovation of all seemed to go to Hubbell as the Giant left-hander started tuning up his mighty arm that pitched eighteen scoreless innings last Sunday.

There was some disappointment when these two aces did not start the game, especially as the two starting hurlers, Hallahan and Gomez, both had pitched in regular league assignments on Tuesday.

July 7, 1933

Dean Fans 17 and Wilson Gets 18 Putouts For Two New Records as Cards Win Twice

By The Associated Press.

ST. LOUIS, July 30.—Two modern baseball records fell today before the brilliant pitching of Jerome (Dizzy) Dean and the stellar catching of Jimmy Wilson of the St. Louis Cardinals. The Cards took both ends of a double-header from the Chicago Cubs, 8 to 2 and 6 to 5.

Dean struck out seventeen men and Wilson made eighteen putouts in the first game for new modern records.

The Cardinals, by their double victory, regained third place in the National League by one point, shoving the Cubs to fourth.

While other pitchers nearly half a century ago struck out more batters in a nine-inning game, Dean set a record for modern baseball. Wilson's eighteen putouts had not been equalled in almost a similar length of time.

The previous modern record of sixteen strikeouts was held jointly by Frank Hahn, Christy Matheson, Rube Waddell and Nap Rucker.

Wilson's figure of eighteen putouts beats the modern National League record (since 1900) of seventeen set by Hank De Berry of the Dodgers on June 17, 1928. The all-time record is held by Vincent Nava of Providence, who had nineteen in a game played June 7, 1884. The American League record is

Times Wide World Photo.
Dizzy Dean, Cardinals.

sixteen, held jointly by Spencer of the Browns, Lapp of the Athletics and Ruel of the Yankees.

Hahn of the Reds made his record against Boston on May 22, 1901. It was equalled by Mathewson of the Giants, pitching against St. Louis on Oct. 3, 1904; by Waddell for the Browns against the Athletics, July 29, 1908, and by Rucker for the Dodgers against St. Louis, July 24, 1909.

The all-time record of nineteen was made in 1884 by Sweeney of Providence and tied the same year by Dailey of Chicago.

The box scores:

FIRST GAME.

CHICAGO (N.)						ST. LOUIS (N.)					
	ab.	r.	h.	po.	a. e.		ab.	r.	h.	po.	a. e.
Koenig, 3b.	4	1	1	1	1 0	Martin, 3b.	5	0	1	1	3 1
W.H'm'n,2b	4	0	2	4	4 1	Watkins, rf.	4	0	1	1	0 0
Cuyler, lf.	3	0	0	1	0 1	Frisch, 2b.	4	0	0	0	2 9
F.Herman,rf	4	0	0	3	0 0	Cr'wford,1b	3	1	0	6	0 0
Demaree, cf.	4	1	1	2	0 0	Medwick, lf.	4	2	4	0	0 0
Campbell, c.	3	0	1	3	1 0	Orsatti, cf.	3	1	1	5	0 0
Hendrick,1b	4	0	0	8	0 0	Wilson, c.	3	1	1	5	0 0
Jurges, ss.	4	0	1	2	4 0	Durocher,ss	4	2	1	1	1 0
Bush, p.	2	0	0	0	2 0	Dean, p.	4	1	3	0	1 0
Grimes, p.	1	0	0	0	1 0						
aMosolf	1	0	0	0	0 0						
Total..	34	2	6	24	14 ..	Total..	33	8	13	27	7 1

aBatted for Grimes in ninth.

Chicago ....100 100 000—2
St. Louis ....100 005 02.—8

Runs batted in—W. Herman, Campbell, Frisch, Orsatti 2. Wilson, Durocher, Dean 2.
Two-base hits—Koenig, Watkins, W. Herman, Dean 2, Campbell, Orsatti, Durocher, Dean 2. Stolen base—Martin. Sacrifices—Orsatti 2. Double plays—Jurges and Hendrick; Jurges, W. Herman and Hendrick. Left on bases—Chicago 7, St. Louis 5. Bases on balls—Off Bush 1, Dean 1. Struck out—By Bush 2, Dean 17, Grimes 1. Hits—Off Bush 10 in 5 1-3 innings, Grimes 3 in 2-3. Hit by pitcher—By Dean (Campbell). Wild pitch—Grimes. Losing pitcher—Bush. Umpires—McGrew and Magerkurth. Time of game—1:42.

SECOND GAME.

CHICAGO (N.)						ST. LOUIS (N.)					
	ab.	r.	h.	po.	a. e.		ab.	r.	h.	po.	a. e.
English, 3b.	4	1	0	0	1 0	Martin, 3b.	3	3	2	0	0 0
W. Her'n,2b.	4	0	1	3	1 0	Watkins, rf.	3	0	1	4	0 0
Cuyler, lf.	2	2	1	5	0 0	Frisch, 2b.	3	0	0	1	4 0
F. Herman,rf	4	0	1	5	1 0	Crawford, 1b.	3	1	1	8	0 0
Demaree, cf.	4	2	2	2	0 0	Medwick, lf.	4	1	1	1	0 0
Hartnett, c.	4	0	1	3	0 0	Orsatti, cf.	3	1	0	5	0 0
Hendrick,1b	4	0	1	7	0 1	O'Farrell, c.	4	0	1	7	1 1
Jurges, ss.	3	0	0	1	3 0	Durocher, ss.	4	0	1	1	2 0
Tinning, p.	2	0	0	1	0 0	Hallahan, p.	0	0	0	0	0 0
Henshaw, p.	0	0	0	0	0 0	Johnson, p.	1	0	0	0	0 0
Root, p.	0	0	0	0	0 0	Haines, p.	1	0	1	0	0 1
aMosolf	1	0	0	0	0 0	Vance, p.	0	0	0	0	0 0
bMolf	1	0	0	0	0 0	cAllen	1	0	0	0	0 0
Total	33	5	7	24	7 1	Total	30	6	8	27	7 2

aBatted for Jurges in ninth.
bBatted for Root in ninth.
cBatted for Johnson in fourth.

Chicago ....300 002 000—5
St. Louis ....361 011 00.—6

Runs batted in—Demaree 2, Hartnett, Medwick 3, Crawford, Watkins, Haines.
Two-base hits—Durocher, Watkins, Haines, Hendrick. Three-base hit—Martin. Home runs—Demaree, Medwick. Stolen bases—English, Cuyler. Sacrifices—Frisch, Cuyler. Left on bases—Chicago 5, St. Louis 5. Bases on balls—Off Tinning 3, Henshaw 1, Hallahan 2, Haines 1. Struck out—By Root 1, Hallahan 1, Johnson 1, Haines 4, Vance 1. Hits—Off Tinning 6 in 4 innings (none out in fifth), Henshaw 1 in 1 1-3, Johnson 2 in 3 1-3, Haines 5 in 4 (none out in ninth), Vance 0 in 1. Winning pitcher—Haines. Losing pitcher—Henshaw. Umpires—Magerkurth and McGrew. Time of game—2:05.

July 31, 1933

Sports of the Times
Reg. U. S. Pat. Off.
By JOHN KIERAN.
The Faultless Pitcher.

HERB PENNOCK, who wore a Yankee uniform through eleven glamourous seasons and five world's series, is now on the roster of the Boston Red Sox. He will be 40 years old in a few weeks. His great left arm isn't what it used to be. Herb is getting along, moving into the twilight of a great pitching career.

Andrea Del Sarto was called the Faultless Painter. Herb Pennock might be called the Faultless Pitcher. There were no chinks in his shining armor; he was the Knight Peerless of the pitching parapet. Waddell was a great left-hander. Possibly the eccentric Rube poured more fire and fury in on a helpless batter than any other southpaw the diamond ever has seen. Bob Grove has been the great fire-ball flinger of recent years, a marvelous left-hander.

But it was Harry M. Stevens who said not long ago when great pitchers were up for discussion:

"Waddell, Walter Johnson, Amos Rusie, Lefty Grove—I've seen them all; great pitchers. But for one game that you had to win, one game with everything at stake, give me Matty!"

Let that stand. Along with it a baseball follower might add: "Pennock is the Matty of left-handers."

Making a Choice.

It's a coincidence that Connie Mack brought out Waddell, Pennock and Grove. He also brought out Eddie Plank. He seems to have possessed a genius for collaring great left-handers. What choice Connie might make among them for a single game is not known at the moment.

But suppose a manager had that important game to face and a left-hander to choose. Could he pick Waddell? Why, no one could tell whether or not the Rube would even show up at the park. He might be riding a hook and ladder truck to a three-alarm fire. There were other reasons why the Rube was unreliable.

Would a manager pick Grove over the others? Lanky Robert was and is a great left-hander, but his control was bad for years and even yet is far from perfect. He might blow the batters down and, again, he might get himself into a deep hole with a sudden flare-back to his old wildness.

A manager could pick Pennock and have no more worries. Herb would show up at the park. He would have all his stuff for a great occasion. His control would be practically perfect. He would never lose his poise or his courage. What more could any manager want from a left-hander?

Every Move a Picture.

For a score of years Pennock has been out there on the mound tossing up curves. fast ones and changes of pace with a graceful motion that has been fascinating to watch. He made it look easy, like the true artist he has been.

That was part of his effectiveness. When the gaunt Mr. Grove heaves himself up to his full height, sticks a right foot toward the clouds and prepares to pour his fire at the batter, the defendant is forewarned. He knows that trouble is coming at him—and swiftly!

But who could suspect the slim, gentlemanly Pennock out there with his graceful, almost languid, motion? There are veteran hitters—and good hitters, too—who never could teach themselves that Herb's fast ball was much faster than it looked to be, his curve just a bit wider than it appeared to a man with a bat in his hand.

There was no puffing and blowing, no clinching of teeth or grunting as the ball was delivered. Burleigh Grimes always looked like a man who was about to commit assault and battery when he threw the ball. Fred Fitzsimmons twists his face even more than he does his arms when winding up. With every pitch, Bullet Joe Bush used to give a grunt that could be heard in the bleachers. Babe Ruth

HERBERT J. (HERB) PENNOCK
OUTSTANDING LEFT HANDED PITCHER IN THE A.L. AND EXECUTIVE OF PHILADELPHIA N.L. CLUB. AMONG RARE FEW WHO MADE JUMP FROM PREP SCHOOL TO MAJORS. SAW 22 YEARS SERVICE WITH PHILADELPHIA BOSTON AND NEW YORK TEAMS IN A.L. RECORDED 240 VICTORIES, 161 DEFEATS. NEVER LOST A WORLD SERIES GAME. WINNING FIVE. IN 1927, PITCHED 7 1/3 INNINGS WITHOUT ALLOWING HIT IN THIRD GAME OF SERIES.

used to stick his tongue out of the corner of his mouth when he was throwing a curve.

Pennock was always a delight to the eye, every move a picture.

A Series Hero.

With Colby Jack Coombs, Pennock shares the record of having won five games and lost none in world's series campaigns. His last effort, though it added nothing to his record of games won, was in the 1932 series between the Yankees and the Cubs. What he did in that series—and why he was picked to do it—is typical of Pennock.

In the third game, with the Yanks leading 7–4 in the ninth and Pipgras pitching, Hartnett led off with a home run. Jurges singled. Pipgras was plainly wavering. Some 51,000 Cub rooters went into a frenzy of cheering. A pinch-hitter, Hemsley, was coming up for the Chicago pitcher.

Joe McCarthy called on Pennock to squelch the rally—Pennock, who had pitched in a world's series eighteen years before that. The pinch-hitter struck out. The next man rolled weakly to Pennock, who tossed him out. The third man hit a grounder to Gehrig. The Old Master had shown them a spot of pitching.

Closing Out the Show.

The final game of that series was a rough-and-tumble performance. The Cubs knocked out Johnny Allen before he had his feet fairly planted on the mound. The Yanks battered several Cub pitchers. When the Yanks finally established a lead, Manager McCarthy once again looked around for the veteran who could be trusted to guard it and give the Yanks a clean sweep in the series. That was Pennock.

Herb pitched the last three innings for the Yankees and it was just a breeze for him. The Cubs were young fellows taking lessons from an artist at his trade.

Some great ball players have been afflicted with "swelled heads." Others have been so bashful that they never were friendly. A few came from so far in the tall timber that they never became accustomed to civilization. Some were diamonds in the rough and one or two, alas, were just roughs on the diamond.

But by a happy coincidence, Herb Pennock had "all the good gifts of nature." He was good-looking, he was friendly, he was courageous. He spoke as he pitched, gracefully, quietly and effectively. In short, wherever he goes, for one observer Herb Pennock will remain the Faultless Pitcher.

January 23, 1934

Baseball Mourns Passing of McGraw

CAREER OF M'GRAW UNIQUE IN SPORTS

His Ten Pennant Victories and Three World's Championships Form Unrivaled Record.

From the early Nineties John Joseph McGraw was one of the greatest figures in organized baseball. In his playing days a brilliant third baseman, whose efforts were not confined to the mere mechanics of the sport, but a player who brought a keen, incisive mind to the national game, a fighter of the old school whose aggressiveness inspired his team-mates of the famous old Baltimore Orioles. McGraw became the most successful figure, perhaps, in all baseball history. His record—ten pennant winners and three world's titles—speaks eloquently of McGraw, the molder of championship clubs, a stickler for discipline and a martinet who saw that his orders were rigidly enforced both on and off the field.

Baseball history does not reveal any record that approaches the achievement of McGraw in capturing ten pennants with his Giants. Connie Mack, veteran pilot of the Athletics, and Miller Huggins, late manager of the Yankees, are the only other leaders whose accomplishments are in any way comparable with those of the fiery McGraw. Mack has won nine flags. Huggins was the Yankee pilot six times for league honors.

Gained Experience on Sand Lots.

McGraw was born in the rural community of Truxton, N. Y., on April 7, 1873, and gained his first knowledge of the game on the sand lots of that tiny village of up-State New York. There were not many boys in the little hamlet of some 300 persons, and decidedly few of any special baseball-playing ability. So it was significant of McGraw's persistency and close application to the task in hand that he was able to attain so much proficiency as a player that in 1890, at the age of 17, he obtained an engagement with the Olean (N. Y.) club, then a member of the original New York and Pennsylvania League.

The next season, 1891, found McGraw transplanted to a far distant field. He had journeyed westward to Iowa, where he signed a contract with the Cedar Rapids (Iowa) club of the Illinois-Iowa League. Reports of McGraw's rapid-fire fielding, his speed on the bases and his solid hitting reached the ears of the officials of the Baltimore club of the old American Association, and in midsummer of that year, Aug. 26, to be exact, McGraw, following his purchase, donned the uniform of the famous old Orioles.

Retained by the Orioles.

McGraw played in thirty-one games during the remainder of the season and showed enough ability to warrant retention. The next year Baltimore became a member of the twelve-club National League. The Orioles had been going badly and Ed Hanlon, who had shown an exceptional faculty for organization and leadership as well as playing

Underwood & Underwood Photo.

As Manager of the Giants in 1912.

ability, was obtained to manage the team.

Hanlon made a number of player deals during the Winter, and in one of them he acquired a youth whose name was to be linked inseparably with McGraw ever thereafter. The new acquisition was a red-headed youngster from Louisville, the late Hughey Jennings.

Jennings and McGraw met on the Orioles' Spring training trip of 1893. The conditioning campaign took the Baltimore club to New Orleans. The year before the Orioles had descended to last place in the twelve-club circuit and Hanlon was determined to lift the club out of the rut. He set to work with the fixed idea of weeding out some of the slipping veterans and replacing them with new blood. McGraw and Jennings got the chance to show what they could do at third base and short and came through with flying colors and clinched these positions.

Robinson a Team-Mate.

The Orioles of that period included many exceptional players, men like Wilbert Robinson, former manager and president of the Brooklyn club, then rated as one of the finest catchers in baseball. His battery mate was the noted pitcher John (Sadie) McMahon. Joe Kelley roamed the outfield.

Hanlon, the George Stallings of another generation, welded the club into a formidable and close-knit unit in the season of 1894 and brought it home in front of the rest of the field, a remarkable performance. By this time, however, the wily pilot had obtained Willie Keeler, Walter Brodie, Kid Gleason and others to supplement the nucleus remaining.

McGraw and Jennings in the Winter previous to the Orioles' first pennant-winning achievement had advanced themselves along another line of endeavor. In one of their long and frank talks they came to the conclusion that their education had largely been neglected and they resolved to overcome the deficiency.

Trade Experience for Schooling.

McGraw proposed taking a course at St. Bonaventure College at Alle-

gany, N. Y., not far from his home and the scene of his first professional baseball experience, and Jennings quickly fell in line with the idea. They were not in a position financially to afford much of an outlay for the education they sought, but with real business acumen arranged with the college authorities to exchange their knowledge of baseball in a coaching capacity for an academic education.

The Orioles from 1894 to 1899 were one of the most formidable and widely discussed clubs in baseball history. Under Hanlon's magic guidance this dashing, aggressive combination captured three National League pennants in succession, then finished second two years in a row and in 1899, the last year of Baltimore's connection with the older major circuit, the club, many of whose famed veteran players had been replaced by that time, dropped to fourth.

Four times the Orioles played for the Temple Cup, the premier trophy of baseballdom of that period, which was annually contended for by the first and second place clubs in the National League. Twice McGraw and his mates captured the annual classic, and their bitter battles with Patsy Tebeau's crack Cleveland club are still vividly remembered by old-time fans.

McGraw gained his first managerial experience in 1899, taking the helm for part of the season, Wilbert Robinson succeeding him. The end of that season witnessed the sale of these two stars to the St. Louis National League Club. However, they preferred to cast their lot with the American League, then in the process of organization.

McGraw and Robinson took over the Baltimore franchise in the new circuit. Then the war between the two major circuits broke out and McGraw became involved in a controversy with Ban Johnson, then president of the American League. The late Andrew Freedman, then president of the New York Giants, had taken a fancy to McGraw and offered him the post of manager. The Giants had been going from bad to worse under several different régimes and Freedman believed that McGraw was the man to put the club on its feet.

Took Charge of the Giants.

On July 19, 1902, McGraw, then a rather stocky, black-haired little fellow, 29 years old, walked out on the old Polo Grounds to take command of the hapless, disorganized Giants. This date is a significant one in the annals of the diamond, and in 1927 was enthusiastically celebrated by a great army of fans and baseball and city officials on the occasion of the twenty-fifth anniversary of McGraw's leadership of the New York National League club.

McGraw undertook the reconstruction of the club, and the success of his efforts is evidenced by the fact that in 1903, his first full year at the helm, the Giants finished in second place. McGraw brought Joe McGinnity, Dan McGann and Roger Bresnahan, three bright young stars, with him from the Baltimore club. He signed Arthur Devlin as his third baseman, Billy Gilbert as his second-sacker. The immortal Christy Mathewson already had joined the club from Bucknell University.

Attendance Rose Quickly.

He was remarkably successful in the development of Mathewson, George Wiltse, Leon Ames and

Dummy Taylor to aid McGinnity and the Giants were made. The attendance figures increased tremendously, and the advent of the New York Highlanders, an opposition club placed in the metropolis by the American League, was scarcely noticed.

In 1904 McGraw's Giants swept through the league, bowling over all opposition and rolling up the huge total of 106 victories, a mark that has been exceeded only twice in the history of the National League. McGraw was hailed as the "Little Napoleon" of organized baseball and baseball followers heaped encomiums on his head as the organizer of one of baseball's most powerful machines.

The previous year the Pittsburgh club, champion of the National League, and the Boston club, title winner in the junior circuit, had met in the first series for the world's championship. But, much to the disappointment of fandom, John T. Brush, who had succeeded Freedman as president of the Giants, stubbornly refused to let his club meet the Boston club, which had captured another pennant. He had been one of the stanch supporters of the National League and could not see that anything was to be gained by recognizing and playing against the champion team of a rival circuit.

The following year the Giants repeated and this year Brush finally consented to allow his club to contend against the champions of the American League, the Philadelphia Athletics. The most brilliantly pitched world's series of all time ensued.

Personnel of Famous Team.

McGraw lined up his team for the opening clash as follows: Mathewson, pitcher; Bresnahan, catcher; McGann, first base; Gilbert, second base; Devlin, third base; Dahlen, shortstop; Mertes, left field; Donlin, centre field, and Browne, right field. It was one of the finest combinations New York fans had ever seen in action.

Connie Mack's Athletics also were formidable, but were no match for the Giants with Mathewson and McGinnity pitching all five games for the National Leaguers. Mathewson established a record for all time of shutting out the opposition in three of the battles. McGinnity blanked the Athletics in another contest and in the other battle, the only one which Philadelphia won, Chief Bender shut out the Giants. All five games were shut-outs, another record for the annual classic.

The Giants then finished second to Frank Chance's sensational Cubs for the next three years, dropping to third in 1909 but rising to second in 1910. McGraw made many bold moves to strengthen his club and invariably had his nine in the running. In 1908 the Giants came within an ace of taking the flag, losing it through defeat in a play-off with the Cubs. The blunder by Fred Merkle in not touching second base and thus giving the Cubs another chance to win out ultimately was one of the most discussed diamond happenings of that decade.

Forgave Merkle for Blunder.

McGraw forgave Merkle and instead of censuring him condoned the fatal oversight, and, moreover, raised his salary for the sake of encouraging the downcast player. Merkle repaid his boss by playing stellar ball for years thereafter and was ranked as one of the most mentally alert players in the game.

In 1911 McGraw finally passed the fighting Cubs and brought his ninth flag to the metropolis. In that year he had Herzog, Fletcher, Doyle and Merkle in his infield; Devore, Snodgrass and Murray in the outfield; Meyers behind the bat and Mathewson, Ames and Wiltse, sole survivors of the 1905 champions, and

As a Member of the Orioles in His Youth.

Marquard and Crandall in the box. The Athletics boasted their "$100,000 infield," whose valuation would have been increased tenfold just a few years later, and Frank Baker's bat, more than any other factor, laid the Giants low in four out of six games.

The Giants repeated in 1912 and this year encountered the Boston Red Sox in the annual classic. The series went to the limit of seven games before Snodgrass made his fatal muff in the tenth inning and Boston pulled out the series.

The Giants captured their third straight pennant in 1913 and again faced Connie Mack's great Athletics. The latter were too much for the Giants once more and took four out of five games. The Giants still had Mathewson, and Big Six pitched the only game the New Yorkers won, but McGraw's hitters could not cope with the brilliant pitching of Coombs, Bender, Plank and Bush.

McGraw built over again, and in 1917, the Giants' next pennant-winning year, many new players were

members of the combination that faced the White Sox. Burns, Kauff and Robertson roamed the outer gardens, Zimmerman, Herzog, Fletcher and Holke held down infield berths, McCarthy and Rariden were behind the bat and Sallee, Schupp, Anderson, Perritt, Tesreau and Rube Benton attended to the pitching duties. Again the Giants were doomed to defeat, the White Sox taking four contests of the six-game series.

The jinx that persistently pursued the Giants in world series was put to rout in 1921, the next year McGraw's club finished on top, and Miller Huggins's Yankees, with Babe Ruth cast in the heavy slugging rôle, could not stop the Giants' dashing, crushing attack.

Giants' Stars of 1921 Triumph.

Dave Bancroft, Frank Frisch, George Kelly, Pep Young, Emil Meusel, George Burns, Johnnie Rawlings, Frank Snyder, Phil Douglas, Arthur Nehf, Earl Smith, Fred Toney and Jess Barnes were members of the McGraw combination of that year. Practically the same players, to whom Heine Groh, Casey Stengel, Bill Cunningham, Jack Scott, Hugh McQuillan and a few others of lesser importance had been added, routed the Yankees, again winners of the American League flag, in five games, the one game the clan of McGraw did not capture being a tie.

For the third consecutive year the two New York clubs clashed in 1923, and this time the Yankees, thanks to a savage batting attack, came out on top, winning the world title by scoring four victories in six starts.

McGraw set a world's record by leading his club to its fourth consecutive pennant in 1924. That year the Giants engaged in an exciting and hard-fought struggle with Bucky Harris's Washington club, whose pitching mainstay was the redoubtable Walter Johnson. There was little to choose between the two clubs, but the Senators finally emerged triumphant, winning the odd game of seven, Johnson stemming the Giants' attack in the late innings of the crucial contest.

Fred Lindstrom, Bill Terry, Hack Wilson, Hank Gowdy, Jack Bentley, Billy Southworth and Rosy Ryan had been added to the pennant-winning ensemble of the previous year.

Victory Under McGraw.

That year, 1924, marked the Giants' last surge to the top in the National League under McGraw's leadership. In 1925 the club finished second after a hard battle with the Pittsburgh Pirates, and again in 1927 McGraw's team, after a slow start, finished with a burst of speed that nearly carried it into another championship, the Giants finally finishing two games rearward of the champion Pirates.

Again rebuilding after falling to fifth place in 1926 and finishing third in 1927, McGraw almost scaled the heights in 1928. Building around Bill Terry, Melvin Ott and Fred Lindstrom as hitters, with Frank Hogan also aiding, and with a pitching staff led by Larry Benton, the Giants carried the fight almost to the last day of the season, only to finish two games behind the St. Louis Cardinals.

In fact, with the season ending on Sunday, Sept. 30, it took defeats at the hands of the Cubs on Friday and Saturday, with a victory by St. Louis on Saturday, to decide the race. McGraw drove his team with all his old-time skill, winning ten and losing five in his last home stand. In 1929 he finished third because Benton failed and in 1930 he was in the same place, practically for the same reason.

The last real effort came in 1931, when he finished second, but far

Highlights in McGraw's Career

Played his first professional game with Olean April, 1890.

Played his first big-league game with Baltimore Orioles Aug. 26, 1891.

Played his last game with the Giants Sept. 12, 1906.

Member of three pennant-winning teams in Baltimore, where he played from 1891 until 1899.

Retired with a lifetime batting average of .334, going over .300 for nine consecutive seasons and reaching .390 in 1899.

Became manager of the Giants in July, 1902, reorganizing an eighth-place club so that he finished second the next year (1903).

Won three world's championships —1905, 1921 and 1922—and ten league pennants.

Set record for consecutive pennants when he won in 1921, 1922, 1923 and 1924—four in a row.

Took teams on foreign tours in 1914 and 1924. The 1914 journey was around the world.

Developed Christy Mathewson and considered him the greatest pitcher of all time.

Retired as manager of the Giants on June 3, 1932.

RECORD OF M'GRAW AS PILOT OF GIANTS

Year.	Position.	Year.	Position.
1903	Second	1918	Second
1904	First	1919	Second
*1905	First	1920	Second
1906	Second	*1921	First
1907	Second	*1922	First
1908	Second	1923	First
1909	Third	1924	First
1910	Second	1925	Second
1911	First	1926	Fifth
1912	First	1927	Third
1913	First	1928	Second
1914	Second	1929	Third
1915	Eighth	1930	Third
1916	Fourth	1931	Second
1917	First		

*World's championships—three.

Recapitulation—First, ten times. Second, twelve times. Third, four times. Fourth, once. Fifth, once. Eighth, once.

WORLD SERIES RESULTS.

1904—No series with Boston Red Sox, American League champions.
1905—Giants 4 games, Athletics 1.
1911—Athletics 4 games, Giants 2.
1912—Red Sox 4 games, Giants 3, tied 1.
1913—Athletics 4 games, Giants 1.
1917—White Sox 4 games, Giants 2.
1921—Giants 5 games, Yankees 3.
1922—Giants 4 games, Yankees 0, tied 1.
1923—Yankees 4 games, Giants 2.
1924—Senators 4 games, Giants 3.

Won three world's championships, ten league championships.

Won 26, lost 28, tied 2 in world series games.

behind the Cardinals, who that year had a superteam, the one which beat the Athletics for the world's championship. The Giants won eighty-seven games, good enough in some years for pennants, but the Cardinals went over the 100 mark.

Then came 1932. McGraw made a few changes, and in the training season in California seemed again to have exercised his magic. On the Coast and on the way East his

men could not lose, compiling one of the best pre-season records ever made. But when the games came that counted they could not win. Through April and May they went, luckless.

Their failure weighed on their leader, and illnesses that he had laughed off and fought off in former years brought him down. He was a sick man, sicker than most people ever knew, when he electrified the baseball world by resigning on June 3 and turning the club over to Bill Terry, whom he had recommended to the officials of the club.

Since his resignation he had acted in an advisory capacity in the selection of young players, something at which his wide acquaintance with baseball club owners and managers had made him invaluable, and gave much counsel to Terry in the campaign which resulted in last year's pennant and world title.

Turbulent Chapters in Career.

There were turbulent chapters in McGraw's career. Several times he became embroiled in altercations with the umpire and once lost an impromptu bout to an arbiter following a heated dispute over the umpire's decision.

A few years ago McGraw was charged with engaging in fisticuffs at the Lambs Club, of which he was a member. John C. Slavin, a comedian, and Wilton Lackaye and William H. Boyd, actors, both received hospital attention and McGraw was expelled from membership in the organization. Later the club reinstated him following the circulation of a petition to which the names of several hundred members were appended. McGraw was indicted on a charge of having liquor in his possession at the time an alleged fight occurred. The Federal court acquitted the Giants' manager.

McGraw also was a baseball missionary to foreign lands, spreading the gospel of baseball to many countries abroad. In 1913, after the Giants and Athletics had met for the world series, McGraw and Charles Comiskey, owner of the White Sox, led two teams on a world tour, embarking at San Francisco and terminating their long journey in New York. The two clubs toured

Japan, China, Australia, Egypt, Italy, France and England, playing their final contest before the King and 35,000 other Britons at London.

Again Led Team Overseas.

In 1924 at the close of the regular season McGraw and Comiskey again took two teams abroad, visiting England and France. Interest in America's national game was kindled anew and many nines were organized abroad as the direct result of this second invasion. The trip, however, was said to have been a financial failure to the extent of some $20,000.

McGraw always said that he did not object to incurring the financial losses his tours abroad cost him provided the journeys had added to the general interest in baseball.

Besides directing the playing of the Giants, since 1919 he had been associated in the business management and ownership of the club. In that year Harry Hempstead sold his interests to Charles A. Stoneham, Judge Francis X. McQuade and McGraw, and the Giants' pilot became vice president of the club. While the club was owned by the late John T. Brush McGraw was reputed to be drawing a salary of $30,000 a year. When he became an official it was generally accepted that he was drawing $65,000. In the early part of the 1928 season McGraw agreed to continue in his managerial capacity for the next two years. This dispelled rumors that he was planning to retire at the end of the 1928 campaign.

During his long management of the Giants McGraw was often accused of buying pennants, meaning that he purchased stars of other clubs to strengthen the Giants and aid them in their pennant fights. The club, however, was in a financial position to acquire players developed by other teams who readily parted with their stars for needed cash.

Always Strong for Fair Play.

McGraw always played the game fairly and his integrity was shown by his prompt dismissal of players who were found to have been involved in sharp practices, no matter how much this weakened the club.

His silver jubilee at the Polo

Grounds in 1927 brought back many memories of his long and successful career. The general feeling of admiration and respect was in Mayor Walker's voice when he presented a huge silver loving cup to baseball's Little Napoleon. Commander Richard E. Byrd and Clarence D. Chamberlin, transatlantic airmen, stood by the Mayor's side as he eulogized the veteran silver-haired leader.

McGraw's playing days undoubtedly would have been extended had it not been for a bad spike wound he suffered as a member of the Orioles. He played only ten years and during this time compiled a grand batting average of .334, while he scored 1,016 runs and stole 443 bases, an excellent offensive record.

Hornsby Episode Recalled.

The Hornsby episode is still fresh in the minds of fandom. McGraw brought the celebrated Rajah to New York in the Spring of 1927 and he played brilliantly for the Giants, only to be traded to the Braves at the close of the season. Rumor had it that enmity had arisen between Hornsby and McGraw, but the claim was never substantiated.

Hornsby himself said after he had been traded that he still esteemed McGraw highly and considered him the greatest manager in the major leagues. McGraw denied there was anything but the most cordial relations between himself and the slugging infielder. Later President Stoneham assumed full responsibility for the disposal of the star player, asserting he had been traded "for the good of the club."

When McGraw took his Giants to Olean for an exhibition contest against St. Bonaventure in the Summer of 1927 he was enthusiastically greeted after thirty-seven years' absence from that town. McGraw's homecoming was one of the biggest events that ever happened in the little city and flags waved from almost every building, while the whole population turned out with several bands to greet him. It was a happy moment for McGraw, who years before had trudged disconsolately through the streets to the railway station after committing those alleged nine errors.

February 26, 1934

STENGEL IS SIGNED AS DODGERS' PILOT

Successor to Carey Receives a Two-Year Contract— Salary Not Revealed.

TO DEMAND BEST EFFORTS

'Boys Have Got to Play for Me,' New Brooklyn Manager Says —Fraser to Be Coach.

By ROSCOE McGOWEN.

Charles Dillon (Casey) Stengel became the ace of a new deal for

the Brooklyn Dodgers yesterday when he signed a two-year contract as manager, succeeding the recently deposed Max Carey.

Sitting at the bedside of Business Manager J. A. Robert Quinn, who has been ill in the Hotel New Yorker for several days, Casey affixed his signature to the document at 8 o'clock yesterday morning.

The only unexpected feature of the whole affair was the fact that Stengel was signed for two years, as Uncle Wilbert Robinson had only a one-year contract before he was dropped in 1931 and Carey also worked on the single-season basis.

No announcement of terms was made, the bare official announcement, signed by President Stephen W. McKeever, merely stating that Stengel has been engaged "for the seasons of 1934 and 1935."

But there was no long discussion of salary, and it is understood Stengel will receive at least as much as his predecessor, who is reported

to have been paid off at the rate of $12,000 a year on his unexpired 1934 contract.

Faces Barrage of Questions.

Following the brief business of signing, Casey adjourned to another suite, where, for more than two hours, he faced a barrage of congratulations and questions from newspaper men, and a battery of photographers.

The genial Stengel acceded to the dozens of demands for poses and answered queries from all sides at the same time, some seriously and some with the quaint wit that has made him famous among baseball men.

"Maybe this means that the Dodgers have gone in for the NRA," he declared once. "You know"——he grinned, "New Riot Act."

But he takes his job with the utmost seriousness, and Brooklyn fans may be assured that, while the club has hired a colorful personality, it has not engaged a clown.

"Every one of the gentlemen directing this club wanted me to be manager," he said. "I will be the manager, too. Darned if I don't think I know a few things about baseball and I think I can teach baseball."

Believes He Has the Men.

"I know I've got ball players who can help the club and help me and I believe I can help them. That's what I want to do. The boys have got to play ball for me. That's all I ask. If they don't give me their best"——. A significant gesture interrupted his speech.

Referring to Hack Wilson, Stengel merely said: "Hack is all right but he'll have to qualify for his job." And that, he intimated, goes for everybody on the club.

The matter of Stengel's assistants is not settled. Chick Fraser, former major league pitcher who has been a valuable scout for Brooklyn, will go to the training camp at Orlando in the capacity of coach.

"If I find that Fraser is more valuable as a coach, in my opin-

Dodgers

ion," said Casey, "he'll stay as a coach. But if I think he'll do us more good as a scout he'll be used in that capacity."

Otto Miller, fellow coach with Stengel under Carey, and who has been with the Dodgers for twenty-two years as catcher and coach, may be retained. But there is also the possibility that Irish Meusel, old Giant star, will get the call, although Stengel definitely mentioned no one.

Listed for Utility Rôle.

Marty McManus, repeatedly mentioned as a candidate for the managership, will be used as a utility infielder, according to Stengel's present plans.

Times Wide World Photo.
NEW BROOKLYN LEADER.
Casey Stengel After Signing Contract Here Yesterday.

Stengel named Mungo, Beck, Benge and Carroll as his first-string hurlers; Leslie, Cuccinello, Frey and Stripp in the infield, and said Danny Taylor was the one man set for the outfield.

"But, gee, fellows," he exclaimed, "you know all this just happened to me and I haven't had time to think. It might be different if I had been looking for this job and had been trying to get it, but I never dreamed of it."

Here Stengel spoke seriously of his relations with Carey.

"Max and I are friends," he said. "I've played this game square and come in here clean—and that's what makes me feel so good about it. I think Max knows that too."

April 24, 1934

50,000 See American League Triumph

AMERICAN LEAGUE VICTOR AGAIN, 9-7

Launches Six-Run Barrage in Fifth to Beat Nationals in All-Star Classic.

HUBBELL DRAWS ACCLAIM

Fans Ruth, Gehrig, Foxx, Simmons, Cronin and Gomez in First Two Innings.

By JOHN DREBINGER.

Packing thrill upon thrill, the foremost professional ball players of the nation battled for two and three-quarter hours at the Polo Grounds yesterday in the 1934 edition of the ball game of the century, with the forces of the American League demonstrating for the second successive year that at this newly devised form of interleague competition they still hold the edge.

For, by uncorking a devastating six-run rally in the fifth inning, the all-stars of the American League carried the day over Memphis Bill Terry and his carefully chosen National League cast by a score of 9 to 7.

A capacity crowd of 50,000 witnessed the struggle. It was a gathering that occupied every seat in the historic arena, jammed the aisles and roared itself purple.

$52,982 to Players' Fund.

About 15,000 more roared, too, when the gates were locked fifteen minutes before game time, shutting all out who had not already purchased reserved seat tickets. The paid attendance totaled 48,363 and the receipts donated to the players' charity fund were $52,982, net.

It was a crowd, too, which at the outset seemed undecided with which side it was to align itself. The National Leaguers were the home team and they were being bossed by Bill Terry. The American circuit had Joe Cronin, boy pilot of the Senators, at the head, and this sort of gave it a renewed setting of last Fall's world's series.

On the other hand, the American Leaguers also had Babe Ruth and Lou Gehrig and no New Yorker could very well be expected to root against either of these two. Whereupon the crowd simply compromised and bellowed unreservedly for whichever side was showing to advantage for the moment.

In rather sharp contrast with the all-star game in Chicago last year, this conflict developed into a titanic struggle of hitters, during which great names in the pitching industry were rudely jostled about.

Contrast With 1933 Game.

In the 1933 conflict a homer by Babe Ruth won the struggle for the American League, 4 to 2, but while the great Bambino, appearing in only five innings yesterday, was held in more or less restraint, others did some thunderous walloping. Frankie Frisch and Joe Medwick hit homers for the National Leaguers, while Earl Averill banged three runs across with a triple and a double in two successive innings.

Of the eight pitchers to step to the mound, three for the American League and five for the National, only two survived with their prestige intact. One, as can readily be imagined, was the invincible Carl Hubbell, who gave a masterful exhibition of his left-handed talents during his assignment for the first three innings.

The other was Mel Harder, trim right-hander of the Cleveland Indians, who checked a National League rally in the fifth after the Americans had swept to the fore, and hurled scoreless baseball for the remainder of the distance.

Gomez Touched for Four Runs.

Vernon Gomez, ace left-hander of the American circuit, who opposed Hubbell for the first three rounds, fell for four runs during his tenure of office on the wings of the homers hit by the two Cardinals, Frisch and Medwick.

His right-handed Yankee colleague, the burly Charlie Ruffing, was routed summarily from the mound in the fifth, while for the National Leaguers, Lon Warneke of the Cubs and Van Lingle Mungo of the Dodgers came down with a grand crash in the fourth and fifth as the forces of the junior circuit amassed a total of eight runs.

In the minutes before the game there was a respectful silence as a memorial tablet to the late John J. McGraw was unveiled in front of the centre-field clubhouse, and a full-throated, hearty cheer went up as the popular Hubbell received a plaque from the Baseball Writers Association for his services last year as the outstanding player of the campaign.

Excitement Starts at Once.

This done, the spectators warmed quickly to the battle at hand. Nor was there much delay in providing them with plenty of provocation for exercising their vocal accomplishments. Charlie Gehringer, leading off the American League batting order, greeted Hubbell with a single to centre and when Wally Berger momentarily fumbled the ball the fleet Tiger swept down to second. Came a pass to Heinie Manush and there was some uneasiness on the National bench.

Hubbell looked around to his infield, apparently awaiting the familiar Giant huddle. However, for this occasion the lean southpaw was not flanked by Blondy Ryan or Hughie Critz. True, he had his manager, Terry, on one side of him, and behind him, at short, was Travis Jackson, his ailing eye sufficiently improved to permit him to play at the last moment. But at second base was Frisch and at third Pie Traynor of the Pirates, both aliens to him during the regular campaign.

So Hubbell merely bore down to his work with renewed vigor and at this point turned on some of the most magnificent flinging seen in years as he mowed down the best of the American League's batting strength.

Ruth was called out on strikes, the Babe looking decidedly puzzled as a screw ball just clipped the outside corner for the third one. Then Gehrig struck out with a grand flourish, and not even the fact that Gehringer and Manush executed a double steal right under Gabby Hartnett's nose as Lou fished for the third one perturbed the long, lean left-hander.

Amid a deafening uproar Hubbell completed the string by fanning Jimmy Foxx, who at the last moment had been inserted in the American League line-up as the third baseman in place of Frank Higgins.

Scarcely had the furor of this master stroke subsided than the crowd was thrown into an another uproar as Frisch, first up for the Nationals, caught one of Gomez's speed balls and lined it into the densely packed upper right tier. Unmindful of this, Gomez retired the next three, and then all eyes again focused on Hubbell.

And once again the famous southpaw held the crowd and American Leaguers spellbound alike as he continued his sweep down the batting order. He fanned the great Al Simmons and also Cronin, making it five in a row. Bill Dickey, the Yankee catcher, clipped him for a single to left, but Gomez was also swept aside on strikes to make it six strike-outs for the first two innings.

Ovation for Hubbell.

For the third, Gehringer flied to Cuyler in right, Manush grounded out, Ruth drew a pass, Gehrig flied out, and as Hubbell marched to the centre-field clubhouse, his afternoon's assignment completed, he was accorded a tremendous ovation from all sides of the packed arena.

Less fortunate was Gomez, who almost got by with nothing worse than the Frisch homer in the first when trouble overtook him with two out in the third. Frisch walked, Traynor singled and Medwick larruped the ball into the upper left tier to give the National League a 4-0 margin.

With the retirement of Hubbell, however, things suddenly took a turn for the worse for the Terry forces. The tall, angular Warneke came on, and the American Leaguers at once bristled with action.

The Cub righthander retired Foxx on a grounder to start the fourth, but Simmons doubled to left and counted on a single by Cronin. Dickey fanned, then Averill, coming into the battle as a pinch hitter for Gomez, hit a tremendous triple which dropped just in front of the bleachers in right centre, and Cronin tallied.

Then came the fifth, in which the fortunes of the National Leaguers toppled like a house of cards. Warneke passed both Ruth and Gehrig, and Terry, after a brief conference with Catcher Hartnett, waved Warneke out and called on Mungo, the ace of Casey Stengel's pitching staff in Brooklyn.

There was no checking the American Leaguers now. Foxx hammered a single to centre and Ruth scored. Jackson made a marvelous stop of Simmons's sharp

Times Wide World Photo.

Averill, American League, Sliding Into Third Base After Hitting Triple in the Fourth Inning. Traynor Is Covering the Bag.

Box Score of the Game

AMERICAN LEAGUE.

	ab.	r.	h.	tb.	2b.	3b.	hr.	bb.	so.	sh.	sb.	po.	a.	e.
Gehringer, Det., 2b...	3	0	2	2	0	0	0	3	0	0	1	2	1	0
Manush, Wash., lf....	2	0	0	0	0	0	0	1	0	0	1	0	0	0
Ruffing, N. Y., p.....	1	0	1	1	0	0	0	0	0	0	0	0	0	0
Harder, Cleve., p.....	2	0	0	0	0	0	0	0	1	0	0	1	0	0
Ruth, N. Y., rf......	2	1	0	0	0	0	0	2	1	0	0	0	0	0
Chapman, N. Y., rf...	2	0	1	3	0	1	0	0	0	0	0	0	1	0
Gehrig, N. Y., 1b....	4	1	0	0	0	0	0	1	3	0	0	11	1	1
Foxx, Phila., 3b.....	5	1	2	3	1	0	0	0	2	0	0	1	2	0
Simmons, Chi., cf, lf..	5	3	3	5	2	0	0	0	1	0	0	3	0	0
Cronin, Wash., ss....	5	1	2	3	1	0	0	0	1	0	0	2	8	0
Dickey, N. Y., c.....	2	1	1	1	0	0	0	2	1	0	0	4	0	0
Cochrane, Det., c....	1	0	0	0	0	0	0	0	0	0	0	1	1	0
Gomez, N. Y., p......	1	0	0	0	0	0	0	0	1	0	0	0	0	0
Averill, Cleve., cf....	4	1	2	5	1	1	0	0	1	0	0	1	0	0
West, St. L., cf......	0	0	0	0	0	0	0	0	0	0	0	1	0	0
Total.............	39	9	14	23	5	2	0	9	12	0	2	27	14	1

NATIONAL LEAGUE.

	ab.	r.	h.	tb.	2b.	3b.	hr.	bb.	so.	sh.	sb.	po.	a.	e.
Frisch, St. L., 2b.....	3	3	2	5	0	0	1	1	0	0	0	0	1	0
aHerman, Chi., 2b....	2	0	1	2	1	0	0	0	0	0	0	0	1	0
Traynor, Pitt., 3b....	5	2	2	2	0	0	0	0	0	0	1	1	0	0
Medwick, St. L., lf...	2	1	1	4	0	1	0	1	0	0	0	0	0	0
Klein, Chi., lf.......	3	0	1	1	0	0	0	0	0	0	0	1	0	0
Cuyler, Chi., rf......	2	0	0	0	0	0	0	0	0	0	0	2	0	0
Ott, N. Y., rf.......	2	0	0	0	0	0	0	0	0	0	1	0	1	0
Berger, Bos., cf......	2	0	0	0	0	0	0	1	0	0	0	0	0	1
P. Waner, Pitt., cf...	2	0	0	0	0	0	0	1	0	0	1	0	0	0
Terry, N. Y., 1b.....	3	0	1	1	0	0	0	1	0	0	0	4	0	0
Jackson, N. Y., ss....	2	0	0	0	0	0	0	1	0	0	0	0	1	0
Vaughan, Pitt., ss....	2	0	0	0	0	0	0	0	0	0	0	4	0	0
Hartnett, Chi., c.....	2	0	0	0	0	0	0	0	0	0	0	9	0	0
Lopez, Brook., c......	2	0	0	0	0	0	0	0	1	0	0	5	1	0
Hubbell, N. Y., p.....	0	0	0	0	0	0	0	0	0	0	0	0	0	0
Warneke, Chi., p.....	0	0	0	0	0	0	0	0	0	0	0	0	0	0
Mungo, Brook., p....	0	0	0	0	0	0	0	0	0	0	0	0	0	0
bMartin, St. L......	0	1	0	0	0	0	0	1	0	0	0	0	0	0
J. Dean, St. L., p....	1	0	0	0	0	0	0	0	0	0	0	0	0	0
Frankhouse, Bos., p..	1	0	0	0	0	0	0	0	0	0	0	0	0	0
Total.............	36	7	8	15	1	0	2	3	5	0	2	27	5	1

a Batted for Hubbell in third, but was permitted to replace Frisch in the seventh. b Batted for Mungo in the fifth.

SCORE BY INNINGS.

American League...... 0 0 0 2 6 1 0 0 0—9
National League....... 1 0 3 0 3 0 0 0 0—7

Runs batted in—American League: Averill 3, Cronin 2, Ruffing 2, Foxx, Simmons. National League: Medwick 3, Frisch, Traynor, Klein.

Left on bases—American League 12, National League 5. Double play—Lopez and Vaughan. Hits—Off Gomez 3 in 3 innings, Ruffing 4 in 1 (none out in fifth), Harder 1 in 5, Hubbell 2 in 3, Warneke 3 in 1 (none out in fifth), Mungo 4 in 1, Dean 5 in 3, Frankhouse 0 in 1. Struck out—By Gomez 3, Harder 2, Hubbell 6, Warneke 1, Mungo 1, Dean 4. Bases on balls—Off Gomez 1, Ruffing 1, Harder 1, Hubbell 2, Warneke 3, Mungo 2, Dean 1, Frankhouse 1. Winning pitcher—Harder. Losing pitcher—Mungo. Umpires—Pfirman (N. L.) at the plate, Owens (A. L.) at first, Stark (N. L.) at second and Moriarty (A. L.) at third, for the first four and one-half innings; Owens (A. L.) at the plate, Stark (N. L.) at first, Moriarty (A. L.) at second and Pfirman (N. L.) at third, for remainder of game. Time of game—2:44.

grounder toward left, but when his hurried toss to second went wide, Simmons received credit for a hit and Gehrig counted, tying the score.

Runs now began to pour over the plate in a torrent. There was a slight pause as Cronin fouled out, but Dickey walked, filling the bases, and Averill, who had remained in the game as the centre fielder, now doubled down the right field foul line, scoring two more.

Gehringer was intentionally passed to fill the bases, again in the hope of enticing Ruffing, now the American League pitcher, to slap into a double play. Ruffing, instead, slapped a single into left and the fifth and sixth runs hustled across the plate.

With Ruth and Gehrig the next hitters, Mungo's troubles loomed almost endless, but at this point the Dodger regained his poise, and ended the inning by retiring the Babe on a grounder and fanning Lou.

National Leaguers Rally.

That seemed to settle the issue quite definitely, but the National League still had a wealth of material on the bench and in this same inning, the fifth, Terry unloaded it. It resulted in a three-run rally that routed Ruffing and was checked just one run short of a tie.

Pepper Martin, the Cardinal thunderbolt, batted for Mungo and walked. Then followed three successive singles by Frisch, Traynor and Chuck Klein, the latter entering the game here as Medwick's successor in the National League outfield.

Two runs had come in during this outburst and Ruffing was asked to withdraw in favor of Harder. The shift brought an abrupt halt to the National charge. For though a third tally was carried in by Traynor on a double steal with Frisch while Paul Waner was striking out, it proved the last marker for the Terry cast.

In the remaining four innings, with Terry hurling all his available man-power into the fray, the National Leaguers obtained just one single off the elusive Cleveland right-hander. That was a double by Billy Herman, Cub second baseman, in the ninth. The sturdy Mel Ott, up twice in the closing stages of the battle, went hitless, as also did Arky Vaughan, who replaced Jackson in the fifth.

One More for the Americans.

As for the American Leaguers, they merely tightened their grip by jamming one more run across off Dizzy Dean in the sixth as this tall and eccentric Cardinal right-hander started on his three innings of labor. A high fly by Simmons in short right which Frisch dropped after a sturdy chase went for a double and a run resulted almost immediately when Cronin pulled a robust two-bagger to left.

The American Leaguers might even have made more, only for the fact that Cronin got himself trapped off second base while Averill was striking out, thereby ending the inning.

Fred Frankhouse, star right-hander of the Braves, went through a commendable ninth for the National League and did his very best to start a rally in the lower half. With no more pinch-hitters available, Terry had to permit Frankhouse to bat for himself in this inning and Fred almost started something with a bunt in front of the plate. But Mickey Cochrane, who had replaced Dickey as the American League catcher, pounced on the ball and caught the Boston pitcher by a step at first.

As a result, the bases were still empty when Billy Herman followed with his double and neither Traynor nor Klein could improve on the situation. Whereupon the crowd filed out well satisfied that it had seen all the baseball that could possibly be crowded into a single afternoon.

July 11, 1934

RUTH HITS 700TH AS YANKS SCORE, 4-2

Reaches Goal of His Career With Mighty Homer in the Third Against Tigers.

GEHRIG, ILL, FORCED OUT

Consecutive-Game Streak May End—Dickey's Two-Bagger Decides the Contest.

By JAMES P. DAWSON.

Special to THE NEW YORK TIMES.

DETROIT, July 13.—The incomparable Babe Ruth reached his goal today with his 700th home run, a wallop that helped in sending the Yankees back into the lead in the American League pennant race.

It came in the third inning, a drive of about 480 feet high over the right-field wall. Earle Combs was on first when Ruth drove the ball out of the lot, fashioning two runs off Tom Bridges, the Detroit pitcher.

It seemed the blow would carry victory for Charley (Red) Ruffing, who was locked in an intense pitching duel with Bridges as 21,000 looked on.

In the end, however, it was a two-base drive off the bat of reliable Bill Dickey in the eighth inning which brought the triumph by a count of 4 to 2 and restored to the Yankees their slender lead over the Tigers in first place.

Wallop Sends Two Home.

Dickey's hit, one of two for the backstop, chased Ruth and Ben Chapman home with the runs that put the game on the Yankees' side of the ledger.

Tonight the Yanks are happy, and Ruth is the happiest of all. They humbled the ace right-hander of the Tigers' hurling staff with a nine-hit attack and can look forward less apprehensively now to the remaining two games in this crucial series.

Times Wide World Photo.

BABE RUTH.

Ruffing, hamered to shelter in his last two championship starts and in his all-star game effort as well, selected the right time to return to his winning ways. He gave the Tigers six scant hits.

A pass and a double, with a high fly, brought the first Tiger run in the third, and the only other score came in the eighth, when Ruffing le the Tigers cluster a single and a triple.

Gehrig's Status in Doubt.

Lou Gehrig, playing in his 1,426th consecutive championship game, was involuntarily withdrawn in the second inning, suffering from an attack of lumbago which may very well bring an end to his unique record. Whether he will play tomorrow was undetermined tonight.

With one out in the third, Combs singled Then, after Saltzgaver had fanned, Ruth, with the count three and two, blasted his fourteenth homer of the season.

That was all the Yankee scoring until the eighth, when, with one out, Ruth drew a pass and took second on Rolfe's single. Rolfe was caught off first, then Chapman walked. Dickey here slashed a double to centre.

Manager McCarthy sent Red Rolfe to short and shifted Saltzgaver to first and Crosetti to third.

The box score:

NEW YORK (A.)	ab.	r.	h.	po.	a.	e.
Combs, cf...	5	1	1	4	0	0
Saltz'r,3b,1b	4	0	0	7	1	0
Ruth, lf...	3	2	1	1	0	0
Byrd, lf...	0	0	0	0	0	0
Gehrig, 1b..	1	0	1	1	0	0
Rolfe, ss...	2	0	1	2	0	0
Chapman, rf.	3	1	1	0	0	0
Dickey, c...	4	0	2	5	0	0
Cros'ti,ss,3b	3	0	1	2	3	0
Heffner, 2b.	4	0	1	6	0	0
Ruffing, p..	4	0	0	0	0	0
Total...	**33**	**4**	**9**	**27**	**6**	**0**

DETROIT (A.)	ab.	r.	h.	po.	a.	e.
Fox, rf......	5	0	0	4	1	0
White, cf...	2	1	0	2	0	0
Goslin, lf...	4	0	1	1	0	0
Ge'inger, 2b.	4	0	1	1	1	0
Rogell, ss...	4	1	1	2	4	0
Gr'nberg, 1b.	4	0	2	8	0	0
Cochrane, c.	3	0	1	8	2	0
Owen, 3b....	3	0	0	1	0	0
Bridges, p..	3	0	0	0	2	0
aWalker...	1	0	0	0	0	0
Total...	**33**	**2**	**6**	**27**	**10**	**0**

aBatted for Bridges in ninth.

New York................0 0 2 0 0 0 0 2 0—4
Detroit ....0 0 1 0 0 0 0 1 0—2

Runs batted in—Ruth 2, Gehringer, Dickey 2, Greenberg. Two-base hits—Greenberg, Goslin, Dickey. Three-base hit—Greenberg. Home run—Ruth. Stolen bases—White, Chapman, Cochrane. Double play—Fox and Gehringer. Left on bases—Detroit 8, New York 6. Bases on balls—Off Bridges 4, Ruffing 4. Struck out—By Bridges 8, Ruffing 3. Wild pitches—Bridges 2. Umpires—Donnelly, McGowan and Owens. Time of game—2:12.

July 14, 1934

Ruth's Record of 700 Home Runs Likely To Stand for All Time in Major Leagues

Special to THE NEW YORK TIMES.

DETROIT, July 13.—A record that promises to endure for all time was attained on Navin Field today when Babe Ruth smashed his seven-hundredth home run in a lifetime career. It promises to live, first, because few players of history have enjoyed the longevity on the diamond of the immortal Bambino, and, second, because only two other players in the history of baseball have hit more than 300 home runs.

In his twenty-first year of play, and what is expected to be his farewell season, Ruth rounded out the record he had set for himself before retiring.

He has another mark he is shooting at and which he should attain before the end of the current campaign. He wants to go out with 2,000 bases on balls to his credit, a reflection of the respect rival pitchers have for him. He is only a few short of the mark.

Lou Gehrig and Rogers Hornsby are the only players who have exceeded 300 home runs in their careers. Gehrig boasts 314 and Hornsby 301. The improbability of a parallel to the Ruth mark is appreciated with the knowledge that Gehrig will have to survive ten more years of play, and then average about forty home runs a year, to equal it.

Today a youth was happy and richer by $20. Even before he circled the bases, Ruth was shouting to mates on the field: "I want that ball! I want that ball!" Emissaries were sent scurrying after the youth who recovered the ball after it cleared the fence, and it was restored to Ruth in the Yankee dugout, in exchange for $20.

Ruth paid $20 for his five-hundredth home-run ball, hit in Cleveland, and a similar amount for the home-run ball that touched the 600 mark three years ago. This one was hit in St. Louis.

Ruth had his greatest home-run year in 1927, when he created the modern season's record of 60. He hit 59 in 1921, and 54 in both 1920 and 1928. In 1930 he smashed 49.

Following is a table of the home runs hit by Ruth in championship games and world's series contests:

CHAMPIONSHIP GAMES.

Year.	Team.	Homers.	Year.	Team.	Homers.
1914..	Red Sox..	0	1926..	Yankees ..	47
1915..	Red Sox..	4	1927..	Yankees ..	60
1916..	Red Sox..	3	1928..	Yankees ..	54
1917..	Red Sox..	2	1929..	Yankees ..	46
1918..	Red Sox..	11	1930..	Yankees ..	49
1919..	Red Sox..	29	1931..	Yankees ..	46
1920..	Yankees ..	54	1932..	Yankees ..	41
1921..	Yankees ..	59	1933..	Yankees ..	34
*1922..	Yankees ..	35	1934..	Yankees ..	14
1923..	Yankees ..	41			
1924..	Yankees ..	46		Total	700
†1925..	Yankees ..	25			

*Out until May 20. suspended for barnstorming after 1921 world's series.
†Out until June with illness after collapsing during training trip.

WORLD'S SERIES GAMES.

Yr.	Against.	Homers.	Yr.	Against.	Homers.
1915..	Phillies	0	1926..	Cardinals ..	4
1916..	Dodgers	0	1927..	Pirates	2
1918..	Cubs	0	1928..	Cardinals ..	3
1921..	Giants	1	1932..	Cubs	2
1922..	Giants	0			
1923..	Giants	3		Total	15

July 14, 1934

PAUL DEAN, CARDS, HURLS NO-HIT GAME

Stops Dodgers, 3-0, After His Brother, Dizzy, Pitches 3-Hit Shutout, 13-0.

GIVES ONE BASE ON BALLS

Just Misses Perfect Performance—18,000 Thrilled by Baseball Drama.

By ROSCOE McGOWEN.

Those highly publicized Dean brothers lived up to every advance notice as they hurled the Cardinals to a double victory over the Dodgers at Ebbets Field yesterday. The elder brother, Dizzy, allowed three safeties, the first coming in the eighth inning, as the Cards took the opener, 13 to 0.

But good as Dizzy was, he went into eclipse behind the extraordinary feat of his youthful brother, who gave 18,000 fans the thrill that comes once in a baseball lifetime by hurling a no-hit game. The Cards made seven safe blows off Ray Benge to win, 3 to 0.

Paul's work was just one point short of perfection. He issued one pass, drawn by Len Koenecke in the first inning after two were out, but thereafter the Stengel athletes just marched to the plate and right back again with monotonous regularity.

Advance in the Race.

By taking two games while the Giants were winning one from the Braves, the Cardinals advanced to within three games of the league-leading New Yorkers.

The tension among the players on the Cardinal bench and among the fans could almost be felt as Paul went to the mound in the ninth. Thousands of fans rose to their feet and leaned forward to watch every move on the field, while two or three Cardinals in the dug-out could be seen holding their fingers crossed.

Stengel gave Paul no break as the youngster was knocking on the door of baseball's hall of fame. Casey sent Jimmy Bucher, a dangerous southpaw hitter, to bat for Al Lopez, and that youth cut viciously at the first pitch. But Paul slipped both the second and third strikes across the outside corner of the plate, and cheers cascaded from the stands.

Then Johnny McCarthy, another portside swinger, was sent in to bat

Times Wide World Photo.

PAUL AND DIZZY DEAN.

for Benge. He connected hard with the ball and for a split second the fans held their breath. But the ball went high in the air and nestled into Frankie Frisch's glove for the second out.

Durocher Pounces on Ball.

Now only Ralph Boyle stood between Paul and his goal, and Buzz came closest to spoiling everything. He drove a slashing grounder toward short that sizzled into Durocher's glove on the short hop and Leo couldn't hold it. But he pounced on the ball like a cat and by a lightning throw just beat Boyle to first to end the game.

As Umpire Sears waved high to signify the put-out, thousands of fans swarmed onto the field and engulfed the young pitcher. But his brother Dizzy and several park policemen were there first and managed to clear a way for him off the field through the Brooklyn dug-out.

Aside from Boyle's last-inning smash, there were only two other occasions when the Dodgers came close to hitting Paul safely. In the first inning Lonnie Frey sliced a drive toward left centre and Joe Medwick ran over fast to snare the ball.

In the seventh it was Sam Leslie who hit the ball hard, driving it close to the barrier in left centre,

but again Medwick saved the day by racing over and making a gloved-hand catch.

Paul fanned six men, three of them in the last two innings, and thirteen other Dodgers were retired on balls not hit out of the infield.

A Great Day for Deans.

It was the greatest day the Dean brothers ever experienced, a day in which one all-time record was smashed and two amazing predictions by Dizzy were fulfilled.

In winning his twenty-seventh game Dizzy broke a mark established by Cy Young in 1899 as a Cardinal hurler to win the most games in a season. Cy won 26 and lost 15 that season. Dizzy has lost only seven.

When Paul won the nightcap it marked his eighteenth victory, and thus made good Dizzy's boast in the Spring that "Paul and I will win forty-five games for the Cardinals this year."

The dizziest prophecy of all which was made good was voiced in the Cardinals' hotel yesterday morning, when the elder Dean told a St. Louis writer that "Zachary and Benge will be pitching against one-hit Dean and no-hit Dean today." Dizzy fell down only on his own assignment by allowing three hits instead of one.

Field Day at Bat.

As for the run-scoring, which was almost lost sight of in the drama of Paul's performance, the Cardinals had a field day at bat in the opener against Tom Zachary, Lefty Clark, Owen Carroll and Walter Beck.

They amassed seventeen hits, six of them for extra bases, including Jim Collins's thirty-fourth homer of the year, made off Carroll in the fourth. They counted twice in the first and five times in the third, when Zachary was driven to cover. Three more in the fourth, two in the sixth and one in the seventh were made off Carroll. One hit and no runs were counted off Beck in the ninth.

Collins, who drove in six runs in the first encounter, batted in two of the three scored in the nightcap. The other was sent home by Pepper Martin and it was Paul Dean who carried it across.

Paul scored in the sixth for the first run of the contest, paving the way by driving a two-bagger to deep left centre for the second hit off Benge.

Medwick doubled in the seventh and scored on Collins's single, and in the ninth banged a three-bagger to the exit gate. He tallied the final run as Collins grounded sharply to Jordan.

Fine Support for Benge.

Some fine support was accorded Benge, Cuccinello making a remarkable leaping catch of Frisch's line drive in the first inning and Jordan coming up with a sparkling play on Rothrock's grounder in the fourth.

The Brooklyn management announced that Catcher Walter Millies, purchased from Dayton, will report today, as Ray Berres is out with a lame arm.

The box scores:

FIRST GAME.

ST. LOUIS (N.).	ab.	r.	h.	po.	a.	e.		BROOKLYN (N.).	ab.	r.	h.	po.	a.	e.
Martin, 3b..	4	1	1	1	1	0		Boyle, rf..	4	0	0	0	0	0
Whiteh'd,2b	1	0	0	0	0	0		Frey, ss..	3	0	0	2	4	1
Rothrock, rf.4		3	2	2	0	0		Koenecke, cf.4		0	0	2	0	0
Frisch, 2b..	4	2	2	6	3	0		Leslie, 1b..	3	0	1	5	1	0
Crawford, 3b.0		0	0	0	0	1		Cuc'nello, 2b..	3	0	0	3	1	0
Medwick, lf.4		2	2	1	0	0		Bucher, 2b..	1	0	0	0	0	0
Collins, 1b..5		3	4	8	1	0		Frederick, lf.4		0	0	0	0	0
V. Das, c..3		1	1	7	1	0		Stripp, 3b..	4	0	1	0	2	0
Fullis, cf..	4	0	1	4	0	0		Lopez, c.....3		0	0	11	0	0
Durocher, ss.	5	0	1	3	1	1		Zachary, p..	0	0	0	0	1	0
J. Dean, p..	5	1	2	1	2	0		Clark, p....	0	0	0	0	0	0
								Carroll, p....1		0	0	0	1	0
Total ..40		13	17	27	14	3		aMcCarthy ..	1	0	0	0	0	0
								Beck, p....	0	0	0	0	0	1
								bTremark ..	1	0	0	0	0	0
								Total ..32		0	3	27	10	3

aBatted for Carroll in eighth.
bBatted for Beck in ninth.

St. Louis	2	0	5	3	0	2	1	0	0—13
Brooklyn	0	0	0	0	0	0	0	0	0—0

Runs batted in—Collins 6, Frisch 2, Davis 3, Medwick, Fullis, Durocher. Two-base hits—Rothrock, Collins 2, Davis. Three-base hit—Martin. Home run—Collins. Stolen base—Frisch. Sacrifice—Rothrock. Double plays—Frey, Cuccinello and Leslie; Frey and Leslie. Left on bases—St. Louis 8, Brooklyn 9. Bases on balls—Off Zachary 2, Carroll 3, J. Dean 4. Struck out—By Zachary 3, Clark 1, Carroll 4, Beck 1, J. Dean 7. Hits—Off Zachary 5 in 2 1-3 innings, Clark 2 in 2-3, Carroll 9 in 5, Beck 1 in 1. Wild pitch—Clark. Losing pitcher—Zachary. Umpires—Bigler, Klem and Sears. Time of game—1:54.

SECOND GAME.

ST. LOUIS (N.).	ab.	r.	h.	po.	a.	e.		BROOKLYN (N.).	ab.	r.	h.	po.	a.	e.
Martin, 3b..	4	1	1	1	1	0		Boyle, rf..	4	0	0	2	0	0
Rothrock, rf.4		0	0	1	0	0		Frey, ss...	3	0	0	4	3	0
Frisch, 2b..	4	0	1	3	0	0		Koenecke, cf.2		0	0	5	0	0
Medwick, lf..4		2	2	4	0	0		Leslie, 1b..	3	0	0	10	1	0
Collins, 1b..	4	0	1	9	1	0		Cuccin'lo, 2b..	3	0	0	0	0	0
DeLancey, c..4		0	1	7	0	0		Frederick, lf.3		0	2	0	0	0
Orsatti, cf..4		0	1	1	0	0		Jordan, 1b..2		0	1	6	1	1
Durocher, ss.3		0	1	3	1	0		Lopez, c....	2	0	0	0	0	0
P. Dean, p..	3	1	2	1	3	0		aBucher ..	1	0	0	0	0	0
								Benge, p..	2	0	0	1	1	0
Total ..33		3	7	27	10	0		bMcCarthy ..	1	0	0	0	0	0
								Total ..27		0	0	27	13	1

aBatted for Lopez in ninth.
bBatted for Benge in ninth.

St. Louis	0	0	0	0	0	1	1	0	1—3
Brooklyn	0	0	0	0	0	0	0	0	0—0

Runs batted in—Martin, Collins 2. Two-base hits—P. Dean, Martin, Medwick (2), Brooklyn 1. Base on balls—Off P. Dean 1. Struck out—By Benge 3, P. Dean 6. Umpires—Klem, Sears and Bigler. Time of game —1:36.

Cards Rout Reds and Win Pennant As Giants Are Beaten by Dodgers

National League Race Comes to Dramatic Close With St. Louis Two Games in Front—Brooklyn Triumphs by 8-5 in Tenth —World Series to Start Wednesday in Detroit.

By JOHN DREBINGER.

The Giants' dream of continued world domination in baseball crumbled almost simultaneously on two fronts yesterday as the curtain rang down on one of the most dramatic finishes in the history of the National League.

Out in St. Louis the Cardinals, who had begun the final day of the race one game ahead, pressed relentlessly on toward their goal as they walloped the last-place Cincinnati Reds for the fourth successive day, with one of their invincible Deans again on the firing line.

But a few seconds before this had come about the National League pennant already had been clinched for them by a vengeful band of Dodgers bent on making Bill Terry regret to the last his ill-fated taunt of last Winter when he asked whether Brooklyn was still in the league.

For in the presence of a gathering of more than 45,000, that almost packed the Polo Grounds to capacity, the Dodgers, after getting bowled over for four runs in the first inning, came back to bag their second and final triumph with a withering three-run blast that brought down the Giants in the tenth inning, 8 to 5.

As a result, the National League pennant goes to the Cardinals, who for the fifth time in the last nine campaigns will carry the banner of the Heydler circuit in the World Series, which opens in Detroit on Wednesday.

As for the Giants nothing now remains for them but the bitter reflection of having been made the victims of one of the most astonishing break-downs in major league baseball.

Two years in a row now Terry's players have confounded critics and public alike. Expected to finish no better than the second division in 1933, they amazed the baseball world by not only winning the National League pennant but the world championship as well.

This year they swept to the fore on June 8, and when by Sept. 7 they were still far in front by a margin of seven full games, it looked an absolute certainty that Terry would again flash home in front.

But then came the break-down, a long, painful affair, which finished in semi-darkness yesterday as the Giants wound up the season two games in back of the Cardinals after losing their fifth straight game. Ironically enough, that happened to be their longest losing streak of the year.

Strangely, too, did this game epitomize with striking likeness the fortunes of the Giants this year. Terry threw into the fray all he had.

He tossed in Freddy Fitzsimmons, Hal Schumacher, and finally Carl Hubbell, once the flower of his pitching staff, but though Fitz went off to an imposing start and further aided his cause with a home run in the fourth, there was no fending off those merciless Dodgers.

In the eighth they routed Fitz and drew abreast. In the tenth they chased Schumacher. They finished off against the arm-weary Hubbell as the stunned Giant sympathizers sat silently in the stands, utterly unable to believe their eyes while a jubilant Brooklyn horde, which had helped swell the paid attendance to 44,055, bellowed its delight.

Fans Storm the Park.

Taking full advantage of a situation which they had never conjectured in their fondest dreams, the Brooklyn fans literally stormed the park. Weeks ago they had visioned nothing more entertaining for the last day of the season than to drop around and spend a pleasant afternoon chiding the remnants of another sixth-place ball club.

But here were their Dodgers—their Dodgers, of all people—occupying a spot with the eyes of the entire baseball world upon them. Rain had cheated the fans on Saturday, when many of them remained away in the full belief no game could possibly be played.

But once the skies cleared at noon yesterday they stampeded across the river in battalions and literally knocked each other down in the wild scramble to get through the turnstiles.

Once inside, they turned on a terrific din, augmented by whistles, horns and bells, thus providing another unprecedented setting for a situation which already had set a record quite unparalleled in all baseball. For this probably marked the first time where a team making a last stand for a pennant came on its home field with as many jeers as cheers ringing in its ears.

Giants Appear Relaxed.

The Giants tore into the battle in a vengeful mood and appeared to be more relaxed than at any other time during the last harrowing month.

Having been relieved of the pressure of keeping themselves on top, nerves which had been kept taut almost to the breaking point finally had loosened up and the Terrymen played with the carefree abandon of a team which no longer had anything to lose but everything to gain.

It was with this spirit that they routed Ray Benge in the first inning and built up a four-run lead for the stoutish Fitzsimmons.

A two-bagger off Joe Moore's bat that hooked just inside the right-field foul line started the Giants on this opening drive. Critz followed with a bunt toward first and when Leslie skidded coming in for the ball, winding up by sitting down, it went for a hit.

That moved Moore around to third and when Terry outgalloped an infield hit to Frey Jo-Jo skipped home with the first run. There was a pause here, as Ott, still in the throes of a fearful batting slump, forced Terry at second and Jackson struck out. But at this point Benge suddenly took an unexpected turn for the worse.

Run is Forced Across.

He walked Watkins, filling the bases, and then passed Mancuso, forcing in the second tally. The Dodgers let out a terrific blast on Umpire Stark's decision on the fourth ball and for a time it looked as though Catcher Lopez, the volatile Spaniard, and Dolly would settle the pennant right then and there at the plate, with or without masks.

When order was finally restored Blondy Ryan sliced a single into right and as Ott and Watkins dashed home the Giants had four for the round, while the Brooklyn contingent sat in a smoldering rage. That last blow also finished Benge and Emil Leonard came on, thereby making it a struggle between two talented exponents of the knuckle-ball mode of pitching.

Leonard checked the rally, but the situation at this point looked pretty bad for Brooklyn. However, the Dodgers have long made a specialty of picking themselves up from a knocked-down position, so that it was no great surprise to anybody when Cuccinello up and tripled over Watkins's head in centre in the second inning and rode home on a single by Taylor.

Two innings later the Dodgers tore into Fitzsimmons, with two former Giant recruits doing the damage. Len Koenecke, for whom the late John McGraw once paid $75,000 in players, only to be dismissed with a wave of the hand by Terry when the latter became manager, cracked a double to left. Behind this shot Sambo Leslie singled to right.

Three-Run Lead Restored.

Fitz, however, wiped out this tally almost at once by belting Leonard for a homer, the ball smacking with a dull thud against the front of the upper balcony. That restored the three-run lead and kept the Flatbush flock quiet until the sixth, when they broke out afresh.

Boyle opened this round by bouncing a single off Fitz's glove, and when Ryan, after fielding the ball, tagged a wild throw to the end of it, Boyle grabbed an extra base. That just put him in the proper position to score as Frey tore off a hit to right.

The Dodgers even threatened to do more damage, for after Koenecke and Leslie had slapped into force plays at second Cuccinello banked a single to centre, sending Leslie to second. At this ticklish point Fitz unfurled a wild pitch that put the runners on second and third. But with a chance to tie the score, Taylor this time grounded out to Critz.

But this delectable dish the Dodgers were merely saving for the eighth, when they routed Fitz and counted twice to draw even. Boyle started this outrage against the Giants' feelings with a single, and after Frey had grounded out, Koenecke laced his second double to left, driving Boyle over the plate and Fitz to the clubhouse.

Fitz, however, had the satisfaction of knowing that he was leaving the game with his homer still giving the Giants a one-run margin.

There was a touch of super-dramatics at this point as Hal Schumacher, coming up from the bullpen, started taking his last warm-up pitches preparatory to relieving Fitz. With the Giants huddled around their pitcher, a sudden roar went up from the crowd. It was a full-throated Brooklyn roar for at that moment the scoreboard revealed a fat "3" for the Cardinals in the fourth, giving St. Louis a 5-0 lead over the Reds. One could almost feel the sinking feeling the Giants must have been experiencing at this trying point.

A moment later the tying Dodger run swirled across the plate. Leslie grounded to Ryan and Koenecke was run down between second and third. But Leslie grabbed second while this was going on and when Schumacher uncorked a wild pitch that rolled toward the Brooklyn dug-out Sambo never stopped running until he had hit the plate while the dazed Giants scrambled madly for the ball. That deadlocked the score.

There was a brief Giant flurry in the last of the eighth when, with one out, Frey fumbled Jackson's grounder and Watkins singled to centre.

But as Manager Terry called on Lefty O'Doul to bat for Mancuso, Manager Stengel supplanted Leonard with the ancient but still crafty Tom Zachary and Terry felt it necessary to make another switch. He sent Harry Danning up to bat in place of O'Doul, but it all came to naught. For Danning ended the inning by slamming into a double play.

Babich Comes to Mound.

With darkness settling down on the field, things now moved hurriedly on to the climax. Johnny Babich, recruit pitcher from the Coast, replaced Zachary in the ninth after Schumacher, palpably worn and tired, staggered through a scoreless round.

In the tenth came the final collapse. Leslie opened fire with a single and when Cuccinello tore off a double to left for his third hit of the day Schumacher went out and the once matchless Hubbell came on the scene.

Hubbell fanned Babich, then purposely passed Stripp to fill the bases. But it was all in vain. Lopez hit a sharp grounder at Ryan, who fumbled the ball and Leslie scored, leaving the bases still full. Came a long fly by Chapman that drove in Cuccinello and when Boyle weighed in behind this with his third single of the day the Dodgers were three up.

To finish the Giants in this condition was but the work of a couple of minutes for the youthful Babich, the only interruption coming when Umpire Stark got cracked in the Adam's apple by a foul tip.

The box score:

BROOKLYN (N).

	ab	r	h	po	a	e
Boyle, rf	6	2	3	4	0	0
Frey, ss	5	0	1	3	5	1
Koenecke, cf	5	1	2	3	0	0
Leslie, 1b	5	1	2	12	2	0
McC'thy, 3b	0	1	0	2	0	0
Cu'nel'o, 2b	4	1	2	1	4	0
Taylor, lf	3	0	1	0	0	0
Babich, p	1	0	0	0	2	0
Stripp, 3b	4	1	0	0	2	0
Lopez, c	5	0	0	4	0	0
Benge, p	0	0	0	0	0	0
Leonard, p	3	0	0	1	2	0
Zachary, p	0	0	0	0	0	0
Chapman, lf	1	0	0	0	0	0
Total	42	8	12	30	17	1

NEW YORK (N).

	ab	r	h	po	a	e
Moore, lf	5	1	1	1	0	0
Critz, 2b	5	1	1	1	5	0
Terry, 1b	4	0	1	11	1	0
Ott, rf	5	1	0	0	0	0
Jackson, 3b	4	0	0	0	3	0
Watkins, cf	3	1	1	4	0	0
Mancuso, c	2	0	1	4	0	0
aO'Doul	0	0	0	0	0	0
Danning, c	1	0	0	3	0	0
Ryan, ss	4	0	1	5	4	2
Fitz'm'ns, p	3	1	1	1	2	0
S'm'cher, p	1	0	0	0	2	0
Hubbell, p	0	0	0	0	0	0
Total	37	5	7	30	17	2

a Batted for Mancuso in seventh.

Brooklyn	0 1 0	1 0 1	0 2 0	3—8
New York	4 0 0	1 0 0	0 0 0	0—5

Runs batted in—Terry, Mancuso, Ryan 2, Taylor, Leslie, Fitzsimmons, Frey, Koenecke, Chapman, Boyle.

Two-base hits—Moore, Koenecke 2, Cuccinello. Three-base hit—Cuccinello. Home run—Fitzsimmon. Stolen base—Boyle. Double plays—Critz, Ryan and Terry; Frey, Cuccinello and Leslie. Left on bases—New York 5, Brooklyn 9. Bases on balls—Off Benge 1, Fitzsimmons 4, Leonard 1, Schumacher 1, Babich 1, Hubbell 1. Hits—Off Benge 4 in 2-3 inning, Leonard 3 in 6 2-3, Zachary 0 in 2-3, Babich 0 in 2, Fitzsimmons 9 in 7 1-3, Schumacher, 2 in 1 2-3 (none out in tenth), Hubbell 1 in 1. Wild pitches—Fitzsimmons, Schumacher. Winning pitcher—Babich. Losing pitcher—Schumacher. Umpires—Stark, Magerkurth and Pfirman. Time of game—2:37.

October 1, 1934

CARDS WIN SERIES, BEAT DETROIT, 11-0; TIGER FANS RIOT

DEAN EASILY THE VICTOR

Six Pitchers Used by the Losers Against Dizzy in Deciding Contest.

7 RUNS SCORED IN THIRD

Frisch's Double With Bases Filled Starts Drive—13 Men Bat in Inning.

WILD SCENES MARK GAME

Landis Banishes Medwick After Aroused Fans Shower Missiles on Player.

By JOHN DREBINGER.

Special to THE NEW YORK TIMES.

DETROIT, Oct. 9.—Amid the most riotous scenes in the history of modern world series play, Frankie Frisch's rip-snorting band of Cardinals today brought an amazing and crushing finish to the seven-game struggle for the world's baseball championship.

The intervention of Commissioner K. M. Landis was made necessary before the Cardinals, who already had achieved unprecedented deeds this year by coming from nowhere to win a pennant in the final leap to the tape, could win the crown.

With their inimitable Dizzy Dean back on the firing line once more to give a final display of his matchless pitching skill, the National League champions fairly annihilated the Tigers, led by their wounded but doughty Mickey Cochrane. The score of the seventh and deciding game was 11 to 0.

Smash Clears the Bases.

Figuratively and literally this most astonishing ball club of modern times tore the game apart. In a whirlwind sweep they blasted seven runs across the plate in the third inning, the first three riding home on a base-clearing two-bagger by the indomitable Frisch himself.

They routed Elden Auker, Schoolboy Rowe, only a short time ago the pride of all Detroit, and two other pitchers.

For a finish, one of their cast, Jersey Joe Medwick, touched off the spark that sent part of the crowd into a raging demonstration that interrupted the game for twenty minutes and for a time threatened to terminate the battle without further play. Commissioner Landis then took a hand and quelled the disturbance by ordering the Cardinal outfielder from the field.

The uproar got its inception during the upper half of the sixth inning. Medwick bounced a triple off the right-field bleachers and finished his dash around the bases with a slide into third base while the disconsolate gathering looked sullenly on.

Lashes Kick at Owen.

Just what provoked Medwick could not be seen as he crashed into the bag in a cloud of dust, with Marvin Owen, the Tiger third baseman, standing over him. Suddenly the St. Louis player was seen to lift his left foot and strike out with his spikes toward Owen's chest.

Medwick missed his mark, but the flare-up was sufficient to arouse the hostile feeling between the rival teams that had been brewing for several days and players of both sides rushed to the spot. However, the four umpires quickly stepped in between the irate players. When Umpire Bill Klem, dean of the National League staff and the arbiter at that base, decided to take no action, the uproar subsided, with only a few minutes delay.

It looked like the end of the disturbance, but it proved only to be the beginning.

With the end of the Cardinal inning, Medwick started out for left field and was greeted by rounds of boos from the 17,000 fans packed solidly in the huge wooden bleachers that had been constructed especially for the series.

Retreats Toward Infield.

Pop bottles, oranges, apples and anything else that came ready to hand were hurled out on the field and the Cardinal player beat a retreat toward the infield while the umpires called time.

Attendants rushed out to clear away the débris and Medwick returned to his post. The din now increased two-fold, more bottles and fruit were showered on the field, and once more the umpires had to call time.

Four times the performance was repeated and each time the anger of the fans, rather than showing any abatement, increased in its intensity. In vain an announcer bellowed through the amplifiers imploring the fans to desist and allow the game to continue. But these Detroit fans were boiling mad and doubtless would have continued the demonstration until the end of time.

Finally, after one more attempt to resume play ended in another deluge of refuse on the playing field, Commissioner Landis rose in his box, a short distance from the Cardinal bench, and waved the umpires to come to him. He ordered Umpire Klem, the two players, Owen and Medwick, and the rival managers, Frisch and Cochrane, to come before him, and there out in full view he held an open court.

Frisch Tries to Protest.

The hearing lasted not more than a minute and the upshot of it was that Landis ordered Medwick to remove himself quickly and quietly from the field. The fiery Frisch attempted to protest, but Landis, with an angry gesture, motioned the St. Louis leader to get out on the field and resume play without further delay.

Chick Fullis, utility outfielder, took Medwick's place in left and the crowd, very much appeased by this turn of events, actually cheered this unassuming St. Louis player as he came trotting out.

Later Commissioner Landis, in explaining his action, stated he primarily ordered Medwick off the field as the only means of continuing the game in the face of the crowd's hostile demonstration.

"Before the series," said baseball's czar, "the umpires are instructed not to put any player off the field unless the provocation is very extreme. I saw as well as everybody what Medwick did, but when Umpire Klem took no action and the players quieted down I hoped the matter was ended.

"But when it became apparent that the demonstration of the crowd would never terminate I decided to take action. I did not call Medwick and Owen in any attempt to patch up the difference between the players."

No Further Action Planned.

"I asked Owen whether he knew of any excuse why Medwick should have made such an attack on him. He said he did not, and with that I ordered Medwick off the field. I do not intend to take any further action."

A few minutes later, after play was resumed, Medwick left the Cardinal bench and crossed over to the Tiger dugout as his only means of exit. There was more jeering, but five policemen rushed out from the boxes in order to discourage any further demonstration on the part of the crowd. This did not prevent one overwrought fan from tossing a final cushion down from the upper tier, the pillow just missing the departing St. Louis player.

The uproar, of course, quite overshadowed all else that happened on the field, even taking the play away from the marvelous Dizzy Dean, who was out to revenge himself in convincing fashion for the beating he had taken in the fifth game in St. Louis last Sunday.

Although he had only one day of rest, the elder Dean was in marvelous form as he shut out the Tigers on six hits to round out the fourth and final victory of the celebrated Dean family. Paul, his 20-year-old brother, had won the third and sixth games of the series. He himself had won the first game, but had suffered a subsequent setback.

Displays Complete Mastery

Now Dizzy was back to display his complete mastery with the only shutout of the entire series. With his brother he had pitched the Cardinals into a pennant when the entire nation deemed the feat impossible. Together the pair had brought to St. Louis its third world's championship since 1926.

Among other things, Dizzy brought to a dramatic close the sixth million-dollar series since interleague warfare began under present rules in 1905.

The paid attendance was 40,902 and the receipts were $138,063, bringing the total for the seven games up to $1,031,341. This was less than $200,000 short of the record gate which the Cardinals and Yankees set in 1926 when their seven games drew $1,207,864.

The total attendance for the series just ended was 281,510, the highest since 1926 when the Cards and Yanks set the record of 328,051.

The conclusion of the struggle marked the third time that the Cardinals had engaged in a million-dollar series. It was also their third appearance in a seven-game tussle. Curiously enough, the Cards were returned the victors in all three.

Try to Rally Around Leader

Against the sort of pitching the elder and greater Dean turned on the Tigers simply had nothing to offer. They strove valiantly, however, to rally around their leader, the stout-hearted Cochrane. Despite the fact that he had spent the night in a hospital nursing a spike wound in his left leg received yesterday, Mickey insisted on playing behind the bat.

When in that torrid third inning the Tiger pitchers crumbled before the fury of that aroused St. Louis host the entire bottom fell out of the game. In all, Cochrane, who pluckily stuck in the battle until the end of the eighth inning, tossed six hurlers into the fray.

All the Detroit pitchers who had appeared previously in the series passed in review. But there was no restraining this remarkable St. Louis team. Shortly after Labor Day these same Cardinals had trailed the New York Giants by eight games in the National League pennant race, only to rout last year's world champions out of the picture on the final two days. They thus gained the right to give the National circuit its second successive world series triumph over the American League.

The crowd, which had been rather tardy in arriving, was still coming through the gates and climbing over one another in the reserved sections of the upper and lower tiers of the grand stand as the rival forces squared off grimly for the important business at hand.

There was something of an embarrassing moment just before the game began when a delegation of loyal and well-meaning Detroit fans rolled a huge floral horseshoe out toward the plate. But its sponsors sadly underestimated the inherent superstitious characteristics of ball players.

Neither Cochrane nor any other member of the Tiger team could be induced to come out of the Detroit dugout and accept the gift. So, after a deal of futile coaxing, the delegation hauled its offering away in silence.

The crowd, however, did not have to wait long for its first chance to cheer. The opening blast came when Auker, after pitching three straight balls to Martin, fanned the overanxious Pepper on his next three deliveries.

This was followed by a touch of uneasiness as Jack Rothrock rammed a double into deep left centre, but the confidence of the gathering returned when Auker, apparently getting a better grip on himself, retired Frisch on a pop fly to Rogell and Medwick on a foul to Owen.

There was even more cheering in the second as the Cards, though they clipped Auker for two more hits, wound up the inning without a run or a man left on base. After Collins singled, De Lancey wiped him off the bases by grounding into a double play, snappily executed by Owen, Gehringer and Greenberg. Orsatti, after sending a hit into right, finished himself by getting thrown out on an attempted steal.

Crowd Cheers Defensively.

However, there was a rather ominous feeling to all this and the cheering itself, while whole-hearted enough, was entirely of a defensive nature. It seemed as though the crowd, expecting only the Cards to do something on the offensive, was delighted over the success with which their battling Tigers were holding the invaders in restraint.

The Tigers themselves had been able to make no headway whatsoever against Dean in those first two innings, only one of their cast reaching first base. He got on only because Collins dropped a low throw by Durocher after Leo had made quite a dashing pick-up of Rogell's awkward bounder in the infield.

Then, in the teeth of a lively gale that swept from the northeast over the right-field wall and made it a bit chilly even though the sun shone brightly in a clear sky, the first explosion came.

It came without warning, as most explosions do, with Durocher opening the third inning by lifting a high fly to White in centre. Nothing still threatened as Dizzy strode to the plate.

Dean lifted a high foul behind the plate and right there, had the usually alert Cochrane been himself, a lot of subsequent disaster might have been avoided. The ball dropped just inside the front row of boxes. Cochrane, had he made a try for it, doubtless could easily have caught it. But he never even looked around to see where the ball was going and allowed it to drop harmlessly for a strike.

The next moment the singular Dean person shot a double to left. Martin outsprinted an infield hit to Greenberg, who delayed too long making up his mind what to do with the ball, Dean going to third. A moment later Martin stole second. Then the charge was on.

Auker, pitching as cautiously as he could, passed Rothrock, filling the bases, and Frisch came up. He ran the count to two and two. He fouled a long shot off to the right, another to the left. Then he hammered a double down the right-field foul line, and as the ball glanced off Fox's glove all the three Cardinals on the bases crossed the plate.

Rowe Replaces Auker.

Frisch's blow finished Auker, and Rowe was called to the mound in an attempt to check the onrushing Cardinals, but didn't stay there long. Schoolboy pitched to three batters and then his day's work was done. He got Medwick on a grounder, but then Collins's sharp single to left chased Frisch across the plate. De Lancey connected for a long two-bagger to right, Col-

lins was in with the fifth run, and Rowe was out.

Elon Hogsett was Cochrane's next selection and the left-hander, too, had a short stay in the box. Orsatti, the first man to face him, walked. Durocher, making his second appearance at the plate during the inning, hit a single to right, and again the bags were filled. Dean scratched a hit along the third-base line and De Lancey came in, leaving the bags still filled.

Martin drew a walk on four straight balls, forcing Orsatti over the plate for the seventh St. Louis run. Now Tommy Bridges, victor over Dizzy Dean in last Sunday's game, relieved Hogsett and managed to bring the inning to a close, Rothrock grounding to Gehringer to force Martin at second for the third out. Thirteen Cardinals came to bat in the inning.

Bridges stopped the scoring until the sixth, although he was clipped for a single by Collins in the fourth.

Martin opened the sixth with a drive to left and raced to second when Goslin handled the ball poorly. Pepper was held at second while Goslin gathered in Rothrock's fly. Frisch then flied to centre, bringing Medwick up and Jersey Joe walloped the triple which brought on his entanglement with Owen after he slid into the base. Martin scored while trouble threatened at third.

Lashes Single to Centre.

After the immediate flare-up had subsided Collins lashed a single to centre, where White fumbled the ball. Medwick came home with the second run of the inning and the ninth of the battle.

Not even the twenty-minute uproar that preceded Medwick's final retirement from the game under orders from Landis interrupted the trend of the engagement. Dizzy, wearing a bright Cardinal windbreaker, stood around the infield while the demonstration was going on in full blast, utterly unmindful of what was going on. Now and then he took a brief warm-up with his catcher.

When play was finally resumed for the last of the sixth the wonder pitcher of the day returned to his task of mowing down the Tigers. Now and then somebody poked him for a hit.

Apparently Dizzy was bent on making this a shutout regardless of how enormous the Cards made the score. Whenever the Tigers threatened Dizzy merely turned on the heat and poured his blazing fast ball and sharp-breaking curve right down the middle.

One could scarcely imagine that this man in the final week of the National League pennant race had pitched his team to victory in three successive starts, that he was making his third appearance in this series and with only forty-eight hours intervening since his last game.

Jokes Through It All.

It was superhuman. Three days ago he had entered a game as a pinch-runner and had received a belt on the head with a thrown ball that might have slain most any other man. But nothing perturbs Dizzy, except when he is in a fit of anger. Then he may tear up uniforms and do all sorts of things. But nothing disturbed his equanimity today. He smiled and joked through it all.

In the seventh the Cards scored two more, probably just for the sheer fun of the thing. Certainly they never needed the runs.

Leo Durocher tripled to the exact spot where he had hit his two-

Box Score of the Seventh Game

ST. LOUIS CARDINALS.

	ab.	r.	h.	tb.	2b.	3b.	hr.	bb.	so.	sh.	sb.	po.	a.	e.
Martin. 3b	5	3	2	2	0	0	0	1	1	0	2	0	1	0
Rothrock, rf	5	1	2	4	2	0	0	1	1	0	0	4	0	0
Frisch, 2b	5	1	1	2	1	0	0	0	0	0	0	3	6	0
Medwick, lf	4	1	1	3	0	1	0	0	0	0	0	1	0	0
Fullis, lf	1	0	1	0	0	0	0	0	0	0	0	1	0	0
Collins, 1b	5	1	4	4	0	0	0	0	0	0	0	7	1	1
De Lancey, c	5	1	1	2	1	0	0	1	0	0	0	5	0	0
Orsatti, cf	3	1	1	1	0	0	0	2	0	0	0	2	0	0
Durocher, ss	5	1	2	4	0	1	0	0	0	0	0	3	4	0
J. Dean, p	5	1	2	3	1	0	0	0	1	0	0	1	0	0
Total	43	11	17	26	5	2	0	4	4	0	2	27	12	1

DETROIT TIGERS.

	ab.	r.	h.	tb.	2b.	3b.	hr.	bb.	so.	sh.	sb.	po.	a.	e.
White, cf	4	0	0	0	0	0	0	0	1	0	0	3	0	1
Cochrane, c	4	0	0	0	0	0	0	0	0	0	0	2	2	0
Hayworth, c	0	0	0	0	0	0	0	0	0	0	0	1	0	0
Gehringer, 2b	4	0	2	2	0	0	0	0	0	0	0	3	5	1
Goslin, lf	4	0	0	0	0	0	0	0	0	0	0	4	0	1
Rogell, ss	4	0	1	1	0	0	0	0	0	0	0	3	2	0
Greenberg, 1b	4	0	1	1	0	0	0	0	3	0	0	7	0	0
Owen, 3b	4	0	0	0	0	0	0	0	0	0	0	1	2	0
Fox, rf	3	0	2	4	2	0	0	0	0	0	0	3	0	0
Auker, p	0	0	0	0	0	0	0	0	0	0	0	0	0	0
Rowe, p	0	0	0	0	0	0	0	0	0	0	0	0	0	0
Hogsett, p	0	0	0	0	0	0	0	0	0	0	0	0	0	0
Bridges, p	2	0	0	0	0	0	0	0	1	0	0	0	0	0
Marberry, p	0	0	0	0	0	0	0	0	0	0	0	0	0	0
Crowder, p	0	0	0	0	0	0	0	0	0	0	0	0	0	0
aG. Walker	1	0	0	0	0	0	0	0	0	0	0	0	0	0
Total	34	0	6	8	2	0	0	0	5	0	0	27	11	3

aBatted for Marberry in eighth.

SCORE BY INNINGS.

St. Louis ....0 0 7 0 0 2 2 0 0—11
Detroit ....0 0 0 0 0 0 0 0 0—0

Runs batted in—St. Louis: Frisch 3, Collins 2, De Lancey, J. Dean, Martin, Medwick, Rothrock.

Left on bases—St. Louis 9, Detroit 7. Struck out—By J. Dean 5, Auker 1, Bridges 2, Crowder 1. Bases on balls—Off Auker 1, Hogsett 2, Marberry 1. Double play—Owen, Gehringer and Greenberg. Hits—Off Auker 6 in 2 1/3 innings, Rowe 2 in 1/3, Hogsett 2 in 0 (none out in third), Bridges 6 in 4 1/3, Marberry 1 in 1, Crowder 0 in 1. Losing pitcher—Auker. Umpires—Geisel (A. L.) at the plate, Reardon (N. L.) at first base, Owens (A. L.) at second base, Klem (N. L.) at third base. Time of game—2:19.

bagger yesterday, the hit which preceded Paul Dean's game-winning blow. Gehringer fumbled Martin's grounder and Leo counted. Martin stole his second base of the day. Then came a long double to left centre by Rothrock and the Wild Horse of the Osage thundered over the plate.

In vain Cochrane tossed in pinch hitters. Fred Marberry pitched the eighth and fell for a hit, but escaped without a score against him. Alvin Crowder, who had started that ill-fated first game when the Tiger infield exploded five errors all around him, pitched the ninth. Perhaps he might have been Cochrane's best bet today. At least, such is the opinion of the vast army of second-guessers.

But what would it have mattered? Crowder at his best could only have obtained a scoreless tie, even though he did retire three Cards in a row in the ninth.

The Tigers had only two scoring chances in the entire battle. They had runners on second and third

with only one out in the fifth. They also had runners on first and second with one out in the ninth. Whereupon Dizzy fanned Greenberg for the third time, turning around even before the third strike reached the plate, and Owen ended the battle with a grounder to Durocher.

And so Detroit, faithful to its Tigers to the last, is still seeking its first world's championship. It won three pennants in a row in the days of Ty Cobb and the immortal Hughie Jennings from 1907 to 1909, but lost all three world series clashes. It waited twenty-five years for another chance.

But an amazing ball club, with two of the most remarkable pitchers baseball ever was to see grow up in one family, blocked the path.

Less than a month ago these Cardinals did not appear to have one chance in a thousand of reaching their present goal. But they edged Bill Terry and his Giants right off the baseball map and today they crushed the Tigers.

October 10, 1934

Gehrig Led American League In Hitting for 1934 With .363

Yankee Star First Baseman Also Recorded Most Home Runs and Was First in Total Bases, Official Averages Show— Gehringer Made Most Hits, Scored Most Runs.

Henry Lou Gehrig, the seemingly invulnerable and tireless first baseman of the New York Yankees, won the individual batting championship of the American League for the 1934 season in addition to making off with several other major hitting honors, according to the official averages released for publication today.

Playing in every contest of his team's 154-game schedule, Gehrig topped the hitters of his circuit with a mark of .363, led the league in home runs, 49, and hit for the most total bases, 409.

Charley Gehringer, star second baseman of the Tigers, finished second to Gehrig in the averages with .356, and led the league in total hits with 214, four more than were credited to Gehrig. Gehringer also led in runs scored with 134.

Hank Greenberg, rangy first baseman of the Tigers, led the league in doubles with 63 two-baggers, while Ben Chapman of the Yankees hit the most triples, 13. But Chapman lost his base-stealing laurels to Bill Werber of the Red Sox, who stole 40 bases and was turned back 15 times. Jo-Jo White of the Tigers finished second with 28, stealing two more than Chapman.

December 3, 1934

REDS' NIGHT GAME DRAWS 25,000 FANS

Many Notables See Contest, First Under Lights in History of Major Leagues.

By The Associated Press.

CINCINNATI, May 24.—Night baseball came up from the minors for its first big league tryout tonight, and 25,000 fans and the Cincinnati Reds liked the innovation. Some of the affection of the Reds for the nocturnal pastime was because they defeated the faltering Phillies, 2 to 1.

The official paid attendance was announced at 20,422, the third largest crowd of the season.

The flood light inaugural, with President Roosevelt switching on the lights from Washington, was staged before a host of baseball notables, including Ford Frick, president of the National League, and Prexy Will Harridge of the American.

The contest was errorless, despite the fact it was the first under lights for practically all the players. The hurlers, Paul Derringer for the Reds and Bowman for the Phils, performed in great style, the former allowing six hits and the visitor only four.

Wilson Gives Approval.

Manager Jimmy Wilson of the Phils said the lights had nothing to do with the low hit total.

"Both pitchers just had all their stuff working, that's all. You can

see that ball coming up to the plate just as well under those lights as you can in daytime."

Jimmy, however, let it be known that he "thinks night baseball is all right, if that fans want it, but I'd rather play in the daytime."

Picture plays were prevalent throughout the game. Myers went far back into left field for Todd's fly in the seventh, Byrd crashed into the centre field wall in the sixth but held on to Camilli's drive, while Camilli snatched several throws out of the dirt from the Phil infield at first.

Myers Comes Home.

Two long flies were dropped by Philadelphia outfielders, but both were scored as hits. The first led to the Red score in the opening frame, Myers pulling up at second when he fell against the left-field wall. Myers came home as Riggs and Goodman grounded out.

Singles by Sullivan and Pool, and Campbell's infield out produced the winning Red marker in the fourth. The Phils got their lone tally in the fifth when Todd singled, took third on Haslin's drive to centre, and counted on Bowman's roller to Myers.

The box score:

PHILADELPHIA (N.)	ab.	r.	h.	po.	a.	e.		CINCINNATI (N.)	ab.	r.	h.	po.	a.	e.
Chiozza, 2b.	4	0	0	1	3	0		Myers, ss.	3	1	1	2	3	0
Allen, cf.	4	0	1	0	0	0		Riggs, 3b.	4	0	0	3	0	0
Moore, rf.	4	0	1	0	0	0		Goodman, rf.	3	0	0	3	0	0
Camilli, 1b.	4	0	1	15	0	0		Sullivan, c.	3	0	1	3	2	0
Vergez, 3b.	4	0	1	0	4	0		Pool, lf.	3	0	1	0	0	0
Todd, c.	3	1	1	3	0	0		Campbell, c.	3	0	0	5	0	0
Watkins, lf.	3	0	0	5	0	0		Byrd, cf.	3	0	0	4	0	0
Haslin, ss.	3	0	1	0	5	0		Derringer, p.	3	0	0	1	2	0
Bowman, p.	2	0	0	0	2	0								
aWilson	1	0	0	0	0	0								
Bivin, p.	0	0	0	0	0	0		Total	28	2	4	27	12	0
Total	32	1	6	21	14	0								

aBatted for Bowman in eighth.

Philadelphia ....0 0 0 0 1 0 0 0 0—1
Cincinnati ....1 0 0 1 0 0 0 0 .—2

Runs batted in—Bowman, Goodman, Campbell. Two-base hit—Myers. Stolen bases—Vergez, Bowman, Myers. Double play—Riggs, Kampouris and Sullivan. Left on bases—Philadelphia 4, Cincinnati 3. Bases on balls—Off Bowman 1. Struck out—By Bowman 1, Bivin 1, Derringer 3. Hits—Off Bowman 4 in 7 innings, Bivin 0 in 1. Losing pitcher—Bowman. Umpires—Klem, Sears and Pinelli. Time of game—1:55.

May 25, 1935

Ruth Hits 3 Homers but Braves Lose, 11-7; Gets an Ovation From Fans in Pittsburgh

By The Associated Press.

PITTSBURGH, May 25.—Rising to the glorious heights of his heyday, Babe Ruth, the sultan of swat, crashed out three home runs against the Pittsburgh Pirates today but they were not enough and the Boston Braves took a 11-to-7 defeat before a crowd of 10,000 at Forbes Field.

The stands rocked with cheers for the mighty Babe as he enjoyed a field day at the expense of Pitchers Red Lucas and Guy Bush, getting a single besides the three circuit blows in four times at bat and driving in altogether six runs.

Ruth left the game amid an ovation at the end of the Braves' half of the seventh inning and after his third home run—a prodigious clout that carried clear over the right-field grandstand, bounded into the street and rolled into Schenley Park. Baseball men said it was the longest drive ever made at Forbes Field.

In his first appearance at the plate the Bambino drove the ball into the stands, scoring Urbanski ahead of him. Lucas was the victim. Again in the third, while Guy Bush was pitching, the Babe found his eye and smashed one that landed on top of the stands. Mallon was on base at the time.

In the seventh Ruth lined out a single to score Mallon again. His last home run drove Bush out of the box and Waite Hoyt finished the game.

Meanwhile, the Pirates pecked away freely at the offerings of three Boston pitchers and managed to keep up with the Babe's tremendous pace in so far as scoring runs was concerned.

The Pirates clinched the game with Tommy Thevenow's double, coming with the bases loaded in the seventh while Ben Cantwell was pitching for the Braves. Pep Young, rookie third baseman, substituting for the ailing Pie Traynor, hit a home run earlier for the Pirates.

The box score:

BOSTON (N.)	ab.	r.	h.	po.	a.	e.		PITTSBURGH (N.)	ab.	r.	h.	po.	a.	e.
Urbanski, ss.	3	1	0	1	1	0		L. Waner, cf.	5	2	3	3	0	0
Mallon, 2b.	4	2	1	4	4	1		Jensen, lf.	4	1	2	1	0	0
Mowry, rf.	1	0	1	0	0	0		P. Waner, rf.	4	2	2	5	0	0
Ruth, rf.	4	3	4	3	0	0		Vaughan, ss.	4	2	2	1	2	0
Berger, cf.	5	1	3	4	0	0		Young, 2b.	3	1	1	3	3	0
Moore, 1b.	4	0	2	6	0	0		Suhr, 1b.	3	2	2	11	0	0
Lee, lf.	5	0	1	3	4	0		Thevenow, 3b	4	1	2	0	4	0
Coscarart, 3b	4	0	2	0	3	0		Grace, c.	4	0	0	3	0	0
Spohrer, c.	4	0	0	3	0	1		Lucas, p.	0	0	0	0	0	0
Betts, p.	2	0	0	0	1	0		Bush, p.	3	0	0	0	3	0
Cantwell, p.	1	0	0	0	1	0		Hoyt, p.	1	0	0	1	0	0
aWhitney	1	0	0	0	0	0								
Benton, p.	0	0	0	0	0	0		Total	35	11	14	27	12	0

Total...38 7 13 24 11 1
aBatted for Cantwell in eighth.

Boston ....2 0 2 0 1 0 2 0 0—7
Pittsburgh ....0 0 0 4 3 0 3 1 .—11

Runs batted in—Ruth 6, Suhr, Thevenow 5, Young 3, Grace, Lee, Vaughan.

Two-base hits—Mallon, Thevenow. Three-base hits—Thevenow, Suhr, L. Waner. Home runs—Ruth 3, Young. Sacrifices—Mallon, Young, Jensen. Double plays—Vaughan, Young and Suhr; Urbanski, Mallon and Moore. Left on bases—Boston 8, Pittsburgh 5. Bases on balls—Off Lucas 1, Betts 1, Bush 2, Cantwell 2. Struck out—By Betts 1, Hoyt 2. Hits—Off Lucas 3 in 1-3 inning, Betts 9 in 4 2-3, Hoyt 2 in 2 2-3, Bush 8 in 6, Cantwell 3 in 2 1-3, Benton 2 in 1. Winning pitcher—Hoyt. Losing pitcher—Cantwell. Umpires—Reardon, Magerkurth and Moran. Time of game—2:14.

May 26, 1935

ESTIMATED YAWKEY HAS SPENT $3,500,000

Huge Sum Expended for Red Sox and Players in Search of Pennant Winner.

CHICAGO, Dec. 10 (AP).—Baseball men today figured that Tom Yawkey had spent more than $3,500,000 since 1932 when he purchased the Boston Red Sox. Reputedly a multimillionaire, most of his wealth inherited from his foster father, Yawkey, unofficial but reliable records show, spent huge sums as follows:

$1,000,000 for purchase of Red Sox.

$1,500,000 to rebuild Fenway Park.

$125,000 for Lefty Grove from the Athletics.

$250,000 for Manager Joe Cronin from Washington.

$35,000 for Lyn Lary from New York.

$25,000 for Julius Solters from Baltimore.

$60,000 for Bill Werber and George Pipgras from Yankees.

$55,000 for Rick Ferrell and Lloyd Brown from St. Louis.

$25,000 for Carl Reynolds from St. Louis.

$25,000 for Wes Ferrell from Cleveland.

$350,000 for Jimmy Foxx, John Marcum, Roger Cramer and Eric McNair from Philadelphia (Foxx and Marcum sale announced. Cramer and McNair reported as made, but will not be announced until January).

$100,000 for miscellaneous, but important, deals.

And yet, his great dream of a pennant for Boston has not been realized.

December 11, 1935

PART III

The Game Matures

1936-1952

Jackie Robinson stealing second against the Yankees in the World Series.
The New York Times

Ty Cobb Achieves Highest Niche In Modern Baseball Hall of Fame

Georgian Gets 222 Votes, 4 Short of Perfect Score and 7 More Than Ruth and Wagner—Mathewson and Johnson Only Others With Enough Ballots to Be Named in Nation-Wide Poll.

By The Associated Press.

CHICAGO, Feb. 2.—Tyrus Raymond Cobb, fiery genius of the diamond for twenty-four years, will be the No. 1 immortal in baseball's permanent hall of fame.

The famous Georgian, who shattered virtually all records known to baseball during his glorious era, won the distinction as the immortal of immortals today by outscoring even such diamond greats as Babe Ruth, Honus Wagner and Christy Mathewson in the nation-wide poll to determine which ten players of the modern age should be represented in the game's memorial hall at Cooperstown, N. Y.

Margin of Seven Ballots.

Only Cobb, Ruth, Wagner, Mathewson and Walter Johnson, probably the speed ball king of them all, received the required majority to win places in the hall of fame, but Cobb had a margin of seven votes over his closest rivals, Ruth and Wagner.

Of 226 ballots cast by players and writers, the Georgia Peach received 222, or four less than a unanimous vote. Ruth and Wagner received 215 each. Mathewson was fourth with 205 and Johnson fifth with 189. Seventy-five per cent of the total votes, or 169, were needed.

Napoleon Lajoie, Tris Speaker, Cy Young, Rogers Hornsby and Mickey Cochrane ran in that order for the other five positions left for the moderns, players who starred from 1900 and on, but as none received 75 per cent of the total vote their cases will be submitted to the Cooperstown committee in charge of the memorial to be erected in time for baseball's centennial in 1939. Their names will be submitted in another poll next year with five or seven places open.

Young Honored in Two Polls.

Their votes were: Lajoie 146, Speaker 133, Young (who also received 32½ votes for the pre-1900 hall of fame) 111, Hornsby 105, and Cochrane 80.

The committee in charge of the vote tabulation, headed by Henry Edwards, secretary of the Baseball Writers Association, figured the struggle for ballots among the moderns would be a two-man battle between Cobb and Ruth. When the first 100 votes were counted, both Cobb and the home run king were unanimous.

Ruth was the first to fall out, losing a vote from a writer who had watched him hang up some of his greatest records. The committee was amazed. Vote counting stopped momentarily for a discussion on how any one could leave the great Ruth off the list of immortals.

The same happened when Cobb missed his first vote. Too, there was some surprise when the usual vote of Cobb, Ruth and Speaker was broken up with a series of ballots for other outfielders.

Times Wide World Photo.
TY COBB.

Sisler Ranked Eleventh.

George Sisler, whose great career with the St. Louis Browns was halted by impairment of vision, ranked eleventh, with 77 votes.

Fifty-one stars, past and present, were named, but few of the present ones received much support, for the reason that the voters figured they would get their chances later, as one or two will be added to the list of immortals each year.

Dizzy Dean, Charley Gehringer and Charles (Gabby) Hartnett, rated as three of the greatest stars of the game today, received only 1 vote apiece. There were many surprises of famous stars receiving only a handful of votes.

The others received votes as follows:

Eddie Collins, 60; Jimmy Collins (former Boston third baseman), 58; Grover Cleveland Alexander, 55; Lou Gehrig, 51; Roger Bresnahan, 47; Willie Keeler (he also received 33 in the old-timer poll), 40; Rube Waddell, 33; Jimmy Foxx, 21; Ed Walsh, 20; Ed Delehanty (also a leader in the old-timer poll), 17; Harold (Pie) Traynor, 16; Frank Frisch, 14; Robert Moses Grove, 12; Hal Chase, 11; Ross Young, 10; Bill Terry, 9; Johnny Kling, 8; Lew Criger, 7.

Johnny Evers, 6; Mordecai Brown, 6; Frank Chance, 5; Ray Schalk, John McGraw and Al Simmons, 4 each; Chief Bender, Eddie Roush and Joe Jackson, 2 each, and 1 vote each to the following: Rube Marquard, William Bradley, Nap Rucker, Jake Daubert, Sam Crawford, Connie Mack, Norm Elberfeld, Frank (Home Run) Baker, Fred Clarke, Dazzy Vance.

February 3, 1936

DIMAGGIO'S 3 HITS HELP YANKS SCORE

Joe Plays Brilliantly in His Big League Debut as Browns Are Beaten by 14-5.

NEW YORK GETS 17 BLOWS

Four Runs in First and Three in Second Clinch Verdict Before 25,000.

By KINGSLEY CHILDS

Considerably more proficient in frequently smacking timely hits of various dimensions to virtually every corner of the ball park, the Yankees climbed back into the winning column yesterday as the Browns invaded the Stadium for the opener of a three-game series.

Although the rival batters furnished the opposing pitchers with anything but sweet music, they provided plenty of harmony for the 25,000 customers, the vast majority of whom were delighted in the 14-to-5 victory recorded by the McCarthymen.

Joe DiMaggio, making his American League début, fared well and got a big hand from the fans. He clouted a triple and two singles in six turns at bat and was the only Yankee to get a hit from Russ Van Atta, who pitched the eighth.

Like the Yankees, who collected seventeen safeties from four moundsmen, the Browns, in dropping their eighth straight contest, also maced the ball hard. The visitors made thirteen good drives, but they were more scattered and did not do as much damage as the Yankee wallops.

Knott Routed in First

They began by routing Jack Knott, starting hurler, with one out in the first session, combining Frank Crosetti's triple and a double by Chapman with three walks and an error by Knott. Earl Caldwell, another right-hander, came to the rescue and tamed the New Yorkers temporarily.

But in the second, the McCarthymen added three counters to the four they obtained in the opening frame, successive singles by Red Rolfe, DiMaggio and Gehrig and a triple by Chapman being the salient factors. Caldwell, however, remained until a pinch hitter batted for him in the sixth, although he yielded another pair of runs in the fourth.

The sixth, with Hogsett twirling, was the big inning for the McCarthymen, for they massed six hits for four counters. Singles by Gehrig, Chapman, George Selkirk and Murphy followed Rolfe's double and DiMaggio's triple.

The Browns feasted principally upon Gomez's slants, belting his deliveries for nine safeties and gaining all their runs during his tenure in the box. They registered three in the first inning and added one each in the third and fifth stanzas.

After successive doubles by Lyn Lary and Ray Pepper in the latter frame, Murphy relieved the southpaw and kept the Browns at bay thereafter.

Prior to that frame, with Ben Chapman and Gehrig leading the attack, the Yankees had counted in all except one inning, generally clustering the markers to demonstrate more impressively their superiority.

New York Pitching Better

The home forces also had the better of the bargain in so far as concerns pitching. Neither Vernon (Lefty) Gomez, who was shelled from the slab in the fifth, nor Johnny Murphy, who finished capa-

---

The box score:

ST. LOUIS (A.)	ab.	r.	h.	po.	a.	e.		NEW YORK (A.)	ab.	r.	h.	po.	a.	e.
Lary, ss	5	1	1	2	9			Crosetti, ss	3	1	1	2	4	3
Pepper, cf	5	1	3	5	1	0		Rolfe, 3b	5	3	2	0	0	1
Solters, lf	5	1	2	3	0			DiMaggio, lf	6	3	3	1	0	0
B'tomley, 1b	3	1	1	4	0			Gehrig, 1b	5	5	4	7	0	0
Bell, rf	4	1	1	2	0	0		Dickey, c	3	1	0	8	1	0
Clift, 3b	3	0	2	0	2	0		Chapman, cf	4	0	4	1	0	0
Hemsley, c	1	0	0	1	1			Hoag, cf	0	1	0	2	0	0
Giuliani, c	3	0	0	6	1	0		Selkirk, rf	5	0	1	4	1	0
Carey, 2b	4	0	3	2	1	9		Lazzeri, 2b	5	0	1	2	2	0
Knott, p	0	0	0	0	0	1		Gomez, p	2	0	0	0	0	0
Caldwell, p	2	0	0	1	0			Murphy, p	3	0	1	0	1	0
aColeman	1	0	0	0	0									
Hogsett, p	0	0	0	0	0	0		Total	41	14	17	27	9	1
bWest	1	0	0	0	0									
Van Atta, p	0	0	0	0	0	0								

Total ... 37 5 13 24 9 1

aBatted for Caldwell in sixth.
bBatted for Hogsett in eighth.

St. Louis .... 3 0 1 0 1 0 0 0 0—5
New York .... 4 3 0 2 0 4 1 0 .—14

Runs batted in—Bell, Clift 2, Chapman 5, Lazzeri 2, Gehrig 2, Dickey, Pepper 2, Lary, DiMaggio, Selkirk.

Two-base hits—Clift, Chapman, Pepper, Rolfe. Three-base hits—Crosetti Chapman 2, DiMaggio. Home run—Pepper. Double plays—Selkirk and Gehrig; Crosetti and Gehrig; Lazzeri, Murphy and Gehrig. Left on bases—New York 11, St. Louis 7. Bases on balls—Knott 3, Caldwell 1, Hogsett 3, Gomez 1, Murphy 1. Struck out—By Gomez 3, Murphy 4, Caldwell 4, Van Atta 1. Hits—Off Knott 2 in 1-3 inning, Caldwell 7 in 4, Hogsett 7 in 2 2-3, Van Atta 1 in 1, Gomez 9 in 4, Murphy 4 in 5. Hit by pitcher—By Hogsett (Hoag). Wild pitch—Hogsett. Winning pitcher—Murphy. Losing pitcher—Knott. Umpires—Summers, Johnston and Owens. Time of game—2:47.

Times Wide World Photo.

DiMAGGIO OF THE YANKEES DRIVING OUT TRIPLE IN THE SIXTH INNING
Giuliani is doing the catching for the Browns, while Summers is the umpire

bly, was quite as generous as the St. Louis twirlers, particularly Elon Hogsett.

It was during the latter's stay in the box that the Yankees obtained their final run in the seventh with a minimum of effort—more specifically, a single by Lou Gehrig after DiMaggio had been retired.

Hogsett, recently obtained by Rogers Hornsby's crew from the Tigers via the trade route, thereupon proceeded to walk Bill Dickey and hit Myril Hoag with a pitched ball. Then the rangy southpaw uncorked a wild pitch that permitted Gehrig to tally.

May 4, 1936

Lazzeri Smashes Four Batting Records

YANKS OVERWHELM ATHLETICS, 25 TO 2

Lazzeri Sets American League Record by Driving In Eleven of the Runs.

CONNECTS FOR 3 HOMERS

Two Come With Bases Filled, New Mark for the Majors— Also Hits a Triple.

By JAMES P. DAWSON
Special to THE NEW YORK TIMES.

PHILADELPHIA, May 24.—Tony Lazzeri hammered his way to baseball fame today with an exhibition of batting unparalleled in American League history as he set the pace in the Yankees' crushing 25-2 victory over the Athletics at Shibe Park.

The 32-year-old veteran of the New York infield blasted three home runs, two of them with the bases loaded, two of them in successive times at bat. He missed a fourth by a matter of inches and had to be content with a triple. With his three-bagger in the eighth with two on Lazzeri erased the American League record for runs batted in by a player in a single game. His homers with the bases filled came in the second and fifth. His third started the seventh.

Tony's hitting today gave him the distinction of driving in eleven runs. The best previous mark was that of Jimmy Foxx, who drove home nine in Cleveland with a double, a triple and a home run in 1933. The National League record is twelve, set by Jim Bottomley in 1924.

Ruth Next in Line

Lazzeri's two homers with the bases filled in a single game created a new major league record. Babe Ruth comes closest to this distinction. He hit homers with the bases loaded in two consecutive

The box score:

NEW YORK (A.)							PHILADELPHIA (A.)						
	ab.	r.	h.	po.	a.	e.		ab.	r.	h.	po.	a.	e.
Crosetti, ss.	6	2	2	3	5	0	Finney, 1b.	3	1	2	5	0	0
Rolfe, 3b.	4	2	0	3	2	0	Dean, 1b.	1	0	1	0	0	.
DiMag'o, lf.	7	2	3	2	0	0	Warstler, 2b.	2	1	1	3	3	0
Gehrig, 1b.	4	3	2	7	0	0	Peters, ss.	1	0	0	1	0	0
Dickey, c.	5	3	2	3	0	1	Moses, rf.	4	0	0	3	0	0
Chapman, rf.	2	4	2	2	0	0	Puccin'i, rf.	3	0	1	1	0	0
Selkirk, rf.	5	3	1	2	0	0	Higgins, 3b.	4	0	1	3	1	0
Lazzeri, 2b.	5	4	4	2	1	0	Johnson, lf.	2	0	0	1	0	0
Pearson, p.	5	2	3	0	1	0	Mailho, lf.	2	0	2	0	0	.
Jorgens, c.	1	0	0	0	1	Ð	New'e, ss-2b.	4	0	1	4	0	
Saltzg'r, 1b.	1	0	0	3	0	0	Berry, c.	4	0	6	6	0	Ð
							Turbev'e, p	0	0	0	0	0	0
Total	45	25	19	27	9	2	Dietrich, p.	1	0	1	0	0	.Ð
							aNiemiec	0	0	0	0	0	0
							Bullock, p.	0	0	0	0	0	0
							Fink, p.	0	0	0	0	0	0
							Upchurch, p.	1	0	0	0	0	0
							bHayes	1	0	0	0	0	0
							Total	33	2	7	27	8	0

aBatted for Dietrich in fourth.
bBatted for Upchurch in ninth.

New York ....0 5 0 5 6 1 2 6 0—25
Philadelphia ....2 0 0 0 0 0 0 0 0— 2

Runs batted in—Higgins, Lazzeri 11, DiMaggio 2, Gehrig, Dickey 2, Selkirk 2, Pearson 2, Crosetti 2. Two-base hits—DiMaggio, Chapman 2, Dean. Three-base hits—Dickey 2, Lazzeri. Home runs—Lazzeri 3, DiMaggio, Crosetti 2. Double plays—Newsome, Warstler and Finney; Crosetti and Gehrig. Left on bases—Philadelphia 7, New York 9 Bases on balls—Off Turbeville 5, Pearson 3, Dietrich 5, Bullock 4, Upchurch 2. Struck out—By Dietrich 2, Pearson 3, Upchurch 2. Hits—Off Turbeville 1 in 1 1-3 innings, Dietrich 6 in 2 2-3, Bullock 1 in 1-3, Fink 3 in 2-3, Upchurch 8 in 4. Wild pitches—Pearson, Bullock 2. Losing pitcher —Turbeville. Umpires—Summers and Johnston. Time of game—2:34.

games, accomplishing the feat twice, once in 1927 and again in 1929.

Lazzeri also set another major league mark with six homers in three consecutive games. He walloped three in yesterday's doubleheader and three today. In addition, he smashed seven in four consecutive games, still another major league record.

The McCarthymen collected nineteen hits today for forty-six total bases, on six homers, three triples, as many doubles and seven singles. Their total of runs scored was three short of the modern record made by the Cardinals in 1929.

Frankie Crosetti hit two homers in successive times at bat with no one on and Joe DiMaggio also smashed one. In addition, Joe had a double and a single.

Fifty-two Runs in Three Games

In the three games of the series the Yanks have clouted thirteen homers, Lazzeri showing the way with his six, five of them in two games. The squad has hit for a total of 107 bases, made 52 runs, 40 in two games, and collected 49 hits. Adding to the general confusion today were sixteen passes issued by five Athletic hurlers, two

TONY LAZZERI

Times Wide World Photo.

short of the all-time mark for a team in a single game.

The New Yorkers established a new major league standard for most homers by one club in two consecutive games. They hit five in yesterday's nightcap and six today for a total of eleven. The Pirates set the old record of ten in 1925. The previous American League mark of nine was made by the Yankees in 1930.

Lazzeri Almost Mobbed

Lazzeri was almost mobbed when his triple gave him a new American League mark for runs batted in and at the conclusion of the game he had to fight his way through a cluster of autograph seekers, without police aid by the way, after 8,000 wildly enthusiastic fans suppressed the disappointment of being unable to see him in a chance to improve on his mark.

Monte Pearson coasted to his sixth victory of the season under protection of the McCarthymen's amazing hitting outburst that blis-

tered the offerings of five Philadelphia hurlers—George Turbeville, Bill Dietrich, Malton Bullock, Herman Fink and Woodie Upchurch.

Mack Not on Hand

Connie Mack wasn't around to see this annihilation of his club. He was in Bridgeport, attending memorial services for the late Mike Flanagan, an old friend who died recently.

A trick of construction robbed Dickey of a home run in the fifth when his tremendous drive bobbled atop the fence over the scoreboard and dropped inside instead of outside the park. Bill had to be content with a triple.

Lazzeri's homers brought him several odd marks. His first four-master today gave him the distinction of three homers in four trips to the plate, for he hit two in his last three times up in yesterday's nightcap. In his last eight times up he drove five homers and a triple and fanned twice.

May 25, 1936

NATIONAL LEAGUE TOPS AMERICAN, 4-3

Cubs' Batters Lead Attack on Grove and Rowe—Warneke Rescues Davis at Boston.

DIZZY DEAN, HUBBELL STAR

Blank Losers for 6 Innings— Galan, Gehrig Hit Homers— Paid Attendance 25,534.

By JOHN DREBINGER
Special to THE NEW YORK TIMES.

BOSTON, July 7.—An irresistible force met an immovable body today and the party of the first part came out second best. The American League, shackled for two-thirds of the way by the matchless pitching of Jerome H. (Dizzy) Dean and Carl Owen Hubbell, and subsequently by still another pitching wizard named Lonnie Warneke, finally succumbed to the National League in the fourth annual all-star game between the two major circuits.

The score was 4 to 3, a result that seemed satisfactory enough to a paid attendance of 25,534, which, though it should have been decidedly bipartisan, nevertheless seemed to lean more strongly toward the under dog. For, as the jovial Charlie Grimm outmasterminded his former world series rival, the taciturn, aggressive-jawed Joe McCarthy, it marked the first time the National League cohorts had been able to record a victory in four tries at this midsummer classic of the diamond.

It was, in fact, a grand day for Uncle Charlie all around, inasmuch as the Cubs, champions of their circuit, contributed perhaps more than any other club to the final triumph. For while the flamboyant Dean of the Cardinals and the silent, retiring Hubbell of the Giants started the National Leaguers on the right track with six innings of super-brilliant pitching, members of the Chicago band played the major part in such offensive manoeuvres as were necessary.

Demaree Gets Single

A single by Frank Demaree and a triple by Gabby Hartnett helped wrench two runs away from the tall and mighty Lefty Bob Grove in the second inning. And in the fifth it was Slim Augie Galan, the agile centerfielder of the Cubs, who started a second National League assault, this time against the towering Schoolboy Rowe, by crashing a home run into the bleachers.

A moment later came another run on a pair of singles by Bill Herman, another Chicagoan, and Joe Medwick of the Cardinals. That tally eventually supplied the winning margin.

For just one brief moment did the National Leaguers lower their guard and it almost proved fatal. That came in the seventh inning, when Curt Davis, tall right-hander of the Cubs, jauntily embarked on

what he hoped would be a clean sweep of the final three innings.

But Curt got no further than two out in the seventh. Lou Gehrig, not to be held in restraint forever, rammed a tremendous home-run clout into the right-field bleachers. Three more singles followed as McCarthy tossed his heaviest gunners into the fray, including Goose Goslin, hero of the 1935 world series, and the redoubtable Jimmy Foxx.

Grimm had one more Cub to save the day, however. He called on the tall, angular Warneke and Lonnie refused to break ground another inch as he turned back the straining American Leaguers the rest of the way.

A Disappointing Feature

There was only one disappointing feature to the contest and all Boston tonight is still pondering the reason. For bright and sunny as it was, and with a park available for 42,000 spectators, the attendance failed to come up to expectations by more than 15,000.

The crowd, therefore, was the smallest to see this clash of the game's greatest players since it was instituted in Chicago in 1933. The largest throng attended at Cleveland last year when 69,812 paid.

The first rift in the struggle came in the latter half of the second when, after Dean had swept majestically through the first two rounds of his three-inning shift, the National Leaguers opened a brief but decisive fire on Grove.

In fact, it was a typical and almost exclusive Chicago drive that enabled the Grimm forces to dash off with a two-run lead. For Demaree, Cub outfielder, started the rush with a clean single to left.

Then came Hartnett, the smiling, affable catcher of the National League champions, exuding good cheer in all directions. All ball games, world series, all-star or mere Spring exhibitions, are a happy picnic for Gabby.

However, his first act upon Grove was decidedly not of the most friendly sort. For he landed solidly on the ball and drove it on a low, deep line to right.

DiMaggio Charges Forward

Joe DiMaggio, the Yankees' spectacular rookie, charged a few steps forward to head off the drive. Perhaps had he played it more cautiously it might not have developed into anything more than a single. Unfamiliar with the National League field here, Joe seemed to have overlooked the fact that there is a lot of territory behind a right fielder in this park should the ball get away from him.

That is exactly what it did. It bounded past like a blue streak in the flashing sunlight and before Joe could retrieve the ball off the distant right field bleachers Demaree had crossed the plate and the broad-shouldered, bulky Hartnett had thundered all the way around to third base for a triple.

A moment later Pinkey Whitney, the Phillies' contribution to the National League troops, hoisted a high fly that chased Earl Averill clear to the centerfield bleachers before he collared the ball and even the slow moving Gabby, by no means a Jesse Owens, had ample time to lumber home with the second run.

For a moment more the National Leaguers threatened to continue the assault on Grove as Leo Durocher, the peppery captain of St. Louis's famed Gas House Gang, whisked a single to center, to which Averill added a slight fumble and Leo, in his best Gas House manner, steamed on for second.

But the fumble proved not as serious as expected. Averill quickly recovered the ball and Leo was thrown out at the halfway mark, with plenty to spare. Grove then swiftly regained his poise, fanning Dean to end the inning.

Fine Catch by Radcliff

The dour Red Sox left-hander also manoeuvred his way through his third and last inning without further trouble, though he did issue one pass and required the help of a fine running catch by Rip Radcliff, who covered quite a piece of ground in hauling down Medwick's wallop down the left-field foul line.

During this same interval, the National League's seemingly invincible Dean gave as near perfect an exhibition of his pitching craft as possible. Although he yielded two passes, only nine American Leaguers faced him for his three rounds, which is par on any course. He walked Luke Appling, the first batter to face him, after running up

the count to three and two, but Dizzy righted this in almost a jiffy. He retired Charlie Gehringer, renowned clouter of the world champion Tigers, on a pop-fly to Durocher and enticed DiMaggio to thump vigorously into a double play.

Opening the second, Dizzy pitched four straight balls to Gehrig, but the wily Cardinal ace was not suffering from any loss of control. He simply was not going to permit Larruping Lou to lean on one of his good offerings and seemed very sure of his ground.

All doubts, in fact, were immediately removed as Dean wiped out Averill on the end of a soft infield fly, slipped a third strike over on Rick Ferrell and craftily trapped Gehrig off first base for the third out.

Dean Fans Higgins

The great Dean in person virtually retired the American Leaguers single-handed in the third, tossing

Times Wide World Photo.

Lefty Grove and Dizzy Dean greeting each other before the contest. Dean pitched to only nine men in his three frames.

Box Score of the Game

AMERICAN LEAGUE

	ab.	r.	h.	tb.	2b.	3b.	hr.	bb.	so.	sh.	sb.	po.	a.	e.
Appling, Chic., ss....	4	0	1	1	0	0	0	1	0	0	0	2	2	0
Gehringer, Det., 2b...	3	0	2	3	1	0	0	2	0	0	0	2	1	0
DiMaggio, N. Y., rf..	5	0	0	0	0	0	0	0	0	0	0	1	0	1
Gehrig, N. Y., 1b...	2	1	1	4	0	0	1	2	0	0	0	7	0	0
Averill, Cleve., cf....	3	0	0	0	0	0	0	0	0	0	0	3	1	0
Chapman, Wash., cf..	0	0	0	0	0	0	0	0	0	0	0	0	0	0
R. Ferrell, Bost., c..	2	0	0	0	0	0	0	2	0	0	0	4	0	0
Dickey, N. Y., c.....	2	0	0	0	0	0	0	0	0	0	0	2	0	0
Radcliff, Chi., lf....	2	0	1	1	0	0	0	0	0	0	0	2	0	0
Goslin, Det., lf.....	1	1	1	1	0	0	0	1	0	0	0	1	0	0
Higgins, Phila., 3b..	2	0	0	0	0	0	0	0	2	0	0	0	1	0
Foxx, Bost., 3b.....	2	1	1	1	0	0	0	0	1	0	0	0	1	0
Grove, Bost., p.....	1	0	0	0	0	0	0	0	1	0	0	1	0	0
Rowe, Det., p.......	1	0	0	0	0	0	0	0	0	0	0	0	0	0
aSelkirk, N. Y......	0	0	0	0	0	0	0	1	0	0	0	0	0	0
Harder, Clev., p.....	0	0	0	0	0	0	0	0	0	0	0	0	1	0
bCrosetti, N. Y......	1	0	0	0	0	0	0	0	1	0	0	0	0	0
Total	32	3	7	11	1	0	1	7	7	0	0	24	7	1

NATIONAL LEAGUE

	ab.	r.	h.	tb.	2b.	3b.	hr.	bb.	so.	sh.	sb.	po.	a.	e.
Galan, Chic., cf......	4	1	1	4	0	0	1	0	2	0	0	1	0	0
W. Herman, Chic., 2b.	3	1	2	2	0	0	0	1	0	0	0	3	4	0
Collins, St. L., 1b...	2	0	0	0	0	0	0	2	0	0	0	9	1	0
Medwick, St. L., lf...	4	0	1	1	0	0	0	0	0	0	0	0	0	0
Demaree, Chic., rf...	3	1	0	0	0	0	0	0	0	0	0	1	0	0
Ott, N. Y., rf......	1	0	1	1	0	0	0	0	0	0	0	0	0	0
Hartnett, Chic., c....	4	1	1	3	0	1	0	0	0	0	0	7	0	0
Whitney, Phila., 3b...	3	0	1	1	0	0	0	1	0	0	0	2	0	0
Riggs, Cinc., 3b....	1	0	0	0	0	0	0	1	0	0	0	0	0	0
Durocher, St. L., ss..	3	0	1	1	0	0	0	0	1	0	0	4	0	0
J. Dean, St. L., p...	1	0	0	0	0	0	0	0	1	0	0	0	2	0
Hubbell, N. Y., p....	1	0	0	0	0	0	0	0	0	0	0	0	2	0
Davis, Chic., p......	0	0	0	0	0	0	0	0	0	0	0	0	1	0
Warneke, Chic., p....	1	0	0	0	0	0	0	0	0	0	0	0	0	0
Total	31	4	9	14	0	1	1	3	6	0	0	27	11	0

aBatted for Rowe in seventh.
bBatted for Harder in ninth.

SCORE BY INNINGS

American League ......0 0 0 0 0 0 3 0 0—3
National League ....0 2 0 0 2 0 0 0 ..—4

Runs batted in—National League: Hartnett, Whitney, Galan, Medwick. American League: Gehrig, Appling 2. Left on bases—American League 9, National League 6. Double plays—Whitney, Herman and Collins; Higgins, Gehringer and Gehrig. Struck out—By J. Dean 3, Hubbell 2, Davis 1, Warneke 2, Grove 2, Rowe 2, Harder 2. Bases on balls—Off J. Dean 2, Hubbell 1, Davis 1, Warneke 3. Grove 2, Rowe 1. Passed ball—Hartnett. Hits—Off J. Dean 0 in 3 innings, Hubbell 2 in 3, Davis 4 in 2/3, Warneke 1 in 2 1/3, Grove 3 in 3, Rowe 4 in 3, Harder 2 in 2. Winning pitcher—J. Dean. Losing pitcher—Grove. Umpires—Reardon (N. L.) at plate, Summers (A. L.) at first base, Stewart (N. L.) at second and Kolls (A. L.) at third for first four and a half innings; Summers at plate, Stewart at first, Kolls at second and Reardon at third for remainder of game. Time of game—2 hours.

out Radcliff and fanning Frank Higgins and Grove, after which he nonchalantly ambled off the field amid a rousing ovation.

With the fourth inning came the second shift of pitchers, the lean but sinewy Hubbell replacing Dean and the elongated Rowe relieving Grove, and the next three innings were almost a repetition of the first three.

The versatile Galan, who had batted right-handed against Grove, now switched to the left side of the plate to face Rowe and launched the National Leaguer's second scoring thrust of the battle by poling a long high drive down the right-field foul line.

The ball struck the tall white flagpole a glancing blow and dropped into the b'eachers. McCarthy, at the head of the American League delegation, came bounding out of his dugout, protesting vigorously that the drive should be called foul, but the four umpires suddenly became stone deaf and Marse Joe presently lapsed into silence, while Augie continued his triumphal jaunt around the bases.

Case of Restraining Sluggers

A few minutes later the National Leaguers had still another run. Herman banged a single into right and DiMaggio, whom luck seemed to have slated for an ill-fated day, fumbled the ball just long enough to permit Herman to grab an extra base. Rowe pitched with extreme care to Jimmy Collins and finally

passed him, only to try conclusions with Medwick with even less satisfactory results. Medwick poked a single to left and Herman counted.

It was now a case of holding those dreaded American League sluggers who in the three previous all-star encounters had completely crushed their rivals.

Hubbell was certainly contributing his full share. His work perhaps was not quite as flawless as Dean's, but it was effective enough.

He allowed only two singles, one by Gehringer in the fourth, the other by Radcliff in the fifth. He walked Gehringer in the sixth and that was all the headway the American Leaguers were able to make against the southpaw ace of New York.

But with the seventh and the advent of Davis to the mound came a squall that almost upset the craft. Gehrig waited only until he had taken one ball and one strike before that lethal bludgeon of his swung into action. It sent the ball in a soaring arch well up in the right-field bleachers.

Averill and Bill Dickey, who now entered the game in place of Ferrell, were retired on infield grounders and for a time it looked as though Davis had regained his bearings.

But McCarthy had still more ammunition in the American League dugout. He called on Goose Goslin to bat for Radcliff, and Goose

Galan crossing plate on his circuit clout in the fifth inning. Herman (left) is congratulating his National League team-mate. Ferrell is the catcher.

Times Wide World Photo.

slammed a hit over second which Herman fielded but could not play.

Foxx, batting for Higgins, similarly bounced a vicious hit off Durocher's glove, and when Davis walked George Selkirk, pinch-hitting for Rowe, the bases were full and the American League charge was in full flight.

Appling Continues Drive

Appling carried on the attack. He smacked a single to right and Goslin and Foxx hustled across the plate. The American League needed only one more to tie, and there was a feeling of apprehension in the National dugout.

Warneke got the call from Grimm and shuffled out to the mound. Selkirk was on third, Appling on first and the powerful-hitting Gehringer at bat. Warneke finally passed the Detroit second-sacker and the American League had the bases full a second time in the inning and DiMaggio up.

He pulled a terrific low liner toward left. But in the next instant the ball landed with a thud in Durocher's glove. It was the third out and the American League's biggest opportunity to carry the day was over.

There was a mild flurry in the eighth, when Warneke issued two passes, but there were two out by the time the second one came along and Lonnie finished off this round with a grand flourish by striking out Foxx, who had remained in the game as third baseman.

With two out in the ninth came the American League's last dying thrust. It was a two-bagger that Gehringer sliced into left field and DiMaggio once again had it within his power to prolong the struggle. But he sent a high pop fly soaring into Herman's hands and the conflict was over.

July 8, 1936

KLEIN'S 4 HOMERS SET MODERN MARK

First Such Feat in National Circuit Since 1896—Phils Top Pirates in 10th, 9-6.

CHUCK'S 4TH DRIVE WINS

He Ties Majors' Record, With Gehrig Only American Leaguer to Match Achievement.

PITTSBURGH, July 10 (P).— Chuck Klein, slugging outfielder,

batted the Phillies to a ten-inning 9-6 victory over the Pirates today by smashing four home runs to set a new modern National League record for one game.

By pounding the ball into the right-field stands in the first, fifth, seventh and tenth innings, Klein equaled the major league record and became the fourth player to do the trick. Lou Gehrig of the Yankees hit four homers on June 3, 1932. Bob Lowe of the Boston Nationals in 1894 and Ed Delehanty of the Phillies in 1896 both turned in the feat, but neither performance is listed in modern records.

Outfielder Bats In Six Runs

The Philly outfielder, who batted in six runs with his wallops, came

Associated Press Photo.
CHUCK KLEIN

close to hitting another homer in the second inning when Paul Waner backed up against the wall in right to pull in his drive.

Klein's fourth smash broke a 6-6 deadlock in the tenth inning and proved to be the winning run, although the Phillies scored two more markers off Bill Swift in the extra frame.

Klein hit his first homer in the opening inning with two on bases. His other three drives, which ran his season total to 14, came with the bases empty.

Trailing by two runs in the ninth, the Bucs tied the score after Leo Norries booted a grounder that would have been the final out.

First Up in Tenth

Klein, first up in the tenth, drove the ball into the stands to decide the game.

Bucky Walter, who relieved Claude Passeau in the ninth, was the winning pitcher and Swift was charged with the loss.

Al Todd, the Pirates' first-string catcher, received a broken finger on his throwing hand in the sixth inning when struck by a foul tip. He will be lost for a month.

The box score:

PHILADELPHIA (N)							PITTSBURGH (N)						
	ab.	r.	h.	po.	a.	e.		ab.	r.	h.	po.	a.	e.
Sulik, cf	5	1	1	5	0	0	Jensen, lf	4	1	1	3	0	0
J. Moore, lf	5	1	1	1	0	0	L. Waner, cf	4	1	1	4	0	1
Klein, rf	5	4	4	5	0	0	P. Waner, rf	4	2	2	1	0	0
Camilli, 1b	4	2	1	10	1	0	Vaughan, ss	5	0	1	2	2	2
Atwood, c	4	0	1	2	0	0	Suhr, 1b	4	0	2	13	1	0
Wilson, c	0	1	0	0	0	0	Young, 2b	3	0	1	1	5	1
Chiozza, 3b	5	0	2	1	1	0	B'haker, 3b	5	0	0	1	1	0
Norris, ss	4	0	1	3	4	2	Lavag'to, 2b	1	1	0	1	1	0
Gomez, 2b	5	0	0	3	2	0	Todd, c	2	0	0	3	0	0
Passeau, p	4	0	1	0	0	0	Padden, c	2	1	0	0	2	0
Walter, p	0	0	0	0	1	0	Weaver, p	1	0	0	0	0	0
							aLucas	1	0	0	0	0	0
Total	41	9	12	30	9	2	Brown, p	1	0	0	0	2	0
							bSchultze	1	0	1	0	0	0
							cFinney	0	0	0	0	0	0
							Swift, p	0	0	0	0	0	0
							Total	38	6	9	30	14	4

aBatted for Weaver in fifth.
bBatted for Brown in ninth.
cRan for Schultz in ninth.

Philadelphia .... 4 0 0   0 1 0   1 0 0   3—9
Pittsburgh .... 0 0 0   1 0 3   0 0 2   0—6

Runs batted in—Klein 6, Norris 2, Suhr 2, Waner, Vaughan, Schulte, L. Waner, Chiozza. Two-base hit—Camilli. Three-base hit—Suhr. Home runs—Klein 4. Sacrifices—Atwood, Norris. Double plays—Chiozza, Gomez and Camilli; Camilli, Norris and Camilli; Vaughan, Lavagetto and Suhr; Walter, Gomez and Camilli. Left on bases—Philadelphia 5, Pittsburgh 7. Bases on balls—Off Weaver 1, Passeau 2, Walter 3. Struck out—By Weaver 2, Passeau 1, Brown 1. Hits—Off Weaver 6 in 5 innings, Brown 2 in 4, Swift 4 in 1, Passeau 8 in 8 2-3, Walter 1 in 1 1-3. Winning pitcher—Walter. Losing pitcher—Swift. Umpires—Sears, Klem and Ballanfant. Time of game—2:15.

July 11, 1936

INDIANS' ROOKIE
FANS 15 TO SCORE

Feller, 17, Is One Short of Modern League Record in Subduing Browns, 4-1.

TROSKY SMASHES 4 HITS

He Leads in Attack Producing 3 Runs in Sixth Inning and Another in Seventh.

CLEVELAND, Aug. 23 (P).—Seventeen-year-old Bob Feller, making his first start for Cleveland, fanned fifteen batters in pitching the Indians to a 4-to-1 victory over the Browns today.

Feller's strike-out was one short of the modern American League record, set by Rube Waddell of Philadelphia in 1908, and two short of Dizzy Dean's National League record set in 1933.

The Adelle, Iowa, rookie, who vaulted into the headlines when he struck out eight Cardinals in three innings during an exhibition game on July 6, restricted the Gashouse Gang's fellow townsmen to six hits. He held St. Louis scoreless except in the sixth inning, when Lyn Lary doubled and Roy (Beau) Bell followed suit.

Hal Trosky led the Indian attack, with four hits. Cleveland reached three pitchers for nine hits and put over three runs in the sixth and one in the seventh inning.

The box score:

ST. LOUIS (A.)							CLEVELAND (A.)						
	ab.	r.	h.	po.	a.	e.		ab.	r.	h.	po.	a.	e.
Lary, ss	4	1	1	3	3	0	Hughes, 2b	4	1	1	0	1	1
Clift, 3b	2	0	1	2	1	0	Hale, 3b	2	1	0	3	1	0
Solters, lf	4	0	0	0	0	0	Averill, cf	3	1	1	1	0	0
Bell, rf	4	0	2	1	0	0	Trosky, 1b	4	1	4	5	0	0
West, cf	4	0	0	0	0	0	Weatherly, rf	3	0	0	2	0	0
Bottomley, 1b	3	0	1	7	1	0	Vosmik, lf	4	0	1	1	0	0
Bejma, 2b	4	0	1	2	1	0	George, c	4	0	1	15	1	0
Guiliani, c	4	0	1	8	1	0	Knckrbckr, ss	4	0	0	0	1	0
Caldwell, p	2	0	0	3	3	0	Feller, p	3	0	1	0	0	0
aColeman	1	0	0	0	0	0	Total	31	4	9	27	4	1
Van Atta, p	0	0	0	0	0	0							
Liebhardt, p	0	0	0	0	0	0							
bPepper	1	0	0	0	0	0							
Total	33	1	6	24	11	1							

aBatted for Caldwell in seventh.
bBatted for Liebhardt in ninth.

St. Louis .... 0 0 0   0 0 1   0 0 0—1
Cleveland .... 0 0 0   0 0 3   1 0 0—4

Runs batted in—Trosky 2, Vosmik 2, Bell. Two-base hits—Lary, Bell, Trosky. Stolen base—Clift. Double plays—Caldwell and Lary. Left on bases—St. Louis 9, Cleveland 7. Bases on balls—Off Caldwell 3, Van Atta 1, Feller 4. Struck out—By Caldwell 4, Van Atta 1, Feller 15. Hits—Off Caldwell 6 in 6 innings, Van Atta 2 in 2, Liebhardt 1 in 1. Wild pitch—Feller. Losing pitcher—Caldwell. Umpires—Geisel, Ormsby and Basil. Time of game—2:20.

August 24, 1936

Lajoie, Speaker, Cy Young Named for Baseball Hall of Fame

ONLY THREE CITED FOR DIAMOND FEATS

Majority of 75% of Vote Won by Lajoie, Speaker and Young in New Poll

JOIN OTHER IMMORTALS

Will Be Honored at Baseball Shrine in Cooperstown— Alexander Near Election

By The Associated Press.

Napoleon Lajoie, Tris Speaker and Cy Young, three of the greatest diamond heroes of the past, have been voted positions in baseball's permanent hall of fame at Cooperstown, N. Y.

The trio, winners of an exacting poll taken from the membership of the Baseball Writers Association of America, will join the "original immortals," Ty Cobb, Babe Ruth, Honus Wagner, Christy Mathewson and Walter Johnson, who were elected in the first poll last year.

Bronze plaques of the "original immortals" already have been hung in the museum at Cooperstown, birthplace of baseball. Those of Lajoie, Speaker and Young will be ordered immediately.

Lajoie, who batted over .300 for fifteen years in the majors when such an average was a mark seldom reached, led the voting in the second poll. The speedy Frenchman, who saw service with the old Phillies, Athletics and Cleveland, received 168 out of a possible 201 votes. Speaker, who reached his greatest stardom with the Red Sox and Indians, was second with 165 votes, as against 153 for Young, one of the greatest "iron man" pitchers of them all.

75 Per Cent Required

Seventy-five per cent of the total, or 151 votes, was necessary to election to the hall of fame. Grover Cleveland Alexander, former Cub and Cardinal pitching star, now reported near death, was twenty-six votes shy of election with 125. In a tie for fourth were Eddie Collins, general manager of the Red Sox and old White ox star, and Wee Willie Keeler, who polled 115 votes each.

Alexander, Collins and Keeler still have a good chance of election, however, as a poll is to be taken each year.

All three of those named today are alive. Lajoie, who ended his major league career in 1917, was living at Daytona Beach, Fla., according to last reports. The daring Frenchman had a lifetime batting average of .338 and a fielding average of .966. He is 60 years old.

Speaker, product of the Texas cow country, has been rated as one of, if not the greatest of center fielders of all time. His best years were 1916-20-25, when he batted .386, .388 and .389, respectively, for the Indians. As manager, he won Cleveland's only world championship in 1920. Speaker is now living in Cleveland, is in the wholesale liquor business and chairman of the Cleveland Boxing Commission. "Spoke" is the youngest of the immortals. He's only 47.

Young Now a Farmer

Young, now on a farm near Peoli, Ohio, pitched more years, pitched more games and won more in the course of his baseball lifetime than any other pitcher in baseball history. He hurled twenty-two years and 874 games and won 511 with the Cleveland Nationals, St. Louis Cardinals, Boston Red Sox, Cleveland Indians and Boston Nationals.

He pitched three no-hit games and once turned in a string of twenty-three consecutive innings of no-hit pitching—an all-time record. In fourteen successive seasons Young won twenty games or more. In 1892 he won thirty-six; in 1893

he took thirty-four, and after a "slump" to twenty-five victories in 1894 he staged a "comeback" in 1895 and won thirty-five games. Young is 68 years old.

Other stars of the past—the vote was limited to those active as players after 1900 but not active today—who received a large number of votes were:

George Sisler 106, Ed Delehanty 70, Jimmy Collins 66, Rube Waddell 67, Big Ed Walsh 56, Rogers Hornsby 53, Frank Chance 49, Johnny Evers 44, Roger Bresnahan 43, and John McGraw 35.

Hornsby Still Active

The comparatively small number of votes polled by McGraw is probably caused by the fact that the voters considered only players, although McGraw was both player and manager. Hornsby, despite the vote he polled, is still on the active player list.

All told, more than 100 stars of yesterday received one or more votes. Mordecai Brown was given 31, Rabbit Maranville 25, Ray Schalk 24, Fred Clarke 22, Johnny Kling 20, and Hal Chase 18.

Among the players receiving five or more votes were Clark Griffith, Lou Criger, Harry Hooper, Eddie Roush, Ross Young, Joe Tinker, Chief Bender, Harry Heilmann, Hugh Duffy, Dazzy Vance, Home Run Frank Baker, Joe Wood, Nap Rucker, Zach Wheat and Iron Joe McGinnity.

January 20, 1937

91

Hubbell Adds No. 24 to String

Giants Capture Sixth in a Row, Ott's Home Run Beating Reds, 3-2

Wallop in Ninth Wins for Hubbell, Who Succeeds Coffman With Score Tied—Mel Also Drives Triple—Bartell Gets Two Doubles—Victors One Game Behind Pirates

By JOHN DREBINGER
Special to THE NEW YORK TIMES.

CINCINNATI, May 27.—Unexpectedly entering a fray which in the beginning was not at all of his choosing, Carl Hubbell today came up with his twenty-fourth consecutive National League victory in a two-year string as the Giants, riding handsomely on the crest of Melvin Ott's seventh homer of the year, brought down the Reds, 3 to 2.

The famous Hub came into the game in the last half of the eighth with the score deadlocked at 2-all, and with no more effort than one would employ in dusting off a shelf, he retired three Reds on infield grounders.

In the upper half of the ninth he sat placidly in the Giant dugout as his no less distinguished roommate, Master Melvin, swung desperately at the slanting shoots served up by the left-handed Lee Grissom. Earlier in the day Mel had cracked a triple off the screening in front of the right-field bleachers, and so the odds were slightly against him on this occasion.

Ball Flies Over 400 Feet

But there is a strange bond of comradeship among these older Giants who date back to the days of John J. McGraw, and Mel swung with tremendous fervor. The result was a towering smash that cleared the screening and dropped into the bleachers more than 400 feet from the plate.

Presently the Giants' inning ended with no further scoring and Hubbell sedately marched out to the mound. He retired three more Reds, this time on pop flies, and it was over. It was as easy as that.

For the screwball maestro it marked his eighth successive pitching victory of 1937 against not a single setback, and this, added to the sixteen straight with which he concluded the 1936 campaign, gives him the amazing all-time mark.

It was also only the second time in this unprecedented string that saw Hubbell receive credit for a game in which he did not start.

Triumph Completes Series Sweep

The victory gave the Giants a clean sweep of the three-game series with the Reds and ran their winning streak to six as they headed back tonight toward the East. It also left them only one game behind the league-leading Pirates, whose game with the Dodgers was called off.

The Box Score

NEW YORK (N.)	ab.	r.	h.	po.	a.	e.	CINCINNATI (N.)	ab.	r.	h.	po.	a.	e.
Bartell, ss..4	4	0	2	4	3	0	Walker, lf..4	4	1	1	1	0	0
Chiozza, 3b.3	3	0	0	0	0	0	Cuyler, cf...4	4	1	1	3	0	0
aDanning ..1	1	0	0	0	0	0	Goodman, rf.4	4	0	1	2	0	0
Hubbell, p..0	0	0	0	0	1	0	Jordan, 1b..4	4	0	1	13	0	0
J. Moore, lf.4	4	0	1	2	0	0	V. Davis, c.4	4	0	0	5	3	0
Ripple, cf..4	4	0	1	1	0	0	Riggs, 3b...3	3	0	1	0	2	0
G. Davis, cf.0	0	0	0	0	0	0	Myers, ss...3	3	0	1	2	4	0
Ott, rf......3	3	1	2	4	0	0	K'pouris, 2b.3	3	0	1	1	5	0
Mancuso, c..4	4	0	1	4	2	0	Grissom, p..3	3	0	0	0	1	0
McC'thy, 1b.3	3	0	0	10	0	0							
Wh'head, 2b.4	4	2	2	1	3	0	Total ..32	32	2	7	27	15	0
Sch'cher, p..2	2	0	0	0	0	0							
Coffman, p..0	0	0	0	0	0	0							
Haslin, 3b..1	1	0	0	0	2	0							
Total ..33	33	3	9	27	11	0							

aBatted for Chiozza in eighth.

New York.................0 0 1 0 0 0 0 1 1—3
Cincinnati...............0 0 0 0 0 2 0 0 0—2

Runs batted in—Bartell 2, Ott, Goodman, Jordan.

Two-base hits—Bartell 2, Whitehead, Riggs, Kampouris. Three-base hit—Ott. Home run—Ott. Sacrifices—McCarthy, Haslin. Double play—Bartell, Whitehead and McCarthy. Left on bases—New York 6, Cincinnati 3. Base on balls—Off Grissom 1. Struck out—By Schumacher 4, Grissom 5. Hits—Off Schumacher 6 in 5 2-3 innings, Coffman 1 in 1 1-3, Hubbell 0 in 2. Winning pitcher—Hubbell. Umpires—Ballanfant, Klem and Sears. Time of game—1:57.

Sharing the spotlight with the spectacular team of Hubbell and Ott was Dashing Dick Bartell, whose bat exploded a pair of doubles which drove in the other two Giant tallies, the second one tying the score in the eighth.

Hal Schumacher started the game on the mound for the Giants and for four innings had a no-hit, no-run effort on the wing. A single by Whitehead and Bartell's first double had given Schumie a one-run lead in the third.

The first Red hit did not come until two had been retired in the fifth. Lew Riggs pumped a blow to right that went for two bases because Ott returned the ball to first instead of second.

Five Hits Rout Schumacher

In the sixth the Reds staged a strenuous uprising that might have been more damaging but for some sleepy work on the bases. Alex Kampouris opened with a double, only to get caught off the bag by the alert Gus Mancuso and Bartell. But after Grissom had grounded out, Harvey Walker, Kiki Cuyler, Ival Goodman and Baxter Jordan weighed in with successive line singles that scored two runs and drove Schumie to cover.

Dick Coffman held the Reds in check until he vacated for a pinch hitter in the eighth, when doubles by Whitehead and Bartell tied the score.

After that it was just a case of the old master stepping up, chalking his cue and continuing his unbroken run.

May 28, 1937

GEHRIG AND GOMEZ STAR IN 8-3 VICTORY

Lou Bats In 4 on Homer and Double to Help American League Beat National

LEFTY EXCELS ON MOUND

But Hubbell Is Routed Quickly —32,000 at Capital See President Start Game

By JOHN DREBINGER
Special to THE NEW YORK TIMES.

WASHINGTON, July 7.—Amid a blazing hot setting which included in its cast President Roosevelt and a sweltering, shirt-sleeve crowd of 32,000 that jammed every available inch of Griffith Stadium, the might of the American League returned to power today as the carefully-chosen forces of Joseph V. McCarthy crushed Bill Terry's hand-picked National League array in major league baseball's fifth annual all-star game.

The final score was 8 to 3, to give the American Leaguers their fourth victory of the five games played to date and the most decisive triumph ever recorded since this mid-Summer classic was inaugurated in 1933.

Financially, the game was a grand success, the gross gate receipts totalling $28,475, the greater part of which will go to a benevolent fund for indigent ball players. The paid attendance numbered 31,391.

President Roosevelt threw out the first ball. But before long, not that ball, but many others, received a terrific cuffing while events in this inter-league struggle reverted sharply to the older order of things.

For where a year ago the flower of the National League's pitching spun back the American circuit's power for its lone victory in the series, the cream of the senior loop's hurling craft was churned to a rich froth today.

Star Pitchers Fail

The invincible Dizzy Dean, the matchless Carl Hubbell and the fireball Van Lingle Mungo all went down in a grand crash as the American Leaguers, paced by four members of the world champion Yanks, literally swept them off their feet.

In fact, more than an American League victory the day proved a smashing individual triumph for Marse Joe's marauding Yanks, leading more than one to remark that there really are in existence now three major leagues, the Yankees, the American and the National.

Of the eight American League runs that came hurtling over the plate seven were driven in by Yankee bludgeons. Columbia Lou Gehrig alone accounted for four. He drove in two with a towering home run drive over the right field wall off Dean in the third inning and three rounds later hammered one of Mungo's blazing shoots into deep center for a double to drive in two more.

Red Rolfe banged in two others with a sweeping triple off Hubbell in the fourth and Bill Dickey banged home the seventh Yankee tally with a two-bagger off Lee Grissom in the fifth.

Charlie Gehringer of the Tigers sent in the only other American League run with a single behind the Rolfe three-bagger that sent the famous screwball maestro of the Giants, Hubbell, out of the arena before he had completed a single inning.

More Help From Yanks

And when to this you add the fact that Vernon (Lefty) Gomez started the American League horde off on the right foot by blasting away from the mound with three scoreless innings, in which he allowed only a single blow, it takes no deep amount of delving into the vital statistics to discover how much part the Yanks played in this one-sided conflict.

Even defensively they flashed, with Joe DiMaggio unfurling a bullet throw from deep right field in the sixth that nipped the one serious threat the National Leaguers made all day.

Against all this Terry fought back stubbornly with all the resources he had at his command. But he had only one man to match the power of those American sluggers.

Jersey Joe Medwick, perhaps the greatest right-handed hitter since the palmy days of Rogers Hornsby, blazed a brilliant trail as he strove almost single handed to keep his colleagues in the fight. In five times up, he uncorked four line-drive hits, two of them doubles.

It was, indeed, pretty much a struggle between the Yanks and Medwick and the celebrated member of St. Louis' famed Gas House Gang simply found himself outnumbered.

Harder Also Hurls Well

In addition to Gomez, Tommy Bridges, the trim right-hander of the Detroit Tigers, and Mel Harder of the Cleveland Indians pitched three innings apiece for the triumphant American Leaguers and it was only of Bridges that the Terry cast was able to make any impression at all.

It was the sort of attack which with gilt-edged pitching might have won, but the McCarthy forces knocked all the gilt off before the conflict had gone more than half way.

In vain Terry flung all six of his hurlers into the fray. With the exception of Cy Blanton, none escaped getting hit in the grand total of thirteen blows, though Bucky Walters, working the eighth, managed to keep from getting scored on.

Thirteen hits also fell to the lot of the National Leaguers, but with the exception of the two Medwick doubles and another two-bagger inserted by Melvin Ott in the rôle of pinch hitter, all were singles. In sharp contrast to this five of the American Leaguers' blows were for extra bases, which rather graphically tells the whole story.

The crowd, which arrived early, jammed traffic in all directions and then amused itself milling around in the general quest for the right seats, got its first thrill at 1:15 o'clock when the portals behind the right wing of the grand stand swung open and the long, sleek

Times Wide World Photo.

President Roosevelt about to throw out the ball. With him, from left to right, are his son, James; Clark Griffith, president of the Washington Senators; Bill Terry, manager of National League forces, and Joe McCarthy, who directed American League players.

open town car of the President rolled out on the playing field.

There were rousing cheers as the Rooseveltian smile beamed on one and all. A military band in square formation at home plate struck up "Hail to the Chief," while the players of both teams lined at attention along the first base foul line.

Griffith Escorts President

Then followed no end of to do as the President was escorted to his box alongside the Washington dugout by Clark Griffith, owner of the Senators, while news photographers jostled each other and clicked their cameras in feverish haste.

Now the scene shifted to the tall flagpole in centerfield, where to the strains of "The Star-Spangled Banner" a detachment of Boy Scouts hoisted Old Glory. More cheers for everybody and again all eyes reverted back to the Presidential box, where the President prepared to toss out the first ball after having it formally presented to him by the rival pilots, McCarthy and Terry.

The Rooseveltian arm swept back, the players surged forward and as the white pellet arched through the air a football scramble ensued that for a few moments resembled that memorable battle of Sportsman's Park.

In this initial skirmish the National League drew its first and what eventually proved its only victory of the day for when the heap of the nation's greatest players untangled themselves Jo-Jo Moore of the Giants had the ball tightly clasped in his fingers.

From then on thrills came fast and furious as the long and lean

Times Wide World Photo.

Gehrig scoring on his third-inning homer, which brought DiMaggio in ahead of him

Box Score of the Game

NATIONAL LEAGUE

	ab.	r.	h.	tb.	2b.	3b.	hr.	bb.	so.	sh.	sb.	po.	a.	e.
Waner, Pitts., rf......	5	0	0	0	0	0	0	0	0	0	0	1	0	0
Herman, Chic., 2b.....	5	1	2	2	0	0	0	0	0	0	0	1	4	0
Vaughan, Pitts., 3b.....	5	0	2	2	0	0	0	0	0	0	0	3	0	0
Medwick, St. L., lf.....	5	1	4	6	2	0	0	0	0	0	0	1	0	0
Demaree, Chic., cf.....	5	0	1	1	0	0	0	0	0	0	0	2	1	0
Mize, St. L., 1b.......	4	0	0	0	0	0	0	0	0	0	0	7	0	0
Hartnett, Chic., c......	3	1	1	1	0	0	0	0	0	0	0	6	0	0
bWhitehead, N. Y.......	0	0	0	0	0	0	0	0	0	0	0	0	0	0
Mancuso, N. Y., c......	1	0	0	0	0	0	0	0	0	0	0	1	0	0
Bartell, N. Y., ss.....	4	0	1	1	0	0	0	0	0	0	0	2	3	0
Dean, St. L., p.......	1	0	0	0	0	0	0	0	0	0	0	0	1	0
Hubbell, N. Y., p......	0	0	0	0	0	0	0	0	0	0	0	0	0	0
Blanton, Pitts., p......	0	0	0	0	0	0	0	0	0	0	0	0	0	0
aOtt, N. Y...........	1	0	1	2	1	0	0	0	0	0	0	0	0	0
Grissom, Cincin., p......	0	0	0	0	0	0	0	0	0	0	0	0	0	0
cCollins, Chic........	1	0	1	1	0	0	0	0	0	0	0	0	0	0
Mungo, Bklyn., p.......	0	0	0	0	0	0	0	0	0	0	0	0	1	0
eMoore, N. Y..........	1	0	0	0	0	0	0	0	0	0	0	0	0	0
Walters, Phila., p......	0	0	0	0	0	0	0	0	0	0	0	0	0	0
Total 41	41	3	13	16	3	0	0	0	0	0	0	24	10	0

AMERICAN LEAGUE

	ab.	r.	h.	tb.	2b.	3b.	hr.	bb.	so.	sh.	sb.	po.	a.	e.
Rolfe, N. Y., 3b.....	4	2	2	4	0	1	0	1	0	0	0	0	2	2
Gehringer, Det., 2b.....	5	1	3	3	0	0	0	0	0	0	0	2	5	0
DiMaggio, N. Y., rf.....	4	1	1	1	0	0	0	1	2	0	0	1	1	0
Gehrig, Cleve., 1b.....	4	1	2	6	1	0	1	0	2	0	0	11	1	0
Averill, Cleve., cf.....	3	0	1	1	0	0	1	1	0	0	0	2	0	0
Cronin, Boston, ss.....	4	1	1	2	1	0	0	0	0	0	0	3	4	0
Dickey, N. Y., c.......	3	1	2	3	1	0	0	1	0	0	0	2	0	0
West, St. L., lf.......	4	1	1	1	0	0	0	0	0	0	0	5	0	0
Gomez, N. Y., p........	1	0	0	0	0	0	0	0	1	0	0	0	0	0
Bridges, Det., p........	1	0	0	0	0	0	0	0	1	0	0	0	0	0
dFoxx, Boston..........	1	0	0	0	0	0	0	0	0	0	0	0	0	0
Harder, Cleve., p.......	1	0	0	0	0	0	0	0	0	0	0	1	1	0
Total 35	35	8	13	21	3	1	1	4	7	0	0	27	15	2

aBatted for Blanton in fifth.
bRan for Hartnett in sixth.
cBatted for Grissom in sixth.
dBatted for Bridges in sixth.
eBatted for Mungo in eighth.

SCORE BY INNINGS

National League...............	0	0	0	1	1	1	0	0	0–3	
American League...............	0	0	2	3	1	2	0	0	..–8	

Runs batted in—Gehrig 4, Medwick, Rolfe 2, Gehringer, Waner, Dickey, Mize. Left on bases—National League 11. American League 7. Double play—Bartell and Mize. Struck out—By Dean 2, Hubbell 1, Blanton 1, Grissom 1, Mungo 1. Bases on balls—Off Dean 1, Mungo 1. Hits—Off Dean 4 in 3 innings. Hubbell 3 in 2-3, Blanton 0 in 1-3, Grissom 2 in 1, Mungo 2 in 2, Walters 2 in 1, Gomez 1 in 3, Bridges 7 in 3, Harder 5 in 3. Winning pitcher—Gomez. Losing pitcher, Dean. Umpires—McGowan (A. L.) behind the plate; Pinelli (N. L.) at first base; Quinn (A. L.) at second base; Barr (N. L.) at third base for first four and one-half innings; Barr behind the plate. Quinn at first, Pinelli at second, McGowan at third for remainder of game. Time of game—2:30.

Dean and the equally slender Gomez started firing away.

Typical Reception for Dean

For most of the capital fans it was their first view of the Gas House Gang's celebrated hurler and they greeted his first appearance with cheers and jeers, indicating they already had acquainted themselves with the manner in which only a Dean is received on an alien ball field.

For two innings, Dean's smooth and effortless delivery kept him abreast of Gomez. He issued a pass to DiMaggio in the first and a pair of singles by Earl Averill and Dickey jolted him in the second.

But the fates had something more disturbing in store for Dizzy. He had retired Rolfe and Gehringer as the first two outs in the third and was within one out of stalking out of there with his customary jauntiness when the blow fell.

DiMaggio singled sharply to center, almost decapitating the great Dean. Then Diz squared off against Gehrig. He had fanned Lou in the first inning and seemed quite sure of himself.

Nor did a resounding foul smack that Gehrig sent flying over the grandstand roof seem to disturb his equanimity. But with the count 3 and 2 there was a terrific jolt and the crowd rose as one to see the ball sail high over the right-field barrier.

Gomez gave the National Leaguers no chance at all. Arky Vaughan singled in the first and was the only one to get on base through all of Lefty's three innings.

With the arrival of Bridges in the fourth, however, the Nationals swung into action, or rather Medwick did. Herman singled, took second on an out and counted on Medwick's first double.

But in the same round with Hubbell sedately stepping on the scene the American Leaguers burst out with even greater fury.

Hubbell's tenure of office was even stormier and far more brief than Dean's. For the American Leaguers, still rankled by the manner in which Hub once had fanned five of their greatest hitters in a row back in 1934, fell on him with a vengeance.

With one out, Dickey walked, and

Sammy West of the Browns rammed a hit through Johnny Mize, the Cardinal first sacker. Bridges fanned for the second out and it looked as though the Hub would survive, but Rolfe unveiled his triple to right center and two scored. Came Gehringer's single to right scoring the Yankee third sacker and a third tally flitted home.

Hubbell was withdrawn by Terry and replaced by Blanton of the Pirates. Cy fanned DiMaggio for the third out and then immediately retired himself for a pinch hitter in the fifth.

Ott Connects in Pinch

That pinch-hitter, Ott, helped the Nationals to their second run off Bridges with a two-bagger to right after Gabby Hartnett had singled. But it took a fly to the outfield by Paul Waner to drive in that run, and the Nationals were still three shy.

Grissom, pitching the fifth for the Nationals, made an imposing entry as he fanned Gehrig and Averill. But then trouble nailed him, too, as Joe Cronin and Dickey cracked him for a pair of doubles, and the Americans had another run, to which they added two more off

Mungo in the sixth when Gehrig hit his mighty two-bagger which just missed being a triple.

This inning, too, saw the National Leaguers make their last desperate stand. In fact, for a few exciting moments it looked as though they would rout Bridges and put themselves back in the fight.

The redoubtable Medwick and Frank Demaree of the Cubs singled. A fly by Mize drove in Jersey Joe. Then, after Hartnett had forced Demaree for the second out, Rolfe fumbled Dick Bartell's grounder and the National Leaguers had two on.

Terry here made another strategic move. He ordered Burgess Whitehead to run for the lumbering Gabby, and Rip Collins, Cubs' slugging first sacker, came to bat for Grissom. Collins singled sharply to right and the Nationals looked to have another run as the fleet Whitehead rounded third.

But the ball thrown by DiMaggio's powerful arm proved even swifter, and Whitey was nailed at the plate for the third out.

Perhaps some day they'll inaugurate a three-cornered all-star struggle, with the Yankees battling as a unit.

July 8, 1937

YORK, TIGERS, SETS HOME-RUN RECORD

Clips Ruth Mark With Nos. 17 and 18 in a Month in 12-3 Conquest of Senators

RUDY HITS IN SEVEN RUNS

He and Gehringer Have Perfect Day at Bat—Lawson Hurls 17th Triumph

DETROIT, Aug. 31 (P).—Rookie Rudy York, hitting his twenty-ninth and thirtieth home runs of the season, topped one of Babe Ruth's records today as he led the Tigers in a 12-to-3 victory over Washington.

Ruth hit seventeen homers in a single month in September, 1927. York's two circuit smashes over the scoreboard at Navin Field were his seventeenth and eighteenth during August.

Times Wide World
RUDY YORK

In addition, York collected two singles for a perfect day at bat, and drove in seven runs. Two mates were on base when York hit each homer, one in the first and another in the sixth. Pete Fox, Detroit right fielder, hit one over the left field fence with the bases empty in the sixth.

Charlie Gehringer, the American League's leading batsman, also had a perfect record at the plate with a double and two singles. Gehringer walked twice and York once.

Both of York's home runs were hit off Pete Appleson, the Senators' starting pitcher. Roxie Lawson, who won his seventeenth game of the season, gave eleven safeties, but scattered them through every inning, and left thirteen Washington runners stranded.

The box score:

WASHINGTON (A.)						DETROIT (A.)					
	ab.	r.	h.	po.	a. e.		ab.	r.	h.	po.	a. e.
Almada, cf..5	0	2	3	0	1	Walker, lf..5	2	1	4	0	0
Lewis, 3b...5	1	2	3	6	0	Fox, rf.....4	2	2	1	0	1
Travis, ss...4	1	0	0	2	0	G'ringer, 2b..3	3	3	2	4	0
Stone, rf...3	0	2	0	1	0	Greenb'g 1b..5	1	2	8	1	0
Kuhel, 1b..5	0	1	10	1	0	York, c.....4	2	4	3	0	0
Myer, 2b...4	0	2	0	0	0	Laabs, cf....3	0	0	5	0	0
Simmons, lf..2	0	1	0	0	0	Owen, 3b....5	0	0	1	0	0
aSington, lf..2	1	0	2	0	0	Gelbert, ss..4	1	1	3	3	0
R. Ferrell, c.4	0	0	6	1	0	Lawson, p...3	1	1	0	2	0
Appleson, p..3	0	1	0	3	0						
bMilles, c...1	0	0	0	0	0	Total...36	12	14	27	10	1
Jacobs, p...0	0	0	0	0	0						
Total...38	3	11	24	14	1						

aRan for Simmons in fourth.
bBatted for Appleson in eighth.

Washington ....1 0 1 1 0 0 0 0 0—3
Detroit ....3 0 0 4 0 4 1 0 .—12

Runs batted in—York 7, Gehringer 2, Fox 2, Greenberg, Almada, Kuhel.
Two-base hits—Walker, Simmons, Lawson, Gehringer, Lewis. Three-base hit—Myer. Home runs—York 2, Fox. Stolen bases—Gehringer 2, Walker. Sacrifice—Lawson. Left on bases—Washington 13, Detroit 8. Bases on balls—Off Lawson 5, Appleson 6, Jacobs 1. Struck out—By Lawson 2, Appleson 4. Hits—Off Appleson 13 in 7 innings, Jacobs 1 in 1. Balk—Lawson. Losing pitcher—Appleson. Umpires—Summers, Geisel and Basil. Time of game—2:00.

September 1, 1937

New York Times

Tris Speaker

Alexander to Hall of Fame

212 OF 262 WRITERS SELECT ALEXANDER

National League Pitcher for 20 Years Only Man Picked by Required 75%

SISLER SECOND WITH 179

Keeler Polls 177, Ed Collins 175 Votes—119 Names Are Included in Balloting

By JOHN DREBINGER

Receiving 81 per cent of a record vote, in addition to being the only one to receive the necessary 75 per cent, Grover Cleveland Alexander, famous National League pitcher for a score of years, became the latest diamond immortal to have his name added to baseball's Hall of Fame at Cooperstown, N. Y. Announcement of Alexander's selection was made yesterday by the Hall of Fame Elections Committee, which had just completed tabulating the Baseball Writers Association's third annual vote.

A total of 262 ballots was cast, thereby making 197 the minimum figure eligible for choice. Alexander's vote was 212.

Three other stars of past years fell slightly under the required 75 per cent. These were George Sisler, brilliant first baseman of the Browns in the last decade, who received 179; Wee Willie Keeler, famous outfielder of the old Orioles and later the New York Highlanders, who polled 177, and Eddie Collins, one-time star second baseman of the Athletics and White Sox and now business manager of the Red Sox, who placed fourth with 175.

Others to receive more than 100 votes were Rube Waddell, Connie Mack's eccentric left-hander of thirty years ago, with 148; Frank Chance, the Chicago Cubs' peerless leader of a quarter of a century ago, 133; Ed Delehanty, forerunner of the great sluggers of today, 132, and Big Ed Walsh, former pitching ace of the White Sox, 110.

Ten Names on Each Ballot

In all, the writers, each of whom was permitted to name ten candidates on his ballot, listed 119 players. The scribes were allowed to vote only for players active after 1900 but no longer playing in 1937.

Alexander thus became the ninth baseball luminary voted into the Hall of Fame by the writers since the practice was inaugurated in 1936. Already named were Ty Cobb, Babe Ruth, Honus Wagner, Christy Mathewson, Walter Johnson,

Times Wide World
GROVER ALEXANDER

Napoleon Lajoie, Tris Speaker and Cy Young.

In addition to these diamond greats the major league owners at their annual meeting in Chicago last month voted to include automatically five others for their long and meritorious services to baseball. These were George Wright, who managed the first professional baseball club, the old Cincinnati Red Stockings; Morgan G. Bulkeley, first president of the National League; Ban Johnson, founder and first president of the American League; John J. McGraw, for thirty years manager of the Giants, and Connie Mack, Athletics' manager since the inauguration of the American League.

Alexander, known to his colleagues as Old Pete, began his major league career in 1911 with the Phillies and almost immediately blazed a trail that for twenty years was to win him renown as one of the greatest right-handers of all time. He won twenty-eight games for the Phillies in his first year, a record no freshman pitcher has matched since, and from 1915 to 1917 turned in three successive

campaigns, in each of which he scored thirty or more victories.

Sergeant in World War

In 1918 Alex was traded to the Cubs, but served nearly all of the year with the A. E. F. in the World War, rising to the rank of sergeant. In 1919 he picked up the thread of his amazing feats with the Cubs, switched to the Cardinals in 1926 and concluded his career in 1930 with the club with which he had started, the Phillies.

He saw active service in three world series, first with the Phillies in 1915 and again with the Cardinals in 1926 and 1927.

Carefree and easy going, with an utter disregard of training rules that frequently had him in difficulties with his managers, Alexander hung up records, some of which are destined to remain on the books for many years. Some of the outstanding ones include: Most National League games pitched, 696; most games won, 373; a league earned-run mark of 1.22 for pitchers working in 250 innings or more; ninety shutouts, a lifetime record, and sixteen shut-outs in one season, a major league record he set in 1916.

The Hall of Fame poll follows:

212—G. C. Alexander		45—Ray Schalk	
179—George Sisler		40—Ross Youngs	
177—Willie Keeler		38—Eddie Plank	
175—Eddie Collins		37—Herb Pennock	
148—Rube Waddell		36—Joe McGinnity	
133—Frank Chance		35—Chief Bender	
132—Ed Delehanty		32—Frank Baker	
110—Ed Walsh		26—Johnny Kling	
91—Johnny Evers		24—Hugh Duffy	
79—Jimmy Collins		23—Hugh Jennings	
73—R. Maranville		18—Addie Joss	
67—R. Bresnahan		17—Wilbert Robinson	
63—Fred Clarke		16—Joe Tinker	
54—Mordecai Brown		14—Harry Heilmann	
48—Miller Huggins		12—Nap Rucker	
46—Rogers Hornsby			

11—Babe Adams, Sam Crawford and Lou Criger.

10—Clark Griffith, Rube Marquard and Dazzy Vance.

9—Ed Roush.

8—Hank Gowdy, Amos Rusie and Fred Tenney.

7—Nick Altrock, Jimmy Archer, Earl Combs, Bill Terry, Bobby Wallace and Zack Wheat.

6—Max Carey and Smoky Joe Wood.

5—Mike Donlin, Duffy Lewis and Art Nehf.

4—Bill Carrigan, Bill Dinneen, Larry Doyle, Harry Hooper and Stuffy McInnes.

3—Jack Barry, George Joseph Burns, Art Fletcher, Heinie Groh, Dick Kerr, Kid Nichols and Pie Traynor.

2—Dave Bancroft, Bill Bradley, Jess Burkett, Jack Chesbro, Jack Coombs, Gavvy Cravath, Kid Elberfeld, Eddie Foster, Joe Judge, Sherwood Magee, Roger Peckinpaugh, Eppa Rixey, Ossie Schreck, Everett Scott and Casey Stengel.

1—Clarence Beaumont, Marty Bergen, Ray Chapman, Andy Coakley, Wilbur Cooper, Stan Coveleskie, Otis Crandall, Walton Cruise, Bill Dahlen, Jake Daubert, Wild Bill Donovan, Charlie Dooin, Joe Dugan, Howard Ehmke, Red Faber, Elmer Flick, Kid Gleason, Eddie Grant, Burleigh Grimes, Bucky Harris, Buck Herzog, Charlie Irwin, Arlie Latham, Hans Lobert, Herman Long, Dolf Luque, Fred Marberry, Bob Meusel, Clyde Milan, Pat Moran, Red Murray, Hub Perdue, Sam Rice, Jimmy Sheckard, Urban Shocker, Jake Stahl, Gabby Street, Ira Thomas, Cy Williams and Chief Zimmer.

January 19, 1938

40,000 See Vander Meer of Reds Hurl Second No-Hit, No-Run Game in Row

DODGERS BOW, 6-0, IN NIGHT INAUGURAL

Vander Meer, Reds' Ace, Makes Baseball History — Hitless String Now 18⅓ Innings

FILLS BASES IN THE NINTH

But Completes Feat Unscathed at Ebbets Field—Fans Rush to Acclaim Young Hurler

By ROSCOE McGOWEN

Last night they turned on the greatest existing battery of baseball lights at Ebbets Field for the inaugural night major league game in the metropolitan area. A record throng for the season there, 40,000, of whom 38,748 paid, came to see the fanfare and show that preceded the contest between the Reds and the Dodgers.

The game, before it was played, was partly incidental; the novelty of night baseball was the major attraction.

But Johnny Vander Meer, tall, handsome 22-year-old Cincinnati southpaw pitcher, stole the entire show by hurling his second successive no-hit, no-run game, both coming within five days, and making baseball history that probably never will be duplicated. His previous no-hitter was pitched in daylight at Cincinnati last Saturday against the Bees, the Reds winning, 3—0. Last night the score was 6—0.

The records reveal only seven pitchers credited with two no-hitters in their careers and none who achieved the feat in one season.

More drama was crowded into the final inning than a baseball crowd has felt in many a moon. Until that frame only one Dodger had got as far as second base, Lavagetto reaching there when Johnny issued passes to Cookie and Dolf Camilli in the seventh.

But Vandy pitched out of that easily enough and the vast crowd was pulling for him to come through to the end.

The Crucial Inning

Johnny mowed down Woody English, batting for Luke Hamlin; Kiki Cuyler and Johnny Hudson in the eighth, fanning the first and third men, and when Vito Tamulis, fourth Brooklyn hurler, treated the Reds likewise in the ninth, Vandy came out for the crucial inning.

He started easily, taking Buddy Hassett's bounder and tagging him out. Then his terrific speed got out of control and, while the fans sat forward tense and almost silent, walked Babe Phelps, Lavagetto and Camilli to fill the bases.

All nerves were taut as Vandy pitched to Ernie Koy. With the count one and one, Ernie sent a bounder to Lew Riggs, who was so careful in making the throw to Ernie Lombardi that a double play wasn't possible.

Leo Durocher, so many times a hitter in the pinches, was the last hurdle for Vander Meer, and the crowd groaned as he swung viciously to line a foul high into the right-field stands. But a moment later Leo swung again, the ball arched lazily toward short center field and Harry Craft camped under it for the put-out that brought unique distinction to the young hurler.

It brought, also, a horde of admiring fans onto the field, with Vandy's team-mates ahead of them to hug and slap Johnny on the back and then to protect him from the mob as they struggled toward the Red dugout.

The fans couldn't get Johnny, but a few moments later they got his father and mother, who had accompanied a group of 500 citizens from Vandy's home town of Midland Park, N. J. The elder Vander Meers were completely surrounded and it required nearly fifteen minutes before they could escape.

Enhances His Record

The feat ran the youngster's remarkable pitching record to eighteen and one-third hitless and scoreless innings and a string of twenty-six scoreless frames. This includes a game against the Giants, his no-hitter against the Bees and last night's game.

Vander Meer struck out seven Dodgers, getting pinch hitters twice, and of the eight passes he issued two came in the seventh and three in the tense ninth.

Added to his speed was a sharp-breaking curve that seldom failed to break over the plate and at which the Dodger batsmen swung as vainly as at his fireball.

On the offense, well-nigh forgot-

Times Wide World

EBBETS FIELD UNDER THE FLOODLIGHTS DURING ITS FIRST NIGHT GAME

ten as the spectacle of Vander Meer's no-hitter unfolded, the Reds made victory certain as early as the third frame, when they scored four times and drove Max Butcher away.

Frank McCormick hit a home run into the left-field stands with Wally Berger and Ival Goodman aboard, while a pass to Lombardi and singles by Craft and Riggs added the fourth run.

Craft's third straight single scored Goodman in the seventh, the latter's blow off Tot Pressnell's right kneecap knocking the knuckleballer out and causing him to be carried off on a stretcher. Berger tripled off Luke Hamlin in the eighth to score Vander Meer with the last run.

The box score:

CINCINNATI (N.)	ab	r	h	po	a	e	BROOKLYN (N.)	ab	r	h	po	a	e
Frey, 2b	5	0	1	2	2	0	Cuyler, rf	2	0	0	1	0	0
Berger, lf	5	1	3	1	0	0	Coscarart, 2b	2	0	0	1	2	0
Goodman, rf	3	2	1	3	0	0	aBrack	1	0	0	0	0	0
McC'mick, 1b	5	1	1	9	1	0	Hudson, 2b	1	0	0	1	0	0
Lombardi, c	3	1	0	9	0	0	Hassett, lf	4	0	0	3	0	0
Craft, cf	5	0	3	1	0	0	Phelps, c	3	0	0	9	0	0
Riggs, 3b	4	0	1	0	3	0	bRosen	0	0	0	0	0	0
Myers, ss	4	0	0	0	1	0	Lavagetto, 3b	2	0	0	0	2	2
V. Meer, p	4	1	1	2	4	0	Camilli, 1b	1	0	0	7	0	0
							Koy, cf	4	0	0	4	0	0
Total	38	6	11	27	11	0	Durocher, ss	4	0	0	1	2	0
							Butcher, p	0	0	0	0	1	0
							Pressnell, p	2	0	0	0	0	0
							Hamlin, p	0	0	0	0	1	0
							cEnglish	1	0	0	0	0	0
							Tamulis, p	0	0	0	0	0	0
							Total	27	0	0	27	8	2

aBatted for Coscarat in sixth.
bRan for Phelps in ninth.
cBatted for Hamlin in eighth.

Cincinnati ....0 0 4 0 0 0 1 1 0—6
Brooklyn ....0 0 0 0 0 0 0 0 0—0

Runs batted in—McCormick 3, Riggs, Craft, Berger.

Two-base hit—Berger. Three-base hit—Berger. Home run—McCormick. Stolen base—Goodman. Left on bases—Cincinnati 9, Brooklyn 8. Bases on balls—Off Butcher 3, Vander Meer 8, Hamlin 1. Struck out—By Butcher 1, Pressnell 3, Vander Meer 7, Hamlin 3. Hits—Off Butcher 5 in 2 2-3, Hamlin 2 in 1 2-3, Pressnell 4 in 3 2-3, Tamulis 0 in 1. Losing pitcher—Butcher. Umpires—Stewart, Stark and Barr. Time of game—2:22.

June 16, 1938

Higgins's 12 Straight Hits Break Big League Mark; Red Sox Divide

Pinky Adds 8 in Twin Bill Against Tigers to 4 Made Sunday—Boston Wins, 8-3, and Bows, 5-4, Before 26,400

By The Associated Press.

DETROIT, June 21.—Frank (Pinky) Higgins, veteran Red Sox third baseman, marched into baseball's hall of fame today by cracking his twelfth consecutive hit while Boston and the Tigers split a double-header.

Even two home runs, with which Rudy York of Detroit entered a tie with Jimmy Foxx of Boston for the major league lead at nineteen each, fell into the background as Higgins, collecting eight hits, broke Tris Speaker's eighteen-year-old big league record. The Sox won the first game, 8 to 3, and Detroit the second, 5 to 4.

Streak Still Intact

Before a tense crowd of 26,400, Higgins banged the big hit, his seventh single of the day, over second base just out of Charley Gehringer's reach in the eighth inning of the second game. It gave him a perfect day at bat and left him a chance to extend the streak tomorrow.

The Sox third-sacker propelled three singles and a double in the first game and four singles in the second, tying Speaker's record of eleven straight hits made in 1920 with a sixth inning single in the nightcap.

Higgins began his streak with a double, three singles, and a walk in a double-header at Chicago Sunday. The Sox were idle yesterday. Higgins walked once in the first game today.

Tigers Outhit In Second

York hit a homer in each game, his drive in the second coming with a man on base and representing the difference between victory and defeat. The Red Sox outhit the Tigers, 10 to 7, in the nightcap, but Dixie Walker and Chet Laabs smashed timely doubles in addition to York's homer, while Ben Chapman's two-bagger was the only Boston drive for an extra base.

Wagner's ineffectiveness at the start caused a parade of four Sox pitchers, McKain and Dickman, who followed him, being removed for pinch-hitters and Bagley finishing. Roxie Lawson lasted until the eighth for Detroit, yielding all ten hits. He also passed seven batsmen, but was aided by three fast double plays and nine stranded Boston base runners. Boots Poffenberger relieved him with none out and retired the last six men in a row.

The split pushed Boston into second place in the American League, a half game ahead of the Yankees.

The Box Scores

FIRST GAME

BOSTON (A.)	ab	r	h	po	a	e	DETROIT (A.)	ab	r	h	po	a	e
Cramer, cf	4	0	2	6	0	0	Rogell, ss	4	1	1	1	4	0
Vosmik, lf	4	0	1	3	0	0	Walker, lf	5	0	1	2	0	0
Chapman, rf	5	0	0	1	0	0	Gehr'ger, 2b	3	1	0	1	2	0
Foxx, 1b	4	0	0	7	0	0	York, c	4	1	2	6	0	0
Cronin, ss	5	2	1	5	2	0	Fox, rf	4	0	1	3	0	0
Higgins, 3b	4	2	4	1	2	1	Greenb'g, 1b	4	0	0	11	0	1
Doerr, 2b	4	2	1	0	3	0	Laabs, cf	3	0	0	2	0	0
DeSautels, c	5	1	1	4	1	0	Ross, 3b	3	0	1	1	2	0
Wilson, p	0	0	0	0	0	0	Bridges, p	3	0	1	0	0	1
Osterm'ler, p	5	1	2	0	0	0	aPiet	0	0	0	0	0	0
Total	40	8	12	27	8	1	Total	33	3	7	27	8	2

aBatted for Bridges in ninth.

Boston ....0 0 1 0 0 3 0 3 1—8
Detroit ....1 0 0 0 0 0 2 0 0—3

Runs batted in—Vosmik, Doerr 2, DeSautels 2, Ostermueller 2, Gehringer, York.

Two-base hits—Ostermueller, Higgins, Rogell, DeSautels. Three-base hit—Doerr. Home run—York. Sacrifice—Doerr. Double play—Cronin and Foxx. Left on bases—Boston 10, Detroit 9. Bases on balls—Off Wilson 3, Ostermueller 3, Bridges 4. Struck out—By Ostermueller 4, Bridges 6. Hits—Off Wilson 2 in 1 inning (none out in 2d), Ostermueller 5 in 8. Winning pitcher—Ostermueller. Umpires—Hubbard, Summers and Grieve. Time of game—2:20.

SECOND GAME

BOSTON (A.)	ab	r	h	po	a	e	DETROIT (A.)	ab	r	h	po	a	e
Cramer, cf	3	0	0	1	0	0	Rogell, ss	3	1	0	2	6	0
Vosmik, lf	4	1	0	1	0	0	Walker, lf	2	2	1	3	0	0
Chapman, rf	5	0	3	0	1	0	G'ringer, 2b	4	0	1	2	3	0
Foxx, 1b	4	1	0	12	1	0	York, c	3	2	1	6	1	0
Cronin, ss	4	1	2	2	5	0	Fox, rf	4	0	0	1	1	0
Higgins, 3b	4	1	4	2	3	0	Gr'berg, 1b	3	0	0	7	2	0
Doerr, 2b	2	0	1	2	3	0	Laabs, cf	4	0	3	5	0	1
Peacock, c	4	0	0	2	0	0	Ross, 3b	3	0	1	0	1	0
Wagner, p	1	0	0	2	0	0	Lawson, p	3	0	0	1	1	0
McKain, p	0	0	0	0	0	0	P'berger, p	1	0	0	0	0	0
aN'nenkamp	1	0	0	0	0	0							
Dickman, p	0	0	0	0	0	0	Total	30	5	7	27	15	1
bGaffke	1	0	0	0	0	0							
Bagby, p	0	0	0	0	0	0							
Total	33	4	10	24	12	0							

aBatted for McKain in seventh.
bBatted for Dickman in eighth.

Boston ....0 0 2 0 0 0 0 2 0—4
Detroit ....2 0 3 0 0 0 0 0 ..—5

Runs batted in—Foxx, Higgins, Peacock, Gaffke, York 2, Fox, Laabs 2.

Two-base hits—Laabs, Walker, Chapman. Home run—York. Stolen base—Foxx. Double plays—Fox and York; Rogell, Gehringer and Greenberg; Gehringer, Rogell and Greenberg; Higgins, Doerr and Foxx. Left on bases—Boston 9, Detroit 7. Bases on balls—Off Wagner 3, McKain 3, Lawson 7. Struck out—By McKain 1, Bagby 1, Lawson 3, Poffenberger 1. Hits—Off Wagner 2 in 2 innings (0 out in third), McKain 2 in 4, Dickman 1 in 1, Bagby 2 in 1, Lawson 10 in 7 (0 out in eighth). Poffenberger 0 in 2. Winning pitcher—Lawson. Losing pitcher—Wagner. Umpire—Summers, Grieve and Hubbard. Time of game—2:06.

June 22, 1938

GREENBERG DRIVES HOMERS 57 AND 58

Detroit Star Needs Three in Five Remaining Games to Eclipse Ruth's Record

TIGERS WIN DOUBLE BILL

Turn Back Browns by 5 to 4 and 10 to 2—Hank Collects Both Blows in Nightcap

By The Associated Press.

DETROIT, Sept. 27.—Hank Greenberg, distance-clouting first baseman of the Tigers, poled two tremendous drives to center for his fifty-seventh and fifty-eighth home runs of the season today as Detroit swept a double-header with the Browns, 5 to 4 and 10 to 2.

With five games left to play, Greenberg is within striking distance of Babe Ruth's 1927 major league record of sixty homers in a single season.

Today's two circuit blows, hit off Pitcher Bill Cox in the first and third innings of the abbreviated nightcap, marked the eleventh time this season Greenberg has hit two or more round-trippers in a single game, thus bettering his own big league record for that feat. Darkness halted the second game after seven innings.

Greenberg's first homer was a 440-foot liner inside the park, and Hank had to slide home to beat the relay from center. Mark Christman, Detroit third baseman, hit a home run inside the park in the first game, and Dixie Walker and Charlie Gehringer also connected. Gehringer's was his twentieth of the season.

The box scores:

FIRST GAME

ST. LOUIS (A.)	ab	r	h	po	a	e	DETROIT (A.)	ab	r	h	po	a	e
Almada, cf	4	0	1	1	0	0	Morgan, cf	5	0	0	0	0	0
McQuinn, 1b	4	0	1	8	0	0	Walker, lf	5	2	2	1	0	0
Mazzera, lf	5	1	1	3	0	0	Gehr'ger, 2b	2	1	0	3	7	0
Clift, 3b	4	1	1	1	1	0	Gre'nb'g, 1b	1	0	1	10	1	0
Grace, rf	5	1	2	4	0	0	Fox, rf	4	0	2	2	0	0
Kress, ss	5	0	1	2	2	1	Rogell, ss	3	1	0	6	2	0
Sullivan, c	2	1	2	4	1	1	Tebbetts, c	4	0	1	4	0	0
Heffner, 2b	3	0	1	1	2	0	Ch'stm'n, 3b	3	1	1	1	1	0
Walkup, p	3	0	2	0	2	0	Benton, p	2	0	0	0	1	0
aBell	1	0	0	0	0	0	Lawson, p	2	0	0	0	1	0
Johnson, p	0	0	0	0	0	1	Total	31	5	7	27	14	0
Total	36	4	12	24	8	3							

aBatted for Walkup in eighth.

St. Louis ....0 0 0 2 0 2 0 0 0—4
Detroit ....2 2 0 0 0 0 0 1 ..—5

Runs batted in—Greenberg, Fox, Christman, Walker, Kress, Sullivan 2, Heffner.

Home runs—Christman, Walker. Stolen bases—Sullivan, Rogell. Sacrifice—Heffner. Double plays—Gehringer, Rogell and Greenberg; Rogell and Greenberg. Left on bases—St. Louis 11, Detroit 9. Bases on balls—Off Walkup 5, Johnson 2, Benton 2, Lawson 3. Struck out—By Walkup 2, Benton 1, Lawson 2. Hits—Off Walkup 6 in 7 innings, Johnson 1 in 1, Benton 9 in 5 2-3, Lawson 3 in 3 1-3. Passed ball—Tebbetts. Winning pitcher—Lawson. Losing pitcher—Johnson. Umpires—Hubbard, Rommell and Kolls. Time of game—2:10.

SECOND GAME

ST. LOUIS (A.)	ab	r	h	po	a	e	DETROIT (A.)	ab	r	h	po	a	e
Almada, cf	4	0	1	1	0	0	Morgan, cf	3	1	0	6	0	0
M'Quinn, 1b	4	0	1	10	0	0	Walker, lf	4	2	3	2	0	0
Mazzera, lf	2	0	1	0	0	0	Geh'ger, 2b	3	2	1	2	1	0
M'Qui'n, lf	1	0	0	4	0	0	Gr'nberg, 1b	4	2	2	2	1	0
Clift, 3b	2	0	0	1	0	0	Fox, rf	4	1	1	2	0	0
Lu'dello, 3b	1	1	1	0	0	0	Rogell, ss	4	0	0	2	3	0
Grace, rf	4	1	3	2	0	1	Tebbetts, c	3	1	1	3	1	0
Kress, ss	4	0	0	1	3	1	Ch'tman, 3b	3	1	1	1	0	0
Ha'shany, c	2	0	1	2	0	0	Coffman, p	3	0	0	1	0	0
Heffner, 2b	3	0	0	0	5	0							
Cox, p	2	0	0	0	2	0	Total	31	10	9	21	5	0
aBell	0	0	0	0	0	0							
Cole, p	0	0	0	0	0	0							
Total	29	2	8	21	10	2							

aBatted for Cox in sixth.

St. Louis ....0 0 0 0 0 1 1—2
Detroit ....2 2 3 0 0 0 3—10

Runs batted in—Greenberg 4, Christman, Coffman, Gehringer 3, Heffner, Grace.

Two-base hit—Lucadello. Three-base hit—Christman. Home runs—Greenberg 2, Gehringer. Double play—Heffner, Kress and McQuinn. Left on bases—St Louis 10, Detroit 2. Base on balls—Off Cox 1, Cole 1, Coffman 4. Struck out—By Coffman 3. Hits—Off Cox 7 in 5 innings, Cole 2 in 2. Losing pitcher—Cox. Umpires—Rommel, Kolls and Hubbard. Time of game—1:40.

September 28, 1938

Hartnett's Homer With 2 Out in 9th Beats Pirates

CUBS HALT PIRATES FOR 9TH IN ROW, 6-5

34,465 See Chicago Supplant Losers in League Lead With a Half-Game Advantage

ROOT WINS IN RELIEF ROLE

Lazzeri's Pinch Double Helps Tie Score in Eighth—Rizzo Connects for Corsairs

By The Associated Press.

CHICAGO, Sept. 28.—In the thickening gloom, with the score tied and two out in the ninth inning today, red-faced Gabby Hartnett blasted a home run before 34,465 cheering fans to give his Cubs a dramatic 6-to-5 victory over the Pirates and a half-game lead in the furious National League pennant battle.

That is the story of one of the most sensational games ever played at Wrigley Field—a game which saw the fighting Chicagoans charge from behind to knot the score and then win on a slashing drive to the left field bleachers to oust Pittsburgh from the No. 1 position it had held since July 12.

Hartnett's smash, against Mace Brown with the count two strikes and no balls, probably saved the Cub pennant chances. Had he failed, the game would have been called because of darkness, necessitating a double bill tomorrow which would have almost insurmountably handicapped the overtaxed Cub pitching staff.

The Chicago manager, whose team was nine games out of first place a little more than a month ago, had to fight his way through a swirling, hysterical mob to touch all the bases and had trouble reaching the dugout. He called the victory and his homer "the two greatest things that ever happened to me."

Bryant Driven to Cover

A hit and two errors helped the Cubs to a run in the second and, with Clay Bryant pitching masterfully, they stayed in front until the sixth. Then the Pirates, combining Johnny Rizzo's twenty-first homer of the season with two other hits and a pair of walks, chased Bryant with a three-run blast. Jack Russell replaced him.

The Bruins came roaring right back to tie the score in their half of the inning on doubles by Hartnett and Rip Collins and a bunt which Billy Jurges beat out.

In the seventh a furiously disputed double play pulled the Cubs out of another hole. The Pirates charged Vance Page, who had replaced Russell, had committed a balk on the pitch Rizzo hit into the double killing, but succeeded only in using up time as darkness gathered.

Battling desperately, the Corsairs went back to work in the eighth. Arky Vaughan walked and Gus Suhr singled. Larry French replaced Page. Heinie Manush batted for Pep Young and singled, scoring Vaughan.

Big Bill Lee, who had finished

Times Wide World
Gabby Hartnett

yesterday's game, went in for French and was greeted by Lee Handley's single which scored Suhr. Manush was nailed at the plate when Al Todd grounded to Jurges, but after wild pitching Handley to third, Lee restored order by forcing Bob Klinger to hit into a double play.

Collins opened the Cub eighth with a single which sent Klinger to the showers, Bill Swift taking his place. Jurges walked and Tony Lazzeri, former Yankee star, slashed a pinch double to right, scoring Collins and putting Jurges on third.

Stan Hack was passed and Billy Herman singled, sending in Jurges with the tying run. However, on the play Joe Marty, running for Lazzeri, was out at the plate, Paul Waner to Todd. Mace Brown replaced Swift and forced Frank Demaree to hit into a double play.

Charlie Root pitched for the Cubs in the ninth and held the Pirates to a single by Paul Waner. Phil Cavarretta and Carl Reynolds were easy outs before Hartnett won the battle and put his team on top for the first time since June 8. It was the Cubs' ninth straight victory and their nineteenth in their last twenty-two games.

Tomorrow, in the concluding game of a thrill-packed series, Lee will be Hartnett's pitching hope, with the jittery Pirates banking on Russ Bauers.

The box score:

PITTSBURGH (N.)	ab.	r.	h.	po.	a.	e.		CHICAGO (N.)	ab.	r.	h.	po.	a.	e.
L.Waner, cf.	4	1	0	2	1	0		Hack, 3b..	3	0	0	3	1	0
P.Waner, rf.	5	0	2	3	1	1		Herman, 2b.	5	0	3	2	2	0
Rizzo, lf..	5	1	1	1	0	0		Demaree, rf	5	0	0	2	0	0
Vaughan, ss.	2	2	1	2	5	1		Cavar'ta,rf	5	0	0	2	0	0
Suhr, 1b...	5	2	2	5	0	0		Reynolds, cf	5	0	1	5	0	0
Young, 2b..	2	0	0	1	1	0		Hartnett, c.	4	2	2	4	1	0
aManush ...	1	0	1	0	0	0		Collins, 1b..	3	1	3	8	5	0
Thevenow,2b	0	0	0	1	3	0		Jurges, ss..	3	1	1	4	4	0
Handley, 3b.	3	0	2	1	1	0		Bryant, p...	2	0	1	0	0	0
Todd, c.....	3	0	0	3	1	1		Russell, p..	0	0	0	0	0	0
Klinger, p.	4	0	0	2	0	0		bO'Dea ...	1	0	0	0	0	0
Swift, p....	0	0	0	0	0	0		Page, p.....	0	0	0	0	0	0
Brown, p...	0	0	0	0	0	0		French, p...	0	0	0	0	0	0
								Lee, p......	0	0	0	0	1	0
Total ...35	5	10	*26	18	4		cLazzeri ..	1	0	1	0	0	0
								dMarty ...	0	0	0	0	0	0
								Root, p.....	0	0	0	0	0	0
								Total ...38	6	12	27	9	0

*Two out when winning run scored.
aBatted for Young in eighth.
bBatted for Russell in sixth.
cBatted for Lee in eighth.
dRan for Lazzeri in eighth.

Pittsburgh ....0 0 0 0 0 3 0 2 0—5
Chicago ....0 1 0 0 0 2 0 2 1—6

Runs batted in—Manush, Rizzo, Handley 3, Hack, Herman, Collins, Hartnett, Lazzeri. Two-base hits—L. Waner, Hartnett, Collins, Lazzeri. Home runs—Rizzo, Hartnett. Double plays—Thevenow and Suhr; Jurges, Herman and Collins; Hack, Herman and Collins; Lee, Jurges and Collins. Left on bases—Pittsburgh 7, Chicago 10. Bases on balls—Off Klinger 2, Swift 2, Bryant 5, Page 1. Struck out—By Klinger 6, Bryant 1, Page 1. Hits—Off Klinger 8 in 7 innings (none out in eighth) ; Swift 3 in 1-3; Brown 1 in 1 1-3; Bryant 4 in 5 2-3; Russell 0 in 1-3; Page 3 in 1 (none out in eighth); French 1 in 0 (pitched to one batter in eighth); Lee 1 in 1; Root 1 in 1. Wild pitch—Lee. Passed ball—Todd. Winning pitcher—Root. Losing pitcher—Brown. Umpires—Barr, Stark, Goetz and Campbell. Time of game—2:37.

September 29, 1938

FELLER SETS MARK BY STRIKING OUT 18

But Indians Bow to Tigers, 4-1, 10-8—Greenberg Finishes With Homer Total 58

CLEVELAND, Oct. 2 (P).—Bob Feller, young Cleveland marvel, enhanced his fame today, but the Indians bowed twice to the Tigers, 4 to 1 and 10 to 8.

Feller fanned eighteen batters in the opener to topple the major league record for strike-outs in one game, but couldn't pull the game out of the fire.

In 1937 Feller fanned seventeen Athletics to set an American League record and tie Dizzy Dean, who was then with the Cardinals, for the major league mark.

Feller's eighteenth victim today was Chet Laabs, who struck out for the fifth time in the ninth. He fanned Pete Fox twice, McCoy twice, Hank Greenberg twice, Tony Piet once, Mark Christman three times and his mound rival, Harry Eisenstat, three times.

Bob allowed seven hits, walked seven men and hit Piet. Detroit scored twice in the seventh on Greenberg's double, Roy Cullenbine's single and George Tebbetts's double. Two walks, a sacrifice and Christman's single gained the other two Detroit runs. There were two men on base when Feller fanned Laabs for strike-out No. 18. He disregarded the runners and pitched with a full wind-up.

Today's feat raised Feller's strike-out total for the season to 240, which leads both major leagues in that department, and gave him a margin of fifteen over Buck Newsom of the Browns, who fanned ten today for a total of 225.

Eisenstat held the Indians scoreless until the ninth of the opener, allowing only four hits.

Greenberg failed to hit a homer and finished the season with fifty-eight, two under Babe Ruth's mark.

The box scores:

FIRST GAME

DETROIT (A.)	ab.	r.	h.	po.	a.	e.		CLEVELAND (A.)	ab.	r.	h.	po.	a.	e.
McCoy, 2b..	3	0	0	1	3	1		Irwin, ss...	3	0	0	0	1	0
Fox, rf.....	4	1	2	0	0	0		Witherly, cf.	4	0	1	1	0	0
Cullnbine, lf	4	2	3	4	0	0		Campbell, rf	4	1	1	1	0	0
Grnberg, 1b	2	1	1	9	0	0		Heath, lf..	4	0	0	0	0	0
Tebbetts, c..	4	0	2	6	0	0		Trosky, 1b..	3	0	1	10	0	0
Laabs, cf...	3	0	2	0	0	0		Pytlak, c...	4	0	1	8	0	0
Piet, 3b...	3	0	1	0	3	0		Keltner, 3b.	3	0	0	0	4	0
Ch'stman, ss.	3	0	1	3	1	0		Grimes, 2b..	3	0	0	2	1	0
Eisenstat, p.	3	0	0	3	0	0		Feller, p...	3	0	0	1	0	0
Total.....33	4	7	27	9	1		Total 30	1	4	27	3	0

Detroit ....0 0 0 0 0 2 0 2 0—4
Cleveland ....0 0 0 0 0 0 0 0 1—1

Runs batted in—Tebbetts 2, Christman 2, Trosky. Two-base hits—Greenberg, Tebbetts. Stolen bases—Cullenbine, Piet. Sacrifice—Tebbetts. Double play—McCoy, Christman and Greenberg. Left on bases—Detroit 11, Cleveland 5. Bases on balls—Off Feller 7, Eisenstat 2. Struck out—By Feller 18, Eisenstat 2. Hit by pitcher—By Feller (Piet). Umpires—Hubbard, Grieve and Moriarty. Time of game—2:07.

SECOND GAME

DETROIT (A.)	ab.	r.	h.	po.	a.	e.		CLEVELAND (A.)	ab.	r.	h.	po.	a.	e.
McCoy, 2b..	4	2	2	2	1	0		Irwin, ss...	3	0	1	1	4	0
Fox, rf....	4	1	2	0	0	0		Witherly, cf.	4	1	1	0	1	1
Cullnbine, lf	3	2	1	1	0	0		Workman, rf.	4	1	2	1	0	1
Grnberg, 1b	3	3	2	6	1	0		Heath, lf..	3	1	1	0	0	0
Tebbetts, c..	4	1	2	6	0	0		Grimes, 1b..	4	2	2	7	0	0
Laabs, cf...	4	1	2	4	0	0		Pytlak, c...	3	0	0	4	1	0
Piet, 3b....	1	0	0	1	3	0		Webb, 3b...	4	0	1	0	2	1
Ch'stman, ss.	3	0	1	2	1	0		Mack, 2b...	4	2	2	4	4	0
Harris, p...	3	1	1	2	0	0		Humphries, p	1	0	0	0	1	0
								Smith, p....	3	0	0	0	1	0
Total.....31	10	13	21	8	1		Total 32	8	11	21	12	2

Detroit ....5 0 1 3 0 0 1—10
Cleveland ....0 0 0 3 1 1 3—8

Runs batted in—Laabs 4, Fox, Cullenbine, Greenberg, Tebbetts, Christman, Grimes 2, Mack 2, Weatherly, Heath. Two-base hits—McCoy, Fox. Three-base hits—Grimes, Mack. Stolen bases—Fox, Cullenbine. Double play—Irwin and Grimes. Left on bases—Detroit 7, Cleveland 7. Base on balls—Harris 4, Humphries 2, Smith 1. Struck out—Harris 6, Humphries 1, Smith 8 in 6. Hits—Off Humphries 5 in 1 inning, Smith 8 in 6. Wild pitch—Harris. Losing pitcher—Humphries. Umpires—Hubbard, Grieve and Moriarty. Time of game—1:37.

October 3, 1938

Foxx Picked as American League's Most Valuable Player

RED SOX SLUGGER NAMED FOR 3D TIME

Foxx Is First in Majors to Be So Honored, Polling 305 of Possible 336 Points

TOPS 19 OF 24 BALLOTS

Dickey Is Second, Greenberg Third, Ruffing Fourth— Team Honors to Yanks

By JOHN DREBINGER

Jimmy Foxx, slugging first sacker of the Boston Red Sox whose spectacular comeback provided one of the highlights of last season, has been chosen the most valuable player in the American League for 1938, it was announced yesterday by the Baseball Writers Association of America, whose committee recently completed its annual poll for The Sporting News Trophy.

The round-faced, popular Double-X, who thus becomes the first player in either major league to win the award three times, scored a smashing victory, compiling a total of 305 points of a possible 336. Bill Dickey, redoubtable catcher of the Yankees, placed second with 196, and Hank Greenberg, the Tigers' home run champion, finished third with 162.

Another Yankee, big Red Ruffing, was ranked next with 146, followed by Buck Newsom, star right-hander of the lowly Browns, who finished with 111.

DiMaggio Sixth on List

Joe DiMaggio, the Yankees' "wonder player" of 1937, who placed second to Charlie Gehringer last year, dropped to sixth place with 106 points. Gehringer, however, took an even more pronounced tumble, polling only 27 points.

JIMMY FOXX

Associated Press

By carrying off top honors Foxx also becomes the first Boston player in either league to gain the prize since the practice was instituted in 1922. In his two previous triumphs, in 1932 and 1933, the one-time Maryland dairy farmer was a member of the Athletics.

Making the same revision in scoring rules as in the National League poll, the writers' committee this year consisted of twenty-four members, three from each city, and each committee ranked ten players with an additional "honor list" of ten which did not count in the scoring.

Foxx's victory was far more decisive than Ernie Lombardi's in the National loop, for where the Cincinnati catcher received only ten first-place ballots, Foxx headed nineteen of the twenty-four ballots

in the American League poll. Of the five who failed to pick him for first, two ranked him second and one each placed him third, fourth and fifth.

Cronin Gets 92 Points

The only others to receive first-place ballots were the two Yanks Dickey and Ruffing, the former being named on top three times and the latter twice. However, the score of these two along with DiMaggio and the fact that, all told, eight members of the world champions received a scattering of votes, enabled the Yanks to carry off team honors with 489 points, as against 411 for the Red Sox, whose manager, Joe Cronin, placed just below DiMaggio with 92.

The honorable mention list for 1938 is headed by Harlond Clift of the Browns, who was named on twelve ballots. Gehringer, Bob Johnson of the Athletics and Rudy York of the Tigers were named on eleven.

The complete list of players receiving one or more votes in the balloting follows:

	Points.
Jimmy Foxx, Boston	305
Bill Dickey, New York	196
Hank Greenberg, Detroit	162
Charley Ruffing, New York	146
Buck Newsom, St. Louis	111
Joe DiMaggio, New York	106
Joe Cronin, Boston	92
Earl Averill, Cleveland	34
Cecil Travis, Washington	33
Charley Gehringer, Detroit	27
Jeff Heath, Cleveland	24
Joe Gordon, New York	23
Hal Trosky, Cleveland	22
Ken Keltner, Cleveland	16
Monty Stratton, Chicago	15
Mel Harder, Cleveland	14
Bob Johnson, Philadelphia	13
Harlond Clift, St. Louis	11
Lou Gehrig, New York	10
Pete Fox, Detroit	9
Joe Vosmik, Boston	7
George McQuinn, St. Louis	7
Lefty Grove, Boston	7
Buddy Lewis, Washington	5
Red Rolfe, New York	5
Buddy Myer, Washington	5
Earle Brucker, Philadelphia	5
Johnny Allen, Cleveland	3
Frank Crosetti, New York	2
Lefty Gomez, New York	1
Doc Cramer, Boston	1

Winners of the most valuable player award in the American League:

Year	Winner	Team
1922	George Sisler	St. Louis
1923	Babe Ruth	New York
1924	Walter Johnson	Washington
1925	Roger Peckinpaugh	Washington
1926	George Burns	Cleveland
1927	Lou Gehrig	New York
1928	Mickey Cochrane	Philadelphia
1931	Lefty Grove	Philadelphia
1932	Jimmy Foxx	Philadelphia
1933	Jimmy Foxx	Philadelphia
1934	Mickey Cochrane	Detroit
1935	Hank Greenberg	Detroit
1936	Lou Gehrig	New York
1937	Charley Gehringer	Detroit
1938	Jimmy Foxx	Boston

(1922-28 league award by baseball writers; 1931-38, Baseball Writers Association award).

Sisler, Collins and Keeler Are Chosen

STARS WHO WERE HONORED YESTERDAY AS THEY APPEARED IN THEIR HEYDAY

Times Wide World
George Sisler

Times Wide World
Eddie Collins

Times Wide World
Wee Willie Keeler

LIST OF IMMORTALS IN BASEBALL GROWS

Sisler, Collins and Keeler Are Elected to National Game's Hall of Fame

ALL WERE GREAT HITTERS

Old Stars Batted Well Over .300 Mark During Careers Covering Many Years

By JOHN DREBINGER

Baseball, entering its centennial year, yesterday added three more names to its list of immortals. George Sisler, one of the game's greatest first baseman; Eddie Collins, outstanding second baseman for more than two decades, and Wee Willie Keeler, whose brilliant career as an outfielder closed several years after the turn of the century, have been elected to the Hall of Fame at Cooperstown.

With a record total of 274 votes cast among the members of the Baseball Writers Association of America in their fourth annual poll, each of the three received more than the 75 per cent of the total necessary for election.

Sisler headed the list with 235 votes. Collins was named on 213 ballots and Keeler received 207, just one above the minimum for qualification.

The three additions swell to nineteen the number of diamond luminaries of the past whose names are being perpetuated on plaques in the Cooperstown shrine. Twelve of these were named by the writers, whose selections are limited to players still active after 1900.

Alexander Named in 1938

The first to be chosen in this group were Ty Cobb, Babe Ruth, Honus Wagner, Christy Mathewson and Walter Johnson. Napoleon Lajoie, Tris Speaker and Cy Young were selected in the 1937 poll and Grover Cleveland Alexander was honored last year.

In addition to these, the Centennial Committee, consisting of Commissioner K. M. Landis, President Will Harridge of the American League and President Ford Frick of the National, chose, a year ago, George Wright, M. G. Bulkeley, Ban Johnson, John J. McGraw, Connie Mack, Henry Chadwick and Alexander Cartwright.

Another group of old-timers, numbering from five to ten, is to be added to the list by the committee between now and the centennial celebration at Cooperstown on June 12.

Sisler, now 45, but still active in the game as high commissioner of semi-professional baseball, ranked for a period as one of the greatest hitters of his time, twice outstripping such renowned sluggers as Cobb and Speaker to win the American League batting crown.

GEORGE EDWARD WADDELL
"RUBE"
COLORFUL LEFTHANDED PITCHER WHO WA
IN BOTH LEAGUES, BUT WHO GAINED FAM
AS A MEMBER OF THE PHILADELPHIA A.
TEAM. WON MORE THAN 20 GAMES IN FIRS
FOUR SEASONS WITH THAT CLUB AND
COMPILED MORE THAN 200 VICTORIES
DURING MAJOR LEAGUE CAREER. WAS
NOTED FOR HIS STRIKEOUT ACHIEVEMENT

Gehrig Voluntarily Ends Streak at 2,130 Straight Games

A University of Michigan star, Sisler, always a quiet, retiring sort of fellow, broke in as pitcher in 1915 with the St. Louis Browns, but was converted into a first baseman the following year and it was at that position he quickly attained stardom.

He ended his services with the Browns in 1927 after serving several years as manager and played with the Senators in 1928. An eye ailment terminated his playing career with Boston in the National League in 1930.

Sisler had a lifetime batting average of .341 and in 1922 reached the peak with .420. That year he also became the first player to win the official award of "most valuable player in the American League."

Collins began his career in 1906, when, fresh from the campus of Columbia University, he joined the Athletics to become a member of Connie Mack's $100,000 infield. When Mack broke up that famous machine at the close of the 1914 season, Collins was traded to the White Sox, with whom he remained until 1926, serving the last two years as manager.

Before closing his long and brilliant career as an active player, Collins returned to Mack in 1927 and remained for three years more under his first mentor, serving chiefly as coach. He is now vice president and general manager of the Boston Red Sox.

An alert base runner and fine hitter, Collins ranked for years as one of the shrewdest "money players" in baseball. He participated in seven world series and three times hit over .400. His lifetime batting average, spanning twenty-five seasons, was .333.

The present generation of fans may only hazily recall Keeler as a star of a bygone era with the early New York Highlanders, now known as the Yankees, and the player who coined the phrase "Hit 'em where they ain't."

But Keeler was a star long before that, first gaining fame with the legendary Baltimore Orioles through the years 1894 to 1898. He then played with Brooklyn from 1899 to 1902, was a member of the Highlanders from 1903 to 1909 and closed his active career in 1910 with the Giants under his one-time Oriole colleague, McGraw. Keeler died in 1923.

He still ranks among old-timers as the greatest bunter the game has ever known and for fourteen years averaged better than .300. He led the National League in 1897 with a mark of .432, second only to the all-time high of .438 established by Hugh Duffy in 1893.

In all, 108 players received votes in this year's poll with twenty-eight nominees drawing more than twenty-five. Heading those who trailed just below the three selected and now looming as logical selections for next year, were Rube Waddell with 179 votes, Rogers Hornsby with 176 and Frank Chance with 158.

The list of those who received more than twenty-five votes follows:

George Sisler	.235	Mordecai Brown	54
Eddie Collins	.213	Wilbert Robinson	46
Willie Keeler	.207	Chief Bender	40
Rube Waddell	.179	Herb Pennock	40
Rogers Hornsby	.176	Ray Schalk	35
Frank Chance	.158	Hugh Duffy	34
Ed Delahanty	.145	Ross Young	34
Ed Walsh	.132	Hugh Jennings	33
Johnny Evers	.107	Joe McGinnity	32
Miller Huggins	97	Home Run Baker	30
Rabbit Maranville	82	Addie Joss	28
Jimmy Collins	72	Eddie Plank	28
Roger Bresnahan	67	Mickey Cochrane	28
Fred Clarke	59	Frank Frisch	26

LOU, NOT HITTING, ASKS REST ON BENCH

Gehrig's String, Started June 1, 1925, Snapped as Yanks Start Series in Detroit

RETURN OF ACE INDEFINITE

But Iron Man Who Holds Many Records Hopes to Regain Form in Hot Weather

By JAMES P. DAWSON
Special to THE NEW YORK TIMES.

DETROIT, May 2.—Lou Gehrig's matchless record of uninterrupted play in American League championship games, stretched over fifteen years and through 2,130 straight contests, came to an end today.

The mighty iron man, who at his peak had hit forty-nine home runs in a single season five years ago, took himself out of action before the Yanks marched on Briggs Stadium for their first game against the Tigers this year.

With the consent of Manager Joe McCarthy, Gehrig removed himself because he, better than anybody else, perhaps, recognized his competitive decline and was frankly aware of the fact he was doing the Yankees no good defensively or on the attack. He last played Sunday in New York against the Senators.

When Gehrig will start another game is undetermined. He will not be used as a pinch-hitter.

The present plan is to keep him on the bench. Relaxing and shaking off the mental hazards he admittedly has encountered this season, he may swing into action in the hot weather, which should have a beneficial effect upon his tired muscles.

Dahlgren Gets Chance

Meanwhile Ellsworth (Babe) Dahlgren, until today baseball's greatest figure of frustration, will continue at first base. Manager McCarthy said he had no present intention of transferring Tommy Henrich, the youthful outfielder whom he tried at first base in the Florida training camp. Dahlgren had been awaiting the summons for three years.

It was coincidental that Gehrig's string was broken almost in the presence of the man he succeeded

Record of Gehrig's Streak

	G.	AB.	R.	H.	RBI.	HR.	PC.
1925	*126	437	73	129	68	21	.295
1926	155	572	135	179	107	16	.313
1927	155	584	149	218	175	47	.373
1928	154	562	139	210	142	27	.374
1929	154	553	127	166	126	35	.300
1930	154	581	143	220	174	41	.379
1931	155	619	163	211	184	46	.341
1932	156	596	138	208	151	34	.349
1933	152	593	138	198	139	32	.334
1934	154	579	128	210	165	49	.363
1935	149	535	125	176	119	30	.329
1936	155	579	167	205	152	49	.354
1937	157	569	138	200	159	37	.351
1938	157	576	115	170	114	29	.295
1939	8	28	2	4	1	0	.143
Total	2,141	7,953	1,880	2,704	1,976	493	.340

*Includes eleven games before consecutive run started.

as Yankee first baseman. At that time Wally Pipp, now a business man of Grand Rapids, Mich., was benched by the late Miller Huggins to make room for the strapping youth fresh from the Hartford Eastern League club to which the Yankees had farmed him for two seasons, following his departure from Columbia University. Pipp was in the lobby of the Book Cadillac Hotel at noon when the withdrawal of Gehrig was effected.

"I don't feel equal to getting back in there," Pipp said on June 2, 1925, the day Lou replaced him at first. Lou had started his phenomenal streak the day before as a pinch-hitter for Peewee Wanninger, then the Yankee shortstop.

This latest momentous development in baseball was not unexpected. There had been signs for the past two years that Gehrig was slowing up. Even when a sick man, however, he gamely stuck to his chores, not particularly in pursuit of his all-time record of consecutive play, although that was a big consideration, but out of a driving desire to help the Yankees, always his first consideration.

Treated for Ailment

What Lou had thought was lumbago last year when he suffered pains in the back that more than once forced his early withdrawal from games he had started was diagnosed later as a gall bladder condition for which Gehrig underwent treatment all last Winter, after rejecting a recommendation that he submit to an operation.

Wired Photo—Times Wide World
VETERAN FIRST BASEMAN AND HIS SUCCESSOR
Lou Gehrig and Babe Dahlgren in Detroit yesterday

The signs of his approaching fade-out were unmistakable this Spring at St. Petersburg, Fla., yet the announcement from Manager McCarthy was something of a shock. It came at the end of a conference Gehrig arranged immediately after McCarthy's arrival by plane from his native Buffalo.

"Lou just told me he felt it would be best for the club if he took himself out of the line-up," McCarthy said following their private talk. "I asked him if he really felt that way. He told me he was serious. He feels blue. He is dejected.

"I told him it would be as he wished. Like everybody else I'm sorry to see it happen. I told him not to worry. Maybe the warm weather will bring him around.

"He's been a great ball player. Fellows like him come along once in a hundred years. I told him that. More than that, he's been a vital part of the Yankee club since he started with it. He's always been a perfect gentleman, a credit to baseball.

"We'll miss him. You can't escape that fact. But I think he's doing the proper thing."

Lou Explains Decision

Gehrig, visibly affected, explained his decision quite frankly.

"I decided last Sunday night on this move," said Lou. "I haven't

been a bit of good to the team since the season started. It would not be fair to the boys, to Joe or to the baseball public for me to try going on. In fact, it would not be fair to myself, and I'm the last consideration.

"It's tough to see your mates on base, have a chance to win a ball game, and be not able to do anything about it. McCarthy has been swell about it all the time. He'd let me go until the cows came home, he is that considerate of my feelings, but I knew in Sunday's game that I should get out of there.

"I went up there four times with men on base. Once there were two there. A hit would have won the ball game for the Yankees, but I missed, leaving five stranded as the Yankees lost. Maybe a rest will do me some good. Maybe it won't. Who knows? Who can tell? I'm just hoping."

Gehrig's withdrawal from today's game does not necessarily mean the end of his playing career, although that seems not far distant. When the day comes Gehrig can sit back and enjoy the fortune he has accumulated as a ball player. He is estimated to have saved $200,000 from his earnings, which touched a high in 1938, when he collected $39,000 as Yankee salary.

When Gehrig performed his duties as Yankee captain today, appearing at the plate to give the batting order, announcement was made through the amplifiers of his voluntary withdrawal and it was suggested he get "a big hand." A deafening cheer resounded as Lou walked to the dugout, doffed his cap and disappeared in a corner of the bench.

Open expressions of regret came from the Yankees and the Tigers. Lefty Vernon Gomez expressed the Yankees' feelings when he said:

"It's tough to see this thing happen, even though you know it must come to us all. Lou's a great guy and he's always been a great baseball figure. I hope he'll be back in there."

Hank Greenberg, who might have been playing first for the Yanks instead of the Tigers but for Gehrig, said: "Lou's doing the right thing. He's got to use his head now instead of his legs. Maybe that Yankee dynasty is beginning to crumble."

Scott Former Record Holder

Everett Scott, the shortstop who held the record of 1,307 consecutive games until Gehrig broke it, ended his streak on May 6, 1925, while he was a member of the Yankees. However, Scott began his string,

once considered unapproachable, with the Red Sox.

By a strange coincidence, Scott gave way to Wanninger, the player for whom Gehrig batted to start his great record.

With only one run batted in this year and a batting average of .143 representing four singles in twenty-eight times at bat, Lou has fallen far below his record achievements of previous seasons, during five of which he led the league in runs driven home.

Some of his more important records follow:

Most consecutive games—2,130.

Most consecutive years, 100 games or more—14.

Most years, 150 games or more—12.

Most years, 100 runs or more—13.

Most consecutive years, 100 runs or more—13.

Most home runs with bases full—23.

Most years, 300 or more total bases—13.

Most years, 100 runs or more driven in—13.

Most games by first baseman in one season—157.

Most home runs in one game—4 (modern record).

Most runs batted in, one season—184 (American League).

May 3, 1939

61,808 FANS ROAR TRIBUTE TO GEHRIG

Captain of Yankees Honored at Stadium—Calls Himself 'Luckiest Man Alive'

By JOHN DREBINGER

In perhaps as colorful and dramatic a pageant as ever was enacted on a baseball field, 61,808 fans thundered a hail and farewell to Henry Lou Gehrig at the Yankee Stadium yesterday.

To be sure, it was a holiday and there would have been a big crowd and plenty of roaring in any event. For the Yankees, after getting nosed out, 3 to 2, in the opening game of the double-header, despite a ninth-inning home run by George Selkirk, came right back in typical fashion to crush the Senators, 11 to 1, in the nightcap. Twinkletoes Selkirk embellished this contest with another home run.

But it was the spectacle staged between the games which doubtless never will be forgotten by those who saw it. For more than forty minutes there paraded in review two mighty championship hosts—the Yankees of 1927 and the cur-

rent edition of Yanks who definitely are winging their way to a fourth straight pennant and a chance for another world title.

Old Mates Reassemble

From far and wide the 1927 stalwarts came to reassemble for Lou Gehrig Appreciation Day and to pay their own tribute to their former comrade-in-arms who had carried on beyond all of them only to have his own brilliant career come to a tragic close when it was revealed that he had fallen victim of a form of infantile paralysis.

In conclusion, the vast gathering, sitting in absolute silence for a longer period than perhaps any baseball crowd in history, heard Gehrig himself deliver as amazing a valedictory as ever came from a ball player.

So shaken with emotion that at first it appeared he would not be able to talk at all, the mighty Iron Horse, with a rare display of that indomitable will power that had carried him through 2,130 consecutive games, moved to the microphone at home plate to express his own appreciation.

And for the final fadeout, there stood the still burly and hearty Babe Ruth alongside of Gehrig, their arms about each other's shoulders, facing a battery of camera men.

All through the long exercises Gehrig had tried in vain to smile, but with the irrepressible Bambino beside him he finally made it. The

Babe whispered something to him and Lou chuckled. Then they both chuckled and the crowd roared and roared.

Late Rally Fails

The ceremonies began directly after the debris of the first game had been cleared away. There had been some vociferous cheering as the Yanks, fired to action by Selkirk's homer, tried to snatch that opener away from the Senators in the last few seconds of the ninth. But they couldn't quite make it and the players hustled off the field.

Then, from out of a box alongside the Yankee dugout there spryly hopped more than a dozen elderly gentlemen, some gray, some shockingly baldish, but all happy to be on hand. The crowd recognized them at once, for they were the Yanks of 1927, not the first Yankee world championship team, but the first, with Gehrig an important cog in the machine, to win a world series in four straight games.

Down the field, behind Captain Sutherland's Seventh Regiment Band, they marched—Ruth, Bob Meusel, who had come all the way from California; Waite Hoyt, alone still maintaining his boyish countenance: Wally Schang, Benny Bengough, Tony Lazzeri, Mark Koenig, Jumping Joe Dugan, Bob Shawkey, Herb Pennock, Deacon Everett Scott, whose endurance record Gehrig eventually surpassed: Wally Pipp, who faded out as the Yankee first sacker the day Columbia Lou took over the

job away back in 1925, and George Pipgras, now an umpire and, in fact, actually officiating in the day's games.

At the flagpole, these old Yanks raised the world series pennant they had won so magnificently from the Pirates in 1927 and, as they paraded back, another familiar figure streaked out of the dugout, the only one still wearing a Yankee uniform. It was the silver-haired Earle Combs, now a coach.

Old-Timers Face Plate

Arriving at the infield, the old-timers strung out, facing the plate. The players of both Yankee and Senator squads also emerged from their dugouts to form a rectangle, and the first real ovation followed as Gehrig moved out to the plate to greet his colleagues, past and present.

One by one the old-timers were introduced with Sid Mercer acting as toastmaster. Clark Griffith, venerable white-haired owner of the Senators and a Yankee himself in the days when they were known as Highlanders, also joined the procession.

Gifts of all sorts followed. The Yankees presented their stricken comrade with a silver trophy measuring more than a foot and a half in height, their thoughts expressed in verse inscribed upon the base. Manager Joe McCarthy, almost as visibly affected as Gehrig himself, made this presentation and hurried back to fall in line with his players. But every few minutes, when he saw that the once stalwart figure they called the Iron Horse was swaying on shaky legs, Marse Joe would come forward to give Lou an assuring word of cheer.

Mayor La Guardia officially ex-

Times Wide World

Members of previous great Yankee teams: Joe Dugan, Waite Hoyt, Herb Pennock, Benny Bengough, Wally Schang, Everett Scott, Wally Pipp, Babe Ruth, George Pipgras, Bob Meusel, Tony Lazzeri, Mark Koenig and Bob Shawkey grouped near flagpole in center field between games.

tended the city's appreciation of the services Columbia Lou had given his home town.

"You are the greatest prototype of good sportsmanship and citizenship," said the Mayor, concluding with "Lou, we're proud of you."

Postmaster General Farley also was on hand, closing his remarks with "for generations to come, boys who play baseball will point with pride to your record."

When time came for Gehrig to address the gathering it looked as if he simply would never make it. He gulped and fought to keep back the tears as he kept his eyes fastened on the ground.

But Marse Joe came forward again, said something that might have been "come on, Lou, just rap out another," and somehow those magical words had the same effect as in all the past fifteen years when the gallant Iron Horse would step up to the plate to "rap out another."

Gehrig Speaks Slowly

He spoke slowly and evenly, and stressed the appreciation that he felt for all that was being done for him. He spoke of the men with whom he had been associated in his long career with the Yankees—the late Colonel Jacob Ruppert, the late Miller Huggins, his first manager, who gave him his start in New York; Edward G. Barrow, the present head of baseball's most power-

ful organization; the Yanks of old who now stood silently in front of him, as well as the players of today.

"What young man wouldn't give anything to mingle with such men for a single day as I have for all these years?" he asked.

"You've been reading about my bad break for weeks now," he said. "But today I think I'm the luckiest man alive. I now feel more than ever that I have much to live for."

The gifts included a silver service set from the New York club, a fruit bowl and two candlesticks from the Giants, a silver pitcher from the Stevens Associates, two silver platters from the Stevens employes, a fishing rod and tackle from the Stadium employes and ushers, a silver cup from the Yankee office staff, a scroll from the Old Timers Association of Denver that was presented by John Kieran, a scroll from Washington fans, a tobacco stand from the New York Chapter of the Baseball Writers Association of America, and the silver trophy from his team-mates.

The last-named present, about eighteen inches tall with a wooden base, supported by six silver bats with an eagle atop a silver ball, made Gehrig weep. President Barrow walked out to put his arms about Lou in an effort to steady him when this presentation was made. It appeared for an instant that Gehrig was near collapse.

On one side of the trophy were the names of all his present fellow-players. On the other was the following touching inscription:

TO LOU GEHRIG

We've been to the wars together,
We took our foes as they came,
And always you were the leader
And ever you played the game.

Idol of cheering millions,
Records are yours by the sheaves,
Iron of frame they hailed you,
Decked you with laurel leaves.

But higher than that we hold you,
We who have known you best,
Knowing the way you came
through
Every human test.

Let this be a silent token
Of lasting friendship's gleam,
And all that we've left unspoken,
Your pals of the Yankee team.

As Gehrig finished his talk, Ruth, robust, round and sun-tanned, was nudged toward the microphone and, in his own inimitable, blustering style, snapped the tears away. He gave it as his unqualified opinion that the Yanks of 1927 were greater than the Yanks of today, and seemed even anxious to prove it right there.

"Anyway," he added, "that's my opinion and while Lazzeri here pointed out to me that there are only about thirteen or fourteen of us here, my answer is, shucks, we only need nine to beat 'em."

Then, as the famous home-run slugger, who also has faded into baseball retirement, stood with his arms entwined around Gehrig's

shoulders, the band played "I Love You Truly," while the crowd took up the chant: "We love you, Lou."

All Tributes Spontaneous

All given spontaneously, it was without doubt one of the most touching scenes ever witnessed on a ball field and one that made even case-hardened ball players and chroniclers of the game swallow hard.

When Gehrig arrived in the Yankee dressing rooms he was so close to a complete collapse it was feared that the strain upon him had been too great and Dr. Robert E. Walsh, the Yankees' attending physician, hurried to his assistance. But after some refreshment, he recovered quickly and faithful to his one remaining task, that of being the inactive captain of his team, he stuck to his post in the dugout throughout the second game.

Long after the tumult and shouting had died and the last of the crowd had filed out, Lou trudged across the field for his familiar hike to his favorite exit gate. With him walked his bosom pal and teammate, Bill Dickey, with whom he always rooms when the Yanks are on the road.

Lou walks with a slight hitch in his gait now, but there was supreme confidence in his voice as he said to his friend:

"Bill, I'm going to remember this day for a long time."

So, doubtless, will all the others who helped make this an unforgettable day in baseball.

July 5, 1939

GAMES ARE TELEVISED

Major League Baseball Makes Its Radio Camera Debut

Major league baseball made its television debut here yesterday as the Dodgers and Reds battled through two games at Ebbets Field before two prying electrical "eyes" of station W2XBS in the Empire State Building. One "eye" or camera was placed near the visiting players' dugout, or behind the right-hand batters' position. The other was in a second-tier box back of the catcher's box and commanded an extensive view of the field when outfield plays were made.

Over the video-sound channels of the station, television-set owners as far away as fifty miles viewed the action and heard the roar of the crowd, according to the National Broadcasting Company.

It was not the first time baseball was televised by the NBC. Last May at Baker Field a game between Columbia and Princeton was caught by the cameras. However, to those who, over the television receivers, saw last May's contest as well as those yesterday, it was apparent that considerable progress has been made in the technical requirements and apparatus for this sort of outdoor pick-up, where the action is fast. At times it was possible to catch a fleeting glimpse of the ball as it sped from the pitcher's hand toward home plate.

August 27, 1939

Feller Opens Season With No-Hit Shutout

INDIANS' ACE BEATS WHITE SOX BY 1-0

Feller Is Only One in Modern Major League History to Hurl Opening No-Hitter

FANS EIGHT, WALKS FIVE

Losers Fill Bases in Second —Single by Heath and Hemsley's Triple Win

By The Associated Press.

CHICAGO, April 16—Bob Feller of the Indians carved a niche for himself in baseball's hall of fame as the American League season opened today, pitching an amazing no-hit game to defeat the White Sox, 1 to 0, before 14,000 roaring fans.

It was the first opening day no-hit contest in modern major league history. It ended after 2 hours and 24 minutes of play as Ray Mack, Cleveland second sacker, made a great knockdown of Taft Wright's grounder and tossed him out at first by a step.

Feller, who struck out eight batsmen and walked five, earned the

BOB FELLER
Times Wide World

decision on two timely Indian safeties in the fourth inning. Jeff Heath singled to left with one out, and after Ken Keltner had flied out, Heath scored on a triple to right by Feller's catcher and friend, Rollie Hemsley.

Three Earlier One-Hitters

It was Feller's first no-hitter, although he has had three one-hit performances in his brilliant major league career. The 21-year-old star won twenty-four games last season.

The White Sox, even though they enjoyed six-hit pitching by the southpaw Edgar Smith, threatened seriously only once. In the second they had the bases filled with two out. Feller, using his blazing fast ball, then struck out rookie Bob Kennedy.

Feller, who put on his great show before his parents, Mr. and Mrs. William Feller, and his sister, Marguerite, retired fifteen men in a row from the fourth inning through the eighth.

He got the first two men in the ninth easily, but Luke Appling,

White Sox shortstop, gave him and the cheering fans several anxious moments. Appling drove four foul smashes to right before drawing a walk on the tenth pitch.

Nice Stop by Mack

Then Mack made his fine play on Wright's drive on the ground. The ball was to Mack's left and the infielder, with a fine stab, knocked it to the ground, picked up the rolling ball and shot it to First Baseman Hal Trosky for the putout.

The last no-hitter in the major leagues was hurled by Monte Pearson of the Yankees, who beat the Indians in the second game of a double-header in New York on Aug. 27, 1938.

The last no-hit game in Comiskey Park was pitched by Bill Dietrich in beating the Browns on June 1, 1937. Records show that Eddie Cicotte of the Sox pitched a no-hitter as early in the season as April 14, in 1917.

The box score:

CLEVELAND (A.)	ab.	r.	h.	po.	a.	e.	CHICAGO (A.)	ab.	r.	h.	po.	a.	e.
Boudreau, ss.	3	0	0	1	2	0	Kennedy, 3b.	4	0	0	1	2	0
Weatherly, cf	4	0	1	2	0	1	Kuhel, 1b.	3	0	0	11	0	0
Chapman, rf.	3	0	0	6	0	0	Kreevich. cf.	3	0	0	3	0	0
Trosky, 1b.	4	0	0	8	0	0	Solters, lf.	4	0	0	2	0	0
Heath, lf.	4	1	1	0	0	0	Appling, ss.	3	0	0	2	0	0
Keltner, 3b.	4	0	1	0	2	0	Wright, rf.	4	0	0	3	0	0
Hemsley, c.	4	0	2	8	0	0	McNair, 2b.	3	0	0	2	2	1
Mack, 2b.	4	0	1	2	3	0	Tresh, c.			2	0	5	0	0
Feller, p.	3	0	0	0	0	0	Smith, p.	1	0	0	0	2	0
							aRosenthal		.1	0	0	0	0
Total	33	1	6	27	7	1	Brown, p.	0	0	0	0	1	0
							Total	28	0	0	27	9	1

aBatted for Smith in eighth.

Cleveland .... 0 0 0 1 0 0 0 0 0—1
Chicago .... 0 0 0 0 0 0 0 0 0—0

Run batted in—Hemsley.
Two-base hit—Mack. Three-base hit—Hemsley. Stolen base—Kuhel. Double play—Kuhel (unassisted). Left on bases—Cleveland 7, Chicago 6. Bases on balls—Off Feller 5, Smith 2. Struck out—By Feller 8, Smith 5. Hits—Of Smith 6 in 8 innings. Brown 0 in 1. Umpires—Geisel. McGowan and Kolls. Time of game—2:24. Attendance 14,000.

April 17, 1940

American League's 4-Run Rally in Ninth Tops National in All-Star Contest

CLIMAX OF THE ALL-STAR GAME IN DETROIT

WILLIAMS'S HOMER DECIDES 7-5 GAME

Ted's Hit With Two On, Two Out in Last of Ninth Wins for American League

VAUGHAN NATIONAL'S HERO

His Two 4-Baggers, All-Star Contest Mark, Tally 4 Runs —54,674 at Detroit

By JOHN DREBINGER
Special to THE NEW YORK TIMES.

DETROIT, July 8—Coming up with a last-minute electrifying charge that floored a foe at the very moment he appeared to have a signal triumph within his grasp, the American League snatched victory from defeat today. Scoring four runs in the last half of the ninth inning, the Harridge forces overcame the National League, 7 to 5, in the ninth annual All-Star game.

A blistering home-run smash by Ted Williams, lanky outfielder of the Red Sox, with two colleagues on base sent the final three tallies hurtling over the plate, while a crowd of 54,674, predominantly American League in its sympathies, acclaimed the shot with a thunderous roar.

Only a few moments before this blow landed with stunning and devastating force, the National League cohorts, led by Deacon Bill McKechnie, Reds' manager, appeared to have the battle tucked away.

Conflict Appears Ended

They had entered the final round leading by two runs, thanks to a pair of circuit blows by Arky Vaughan. When, with one out and the bases full, Claude Passeau, Chicago Cubs' pitcher, appeared to have induced the mighty Joe DiMaggio to slam vigorously into a double play, the contest, played for the benefit of the United Service Organizations, looked to be over.

But a rather hurried peg to first base by Billy Herman, Dodger second sacker, went a trifle wide of its mark and Jolting Joe escaped by a stride. It left Passeau still striving for one more out to clinch the struggle, but Claude never caught up with it. For a few seconds later Williams, leading bats-

Williams of Red Sox crossing plate on ninth-inning homer that gave American League three runs. DiMaggio of Yankees (5) and Coach Shea (30) of Tigers are the first to congratulate him.

man of the American League, bashed the ball almost on a line against the upper parapet of the right-field stands of Briggs Stadium.

Thus the squad directed by Del Baker, Tiger pilot, brought to the American League its sixth triumph in the nine All-Star games played since 1933.

Up to the time of this culminating assault, however, the National Leaguers certainly looked to be riding high, wide and handsome. Joe DiMaggio, though his current forty-eight-game hitting streak was not at stake, nevertheless had to wait until the eighth inning before he lashed out with a double to save, at least, his prestige.

Employs 1940 Tactics

Resorting to much the same tactics that he employed at St. Louis a year ago when he fired the National League's vaunted pitching talent into the foe with bewildering rapidity for a shut-out victory, McKechnie, for the first six innings, again hurled three crack

Ted Williams, whose circuit blow with two on won the game.

moundsmen—Whitlow Wyatt, Paul Derringer and Bucky Walters—at the foe, each working only two innings apiece.

But in the home stretch, McKechnie veered from his course. Perhaps the two homers which Vaughan, the Pirate shortstop, had unleashed in the seventh and eighth innings, each with a man on base, lulled the National League skipper into a feeling of false security.

Bill permitted Passeau, who had entered the fray in the seventh, to remain on the mound through the ninth, and with this, by the margin of Williams's staggering clout, the wily Cincinnati leader overreached himself.

Passeau had seen one run shot away from him in the eighth when Joe DiMaggio unfurled his double for his first and only hit and presently scored when brother Dominic DiMaggio, who had entered the battle in its later stages, whistled a single to right.

This still left Passeau with a

two-run margin. When Claude concluded the eighth by fanning the renowned Jimmy Foxx with two aboard the bases, McKechnie apparently saw no reason why the Chicago right-hander could not safely navigate through the ninth as well.

As the last of the ninth opened with Frank Hayes popping out, there still seemed no danger lurking around in the last few strides to the wire.

Pass Fills the Bases

But Ken Keltner, batting for Edgar Smith. the fourth and last American League hurler, bounced a single off Eddie Miller, the Braves' shortstop who had just replaced Vaughan in the field. Joe Gordon of the Yankees singled to right, and when Cecil Travis drew a pass, filling the bases, a feeling that something dramatic was about to come to pass gripped the crowd.

Joe DiMaggio stepped to the plate. But Joe's best was a grounder at Miller that just missed ending the struggle, but Herman's wide peg, though not an error, let in one tally and missed DiMaggio at first for what would have been the final out, and Williams did the rest.

Despite the early fine pitching efforts of Wyatt, Walters and Derringer, the National Leaguers also had to wait until the struggle moved well on its way before they assumed what promised to be a commanding lead. For during the first six rounds the American Leaguers likewise flashed some brilliant hurling.

Bobby Feller, youthful Cleveland ace and ranked as the foremost pitcher of his time, blazed through the first three rounds to face only nine men. He allowed one single and that was all. The hitter was trapped off first.

Then came the left-handed Thornton Lee of the White Sox to hurl the next three rounds and it was not until the sixth that the National Leaguers managed to break through with their first tally.

Walters sparked this one by banging a double to left, advancing to third on Stanley Hack's sacrifice and then skipping home on Terry Moore's long fly to Williams in left.

That matched the run which the American Leaguers had marked up in the fourth off Derringer, although the tally was scarcely big Paul's fault. Travis, crack third sacker of the Senators, had doubled with one out and moved to third on Joe DiMaggio's fly to deep right.

Catches Spikes in Turf

Williams then followed with a sharp liner toward right that seemed to be moving straight for where Bob Elliott, Pirate outfield-

er, was standing, for the third out. But Elliott momentarily misjudged the ball, rushed in a few steps, caught his spikes in the turf as he tried to back-track and wound up rather inelegantly sprawled on the grass. The ball shot over his head against the stand for a double and Travis scored.

However, though Walters managed to erase this run in the sixth, the American League went ahead again in the same inning by clipping Bucky for a tally. The Cincinnati ace right-hander paved the way for his own difficulties here by walking Joe DiMaggio and Jeff Heath, and then Lou Boudreau smacked a single to center, scoring DiMaggio.

In the seventh the tide veered sharply toward the National League legions. Sid Hudson, youthful right-hander of the Senators, came on to pitch for the American Leaguers and for a few minutes threatened to have himself annihilated.

Enos Slaughter, who had replaced the hapless Elliott in the McKechnie outfield, singled to left and grabbed an extra base when Williams stumbled over the ball for an error. The misplay, however, had no bearing on what followed, for Vaughan arched his first homer into the upper right tier of the grand stand.

Herman followed with a double and it promised another tally when Al Lopez deftly sacrificed Billy to third and Joe Medwick came up to bat for Walters. Just to show that seven long years scarcely tax the memory of a baseball fan, there was again a fine round of boos for Muscles Joe, who, as a Cardinal on this same field in the 1934 world series, had seen himself shelled from the arena with a barrage of vegetables.

But though Medwick tried hard to add a little more to the general discomfiture of his old friends, he grounded to the infield and Hudson luckily escaped without any further scoring being charged against him.

However, with the eighth, the National Leaguers jacked up their lead with another pair of runs and again it was the booming bat of Vaughan that jarred the opposition.

The southpaw Smith had supplanted Hudson on the mound as this round opened and fanned Pete Reiser for a starter. But Johnny Mize, silenced up to now, rifled a two-bagger to right. His Cardinal team-mate, Slaughter, struck out, but Vaughan again belted the ball into that inviting target offered by the upper right stand and the National lead was now 5 to 2.

Hero of the Hour

It marked the first time a player ever had managed to belt two homers in an All-Star game and Vaughan decidedly was the hero of the hour.

And he still was all of that until

Box Score of the Game

NATIONAL LEAGUE

	ab.	r.	h.	tb.	2b.	3b.	hr.	sh.	sb.	bb.	so.	po.	a.	e.
Hack, Chicago, 3b	2	0	1	1	0	0	0	1	0	1	1	3	0	0
Lavagetto, Brooklyn, 3b	1	0	0	0	0	0	0	0	0	0	0	0	0	0
Moore, St. Louis, lf	5	0	0	0	0	0	0	0	0	0	1	0	0	0
Reiser, Brooklyn, cf	4	0	0	0	0	0	0	0	0	0	2	6	0	2
Mize, St. Louis, 1b	4	1	1	2	1	0	0	0	0	0	0	5	0	0
McCormick, Cincinnati, 1b	0	0	0	0	0	0	0	0	0	0	0	0	0	0
Nicholson, Chicago, rf	1	0	0	0	0	0	0	0	0	0	1	1	0	0
Elliott, Pittsburgh, rf	1	0	0	0	0	0	0	0	0	0	0	0	0	0
Slaughter, St. Louis, rf	2	1	1	0	0	0	0	0	0	0	1	0	0	0
Vaughan, Pittsburgh, ss	4	2	3	9	0	0	2	0	0	0	0	1	2	0
Miller, Boston, ss	0	0	0	0	0	0	0	0	0	0	0	1	0	0
Frey, Cincinnati, 2b	1	0	1	1	0	0	0	0	0	0	0	1	3	0
Herman, Brooklyn, 2b	3	0	2	3	1	0	0	0	0	0	0	3	0	0
Owen, Brooklyn, c	1	0	0	0	0	0	0	0	0	0	0	0	0	0
Lopez, Pittsburgh, c	1	0	0	0	0	0	0	1	0	0	0	3	0	0
Danning, New York, c	1	0	0	0	0	0	0	0	0	0	0	3	0	0
Wyatt, Brooklyn, p	0	0	0	0	0	0	0	0	0	0	0	0	0	0
aOtt, New York	1	0	0	0	0	0	0	0	0	0	1	0	0	0
Derringer, Cincinnati, p	0	0	0	0	0	0	0	0	0	0	0	1	0	0
Walters, Cincinnati, p	1	1	1	2	1	0	0	0	0	0	0	0	0	0
cMedwick, Brooklyn	1	0	0	0	0	0	0	0	0	0	0	0	0	0
Passeau, Chicago, p	1	0	0	0	0	0	0	0	0	0	0	0	0	0
Total	35	5	10	19	3	0	2	2	0	1	7	*26	7	2

AMERICAN LEAGUE

	ab.	r.	h.	tb.	2b.	3b.	hr.	sh.	sb.	bb.	so.	po.	a.	e.
Doerr, Boston, 2b	3	0	0	0	0	0	0	0	0	0	1	0	0	0
Gordon, New York, 2b	2	1	1	1	0	0	0	0	0	0	0	2	0	0
Travis, Washington, 3b	4	1	1	2	1	0	0	0	0	1	0	1	2	0
J. DiMaggio, New York, cf	4	3	1	2	1	0	0	0	0	1	0	1	0	0
Williams, Boston, lf	4	1	2	6	1	0	1	0	0	1	1	3	0	1
Heath, Cleveland, rf	2	0	0	0	0	0	0	0	0	1	1	1	0	1
D. DiMaggio, Boston, rf	1	0	1	1	0	0	0	0	0	0	0	1	0	0
Cronin, Boston, ss	2	0	0	0	0	0	0	0	0	0	1	3	0	0
Boudreau, Cleveland, ss	2	0	2	2	0	0	0	0	0	0	0	0	1	0
York, Detroit, 1b	3	0	1	1	0	0	0	0	0	0	0	6	2	0
Foxx, Boston, 1b	1	0	0	0	0	0	0	0	0	0	1	2	2	0
Dickey, New York, c	3	0	1	1	0	0	0	0	0	0	0	4	2	0
Hayes, Philadelphia, c	1	0	0	0	0	0	0	0	0	0	0	2	0	0
Feller, Cleveland, p	0	0	0	0	0	0	0	0	0	0	0	0	1	0
bCullenbine, St. Louis	1	0	0	0	0	0	0	0	0	0	0	0	0	0
Lee, Chicago, p	0	0	0	0	0	0	0	0	0	0	0	0	1	0
Hudson, Washington, p	0	0	0	0	0	0	0	0	0	0	0	0	0	0
dKeller, New York	1	0	0	0	0	0	0	0	0	0	1	0	0	0
Smith, Chicago, p	0	0	0	0	0	0	0	0	0	0	0	1	0	1
eKeltner, Cleveland	1	1	1	1	0	0	0	0	0	0	0	0	0	0
Total	36	7	11	17	3	0	1	0	0	4	6	27	11	3

*Two out when winning runs were scored.
aBatted for Wyatt in third.
bBatted for Feller in third.
cBatted for Walters in seventh.
dBatted for Hudson in seventh.
eBatted for Smith in ninth.

SCORE BY INNINGS

National League.....................0 0 0 0 0 1 2 2 0—5
American League.....................0 0 0 1 0 1 0 1 4—7

Runs batted in—Williams 4, Moore, Boudreau, Vaughan 4, D. DiMaggio, J. DiMaggio. Earned runs—National League 5, American League 7. Left on bases—National League 6, American League 7. Double plays—Frey, Vaughan and Mize; York and Cronin. Struck out—By Feller 4 (Hack, Reiser, Nicholson, Ott); by Derringer 1 (Heath); by Walters 2 (Cronin, Doerr); by Hudson 1 (Moore); by Smith 2 (Reiser, Slaughter); by Passeau 3 (Keller, Williams, Foxx). Bases on balls—Off Wyatt 1 (Williams); off Walters 2 (J. DiMaggio, Heath); off Hudson 1 (Hack); off Passeau 1 (Travis). Hits—Off Feller, 1 in 3 innings; off Lee, 4 in 3 innings; off Hudson, 3 in 1 inning; off Smith, 2 in 2 innings; off Wyatt, 0 in 2 innings; off Derringer, 2 in 2 innings; off Walters, 3 in 2 innings; off Passeau, 6 in 2 2-3 innings. Winning pitcher—Smith. Losing pitcher—Passeau. Umpires—Summers (A. L.), Jorda (N. L.), Grieve (A. L.) and Pinelli (N. L.). Time of game—2:23. Attendance—54,674.

the DiMaggio brothers whittled one tally away from Passeau's lead in the last of the eighth and Williams swept away the rest with his closing smash in the ninth.

Wyatt's pitching in the first two innings was practically as flawless as was Feller's work in the first three. The slim Brooklyn right-hander faced only six batters and, though he gave one a pass, he immediately snuffed this fellow off the base line by inducing the next man to slap into a double play.

Feller, fanning four during his three scoreless rounds, was equally invincible. Lonnie Frey opened the third with a single, but almost immediately got himself trapped off first base because somebody apparently had failed to tell Lonnie that Rapid Robert no longer is the easy mark for base runners that he used to be.

July 9, 1941

DiMaggio's Streak Ended at 56 Games

SMITH AND BAGBY STOP YANKEE STAR

DiMaggio, Up for Last Time in Eighth, Hits Into a Double Play With Bases Full

M'CARTHYMEN WIN BY 4-3

Stretch Lead Over Indians to 7 Lengths Before Biggest Crowd for Night Game

By JOHN DREBINGER

Special to THE NEW YORK TIMES.

CLEVELAND, July 17 — In a brilliant setting of lights and before 67,468 fans, the largest crowd ever to see a game of night baseball in the major leagues, the Yankees tonight vanquished the Indians, 4 to 3, but the famous hitting streak of Joe DiMaggio finally came to an end.

Officially it will go into the records as fifty-six consecutive games, the total he reached yesterday. Tonight in Cleveland's municipal stadium the great DiMag was held hitless for the first time in more than two months.

Al Smith, veteran Cleveland lefthand and a Giant cast-off, and Jim Bagby, a young right-hander, collaborated in bringing the DiMaggio string to a close.

Jolting Joe faced Smith three times. Twice he smashed the ball down the third-base line, but each time Ken Keltner, Tribe third sacker, collared the ball and hurled it across the diamond for a put-out at first. In between these two tries, DiMaggio drew a pass from Smith.

Then, in the eighth, amid a deafening uproar, the streak dramatically ended, though the Yanks routed Smith with a flurry of four hits and two runs that eventually won the game.

Double Play Seals Record

With the bases full and only one out Bagby faced DiMaggio and, with the count at one ball and one strike, induced the renowned slugger to crash into a double play. It was a grounder to the shortstop, and as the ball flitted from Lou Boudreau to Ray Mack to Oscar Grimes, who played first base for the Tribe, the crowd knew the streak was over.

However, there were still a few thrills to come, for in the ninth, with the Yanks leading, 4 to 1, the Indians suddenly broke loose with an attack that for a few moments threatened to send the game into extra innings and thus give DiMaggio another chance.

Gerald Walker and Grimes singled, and, though Johnny Murphy here replaced Gomez, Larry Rosenthal tripled to score his two colleagues. But with the tying run on third and nobody out the Cleveland attack bogged down in a mess of bad base-running and the Yanks' remaining one-run lead held, though it meant the end of the streak for DiMaggio, who might have come up fourth had there been a tenth inning.

Started May 15

It was on May 15 against the White Sox at the Yankee Stadium

Jim Bagby Jr.

that DiMaggio began his string, which in time was to gain nationwide attention. As the great DiMag kept clicking in game after game, going into the twenties, then the thirties, he became the central figure of the baseball world.

On June 29, in a double-header with the Senators in Washington, he tied, then surpassed the American League and modern record of forty-one games set by George Sisler of the Browns in 1922. The next target was the all-time major league high of forty-four contests set by Willie Keeler, famous Oriole star, forty-four years ago under conditions much easier then for a batsman than they are today. Then there was no foul-strike rule hampering the batter.

But nothing hampered DiMaggio as he kept getting his daily hits, and on July 1 he tied the Keeler mark. The following day he soared past it for game No. 45, and he kept on soaring until tonight. In seeking his fifty-seventh game, he finally was brought to a halt.

Actually, DiMaggio hit in fifty-seven consecutive games, for on July 8 he connected safely in the All-Star game in Detroit. But that contest did not count in the official league records.

Did Better on Coast

DiMaggio's mark ends five short of his own Pacific Coast League record of sixty-one consecutive games, which he set while with San Francisco in 1933. The all-time minor league high is sixty-seven, set by Joe Wilhoit of Wichita in the Western League in 1919.

The contest tonight was a blistering left-handed mound duel between Gomez and Smith, with Gomez going ahead one run in the first on Red Rolfe's single and Tommy Henrich's double.

A tremendous home run inside the park, which Walker outgalloped, tied the score in the fourth and the battle remained deadlocked until Joe Gordon untied it with his fifteenth homer of the year into the left-field stand in the seventh.

In the eighth the Yanks seemingly clinched victory when Charlie Keller rifled a triple to center past Roy Weatherly, who played the ball badly, needlessly charging in when he might just as well have played it safe for a single.

In its wake came singles by Gomez and Johnny Sturm. A double by Rolfe and two runs were in. Smith walked Henrich to fill the bases, and in this setting, with one out, the result of a harmless grounder by Phil Rizzuto and Bagby stepped in to face the great DiMag. A moment later the streak was over.

Traffic Snarl on Bases

The Indians were guilty of atrocious work on the bases in the ninth after Rosenthal had cracked Murphy for a triple to drive in two. Hal Trosky, pinch hitting, grounded out to first. Then Soup Campbell, batting for Bagby, splashed a grounder to Murphy. Rosenthal tried to score, was run down between third and home.

To make matters worse, Campbell, dashing past first base, never looked see what was going on and so made no attempt to grab second during the run-up. Weatherly, amid no end of hoots and jeers, grounded out for the final play.

The victory was Gomez's eighth, his sixth in a row. It was the Yanks' seventeenth in their last eighteen games and thirty-first in their last thirty-six contests. Their lead over the thoroughly demoralized Tribe was stretched to seven games.

July 18, 1941

DiMaggio's Record Streak

Date	Opponent	ab.	r.	h.	2b.	3b.	hr.	Date	Opponent	ab.	r.	h.	2b.	3b.	hr.
May 15	White Sox	4	0	1	0	0	0	June 17	White Sox	4	1	1	0	0	0
May 16	White Sox	4	2	2	0	1	1	June 18	White Sox	3	0	1	0	0	0
May 17	White Sox	3	1	1	0	0	0	June 19	White Sox	3	2	3	0	0	1
May 18	Browns	3	3	3	1	0	0	June 20	Tigers	5	3	4	1	0	0
May 19	Browns	3	0	1	0	0	0	June 21	Tigers	4	0	1	0	0	0
May 20	Browns	5	1	1	0	0	0	June 22	Tigers	5	1	2	1	0	1
May 21	Tigers	5	0	2	0	0	0	June 24	Browns	4	1	1	0	0	0
May 22	Tigers	4	0	1	0	0	0	June 25	Browns	4	1	1	0	0	1
May 23	Red Sox	5	0	1	0	0	0	June 26	Browns	4	0	1	1	0	0
May 24	Red Sox	4	2	1	0	0	0	June 27	Athletics	3	1	2	0	0	1
May 25	Red Sox	4	0	1	0	0	0	June 28	Athletics	5	1	2	1	0	0
May 27	Senators	5	3	4	0	0	1	June 29	Senators	4	1	1	1	0	0
May 28	Senators	4	1	1	0	1	0	June 29	Senators	5	1	1	0	0	0
May 29	Senators	3	1	1	0	0	0	July 1	Red Sox	4	0	2	0	0	0
May 30	Red Sox	2	1	1	0	0	0	July 1	Red Sox	3	1	1	0	0	0
May 30	Red Sox	3	0	1	0	0	0	July 2	Red Sox	5	1	1	0	0	1
June 1	Indians	4	1	1	0	0	0	July 5	Athletics	4	2	1	0	0	1
June 1	Indians	4	1	1	0	0	0	July 6	Athletics	5	2	4	1	0	0
June 2	Indians	4	2	2	1	0	0	July 6	Athletics	4	0	2	0	1	0
June 3	Tigers	4	1	1	0	0	1	July 10	Browns	2	0	1	0	0	0
June 5	Tigers	5	1	1	0	0	0	July 11	Browns	5	1	4	0	0	1
June 7	Browns	5	2	3	0	0	0	July 12	Browns	5	1	2	1	0	0
June 8	Browns	4	3	2	0	0	2	July 13	White Sox	4	2	3	0	0	0
June 8	Browns	4	1	2	1	0	1	July 13	White Sox	4	0	1	0	0	0
June 10	White Sox	5	1	1	0	0	0	July 14	White Sox	3	0	1	0	0	0
June 12	White Sox	4	1	2	0	0	1	July 15	White Sox	4	1	2	1	0	0
June 14	Indians	2	0	1	1	0	0	July 16	Indians	4	3	3	1	0	0
June 15	Indians	3	1	1	0	0	1								
June 16	Indians	5	0	1	1	0	0	Total		223	56	91	16	4	15

Cardinals Subdue Braves, 6-1, 3-2; Crabtree's Homer Takes Nightcap

His Round-Tripper in 9th Is Duplicate of One Hit in First Game—Five Unearned Runs Decide Opener—Pollet, Lanier Win

By JAMES P. DAWSON
Special to THE NEW YORK TIMES.

ST. LOUIS, Sept. 17—Adjusting themselves to both the ridiculous and the sublime, the Cardinals annexed a double-header from the Braves at Sportsman's Park today to cut half a game from Brooklyn's lead in the torrid National League pennant fight and advance to within one length of the Dodgers.

Jumping quickly to take advantage of a pair of errors by Tom Earley and Buddy Hassett in the eighth inning of the opener, Billy Southworth's band crowned an uphill battle with a cluster of five unearned runs that gave them the game, 6 to 1.

Estel Crabtree's third homer of the campaign, opening the seventh inning, squared a run the Braves scored on Marty Marion's error in the fifth inning. The late outburst gave the left-handed rookie, Howard Pollet, his fourth victory.

A Majestic Wallop

When the teams came down to the home half of the ninth deadlocked at 2-all in the nightcap, Crabtree settled the issue with another homer, a majestic drive that bounced off the right-field roof and gave the Cards the spoils, 3 to 2.

A ladies' day crowd of 7,712 left the scene joyous not only in the knowledge that the Cards had shortened the gap between the Dodgers and themselves but also in the fact that the club had maintained an even balance with the Brooks on the losing side and is two games short on the winning side in the season's play.

The left-handed Max Lanier notched his ninth victory in the nightcap as Jim Tobin bowed in his ninth defeat. Stanley Musial, a 20-year-old rookie up from the Rochester farm, celebrated his first major league game with a double that sent the Cards two runs in front in the third inning.

Error Helps Braves

Then, when the Braves leaped on Lanier for two runs in the seventh with the aid of an error by Creepy Crespi, the 37-year-old Crabtree took command and kept his club snapping at the heels of the Dodgers.

Musial came up for the second time with two out in the third. Lanier was on second after scratching a single before Johnny Hopp walked. Then Musial crashed a double to the fence in right center that chased in both runs.

Lanier didn't yield a hit until the fourth, when Dudra singled after the Card southpaw had bowled over eleven men in a row. Lanier then

disposed of eight more before Crespi fumbled Frank Demaree's grounder with one out in the seventh. Eddie Miller tripled Demaree home and Gene Moore's single chased in Miller, tying the score.

Boston threatened in the ninth when Carvel Rowell opened with a double. But Lanier then turned the Braves back with two on.

Tobin had no reason for apprehension as the last half opened. He had turned the Cards back through three straight innings in which he pitched to nine men and permitted them to hit the ball out of the infield once.

The husky Hub hurler whizzed a strike past Crabtree. Then Estel leaned against the next pitch and the game was over.

Six of the runs in the opener were unearned. The single untainted tally was Crabtree's round-tripper, a drive beyond the right-field roof in the seventh which pulled the Cards even.

Earley contributed to his own downfall in the eighth. His error in failing to touch first as Hassett fielded Jimmy Brown's grounder with one out gave Brown a life. Hopp banged a double to right and, after Terry Moore skied to Gene Moore, Johnny Mize was intentionally passed, filling the bases.

Hassett here booted Crabtree's grounder and then handled it like a hot coal, two runs scoring. Crespi walked, filling the bases, and Marion's single chased in two more. Gus Mancuso came up to drive in Crespi from third with a single that also knocked Earley out—too late. Art Johnson got the side out—too late.

Marion paved the way for the run that robbed Pollet of a shutout. Marty booted Phil Masi's grounder opening the fifth. A wild pitch let the Hub backstop

reach second with two out. He scored when Earley hit a single to right.

September 18, 1941

The Box Scores

FIRST GAME

BOSTON (N.)						ST. LOUIS (N.)					
	ab.	r.	h.	po.	a. e.		ab.	r.	h.	po.	a. e.
Sisti, 3b	4	0	2	1	2 0	Brown, lf	4	1	2	0	2 0
Cooney, cf	3	0	0	0	0 0	Hopp, lf	4	1	1	3	0 0
Hassett, 1b	3	0	0	7	2 1	T. Moore, cf	3	0	0	3	0 0
Demaree, lf	4	0	0	1	0 0	Mize, 1b	3	1	1	10	0 0
Miller, ss	4	0	3	5	0 0	Crabtree, rf	4	2	1	1	0 0
Masi, c	4	1	1	4	2 0	Crespi, 2b	2	0	5	3	3 0
Rowell, 2b	3	0	1	3	2 0	Marion, ss	3	0	1	2	1 1
E. Moore, rf	3	0	0	3	6 0	Mancuso, c	4	0	1	3	2 0
aDudra	0	0	0	0	0 0	Pollet, p	4	0	0	0	3 0
Earley, p	2	0	1	0	1 1						
Johnson, p	0	0	0	0	1 0						
bMontgom'ry	1	0	0	0	0 0	Total	30	6	7	27	11 1
Total	31	1	8	24	10 2						

aBatted for E. Moore in ninth.
bBatted for Johnson in ninth.

Boston .... 0 0 0 0 1 0 0 0 0—1
St. Louis .... 0 0 0 0 0 0 1 5 .—6

Runs batted in—Earley, Crabtree, Marion 2, Mancuso.
Two-base hit—Hopp. Home run—Crabtree. Sacrifices—Earley, Marion, Hassett. Double plays—Mize (unassisted); Sisti, Hassett and Sisti. Left on bases—Boston 9, St. Louis 6. Bases on balls—Off Earley 1, Pollet 4. Struck out—By Earley 4, Pollet 1. Hits—Off Earley 7 in 7 2-3 innings, Johnson 0 in 1-3. Hit by pitcher—By Earley (Crespi). Wild pitch—Pollet. Losing pitcher—Earley. Umpires—Conlan, Goetz and Beardon. Time of game—2:12.

SECOND GAME

BOSTON (N.)						ST. LOUIS (N.)					
	ab.	r.	h.	po.	a. e.		ab.	r.	h.	po.	a. e.
Sisti, 3b	4	0	0	1	1 0	Brown, 3b	4	0	1	0	3 0
Rowell, lf	4	0	1	2	0 0	Hopp, cf	3	1	0	4	0 0
Dudra, 1b	4	0	1	8	1 0	Musial, rf	4	0	2	1	0 0
Demaree, rf	1	1	0	1	0 0	Mize, 1b	4	0	0	13	2 0
Miller, ss	3	1	1	3	2 0	Crabtree, lf	4	1	1	0	0 0
E. Moore, cf	3	0	1	4	2 0	Marion, ss	2	0	0	1	3 0
Cooney, cf	1	0	0	0	0 0	Crespi, 2b	3	0	1	4	4 1
Roberge, 2b	3	0	0	1	6 0	Mancuso, c	2	0	0	3	0 0
Berres, c	3	0	0	2	0 0	Lanier, p	3	1	1	1	1 0
Tobin, p	3	0	1	2	2 0						
Total	32	2	5	*24	13 0	Total	29	3	6	27	13 1

*None out when winning run was scored.

Boston .... 0 0 0 0 0 0 2 0 0—2
St. Louis .... 0 0 2 0 0 0 0 0 1—3

Runs batted in—Musial 2, Miller, E. Moore, Crabtree.
Two-base hits—Musial, Rowell. Three-base hit—Miller. Home run—Crabtree. Double plays—E. Moore, Miller and Dudra; Marion and Mize. Left on bases—Boston 4, St. Louis 5. Bases on balls—Off Tobin 3, Lanier 1. Struck out—By Tobin 2, Lanier 3. Umpires—Goetz, Beardon and Conlan. Time of game—1:37. Attendance—7,712.

Boston Red Sox

New York Yankees

Batting Mark of .4057 for Williams

STAR GETS 6 HITS AS RED SOX SPLIT

Williams Becomes First Big Leaguer in 11 Years to Bat .400 or Better

WALLOPS 37TH HOME RUN

Adds Three Singles in 12-11 Victory Over Athletics, Who Take Nightcap, 7-1

PHILADELPHIA, Sept. 28 (UP)— Ted Williams of the Red Sox today became the first American Leaguer to hit .400 or higher for a season since 1923, when Harry Heilmann batted .403 for Detroit. Bill Terry was the last National League player to turn the trick. He batted .401 for the Giants in 1930.

Making six hits in eight times at bat while Boston and the Athletics split a double-header, Williams finished with a mark of .4057. He started the twin bill with an average of .39955. Williams played in 143 games this season, getting 185 hits in 456 times at bat.

Boston won the first game, 12 to 11, and the second was called on account of darkness after eight innings, with Philadelphia on top, 7 to 1.

Williams made his thirty-seventh home run and three singles in five chances in the opener, and a double and single in three attempts in the second encounter.

For the season he batted in 120 runs, scored 135 and walked 151 times. He struck out twenty-six times. Williams is the sixth American Leaguer to bat .400. Nap Lajoie, Ty Cobb, George Sisler, Joe

Jackson and Heilmann were the others. Jackson hit .408 for Cleveland in 1911, but lost the batting title to Cobb, who finished with .420.

The first game saw the Sox rally after the Mackmen had scored nine runs in the fifth inning.

In the nightcap Fred Caliguiri held the Sox to six hits, one a homer by Frank Pytlak. Hal Wagner homered for the Athletics.

FIRST GAME

BOSTON (A.)	ab.r.h.po.a.e.	PHILADELPHIA (A.)	ab.r.h.po.a.e.
DiMag'o, cf.5	1 3 4 0 1	Collins, rf..5	2 2 3 0 0
Finney, rf...4	1 0 3 0 1	Valo, lf....5	3 2 2 0 0
Flair, 1b....5	2 1 5 0 0	Richmond,3b.5	2 3 0 3 0
Williams, lf.5	3 4 3 0 0	Johnson, 1b.4	1 2 15 1 0
Tabor, 3b...4	2 2 1 2 1	Chapman, cf.5	0 2 1 0 0
Doerr, 2b...5	3 2 3 3 0	Davis, 2b...4	1 1 2 6 2
L.News'e, ss.3	0 1 2 2 0	Suder, ss...5	1 2 2 4 1
aFoxx 0	1 0 0 0 0	Hayes, c...3	0 0 1 0 0
Carey, ss...2	0 0 0 0 0	Fowler, p...2	0 0 0 2 0
Pytlak, c...4	0 1 6 1 0	bMiles 1	1 1 0 0 0
H.News'e, p.2	0 1 0 1 0	Vaughan, p..1	0 0 1 0 0
Wagner, p...3	0 1 0 0 0	Shirley, p...0	0 0 0 2 0
		cMcCoy 1	0 0 0 0 0
Total....40	12 16 27 9 3	Total...41	11 15 27 18 3

aBatted for L. Newsome in ninth.
bBatted for Fowler in fifth.
cBatted for Shirley in ninth.
Boston ....0 0 0 0 3 1 6 0 2—12
Philadelphia ....0 0 2 0 9 0 0 0 0—11
Runs batted in—Richmond, Johnson 2, Williams 2, Tabor, Pytlak, Chapman, Davis, Miles, Collins, Valo 2, Doerr 3, Flair 2, L. Newsome, Wagner 2. Two-base hits—Johnson, Tabor. Three-base hits—Richmond, Valo, Flair, Doerr. Home runs—Williams, Tabor. Sacrifices—L. Newsome, Davis. Double plays—Suder and Johnson; Richmond, Davis and Johnson 2; Davis, Suder and Johnson. Left on bases—Boston 7, Philadelphia 9. Bases on balls—Off H. Newsome 3, Wagner 1, Vaughan 3. Struck out—By H. Newsome 5. Hits—Off H. Newsome 13 in 4 2-3 innings, Vaughan 1 in 1 2-3, Shirley 3 in 2 1-3. Winning pitcher—Wagner. Losing pitcher—Shirley. Umpires—McGowan, Quinn and Grieve. Time of game—2:02.

SECOND GAME

BOSTON (A.)	ab.r.h.po.a.e.	PHILADELPHIA (A.)	ab.r.h.po.a.e.
DiMaggio, cf.4	0 1 4 0 1	Valo, lf....3	1 1 1 0 0
Finney, rf...2	0 0 0 0 0	Mack'wicz, cf4	1 1 1 0 0
Fox, rf.....2	0 1 0 0 0	Miles, rf....4	1 2 2 0 0
Flair, 1b....4	0 0 11 1 0	Davis, 1b...3	1 0 11 0 0
Williams, lf.3	0 2 0 0 0	McCoy, 2b...3	1 2 3 3 0
Tabor, 3b...4	0 0 0 1 0	Brancato, 3b.4	0 2 2 2 0
Carey, 2b...3	0 1 2 3 0	Suder, ss...3	1 1 1 4 0
Newsome, ss.3	0 0 3 4 0	Wagner, c...4	1 2 3 0 0
Peacock, c...1	0 0 1 2 0	Caliguiri, p..4	0 0 0 0 0
Pytlak, c...1	1 1 2 0 0		
Grove, p...0	0 0 0 0 0	Total.....32	7 11 24 9 0
Johnson, p..2	0 0 1 2 0		
Total....29	1 6 24 13 1		

Boston ....0 0 0 0 0 0 0 1—1
Philadelphia ....3 1 0 1 1 0 1 0—7
Runs batted in—Miles, Brancato 2, Wagner 2, Pytlak. Two-base hit—Williams. Three-base hits—Suder, Mackiewicz. Home runs—Wagner, Pytlak. Double plays—Tabor, Carey and Flair; McCoy, Suder and Davis. Left on bases—Boston 5, Philadelphia 5. Struck out—By Johnson 4, Caliguiri 1. Bases on balls—Off Johnson 2, Caliguiri 1. Hits—Off Grove 4 in 1 inning, Johnson 7 in 7. Wild pitches—Grove, Johnson. Losing pitcher—Grove. Umpires—Quinn, Grieve and McGowan. Time of game—1:21. Attendance—10,268.

September 29, 1941

YANKS WIN IN 9TH, FINAL 'OUT' TURNS INTO 4-RUN RALLY

Game-Ending Third Strike Gets Away From Dodger Catcher, Leading to 7-4 Victory

KELLER IS BATTING HERO

Double, His Fourth Safety, Puts New York in Front—Victors Now Lead in Series, 3-1

By JOHN DREBINGER

It couldn't, perhaps, have happened anywhere else on earth. But it did happen yesterday in Brooklyn, where in the short space of twenty-one minutes a dazed gathering of 33,813 at Ebbets Field saw a world series game miraculously flash two finishes before its eyes.

The first came at 4:35 of a sweltering afternoon, when, with two out and nobody aboard the bases in the top half of the ninth inning, Hugh Casey saw Tommy Henrich miss a sharp-breaking curve for a third strike that for a fleeting moment had the Dodgers defeating the Yankees, 4 to 3, in the fourth game of the current classic.

But before the first full-throated roar had a chance to acclaim this brilliant achievement there occurred one of those harrowing events that doubtless will live through all the ages of baseball like the Fred Snodgrass muff and the failure of Fred Merkle to touch second.

Makes Frantic Dash

Mickey Owen, topflight catcher of the Dodgers, let the ball slip away from him and, before he could retrieve it in a frantic dash in front of his own dugout, Henrich had safely crossed first base.

It was all the opening Joe McCarthy's mighty Bronx Bombers, shackled by this same Casey ever since the fifth inning, needed to turn defeat for themselves into an amazing victory which left a stunned foe crushed.

For in the wake of that excruciating error came a blazing single by Joe DiMaggio, a two-base smash against the right-field barrier by Charley Keller, a pass to Bill Dickey by the now thoroughly befuddled Casey and another two-base clout by the irrepressible Joe Gordon.

Flatbush's Darkest Hour

Four runs hurtled over the plate and, though the meteorological records may still contend that this was the brightest, sunniest and warmest day in world series history, it was easily the darkest hour that Flatbush ever has known.

For this astounding outburst gave the Yankees the game, 7 to 4, and with this victory McCarthy's miraculous maulers moved to within a single stride of another world championship. Their lead, as the series enters the fifth encounter at Ebbets Field today, now stands at three games to one. and the Bombers need to touch off only one more explosion to bring this epic interborough struggle to a close.

Almost from the moment Mayor La Guardia threw out the first ball this battle was one that had the crowd seething and sizzling under an emotional strain that at times threatened to burst out the sides of the arena in the heart of Flatbush.

Higbe First to Go

Neither of the starting pitchers, Kirby Higbe for the Dodgers and Atley Donald, survived the fierce fighting under the blistering midsummer sun. Kirby, twenty-two-game winner of the National League champions, making his delayed first appearance in the series, was the first to go. He was driven to cover in the fourth inning, by which time the Yanks had run up a lead of 3 to 0.

But this merely provided the setting for the making of a couple of Brooklyn heroes who last night would have been the toast of the borough had victory remained momentarily perched at 4:35 o'clock.

One was Jimmy Wasdell, who hit a pinch double in the last of the fourth to drive in two runs. The other was Pete Reiser, freshman star of the Dodgers, who, finally coming into his own, whacked a homer over the rightfield wall with Dixie Walker on base in the fifth inning to give the Brooklyn host its 4-to-3 lead.

That blow finished Donald and, though Relief Pitchers Marvin Breuer and Johnny Murphy gave the Dodgers no more runs, they appeared to need no more to clinch this victory that would have squared the series at two games apiece. For Casey, the same round-faced Hugh whose brief relief turn had opened the floodgates for a Yankee triumph in Saturday's third game, looked this time to have the Bombers firmly in hand.

Casey replaced a wavering Johnny Allen in the fifth inning to repulse the Yanks with the bases full and he kept repelling them right on and up through the ninth until Owen's crowning misfortune turned the battle and the arena upside down.

Johnny Sturm, Yankee lead-off man, had opened that last-ditch stand in the ninth by grounding out to Pete Coscarart, who again was at second base for Brooklyn in place of the injured Billy Herman. Red Rolfe proved an even easier out. He bounced the ball squarely into Casey's hands and was tossed out at first with yards to spare.

Two were out, nobody was on. the Yanks looked throttled for the second time in the series and the Brooklyn horde scarcely could contain itself as it prepared to hail the feat with a tumultuous outburst of pent-up enthusiasm.

A Swing and a Miss

Casey worked carefully on Henrich and ran the count to three balls and two strikes. Then he snapped over a low, sharp-breaking curve. Henrich swung and missed. A great Flatbush triumph appeared clinched. But in the twinkling of an eye the victory was to become an even greater illusion.

As the ball skidded out of Owen's mitt and rolled toward the Dodger bench with Mickey in mad pursuit, police guards also came rushing out of the dugout to hold back the crowd which at the same moment was preparing to dash madly out on the field.

Owen retrieved the ball just in front of the steps, but Henrich, who the moment before had been at the point of throwing his bat away in great disgust, now was tearing like wild for first and he made the bag without a play.

The Yanks, of course, had not yet won the game. They were still a run behind and, though they had a man on first, Casey needed to collect only one more out to retain his margin.

But there was an ominous ring to the manner in which DiMaggio bashed a line-drive single to left that sent Henrich to second. A moment later Keller belted the ball high against the screening on top of the right-field fence. It just missed being a home run.

It was recovered in time to hold the doughty King Kong on second for a double, but both Henrich and DiMaggio streaked around the bases and over the plate. The dreaded Yanks were ahead, 5—4. To make matters even more excruciating, Casey had had a count of two strikes and no balls on

Keller when King Kong pasted that one.

Down in the Brooklyn bullpen Curt Davis was warming up with great fury, but the Dodger board of strategy appeared paralyzed by the cataclysm and Manager Leo Durocher did nothing.

Casey pitched to Dickey and walked him. Again the Yanks had two on base. Casey stuck two strikes over on Gordon, then again grooved the next one. Ironically, Joe the Flash smacked the ball into left field, where Wasdell, who might have been one of the heroes, was left to chase it while Keller and Dickey raced for home with two more runs to make it four for the round.

This was enough, more than enough. Few clubs in major league history have ever had an almost certain victory snatched from them under more harrowing circumstances.

Snuffing out the final three Dodgers in the last half of the ninth was almost child's play for the relief hurler whom the Yanks affectionately call Grandma Murphy. Indeed, the kindly Grandma appeared motivated by only the most humane feelings as he put those battered Dodgers out of their misery.

Like Casey in the top half of that ninth, Murphy had to face the head of the batting order. But at that moment the Dodgers didn't know whether they were standing on their heads or their heels. Peewee Reese fouled out to Dickey and Walker and Reiser ended the game by never getting the ball out of the infield.

At the outset of the conflict, as Donald and Higbe squared away on the mound, evidence came early as to why Durocher had deferred starting his so-called second ace as long as he had. Higbe went down a run in the very first inning on a single by Rolfe, a pass to DiMaggio and another sharp single to right by Keller.

Slaps Into Force Play

Keller, by far the batting star of the day with four hits, two of them doubles, started Higbe on his final downfall in the fourth by polling his first two-bagger against the right-field barrier. A walk to Dickey and a Gordon single filled the bases with none out. For a moment Higbe promised to squirm out of the difficulty by inducing Phil Rizzuto to slap into a force play at the plate and striking out Donald.

But Sturm, one of those lesser lights in the Yankee attack who occasionally strike damaging blows, struck one now. He drove a sharp single to center. Dickey and Gordon scored and Higbe gave way to Larry French who, in facing only one batter, had checked the Yanks' eighth-inning victory rally on Saturday.

This time the veteran left-hander of the National League did even better. He delivered only one ball to Rolfe. It was almost a wild pitch, Owen blocking it with con-

---

Box Score of the Fourth Game

NEW YORK YANKEES

	ab.	r.	h.	tb.	2b.	3b.	hr.	bb.	so.	sh.	sb.	po.	a.	e.
Sturm, 1b	5	0	2	2	0	0	0	0	0	0	0	9	1	0
Rolfe, 3b	5	1	2	2	0	0	0	0	0	0	0	2	0	0
Henrich, rf	4	1	0	0	0	0	0	1	0	0	0	3	0	0
DiMaggio, cf	4	1	2	2	0	0	0	1	0	0	0	2	0	0
Keller, lf	5	1	4	6	2	0	0	0	0	0	0	1	0	0
Dickey, c	2	2	0	0	0	0	0	3	0	0	0	7	0	0
Gordon, 2b	5	1	2	3	1	0	0	0	0	0	0	2	3	0
Rizzuto, ss	4	0	0	0	0	0	0	1	0	0	0	2	3	0
Donald, p	2	0	0	0	0	0	0	0	1	0	0	0	1	0
Breuer, p	1	0	0	0	0	0	0	0	0	0	0	0	1	0
aSelkirk	1	0	0	0	0	0	0	0	0	0	0	0	0	0
Murphy, p	1	0	0	0	0	0	0	0	0	0	0	1	0	0
Total	39	7	12	15	3	0	0	5	2	0	0	27	11	0

BROOKLYN DODGERS

	ab.	r.	h.	tb.	2b.	3b.	hr.	bb.	so.	sh.	sb.	po.	a.	e.
Reese, ss	5	0	0	0	0	0	0	0	0	0	0	2	4	0
Walker, rf	5	1	2	3	1	0	0	0	0	0	0	5	0	0
Reiser, cf	5	1	2	5	0	0	1	0	1	0	0	1	0	0
Camilli, 1b	4	0	2	3	1	0	0	0	0	0	0	10	1	0
Riggs, 3b	3	0	0	0	0	0	0	1	1	0	0	2	0	0
Medwick, lf	2	0	0	0	0	0	0	0	0	0	0	1	0	0
Allen, p	0	0	0	0	0	0	0	0	0	0	0	0	0	0
Casey, p	2	0	1	1	0	0	0	1	0	0	0	3	0	0
Owen, c	2	0	0	0	0	0	0	2	0	0	0	2	1	1
Coscarart, 2b	3	1	0	0	0	0	0	1	2	0	0	4	2	0
Higbe, p	1	0	1	1	0	0	0	0	0	0	0	0	1	0
French, p	0	0	0	0	0	0	0	0	0	0	0	0	0	0
Wasdell, lf	3	0	1	2	1	0	0	0	0	0	0	2	0	0
Total	35	4	9	15	3	0	1	4	5	0	0	27	14	1

aBatted for Breuer in eighth.

SCORE BY INNINGS

New York Yankees	1	0	0	2	0	0	0	0	4—7
Brooklyn Dodgers	0	0	0	2	2	0	0	0	0—4

Runs batted in—Keller 3, Sturm 2, Wasdell 2, Reiser 2, Gordon 2.

Earned runs—Yankees 3, Dodgers 4.

Left on bases—Yankees 11, Dodgers 8. Double play—Gordon, Rizzuto and Sturm. Struck out—By Donald 2, Higbe 1, Breuer 2, Casey 1, Murphy 1. Bases on balls—Off Higbe 2, Casey 2, Donald 3, Breuer 1, Allen 1. Pitching summary—Off Higbe 6 hits, 3 runs in 3 2-3 innings; French 0 hits, 0 runs in 1-3; Allen 1 hit, 0 runs in 2-3; Casey 5 hits, 4 runs in 4 1-3; Donald 6 hits, 4 runs in 4 (none out in fifth); Breuer 3 hits, 0 runs in 3; Murphy 0 hits, 0 runs in 2. Hit batsman—By Allen (Henrich). Winning pitcher—Murphy. Losing pitcher—Casey. Umpires—Goetz (N. L.), plate; McGowan (A. L.), first base; Pinelli (N. L.), second base; Grieve (A. L.), third base. Time of game—2:54.

siderable difficulty, but it ended the inning, for the two Yanks on the bases cut loose from their moorings and Rizzuto was trapped and run down between second and third.

However, the Yanks were ahead, 3 to 0, and with Donald working smoothly, the rest of the blistering afternoon held little excitement in prospect.

But in the last of the fourth came the first jolt when Donald, after retiring two batters, walked Owen and Coscarart. Wasdell was sent in to pinch hit for French. He caught an outside pitch on the end of his bat and the ball soared high down the left-field foul line. It fell safely in the extreme left-hand corner of the playing field, just

out of Keller's desperate reach, and the stands swayed as Owen and Coscarart dashed around the bases and scored. The Yanks were now leading by only 3 to 2.

Nor was this a patch to the uproar that went up in the Dodger fifth when the aroused Flatbush Flock routed Donald before he had retired a man. Walker banged a double to left and the next instant the arena became an outdoor madhouse as Reiser, batting champion of the National League in his freshman campaign, rammed the ball over the right-field wall. It was the first Dodger home run hit in a world series in Brooklyn since 1916, when Hy Myers clouted one for the late Wilbert Robinson, and

THE BREAK IN THE NINTH INNING WHICH GAVE THE YANKEES THEIR CHANCE

Mickey Owen chasing the ball (designated by arrow) after the sharp-breaking curve which Pitcher Hugh Casey threw for a third strike on Tommy Henrich got away from the Dodger catcher. Henrich, the bat still in his hand, is starting for first. Umpire Larry Goetz's hand is up after calling the strike.

the folks really went to town on this shot.

At the same time Donald went to the clubhouse and Breuer took the mound for the McCarthy forces. He put a quietus on the show in short order and kept things quiet until he vacated for a futile pinch hitter, George Selkirk, in the eighth.

Casey Does His Share

In the meantime, Casey, who had replaced Allen in the upper half of the fifth with the bases full and then retired Gordon on an easy fly for the third out, was doing his share to keep the Yankees quiet.

But this game apparently was never meant to remain quiet and the uproar and events in that bizarre ninth will doubtless remain a nightmare in Flatbush in all the years to come.

And so the Yanks once again stand poised as they have stood in every world series they have played since 1927—seven in all. They have three victories in the bag, their opponents on the ropes and only one more encounter is needed to haul down the lion's share of the spoils.

As usual, McCarthy can continue to gamble with his inexhaustible supply of mound talent. He used three hurlers yesterday, with Murphy the winner. In the first three games he started Charley Ruffing, Spud Chandler and Marius Russo. Today, at Ebbets Field, still a fifth starter will make his debut, the husky Tiny Bonham, a strapping right-hander with a tantalizing fork ball.

Tiny came up from the farm system in August of 1940. He has never pitched a world series game before. But then neither had Russo, who spun a masterful four-hitter to win on Saturday.

In contrast with this, Durocher is strictly up against it. He must call on the veteran Whit Wyatt to keep the fading Dodgers in the struggle. And though Whit scored the only Brooklyn victory to date when he won the second game on Thursday, he has had, even with a day of postponement, only three full days of rest since.

The Flock, then, indeed is in a mighty tight spot, and all because it had a pitcher yesterday who threw such a curve it not only fooled the batter but his catcher as well.

October 6, 1941

111

Hornsby Enters Baseball Hall of Fame

BRILLIANT HITTER PICKED BY WRITERS

Hornsby, Listed on 182 of 233 Ballots, Is Lone Eligible Named to Hall of Fame

BATTED .358 IN MAJORS

Champion of National League Seven Times—Now Pilot of Fort Worth Club

By JOHN DREBINGER

One by one the names of the diamond's immortals are finding their way into baseball's Hall of Fame, and the latest to make his entry is Rogers Hornsby, brilliant batsman and stormy petrel of the major leagues for close to a quarter of a century.

Announcement of his selection was made yesterday and, to add still further to the luster of his choice, he is the only one to have qualified in the recent election of the Baseball Writers Association of America. As a result of the vote, the first to be taken by the writers in three years, a plaque with Hornsby's head in bas-relief will be installed in the baseball shrine at Cooperstown, N. Y.

According to Bill Brandt of the National League's Service Bureau, who conducted the tabulating of the poll, the peerless Rajah was named on 182 of the 233 ballots and was the only one to scale the required 75 per cent of the total vote necessary for election.

136 Votes for Chance

Trailing on Hornsby's heels but failing to obtain the necessary 175 votes were such diamond luminaries as Frank Chance with 136, Rube Waddell, 126; Ed Walsh, 113; Miller Huggins, 111, and Ed Delahanty, 104.

These were the only ones to pass the 100-mark, while just outside this group came Johnny Evers with 91, Wilbert Robinson, 89; Mickey Cochrane, 88, and Frankie Frisch, 84.

Thus, more than four years after he went storming out of his last major league job, the graying, 46-year-old Texan finds himself showered with new honors, considered by many the highest the game has to offer. He becomes only the fourteenth chosen by writers' polls, although the list, which is headed by Ty Cobb, Babe Ruth and Honus Wagner, was several years ago

RECEIVES ONE OF BASEBALL'S HIGHEST HONORS

Rogers Hornsby, named yesterday to the Hall of Fame, ponders the future from the January solitude of the stands in the Fort Worth Cats' park. He is pilot and general manager of the club.

Associated Press Wirephoto

The result of this year's balloting:

182 Rogers Hornsby	45 Pie Traynor
136 Frank Chance	44 Ross Youngs
126 Rube Waddell	39 Home Run Baker
113 Ed Walsh	37 Dazzy Vance
111 Miller Huggins	36 Bill Terry
104 Ed Delahanty	36 Joe Tinker
91 Johnny Evers	33 Addie Joss
89 Wilbert Robinson	15 Nap Rucker
88 Mickey Cochrane	15 John Kling
84 Frank Frisch	11 Babe Adams
77 Hugh Duffy	8 Hank Gowdy
72 Herb Pennock	5 Kid Nichols
71 Clark Griffith	4 Jess Burkett
68 Jimmie Collins	4 Harry Heilmann
66 Rabbit Maranville	3 Eddie Grant
64 Hugh Jennings	3 Branch Rickey
63 Mordecai Brown	2 Zack Wheat
63 Eddie Plank	2 Donie Bush
59 Iron Man McGinnity	2 Sam Crawford
58 Fred Clarke	2 Pepper Martin
57 Roger Bresnahan	2 Roger Peckinpaugh
55 Chief Bender	2 Rhoddy Wallace
53 Ray Schalk	

1—Ginger Beaumont, Jake Beckley, Joe Boley, Bill Bradley, Lave Cross, Bill Dinneen, Jack Dunn, Kid Elberfeld, Red Faber, Billy Hamilton, Babe Herman, Waite Hoyt, Joe Kelley, Dick Kerr, Arlie Latham, Bobby Lowe, Sherwood Magee, Deacon Philippe, Edd Roush, Amos Rusie, Germany Schaefer, Everett Scott, Harry Steinfeldt, Fred Tenney, Bill Wambsganss, Hack Wilson and Smoky Joe Wood.

augmented by thirteen more names automatically chosen by the Hall of Fame Committee.

Batting champion of the National League seven times, six of these in succession, and with a lifetime average of .358 in the majors, Hornsby ranked during his playing years as perhaps the greatest right-handed hitter of all time. In three of the years in which he won the batting crown he hit over .400, with his mark of .424 in 1924 still standing as the league's modern record. In addition to this he was named the circuit's most valuable player in 1925 and 1929.

A St. Louis Hero

A star second baseman, he spent most of his active playing years with the Cardinals, with whom he broke in in 1915. In 1925 he succeeded Branch Rickey as manager of the St. Louis club and the following year became the Mound City's greatest hero by not only winning the National League pennant, the first to go to St. Louis, but by conquering the Yankees in the ensuing world series as well. And that, incidentally, was also to mark the last defeat ever suffered by the Yanks in world series play.

However, a bitter salary dispute with Owner Sam Breadon was to follow this achievement and that Winter, in a sensational deal, Hornsby was traded to the Giants for Frankie Frisch and Jimmy Ring. That deal was also to mark the beginning of a stormy trail for the Rajah, who, blunt and outspoken to a fault, somehow could never keep his peace with the so-called "stuffed shirts" in baseball "front offices."

At present he is pilot and general manager of the Fort Worth club.

HORNSBY IS APPRECIATIVE

But Says That Winning the War Is No. 1 in His Thoughts Now

FORT WORTH, Jan. 20 (UP)— Baseball's mighty rajah—candid, friendly Rogers Hornsby—pushed aside the glory of his election to Cooperstown's hall of fame today to "talk about more important business."

"It's quite a distinction," Hornsby said, "but right now there's a couple of things more important:

"First, winning the war.

"Second, baseball."

January 21, 1942

Cards Win Pennant on Final Day; Series Starts in St. Louis

By JOHN DREBINGER
Special to THE NEW YORK TIMES.

ST. LOUIS, Sept. 27—Sweeping inexorably on toward their goal, the Cardinals, on this, the final day of the championship season, brought to a triumphant close their spectacular seven-week pennant drive by clinching the National League flag with a smashing victory over the Cubs in the first game of the afternoon's double-header.

The end came at 3:12 o'clock, amid the thunderous roars of 32,-330 frenzied enthusiasts. Billy Southworth's high-flying Redbirds, behind the steady hurling of Ernie White and after routing Lon Warneke with a four-run blast in the fifth inning, crushed the Chicagoans, 9 to 2.

After that it no longer mattered how the still desperately striving Dodgers fared in Philadelphia or what the outcome of the second game here would be. Just to keep the records, however, it might be added that the forlorn flock of Flatbush went on to win that final game, while the Cards, with most of their regulars on the sidelines, won again, 4 to 1, to give Johnny Beazley, their freshman star right-hander, his twenty-first victory. That made it a two-game lead to the finish line.

And so, with all speculation at an end, arrangements for the forthcoming world series, in which the new National League titleholders will face the formidable Yankees of the American League, moved ahead tonight with feverish haste.

The first wartime classic since 1918, in which the United Service Organizations are to share in the receipts, will start here on Wednesday. The second game also will be staged at Sportsman's Park, which has a seating capacity of 34,000.

Following an open date Friday for traveling, the struggle will switch to the Yankee Stadium in New York for the third game on Saturday, as well as the fourth Sunday and the fifth, if needed, on Monday. If by then neither side has gained the required four victories, the conflict will return here for the sixth game on Oct. 7 and the seventh on Oct. 9.

Caps Sensational Battle

The triumph of the Redbirds today capped one of the most sensational uphill pennant battles the National League, rich in struggles of this sort, has seen in some years. Not since 1934 has a major league race been in doubt until the final day, and that year, oddly, saw the Cardinals win their last pennant as they swept by the faltering Giants.

Trailing by ten games on the morning of Aug. 6 last and still nine and a half lengths back of the front-running Dodgers as late as Aug. 15, the Cards were given little chance of making even a close race of it.

But day after day they kept hammering away until on Sept. 12 they drew even by sweeping a two-game series with the now thoroughly panic-stricken leaders in Brooklyn. On the following day St. Louis forged ahead.

From then on the Cards were never headed, and even when the Dodgers regained their stride to close with an eight-game winning string these surprising young men, directed by the quietly efficient Southworth, never took their eyes off that flag. From the day they moved into the lead on Sept. 13 until they clinched it they won ten out of eleven games.

An Amazing Record

But most amazing of all was their record for their last fifty-three games, more than a third of a season, in which they won forty-three, lost only nine and tied one.

Thus to the Mound City comes its first National League pennant in eight years and its sixth in the history of the senior loop. It was in 1926, under the leadership of Rogers Hornsby, that the Cardinals won their first flag. That year the Cards also vanquished the Yankees in a memorable seven-game world series which also was to remain as the last Yankee defeat in an October classic.

With Hornsby traded to the Giants in 1927, the Cards did not repeat that year, but in 1928, under Bill McKechnie, they won their second flag. With Gabby Street in command they bagged two more pennants in 1930 and 1931, topping the 1931 victory with another world series triumph in seven games over the formidable Athletics of that era.

In the two following campaigns the Redbirds were vanquished for the flag by the Cubs and then the Giants, but in 1934, with the dynamic Frankie Frisch in the driver's seat, the Cards came roaring back. That was the famous Gas House Gang which, with the two pitching Deans almost incessantly on the firing line, shot by the staggering Giants and then went on to wrest the world championship from the Tigers in a tempestuous seven-game series.

With the Cardinals' famed chain-store farm system then operating at its peak, many feared at the time that the Redbirds would remain invincible for many years. But for one reason or another, no pennants flew at Sportsman's Park for the next seven years.

With the possibility looming that the pennant race still would be plunged into a deadlock by nightfall, there were just a few anxious moments in the first game today when the Cubs forged a run ahead in the fourth on a pair of singles by Stanley Hack and Dom Dallessandro and an overthrow to the plate by Jimmy Brown.

But in the next round there again came one of those brief rifts in the enemy defenses which seem all these swift-moving Redbirds ever need, and when old Warneke went down under four runs every one knew the fight was over. Whitey Kurowski walked, Len Merullo booted Marty Marion's sharp grounder and in the wake of that came a trio of singles by White, Terry Moore and Enos Slaughter.

In the seventh the Cub defenses cracked again and, off Hiram Bithorn and Vern Olsen, the pennant-bound Redbirds grabbed four more runs and that more than settled it.

As Clyde McCullough ended it with a long fly to Stan Musial in left, a jubilant band of Redbirds dashed from the bench and joined their comrades on the field in hoisting White on their shoulders while the crowd cheered for several minutes.

FIRST GAME

CHICAGO (N.)							ST. LOUIS (N.)					
	ab.	r.	h.	po.	a.	e.		ab.	r.	h.	po.	a.	e.
Hack, 3b.	4	1	2	3	2	0	Brown, 2b.	3	1	1	2	1
Merullo, ss.	1	0	0	2	4	1	Moore, cf.	5	2	3	1	0	0
Nicholson, rf.	3	0	0	0	0	Slaughter, rf.	5	1	2	2	0	0
Dal's'dro, cf.	3	1	2	2	0	1	Musial, lf.	4	0	1	4	0	1
McCull'gh, c.	4	0	0	2	2	1	W. Cooper, c.	3	0	0	10	1	0
Novikoff, lf.	3	0	0	0	0	0	Hopp, 1b.	4	0	1	5	0	0
Cacar'tta, 1b.	3	0	1	6	3	0	Kurowski, 3b.	3	1	1	1	3	0
Sturgeon, 2b.	3	0	0	7	3	1	Marion, ss.	4	2	0	2	0
Warneke, p.	1	0	0	1	1	0	White, p.	3	2	2	0	0	0
Bithorn, p.	1	0	0	0	0							
Olsen, p.	0	0	0	1	0	0							
aRussell	1	0	0	0	0		Total....	34	9	11	27	5	2
Mooty, p.	0	0	0	0	1	0							
Total....	31	2	5	24	16	4							

aBatted for Olsen in eighth.

Chicago	0 0 0	1 0 0	1 0 0—2
St. Louis	0 0 0	0 4 0	4 1 .—9

Runs batted in—White, Moore 3, Musial, Cavarretta, Dalessandro, Slaughter, W. Cooper, Hopp. Two-base hit—Cavarretta, Musial. Sacrifices—Brown, White. Double play—Sturgeon, Merullo and Cavarretta. Left on bases—Chicago 3, St. Louis 6. Bases on balls—Off Warneke 1, White 1. Struck out—By Bithorn 2, White 8. Hits—Off Warneke 6 in 4 1-3 innings, Bithorn 3 in 2, Olsen 1 in 2-3, Mooty 1 in 1. Losing pitcher—Warneke. Umpires—Barlick, Ballanfant, Conlan and Reardon. Time of game—2:13.

SECOND GAME

CHICAGO (N.)							ST. LOUIS (N.)					
	ab.	r.	h.	po.	a.	e.		ab.	r.	h.	po.	a.	e.
Block, 3b.	3	1	2	0	0	0	Crespi, 2b.	3	1	2	3	3	1
Russell, 3b.	1	0	0	0	0	0	Walker, cf.	4	0	1	4	0	0
Merullo, ss.	4	0	0	4	1	0	Musial, rf.	4	0	1	1	0	0
Nich'ls'n, rf.	4	0	1	1	0	0	Sanders, 1b.	4	1	9	0	0
Dal's'dro, cf.	3	0	1	0	0	0	O'Dea, c.	4	0	2	6	0	0
Scheffing, c.	3	0	0	8	1	0	Triplett, lf.	3	1	1	0	0
Novikoff, lf.	4	0	2	3	0	0	Dusak, 3b.	4	2	2	0	5	0
Cavar'tta, 1b.	3	0	0	6	0	0	Cross, ss.	4	0	1	3	0
Foxx, 1b.	1	0	0	1	0	0	Beazley, p.	3	1	0	1	0
Stringer, 2b.	3	0	1	2	3	0							
Passeau, p.	3	0	0	0	2	0	Total..	33	4	11	27	12	1
aGilbert	1	0	0	0	0	0							
Total..	34	1	7	24	7	0							

aBatted for Passeau in ninth.

Chicago	1 0 0	0 0 0	0 0 0—1
St. Louis	1 2 0	0 0 1	0 0 .—4

Runs batted in—Dalessandro, Sanders, Cross, Crespi, Beazley. Two-base hits—Walker, O'Dea, Musial, Dusak, Beazley. Double play—Dusak, Crespi and Sanders. Left on bases—Chicago 8, St. Louis 8. Bases on balls—Off Passeau 2, Beazley 2. Struck out—By Passeau 6, Beazley 3. Passed ball—O'Dea. Umpires—Ballanfant, Conlan, Reardon and Barlick. Time of game—1:49. Attendance—32,386.

September 28, 1942

No Errors for Litwhiler
PHILADELPHIA, Sept. 28 (AP)—Danny Litwhiler of the last-place Phils, set a new major league fielding record for outfielders by playing the entire season without making an error, Phils' officials said tonight. The previous record for outfielders for fewest boots in a season is two, made jointly by Edgar Hahn of the White Sox in 1907, and equaled by Pete Fox of Detroit in 1938.

September 29, 1942

Gordon Tops Williams for Award as American League's Most Valuable Player

YANKEE INFIELDER IS SURPRISE CHOICE

Batting, Defense Skill, Team Play Figured in Selection of Gordon for Honor

---

GETS 270 POINTS IN VOTE

---

249 for Williams, Runner-Up Again—Pesky, Red Sox, Third —Stephens, Browns, Fourth

---

By ARTHUR DALEY

Joe Gordon was named the most valuable player of 1942 in the American League, it was disclosed yesterday. The surprise selection will leave Boston fans in general, and Ted Williams in particular, startled. The Yankee infielder follows Joe DiMaggio as recipient of one of baseball's highest honors, and again Williams is runner-up.

The Flash beat the angular Red Sox outfielder, 270 points to 249, in one of the closest ballots in the history of the award. A committee of twenty-four members of the Baseball Writers Association made the selections.

A year ago Williams batted .406, but DiMaggio's fifty-six-game hitting streak and all-around play gave Jolting Joe the call. This season Williams fell off in his batting —if a .356 average needs any apology—but he still led both leagues in hitting, in runs batted in, with 137, and in homers, with 36. Thus he gained the famed "triple crown," the first time any one performed this feat since Lou Gehrig in 1934.

Finished With .321

Gordon, however, practically carried the Yankees in the early part of the campaign. He led the league in batting through July at a time when DiMaggio, Charlie Keller and the rest of the Yanks had feeble averages. The Flash finished with an eminently respectable .321. His fielding was dazzling all year.

Johnny Pesky, Red Sox freshman shortstop, received two first places;

THE GORDONS ARE MIGHTY PROUD OF THE FLASH

Joe Gordon, second baseman of the New York Yankees, at his home in Eugene, Ore., reading the news to his wife and two children after he had been named the most valuable player in the American League.
Associated Press Wirephoto

Verne Stephens, the Browns' freshman shortstop, got one and the other two shared the rest.

Gordon received twelve top nominations to nine for Williams. Two more first-place votes would have enabled the Boston star to climb past the Yankee ace for the award. Pesky edged out Stephens, 143 points to 140, for third place.

Others Far Behind

All others were far behind. Ernie Bonham of the Yanks was fifth with 102, Tex Hughson of the Red Sox sixth with 92, and then came DiMaggio, Stan Spence of Washington, Phil Marchildon of Philadelphia and Manager Lou Boudreau

of Cleveland to fill out the first ten.

The committee undoubtedly was influenced by the fact that the Yanks would not have been able to win their sixth pennant in seven years if it had not been for Gordon. The rock of the New York infield never had a better year than in 1942. He not only batted about 40 points higher than ever before, but his fielding was so phenomenal that he now ranks with the greatest second basemen of all time.

THE VOTING

(First-Place Votes in Parentheses)
Player and Club.

Player and Club	Pts
1—Joe Gordon, New York (12)	270
2—Ted Williams, Boston (9)	249
3—John Pesky, Boston (2)	143
4—Vernon Stephens, St. Louis (1)	140
5—Ernie Bonham, New York	102
6—Cecil Hughson, Boston	92
7—Joe DiMaggio, New York	86
8—Stanley Spence, Washington	65
9—Phil Marchildon, Philadelphia	39
10—Lou Boudreau, Cleveland	31
11—Bobby Doerr, Boston	24
12—Ted Lyons, Chicago	23
13—George Case, Washington	17
14—Ken Keltner, Cleveland	15
14—Charles Keller, New York	15
16—Walter Judnich, St. Louis	14
17—Bill Dickey, New York	12
17—Don Gutteridge, St. Louis	12
19—Phil Rizzuto, New York	9
19—Chester Laabs, St. Louis	9
21—Rick Ferrell, St. Louis	8
21—Henry Borowy, New York	8
23—James Bagby, Cleveland	6
23—Taft Wright, Chicago	6
25—Tony Lupien, Boston	4
25—Les Fleming, Cleveland	4
27—Spurgeon Chandler, New York	3
27—Rudy York, Detroit	3
29—Barney McCosky, Detroit	1

November 4, 1942

BIG LEAGUE TEAMS TO TRAIN NEAR HOME

Potomac and Ohio Rivers in South, Mississippi in West Fixed as Camp Limits

---

EASTMAN PRAISES ACTION

Majors, Meeting With Landis, Retain 154-Game Schedule While Revising Dates

---

By The Associated Press

CHICAGO, Jan. 5—The major leagues, in emergency joint session with Commissioner Kenesaw Mountain Landis, decided today to set back the opening of the 1943 baseball season eight days to April 21, but voted to extend the playing period one week, closing on Oct. 3, instead of Sept. 26.

They also drew up a sharply defined area in which they may do their Spring training, with the understanding each club would condition at home, or as close as possible, in the interest of curtailing rail travel.

Teams, they decided, must train north of the Potomac and Ohio Rivers and east of the Mississippi, with the exception of the two St. Louis clubs, which have the option of using Missouri as a site. This decision ruled out as training bases the South Atlantic seaboard States and Hot Springs, Ark., mentioned as possible alternate sites after Florida and California

earlier had been listed as "out of bounds."

Statement by Eastman

In Washington, Director Joseph B. Eastman of the Office of Defense Transportation was "greatly pleased by the action which the major leagues have taken." His statement, released here by the Office of War Information, follows:

"I am greatly pleased with the action which the major leagues have taken today to reduce their travel requirements for the coming season. The only request I made of them was, in effect, a general request that they hold travel to the necessary minimum. At no time have I undertaken to say what the minimum is, because I do not know enough about the baseball industry to pass judgment on that matter.

"In these circumstances, the action which the major leagues have taken on their own initiative is most gratifying. It shows a real and keen appreciation of the very troublesome travel problem which our country has under present war conditions, a problem which is bound to grow in difficulty and seriousness.

"The example which such an important national industry has thus set will have, I am sure, a most beneficial influence throughout the nation. I hope and believe there will be many who will follow this fine example."

Meeting Delayed Two Hours

The meeting, hailed as baseball's most important since Landis quit the Federal bench in 1921 to become commissioner after the 1919 world series scandal, was delayed nearly two hours because representatives of several Eastern clubs were aboard trains late in arriving.

Landis personally announced results of the two-hour parley. He said the 154-game schedule would

remain in effect, including three East-West trips, previously agreed upon. Since 1936, each club has made the cross-country junket four times.

"Transportation during Spring training will be held to a minimum," Landis said, "and after Spring training there will be need for utmost cooperation on the part of the various clubs to cut man-mileage as much as possible."

He said the question of reduced personnel on road trips would be left up to the individual clubs. The player limit for each club still is 25, but there have been suggestions that each team take fewer men on trips, possibly no more than 20.

The commissioner, who had conferred last week in Washington with Eastman, presided over the meeting, which was attended by men from fifteen of the sixteen major league clubs.

Washington was the only team without a representative, although Joe Cambria, head scout, was in the anteroom waiting to report back to President Clark Griffith of the Senators.

The determination of a set area wherein clubs may train makes it possible for all to proceed at once with Spring workout plans. The Chicago Cubs and White Sox, already set to go to French Lick Springs, Ind., and the Boston Red Sox, who will train at Tufts College, Medford, Mass., are the only ones certain where they are going.

The decision to open the season approximately one week later apparently was a compromise between the American League, understood to have wanted an April 27 start, and the National, which had favored retaining the original April 13 opening.

Traditionally the major league season has opened on a Tuesday, with Washington getting a one-day start every other year, but the new schedule will call for the cam-

paign to open on a Wednesday. No reason was announced for this shift.

Landis was "utterly astounded at the number of miles saved by condensing Spring training trips within a specific radius." He did not reveal precisely how many man miles would be saved by the new restricted travel program.

Some of the team representatives, before scurrying home to set up their Spring camps, drew this sketchy picture:

The two Philadelphia teams will train "right around home," said President Gerry Nugent of the Phils and Connie Mack of the Athletics.

The St. Louis Cardinals will look around, but may explore Excelsior Springs, Mo., Owner Sam Breadon said.

The Boston Braves will hunt for a college field house near home, Secretary John J. Quinn hinted.

The Cleveland Indians "are looking around," commented President Alva Bradley.

The Pittsburgh Pirates are "uncertain," President Bill Benswanger reported.

The Brooklyn Dodgers probably will work out at Yale University, New Haven, Conn., said General Manager Branch Rickey.

The Detroit Tigers may do part of their conditioning at Benton Harbor, Mich., General Manager Jack Zeller stated.

The Cincinnati Reds are in a spot, President Warren Giles lamented. The new training zone limits clubs to areas north of the Ohio River. "Right now," Giles said, "our ball park is precisely three feet u-n-d-e-r the Ohio River because of flood waters."

January 6, 1943

'HELP WANTED' SIGN OUT

Baseball 'Ad' Reveals Openings on Cards' Farm Clubs

ST. LOUIS, Feb. 23 (P)—The

world champion Cardinals, who once did a booming business selling surplus players from their far-flung farm system, today put out a "help wanted" sign.

An advertisement, probably without precedent in the history of baseball, said the Cardinals had openings on their minor league clubs for free agents with previous

professional experience. It appeared in this week's issue of The Sporting News, national baseball weekly.

"These are unusual times," said President Sam Breadon in explanation of the unusual advertisement.

The Cardinal organization, which formerly supplied nearly all major league teams with players, has had a different customer since the war.

The armed forces have taken more than 265 athletes from the team's coast-to-coast system.

Memphis of the Southern Association and Toronto of the International League also had advertisements for players in The Sporting News.

February 24, 1943

115

Tobin Hurls 1st No-Hit Game in Majors Since 1941

VETERAN SUBDUES BROOKLYN, 2 TO 0

Tobin First Brave to Pitch No-Hit Game Since Hughes' Performance in 1916

AIDS CAUSE WITH HOMER

Connects Off Ostermueller in Eighth—Ryan's Double Leads to Third-Inning Tally

By ROSCOE McGOWEN
Special to THE NEW YORK TIMES.

BOSTON, April 27—Jim Tobin pitched himself into baseball immortality today against the Dodgers when he hurled the first no-hitter turned in by a Braves pitcher since Tom Hughes turned the trick against the Pirates here on June 16, 1916, and the Braves won by the same score, 2—0, this afternoon as in the Houghes classic.

Just after the 31-year-old knuckleball expert made his final pitch and watched Steve Shemo go over close to second base to scoop up Dixie Walker's hot grounder and throw him out he became the center of a mob of back-slapping and hugging team-mates.

Dozens of fans, from the small crowd of 1,984, galloped onto the field and added their plaudits for Jim to those of the Braves, while Tobin struggled happily to reach the dugout.

Tobin Opens Game With Pass

Tobin walked Big Poison Waner to start the game, then turned back every Dodger, including Frenchy Bordagaray as a pinch hitter for Fritz Ostermueller, until there were two out in the ninth. Then Jim walked the dangerous Paul again on four pitches before facing Walker for the final test.

It was the elder Waner, incidentally, who came closest to spoiling Tobin's no-hitter with a solid smash. With two away in the third frame Big Poison slashed a hard bounder a little to Tobin's left and Jim knocked the ball down and recovered it in time to throw Paul out.

One more close shave came in the second inning when Bill Hart dumped what looked like a perfect bunt down the third-base line. But the ball rolled foul a few feet short of the bag and Tobin pounced on it the moment it crossed the line. Hart had it beaten easily had it remained fair.

Tobin added to the acclaim he was later to receive by whacking a tremendous home run over the left-field wall to start the eighth inning and thus give himself a bit of insurance of victory.

Connie Ryan was chiefly responsible for the first Boston run, which came in the third inning, which he opened with a long double to right center. Ryan advanced on Tommy Holmes' fly to Paul Waner and rode home on Chuck Workman's solid single to right through the drawn-in Dodger infield.

Ryan Has Batting Eye

That was the last hit off Ostermueller until Tobin's big blow, four of the five Boston hits coming in the first three frames, including a double in the first by Ryan.

The most recent no-hitter prior today was one hurled by Lon Warneke for the Cardinals Aug. 30, 1941.

Today's achievement tasted all the sweeter to Tobin, first because Leo Durocher wanted so badly to beat him, and second because a knee injury in an exhibition game in Washington in 1940 had brought a doctor's verdict that he never would play ball again.

When Durocher was told Tuesday night that Tobin was slated to pitch the second game because Al Javery had a sore shoulder, Leo said:

"That's fine with me. I'd rather hit against Tobin any time than Javery. That guy (meaning Javery) can throw that ball hard."

And before the game Durocher said in the dugout that he'd be willing "not to eat for a week if I can just win this game." Leo was on the first base coaching line yelling his head off in encouragement to his men until the Braves scored in the third. Then he turned the task over to Red Corriden and retired to the bench.

The box score:

BROOKLYN (N.)	ab.	r.	h.	po.	a.	e.		BOSTON (N.)	ab.	r.	h.	po.	a.	e.
P. Waner, rf.	2	0	0	5	0	0		Ryan, 2b.	4	1	2	1	3	0
Walker, lf.	4	0	0	3	0	0		Holmes, cf.	4	0	0	2	0	0
Olmo, 2b.	3	0	0	2	3	0		Workman, rf.	3	0	1	2	0	0
Galan, cf.	3	0	0	4	0	0		Ross, lf.	3	0	0	2	0	0
Schultz, 1b.	3	0	0	6	1	0		Clemens, lf.	0	0	0	0	0	0
English, ss.	3	0	1	2	0		Masi, c.	3	0	0	7	0	0
Hart, c.	3	0	0	3	2	0		Etchison, 1b.	3	0	0	10	0	0
Bragan, ss.	3	0	0	2	0	0		Wietelmann, ss.	3	0	0	1	1	0
O'mueller, p.	2	0	0	1	0	0		Shemo, 2b.	3	0	1	2	4	0
aBordagaray	1	0	0	0	0	0		Tobin, p.	3	1	1	0	1	0
Total	27	0	0	24	9	2		Total	29	2	5	27	9	0

aBatted for Ostermueller in ninth.

Brooklyn	0	0	0	0	0	0	0	0	0—0
Boston	0	0	1	0	0	0	0	1	x—2

Runs batted in—Workman, Tobin. Two-base hits—Ryan 2. Home run—Tobin. Double play—Hart, Olmo and Schultz. Left on bases—Brooklyn 2, Boston 5. Bases on balls—Off Tobin 2, Ostermueller 2. Struck out—By Tobin 6, Ostermueller 2. Umpires—Stewart, Jorda and Magerkurth. Time of game—1:30. Attendance—1,984.

April 28, 1944

Negroes Allowed in Grandstand

ST. LOUIS, May 4 (AP)—The St. Louis major league baseball teams, the Cardinals and Browns, have discontinued their old policy of restricting Negroes to the bleachers and pavilion at Sportsman's Park. Negroes now may purchase seats in the grandstand.

May 5, 1944

NATIONAL ANNEXES ALL-STAR GAME, 7-1

Victory Margin Record Is Set for 12-Year-Old Series as American Loop Is Routed

WINNERS POUND HUGHSON

Reach Tex for 4 Runs in Fifth and Clinch Contest—29,589 Attend at Pittsburgh

By ROSCOE McGOWEN
Special to THE NEW YORK TIMES.

PITTSBURGH, July 11—Even hotter than the torrid temperature, the National League All-Stars, led by Manager Billy Southworth, tonight blazed through the American Leaguers, piloted by Joe McCarthy, for the widest victory margin in the history of the twelve-year-old classic.

The score, 7-1, topped the largest previous difference, which was in 1937 at Washington in the fifth game when the junior loop outscored the Nationals by five runs, 8 to 3.

A crowd of 29,589 at Forbes Field, considerably under the pregame estimates, paid $81,275 into the Service Men's Bat and Ball Fund and got thrills that were more than worth the price of admission. In addition, the $25,000 paid for the radio rights went to the fund, boosting the total to $106,275.

Fans Roar Acclaim

Most of the fans were strongly National League and their roars of acclaim were tremendous when the Southworth men, trailing by 1—0 as they came up in the fifth inning, blasted Tex Hughson, Red Sox ace, for four runs on five hits to take a lead that never was threatened thereafter.

That scoring spree set another record for the senior league, marking the most runs it has ever counted in one inning since the first All-Star game was played in Comiskey Park, Chicago, in 1933.

First hero to the crowd was Bad Bill Nicholson, the Cubs' home-run hitter, who batted for Ken Raffensberger in the fifth and drove a double off the right-field wall to score Connie Ryan, who had singled and stolen second, with the tying run.

Disaster for the McCarthy forces descended rapidly then. Augie Galan bounced a single high over Vern Stephens' head near second to bring Nicholson across with the run that put the National Leaguers ahead.

McQuinn Drops Throw

But it didn't stop there. Phil Cavarretta, who had seen his long triple go to waste in the third, walked and Stan Musial was safe when George McQuinn dropped Bobby Doerr's fast throw for an error. Walker Cooper promptly shot a single between Ken Keltner and Stephens, scoring Galan, but Cavarretta was cut down at the plate on Bob Johnson's throw to Frankie Hayes.

Here Dixie Walker, who had been in a slump during the late stages of the Dodgers' long losing streak, slammed his second single to right, scoring Musial and sending Hughson away. Bob Muncrief of the St. Louis Browns came in to end the surge by getting Bob Elliott on a foul to Johnson.

RIVAL MANAGERS BEFORE GAME

Billy Southworth and Joe McCarthy at Forbes Field, Pittsburgh, last night

All-Star Box Score

AMERICAN LEAGUE

	ab.	r.	h.	po.	a.	e.
Tucker, Chi., cf..	4	0	0	1	0	0
Spence, Wash., rf.	4	0	2	2	1	0
McQuinn, St.L., 1b.	4	1	3	5	1	1
Stephens, St.L., ss.	4	0	1	1	0	0
Johnson, Bost., lf.	3	0	0	2	1	0
Keltner, Clev., 3b.	4	1	1	0	4	0
Doerr, Bos., 2b..	3	0	0	4	1	1
Hemsley, N. Y., c.	2	0	0	2	0	0
Hayes, Phila., c..	1	0	0	3	0	1
Borowy, N. Y., p.	1	0	1	0	0	0
Hughson, Bos., p.	1	0	0	0	0	0
Muncrief, St. L., p.	0	0	0	1	0	0
aHiggins, Det....	1	0	0	0	0	0
Newhouser, Det., p.	0	0	0	0	1	0
Newsom, Phila., p.	0	0	0	0	0	0
Total	32	1	6	24	9	3

NATIONAL LEAGUE

	ab.	r.	h.	po.	a.	e.
Galan, Bkn., lf..	4	1	1	2	0	0
Cavar'ta, Chi., 1b.	2	1	2	12	0	0
Musial, St.L., rf.	4	1	1	2	1	0
W. Cooper, St.L.,c.	5	1	2	5	2	0
Mueller, Cin., c..	0	0	0	6	0	0
Walker, Bkn., rf..	4	0	2	0	0	0
DiMaggio, Pitts., cf.	0	0	0	0	0	0
Elliott, Pitts., 3b..	3	0	0	0	3	0
Kurowski, St.L., 3b.	1	0	1	0	1	0
Ryan, Bos., 2b..	4	1	2	4	4	1
Marion, St.L., ss..	3	1	0	2	3	0
Walters, Cin., p.	0	0	0	0	1	0
bOtt, N.Y..........	1	0	0	0	0	0
Raff'sb'g'r, Phil.,p.	0	0	0	0	0	0
cNicholson, Chi...	1	1	1	0	0	0
Sewell, Pitts., p..	1	0	0	0	0	0
dMedwick, N.Y...	0	0	0	0	0	0
Tobin, Bos., p.....	0	0	0	0	0	0
Total	33	7	12	27	15	1

aBatted for Muncrief in seventh.
bBatted for Walters in third.
cBatted for Raffensberger in fifth.
dBatted for Sewell in eighth.

Americans ......0 1 0 0 0 0 0 0 0—1
Nationals ....0 0 0 0 4 0 2 1 ..–7

Runs batted in—Borowy, Nicholson, Galan, W. Cooper, Walker, Kurowski 2, Musial.

Two base hits—Nicholson, Kurowski. Three-base hits—Cavarretta. Stolen bases—Ryan. Sacrifices—Marion, Musial, Medwick. Double plays —Spence and Hemsley; Marion, Ryan and Cavarretta. Earned runs—Americans 1, Nationals 5. Left on bases— Americans 5, Nationals 9. Bases on balls—Off Borowy 1 (Cavarretta), Hughson 1 (Cavarretta), Sewell 1 (Johnson), Newhouser 2 (Galan, Cavarretta). Struck out—By Walters 1 (Johnson), Raffensberger 2 (Doerr, McQuinn), Hughson 2, (W. Cooper, Marion), Sewell 2 (Stephens, Hayes), Muncrief 1 (Sewell), Newhouser 1 (Marion).

Pitching summary—Off Walters, 5 hits 1 run in 3 innings; Raffensberger, 1 hit 0 runs in 2 innings; Sewell, 0 hits 0 runs in 3 innings; Tobin, 0 hits 0 runs in 1 inning; Borowy, 3 hits 0 runs in 3 innings; Hughson, 5 hits 4 runs in 1 2-3 innings; Muncrief, 1 hit 0 runs in 1 1-3 innings; Newhouser, 3 hits 3 runs in 1 2-3 innings; Newsom, 0 hits 0 runs in 1-3 inning. Wild pitch—Muncrief. Winning pitcher—Raffensberger. Losing pitcher—Hughson. Umpires—Barr, N. L. (plate); Berry, A. L. (first base); Sears, N. L. (second); Hubbard, A. L. (third), for first 4½ innings; Hubbard, A. L. (plate); Sears, N. L. (first); Berry, A. L. (second); Barr, N. L. (third), thereafter. Attendance—29,589 paid. Time of game —2:11.

The halt was only temporary, however, the Nationals breaking out again in the seventh with Detroit's left-hander Hal Newhouser on the mound. Cavarretta opened with a single. Musial sacrificed. Cooper beat out a hit to Doerr over second and, after Walker had been robbed of a hit by Stephens' glittering catch of his low looper into short left. Whitey Kurowski belted a long double into the left-field corner to score both runners.

The other run for the victors came in the eighth off Newhouser. Slats Marion reached first after striking out when Hayes let the ball through for an error and got around on Muscles Medwick's sacrifice, passes to Galan and Cavarretta and Musial's scoring fly to Johnson.

Newsom Goes to Mound

This was enough to send Newhouser out and bring in the great Bobo Newsom, who pitched only to Walker Cooper and got him out on a pop to Doerr.

On the American League side, the junior loopers made their only threats and scored their only run against Bucky Walters, ace of the Cincinnati Reds. When Bucky left the game after his three-inning stint he was the losing pitcher of the moment—but fortunately for Ford Frick's pride and peace of mind, only the moment.

McQuinn and Stephens got successive singles off Bucky with two out in the first frame, but he fanned Johnson, and when the losers scored in the second it was not on a devastating blow.

Ken Keltner led off that frame with a solid single to left and moved to third as Doerr and Hemsley grounded to Ryan and Marion. Here Hank Borowy, who shut out the Nationals with three hits in three innings, bounced one over second base. Ryan made a great stop, but his hurried, off-balance throw wasn't good enough to get Hank.

The blow went for a single and Borowy had the minor distinction of driving in the only American League tally.

Raffensberger the Winner

Raffensberger, who was the pitcher of record during the big fifth and therefore the winner, stopped the Americans in the fourth and fifth, allowing only a single by Stan Spence. Then Rip Sewell took over and not only faced but nine men in three innings but set the local fans into an uproar of delight by serving several of his famous "ephus" pitches.

In the eighth, with two out, Rip threw two perfect rainbow strikes to McQuinn. George trying to bunt the second one and getting tossed out by Cooper. Jim Tobin, Boston's veteran no-hit knuckleballer, disposed of Stephens, Johnson and Keltner in the ninth and the National League's fourth victory in a dozen games was more than safe.

Stephens had no assists and only one chance, his spectacular catch of Walker's looper in the seventh. . . . Mel Ott got into the game as a pinch-hitter for Walters but exposed no dynamite, flying to center. . . . George Barr was behind the plate until the start of the home fifth, when Cal Hubbard replaced him and the other arbiters also switched positions.

July 12, 1944

RULING ON GRAY CATCHES

Umpires Get Instructions on Browns' One-Armed Player

ST. LOUIS, March 14 (AP)—Special instructions for ruling on catches by Pete Gray will be given to umpires if the one-armed outfielder makes the grade this year with the Browns, President Will Harridge of the American League has advised The Post-Dispatch.

After making a catch, Gray places the ball against his chest and moves his left hand to the stub of his right arm. In this motion the ball rolls out of his glove and up his wrist as if it were a ball-bearing between the arm and body. When the glove is tucked under the stub, Gray draws his arm back across his chest until the ball rolls back into his hand, ready for a throw.

Harridge said umpires would be instructed to give credit to Gray for momentary catches. In the event he drops the ball after starting the process of removing his glove, the catch will not be ruled out.

This is the same regulation umpires in the Southern Association used in governing plays by Gray when he was with Memphis last season.

March 15, 1945

SENATOR CHANDLER GETS BASEBALL POST

'Immediately Available,' New Commissioner Accepts for Seven Years at $50,000

NAMED ON FIRST BALLOT

M'Phail, Stoneham Lead Fight for Choice of 46-Year-Old Successor to Landis

CLEVELAND, April 24 (AP)—Baseball's five-month quest for a commissioner ended today with election of Senator Albert B. (Happy) Chandler of Kentucky to fill the position vacated by the death of Kenesaw Mountain Landis.

By unanimous vote of the sixteen major league club owners or their representatives, and on the first ballot, the 46-year-old junior Senator from the Bluegrass State was named for a seven-year term at an annual salary of $50,000.

Leslie M. O'Connor, secretary to the late commissioner and chairman of the three-man advisory council that has ruled the sport since the death of Judge Landis last Nov. 25, said Senator Chandler would take office within a reasonable time. In Washington, however, Mr. Chandler said he would be "immediately available."

The former Governor of Kentucky from Versailles was selected after a four-hour discussion in which expected fireworks failed to materialize. The group that favored naming a commissioner at once, and ready to prolong the argument as long as necessary, found enough support without extended debate after the major leagues' steering committee of four —Alva Bradley of Cleveland, Don Barnes of the St. Louis Browns, Sam Breadon of the St. Louis Cardinals and Phil Wrigley of the Chicago Cubs—had made its report.

Others Considered for Post

Other men were discussed but club owners declined to identify them, pointing out that Senator Chandler was their man from the time they knew that he was available. From another source, however, it was learned that the names of Gov. Frank J. Lausche of Ohio; Bob Hannegan, chairman of the Democratic National Committee; former Postmaster General James A. Farley and President Ford C. Frick of the National League had been mentioned prominently.

Selection of Mr. Chandler as baseball's second commissioner since the office was established in 1920 was in line with the contention of many baseball men that they should go outside their ranks to fill so important a position.

Senator Chandler, a graduate of the University of Kentucky and Harvard Law School, also is baseball's second lawyer commissioner. Judge Landis was picked off the Federal bench to take over the job following the Chicago White Sox scandal in 1919.

One group of club representatives went into the meeting with the idea of retaining the three-man commission composed of Messrs. O'Connor and Frick and President Will Harridge of the American League, or the selection of a duration commissioner.

They found themselves outnumbered, however, as Larry MacPhail of the Yankees and Horace Stoneham of the Giants rallied a force that called for immediate action.

War Situation Guides Action

At first, Senator Chandler had said he couldn't leave his present job, but, after accepting the position in a telephone conversation, he added: "Now that the war with Germany is virtually over I can conscientiously leave my other duties."

Before the club representatives got down to the task of selecting Mr. Chandler, they arranged for eight games to be played for the benefit of the Red Cross and National War Fund on July 9, 10 or 11. To save all travel possible and subject to approval of the Office of Defense Transportation, there will be five games in cities having more than one big league club and the other teams will play in towns en route to regularly scheduled games.

In New York it will be the Giants and Yankees; in Boston, Braves and Red Sox; in Chicago, Cubs and White Sox; in Philadelphia, Athletics and Phils, and in St. Louis, Cards and Browns. Detroit will play at Pittsburgh, Brooklyn at Washington and Cincinnati at Cleveland.

Senator Albert B. Chandler

At an earlier business session the owners decided that a player reinstated from the National Defense List who had participated in one league game could be retained on the roster for fifteen days without affecting the player limit. Previously a player who had participated in one game was considered a member of the team.

The magnates also agreed that an athlete undecided about playing baseball this year would be permitted to apply for the voluntary retired list so as not to be included in a club's player limit.

MacPhail Notifies Chandler

WASHINGTON, April 24 (U.P.)—Senator Chandler tonight was informed of his appointment as Baseball Commissioner by Larry MacPhail, who telephoned from Cleveland. The Yankee president put Ford Frick, Will Harridge and representatives of the sixteen major league clubs on the telephone and Mr. Chandler talked to them one by one.

The Senator said that he expected Mr. Frick in Washington within the next few days to discuss when he could take over. He added that league officials had given from thirty to sixty days for him to get his affairs straightened.

Mr. Chandler's hotel room was a bedlam as well-wishers dropped in to extend best wishes and reporters flocked in for an interview. Conversation was interrupted continually by telephone calls. Relating how Mr. MacPhail had broken the news, the Senator said:

"Larry told me that the decision finally was made on the basis of who among all the candidates loved baseball the best. They decided on me. I'm tickled to death and think that is one of the highest tributes ever paid to me in my life."

He said he expected to have full authority as commissioner: that he would not accept if there were any strings attached. "It never occurred to me that it would be anything less," he added. "I can't go in there standing in the shadow of Judge Landis and not have authority to do a good job."

Another telephone call was from Leslie O'Connor, Judge Landis' secretary. Senator Chandler said he had asked Mr. O'Connor to "stand by and we'll do the job."

April 25, 1945

It's the Old Game
With a New Line-up

Not even the war could put a damper on baseball or on the enthusiasm of fans.

Out at home—Cronin of the Boston Red Sox tagged as he slides for the plate.

By ARTHUR DALEY

A STRONG-ARMED young man wheels on the pitcher's mound, his arm flashes and a baseball blazes to the plate. A strong-backed young man wheels in the batter's box, his bat flashes and a baseball rides the summer air before crashing in the grandstand for a home-run. The year could be 1935, long before the war stripped the major leagues of most of their talent. Yet the year could just as easily be 1945, the fourth (possibly the last) wartime season. The fundamentals of the game—and hence its tremendous inherent appeal—haven't changed one iota, war or no war, talent or no talent.

For baseball is still baseball, the great American national game. The sport not only has endured under wartime strictures and the twin losses of most of its players and most of its regular fans; it actually has prospered. Despite a lop-sided pennant race last season the National League

gained almost a quarter of a million spectators while the American League gained more than a million.

Those statistics are even more impressive when you place them side by side with others — mathematically impossible though they sound. When the war came there were about 400 young men wearing major league baseball uniforms. At the last reliable count 565 of them had traded in diamond spangles for khaki or blue!

The reader has a perfect right to blink twice at these figures and conclude that the big-league ball parks these days must be populated by nothing but minus signs. The explanation is that the calls to the colors didn't come in wholesale lots; they came so gradually that there always was a replacement available for each departing diamond hero until finally it was a case of replacements replacing replacements. Some were minor leaguers being brought up before they were ready.

Others were retired veterans put back into harness. The solid core, however, was some 200 or so 4-F operatives who gave substance and body to the entire organization.

THEY were the key men who kept baseball going—by courtesy of their draft boards—and they also were the key men for keeping alive the interests of the fans. Certainly, you've seen a lot of strangers out on the field in familiar uniforms. But you've also seen enough old favorites to make you feel that the changes haven't been so great after all.

Two things saved America's national game. One was Selective Service whose unquestioned honesty was the bulwark on which the 4-F athletes relied. As a corollary to that was an awakened public consciousness of the fact that an apparently healthy baseball player depended on adhesive tape, diathermy, massages, sun

119

lamps, whirlpool baths and other artificial aids to go full clip for the couple of hours a game required.

The second savior was the armed forces. Our boys in the foxholes not only didn't resent professional sports; they demanded them to such an extent that General Eisenhower actually took time out in October, 1943, to order full broadcasts of the Yankee-Cardinal World Series as a morale-builder for the troops in Europe.

When a sport gets the whole-hearted support of the home front and the battle-front it is resting on solid ground. It stands up of itself, even if it has to reach so far in its search for talent as to take in a one-armed outfielder like Pete Gray of the St. Louis Browns. And nothing, by the way, has done more to encourage our disabled veterans than his presence in the line-up.

BUT baseball is more than players; it is also fans. The true aficionado's devotion to the sport is also a partial explanation of its wartime survival. To be sure, about 12,000,000 youngsters of the "rabid fan" age have gone to war. But new fans, with high wages in their pockets, have been able to attend more games than the old fans, and a flood of night baseball has brought in people never before able to attend.

The quality of wartime baseball has not greatly affected its popularity. Though every fan imagines himself a super-expert with an inherent right to second-guess the manager, he really isn't an expert at all. Slight mechanical transgressions are entirely beyond his ken and not at all visible to the naked eye.

It's not easy to discern that the current centerfielder missed catching the ball by the extra step a Joe DiMaggio would have taken or that the batter missed making a hit by the fraction of an inch which would not have eluded a Ted Williams or a Stan Musial. The spectator takes what he gets, asks no questions and seems eminently satisfied with it.

WHY is it that a fan, seemingly sated with five hours of top-flight baseball during a Sunday double-header at the Yankee Stadium, will instinctively stop on his way to the subway to watch a sandlot game across the street? There can be no logical explanation. The game is in his blood and the finer points of it are submerged in the thrill of action and the spice of competition.

Other games have action and competition. How then does baseball differ? The answer most probably lies in that most ancient of diamond axioms:

"The game's never over until the final out." In this respect baseball is apart from all other sports. If you come to the final few minutes of football or basketball, for instance, and one team or the other has a big lead, the battle to all intents and purposes is over.

BASEBALL is not like that. Suppose we take that very famous encounter between the Cincinnati Reds and the New York Giants at the Polo Grounds one summer night in 1940. Pitching for the Reds was that master craftsman, Bucky Walters. With two out in the ninth inning he had a lead of 3 to 0. On four distinct occasions he was one pitch away from victory. He never made it.

This was something ripped right from the pages of Frank Merriwell. Bucky reached three balls and two strikes on Bob Seeds—and walked him. He reached three and two on Burgess Whitehead—and Whitehead hit a home run. He reached three and two on Master Melvin Ott—and walked him. He whistled over two strikes on Harry (the Horse) Danning and that inconsiderate individual belted a juicy offering into the stands for a game-winning homer.

So much for the perennial appeal of America's grand old game. What, we may ask now, about it's future? Can baseball's former greats, now playing on Uncle Sam's teams, get back on the diamond? And what of the veterans and the very young who make up the teams of today?

To answer the last question first, it is certainly likely that the majority of those about whom baseball writers are singing the popular tune, "They're Either Too Young or Too Old," are destined to be discarded once the service men return. After all, there will be a total of 965 men—565 in the armed forces and 400 still in the big leagues—battling for those 400 berths once the last man is discharged. They will return to baseball as they left it—in dribs and drabs. A real star actually can turn a pennant race topsy-turvy overnight, which adds considerable spice to the current situation.

A campaign ago, for instance, Dick Wakefield was discharged from Navy Pre-Flight in mid-season. He returned to the faltering Detroit Tigers and his big bat spoke so eloquently in the final seventy-eight games that the Bengals almost overhauled the Browns for the American League pennant.

Wakefield clicked and so have some others. But every service man restored to a major league roster will be a question mark until he proves himself again. The older ones are going to find that their reflexes aren't quick enough in a game where quick reflexes are absolutely demanded. They are also going to find that in baseball a man is "old" at 34.

THE majority, however, will discover when they return that they will have few problems of reconversion (except maybe personal ones) facing them. The younger players won't need much more preparation than a shave and a haircut. And all will return to see the grand old game as flourishing and as strongly entrenched as when they left it.

Baseball has been advancing in the esteem of the American public with steady strides for the past 106 years. During that time it has enjoyed the most robust kind of health. It's a hardy old cuss. If the war couldn't kill it, nothing will. It has more lives than a cat.

June 17, 1945

Chicago Cubs

Phil Cavarretta

CUBS, INDIANS TOP ALL-STAR CHOICES

Chicago Places 7 on Mythical National League Squad and Cleveland 5 on American

The Cubs and Indians led their respective leagues in men selected for the mythical 1945 all-star game yesterday by vote of thirteen of the sixteen big league managers in a poll conducted by The Associated Press.

Seven Cubs were picked on the National League's twenty-five-man squad and five Indians surprisingly made the American list for the game that never will be played. The contest scheduled to have been played Tuesday in Boston's Fenway Park was called off in cooperation with the Office of Defense Transportation and replaced by a two-day schedule of exhibitions for war relief.

Reversing the usual procedure, the national team would have leaned heavily on power-hitting from the bats of Tommy Holmes of Boston, who leads both circuits with .401 and has hit in thirty-seven consecutive games, and Chicago's Phil Cavarretta, batting .372.

Luke Sewell of the Browns, who would have bossed the American League entry against Billy Southworth of the Cardinals, would have been able to call on such pitching stars as Dave Ferriss of Boston, Hal Newhouser of Detroit and Russ Christopher of Philadelphia, backed by Hank Borowy of New York, Steve Gromek and Allie Reynolds of Cleveland, Dutch Leonard of Washington and Thornton Lee of Chicago.

Managers Sewell and Southworth and Joe McCarthy of the Yankees declined to name teams on short notice.

The unofficial all-stars, with pitchers' won and lost records and batters' averages in parentheses:

NATIONAL LEAGUE

PITCHERS—Cooper (8–1), Boston: Gregg (10–5), Brooklyn: Passeau (10–2) and Wyse (10–5), Chicago: Sewell (9–7) and Roe (6–6), Pittsburgh: Barrett (10–6), St. Louis: Mungo (9–4), New York.
CATCHERS—Lombardi (.296), New York: Masi (.335), Boston: O'Dea (.263), St. Louis.
INFIELDERS—Cavarretta (.372), Johnson (.309), and Hack (.327), Chicago: Verban (.281), Marion (.253) and Kurowski (.330), St. Louis: McCormick (.293), Cincinnati: Elliott (.281), Pittsburgh.
OUTFIELDERS—Holmes (.401), Boston: Walker (.299) and Rosen (.363), Brooklyn: Ott (.325), New York: Pafko (.301) and Nicholson (.259), Chicago.

AMERICAN LEAGUE

PITCHERS—Newhouser (13–5), Detroit: Ferris (14–2), Boston: Christopher (11–5), Philadelphia: Borowy (10–5), New York: Reynolds (8–7) and Gromek (9–5), Cleveland: T. Lee (9–6), Chicago: Leonard (9–3), Washington.
CATCHERS—Ferrell (.238), Washington: Tresh (.253), Chicago: Hayes (.240), Cleveland.
INFIELDERS—Etten (.294), New York: Stirnweiss (.309) and Grimes (.276), New York: Mayo (.292), Detroit: McQuinn (.265) and Stephens (.318), St. Louis: Boudreau (.274), Cleveland: Cuccinello (.328), Chicago.
OUTFIELDERS—Case (.327), Washington: Cramer (.278) and Greenberg (.286), Detroit: Johnson (.297), Boston: Moses (.278), Chicago: Heath (.315), Cleveland.

July 12, 1945

TIGERS ANNEX FLAG ON FOUR-RUN HOMER

Greenberg's Blow With Bases Filled in 9th Tops Browns, 6-3, to Clinch Pennant

NEWHOUSER WINS NO. 25

Relieves Trucks and Receives Credit for Victory—Second Contest Is Washed Out

ST. LOUIS, Sept. 30 (AP)—A mighty home run by Hank Greenberg with the bases filled in the ninth inning proved the championship punch for the Tigers today as they beat the Browns by 6 to 3 in the first game of a concluding double-header at Sportsman's Park and sewed up the American League pennant.

Never was a title won in more dramatic fashion. Premature darkness was settling over the field and a light mist was falling as big Hank stepped up with his team a run behind and gave one of Nelson Potter's screwballs a tremendous ride into the bleachers just inside the left-field foul line.

The Tigers, the long strain of the flag race suddenly ended by Hank's big whack, raced out of their dugout in a body to meet the tall fellow as he trotted across the plate. One after another they wrung his hand and pounded his broad back as they escorted him joyously to the bench. It was Hank's thirteenth circuit blow since he rejoined the club in July and probably was the most important one he ever has hit.

Play on Muddy Field

It came just in time, too, as the clubs barely had begun the second game a few minutes later when the rain, which had delayed the opener nearly an hour, started coming down in sheets and washed out any further play for the day. It rained off and on throughout the decisive contest and the field was so muddy at times the players had difficulty wading around. Greenberg's wallop buried the Senators' last hope of finishing in a tie and squared the Tigers away for the opening game of the world series against the Cubs Wednesday in Detroit. After having "backed" close to the title in recent weeks, the Bengals finally won it like true champions, coming from behind to assert their leadership.

Hal Newhouser was credited with the triumph, his twenty-fifth of the season against nine defeats. He relieved Virgil Trucks in the sixth inning after the recent Navy dischargee got into trouble.

Double Play Helpful

Al Benton hurled the last inning for the champions and, with the aid of a slick double play, easily protected the club's lead.

It was a tense battle all the way until Hank hit the jackpot, with first one club and then the other forging ahead. The Browns jumped into the lead in the first inning, when Don Gutteridge and Lou Finney, first two batters to face Trucks, ganged on him for a double and a single before he could get his bearings.

The Tigers clawed back to score one off Potter in the fifth on a walk to Trucks and successive singles by Skeeter Webb and Eddie Mayo, and they pulled ahead, 2—1, in the sixth on a pair of walks and Catcher Paul Richards' clean single to left.

When Trucks weakened in the last of the sixth, giving up a double to Potter and a walk to Gutteridge, Newhouser was rushed in from the bullpen. Hal escaped damage as he struck out Milt Byrnes and caused George McQuinn to fly out to center, but the Browns got to him for the tying run in the seventh on Gene Moore's double off the rightfield wall and Vernon Stephens' single.

Two-Bagger by McQuinn

After the Tigers had failed to score off Potter in the eighth, even though their first two batters singled, the Browns pushed over another run in their half on Finney's single and McQuinn's two-base blast off the screen in deep right center.

Things looked extremely gloomy for Manager Steve O'Neill's champions when they came up for the last time. Hub Walker batted for Newhouser and plunked a single into center field. Webb laid down a bunt toward first, and both runners were safe when the throw to

second was not in time to get Walker, though the Browns kicked hard on the decision. Red Borom went in to run for Walker.

Mayo sacrificed, moving both runners along, and then, after a mid-diamond conference, the Browns decided to pass Roger Cramer purposely to get to Greenberg. It was a fatal mistake. The big man rubbed his bat vigorously with a hunk of bone he had carried out to the plate for the purpose, looked at a ball and then got the one he wanted.

There was never a doubt the wallop was going into the stands, but it was so close to the foul line that the crowd of 5,582 paid admissions gave the umpires a rousing raspberry for calling it a fair ball. The drive gave the Tigers the game they needed for the championship.

The box score:

DETROIT (A.)	ab.r.h.p.a.e.		ST. LOUIS (A.)	ab.r.h.p.a.e.
Webb, ss	.3 1 1 3 3 0		Gutte'ge, 2b.3 1 1 6 3 0	
Mayo, 2b	..4 0 1 3 3 0		Finney, lf. .2 0 2 1 0 0	
Cramer, cf.5 1 2 2 0 0			Byrnes, cf..2 0 0 2 0 0	
Greenb'g, lf.5 1 2 1 1 0			Christman .1 0 0 0 0 0	
Cullen'e, rf.4 1 1 0 0 0			Gray, cf. .1 1 0 2 0 0	
York, 1b..5 0 0 6 1 0			McQui'n, 1b.4 0 1 3 2 0	
Outlaw, 3b..2 0 1 1 1 0			Moore, rf. .4 1 1 0 0 0	
Richards, c.4 0 1 10 1 0			Stephens, ss.4 0 2 2 2 0	
Trucks, p..2 1 1 0 1 0			Mancuso, c. .4 0 0 5 0 0	
Newhou'r, p..0 0 0 0 0 0			Schulte, 3b.4 0 0 3 4 0	
aWalker ..1 0 1 0 0 0			Potter, p..3 0 1 1 0 0	
bBorom ...0 1 0 0 0 0				
Benton, p...0 0 0 0 0 0				
Total ...35 6 9 27 11 0			Total ...32 3 8 27 11 0	

aBatted for Newhouser in ninth.
bRan for Walker in ninth.
cBatted for Byrnes in sixth.

Detroit ....0 0 0 0 1 1 0 0 4—6
St. Louis ....1 0 0 1 0 0 1 0 0—3

Runs batted in—Finney, Mayo, Richards, Stephens, McQuinn, Greenberg (4). Two-base hits—Gutteridge, Potter, McQuinn, Moore. Home run—Greenberg. Sacrifice hits—Webb, Mayo. Double plays—Richards and Mayo; Outlaw, Mayo and York. Left on bases—St. Louis 5, Detroit 9. Bases on balls—Off Trucks 2, Potter 5, Newhouser 1. Struck out—By Trucks 3, Potter 4, Newhouser 5. Hits—Off Trucks 3 in 5 1-3 innings, Newhouser 4 in 2 2-3, Benton 1 in 1. Winning pitcher—Newhouser. Umpires—Pipgras, Berry, Rue and Hubbard. Time of game—2:23. Attendance—5,582.

October 1, 1945

Players Who Jumped Contracts Ruled Automatically Suspended

Chandler Acts Against Those Who Did Not Return by Opening Day—Must Wait Five Years to Seek Reinstatement

CINCINNATI, April 16 (AP)—Baseball Commissioner A. B. Chandler today announced the automatic suspension of players who jumped their American contracts to play in foreign leagues.

Chandler, who had declared at a meeting in Havana, Cuba, on March 20 that he would slam the door of organized ball on all such players, said today as he watched the Cincinnati Reds-Chicago Cubs opener: "Those who did not return by opening day are now out."

"They can't even petition for a return to American organized baseball for five years," he added.

The baseball commissioner said he was willing to "go along" with any foreign country wanting to play baseball that "would establish

decent and regulation contracts and have respect for the rights of others."

Earlier, the commissioner had invited all contract "jumpers" to return to their teams before the major league season opened. Then he ruled that those who did not return by that date would not be permitted to apply for reinstatement for a five-year period.

Chandler would not comment today on what action he might take if the players apply for reinstatement after five years.

Players in Agreement

MEXICO CITY, April 16 (AP)—The American colony of ex-big leaguers, isolated here in the heart of tamale land, weren't the least

bit homesick tonight as they read stories of the colorful opening of the United States' big league baseball seasons, an event in which most of them had participated many times.

The consensus among the seven former major leaguers who were around town waiting for Thursday's games, was that "the boys up North can play for peanuts and like it; but we're playing for real money and we love it."

Catcher Mickey Owen, former star Dodger catcher and the one player who should have missed the traditional opening most of all, was the happiest of the lot. The curly-haired veteran, who said he had been through eight National League openings, declared:

"I'm perfectly happy here. My wife likes Mexico and we moved into this super-modern apartment today and everything is dandy."

Owen, 30-year-old Missouri-born star, is scheduled to make his debut with Veracruz on Thursday at mile-high Delta Park where a well-hit ball takes off like a rabbit in the rarefied atmosphere.

Outfielder Danny Gardella, who deserted the Giants after a row with Manager Mel Ott, still was sore at his former boss. Dangerous Dan, firmly intrenched here as a star, was questioned as to his feelings on missing the big leagues'

opening day up North and snapped: "I assure you I'm just as happy as Ott and probably less confused."

Alex Carrasquel, 32-year-old Venezuelan pitcher who jumped the White Sox, said:

"I have no regrets—who would, leaving the White Sox?"

Echoes the Sentiments

Myron Hayworth, former Browns catcher and the latest addition to the Mexican League, echoed the others' sentiments. The receiver, who is drawing one of the top salaries, emphasized that he was "perfectly happy," after taking his second workout today.

It was the same with Frank Scalzi, one-time member of the Indians and Giants, who plays under the name of Rizutti here, and Roberto Ortiz, ex-Senator.

The one possible exception was Luis Olmo, who probably would have won a starting outfield berth with the Dodgers if he had stuck in the National League. The 26-year-old Puerto Rican spent most of the day in his hotel room, with his injured knee in a cast.

"Oh, it's all right and I like it here," Olmo said, "but you might say I'm just a trifle lonely. Who wouldn't be, in a hotel room, all alone?"

April 17, 1946

AMERICAN LEAGUE WINS IN ROUT, 12-0

Williams, With 2 Homers and 2 Singles, Belts in 5 Runs Against National Rivals

KELLER CLOUTS 4-BAGGER

Feller, Newhouser, Kramer Fan 10 for 3-Hit Shut-Out Before 34,906 at Boston

By JOHN DREBINGER
Special to THE NEW YORK TIMES.

BOSTON, July 9—Putting on an amazing exhibition of offensive strength, the American League, with beanpole Ted Williams spearheading an overpowering fourteen-hit attack, trampled underfoot the National League today to win baseball's thirteenth midsummer All-Star game, 12 to 0.

The victory, witnessed by a crowd of 34,906 that packed historic Fenway Park to capacity and paid a gross of $111,338 and a net of $89,071 for baseball's welfare fund and the families of Spokane players killed in a bus accident, was the most decisive ever recorded in the classic.

Before an admiring home throng, Williams fairly outdid himself. Unabashed by the fact that the Yankees' Charlie Keller tried to steal his thunder by touching off a first-inning homer, the Red Sox problem child went on fairly to murder the National pitching selections that Manager Charlie Grimm so desperately tossed in his way.

"Blooper" Ball No Puzzle

He exploded four hits, two of them tremendous homers, and belted in five runs. Nothing whatever seemed to puzzle him, least of all Rip Sewell's renowned "blooper" pitch which Ted the Terrific walloped into the bleachers with two aboard to climax a four-run eighth inning.

Behind this devastating attack, Steve O'Neill's American Leaguers, by way of making their display of superiority utterly complete, tossed three hurlers into the fray that baffled the Nationals just as thoroughly.

Starting with Cleveland's Bob Feller and following with Detroit's Hal Newhouser and the Browns' Jack Kramer, the junior circuit allowed its rivals only three hits, all singles and only one escaping the infield. Working three innings apiece, Feller gave two hits, Newhouser the other and Kramer gave nothing except one walk.

That came in the eighth, by which time the harried Nationals doubtless would like to walk out

Their Batting and Pitching Brought Victory

Kramer (left) Newhouser (center) and Feller in the clubhouse after the contest

on the show in a body. Only one of their number got as far as third and then as the result of a first-inning error. From the second inning on not one got so far as second. Ten struck out.

Higbe Batted From Box

Contrasting sharply with this, the National League hurlers scarcely enjoyed a moment of free breathing. Claude Passeau was the victim of the Keller homer. The Dodgers' Kirby Higbe went down for Williams' first homer in the fourth and then was put to rout with a three-run, four-hit barrage in the fifth. The Reds' Ewell Blackwell was stung for two tallies in the seventh and in the eighth Pittsburgh's Sewell served as Williams' foil for a final record assault.

With this second homer Williams became the first player ever to drive three homers in all-star competition. He hit his first four years ago and also tied Arky Vaughan's 1941 record of two in one game.

With four Red Sox in the starting line-up as Feller and Passeau opened on the firing line the crowd, as expected, appeared predominantly American League. It therefore must have been something of a shock when Stan Musial bounced a one-hopper at Johnny Pesky who, with all the time in the world to make the put-out, tossed a one-hopper to first for an error.

On the heels of that Johnny Hopp dribbled one down the third-base line for an infield hit, putting National Leaguers on first and second, but Feller appeared unperturbed. During the course of a season in Cleveland he encounters a lot of that.

Walker Advances Runners

So he concentrated on Dixie Walker, subdued the Flatbush favorite on a grounder to Bobby Doerr that advanced the runners to second and third, and then fanned Whitey Kurowski. That produced a deal of cheering, but it was barely a whisper to what followed a few minutes later.

After Passeau had retired the first two American League batters, Dom DiMaggio and Pesky, the Cub ace right-hander, hero of that famous world series one-hitter last October, faced Williams. It was their first meeting since that memorable All-Star game in Detroit in 1941, when Ted smacked Claude for a homer that gave the American Leaguers a spectacular ninth-inning victory.

Doubtless Passeau held that well in mind, for he pitched cautiously and passed the lanky Sox outfielder. Before Claude had a chance to decide whether he had made the best move, he fed one a little too good to Keller and the next moment the crowd let out an ear-splitting roar as doughty King Kong sent the ball soaring over the railing in right center and into the National League bullpen.

With an immediate two-run margin, the American League's fireball ace needed no more help. For his three innings, all that rules of the competition allow to a pitcher, Feller gave two hits, the second also being an infield blow

by the Giants' Walker Cooper, in the second inning. He walked none and fanned three.

Passeau likewise swept through the second and third innings without any further slip. He yielded one more hit, a single by DiMaggio, which pleased the crowd immensely, and a pass, but snappy work by an infield that included three Cardinals—Kurowski, Marty Marion and Red Schoendienst—kept him out of trouble.

However, the American Leaguers were leading by two as Newhouser and Higbe appeared as the rival pitchers in the fourth. This margin immediately was increased by one as Williams, first batter to face the Brooklyn right-hander, lifted a towering 400-foot smash into the bleachers in dead center.

Higbe got by the remainder of the fourth without difficulty, but in the fifth it caught him head-on as Buddy Rosar singled and galloped around to third on a single by Newhouser. The latter took second on Johnny Hopp's futile throw to the far corner.

Stephens Bats in Two

This induced Higbe to pass Stan Spence intentionally, filling the bases, but it scarcely improved the situation. For Vern Stephens, who had just replaced Pesky at short, dropped a two-bagger just inside the right-field line and two scored.

Then came a single off the redoubtable Williams' bat to drive in Spence, and that made it three for the round. It also ended Higbe's stay and Blackwell, the Reds' long and lean right-hander, emerged to restrain the American Leaguers for a little while.

Newhouser, in the meantime, was mowing down the National Leaguers with machine-gun precision. The Detroit southpaw wizard, who only last Sunday had racked up his sixteenth victory with a shutout, faced ten batters in his three innings, fanned four and allowed only one hit, a single by Peanuts Lowrey after two had been retired in the sixth.

Blackwell, replacing Higbe, did quite well for a time, but no National League pitcher was to escape the fury of the aroused American Leaguers. After getting two out of the way in the seventh, Blackwell saw Williams push a single past Phil Cavarretta at first. Keller walked and both scored when Joe Gordon slapped a double against the left-field wall.

In the eighth came the boisterous finale as O'Neill's larruping crew mauled Sewell for four blows and an equal number of tallies. Singles by George Stirnweiss and Kramer and a fly by Sam Chapman had produced one tally when Sewell decided to regale his rivals with his "blooper" pitch.

Stephens sliced one just beyond Frankie Gustine's reach for a single. Then Rip tossed another to Williams.

The ball arched high in the air as it floated to the plate, when it got there thumping Ted really gave it altitude. He sent it sailing high into the right-field bleachers for a final cluster of three that threw the gathering into a paroxysm of laughter.

That closing outburst also overshadowed the American League's concluding pitching effort by Kramer, which surpassed even that of his two predecessors. By then, however, the National Leaguers were so thoroughly bewildered they scarcely seemed aware of what was going on.

The Browns' right-hander hurled three hitless as well as scoreless innings and allowed only one man to reach first base. In the eighth, with two down, Gustine walked.

The result gave the jubilant American Leaguers a lead of nine games to four in the All-Star competition. Each side used twenty-one players. It was the only phase of the battle in which the National Leaguers held their own.

All-Star Box Score

NATIONAL LEAGUE

	a.b.	r.	h.	po.	a.	e.
Schoendienst, St. L., 2b	2	0	0	0	2	0
Gustine, Pitt., 2b	1	0	0	1	1	0
Musial, St. L., lf	2	0	0	0	0	0
Ennis, Phil., lf	2	0	0	0	0	0
Hopp, Bost., cf	2	0	1	0	0	0
Lowrey, Chi., cf	2	0	1	3	0	0
Walker, Bkn., rf	3	0	0	1	0	0
Slaughter, St. L., rf	1	0	0	0	0	0
Kurowski, St. L., 3b	3	0	2	1	0	0
bVerban, Phil	1	0	0	0	0	0
Mize, N. Y., 1b	1	0	0	7	0	0
McCormick, Phil., 1b	1	0	1	1	0	0
Cavarretta, Chi., 1b	1	0	0	1	0	0
W. Cooper, N. Y., c	1	0	1	0	0	0
Masi, Bost., c	2	0	0	4	1	0
Marion, St. L., ss	3	0	0	4	6	0
Passeau, Chi., p	1	0	0	0	3	0
Higbe, Bkn., p	1	0	0	0	0	0
Blackwell, Cin., p	1	0	0	0	0	0
aLamanno, Cin	1	0	0	0	0	0
Sewell, Pit., p	0	0	0	0	0	0
Total	31	0	3	24	13	0

AMERICAN LEAGUE

	a.b.	r.	h.	po.	a.	e.
D. DiMaggio, Bost., cf	2	0	1	1	0	0
Spence, Wash., cf	0	1	0	1	0	0
Chapman, Phil., cf	2	0	0	1	0	0
Pesky, Bost., ss	2	0	0	1	0	1
Stephens, St. L., ss	3	1	2	0	4	0
Williams, Bost., lf	4	4	4	1	0	0
Keller, N. Y., rf	4	2	1	1	0	0
Doerr, Bost., 2b	2	0	0	1	1	0
Gordon, N. Y., 2b	2	0	1	0	1	0
Vernon, Wash., 1b	2	0	0	2	1	0
York, Bost., 1b	2	0	1	5	0	0
Keltner, Cleve., 3b	0	0	0	0	0	0
Stirnweiss, N. Y., 3b	3	1	1	0	0	0
Hayes, Cleve., c	1	0	0	3	0	0
Rosar, Phil., c	2	1	1	5	0	0
Wagner, Bost., c	1	0	0	4	0	0
Feller, Cleve., p	0	0	0	0	0	0
cAppling, Chi	1	0	0	0	0	0
Newhouser, Det., p	1	1	1	1	0	0
dDickey, N. Y	1	0	0	0	0	0
Kramer, St. L., p	1	1	1	0	0	0
Total	36	12	14	27	7	1

aBatted for Blackwell in eighth.
bBatted for Kurowski in ninth.
cBatted for Feller in third.
dBatted for Newhouser in sixth.

Nationals ......0 0 0 0 0 0 0 0 0— 0
Americans ......2 0 0 1 3 0 2 4 ..—12

Runs batted in—Keller 2, Williams 5, Stephens 2, Gordon 2, Chapman. Two-base hits — Stephens, Gordon. Home runs — Keller, Williams 2. Double plays — Marion and Mize; Schoendienst, Marion and Mize. Earned runs—Nationals 0, Americans 12. Left on bases—Nationals 5, Americans 4. Bases on balls—Off Passeau 2 (Williams, Keltner), Higbe 1 (Spence), Blackwell 1 (Keller), Kramer 1 (Gustine). Struck out—By Feller 3 (Kurowski, Marion, Passeau), Newhouser 4 (Kurowski, Higbe, Gustine, Ennis), Higbe 2 (Keller, Stirweiss), Blackwell 1 (Dickey), Kramer 3 (Cavarretta, Marion, Ennis).

Pitching summary—Off Feller, 2 hits 0 run in 3 innings; Newhouser, 1 hit 0 run in 3 innings; Kramer, 0 hit, 0 run in 3 innings; Passeau, 2 hits, 2 runs in 3 innings; Higbe, 5 hits 4 runs in 1 1/3 innings; Blackwell, 3 hits 2 runs in 2 2/3 innings; Sewell, 4 hits 4 runs in 1 inning. Wild pitch—Blackwell. Winning pitcher—Feller. Losing pitcher—Passeau.

Umpires—Summers (A.L.), plate; Boggess (N.L.), 1b; Rommel (A.L.). 2b; Goetz (N.L.), 3b (first four and a half innings). Goetz (N.L.), plate; Rommel (A.L.), 1b; Boggess (N.L.). 2b; Summers (A.L.), 3b (last four and a half innings). Attendance—34,906. Gate receipts (less taxes)—$89,701. Time of game—2:18.

July 10, 1946

RED SOX TAKE PAIR AS WILLIAMS STARS

Ted's 3 Homers Bat in 8 Runs in 11-10 Opening Fray, Then Indians Drop Second, 6-4

BOSTON LEAD IS 11 GAMES

Boudreau Slams 4-Bagger and 4 Doubles in First—Hughson and Ferriss Save Mates

BOSTON, July 14 (P)—On the

Ted Williams being greeted by team-mates Bobby Doerr (1) and Johnny Pesky (6) after he connected for the circuit with the bases filled in the third inning of the first game with the Indians at Boston. He also hit two other four-baggers and a single in the contest. The Cleveland catcher is Jim Hegan and the umpire Ed Rommel.

Associated Press Wirephoto

strength of Ted Williams' thumping bat, the not-to-be-denied Red Sox outscored the Indians, 11—10, in the first game of a twin bill today and then went on to take the second by a more moderate score, 6—4. The double triumph stretched Boston's American League lead to 11 games over the second-place Yankees.

All Theodore Samuel Williams did in the first game was clout three homers and a single, drive in eight runs and score four times. Ted the Kid thus joined a large group of sluggers who have belted three homers in a single contest.

Lou Boudreau, Cleveland pilot who in the nightcap set up the most unusual defense against Williams ever seen in Fenway Park, also had himself a time in the opener. Boudreau hit a homer and four successive doubles in that first game during which the two teams sprayed hits all over and out of the field.

Passes to Williams Total 96

When Williams went to bat in the second game, during which he received his ninety-fifth and ninety-sixth bases on balls, Shortstop Boudreau concentrated six men in right field.

The Cleveland manager played back on the grass midway between first and second. Jimmy Wasdell, the first sacker, posted himself on the grass near the foul line.

The third baseman was on the grass on the right side of second base and the right and center fielders patrolled as deep as possible in that sector. The set-up was successful once when Boudreau snagged a hot grounder and threw Thumpin' Theodore out at first.

The first time Williams batted in the second contest he lined a double down the right field foul line. The smash was just too high for Wasdell, who leaped with his gloved hand outstretched.

The Sox really wanted these two games. Joe Cronin used Tex Hughson and Dave Ferriss, two of his aces, to finish, Tex in the opener and Boo in the second.

Gromek Yields First Homer

Williams' first four-sacker, on a one-and-nothing pitch off Steve Gromek, was a tremendously high smash which bounded off the top of the wall between the bull pen and the right field bleachers, more than 400 feet from the plate. His

The box scores:

FIRST GAME

CLEVELAND (A.)							BOSTON (A.)						
	ab.	r.	h.	po.	a.	e.		ab.	r.	h.	po.	a.	e.
Case, lf	6	1	2	3	0	0	Culb's'n, rf	5	2	3	0	0	0
Conway, 2b	6	0	2	5	2	0	P'esky, ss	4	2	0	1	7	0
Seerey, cf	3	2	2	0	0	0	DiMag'o, cf	5	0	1	2	0	0
Edwards, rf	6	1	1	5	0	0	Will'ms, lf	5	4	4	2	0	0
Boudr'u, ss	5	3	5	0	3	1	Doerr, 2b	5	1	4	6	3	0
Keltner, 3b	3	1	2	1	2	0	York, 1b	5	0	1	11	1	0
Wasdell, 1b	5	0	1	5	1	2	Russell, 3b	4	0	0	1	2	0
Hegan, c	5	2	2	5	0	0	Partee, c	4	2	3	2	0	0
Gromek, p	2	0	0	0	1	0	Wagner, c	0	0	0	1	0	0
Black, p	2	0	1	0	2	0	Dobson, p	1	0	0	0	1	0
Berry, p	0	0	0	0	0	0	Dre'werd, p	1	0	0	0	3	0
aMank'w'z	1	0	0	0	0	0	Bagby, p	1	0	0	1	0	0
							bLazor	1	0	0	0	0	0
Total	44	10	18	24	11	3	Hughson, p	0	0	0	0	1	0
							Total	40	11	16	27	17	0

aBatted for Berry in ninth.
bBatted for Bagby in eighth.

| Cleveland | 4 0 1 | 0 3 1 | 1 0 0—10 |
| Boston | 0 0 5 | 1 1 0 | 1 3 .—11 |

Runs batted in—Edwards, Boudreau 4, Keltner 3, Case, Black, Williams 8, York.
Two-base hits—Case, Boudreau 4, Hegan, Black, York, DiMaggio. Three-base hits—Hegan, Conway, DiMaggio. Home runs—Boudreau, Keltner, Williams 3. Stolen base—Pesky. Sacrifice—Dreisewerd. Double plays—Wasdell, Conway and Wasdell; Pesky, Doerr and York. Left on bases—Cleveland 12, Boston 7. Bases on balls—Off Gromek 1, Dobson 1, Dreisewerd 1, Bagby 3. Struck out—By Gromek 3, Berry 1, Dreisewerd 1, Bagby 1, Hughson 1. Hits—Off Gromek 6 in 2 2-3 innings, Black 7 in 3 1-3, Berry 3 in 2, Dobson 4 in 2-3, Dreisewerd 7 in 4, Bagby 5 in 3 1/3, Hughson 2 in 1. Winning pitcher—Bagby. Losing pitcher—Berry. Umpires—Rommel, Boyer and Grieve. Time of game—2:32.

SECOND GAME

CLEVELAND (A)							BOSTON (A)						
	ab.	r.	h.	po.	a.	e.		ab.	r.	h.	po.	a.	e.
Case, lf	5	2	2	0	0	0	C'berson, rf	3	0	1	0	0	0
Conway, 2b	1	1	0	1	5	0	McBride, lf	0	0	0	1	0	0
Seerey, cf	4	0	1	2	0	0	Pesky, ss	4	0	2	2	2	0
Edwards, rf	5	1	3	4	0	0	Williams, lf	2	2	1	0	0	0
Boudreau, ss	4	0	1	3	4	0	DiM'gio, cf	4	0	1	5	0	0
Keltner, 3b	4	0	1	3	0	0	Doerr, 2b	3	2	1	2	1	0
Wasdell, 1b	3	0	1	12	0	0	York, 1b	3	1	2	2	0	0
Lollar, c	3	0	0	2	0	0	Russell, 3b	4	0	1	3	1	0
Jordan, c	1	0	1	0	0	0	Wagner, c	4	0	0	11	0	0
Embree, p	2	0	0	0	0	0	Zuber, p	2	1	0	0	0	0
aWoodling	1	0	0	0	0	0	Ferriss, p	0	0	0	0	0	0
Lemon, p	0	0	0	3	0	0	Total	29	6	9	27	4	0
bMeyer	1	0	0	0	0	0							
Gassaway, p	0	0	0	0	0	0							
Total	34	4	8	24	15	0							

aBatted for Embree in seventh.
bBatted for Lemon in eighth.

| Cleveland | 0 0 1 | 0 0 0 | 1 1 1—4 |
| Boston | 0 3 0 | 0 0 2 | 1 0 .—6 |

Runs batted in—Edwards, Case, Boudreau, Jordan, York 2, Russell, Wagner, DiMaggio.
Two-base hits—Edwards, Russell, Williams. Home run—Case. Stolen bases—Case, Conway. Sacrifice—McBride. Double plays—Conway, Boudreau and Wasdell; Keltner, Conway and Wasdell; Russell, Doerr and York. Left on bases—Cleveland 11, Boston 5. Base on balls—Off Embree 3, Lemon 2, Zuber 7, Ferriss 3. Struck out—By Embree 1, Zuber 7, Ferriss 1. Hits—Off Embree 5 in 6 innings, Lemon 2 in 1, off Gassaway 0 in 1, Zuber 5 in 7 2-3, Ferriss 3 in 1 1-3. Winning pitcher—Zuber. Losing pitcher—Embree. Umpires—Boyer, Grieve and Rommel. Time of game—2:12. Attendance—31,581 paid.

July 15, 1946

Bob Feller
The New York Times

Feller's Speed Measured At 98.6 Miles Per Hour

By The United Press.

WASHINGTON, Aug. 20—Bob Feller threw a baseball 98.6 miles per hour tonight in a special throwing test, judged by an Army measuring device.

Preliminary to tonight's Indians-Washington Senators game, the Cleveland ace went into a long windup and uncorked the ball with his right arm at a speed of 145 feet per second to better the former record of 139 feet per second, or 94 miles per hour, set by Atley Donald.

The Army test machine measured the speed of the pitch, from the mound to the plate, to within 1/10,000th of a second.

August 21, 1946

Cards Win Pennant

BROOKS LOSE, 8-4, DESPITE 3-RUN 9TH

Dickson Pitches 2-Hitter Till Last Inning, When Brecheen Saves Game for Cards

LONG BLOWS ROUT HATTEN

Redbirds, Taking 9th Flag in 20 Years, Meet Red Sox in Series Opener Sunday

By JOHN DREBINGER

Incredible as it may sound, the National League's pennant race finally has ended.

It drew to a close about 15 minutes after 4 o'clock yesterday afternoon at Ebbets Field when the Cardinals, after battering their foe with a bruising thirteen-hit attack, smothered a last-ditch demonstration by a desperate band of Dodgers to finish on top, 8 to 4.

That gave the Redbirds from St. Louis the first pennant play-off series in major league history in two straight victories and the right to engage the American League's champion Red Sox in the long deferred and almost forgotten World Series, which will get under way in St. Louis next Sunday.

Remaining in character to the end, the Flatbush Flock went down swinging with one last despairing, electrifying flourish. Held to one run and two hits by Murry Dickson, crack right-hander, for eight innings—with both the run and the hits coming in the first—Brooklyn's Beloved Bums thrilled what was left of a gathering of 31,437 of the faithful in the ninth inning by routing Dickson and continuing their attack against Harry Brecheen until they had three tallies in and the bases full.

Two Strike-Outs End Game

With the tying run at the plate and only one out, Brecheen hung up two searing strike-outs that doubtless will leave their scars for years to come. Then it was that the Bums, who had escaped seemingly inevitable extinction so many times this year, finally breathed their last.

Starting with left-handed Joe Hatten, who was blasted out inside of five rounds, by which time he had given as many runs, Leo Durocher hurled six pitchers into the struggle, but all to no avail.

So the Cardinals bagged their ninth National League pennant over a span of twenty years and for the sixth time under a different manager. Rogers Hornsby was the first one for the Redbirds in 1926. Two years later Bill McKechnie piloted them home in front. In 1930 and 1931, Gabby Street, who came all the way from St. Louis to see yesterday's encounter, was the winning skipper. Frankie Frisch led the famed Gashouse Gang in 1934 and then came Billy Southworth's three straight winning campaigns from 1942 to 1944.

Now quiet, soft-spoken Eddie Dyer, who used to operate the Cardinal farm system, retired a few years ago and returned when Southworth left for Boston, has guided St. Louis home in front in his first year as a major league manager and after one of the most thrilling campaigns in history.

Good World Series Record

Five of eight previous Cardinal pennant winners went on to take world championships, if that is of any encouragement to the present Redbirds as they prepare for the redoubtable Red Sox, who for weeks and weeks have been waiting for this big moment.

As yesterday's battle got under way under a cloudless sky, the crowd, doomed to spend most of the afternoon in stony silence, got an early chance to whoop it up a bit when the Dodgers in a surprise foray after their first two batters had been retired tore into Dickson for a run.

Augie Galan, who in a last-minute switch was moved to third while Dick Whitman started in left, outgalloped an infield hit to Red Schoendienst. On the heels of this came a pass to Dixie Walker and when Ed Stevens lashed a single through the mound and into center field Galan romped home amid considerable noise.

At that, it didn't sound quite like a genuine Flatbush roar, giving rise to the suspicion that in the general shuffle for reserved seats most of the faithful must have suffered a complete shut-out. It seemed more like a sedate world series gathering than the boisterous Flatbush host one might have expected for the occasion.

Marion Drives in Dusak

Then the Dodger lead vanished almost as quickly as the cheers in that first inning had subsided. With one out in the second, Erv (four-sack) Dusak smacked one against the left-field wall and while he didn't get all four sacks on that shot he did get three. Came a fly by Marty Marion to Carl Furillo in center and Dusak scored.

A moment later two surprise blows snapped the tie almost in the twinkling of an eye. Clyde Kluttz, whom the Giants had tossed away last May for something less than a song, considering the fact that Vince DiMaggio never could sing, slammed a single into center. That, of course, didn't seem so damaging, as the next batter was Dickson.

But the slim right-hander has a habit of producing a damaging blow when least expected. He won one of those important Cub games in the West with a single and this time he did infinitely better. He belted a line triple into right center. It fetched home Kluttz and the Cards were in front to remain there.

To be sure, the margin at that point was only 2 to 1, but somehow the folks seemed to feel it was all over and when the Redbirds went on another rampage in the fifth, routing Hatten with a three-run blast, even the last die-hard on the premises realized the Bums had run out their string of miraculous achievements. They were just in there to take a beating and they absorbed it, one must say, with exceptionally good grace.

It was quite an unexpected blow that leveled the flock in the first round, for there were two out and the bases were empty when Stan Musial, batting champion of the league, banged a double over Dixie Walker's head in right. Hatten then was instructed to pass Whitey Kurowski, but this was to prove a sad day for Durocher's usually successful strategems.

Enos Slaughter, who isn't a fellow to take lightly the imputation that he can't hit a left-hander as well as any right-handed batsman, smashed a terrific drive into deep right center and by the time the ball had been retrieved Slaughter was on third for another Redbird triple while Musial and Kurowski were over the plate.

Next came a single to center by Dusak, Slaughter raced in with the third tally of the inning and Hatten went out to be replaced by Hank Behrman, who finally brought the round to a close without further damage.

There was no checking those Redbirds for long, though. With Behrman passing out almost immediately for the first of four pinch-hitters Durocher tossed into the battle, little Vic Lombardi appeared in the sixth.

Lombardi Loses Control

The diminutive southpaw got by well enough in that inning, but he walked Kurowski and Slaughter to open the seventh. After a sacrifice by Dusak, Durocher made another frantic wave to the Dodger bull pen.

It called out the indefatigable Kirby Higbe and his familiar "13," but the numeral brought no particular luck on this momentous occasion. Marion executed a deft sacrifice squeeze bunt that sent Ku-

rowski streaking home from third and while this was the only tally the Redbirds got in this round, they smacked Higbe lustily in the eighth, routing him with a three-hit splurge that accounted for their final pair of tallies.

Many Fans Leave Before Rally

Schoendienst opened this brisk assault with a single and a moment later swept around to third on a double to left by Terry Moore. Again came an intentional pass, this time to Musial, and again the move failed to meet requirements.

Kurowski, walked three times in a row, slammed a single into right and Schoendienst and Moore counted. The Redbirds now had eight runs, while the Dodgers, though still on their feet, appeared hopelessly out.

After their brief first inning demonstration against Dickson, they had been utterly unable to do a thing for seven tortuous rounds. In fact, in that stretch they got only one ball beyond the confines of the infield, a fly to left by Stevens in the fourth. They never were close to a hit, drew three passes and not a Dodger advanced to second.

It was too much for even the hardiest of Flatbush habitues and so it was that when the Dodgers, with an effort born of despair, launched their belated ninth-inning rally the stands were almost one-quarter empty.

The attack began with Galan ramming a double into right, but when the beloved Dixie Walker, hitless throughout this play-off series, flied harmlessly to centre, the folks just knew this was the bitter end. Even when Stevens followed with a three-base smash to center, scoring Galan, it caused only a feeble cheer, but soon it became evident that both the Dodgers and the noise were not to be shut down with this for a final gesture.

Furillo plunked a single in centre driving in Stevens. Then Dickson unfurled a wild pitch and walked Peewee Reese and the folks plucky enough to remain let out a full-throated roar.

Ideal Setting for Homer

Dyer, unable to stand the suspense any longer, bustled out of his dugout for the second time in the inning and called in Brecheen, a left-hander, but the Cat wasn't to solve the problem at once. Bruce Edwards greeted Brecheen with a single to left, driving in Furillo with the third run of the inning, and when Cookie Lavagetto, batting for Harry Taylor, walked, filling the bases, Flatbush could not have asked for a better setting.

There was the tying run at the plate and a homer into the stands really would have turned things upside down, but at that point the fates must have decided that Brooklyn's hour of miraculous

deeds had run far enough. Either that, or Brecheen decided he had better put a little more stuff on the ball.

Stanky fanned, taking the third strike and then tall Howie Schultz, who had hit a homer in that first play-off game on Tuesday in St. Louis, batted for Dick Whitman. He swung with tremendous fervor but disturbed nothing save the atmosphere, for his strike-out ended the struggle. The Flock, at least, went down swinging to provide some measure of comfort for those who remained to the last.

With this triumph the Cards closed the season's book against their most determined foes with a record of sixteen triumphs against eight for the Flock. Never conceded the barest pennant chance at the outset of the race last April, Brooklyn remained in the running until battered down in this unprecedented play-off series.

The victory was Dickson's fifteenth against only six setbacks. It was also his fourth over the Brooks, who beat him once. Hatten, going into the battle seeking his fifteen triumph and with a six-game winning streak, went down for his eleventh reverse and fourth at the hands of the Redbirds.

Dodgers' Box Score

ST. LOUIS (N.)	ab.	r.	h.	po.	a. e.
Schoen't, 2b.	5	1	1	1	5 0
Moore, cf.	5	1	2	2	0 0
Musial, 1b.	4	1	1	14	1 0
Kurow'i, 3b.	2	2	1	1	1 0
Slaugh'r, rf.	3	1	1	0	0 0
Dusak, lf.	3	1	2	1	0 0
H. Wal'r, lf.	1	0	0	0	0 0
Marion, ss.	3	0	1	4	3 0
Kluttz, c.	5	1	2	3	2 0
Dickson, p.	5	0	2	1	5 0
Brecheen, p	0	0	0	0	0 0
Total	36	8	13	27	17 0

BROOKLYN (N.)	ab.	r.	h.	po.	a. e.
Stanky, 2b.	5	0	0	3	4 0
Whitman, lf.	4	0	0	2	0 0
dSchultz	1	0	0	0	0 0
Galan, 3b.	4	2	2	0	4 0
F. Wal'r, rf.	3	0	0	0	0 0
Stevens, 1b.	4	1	2	11	0 0
Furillo, cf.	4	1	1	4	0 0
Reese, ss.	2	0	0	2	3 0
Edwards, c.	2	0	1	3	1 0
Hatten, p.	1	0	0	0	1 0
Behrman, p.	0	0	0	0	0 0
aHerm'ski	1	0	0	0	0 0
Lomb'rdi, p.	0	0	0	0	1 0
Higbe, p.	0	0	0	1	0 0
Melton, p.	0	0	0	0	0 0
bMedwick	1	0	0	0	0 0
Taylor, p.	0	0	0	0	0 0
cLavagetto	0	0	0	0	0 0
Total	32	4	6	27	14 0

aBatted for Behrman in fifth.
bBatted for Melton in eighth.
cBatted for Taylor in ninth.
dBatted for Whitman in ninth.

St. Louis ....0 2 0 0 3 0 1 2 0—8
Brooklyn ....1 0 0 0 0 0 0 0 3—4

Runs batted in—Stevens 2, Marion, Dickson, Slaughter 2, Dusak, Kurowski 2, Furillo, Edwards.

Two-base hits—Musial, Moore, Galan. Three-base hits—Dickson, Slaughter, Stevens. Sacrifices—Schoendienst, Dusak, Marion. Double plays—Dickson, Marion and Musial; Stanky, Reese and Stevens. Left on bases—St. Louis 11, Brooklyn 7. Bases on balls—Off Dickson 5 (F. Walker, Edwards 2, Reese 2); Hatten 3 (Kurowski 2, Marion); Lombardi 2 (Kurowski, Slaughter); Brecheen 1 (Musial, Slaughter); Brecheen 1 (Lavagetto). Struck out—By Dickson 3 (Stanky, Reese, Hermanski); Brecheen 2 (Stanky, Schultz); Higbe 1 (Dickson); Taylor 1 (Dickson).

Pitching summary—Hatten 7 hits 5 runs in 4 2-3 innings; Behrman 1 hit 0 runs in 1-3; Lombardi 1 hit 1 run in 1 1-3; Higbe 3 hits 2 runs in 1; Melton 0 hits 0 runs in 2-3; Taylor 1 hit 0 runs in 1; Dickson 5 hits 3 runs in 8 1-3 innings; Brecheen 1 hit 1 run in 2-3. Wild pitch—Dickson. Winning pitcher—Dickson. Losing pitcher—Hatten.

Umpires—Pinelli (plate); Goetz (1b); Boggess (2b); Reardon (3b). Time of game—2:44. Attendance—31,487.

October 4, 1946

PENSION PROGRAM FOR PLAYERS VOTED BY MAJOR LEAGUES

Veterans, on Reaching 50, Will Be Assured of Payments of $50 to $100 a Month

---

$675,000 YEARLY NEEDED

Dues Required From Those in Plan—Minimum World Series Pool of $250,000 Set

---

By JOHN DREBINGER

The most elaborate and complicated pension program ever undertaken by a professional sport was adopted yesterday when the National and American Leagues, sitting in joint session in the Waldorf-Astoria Hotel, agreed to a plan assuring veteran baseball players an income ranging from $50 to $100 a month on reaching fifty years of age.

In making the announcement Commissioner A. B. (Happy) Chandler, who presided at the meeting, said the two leagues approved in full the plan worked out by a special committee. Dixie Walker of the Dodgers and Johnny Murphy of the Yankees sat as player representatives on the committee. It meets, Chandler said, virtually all the original requests made by the players.

Under the provisions of the program a player, after serving five seasons in the major leagues, shall receive, on reaching 50, an income of $50 a month for the rest of his life. Each additional year of service will increase the pension amount $10 a month until a maximum of $100 a month is reached for ten-year men and over.

Those Who Are Eligible

All players, coaches and trainers on the rosters of the sixteen major league clubs on opening day of the 1947 season shall be eligible. Also, all players who served in the war shall be permitted to include that time in service, provided they were in the major leagues for three years prior to their entrance into the armed forces.

To insure this huge pension program, which within a few years will involve several thousand players, it is estimated by its underwriters, the Equitable Life Assurance Society of the United States, that an annual pool of approximately $675,000 will be required.

This amount will be raised by dues from players, contributions by the ball clubs, the total receipts from the annual All-Star game and the $150,000 which some sponsor pays annually for the world series radio broadcasting rights.

Victory For the Players

It was estimated yesterday that the ball clubs will carry approximately 80 per cent of the burden of upkeep, thereby yielding another signal victory to the players who, when they started their movement for better working conditions last year, included a pension request among their demands.

Dues from players will operate on a sliding scale. A player must pay $45.45 the first year he subscribes to the plan, and $90.90 the second year. Thereafter the payments increase each year until the tenth year when the fee will be $454.75. However, when a player's total payments aggregate $2,500, his yearly payments shall be reduced to $250 annually.

In the event a player does not remain in the majors at least five years to qualify for the lowest income the money he has put in shall be returned to him. Also, should a player die before drawing any benefits, a group insurance plan provides that his beneficiaries shall be paid for 120 months at the rate applying to the player.

Obligation of Owners

The club owners' contributions shall consist of a flat payment of $250 by each club for every player on its roster subscribing to the plan and there will be no refunds on these subscriptions. The owners further committed themselves to make up the difference should there still be insufficient funds on hand to finance the plan. There is at present $352,000 being held in escrow by Commissioner Chandler for the fund, part of this amount including last year's All-Star receipts and the money from the sale of the world series radio rights.

It is stipulated, however, that for the plan to operate a 75 per cent membership will be required from an entire league, and each club must have at least 60 per cent of its players participating. If less than this quota on a club takes part, none can be permitted to do so.

Feeling in a surprisingly magnanimous mood, the club owners also adopted a rule which provides a minimum world series players' pool of $250,000 whenever the receipts do not come up to that amount. Last fall the players of the Cardinals and Red Sox shared in only $212,000, with the result that the individual players of the losing Boston club received less money than the umpires. Under the new arrangement a player on a winning team will be guaranteed approximately $5,000.

Slight Curb Adopted

At the same time the owners moved to put a slight curb on post-season barnstorming with the adoption of a rule which prohibits barnstorming games to start until the conclusion of the world series. The 30-day limit, however, still prevails.

At the insistence of the Commissioner, the magnates also acted to curb the practice of a club rewarding its pennant winning players with a bonus such as Owner Tom Yawkey conferred on his Red Sox players last season. Actually, a rule barring the practice has been on the books but it failed to carry a penalty. Now teeth have been added and any club giving its players such group awards shall be fined the equivalent of the total bonus.

Official recognition also was given to the "bonus player" clause which provides that any free agent player who receives more than $5,000 for signing a contract shall be known as a "bonus player" and thus subjected to numerous restrictions. Actually, the leagues adopted the rule last year, but numerous changes had to be made to make it conform with the demands of the minor leaguers.

Just before the joint meeting went into session George Trautman, new president of the National Association, governing body of the minors, appeared before the owners. He assured them that the vigorous campaign launched by his predecessor, William G. Bramham, to stamp out gambling evils would be continued and that he was confident present plans would meet the situation fully.

February 2, 1947

Chandler Bars Durocher For 1947 Baseball Season

By LOUIS EFFRAT

Leo Durocher, manager of the Brooklyn Dodgers, yesterday was suspended for the 1947 season by Commissioner A. B. (Happy) Chandler in the most drastic action ever taken against a major league baseball pilot.

From his offices in Cincinnati, where the diamond czar had been weighing evidence, Chandler announced also that Charley (Chuck) Dressen, New York Yankee coach, had been suspended for thirty days. Fines of $2,000 each were levied against the Dodger and Yankee clubs and one of $500 against Harold Parrott, Brooklyn road secretary.

The Durocher and Dressen suspensions are effective next Tuesday.

All Quiet in Brooklyn

The outgrowth of a feud that has been seething between the Brooklyn and Yankee organizations since L. S. (Larry) MacPhail, former Dodger president, moved over to the Yankees in the rival American League, the ruling by Chandler brought a strange stillness to Brooklyn yesterday. In Durocher case the severity of the penalty was without precedent in all-time baseball history, covering more than a century.

Durocher, oft-entangled, fiery field manager who in eight seasons at the helm of the Dodgers master-minded his team into first-division finishes seven times and won Brooklyn's first National League pennant in twenty-one years in 1941, was charged by Commissioner Chandler with being guilty of "conduct detrimental to baseball."

Durocher and President Branch Rickey of the Dodgers had accused MacPhail, Leo's one-time boss and friend, of having alleged gamblers in his box at an exhibition game between the Dodgers and Yankees at Havana last month. MacPhail, perturbed, to put it mildly, filed charges against both and the commissioner held hearings at Sarasota and at St. Petersburg. Chandler listened to testimony from numerous baseball persons, but did not disclose his decision until yesterday.

Standards Not Met

The commissioner, in his decision at Cincinnati, said:

"Durocher has not measured up to the standards expected or required of managers of our baseball teams.

"This incident in Havana, which brought considerable unfavorable comment to baseball generally, was one of a series of publicity-producing affairs in which Mana-

ger Durocher has been involved in the last few months.

"Managers of baseball teams are responsible for the conduct of players on the field. Good managers are able to insure the good conduct of the players on the field and frequently their example can influence players to be of good conduct off the field.

"As a result of the accumulation of unpleasant incidents detrimental to baseball, Manager Durocher is hereby suspended from participating in professional baseball for the 1947 season."

Dressen was suspended because in Chandler's opinion, the crafty coach, himself a former major-league pilot, had broken a verbal agreement to remain with the Dodgers as aide to Durocher, Chuck now serves in a similar capacity under Stanley (Bucky) Harris of the Yankees.

Reason for Parrott Fine

Parrott, ex-baseball writer for The Brooklyn Daily Eagle, was fined because, as Durocher's "ghost writer," he had written derogatory statements in Durocher's column in the Eagle. Incidentally, he was ordered by Chandler to stop writing the column at once.

The $2,000 fines against each club were "because their officials engaged in a public controversy damaging to baseball."

Dejected, confused, bewildered in fact, Durocher received the news in Rickey's office yesterday morning. Aside from a "For what?" outburst, The Lip, as he is called, remained quiet, as it were. That Leo is to be sidelined for the season was a shock to everyone in Brooklyn—the front office and the man-on-the-street.

Durocher, President Rickey, coaches and other executives were in conference in the Brooklyn offices early yesterday. They were engaged in a round-table discussion concerning the immediate future of Jackie Robinson, Negro star with the Montreal farm club. Rickey's phone rang. It was a long distance emergency call from Cincinnati and Commissioner Chandler was on the opposite end.

Silent on His Plans

The commissioner informed Rickey of his action and when the Dodger president told Durocher, the latter's reaction was "For what?" Throughout the afternoon,

Leo's only remarks were repeatedly "For what?" He had nothing to say about future plans, how long he would remain here, where he would go or what his next move might be. He just didn't know. Nor did Rickey.

Would there be an appeal?

"To whom?" Rickey replied. "Mr. Chandler is the commissioner. No, I don't think we will appeal."

Will Durocher's salary—estimated to be in the neighborhood of $75,000 annually, including bonuses —be paid during the period of suspension?

"I haven't gone into that," Rickey said.

Will Durocher be returned as manager in 1948?

"Obviously, I can't talk about that now," Rickey answered.

It was evident that none directly or indirectly concerned in the most spectacular off-the-field baseball development in years was in the mood to talk about it. At the offices of the Yankees, MacPhail had "nothing at all to say." Instead, he scheduled a press conference for 11 A.M. today at the midtown offices of the Yankees.

No Comment From Frick

Ford Frick, National League president, hastily summoned to Brooklyn by Rickey, had no comment, and at Chicago, Will Harridge, American League head, was similarly noncommittal. Anyway, Commissioner Chandler had warned:

"All parties to this controversy are silenced from the time this order is issued."

Totally unexpected, Chandler's action was most stunning. It left the Dodgers without a manager a week before the regular season's start. Four exhibition games are to be played at Ebbets Field, one with Montreal today and three with the Yankees over the weekend. For today only, Clyde Sukeforth, one of Durocher's trio of coaches, will handle the Dodgers against the Royals.

Of Durocher's successor, Rickey merely said: "We'll have a manager on the field next Tuesday." Who that person will be still is a matter of conjecture. Among the experts, there was considerable speculation yesterday. The names of Ray Blades, currently a Brooklyn coach and former manager of St. Louis Cardinals; Dixie Walker, veteran outfielder of the Dodgers; Bill Terry, former Giant leader; Frankie Frisch, ex-St. Louis Cardinal and Pittsburgh Pirate pilot, now a radio broadcaster, and three or four others were mentioned as possibilities.

Target of Criticism

Commissioner Chandler, who exonerated MacPhail and Rickey in yesterday's action, showed that he is determined to rule with a firm hand. The target of much criticism since he succeeded the late Judge Kenesaw Mountain Landis two years ago, the former Governor and Senator from Kentucky made his biggest and certainly his most important decision yesterday.

Not even Landis, who once suspended Babe Ruth and Bob Meusel for forty days back in 1921, dealt so heavily with a suspended player. The judge later barred Jimmy O'Connell and Cozy Dolan of the Giants for life, but on the matter of suspension yesterday's move was tops.

Durocher celebrated his fortieth birthday last July. He was involved in a fracas with a fan at Ebbets Field last season, but was cleared in court of fracturing the man's jaw. Durocher and Chandler had a long chat after the season and it is rumored that the commissioner warned Leo to watch his step, to choose his company.

Last winter Durocher married Laraine Day, movie star, and legal complications followed. Miss Day, here now, was scheduled to fly to Hollywood last night, but delayed the trip after learning of her husband's suspension.

Some persons — none officially connected with baseball—yesterday were inclined to remove Durocher permanently from the picture. They, however, were strictly guessing. It is not that easy to read Rickey's mind.

Leo Durocher, suspended for the coming season, with Branch Rickey, president of the Brooklyn Dodgers, at the club's headquarters on Montague Street.   The New York Times

Dodger players discussing the ruling in their dressing room at Ebbets Field. Left to right: Catcher Bruce Edwards, Shortstop Pee Wee Reese and Pitcher Rube Melton.   Associated Press

April 10, 1947

Dodgers Purchase Robinson, First Negro in Modern Major League Baseball

ROYALS' STAR SIGNS WITH BROOKS TODAY

International League Batting Champion Will Bid for Job in Big League Infield

MONTREAL TRIPS DODGERS

Lund and Campanis Hit 2-Run Homers Against Branca in Fourth for 4-3 Triumph

By LOUIS EFFRAT

Jackie Robinson, 28-year-old infielder, yesterday became the first Negro to achieve major-league baseball status in modern times. His contract was purchased from the Montreal Royals of the International League by the Dodgers and he will be in a Brooklyn uniform at Ebbets Field today, when the Brooks oppose the Yankees in the first of three exhibition games over the week-end.

A native of Georgia, Robinson won fame in baseball, football, basketball and track at the University of California at Los Angeles before entering the armed service as a private. He emerged a lieutenant in 1945 and in October of that year was signed to a Montreal contract. Robinson's performances in the International League, which he led in batting last season with an average of .349, prompted President Branch Rickey of the Dodgers to promote Jackie.

The decision was made while Robinson was playing first base for Montreal against the Dodgers at Ebbets Field. Jackie was blanked at the plate and contributed little to his team's 4-3 victory before 14,282 fans, but it was nevertheless, a history-making day for the well-proportioned lad.

An Inopportune Moment

Jackie had just popped into a double-play, attempting to bunt in the fifth inning, when Arthur Mann, assistant to Rickey, appeared in the press box. He handed out a brief, typed announcement: "The Brooklyn Dodgers today purchased the contract of Jackie Rosevelt Robinson from the Montreal Royals."

Robinson will appear at the Brooklyn offices this morning to sign a contract. Rickey does not anticipate any difficulty over terms.

According to the records, the last Negro to play in the majors was one Moses Fleetwood Walker, who caught for Toledo of the American Association when that circuit enjoyed major-league classification back in 1884.

The call for Robinson was no surprise. Most baseball persons had been expecting it. After all, he had proved his right to the opportunity by his extraordinary work in the AAA minor league, where he stole 40 bases and was the best defensive second baseman. He sparked the Royals to the pennant and the team went on to annex the little world series.

Robinson's path in the immediate future may not be too smooth, however. He may run into antipathy from Southerners who form about 60 per cent of the league's playing strength. In fact, it is rumored that a number of Dodgers expressed themselves unhappy at the possibility of having to play with Jackie.

Robinson Is "Thrilled"

Jackie, himself, expects no trouble. He said he was "thrilled and it's what I've been waiting for." When his Montreal mates congratulated him and wished him luck, Robinson answered: "Thanks, I'll need it."

Whether Robinson will be used at first or second base is not known. That will depend upon the new manager, yet to be named by Rickey.

Rickey, in answer to a direct query, declared he did not expect trouble from other players, because of Robinson. "We are all agreed," he said, "that Jackie is ready for the chance."

Several thousand Negroes were in the stands at yesterday's exhibition. When Robinson appeared for batting practice, he drew a warm and pleasant reception. Dixie Walker, quoted in 1945 as opposed to playing with Jackie, was booed on his first turn at bat. Walker answered with a resounding single.

If, however, Robinson is to make the grade, he will have to do better than he did against the Brooks. Against Ralph Branca, Jackie rolled meekly to the mound, walked and then popped an intended sacrifice bunt into a double play. At first base—a new position for him —he handled himself flawlessly, but did not have a difficult chance.

Six Hits for Each Club

The biggest crowd to watch the Dodgers this spring saw the Brooks, under Clyde Sukeforth (he's the pro tem manager, Rickey said), go down to defeat before the sound pitching of Ervin Palica and Jack Banta, who combined for a six-hit effort. The Royals collected the same number of safeties against Branca, Hank Behrman and Lefty Paul Minner, but two were round-trippers.

The homers, both in the fourth inning at the expense of Branca, accounted for all the Montreal runs. After Robinson had walked and Jack Jorgensen had flied out, Don Lund blasted a liner into the lower left-field stand. Then a pass to Earl Naylor and a longer four-bagger to left center by Al Campanis made it 4—0.

The Dodgers retrieved two runs in the same stanza. Walker walked and Duke Snider doubled to center. Walker tallied and when Lou We-

THE DODGERS ACQUIRE A NEW INFIELDER

Jackie Robinson being congratulated by Clay Hopper, manager of the Montreal Royals, at Ebbets Field yesterday after it was announced that the Brooklyn club had purchased the Negro from its farm team.

Associated Press

laj, Montreal shortstop, threw wild on the relay, Snider went all the way arour 1. A walk to Stan Rojek and Gene Hermanski's double netted the last Brooklyn run in the seventh.

While Lund's and Campanis' round-trippers were well tagged, both would have been caught last year. The walls are fourteen feet closer to home plate this season.

"I'm for Robinson" buttons were sold outside the park.

The box score:

MONTREAL

	ab.	r.	h.	po.	a.	e.
Welaj, ss	3	0	0	2	1	1
Rob'son, 1b	3	1	0	7	0	0
Jorg'sen, 3b	4	0	1	0	1	0
Lund, rf	3	1	1	1	0	0
Naylor, cf	3	1	1	3	0	0
Pluss, lf	2	0	1	1	1	0
C'panis, 2b	4	1	1	3	3	0
Sandlock, c	2	0	0	7	0	0
C'p'an'la, c	1	0	0	3	1	0
Palica, p	2	0	1	0	0	0
aShuba	1	0	0	0	0	0
Banta, p	1	0	0	0	3	0
Total	29	4	6	27	10	1

DODGERS (N.)

	ab.	r.	h.	po.	a.	e.
Stanky, 2b	3	0	0	3	2	0
Mauch, 2b	2	0	0	0	2	0
Lav'g'to, 3b	2	0	0	3	1	0
Rojek, 3b	1	1	0	1	0	0
Herm'ki, lf	5	0	2	5	0	0
Walker, rf	2	1	1	1	0	0
Woyt, rf	1	0	0	0	0	0
Snider, cf	4	1	2	0	0	0
Stevens, 1b	1	0	0	8	0	0
cTatum	0	0	0	0	0	0
Schultz, 1b	0	0	0	0	0	0
Miksis, ss	2	0	0	3	3	0
Bragan, c	3	0	0	2	2	0
dReiser	0	0	0	0	0	0
Anderson, c	0	0	0	1	0	0
Branca, p	2	0	0	0	2	0
bWhitman	1	0	0	0	0	0
Behrman, p	0	0	0	0	0	0
eVaughan	1	0	1	0	0	0
Minner, p	0	0	0	0	1	1
Total	30	3	6	27	13	1

aGrounded out for Palica in seventh.
bFanned for Branca in seventh.
cRan for Stevens in eighth.
dWalked for Bragan in eighth.
eSingled for Behrman in eighth.

Montreal	000	400	000	—4
Brooklyn	000	200	100	—3

Runs batted in—Lund 2, Campanis 2, Snider, Hermanski.

Two-base hits—Hermanski 2, Snider, Jorgensen. Home runs—Lund, Campanis. Sacrifices—Miksis, Pluss. Double plays—Lavagetto and Miksis; Mauch, Miksis and Stevens; Banta, Campanella and Robinson. Left on bases—Montreal 5, Brooklyn 10. Bases on balls—Off Palica 4, Branca 6, Banta 4. Struck out—By Palica 6, Branca 2, Banta 3, Minner 1. Hits—Off Palica 4 in 6 innings, Banta 2 in 3, Branca 4 in 7, Behrman 1 in 1, Minner 1 in 1. Winning pitcher—Palica. Losing pitcher—Branca. Umpires—Tabachi and Goetz. Time of game—2:20. Attendance—14,282.

April 11, 1947

Says Cards' Strike Plan Against Negro Dropped

Ford Frick, National League president, said last nig a threatened strike by the St. Louis Cardinals against the presence of Negro First Baseman Jackie Robinson in a Brooklyn Dodger uniform has been averted, The Associated Press reported.

Frick said that Sam Breadon, owner of the Cardinals, came to New York last week and informed him that he understood there was a movement among the Cardinals to strike in protest during their just-concluded series with the Dodgers if Robinson was in the line-up.

"I didn't have to talk to the players myself. Mr. Breadon did the talking to them. From what Breadon told me afterward the trouble was smoothed over. I don't know what he said to them, who the ringleader was, or any other details," Frick said.

Asked if he intended to take any action, Frick said he would have to investigate further before he could make any decision.

The National League president said he had not conferred with Baseball Commissioner A. B. (Happy) Chandler concerning the matter.

May 9, 1947

SENIOR LOOP BOWS AT CHICAGO BY 2-1

Doerr Scores Winning Run for American Circuit on Pinch Single by Spence in 7th

MIZE DRIVES FOUR-BAGGER

Solves Shea to Give Nationals Lead—Blackwell, Newhouser Excel—41,123 at Game

By JOHN DREBINGER

Special to The New York Times.

CHICAGO, July 8—In picturesque Wrigley Field today the American League demonstrated once again that, when it comes to grappling with its rival loop in baseball's annual midsummer classic, it still knows how to play the winning hand.

Jarred for a thundering home run by big Jawn Mize in the fourth inning, Joe Cronin's cohorts contrived to keep the National League's vaunted newborn power tightly throttled he rest of the way and then came on to win the 1947 All-Star game, 2 to 1.

The victory, acclaimed by a gathering of 41,123, marked the tenth triumph for the junior loop in the fourteen games played since 1933. The net receipts were $105,-314.90. Of this amount, seventy-five per cent will go to the players' pension fund.

Four hurlers, starting with Hal Newhouser and continuing with Frank Shea, Walter Masterson and Joe Page, went to the mound in the American League's determined effort to hold in check the high-powered offensive which the senior loop had marshaled under the direction of Eddie Dyer.

With the exception of one pitch by the Yankees' Shea which Mize, the mighty mauler of the Giants, bashed for a resounding circuit blow with the bases empty, this quartet succeeded admirably. In all, the four yielded only five hits, Mize getting another when he singled to keep a despairing National rally alive in the eighth.

At that, victory did not come to the American Leaguers as easily as it did in other years. For the Nationals tossed some pretty fair pitching into this fray, too.

Slams Into Double Play

Ewell Blackwell handcuffed the Americans for the first three innings and for two more Harry Brechenn, hero of last October's world series, continued the good work. But in the sixth, Harry the Cat skidded momentarily and let in the tying run.

It came on a pair of singles by Luke Appling and Ted Williams, with Joe DiMaggio rather inelegantly pushing the tally across while slamming into a double play.

In the seventh Cronin's men jammed through what eventually proved the decisive tally when the Nationals again momentarily let down their guard.

The decisive push started when, with one down, Bobby Doerr cracked a single into left off Johnny Sain and stole second on Brooklyn's catcher, Bruce Edwards who, along with two other Dodgers, Peewee Reese and Eddie Stanky, had just entered the game.

Sain, though he succeeded in striking out Buddy Rosar, made two sad mistakes. Trying to trap Doerr off second, the Braves' right-hander succeeded only in hitting the runner and as the ball trickled out into center field, Doerr raced on to third.

Two Sweeping Strikes

Then, facing Stan Spence, who here entered as pinch hitter for the retiring Shea, Sain curved over two sweeping strikes. But with the count "two and nothing" on the batter, Johnny now tossed up a rather fat pitch which the Washington outfielder promptly whacked into center field for a single.

It scored Doerr easily and that, despite no end of huffing and puffing by the Nationals in the two closing rounds, decided the ball game.

There was a cloudless sky overhead and a cooling breeze blowing in off Lake Michigan as the battle got under way. The breeze made the temperature just right although it didn't augur well for the long-range clouters, particularly the right-handed swingers who had to drive their shots directly into it.

Following the customary round of perfunctory cheers and jeers that greeted the announcement that baseball's high commissioner, A. B. (Happy) Chandler, would toss out the first ball, the crowd lost no time making it clear that its sympathies were dominantly National League.

Not For South Siders

This may seem surprising inasmuch as Chicago is a two-league city. But it must be held in mind that this game was played in the National League end of the town and there are South Side fans who would sooner jump in the lake than travel north for a ball game unless the White Sox were involved.

With the exception of the two National League players, Eddie Miller and Bob Elliott, who had been withdrawn because of injuries, each side started the top performers who had been chosen in the nationwide poll of fans, although the American made a last-minute shift in its pitching plans. On being told that Spud Chandler's arm did not feel up to the mark, Manager Cronin eliminated the veteran Yankee right-hander and elected to start Detroit's ace southpaw, Newhouser.

Cincinnati's brilliant young right-hander, Blackwell, and the Tiger mound luminary immediately put on a dazzling show of pitching mastery as they swept through the first three innings which, under the rules, was all they were allowed to go. Each yielded one single. Not another batter got on base.

All-Star Box Score

AMERICAN LEAGUE

	ab.	r.	h.	po.	a.	e.
Kell, Detroit, 3b	4	0	0	0	0	0
Johnson, N. Y., 3b	0	0	0	0	0	0
Lewis, Wash., rf	2	0	0	1	0	0
aAppling, Chicago	1	1	1	0	0	0
Henrich, N. Y., rf	1	0	0	3	0	0
Williams, Boston, lf	4	0	2	3	0	0
DiMaggio, N. Y., cf	3	0	1	1	0	0
Boudreau, Cleve., ss	4	0	1	4	4	0
McQuinn, N. Y., 1b	4	0	0	9	1	0
Gordon, Cleve., 2b	2	0	1	0	4	0
Doerr, Boston, 2b	2	1	1	0	2	0
Rosar, Phila., c	4	0	0	6	0	0
Newhouser, Det., p	1	0	0	0	0	0
Shea, N. Y., p	1	0	0	0	0	0
bSpence, Wash.	1	0	1	0	0	0
Masterson, Wash., p	0	0	0	0	0	0
Page, N. Y., p	0	0	0	0	0	0
Total	34	2	8	27	11	0

NATIONAL LEAGUE

	ab.	r.	h.	po.	a.	e.
H. Walker, Phila., cf	2	0	0	1	0	0
Pafko, Chicago, cf	2	0	1	2	0	0
F. Walker, Bklyn., rf	2	0	0	2	0	0
Marshall, N. Y., rf	1	0	0	3	0	0
Cooper, N. Y., c	3	0	0	6	0	0
Edwards, Bklyn., c	0	0	0	2	0	0
Cavarretta, Chi., 1b	1	0	0	1	0	0
Mize, N. Y., 1b	3	1	2	8	0	0
Masi, Boston, c	0	0	0	0	0	0
Slaughter, St. L., lf	3	0	0	0	0	0
Gustine, Pitts., 3b	2	0	0	0	2	0
Kurowski, St. L., 3b	2	0	0	0	1	0
Marion, St. Louis, ss	2	0	1	0	1	0
Reese, Bklyn., ss	1	0	0	0	2	0
Verban, Phila., 2b	2	0	0	0	0	0
Stanky, Bklyn., 2b	2	0	0	2	2	0
Blackwell, Cin., p	0	0	0	0	0	0
cHaas, Cincinnati	1	0	1	0	0	0
Brecheen, St. L., p	1	0	0	0	1	0
Sain, Boston, p	0	0	0	0	0	1
dMusial, St. Louis	1	0	0	0	0	0
Spahn, Boston, p	0	0	0	0	0	0
eRowe, Phila.	1	0	0	0	0	0
Total	32	1	5	27	9	1

aSingled for Lewis in Sixth.
bSingled for Shea in seventh.
cSingled for Blackwell in third.
dGrounded out for Sain in seventh.
eFlied out for Spahn in ninth.

Americans	000	001	100	—2
Nationals	000	100	000	—1

Runs batted in—Mize, Spence.

Two Base Hits—Williams, Gordon. Home run—Mize. Stolen base—Doerr. Double Play—Reese, Stanky, and Mize. Earned runs—Americans 1, Nationals 1. Left on bases—Americans 6, Nationals 8. Bases on balls—Off Shea 2 (Slaughter, Mize), Spahn 1 (DiMaggio), Masterson 1 (Marshall), Page 1 (Reese). Struck out—By Blackwell 4 (Kell, Williams, Boudreau, Gordon), Newhouser, 2 (Cooper, H. Walker), Brecheen 2 (McQuinn, Kell), Shea 2 (Marshall, Kurowski), Sain 1 (Rosar), Masterson 2 (Reese, Cavarretta), Spahn 1 (Henrich).

Pitching Summary—Off Blackwell, no runs, 1 hit in 3 innings; Brecheen, 1 run, 5 hits in 3; Sain, 1 run, 2 hits in 1; Spahn, no runs, no hits in 2. Newhouser, no runs, 1 hit in 3; Shea, 1 run, 3 hits in 3; Masterson, no runs, no hits in 1-2/3; Page, no runs, 1 hit in 1-1/3. Wild Pitch – Blackwell. Passed ball—Cooper. Winning pitcher—Shea. Losing pitcher—Sain.

Umpires—Conlan (N. L.), Plate—3b; Boyer (A. L.), 1b-2b; Henline (N. L.), 2b-1b; Passarella (A. L.), 3b-Plate. Time of game—2:19. Attendance—41,123. Net receipts—$105,314.90.

The Nationals, though directed by Dyer, didn't bother to use the famed "overshift defense" against Williams in the first inning. It really made no difference, for Blackwell, after fanning George Kell and retiring Buddy Lewis on a grounder to Mize, slipped a third strike over on Thumping Theodore that produced deafening cheers.

DiMaggio Reaches Third

To DiMaggio went the distinction of coming up with the first hit of the afternoon, a ringing single to center that opened the second for the American League. The Yankee Clipper advanced to third on two surprising battery slips, a passed ball by the Giants' star catcher, Walker Cooper, and a wild pitch.

But Blackwell appeared oblivious to all this. He fanned Lou Boudreau, retired George McQuinn on a fly to Slaughter in left, which came before DiMaggio had reached third, and Joe Gordon also went down a victim on strikes.

Newhouser, however, was no less effective, although he registered only two strikeouts to Blackwell's four. He retired eight National Leaguers in a row to make it two down in the last of the third before Bert Haas, pinch-hitting for Blackwell, hammered a single into left for the first and only blow off the Detroit lefty.

There was a boisterous ovation for both hurlers as they left the field for the gathering by now was in an expansive mood and cheered most everybody.

Earlier there had been some very hearty applause for Emil Verban, the Philly second sacker who, with his manager, Ben Chapman, had been badly shaken up in a train crack-up last night. Verban felt sufficiently recovered to start as scheduled at second base while Chapman likewise ignored his bruises and, as aide to Dyer, alternated with the Giants' Mel Ott in coaching on the base lines.

With the Cardinals' left-handed Brecheen and the Yankees' freshman star, Shea, taking over the pitching for the next three innings, things began to pick up and for a few minutes it looked as though the American Leaguers would come up with the first run.

For with one down in the fourth, Williams this time lashed a double down the right-field foul line and though DiMaggio grounded to Frankie Gustine at third, Boudreau got a scratch single in the same sector that put Williams on third. Brecheen, however, craftily whiffed McQuinn for the third out and so it remained for the National Leaguers to strike the first telling blow.

It fell in the fourth when, with two out and the bases empty, Mize, author of twenty-four home runs in the senior loop this season, put the full weight of his powerful frame into one of Shea's swift pitches. The ball went soaring into the teeth of the spanking breeze and

into the right-field bleachers. The National Leaguers were jubilant.

But in the sixth came ominous sounds as Appling, veteran White Sox shortstop, went in to pinch hit for Lewis. He singled sharply to left and a moment later was on third when Williams, with the Nationals still disdaining to indulge in any overshifting of their inner defense, larruped a single into right.

Scores Tying Marker

Brecheen definitely was now in a tight spot and though he righted himself in time to induce DiMaggio to slap into a double play by way of Reese to Stanky to Mize, Appling scored and the battle was deadlocked.

In the next round the Americans unlocked it at the expense of Sain, and although Johnny's Boston colleague, the left-handed Warren Spahn, then came on to continue the fine pitching in the eighth and ninth, the mischief had been done. There was nothing the Nationals could do to offset Doerr's damaging steal and Spence's pinch single in the seventh. In all the Americans collected eight hits.

There were still a few thrills for the crowd, however. Masterson, after retiring three Nationals in the seventh, had two out in the eighth and only Willard Marshall on first, the result of a pass, when Cronin elected to do a bit of extra, superfine masterminding that nearly backfired.

Cronin called on the Yankees' left-hander, Joe Page, to oppose the highly respected Mize and it almost upset the cart. For Mize rammed a single into right that swept Marshall around to third.

But Page was determined not to blow this hard-earned triumph for the junior loop. He retired Enos Slaughter on a grounder for the third out and the rest was pretty smooth sailing. The Yankee southpaw walked Reese with one out in the ninth, but a sharp fielding play by Doerr, who collared Stanky's grounder and executed a fine force play at second, lent a helping hand here.

Then Schoolboy Rowe, another Philly survivor of last night's train wreck, came up to pinch hit for Spahn and hit a high, twisting fly that for a moment threatened to drop safe in right. But the Yanks had one more star in this combat. Tommy Henrich, entering in the late innings, followed the ball's windblown gyrations and finally caught it for the final out.

Only at one other stage had the Nationals threatened to break through. That came in the fifth when Marty Marion singled and presently Andy Pafko's line hit fell for a single in center, DiMaggio slightly misjudging the ball and coming up to it too late. But Shea here fanned the Giants' Marshall for the third out.

July 9, 1947

ROBINSON 'ROOKIE OF YEAR'

Sporting News Honors Dodgers' Negro for 'Team Value'

ST. LOUIS, Sept. 12 (AP) — Jackie Robinson, the Brooklyn Dodgers' 28-year-old Negro first baseman, received The Sporting News rookie of the year award to-day.

The choice of Robinson, described by editor J. G. Taylor Spink as "spectacularly outstanding," was on the basis of "stark baseball values," the baseball weekly said.

"Robinson was rated and examined solely as a freshman player in the big leagues—on the basis of his hitting, his running, his defensive play, his team value," Spink wrote. "The sociological experiment that Robinson represented, the trail-blazing he did, the barriers he broke down did not enter into the decision."

Robinson joined the Dodgers last April from Montreal. He has laid down 42 successful bunts, 14 of them beaten out for hits and 28 sacrifices. His stolen base total is 25 and he has hit 10 home runs. He ran his batting average up to .317 in June when he exhibited a 21-game hitting streak, dropped to .253 in July and during August hit at a .311 clip. His present average is .297.

September 13, 1947

DODGERS' ONLY HIT BEATS YANKEES, 3-2, WITH 2 OUT IN NINTH

Lavagetto's Pinch Double Bats in 2 Runs, Evens Series and Spoils Bevens' No-Hitter

---

10 WALKS HELP BROOKLYN

Casey Wins in Relief Second Day in Row With Lone Pitch Resulting in Double Play

---

By JOHN DREBINGER

With the first no-hitter in world series history in the making at Ebbets Field yesterday, Cookie Lavagetto rewrote the script with two out in the ninth inning to establish the Dodgers as the first club in baseball's autumnal classic ever to win a game on just one hit.

In his familiar role of pinch hitter, the veteran Lavagetto slammed a two-bagger off the right-field wall against Floyd (Bill) Bevens that drove in two runners put on by walks. That floored the Yankees on the spot for a 3-to-2 Brooklyn triumph, tied the series at two victories apiece, stunned about half the crowd of 33,443 and sent the other half—the faithful of Flatbush—screaming hysterically on to the field in an endeavor to lay fond hands on their hero.

Bevens, stalwart right-hander, was within one short stride of baseball immortality until he lost all in the twinkling of an eye to Burt Shotton's unpredictable Dodgers.

For eight and two-thirds innings of this nerve-tingling fourth game Bevens, a strong, silent man from Salem, Ore., held the bats of Brooklyn's Bums even more silent than a tomb. No series pitcher ever had gone that far without allowing a hit.

An Unenviable Record

On the way, Bevens established another world series mark, though he will never reflect upon that one in his later years with any feeling of gratification. He gave ten bases on balls, one more than Colby Jack Coombs of the Athletics permitted in 1910.

Two of those passes helped the Dodgers to their first run in the fifth inning to whittle away one of two tallies the Yanks had counted earlier. And the final two were indirectly to cause his defeat, though the last one was not wholly of his choosing. It was ordered by Manager Bucky Harris, who by that decision left himself open to sharp criticism. Most observers seemed to feel the usually astute Yankee skipper had pulled something of a strategic "rock."

As the final half of the ninth opened, with the Bombers leading, 2 to 1, Bruce Edwards went out when Johnny Lindell hauled down his lofty shot in front of the left-field stand with a leaping catch. But Carl Furillo walked for Bevens' ninth pass before Shotton fairly sprayed the summery afternoon with a maze of masterminding.

Jorgensen Fouls Out

After Spider Jorgensen had fouled out to George McQuinn back

Gionfriddo stealing second in ninth inning as Rizzuto takes Berra's throw. Pinelli is the umpire.

of first, Shotton sent Al Gionfriddo, rookie outfielder, to run for Furillo. Only one more batter need be retired then to clinch the victory for Bevens as well as that world series no-hit goal which has eluded some of baseball's greatest hurlers since 1903.

The batter was Pete Reiser, whom Shotton sent up for Hugh Casey, relief ace who had entered the contest in the top half of the ninth with the bases full and one out to end the inning on one pitch. Pistol Pete, limping painfully on a swollen ankle which he had sprained the previous day, had sat this one out up to that moment.

Shotton's strategy flashed again with one strike and two balls on Reiser as Gionfriddo streaked for second and stole the bag on an eyelash play. That pitch, too, was wide, making the count three and one.

There Harris made his questionable move. He ordered Bevens to toss the next one wide, thereby walking the lame Reiser. It seemed a direct violation of one of baseball's fundamental precepts which dictates against putting the "winning run" on base in such a situation.

Shotton followed with two more moves on the field, which seemed suddenly converted into a chessboard. He sent Eddie Miksis in to run for Reiser, an obvious shift,

and then called on Lavagetto to bat for Ed Stanky.

The swarthy-complexioned veteran, a right-handed batter, swung viciously at the first pitch and missed. Then he swung again and connected, the ball sailing toward the right-field wall.

Over raced Tommy Henrich. The previous inning the brilliant Yankee gardener had made a glittering leaping catch of a similar fly ball to rob Gene Hermanski of a blow and keep the no-hitter alive.

There was nothing Tommy could do about this one, though it soared over his head and struck the wall. Desperately he tried to clutch the ball as it caromed off the boards in order to get it home as quickly as possible, but that sloping wall is a tricky barrier and as the ball bounced to the ground more precious moments were lost.

Finally Henrich hurried the ball on its way. McQuinn caught it and relayed it to the plate, but all too late. Gionfriddo and Miksis already were over the plate while in the center of the diamond Dodger players and fans were all but mobbing Lavagetto in their elation.

First to Lose One-Hitter

While that was going on Bevens, the silent man from the northwest, was walking silently from the field. In a matter of seconds a priceless no-hit victory had been wrenched from his grasp and converted into a galling one-hit defeat. Only two other pitchers had tossed world series one-hitters before with both, of course, winning. They were Ed

Reulbach of the Cubs in 1906 and Claude Passeau, a later day Cub, in 1945.

Big Casey, relief pitcher who had won for the Flock in that stirring 9-8 game the previous day, also was returned the winner of this one, though he pitched only one ball. The Flock was still behind when he went in and under the rules he automatically became the victor, the first pitcher in world series history to take two games on successive days.

Huge Hughey entered the struggle when Hank Behrman, third of Shotton's hurlers in this extraordinary conflict, got into trouble. A single by Lindell, a belated throw to second by Edwards on Bevens' sacrifice and a single by George Stirnweiss filled the bases with one out in the ninth.

Casey Replaces Behrman

Casey replaced Behrman. Henrich slapped his first pitch right back into Casey's hands. Hughey fired to Catcher Edwards at the plate for one out and Edwards winged to Jackie Robinson at first for the double play.

That inning, too, was typical of the Yanks' play throughout. Actually they lost by wasting myriad chances to sew it up decisively. In the opening round, Harry Taylor, an experimental starter for the Dodgers, offered to roll up the series on the spot for the Bombers when he faced only four batters and forced in a run with a walk.

That tally was all the Yanks made out of their flying start. They didn't get another until the

fourth when Bill Johnson cracked Hal Gregg for a triple to open the inning and Lindell followed with a double. They never did get another with Gregg pitching brilliantly from the first through the seventh and though they totaled eight blows they lost when their hurler allowed only one.

The Yanks started as if they meant to annihilate the Dodgers piecemeal and mesh the parts into the Gowanus. The opportunity lay before them to tear the game wide open as the youthful Taylor, carrying for the moment Shotton's despairing hopes, faced four batters and got none out, although he would have retired one except for a misplay.

Rookie Sensation Fails

Taylor had been one of the rookie sensations of the National League, winning ten and losing five until he tore a tendon in his right elbow in the process of beating the Cardinals. Handsome Harry, however, simply had nothing to carry into this combat beyond the best wishes of the Flatbush faithful and about the only mystifying feature was the fact that the Brooks' board of strategy never became aware of that until he started laboring on the mound.

Stirnweiss greeted Taylor's first pitch with a sharp single into left field. Henrich allowed the count to reach two and two before he smacked a single into center, Snuffy holding up at second.

Then followed a play that might have helped Taylor over the rough spot but instead put him deeper in the hole. Larry Berra, back behind the plate as the Yanks' starting catcher, slapped a grounder to Robinson. Jackie fired the ball to Reese for a force play on Henrich, but Peewee dropped the throw.

The error filled the bases so that Taylor, within a few minutes of the start, was up to his elbows in trouble. Moreover, he was confronted by the wholly uninviting situation of facing Joe DiMaggio with the bases full and nobody out.

At that, it is quite possible he did about the best circumstances would permit. He tossed four wide pitches for a base on balls and while that forced in a run it could have been a lot worse.

With that walk Taylor was asked to walk out himself under orders from the bench, and Gregg, who had started warming up on

Series Box Score

FOURTH GAME
NEW YORK YANKEES

	AB.	R.	H.	PO.	A.	E.
Stirnweiss, 2b	4	1	2	2	1	0
Henrich, rf	5	0	1	2	0	0
Berra, c	4	0	0	6	1	1
DiMaggio, cf	2	0	0	2	0	0
McQuinn, 1b	4	0	1	7	0	0
Johnson, 3b	4	1	1	3	2	0
Lindell, lf	3	0	2	3	0	0
Rizzuto, ss	4	0	1	1	2	0
Bevens, p	3	0	0	0	1	0
Total	33	2	8	*26	7	1

BROOKLYN DODGERS

	AB.	R.	H.	PO.	A.	E.
Stanky, 2b	1	0	0	2	3	0
eLavagetto	1	0	1	0	0	0
Reese, ss	4	0	0	3	5	1
Robinson, 1b	4	0	0	11	1	0
Walker, rf	2	0	0	1	0	0
Hermanski, lf	4	0	0	2	0	0
Edwards, c	4	0	0	7	1	1
Furillo, cf	3	0	0	2	0	0
bGionfriddo	0	1	0	0	0	0
Jorgensen, 3b	2	1	0	0	1	1
Taylor, p	0	0	0	0	1	0
Gregg, p	1	0	0	0	1	0
aVaughan	0	0	0	0	0	0
Behrman, p	0	0	0	0	1	0
Casey, p	0	0	0	0	1	0
cReiser	0	0	0	0	0	0
dMiksis	0	1	0	0	0	0
Total	26	3	1	27	15	3

*Two out when winning run scored.
aWalked for Gregg in seventh.
bRan for Furillo in ninth.
cWalked for Casey in ninth.
dRan for Reiser in ninth.
eDoubled for Stanky in ninth.

New York ...... 1 0 0 1 0 0 0 0 0—2
Brooklyn .... 0 0 0 0 1 0 0 0 2—3

Runs batted in—DiMaggio, Lindell, Reese, Lavagetto 2.

Two-base hits—Lindell, Lavagetto. Three-base hit—Johnson. Stolen bases—Rizzuto, Reese, Gionfriddo. Sacrifices—Stanky, Bevens. Double plays—Reese, Stanky and Robinson; Gregg, Reese and Robinson; Casey, Edwards and Robinson. Earned runs—New York 1, Brooklyn 3. Left on bases—New York 9, Brooklyn 8. Bases on balls—Off Taylor 1 (DiMaggio), Gregg 3 (DiMaggio, Lindell, Stirnweiss), Bevens 10 (Stanky 2, Walker 2, Jorgensen 2, Gregg, Vaughan, Furillo, Reiser). Struck out—By Gregg 5 (Stirnweiss 2, Henrich, McQuinn, Bevens), Bevens 5 (Edwards 3, Gregg, Robinson).

Pitching summary—Off Taylor 1 run, 2 hits in 0 innings (none out in first); Gregg 1 run, 2 hits in 7; Behrman 0 runs, 2 hits in 1 1-3; Casey 0 runs, 0 hits in 2-3. Wild pitch—Bevens. Winning pitcher—Casey.

Umpires—Goetz (NL), plate; McGowan (AL), first base; Pinelli (NL), second base; Rommel (AL), third base; Boyer (AL), left field; Magerkurth (NL), right field. Time of game—2:20. Attendance—33,443.

Taylor's third pitch, took over. McQuinn popped to Reese for the first out and a moment later Johnson slapped a grounder at Reese. In a flash, Peewee, Stanky and Robinson completed one of their gilt-edged double plays.

One run was all the vaunted Bombers extracted from that wide open position and in the third they blew another opportunity. With two down, DiMaggio drew his second pass and McQuinn tapped a ball in front of the plate. Edwards grabbed it and when his fast peg shot wide of first to bounce off the temporary boxes running down the right-field side, DiMaggio and McQuinn tore around the bases.

Rounding third, DiMaggio was waved on by the usually coldly calculating Coach Chuck Dressen, who miscued this time. Out in right Dixie Walker, who otherwise played an inconspicuous role, collared the ball and fired it to the plate in ample time for the third out.

Behrman Gives Two Hits

After the extra-base blows by Johnson and Lindell in the fourth, the Yanks got no more hits until the ninth. Then Behrman, who had started pitching in the eighth, gave up two.

In the meantime Bevens was weaving in and out of trouble, but only because of the endless walks he kept serving up. Only a few fine plays were needed to help him, so invincible was his stuff. Lindell made a miraculous diving catch of a foul fly off Robinson in the third and DiMaggio faded way back to haul down a shot in dead center by Hermanski in the fourth.

Bevens walked two in the first, one in the second and another in the third, to which he added a wild pitch. When he passed two in the fifth, they led to the Dodgers' first tally.

Jorgensen received the first of those to open the round and Gregg followed with the next. Stanky sacrificed the runners to second and third and on Reese's grounder to Phil Rizzuto, which resulted in Gregg being tossed out at third on a fielder's choice, Jorgensen counted.

Bevens walked one in the sixth and one in the seventh. Not until the eighth, which Henrich ended with his great catch off Hermanski, did big Bill pitch a perfect inning. Then he walked two more in the ninth, inviting disaster just once too often. He opened four of the nine innings with passes.

So this most amazing series, starting as a gay jaunt for the Yanks, threatens to develop into a real dog fight that must return to the Yankee Stadium for final decision after today's fifth game at Ebbets Field. Frank Shea, who won the opener for the Bombers, though he tossed only five innings, is slated to make his second start today. Viv Lombardi, mite southpaw whom the American Leaguers belted out in the second game, is Shotton's mound choice.

October 4, 1947

DODGERS SET BACK YANKEES BY 8 TO 6 FOR 3-3 SERIES TIE

Rout Page With Four in Sixth to Win Before 74,065, New Crowd Mark for Classic

38 PLAYERS IN THE GAME

Gionfriddo's Great Catch of DiMaggio's Drive Prevents Losers From Tying Score

By JOHN DREBINGER

Incredible as it may seem to a bewildered world at large, the 1947 world series is still with us, and so are the Dodgers.

For in one of the most extraordinary games ever played, one that left a record series crowd of 74,065 limp and exhausted, Burt Shotton's unpredictable Flock fought the Yankees in a last-ditch stand at the Stadium yesterday and defeated them, 8 to 6.

As a consequence, the classic, which in this same park last Tuesday had started as a soft touch for Bucky Harris' American League champions, now stands tied at three victories apiece. The seventh and deciding game will be played at the Stadium today.

It was a conflict that lasted three hours and nineteen minutes, the longest on record for nine innings in a world series. Had it gone into an extra inning, another series precedent would have been set, as permission had been obtained to turn on the floodlights.

As for the gathering, which had shelled out record gross receipts of $393,210, it was to thrill to a show that scarcely left a moment's breathing spell. The Yanks tossed twenty-one players into the fray, six of them hurlers, while the battling Bums countered with seventeen, four of them flingers, the last of all being the astounding Hugh Casey.

The game also was marked by one of the greatest catches in series history—Al Gionfriddo's collaring of Joe DiMaggio's 415-foot drive in the sixth inning.

The fans saw the aroused Dodgers fighting to keep the series alive, rout Allie Reynolds inside of three

rounds, getting two runs in the first and two in the third. It saw the Bombers roar back in the lower half of the third to blast Vic Lombardi from the mound with a four-run demonstration.

The Yanks added one more tally off Ralph Branca in the fourth to take a 5-4 lead, while the Bums screamed to the high heavens that the umpires were blind in calling Yogi Berra's single down the right-field foul line a fair ball.

This was not a patch to what followed as the Flock, in the sixth, crushed the incomparable Yankee relief hurler. Joe Page, with a withering four-run attack, a single by Peewee Reese off Bobo Newsom driving in the final pair.

In the lower half of the same round the crowd was to witness the Bombers come within an eyelash of tying the score again. With two on, DiMaggio sent a tremendous smash in the direction of the left-field bullpen only to see Gionfriddo, a rookie outfielder, rob Jolting Joe of his greatest moment.

Dashing almost blindly to the spot where he thought the ball would land and turning around at the last moment, the 25-year-old gardener, who had been merely tossed as an "extra" into the deal that shipped Kirby Higbe to the Pirates earlier this year, leaned far over the bullpen railing and, with his gloved hand, collared the ball.

It was a breathtaking catch for the third out of the inning. It stunned the proud Bombers and jarred even the usually imperturbable DiMaggio. Taking his position in center field with the start of the next inning, he was still walking inconsolably in circles, doubtless wondering whether he could believe his senses.

Casey Takes the Mound

And then came the last of the ninth when the Yanks, still three runs in arrears, sought desperately to make their last-ditch stand. Joe Hatten, the southpaw who had come in for the Flock in the sixth, had managed to squirm out of one difficulty when the Bombers filled the bases in the seventh. However, when Bill Johnson opened the Yankee ninth with a single and George McQuinn walked, big Casey came out of that left-field bullpen to make his fifth appearance in the series.

Casey retired Phil Rizzuto on a fly to center, but Aaron Robinson plunked a single into left, filling the bases, and the already exhausted fans rallied once more to this last dramatic surge. Lonnie Frey, pinch-hitting, grounded to Jackie Robinson, who threw to second for a force play while Johnson scored.

The tying runs were still on base, but they never got any farther. Casey in person handled George Stirnweiss' feeble grounder to the mound, tossed the ball to Jackie Robinson and the epic struggle was over.

The Yankees, setting a series record with their twenty-one players and tying another with their six pitchers, had amassed fifteen hits. But they left thirteen men stranded on the bases, one short of the record, and this is where they left the battle. The southpaw Page, who had saved and won so many games for them this year, failed them at a most vital moment to become the losing pitcher.

Another casualty was Johnny Lindell who, after getting two singles, had to leave the field when it was discovered he was suffering from a fractured rib. That forced Harris, who had started so confidently with Sherman Lollar behind the plate and the rookie Jack Phillips on first, to throw in all his manpower, winding up with Berra, his jittery catcher, in right and Tommy Henrich in left.

Collect Five Doubles

As for the Dodgers, the battle was of a sort in which they reveled all summer as they out-scrambled their National League rivals so many times. They collected twelve blows. These included a trio of doubles by Reese, Robinson and Dixie Walker that sank Reynolds in the third and the pair of two-baggers by Carl Furillo and pinch-hitter Bob Bragan that sparked the four-run rally which brought down Page in that hysterical sixth.

Their winning pitcher was Ralph Branca, who, relieving little Lombardi in the Yanks' explosive third, hurled only two and one-third innings. He yielded six hits, not to mention the tally that put the Yanks ahead for the only time in the fourth. However, the four runs with which the Flock tore off the roof in the sixth went to his credit and that gave him the triumph.

Other Yankee hurlers to get into the fray were Karl Drews, who relieved Reynolds in the third; Vic Raschi and Charlie Wensloff who, all too late, held the Dodgers hitless and runless in the final three rounds. The ten hurlers for the two teams set another series mark.

It was again a cloudless, summery day such as had prevailed in the games in Brooklyn. When the first three batters got on base the picture bore an even closer resemblance to that of the two previous afternoons in Flatbush.

Phil Rizzuto

Jammed to Capacity

This time, however, it was the Brooks who looked as though they meant to rip things wide open at the outset. Though they didn't quite extract all that the situation invited, they did do a little better than the Bombers. For where the Yanks had squeezed only one run from a similar first-inning set-up on Friday and none at all on Saturday, the Flock came up with two tallies, although neither was scored with any particular degree of elegance.

The strains of "The Star-Spangled Banner" had scarcely floated away over the adjoining Bronx housetops, which also were jammed to capacity, than Eddie Stanky brought the crowd up with a roar as he rammed a single into left. On the heels of that Reese stroked a one-base thump into center, and at that moment it seemed

everyone in the park was for the underdog Dodgers.

Then Jackie Robinson sent a towering fly down the left-field foul line. Lindell seemed at first to have trouble sighting the ball, got it and then lost it in the blinding sun. It fell to the ground but, as both runners had remained tagged up, Robinson got only a single, filling the bases.

Reynolds, an easy mound victor in the second game, was really up to his neck in trouble and yet, like Harry Taylor and Rex Barney in the previous two encounters, he almost managed to make a similar escape.

Walker swung vigorously but succeeded only in thumping into a double play that rubbed out himself and Robbie at second. However, Stanky counted and Reese moved to third on the play which was further enlivened by Jackie

Robinson crashing heavily into Rizzuto at the midway bag. It knocked the wind out of Li'l Phil and it required almost five minutes for him to get it back.

Yanks Go on Rampage

Then came a passed ball as Lollar failed to block one of Reynolds' shots, and Reese raced over with the second tally. The Flock had come up with only two runs but it grabbed two more in the third for a 4-0 lead as Reese, Robinson and Walker hit successive two-baggers that sent Reynolds to the showers.

But the hub-bub caused by the Flatbush faithful had barely subsided than the Yanks went on a rampage in the third and finished Lombardi. Lollar opened with a double. Drews, left to bat for himself, fanned, but Spider Jorgensen's

fumble of Stirnweiss' grounder, and singles by Henrich, Lindell and DiMaggio followed for three runs. Then Branca replaced Lombardi, the mite left-hander. Bill Johnson greeted him with a single that drove in the fourth run before the big right-hander could get things under control.

In the fourth, however, Branca faltered and was nicked for singles by Aaron Robinson, who had now become the Yankee backstop; Henrich and Berra. The Dodgers put up a terrific uproar when Umpires Pinelli and Rommel, who at first made no signal at all, ruled the Berra hit a fair ball.

That shot put the Yanks in front by a tally, but the margin endured only until the Dodgers swung into action with their tempestuous sixth. Bruce Edwards opened it with a single and moved to third on Furillo's double.

Composite Score of World Series Games

BROOKLYN DODGERS

	G	AB	R	H	2B	3B	HR	RBI	BB	SO	Bat Avg	PO	A	E	Fldg Avg
Stanky, 2b	6	21	4	5	1	0	0	2	3	2	.238	15	18	1	.971
J. Robinson, 1b	6	23	3	7	2	0	0	3	3		.304	46	4	0	1.000
dReiser, cf-lf	5	8	1	2	0	0	0	3	1		.250	7	0	1	.875
Walker, rf	6	24	1	6	1	0	1	4	2	1	.250	6	1	0	1.000
Hermanski, lf	6	17	3	2	0	0	1	3	3		.118	13	0	0	1.000
Furillo, cf	6	14	2	5	2	0	0	3	3	0	.357	10	1	1	.917
Edwards, c	6	23	4	4	1	0	0	1	2	7	.174	39	4	1	.977
Jorgensen, 3b	6	18	1	3	1	0	0	2	2	4	.167	8	11	2	.905
eLavagetto, 3b	4	6	0	1	1	0	0	3	0	2	.167	0	1	0	1.000
Reese, ss	6	20	5	7	1	0	0	4	5	2	.350	8	14	1	.957
Branca, p	3	5	0	0	0	0	0	0	0	1	.000	0	1	0	1.000
Behrman, p	4	0	0	0	0	0	0	0	0	0	.000	0	3	0	1.000
Casey, p	5	1	0	0	0	0	0	0	0	1	.000	2	3	0	.000
fLombardi, p	3	2	0	0	0	0	0	0	0	0	.000	0	0	0	.000
Gregg, p	2	1	0	0	0	0	0	0	0	1	.000	0	3	0	1.000
Barney, p	2	1	0	0	0	0	0	0	0	0	.000	0	1	0	1.000
Hatten, p	3	3	1	1	0	0	0	0	0	0	.333	0	1	0	1.000
aMiksis, 2b-lf	4	2	1	0	0	0	0	0	0	1	.000	1	1	1	.667
bVaughan	3	2	0	1	0	0	0	0	1	0	.500	0	0	0	.000
gBragan	1	1	0	1	1	0	0	1	0	0	1.000	0	0	0	.000
cGionfriddo, lf	3	3	2	0	0	0	0	0	1	0	.000	1	0	0	1.000
hBankhead	1	0	1	0	0	0	0	0	0	0	.000	0	0	0	.000
Total		195	27	45	12	0	1	24	28	29	.231	156	66	8	.965

NEW YORK YANKEES

	G	AB	R	H	2B	3B	HR	RBI	BB	SO	Bat Avg	PO	A	E	Fldg Avg
Stirnweiss, 2b	6	25	3	7	0	1	0	3	5	8	.280	13	17	0	1.000
Henrich, rf	6	26	2	9	2	0	1	4	2	2	.346	10	0	0	1.000
Berra, c-rf	5	16	2	3	0	1	2	1	2	1	.188	20	2	2	.917
DiMaggio, cf	6	23	4	6	0	0	2	5	5	2	.261	19	0	0	1.000
McQuinn, 1b	6	21	2	3	0	0	0	1	4	7	.143	41	4	1	.978
Johnson, 3b	6	23	6	6	0	2	0	2	4		.261	10	13	0	1.000
Lindell, lf	6	18	3	9	3	1	0	7	5	2	.500	11	0	0	1.000
Rizzuto, ss	6	22	1	5	1	0	0	1	4	0	.227	16	13	0	1.000
Lollar, c	2	4	3	3	2	0	1	0	0	0	.750	2	1	0	1.000
A. Robinson, c	2	7	2	2	0	0	0	1	0		.286	9	0	1	.900
Shea, p	2	5	0	2	1	0	0	1	0	2	.400	1	3	0	1.000
Page, p	3	3	0	0	0	0	0	0	0	0	.000	1	2	0	1.000
Reynolds, p	2	4	2	2	0	0	0	1	0	0	.500	1	0	0	1.000
Newsom, p	2	0	0	0	0	0	0	0	0	0	.000	0	1	0	1.000
Raschi, p	2	0	0	0	0	0	0	0	0	0	.000	0	0	0	.000
Drews, p	2	2	0	0	0	0	0	0	0	1	.000	0	3	0	1.000
Chandler, p	1	0	0	0	0	0	0	0	0		.000	0	1	0	1.000
Bevens, p	1	3	0	0	0	0	0	0	0	1	.000	0	1	0	1.000
Wensloff, p	1	0	0	0	0	0	0	0	0	0	.000	0	0	0	.000
iBrown	3	2	2	2	1	0	0	2	1	0	1.000	0	0	0	.000
jClark	2	1	1	0	0	0	0	0	1	0	.000	0	0	0	.000
kPhillips, 1b	2	2	0	0	0	0	0	0	0	0	.000	4	0	0	1.000
lHouk	1	1	0	1	0	0	0	0	0	0	1.000	0	0	0	.000
mFrey	1	1	0	0	0	0	0	0	0	0	.000	0	0	0	.000
Total		208	33	60	10	4	4	30	31	32	.288	158	61	4	.982

a Struck out for Behrman in seventh of first game and ran for Reiser in ninth of fourth game.

b Flied out for Gregg in seventh of second game, walked for Gregg in seventh inning of fourth game, and doubled for Behrman in seventh of fifth game.

c Forced Jorgensen for Barney in ninth of second game, ran for Furillo in ninth of fourth game, and walked for Hatten in sixth of fifth game.

d Walked for Casey in ninth of fourth game, and walked for Stanky in seventh of fifth game.

e Doubled for Stanky in ninth of fourth game, and fanned for Casey in ninth of fifth game.

f Ran for Edwards in ninth of fifth game.

g Doubled for Branca in sixth of sixth game.

h Ran for Bragan in sixth of sixth game.

i Walked for Shea in fifth of first game, doubled for Chandler in sixth of third game, and singled for Phillips in third of sixth game.

j Walked for Raschi in third of third game, and lined out for Newsom in sixth of sixth game.

k Flied out for Drews in fourth of third game.

l Singled for Raschi in seventh of sixth game.

m Forced A. Robinson for Wensloff in ninth of sixth game.

COMPOSITE SCORE BY INNINGS

Brooklyn	3	6	4	3	1	6	1	0	3	—27
New York	2	0	7	6	10	2	5	0	1	—33

PITCHING SUMMARY

	G	CG	IP	H	R	ER	BB	SO	HB	WP	W	L	Pct	Era
Casey	5	0	8 1/3	4	0	0	1	2	1	0	2	0	1.000	0.00
Branca	3	0	8 1/3	12	8	8	5	9	1	0	1	1	.500	8.64
Lombardi	2	0	6 2/3	14	9	9	1	5	0	1	0	1	.000	12.15
Barney	2	0	6 1/3	4	2	2	10	3	0	2	0	1	.000	2.84
Behrman	4	0	4 2/3	7	4	4	2	2	1	0	0		.000	7.27
Hatten	3	0	8 2/3	11	7	7	7	4	0	0	0	0	.000	7.27
Gregg	2	0	9	6	2	2	4	4	0	0	0	0	.000	2.00
Taylor	1	0	2	1	0	1	0	0	0	0	0	0	.000	0.00
Shea	2	1	14	6	2	2	7	10	0	0	2	0	1.000	1.29
Reynolds	2	1	11 1/3	15	7	6	3	6	0	0	1	0	1.000	4.74
Bevens	1	1	8 2/3	10	3	3	10	5	0	1	0	1	.000	3.12
Newsom	2	0	2 1/3	6	5	5	2	0	0	0	0	1	.000	19.29
Page	3	0	8	11	6	6	2	6	0	0	1	0	.000	6.75
Raschi	2	0	1 1/3	2	1	1	0	1	0	0	0	0	.000	6.75
Drews	2	0	3	3	1	1	1	0	0	0	0	0	.000	3.00
Chandler	1	0	2	2	2	2	4	1	0	0	0	0	.000	9.00
Wensloff	1	0	2	3	0	0	0	0	0	0	0	0	.000	0.00

Earned runs—Brooklyn 26, New York 32. Left on bases—Brooklyn 42, New York 54. Stolen bases—J. Robinson 2, Reese 3, Walker, Rizzuto, Gionfriddo. Sacrifices—Henrich, J. Robinson, Stanky, Bevens, Furillo. Double plays—Johnson and McQuinn; Jorgensen, Stanky and J. Robinson; Stirnweiss, Rizzuto and McQuinn; Stanky and J. Robinson 3; Stanky and J. Robinson; Gregg, Reese and J. Robinson; Casey, Edwards and J. Robinson; Reese, Miksis and J. Robinson; Rizzuto and Phillips. Hit by Pitcher—By Branca (Johnson); Drews (Hermanski); Casey (Lindell). Balk—Shea. Passed balls—Lollar 2, Edwards 2. Umpires—McGowan (AL); Pinelli (NL); Rommel (AL); Goetz (NL); Magerkurth (NL) and Boyer (AL). Attendances—First game, 73,365; second game, 69,865; third game, 33,098; fourth game, 33,443; fifth game, 34,379; sixth game, 74,065. Times of games—2:20, 2:36, 3:05, 2:20, 2:46, 3:19.

Scores Tying Run

Here, for the third successive day, Cookie Lavagetto was called on to pinch hit. Friday he had delivered his epic two-run two-bagger that had sunk the Yanks in the ninth and robbed Bill Bevens of a no-hitter. Saturday, in an almost similar ninth-inning situation, he had fanned. This time he came sort of "in between." He lifted a fly to Berra in right and Edwards galloped in with the tying run.

Then Bragan, a catcher, slammed a pinch double to left to score Furillo. Dan Bankhead, the Dodgers' Negro pitcher, entered the struggle as a runner for Bragan.

Page, who had entered the game the previous round to relieve Drews, now appeared visibly shaken. Stanky pounded a single into right and as Berra fired the ball home, Bankhead skidded back to third. But here Aaron Robinson fumbled it and that enabled Stanky to take second on the misplay. It was a slip that was to provide the Flock with an additional run.

For after Newsom replaced the stunned and crestfallen Page, Reese promptly greeted Bobo with a single, his third hit of the afternoon, and both Bankhead and Stanky scored. That made it four for the round and an 8-5 lead.

After that it became a matter of hanging on for dear life, and this the Dodgers did with the help of their amazing Casey. In this unprecedented struggle of the bullpens Hugh seemed to score a great personal triumph over his American League rival, Page.

And so, with the classic all even once more, the Dodgers, though still not favorites in the betting, nevertheless have precedent heavily in their corner for the first time. This marks the eleventh time the struggle has gone down to the final encounter of a seven-game series. Of the ten already played, the National Leaguers have won seven.

Also to be remembered is the fact that Harris must counter today with Bevens, who has had only two days' rest since losing that heart-breaking one-hitter Friday. As for Shotton, his hurling staff seems no more badly scrambled than at any time in the series. He will start with Hal Gregg and doubtless follow with a string of others that eventually will get down to one more appearance for the inimitable Casey.

October 6, 1947

YANKEE STAR LEADS WILLIAMS BY POINT

DiMaggio Selected for Player Award With Score of 202 by Baseball Writers

By JOHN DREBINGER

By the slender margin of a single point, Joe DiMaggio, star centerfielder of the Yankees has been named the American League's most valuable player for 1947, it was announced yesterday by the Baseball Writers Association of America.

In being voted the Kenesaw Mountain Landis Memorial award, Jolting Joe received 202 points in the poll of the scribes' twenty-four-man committee as against 201 for Ted Williams, Red Sox star slugger and winner of the prize last year.

Third ranking also was gained by only a single point with Lou Boudreau, manager-shortstop of the Indians, scoring 168 points to 167 for Joe Page, the tireless left-hander who did an amazing relief job for the Yankees last summer. Fifth place went to George Kell, Tiger third sacker, who scored 132.

It marked the third time that DiMaggio had finished on top, the Yankee clipper having first captured the award in 1939 and again in 1941. And for Williams it was the third time Boston's temperamental "problem child" had failed to win the prize despite a distinguished personal record.

In 1941 Williams hit .406, yet bowed to DiMaggio who that year had set his spectacular fifty-six-game hitting streak. In 1942 Williams again won the batting crown with .356 but trailed behind Joe

New York Yankees

Joe DiMaggio

Gordon, then with the Yanks, for the MVP award.

The past season again saw Williams lead individual batting as well as top the field in homers and runs batted in. But the scribes apparently estimated DiMaggio the more valuable team worker.

Jolting Joe polled eight first place ballots as against only three for Williams who drew most of his points from ten second place ratings. As in the National League vote, points were distributed on a basis of 14 for first place, 9 for second, 8 for third and so on down to one for tenth.

McQuinn Rated Sixth

Curiously Page, whom his manager, Bucky Harris, openly named as the year's most important factor in the Yanks' pennant victory, had the second highest first place votes to DiMaggio, the lefty appearing No. 1 on seven ballots.

George McQuinn, the veteran Mack cast-off, whose astonishing comeback at first base also played a strong role in the Yankee victory, received three first-place votes which helped him finish sixth with 77 points. In all, eighteen of the twenty-four writers named a Yankee for the No. 1 spot. Eddie Joost of the Athletics got two of the remaining first ballot votes, while Boudreau got the other.

The Bombers, in fact, did exceptionally well, placing eight men among the thirty-four who received points. Tommy Henrich, Frank, Shea, Yogi Berra and Allie Reynolds are bunched between 33 and 18 points, while a little further down the line Bill Johnson appears with 9.

That it was a tough year for old favorites was indicated when Hal Newhouser, winner in 1944 and 1945, this year had to be satisfied with honorable mention, for which no points are awarded. But Joe Gorden, who as a Yank had won in 1942, still was able to make a presentable showing as an Indian. He placed seventh with 59 points, one more than Cleveland's Bob Feller received.

The complete point score follows:

DiMaggio, Yankees, 202; Williams, Red Sox, 201; Boudreau, Indians, 168; Page, Yankees, 167; Kell, Tigers, 132; McQuinn, Yankees, 77; Gordon, Indians, 59; Feller, Indians, 58; Marchildon, Athletics, 47; Appling, White Sox, 43; Joost, Athletics, 35; McCosky, Athletics, 35; Henrich, Yankees, 33; Shea, Yankees, 23; Berra, Yankees, 18; Reynolds, Yankees, 18; Dillinger, Browns, 13; Pesky, Red Sox, 11; Fain, Athletics, 9; W. Johnson, Yankees, 9; Spence, Senators, 9; Hutchinson, Tigers, 8; Wynn, Senators, 8; Doerr, Red Sox, 6; Rosar, Athletics, 6; Christman, Browns, 4; McCahan, Athletics, 4; Mitchell, Indians, 4; Cullenbine, Tigers, 3; Dobson, Red Sox, 3; Heath, Browns, 1; Lopat, White Sox, 1; Stephens, Browns, 1; Wright, White Sox, 1.

Honorable Mention—Red Sox: D. DiMaggio, Murrell Jones. White Sox: Finney, Haynes, Tresh. Tigers: Newhouser, Evers, Overmire. Yankees: Rizzuto, Newsom, Keller, Stirnweiss, Lindell. Athletics: Valo, Suder, Majeski, Fowler. Browns: Lehner, Judnich. Senators: Vernon, Yost.

November 28, 1947

CARDS TRIM BROOKS FOR 6TH IN ROW, 13-4

Pollet Coasts Behind 15-Hit Attack—Dodgers Drop Fifth Straight at Ebbets Field

By JOSEPH M. SHEEHAN

If the Dodgers ever again see the Cardinals, with emphasis on Stan Musial and Enos Slaughter, it will be too soon. In a manner that severely shook the faith of 11,953 Ebbets Field loyalists, Eddie Dyer's wrecking crew yesterday completed the deflation of Flatbush's erstwhile favorites.

Behind a smooth pitching performance by Howie Pollet, St. Louis blasted Joe Hatten, Hugh Casey and Clyde King for fourteen hits. Combined with ten walks, two hit batsmen and two errors, they added up to a 13-4 defeat for Brooklyn, which has dropped five straight games, all at home.

Traveling at a blistering pace, the league-leading Cardinals have won six games in a row and thirteen of their last sixteen. As groggy Dodger pitchers can attest, the Redbirds will continue to fly high until someone clips the wings of Musial and Slaughter.

Musial Bats .733 for Series

This slugging duo again went berserk. Musial had a four-for-six day, with a single, two doubles and a homer, to run his batting average for the series up to an incredible .733. Slaughter settled for a series mark of .500 on the strength of two singles and a double in five official trips to the plate.

Del Rice, with a brace of doubles that drove in four runs; Nippy Jones, with two singles that produced three tallies, and Ernie Dusak, who also singled twice, joined the fun at the expense of a Dodger staff so destitute that Manager Leo Durocher felt obliged to let Hatten stay through to the bitter end of the six-run Cardinal fifth inning.

Until that stanza, the Brooklyn southpaw matched the pace set by his St. Louis counterpart. Each team had scored once, the Cardinals in the third on a single by Dusak and Musial's double, the Dodgers in the fourth on a walk to Bruce Edwards, two infield outs and Dick Whitman's single.

Twelve Cards Bat in Fifth

However, Lefty Joe fell all to pieces in the fifth. Before he ended the horrendous frame by surprisingly fanning Musial with the bases full, twelve Cardinals batted. Half of them scored as the net result of three hits, six walks, two wild pitches and an error. Musial, Slaughter and Rice were the hitters.

A pinch-hitter paved the way for the entrance of Casey in the sixth. The suddenly ineffective relief ace was shelled for three hits and three runs in that inning and, with the bases empty in the seventh, served Musial a fat pitch that Stan propelled across Bedford Avenue for his fifth home run. King worked the ninth and gave two runs on two hits and a walk.

With the heat off, Pollet eased up a bit, but the Dodgers got to him too late with too little. Three Brooklyn runs on three solid hits in the eighth failed to ruffle the Redbird star, who proceeded smoothly to his third triumph against no defeats. The setback was Hatten's second in four starts.

The box score:

ST. LOUIS (N.)	ab.	r.	h.	po.	a.	e.		BROOKLYN (N.)	ab.	r.	h.	po.	a.	e.
Lapointe, 2b.	4	1	0	4	1	0		Miksis, 2b.	5	0	1	1	2	0
Dusak, cf.	5	1	2	0	0	0		Robinson,1b	5	0	1	10	1	1
Musial, lf.	6	3	4	2	0	0		Lund, lf	3	1	2	2	0	0
Kurowski,3b	3	2	0	0	0	0		Furillo, cf	3	1	0	4	1	0
Lang, 3b	0	0	1	0	0	0		Edwards, c.	3	1	0	0	1	0
Slaughter,rf	5	2	3	5	0	0		Reese, ss	4	0	1	2	5	0
Jones, 1b	4	2	2	7	0	0		Brown, 3b.	4	1	1	3	1	1
Marion, ss	5	1	1	3	2	1		Whitman, rf.	4	0	2	0	0	0
Rice, c	4	1	2	4	1	0		Hatten, p.	1	0	1	1	3	0
aSchoen'st	0	0	0	0	0	0		bMauch	1	0	0	0	0	0
Garagiola, c	0	0	0	2	0	0		Casey, p	0	0	0	0	0	0
Pollet, p	4	0	0	0	1	0		cHodges	1	0	0	0	0	0
								King, p	0	0	0	0	2	0
Total	40	13	14	27	6	1		Total	36	4	9	27	15	2

aRan for Rice in eighth.
bFanned for Hatten in fifth.
cFanned for Casey in eighth.

St. Louis ... . 0 0 1 0 6 3 1 0 2—13
Brooklyn ... . 0 0 0 1 0 0 3 0—4

Runs batted in—Musial 2, Whitman 3, Slaughter 3, Rice 4, Jones 3, Brown.

Two-base hits—Musial 2, Rice 2, Robinson, Slaughter, Reese, Lund 2, Whitman. Home run—Musial. Double play—Miksis, Reese and Robinson. Left on bases—St. Louis 12, Brooklyn 9. Bases on balls—Off Pollet 4, Hatten 8, Casey 1, King 1. Struck out—By Pollet 5, Hatten 3. Hits —Off Hatten 8 in 5 innings, Casey 4 in 3, King 2 in 1. Hit by pitcher—By Casey (Kurowski, Rice). Wild pitches—Hatten 2. Losing pitcher—Hatten. Umpires—Gore, Robb and Pinelli. Time of game—2:53. Attendance—11,953.

May 21, 1948

DiMaggio's 5 Blows Highlight Yank Victory

BOMBERS CONQUER WHITE SOX BY 13-2

DiMaggio Smashes 2 Homers, Triple, Double and Single to Top 22-Hit Attack

LINDELL ALSO CONNECTS

Drives 4-Bagger, Two Singles for Yanks—Raschi Coasts to His Third Victory

By JAMES P. DAWSON

Special to THE NEW YORK TIMES.

CHICAGO, May 20—Inspired by the greatest batting day Joe DiMaggio has enjoyed since pre-war times, the Yankees touched record heights in the vital statistics department at Comiskey Field today when they overwhelmed the hapless White Sox, 13 to 2.

The Bombers from the Bronx slugged four of Ted Lyons' throwers for twenty-two hits, good for thirty-eight bases, exceeding their previous high in hits by six and their best previous accumulation of total bases by twelve. Their thirteen runs bettered by one the dozen accumulated in the season's opener April 19 against Washington, when they banged out sixteen hits, good for twenty-six bases.

In today's slugging orgy DiMaggio hammered out two homers, a triple, a double and a single. He pounded in six runs and was deprived of a "6 for 6" day when Ralph Hodgin backed to the left-field wall in the eighth to pull down what would have been another extra-base blow.

Big John Lindell exploded a homer and contributed two singles to the cannonade that rang about the ears of the futile Sox hurlers. Billy Johnson had a three-hit day, with one double. Bobby Brown stroked three singles. All told the Yanks got three homers, one triple, five doubles and thirteen singles in the explosion that entertained a meager 5,001 cash customers and brought immeasurable pain to Ted Lyons.

Stirnweiss Is Hitless

Only George Stirnweiss failed to get a hit in this slugfest, and Ike Pearson was the only one of the five hurlers Lyons tossed into the fray to escape the barrage. The veteran right-hander got the call with two out in the four-run ninth, just in time to make Stirnweiss bang into a force play that dropped the curtain on the worst beating the Sox have absorbed this campaign.

Vic Raschi picked up his third straight triumph, though his performance held room for improvement. He walked in a run on four passes in the fourth. He was clubbed for three hits by Taft Wright, one a home run in the eighth, and allowed seven hits in all.

Lyons started Orval Grove, who got into trouble by messing up an easy double play in the first and finished in the fifth after being clubbed for nine hits and five runs. Fred Bradey appeared with the sixth, but was hammered to shelter with one man away and four runs in. Earl Harrist checked the scoring without interfering with the hitting. And in the ninth the aging Earl Caldwell was moved out of the contest under a six-hit salvo that included Lindell's homer and produced four more runs.

Both Wallops Off Grove

Grove was the victim of DiMaggio's two homers. Walloping Joie exploded the first with two aboard in the first inning. After the Yanks had added another run in the second on three hits, DiMaggio opened the fifth with his second homer, his sixth of the campaign. Singles by Raschi and Lindell with DiMaggio's triple finished Bradley quickly in the sixth, and a double by Yogi Berra greeted Harrist as the Yanks collected four more.

That was all until the ninth, when Bobby Brown singled, Cliff Mapes doubled, Lindell hit his homer with one on, DiMaggio doubled, Berra walked, Johnson doubled and George McQuinn singled, all for four more before Pearson came on to end the slaughter.

The home-run production boosted the Yankee total to thirty. Sox pitchers have now been clubbed for thirty-one this season.

Have Used 69 Pitchers

Illustrating the sorry condition of Lyons' pitching squad is the fact that in twenty-four games, including a tie, the Southsiders have had sixty-nine in action.

Until today Grove enjoyed the distinction of being the only Sox hurler to go the route, in spring exhibitions and regular play.

The Yanks could do nothing wrong today. Contrarily, nothing went right for the Sox.

Johnson tripped and fell under Luke Appling's pop in the seventh but stuck out his glove to make the catch while lying on the ground.

The box score:

NEW YORK (A.)

	ab.	r.	h.	po.	a.	e.
Brown, ss.	5	0	3	2	3	0
Keller, lf.	4	2	1	1	0	0
Mapes, lf.	1	1	1	1	0	0
Lindell, rf.	6	3	3	4	0	0
DiMa'io, cf.	6	4	5	3	0	0
Berra, c.	5	1	2	2	0	0
Johnson, 3b.	6	0	3	1	1	0
M'Qu'n, 1b.	4	0	2	10	1	0
Stirn'ss, 2b.	6	0	0	2	5	0
Raschi, p.	5	2	2	1	1	0
Total	48	13	22	27	11	0

CHICAGO (A.)

	ab.	r.	h.	po.	a.	e.
Baker, 2b.	3	0	0	3	1	0
Lupien, 1b.	5	0	2	6	1	0
Appling, 3b.	4	1	0	3	2	0
Hodgin, lf.	3	0	1	3	2	0
Wright, rf.	4	1	3	4	0	0
Robinson, c.	3	0	1	3	1	0
Philley, cf.	3	0	0	3	0	0
Michaels, ss.	3	0	0	2	7	0
Grove, p.	1	0	0	0	0	1
aKolloway	1	0	0	0	0	0
Bradley, p.	0	0	0	0	0	0
Harrist, p.	0	0	0	0	0	0
bWallaesa	1	0	0	0	0	0
Caldwell, p.	0	0	0	0	0	0
Pearson, p.	0	0	0	0	0	0
cWeigel	1	0	0	0	0	0
Total	32	2	7	27	14	1

APopped out for Grove in fifth.
bFlied out for Harrist in seventh.
cGrounded out for Pearson in ninth.

New York	3	1	0	0	1	4	0	0	4	—13
Chicago	0	0	0	1	0	0	0	1	0	— 2

Runs batted in—DiMaggio 6, Keller, Lindell 3, Philley, Berra, Wright, Johnson, McQuinn.

Two-base hits—McQuinn, Berra, Mapes, DiMaggio, Johnson. Three-base hit—DiMaggio. Home runs—DiMaggio 2, Wright, Lindell. Double plays—Johnson, Stirnweiss and McQuinn; Stirnweiss, Brown and McQuinn. Left on bases—New York 13, Chicago 10. Bases on balls—Off Grove 1, Bradley 1, Harrist 1, Caldwell 2, Raschi 7. Struck out—By Raschi 2, Harrist 1. Hits—Off Grove 9 in 5 innings, Bradley 3 in 1-3, Harrist 2 in 1 2-3, Caldwell 8 in 1 2-3, Pearson 0 in 1-3. Wild pitch—Grove. Losing pitcher—Grove. Umpires—Rommel, Passarella and Boyer. Time of game—2:26. Attendance—5,001.

May 21, 1948

WHITE SOX IN SPLIT AS SEEREY EXCELS

Pat Blasts 4 Homers in 12-11 Victory Over Athletics—McCahan Wins 2d, 6--1

PHILADELPHIA, July 18 (AP)—The White Sox split a pair of games with the Athletics today, winning by 12—11 in eleven innings and then losing, 6—1, in the five-inning nightcap cut short by Pennsylvania's Sunday curfew law.

Pat Seerey, the stocky left fielder of the White Sox, blasted four home runs in the first game to equal a long-standing major league record.

Not since Chuck Klein of the Phillies turned the trick in a ten-inning game in 1936 has a batter hit four homers in one game. Only four other players have driven four out of the park in a single contest.

The first game, one of the wildest contests of the year, took 3 hours and 44 minutes to complete and saw ten pitchers parade to the mound.

Philadelphia reeled off five quick runs, but lost the lead in the middle of the game when Seerey hit homers in three straight innings—the fourth, fifth and sixth—and Chicago gained an 11-7 lead.

But the Athletics surged back as Eddie Joost cracked for the circuit with two on and the score was tied, 11—11, at the end of the regulation nine innings.

The score stood until Seerey unlimbered his fourth circuit smash in the eleventh with no one on base. That swat earned Howie Judson the victory and gave Lou Brissie the defeat.

The Mackmen loaded the bases in the last of the eleventh, but Mario Pieretti came in and retired Ferris Fain for the final out.

Bill McCahan won his first game of the season in the nightcap and knocked in the winning runs himself off Bill Gillespie. McCahan singled home two runs in the fifth and final inning. The Athletics went on to score three more times before the contest was called.

The box scores:

FIRST GAME

CHICAGO (A.)

	ab.	r.	h.	po.	a.	e.
Kol'way, 2b.	7	2	5	5	2	0
Lupien, 1b.	7	1	1	8	2	0
Appling, 3b.	7	1	3	2	5	0
Seerey, lf.	6	4	4	3	0	0
Robinson, c.	6	0	3	4	1	0
Wright, rf.	6	0	2	0	0	0
Philley, cf.	6	1	2	5	0	0
Michaels, ss.	6	3	4	6	3	1
Papish, p.	0	0	0	0	1	0
Moulder, p.	1	0	0	0	0	0
aHodgin	1	0	0	0	0	0
Caldwell, p.	0	0	0	0	0	0
bBaker	1	0	0	0	0	0
Judson, p.	3	0	0	0	0	0
Pieretti, p.	0	0	0	0	0	0
Total	57	12	24	33	14	1

PHILADELPHIA (A.)

	ab.	r.	h.	po.	a.	e.
Joost, ss.	7	4	4	1	2	0
McCosky, lf.	2	2	1	3	1	0
White, cf.	4	1	2	2	0	0
Brissie, p.	0	0	0	0	0	0
cChapman	0	0	0	0	0	0
Fain, 1b.	5	0	0	13	0	0
Majeski, 3b.	5	0	1	0	3	0
Valo, rf.	3	0	1	4	0	0
Rosar, c.	3	0	0	5	0	0
Guerra, c.	3	0	0	3	0	0
Suder, 2b.	5	2	1	2	1	0
Scheib, p.	1	1	0	0	4	0
Savage, p.	1	0	0	0	0	0
Harris, p.	1	1	1	0	0	1
J.Coleman, p	0	0	0	0	0	0
R.C'eman, cf	2	0	1	0	0	0
dDemars	0	0	0	0	0	0
Total	42	11	12	33	11	1

aFlied out for Moulder in fourth.
bFlied out for Caldwell in sixth.
cWalked for Brissie in eleventh.
dRan for Chapman in eleventh.

Chicago	0	0	1	1	2	5	2	0	0	0	1	—12
Philadelphia	1	4	0	1	1	0	4	0	0	0	0	—11

Runs batted in—Kolloway 3, Appling, Seerey 7, Baker, Joost 5, McCosky, Fain 2, Majeski.

Two-base hits — Robinson, Wright, Kolloway, Philley, Joost 2, Majeski. Three-base hit—Kolloway. Home runs—Seerey 4, Joost. Sacrifices—McCosky, White 2. Double plays—McCosky and Rosar; Kolloway, Michaels and Lupien. Left on bases—Chicago 15, Philadelphia 14. Bases on balls—Off Scheib 1, Savage 1, J. Coleman 1, Papish 4, Caldwell 1, Judson 7. Struck out—By Scheib 2, J. Coleman 1, Brissie 1, Moulder 1, Caldwell 1, Judson 2. Hits—Off Scheib 9 in 4 2-3 innings, Savage 5 in 1, Harris 4 in 1 2-3, J. Coleman 3 in 1 2-3, Brissie 3 in 2, Papish 3 in 1, Moulder 0 in 2, Caldwell 4 in 2, Judson 3 in 5 2-3, Pieretti 0 in 1-3. Hit by pitcher—By Papish (Valo). Wild pitches—Papish, Moulder, Savage. Balk—Judson. Winning pitcher—Judson. Losing pitcher — Brissie. Umpires — Hurley, Berry and Grieve. Time of game—3:44.

SECOND GAME

CHICAGO (A.)

	ab.	r.	h.	po.	a.	e.
Kolloway, 2b	3	0	1	2	3	0
Lupien, 1b.	3	0	0	9	0	0
Baker, 3b.	3	0	2	1	1	0
Seerey, lf.	2	1	0	1	0	0
Wright, rf.	2	0	1	0	0	1
Philley, cf.	2	0	0	2	1	0
Michaels, ss.	2	0	1	0	5	0
Tresh, c.	2	0	1	0	0	0
Gillespie, p.	2	0	0	0	1	0
Total	21	1	6	15	11	1

PHILADELPHIA (A.)

	ab.	r.	h.	po.	a.	e.
Joost, ss.	2	0	0	2	0	0
McCosky, lf.	2	2	1	1	0	0
R.Cole'an, cf	2	1	0	1	0	0
Fain, 1b.	3	0	2	6	0	0
Majeski, 3b.	3	0	0	1	4	0
Valo, rf.	2	0	0	0	0	0
Guerra, c.	2	1	1	3	0	0
Suder, 2b.	2	1	2	1	3	0
McCahan, p.	2	1	1	0	0	0
Total	20	6	7	15	7	0

Chicago	0	1	0	0	0	—1
Philadelphia	1	0	0	0	5	—6

Called, Sunday curfew law.

Runs batted in—Philley, Fain 3, Majeski, McCahan 2.

Two-base hits—Baker, Suder. Left on bases—Chicago 6, Philadelphia 2. Sacrifice—Joost. Bases on balls—Off McCahan 1, Gillespie 2. Struck out—By McCahan 1. Wild pitch—Gillespie. Umpires—Berry, Grieve and Hurley. Time of game—1:10. Attendance—17,296.

July 19, 1948

Personalities of Baseball

Tribute Paid to General Doubleday, Founder of Our National Game

To the Editor of The New York Times:

The nation-wide grief occasioned by the passing of a great exponent of baseball prompts me to offer a thought which seems fitting at such a time. The general public knows little, indeed, about the origin of the game of baseball, and it is safe to say that a very small percentage of the fans could, if called upon, give the name of its inventor. It is probable that equally few could give the approximate date when the game was devised.

If a game can produce such a figure as Babe Ruth, and such emotions in connection with any player of the game, then should we not at least make passing mention of Abner Doubleday, and the fact that if he had not devised a game that could so capture the fancy of the American people, then there could have been no Babe Ruth? So, while we are at it, how about a hand for little Abner, playing One o' Cat in the lots of Cooperstown, N. Y., and as he played, pondering the matter of how it might somehow be made into more of a game.

Watching the Play

It is probable that old Fenimore Cooper while taking taking his constitutionals used to pass by Abner and the boys at play with a ball and some form of a bat, and anyone who had read his works would imagine that he would have tarried, and looked on for awhile with benign amusement. The fact that the boy Abner went on to be a distinguished American soldier should hardly lessen the thanks that are due him by the baseball-loving public.

General Doubleday (who, while a West Point cadet on furlough devised the game at Cooperstown in 1839) served in three wars—Mexican, Seminole and Civil, and was one of the better-known Civil War generals, commanding a division at Chancellorsville and a corps at Gettysburg. In the early part of the Battle of Gettysburg he commanded the entire Federal force participating before the arrival on the scene of General Meade.

At the outbreak of the war he was, as a captain of artillery, in the garrison of Fort Sumter, when it was fired on, and it was his battery which was the first to return the Confederate fire.

He was a man of many interests—an author, and an accomplished linguist. Happily, he lived to a good age, and saw his game well launched, dying in 1893 at the age of 73. He saw the National League organized and seventeen years on its way, though he missed by seven years seeing the organization of the American League.

Name Little Known

Needless to say, people whose business is baseball, well know the name of Abner Doubleday, and he has been honored by the establishment of the Baseball Hall of Fame at Cooperstown. But his name, when mentioned, will ring a bell with but very few of the millions of ardent devotees of his game. It would be a good thing if the name of the inventor of the game could somehow be more impressed upon the consciousness of the thousands of persons—particularly the growing boys—whose interest in it amount almost to an obsession. It is an interesting point that the positon of the bases, and the distance between the bases, has never been changed.

I like to think of the old General in his billet on high, stroking his handlebar mustache and looking down on the solicitude of the American public for this produce of his game, and then upon the mourning for this man, which is almost national in character.

Perhaps he has just greeted the Babe, as though upon his arrival at home plate, throwing an arm around the big shoulders, and saying, "Well done, my boy: We could have used you at Cooperstown." At any rate, it is a pleasant thought to dwell upon.

R. W. HUBBELL.
Englewood, N. J., Aug. 20, 1948.

August 28, 1948

Origins of Baseball

Inventor Said to Have Been Alexander Joy Cartwright, in New York

To the Editor of The New York Times:

In your letter column of Aug. 28, R. W. Hubbell pays tribute to Gen. Abner Doubleday as the inventor of baseball and adds a little nonsense of his own to the groundless legend that has grown up about the general, who earned fame enough as a soldier without begging any he does not deserve.

A number of people in the past few years have tried (as I did in my book "Baseball") to tell the simple truth about Abner Doubleday. Yet no one, not even the learned Robert W. Henderson, has been able to catch up with the myth that has been systematically spread by the guardians of the professional game.

Abner Doubleday did not invent baseball. As far as any earnest research can reveal, he never played the game, watched the game, or talked about the game, and certainly never wrote about it. Mr. Hubbell says that Abner invented the game "when he was on furlough" from West Point in 1839. The records of the War Department will show that the good general was a plebe at West Point in 1839 and, as such, not even eligible for a furlough. And, inasmuch as the original story about the game's invention held that Doubleday in 1839 was "a student at Green's Select School in Cooperstown," this furlough story must be an invention of Mr. Hubbell's.

It may give Mr. Hubbell pleasure to dream about Abner Doubleday in his billet on high "stroking his handlebar mustache" (he never wore one in his term on earth which could properly be called "handlebar"), but that is no reason for misleading the youth of the nation. Let the "people whose business is baseball" mislead themselves and Mr. Hubbell if they wish. But let the rest of us, in the name of accuracy, recognize the facts.

"The position of the bases and the distance between the bases," says Mr. Hubbell, "has never been changed." I suppose he means "changed from the way Doubleday had them." Well, if Mr. Hubbell will look into this matter (he might even read my book, or Frank Menke's, or, better still, Robert W. Henderson's), he will learn that even the game Doubleday was supposed to have invented had four bases in addition to the batter's point. In short, it was not a diamond square at all, but an oblong town ball field such as had been used in Massachusetts and Philadelphia (and in the English game of rounders) for many, many years before young Doubleday could distinguish between a baseball and an egg.

The man who really invented baseball, who put nine men on a side (Doubleday's game, even the legend admits, had eleven), who set the bases "forty-two paces apart" (a fair approximation of the regulation distance) and who removed from the game the rule which permitted putting a man out by bouncing the ball off his anatomy was Alexander Joy Cartwright of New York City. And the true birthplace of baseball is not Cooperstown but the corner of Thirty-fourth Street and Lexington Avenue—or, if the first formal presentation of the game is considered, Hoboken, N. J.

May I suggest, too, that if, as Mr. Hubbell imagines, Fenimore Cooper ever saw young Doubleday playing one-hole cat (that's the correct name) in Cooperstown he was probably having hallucinations? For one-hole cat was a poor man's version of cricket and played more in the city than in the small towns, where there was always room for the rowdier game of town ball.

I do agree with Mr. Hubbell that the general public knows very little about the origin of the game of baseball. But I am afraid he must count himself among those who could not come close to telling the approximate date when the game was devised.

ROBERT SMITH.
Lenox, Mass., Sept. 1, 1948.

September 14, 1948

Slaughter Hurt, Musial Sets Mark As Cardinals Check Braves, 8 to 2

Enos, on Base, Has Nose Broken by Liner—Stan Hits 5 for 5 Fourth Time in 1948—Boston Victory Skein Ends at 8

BOSTON, Sept. 22 (AP)—Those never-say-die Cardinals stymied the pennant aspirations of the Braves at least temporarily today by thumping Boston, 8—2, with a 17-hit attack before 10,937 disappointed patrons.

So the pennant party—first in 34 years for the Braves—must be delayed at least until Saturday as the Tribe is idle until then and St. Louis will not play again until Friday. The Braves can clinch the flag if they win two games. They have eight to play.

The victory did move the Cardinals into second place, a half game ahead of the Dodgers, who were beaten, but it cost them the services of Enos (Country) Slaughter, classy outfielder.

Slaughter, racing toward second on a hit and run play in the fourth inning, was struck hard on the bridge of the nose by Nippy Jones' liner. Although he remained conscious, Slaughter was knocked to the ground.

Slaughter in Hospital Overnight

Carried from the field on a stretcher, he was removed under a physician's care to St. Elizabeth's Hospital, where his injury was diagnosed as a fractured nose with accompanying hemorrhage. Although Slaughter wanted to leave the hospital as soon as possible, he was ordered held overnight to be examined tomorrow by a nose-and-throat specialist, Dr. Vincent Kelley.

Stan Musial, leading hitter of both major leagues, led the attack on five Boston pitchers and put himself in the record books. Stan got five hits in one game for the fourth time this season, a new National League record. Musial also equaled the major league mark of five hits in each of four games in one season which the famous Ty Cobb of the Tigers established in 1922.

Musial's hit production included his thirty-eighth home run, a double and three singles. The left-handed slugger poked his double and two of his singles into left field.

The loss, charged to Lefty Warren Spahn, who had won his last four in succession, snapped a Boston victory string of eight games.

St. Louis Scores in Second

Three singles gave the Cards a run in the second inning and they got two more on Musial's double, Slaughter's single, an error by Tommy Holmes and a fly in the third.

The Box Score

ST. LOUIS (N.)	ab.	r.	h.	po.	a.	e.		BOSTON (N.)	ab.	r.	h.	po.	a.	e.
Sch'd'nst,2b	5	1	1	2	1	0		Holmes, rf.	3	0	1	1	0	1
Marion, ss.	5	0	1	2	6	0		Dark, ss	4	0	0	2	2	0
Musial,rf-lf	5	3	5	4	0	1		M.McC'mk lf	4	0	0	4	4	0
Slaughter, lf.	2	1	1	0	0	0		Elliott, 3b	4	0	0	1	1	0
Dusak, rf.	0	0	0	1	0	0		F.M'Cmk,1b.	4	0	0	8	2	0
Jones, 1b.	5	1	2	12	0	1		Conatser, cf.	4	1	2	3	0	0
Moore, cf	5	0	1	2	0	0		Masi, c.	4	0	2	4	0	0
Lang, 3b.	5	1	3	0	3	0		Sisti, 2b.	4	0	2	0	0	0
Rice, c.	4	0	1	4	0	0		Spahn, p.	0	0	0	0	1	0
Brazle, p.	4	1	1	0	4	0		aSturgeon	1	1	1	0	0	0
								Barrett, p.	0	0	0	0	0	0
								Hogue, p.	0	0	0	0	1	0
								bRyan	1	0	0	0	0	0
								Shoun, p.	0	0	0	0	1	0
								Lyons, p.	1	0	0	2	1	0
Total	42	8	17	27	14	2		Total	34	2	6	27	9	1

aTripled for Spahn in third.
bPopped out for Hogue in fifth.

St. Louis ....0 1 2 4 0 1 0 0 0—8
Boston ....0 0 1 0 0 0 1 0 0—2

Runs batted in—Rice, Slaughter, Jones, Brazle, Marion, Musial 2, Northey, Dark, Masi. Two-base hits—Musial, Lang 2, Schoendienst, Northey, Conatser, Masi. Three-base hit—Sturgeon. Home run—Musial. Double play—Hogue, Elliott and F. McCormick. Left on bases—St. Louis 9, Boston 6. Bases on balls—Off Brazle 1, Barrett 1, Hogue 1. Struck out—By Brazle 4, Spahn 1, Barrett 1, Shoun 1. Hits—Off Spahn 6 in 3 innings, Barrett 4 in 2/3, Hogue 2 in 1 1/3, Shoun 3 in 2, Lyons 2 in 2. Wild pitch—Shoun. Losing pitcher—Spahn. Umpires—Robb, Pinelli and Gore. Time of game—1:54. Attendance—10,937.

Bob Sturgeon's pinch triple, on which he just made third with a head-first slide, and an infield out gave the Braves one run in the third, but the Cards went to town for four in the fourth inning, which ended when Slaughter was struck by Jones' liner. It was in that inning that San the Man poled his home run into the bull pen in right.

Red Schoendienst, who had doubled, scored ahead of Musial. Don Lang started the inning with a two bagger and scored on Lefty Al Brazle's single after Del Rice had been called out on strikes. Then came Schoendienst's double and a long fly before Musial's four bagger.

Musial swung his red-hot bat for a single after two were out in the sixth and raced home with the eighth St. Louis run on Ron Northey's double to the left-field fence.

The Braves got their other run in the seventh on Clint Conatser's two-base blow high off the left-field wall and Phil Masi's two-base hit between the right and center fielders.

It was Brazle's sixth victory of the season, his third against one loss over the Braves. It was Spahn's third loss to the Cardinals, whom he has beaten thrice. The game ended the season play between the two clubs, with each having won eleven games.

Indians Win American League Flag, Beating Red Sox in Play-Off, 8-3

By JOHN DREBINGER
Special to The New York Times.

BOSTON, Oct. 4—Cleveland is to have its first world series in twenty-eight years.

This became an actuality today as the Indians, fired by the inspirational leadership of their talented skipper, Lou Boudreau, crushed Joe McCarthy's Red Sox in the single game that had been found necessary to break the deadlock in the American League 1948 pennant scramble.

The play-off, first in the history of the junior circuit and witnessed by a crowd of 33,957 shivering fans, most of whom watched it in glum silence, was decided by an 8-to-3 score, and as a consequence the Indians will oppose the National League champion Braves when the world series opens here Wednesday.

It marked only the second American League flag to be won by Cleveland and the first since 1920, when Tris Speaker, the famed Grey Eagle, led another band of Indians to a pennant as well as a subsequent world championship.

There never was much doubt of the outcome on this crisp autumnal afternoon. For the Tribe, which in the last few days of one of the most thrilling pennant races in major league history, had flubbed a couple of chances to win the flag outright over the regular 154-game schedule, this time shot straight for the mark.

Behind the stout-hearted five-hit hurling of Gene Bearden, 27-year-old southpaw freshman who last year was toiling on the Pacific Coast, Manager Boudreau blazed the trail with two home runs. Ken Keltner blasted another with two comrades aboard to spark a bruising four-run fourth inning, and that about tells the story.

Boudreau's play throughout was truly phenomenal. The personable graduate of the University of Illinois who in 1942 at the age of

Gene Bearden (left). Boudreau (center) and Ken Keltner, who played leading roles in the triumph, in dressing room after the game.
Associated Press Wirephotos

Play-off Box Score

CLEVELAND INDIANS

	AB.	R.	H.	PO.	A.	E.
Mitchell, lf	5	0	1	1	0	0
Clark, 1b	2	0	0	5	0	0
Robinson, 1b	2	1	1	9	0	0
Boudreau, ss	4	3	4	3	5	0
Gordon, 2b	4	0	0	0	0	0
Keltner, 3b	5	1	3	0	6	0
Doby, cf	5	1	2	1	0	0
Kennedy, rf	2	0	0	0	0	0
Hegan, c	3	1	0	6	1	0
Bearden, p	3	0	1	0	2	0
Total	35	8	13	27	17	1

BOSTON RED SOX

	AB.	R.	H.	PO.	A.	E.
D. DiMaggio, cf	4	0	0	3	0	0
Pesky, 3b	4	1	1	3	4	0
Williams, lf	4	1	1	3	0	1
Stephens, ss	4	0	1	2	4	0
Doerr, 2b	4	1	1	5	2	0
Spence, rf	1	0	0	1	0	0
aHitchcock	0	0	0	0	0	0
bWright	0	0	0	0	0	0
Goodman, 1b	3	0	0	7	1	0
Tebbetts, c	4	0	1	3	1	0
Galehouse, p	0	0	0	0	1	0
Kinder, p	2	0	0	0	1	0
Total	30	3	5	27	14	1

aHitchcock walked for Spence in ninth.

bWright ran for Hitchcock in ninth.

Cleveland . 1 0 0 4 1 0 0 1 1—8
Boston ...1 0 0 0 0 2 0 0 0—3

Runs batted in—Boudreau 2, Keltner 3, Hegan, Stephens, Doerr 2. Two-base hits—Doby 2, Keltner, Pesky. Home runs—Boudreau 2, Keltner, Doerr. Sacrifices—Kennedy 2, Robinson. Double plays: Gordon, Boudreau and Robinson; Bearden, Gordon and Robinson; Stephens, Doerr and Goodman 2. Left on bases—Cleveland 7, Boston 5. Bases on balls—Off Bearden 5 (Spence 2, Galehouse, Goodman, Hitchcock); Galehouse 1 (Bearden); Kinder 3 (Boudreau, Hegan, Gordon). Struck out—By Bearden 5 (Goodman, Doerr, Stephens, Spence, Pesky); Galehouse 1 (Hegan); Kinder 2 (Hegan, Doby). Hits—Off Galehouse 5 in 3 innings (none out in fourth); Kinder 8 in 6. Wild pitch—Kinder. Losing pitcher—Galehouse. Umpires—McGowan (plate); Summers (first base); Rommel (second base); Berry (third base). Time of game—2:24. Attendance—33,957.

---

25 became the youngest manager ever to direct a major league club, gave a performance seldom matched by any player in a struggle of such importance.

Playing his own position at shortstop flawlessly, maneuvering his men hither and yon with rare judgment and watching like a hawk every pitch of his youthful moundsman, Lou still found time not only to larrup two homers over the left field barrier, but added two singles, each of which figured in further scores.

Against this demonstration Joe McCarthy, completing his first year as manager of the Red Sox, and winner of eight American League pennants as field general of the Yankees, suddenly found himself completely out of ammunition.

For the battering Bosox, whose electrifying spurt in the last two days of the regular campaign had overcome a two-game deficit, failed Marse Joe rather badly.

Denny Routed In Fourth

In a surprise move McCarthy started his veteran righthander, Dennis Galehouse, and lived to regret it within four innings, for Denny was put to rout with the Keltner three-run homer. Then he followed with Ellis Kinder, who fell victim of the final fourth-inning tally, gave up three more in the fifth, eighth and ninth.

Even the renowned Ted Williams cast a rather sorry figure in this sudden-death struggle which the pleading Hub fans had hoped would produce the first All-Boston world series in history.

The Kid's mighty bat, which the two previous days had helped blast the Yankees out of the race, connected for only one single in four tries today. To add further to the woes of the disconsolate Boston fans, Williams capped his day by muffing a fly ball that gave the Clevelanders their tally in the eighth.

Of all the Sox, Bobby Doerr alone remained about the only "hero in defeat." With Williams on base, the result of the Indians' only misplay of the day, Doerr whacked his twenty-seventh homer of the year in the sixth.

But after this slip, Bearden kept the Sox tightly bottled the rest of the way.

Seventh Victory in Row

Inasmuch as all records compiled today go into the season's final statistics, this also marked the twentieth mound victory for the tall Coast southpaw against only seven defeats, and his seventh triumph in row.

Amid a world series setting which saw Commissioner A. B. Chandler in a "ringside" box and correspondents on hand from virtually all major league towns, the conflict had progressed only a few minutes when the indomitable Boudreau fired his first shot.

On his arrival this morning with his team from Cleveland, where the Indians had suffered an excruciating Sunday defeat at the hands of the Tigers to plunge the race into a last-day tie, Boudreau appeared a bit drawn and tired.

But there was nothing wrong with his flashing, clear eyes as he whipped into a Galehouse pitch and sent it sailing over the left-field barrier for his seventeenth homer of the year. It came with two out and nobody on and gave the Indians a one-run lead.

The margin was wiped out almost immediately when Johnny Pesky doubled in the lower half of the first and galloped home on Vern Stephens' single just inside the third-base line.

For the next two rounds Bearden and Galehouse kept the one-all deadlock intact. But in the fourth the Indians struck again and once more it was Boudreau who showed the way. This time the Cleveland pilot plunked a single into left. Joe Gordon followed with another into the same sector and a feeling of uneasiness swept through the crowd.

A moment later Keltner exploded a towering shot and as the ball streaked against the clear blue sky the Hub fans, who so often have seen enemy hopes dashed against the perilous left-field wall of historic Fenway Park, knew on the spot the worst was about to happen.

No. 31 Over the Wall

The ball soared over the wall for Keltner's thirty-first homer of the campaign and three Tribal runs scored. That was all for Galehouse and Kinder, one of the lesser lights on the Bosox staff, acquired from the St. Louis Browns last winter, emerged from the bullpen.

The former Brownie righthander didn't quell the uprising at once. Lary Doby, the Negro star, rifled a double off the wall in left center, the first of two two-baggers he was to hit during the afternoon. A sacrifice bunt by Bob Kennedy advanced Doby to third and he streaked over the plate while Stephens was tossing out Jim Hegan at first.

The Indians were four tallies in front and the stunned gathering, now looking on in stony silence, seemed to sense that final disaster was not far away.

The fifth was almost a repetition of the first. Kinder had just retired the top two batters of the Cleveland line-up when Boudreau unfurled his second circuit smack of the afternoon and eighteenth of the campaign. That made it 6—1.

Gordon Muffs Ted's Fly

In the last of the sixth, however, came a faint flurry of Boston hope. With one out, Williams, who had grounded out in the first and fouled out in the third, lifted a towering fly back of second base.

The crowd groaned but cheered a moment later as Gordon, staggering under the ball as he tried to sight it against a blinding sun, momentarily caught it, then dropped it for an error.

Unruffled, Bearden fanned Stephens for the second out, but Doerr was not to be disposed of so easily. He, too, sent the ball winging over the left field wall and as the two runners jogged around the basepaths. Boston spirits flared again. The score was now 6 to 3.

But the Bosox were never to get any closer. Bearden quickly brought the sixth to a close by fanning Stan Spence and in the seventh the chilled spectators were to put in another harrowing period as a pair of singles by Bearden and Dale Mitchell, a sacrifice and an intentional pass to Boudreau filled the bases for Cleveland with only one out.

More Trouble in Eighth

But Kinder revived hopes by retiring Gordon on the end of an infield pop-up and holding Keltner to a fly that Williams caught in left. The folks breathed again, but not for long. For there was more trouble in the eighth. Doby lashed another double into left center. Kennedy sacrificed him to third and Hegan drew a pass.

For an instant it looked as though Kinder would again effect a miraculous escape when Doby got himself picked off third for the second out, Hegan taking second during the run-up.

But on the heels of that Bearden lifted a high fly to left center which Williams, verging on the ball with Dom DiMaggio, elected to take. Ted, however, dropped it and Hegan scored easily.

In the ninth came the Tribe's final thrust. Ed Robinson singled and so did Boudreau for his fourth hit in four official times at bat. Came a wild pitch that advanced the runners to second and third and this forced an intentional pass to Gordon.

At that, only one run scored, Robinson skipping home while Keltner was pounding into a double play. But the Indians needed no more.

There was nothing the Sox could do with Bearden's baffling slider and knuckler. Bill Goodman drew a pass in the seventh only to see Birdie Tebbetts ground into a twin killing.

After Dom DiMaggio, hitless all day, had grounded out in the eighth and Pesky had fanned, Williams connected with a well-placed single into left. But Stephens ended this threat by forcing Ted at second.

In the ninth came one more pass, the fifth to be given up by Bearden. But the tall lefty made Goodman his sixth strike-out victim. Then Tebbetts grounded to Keltner and the American League's thrilling flag race, which early in August had seen four entries virtually locked in a tie and which still had three in the running up to the next to the last day of the regular season, finally had come to an end.

And so the Indians, after nearly three decades of bitter disappointments and in the third year of Bill Veeck's spectacular tenure as club president, at long last brought a second pennant to Cleveland.

Veeck, whose glamorous feats of showmanship produced attendance figures in the lakefront city which surpassed even the fabulous record of the Yankees, had once threatened this summer to jump off the "highest bridge in Cleveland" if the Indians failed to win the flag. Tonight he was all smiles as jubilant American Leaguers showered him with congratulations and best wishes for success in the forthcoming world series.

October 5, 1948

Musial of Cardinals Again Is Voted 'Most Valuable' in National League

Outfielder, First Player Ever to Capture Award Three Times, Gets 303 Points— Sain of Braves Second With 223

By JOHN DREBINGER

Stanley F. Musial, brilliant Cardinal outfielder who swept all but one of the National League's batting laurels last summer, has been named the most valuable in his circuit for 1948, according to announcement made yesterday after a poll of the twenty-four-man committee chosen from the ranks of the Baseball Writers Association of America.

Thus, Stan the Man, in winning the Kenesaw Mountain Landis Memorial plaque, becomes the first player in National League history to gain the MVP award three times. The 28-year-old star from Donora, Pa., who has had only six full seasons of major league ball, first won it in 1943 and repeated in 1946, after two years of service in the Navy.

As in the case of Lou Boudreau's triumph in the American League, Musial scored in hollow fashion in the balloting, in which each committeeman ranks ten players, first place receiving 14 points; second place, 9; third place, 8, and so on down to 1 point for tenth.

Dark in Third Place

Musial, named first on eighteen of the twenty-four ballots, scored a total of 303 points, with second honors going to Johnny Sain, ace righthander of the Braves. Boston's twenty-four-game winner totaled 223 points but drew only five first-place ballots.

Alvin Dark, star rookie shortstop of the Braves, received the only other first-place vote. Dark, who hit a snappy .322 in helping the Braves win their first pennant in thirty-four years finished third in the point score with 174 points, the only other player to top the 100-mark.

So thoroughly did Musial dominate the voting that only one ballot placed him as low as fourth. One other ranked him third and four named him second.

The flashy Cardinal who, handicapped by an attack of appendicitis suffered an off-year in 1947, came back with a dazzling display that almost single-handedly kept the Redbirds in the pennant race throughout the 1948 campaign. He captured the batting crown with .376 and also finished as league leader with 135 runs, 230 hits, 131 runs-batted-in, 46 doubles and 18 triples.

Only the home run title eluded him and this by the narrowest margin. He hit 39 round-trippers. The Pirates' Ralph Kiner and the Giants' Johnny Mize finished in a tie for the lead with 40 apiece.

Home Run Stars Trail

Both home run sluggers, however, were far outdistanced in the MVP balloting. Kiner polled 55 points to finish in a seventh place tie with the Cardinal's Enos Slaughter while Mize scored only 22 to place seventeenth.

Sid Gordon, who drove in 109 runs and batted .299 at third base for the Giants, finished fourth behind Dark with 72 points, followed by Harry Brecheen, the Cards' crack southpaw, with 61.

Pee Wee Reese is the first Dodger to show, with 60 points for sixth place, while two players who helped the Pirates make their surprising pennant run round out the first ten, Danny Murtaugh, a former Philly cast-off, scoring 52 points and Stan Rojek, sold by the Dodgers, coming up with 51 to top all his other former Brooklyn teammates except Reese.

In all, thirty-two players received one or more points with Bob Elliott of the Braves, last year's winner, placing thirteenth with 33.

The complete point score follows:

Stan Musial, St. Louis, 303; Johnny Sain, Boston, 223; Alvin Dark, Boston, 174; Sid Gordon, New York, 72; Harry Brecheen, St. Louis, 61; Pee Wee Reese, Brooklyn, 60; Ralph Kiner, Pittsburgh, 55; Enos Slaughter, St. Louis, 55; Danny Murtaugh, Pittsburgh, 52; Stan Rojek, Pittsburgh, 51; Richie Asburn, Philadelphia, 48; Johnny Schmitz, Chicago, 37; Bob Elliott, Boston, 33; Warren Spahn, Boston, 31; Jackie Robinson, Brooklyn, 30; Andy Pafko, Chicago, 25; Johnny Mize, New York, 22; Rex Barney, Brooklyn, 15; Johnny Vander Meer, Cincinnati, 9; John Wyrostek, Cincinnati, 9; Ralph Branca, Brooklyn, 8; Bob Chesnes, Pittsburgh, 8; Roy Campanello, Brooklyn, 8; Phil Cavaretta, Chicago, 6; Eddie Miller, Philadelphia, 4; Del Ennis, Philadelphia, 3; Grady Hatton, Cincinnati, 3; Larry Jansen, New York 2; Dixie Walker, Pittsburgh, 2; Gil Hodges, Brooklyn, 2; Whitey Lockman, New York, and Hank Sauer, Cincinnati, each 1.

December 3, 1948

Ban on Major Leaguers Who Jumped to Mexico Lifted by Chandler

WELCOME ASSURED ON EXILES' RETURN

Players May Be Reinstated Immediately, Baseball Head Tells Them in Letter

18 WERE SUSPENDED IN '46

Chandler Cites Recent Court Decisions as One Basis for Ending Ban on Stars

WASHINGTON, June 5 (AP)—Major league baseball tonight welcomed back all players who presently are under five-year suspensions for jumping to the outlawed Mexican League in 1946.

Commissioner A. B. (Happy) Chandler said he was forwarding by mail an offer to reinstate all players "who were placed on the ineligible list in 1946 for breaking their player contracts and jumping to Mexico."

Chandler said that all the league jumpers have to do is apply in writing to the president of their league—the American or the National as the case may be. In each case, he said, reinstatement will be automatic.

"Application for reinstatement," he told a reporter, "is tantamount to reinstatement itself."

"In fact, I just talked with Mickey Owen, who is in Winner, S. D., and he's leaving immediately to join the Brooklyn Dodgers."

Told to Pack His Bag

Owen, one of the best-known players who jumped to Mexico, talked with Chandler by telephone in the presence of newsmen. The commissioner was heard to tell Owen:

"Get your bag packed, boy, and get to your club right away."

Owen replied that he would join the Dodgers within 48 hours.

In reply to questions, Chandler said the reinstatement action had been talked over between all the club owners in both leagues and all are willing to take their players back.

"That is why application is automatic reinstatement," Chandler said.

"This is being done at this time because, under all the circumstances, it seems a fair thing to do, and because the threat of compulsion by court action has now been removed by recent unanimous decisions of the Circuit Court of Appeals in New York."

Judge Conger's Decision

In the New York court last Thursday, the Appeals bench unanimously affirmed District Court Judge Conger's decision of last April pointing out that to compel reinstatement of the players through the court "would restore them to positions they resigned voluntarily."

The Court ruled that in jumping to the Mexican League in the spring and summer of 1946, the players thereby violated their contracts, in effect resigning from their positions.

This verdict was rendered in the case of two former St. Louis Cardinal pitchers—Rookie Fred Martin and Max Lanier.

Former New York Giant outfielder Danny Gardella also has an action before the courts. Both cases are new pending before the Federal District Court in New York and no time has been set as to when they will be heard.

In addition to the four, mentioned the outstanding players affected by the ruling are:

Second baseman Lou Klein of the St. Louis Cardinals; Napoleon Reyes and hurler Adrian Zabala of the New York Giants; outfielder Roberto Ortiz and Chile Gomez of the Washington Senators; Luis Olmo of the Brooklyn Dodgers; Bobby Estalela of the Philadelphia Athletics; Chico Hernandez of the Chicago Cubs and Rene Monteagudo of the Philadelphia Phillies.

Lanier, reached by telephone in Canada, said he was "delighted" by Chandler's action and would apply for reinstatement immediately. Lanier is playing with Drummondville in the Quebec Provincial League.

Letter to the Players

Chandler's letter to each of the players concerned read as follows:

"This is to notify you that I have decided to permit you and other players placed on the ineligible list for violation of contractual obligations to apply for reinstatement. Accordingly, if you desire to be reinstated you should file your application at once with the president of your league in accordance with the provisions of major league rule 16."

In a statement to reporters, Chandler added:

"In 1946 when our players were being induced to break their contracts and jump to Mexico by glowing promises and enormous cash bonuses, I announced that I would suspend for five years those players who violated their player contracts by jumping to Mexico and who did not return to their clubs before the beginning of the season.

"In Havana, Cuba, in March I personally told those players who had jumped to come back to the majors and report to their clubs or they would be suspended.

"This action (suspension for five years) was then necessary in order to make these young men fully realize the serious nature of their contractual obligations and because of the threat to the integrity of the game resulting from their wrongful action.

"Some eighteen men in all were nevertheless persuaded to break their contracts and to play baseball in the Mexican League, and I accordingly notified each of these men that he would be placed on the ineligible list for five years. Shortly afterwards, Major league rule 15 (A) was enacted to make compulsory the five year ineligibility of players who jumped their contracts after that time. No more did so.

(To support Chandler's action, the American and the National League adopted the five-year rule in July of 1946 at their annual meeting.)

"Following the failure of the Mexican League to live up to the glowing promises made for it, many of these men petitioned me for reinstatement. In fairness to those players who had, in spite of large cash offers. remained with their clubs and carried out their obligations, I refused to reinstate them at that time. I always intended to give consideration for their reinstatement at a later date, after I had become convinced that the seriousness of their action in disregarding solemn obligations had been sufficiently brought home.

"In October, 1947, however, the Gardella suit was filed for the purpose, among others, of forcing the reinstatement of these players on the ground that baseball's contracts and in fact its entire structure was an illegal violation of the anti-trust laws. Another action was later filed by Martin and Lanier.

"If these suits had been successful in compelling the immediate reinstatement of these players, my authority, as commissioner, to enforce rules designed to preserve the honesty and integrity of the game would have been seriously impaired, if not destroyed. I have been confident throughout that no court would order the immediate reinstatement of these players,

who have properly been declared ineligible for contract violation.

"While this question was still before the courts and could be interpreted as a threat, however, I could not even consider taking such action voluntarily. Baseball will not ever surrender to threats of force, and it cannot afford to take any action which could be interpreted as such a surrender."

Forcing Action Fails

"The attempt to force immediate reinstatement through the courts has now failed. In denying the plaintiffs this relief in April, Judge Conger pointed out that to compel reinstatement of these players 'would restore them to positions they resigned voluntarily.' On appeal the Circuit Court of Appeals last Thursday unanimously affirmed this decision. This is a definite determination that baseball cannot be compelled to reinstate these players now, and it accordingly appears to remove the possibility that a court will order any change in their status during the term of the five-year ineligibility period originally ordered.

"The threat of compulsion by a court order having been ended, I feel justified in tempering justice with mercy in dealing with all of

these players. They have been ineligible for more than three years, and nearly all of them have admitted their original mistake and have expressed regret at their submission to the temptation to violate their contracts. In addition, the president of the Mexican

League has met with me in Cincinnati, and satisfactory relations have been established which should end the efforts of that league to induce our players to break their contracts.

"In the interest, therefore, of fair play to all and in the hope that the misguided young men who once so lightly disregarded their obligations will now be able to make a fresh start, I have decided to permit them to be restored, on application, to the eligible list."

Chandler pointed out that the major league clubs concerned are not bound to keep the reinstated players in the big time.

They will be reinstated to all the rules of baseball and under such can be optioned and waivered to the minor leagues, he said.

Chandler said that if any of the players don't ask for reinstatement now, they will automatically be reinstated in July, 1951, when the five-year suspension ends.

June 6, 1949

American League Defeats National for 12th Time in 16th All-Star Contest

32,577 SEE RASCHI SAVE 11-7 VICTORY

Yankee Ace Blanks Nationals in Last 3 Innings—18 Runs New All-Star Game High

AMERICANS DRIVE 13 HITS

Rivals' 5 Errors Also Help— Musial, Kiner Get Homers— Joe DiMaggio Bats In 3

By JOHN DREBINGER

In a most extraordinary exhibition, during which baseball was displayed at times at its best but more often at its worst, the American League yesterday at Ebbets Field demonstrated once again that, regardless of the going, it still could bludgeon its National League rivals into submission.

Exploding thirteen hits and profiting considerably by the amazing total of five errors on the part

of their inept adversaries, the cohorts of the junior circuit, led by Lou Boudreau, walloped Billy Southworth's array of assorted talent from one end of Flatbush to the other to win the major league All-Star game, 11 to 7.

The encounter, which consumed more than three hours and produced a parade of forty-two performers, was witnessed by a gathering of 32,577 that contributed a net of $79,225.02 to the players' pension fund.

Sixteen Runs Previous High

It marked the twelfth victory for the American League in the sixteen "dream" games played since 1933 and fourth in a row for the Will Harridge circuit. The total of eighteen runs for the two teams set a new record for the classic, topping the 9-7 score by which the American Leaguers triumphed in 1934. The five fielding blunders by the Nationals also set a stunning high.

At that, the Southworth squad fought back valiantly enough to make it a stirring if not at all times a glittering contest. Floored for four tallies in the opening round when two ghastly misplays wrecked what could have been a perfect first inning by Warren Spahn, the National Leaguers picked themselves up and, with the aid of two-run homers by Stan Musial and Ralph Kiner, elbowed their way back into the struggle.

They even led briefly at the end of the third and at the end of six

Joe DiMaggio scoring the second run for the American League on a single by Eddie Robinson of the Senators. The catcher is Andy Seminick of the Phillies.

141

innings were trailing by only one run. In the seventh, though, Howie Pollet, stylish southpaw of the Cardinals, was whacked for three runs and that clinched the battle.

Oddly, the American Leaguers included no homers in their offensive. However, they inserted no end of damaging blows to take advantage of their opponents' sad fielding lapses.

Williams Ignores Broken Rib

Joe DiMaggio, playing in his tenth classic, lashed a single and double that drove in three tallies, top figure for the day. Eddie Joost banged a two-run single off Gil Hodges' bare hand in the fourth to wipe out a 5-4 National League lead, and even though Ted Williams, playing with a fractured rib, was able to do no better than draw two passes and strike out once, it mattered little.

Four hurlers were used by the American League. Mel Parnell, Red Sox southpaw, was belted out in the second to be relieved by the Tigers' Virgil Trucks who, though roughed up for two runs in the third, nevertheless became the winner.

Lou Brissie, hurling the middle three innings, gave two tallies on Kiner's sixth-inning homer. In the final three the Yankees' big Vic Raschi blanked the baffled National Leaguers with one hit, a ninth-inning single by Andy Pafko.

Southworth, on the other hand, drew nothing save ill luck in his mound selections which reached a total of seven, another All-Star record. After Spahn's disastrous first round, the Dodgers' Don Newcombe fell victim of Joost's fourth-inning single that put the American Leaguers ahead for the balance of the long afternoon and as a consequence the young Negro righthander was charged with the defeat.

Munger Effective in Fifth

George Munger tossed a hitless and runless fifth but was asked to vacate for a pinch-hitter who, ironically, struck out, and that led only to more trouble. For in the sixth the Braves' Vern Bickford got thumped for two runs and then Pollet permitted the cluster of three in the seventh.

All too late the Reds' beanpole Ewell Blackwell and the Dodgers' Preacher Roe appeared for the eighth and ninth, respectively, to retire three batters apiece. Those were the only perfectly pitched innings of the game.

Particularly poignant were the day's doings for Brooklyn fans in the gathering. Though six of their Beloved Bums took part in the spectacle none distinguished himself too highly beyond Roe's ninth-inning mound splurge and the fact that Jackie Robinson and Peewee Reese, along with the Cards' Musial and the Pirates' Kiner, were the only players to play the full game.

Robinson became the first Negro to appear in an All-Star contest, though later three others, his team mates, Roy Campanella and Newcombe, and the Indians' Larry Doby, took part. Robinson touched off a noisy first-inning double, but thereafter his bat remained silent.

As for Reese, the Dodger captain had a particularly unhappy time of it. He went hitless in five official times at bat, ended a second-inning rally by slapping into a double play and committed one of the most damaging misplays.

The gathering barely had settled down under a cloudy sky, that later in the sixth inning interrupted play for eleven minutes with a sprinkle of rain, when the fireworks began. Spahn fanned the first batter, Dom DiMaggio, and looked to have George Kell snuffed out on an easy grounder to Eddie Kazak, but the Card third-sacker made a bad throw to Johnny Mize on first and difficulties followed thick and fast for Spahn.

Though the Boston lefty fanned Williams, Kell stole second with the help of a bad throw by Catcher Andy Semenick and Joe DiMaggio punched a solid single into left for the first tally.

A pass to Joost and a single by Eddie Robinson followed for another run. Then Reese fumbled Cass Michaels' hard grounder to let a third runner streak home and when Birdie Tebbetts singled to left the jubilant American Leaguers had four.

Nationals Strike Back

The National Leaguers weren't curling up, though, as they had in 1946 when their rivals set an all-time high for one team with their memorable 12-0 triumph. They lashed right back in the same round, Jackie Robinson's double and Musial's clout over the right-field wall producing two against Parnell.

In the second the aroused senior league finished Parnell, who vacated after a pass to Will Marshall, Kazak's single and a hit batsman had filled the bases. Trucks took over and one tally was all that followed, Newcombe belting that home with a long fly to left on which Williams made a dazzling catch.

Two more runs crossed in the third against Trucks and Southworth's band was in front, 5 to 4. The first resulted when Jackie Robinson walked, dashed to third on Musial's single and scored while Kiner was pounding into a double play. Despite this annoying setback, another tally followed in the

All-Star Box Score

AMERICAN LEAGUE

	ab.	r.	h.	po.	a.	e.
D. DiMaggio, Bos, rf-cf	5	2	2	2	0	0
Raschi, N. Y., p.	1	0	0	0	1	0
Kell, Detroit, 3b.	3	2	2	0	1	0
Dillinger, St. L., 3b.	1	2	1	0	2	0
Williams, Boston, lf.	2	1	0	1	0	0
Mitchell, Cleve., lf.	1	0	1	1	0	1
J. DiMaggio N. Y., cf.	4	1	2	0	0	0
Doby, Cleve., rf-cf.	1	0	0	2	0	0
Joost, Phila., ss.	2	1	1	2	2	0
Stephens, Boston. ss.	2	0	0	2	0	0
E. Robinson, Wash.. 1b	5	1	1	8	0	0
Goodman, Boston, 1b..	0	0	0	1	1	0
Michaels, Chicago, 2b..	2	0	0	1	3	0
J. Gordon, Cleve., 2b..	2	1	1	3	3	0
Tebbetts, Boston, c....	2	0	2	2	0	0
Berra, N. Y., c.	3	0	0	2	1	0
Parnell, Boston, p.	1	0	0	0	1	0
Trucks, Detroit, p.....	1	0	0	0	0	0
Brissie, Phila., p.....	1	0	0	0	0	0
Wertz, Detroit, rf.....	2	0	0	0	0	0
Total	**41**	**11**	**13**	**27**	**15**	**1**

NATIONAL LEAGUE

	ab.	r.	h.	po.	a.	e.
Reese, Brooklyn, ss....	5	0	0	3	3	1
J. Robinson, B'klyn, 2b	4	3	1	1	0	
Musial, St. L., cf-rf..	4	1	3	2	0	0
Kiner, Pittsburgh, lf..	5	1	1	3	0	0
Mize, N. Y., 1b..	2	1	0	1	0	0
Hodges, B'klyn, 1b..	3	1	1	8	2	0
Marshall, N. Y., rf....	1	1	0	1	0	1
Bickford, Boston, p....	0	0	0	0	0	0
bThomson, N. Y....	1	0	0	0	0	0
Pollet, St. Louis, p....	0	0	0	0	1	0
Blackwell, Cinc'nati, p.	0	0	0	0	0	0
Slaughter, St. L., rf..	1	0	0	0	0	0
Roe, Brooklyn, p.......	0	0	0	0	0	0
Kazak, St. Louis, 3b.	2	0	2	0	0	1
S. Gordon, N. Y., 3b...	2	0	1	0	4	0
Seminick. Phila., c.....	1	0	0	3	0	1
Campanella, B'klyn, c.	2	0	0	2	0	1
Spahn, Boston, p.......	0	0	0	0	0	0
Newcombe, B'klyn, p..	1	0	0	0	0	0
aSchoendienst, St. L..	1	0	1	0	0	0
Munger, St. Louis, p..	0	0	0	0	0	0
Pafko, Chicago, cf....	2	0	1	2	0	0
Total	**37**	**7**	**12**	**27**	**10**	**5**

aSingled to center for Newcombe in fourth.

bFlied out for Bickford in Sixth.

Amer. League...4 0 0 2 0 2 3 0 0—11
Nat'l League....2 1 2 0 0 2 0 0 0— 7

Earned runs—American League 7, National League 7.

Runs batted in—J. DiMaggio 3, E. Robinson, Tebbetts, Musial 2, Newcombe, Kazak, Joost 2, Kiner 2, D. DiMaggio, Dillinger, Mitchell.

Two-base hits—J. Robinson, Tebbetts, Gordon, D. DiMaggio, J. DiMaggio, J. Gordon, Mitchell. Home runs—Musial, Kiner. Stolen base—Kell. Double plays—Michaels, Joost and E. Robinson; Joost, Michaels and E. Robinson; J. Robinson, Reese and Hodges. Left on bases—American League 8, National League 12. Bases on balls—Off Spahn 2 (Joost, Williams), Parnell (Marshall), Newcombe (Williams), Trucks 2 (J. Robinson, Marshall), Munger (Michaels), Bickford (Kell), Brissie 2 (Campanella, Reese), Raschi 3 (S. Gordon, Pafko, Musial). Struck out—By Spahn 3 (D. DiMaggio, Williams, Parnell), Parnell (Mize), Brissie (Pafko), Blackwell 2 (J. Gordon, Stephens), Raschi (Campanella).

Pitching summary—Off Spahn 4 hits and 4 runs in 1 1/3 innings, Parnell 3 and 3 in 1 (none out in 2d). Newcombe 3 and 2 in 2 2/3, Trucks 3 and 2 in 2, Munger 0 and 0 in 1, Bickford 2 and 2 in 1, Brissie 5 and 2 in 3, Pollet 4 and 3 in 1, Blackwell 0 and 0 in 1, Roe 0 and 0 in 1, Raschi 1 and 0 in 3. Hit by pitcher—By Parnell (Seminick). Winner—Trucks. Loser —Newcombe.

Umpires—Barlick (N) plate, Hubbard (A) 1B, Gore (N) 2B, Summers (A) 3B, Ballanfant (N) LF, Grieve (A) RF. Time of game—3:04. Attendance—32,577 (paid). Receipts—$79,225.02.

inning when Mize and Kazak surrounded another pass to Marshall with a pair of singles.

In the fourth the Americans worked runners around to second and third with two out on Kell's single and a pass to Williams. In this spot, Newcombe directly after checking Joe DiMaggio, suffered a tough break.

Two Score on Single

Joost sent a scorching one-hopper toward right field. Hodges, who had just taken over first base for the Nationals, tried to collar the ball with his bare hand, but the thing caromed off his fingers and into the outfield for a single on which Kell and Williams scored.

In front, 6 to 5, the Americans never again were headed. They looked to have it tucked away in the sixth when Dom DiMaggio doubled, Kell walked and Joe DiMaggio drove in his final pair of tallies with a double into left center.

The Nationals, however, had one more round of ammunition and they fired it in the same round. With a runner aboard, the result of a pass to Reese, who promptly had been forced by Robinson, Kiner wafted a towering homer into the lower stand in left to cut the American lead to a lone tally.

All further hope for the Ford Frick circuit crashed in the seventh when Pollet was pounded for three runs on a Joe Gordon double, singles by Dom DiMaggio and Bob Dillinger and another two-bagger by Dale Mitchell. There would have been more had not Pafko torn in to make a spectacular sliding catch of Vic Wertz's low liner to center for the second out.

After that final splurge of American League power, the Nationals had nothing further to offer in rebuttal. In the last three rounds they bowed to Raschi's effective hurling although the big Yankee thirteen-game winner did try to give a little encouragement to them with three passes.

Not until two were out in the ninth with the bases empty did Pafko single. Andy even raced to second when the ball got away from Mitchell in left for the only American League error, but the luckless Reese ended the struggle with an easy pop fly that fell for the final out into the waiting hands of Joe Gordon.

In all, the triumphant American Leaguers tossed twenty players into the fray. Nationals used twenty-two in another thwarted effort to wrench interleague supremacy from their rivals.

July 13, 1949

Ralph Kiner

Pittsburgh Pirates

KINER HITS NO. 50, SETS LOOP RECORD

But Giants Nip Pirates, 6-4, as Williams Gets a 2-Run Homer in the Tenth

PITTSBURGH, Sept. 19 (P)—Ralph Kiner, Pittsburgh left fielder, smashed his fiftieth home run of the year tonight to establish a National League record but the Giants nipped the Pirates, 6--4, as Dave Williams hit a homer in the first of the tenth with one on.

Kiner, who got his circuit clout in the second inning, became the first player in the National League twice to hit fifty or more homers in a season.

Williams' homer came off relief pitcher Harry Gumbert, the fourth Buc hurler.

A rhubarb developed in the seventh after the Bucs had gone into a 4-3 lead. Tom Saffell was caught in a rundown by Infielder Bill Rigney and Pirate players rushed onto the field when they thought Rigney pushed the ball into Saffell's face. However, order was restored quickly.

A crowd of 11,452 was on hand to see Kiner hit his homer. He now is only one behind his own record of fifty-one established in 1947.

The box score:

NEW YORK (N.)	ab.	r.	h.	po.	a.	e.
Will'ms, 2b	4	1	2	1	4	0
Lockman, lf	4	0	1	0	0	1
Hopp, 1b	5	0	0	10	0	0
Marshall, rf	5	1	1	2	0	0
Thom'on, cf	2	1	1	0	0	0
Lafata, 1b	3	1	0	9	0	0
Rigney, ss	4	2	0	3	2	0
Westrum, c	3	0	1	5	1	0
Highe, p	3	0	2	0	1	0
aThompson	1	0	0	0	0	0
Jones, p	1	0	0	0	0	0
Total	**35**	**6**	**7**	**30**	**14**	**1**

PITTSBURGH (N.)	ab.	r.	h.	po.	a.	e.
Rojek, ss	4	0	0	1	3	0
Saffell, rf	5	1	1	2	1	0
Hopp, 1b	3	1	2	7	0	0
Kiner, lf	5	1	2	4	0	0
Westlake, cf	4	0	3	1	0	0
Castleman, 2b	4	0	0	3	2	0
McC'llough, c	4	1	1	5	1	0
Walsh, p	2	0	0	0	1	0
bWalker	1	0	0	0	0	0
Post, p	0	0	0	0	0	0
Sewell, p	0	0	0	0	0	0
Gumbert, p	1	0	0	1	1	0
Total	**36**	**4**	**8**	**30**	**14**	**1**

aSingled for Highe in eighth
bSacrificed for Post in seventh.

New York .... 0 2 0 0 0 1 0 1 0 2—6
Pittsburgh .... 0 1 0 0 0 1 2 7 0 0—4

Runs batted in—Westrum 2, Kiner, Highe, Westlake, McCullough, Saffell, Williams 2. Two-base hits—Westlake, Kiner. Home runs—Kiner, Williams. Stolen bases—Thomson, Hopp, Lockman. Sacrifice—Walker, Jones, Lafata. Double play—Rojek, Bragall and Hopp. Left on bases—New York 11, Pittsburgh 6. Bases on balls—off Walsh 4, Highe 2, Post 4, Sewell 1, Jones 1, Gumbert 1. Struck out—By Highe 4, Walsh 3, Post 1, Jones 1. Hits—off Walsh 2 in 4 1-3 innings, Post 2 in 2 2-3, Sewell 1 in 0, Gumbert 2 in 3, Highe 5 in 7, Jones 1 in 2. Passed ball—Westrum. Winner—Jones (11-16). Loser Gumbert (5-7). Umpires—Goetz, Reardon and Jorda. Time of game—2.41. Attendance—11,342.

YANKEES AND DODGERS WIN PENNANTS IN FINAL GAMES; 68,055 CHEER IN STADIUM

RED SOX DEFEATED

Raschi Pitches Yanks to American League Flag With 5-3 Triumph

BROOKLYN VICTOR BY 9-7

Conquers Phillies in 10th for National Loop Title—World Series Opens Wednesday

By WILLIAM J. BRIORDY

It will be the New York Yankees against the Brooklyn Dodgers in the 1949 edition of the world series starting Wednesday at Yankee Stadium.

In pulse-quickening finishes to the keenest major-league races in forty-one years, the battered Yanks staved off a last-inning rally to beat the Boston Red Sox, 5—3, to win the American League pennant before 68,055 Yankee Stadium on-lookers, while the Dodgers collared the National League flag by halting the Phillies, 9—7, in ten innings at Philadelphia's Shibe Park yesterday.

When the Yanks and Dodgers come to grips Wednesday, it will mark the third world series meeting of the interborough rivals and the second in three years. The Yanks won both previous series—in 1941 and 1947. The triumph was the sixteenth in the American League for the Yanks. Starting with 1890, the Dodgers have annexed the National League championship eight times. The Yanks' margin over the Dodgers in 1941 was 4—1 and in 1947 it was 4—3.

The Yanks and Red Sox were in a flat-footed tie when the teams took the field at the Stadium yesterday. The Dodgers entered the final day with a one-game lead over the St. Louis Cardinals, who snapped out of a four-game losing streak to beat the Chicago Cubs, 13—5.

Vic Raschi

Belated Card Victory

The Cards pulled out of their tailspin too late to catch the Brooks. The Yanks and Dodgers annexed their respective league titles by one game and, interestingly enough, the winners and runners-up in each circuit finished with identical records, 97 and 57 for the champions and 96 and 58 for the second-place clubs.

The Dodgers will be at Yankee Stadium Wednesday and Thursday and then the Brooks will be hosts to the Bombers Friday, Saturday and Sunday, at Ebbets Field, barring a sweep. In the event the series lasts that long, the final two games are listed for the Stadium on Monday and Tuesday, Oct. 10 and 11.

Stout-hearted hurling by their big righthander, Vic Raschi, enabled the gallant Yanks to defeat Joe McCarthy's Red Sox. It was a bitter pill, too, for the 62-year-old McCarthy, who saw his pennant hopes smashed in the same stadium where he led the Bombers to eight American League pennants and seven world championships. Moreover, it was the second straight season the Bosox were beaten out in the last stage of the campaign. Last year the Red Sox lost in a play-off with Cleveland.

Raschi held Boston in check for eight innings behind a one-run lead

which a triple by Phil Rizzuto had given him in the first inning. The Bomber hurler, up to the ninth, had the Bosox blanked on two hits in a tense mound battle with Ellis Kinder, who was trying for his twenty-fourth decision of the year.

Game Decided in Eighth

In the last of the eighth the Yanks put on the rally that won the flag. With Kinder going out for a pinch-hitter, the desperate McCarthy nominated Mel Parnell, his 25-game winning southpaw, to hold the Bombers until his own power hitters could have one last fling at Raschi.

Old Reliable Tommy Henrich greeted Parnell with a home run into the right field stands. Yogi Berra singled and Tex Hughson was called on to relieve Parnell. Joe DiMaggio hit into a double play but the Yanks proceeded to fill the bases. Then Jerry Coleman, rookie second baseman, cleared them with a pop fly two-bagger to short right field. That four-run outbreak carried the day, for the

aroused Bosox lashed back for three runs in the ninth.

The first two Red Sox runs in the ninth came in on Bobby Doerr's triple over the head of Joe DiMaggio, running on shaky legs. The Clipper then called time and dramatically took himself out of the game. Joltin' Joe, a sick man these past three weeks, received a great ovation as he walked off the field.

BOSTON (A.)	ab.	r.	h.	po.	a.	e.
D.DiM'gio,cf	4	0	0	5	0	0
Pesky, 3b.	3	0	0	1	0	0
Williams, lf.	2	1	0	0	0	1
Stephens, ss.	4	1	1	2	3	0
Doerr, 2b.	4	1	2	0	5	0
Zarilla, rf.	4	0	1	1	0	0
Goodman, 1b.	3	0	1	9	1	0
Tebbetts, c.	4	0	0	6	0	0
aWright	1	0	0	0	0	0
Parnell, p.	0	0	0	0	0	0
Hughson, p.	0	0	0	0	0	0
Total	**30**	**3**	**5**	**24**	**12**	**1**

NEW YORK (A.)	ab.	r.	h.	po.	a.	e.
Rizzuto, ss.	4	1	2	1	7	0
Henrich, 1b.	3	1	1	10	0	0
Berra, c.	4	0	1	5	0	0
J.DiMa'gio,cf	4	0	1	3	0	0
Woodling lf.	0	0	0	0	0	0
Lindell, lf.	2	0	1	1	0	0
Bauer, lf-rf.	1	0	0	0	0	0
Johnson, 3b.	4	1	2	0	6	0
Mapes, rf-cf.	3	1	0	3	0	0
Coleman, 2b.	4	0	1	3	1	0
Raschi, p.	3	0	0	1	0	0
Total	**31**	**5**	**9**	**27**	**6**	**0**

aWalked for Kinder in eighth.

Boston	0	0	0	0	0	0	0	0	3—3
New York	1	0	0	0	0	0	0	4	.—5

Runs batted in—Henrich 2, Coleman 3, Doerr 2, Goodman.

Two-base hit—Coleman. Three-base hits—Rizzuto, J. DiMaggio, Doerr. Home run—Henrich. Stolen bases—Goodman, Lindell. Double plays—Coleman and Henrich; Rizzuto and Coleman; Stephens and Goodman. Left on bases—Boston 5, New York 6. Bases on balls—Off Raschi 5, Kinder 3, Hughson 1. Struck out—By Raschi 4, Kinder 5. Hits—Off Kinder 4 in 7 innings, Parnell 2 in 0 (pitched to 2 batters); Hughson 3 in 1. Wild pitch—Raschi. Passed ball—Berra. Winner—Raschi (21—10). Loser—Kinder (23—6). Umpires—Hubbard, Rommel, Berry, Summers, Honochick and Hurley. Time of game—2:30. Attendance—68,055.

MANAGERS OF THE CHAMPIONS

Casey Stengel, Yankees

Burt Shotton, Dodgers

The New York Times

Dusk was settling over Shibe Park as the Dodgers put over their rousing tenth-inning rally to down the Phillies. Jack Banta, young relief pitcher, handcuffed the dangerous Philadelphia hitters for four innings after the Brooks had dissipated a 5-0 bulge.

Peewee Reese, who in five previous visits to the plate hadn't hit the ball out of the infield, dropped a single into left to open the top half of the tenth. Then the Dodgers proceeded to rush their two tallies across like real champions. Reese moved to second on Eddie Miksis' sacrifice and big Duke Snider sent the Dodger captain home when he rapped a sizzler through the legs of Pitcher Ken Heintzelman, nemesis of the Brooks all season.

With 36,765 fans cheering them on, the Brooks sewed it up. After Jackie Robinson had been purposely passed, Luis Olmo smashed a single past Willie Jones into left field to drive Snider across. Duke had taken second on the throw to the plate as Reese counted.

The jubilant Dodgers mobbed Banta at the end of the game. It was the tenth victory of the season for the big righthander, but none of his successes was as important as this one. He had come into the game after Don Newcombe and Rex Barney had been driven to the showers.

The Box Score

BROOKLYN (N.)   PHILADELPHIA (N.)

	ab.	r.	h.	po.	a.	e.		ab.	r.	h.	po.	a.	e.
Reese, ss...	5	1	1	0	1	0	Ashburn, cf.	6	0	2	4	0	0
Jorg'sen, 3b	3	1	1	2	2	0	eSanicki...	1	0	0	0	0	0
aEdwards..	1	0	0	0	0	0	Hamner, ss.	5	1	1	4	5	0
Miksis, 3b..	0	0	0	1	2	0	Sisler, 1b...	4	0	1	11	2	1
Snider, cf..	4	1	1	2	0	0	Ennis, lf...	4	2	2	0	0	0
Robi'son, 2b.	3	1	1	1	2	0	Seminick, c.	5	0	0	1	1	1
H'm'nski, lf.	3	1	0	0	0	0	Nich'son, rf.	4	1	1	2	0	0
Olmo, lf....	2	0	1	2	0	0	Jones, 3b...	5	1	1	1	4	0
Furillo, rf..	6	2	4	4	0	1	Goliat, 2b..	5	1	2	6	0	0
Hodges, 1b.	4	2	2	10	1	0	Meyer, p....	0	0	0	1	2	0
Camp'ella, c.	3	0	1	7	0	0	Roberts, p..	0	0	0	0	0	0
N'combe, p..	2	0	1	1	0	0	bBlatner..	0	0	0	0	0	0
Barney, p...	1	0	0	0	0	0	Th'mpson, p.	0	0	0	0	0	0
Banta, p....	1	0	0	0	1	0	cHollmig	1	0	1	0	0	0
							Stimmons, p.	0	0	0	0	0	0
							K'nstanty, p.	0	0	0	0	2	0
							dBlatnik	1	1	1	0	0	0
							H'zelman, p.	1	0	0	0	2	0
							Trinkle, p..	0	0	0	0	0	0
Total ...	**38**	**9**	**13**	**30**	**9**	**1**							
							Total ...	**42**	**7**	**12**	**30**	**14**	**2**

aFlied out for Jorgensen in seventh.
bWalked for Roberts in third.
cDoubled for Thompson in fourth.
dSingled for Konstanty in sixth.
eStruck out for Trinkle in tenth.

Brooklyn ....0 0 5   0 2 0   0 0 0   2—9
Philadelphia ....0 0 0   4 1 2   0 0 0   0—7

Runs batted in—Robinson, Furillo, Hodges, Newcombe 2, Campanella 2, Snider, Olmo, Jones 3, Ashburn, Nicholson, Hamner, Ennis.

Two-base hits—Hollmig, Campanella, Nicholson. Home run—Jones. Sacrifices—Banta, Robinson, Miksis. Stolen bases—Robinson 2. Double play—Hamner and Sisler. Left on bases—Brooklyn 12, Philadelphia 9. Bases on balls—Off Meyer 3, Roberts 1, Newcombe 2, Barney 1, Konstanty 1, Heintzelman 4. Banta 1. Struck out—By Newcombe 2, Barney 1, Konstanty 1, Banta 3. Hits—Off Meyer 5 in 2 2-3 innings, Roberts 1 in 1-3, Thompson 0 in 1, Simmons 2 in 0, Newcombe 6 in 3 1-3, Barney 4 in 2 1-3, Banta 2 in 4 1-3, Konstanty 1 in 2, Heintzelman 4 in 2 1-3, Trinkle 0 in 2-3. Wild pitch—Meyer 2. Winner—Banta (10—6). Loser—Heintzelman (17—10). Umpires—Goetz, Reardon, Barlick and Jorda. Time of game—3:17. Attendance—36,765.

October 3, 1949

National League Beats American

Ralph Kiner, left, whose homer in the ninth inning tied up the game, and Red Schoendienst, right, whose four-bagger won it in the fourteenth, in the clubhouse with Manager Burt Shotton after the contest.

LONG HITS DECIDE ALL-STAR GAME, 4-3

Kiner's Homer in Ninth Ties Score and Nationals Win in 14th Before 46,127 Fans

---

KEY TRIPLE BY SLAUGHTER

Blackwell Victor, but Jansen Holds Foe to One Safety for Five Innings, Fans Six

---

By JOHN DREBINGER
Special to THE NEW YORK TIMES.

CHICAGO, July 11 — Baseball's mid-summer classic, the All-Star game, conceived in 1933, began its second turn of the wheel today and after seventeen long years it finally looks as if something new is about to be added.

For on this steaming afternoon in the presence of 46,127 onlookers, the National League, so often the underdog in this annual fixture, turned on its arch tormentor to topple the American League in fourteen blistering innings with a pair of electrifying home runs.

Ralph Kiner, the Pirates' renowned slugger, hit the first with the bases empty in the top half of the ninth to deadlock the battle at 3-all. In the fourteenth, the Cardinals' Al (Red) Schoendienst exploded the other to give the senior circuit the battle, 4 to 3.

Ironically, two hurlers from the American League's leading Tigers were the victims. Art Houtteman yielded the homer by Kiner. Ted Gray was the one whom Schoendienst felled to become the losing pitcher.

Back to Original Site

Thus, as the classic returned to Comiskey Park, scene of the first encounter, the National Leaguers, beaten in twelve of the first sixteen games, gained their fifth triumph and with it the hope that as the spectacle swings around its orbit of major league parks a second time their luck will be better.

Most jubilant of all National Leaguers was old Burt Shotton who as director of the senior loop's forces gained some measure of revenge on the American League skipper, Casey Stengel, whose Yankees had topped Shotton's Dodgers in last October's World Series.

It was a nerve tingling exhibition the rival camps put on in this longest of All-Star games. In fact it was the first ever to go into extra innings.

In the fifth the American Leaguers went ahead, 3-2, on a pair of tallies wrenched from the Dodgers'

Don Newcombe. After those two runs, Shotton dug into the reserve trough of his National League pitching talent for nine scoreless innings.

Most brilliant of all the hurling was that which Larry Jansen, tall right-hander of the sixth-place Giants, contributed to the National's hard earned triumph. He wheeled in with five scoreless innings, from the seventh to the eleventh, inclusive, in which he allowed one hit and fanned six.

Fain Singles in Fourteenth

Then came Ewell Blackwell, the Reds' beanpole righthander, to put on the crusher in the closing three innings during which he allowed only one hit. That was a single by Ferris Fain with one out in the fourteenth. A moment later Joe DiMaggio ended it by splashing into a double play and that returned Blackwell the winner.

Stengel, too, got some fine hurling after his Vic Raschi had yielded two runs in the second, but when he called on Gray, only lefty to appear in the encounter, to start the thirteenth, he paved the way to his undoing. For in the fourteenth Schoendienst, a switch hitter, stepped to the right side of the plate and while Red normally does his heaviest hitting from the left side, this game-winning shot soared high in the upper left deck.

Gray never finished the round, for when another single, a strikeout and a passed ball followed, Stengel called on one of the heroes of bygone All-Star games, Bob

Feller, to prevent any further damage.

A sizzling sun beat down on the arena through fleecy white clouds as the starting hurlers, the Yanks' Raschi and the Phils' Robin Roberts, got the struggle under way and the sweltering crowd did not have to wait long for its first thrill.

Williams Makes Fine Catch

The National League's second batter, Kiner, slammed into one of Raschi's swift pitches and sent the ball riding toward the scoreboard in left center for what looked like an extra base hit. But Ted Williams, who some folks think specialize exclusively in getting his bat on a ball, got his glove on this one for a spectacular running catch that sent him careening off the wall.

For a moment it looked as if the Boston kid had hurt himself as his left elbow crashed into the barrier, but after some vigorous rubbing Ted signaled he was still sound in wind and limb.

Only three National Leaguers faced Raschi in that opening round and the Americans also were held scoreless in the lower half although the Yanks' Phil Rizzuto, playing in his first All-Star game after a long and patient wait, signalized the event by slapping Roberts' first pitch into left field for a single.

However, in the second the Nationals moved in front to score two runs in almost less time than it takes to say Jack Robinson, which was exactly the fellow's name who started it.

The Dodgers' brilliant Negro second sacker, playing his third successive All-Star encounter, opened with a single to right and a moment later was streaking over the plate as Enos Slaughter, the Cards' redoubtable veteran, larruped a triple into left center. Next came a long fly to right by the Cubs' Hank Sauer which produced an extra heavy cheer from the Chicago fans in addition to the second tally that Slaughter fetched home from third after the catch.

In the last of the second it looked as if the Americans would get one of these markers right back when Walt Dropo, the Red Sox' slugging rookie first-sacker, drove one down the center of the fairway that threatened to fall into the bullpen 415 feet away. But Slaughter, whom Shotton at the last moment had shifted to center in place of Sauer, who opened in right, hauled down the ball with his glove hand directly in front of the low barrier.

However, there was no checking the Americans in the third, which saw them clip Roberts for their first tally. Cass Michaels, batting for Raschi, who had just finished his three-inning stint, all that the rules allowed at that stage, got the junior circuit off its mark with a drive that bounced into the bullpen for a ground-rule double.

Rizzuto then pulled a neat bunt down the third-base line. It is possible Li'l Phil meant it mainly for a sacrifice, but when Willie Jones, the Phils' third-sacker, let it roll in the hope it would stray foul, the Yanks' Mighty Mite had his second hit.

It also moved Michaels to third, from where the Senators' second

All-Star Box Score

NATIONAL LEAGUE

	AB	R	H	PO	A	E
Jones, Phila., 3b	7	0	1	2	3	0
Kiner, Pitts., lf	6	1	2	1	0	0
Musial, St. L., 1b	5	0	0	11	1	0
Robinson, Bklyn., 2b	4	1	1	3	2	0
Wyrostek, Cinc., rf	2	0	0	0	0	0
Slaughter, St. L., cf-rf	4	1	2	3	0	0
Schoend'nst, St. L., 2b	1	1	1	1	1	0
Sauer, Chic., rf	2	0	0	1	0	0
Pafko, Chic., cf	4	0	2	4	0	0
Campanella, Bklyn, c	6	0	0	13	2	0
Marion, St. L., ss	2	0	0	3	2	0
Konstanty, Phila., p	0	0	0	0	1	0
Jansen, N. Y., p	2	0	0	1	0	0
cSnider, Bklyn	1	0	0	0	0	0
Blackwell, Cinc., p	1	0	0	0	1	0
Roberts, Phila., p	1	0	0	0	0	0
Newcombe, Bklyn., p	0	0	0	0	1	0
bSisler, Phila	1	0	1	0	0	0
Reese, Bklyn., ss	3	0	0	2	4	0
Totals	52	4	10	42	17	0

AMERICAN LEAGUE

	AB	R	H	PO	A	E
Rizzuto, N. Y., ss	6	0	2	2	2	0
Doby, Cleve., cf	6	1	2	9	0	0
Kell, Det., 3b	6	0	0	2	4	0
Williams, Bost., lf	4	0	1	2	0	0
D. DiMaggio, Bost., lf	2	0	0	1	0	0
Dropo, Boston, 1b	3	0	1	8	1	0
...in, Phila., 1b	3	0	1	2	1	0
Evers, Det., rf	2	0	0	1	0	0
J. DiMaggio, N. Y., rf	3	0	0	3	0	0
Berra, N. Y., c	2	0	0	2	0	0
Hegan, Cleve., c	3	0	0	7	1	0
Doerr, Boston, 2b	3	0	1	4	0	0
Coleman, N. Y., 2b	2	0	0	0	0	1
Raschi, N. Y., p	0	0	0	0	0	0
aMichaels, Wash.	1	1	1	0	0	0
Lemon, Cleve., p	0	1	0	1	0	0
Houtteman, Det., p	1	0	0	1	0	0
Reynolds, N. Y., p	1	0	0	0	0	0
dHenrich, N. Y.	1	0	0	0	0	0
Gray, Det., p	0	0	0	0	0	0
Feller, Cleve., p	0	0	0	0	0	0
Total	49	3	8	42	13	1

aDoubled for Raschi in third.
bSingled for Newcombe in sixth.
cFlied out for Jansen in twelfth.
dFlied out for Reynolds in twelfth.

National ..020 000 001 000 01—4
American ..001 020 000 000 00—3

Runs batted in—Slaughter, Sauer, Kell 2; Williams, Kiner, Schoendienst.
Two-base hits—Michaels, Doby, Kiner. Three-base hits—Slaughter, Dropo. Home runs—Kiner, Schoendienst. Double plays—Jones, Schoendienst and Musial. Left on bases—National League 9, American League 6.
Bases on balls—Off Roberts 1 (Evers), Newcombe 1 (Lemon), Houtteman 1 (Slaughter), Reynolds 1 (Musial). Feller 1 (Reese). Struck out—By Raschi 1 (Roberts), Roberts 1 (Doby), Lemon 2 (Campanella, Kiner), Newcombe 1 (Rizzuto), Konstanty 2 (Evers, Hegan), Jansen 6 (Houtteman, Doby, Kell, Williams, Hegan, Coleman), Reynolds 2 (Jansen, Reese), Blackwell 2 (Hegan, Coleman), Gray 1 (Campanella), Feller 1 (Blackwell).
Hits—Off Raschi 2 in 3 innings, Roberts 3 in 3, Newcombe 3 in 2, Lemon 1 in 3. Konstanty 0 in 1, Houtteman 3 in 3, Jansen 1 in 5, Reynolds 1 in 3, Gray 3 in 1 1/3, Feller 0 in 2/3, Blackwell 1 in 1. Wild Pitch—Roberts. Passed ball—Hegan. Winning pitcher—Blackwell. Losing pitcher—Gray.
Umpires—Bill McGowan (A. L.), plate; Ralph Pinelli (N. L.), first base; Ed Rommel (A. L.), second base; John Conlan (N. L.), third base; John Stevens (A. L.), and Doug Robb (N. L.), alternates. Time of game—3:19. Attendance—46,127 (paid). Receipts—$126,179.51.

sacker presently scored on George Kell's fly to Slaughter in deep center.

As the second pair of hurlers appeared in the fourth, Bob Lemon for the Americans and Newcombe for the Nationals, the junior loop launched an immediate threat as Dropo greeted Newcombe with a three-base slam that caromed off the bull pen wall at a crazy angle. But big Newcombe squirmed out of this jam neatly enough. After Hoot Evers had grounded out, Dropo erased himself by getting caught in a run-up between third and home on Yogi Berra's grounder to the mound.

In the fifth, however, Newcombe's luck ran out on him almost before he knew it and the Americans were in the lead with a pair of tallies. An odd feature of the thrust came in the fact that of the four Negro players on the field at the time three of them, Newcombe, Robinson and the Indians' Larry Doby, figured in its key play.

Lemon Draws a Pass

After Lemon had drawn a pass and Rizzuto had fanned, Doby lashed a sharp bounder through the mound and over second. For a instant it looked as if Robinson would collar the ball, but it caromed off his glove for a hit and as the white pill trickled into centerfield, Lemon not only tore around to third, but Doby, flashing some of his dazzling speed on the basepaths, slid into second for an extraordinary two-bagger.

Two American League runs followed. The first crossed as Kell again flied to deep center to drive in his second tally. The second resulted from Williams' lone hit, a resounding single to right.

With the Americans in front, defenses on both sides tightened and with the exception of the Kiner homer in the ninth neither party made any headway until the struggle was ended in the fourteenth by Schoendienst, who had replaced Robinson at second base in the eleventh.

Jim Konstanty, the Phils' relief specialist, blanked the Americans in the sixth, getting two on strikes. Jansen followed in the seventh with five innings of some of the finest hurling any All-Star classic has seen.

Permitted to go more than three because of the tie at the close of nine innings, the tall Giant right-hander allowed only one American Leaguer to reach first base in his long stretch through the eleventh.

This was Doby, who singled in the tenth.

In the meantime, the American League hurlers were doing quite all right, too. Lemon swept through his three innings, from the fourth through sixth, allowing one hit, a pinch single by Dick Sisler.

Then Houtteman held the Nationals at bay until Kiner, first up in the ninth, sent a lofty shot that dropped into the lower left stand. It was the Pirate slugger's second homer in All-Star competition.

From the tenth through the twelfth, the Yanks' Allie Reynolds kept the Nationals bottled, although the Chief had a close call in the eleventh when the Nationals filled the bases on a Kiner double, an intentional pass to Stan Musial and an error by Jerry Coleman, who had entered the encounter two innings previously to tighten his side's defense.

But Dom DiMaggio, who, along with Brother Joe, also had entered the game in the ninth, ended this threat with a fine catch of Andy Pafko's lusty slam to the left field wall.

In all, forty players appeared in the struggle, nineteen for the Nationals, twenty-one for the Americans. Seven went all the way, and Jansen's five-inning stint was the longest stretch by an all-star hurler since 1935 when, prior to the three-inning rule, Lefty Gomez started and reeled off six innings on the mound.

In addition to losing the ball game, the American League may have lost the services of its two hitting stars. Williams severely jarred the ligaments of his left elbow pulling down Kiner's mighty blast and banging into the left field scoreboard in the first inning, and Joe DiMaggio pulled some abdominal muscles streaking to first trying to beat the double play which ended the game.

Whether either will be able to resume the championship season Thursday remains to be determined.

July 12, 1950

Philadelphia Phillies

BROOKLYN SLUGGER TIES MAJOR RECORD

Hodges' Four Homers, Batting In Nine Runs, Pace 19-3 Victory Over Braves

By ROSCOE McGOWEN

Gil Hodges made baseball history as the Dodgers made merry with the Braves by beating them, 19—3, at Ebbets Field last night.

The big Brooklyn first baseman hit·four home runs and thus became the second major leaguer and first National Leaguer in modern annals to perform the feat in a nine-inning game.

The late Lou Gehrig was the man Hodges tied. The only difference was that the Yankee iron man hit his consecutively, his final one in the seventh inning, against the Athletics in 1932.

Gil hit his fourth one in the eighth inning into the upper leftfield stand off Johnny Antonelli. His first was in the second inning off Warren Spahn, the second in the third inning off Normie Roy and the third off Bob Hall in the sixth. In the fourth gil grounded to the third baseman and in the seventh he singled.

All homers save the last went into the lower left-field stands. Altogether Gil hit for seventeen total bases and he drove in nine runs, all with his homers. Carl Furillo was on base in each instance and in the third inning Jackie Robinson also was aboard.

Before the turn of the century Bobby Lowe, Boston Nationals, hit four consecutive homers within nine innings in 1894 and Ed Delehanty hit four with the Phils in 1896.

Two moderns, Chuck Klein with the Phils in 1936 and Pat Seerey with the White Sox in 1948, required ten and eleven innings, respectively, to get four in one game.

Total Bases Tie Record

Hodges also tied an all-time record with his seventeen total bases. This also was set by Lowe and Delehanty when they hit their quartets of homers.

There were only 14,226 cash customers present to see Hodges' almost unprecedented feat—certainly unprecedented for a Dodger—but they enjoyed every minute of the entire performance by the Brooks, who hadn't beaten any team so humiliatingly in many a moon.

They scored seven times in the third inning, with Duke Snider also tuning in with a terrific two-run homer over the scoreboard in right, his No. 24.

Hodges' total now is 23, which gives him a tie for the second time in two seasons with the old record for most homers hit by a right-handed Dodger, first set by Hack Wilson in 1932. Of course Roy Campanella, with his 28, already has exceeded that this season.

As the third player on the team to hit three or more homers in one game this season, Hodges also helped the Dodgers establish another major league record. Previously both Snider and Campanella had driven for the circuit thrice in a single contest.

The most lonesome home run was struck by Sid Gordon and, believe it or not, it gave the Braves a 1-0 lead. Sid clouted his No. 24 into the lower left-center-field stand off Carl Erskine in the second inning. Then Hodges started the Brooks on their spree in the Brooklyn half.

Erskine went all the way for his second triumph—both over the Braves—and until Gordon singled in the seventh, personally outhit the entire Boston team. Carl made four straight· singles—in the second, third, fifth and sixth innings —and was hit by an Antonelli pitch in the seventh. They didn't get Erskine out until the eighth when he sent a long drive to Gordon.

Spahn, searching for his seventeenth triumph, instead took his fifteenth setback. He has been whipped by the Broks four· times, while beating them only twice.

The box score:

BOSTON (N.)	ab.	r.	h.	po.	a.	e.		BROOKLYN (N.)	ab.	r.	h.	po.	a.	e.
Hartsf'd, 2b.	5	0	1	4	1	3		Brown, lf.	4	0	1	1	0	0
Jethroe, cf.	5	0	0	1	0	0		Reese, ss.	5	1	2	1	4	1
Torgson, 1b.	4	1	1	7	0	0		Snider, cf.	5	1	1	4	0	0
Elliott, 3b.	3	0	1	1	4	0		Robinson, 2b.	5	1	1	2	1	0
Cooper, c.	3	0	2	0	0	0		Morgan, 2b.	0	0	0	0	1	0
Crandall, c.	1	1	0	2	0	1		Furillo, rf.	5	4	3	1	0	0
Gordon, lf.	4	1	3	4	0	0		Hodges, 1b.	6	4	5	9	0	0
Marshall, rf.	4	0	2	1	0	0		Campanella, c	2	2	4	0	0	0
Kerr, ss.	4	0	0	1	4	0		Edwards, c.	1	1	1	2	0	0
Spahn, p.	1	0	0	0	0	0		Cox, 3b-2b.	5	3	3	2	3	0
Roy, p.	0	0	0	0	1	0		Erskine, p.	5	1	4	0	0	0
Haefner, p.	0	0	0	0	0	0								
aReiser	1	0	0	0	0	0		Total	65	19	21	27	10	1
Hall, p.	0	0	0	0	1	0								
Antonelli, p.	1	0	0	0	0	0								
bHolmes	1	0	0	0	0	0								
Total	36	3	5	24	11	4								

aStruck out for Haefner in fifth.
bLined out for Antonelli in ninth.

Boston .... 0 1 0 0 0 0 2 0 — 3
Brooklyn .... 0 3 7 0 0 4 3 2 .—19

Runs batted in—Hodges 9, Reese 3, Gordon 2, Snider 3, Brown 2, Marshall.
Two-base hits—Reese, Marshall 2. Home runs— Hodges 4, Gordon, Snider. Sacrifice—Cox. Left on bases—Boston 9, Brooklyn 11. Bases on balls —Off Spahn 3, Haefner 1, Hall 3, Antonelli 2, Erskine 2. Struck out—By Spahn 2, Hall 1, Antonelli 2, Erskine 6. Hits—Off Spahn 7 in 2 innings (none out in third); Roy 3 in 1-2-3; Haefner 1 in 1-2-3; Hall 6 in 1-2-3; Antonelli 4 in 7 - 3. Hit by pitcher—By Antonelli (Erskine). Winning pitcher—Erskine (2—3). Losing pitcher—Spahn (16—15). Umpires—Conlan, Gore and Stewart. Time of game—2:56. Attendance—14,226.

September 1, 1950

Phils Beat Dodgers for Flag; Win 4-1 on Homer in Tenth

By ROSCOE McGOWEN

The Philadelphia Whiz Kids, who came so close to winning the ignominious title of the Fizz Kids, captured the first National League pennant for the Quaker City in thirty-five years when they beat the Dodgers, 4—1, yesterday at Ebbets Field before the greatest outpouring of Flatbush fans—35,073—of the 1950 season.

The Brooklyn pennant bubble exploded in the top of the tenth inning when Dick Sisler, son of the Hall of Fame fellow who has been a Branch Rickey employe for years, swung with a mixture of power and desperation and drove a three-run homer into the lower left field stands.

Don Newcombe, who pitched and lost the first game of the 1950 campaign in Philadelphia, was the victim of Sisler's flag-winning wallop and Robin Roberts, the same chap who bested Newk in the season's opener, was the winning pitcher.

Roberts gained his twentieth triumph—the most important No. 20 he'll ever win — and became the first Phil hurler to win that many since the great Grover Cleveland Alexander turned in his third straight thirty-game season in 1917.

The courageous young righthander, who had failed in six previous starts to nail down No. 20, although pitching some fine games, deserved this big triumph, for he held the Brooks to five hits and would have had a shut-out but for a freakish home run by Peewee Reese, the gallant Brooklyn captain and shortstop.

In the sixth inning, with two out and the Phils leading, 1—0, Reese hit a towering fly to right field and the ball came down to the top of the wall and lodged in the screen.

Reese, assuming the ball had bounced off the screen or wall, raced around to third before he learned that the ball was out of play, while the crowd screamed its delight. That, they thought, would send the Brooks on to victory—and they were wrong only by a little bit, at that.

In the ninth inning the Dodgers

HAILING A HERO: Sisler (8) is joyously greeted after game-winning homer. Philadelphia regulars are Miller (center, wearing windbreaker), Heintzelman (third from left) and Goliat (hatless, rear). At left is Coach Bengough.   Associated Press

appeared certain to push over the winning tally, but it was thrown out at the plate, and from now on through the winter it will be hard to convince a lot of Flatbush fanatics that Coach Milt Stock didn't make a bad decision.

That momentous inning started with Cal Abrams, the lead-off man, drawing his second pass from Roberts on a three-and-two pitch. Reese tried twice to bunt and, with two strikes against him, lined a clean single into left center field, Abrams stopping at second.

Naturally, the Phils had to look for a bunt from Duke Snider, and were playing fairly close, but Duke rifled the first pitch into center—and the stands exploded in a vast roar. This was it.

But Richie Ashburn, coming in fast, fielded the hit clearly and fired it with deadly accuracy to Stan Lopata at the plate. Meanwhile, Stock was waving Abrams around third, with the disappointing, but certainly not unexpected result that Lopata was waiting with the ball when Cal arrived.

Robinson Purposely Passed

Even then, since Reese and Snider had advanced on the throw, the Dodgers had a big chance for the victory that would have sent them into a play-off today.

Jackie Robinson, of course, was purposely passed to fill the bases. Then Carl Furillo swung at the first pitch and the fans groaned as Eddie Waitkus camped under the feeble foul near first base.

The last hope faded when Gil Hodges, the Brooks' leading home run hitter, drove a high fly to right that Del Ennis took near the center field side of the scoreboard.

Then came the Phils' tenth and one could almost sense the feeling in the stands that this was all for the Dodgers. This feeling became more pronounced when Roberts started the winning frame with a single through the middle.

Waitkus, making one attempt to bunt, then swung and dropped a pop-fly single into short center out of everybody's reach, Roberts stopping at second. The bunt was on again but Ashburn, a good bunter and a fast runner, bunted into a force out at third, Newcombe making a good play on the attempted sacrifice.

Up came the extremely dangerous Sisler, who already had driven three consecutive singles to right field off Newcombe's slants. Dick swung at the first two pitches, missing one and fouling one, then looked at a wide one.

Biggest and Shortest

When he let go at the next one and the ball arched high toward left field, Abrams stood for a split second, then ran madly toward the wall. But it was no use. The biggest home run—and possibly one of the shortest—the stands are only 348 feet from home plate—that young Sisler ever hit, was on the records and the Whiz Kids had won the pennant that had been eluding them so exasperatingly for the longest week of their lives.

What followed was anticlimax. Newcombe striking out Ennis and getting Puddin' Head Jones on a simple grounder to Reese.

The Dodger tenth was a breeze for Roberts. Roy Campanella hit a

solid liner to deep left but it was caught easily by Jack Mayo, who had just been sent into left field in place of Sisler as a defensive move —one which Manager Eddie Sawyer frequently has made this year.

Then Jim Russell, pinch-hitting for Billy Cox, struck out and Tommy Brown, taking Newcombe's place at bat, lifted a high one to Waitkus at first.

The first break for the Phils came in the fifth inning, when they scored their first and all-important run, which might have been averted.

Waitkus and Ashburn had been retired on a couple of fine plays by Hodges, with Newcombe covering first base in each instance, when the tough young Sisler slashed his second single just out of Gil's reach.

Here Ennis lifted a high fly to right center and it appeared it could be caught. But Snider, playing deep for the Phil slugger in left center, couldn't race in fast enough, and Jackie Robinson didn't get out under the ball.

Whether Jackie could have made the catch is something that won't be known. Certainly Robby must have thought Snider would get under it, because Del was running at top speed all the way.

Anyway, immediately following that, Sisler, having moved around to third, Jones swung at Newcombe's first pitch and rifled the ball through to Reese's left for the single that brought in the run.

Reese delivered three of the five Brooklyn hits, opening the fourth inning with a line double to left that bounced around in the densely populated Phil bullpen. But here the Dodgers got a bad break when Snider tapped a ball toward first that he probably would have beaten out for a hit.

Marooned at Second

That would have put men on first and third with none out, but the ball just brushed Duke's leg as he dashed for first and the alert Larry Goetz, calling balls and strikes for the second straight day, promptly called Duke out and Reese had to return to second.

That's where the Little Colonel stayed, for Robinson bounced out to Roberts and Furillo lifted one of the few flies to the outfield hit by the Brooks, Ashburn taking it in right center.

As an indication of the caliber of Roberts' pitching, the big bonus boy had six assists and one put-out, while his first baseman had seventeen putouts.

Newcombe, on the other hand, was rather soundly smacked, even when he got his man out. A double play following Ennis' single to open the second frame, started by Reese, got Don out of trouble then, and at the start of the Phils' ninth Abrams made a spectacular leaping catch of Gran Hamner's drive against the left-field wall.

When Andy Seminick followed with a single and the fleet Ralph Caballero ran for him, Newcombe was helped out again by the fine collaboration of Campanella and Robinson, who nailed Ralph trying to steal.

Altogether the Phils made eleven hits, which helps to indicate that, on one important day, at least, the better pitcher and the better team won.

Thirteenth for Dick

A touch of irony may be noted in the fact that Sisler's homer was his thirteenth of the year, his third off Brooklyn pitching, and that all three were struck at Ebbets Field.

Seminick came into second with considerable vigor in the seventh when Mike Goliat bunted into a force play, Campanella to Reese, and Pee Wee had his right foot spiked slightly. Robinson was observed making a few comments to the big Phil catcher as Andy was heading for the dugout.

A small boy risked life and limb to clamber atop the right-field wall to get Reese's home-run ball. The kid tossed it to a friend in the stands below, apparently fearing a cop would take it away from him.

For the record, which doesn't matter much now, the Dodgers, starting from third place nine games back on Sept. 19, won 13 of 16 games to come close to the Phils, who won only three of twelve in that period.

The box score:

PHILADELPHIA (N.)							BROOKLYN (N.)						
	ab.	r.	h.	po.	a.	e.		ab.	r.	h.	po.	a.	e.
Waitkus, 1b.	5	1	1	18	0	0	Abrams, lf.	2	0	0	2	0	0
Ashburn, cf.	5	1	0	2	1	0	Reese, ss.	4	1	3	3	5	0
Sisler, lf.	5	2	4	0	0	0	Snider, cf.	4	0	1	3	0	0
Mayo, lf.	0	0	0	1	0	0	Rob'son, 2b.	3	0	0	4	3	0
Ennis, rf.	5	0	2	2	0	0	Furillo, rf.	4	0	0	3	0	0
Jones, 3b.	5	0	1	0	3	0	Hodges, 1b.	4	0	0	9	3	0
Hamner, ss.	4	0	0	1	2	0	Camp'lla, c.	4	0	1	2	4	0
Seminick, c.	3	0	1	3	1	0	Cox, 3b.	3	0	0	0	2	0
aCaballero	0	0	0	0	0	0	bRussell	1	0	0	0	0	0
Lopata, c.	0	0	0	1	0	0	N'combe, p.	3	0	0	0	3	0
Goliat, 2b.	4	0	1	3	3	0	cBrown	1	0	0	0	0	0
Roberts, p.	2	0	1	1	6	0							
Total.	38	4	11	30	16	0	Total.	33	1	5	30	17	0

aRan for Seminick in ninth.
bStruck out for Cox in tenth.
cFouled out for Newcombe in tenth.

Philadelphia ....0 0 0 0 0 1 0 0 0 3—4
Brooklyn ....0 0 0 0 0 1 0 0 0 0—1

Runs batted in—Jones, Reese, Sisler 3. Two-base hit—Reese. Home runs—Reese, Sisler. Sacrifice—Roberts. Double plays—Robinson and Hodges; Roberts and Waitkus. Left on bases—Philadelphia 7, Brooklyn 5. Bases on balls—Off Roberts 3, Newcombe 2. Struck out—By Roberts 2, Newcombe 3. Winning pitcher—Roberts (20—12). Losing pitcher—Newcombe (19—11). Umpires—Goetz, Dascoli, Jorda and Donatelli. Time of game—2:35. Attendance—35,073.

October 2, 1950

Mack Quits as Athletics' Manager After 50 Years; Dykes Gets Post

By WILLIAM G. WEART
Special to THE NEW YORK TIMES

PHILADELPHIA, Oct. 18— Connie Mack, known the world over as the grand old man of baseball, retired today as manager of the Athletics, the Philadelphia team he founded and managed since he helped organize the American League in 1901.

After sixty-seven years of playing the game and leading his White Elephants, the genial 87-year-old patriarch of the national game announced his resignation as field boss of the club at a hastily called luncheon press conference.

As two score newspaper men and sportscasters sat in stunned silence, Mr. Mack revealed that Jimmy Dykes, one of his most famous protégés, had been selected to succeed him in the dugout and that Arthur Ehlers, as general manager, would be in complete charge of the club's business affairs.

Speaking from his place at the center of the head table, with Dykes on one side and Ehlers on the other, Connie, tall and erect, smiled and said:

"It's a pleasure for me to be here today. I'm retiring from baseball and this is the way I'm retiring— as manager of the baseball club. I'm not quitting because I'm too old, but because I think the people want me to."

Continuing without the usual

long pauses and "ah's," Mr. Mack added:

"I know you realize I have been connected with the game for a long time. There are two men sitting here beside me—one is the new general manager. The other is the real (team) manager." He pointed to Ehlers and Dykes in turn and then went on:

"It is a pleasure for me to make the announcement. While I have not given Philadelphia all that was expected of me, I do know your future manager will do a great job if we get him the players—with the material he will have."

Although he will remain as president of the club, Mr. Mack emphasized that Ehlers would handle all future deals and, in the future, also would give out all news concerning the team.

Even in retiring, Connie still hopes for that "one more" pennant for the A's. During his half-century as manager, the team captured nine pennants and won five world series, among his golden years were 1929, 1930 and 1931 when the club, on which Dykes was the third baseman, came roaring home with successive pennants.

"You know," Connie observed, "we all like a winner and I feel that in our new manager we are going to have a winner—at least we are going after the material to make a winner."

CONNIE MACK AND HIS SUCCESSORS WHO WILL RUN ATHLETICS

The retiring manager of the Philadelphia team, center, with Jimmy Dykes, left, who will be the new manager, and Arthur Ehlers, who becomes general manager of the organization. Associated Press Wirephoto

Rumors that Mr. Mack would retire have been prevalent over the last decade, but each time he spiked them by saying that he would manage the Athletics as long as he was physically able.

His retirement from the bench follows closely the reorganization of the club, both officially and financially. Two of his sons, Roy and Earle, gained control of the club recently by buying out Connie Mack Jr., a half-brother, and other stockholders, excepting the interest held by Connie himself.

Mr. Mack's decision to retire as manager, it was learned, was reached on Monday after a series of discussions with Roy and Earle, who are vice president and secretary-treasurer, respectively.

The sons did not bring any pressure to force their father to withdraw from the bench. On the contrary, they announced a few weeks ago that their father would remain in the dugout as long as he wanted to. He will retain his post as club president and plans to make some of the road trips with the team, "because that's a habit hard to break."

In expressing thanks for his appointment as general manager, Ehlers said he intended to call upon Mr. Mack and his sons for advice "whenever I need it."

"I'm no different from any other person in baseball," he added. "I have the deepest respect and admiration for Mr. Mack. He is the most lovable and kindly man I ever knew and it is an honor to be associated with him.

Dykes then warned that he would tolerate no loafing on the ball club next season. "If any of the players read what I say," he added, "I want them to know that the honeymoon is over."

"Until last night," Jimmy said. "I had no idea where I'd be next year. In fact I was dickering for a job with Detroit.

"If as manager of the Athletics. I can ever receive one-millionth of the praise and respect that Mr. Mack has, I'll think I have acquired something."

WON FIRST FLAG IN 1902

Mackmen Beat Cubs for Initial Series Triumph in 1910

Connie Mack was born Dec. 23, 1862, in East Brookfield. Mass. His name then was Cornelius McGillicuddy, but sports writers whittled that down to Connie Mack. It fitted better in the box scores. The telephone directory still lists his name as "McGillicuddy."

The 6 foot 2 'string bean' quit a factory job in 1883 to play professional baseball. He was a catcher for eighteen years before organizing the Athletes in the newly formed American League in 1901.

As the "tall tactician" of baseball, Mack brought Philadelphia its first league title in 1902. Again in 1905, with Chief Bender and Eddie Plank as the leading pitchers, the Mackmen dominated baseball's junior circuit.

The first Mack victory in a world series came in 1910 when the Athletes turned back the Chicago Cubs. They retained the world title in 1911, whipping the New York Giants.

Again in 1913 and 1914 the Athletics won the American League flag, taking the world series in 1913. But in 1914 George Stallings' amazing Boston Braves defeated the Athletics in the post-season series.

Scraps $100,000 Infield

Mack then sold many of his stars, including Eddie Collins and the remainder of the fabulous $100,000 infield.

After finishing seven successive years in the cellar, Mack began rebuilding. Gradually the Athletics moved into contention, until in 1929 they won the first of three straight pennants.

Spearheads of what Mack has often called his greatest team were such great players as Lefty Grove, George Earnshaw, Rube Walberg. Jimmy Foxx, Al Simmons, Mule Haas, Bing Miller, Max Bishop, Joe Boley, Mickey Cochrane and Dykes.

Mack then unloaded his entire team in another sale. Since then

Connie's efforts to build another serious pennant contender have proved futile.

Won Edward Bok Prize

One of the most respected men connected with sports, Connie was awarded the $10,000 Edward W. Bok prize for distinguished service to Philadelphia in 1929. Before that, the award had gone only to artists, scientists, educators and philanthropists.

He was wined and dined in countless pre-season gatherings before the opening of the 1950 season. All were focused on another pennant in Mack fiftieth year of managing.

The pitching staff, a bulwark for several years, fell apart, however, and the club was unable to make up for the mound deficiency at the plate.

Connie Mack's Record

By The United Press.

PLAYER

Year, Club and League.	Pos.	G.	AB.	R.	H.	BA.	FA.
1884, Meriden (Ct.St.)	.c.	..	..	..	..	..	..
1885, Hartford (So.N E.,							
Conn. St.)	.c.	1	4	1	2	.500	.917
1886, Hartford (E.)	c.inf.	69	278	44	69	.248	.953
'86, Wash. (Nat.)	.c	10	36	4	13	.361	.932
'87, Wash. (Nat.)	c	60	322	35	71	.220	.904
1888, Wash. (Nat.)	.c.	85	300	49	56	.187	.916
889, Wash. (Nat.)	.c.inf.	97	386	51	113	.292	.903
1890, Buff.(Plyrs)	.c,inf.	123	506	95	136	.268	.939
1891, Pitt. (Nat.)	.c.	71	271	41	57	.210	.933
1892, Pitt. (Nat.)	.c.	86	338	39	87	.257	.949
1893, Pitt. (Nat.)	.c.	36	120	22	39	.325	.885
1894, Pitt. (Nat.)	.c.	63	230	32	59	.257	.938
1895, Pitt. (Nat.)	.c.	14	47	12	17	.362	.916
1896, Pitt. (Nat.)	.c.	30	116	7	24	.207	.981
1897, Milw. (West.)	.c,1b.	27	71	12	18	.254	.963

Major league total....695 2,672 387 672 .251 .925
(Mack hit only two home runs during his playing career, both for Pittsburgh in 1892).

MANAGER

			Games	
Year, Club and League.	Fin.	W.		L.
*1894, Pittsburgh (Nat.)	7th	11		11
1895, Pittsburgh	7th	71		61
1896, Pittsburgh	6th	66		63
1897, Milwaukee (West.)	4th	85		51
1898, Milwaukee	3d	82		57
1899, Milwaukee	6th	55		68
1900, Milwaukee (Amer.)	2d	79		58

(American League)

Year Club	Fin.(W.L.)		Year Club	Fin.(W.L.)	
1901. Phila.	4th 74 62		1926. Phila.	3d 83 67
1902. Phila.	1st 83 53		1927. Phila.	2d 91 63
1903. Phila.	2d 75 60		1928. Phila.	2d 98 55
1904. Phila.	5th 81 70		1929. Phila.	1st 104 46
1905. Phila.	1st 92 56		1930. Phila.	1st 102 52
1906. Phila.	4th 78 67		1931. Phila.	1st 107 45
1907. Phila.	2d 88 57		1932. Phila.	2d 94 60
1908. Phila.	6th 68 84		1933. Phila.	3d 79 72
1909. Phila.	2d 95 58		1934. Phila.	5th 68 82
1910. Phila.	1st 102 48		1935. Phila.	8th 58 91
1911. Phila.	1st 101 50		1936. Phila.	8th 53 100
1912. Phila.	3d 90 62		1937. Phila.	7th 54 97
1913. Phila.	1st 96 57		1938. Phila.	8th 53 99
1914. Phila.	1st 99 53		1939. Phila.	7th 55 97
1915. Phila.	8th 43 109		1940. Phila.	8th 54 100
1916. Phila.	8th 36 117		1941. Phila.	8th 64 90
1917. Phila.	8th 55 98		1942. Phila.	8th 55 99
1918. Phila.	8th 52 76		1943. Phila.	8th 49 105
1919. Phila.	8th 36 104		1944. Phila.	5th 72 82
1920. Phila.	8th 48 106		1945. Phila.	8th 52 98
1921. Phila.	8th 53 100		1946. Phila.	8th 49 105
1922. Phila.	7th 65 89		1947. Phila.	5th 78 76
1923. Phila.	6th 69 83		1948. Phila.	4th 84 70
1924. Phila.	5th 71 81		1949. Phila.	5th 81 73
1925. Phila.	2d 88 64		1950. Phila.	8th 52 102

*Took over as manager on Sept. 3 with club in seventh place.

WORLD SERIES
(ALL WITH PHILADELPHIA)

Year and Opponent.	Games		Year and Opponent.	Games	
	W.	L.		W.	L.
1905. New York.1		4	1914. Boston...0		4
1910. Chicago..4		1	1929. Chicago..4		1
1911. New York.4		2	1930. St. Louis..4		2
1913. New York.4		1	1931. St. Louis..3		4

3 YANKEE ROOKIES LIKELY TO REMAIN

Mantle, Morgan, McDougald Bright Prospects—Bombers Lose to Oakland, 9-6

By JAMES P. DAWSON
Special to The New York Times.

OAKLAND, Calif., March 24—Out of the substantial squad of rookies Casey Stengel took to the Yankee training camp at Phoenix when the club launched its 1951 preparatory campaign at least three today were reasonably assured of berths as regulars.

They are Mickey Mantle, the spectacular 19-year-old from Commerce, Okla., who is pretty well established as the replacement the club has been seeking against the day when Joe DiMaggio discards his glove and spikes; Tom Morgan, a right-hand pitcher from El Monte, Calif., and Gil McDougald, San Francisco product who appears to fit in perfectly with Manager Stengel's scheme of an adjustable infielder.

Mantle, hailed on all sides for his speed, hitting, throwing arm and instinctive natural ability, undoubtedly will accompany the Yankees to New York regardless of whether he is retained as a regular or shipped down to the minors for another year of preparation. The tremendous amount of

Mickey Mantle, the Yankees' nineteen-year-old rookie
Associated Press Wirephoto

publicity he has received dictates this, although Stengel wavers from day to day on the subject of whether to keep the youngster.

Morgan is a pitcher who is expected to take up some of the slack left by the departure of Whitey Ford for war service. McDougald will fill the gap left by the absence of Bobby Brown, who is frozen to his internship in a hospital here.

No official announcement has been forthcoming about the retention of these three players. Distribution of rookies at a training camp is always a top secret. As a matter of fact, the indications today were that the Bomber squad which came here will return intact

to Phoenix, disappointing Frank O'Doul of the Seals, who had expected some of the rookies would be cut adrift here for further seasoning.

Morgan is one of the most solidly recommended players on the rookie list. A good hitting pitcher, a fair fielder, he has a good sinking fast ball, a curve that is baffling at times, a good change-up pitch and, most important, good control.

McDougald, too, is highly recommended in the advance reports of scouts. In three years of schooling he has never hit under .330. At Twin Falls in 1948 his mark was .340. The following year at Victoria he slammed .344. With Beaumont last year his average was .336. His 187 hits, including 13 homers, 13 triples and 21 doubles, with 115 runs batted in, brought him distinction as the Texas League's most valuable player.

Such an authority as Rogers Hornsby, who should know, unhesitatingly recommended McDougald as major league material, saying without equivocation he was doing everything in major league style last year with Beaumont, where the Rajah managed.

McDougald started with the training squad as a third baseman, although at Beaumont he played second. The object, obviously was a replacement for Brown. The impression McDougald made with his natural ability at scooping grounders, ferrying the ball across the field, and hitting, led Manager Stengel to use the rookie at second in several recent games, with the express purpose of having the Frisco lad ready to step in should anything happen to Phil Rizzuto. This experiment saw Jerry Coleman shifted over to short, where he is thoroughly at home. And, as the recommendation said, McDougald fitted right smartly into the double-play combination around second.

March 25, 1951

MAYS, NEGRO STAR, JOINS GIANTS TODAY

Rookie to Play Center Field Against Phils—Wilson Is Optioned to Ottawa

Willie Mays, 20-year-old Negro outfielder, will start in center field for the Giants in the game with the Phillies in Shibe Park tonight.

Purchase of the youngster from the Minneapolis Club was completed at the Giants' offices yesterday. Leo Durocher, who had seen him play once, and Carl Hubbell, who had watched him often, were positive they had acquired an exceptional player.

Backing a press release saying "no minor league player in a generation has created so great a stir as has Mays at Minneapolis" was a batting average of .477 for thirty-five games with the Millers. He was in Sioux City yesterday for an exhibition game and was being flown here.

To make room on the roster for Mays, Artie Wilson, infielder, was optioned to Ottawa of the International League.

Tommy Heath, Minneapolis manager, advised Durocher over the telephone to keep Mays in center field, the only position he has ever played. He said he could "cover it like a tent," and that the Polo Grounds was made to order for him.

That's where the newcomer will play, at least for the present, displacing Bobby Thomson, who will resume his old position in left field. Mays will bat third in the line-up. Monte Irvin will be in

Willie Mays

right field and Whitey Lockman at first.

In his thirty-five games with Minneapolis, Mays made twenty-nine extra-base hits, eight of them homers, and batted in thirty-nine. He got seventy-one hits in 149 times at bat. A fast man on the bases, he had stolen eight. He's a 5 foot 11 inch 170-pounder who bats and throws right-handed.

Mays was signed by the Giants organization last June upon his graduation from high school. He was assigned to Trenton of the International League, where he hit .353 in eighty-one games.

The player was born at Fairfield, Ala., outside Birmingham. While in school he played some games for the Birmingham Black Barons.

May 25, 1951

Feller Hurls Third No-Hitter for Indians

ACE HELPS TRIBE TAKE TWO, 2-1, 2-0

Errors Enable Tigers to Tally in Feller's No-Hitter That Makes Baseball History

CLEVELAND, July 1 (UP) — Bobby Feller, who had to talk a coach into letting him stay in the game, pitched the third no-hitter of his career — and became the first pitcher in modern times to do so — as the Indians beat the Tigers, 2—1, today. The Indians also won the second game of the double-header, 2—0, on Bob Chakales' four-hitter.

The venerable fireballer, who was tossed aside as "through" only a few months ago and left off the American League All-Star team, said he was never better than when he set down the Tigers this afternoon. The one run he gave up was the result of two errors, one of them Feller's.

In the third inning Coach Mel Harder went out to the mound and asked Feller, "Do you feel okay? You don't look too good."

But Feller insisted that he was good enough to stay in — and then he proved it in historic fashion. Only four men reached base — three on walks, one on an error.

Throws Sliders, Curves

"I didn't even have a very good fast ball," Feller mused after the game. "I threw mostly sliders and curves. It was a wonderful thrill, but I still think my second no-hitter — against the Yankees — was better."

He is the first modern pitcher in history to throw three no-hitters. The legendary Cy Young pitched one in 1897, another in 1904 and the third in 1908.

Feller pitched his first no-hitter against the White Sox on opening day in 1940, his second against the Yankees on April 30, 1946, and then today he did it again before 42,891 nearly hysterical fans.

The Tigers got their run in the fourth inning. It came as the result of Ray Boone's error, a stolen base, a wild pick-off throw and a fly ball.

It's all part of a monumental comeback for the Iowa farm boy

who broke into the majors in 1936 at the age of 17. He had a 16-11 record last season and that—for him—was dismal.

His No. 219 in Majors

But he started like a whirlwind this season, winning four straight, losing a game, then winning six straight. The triumph today was his eleventh of the season against two losses, and the 219th of his career—more than any other active major league pitcher. Both of his previous no-hitters were by 1—0 scores.

The crowd rocked huge Cleveland Stadium as Feller slipped a third strike past Vic Wertz with the count 3—2 for the last out of the game.

Feller was forced to go at top form all of the way against Bob Cain, who threw a six-hitter, and the Indians did not win until the eighth when Sam Chapman tripled and Luke Easter slashed a single off Dick Kryhoski's glove to score Milt Nielsen who ran for Chapman.

The Tigers hit only five flies to the outfield and Feller struck out five. He walked only three men and retired the first nine hitters in order.

Cain allowed a run in the first inning on singles by Dale Mitchell and Bob Avila and Easter's infield out. The last time Cain pitched against Cleveland Bob Lemon beat him with a one-hitter.

Second No-Hitter of Year

Feller's no-hitter was the second of the year in the majors. Cliff Chambers pitched one for the Pirates against the Boston Braves on May 6. The last no-hitter by an American League pitcher was turned in by Lemon on June 30, 1948, and the victims were the same Tigers.

The Indians completed the humiliation of the Tigers in the second game as they made it ten victories in a row for the season. In the ten games, the Tigers have scored a total of eight runs against Cleveland pitching. They were shut out three times, scored one run in six games and two runs in one game.

The Indians collected seven hits off Ted Gray and Virgil Trucks and scored their runs in the sixth on a walk to Avila, singles by Chapman and Easter and a double by Bob Kennedy.

In New York, Yankee Manager Casey Stengel, who will pilot the American League All-Stars in the annual dream game with the National League, said he left Feller

off the team "because I think Lemon would relieve better."

Casey shook his head and added: "That cooks me. How could I know the guy was gonna pitch a no-hitter?" The box scores:

FIRST GAME

DETROIT (A.)	ab.	r.	h.	po.	a.
Lipon, ss	3	1	0	1	3
aHutchinson	1	0	0	0	0
Priddy, 2b	2	0	0	0	0
bKeller	1	0	0	0	0
Kell, 3b	4	0	0	1	1
Wertz, rf	3	0	0	1	0
Evers, lf	3	0	0	5	0
Kryhoski, 1b	3	0	0	8	1
Ginsberg, c	3	0	0	3	1
Groth, cf	2	0	0	2	0
Cain, p	2	0	0	1	1
Total	28	1	0	24	8

CLEVELAND (A.)	ab.	r.	h.	po.	a.
Mitchell, lf	3	1	1	3	0
Avila, 2b	4	0	1	0	3
cNielsen	0	0	0	0	0
Doby, cf	0	0	0	0	0
Easter, 1b	4	0	1	13	0
Simpson, 1b	0	0	0	0	0
Rosen, 3b	4	0	0	0	4
Kennedy, rf	4	0	0	3	0
Boone, ss	2	0	0	2	5
Hegan, c	3	0	2	5	0
Feller, p	2	0	0	0	0
Total	30	2	6	27	12

aFlied out for Lipon in eighth.
bFlied out for Priddy in eighth.
cRan for Chapman in eighth.

Detroit .... 000 100 000—1
Cleveland .... 100 000 01.—2

Errors—Boone, Feller. Runs batted in—Easter, Kell. Three-base hit—Chapman. Stolen base—Lipon. Left on bases—Detroit 3, Cleveland 7. Bases on balls—Off Cain 3, Feller 3. Struck out—By Cain 3, Feller 5. Winning pitcher—Feller (11-2). Losing pitcher—Cain (6-6). Umpires—Berry, Napp, Hurley and Passarella. Time of game—2:05.

SECOND GAME

DETROIT (A.)	ab.	r.	h.	po.	a.
Lipon, ss	4	0	0	1	4
Priddy, 2b	4	0	1	5	5
Kell, 3b	4	0	0	1	2
Wertz, rf	4	0	0	2	1
Evers, lf	4	0	1	0	1
Kryhoski, 1b	3	0	0	10	0
Groth, cf	3	0	0	3	0
Robinson, c	2	0	0	3	0
Gray, p	2	0	1	1	2
aGinsberg	1	0	1	0	0
Trucks, p	0	0	0	0	1
Total	29	0	4	24	16

CLEVELAND (A.)	ab.	r.	h.	po.	a.
Mitchell, lf	4	0	2	1	0
Avila, 2b	4	0	1	5	5
Chapman, cf	4	1	2	1	0
Easter, 1b	3	0	2	8	0
Simpson, 1b	0	0	0	0	0
Rosen, 3b	3	0	0	2	3
Kennedy, rf	2	0	1	3	0
Boone, ss	3	0	0	4	2
Tebbetts, c	2	0	0	5	0
Chakales, p	3	0	0	0	1
Total	26	2	7	27	8

aSingled for Gray in eighth.

Detroit .... 000 000 000—0
Cleveland .... 000 002 00.—2

Runs batted in—Easter, Kennedy. Two-base hit—Kennedy. Sacrifices—Kennedy, Avila. Double plays—Gray and Kryhoski; Avila, Boone and Easter 2. Left on bases—Detroit 5, Cleveland 6. Bases on balls—Off Gray 3, Trucks 1, Chakales 3. Struck out—By Gray 1, Trucks 1, Chakales 4. Hits—Off Gray 6 in 7 innings, Trucks 1 in 1. Winning pitcher—Chakales (3-2). Losing pitcher—Gray (3-6). Umpires—Napp, Hurley, Passarella and Berry. Time of game—1:41. Attendance—42,891.

July 2, 1951

National League All-Stars Win, 8-3

By JOHN DREBINGER
Special to THE NEW YORK TIMES.

DETROIT, July 10—The power of the home run, long exploited by the American League, rode with the rival loop today as the' National circuit, directed by Eddie Sawyer, romped off with the eighteenth All-Star game. The score was 8 to 3, a result that stunned a preponderantly American League gathering of 52,075.

Six of the Nationals' eight tallies came as the result of four circuit blows hit by Stan Musial, Bob Elliott, Gil Hodges and Ralph Kiner.

Not to be completely outshone in a method of attack which once was their greatest stock in trade, Casey Stengel's American League cohorts came up with two. One of these was by Vic Wertz, the other by George Kell, and since these were struck by a couple of hometown boys, both being members of the Tigers, they were received more enthusiastically than any of the others in this strictly American League bailiwick. But otherwise they had little effect.

This triumph was only the sixth for the Nationals as against twelve for the junior loop. But since this marked the second in a row, the longest "winning streak" ever compiled by the senior circuit, National Leaguers tonight were visualizing a definite swing in the pendulum which next fall could bring them a world-series victory as well.

Last year, at Comiskey Park in Chicago, the Nationals also won with the aid of the four-bagger,

Kiner's homer deadlocking the battle in the ninth and Red Schoendienst's clout sealing a 4-3 triumph in the fourteenth.

On this sweltering afternoon, however, the Nationals had power in abundance. Their four homers set a new high for a team in the mid-summer classic, and the total of six also was a record. They belted five of Stengel's hurlers for an even dozen hits.

And behind this heavy cannonading, Sawyer was able to muster mound talent that more than adequately met all requirements.

His own Robin Roberts of the champion Phils went the first two innings and gave up a tally. Then the Giants' Sal Maglie hurled the next three. He served up the home-run blast hit by Wertz and Kell in the fourth and fifth, but it was during his tenure on the hill that the Nationals, with a three-run splurge in the top of the fourth, swept to the fore.

Blackwell Finishes Game

As a consequence, the famed barber of the Polo Grounds received credit for the victory, although the Dodgers' Don Newcombe provided the day's best mound pyrotechnics. The giant Negro right-hander blanked the straining American Leaguers through the sixth, seventh and eighth on just two hits, one a triple by Ted Williams, after which the Reds' Ewell Blackwell came on to snuff out the Americans' last lingering hopes in the ninth.

In all Sawyer called on twenty players, six of them from the league-leading Dodgers, and all acquitting themselves in grand manner. Chubby Roy Campanella caught the entire nine innings, while Jackie Robinson, by way of demonstrating the versatility of the National's attack, drove in one

Feller's Pitching Masterpieces

NO-HIT GAMES

Date	Opponent	Score	Strikeouts	Walks	*Spoiler
April 16, 1940	Chicago	1—0	8	5	—
April 30, 1946	New York	1—0	11	5	—
July 1, 1951	Detroit	2—1	5	3	—

ONE-HIT GAMES

Date	Opponent	Score	Strikeouts	Walks	*Spoiler
April 20, 1938	St. Louis	9—0	6	6	Sullivan
May 25, 1939	Boston	11—0	10	5	Doerr
June 27, 1939	Detroit	5—0	13	6	Averill
July 12, 1940	Philadelphia	1—0	13	2	Siebert
Sept. 26, 1941	St. Louis	3—2	6	7	Ferrell
Sept. 19, 1945	Detroit	2—0	7	4	Outlaw
July 31, 1946	Boston	4—1	9	9	Doerr
Aug. 8, 1946	Chicago	5—0	5	3	Hayes
April 22, 1947	St. Louis	5—0	10	1	Zarilla
May 2, 1947	Boston	2—0	10	6	Pesky

*All hits were singles.

of the runs with a beautifully executed bunt down the third-base line.

Stengel, on the other hand, spent a trying afternoon. Victor in two successive world series, the crafty Casey plunged to his second straight All-Star defeat chiefly because the pitching strength at his disposal failed rather badly after Ned Garver's opening three innings.

The talented right-hander of the tail-end Browns did an admirable job, yielding only one hit and one run and that largely the result of a first-inning error.

But to add to Casey's woes, it was his own Yankee southpaw ace, Eddie Lopat, who virtually sank the cause of the American Leaguers in his only inning on the mound.

Parnell Yields Homer

Coming on in the fourth with the score deadlocked at 1-all, Lopat was stung for three runs on homers by Musial and Elliott and from the jolting effects of these two shots the Stengel forces never recovered. That barrage also made Lopat the loser, although the Nationals went on to crack the Tigers' Fred Hutchinson for three more tallies in the next three rounds in addition to picking up one more on Kiner's booming shot off Mel Parnell in the eighth.

Preliminary ceremonies, as usual, were brief. Just before the battle, the players of the rival squads strung out along the two foul lines while the crowd stood for a minute of silent tribute to the late Harry Heilmann, famed Detroit player of another era who had died yesterday morning.

Then the greatest of all Tigers, the matchless Tyrus Raymond Cobb, standing in Commissioner A. B. Chandler's box, tossed out the first ball that sent the struggle under way. And immediately the National Leaguers were on their way.

Richie Ashburn, the nimble outfielder of the Phils, drove Garver's first pitch into left field for a double and a moment later raced to third on Alvin Dark's fly to right.

Had there been perfect play, Ashburn would not have advanced further, for though Musial drew a pass, Robinson popped out in front of the plate to Yogi Berra, the doughty Yankee backstop who, like Campanella, caught the full game.

That made it two out, but before Hodges grounded out and retired the side, Musial raced for second on an attempted steal. Berra's peg had him, but Nelson Fox dropped the throw and before the ball could be retrieved, the fleet Ashburn was over the plate.

Fain Smashes Triple

Garver faced only six batters in the next two innings and in the second the Stengel cast drew even against Roberts on Berra's single and a triple off the right field wall by Ferris Fain, which Del Ennis fielded none too swiftly.

For a moment it looked as if the Americans would make off with still another tally as Chico Carrasquel dropped a single in short center. But Fain held up at third too long before heading home and was an easy victim of Ashburn's swift peg to the plate. That

The four National Leaguers who hit home runs celebrating the victory in the clubhouse. They are, left to right, Bob Elliott, Gil Hodges, Ralph Kiner and Stan Musial.

was the closest the Americans ever came to gaining the lead.

Lopat had just come on in the fourth when the Nationals really opened up. Musial greeted the southpaw with a drive into the upper right deck. The homer was Stan the Man's third in All-Star competition, a mark equaled by Kiner several innings later.

Before the fourth was over, Hodges banged a single off Kell's glove and galloped home ahead of Elliott's swat into the lower left

All-Star Box Score

NATIONAL LEAGUE

	AB.	R.	H.	PO.	A.	E.
Ashburn, cf.	4	2	2	4	1	0
Snider, cf.	0	0	0	0	0	0
Dark, ss.	5	0	1	0	3	0
Reese, ss.	0	0	0	0	1	0
Musial, lf., rf.	4	1	2	0	0	0
Westlake, lf.	4	1	2	3	1	1
J. Robinson, 2b.	4	1	1	3	1	0
Schoendienst, 2b.	0	0	0	0	0	0
Hodges, 1b.	5	2	2	6	0	0
Elliott, 3b.	2	1	1	1	1	0
Jones, 3b.	2	0	0	3	0	0
Ennis, rf.	2	0	0	0	0	0
Kiner, lf.	2	1	1	1	0	0
Wyrostek, rf.	1	0	0	0	0	0
Campanella, c.	4	0	0	9	1	0
Roberts, p.	0	0	0	0	0	0
aSlaughter	1	0	0	0	0	0
Maglie, p.	1	0	0	0	0	0
Newcombe, p.	2	0	1	0	1	0
Blackwell, p.	0	0	0	0	0	0
Total	39	8	12	27	9	1

AMERICAN LEAGUE

	AB.	R.	H.	PO.	A.	E.
D. DiMaggio, cf.	5	0	1	1	0	0
Fox, 2b.	3	0	1	3	1	1
Doerr, 2b.	1	0	1	1	0	0
Kell, 3b.	3	1	1	4	2	0
Williams, lf.	3	0	1	3	0	0
Busby, lf.	0	0	0	0	0	0
Berra, c.	4	1	1	4	2	1
Wertz, rf.	3	1	1	2	0	0
Rizzuto, ss.	1	0	0	1	2	0
Fain, 1b.	3	0	1	5	0	0
E. Robinson, 1b.	1	0	0	1	0	0
Carrasquel, ss.	2	0	1	0	3	0
Minoso, rf.	2	0	0	2	0	0
Garver, p.	1	0	0	0	0	0
Lopat, p.	0	0	0	0	0	0
bDoby	1	0	0	0	0	0
Hutchinson, p.	0	0	0	0	0	0
cStephens	1	0	0	0	0	0
Parnell, p.	0	0	0	1	0	0
Lemon, p.	0	0	0	0	0	0
dHegan	1	0	1	0	0	0
Total	35	3	10	27	11	2

aFlied out for Roberts in third.
bPopped out for Lopat in fourth.
cStruck out for Hutchinson in seventh.
dDoubled for Lemon in ninth.

National ....1 0 0 3 0 2 1 1 0—8
American ......0 1 0 1 1 0 0 0 0—3

Runs batted in—Fain, Musial, Elliott 2, Wertz, Kell, Hodges 2 Robinson, Kiner.

Two base hits—Ashburn, Hegan. Three base hits—Fain, Williams. Home runs—Musial, Elliott, Wertz, Kell, Hodges, Kiner. Sacrifice—Kell. Double play—Berra and Kell. Left on bases—National 8, American 9.

Bases on balls—Off Garver 1 (Musial), Hutchinson 2 (Robinson, Ashburn), Parnell 1 (Jones), Roberts 1 (Kell), Maglie 1 (Williams), Blackwell 1 (Doerr). Struck out—By Garver 1 (Ennis), Parnell 1 (Jones), Lemon 1 (Hodges), Roberts 1 (Garver), Maglie 1 (Williams), Newcombe 3 (Fain, Stephens, D. DiMaggio), Blackwell 2 (D. DiMaggio, Kell). Hits—Off Roberts 4 in 2 innings, Garver 1 in 3, Lopat 3 in 1, Maglie 3 in 3, Hutchinson 3 in 3, Parnell 3 in 1, Newcombe 2 in 3, Lemon 2 in 1, Blackwell 1 in 1. Passed ball—Campanella. Winning pitcher—Maglie. Losing pitcher—Lopat.

Umpires—Art Passarella (A. L.), Scotty Robb (N. L.), Ed Hurley (A. L.), Lou Jorda (N. L.). Alternates— Jim Honochick (A. L.) and Frank Dascoli (N. L.). Time of game —2:41. Attendance—52,075. Receipts —$124,294.07.

field seats. Lopat had given only three hits but they had put the Nationals ahead, 4 to 1.

One tally was whittled away when Wertz homered off Maglie in the fourth and Kell chopped away another with his blow in the lower left deck in the fifth. But with the sixth, the Nationals put on more pressure.

Hutchinson walked Robinson, opening the inning, and a moment later Hodges, leading home run clouter of his league with 28, rifled a drive into the lower left stand. Hutchinson had given up only one blow but it counted for two.

Surprise of the Day

In the seventh, with Hutch still pitching, Ashburn walked and Dark singled. Musial here forced Dark at second for the second out while Ashburn moved to third. At this point the Nationals pulled perhaps their biggest surprise play of the day.

With Robinson at the plate and the Americans apparently braced for another powerful thrust, Robbie confounded the opposition with a swinging bunt that stayed just inside the third-base line with all the artistry of a billiard shot. It caught Kell flat footed and Ashburn scored with ease.

In the eighth, with southpaw Parnell on the mound, the Nationals again switched tactics as Kiner lofted his all-star homer No. 3 into the upper left deck. That closed the Nationals' scoring for the day though they picked up two more singles off Bob Lemon in the ninth.

The Americans' attack folded completely after the ponderous Newcombe strode to the mound for the sixth. A great catch by Ashburn of Wertz's liner off the wall in deep right center saved possible trouble in the sixth, but after that nothing threatened until Williams belted a triple to the same sector to lead off the Americans' eighth. Duke Snider, just in the game, got a glove on the ball, but couldn't hold it and Ted got his only hit of the afternoon.

But though there were none out, the Americans could not get the run home as Big Newk retired the next three batters without allowing the ball out of the infield.

Doerr Draws Pass

In the ninth, Blackwell would have rubbed out three more in a row had not pinch-hitter Jim Hegan's pop fly fallen for a fluke double in short left. That prolonged matters a bit, for Bobby Doerr drew a pass after Dom DiMaggio struck out, but Blackwell fanned Kell for the final out.

The Little Professor, by the way, played the entire game for the Americans as did Kell along with Berra. Joe DiMaggio, though present, did not get into the encounter.

Hodges was the only National Leaguer beside Campanella to play the nine innings for his side. And, like every other National Leaguer on the premises, enjoyed every minute of the contest which drew $124,294.07 for the players' pension fund,

Sports of The Times
By ARTHUR DALEY
The Old Arbitrator

BILL KLEM was more than just another umpire. He was the best. John McGraw said so, although he and Klem fought like a couple of Kilkenny cats. All the ballplayers said so. All the baseball writers said so. By way of making it unanimous, Bill Klem said so.

The Old Arbitrator died the other day and baseball is the sadder for his departure. It wasn't only because he was a wonderful person who was held in affectionate esteem by all who crossed his path. He symbolized his profession with his uncompromising honesty, his perpetual alertness and his wistful claim of infallibility. More than that, though, he revolutionized the umpiring trade and had a more profound effect on it than any other man, an umpirical Babe Ruth as it were.

"I never missed one in my life" is a catchword that will endure as long as baseball is played. Old Bill actually didn't mean it when he said it and eventually was to modify it a mite by tapping his heart and adding softly, "in my heart." But when he first uttered it, it was in thunderous defiance of his on-the-field enemy and off-the-field friend, John Joseph McGraw. And the Little Napoleon was impressed.

Tough Decision

The Giants lost a tight one to the Cubs as a result of a ruling by Klem. Part of the scoreboard was in foul territory and part of it in fair territory. The paint line designating the foul line stopped at the bottom of the scoreboard and continued atop it. And a Cub batter hit one where no line was marked.

"Fair ball!" bellowed the Foghorn, unhesitatingly.

McGraw turned purple with rage. The Old Arbitrator was his usual picture of composure, heedless of the Little Napoleon's blistering invective. But the park superintendent, obeying or-

ders from McGraw, examined the scoreboard until he found the dent where the ball had struck. It was in fair territory—by no more than an inch.

The Old Arbitrator took that discovery in stride. "Naturally it was fair," he roared at McGraw, "I never missed one in my life." Thus was a legend born.

Once when Klem was a young umpire, new to the league and to McGraw's browbeating tactics, the great Giant manager threatened to have Bill stripped of his job.

Declaration of Principles

"Mister Manager," said Klem quietly, "if it's possible for you to take my job away from me, I don't want it."

The Old Arbitrator brought to that job a dignity it never had had before. He brought it respect and authority. He loved it with a consuming passion.

"Baseball is more than a game to me," he once proclaimed with all the fervor of his heart. "It's a religion." And Old Bill was always a God-fearing man who practiced his religion with scrupulous devotion.

Before he came along, umpires always dressed in their hotel rooms and left the game with the departing crowd. But Klem reasoned that this was improper. Not only might hot-tempered spectators assail the Men in Blue, verbally or physically, but weaker-willed members of his profession might lean toward home-town decisions. So he dressed for work at the ball park, even though he had to use the groundkeeper's shed, with a bucket of water instead of a shower.

So vehemently did he insist on separate dressing rooms for umpires that every ball park in the country eventually built them separate quarters. He even had architects scrap plans and go to what they deemed needless extra expense in order to have umpires' rooms far removed from the players.

Totally Unawed

No one ever awed him, not even Judge Landis. When the Old Jedge hauled him on the carpet to discuss the charge that Klem had been betting on horses, the ever-forthright Old Arbitrator never quailed.

"I've been betting them for nigh on to thirty years, Judge," he roared, "and I've always paid off a hundred cents on the dollar."

His relationship with McGraw was the strangest thing. They were the bitterest of enemies on the field but off it they were such friends that they frequently had dinner together. "The greatest manager who ever lived," said Klem of McGraw. "If there ever was a good umpire," said McGraw. "he was Bill Klem."

The Little Napoleon may have called him a blind so-and-so but whenever there was a crucial game, he always hoped the Old Arbitrator would be the umpire. It meant fair and accurate calls, because Klem was on top of every play and in the best possible position to see it. That was a phobia with him and he hammered it into every young umpire he ever taught.

Eighteen times he was chosen to umpire in the world series. Only the best should be in a world series and everyone knew that Klem was the best. So did he. Maybe that's why he was.

September 18, 1951

Frick Elected Commissioner Of Baseball for Seven Years

National League Head Gets Job at $65,000 Annually When Giles Withdraws

By JOSEPH M. SHEEHAN
Special to THE NEW YORK TIMES.

CHICAGO, Sept. 20—Ford C. Frick, 56-year-old president of the National League, tonight was elected commissioner of baseball.

His appointment, accepted over the phone from Bronxville, N. Y., was for a seven-year term at an annual salary of $65,000. It was to go into effect at midnight.

Warren C. Giles, president of the Cincinnati Reds and chief rival of Mr. Frick for the post vacated last July 15 by Albert B. (Happy) Chandler, withdrew his name from consideration after an around-the-clock voting deadlock between two career baseball men.

So on the final ballot of a number that reached at least fifty, Mr. Frick was the unanimous choice of the voting representatives of the sixteen major league clubs. The decision was announced shortly after 11 P. M. (New York time) following morning and afternoon sessions that had failed to produce a result. The vacancy left by the necessary resignation of Mr. Frick as president of baseball's senior circuit will be dealt with in the near future by the National League owners, probably during the world series, scheduled to open Oct. 3 or 4. An excellent guess is that Mr. Giles will get that job.

The choice of Mr. Frick, a teacher, sports writer, newspaper columnist and radio commentator before he became president of the National League in 1934, marks the first time that the sport has named a baseball man to the national pastime's highest administrative post.

The first commissioner was the late Judge Kenesaw Mountain Landis, nominated to the office in 1921 after the infamous Chicago Black Sox scandal had rocked the spot to its foundations. In 1945, following the death of Judge Landis, Mr. Chandler, then United States Senator from Kentucky, was voted into the job.

After a tempestuous reign, Mr. Chandler failed by three votes to muster the twelve votes required for re-election at St. Petersburg, Fla., last December. He was repudiated again in Miami last March, and he stepped down last July.

In considering a successor, the owners weighed the qualifications of many prospective candidates from all walks of life. There was much debate concerning whether another outsider of public stature and administrative experience would not be the wisest choice.

Ford C. Frick
The New York Times

In Family Circle

However, the final showdown was between two members of baseball's family circle—Mr. Frick and Mr. Giles.

No other names, of all those that have been bandied about for the last few months, figured in the picture in this executive session at the Palmer House, the first and only official joint meeting of the leagues on the commissionership since Mr. Chandler lost out.

Going into today's marathon session, Mr. Giles was generally considered to have the edge. The personable 55-year-old Cincinnati president had the backing of the owners who had supported Mr. Chandler, which gave him a nine-vote start toward the required twelve votes.

However, Mr. Frick had strong support also and some of those who were for Mr. Giles were satisfied that the National League president, who had run the affairs of his circuit with smooth efficiency, was equally qualified for the big job.

With the voting conducted on an "aye" and "nay," rather than man-against-man basis, with Mr. Giles and Mr. Frick considered alternately, neither man was able to muster a three-fourths majority. It was learned after the meeting that ten votes was the highest either polled on any ballot, and their fortunes fluctuated throughout.

Webb Only Non-Voter

Asked how many ballots were taken, Del Webb said, "a lot of them," then added, "at least fifty."

The vice president of the New York Yankees served as non-voting chairman of the joint meeting. As chairman of the screening committee, he had devoted months of laborious effort to narrowing the field of candidates to workable proportions.

After disposing of a few routine matters, the club officials went into executive session at 12:30 P. M. (New York time). Attendance was restricted to voting representatives, except for Mr. Webb.

As a large corps of lobby-watchers roamed restlessly about the corridors, the meeting dragged on behind locked doors. Now and then officials would pop out but only to cancel transportation reservations.

Announcement by Mr. Webb, before the dinner-time break, that "numerous ballots were taken on two candidates, Mr. Frick and Mr. Giles" without decisive result marked the first official identification of candidates.

Identity of the survivors after the narrowing of the field to eleven, then five at informal joint meetings in New York on Aug. 7 and 21, had been carefully guarded, although subsequent leaks had brought most of the names out into the open.

Other prospective candidates prominently mentioned along the tortuous route to selecting a successor to Mr. Chandler were Gen. of the Army Douglas MacArthur, James A. Farley, former Postmaster General and currently chairman of the board of the Coca Cola Export Company, and Gov. Frank Lausche of Ohio.

Vice President Gabe Paul represented Cincinnati, Mr. Giles withdrawing to await the decision at a neighboring hotel. However, the president of the Reds was recalled to the meeting at the start of the night session.

Shortly after he had entered the room, a burst of applause was heard. This first was taken to mean that he had been elected. It later proved to have been an accolade in appreciation of his sportsmanship in stepping down and thus ending the long deadlock.

Earl Hilligan and Charles Segar, respective publicity directors of the American and National Leagues, then were called into the room. In a short while Mr. Hilligan emerged to read the official announcement of Mr. Frick's election.

Representing the National League clubs were Horace Stoneham, Giants; Walter O'Malley, Dodgers; Robert Carpenter, Phillies; Lou Perini, Braves; Philip K. Wrigley, Cubs; Fred Saigh, Cardinals; John Galbreath, Pirates, and Gabe Paul, Reds.

American League electors were Dan Topping, Yankees; Roy Mack, Athletics; Tom Yawkey, Red Sox; Calvin Griffith, Senators; Walter O. Briggs Jr., Tigers; Ellis Ryan, Indians; Charles Comiskey, White Sox, and Bill DeWitt, Browns.

September 21, 1951

Yanks Clinch Flag, Aided by Reynolds' No-Hitter

BOMBERS CONQUER RED SOX, 8-0, 11-3

Yanks Take 3d Flag in Row, Reynolds' 2d No-Hitter of Year Winning Opener

RASCHI'S 21ST IS CLINCHER

7-Run Second Inning Decides Second Game—Joe DiMaggio Drives 3-Run Homer

By JOHN DREBINGER

In a brilliant display of all-around skill that included a nerve tingling no-hitter in one encounter and a seven-run explosion in the other, the Yankees yesterday clinched the 1951 American League pennant. It was their third flag in a row and eighteenth in thirty years.

With Allie Reynolds tossing his second no-hitter of the year—a feat previously achieved by only one other hurler in history—the Bombers vanquished the Red Sox in the opener of the double-header at the Stadium, 8 to 0.

Then, behind big Vic Raschi, the Stengeleers crushed the already eliminated Bosox, 11 to 3, to the cheers of 39,038 fans. Joe DiMaggio further embellished the triumph with a three-run homer as another flag was nailed to the Yankee masthead.

Tribe Clinches Second

Even were the Bombers to lose their three remaining games to the Steve O'Neill's Red Sox, they could not be overtaken by the last to survive. Cleveland's doleful Indians who, three and a half games out, have only two more encounters to play. The Tribe clinched second place as a result of Boston's two defeats.

Thus there remains nothing more for the Bombers to do now but await the outcome of the seething National League race between the Giants and the Dodgers to determine which club they shall meet in the world series. Unless the National's struggle ends in a deadlock tomorrow, necessitating a best-two-out-of-three game play-off, the big series will start at the Stadium on Wednesday.

In yesterday's smashing Yankee triumph, Reynolds' masterful performance provided most of the thrills, making even the clinching of the pennant somewhat anticlimactic.

Those who sat in on the show are not likely to forget those last tense moments when Reynolds, who had walked four batters during the game, had to collect "twenty-eight outs" before reaching his goal.

Berra Goes Sprawling

With two out in the ninth and the still fearsome Ted Williams at bat, a high foul was struck back of home plate. Yogi Berra, usually sure on these, scampered under it, but in the next agonizing moment the ball squirmed out of his glove as the Yankees chunky backstop went sprawling on his face.

It meant Williams would have to be pitched to some more. But Reynolds, an amazingly good-natured competitor under the most trying circumstances, patted Berra consolingly on the back and said, "Don't worry, Yogi, we'll get him again."

And, sure enough, up went another high, twisting foul off to the right side of the plate. It looked tougher than the first one. But Yogi meant to catch this one if it burst a girth rope and as he finally froze to the ball directly in front of the Yankee dugout, Reynolds first, and virtually all the other Yanks jubilantly piled on top of him. For a moment it looked as if Berra, not Reynolds, was the hero of the occasion.

Only one other major league hurler has ever fired two no-hitters in one season, and none ever in the American League. In 1938, Johnny Vander Meer, Cincinnati southpaw, turned in two on successive mound appearances, holding the Braves hitless on June 11 and repeating the trick on June 15 against the Dodgers in the first night game played in Ebbets Field.

This was the fourth no-hitter recorded in the majors this season. Aside from Reynolds, Bob Feller of the Indians hurled one against the Tigers on July 1, and Cliff Chambers of the Pirates posted one on May 6 against the Braves.

Reynolds' first no-hitter this year was tossed on the night of July 12 against the Indians at Cleveland. After the forthcoming world series, the Chief expects to undergo an operation on his right elbow.

Apart from the four batters who drew walks, the passes coming singly in the first, fourth, seventh and ninth innings, no other member of the Sox reached first base. No one reached second. The ace right-hander struck out nine and not one Boston batter seemed to come even close to a hit.

Behind this superlative hurling, which gave Reynolds his seventeenth triumph of the season against eight defeats, the Yanks lost no time getting the upper hand. They counted twice in the first off Mel Parnell, their conqueror in Boston last week, and added two more in the third with the help of a Dom DiMaggio error.

Then Ray Scarborough came on to be clubbed for a two-run homer

by Joe Collins in the sixth and in the eighth Gene Woodling larruped his No. 15 into the right field seats off Harry Taylor.

With this victory, the Yanks were assured of at least a first-place tie. Then they went after the clincher.

Some Anxious Moments

At the start there were some anxious moments as the Sox, with Williams out of their line-up, clipped Raschi for two runs in the first and another in the second with the aid of two surprising wild pitches. Williams, it was explained, had suffered a painful bruise when hit by a foul tip on the right leg in the first game.

Trailing by three, the Bombers made their move in the last of the second. With Commissioner-elect Ford C. Frick looking on, they crushed the Bosox with a seven-run demonstration, raking Bill Wight and Walt Masterson for five blows, the last a tremendous triple by Gil McDougald.

Commissioner Frick had missed the no-hitter, but he was in at the "kill" of the flag race. It probably marked the first time since his days as a baseball scribe covering the Yankees that the man who for seventeen years has been the National League president, saw an American League pennant decided.

From the third inning on, Raschi swung into his usually flawless style and so rolled on to his twenty-first victory against ten defeats. The closing crusher for the crestfallen Bosox came in the sixth, when Joe DiMaggio, not to be denied a share in the final spotlight, belted Chuck Stobbs for his twelfth homer with two runners aboard.

And so, to this most successful organization in baseball history not only comes its eighteenth pennant but for the fourth time the Bombers have annexed three in a row. Once they stretched the string to four and the chance to repeat this feat lies before them in 1952.

Also to the astounding Charles Dillon Stengel, who never had ~~~ ~ ~~~ in the American League prior to 1949, when he succeeded Bucky Harris as Yankee manager, comes the distinction of being the third pilot to win pennants in his first three years in a league. The fabulous Frank Chance did it with the Cubs in 1906-07-08. In the American League Hughey Jennings did it with the Tigers in 1907-08-09.

It was on this same corresponding Friday date that Bombers clinched their pennant last year, although on that occasion they had it much easier. The Yanks sitting idly in their hotel quarters in Boston while the runner-up Tigers were eliminated by the Indians. The most difficult victory came in 1949, when the Yanks, trailing the Red Sox by one with two games to go, vanquished the Sox in both games to win on the last day.

The span of Yankee triumphs covers only three decades. They won their first pennants under the late Miller Huggins in 1921-22-23, and with the little Miller still added three more in 1926-27-28.

After Huggins' death in 1929, the Bombers lapsed for a few years, but Joe McCarthy had them back with a flag in 1932 and then with 1936 followed the greatest sustained effort of winning in baseball history.

The Bombers, under McCarthy, won four in a row from 1936 through 1939. They were nosed out in a close finish in 1940. But in 1941 were back to reel off three more through 1943. In eight years, Marse Joe had bagged seven flags, a feat without precedent in the majors. But Professor Casey, with three victories in three tries, may give that record a terrific go.

The Box Scores

FIRST GAME

BOSTON (A.)	ab.	r.	h.	po.	a.
D.DiM'gio, cf.	2	0	0	2	0
Pesky, 2b.	4	0	0	1	2
Williams, lf.	3	0	0	3	0
Vollmer, rf.	2	0	0	0	0
Goodman, 1b.	3	0	0	1	0
Boudreau, ss.	3	0	0	0	1
Hatfield, 3b.	3	0	0	3	2
Robinson, c.	3	0	0	3	0
Parnell, p.	1	0	0	0	2
Scarb'gh, p.	0	0	0	0	1
Taylor, p.	0	0	0	0	2
aMaxwell	1	0	0	0	0
Total	26	0	0	24	10

NEW YORK (A.)	ab.	r.	h.	po.	a.
Rizzuto, ss.	5	1	1	1	2
Coleman, 2b.	5	2	1	2	3
Bauer, rf.	4	0	1	5	0
J.DiM'gio, cf.	4	0	1	0	0
McD'gald, 3b.	3	1	1	0	1
Berra, c.	4	0	1	9	1
Woodling, lf.	4	2	2	2	0
Collins, 1b.	4	2	2	8	0
Reynolds, p.	3	0	0	0	1
Total	34	8	10	27	8

aGrounded out for Taylor in ninth.

Boston .... 000 000 000—0
New York .... 202 102 01x—8

Errors—D. DiMaggio, Vollmer, Hatfield, Berra. Runs batted in—Bauer, Berra, McDougald, Coleman, Collins 3, Woodling. Two-base hit—Collins. Home runs—Collins, Woodling. Stolen base—Coleman. Sacrifice—Reynolds. Double plays—Hatfield and Goodman; Rizzuto and Collins. Left on bases—Boston 3, New York 5. Bases on balls—Off Parnell 2, Reynolds 4. Struck out—By Parnell 2, Reynolds 9. Hits—Off Parnell 5 in 3 innings, Scarborough 3 in 3, Taylor 2 in 2. Winning pitcher—Reynolds (17-8). Losing pitcher—Parnell (18-11). Umpires—Hubbard, McGowan, Berry and Hurley. Time of game—2:12.

SECOND GAME

BOSTON (A.)	ab.	r.	h.	po.	a.
D.D.M'gio, cf.	5	2	2	4	0
Pesky, 2b.	4	1	1	2	3
Maxwell, lf.	3	0	0	2	0
Vollmer, rf.	4	0	0	1	0
Goodman, 1b.	3	0	0	5	0
Boudreau, ss.	4	0	2	1	2
Hatfield, 3b.	3	0	1	1	1
Moss, c.	3	0	0	7	0
aRichter	1	0	0	0	0
Wright, p.	1	0	0	0	0
Masterson, p.	1	0	0	0	0
Stobbs, p.	2	0	0	1	0
Nixon, p.	0	0	0	0	0
bWright	0	0	0	0	0
Total	33	3	6	24	6

NEW YORK (A.)	ab.	r.	h.	po.	a.
Rizzuto, ss.	5	1	3	1	4
Coleman, 2b.	5	1	3	1	2
Bauer, rf.	5	2	3	2	0
J.D.M'gio, cf.	5	1	1	4	0
McD'gald, 3b.	5	0	1	2	3
Berra, c.	4	1	2	5	0
Woodling, lf.	4	1	0	6	0
Collins, 1b.	4	1	2	6	0
Raschi, p.	3	1	0	0	0
Total	36	11	13	27	6

aFouled out for Moss in ninth.
bWalked for Nixon in ninth.

Boston .... 210 000 000—3
New York .... 070 003 01.—11

Errors—Goodman, Boudreau. Runs batted in—Boudreau, Hatfield, McDougald 2, Rizzuto 2, Bauer 2, J. DiMaggio 4, Collins. Two-base hits—Bauer, Coleman. Three-base hit—McDougald. Home run—J. DiMaggio. Stolen base—D. DiMaggio. Sacrifice—Coleman. Double plays—Boudreau, Pesky and Goodman 2. Left on bases—Boston 7, New York 6. Bases on balls—Off Wight 3, Stobbs 1, Raschi 4. Struck out—By Stobbs 2, Nixon 4, Raschi 5. Hits—Off Wight 4 in 1 1-3 innings, Masterson 2 in 1-3, Stobbs 5 in 4 1-3, Nixon 2 in 3. Wild pitches—Raschi 2, Nixon 2. Passed ball—Moss. Winning pitcher—Raschi (21—10). Losing pitches—Wight (7-7). Umpires—McGowan, Berry, Hubbard and Huly. Time of Game—2:32.

BROOKS BEAT PHILS IN FOURTEENTH, 9-8

Robinson's Homer With 2 Out Decides Thrilling Uphill Struggle for Dodgers

SCORE IS TIED IN EIGHTH

Flatbush Club Fights to 8-8 Deadlock After Trailing 6-1 —Defense Is Superb

By ROSCOE McGOWEN
Special to THE NEW YORK TIMES.

PHILADELPHIA, Sept. 30 — Jackie Robinson made the most vital put-out of his career in the twelfth inning today, then hit the most important home run of his life in the fourteenth to give the embattled Dodgers a 9-8 triumph over the Phils and put the Brooks into a pennant play-off with the Giants.

Two more dramatic events probably never have been seen in such a ball game, and the record Shibe Park crowd of 31,755—thousands of them from Brooklyn—reacted accordingly.

Don Newcombe, the sixth pitcher Manager Chuck Dressen had tossed into the game, had the bases filled and two out in the twelfth when a hit would have sent the Dodgers tumbling into the most disastrous flag loss in National League history.

Eddie Waitkus apparently had made that hit with a low line drive to the right field side of second base. But Robinson raced over, dived to clutch the ball just off the ground and Umpire Lon Warneke's arm went up signaling the saving put-out.

Robbie fell hard on his shoulder and collapsed after tossing the ball weakly toward the infield. Anxious Dodgers clustered around the second baseman and several minutes later he rose groggily and walked slowly and uncertainly toward the dugout, while fans in every part of the stands rose and cheered him.

Out After Passing Two

The game went on, with both Robin Roberts, third Phil pitcher, and Newcombe constantly threatened. Roberts was having something the better of the tense duel. In the thirteenth Newcombe walked two after two were out and Dressen took him out and brought in Bud Podbielan. Bud ended the inning easily.

Roberts set the Dodgers down in the thirteenth and had retired Pee Wee Reese and Duke Snider on pop-ups in the fourteenth when Robinson came to the plate.

Roberts got one ball and one strike on Robby, then Jack swung with all his power and the ball sailed high into the upper left field stands. Jackie trotted slowly around the bases and was overwhelmed by the entire Brooklyn team as he approached the dugout.

President Walter O'Malley, his wife, General Manager Buzzie Bavasi and his wife, who had been alternately despairing and hopeful throughout the game, rose from their rail box and became as nearly hysterical as such normally composed people can be.

But the tension wasn't ended. Podbielan, who previously had won one game and lost two, still had to get the Phils out in their half. Bud was threatened immediately by the best hitter among the Phils, Richie Ashburn, who lined a single to left just a few inches from Reese's gloved hand and was promptly

Robinson making game-saving diving catch of a low line drive by Eddie Waitkus which came with the bases filled in the twelfth inning. Umpire Lon Warneke has his hand up calling it a fair catch. Willie Jones (6) of Phils is running toward second.

Peewee Reese heads for Robinson, who collapsed after making the put-out. Jones stands on the bag. The ball, which Robinson tossed, is at Umpire Warneke's feet.

sacrificed to scoring position by Puddin' Head Jones.

Easy Pop to Hodges

Podbielan went to a full-count against Del Ennis and a great sigh of relief came from the Dodger fans when Del lifted an easy pop to Gil Hodges.

Waitkus, the fellow who almost won the game in the twelfth, didn't prolong the agony. Eddie lifted a simple fly to Andy Pafko, and there was a wild scene around the Brooklyn dugout.

Hundreds of fans swarmed out of the stands and Dodgers in the field had to fight their way through to get to their dressing rooms.

The feeling of relief for the Dodgers and for their harried supporters was terrific, considering the handicap the Brooks had to overcome even to get into the ball game.

By the end of the third inning they were trailing, 1—6, with Preacher Roe knocked out in the second and Ralph Branca giving up two runs in the third.

Robinson had been an early "bust," slapping into an inning-ending double play in the first inning with Reese on third and Duke Snider on first base, and looking at a third strike from Bubba Church in the fourth. Jackie also had failed to snare a grounder from Ashburn in the Phils' four-run second inning, which became a two-run single—but not in Jackie's book. He thought he should have had the ball.

Driven Home by Pafko

Robbie redeemed himself in the fifth with a triple to right that drove in Snider and sent Church away, and Pafko singled Robby

home with the third run of the inning that reduced the Phils' lead to 6—5.

But in the fifth Brooklyn hopes suffered another blow when Clyde King, who had taken over at the start of the fourth, was knocked out by Gran Hamner's bad-hop triple, which led to two more runs.

Bill Nicholson had opened with a single to right and Hamner hit what appeared to be another one. But the ball took a sudden hop over Carl Furillo's head and went for three bases, scoring Nicholson.

With Clem Labine pitching, Ed Pellagrini singled the second run across and the Dodgers faced another struggle to get even.

Meanwhile the scoreboard, showing the Giants leading the Braves, 3—1, continued to drop a row of ciphers in the Boston column and the Dodgers, who couldn't avoid noticing this, more and more were being put in a hopeless position.

It was 3:35 by the scoreboard clock and Jones was at bat against Carl Erskine in the sixth inning when the final score at Boston was posted. At the roar of the Phils' partisans Robinson looked over his shoulder and he—and every other Dodger—knew certainly then that they had to win this one, or else.

Erskine did his job competently for two innings, preventing any scoring, then left to let Rube Walker bat for him in the all-important eighth—when the Brooks really got into the game for the first time by tying the score at 8-all.

Walker came through nobly, walloping a long double to left center off Karl Drews after the pitcher had two strikes against

him. This blow scored Hodges, who had beaten out a hit to Hamner, and Cox, who had dumped a single just inside the right-field foul line.

At this point Roberts replaced Drews and Furillo, who perhaps should be rated the gilt-edged hero ahead of Robinson, lined a one-and-one pitch into left center for the single that scored Don Thompson, running for Walker, with the run that tied the count.

Newcombe came out amid a tremendous burst of cheers to start pitching in the eighth and, while he was constantly threatened in every inning, still allowed only one hit. That was a single to center by Ashburn, the first man he faced.

Don had put two strikes over on Ashburn and the next pitch sent Richie into the dirt, which brought a warning from Plate Umpire Lou Jorda. Dressen came from the dugout on the double-quick to protest the umpire's action. But Newcombe emerged safely from that and every succeeding inning until, apparently, his arm stiffened or tired and Dressen finally took him out.

The Dodgers had Roberts wobbling a bit in the ninth, which Snider opened with a single, and in the tenth, which Hodges started with a single. But the Brooks couldn't score. Following Hodges' blow Cox bunted into a double play—second time in two games a Dodger had done that.

Reese bounced a single through the middle with one out in the eleventh but neither Snider nor Robinson could harm Roberts then and Robin had retired ten Dodgers in a row when Robinson connected for what could be a $165,000 home run—an estimate of a world series winning pot.

Pafko also came through with a game-saving catch on Seminick in the eleventh inning with Hamner on via a pass and two out. Andy raced toward the left-field foul line and made a gloved-hand grab of the vicious liner that seemed ticketed for two bases.

The box score:

BROOKLYN (N.)	ab.	r.	h.	po.	a.
Furillo, rf	7	1	2	2	0
Reese, ss	6	0	3	3	3
Snider, cf	7	1	3	3	0
Robinson, 2b	6	2	2	6	5
Campanella, c	7	1	2	8	0
Pafko, lf	7	0	1	7	2
Hodges, 1b	5	1	2	10	5
Cox, 3b	6	1	1	2	3
Roe, p	0	0	0	0	0
aRussell	1	0	0	0	0
King, p	0	0	0	0	0
Labine, p	0	0	0	0	0
bBelardi	1	0	0	0	0
Erskine, p	0	0	0	0	0
cWalker	1	0	1	0	0
dThompson	0	1	0	0	0
Newcombe, p	2	0	0	1	0
Podbielan, p	0	0	0	0	0
Total	56	9	17	42	18

PHILADELPHIA (N.)	ab.	r.	h.	po.	a.
Pellagrini, 2b	6	1	2	5	5
Ashburn, cf	8	0	4	2	0
Jones, 3b	4	0	1	3	3
Ennis, lf	8	0	1	6	1
Brown, 1b	2	1	1	3	1
Waitkus, 1b	6	0	0	10	1
Clark, rf	1	0	0	1	0
Nicholson, rf	6	2	2	2	0
Hamner, ss	5	3	2	2	6
Seminick, c	2	1	0	7	1
Church, p	2	0	1	1	0
Drews, p	2	0	1	0	0
Roberts, p	1	0	0	0	1
Total	53	8	15	42	21

aStruck out for Branca in fourth.
bStruck out for Labine in sixth.
cDoubled for Erskine in eighth.
dRan for Walker in eighth.

Brooklyn ......0 0 1 1 3 0 0 3 0 0 0 0 1—9
Philadelphia ..0 0 4 2 0 0 0 0 0 0 0 0 0—8
Errors—Jones, Robinson.

Runs batted in—Brown, Pellagrini 2, Ashburn 2, Church 2, Hamner, Reese, Pafko 2, Snider, Robinson 2, Walker 2, Furillo. Two-base hits—Jones, Hamner, Pellagrini, Snider, Walker, Campanella. Three-base hits—Reese, Campanella, Robinson, Hamner. Home runs—Brown, Robinson. Sacrifices—Jones 2, Robinson, Pellagrini. Double plays—Hamner, Pellagrini and Brown; Ennis, Pellagrini and Waitkus; Seminick, Hamner and Pellagrini. Left on bases—Brooklyn 9, Philadelphia 18. Bases on balls—Off Church 3, Roe 1, Branca 2, Labine 1, Newcombe 6. Struck out—By Church 3, Drews 2, Roberts 1, Roe 1, Branca 2, Labine 2, Newcombe 3. Hits—Off Roe 5 in 1 2-3 innings, Branca 2 in 1 1-3, King 3 in 1 (none in fifth), Labine 1 in 1, Church 6 in 4 1-3, Drews 5 in 3, Roberts 6 in 6 2-3, Erskine 2 in 2, Newcombe 1 in 5 2-3, Podbielan 1 in 1 1-3. Hit by pitcher—By King (Jones), Newcombe (Pellagrini). Wild pitch—Branca. Winning pitcher—Podbielan (2-2). Losing pitcher—Roberts (21-15). Umpires—Jorda, Gore, Warneke and Goetz. Time of game—4:30. Attendance—31,755.

October 1, 1951

GIANTS CAPTURE PENNANT, BEATING DODGERS 5-4 IN 9TH ON THOMSON'S 3-RUN HOMER

BROOKLYN'S BRANCA LOSER

Yields Homer on Second Pitch After Relieving Newcombe in the Play-Off Final

---

By JOHN DREBINGER

In an electrifying finish to what long will be remembered as the most thrilling pennant campaign in history, Leo Durocher and his astounding never-say-die Giants wrenched victory from the jaws of defeat at the Polo Grounds yester-

day, vanquishing the Dodgers, 5 to 4, with a four-run splurge in the last half of the ninth.

A three-run homer by Bobby Thomson that accounted for the final three tallies blasted the Dodgers right out of the world series picture and this afternoon at the Stadium it will be the Giants against Casey Stengel's American League champion Yankees in the opening clash of the world series.

Seemingly hopelessly beaten, 4 to 1, as the third and deciding game of the epic National League play-off moved into the last inning, the Giants lashed back with a fury that would not be denied. They

routed big Don Newcombe while scoring one run.

Then, with Ralph Branca on the mound and two runners aboard the bases, came the blow of blows. Thomson crashed the ball into the left-field stand. Forgotten on the instant was the cluster of three with which the Brooks had crushed Sal Maglie in the eighth.

For a moment the crowd of 34,320, as well as all the Dodgers, appeared too stunned to realize what had happened. But as the long and lean Scot from Staten Island loped around the bases behind his two team-mates a deafening roar went up, followed by some of the wildest scenes ever wit-

nessed in the historic arena under Coogan's Bluff.

Mobbed at Home Plate

The Giants, lined up at home plate, fairly mobbed the Hawk as he completed the last few strides to the plate. Jubilant Giant fans, fairly beside themselves, eluded guards and swarmed on the field to join the melee.

When the players finally completed their dash to the center-field clubhouse, the fans, thousands deep on the field, yelled themselves purple as Thomson repeatedly appeared in the clubhouse windows in answer to the most frenzied "curtain calls" ever accorded a ballplayer.

And so, as this extraordinary campaign moves on in a flow of diamond drama, it will be the Giants and Yankees meeting for the sixth time in world series history. They last were rivals in the classic of 1937.

The second game also will be staged in the Bronx arena that so quietly looked down on the scene yesterday from the other side of the Harlem.

On Saturday the action will shift to the Polo Grounds, where the third and fourth games will be played, as well as the fifth, if necessary. Should neither side have four victories racked up by then, the struggle will return to the Stadium for the sixth and seventh games.

A Long Uphill Battle

As soon as Durocher was able to regain his voice he announced that Dave Koslo, his lone southpaw of any account, will be the starter against the Bombers today. Casey Stengel announced, following the clinching of the American League pennant last Friday, that Allie Reynolds, hero of two no-hitters the past season, would be his mound choice for the opener.

The pennant, which the Giants so dramatically won in the second play-off series in National League history and the first to go the full three games, brought to a climax one of the most astonishing uphill struggles ever waged in the annals of the sport.

Off to an atrocious start in the spring when they blew eleven in a row, the Giants plugged away grimly for weeks to make up the lost ground. But as late as Aug. 11 they were still thirteen and a half games behind the high-flying Brooks who, hailed by experts as the "wonder team" of the modern age, threatened to win by anywhere from fifteen to twenty lengths.

Then, on Aug. 12 began the great surge. Sixteen games were won in a row and from there the Polo Grounders rolled on to finish in a deadlock with the Dodgers at the close of the regular schedule. Majestically they swept ahead on Monday in the opener of the three-game play-off series in Brooklyn. Then disaster engulfed them as they came to the Polo Grounds Tuesday to be buried under a 10-0 score.

And they were still struggling to get out from under as late as the ninth inning yesterday when Thomson, whose two-run homer had won on Monday, exploded his No. 32 of the year that ended it all.

In the stretch from Aug. 12 until yesterday's pennant-clincher Durocher's minions hung up the almost incredible record of thirty-nine victories, against only eight defeats, an achievement to match that of the Miracle Braves of 1914.

The pennant is the sixteenth in the long history of the Giants, who captured their first two flags back in the late Eighties under Jim Mutrie, who also gave them their nickname. Under John J. McGraw they won ten in a span that began in 1904 and ended in 1924, when

The Box Score

BROOKLYN DODGERS

	AB.	R.	H.	PO.	A.
Furillo, rf.	5	0	0	0	0
Reese, ss.	4	2	1	2	5
Snider, cf.	3	1	2	1	0
Robinson, 2b.	2	1	1	3	2
Pafko, lf.	4	0	1	4	1
Hodges, 1b.	4	0	0	11	1
Cox, 3b.	4	0	2	1	3
Walker, c.	4	0	1	2	0
Newcombe, p.	4	0	0	1	1
Branca, p.	0	0	0	0	0
Total	34	4	8	*25	13

NEW YORK GIANTS

	AB.	R.	H.	PO.	A.
Stanky, 2b.	4	0	0	0	4
Dark, ss.	4	1	1	2	2
Mueller, rf.	4	0	1	0	0
cHartung	0	1	0	0	0
Irvin, lf.	4	1	1	1	0
Lockman, 1b.	3	1	2	11	1
Thomson, 3b.	4	1	3	4	1
Mays, cf.	3	0	0	1	0
Westrum, c.	0	0	0	7	1
aRigney	1	0	0	0	0
Noble, c.	0	0	0	0	0
Maglie, p.	2	0	0	1	2
bThompson	1	0	0	0	0
Jansen, p.	0	0	0	0	0
Total	30	5	8	27	11

*One out when winning run scored
aStruck out for Westrum in eighth
bGrounded out for Maglie in eighth
cRan for Mueller in ninth.

Brooklyn ....1 0 0 0 0 0 0 3 0—
New York ....0 0 0 0 0 0 1 0 4—

Runs batted in—Robinson, Thomson 4, Pafko, Cox, Lockman (Reese scored on Maglie's wild pitch in eighth.

Two-base hits—Thomson, Irvin, Lockman. Home run—Thomson. Sacrifice—Lockman. Double-plays—Cox, Robinson and Hodges; Reese, Robinson and Hodges. Left on bases—Brooklyn 7, New York 3. Bases on balls—Off Maglie 4 (Reese, Snider, Robinson 2), Newcombe 2 (Westrum 2). Struck out—By Maglie 6 (Furillo, Walker 2, Snider, Pafko, Reese), Newcombe 2 (Mays, Rigney). Hits—Off Maglie 8 in 8 innings, Jansen in 1, Newcombe 7 in 8 1/3, Branca 1 in 0 (pitched to one batter in ninth). Wild pitch—Maglie. Winning pitcher—Jansen (23-11). Losing pitcher—Branca (13-12). Umpires—Lou Jorda (plate), Jocko Conlan (first base), Bill Stewart (second base) and Larry Goetz (third base). Time of game—2:28. Attendance—34,320 (paid).

the Little Napoleon became the first manager in history to win four in a row.

In 1933 Bill Terry, a spectator at yesterday's game, piloted the Giants to the top again and repeated it in 1936 and 1937. Since then, however, the years have been lean and bleak, until the fiery Leo the Lip came through for them this year. The Giants thus tied the sixteen-pennant record of the Chicago Cubs in the National League.

The clincher was a struggle that should live long in the memory of the fans who saw it, as well as those who had it portrayed for them by radio and television in a coast-to-coast hook-up.

And many a night will Bob Thomson recall that, despite his game-winning homer, his third hit of the day, he might well have wound up the "goat" of the game by reason of some blind base running back in the second inning, when the Giants were trailing, 1—0.

Nor will Sal Maglie, the Barber, soon forget those agonizing moments he spent directly after the Giants had wrenched a run away from Newcombe in the seventh to tie the score at one-all. The Dodgers laced him for three runs in the top of the eighth, the first coming in on a wild pitch.

Bobby Thomson following through on his home run. The catcher is Al Walker and the umpire Lou Jorda. *The New York Times*

But the most poignant memory of all will be that which hapless Chuck Dressen, the Brooks' pilot, will carry with him for years to come. His club had blown a thirteen-and-a-half game lead. But all this would have been forgotten and forgiven had Branca held that margin in the last of the ninth.

He Follows the "Book"

But with one out and runners on second and third Dressen, as daring a gamester as Durocher, chose to follow the "book." He refused to walk Thomson because that would have represented the "winning run." Yet behind Bobby was Willie Mays, a dismal failure throughout the series and behind that the Giants had even less to offer. It's something the second guessers will hash over through many a winter evening.

For seven innings this was a bitter mound duel between Newcombe, seeking his twenty-first victory, and Maglie, gunning for his twenty-fourth. In the end neither figured in the decision. For it was Branca who was tagged with the defeat while the triumph went to Larry Jansen, who pitched for the Giants in the ninth when the cause seemed lost.

Larry retired three batters in

a row and the Dodgers, three runs in front, thought absolutely nothing of it. They were certain they had this one in the bag.

But a few minutes later Jansen was jubilantly stalking off the field in possession of his twenty-third triumph, fitting tribute at that, considering that the tall right-hander from Oregon had pitched the 3-2 victory over the Braves last Sunday to send the race into the play-offs.

A momentary break in control put Maglie a run behind in the first inning when, with one out, he walked Pee Wee Reese and Duke Snider, the latter on four straight pitches. Jackie Robinson followed with a single to drive in the Dodger captain.

From then through the seventh, Maglie pitched magnificently. But not until the last of the seventh were the Giants able to match that Brooklyn run that kept taunting them on the scoreboard. With one out in the second, Whitey Lockman singled and Thomson blasted a line drive down the left field line.

Lockman had to pull up at second, but Thomson kept on running until he, too, was almost on top of second. He was promptly run down and that wrecked that rally.

In the fifth the indomitable

AFTER THE GAME WAS OVER

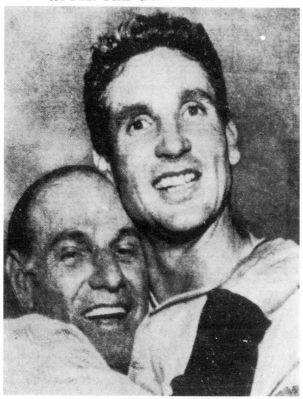

Bobby Thomson and Manager Leo Durocher of the Giants in the clubhouse after the victory over the Dodgers. *Associated Press*

Thomson got a double because there was no one in front of him to watch. But that availed nothing. For there was one out and Mays fanned. After Wes Westrum walked, Maglie grounded out.

Finally in the seventh the Giants made it and again it was Thomson's bat that played the decisive stroke.

Monte Irvin opened with a double. He advanced to third on Whitey Lockman's attempted sacrifice on which the Dodgers retired nobody and a moment later Thomson lifted a high fly to Snider in dead center to bring Irvin over the plate.

The Giants at long last were even, but victory was shunted far into the background when Maglie faltered in the eighth. Reese singled, went to third on Snider's single and scored on a wild pitch.

Following an intentional pass to Robinson came a scratch hit off Thomson's glove by Andy Pafko to drive in another run and then Bill Cox rifled one past Thomson to fetch in the third tally of the inning.

The Scot, converted into a third baseman by Durocher in midseason, certainly seemed to be moving in the center of everything in this great struggle.

In the last of the eighth the stunned Giants were three easy outs for Newcombe, who had a four-hitter going. In the top of the ninth hardly anyone paid attention as Jansen polished off three Dodgers in a row.

Wait for Final Outs

Through eight innings the Dodgers gave Newcombe brilliant support afield. Cox was a stone wall at third. Reese was an artist at short. Robinson made a great play on a wide throw from left by Pafko to save a run. Hodges made a leaping catch of a rifled shot over first. In the ninth of course, the Dodgers couldn't do much about it. There's no defense against home runs.

Jubilant Brooklyn fans were waiting for just "three more outs." Even the most devout of Giant diehards were preparing to slink out as quietly as possible. Their pets had waged a great uphill fight, but to win it all, perhaps, was just a trifle too much to expect.

Then Alvin Dark raised a feeble hope as he opened this last ditch stand by banging a sharp single off Gil Hodges' glove. Don Mueller, who was to wind up a casualty in the inning, slammed another single into right. To a deep groan, Monte Irvin popped out. But Whitey Lockman rammed a double into left, with Mueller racing to third. As Don slid into the bag he sprained his left ankle and the Giant outfielder had to be carried off the field on a stretcher.

At this point Dressen made his two most momentous decisions. Deciding that Newcombe, who had hurled fourteen and two-third innings to keep the flock in the race over Saturday and Sunday in Philadelphia, could go no further, he called in Branca.

Then, following a further consultation, it was decided that though first base was open, Big Ralph was to pitch to the Scot.

It was a decision that in a few more minutes was to bring to a suprising end the tremendous struggle which had been going on for 157 games.

Branca fearlessly fired the first strike past Robert.

What he tossed on the next pitch brought a varied assortment of opinion even from those most involved. But there was no doubt about where it went.

It sailed into the lower left-field stand a little beyond the 315 foot mark. The ball, well tagged, had just enough lift to clear the high wall.

And with that Leo Durocher almost leaped out of his shoes as he shrieked and danced on the coaching line.

Now Leo the Lip, who as manager of the Dodgers fought the Yankees in 1941 in a world series and lost, will try it again, and with one of the most extraordinary Giant teams in the long history of baseball on the banks of the Harlem.

October 4, 1951

Heilmann and Paul Waner Named to Baseball's Hall of Fame

ELECTED TO SHRINE OF DIAMOND SPORT

The New York Times

Harry Heilmann
(in a Detroit uniform in 1923)

Paul Waner
(as he appeared in 1940)

EX-BATTING STARS ATTAIN HIGH HONOR

Heilmann, Who Died Last July Believing He Had Made It, Named to Hall of Fame

203 VOTES FOR TIGER ACE

Waner, 'Big Poison' of the Pirates, Is Chosen on 195 Ballots Cast by Writers

By JOHN DREBINGER

The late Harry Edwin Heilmann, regarded by many as one of the diamond's least appreciated stars of the past, and Paul Glee Waner, an outstanding hitter, are the latest to move into baseball's Hall of Fame at Cooperstown, N. Y. They are the sixty-first and sixty-second players to be so honored.

Announcement of their election was made yesterday by Kenneth D. Smith, national secretary of the Baseball Writers' Association of America, whose membership had just completed its annual survey. Only members of twenty years or more standing were eligible to vote and they were limited to vote only for players active in the past twenty-five years but who did not play in 1951.

Heilmann, former Detroit slugger who died last July on the eve of the All-Star Game, made it with 203 votes. A total of 234 ballots were cast, with 176 the necessary 75 per cent for election.

With Votes to Spare

Waner, who had missed out by 8 votes a year ago, this time was chosen with ballots to spare, the once mighty "Big Poison" of the Pirates polling 195.

Falling short by 21 was Bill Terry. The former Giant manager and star first baseman was named on 155 ballots, followed by Dizzy Dean, with 152; Al Simmons 141; Bill Dickey 139; Rabbit Maranville 133; Dazzy Vance 105, and Ted Lyons 101.

Heilmann, who was generally conceded to rank almost directly behind Rogers Hornsby as one of the game's greatest right-handed hitters, was born in San Francisco on Aug. 3, 1894, broke in with the Tigers in 1914 and by 1916 became a regular outfielder, teaming with Ty Cobb.

Heilmann topped the American League hitters four times, in 1921 with .394; in 1923 with .403, in 1925 with .393, and in 1927 with .398. From 1919 through 1930 he hit better than .300 for twelve successive seasons. He ended his major league career with the Reds in 1932, by which time he had compiled a lifetime average of .342.

Upon his retirement as a player, Heilmann returned to Detroit, where he enjoyed wide popularity as a radio baseball commentator,

a vocation he followed until stricken by lung cancer. When it was learned early last summer that Heilmann had no chance to recover, an effort was made to hold a special Hall of Fame election but the plan came too late.

Congratulated by Cobb

Heilmann died in the belief that he had made it, for as he lay on his deathbed, Ty Cobb, under the impression a special Old Timers Committee had voted Heilmann in, came to congratulate his old teammate.

Waner, a fun-loving little fellow, was born April 16, 1903 in Harrah, Okla. Standing only 5 feet 8½ inches in height and never weighing more than 155 pounds, he became one of only seven players who compiled a total of 3,000 or more hits.

In fact, he made the 3,000th one twice. The first was on a questionable fumble that the official scorer obligingly called a hit. "No, no," shouted Waner from the field as the signal went up, "please call that an error, I want that 3,000th hit to be a real one."

His wish granted, he presently made it "a real one" and went on to amass 3,152 blows in a career that ended in 1945 with the Yankees. It was with the Pirates that he attained his greatest fame. He broke in with the Bucs in 1926 and, joined a year later by his brother Lloyd, gave the Corsairs one of the greatest "brother acts" in baseball.

In 1927, Paul won the National League batting crown with .380, repeated in 1934 with .362 and won again in 1936 with .373. He was voted the National League's most valuable player in 1927.

Overjoyed at News

For all that, he never made a secret of his training laxities. He stretched his active career to an amazing length of twenty campaigns, hit better than .300 twelve straight seasons and compiled a lifetime average of .333. After 1940 he spent his closing years with the Braves and Dodgers and finished in 1944 and 1945 with the Yankees.

Now living in Sarasota, where he operates a batting range at the airport, Waner, according to a United Press report, was overjoyed last night at the news of his election.

"I had given up hope," he said, "but at last I have realized my life's ambition. This is what I have been looking for for a long time. It looked as if I was going to have to die before I could get into the Hall of Fame. Thank God I have lived to see the day."

Those who received 100 or more follow:

Harry Heilmann (elected) 203
Paul Waner (elected) 195
Bill Terry 155
Dizzy Dean 152
Al Simmons 141
Bill Dickey 139
Rabbit Maranville 133
Dazzy Vance 105
Ted Lyons 101

Others who received 10 or more: Gabby Hartnett 77, Hank Greenberg 75, Chief Bender 70, Joe Cronin 48, Ray Schalk 44, Max Carey 36, Hank Goudy 34, Ross Youngs 34, Pepper Martin 31, Zach Wheat 30, Lefty Gomez 29, Tony Lazzeri 29, Casey Stengel 27, Ed Rousch 24, Hack Wilson 21, Chuck Klein 19, Bucky Harris 12, Waite Hoyt 12, Dave Bancroft 11, Duffy Lewis 11, Kiki Cuyler 10, Mel Harder 10, Steve O'Neill 10, Charley Ruffing 10.

February 1, 1952

CAIN, FELLER YIELD ONLY 1 BLOW EACH

Browns Score by 1-0 to Take First Place From Indians and Drop Tribe to Third

NEW LEAGUE RECORD SET

Young's Triple in 1st Helps Win as Two One-Hitters Establish a Low Total

ST. LOUIS, April 23 (AP)—Bobby Cain outpitched Bob Feller tonight in a unique duel in which the Browns defeated the Indians, 1 to 0, and took over first place in the American League.

Feller, like Cain, allowed only one hit, but the safety off the Cleveland veteran was a first-inning triple by Bobby Young, good for a run, whereas the only hit off Cain's delivery was a harmless single by Luke Easter in the fifth.

Young's triple opened the Brown's first inning and when the third baseman, Al Rosen, fumbled Marty Marion's grounder, Young scored the only run of the game.

It was Feller's eleventh one-hit game and the only one-hitter he ever lost. The game was played in 50 degree cold, before 7,110 shivering and delighted fans.

Second Victory for Cain

Cain, who came to the Browns last Valentine's Day in a seven-player deal with the Tigers, hasn't known a winning season as a major leaguer since breaking in with the White Sox in 1949. With tonight's excellent performance he now has a 2-0 record, one of three Browns as yet undefeated.

In two games the Browns have toppled the Indians out of a one-and-a-half game lead, breaking the Tribe's seven-game winning streak and reducing Cleveland to third place.

Ironically, Cain was Feller's victim when Bob pitched his third no-hitter last year. On July 1 the Cleveland right-hander defeated Cain and Detroit, 2—1, holding the Tigers hitless. Cain allowed six hits.

Tonight's game marked the second time in modern baseball history that each pitcher allowed the opposition only one hit. On July 4, 1906, Mordecai (Three-Fingered) Brown of Chicago and Lefty Leifield of Pittsburgh permitted only one hit each as the Cubs defeated the Pirates, 1—0.

On May 2, 1917, Jim Vaughn of Chicago and Fred Toney of Cincin-

nati hurled a no-hitter each through nine innings. The Reds, however, nicked Vaughn for two hits and a run in the tenth to win, 1—0, as Toney hurled a ten-inning no-hitter.

The 33-year-old Feller and Cain, 27, battled on even terms all the way through the duel which goes into the record books as the lowest-hit game in the fifty-one-year history of the American League.

1913 Record Is Erased

The former American League record for the least amount of hits by both teams in one game was three, set by Washington, with one safety, and Detroit, with two, on June 10, 1913, and equaled by Washington (2) and Cleveland (1) July 27, 1915.

Cain, a southpaw, fanned seven and walked three. Feller struck out five and gave up two passes. The big strikeout for Cain came when he fanned Harry Simpson to end the game.

Only four Browns reached base. The Tribe put men on base the same number of times.

It was a stunning defeat for Cleveland, still staggered by Tuesday night's 8-3 Brownie victory.

There was much debate about whether Young's all-important triple could have been caught. Most writers believed it could have been.

Perhaps figuring that the wind would stall the ball in flight, Rookie Jim Fridley moved to his left in left field and stood hopeless as the ball sailed over his head.

The lone run was ruled an earned tally by the official scorekeeper despite the fact Rosen muffed Marion's grounder to allow Young to cross the plate. According to the official scorer, Young would have been able to score with or without Rosen's assistance.

The box score:

CLEVELAND (A.)	ab.	r.	h.	po.	a.	ST. LOUIS (A.)	ab.	r.	h.	po.	a.
Simpson, rf.	4	0	0	1	0	Young, 2b.	4	1	1	2	4
Berardino, 2b.	2	0	0	1	5	Marion, ss.	2	0	0	2	3
Reiser, cf.	3	0	0	3	0	Rivera, cf.	2	0	0	4	0
Easter, 1b.	3	0	1	10	0	Wright, lf.	3	0	0	1	0
Rosen, 3b.	2	0	0	0	0	Rapp, rf.	3	0	0	1	0
Fridley, lf.	3	0	0	3	0	Delsing, rf.	0	0	0	0	0
Boone, ss.	3	0	0	0	2	Goldsb'ry, 1b.	3	0	0	8	0
Tebbetts, c.	2	0	0	5	0	Thomas, 3b.	3	0	0	1	3
Feller, p.	2	0	0	1	1	Courtney, c.	3	0	0	8	1
aAvila	1	0	0	0	0	Cain, p.	3	0	0	0	0
Total	25	0	1	24	8	Total	26	1	1	27	11

aFlied out for Feller in ninth.

Cleveland ....000 000 000—0
St. Louis ....100 000 00.—1

Error—Rosen.
Run batted in—Marion.
Three-base hit—Young. Double plays—Courtney and Young; Young, Marion and Goldsberry; Marion, Young and Goldsberry. Left on bases—Cleveland 1, St. Louis 3. Bases on balls—Off Cain 3, Feller 2. Struck out—By Cain 7, Feller 5. Runs and earned runs—Feller 1 and 1. Winning pitcher—Cain (2—0). Losing pitcher—Feller (1—1). Umpires—Horochick, Rommel and Berry. Time of game—1:58. Attendance—7,110.

April 24, 1952

Trucks of Tigers Hurls No-Hitter, His Second of Season

DETROIT STAR WINS AT STADIUM, 1 TO 0

Trucks Becomes Third Player in Major Leagues to Pitch 2 No-Hitters in Season

RIZZUTO 'HIT' DISPUTED

Official Scorer Changes Call to Error When Pesky Says Ball Spun Out of Glove

By JOHN DREBINGER

Virgil Trucks, 33-year-old right-hander of Detroit's last-place Tigers, moved himself among the ultra select of the pitching craft at the Stadium yesterday when he blazed a no-hitter against the Yankees as the Bengals tripped the Bombers in the second and last game of their series, 1 to 0.

It marked the second time this year that the husky Alabaman, who is of Irish-Indian ancestry, has tossed a no-hitter, thus becoming the third player in major league history to achieve the feat of turning the trick twice in one season.

And since his first one this season, hurled on May 15 against the Senators in Detroit, was a day game, this brings to Trucks the added distinction of being the first to turn the trick in afternoon encounters.

Last summer Allie Reynolds hurled one against the Indians in Cleveland on July 12 and against the Red Sox at the Stadium on Sept. 28 but the Cleveland game was under lights. And when Johnny Vander Meer of the Reds fired his memorable two successive no-hitters in 1938, the first on June 11 against the Braves was a day game, but the second on June 15 was at night against the Dodgers in Brooklyn. In fact, that was the first night contest ever played at Ebbets Field.

A Bit of a Tight Fit

At that, this last performance of Trucks was a bit of a tight fit, inasmuch as for a time there was considerable uncertainty whether there was a no-hitter at all in the making.

For in the third inning Phil Rizzuto slapped a ground ball at Johnny Pesky, who appeared to be having trouble getting the ball out of his glove and when he finally got it away the throw to first arrived low and late.

This reporter, who was the game's official scorer, immediately called it an error, but upon the insistence of several colleagues that the ball had stuck in the webbing of the player's glove, which technically makes it a hit, the verdict was changed.

However, that still did not satisfy the official scorer, who then had Pesky himself queried on what had happened. Pesky emphatically declared that the ball had not stuck in his glove, that it had spun out and as a result he had trouble closing his right hand on it in time to make a proper throw. "I just messed it up," said Pesky.

Final Decision Made

That clearly made it an error and that became the final decision.

The top half of the seventh inning had just been completed when this verdict was made known to the crowd of 13,442 and a rousing cheer went up from the fans who didn't seem to like the "hit" decision from the beginning.

The pressure on Trucks, of course, now became terrific, as he still had three more innings to go against the straining Bombers. But Trucks swept majestically through the remaining nine batters to receive an even more thunderous ovation when he posted the final out.

To add to the pressure, the Tigers, at the very moment the final decision was being made, were in the process of wrenching the game's only tally from Southpaw Bill Miller, who did a fine piece of hurling himself. In fact, for six innings the Yanks' rookie had allowed only one hit, an infield blow that Rizzuto dug up to his right in deep short but too late to make a play.

There was no question of this being a safe blow but it was the only one off Miller until, with one out in the seventh, Walter Dropo blasted an honest-to-goodness double down the left-field foul line. On the heels of that Steve Souchock hammered a single down the same line, scoring Dropo, and with that went eventual victory.

Three Big Innings to Go

There were still three big innings to go for Trucks. Through no fault of his he had seen a Yank get on base in the first inning when he struck out Hank Bauer only to see the third strike go right through Catcher Matt Batts, Hank taking first on the error.

In the wake of the Rizzuto third-inning incident, Miller followed with a sacrifice and Mickey Mantle walked. But from that point on not another Bomber got on base

In the fifth Rizzuto almost came up with what could have been a legitimate blow, a vicious low line drive that threatened to zoom right through the box. But the ball never got beyond the mound as it stuck fast in Trucks' glove.

On and on went Trucks, the ball now catapulting off his right arm as if driven by a machine. With the electrical scoreboard revealing that the no-hitter was still intact the Detroit hurler seemed to redouble his efforts.

He had two close calls in the ninth. After Mantle fanned for the second time, Joe Collins stroked a powerful drive that threatened to go for extra bases in left center. But Centerfielder Johnny Groth hauled it down. Then Bauer came up for the final play.

Hank took a terrific cut at a pitch and sent a sizzling one-hopper squarely at Al Federoff. It almost knocked the Tiger second sacker down. But he froze to the ball, tossed it to Dropo at first for the final out and the crowd let out a deafening roar as Trucks' jubilant team-mates pounded him on the back. After seeing three Yanks reach first in the first three innings, Trucks retired twenty batters in a row. He fanned eight.

Ironically, this was only Trucks' fifth victory of the season against fifteen defeats and only five of his games have been complete. On May 21, six days after he had tossed his first no-hitter. Trucks went six and two-thirds innings against the Athletics in a bid that would have duplicated Vander Meer's feat of tossing two successive no-hitters. But in the seventh inning, with two out, the spell was broken although he went on to win a two-hitter.

On July 22 he tossed a one-hitter with the Senators again his victims. He won that one, 1—0, the same score he achieved in both his no-hitters.

Trucks also is the only American Leaguer with a no-hitter to his credit this year. In the National League on June 19 Carl Erskine of the Dodgers held the Cubs hitless to gain a 5-0 victory.

In going down to his fifth defeat, Miller gave up only four hits in eight innings. With Miller vacating for a pinch hitter in the last of the eighth, Ray Scarborough, recently acquired from the Red Sox, made his debut as a Yankee in the ninth and gave up the Tigers' fifth and final hit of the day.

Yankee Box Score

DETROIT (A.)	ab.r.h.po.a	NEW YORK (A.)	ab.r.h.po.a
Groth, cf.	4 0 0 2 0	Mantle, cf.	3 0 0 3 0
Pesky, ss.	4 0 0 3 2	Collins, 1b.	4 0 0 10 1
Hatfield, 3b.	3 0 1 2 0	Bauer, rf.	4 0 0 0 1
Dropo, 1b.	4 1 2 5 3	Berra, c.	3 0 0 7 0
Souchock, rf.	4 0 1 3 0	Woodling, lf.	3 0 0 3 0
Delsing, lf.	4 0 0 2 1	Babe, 3b.	3 0 0 3 2
Batts, c.	2 0 1 6 2	Martin, 2b.	3 0 0 1 4
Federoff, 2b.	3 0 0 0 1	Rizzuto, ss.	2 0 0 0 5
Trucks, p.	2 0 0 4 2	aMize	1 0 0 0 0
		Bridew'er, ss.	0 0 0 0 0
Total	30 1 5 27 11	Miller, p.	1 0 0 0 0
		bNoren	1 0 0 0 0
		Scarbor'gh, p.	0 0 0 0 0
		Total	28 0 0 27 14

aFouled out for Rizzuto in eighth.
bFlied out for Miller in eighth.

Detroit .... 0 0 0 0 0 0 1 0 0—1
New York .... 0 0 0 0 0 0 0 0 0—0

Errors—Batts, Pesky.
Two-base hit—Dropo. Sacrifice—Miller. Double play—Babe, Martin and Collins. Left on bases—Detroit 5, New York 3. Bases on balls—Off Trucks 1, Miller 2. Struck out—By Trucks 8, Miller 7. Hits—Off Miller 4 in 8 innings, Scarborough 1 in 1. Runs and earned runs—Off Miller 1 and 1. Hit by pitcher—By Miller (Batts). Winning pitcher—Trucks (5-15). Losing pitcher—Miller (3-5). Umpires—Robb, Grieve, Honochick and Passarella. Time of game—2:03. Attendance—13,442.

Russians Say U. S. Stole 'Beizbol,' Made It a Game of Bloody Murder

Special to The New York Times.

MOSCOW, Sept. 15—The magazine Smena, under the title "Beizbol," explained to its readers today that baseball, the American national sport, was a "beastly battle, a bloody fight with mayhem and murder" and furthermore nothing but a Yankee perversion of an ancient Russian village sport called lapta.

Smena presented a vivid description of the American national sport for its readers, declaring that, far from being "amusing," "noble" or "safe," beizbol actually was a dangerous game in which both players and spectators frequently suffered terrible wounds or even death.

[The carnage in the National League was unabated yesterday. The Giants slaughtered the St. Louis Cardinals, 12 to 1, only one day after the Cardinals had slaughtered the Giants. The Dodgers maintained their three-game lead by ruthlessly putting down Cincinnati's non-political Reds, 11 to 5.]

"Let us leave to one side the national American origin of this game." said Smena. "It is well known that in Russian villages they played lapta, of which beizbol is an imitation. It was played in Russian villages when the United States was not even marked on the maps."

The Soviet Encyclopedia describes lapta in the following terms:

"At opposite ends of a broad square there are marked 'cities.' The players are divided into two teams. The players in turn with a blow of a round stick knock a ball up and ahead, and during its flight run around to the 'city' of the opposing team and back. The latter tries to catch the ball and strike the runner with it."

To illustrate the bloody nature of beizbol, Smena published a photograph described as revealing "an episode in the play of 'Sen Louis' and the 'Rodjers,' Del Rois having received a blow on the head is carried unconscious from the field."

The article quoted the memoirs of the famous American player, Tai Kopb, published last March in the magazine Laif, which reported that after years of play his body was covered from head to foot with scars.

'A Surplus of Rough Play'

The article said American businessmen "intensively implanted" this bloody sport among 14-year-old and 15-year-old adolescents who "supplement their lack of technique by a surplus of rough play."

The article explained that the "New York club Rodjers" had a special training camp to train youths in this "beastly battle."

The article said that baseball betting annually in the United States ran to $5,000,000,000 and baseball admissions to 14,000,000 or 15,000,000 and that advertising was also a source of big income.

Indication of the bloody character of the game, said Smena, is provided by the names of some of the teams, such as "Tigrov" and "Piratov."

Despite the huge profits, said Smena, the players "are in a situation of slaves: as in football, baseball and other sports they are bought and sold and thrown out the door when they become unnecessary."

It revealed that the "most famous American baseball player, Babis Rut," was sold against his wishes to another club for $150,000.

The life of a big league player, it said, was only six or seven years, "after which, with ruined health and often also crippled, he increases the army of American unemployed."

Typical of the fate of discarded veterans of this cruel and bloody sport, said Smena, is what happened to the famous player, Garri Kellman. "For several years he played on the best teams," said Smena, "and having gone into retirement, he died of starvation."

September 16, 1952

Roberts Beats Giants for No. 28

12-BLOW ASSAULT TAKES FINALE, 7-4

Phils Rout Harshman of the Giants and Roberts Equals Dean's Record of 1935

JONES, NICHOLSON EXCEL

Their Homers Spark Winners' Drive at Polo Grounds—Thompson Also Hits One

By JAMES P. DAWSON

The Giants closed the 1952 championship season at the Polo Grounds yesterday by serving as the victims of Robin Roberts' twenty-eighth triumph of the campaign.

This gave the right-handed stalwart of the Phillies the distinction of being the first National League pitcher to count so many successes since Dizzy Dean won twenty-eight and lost twelve for the Cards in 1935. The score was 7 to 4.

A twelve-hit assault, topped by home-runs by Willie Jones and Bill Nicholson, aided Roberts to his victory. Three Giant hurlers were pounded.

The loser was Jack Harshman. He gave up nine of the Phillies' hits and six of their runs in his second unsuccessful attempt to prove that he was a better pitcher than he was a first baseman.

Hit by Batted Ball

Harshman hobbled off the field with one out in the fifth after Stan Lopata had caromed a freak double off his left leg. Al Corwin checked the Phils briefly. The left-handed Montia Kennedy, hurling the last four innings, was around long enough to yield Nicholson's homer in the ninth.

Henry Thompson walloped a homer for the Giants in the second inning. A gift run followed when Jones booted Bobby Thomson's rap. But this lead was short-lived.

After Harshman had fanned six while blanking the Phils with two hits through three innings, he weakened. Del Ennis opened the fourth with a single. Granny Hamner tripled. With one out Jones sent his eighteenth homer into the upper left field stand.

In the fifth Dick Young opened with a walk and stole second. Richie Ashburn sacrificed. Successive singles by Nicholson, Ennis and Hamner preceded the Lopata double. That finished Harshman.

One Hit in Five Innings

Robert steadied after the second and yielded but one hit in the next five innings. In the eighth, however, he wavered and the Giants got a run on two singles, a pass and a force out. They clustered three singles for their final run in the ninth.

A crowd of 5,933 turned out for the finale, boosting Giant home attendance for the season to 985,011.

Whitney Lockman rounded out the entire 154-game schedule by playing the first inning. He was the only Giant to do so.

The box score:

PHILADELPHIA (N.)	ab	r	h	po	a		NEW YORK (N.)	ab	r	h	po	a
Ryan, 2b	0	0	0	0	0		Mueller, rf	5	1	3	1	0
Young, 2b	3	1	0	2	1		D.Spencer, ss	5	0	3	1	4
Ashburn, cf	4	0	1	1	0		Lockman, 1b	1	0	0	0	0
Nicholson, rf	5	2	2	2	0		Wilson, 1b	4	0	0	11	0
Ennis, lf	3	2	2	0	0		Thompson, 3b	3	1	1	1	1
Hamner, ss	5	1	3	2	3		Thomson, cf	4	1	0	2	0
Lopata, c	5	0	2	6	1		Rhodes, lf	4	0	1	2	0
Jones, 3b	5	1	1	2	2		Williams, 2b	2	0	0	0	1
Waitkus, 1b	3	0	0	11	1		Hofman, 2b	1	0	0	2	4
Roberts, p	4	0	1	1	1		Katt, c	4	1	1	7	3
							Harshman, p	1	0	0	0	1
Total	37	7	12	27	9		Corwin, p	0	0	0	0	0
							aHartung	1	0	0	0	0
							Kennedy, p	1	0	0	0	1
							bIrvin	1	0	0	0	0
							Total	37	4	9	27	15

aStruck out for Corwin in fifth.
bStruck out for Kennedy in ninth.

Philadelphia ....0 0 0 3 3 0 0 0 1—7
New York ....0 2 0 0 0 0 0 1 1—4

Errors—Jones, Young. Runs batted in—Thompson, Williams, Hamner 2, Jones 2, Nicholson 2, Lopata, Thomson, D. Spencer. Two-base hit—Lopata. Three-base hit—Hamner. Home runs—Thompson, Jones, Nicholson. Stolen base—Young. Sacrifice—Ashburn. Double play—Hamner and Waitkus. Left on bases—New York 5, Philadelphia 9. Bases on balls—Off Harshman 2, Corwin 1, Roberts 1, Kennedy 2. Struck out—By Harshman 6, Kennedy 2, Roberts 6. Hits—Off Harshman 9 in 4 1-3 innings, Corwin 0 in 2-3, Kennedy 3 in 4. Runs and earned runs—Harshman 6 and 6, Kennedy 1 and 1, Roberts 4 and 3. Hit by pitcher—By Roberts (Hofman). Winning pitcher—Roberts (28-7). Losing pitcher—Harshman (0-2). Umpires—Boggess, Jackowski, Pinelli and Engeln. Time of game—2:31. Attendance—5,933.

September 29, 1952

Robin Roberts (left) and Dick Sisler in the dressing room

The New York Times

PART IV

Baseball On The Move

1953-1964

Willie Mays beating Johnny Podres to first base—the hard way.
The New York Times

Braves Move to Milwaukee; Majors' First Shift Since '03

National League Lets Perini Transfer Club From Boston After 77 Years' Stay

By LOUIS EFFRAT
Special to The New York Times.

ST. PETERSBURG, Fla., March 18—Unlike Bill Veeck, who had failed to effect an American League transfer of his Browns from St. Louis to Baltimore two days ago, Lou Perini succeeded today in shifting his National League baseball franchise from Boston to Milwaukee.

After a meeting of senior circuit club owners, Warren Giles, the league president, announced the unanimous approval of Perini's plan. Although the discussions lasted three and a half hours, Giles said "there was no real opposition" to the first shift of a major-league baseball franchise in half a century.

Minor details, including the rescheduling of night games, remain; but the package was wrapped, sealed and delivered to Perini. To gain his point, the contractor-sportsman, a native New Englander, had to receive all eight votes of the National League club owners.

One negative ballot would have brought rejection, but once Walter O'Malley of the Dodgers had moved for approval of the Braves' transfer and Horace Stoneham of the Giants had seconded the motion, every hand, including Perini's, went up in approval in the open vote.

It then became necessary to satisfy and compensate the American Association, the Triple-A minor league in which the Milwaukee Brewers had been playing and from which they would have to be moved. Perini convinced the association's leaders that Toledo, Ohio, an "open city," was ready to welcome the Milwaukee club, which he owns, in the same association, and agreed to pay the group $50,000. The vote to accept Perini's proposition was 7–1 in favor of the move. Only Kansas City, the Yankees' farm, voted "no."

At 2:39 P. M., Giles emerged from the meeting room with the following announcement:

"The National League has unanimously approved the transfer of the Boston franchise to Milwaukee

Associated Press Wirephoto
Lou Perini, Braves president, after the decision yesterday.

on condition that the American Association takes the necessary steps, so that the move can be made."

Within a half hour, the "necessary steps" were taken and for the first time since 1901, when the Red Sox set up American League business at the Hub, Boston became a one-team city. The Braves, who, along with the Cubs, are uninterrupted charter members of the National League, had been there since 1876. For five years prior to 1876 Boston had been in the National Association of Professional Baseball Clubs.

The nickname of the team will continue to be the "Braves." However, it no longer will be an Eastern outfit. It was agreed that Pittsburgh would hereafter be in the Eastern Division, while Milwaukee would be in the Western Division. Each will absorb the other's original schedule, with only the night game dates to be shuffled. Thus, opening day, April 13, will find Milwaukee at Cincinnati and on the following afternoon it will be Pittsburgh at Brooklyn.

'Fine Standing' Held Factor

Some observers thought Perini's success was almost as great a surprise as was Veeck's failure. It had been felt that the American League had set the precedent at

Tampa Monday, when the Browns' plea was turned down. But Perini never lost confidence and Giles later declared that "the fine standing and prestige of Perini in our league was a great factor." The president conceded that questions were asked, but these mostly concerned schedules, commitments and other minor matters.

"These were answered most satisfactorily by Perini," Giles said. "He has received written releases from radio and television contracts and all is cleared. It is a good move for our league to go into as thriving a Midwestern city as Milwaukee. We wanted to do what Perini wanted to do. The time element is inconvenient, but if it's right, it's right."

At Milwaukee, the Braves' new home will be in County Stadium, a $5,000,000 structure that at the moment has 28,011 grandstand seats and 7,900 bleachers.

According to 1950 census figures, Milwaukee has a total population of 871,047 in its metropolitan district, with 637,392 in the city area. However, there is a potential of 1,500,000 fans within a radius of a hundred miles.

Perini expressed appreciation for the "vote of confidence" extended to him by the National League and for the cooperation of the American Association. He had taken active control of the Braves at Boston in 1945 and in 1948, the year his club won the pennant, 1,455,439 fans saw the home games.

Last year, though, the fans did not support the Braves, who finished seventh, and attracted only 281,000. It was said that Perini had lost more than $700,000 in 1952. That financial loss, however, was not the motivating factor in Perini's decision to move.

"I definitely feel that since the advent of television Boston has become a one-team city," Perini said, "and the enthusiasm of the fans for the Boston National League club has waned. The interests of baseball can best be served elsewhere and Milwaukee

has shown tremendous enthusiasm."

He said that he had foreseen the trend of transferring franchises and that "other cities can take a page from the Milwaukee book by providing for major-league facilities."

Perini said "naturally, I regret having to disappoint a great many New England fans and apologize for discommoding so many members of the press and radio."

Perini was congratulated by all of the baseball men present, including Bill Dewitt, vice president of the Browns. O'Malley said he was "dubious at first, but I have high regard for Perini's judgment and went with him." Stoneham said, "I was with him all the way."

Gabe Paul, the vice president of the Reds, also voiced confidence in Perini.

The all-star game, listed for July 14 at Braves' Field, will be played at Crosley Field, Cincinnati, on the same date. Cincinnati's turn would have come in 1954, but today's action moved the Ohio city up. The game was last played there in 1938. The American Association had gone into session this morning before the National League owners assembled. At the request of Giles the minors group recessed until the completion of the big league's session. Then the association members completed their business.

Branch Rickey, who flew here from Havana, where his Pirates are training, agreed to absorb the original Boston schedule, though his team's first fifteen games will be against the Dodgers, Giants and Phillies.

Before today the last change in the major-league map occurred in 1903, when the Baltimore Orioles became the New York Highlanders, now the Yankees. In 1902 Milwaukee, then in the American League, became the St. Louis Browns and in 1898 Louisville moved to Pittsburgh.

March 19, 1953

Milwaukee Braves

Associated Press Wirephoto

MANTLE PIECE: If Mickey Mantle didn't quite knock the cover off the ball with that 565-foot home run yesterday in Washington, he gave it a clobbering at any rate. The ball, which Mickey holds, was scuffed in two spots by the time it came to rest in the backyard of a house near Griffith Stadium.

Towering Drive by Yank Slugger Features 7-3 Defeat of Senators

Mantle's 565-Foot Homer at Capital Surpassed Only by Mighty Ruth Wallops

By LOUIS EFFRAT
Special to THE NEW YORK TIMES.

WASHINGTON, April 17—Unless and until contrary evidence is presented, recognition for the longest ball ever hit by anyone except Babe Ruth in the history of major league baseball belongs to Mickey Mantle of the Yankees. This amazing 21-year-old athlete today walloped one over the fifty-five-foot high left-field wall at Griffith Stadium. That ball, scuffed in two spots, finally stopped in the backyard of a house, about 565 feet away from home plate.

This remarkable homer, which helped the Yankees register a 7-3 victory over the Senators, was Mickey's first of the season, but he will have to go some, as will anyone else, to match it.

Chuck Stobbs, the Nat southpaw, had just walked Yogi Berra after two out in the fifth, when Mantle strode to the plate. Batting right-handed, Mickey blasted the ball toward left center, where

the base of the front bleachers wall is 391 feet from the plate. The distance to the back of the wall is sixty-nine feet more and then the back wall is fifty feet high.

Bounces Out of Sight

Atop that wall is a football scoreboard. The ball struck about five feet above the end of the wall, caromed off the right and flew out of sight. There was no telling how much farther it would have flown had the football board not been there.

Before Mantle, who had cleared the right-field roof while batting left-handed in an exhibition game at Pittsburgh last week (only Babe Ruth and Ted Beard had ever done that) had completed running out the two-run homer, Arthur Patterson of the Yankees' front-office staff was on his way to investigate the measure.

Patterson returned with the following news:

A 10-year-old lad had picked up the ball. He directed Patterson to the backyard of 434 Oakdale Street and pointed to the place where he had found it, across the street from the park. The boy, Donald Dunaway of 343 Elm Street N. W., accepted an undisclosed sum of money for the prize, which was turned over to Mantle. The Yankee was to send a substitute ball, suitably autographed to the boy.

Until today, when Mantle made it more or less easy for Lefty Ed Lopat, who worked eight innings, to gain his first triumph, no other batter had cleared the left-field wall here. Some years ago, Joe DiMaggio bounced a ball over, but Mickey's accomplishment was on the fly.

Longest Bunt as Well

Later in the contest, Mickey dragged a bunt that landed in front of second base and he outsped it for a single. Thus, in the same afternoon, it would appear, the young man from Commerce, Okla., fashioned one of the longest homers and the longest bunt on record.

Everything else that occurred in this contest was dwarfed by Mantle's round-tripper, which traveled 460 feet on the fly. There was a third-inning homer by Bill Martin, which gave the Yankees' the lead.

The Nats tied it against Lopat in the same frame on a single by Wayne Terwilliger, a sacrifice by Stobbs and Eddie Yost's single to left.

However, Hank Bauer doubled and counted on a single by Joe Collins for a 2-1 edge in the fourth then it was that Mickey connected with a fast ball and wrote diamond history. Other things happened, including Tom Gorman's appearance for the last inning, but no one appeared to be interested.

The Box Score

NEW YORK (A.)						WASHINGTON (A.)					
	ab.	r.	h.	po.	a		ab.	r.	h.	po.	a
Martin, 2b..	4	1	2	3	4	Yost, 3b......	5	0	2	1	4
Rizzuto, ss..	5	0	1	3	3	Busby, cf.....	4	0	1	4	1
Berra, c......	4	1	1	2	2	Vernon, 1b...	3	0	0	13	1
Mantle, cf...	3	1	2	0	0	Jensen, rf...	4	0	0	3	0
Bauer, rf....	4	2	1	2	0	Runnels, ss...	3	1	1	0	2
Woodling, lf.	5	1	2	5	0	Wood, lf......	4	0	1	2	0
Collins, 1b..	4	0	1	11	1	Ter'liger, 2b..	4	2	3	2	5
Carey, 3b....	4	1	1	1	1	Peden, c.....	4	0	1	0	1
Lopat, p.....	4	0	1	0	4	Stobbs, p.....	1	0	0	2	1
Gorman, p...	0	0	0	0	0	aHoderlein ..	1	0	1	0	0
						Moreno, p...	0	0	0	0	0
Total ...	37	7	12	27	15	bVerble	1	0	0	0	0
						Total ...	34	3	10	27	15

aSingled for Stobbs in seventh.
bFlied out for Moreno in ninth.

```
New York .............. 0 0 1 1 2 0  0 3 0—7
Washington .............. 0 0 1 0 0 0  1 1 0—3
```
Errors—None.
Runs batted in—Martin 2, Yost, Collins, Mantle 2, Hoderlein, Carey, Woodling, Terwilliger. Two-base hits—Bauer, Terwilliger, Woodling. Home run—Martin, Mantle. Stolen base—Martin and Collins. Double play—Lopat, Martin and Collins. Left on bases—New York 9, Washington 8. Bases on balls—Off Stobbs 4, Lopat 3, Moreno 2. Struck out—By Lopat 2. Hits—Off Lopat 10 in 8 innings, Stobbs 7 in 7, Gorman 0 in 1, Moreno 5 in 2. Runs and earned runs—Stobbs 4 and 4, Lopat 3 and 3, Moreno 3 and 3. Winning pitcher—Lopat (1-0). Losing pitcher—Stobbs (0-1). Umpires—Honochick, McGowan, Paparella and McKinley. Time of game—2:27. Attendance—4,206.

WILD PITCH IN NINTH TRIPS NEW YORK, 3-2

Adcock of Braves Is First in Majors to Hit 475 Feet Into Polo Grounds Bleachers

By JOSEPH M. SHEEHAN

Joe Adcock hit a ball into the center-field bleachers of the Polo Grounds — the first time this feat has been achieved in a major league contest — as the slump-shackled Giants dropped a second straight decision to the Braves, 3—2, yesterday.

With Andy Pafko on base in the third inning, the towering Milwaukee first baseman lashed into a high, fast pitch by Jim Hearn. The ball took off in a high arc toward center, with Bobby Thomson in pursuit.

Hopefully, Bobby chased the soaring drive all the way to the four-foot wall in front of the open stand to the left of the clubhouse exit corridor. His chase was in vain. There was no catching this prodigious smash.

Ball Clears Fence Easily

Not until it had cleared the five-foot wire fence atop the bleacher wall with something to spare did the ball Adcock clouted come to rest. It landed ten rows up in the stand, after carrying approximately 475 feet. The 483-foot sign on the center-field flagpole supplied the basis for this distance estimate.

Two other batters have hit into the center-field bleachers since the present Polo Grounds boundaries were established in 1923—but neither blow was struck in an official major league game.

Schoolboy Rowe, the Detroit pitcher, hit one about where Adcock's blow landed in batting practice prior to a 1933 exhibition game between the Giants and Tigers. And, in a Negro League contest in 1948, Luke Easter, now with the Indians, deposited a drive in the right-field sector of the divided stand.

However, having come under less stringent circumstances, these rightfully don't count. In reaching a target that has defied the aim of many of baseball's mightiest sluggers for thirty years, Adcock made history.

While it supplied the chief talking point for the 3,927 spectators, Adcock's wallop was only part of the story of another heart-breaking defeat for the Giants, who can't seem to get going.

Ways to Defeat Are Many

"Every day we find a new way

to lose," Manager Leo Durocher moaned disconsolately afterward.

With Hoyt Wilhelm the innocent victim, the Giants contrived to lose this one in the ninth, after catching up to Warren Spahn, as the result of a weird series of misadventures.

A high throw by Alvin Dark put Adcock on first to set Milwaukee's winning rally in motion. Wilhelm then whipped a third strike past Jack Dittmer. Adcock broke for second with the pitch, so Catcher Sam Calderone stepped forward to throw.

As Calderone released the ball, his hand smashed into Dittmer's bat, splitting open the nail on his little finger. The ball flew far to the left of second base, and when Thomson missed a swooping stab at it, Adcock continued to third.

Jim Pendleton, running for Adcock, then came scooting home with the winning run, when one of Wilhelm's knucklers, delivered to Pinch-hitter George Crowe, got away from Sal Yvars, who had replaced Calderone. Although Yvars had his glove in front of the ball, it was scored as a wild pitch.

To cap matters, in the Giants' last turn, Monte Irvin, trying to score the tying run from second on Don Mueller's single, was cut down at the plate for the game's final out on Bill Bruton's perfect one-hop throw to Walker Cooper.

The box score:

MILWAUKEE (N.)						NEW YORK (N.)					
	ab.r.h.po.a						ab.r.h.po.a				
Bruton, cf	3 0 1 0 1					Williams, 2b	4 1 2 4 4				
Logan, ss	4 0 0 3 1					Dark, ss	4 0 0 2 4				
Mathews, 3b	4 0 3 0 3					Thomson, cf	4 0 0 1 0				
Gordon, lf	4 0 1 3 0					Irvin, lf	4 0 1 4 0				
Pafko, rf	4 1 1 3 0					Lockman, 1b	3 0 1 6 1				
Adcock, 1b	3 1 1 10 0					Spencer, 3b	4 0 0 0 3				
dPendleton	0 1 0 0 0					Mueller, rf	4 0 2 0 0				
Cooper, c	0 0 0 1 0					Westrum, c	2 0 0 8 0				
Dittmer, 2b	2 0 0 2 3					aHofman	0 0 0 0 0				
Crandall, c	3 0 0 4 0					bThompson	0 0 0 0 0				
eCrowe, 1b	1 0 0 1 0					Calderone, c	0 0 0 1 0				
Spahn, p	4 0 0 0 4					Yvars, c	0 0 0 0 0				
						Hearn, p	2 0 0 0 0				
Total	32 3 7 27 16					cRigney	1 1 0 0 0				
						Wilhelm, p	0 0 0 1 0				
						Total	32 2 6 27 12				

aWalked for Westrum in eighth.
bRan for Hofman in eighth.
cGrounded into force out for Hearn in eighth.
dRan for Adcock in ninth.
eGrounded out for Crandall in ninth.

Milwaukee .... 0 0 2 0 0 0 0 0 1—3
New York .... 0 0 0 1 0 0 0 1 0—2

Errors—Spahn, Logan, Dark, Calderone. Runs batted in—Adcock 2, Lockman, Williams.
Home run—Adcock. Stolen base—Adcock. Sacrifice—Lockman. Double plays—Spencer, Williams and Lockman; Dark and Lockman; Dark, Williams and Lockman. Left on bases—Milwaukee 6, New York 5. Bases on balls—Off Spahn 1, Hearn 4. Struck out—By Spahn 2, Hearn 7, Wilhelm 1. Hits—Off Hearn 7 in 8 innings, Wilhelm 0 in 1. Runs and earned runs—Hearn 2 and 2, Wilhelm 1 and 0, Spahn 2 and 1. Wild pitch—Wilhelm. Winning pitcher—Spahn (2-1). Losing pitcher—Wilhelm (1-1). Umpires—Dixon, Goetz, Dascoli and Conry. Time of game—2:14. Attendance—3,927.

April 30, 1953

Baltimore Gets St. Louis Browns As Syndicate Buys Veeck Interest

American League Unanimously Approves Move—Controlling Stock Brings $2,475,000

By JOSEPH M. SHEEHAN

The major league baseball map, unchanged for fifty years, underwent its second revision in a little more than six months last night when the American League unanimously approved the transfer of the St. Louis Browns to Baltimore.

To effect the American League's first franchise shift since 1903, when Baltimore dropped out and New York was admitted, a Baltimore syndicate paid $2,475,000 to buy Bill Veeck's controlling interest in the Browns.

At Tampa, Fla., last March 15, two days before the National League had approved the transfer of the Braves from Boston to Milwaukee, and here only last Sunday, the American League had rejected the Browns-to-Baltimore proposals in which Veeck would have retained administrative control and considerable financial interest in the franchise he acquired in July, 1951.

The decisive action that will return to big league baseball one of its most glamorous names of the past—that of the Baltimore Orioles—was accomplished behind locked doors at the Hotel Commodore within the space of ninety minutes. This was in sharp contrast to proceedings of Sunday and Monday, when the American League owners had grappled for hours without effective result with the problem of what to do with the moribund Browns, who had a checkered past and a completely hopeless future in St. Louis.

Baltimore won its unflagging battle to take over the Browns, who finished last in the campaign that just closed with fifty-four victories and 100 defeats, because it alone of the numerous cities under consideration had the enthusiasm, the resources and the facilities to swing the deal.

When it became obvious after last Sunday's adverse 4-4 vote (six affirmative votes are needed to approve a franchise shift) that his fellow-owners wanted nothing more to do with Veeck, the Baltimore syndicate headed by Clarence W. Miles went to work and raised the additional money to buy Veeck out.

Originally, the Miles syndicate had proposed to acquire, for $1,-115,000, half of the 79 per cent stock interest in the Browns that

Associated Press
Clarence Miles after closing deal yesterday to buy Browns.

Veeck controlled for Chicago and St. Louis interests. In this situation, Veeck was to continue in the picture as general manager of the club.

There were objections to Baltimore's entry also on the grounds that it was situated too close to Philadelphia and Washington, none too secure financially themselves, and that the traditional East-West balance of the league would be upset.

Mayor Plays Key Role

These objections foundered in the face of the fact that "Baltimore is ready to play ball," as Mayor Thomas D'Alesandro, who played a key role in his city's winning fight, succinctly put it the other day. No other candidate city could make that claim.

Baltimore's reconstructed municipal stadium, on which the Orioles already hold a lease-option at favorable terms, is now being double-decked and will be ready for baseball use, with nearly 52,000 seats, next April. Only Cleveland's Municipal Stadium (73,500) and New York's Yankee Stadium (67,000) and the Polo Grounds (55,000), of the present major league parks have a larger seating capacity.

Despite Baltimore's location between Philadelphia and Washington, both of which are in the Eastern division, the Orioles will be a "Western club" in the American League. Every effort will be made not to have Baltimore and Washington playing at home at the same time, since it is felt many persons living between the two cities may

be attracted to games in both.

Los Angeles, San Francisco, Kansas City, Minneapolis, St. Paul, Montreal and Toronto, the other cities most prominently mentioned before yesterday as possible new homes for the Browns, did not have the existing facilities to stage major league baseball properly. Nor were they, in the showdown, willing to put up the cash necessary to acquire the St. Louis franchise.

However, the American League made clear its continuing interest in acquiring Pacific Coast representation. Simultaneously with the news of the shift of the Browns, the circuit announced the adoption of a constitutional amendment providing for expansion to a ten-club league "in the event it should become desirable to bring major league baseball to the Pacific Coast."

Concession to Webb

This amendment, duplicating similar action taken by the National League several years ago, represented a concession to the views of Del E. Webb. The vice president and co-owner of the Yankees, convinced that the future of the American League lies to the West, had fought a successful delaying action against the admission of Baltimore in the hope of bringing Los Angeles into the circuit.

When Los Angeles' financial support failed to materialize, Webb bowed to the exigencies of the situation and withdrew his objections to Baltimore and, in fact, made the motion to admit that city with the ten-club rider, which was accepted.

The news break came shortly before 6 P. M., when Earl Hilligan, director of the American League Service Bureau, emerged from the conference room, into which the owners had closeted themselves at 4:30 P. M.

Surrounded by reporters, camera men and radio people, Hilligan read this statement: "The American League today approved the transfer of the St. Louis franchise to Baltimore. At the same time, the American League constitution was amended to provide for a ten-club league in the event it should be desirable to expand major league baseball to the Pacific Coast."

With the announcement that Baltimore at last had been accepted, a spontaneous cheer broke out from the corps of newspaper men from that city, who had waited three anxious days with their delegation. They were joined by others whose sympathies had been won over by the gallant fight, against odds that seemed overwhelming, of the Miles group and Mayor D'Alesandro.

Pennant for Team Forecast

Probably the happiest man of all was Mayor D'Alesandro. Spotting Webb after the break-up of the meeting, he approached the Yankee executive and exclaimed, "Mr. Webb, I promise you when the Yankees come to Baltimore we'll have a record crowd out to see them. But I must warn you that we're out to break your monopoly on winning pennants.

We are going to be in the World Series in 1954."

Then turning to the assembled newsmen, he said, "This is a great day for Baltimore and the big leagues. We have been fighting a long time to bring this about and it was worth it. I want to thank all my friends who supported me and helped bring it about."

The jubilation of Mayor D'Alesandro was echoed in Baltimore. Wire service reports from the nation's sixth-ranking city (population 940,000) carried exultant quotes by civic leaders and the "man-in-the-street" on the rebirth of the Orioles.

As organizer of the purchasing syndicate, Miles, an attorney who is chairman of the Maryland State Bar Association, will become chairman of the Orioles' board of directors. His associates, not identified yesterday, include a number of Baltimore's leading industrialists and business men.

While neither Miles nor any of his group have previously been identified with baseball, "we are all sports-minded and intensely interested," he said.

"I feel confident that this will be a successful operation because of the tremendous public interest our efforts have aroused. There is a keen appetite and desire for major league baseball in Baltimore."

Without specifying any figure, Miles said that his group was prepared to spend "as much as we can" to make the Browns a contender. Under the terms of the sale, Baltimore acquires all the St. Louis players and minor league properties.

To clear the way for the American League to come into Baltimore, the Miles syndicate purchased the Baltimore Orioles International League franchise from Jack Dunn for $350,000. Dunn has been invited to join the new organization.

Miles will meet soon with Frank Shaughnessy, president of the International League, to decide what will become of the Baltimore franchise in that circuit. The belief is that the International League will operate as a six-team circuit, with Springfield as well as Baltimore out.

Veeck Expresses Satisfaction

Although the transaction knocked him out of baseball, Veeck expressed satisfaction with the results of the meeting.

"Yes, I sold everything—lock, stock and barrel," he said. "It was the only satisfactory solution and the only way we could fulfill our promises and bring the club to Baltimore.

"The Browns obviously were in bad shape and these people, with strictly local backing, are in a much better position to do a job than we were."

Although he admittedly was in desperate financial straits after reportedly losing nearly a million dollars in two and a half seasons at St. Louis, Veeck insisted that he had not made a "distress sale." "The price obviously was satisfactory or it would not have been accepted," he said.

There was no stipulation that

Veeck remain out of baseball. "In fact, like a bad penny, I'll probably turn up again somewhere," he quipped. In response to queries as to whether he believed that anyone had been "out to get him," Veeck replied "I do not choose to think so—which is my privilege."

The former owner of the Browns has no immediate plans except to stay here for the world series and then "sneak off and spend some of my ill-gotten gains, which aren't much, I can assure you."

Before his ill-fated venture in St. Louis, Veeck had spectacular success at Milwaukee, then in the American Association, from 1941 through 1945, and with the Cleveland Indians of the American League, from 1946 through 1949.

The curly haired ex-Marine, who affects open-collared sport shirts, was a dynamic baseball executive, who kept things hummig on and off the field. He specialized in daring trades and bizzare promotion stunts. At Cleveland, he gave out orchids to female fans, hired baby sitters for ticket-purchasers, put on colorful sideshows on special occasions, etc. Under his direction, the Indians set a major league attendance record of 2,620,627 in 1948.

Even at St. Louis, long since discredited as a two-team city, attendance rose from 293,790 in 1951 to 518,796 in 1952 under his guidance. However, when his attempt to move the Browns to Baltimore last spring backfired, he was dead in St. Louis—and knew it. Playing out the string, as Veeck described it, the Browns drew 310,914 this season.

Three Two-Club Cities

With the demise of the Browns as a St. Louis entry, New York, Chicago and Philadelphia (where the days of the Athletics may be numbered) are the only two-club cities remaining in major league baseball.

The shift of the Braves to Milwaukee (a step taken in part out of desperation by Owner Lou Perini and in part to block Veeck's entry into a city where he was known and respected), looms more than ever as the touch-off of a chain-reaction. Additional changes in the set-up of the two major leagues seem inevitable in the near future.

Milwaukee demonstrated the crowd-drawing potential of new territory by establishing a National League attendance record of 1,826,397 in its first season of operation.

It is somewhat coincidental that St. Louis, Milwaukee and Baltimore all were involved in the only previous franchise shifts since the two present major leagues shook down into stable form with the organization of the American League in 1901.

St. Louis joined the junior circuit in 1902, as a replacement for Milwaukee, an original member. Baltimore, as previously cited, dropped out in 1903 and Milwaukee, of course, came back into the majors, as a National League team, last spring.

In its fifty-two years in the American League, St. Louis won only one pennant, in the World War II season of 1944, and managed only twelve first-division finishes.

JOHN J. McGRAW
STAR THIRD-BASEMAN OF THE GREAT BALTIMORE ORIOLES, NATIONAL LEAGUE CHAMPIONS IN THE '90'S, FOR 30 YEARS MANAGER OF THE NEW YORK GIANTS STARTING IN 1902. UNDER HIS LEADERSHIP THE GIANTS WON 10 PENNANTS AND 3 WORLD CHAMPIONSHIPS.

Baltimore
Orioles

Despite its long absence from the major league scene, Baltimore has a rich and glowing baseball tradition. Identified with professional baseball since 1871, the Maryland city was the home of one of the famous teams of history, the Orioles of 1894-96.

This swaggering group, which included such Hall of Famers as John J. McGraw, Wee Willie Keeler, Wilbert Robinson, Hughey Jennings and Fred Clarke, won three straight National League pennants and twice beat American Association rivals in the Temple Cup competition, which was a forerunner of the modern world series. Even today the description

"old Oriole" typifies the peak of dash and spirit in a player.

It also was in Baltimore that baseball's most famous player of all, Babe Ruth, was born and made his start.

The return of major league baseball to Baltimore marked that city's second big sports success of the year. In January, Baltimore won a battle to be readmitted to the National Football League. With the completion of its new stadium, the city also looks to staging such big football attractions as Navy-Notre Dame and perhaps major fights.

September 30, 1953

Yanks Take 5th Series in Row, a Record; Martin's Hit in 9th Beats Dodgers, 4 to 3

The Box Score

SIXTH GAME
BROOKLYN DODGERS

	AB.	R.	H.	PO.	A.
Gilliam, 2b	4	0	0	4	4
Reese, ss	4	0	1	1	4
Robinson, lf	4	1	2	3	0
Campanella, c	4	0	1	4	0
Hodges, 1b	4	0	0	7	0
Snider, cf	3	1	0	4	1
Furillo, rf	4	1	3	2	0
Cox, 3b	4	0	1	0	1
Erskine, p	1	0	0	0	1
aWilliams	0	0	0	0	0
Milliken, p	0	0	0	0	0
bMorgan	1	0	0	0	0
Labine, p	1	0	0	0	1
Total	34	3	8x	25	11

NEW YORK YANKEES

	AB.	R.	H.	PO.	A.
Woodling, lf	4	1	2	1	0
Collins, 1b	3	0	1	5	1
cMize	1	0	0	0	0
Bollweg, 1b	0	0	0	0	0
Bauer, rf	3	2	1	3	0
Berra, c	5	0	2	10	0
Mantle, cf	4	0	1	5	0
Martin, 2b	5	0	2	1	0
McDougald, 3b	4	0	0	0	0
Rizzuto, ss	4	1	2	2	2
Ford, p	3	0	1	0	1
Reynolds, p	1	0	1	0	0
Total	37	4	13	27	4

xOne out when winning run scored.
aWalked for Erskine in fifth.
bFlied out for Milliken in seventh.
cGrounded out for Collins in eighth.

Dodgers ....000 001 002—3
Yankees ....210 000 001—4

Errors—Gilliam, Erskine, Cox.

Runs batted in—Berra, Martin 2, Woodling, Campanella, Furillo 2. Two-base hits—Berra, Furillo, Martin, Robinson. Home runs—Furillo. Stolen base—Robinson. Double plays—Cox, Gilliam and Hodges; Snider, Gilliam and Campanella; Labine, Gilliam and Hodges. Left on bases—Dodgers 6, Yankees 13. Bases on balls—Ford 1 (Williams), Reynolds 1 (Snider), Erskine 3 (Woodling, Mantle, Bauer), Milliken 1 (Collins), Labine 1 (Bauer). Strike outs—Ford 7 (Snider 3, Cox, Erskine, Campanella, Gilliam), Reynolds 3 (Campanella, Cox, Labine), Erskine 1 (Collins), Labine 1 (McDougald). Hits—Off Erskine 6 in 4 innings, Milliken 2 in 2, Ford 6 in 7, Labine 5 in 2 1/3, Reynolds 2 in 2. Runs and earned runs—Erskine 3 and 3, Milliken 0 and 0, Ford 1 and 1, Labine 1 and 1, Reynolds 2 and 2. Winning pitcher—Reynolds. Losing pitcher—Labine. Umpires—Bill Stewart (N. L.), plate; Ed Hurley (A. L.), first base; Art Gore (N. L.), second base; Bill Grieve (A. L.), third base; Frank Dascoli (N. L.), left field; Hank Soar (A. L.), right field. Time of game—2:55. Paid attendance—62,370.

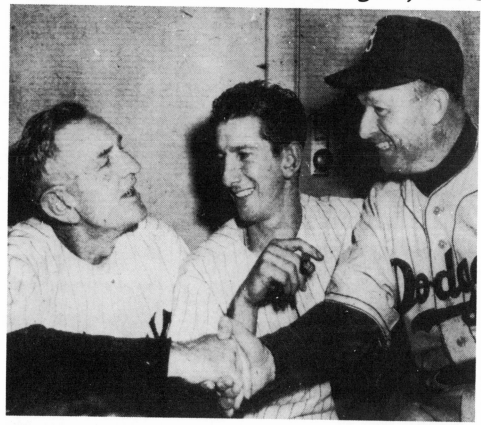

With a brave smile, Chuck Dressen congratulates Casey Stengel on the Yankees' fifth straight world series victory. In center is Billy Martin, who won last game with ninth-inning hit.

The New York Times

Furillo's Last-Inning Homer Ties Score, Then Bomber Star Gets 12th Safety

By JOHN DREBINGER

In a whirlwind, breath-taking finish that doubtless will be remembered as long as baseball is played, Casey Stengel's Yankees yesterday became the first club in history to win five world series championships in a row.

The extraordinary feat was achieved at the Stadium before a crowd of 62,370 roaring fans. They saw the American League's amazing Bombers vanquish a fighting band of Dodgers, 4 to 3, to clinch the 1953 classic by a margin of four games to two.

For one throbbing moment in a thrill-packed ninth inning, Chuck Dressen's Flatbush Flock stood even. This came when Carl Furillo blasted a two-run homer off Allie Reynolds. It deadlocked the score at 3-all.

Minutes later, in the last half of the ninth, amazing Bill Martin,

doubtless cast from the start to fill the hero's role, slammed a single into center field off relief hurler Clem Labine. That shot, which gave Billy a series record of twelve hits, sent Hank Bauer racing over the plate with the decisive tally.

Sixteen in Thirty Years

And so to 63-year-old Charles Dillon Stengel, who in some forty-odd years has just about touched all the bases in an astounding career, now goes the distinction of becoming the first manager to match five straight pennants with five successive world titles. He did it, too, in his first five years in the American League. For prior to 1949 the Ol' Perfessor, as the gravel-voiced philosopher, sage and wit of the diamond is fondly known, had never so much as played, coached or managed a single inning in the junior circuit.

As a fitting climax to the classic's fiftieth anniversary, the Yankees chalked up their sixteenth world championship against only four defeats. This achievement is

all the more remarkable in that all sixteen triumphs were gained in a span of thirty years. Also, it boosted the American League's lead over the rival loop to a margin of thirty-three series victories to seventeen.

On the other hand, Brooklyn's record of gloom took on an even darker hue. For this was the seventh time that a Dodger team had tried and failed to bring to that hotbed of diamond fanaticism its first world series crown. But even the most sorely disappointed Flatbush fan could not complain about the way Dressen's National Leaguers, on this occasion, fought off defeat until the last gasp.

Chuck had started Carl Erskine, the trim righthander who on Friday had set a world series record with fourteen strikeouts to win the third game in Ebbets Field. But Carl had only two days of rest and the Bombers got a three-run lead in the first two rounds behind their own Whitey Ford.

If there were any mistakes up to now it was the Yanks who made them. They tossed away an extra tally in the second inning when Ford, in an astounding mental lapse, failed to score on a fly ball

that traveled almost 400 feet.

Though Dressen was later to get superb relief hurling from Bob Milliken and Labine until Clem's final cave-in the last of the ninth, overhauling that three-run deficit proved a herculean effort. Off Ford the Dodgers never did make it.

One Tally In the Sixth

They knicked the young southpaw from Astoria for one tally in the sixth which Jackie Robinson personally conducted around the paths by stroking a two-bagger, stealing third and scoring on an infield out. But the pair that tied it in the ninth on Furillo's homer was not made off Ford at all.

Actually, all that final drama began with the eighth inning. It was then that Stengel, in a move as startling as any in his brilliant managerial career, withdrew Ford.

The bull-pen gates opened to reveal the confidently striding figure of Reynolds. The redoubtable Chief, who had started the opener for the Yanks, had strained a muscle in his back in that game. He came back to stop the Flock in its tracks in the ninth inning of the fifth game in Brooklyn Sunday. Now he was being called upon to lock up the clincher.

Ford, in his seven innings, had given up only six hits. He was leading 3 to 1, and there seemed to be no particular reason for making a change. Still, the Ol' Perfessor often makes alterations that defy analysis by baseball's outstanding academic minds.

Ford had made a spectacular comeback after his ill-starred one-inning effort which had cost the Bombers the fourth game. Perhaps the shot which pinch hitter Bob Morgan had streaked toward the right field stands in the seventh with a runner aboard helped Casey to make up his mind.

Bauer had caught that one off Morgan's bat as it was about to fall into the seats. Anyway, little did anyone suspect that Reynolds, now entering the game simply to save it for the youthful Ford, would wind up the winner himself, for it was his seventh world series mound triumph, tying the record of another Yankee stalwart of another period, Red Ruffing.

Robinson singled in the eighth, but there were two out and Roy Campanella, striving desperately to answer the prayers of the Flatbush faithful, went down swinging on a third strike.

Big Jawn Called to Bat

In the last of the eighth Stengel made another move, startling, yet withal a nice gesture. Phil Rizzuto and Reynolds had singled with one out. A close play at the plate had rubbed out Rizzuto when he tried to score on Gene Woodling's grounder, but there were still two on base.

So the Ol' Perfessor called in Johnny Mize to pinch hit. A year ago the big Georgian had been the hero. This year there had not been much occasion to call on him and at the age of 41 this easily could prove his farewell as an active player. His best was a grounder down the first base line that ended the round.

But the Yanks were still two in front and they were still that way when Gil Hodges, first Dodger up in the ninth, flied out. But Duke Snider, whom Ford had fanned three times earlier in the battle, now worked Reynolds for a pass after running the count to three and two.

Then came Furillo. He, too, worked it to three and two. Then he lashed one on a line into the lower right field stand and the Flatbush host was beside itself. The score was deadlocked and one could see Reynolds felt keenly disappointed.

The Chief fairly burned the ball across the plate as he next struck out Billy Cox and Labine to end the inning. But the score was tied.

Now the grand finale. Bauer, first up in the last of the ninth, walked. Yogi Berra flied out but Mickey Mantle topped a ball to the left of the diamond which skipped off Cox's glove and went

for a hit. This set up the break in the game.

For up came that incredible 25-year-old star. Martin, a .257 hitter through the regular season who was now emerging as the grand hero. His base clearing first inning triple had sent the Yanks off to a flying start at the outset of the series. He later was to hit two homers and up to this moment he had made eleven hits, tops for the series.

One Smack to Glory

Labine worked carefully, got the count to one and one. Then Billy smacked it. Right over second base it went and that was all.

It was the twelfth hit of the series for the peppery Californian who once played for Stengel when the latter managed Oakland in the Coast League before coming to the Yanks. In fact, it was largely on the insistance of Casey that Martin came to the Yanks at all. They never did think too much of him. Now he can name his own price. Those twelve hits gave Martin the record for a six-game series and tied the mark of a dozen blows made in a seven-game classic.

For the first time since the series began, the weatherman, who so obligingly had provided a mid-summer setting for the first five games, walked out on the show. A gray sky that threatened rain almost from the first, blotted out every trace of the sun, so that the fielders had nothing to worry about on that score. Shirt sleeves also went out of fashion overnight for the fans. It was, in fact, more than a trifle chilly.

However, though the weather slumped, not so those toughened pioneers of that first world series fifty years ago who have been rotating in tossing out the first ball. Yesterday it was Fred Parent, 1903 Red Sox shortstop, who took his turn. Fred really put something on it as he fired into Berra's big mitt. Then the stars of today took over.

It soon became evident that Erskine wasn't the pitcher of the third game of last Friday and that the two intervening days had not given him sufficient rest.

In Trouble From the Start

He was in trouble right from the start and but for some blundering by the Bombers on the basepaths in the second inning, the handsome Hoosier righthander would have plunged deeper in the hole.

He walked Woodling, who again was leading off in the Stengel batting order. He fanned Joe Collins, one of his four-time victims last Friday at Ebbets Field, but Bauer lined a single to left and Berra hammered a drive down the right field line that hopped by Furillo and bounced into the stand for an automatic two-bagger.

In a way that helped the Dodgers since Bauer, who almost certainly would have scored had the ball remained in play, had to hold up at third, while only Woodling was permitted to count. The break didn't help much, however.

Erskine, who also fanned Mantle four times the last time he faced him, was not permitted to embellish that record. He was in-

The New York Times

Furillo, leading hitter in the National League, whose dramatic home run gave Dodgers a lease on life in the ninth, walks slowly back to Brooklyn dressing room after the game.

structed to pass the Oklahoma Kid intentionally and that filled the bases.

This strategy might have paid off. Martin sent a blistering one hopper to the right of second base. Junior Gilliam momentarily collared the ball only to let it get away. Had he held it, it most likely would have resulted in an inning-ending double play.

Scored as an Error

Instead, it was scored an error, although this verdict did not meet with the general approval of the press box occupants. Quite a few of the experts were of the opinion it should have been called a hit, since it looked to have Gilliam handcuffed all the way.

Be that as it may, it allowed Bauer to come home with the second tally and though Gil McDougald here slapped into a double play, the Bombers for the fourth time in the series had skipped off to a first inning lead.

And in the second they got with another run. They should have had two, but lost one on an

incredible bit of base running—or lack of it—on the part of Master Ford.

Rizzuto opened the inning with a single to center and Whitey lined one into right that swept Li'l Phil around to third. Woodling followed with a long fly to Jackie Robinson in left and Rizzuto scampered over the plate with one run.

Now came some harrowing moments for the Dodgers. They seemed about to blow sky high. But the Bombers themselves bungled it. Collins, in backing away from a pitch, accidentally bunted one down the third-base line that could not have been more scientifically placed.

Erskine tracked it down and fired the ball to first, but too late and too wide. In fact, Carl threw the ball right over Hodges' head and it went for a hit and an error, the play winding up with Ford on third, Collins on second and still only one out.

Pitching cautiously to Bauer, Erskine walked him to fill the bases. Then Berra lifted a towering fly that Snider caught in deep right center. It was so deep that no one even thought Ford would fail to score from third. All eyes were focused on Collins as he tagged up at second and lit out for third the moment the ball landed in Duke's glove.

But as Gilliam received Snider's throw-in someone in the infield yelled, "Home, home, throw it home." Gilliam whirled around, fired the ball to Campanella at the plate and there, lo and behold, was Ford, still leisurely jogging home and never making it. For Campy tagged him with the ball for the third out. That "lost" run was almost to come up and haunt the Bombers in the end.

It probably was destined right from the beginning that the Yanks should win this series if only in response to an overwhelming force of habit.

It was in 1923 that the Yanks won their first world title under the late Miller Huggins. They had won their first league pennants in 1921 and 1922, but had been turned back by the Giants in the series. Since 1923 they have been stopped only twice, by the Cardinals in 1926 and again by the Redbirds in 1942.

After '23 they triumphed again under Huggins in 1927 and 1928. They won next in 1932 under Joe McCarthy, who then led them through four successive series triumphs from 1936 to 1939, a mark that stood until Stengel tied it last year and surpassed it this year.

Two more titles went to the Yanks under McCarthy in 1941 and 1943. Then Marse Joe stepped out, but in 1947 the Yanks were back with another world crown under Bucky Harris and in 1949 there began the present act of five in a row under Stengel.

For Brooklyn, the defeat was the seventh in world series play. The Dodgers of Uncle Wilbert Robinson's day bowed to the Red Sox in 1916 and to the Indians in 1920. Since then it's been five setbacks in a row at the hands of the Yankees, in 1941, 1947, 1949, last October and finally the one in yesterday's cold and biting wind.

October 6, 1953

Dodgers Sign Alston As Manager in 1954

By JOHN DREBINGER

The Flatbush mystery has finally been solved. Walter Emmons (Smokey) Alston, a tall, scholarly sort of fellow who will be 42 next Tuesday, is the new manager of the Dodgers.

The skipper for the last four seasons at Montreal, Brooklyn's top farm club, Alston was officially appointed yesterday as the new Flock pilot by Walter F. O'Malley, Dodger president.

Alston succeeds Charlie (Chuck) Dressen, who managed the Dodgers to two successive pennants and left in a huff a few days after the world series when the club refused him more than a one-year contract.

Alston also moves into the job that the club originally had planned for Peewee Reese but which the brilliant and popular Dodger shortstop declined because he did not believe a manager should play at the same time.

Alston, a native of Hamilton, Ohio, but now a resident of Oxford, Ohio, signed a one-year contract and while salary terms were not revealed it was understood he would receive about $25,000. "It always will be a one-year contract, but I hope it will be renewed for many years to come," said O'Malley.

As for his coaching staff, Alston said it would take him a few days to make up his mind. "After all," he said, "I only got word of this over the telephone from Mr. O'Malley at my home yesterday. I'll need a little time to think this out."

Staff May Remain

However, he was assured that he would have a free hand in all matters. The coaches under Dressen

Chuck Dressen

were Billy Herman, Cookie Lavagetto and Jake Pitler. Asked whether any or all of these might be retained, Alston replied "that also might be a possibility." One report last night already had Lavagetto named as Alston's successor at Montreal, but this was denied by O'Malley.

Almost smothered by a battery of newsreel and press photographers and a rapid-fire broadside of questions from the press, Alston handled himself with rare dexterity for one supposedly unfamiliar with major league surroundings.

He admitted that, though in the Dodger organization ten years, he had seen Ebbets Field only once and, in fact, had seen very few major league games in any park. Yet, far more important, he has had a hand in developing some twenty-five of the Dodgers' present top-flight players, the most notable being Don Newcombe and Roy Camapanella who were his battery when he managed Nashua in 1946.

Other Dodgers with whom Alston is thoroughly familiar include Carl Erskine, Joe Black, Johnny Podres, Junior Gilliam, Clem Labine, Wayne Belardi, Bobby Morgan, Don Thompson, Dick Williams and George Shuba.

A strapping fellow who stands 6 feet 2 inches and weighs 210 pounds, Alston was a first baseman in his playing days but ruefully admits his "major league career" was brief. As a Cardinal in 1936 he came to bat once. "I fouled off a couple, then struck out." Lon Warneke of the Cubs was the pitcher. Alston can boast of one more inning of major league play than did Joe McCarthy, who was quite a success as manager of the Yankees without having played.

Big Success in Minors

As manager in the minors, however, Alston has been strikingly successful, his most recent triumph having been in leading the Montreal Royals to victory in the 1953 little world series over the Yankee-owned Kansas City club.

Asked whether this might also have influenced his final choice on Alston, O'Malley laughed and said, "you might call it the clincher."

O'Malley then made the surprising admission that Alston had not been his personal choice. He explained that a staff of five men had comprised the board of strategy: O'Malley, his two vice presidents, Buzzy Bavasi and Fresco Thompson, and two top scouts, Andy High and John Corriden.

"My four colleagues were for Alston practically from the start," said O'Malley. "I had another candidate." O'Malley here paused, turned in his chair and looked sharply around at Thompson.

O'Malley made it clear he was now solidly behind his new manager.

"I want you to feel," said O'Malley to Alston, "the job is yours as long as you are happy with it and we are happy with you.

"There will be no looking over the shoulder while you are doing your work. This is no interim job. No Brooklyn manager was ever fired by us for losing, though, naturally, we want to win, and my greatest ambition is to win the world series."

O'Malley then switched to Reese

by way of also setting Alston right on this score.

"Peewee had been in our minds as a coming manager for many years," said O'Malley, "but he informed us he did not care to manage while still playing. When his playing days are over and he then cares to take up managing, I am pretty certain we'll be able to place him somewhere in our organization.

"However, this has nothing to do with you, Walter. The job is yours. The players will be solidly behind you and no one will be more loyal than Reese, a fine gentleman and a fine player who only wants to win and will tell you so the first time he sees you."

Oddly, the fine hand of Branch Rickey can still be detected in this latest Dodger managerial move. It was under Rickey, then head of the Cardinal chain, that Alston broke in professionally.

He came from a baseball-minded family, his father and two uncles at one time having played with him on the same semi-pro team in Ohio. After his graduation from the University of Miami, in Ohio in 1934 he signed with Greenwood in the St. Louis farm system as a slugging first sacker.

However, apart for his brief 1936 trial with the Cards, his playing skill never rose above minor league level, and in 1947 his active career ended.

Managed Trenton Club

As a skipper, though, he made far more headway. His first job as manager was with Portsmouth in 1940, followed by two years with Springfield in the Mid-Atlantic League. Following Rickey to Brooklyn in 1943, he then managed Trenton for the next two seasons and from here on his managerial star in the minors rose rapidly.

He won the New England League play-offs for Nashua in 1946 with Newcombe and Campanella as his star battery. The next year he bagged the Western League play-offs with Pueblo. In 1948 he finished third with St. Paul in the American Association but won the play-offs and the following year won the pennant with the Saints.

His next stop was Montreal, where he won pennants in 1951 and 1952. Although his team finished second the past season, it nevertheless topped Rochester and Buffalo in the play-offs and went on to a 4-to-1 victory over Kansas City in the little world series.

Soft spoken but never at a loss for words, Alston gives the impression of being an efficient, studious worker of the Eddie Sawyer type.

Asked what style of play he preferred from his teams, he replied: "The matter of technique is something that can only be determined by the type of ball club. I would never try asking my players to do something for which they are not fitted."

When asked whether he was a strict disciplinarian or more of the "honor type" manager, Alston said that this also would depend upon future developments.

"In fact," he said, "there is little I can say until I have had time to inspect things at the training camp. Will Jackie Robinson play in 1954? I'm pretty sure Jackie

will be playing somewhere in our line-up."

Another odd feature was a frank admission that he wanted this Dodger job from the moment it was declared open with the departure of Dressen. He even had thought once or twice of writing to O'Malley and making formal application.

"But then I decided I wouldn't," he said. "The club had watched me work for ten years in the minors and if they thought enough of me to give me the big job I decided they'd do it without me reminding them of my qualifications."

Alston admitted that except for an occasional glimpse on television he had never seen a world series. But he is hopeful of getting a closer look next October.

Thus ended a guessing contest that had all Brooklyn in a dither ever since Dressen walked out on the job. At one time or another many big-time names in the baseball world were mentioned as candidates, including such past and present diamond luminaries as Bill Terry, Lefty O'Doul, Bucky Harris and Tommy Henrich.

Alston is married, has a married daughter of 21 and also is a grandfather. He neither drinks nor plays poker.

Carey Dropped in 1934

Twice the Brooklyn club found itself in the unusual position of paying two managers at the same time. O'Malley cited this as the chief reason the present regime intended to adhere with such fervor to the one-year contract.

After Wilbert Robinson, who began his term in 1914, stepped down in 1931, Max Carey managed in 1932 and 1933. But though Max had still another year to go on his contract, he was dismissed in the spring of 1934 and Casey Stengel, his coach, was named.

But Casey, who this year led the Yankees to their fifth straight world championship, suffered a fate similar to the one that had befallen Carey. Still under contract through 1937, Stengel was dropped at the close of the 1936 season and Burleigh Grimes was installed to lead through 1938.

In 1939 Leo Durocher began his tempestuous career in Brooklyn, which was interrupted in 1947 when, with Leo under one-year suspension by order of the former commissioner, A. B. Chandler, Burt Shotton managed the Dodgers to a pennant. Leo returned in 1948 but lasted only until midseason, when he supplanted Melvin Ott as manager of the Giants while Shotton returned to lead the Flock.

Shotton won another pennant in 1949, but slipped up in 1950 and Dressen became his successor, losing to the Giants in the memorable 1951 pennant play-off but winning flags in 1952 and 1953.

November 25, 1953

Terry, Dickey and Maranville
Are Elected

EX-PILOT OF GIANTS IS THIRD IN BALLOT

Controversial Terry Trails Rabbit and Yanks' Dickey— 73 in Cooperstown Shrine

By **ROSCOE McGOWEN**

Walter (Rabbit) Maranville, William (Bill) Dickey and William H. (Memphis Bill) Terry yesterday were voted into baseball's Hall of Fame at Cooperstown, N. Y., by the senior baseball writers of the country.

The little Rabbit, who died suddenly of a heart attack in New York on Jan. 5, was the top man with 209 of a possible 252 votes cast. Dickey, the one-time great Yankee catcher, ran second with 202 votes. Terry, former first baseman and manager of the Giants, finished third with 195.

The trio's election brought to seventy-three the number of players enshrined at Cooperstown. There were votes for fifty-three players in the 1954 balloting.

Joe DiMaggio led the group that failed to make the grade in the balloting. The former Yankee Clipper received 175 votes, missing election by fourteen. Ted Lyons, former Chicago White Sox ace and now pitching coach for the Dodgers, was next with 170, followed by Dazzy Vance (158), one-time Dodger hurling great, and Gabby Hartnett (151), once the catching pride of the Chicago Cubs.

Maranville's widow, who is under a doctor's care, said:

"I am thankful for the nomination and want to thank all the baseball writers who participated in the voting. It is something I will treasure for the rest of my life."

Sentiment Plays Role

There is no doubt that sentiment played a part in the Rabbit's election, although he had been running fairly high in the voting in recent years.

On the other hand, the election of Terry came in spite of adverse sentiment. The forthright Memphis Bill had not endeared himself to numerous baseball writers, especially in New York, during his managerial years.

Bill was chosen strictly on his record as a player — a lifetime batting average in fourteen years, all with the Giants, of .341, which

Trio Named to Baseball's Shrine at Cooperstown, N. Y.

The New York *Times*

Bill Terry   **Bill Dickey**   **Rabbit Maranville**

Pictures of players as they appeared in their prime

was topped by a .401 mark in 1930. Obviously some writers still were reluctant to vote for the 55-year-old Terry.

Terry replaced the late John McGraw as manager of the Giants in 1932. The next year the Giants won the pennant and the world series from the Washington Senators. They repeated as pennant winners in 1936 and 1937, but on each occasion the Giants were beaten by the Yankees subsequently.

Bill was a terrific line-drive hitter, his greatest power being to left center field. Although a left-handed hitter, he never tried to pull the ball for home runs. He went for base hits.

Because of his Puckish spirit and his many pranks, both on and off the field, Maranville was an almost legendary character in the game. But he was a fine shortstop and second baseman, with a competitive spirit exceeded by none.

Joining the Boston Braves in 1912, the Rabbit was a sparkplug in the so-called Miracle Braves of 1914, who won the pennant after being in last place on July 4 and then beat the Athletics

four straight in the world series.

In 1921 the Braves traded him to Pittsburgh, whence he went to the Chicago Cubs. He managed the Cubs briefly (and somewhat hilariously) in 1925. Later he played, quite appropriately, for the Dodgers, then with the St. Louis Cardinals.

He returned to the Braves in 1935, when his career virtually ended when he broke his leg sliding home in an exhibition game at St. Petersburg, Fla.

The Rabbit had managed the Braves for a short time in 1929. Later he was a pilot in the minors. At the time of his death he was director of The New York Journal-American's sandlot baseball program.

The 46-year-old Dickey, born in Bastrop, La., finished seventeen active seasons with the Yankees in 1946. That same year he had his wry adventure of managing the Yanks under Larry MacPhail. Dickey had returned to baseball after two years as an officer in the Navy.

Bill set a major league record by catching 100 or more games for thirteen consecutive years. He played in eight world series and seven major league All-Star games.

Dickey's lifetime batting average was .313. Some rated him the most dangerous clutch hitter of the devastating Bombers of that period.

Bombers' Manager Briefly

On May 24, 1946, Dickey replaced the ailing Joe McCarthy as the Yankee pilot. Johnny Neun succeeded Dickey on Sept. 12. Bill subsequently managed Little Rock, dropped out of baseball for a year, and then returned to the Yankees as a coach under Casey Stengel.

At his home in Little Rock, Dickey told The United Press:

"I don't know what to say. I've wanted to get in there a long time and finally made it. I'm sure happy."

Terry's reaction will be regarded as typical by both his friends and foes.

"I have nothing to say about it," he told The Associated Press. "Nothing at all?"

"I have no comment to make."

January 21, 1954

20 HITS BY CUBS ROUT CARDS, 23-13

3-Hour 43-Minute Test Sets Mark as Longest 9-Inning Encounter in League

By The Associated Press.

CHICAGO, April 17—The Chicago Cubs, blasting six opposing pitchers for twenty hits, today ran up their highest score in thirty-two years, crushing the St. Louis Cardinals, 23—13. The contest was the longest nine-inning game in National League history—3 hours 43 minutes.

The Cubs, who battered St. Louis, 13—4, in the season's opener, produced their most runs since defeating the Phillies, 26—23, in 1922.

The previous longest regulation game was the 3:38 contest between the Brooklyn Dodgers and the New York Giants on Sept. 6, 1952. The major league record of 3:52 was set by the New York Yankees and the Boston Red Sox last May.

Cubs Clout Seven Doubles

The contest, witnessed by 14,609 Wrigley Field fans, was played in a brisk wind. Thirty-five hits were made, sixteen of them for extra bases.

The Cubs contributed seven of the ten doubles hammered. There also was one triple, by the Cardinals' Wally Moon, and five homers. Hitting for the circuit were the Cards' Rip Repulski, Sol Yvars and Rookie Tom Alston, who made his first major league hit a four-bagger.

The Cubs went ahead to stay with five runs in the third when Ransom Jackson and Hal Jeffcoat hit homers. They tallied ten runs in the fifth when sixteen men took their turns and pounded seven blows. Eight of the runs in the big inning were earned.

There were six errors in the game. Five were made by the Cardinals—three by Third Baseman Ray Jablonski.

21 Passes Are Issued

The Cardinals' six hurlers and the Cubs' three allowed twenty-one walks. Jim Brosnan, who entered the game in the fifth, was the winner and Gerry Staley the loser.

The Cubs' score was one run shy of equaling the worst pound-

ing ever administered to a Card team—a 24-6 licking by Pittsburgh in 1925.

Both the Cubs' and the combined run totals fell short of National League records. The Cards set the record for one team, scoring twenty-eight runs in a 1929 game. The Cubs figured in the combined scoring record, whipping Philadelphia, 26—23 in 1922.

Before the contest was two innings old Repulski had appeared in all three outfield positions for the Cards. He started in right and when the Cubs batted in the second Repulski shifted to left as Stan Musial moved from left to right.

Just before Bob Talbot, the Cubs' center fielder, batted in the second inning, Repulski went to center and Moon to left field as Rip's successor.

The box score:

ST. LOUIS (N.)	ab.r.h.po.a	CHICAGO (N.)	ab.r.h.po.a
Rep'ki.rf.lf.cf	5 3 2 3 0	Talbot, cf	.6 1 2 0 0
Moon, cf.lf	4 2 3 1	Fondy, 1b	.6 2 1 11 2
Sch'd'nst.2b	3 1 2 4 5	Kiner, lf	.2 1 1 2 0
Hemus, 2b	.2 0 2 0 2	dB'mholtz,lf	1 0 0 0 6
Musial, lf.rf	.2 0 1 0 0	Sauer, rf	.4 3 3 1 2 0
Burgess, rf	..2 0 0 1 0	Jackson, 3b	.5 4 4 0 5
Jablonski,3b	6 0 1 2 1	Banks, ss	..5 2 1 2 2
Alston, 1b	..5 1 1 9 1	Baker, 2b	..5 4 3 4 5
Yvars, c	..4 3 3 1 0	Garagiola, c	.3 2 3 2 0
Sarni, c	....0 0 0 1 0	bEdwards	..0 1 0 0 0
Grammas,ss	1 2 0 0 2	McC'lough,c	1 0 1 3 0
cSchoff'd,ss	1 0 0 0 0	Klippstein,p	0 0 0 0 0
Staley, p	...1 0 0 0 0	Jeffcoat, p	.3 2 2 2 0
White, p	...0 0 0 0 0	Brosnan, p	3 1 1 0 1
Lint, p	....0 0 0 0 0		
aFrazier	.1 1 1 0 0	Total.. 44 23 20 27 13	
Wright, p	..0 0 0 0 0		
Brazle, p	...0 0 0 0 0		
Deal, p	....2 0 0 0 0		
Total.. 39 13 15 24 12			

aSingled for Lint in fifth.
bWalked for Garagiola in fifth.
cRan for Grammas in sixth.
d Ran for Kiner in sixth.

St. Louis ....0 5 1 0 .4 0 0 1 2—13
Chicago ....2 2 5 3 1 0 0 1 0 .—23

Errors—Jablonski 3, Schoendienst, Grammas, Brosnan.

Runs batted in—Sauer 2, Jeffcoat 3, Fondy 2, Jackson 3, Garagiola 3, Banks 3, Baker 3, Edwards, Brosnan 2, Talbot, McCullough, Moon 2, Schoendienst 2, Jablonski, Hemus, Yvars, Repulski 3, Alston.

Two-base hits—Garagiola, Jeffcoat, Kiner, Yvars, Musial, Moon, Baker, Jackson, McCullough. Three-base hit—Moon. Home runs—Jackson, Jeffcoat, Yvars, Repulski, Alston. Stolen bases — Yvars. Sacrifices—Staley. Schoendienst. Sacrifice fly—Fondy. Double plays—Jablonski, Schoendienst and Alston; Schoendienst and Alston; Banks and Fondy. Left on bases—St. Louis 10, Chicago 10. Bases on balls—Off Klippstein 5, Jeffcoat 1, Brosnan 3, Staley 2, White 1, Lint 2, Wright 3, Brazle 2, Deal 2. Struck out—By Klippstein 1, Brosnan 3, Staley 1, Hits—Off Klippstein 2 in 11-3 innings, Jeffcoat 7 in 4 2-3, Brosnan 4 in 4 2-3, Staley 7 in 2, White 2 in 1-3, Lint 2 in 1 2-3. Wright 2 in 1-3, Brazle 4 in 1 1-3, Deal 3 in 3 1-3. Runs and earned runs—Off Klippstein 4 and 4. Jeffcoat 6 and 6, Brosnan 3 and 3, Staley 7 and 7, White 2 and 2. Lint 3 and 2, Wright 3 and 3, Brazle 5 and 3, Deal 1 and 1. Wild pitches—Lint 2. Winning pitcher—Brosnan (1—0). Losing pitcher—Staley (0—1). Umpires—Warneke, Donatelli, Ballanfant and Barlick. Time of game—3:43. Attendance—14,609.

April 18, 1954

Musial Sets Record With 5 Homers

ST. LOUIS SLUGGER PACES 10-6 VICTORY

Musial Belts 3 Homers, Then Adds 2 for Twin-Bill Mark as Giants Triumph, 9-7

By JOHN DREBINGER
Special to The New York Times.

ST. LOUIS, May 2—Stan Musial set one major league record and tied another today as he walloped five home runs in the course of a double-header. But all it got the Cardinals was an even break with the Giants in a bruising twin bill that kept 26,662 roaring fans in a dither for the better part of seven hours.

In the opener the Redbirds downed the Polo Grounders, 10 to 6, with an outburst of five circuit drives to three for the New Yorkers. Stan the Man hit three in this game, his final blast, off Jim Hearn, coming with two aboard in the last of the eighth to break a 6-all tie.

Then, in the nightcap, practically all of it played under lights, Musial hit two more. But Leo Durocher's minions, erupting for eight runs in the fourth inning, managed to hang on to win this one, 9 to 7.

Cards Get 12 Homers

In all the Cards hit three homers in the second encounter to one for the Giants, making a grand total of twelve round trippers for the day.

Musial set a new mark with his five for the twin bill, the previous high for most homers in a double-header being four.

Musial also tied the major league record of five homers for two consecutive games.

The second game was, indeed, a bruising affair. When it wound up, Musial had a season's total of eight home runs.

At the outset it looked as though the Giants were headed for another drubbing when Tom Alston clubbed Don Liddle for a base-clearing double in the first inning. But in the fourth, the Polo Grounders came back with their cluster of eight as they battered Joe Presko, Royce Lint and Mel Wright for eight hits.

Mueller, who came up with five blows in this game, got two in this inning, one a triple, while Bobby Hofman contributed a three-run homer. But Hoyt Wilhelm, who replaced Liddle, ran into a three-run squall in the fifth on homers by Musial and Ray Jablonski and in the seventh Musial whacked him for another.

Both of the shots by Stan were tremendous wallops clear out of the park into Grand Avenue. They drove in three runs which, along with six in the first game, gave Musial a total of nine runs-batted-in for the day.

But at this point, Larry Jansen came on to stop the Redbirds cold. He blanked them through the eighth and ninth, and for good measure drove in an extra run for the Giants in the top of the ninth with a single.

Brazle Gains Victory

Stan the Man was pretty much the whole show in the opener, which saw Alpha Brazle, the ancient southpaw replace Starter Gerry Staley in the sixth inning to notch his first victory of the season.

Warming up on a base on balls off Johnny Antonelli in the first inning, Musial then proceeded to ring up a perfect game at bat for himself.

He hit homers in successive times at bat off Antonelli in the third and fifth, the first of these shots coming with the bases empty, the second with one on. He singled off Hearn in the sixth and in the eighth whacked the big right-hander for his game-clinching clout with two runners aboard.

It was, in fact, pretty much a home-run or no count affair most of the way, with eight of the ten tallies by the Cards coming as the result of circuit clouts.

Antonelli was slapped for six runs and four homers before being belted out in the fifth. In addition to Musial's first two, the former Brave lefty saw Wally Moon hit his third four-bagger of the season in the first and Tom Alston his third in the fourth.

The Giants, however, weren't exactly standing still. They reached Staley for three runs in the fourth with the aid of a couple of doubles by Henry Thompson and Irvin. Successive homers by Lockman and Westrum produced two more tallies in the fifth and in the sixth Irvin's No. 4 off Brazle deadlocked the score at 6-all.

From here on Brazle held firm while Hearn blew wide open in the eighth and went down to his second setback of the year.

Giants' Box Scores

FIRST GAME

NEW YORK (N.)						ST. LOUIS (N.)					
	ab.	r.	h.	po.	a.		ab.	r.	h.	po.	a.
Williams, 2b	4	1	1	2	1	Moon, cf	.5	2	2	2	0
Dark, ss	..4	0	1	0	2	S'dienst, 2b	3	3	0	3	3
Tho'son, 3b	.4	1	1	1	4	Musial, rf	.4	3	4	4	0
Irvin, lf	3	2	2	2	0	Jab'ski, 3b	.5	0	1	0	2
Mueller, rf	.4	0	1	0	0	Repulski, lf	.5	1	2	2	0
Mays, cf	...3	0	0	2	0	Alston, 1b	..4	1	4	8	1
Lockm'n, 1b	.4	1	1	9	1	Gram'as, ss	..2	0	0	1	1
Westrum, c	.4	1	2	7	2	aHemus, ss	.3	0	1	0	0
An'nelli, p	.2	0	0	1	1	Rice, c	3	0	0	6	1
Hearn, p	0	0	0	0	0	Staley, p	...1	0	0	1	2
Picone, p	...0	0	0	0	0	bLowrey	..1	0	0	0	0
cHofman	.1	0	0	0	0	Brazle, p	..1	0	0	0	0
Total	...33	6	9	24	11	Total	.37	10	14	27	10

aHit into force out for Grammas in fifth.
bStruck out for Staley in fifth.
cStruck out for Picone in ninth.

New York ....000 321 000—6
St. Louis 201 120 04.–10

Errors—Thompson, Dark.
Runs batted in—Moon, Alston 2, Musial 6, Hemus, Thompson, Irvin 2, Mueller, Lockman, Westrum.
Two-base hits—Thompson, Irvin, Repulski. Home runs—Moon, Musial 3, Alston, Lockman, Westrum, Irvin. Sacrifices—Staley, Hearn. Double plays—Schoendienst, Grammas and Alston; Jablonski, Schoendienst and Alston. Left on bases—New York 3, St. Louis 9. Bases on balls—Antonelli 3, Hearn 2, Brazle 2. Struck out—By Antonelli 4, Hearn 2, Staley 3, Brazle 3. Hits—Off Antonelli 6 in 4 innings (faced three men in fifth), Hearn 8 in 3 1-3, Picone 0 in 2-3, Staley 7 in 5, Brazle 2 in 4. Runs and earned runs—Off Antonelli 6 and 5, Hearn 4 and 4, Staley 5 and 5, Brazle 1 and 1. Winning pitcher—Brazle (1–0). Losing pitcher—Hearn (0–2). Umpires—Donatelli, Ballanfant, Barlick and Warneke. Time of game—2:48.

SECOND GAME

NEW YORK (N.)						ST. LOUIS (N.)					
	ab.	r.	h.	po.	a.		ab.	r.	h.	po.	a.
Lockman, 1b	2	1	0	10	1	Moon, cf	..4	0	1	2	0
Dark, ss	...5	0	0	2	1	Sch'ienst,2b	5	2	2	2	2
Thompson,3b	4	1	1	0	2	Musial, rf	.4	3	2	4	1
Irvin, lf	4	1	1	0	0	Jablonski,3b	5	1	3	1	0
Mueller, rf	.5	3	5	2	0	Repulski, lf	.4	1	0	3	0
Mays, cf	..4	0	1	6	0	Alston, 1b	..2	0	1	7	0
St. Claire, c	.4	1	2	3	1	Grammas,ss	3	0	0	2	3
bAmalsitano	.0	0	0	0	0	Poholsky, p	0	0	0	0	1
Westrum, c	..0	0	0	1	0	gLowrey	..0	0	0	0	0
Samford, 2b	.1	0	0	0	1	Deal, p	...0	0	0	0	0
aRhodes	1	1	1	0	0	Sarni, c	...2	0	0	2	0
Wilhelm	..1	0	0	0	1	dHemus, ss	.2	0	0	0	0
Jansen, p	..2	0	1	0	2	Presko, p	..1	0	0	0	1
Liddle, p	...1	0	0	1	0	Lint, p	0	0	0	0	0
bTaylor	..0	0	0	0	0	Wright, p	..1	0	0	0	0
cHofman,2b	4	1	1	2	3	eFrazier	...1	1	0	0	0
						fMiller	0	0	0	0	0
Total	..38	9	13	27	12	Rice, c	1	0	0	4	0
						Total	...35	7	10	27	8

aSingled for Samford in fourth.
bWalked for Liddle in fourth.
cHit home run for Taylor in fourth.
dFlied out for Sarni in sixth.
eDoubled for Wright in sixth.
fRan for Frazier in sixth.
gWalked for Poholsky in seventh.
hRan for St. Claire in ninth.

New York 000 800 001–9
St. Louis 300 030 100–7

Errors—None.
Runs batted in—Alston 3, Musial 3, Jablonski, Mays 3, Hofman 3, Mueller 2, Jansen. Two-base hits—Schoendienst, Alston, Mueller, Thompson. Three-base hits—Mueller. Schoendienst. Home runs—Musial 2, Jablonski, Hofman. Stolen base—Jablonski. Sacrifice fly—Mays. Double plays—Thompson, Hofman and Lockman; Jansen, Dark and Lockman. Left on bases—New York 9, St. Louis 7. Bases on balls—By Wilhelm 3, Jansen 2, Presko 3, Lint 2. Struck out—By Wilhelm 3, Jansen 1, Presko 3. Hits—Off Liddle 3 in 3 innings, Wilhelm 6 in 3 (none out in seventh), Jansen 1 in 3, Presko 4 in 3 1-3, Lint 3 in 1-3, Wright 4 in 2 1-3, Poholsky 0 in 1, Deal 2 in 2. Runs and earned runs—Off Liddle 3 and 3, Wilhelm 4 and 4, Presko 3 and 3, Lint 5 and 5, Deal 1 and 1. Hit by pitcher—By Moon (Liddle); St. Claire (Deal). Winning pitcher—Jansen (1–0). Losing pitcher—Lint (1–1). Umpires—Ballanfant, Barlick, Warneke and Donatelli. Time of game—2:58. Attendance—26.662.

May 3, 1954

PLAYERS ORGANIZE AND RETAIN LEWIS

But Attorney Denies Major League Representatives Have Formed a Union

CLEVELAND, July 12 (P)— Big league baseball players today organized formally into a group known as the Major League Baseball Players Association. They also adopted by-laws and a constitution.

J. Norman Lewis, the players' attorney, will be paid a reported $30,000 for services rendered while helping the players negotiate revisions in their pension set-up with the owners. The money, to come from the majors' central fund, will cover the lawyer's fee through October, 1954.

Lewis said the matter of any retaining fee after October was not discussed.

The sixteen-player representatives from the American and National League clubs met for three and a half hours.

The group will elect player representatives from each of the sixteen clubs beginning in July, 1955. These men in turn will elect a league representative from each circuit.

Lewis denied that the player action could be construed as the forming of a union. He pointed out that no dues would be paid into the association. Previously, the player representatives group, which was formed informally in 1946, preferred to be known as a "players' fraternity."

There will be four meetings a year of the new organization—the second week of April; All-Star game week; world series time and the first week of December.

All expenses, including the attorney's salary will be paid from baseball's central fund. This fund consists of the gate receipts of the All-Star game and the TV-radio receipts of the All-Star game and the world series.

The present league player representatives, Ralph Kiner of the Chicago Cubs and Allie Reynolds of the New York Yankees, and the current player representatives from each major league club, will continue to serve until the new delegates are elected in 1955.

Lewis will meet tomorrow with the American and National League attorneys to discuss the question of preparing contracts on a revised pension agreement.

The central fund, after the present contract on the players' pension expires in 1955, will earmark 60 per cent of the money for the players and 40 per cent for the owners.

The player discussions brought up these proposals to be submitted at the July 26 meeting of club owners in New York:

¶That players be permitted to deal directly for winter league baseball play themselves and that no limit be placed on the number of players in winter ball.

¶That the owners start spring training no earlier than March 1, play no games earlier than March 10 and keep one day per week open in the spring training.

¶That the clubs pay their players on a monthly basis over 12 months instead of the general practice of five and a half months a year.

July 13, 1954

American League's 17 Hits End National's All-Star Game Streak

BATTING OF ROSEN PACES 11-9 VICTORY

Indian Slugger Hits 2 Homers and Drives In 5 Runs for American League Stars

By JOHN DREBINGER
Special to The New York Times.

CLEVELAND, July 13—In a slugfest that had a crowd of 68,751 fans roaring for more than three hours, the American League today brought to an end the National League's four-year reign in baseball's mid-summer classic.

Unloading an attack such as the junior loop had not known since its more pristine days of power, Casey Stengel's cohorts beat the National Leaguers, led by the Dodgers' rookie skipper, Walter Alston, 11 to 9, in the 1954 All-Star game.

Thus to Stengel came his last sought prize. Four times had the pilot of the five-time world champion Yankees been thwarted in his bid to direct his league to an All-Star triumph. But today, under a broiling sun in the huge arena on Cleveland's lakefront, the American Leaguers, short-enders in the betting, finally came through for the Ol' Professor.

All sorts of records for the event were broken or tied. The victors exploded seventeen hits, a new high, which included four homers, equaling a former record.

Home Star Applauded

Two of those circuits clouts were delivered by Cleveland's own Al Rosen and produced a terrific din. They drove in five runs to tie another mark and behind them was an even more touching story. For just before the game, Rosen, plagued since May 25 with a broken right index finger, had told Stengel he was willing to withdraw from the starting line-up.

Though Commissioner Ford Frick gave permission to Stengel to withdraw Rosen who, as one of the starters chosen in a nationwide poll of fans, was supposed to go at least three innings, Casey left it up to the player. Rosen wound up playing the entire game, added a single to his two homers, and finished playing third base after covering first base for eight innings.

Ray Boone also blasted a homer for the victors but perhaps the noisiest clout was one that another Indian, Larry Doby, unloaded in the role of pinch hitter in the eight. For that shot came with the Nationals leading, 9—8, and tied the score.

Before the round ended the Americans filled the bases on Gene Conley, Milwaukee's six-foot-eight right-hander. A few moments later, with the Dodgers' Carl Erskine, the Nationals' sixth pitcher of the afternoon on the mound, Chicago's Nelson Fox popped a single just over the infield.

Series Margin Now 13-8

It scored two to give the jubilant American leaguers their margin of victory and their thirteenth triumph in the event against eight setbacks.

The Nationals, however, were by no means idle. They touched off fourteen blows, including two homers. Ted Kluszewski hit one in the fifth, and in the eighth another Cincinnati Redleg, Gus Bell, as pinch hitter, belted the other for two runs, which momentarily put the Nationals one in front.

In all thirteen pitchers went into the fray, the Americans using seven. The most bizarre touch of all was that the winning hurler had to be the Senators' young southpaw, Dean Stone, even though he tossed only three pitches and did not retire a batter.

With Red Schoendienst on third and Alvin Dark on first, Stone took over in the eighth as a replacement for Chicago's Bob Keegan, who had just been the victim of the Kluszewski homer. The batter was Duke Snider, but with the count one-and-one, Schoendienst tried to steal home and was tagged out.

Leo Durocher and Charlie Grimm, the baseline coaches, stormed upon Umpire Bill Stewart, claiming to no avail that Stone had committed a balk. Since the Americans then swept ahead in the eighth with their final cluster of three, Stone, as "the pitcher of record," received credit for the game. The loser, of course, was Conley.

Roberts Batted Hard

There were other jolts earlier for the Nationals. In the third Robin Roberts, pride of the senior loop's pitching talent, was raked

for four runs on the Rosen and Boone homers.

After the Nationals had struck back with a five-run fourth, other disappointments were to follow. Perhaps the most poignant of all was in the ninth as the Nationals made a despairing bid to reclaim the battle. With a runner on base, the Cardinals' renowned Stan Musial twice missed a score-tying homer as his drives into the right-field stand went foul.

Then he went out as did the next two, leaving the Giants' Willie Mays on deck. Willie had appeared midway in the conflict as a replacement for Jackie Robinson. All he was able to contribute was a single, which preceded the Bell homer.

Just two of Stengel's seven hurlers did manage to distinguish themselves. The first was Casey's own Whitey Ford, who blanked the Nationals on one hit in the first three innings. Finally Virgil Trucks of the White Sox went in to protect the Americans' two-run advantage in the ninth.

The crowd, just 1,061 short of the All-Star attendance record of 69,812, set in this same arena in 1935, nevertheless set a high for net receipts of $259,204. This erased the former mark of $155,654 set last July in Cincinnati.

The crowd arrived early to see fireworks and it did not have long to wait. Oddly, though, the American League's most famous slugger, Ted Williams, got into

quite a stretch of the encounter without contributing much to the triumph. He fanned twice, walked once.

Roberts, who was starting his fourth All-Star game for the National Leaguers in the last five classics, did not appear his old self from the beginning, although he went through two scoreless rounds. In his nine previous innings of All-Star hurling the Phillies' fireballing right-hander had yielded only two runs.

He labored through the first inning in which Bob Avila tagged him for a single and Yogi Berra drew a pass. Then Hank Bauer clipped him for a single in the second.

Avila Singles Second Time

Despite all this, Roberts was within one out of completing his three innings without a score when the roof fell in. Though Minnie Minoso walked to open the third and Avila, the Indians' second sacker, drew cheers with his second successive single. Mickey Mantle fanned and Berra grounded out, the runners advancing to second and third.

Roberts had whiffed Rosen in the first inning for the third out with two aboard, but this time the Phillie ace got only one strike across on the American League's most valuable player. The next went soaring over the outfield barrier a little to the left of center and the American Leaguers were three in front.

A moment later it was four as Boone of the Tigers stroked his homer into the same sector.

This also spurred the Nationals to action and in the fourth they lashed back for five runs. They routed Sandy Consuegra with five straight hits, the last a two-run two-bagger by Robinson, who scored on Don Mueller's pinch double against Bob Lemon. They added two in the fifth when Kluszewski smacked Bob Porterfield for his homer with one on.

Meanwhile, Johnny Antonelli, the Giants' southpaw, was having his troubles. He pitched only the fourth and fifth, giving three tallies, the last two on Rosen's second homer. Rosen thus became the third player in All-Star history to hit two four-baggers in one game. The first two players were Arky Vaughan in 1941 and Williams in 1946.

Spahn Routed Quickly

That had the battle tied at 7—all, but with the sixth the Americans went one ahead when Milwaukee's Warren Spahn got into a peck of trouble. The Giants' fine reliever, Marvin Grissom, saved this situation by turning back Boone with the bases full.

Cleveland Indians

Al Rosen

Grissom then had to go out in the eighth for a pinch-hitter, Bell, who put the Nationals in front again with his homer behind the Mays single. After that Alston's pitching again went completely sour.

Doby cracked Conley for his game-tying homer in the eighth, Mantle and Berra singled and Rosen walked to fill the bases. Erskine went in to fan Mickey Vernon, but Fox followed with his soft tap that fell in short center just beyond Dark's reach.

The Americans' 17-hit total surpassed the All-Star mark of 14 for one club set by the American League in 1934 and repeated in 1936. The two clubs together totalled 31 hits and that topped the former mark of 26 set in the game of 1937. Also, the total of 20 runs bettered the old mark of 18 established in 1949.

The four American League homers tied the record set by the Nationals in 1951, and the six for the two clubs also tied the mark made in the 1951 contest. Rosen's five runs batted in matched the All-Star high by Williams in 1946.

Box Score of All-Star Game

NATIONAL LEAGUE	ab.	r.	h.	po.	a.	e.
Hamner, 2b	3	0	0	0	0	0
Schoendienst, 2b	2	0	1	0	0	0
Dark, ss	5	0	1	1	2	0
Snider, cf, rf	4	2	3	2	0	0
Musial, rf, lf	5	1	2	2	1	0
Kluszewski, 1b	4	2	2	5	0	0
Hodges, 1b	1	0	0	1	0	0
Jablonski, 3b	3	1	1	0	1	0
Jackson, 3b	2	0	0	1	1	0
Robinson, lf	2	1	1	0	0	0
Mays, cf	2	1	1	1	0	0
Campanella, c	3	0	1	9	0	0
Burgess, c	0	0	0	1	0	0
Roberts, p	1	0	0	0	1	0
aMueller	1	0	1	0	0	0
Antonelli, p	0	0	0	0	0	0
cThomas	1	0	0	0	0	0
Spahn, p	0	0	0	0	0	0
Grissom, p	0	0	0	0	0	0
eBell	1	1	1	0	0	0
Conley, p	0	0	0	0	0	0
Erskine, p	0	0	0	0	0	0
Total	**40**	**9**	**14**	**24**	**5**	**0**

AMERICAN LEAGUE	ab.	r.	h.	po.	a.	e.
Minoso, lf, rf	4	1	2	1	0	1
Piersall, rf	0	0	0	0	0	0
Avila, 2b	3	1	3	1	1	0
Keegan, p	0	0	0	0	0	0
Stone, p	0	0	0	0	1	0
fDoby, cf	1	1	1	0	0	0
Trucks, p	0	0	0	0	0	0
Mantle, cf	5	1	2	2	0	0
Berra, c	4	2	2	5	0	0
Rosen, 1b, 3b	4	2	3	7	0	0
Boone, 3b	4	1	1	1	3	0
gVernon, 1b	1	0	0	1	0	0
Bauer, rf	2	0	1	1	0	0
Porterfield, p	1	0	0	0	0	0
dFox, 2b	2	0	1	1	0	0
Carrasquel, ss	5	1	1	5	4	0
Ford, p	1	0	0	0	0	0
Consuegra, p	0	0	0	0	0	0
Lemon, p	0	0	0	0	0	0
bWilliams, lf	2	1	0	2	0	0
Noren, lf	0	0	0	0	0	0
Total	**39**	**11**	**17**	**27**	**9**	**1**

aDoubled for Roberts in fourth.
cStruck out for Antonelli in fifth.
eHit homer for Grissom in eighth.

bStruck out for Lemon in fourth.
dStruck out for Porterfield in seventh.
fHit homer for Stone in eighth.
gStruck out for Boone in eighth.

National League	0 0 0	5 2 0	0 2 0— 9
American League	0 0 4	1 2 1	0 3 .—11

Runs batted in—Rosen 5, Boone, Avila 2, Doby, Fox 2, Kluszewski 3, Jablonski, Robinson 2, Mueller, Bell 2.

Two-base hits—Robinson, Mueller, Snider. Home runs—Rosen 2, Boone, Kluszewski, Bell, Doby. Sacrifice fly—Avila. Double plays—Avila, Carrasquel and Rosen. Left on base—National 6, American 9. Bases on balls—Off Roberts 2, Spahn, Conley, Ford, Trucks. Struck out—By Roberts 5, Antonelli 2, Grissom 2, Erskine 1, Porterfield 1.

Hits—Off Ford 1 in 3 innings, Consuegra 5 in 1/3, Lemon 1 in 2/3, Porterfield 4 in 3, Keegan 3 in 2/3, Stone 0 in 1/3, Trucks 0 in 1, Roberts 5 in 3, Antonelli 4 in 2, Spahn 4 in 2/3, Grissom 0 in 1 1/3, Conley 3 in 1/3, Erskine 1 in 1/3. Runs and earned runs—Off Roberts 4 and 4, Antonelli 3 and 3, Spahn 1 and 1, Conley 3 and 3, Consuegra 5 and 5, Porterfield 2 and 2, Keegan 2 and 2. Winning pitcher—Stone. Losing pitcher—Conley. Umpires—Rommel (A.), plate and third base; Ballanfant (N.), first base; Honochick (A.), second base; Stewart (N.), third base and plate; Gorman (N.), left field; Paparella (A.), right field. Time—3:10. Attendance—68,751.

July 14, 1954

ADCOCK'S 4 HOMERS HELP BRAVES ROUT DODGERS, 15-7

TEN 4-BAGGERS HIT

Mathews Adds Pair to Adcock's 4—Records Fall in Brooklyn

By ROSCOE McGOWEN

Joe Adcock, the Braves' first baseman, hit four home runs and a double at Ebbets Field yesterday to tie three major league records and establish two others.

The Braves won the game, 15—7, running their winning streak to nine. Milwaukee is only five games out of second place and the Brooks are four games back of the first-place Giants.

Adcock was the seventh player to hit four homers in a game. Bobby Lowe of Boston in 1894, Ed Delahanty of Philadelphia in 1896, Chuck Klein of the Phils in 1936 and Gil Hodges of the Dodgers in 1950 were the National Leaguers sharing the record previously. Lou Gehrig of the Yankees in 1932 and Pat Seerey of the Chicago White Sox in 1948 were the American League players to turn the trick.

Klein and Seerey required extra innings to match the mark. Klein belted his fourth homer in the tenth inning and Seerey connected for No. 4 in the eleventh.

The Braves' star, who connected in the fourth inning on Friday against the Brooks, equalled the major league mark for five homers in two consecutive games.

Joe's total of eighteen bases put a new record in the book, the seventeen-base total previously having been shared by Lowe, Delahanty and Hodges. Adcock's other mark was for the most extra bases on long hits, thirteen.

The two teams tied the National League record for homers by both clubs, ten, the Braves belting seven and the Brooks three. The American League record is eleven, set by the Yankees (six) and Detroit (five), in 1950.

Four Pitchers Belted

Adcock's homers were made

off four pitchers, Don Newcombe, the loser; Erv Palica, Pete Wojey and Johnny Podres. His two-bagger was belted off Palica on Joe's second trip to the plate in the third inning.

Two of his homers and the double were hit on first pitches, the other two big blows on second pitches. The second homer bounced off the façade, but the others went into the lower stands in left center field.

The other major league record tied by Adcock was five extra base hits in a nine-inning game. Lou Boudreau, with Cleveland in 1946, set the modern record with four doubles and a homer in one game.

The other Milwaukee home run hitters were Eddie Mathews, who hit two in a row off Newcombe and Palica, in the first and third innings; and Andy Pafko, who hit his into the left field stands in the seventh off Wojey.

For the Dodgers, Don Hoak and Gil Hodges smacked solo homers in the sixth and eighth and Rube Walker a two-run blast in the eighth, all off Lew Burdette. The Braves' hurler gained

ASSOCIATED PRESS

SEVEN HOMERS AMONG THEM: Milwaukee players hold up fingers to indicate home runs hit by each one of them in game with Dodgers. Left to right: Ed Mathews, Joe Adcock, who tied a major league record with four homers in a nine-inning game, and Andy Pafko.

The Box Score

MILWAUKEE (N.)	ab.	r.	h.	po.	a.
Bruton, cf.	5	0	4	4	0
O'C'nell, 2b.	5	0	0	4	4
Mathews, 3b.	4	3	2	3	2
Aaron, lf.	5	2	2	0	0
Adcock, 1b.	5	5	5	10	0
Pafko, rf.	4	2	3	0	0
P'ndleton, rf.	1	1	0	0	0
Logan, ss.	2	1	1	1	1
Smalley, ss.	2	1	1	0	1
Crandall, c.	4	0	0	3	1
Calderone, c.	1	0	1	2	0
Wilson, p.	1	0	0	0	0
Burdette, p.	4	0	0	0	4
Buhl, p.	0	0	0	0	0
Jolly, p.	0	0	0	0	0
Total	44	15	19	27	13

BROOKLYN (N.)	ab.	r.	h.	po.	a.
Gilliam, 2b.	4	1	4	3	1
Reese, ss.	3	0	1	1	1
Zimmer, ss.	1	0	0	1	1
Snider, cf.	4	0	1	0	0
Shuba, lf.	1	0	0	0	0
Hodges, 1b.	5	1	1	7	0
Amoros lf-cf.	5	2	3	6	0
Robins'n, 3b.	0	0	0	0	0
Hoak, 3b.	2	1	1	0	1
Furillo, rf.	5	1	2	3	0
Labine, p.	0	0	0	0	0
Walker, c.	5	1	1	6	1
Newc'mbe, p.	0	0	0	0	0
Palica, p.	1	0	0	0	0
aMoryn	1	0	0	0	0
Palica, p.	0	0	0	0	0
Wojey, p.	1	0	0	0	1
bPodres, p.	2	0	2	0	1
Total	39	7	16	27	7

aHit into double play for Labine in second.
bSingled for Wojey in seventh.

Milwaukee .... 1 3 2 0 3 0 3 0 3—15
Brooklyn .... 1 0 0 0 0 1 0 4 1—7

Error—Hoak.
Runs batted in—Mathews 2, Snider, Adcock 7, Logan, Hoak 2, Pafko 2, Hodges, Furillo, Walker 2.
Two-base hits—Gilliam, Pafko, Bruton 3, Amoros, Adcock, Aaron. Three-base hit—Amoros. Home runs—Mathews 2, Adcock 4, Hoak, Pafko, Hodges, Walker. Sacrifice—O'Connell. Sacrifice fly—Hoak. Double plays —Mathews, O'Connell and Adcock; O'Connell, Logan and Adcock; Zimmer, Gilliam and Hodges. Left on bases—Milwaukee 6, Brooklyn 10. Bases on balls—Off Burdette 2, Jolly 1, Palica 2. Struck out—By Burdette 3, Jolly 1, Palica 1, Wojey 3, Podres 1. Hits—Off Wilson 5 in 1 inning (pitched to three batters in second), Burdette 8 in 6 1-3, Buhl 2 in 0 (pitched to two batters in eighth), Jolly 1 in 1 2-3, Newcombe 4 in 1 (pitched to three batters in second), Labine 1 in 1, Palica 5 in 2 1-3, Wojey 4 in 2 2-3, Podres 5 in 2. Runs and earned runs—Off Wilson 1 and 1, Burdette 5 and 5, Jolly 1 and 1, Newcombe 4 and 4, Palica 5 and 5, Wojey 3 and 3, Podres 3 and 2. Wild pitch—Podres. Hit by pitcher—By Wilson (Robinson). Winning pitcher—Burdette. Losing pitcher—Newcombe (6-6). Umpires—Boggess, Engeln, Stewart and Pinelli. Time of game—2:53. Attendance—12,263.

his ninth triumph, but had to be relieved in the Brooks' four-run eighth.

Burdette had taken over for Charley Grimm's undefeated starter, Jim Wilson, in the second inning. And in the first two innings, the Dodgers gave their season's greatest exhibition of futility.

In both innings they had the bases filled with none out and managed to score only one run in the first inning. Thereafter, Burdette held the Brooks at bay until Hoak broke through with his homer. Probably the intense heat—the mercury officially registered 95.3—took its toll from Burdette.

Adcock drove in seven runs, his second homer in the fifth being belted with two on, his third in the seventh with one aboard. All other Milwaukee homers were solo shots. One run, in the ninth, when Podres was on the mound, scored on a wild pitch and another when Dave Jolly, the final Braves' pitcher, hit into a double play.

Although the Dodgers made sixteen hits, only three under the Milwaukee output, they never were really in the ball game after being frustrated in the first two innings.

With four runs across in the eighth, they had the bases filled on Podres' second straight single, another by Junior Gilliam and a pass to Don Zimmer.

But with the 17,263 fans, including 5,000 Knothole kids—excepting 460 Milwaukeeans who came here on an excursion to root for their heroes—pleading

Cleveland Indians

Indians Take 111th For Record Season

By The United Press.

CLEVELAND, Sept. 25—Early Wynn missed a no-hitter in the ninth but the Cleveland Indians set an American League record of 111 victories in a single season by defeating the Detroit Tigers 11 to 1, today.

Wynn missed what would have been the first American League no-hitter of the season when Fred Hatfield singled to open the ninth inning. Steve Souchock tripled one out later to deprive Wynn of a shutout.

It was Wynn's fourth two-hitter of the year and he remains a possibility to open the world series against the Giants. He was pitching today with a sore left foot, the result of an ingrown toenail on the big toe of that leg. By gaining his twenty-third triumph, Wynn tied his teammate, Bob Lemon, for the league lead in victories. Either Wynn or Lemon will face the Giants at the Polo Grounds next Wednesday.

Today's 111th victory broke the league record of 110, established in 1927 by the New York Yankees.

The Indians pounded three Tiger pitchers, starting with George Zuverink, for fourteen hits. These included three by Bob Avila, who improved his average to .340 and who is certain

for a grand slam, George Shuba popped to Mathews and Hodges grounded out to short.

Newcombe suffered his sixth loss and now has two straight knockouts.

August 1, 1954

to be crowned batting champion of his league.

Larry Doby drove in a run to increase his runs-batted-in total to 125, giving him the lead over Yogi Berra of the Yankees.

Wynn had a perfect game until one man was out in the sixth, but then he walked Red Wilson on a 3-2 pitch. He passed four men in all, and struck out four.

Hatfield ran the count to 3—1 before he rapped his clean single to right field.

The box score:

DETROIT (A.)					CLEVELAND (A.)				
	ab.r.h.po.a					ab.r.h.po.a			
Kuenn, ss.	3 0 0 0 3				Smith, lf.	rf.4 3 3 0 0			
Herbert, p.	0 0 0 0 0				Avila, 2b.	4 3 3 5 2			
dNieman	1 0 0 0 0				Doby, cf.	3 1 2 3 0			
Marlowe, p.	0 0 0 0 0				Rosen, 3b.	1 0 1 1 0			
Hatfield, 2b.	3 1 1 1 4				aRega'do,3b	1 0 1 1 2			
Delsing, lf.	3 0 0 1 0				bMitchell	1 1 1 0 0			
Boone, 3b.	2 0 0 0 1				Majeski, 3b.	2 0 0 0 2			
Souchock,3b	2 0 1 0 3				Glynn, 1b.	5 1 1 7 0			
Belardi, 1b.	4 0 0 12 0				Philley,rf,lf	5 1 1 2 0			
Kaline, rf.	4 0 0 1 1				Str'kland,ss	2 1 1 2 1			
Tuttle, cf.	3 0 0 1 0				Hegan, c.	4 0 0 6 0			
Wilson, c.	1 0 0 3 2				Wynn, p.	4 0 0 0 1			
Streull, c.	0 0 0 1 0								
Zuverink, p.	1 0 0 1 1				Total	36 11 14 27 8			
Lary, p.	0 0 0 0 0								
cKing	1 0 0 0 0								
Bullard, ss.	1 0 0 2 2								
Total	29 1 2 24 17								

aRan for Rosen in first.
bDoubled for Regalado in fifth.
cFlied out for Lary in sixth.
dHit into force play for Herbert in eighth.
Detroit .... 0 0 0 0 0 0 0 0 1—1
Cleveland .... 1 0 2 0 4 0 4 0 .—11
Errors—Kaline, Bullard.
Runs batted in — Regalado 2, Mitchell 2, Philley 2, Strickland, Wynn, Smith, Souchock, Doby.
Two-base hits—Doby, Avila, Mitchell, Philley. Three-base hit—Souchock. Double play—Wilson and Hatfield. Left on bases—Detroit 5, Cleveland 7. Bases on balls—Off Zuverink 3, Lary 1, Herbert 2. Wynn 4. Struck out—By Zuverink 2, Marlowe 1, Wynn 4. Hits—Off Zuverink 7 in 4 1-3 innings, Lary 2 in 2-3, Herbert 5 in 2, Marlowe 0 in 1. Runs and earned runs—Off Zuverink 6 and 6, Lary 1 and 1, Herbert 4 and 0, Wynn 1 and 1. Wild pitch—Wynn. Winning pitcher—Wynn (23—11). Losing pitcher—Zuverink (9—13). Umpires—Runge, Summers, McKinley and Hurley. Time of game—2:28. Attendance—8,647.

September 26, 1954

GIANTS WIN IN 10TH FROM INDIANS, 5-2, ON RHODES' HOMER

Pinch-Hitter Decides World Series Opener With 3-Run Wallop at Polo Grounds

52,751 SEE LEMON LOSE

Grissom Is Victor in Relief—Mays' Catch Saves Triumph —Wertz Gets 4 Hits

By JOHN DREBINGER

At precisely 4:12 o'clock by the huge clock atop the center-field clubhouse at the Polo Grounds yesterday afternoon, Leo Durocher peered intently at his hand and decided it was time to play his trump card.

It was the last half of the tenth inning in the opening game of the 1954 world series. The tense and dramatic struggle had a gathering of 52,751, a record series crowd for the arena, hanging breathlessly on every pitch.

The score was deadlocked at 2-all. Two Giants were on the base paths and on the mound was Bob Lemon, twenty-three-game winner of the American League, who had gone all the way and was making a heroic bid to continue the struggle a little further. Then Leo made his move.

He called on his pinch-hitter extraordinary, James (Dusty) Rhodes from Rock Hill, S. C., to bat for Monte Irvin. Lemon served one pitch. Rhodes, a left-handed batsman, swung and a lazy pop fly sailed down the right-field foul line.

Ball Just Clears Wall

The ball had just enough carry to clear the wall barely 270 feet away. But it was enough to produce an electrifying three-run homer that enabled the Giants to bring down Al Lopez' Indians, 5 to 2.

It was a breath-taking finish to as nerve-tingling a struggle as any world series had ever seen. The game had started as a stirring mound duel between 37-year-old Sal Maglie and the Tribe's brilliant Lemon.

It saw Vic Wertz, sturdy first sacker, rake Giant pitching for four of the Indians' eight hits. His first one was a triple that

drove in two first-inning runs off Maglie. In the third the Polo Grounders wrenched those two tallies back from Lemon.

Then, in the eighth, Maglie faltered and Don Liddle, a mite of a southpaw, went in, almost to lose the game on the spot. With two runners on base, Wertz connected for another tremendous drive that went down the center of the field 450 feet, only to have Willie Mays make one of his most amazing catches.

Traveling on the wings of the wind, Willie caught the ball directly in front of the green boarding facing the right-center bleachers and with his back still to the diamond.

That brought on Marvin Grissom, another Giant relief ace, who was to go the rest of the way fending off one Cleveland threat after another. And in the tenth it was Willie the Wonder who again moved into the picture.

Mays Gets a Walk

For though Mays was to go hitless throughout the afternoon, here he made an offensive maneuver that presently was to set the stage for Rhodes' game-winning homer. With one out, Mays drew a pass, his second walk of the day.

Then, with Lemon pitching carefully to Henry Thompson, Willie stole second. That immediately changed Cleveland's strategy. Thompson received an intentional pass, doubtless in the hope that Irvin, whom Durocher had insisted on playing in left field and who had been ineffective, would obligingly slap into a double play. But Monte never went to bat.

Instead, up went Dusty. An instant later he leaned into the first pitch and produced a shot that doubtless was heard around the world, though for distance it likely could go as one of the shortest homers in world series history.

The ball hit the chest of a fan in the front row about seven feet from the foul line and bounced back on the playing field. It would have made no difference if the ball had been ruled in play, for Mays undoubtedly would have scored the winning run on the blow.

At any rate, the clout, which was only the fourth pinch homer hit in a modern fall classic, served its purpose. It sent the National Leaguers roaring out of the arena.

It was a steaming, summery afternoon right out of a July calendar. As Perry Como, accompanied by Artie White's orchestra, led the crowd in the singing of the national anthem, white

Mays making sensational catch

Associated Press

The Box Score

FIRST GAME

CLEVELAND INDIANS

	AB	R	H	PO	A
Smith, lf	4	1	1	1	0
Avila, 2b	5	1	1	2	3
Doby, cf	3	0	1	3	0
Rosen, 3b	5	0	1	1	3
Wertz, 1b	5	0	4	11	0
dRegalado	0	0	0	0	0
Grasso, c	0	0	0	1	0
Philley, rf	3	0	0	1	0
aMajeski	0	0	0	0	0
bMitchell	0	0	0	0	0
Strickland, ss	3	0	0	2	3
Dente, ss	0	0	0	0	0
cPope, rf	1	0	0	0	0
Hegan, c	4	0	0	6	1
eGlynn, 1b	1	0	0	0	0
Lemon, p	4	0	0	1	1
Total	**38**	**2**	**8**	***28**	**12**

NEW YORK GIANTS

	AB	R	H	PO	A
Lockman, 1b	5	1	1	9	0
Dark, ss	4	0	2	3	2
Mueller, rf	5	1	2	2	0
Mays, cf	3	0	0	5	0
Thompson, 3b	3	1	1	3	3
Irvin, lf	3	0	0	5	0
fRhodes	1	1	1	0	0
Williams, 2b	4	0	0	1	1
Westrum, c	4	0	2	5	0
Maglie, p	3	0	0	0	2
Liddle, p	0	0	0	0	0
Grissom, p	1	0	0	0	0
Total	**36**	**5**	***9**	**30**	**8**

*One out when winning run scored.

aAnnounced as batter for Philley in eighth.
bWalked for Majeski in eighth.
cCalled out on strikes for Strickland in 8th.
dRan for Wertz in tenth.
eStruck out for Hegan in tenth.
fHit home run for Irvin in tenth.

Cleveland	2 0 0	0 0 0	0 0 0	0-2
New York	0 0 2	0 0 0	0 0 0	3-5

Errors—Mueller 2, Irvin.
Runs batted in—Wertz 2; Mueller, Thompson, Rhodes 3.
Two-base hit—Wertz. Three-base hit—Wertz. Home run—Rhodes. Stolen base—Mays. Sacrifices—Irvin, Dente. Left on bases—Cleveland 13, New York 9. Bases on balls—Lemon 5 (Dark, Mays 2, Thompson 2), Maglie 2 (Lemon, Doby), Grissom 3 (Mitchell, Doby, Pope). Struck out—Maglie 2 (Strickland, Smith), Grissom 3 (Pope, Glynn), Lemon 6 (Maglie 2, Irvin, Thompson, Grissom, Mueller). Hits—Off Maglie 7 in 7 innings (none out in 8th), Liddle 0 in 1/3, Grissom 1 in 2 2/3. Runs and earned runs—Off Maglie 2 and 2, Lemon 5 and 5. Hit by pitcher—By Maglie (Smith). Wild pitch—Lemon. Winning pitcher—Grissom. Losing pitcher—Lemon.
Umpires—Al Barlick (N.), plate; Charlie Berry (A.), first base; Jocko Conlan (N.), second base; John Stevens (A.), third base; Lou Warneke (N.), left field; Larry Napp (A.), right field. Time of game—3:11. Paid attendance—52,751.

---

shirts were the fashion in the sun-bathed seats along the left side of the park. Then the spotlight turned on 12-year-old Jimmy Barbieri, captain of Schenectady's champion team of Little Leaguers, who at this moment doubtless was the proudest youngster in all the land.

Youngster Tosses First Ball

They had conferred the honor of tossing out the first ball upon Jimmy and there were lusty cheers as he fired it with a thud into the big mitt of Wes Westrum, the Giants' catcher. A moment later the fifty-first modern world series was on its way and in no time at all it became evident that not all in the packed stands were Giant partisans.

The American League had its representation, too, including disgruntled Yankee fans, not to mention a few disguised National Leaguers from Brooklyn.

And they made their presence known in no mistaken tones as Maglie got off to a shaky start that sent the Indians off to a two-run lead.

The Barber, whose control is his chief stock in trade and is usually razor sharp, confounded nearly everyone by serving three wide pitches to Al Smith, Cleveland's lead-off batter.

The fourth pitch was even wider, hitting Smith in the side, and the first man up was on. Bobby Avila, the American League's batting champion, followed. Maglie served another ball, making it five in a row that missed the plate. A feeling of uneasiness swept through the stands.

Finally Maglie sent over a strike. It brought a cheer, but the applause was short-lived. For Avila stroked the next one into right field for a single and when

Don Mueller, charging the ball, fumbled it, Smith raced to third. The Indians had runners on first and third with nobody out.

Here, the Barber of old asserted himself. He snuffed out Larry Doby, the American League's top home-run clouter, on the end of a pop foul that Thompson gobbled up back of third, and the slugging Al Rosen went out on an infield pop-up to Whitey Lockman.

But Maglie's opening-round troubles weren't over yet and a moment later the situation became serious as Wertz lined a powerful drive over Mueller's head in deep right-center. The ball caromed off the wall and bounded gaily past the Giant bullpen before the fleet-footed Mays collared it and started it on its way toward the infield.

Liddle Warms Up

When order was restored, Wertz was on third with a triple, Smith and Avila had crossed the plate to put the Tribe two in front and Liddle started warming up with feverish haste in the Giant bullpen. But Maglie wasn't needing any help yet. He got Dave Philley to line the ball to Mueller for the third out, and Giant fans breathed again.

In fact, in a few more minutes the New York fans were setting up quite a din of their own as, in the lower half of the first, the Polo Grounders launched their first threat against Lemon. With one down, Alvin Dark drew a pass and Mueller punched a single to right, sweeping Dark around to third.

But Lemon quickly quelled the uprising. With the crowd imploring Mays to square matters, Willie went out on a pop fly to George Strickland, Cleveland shortstop, and Thompson ended

it by grounding to Wertz down the first-base line.

With the third, however, the Giants did draw even as they lashed into Lemon for three singles which, along with a pass, gave them two tallies. Lockman, the blond North Carolinian, opened the assault on the Cleveland right-hander with a single to right and a moment later was on his way to third as Dark blasted a single through the mound and into center field.

Mueller followed with a grounder to Avila that resulted in a force play at second, but it permitted Lockman to score. Mays walked and Thompson singled to right to drive in Mueller, and the contest was tied at 2—all.

What is more, the Giants had

runners on first and third, there was only one out and it was now Cleveland's turn to show uneasiness in the dugout. In the Tribe bullpen Art Houtteman started warming up.

But Lemon stopped the assault himself. He fanned Irvin, who patrolled left field in place of Rhodes, and Davey Williams ended matters with a grounder to short.

But the Giant fans were happy. Maglie was back on an even footing with the American League's top winning pitcher and from here on it was touch and go.

Westrum Gets Two Hits

For a time both hurlers steadied. There were two Giant singles in the fourth. One was by Westrum, the Polo Grounders' supposedly weak-hitting receiver, who contributed two blows to the New York final total of nine. But the second safety of the inning by Dark fell with two out, and Lemon got out of that spot.

Meanwhile, Maglie was staging a fine recovery, even though Wertz clipped him for a single to left in the fourth, and it wasn't until the sixth that the Barber seemed headed for more trouble.

Again his tormentor was Wertz, who this time singled to right, with Mueller adding another error. Don tried to nip the runner off first, but his throw shot by Lockman and Vic wound up on second. An infield out put him on third with one down.

But Maglie got Strickland to pop up and then was saved when Thompson came up with the first of several sparkling plays he made at third. Knocking down Jim Hegan's hard smash over the bag, Henry had to recover the ball in foul territory. Yet he fired it to first in time to make the third out, and in the seventh Thompson again made a fine stop. Henry was really playing a great defensive game at the hot corner.

In the eighth, however, Maglie faltered again. He walked Doby, and Rosen, hitless to this point, banged a scorching single off Dark's bare hand. That brought in Liddle, who saw Wertz almost wreck everything with his tremendous bid for a fourth straight hit. Mays alone saved Don with his miraculous catch in center.

Grissom went in immediately as both managers now surcharged the air with masterminding maneuvers. Lopez already had sent up Hank Majeski to pinch-hit for Philley, but when Leo switched to the right-handed Grissom, Lopez countered with Dale Mitchell, a left-handed batter. This duel of wits ended with Mitchell drawing a pass, filling the bases with one out.

The Indians were poised for a big killing, and as another lefty swinger, Dave Pope, capable of hitting a long ball, stepped up to bat for Strickland, the National League enthusiasts scarcely were able to breathe.

Grissom Fans Pope

But Grissom slipped a third strike over on an astonished Indian and that doubtless was the turning point of the battle. A moment later the inning and big threat ended with Hegan flying out.

In the last of the eighth the Giants crowded Lemon for the first time since the third. Thompson walked and presently got around to third on a sacrifice and a wild pitch. But Westrum ended this threat with a long fly to Doby in center.

In the ninth Giant hearts stopped beating when, with two out, Irvin, dropped Avila's pop fly for a two-base error. That put Grissom in a jam again, but he got out of it by giving Doby an intentional pass and rubbing out Rosen on another fly to left, which Irvin this time froze to with a great sigh of relief.

In the top of the tenth the desperately straining Clevelanders made another bid and once more Wertz started it. Vic blasted a double into left-center that even Mays couldn't track down. As Wertz jogged off the field after being replaced by a pinch-runner, Rudy Regalado, the crowd generously gave him an ovation.

Sam Dente's sacrifice put Regalado on third with only one out. But Grissom fanned Glynn after Pope walked, and Lemon, striving to win his own game, lined the ball squarely into Lockman's glove inches off the ground.

That was to prove the Indians' last threat, for in the last of the tenth it all vanished on the end of Rhodes' poke.

The pinch home run, which so spectacularly had won for the Giants all summer, had paid off again. During the regular season the Polo Grounders had set a major league record with ten pinch home runs. Rhodes contributed two of these.

In world series play the only previous pinch homers ever hit were those by Yogi Berra of the Yanks in 1947, Johnny Mize, another Yank, in 1952 and George Shuba of the Dodgers last year. And yesterday's game was the first extra-inning affair since Oct. 5, 1952, when the Dodgers beat the Yankees, 6—5, in eleven innings.

And so Leo the Lip considered himself sitting pretty last night as he prepared to fire his south-paw ace, Johnny Antonelli, against the Clevelanders in the second game at the Polo Grounds this afternoon.

There were, to be sure, some critics unkind enough to remark that had Leo played Rhodes in left field from the beginning, victory might have come easier. Perhaps so, but then just look at the tremendous thrill the crowd, which had to pay a net sum of $316,957 into the till, would have missed.

As for Lopez, the Cleveland skipper's big hope was that his other twenty-three-game winner, Early Wynn, would fare better than Lemon and square the series before it moves to Cleveland tomorrow.

Kansas City's American League Bow a Success

Associated Press Wirephoto

A PRESIDENTIAL CUSTOM: Former President Truman as he prepared to throw out the first ball at Athletics' and Tigers' opener at Kansas City yesterday. Watching in uniform are Lou Boudreau, left, manager of Athletics, and Bucky Harris, pilot of the Detroit club.

32,844 FANS WATCH TEAM TRIUMPH, 6-2

Transplanted A's Top Tigers With 3-Run Sixth—Truman Makes Opening Pitch

By JOSEPH M. SHEEHAN
Special to The New York Times.

KANSAS CITY, April 12—Kansas City made a festive, happy bow into major league baseball today. To the boundless delight of an overflow crowd of 32,844 at the sparkling new Municipal Stadium, the transplanted Athletics turned back the Detroit Tigers, 6—2, in their opening game.

A three-run rally in the sixth settled matters in favor of Lou Boudreau's charges. Don Bollweg's pinch single with the bases full brought home the last two runs after Elmer Valo, also up as a pinch-hitter, had worked a pass to force home Bill Renna with the tally that put the Athletics in front.

Ewell Blackwell, recently purchased from the New York Yankees, preserved the lead for Kansas City with three scoreless innings of relief pitching. However, the official credit for the victory went to Alex Kellner, who started for the Athletics and was still the pitcher of record when they moved ahead to stay.

Many notables were on hand to join in the celebration of Kansas City's entrance into the big leagues. Former President Harry S. Truman made the ceremonial first pitch. It was a sizzling, left-handed fast ball that smacked into Joe Astroth's mitt.

Kansas Governor at Game

Gov. Fred Hall of Kansas, Lieut. Gov. James C. Blair of Missouri, Mayor H. Roe Bartle of Kansas City, the mayors of numerous surrounding communities and other high state and city officials also attended.

Ford C. Frick, the commissioner of baseball; Will Harridge, president of the American League, and Earl Hilligan, his assistant, looked on.

So did Walter O. (Spike) Briggs Jr., president of the Tigers, and Del E. Webb, co-owner of the Yankees and co-builder of the handsome new stadium here.

A particularly warmly received guest of Arnold Johnson, the new owner of the Athletics, was 92-year-old Connie Mack, under whose direction the club had operated in Philadelphia for more than half a century. Roy Mack and other members of the Mack family also came on from Philadelphia for the historic event.

Reacting to the situation, the Athletics, rather an apathetic crew in finishing last, with a 51-103 won-lost record in Philadelphia last season, put on a

Athletics' Box Score

DETROIT (A.)						KANSAS CITY (A.)					
	ab.	r.	h.	po.	a.		ab.	r.	h.	po.	a.
Kuenn, ss	4	0	1	2	1	Power, 1b	3	0	0	6	1
Hatfield, 2b	4	0	1	2	1	bBollweg, 1b	1	0	1	3	0
Kaline, rf	4	0	2	3	1	Suder, 2b	5	0	0	4	4
Boone, 3b	3	0	1	0	2	Finigan, 3b	4	1	1	0	3
Porter, 1b	4	0	1	7	0	Zernial, lf	4	0	1	2	0
Tuttle, cf	3	0	0	1	0	Renna, rf	4	1	1	3	0
B. Phil'ps, lf	3	0	0	2	0	W. Wilson, cf	3	3	3	3	0
eDelsing	0	0	0	0	0	Dema'tri, ss	4	0	2	2	1
R. Wilson, c	4	1	3	4	1	Astroth, c	1	1	0	4	0
Garver, p	2	0	0	0	0	Kellner, p	2	0	0	0	4
cFain	0	0	0	0	0	aValo	0	0	0	0	0
dMalmberg	0	0	0	0	0	Blackwell, p	0	0	0	0	0
Fletcher, p	0	0	0	1	0						
Total	30	2	8	24	9	Total	31	6	9	27	13

aWalked for Kellner in sixth.
bSingled for Power in sixth.
cWalked for Garver in seventh.
dRan for Fain in seventh.
eWalked for Phillips in ninth.

Detroit ....0 0 0 1 1 0 0 0 0—2
Kansas City ....0 1 1 0 0 3 0 1 .—6
Error—Boone.
Runs batted in—Tuttle. R. Wilson, Demaestri, Zernial, Valo, Bollweg 2, W. Wilson.
Two-base hits—Hatfield, W. Wilson, Finigan Porter, Renna. Home runs—R. Wilson, W. Wilson. Sacrifice—Blackwell. Sacrifice fly—Tuttle. Double play—Hatfield and Kuenn, Demaestri, Zernial, Valo, Bollweg: Suder and Bollweg. Left on bases—Detroit 6, Kansas City 8. Bases on balls—Off Garver 4, Fletcher 1, Kellner 1, Blackwell 3. Struck out—By Garver 3, Kellner 4. Hits—Off Garver 7 in 6 innings, Kellner 6 in 6; Fletcher 2 in 2, Blackwell 2 in 3. Runs and earned runs—Off Garver 5 and 5. Kellner 2 and 2, Fletcher 1 and 1. Hit by pitcher—By Garver (Astroth). Winning pitcher—Kellner (1–0). Losing pitcher—Garver (0–1). Umpires—Summers, Hurley, Runge and Soar. Time of game—2:38. Attendance—32,147 (paid).

sprightly show for their new followers.

Kansas City has no illusions about the merits of the ball club it has adopted. But there was obvious elation in the stands that, on this occasion at least, the home athletes gave a major-league performance.

'Big' Inning a Hit

Certainly Boudreau, who took over the management of the Athletics after the transfer of the franchise, won friends and influenced people here by his unhesitating decision to go for the "big" inning with the score tied in the sixth.

The Athletics had scored first. A double by Bill Wilson, who had a perfect day at bat with a homer, single and a walk in addition, and a single by Joe DeMaestri gave them a run in the second. They picked up another in the third on a double

by Jim Finigan and a single by Gus Zernial.

But the Tigers quickly caught up. Ray Boone's walk, a double by J. W. Porter and a long fly to right by Bill Tuttle produced a run for the visitors in the fourth. They tied the score in the fifth on Bob Wilson's homer over the left-field wall.

There will be a lot of homers hit over this twelve-foot barrier, only 330 feet from the plate at the foul line and 375 feet in left center.

In the decisive sixth, Renna greeted Ned Garver with a line double off the left-field wall. Bill Wilson walked and, after De-Maestri had advanced both runners with a grounder to third that Boone boobled, a pass to Astroth filled the bases.

Here Boudreau made his move. He sent Valo to hit for Kellner and Elmer worked Garver for a pass. Lou then called on Bollweg, another left-handed hitter, to bat for Vic Power. Don responded with a solid single to right that drove in Wilson and Astroth.

The Athletics added a security tally in the eighth when Bill Wilson smashed his homer, also a left-field wallop, off Van Fletcher, who had succeeded Garver in the seventh.

Keeping the Tigers off balance with assorted sweeping side-arm curves, Blackwell did the rest for Kansas City. The big right-hander, out of action all last season with a dead arm, yielded two singles and three walks, but wrapped up each of his three innings by inducing an unwary Tiger to hit into a double play.

April 13, 1955

Sports of The Times

By ARTHUR DALEY

Typographical Error

FOR thirty-eight years the statisticians have been short-changing Napoleon Lajoie on his batting average. But the Big Frenchman has just received a rebate and all is serene again. Instead of hitting a miserable .405 in 1901, he actually batted .422, a figure that now becomes the highest in American League history and that now supersedes the .420 jointly held by Ty Cobb and George Sisler. It's an odd story.

It involves a typographical error and an astonishing amount of laborious research. Even the telling of the tale requires considerable backtracking. It started, properly enough, in 1901 when Lajoie won the American League batting championship with a mark of .422. This was gained through 229 hits in 543 times at bat. So far, so good.

But some rascal of a printer struck the wrong key when he was making a tabulation of the American League batting averages for the Reach Guide of 1902. The Lajoie hit total landed in the book as 220 instead of 229. Just a minute, though. If the pronunciation of that name bothers you, it strikes the ears as if it were La-joe-way—with the emphasis on the first syllable.

The First Recheck

When the great second baseman retired after the 1916 season, some figger filbert for the Spalding Record Book went to work on Lajoie's lifetime averages and kept falling on his face over a discrepancy. He found it—or so he thought—in the 220 hits for 1901. Therefore, the .422 average was arbitrarily reduced to .405 for the 1917 compendium. What made this move excusable was that the official American League records had been lost or destroyed.

Even more strange was the fact that Lajoie never made a peep, which is virtually a violation of union rules. A ballplayer will scream like a wounded elephant if he's cheated out of even one-thousandth of a point in his batting average.

Yet Lajoie never uttered a complaint. It seems incomprehensible to a fellow who has

Napoleon Lajoie
His missing hits have been found

always been told that all ballplayers keep their up-to-date batting average penciled on the cuffs of their sleeves.

The Second Recheck

Two years ago The Sporting News, baseball's bible, ran a feature on Lajoie and casually mentioned the discrepancy that was to be found in his twin statistics for 1901, his original .422 and his later .405. But there are baseball fans who can devour statistics alive, no matter how indigestible they seem to be. And this one was quite a swallow.

A Philadelphia fan, John G. Tattersall, perked up both ears at the challenge and eagerly went to work. The Seven Labors of Hercules were no more herculean than the task he undertook. First he went through the record books for 1901 and 1902 in order to confirm the impression that there had been a slip of some sort. The 1901 book listed 229 hits and the 1902 book had the total at 220. But that still wasn't proof.

So the tireless Mr. Tattersall went about proving his point. He got out the old newspaper files. Have you ever checked ancient and yellowing newspaper files? It's exhausting, frustrating work, especially since the sports pages of that era weren't pages at all but a few scattered columns that could be anywhere in the paper.

It must have been like trying to run uphill in sand. But he went through the day-by-day box scores and triumphantly emerged with the proof he needed. Lajoie had hammered out 229 hits, not 220. But what to do with his proof?

Final Rechecks

Tattersall sent news of his discovery to Ernest J. Lanigan, the official historian for baseball's Hall of Fame at Cooperstown. Naturally, Lajoie is a member of the Hall of Fame. He was elected in 1937 with the second batch of diamond immortals. But because he's one of the prides of white-haired Ernie, the energetic Mr. Lanigan also checked his records. Tattersall was correct. However, the cautious Ernie insisted on further confirmation.

So he asked Seymour Siwoff, the manager of the Al Munro Elias Baseball Bureau and the editor of The Little Red Book, to make independent checks of his own. Siwoff enlisted Hy Turkin, editor of the Encyclopedia of Baseball, and those two expert jugglers of diamond statistics went over box scores for the entire 1901 season. Lanigan was right. Tattersall was right and Lajoie was a .422 hitter.

So lengthy an operation was the rechecking that it wasn't completed in time for the 1954 edition of The Little Red Book. But it is in the 1955 edition and, eventually, will be incorporated in all official American League listings. The odd part of it all is that the extra nine hits, missing for these many years, only lift Lajoie's lifetime mark from .338 to .339. Nine hits, you see, can't make much of a dent when a man makes 3,251 in his career.

He was of the truly great ones was Napoleon Lajoie. But we're running out of space and that will have to wait for another day.

May 22, 1955

National All-Stars Win in Twelfth, 6-5

By JOHN DREBINGER
Special to The New York Times.

MILWAUKEE, July 12— Short of winning a world championship, which it some day hopes to achieve, this seething baseball metropolis of the Midwest experienced its greatest baseball thrill today.

A gathering of 45,314 roaring fans watched a grimly fighting band of National Leaguers rally to draw even with the American League and carry the 1955 All-Star game into extra innings.

The fans saw, in the top half of the twelfth, their own Gene Conley, the beanpole right-hander of the Braves, step to the mound to fan three batters in a row.

In the last half of the inning they saw Stan Musial of the St. Louis Cardinals blast a home run into the right field bleachers.

The blow gave the Nationals the game, 6 to 5. It also gave Leo Durocher, who directed the National League forces, another signal triumph over Cleveland's skipper, Al Lopez, who led the American Leaguers and who last October bowed to Leo in the world series.

Lopez, during the early stages of the battle, had directed his forces well. But then he seemed to lose command in the closing rounds as the Nationals closed with a rush.

The Americans had ripped into Robin Roberts for four runs in the opening round. Three tallies rode in on a homer by the Yankees' Mickey Mantle. By the sixth the Americans had increased the advantage to 5—0.

But as the game progressed, Durocher, who hadn't been doing so well with the starting line-up the fans had voted him in the nationwide poll, began making changes of his own. The Giant manager inserted his own Willie Mays, who in the seventh inning made an electrifying catch that robbed Ted Williams of a homer, which would have given the Americans two additional runs.

On the heels of that, the Say Hey Kid, with a pair of singles,

Box Score of All-Star Game

AMERICAN LEAGUE	ab.	r.	h.	po.	a.	e.	NATIONAL LEAGUE	ab.	r.	h.	po.	a.	e.
Kuenn, ss	3	1	1	1	0	0	Schoendienst, 2b.	6	0	2	3	2	0
Carrasquel, ss	3	0	2	1	3	1	Ennis, lf	1	0	0	1	0	0
Fox, 2b	3	1	1	2	0	0	cMusial, lf	4	1	1	0	0	0
Avila, 2b	1	0	0	1	2	0	Snider, cf	2	0	0	3	0	0
Williams, lf	3	1	1	1	0	0	Mays, cf	3	2	2	3	0	0
Smith, lf	1	0	0	0	0	0	Kluszewski, 1b	5	1	2	9	1	0
Mantle, cf	6	1	2	3	0	0	Mathews, 3b	2	0	0	0	3	1
Berra, c	6	1	1	8	2	0	Jackson, 3b	3	1	1	0	0	0
Kaline, rf	4	0	1	6	0	0	Mueller, rf	2	0	1	0	0	0
Vernon, 1b	5	0	1	8	0	0	dAaron, rf	2	1	2	0	0	0
Finigan, 3b	3	0	0	2	0	0	Banks, ss	2	0	0	2	1	0
Rosen, 3b	2	0	0	0	1	0	Logan, ss	3	0	1	1	1	0
Pierce, p	0	0	0	0	0	0	Crandall, c	1	0	0	1	0	0
bJensen	1	0	0	0	0	0	eBurgess, c	1	0	0	2	0	0
Wynn, p	0	0	0	0	0	1	hLopata, c	3	0	0	10	0	0
gPower	1	0	0	0	0	0	Roberts, p	0	0	0	1	1	0
Ford, p	1	0	0	0	0	1	aThomas	1	0	0	0	0	0
Sullivan, p	1	0	0	0	0	0	Haddix, p	0	0	0	0	2	0
							fHodges	1	0	1	0	0	0
Total	44	5	10	*33	9	2	Newcombe, p	0	0	0	0	0	0
							iBaker	1	0	0	0	0	0
							Jones, p	0	0	0	0	0	0
							Nuxhall, p	2	0	0	0	1	0
							Conley, p	0	0	0	0	0	0
							Total	45	6	13	36	12	1

*None out when winning run was scored.
aPopped out for Roberts in third.
bPopped out for Pierce in fourth.
cStruck out for Ennis in fourth.
dRan for Mueller in fifth.
eHit into force out for Crandall in fifth.
fSingled for Haddix in sixth.
gPopped out for Wynn in seventh.
hSafe on error for Burgess in seventh.
iFlied out for Newcombe in seventh.

```
American .............4 0 0   0 0 1   0 0 0   0 0 0—5
National .............0 0 0   0 0 0   2 3 0   0 0 1—6
```

Runs batted in—Mantle 3, Vernon, Logan, Jackson, Aaron, Musial. Two-base hits—Kluszewski, Kaline. Home runs — Mantle, Musial. Sacrifices — Pierce, Avila. Double plays—Kluszewski, Banks and Roberts; Wynn, Carrasquel and Vernon. Left on bases—American 12, National 8. Bases on balls—Roberts 1 (Williams), Ford 1 (Aaron), Jones 2 (Vernon, Rosen), Nuxhall 3 (Smith, Kaline, Avila), Sullivan 1 (Musial). Strike outs—Pierce 3 (Ennis, Snider, Banks), Haddix 2 (Kaline, Finnigan), Wynn 1 (Musial), Newcombe 1 (Avila), Jones 1 (Mantle), Nuxhall 5 (Ford, Vernon, Rosen, Sullivan, Smith), Sullivan 4 (Mays, Jackson, Logan, Lopata), Conley 3 (Kaline, Vernon, Rosen). Hits—Off Roberts 4 in 3 innings, Pierce 1 in 3, Haddix 3 in 3, Wynn 3 in 3, Newcombe 1 in 1, Jones 0 in 2-3, Ford 5 in 1 2-3, Nuxhall 2 in 3 1-3, Sullivan 3 in 3 1-3 (faced one batter in twelfth), Conley 0 in 1. Runs, earned runs—Roberts 4 and 4, Haddix 1 and 1, Ford 5 and 5, Sullivan 1 and 1. Hit by pitcher—By Jones (Kaline). Wild pitch—Roberts. Passed ball—Crandall. Winning pitcher—Conley. Losing pitcher—Sullivan. Umpire—Barlick (N.), Soar (A.), Boggess (N.), Summers (A.), Secory (N.), Runge (A.). Time—3:17. Attendance—45,314. Receipts (gross)—$179,545.50.

Duke Snider watches Mickey Mantle's three-run homer for the American Leaguers disappear over the fence in the first inning.

helped ignite two rallies that enabled the Nationals to draw even. They counted twice in the seventh and three times in the eighth to make it 5-all.

Meanwhile, Don Newcombe blanked the Americans in the seventh. In the eighth, the Cubs' Sam Jones got into difficulties and filled the bases with two out. But here Cincinnati's left-hander, Joe Nuxhall, entered the struggle to turn in some of the day's best pitching.

The Redlegs' hurler struck out Whitey Ford of the Yanks, a development that later was to cause some more second guessing on Lopez. Most experts seemed to feel Lopez, even though still three runs ahead, should have called on a pinch hitter, since he had ample pitching strength in Bob Turley, Herb Score and Dick Donovan.

Nuxhall held the Americans scoreless through the ninth, tenth and eleventh. Then Conley put on his magnificent performance in the twelfth as he fanned Kaline, Mickey Vernon and Al Rosen to become the eventual winner.

Sullivan Yields Homer

In gaining their winning tally, which Musial hammered out of bounds, the Nationals had to overcome an equally rugged foeman. Frank Sullivan, the Red Sox right-hander, after relieving Ford in the eighth, had held the Nationals at bay through three and one-third innings before Musial's blow laid him low.

It was the fourth All-Star home run of his career for Stan the Man, a record for the competition. Like Mays, Musial was a late starter in the game, since he was not one of the originals chosen by the fans. Although a first sacker all this season, Stan replaced the Phils' Del Ennis in left field to allow Cincinnati's mighty Ted Kluszewski to play the entire game at first.

Musial's appearance also made him the dean of all present-day active players in All-Star competition. This was his twelfth classic, one more than Williams, who today played in his eleventh.

Williams, however, did not finish and the move doubtless was one that Lopez long will regret. He permitted the Red Sox slugger, who had singled earlier in the day, to retire after Mays made his spectacular catch to end the Americans' seventh. The Americans were still leading by five and the victory seemed safe.

Just before the battle got under way the crowd, which had tossed $179,545.50 into the till, stood in silent tribute to the memory of Arch Ward, the Chicago Tribune sports editor, who had founded the All-Star game in 1933. Funeral services for Ward were held in Chicago this morning.

Then, scarcely had the fans settled back in their seats after the singing of the National Anthem, than the American Leaguers opened fire on Roberts. The right-handed ace of the Phillies was starting his fifth mid-summer classic.

Harvey Kuenn singled to left. Nellie Fox singled to right and runners were on first and third. Next occurred a wild pitch as Roberts worked on Williams. Kuenn scored on the slip.

Williams Draws Walk

Roberts, who seemed to be having unusual trouble with his control, wound up walking Williams. A moment later, Mantle sent a tremendous smash straight down the middle. It cleared the barrier between the bleachers and bullpens, more than 400 feet away. It also gave the American Leaguers a 4-0 lead.

For all of five innings after that, the game became one of the most silent All-Star struggles in history. The crowd, predominantly National League in its sympathies, watched the futile efforts of its favorites to cut down the margin.

Billy Pierce, the crack southpaw of the White Sox, blanked the Nationals and allowed only one hit in the first three innings. In fact, he faced only nine batters.

Red Schoendienst, leading off the Durocher batting order, singled in the first. But the Cardinal second sacker was then rubbed out trying to steal second on a pitch that bounced out of Catcher Yogi Berra's glove.

Early Wynn, the star right-hander of Lopez' Indians, then blanked the Nationals for three more innings. He gave up three blows. In the fifth, Kluszewski doubled and Don Mueller singled to left. But Kluszewski couldn't score on the hit and Wynn worked his way out of the jam.

In the sixth, the gloom of the Milwaukee fans went even a shade deeper. Harvey Haddix, a Cardinal left-hander, yielded a tally after blanking the American Leaguers in the fourth and fifth.

Berra singled and Al Kaline banged a double off Ed Mathews' wrist. The injury later sent the Braves' third sacker to the hospital for X-rays. The examination showed no fracture.

Berra went to third on Kaline's blow. Vernon bounced a grounder to Kluszewski and Yogi scooted home. The Americans were ahead, 5 to 0.

Mays Takes Over

With the seventh, however, the Nationals began to bestir themselves. The Dodgers' Duke Snider had not overly distinguished himself when he gave way in center field to Mays. Willie made his presence felt almost immediately.

Two were out and Chico Carrasquel was on first in the American's seventh when Williams stroked a powerful smash toward right center. But Willie gave chase and just as the ball appeared to clear the wire railing, the Say Hey Kid leaped up to snare the ball in his glove.

First up in the last of the seventh, Mays greeted Ford with a single to left. The Yankee southpaw had just taken the mound. He got the next two, but Hank Aaron of the Braves, in as the result of another belated, though popular, move by Durocher, drew a pass.

A moment later the Braves' Johnny Logan singled to right and one run scored. Then Stan Lopata grounded to Carrasquel, who had just taken over at short for the Americans. Chico booted the ball, threw wide to second and a second run scored on the error.

Two were out in the eighth when the Nationals launched another offensive against Ford. Again it was Mays who started it with a single. Kluszewski and Randy Jackson, who had replaced Mathews, also singled. That scored Willie and Ford went out for Sullivan.

Before the Red Sox right-hander got matters under control, Lopez was to receive another jolt as two runs tallied to tie the score.

Aaron blasted a single to right and when Kaline's throw toward third got away from Rosen for an error, both Kluszewski and Jackson tallied. The Indians' Rosen had been another delayed entry by Lopez that did not pan out so well.

The aroused Nationals appeared set for a killing in the ninth when, with two down, Schoendienst singled and Musial walked. But Sullivan this time mastered Mays and got him on a third strike.

Nuxhall drew thunderous cheers when, after walking Kaline in the tenth, he fanned three in a row, but he had a close call in the eleventh. A pass to Avila and a single by Mantle had two on with two out when Berra bounced a grounder over second.

Schoendienst made a miraculous stop and fired the ball over his shoulder toward first. A mighty close play followed and when Yogi was called out, he protested vehemently. That, too, was to prove the American Leaguers' last gasp.

The cheering for Conley in the twelfth had barely subsided when Musial hit Sullivan's first pitch in the lower half. With that, another stirring interleague classic had gone into the records. The Americans still lead in the series, thirteen games to nine, but the Nationals have won five of the last six contests.

For the vanquished, Berra set a record by becoming the first catcher to work five complete All-Star games. He had previously been tied with Roy Campanella at four. Three other American Leaguers went all the way today, Mantle, Kaline and Vernon. Kluszewski and Schoendienst were the two "iron men" for the triumphant National League.

July 13, 1955

Banks Breaks Majors' Record for Shortstops With 40th Homer as Cubs Crush Cards, 12-2

Stephens' Mark of 39 Circuit Blows for Red Sox in 1949 Season Is Surpassed

CHICAGO, Sept. 2 (UP)—Ernie Banks broke the major league record for home runs by a short-stop today. He walloped his for-tieth homer of the year to lead the Chicago Cubs to a 12-2 tri-umph over the St. Louis Cardinals. A ladies' day crowd of 14,693 saw the game.

Banks' blow, his first homer in eighteen games since Aug. 11, came with Dee Fondy and Gene Baker on base and capped the Cubs' eight-run second in-ning against Tom Poholsky and Paul LaPalme. The hit was made off LaPalme on a 2-and-1 pitch and it went into the wire net behind the left-field runway.

The previous record for hom-ers by a shortstop was thirty-

nine set by Vern Stephens with the Boston Red Sox in 1949. Banks hit his thirty-ninth against the Cincinnati Redlegs.

Chicago Home Stand Opens

The game today opened a Cubs' home stand in Wrigley Field after a fifteen-game road trip.

The victory went to Paul Minner. It was his sixth without defeat against the Cardinals this season and the twenty-first of his career over St. Louis, against seven losses.

The Cubs clinched the deci-sion in the second when Banks, Ransom Jackson and Eddie Mik-sis opened with singles. Two runs scored when Alex Gram-mas bobbled Jim Bolger's ground ball and the bases were full again when Walker Cooper was safe on a fielder's choice.

Miksis scored on Fondy's in-field single and Baker doubled for two more runs before Banks batted for the second time and knocked the ball over the fence.

The three runs batted in lifted Ernie's season total to 101.

Jackson later collected his eighteenth homer and Cooper his seventh. The triumph was the sixth for the Cubs in the last seven games and the Cards' fourth straight loss.

Poholsky suffered his tenth defeat against seven successes.

Tight Inside Pitch

After the game, Banks said, "I had a feeling that I ought to get one today. All the time we were on the road they were pitching me outside and I was hitting the ball to center field or right field.

"But the Cardinals always pitch me tight inside, and that's where LaPalme threw it. I was tired out on the road and I couldn't get around well on the outside pitches. Maybe the half-day rest before today's game did me some good."

The homer was Banks' eighth of the year off Cardinal pitch-

ing, but his first off LaPalme.

Banks has collected four grand-slam homers this season to tie the major league record.

September 3, 1955

The Box Score

ST. LOUIS (N.)	ab.	r.	h.	po.	a.		CHICAGO (N.)	ab.	r.	h.	po.	a.
Boyer, 3b.	4	1	4	2	2		Fondy, 1b.	5	1	4	10	0
S'dienst, 2b.	2	0	1	0	1		Baker, 2b.	5	1	1	3	5
Steph'n, 2b.	2	0	1	1	3		B'mholtz, lf.	4	0	0	1	0
Musial, rf.	2	0	1	0	0		Merriman,lf	1	0	0	0	0
Elliott, rf.	1	0	0	2	0		Jackson, 3b.	5	2	2	0	1
Wh'nant, lf.	4	0	0	3	0		Banks, ss.	4	2	3	5	3
Sarni, c.	2	0	0	3	1		Miksis, rf.	4	1	1	0	0
Burbrink, c.	2	0	0	1	1		Bolger, cf.	4	2	1	2	0
Virdon, cf.	4	0	1	2	0		Cooper, c.	4	2	1	5	0
Moon, 1b.	3	3	1	10	0		Minner, p.	4	1	1	1	4
Grammas,ss	4	0	2	0	3							
Poholsky, p.	1	0	0	0	0		Total	40	12	14	27	13
LaPalme, p.	0	0	0	0	1							
Mack'son, p.	0	0	0	0	0							
aRepulski	1	0	0	0	0							
McDaniel, p.	0	0	0	0	0							
bHemus	1	0	0	0	0							
Total	34	2	11	24	12							

aPopped out for Mackinson in seventh.
bGrounded out for McDaniel in ninth.

St. Louis ....0 0 1 0 0 0 0 0 1—2
Chicago ....0 8 2 0 0 1 0 .—12

Errors—Grammas, Moon.
Runs batted in—Bolger, Fondy 3, Baker 2, Banks 3, Jackson, Cooper, Moon.
Two-base hits—Boyer, Musial, Baker. Bol-zer, Fondy 2, Grammas. Home runs—Banks, Jackson, Cooper, Moon. Double plays—Min-ner and Baker; Baker, Banks and Fondy 2; Baker and Fondy. Left on bases—St. Louis 7, Chicago 5. Bases on balls Minner 2, McDaniel 1. Struck out—By Minner 5, Poholsky 2, Mackinson 1. Hits—Off Pohol-sky 5 in 1 1-3 innings, La Palme 1 in 2-3, Mackinson 6 in 4, McDaniel 2 in 2. Runs and earned run—Off Minner 2 and 2, Po-holsky 7 and 4, La Palme 1 and 0, Mackin-son 3 and 3, McDaniel 1 and 1. Winning pitcher—Minner (9-8). Losing pitcher—Poholsky (7–10). Umpires Pinelli, Gorman, Boggess and Engeln. Time of game—2:20. Attendance—8,160 (paid).

DODGERS CAPTURE 1ST WORLD SERIES; PODRES WINS, 2-0

He Beats Yanks Second Time as Team Takes Classic in 8th Try, 4 Games to 3

HODGES DRIVES IN 2 RUNS

Single in 4th and Sacrifice Fly in 6th Decide—Amoros Catch Thwarts Bombers

By JOHN DREBINGER

Brooklyn's long cherished dream finally has come true. The Dodgers have won their first world series championship.

The end of the trail came at the Stadium yesterday. Smokey Alston's Brooks, with Johnny Podres tossing a brilliant shut-

out, turned back Casey Stengel's Yankees, 2 to 0, in the seventh and deciding game of the 1955 baseball classic.

This gave the National League champions the series, 4 games to 3. As the jubilant victors almost smothered their 23-year-old left-handed pitcher from Witherbee, N. Y., a roaring crowd of 62,465 joined in sounding off a thun-derous ovation. Not even the stanchest American League die-hard could begrudge Brooklyn its finest hour.

Seven times in the past had the Dodgers been thwarted in their efforts to capture base-ball's most sought prize—the last five times by these same Bombers.

When the goal finally was achieved the lid blew off in Brooklyn, while experts, poring into the records, agreed nothing quite so spectacular had been accomplished before. For this was the first time a team had won a seven-game world series after losing the first two games.

Victor in Third Game

And Podres, who had van-quished the Yankees in the third game as the series moved to Eb-bets Field last Friday, became

the first Brooklyn pitcher to win two games in one series.

Tommy Byrne, a seasoned campaigner who was the Yanks' "comeback hero of the year," carried the Bombers' hopes in this dramatic struggle in which victory would have given them their seventeenth series title. But Byrne, whose southpaw slants had turned back the Dodgers in the second encounter, could not quite cope with the youngster pitted against him.

In the fourth inning a two-bagger by Roy Campanella and a single by Gil Hodges gave the Brooks their first run.

In the sixth a costly Yankee error helped fill the bases. It forced the withdrawal of Byrne, though in all he had given only three hits.

Stengel called on his right-handed relief hurler, Bob Grim.

Bob did well enough. But he couldn't prevent Hodges from lifting a long sacrifice fly to center that drove in Pee Wee Reese with the Brooks' second run of the day.

Fortified with this additional tally, Podres then blazed the way through a succession of thrills while a grim band of Dodgers fought with the tenacity

of inspired men to hold the ad-vantage to the end.

Fittingly, the final out was a grounder by Elston Howard to Reese, the 36-year-old shortstop and captain of the Flock. Ever since 1941 had the Little Colonel from Kentucky been fighting these Yankees. Five times had he been forced to accept the loser's share.

Many a heart in the vast arena doubtless skipped a beat as Pee Wee scooped up the ball and fired it to first. It was a bit low and wide. But Hodges, the first sacker, reached out and grabbed it inches off the ground. Gil would have stretched halfway across the Bronx for that one.

Thus to the 43-year-old Walter E. Alston of Darrtown, Ohio, goes the distinction of piloting a Dodger team to its first world title. As a player, Smokey had appeared in the majors only long enough to receive one time at bat with the Cardinals. What is more, he ruefully recalls, he struck out.

Dropped back to the minors soon after that, Alston didn't appear in the majors again until he was named manager of the Brooks in 1954.

Yet, in his second year he not only led the Dodgers to an over-whelming triumph for the Na-tional League pennant but also attained a prize that had eluded such managerial greats as the late Uncle Wilbert Robinson, Leo

The New York Times

BATTERY IS CHARGED WITH VICTORY: Johnny Podres is hoisted aloft by Catcher Roy Campanella after pitching the Dodgers to triumph over Yankees yesterday in seventh game of the world series. Don Hoak, third baseman, rushes over to join the festivities.

Durocher, Burt Shotton and Chuck Dressen.

The Dodgers made their first world series appearance in 1916. They lost to the Boston Red Sox. In 1920 they bowed to the Cleveland Indians. Then in 1941, '47, '49, '52 and '53 they went down before the mighty Bombers.

As for the Yanks, the defeat brought to an end a string of world series successes without parallel. Victors in sixteen classics, they suffered only their fifth setback. It was their first defeat under Charles Dillon Stengel, who bagged five in a row from 1949 through 1953.

Giants, Cards Did Trick

Back in 1921 and 1922 the Bombers lost to John McGraw's Giants. Until yesterday the Cardinals had been the only other National League champions to stop them. St. Louis won in 1926 and again in 1942. Since then the Yankees had bagged seven classics until the Brooks broke their spell.

Perfect baseball weather again greeted the belligerents as the battle lines were drawn for this final conflict.

The crowd, though smaller than for the three previous Stadium games, contributed $407,549 to the series pool, to help set a world series "gate" total of $2,337,515. This, of course, is apart from the addition revenues derived from radio and television.

As the players took the field there was a final check on the invalids, of whom both sides provided more than a fair share. Duke Snider was back in the Dodger line-up. Duke had gone out of the sixth game on Monday with a twisted knee when he stepped in a small hole fielding a pop fly in center field.

But Jackie Robinson, who had fought so valiantly for the Brooks in the three straight games they won in Ebbets Field, had to remain on the sidelines. He was suffering from a strained Achilles tendon in his right leg. So Don Hoak played third.

Bauer in Right Field

In the Yankee camp, Hank Bauer, the ex-marine, was in right field again despite a pulled thigh muscle. But Mickey Mantle, a serious loss to the Bombers throughout the series, was still out with his painfully torn leg muscle. He did manage to get into the game for one pinch-hit performance. His best was a towering, though harmless, pop fly.

Since the Yanks, who on Monday had squared the series by crushing the left-handed Karl Spooner with a five-run first-inning blast, were again being confronted by a southpaw, Stengel strung along with his right-handed batting power. But defensively this was to prove costly. For it was Bill Skowron, his first-sacker, who made the damaging fielding slip in the sixth.

For three innings Podres and Byrne maintained a scoreless deadlock. Skowron, a right-handed hitter who had stunned

the Brooks with his three-run homer into the right-field stands Monday, gave them another mild jolt in the second.

This time he bounced a ground-rule double into the same stands. But there already were two out and Podres quickly checked this scoring bid.

There again were two out when the Yanks strove to break through in the third with a threat that had a freakish end. Phil Rizzuto walked. Incidentally, this was Li'l Phil's fifty-second world series game, topping by one the record held by Joe DiMaggio.

Behind that pass Billy Martin singled to right, Rizzuto pulling up at second. Gil McDougald then chopped a bounding ball down the third-base line. Had Hoak fielded it he doubtless would have been unable to make a play anywhere.

But Don didn't get his hands on it. The ball struck Rizzuto at the moment L'il Phil was sliding into third base. McDougald, of course, received credit for a hit. But Rizzuto was declared out for getting hit by a batted ball and the inning was over.

In the fourth the Dodgers broke through for the first run and they did it with their first two hits off Byrne.

The 35-year-old lefty from Wake Forest, N. C., had just fanned Snider for the first out when Campanella slammed a double into left. Roy moved to third on Carl Furillo's infield out and a moment later Campy was over the plate on Hodges' solid single into left.

In the last of this round Podres had to turn back a serious Yankee threat. A mix-up of signals in the usually smooth operating Dodger outfield had Johnny in a hole.

Yogi Berra lifted an easy fly slightly to the left of center. It appeared to be a simple catch for Snider. But Junior Gilliam, who had started the game in left, also dashed for the ball. As a result the Duke at the last second shied away from the ball and it fell to the ground for a flukey two-bagger.

Work Cut Out for Podres

Since this happened on the first play of the Yankee inning, Podres had his work cut out for him. But he got Bauer on a fly to right. Skowron grounded to Zimmer and Bob Cerv ended it with a pop to Reese.

A single by Reese started the drive against Byrne in the sixth. Ill fortune then overtook Tommy in a hurry. Snider laid down a sacrifice bunt. Byrne fielded it and flipped it to Skowron, who had an easy out at first. But Moose, who had been the big hero on Monday, now became the goat.

Seeking to make the out on Snider by way of a tag, Skowron had the ball knocked out of his hand and the Dodgers had two aboard. Campanella then sacrificed and the runners were on second and third.

Byrne was allowed to remain long enough to give Furillo an

intentional pass. Then Tommy gave way to Grim. Bob couldn't keep Hodges from hitting a long fly to center that scored Reese with the second run of the game.

For a moment it looked as if the Dodgers would pile up more since Grim, before steadying, unfurled a wild pitch and gave a pass to Hoak to fill the bases a second time.

But here Alston called on Shotgun George Shuba to pinch-hit for Zimmer. George grounded to Skowron to end the round.

However, this maneuver indirectly was to play a prominent part in what followed. For, just as on Monday Stengel's move to replace Skowron by the better-fielding Joe Collins at first had resulted in the nipping of a Dodger threat, something of the sort now worked for Alston.

For with Zimmer out, Gilliam was switched to second base and Sandy Amoros went in as the left fielder. Minutes later Sandy was to make a glittering catch and throw that were to save the Brooks some mighty bad moments.

Martin walked in the last of the sixth and McDougald outgalloped a bunt for a hit to put two on with nobody out. Berra then stroked an outside pitch, the ball sailing down the left-field foul line.

It appeared to be a certain hit. But Amoros, racing at top speed, stuck out his glove and caught the ball in front of the stand. Martin, meanwhile had played it fairly safe and was only a few feet up from second.

But McDougald had gone well down from first, with the result that when Sandy fired the ball to Reese, who in turn relayed it to Hodges at first, McDougald was doubled off the bag by inches. It was a killing play for the Yanks.

Then in the eighth the Bombers made their last bid. Rizzuto, fighting heroically to the last, singled to left. Martin flied out. But McDougald slashed a fierce hopper down the third-base line that struck Hoak on the shoulder and bounded away for a single.

The Yanks again had two on and with the still dangerous Berra and Bauer the next two batters. Podres now turned on his finest pitching of the afternoon. He got Berra on a short pop-up that Furillo snared in right. He then fanned Bauer amid a deafening salvo of cheers.

That about clinched it. For even though Bob Turley tossed two scoreless rounds for the Yanks in the eighth and ninth, Stengel's best stretch of relief pitching in the entire series had come too late and to no purpose.

Podres, who had just turned 23 on Friday when he tripped the Yanks the first time in this series, made short work of the Bombers in the last of the ninth. He allowed eight hits in bagging his second triumph of the series but he was always in command.

The Box Score

SEVENTH GAME

BROOKLYN DODGERS

	AB.	R.	H.	PO.	A.
Gilliam, lf., 2b.....	4	0	1	2	0
Reese, ss.........	4	1	1	2	6
Snider, cf.........	3	0	0	2	0
Campanella, c.....	3	1	1	5	0
Furillo, rf.........	3	0	0	3	0
Hodges, 1b........	2	0	1	10	0
Hoak, 3b..........	3	0	1	1	1
Zimmer, 2b........	2	0	0	0	2
aShuba...........	1	0	0	0	0
Amoros, lf........	0	0	0	2	1
Podres, p.........	4	0	0	0	1
Total	29	2	5	27	11

NEW YORK YANKEES

	AB.	R.	H.	PO.	A.
Rizzuto, ss........	3	0	1	1	3
Martin, 2b........	3	0	1	1	6
McDougald, 3b....	4	0	3	1	1
Berra, c..........	4	0	1	4	1
Bauer, rf.........	4	0	0	1	0
Skowron, 1b......	4	0	1	11	1
Cerv, cf..........	4	0	0	5	0
Howard, lf........	4	0	1	2	0
Byrne, p..........	2	0	0	0	2
Grim, p...........	0	0	0	1	0
bMantle..........	1	0	0	0	0
Turley, p.........	0	0	0	0	0
Total	33	0	8	27	14

aGrounded out for Zimmer in sixth.
bPopped out for Grim in seventh.

Brooklyn ......0 0 0 1 0 1 0 0 0—2
New York......0 0 0 0 0 0 0 0 0—0

Error—Skowron.
Runs batted in—Hodges 2.
Two-base hits—Skowron, Campanella, Berra. Sacrifices—Snider, Campanella. Sacrifice fly—Hodges. Double play—Amoros, Reese and Hodges. Left on bases—Brooklyn 8, New York 8. Bases on balls—Off Byrne 3 (Hodges, Gilliam, Furillo), Grim 1 (Hoak), Turley 1 (Amoros), Podres 2 (Rizzuto, Martin). Struck out—By Byrne 2 (Snider, Zimmer), Grim 1 (Reese), Turley 1 (Snider), Podres 4 (McDougald), Byrne 2, Bauer). Hits—Off Byrne 3 in 5 1/3 innings, Grim 1 in 1 2/3, Turley 1 in 2. Runs and earned runs—Off Byrne 2 and 1. Wild pitch—Grim. Losing pitcher—Byrne.

Umpires—Honochick (A.), plate; Dascoli (N.), first base; Summers (A.), second base; Ballanfant (N.), third base; Flaherty (A.), left field; Donatelli (N.), right field. Time of game—2:44. Paid attendance—62,465.

This also was only the third time a Brooklyn pitcher had scored a series shutout. Burleigh Grimes did it in 1920 against the Indians and Preacher Roe tossed one against the Yanks in 1949.

Thus an amazing season came to a close for Brooklyn. Earlier in the year those beloved "Bums" had ripped the National League flag race apart by winning twenty-two of their first twenty-four games. It was a runaway pace that enabled them to clinch the flag on Sept. 8 by a margin of seventeen games.

And now the Dodgers are the world champions after as extraordinary a series as has been played. For six days the home team won. The Yanks won the first two games with their left-handed pitchers, Whitey Ford and Byrne, at the Stadium. Then the Brooks tore off three in a row in Brooklyn.

But when Stengel tried to make it again with his two lefties he slipped up. Ford came through to win a second time on Monday to square it at 3-all. But in this final test, Byrne, a tower of strength to the Yanks in their stirring pennant fight, wasn't up to taking the youthful Podres.

Johnny, recovering from a sore arm, which had plagued him in midseason, more than took up the slack caused by the loss of Don Newcombe's services.

Far into the night rang shouts of revelry in Flatbush. Brooklyn at long last has won a world series and now let someone suggest moving the Dodgers elsewhere!

National Leaguers, too, were rejoicing. For, coming after the Giants' triumph over the Indians last October, this marks the first time since 1933 and 1934 that the senior loop has been able to put together two successive series winners. In 1933 and 1934 the Giants and Cardinals did it.

October 5, 1955

BERRA IS NAMED MOST VALUABLE IN LEAGUE AGAIN

Yankee Catcher Becomes 3d in American Loop History to Gain Award 3 Times

---

KALINE SECOND IN POLL

Detroit Outfielder Gets 201 Points to Bomber's 218— Smith of Indians at 200

By JOHN DREBINGER
Special to The New York Times.

CHICAGO, Dec. 3—Yogi Berra, a potent factor in the seven pennants the Yankees have won in the last nine campaigns, again has been named the American League's most valuable player.

The Bombers' stout-hearted and strong-armed catcher was declared the winner today of the twenty-four-man-committee poll of the Baseball Writers Association that decided the disposition of the Kenesaw Mountain Landis Trophy for 1955.

The election, however, was a tight one. Yogi finished on top with 218 points. Second place went to Al Kaline, the Detroit Tigers' slugging young outfielder and the season's American League batting champion.

Kaline polled 201 points against an even 200 for Al Smith, the Cleveland Indians' fine outfielder and utility infielder.

Each member of the committee rated ten players on his ballot, points being scored on a basis of 14 for first place, 9 for second, 8 for third and so on down to one for tenth.

Foxx Pioneer in Feat

Berra thus becomes the third player in American League history to win the award three times. Jimmy Foxx, powerful home run clouter of the then Philadelphia Athletics, won it in 1932 and 1933 and again in 1938 as a member of the Boston Red Sox.

That mark was not equaled until Joe DiMaggio, the Yankee Clipper, came along to win the prize in 1939, 1941 and 1947. Berra gained his previous crowns in 1951 and 1954. Only one other player, besides Foxx and Berra, has won the award in two successive years. The Tigers' Hal Newhouser made it in 1944 and 1945.

The first writers' poll was conducted in 1931, with the Athletics' Bob Grove the American League victor. In the National League, only one player has captured the award three times, the Cardinals' Stan Musial having taken it in 1943, 1946 and 1948.

Ted Williams, famed Red Sox player and a former winner, placed fourth in the 1955 poll with 143, followed by the Yankees' Mickey Mantle with 113 points.

Rounding out the first ten were Ray Narleski, the Indians'

indefatigable relief hurler, with 90; Nellie Fox, Chicago White Sox, 84; Hank Bauer, Yankees, 64; Vic Power, Kansas City Athletics, 53, and Jackie Jensen, Red Sox, 39. In all, twenty-nine players received votes.

Berra, Kaline and Smith were the only candidates to be named on all twenty-four ballots. Oddly, though Smith finished only third in the point score, he tied Berra for first-place ballots with seven apiece. Kaline drew four first-place votes, but rolled up points with six seconds and six fourths.

Berra received only two second-place counts, but followed with six thirds, four fourths, three fifths, one sixth and one eighth.

In addition to the first three, the only players to receive first-place ballots were Williams, Narleski, Bauer and Power, each of whom was named once, and Gil McDougald. Gil had a cu-

rious count. The Yankee infielder picked up two first-place ballots, but was named on only one other, for fifth place.

The 30-year-old Berra has been a New York stalwart since 1947. In the ensuing years he has compiled a lifetime batting average of .293, with a total of 208 home runs and 898 runs batted in for an even 1,200 games. Last season, catching 147 games, Yogi's batting mark slipped to .272, his lowest since he entered the majors.

But there was no denying he was still the great driving force of the American League champions, their most dependable clutch hitter, in addition to being an almost flawless receiver. He hit twenty-seven homers and drove in 108 runs to make 1955 his fourth year over the 100 mark.

In Service Two Years

Berra, who was born in St. Louis, began his professional career in 1943 with Norfolk in the Yankee farm system. He just

missed becoming a St. Louis Cardinal because Branch Rickey, then head man of the Redbirds, refused to pay him an additional $500. Following two years in service, Yogi was promoted to the Newark club in 1946 and in 1947 was a full-time Yankee.

He was also a part-time outfielder, but he soon established himself as a receiver and as such has been rated tops in the American League since 1949.

Last October saw Yogi in his seventh world series. He has been the American League's catcher in seven All-Star games.

The point totals in the voting:

Yogi Berra, New York, 218; Al Kaline, Detroit, 201; Al Smith, Cleveland, 200; Ted Williams, Boston, 143; Mickey Mantle, New York, 113; Ray Narleski, Cleveland, 90; Nellie Fox, Chicago, 84; Hank Bauer, New York, 64; Vic Power, Kansas City, 53; Jackie Jensen, Boston, 39; Sherman Lollar, Chicago, 37; Gil McDougald, New York, 34; Billy Klaus, Boston, 27; Tommy Byrne, New York, 24; Whitey Ford, New York, 21; Ray Boone, Detroit, 16; Roy Sievers, Washington, 9; Harvey Kuenn, Detroit, 8; Billy Pierce, Chicago, 8; Dave Philley, Cleveland and Baltimore, 6; Early Wynn, Cleveland, 6; Elmer Valo, Kansas City, 5; Mickey Vernon, Washington, 4, and Billy Hoeft, Detroit; Don Mossi, Cleveland; Frank Sullivan, Boston; Gus Triandos, Baltimore; Jose Valdivielso, Washington, and Sammy White, Boston, 1 each.

December 4, 1955

Campanella Is Named as Most Valuable in National League

DODGERS' CATCHER PICKED THIRD TIME

Campanella Captures Honors by 5 Points Over Snider— Banks of Cubs Is Next

By ROSCOE McGOWEN

For the third time in his eight-year National League career, Roy Campanella won the most valuable player award yesterday. The other great local catcher, Yogi Berra of the Yankees, recently gained the American League honors for 1955, also his third such citation.

It was a close race between the star Brooklyn catcher and his center-field team-mate, Duke Snider. Each received eight first-place votes, but the balloting by the twenty-four-member committee of the Baseball Writers Association from second place on down decided the issue.

Campanella's total was 226 points and the Duke received

221. The point system was based on 14 for a first-place ballot, 9 for second, 8 for third and so on, down to 1 for tenth.

Campanella received six second-place votes, three third-place, four for fifth and three for seventh place. Snider, who, amazingly, was omitted from one ballot, drew four seconds, two thirds, five fourths, three fifths and one seventh.

Reese and Roberts Cited

Ernie Banks of the Chicago Cubs, who set a record for home runs by a shortstop with 44, drew six first-place ballots. The other candidates who received first-place votes were Robin Roberts, right-handed pitcher of the Phillies, and Pee Wee Reese, captain and shortstop of the Dodgers, who drew one each.

Banks finished third with 195 points and the Giants' Willie Mays was fourth with 165. Roberts finished fifth with 159 and Reese tied for ninth with Henry Aaron, Milwaukee Braves' outfielder, at 36.

Brooklyn's twenty-game winning pitcher, Don Newcombe, had 89 points in seventh place, behind Ted Kluszewski, Cincinnati Redlegs' first baseman, who scored 111.

Three players, in addition to Campanella and Berra, have been three-time winners of the most valuable player award in the majors. In the American League Jimmy Foxx of the then Philadelphia Athletics won it in 1932, 1933 and 1938, and Joe DiMaggio of the Yankees in 1939, 1941 and 1947. Stan Musial, St. Louis Cardinal star, was the National League winner in 1943, 1946 and 1948.

Berra and Campy both captured the honors in 1951. Berra repeated in 1954 and Campanella in 1953.

Campy had a sad season in 1954. His injured left hand reduced him to a .207 batting average, with only nineteen homers and fifty-one runs batted in, and he didn't receive a single vote for the award that year. His hand was operated on twice in 1954, in May and after the season ended.

Despite an injury to his left kneecap, which put him out of action for more than two weeks in midseason, Roy caught in 123 games and was one of the big reasons the Dodgers won the 1955 flag.

He finished fourth in the National League batting averages with a mark of .318, a fraction of a point behind Musial and

Mays, but all were several points below the batting champion, Richie Ashburn, Philly outfielder.

Scored Decisive Series Run

Campy belted thirty-two home runs in 1955. That put his major league total at 209, twenty-seven below the mark for catchers set by Gabby Hartnett of the Cubs.

Roy whacked twenty doubles and one triple and batted in 107 runs this year. Perhaps his most important double, however, was one that didn't figure in the season statistics. That two-bagger came in the seventh and deciding game of the world series against the Yankees.

Following that blow Campy scored on a single to left by Gil Hodges. It proved enough to win for the glittering young pitching hero of the series, Johnny Podres.

Campy scored eighty-one runs during the regular season and his hits totaled 142.

Roy has had three seasons with Brooklyn in which he has batted in 100 or more runs and four campaigns in which he has hit thirty or more homers.

It was in 1953 that Campanella set a record for runs batted in by a catcher with 142.

December 9, 1955

ERSKINE'S NO-HITTER BEATS GIANTS, 3-0

TWO REACH BASE

Passes to Mays, Dark Spoil Erskine's Bid for Perfect Game

By JOHN DREBINGER

Carl Erskine, pitching stylist of the Dodgers, moved for the second time among baseball's elite at Ebbets Field yesterday when he fired a no-hitter against the Giants.

The world champions won the encounter, 3 to 0, as Erskine himself fielded the last play, a roller to the mound. As he fired the ball to Gil Hodges at first base for the final out, a deafening roar went up from a gathering of 24,588.

Even Giant enthusiasts were seen to join in the cheers although this meant the second straight defeat of the current three-game series for the Polo Grounders.

For Erskine it marked the second no-hitter of his career. The 29-year-old trim little Hoosier right-hander tossed his first one, also at Ebbets Field, on June 19, 1952, against the Cubs. He won that day, 5 to 0.

Curiously, the last no-hitter in the National League was hurled exactly one year ago to the day when the Cubs' Sam Jones beat the Pirates.

Two Bases on Balls

Two bases on balls were all that kept Erskine from pitching a perfect game. No other Giant reached first base as the Dodgers played errorless ball.

Willie Mays drew the first pass with two out in the first inning. Alvin Dark received the other to open the Giant fourth. Both walks came after the count had reached three balls and two strikes. Neither Giant advanced beyond first base.

Erskine had his two closest calls, in the fourth. For directly after Dark walked, Mays sent a screaming low liner heading toward left field.

But Jackie Robinson, Dodger third sacker, hurled himself at the ball and held it in his gloved hand as he staggered to his knees from the force of the blow.

Then, after Dusty Rhodes had gone out on a foul to Roy Campanella behind home plate, Daryl Spencer drove the ball on a line to deep right center. It looked good for extra bases, but Carl Furillo, racing at top speed toward the fence, hauled down the ball for the third out of the inning.

Few Feet Save No-Hitter

After that came two more narrow squeaks for the Dodger right-hander. In the eighth inning, Don Mueller, pinch-hitting for Foster Castleman, took dead aim at left field and stroked an outside pitch in that direction. But Don's liner went squarely into the hands of the Brooks' shortstop, Pee Wee Reese.

In the ninth, with one out and the crowd hanging breathlessly on every pitch, Whitey Lockman, Giant lead-off man and a left-handed swinger, pulled around on a pitch to send a towering fly scaling the right field barrier. But at the last moment the ball hooked foul by a few feet.

Lockman then went out on a hard smash to the mound, Erskine stopping the ball with the back of his glove, picking it up and tossing to Hodges for the second out. Minutes later Carl retired Dark the same way, and the Giants breathed their last. Only three Polo Grounders fanned.

Brilliant as was the performance, however, it didn't quite match Erskine's 1952 no-hitter. On that occasion only one batter reached first base. Willie Ramsdell, Erskine's mound adversary that day, drew a base on balls to spoil a perfect game.

Al Worthington, young right-hander of the Giants, drew the misfortune of bucking yesterday's superlative effort. In fact, for six rounds he held the Brooks to two hits, but fell a run behind in the third when he suffered a momentary lapse in control.

Tagged for a single by Duke Snider, Worthington walked three batters in this inning, the third one, to Robinson, forcing in the run.

A Tremendous Play

In the sixth Worthington almost gave up another run. He was saved by another one of those electrifying throws by Mays. With two out and Furillo on first, the result of a pass, Erskine belted a liner into left center. Lockman, playing left field, flagged it down but, being in no position to make a throw, Whitey flipped the ball to Mays.

Willie spun around and made a tremendous peg to the plate, the ball arriving just in time to nail Furillo trying to score. A fine tag by Catcher Ray Katt also made the out possible.

In the seventh, however, the Dodgers lashed into Worthington in earnest and scored two runs that put the Giant hurler to rout.

Reese singled, and Snider clubbed a long double to left center that enabled Pee Wee to score all the way from first. When Hodges singled to drive in the Duke, Worthington was replaced by Marv Grissom. The latter retired the next five Dodgers.

By his feat yesterday Erskine became the ninth hurler to pitch two no-hitters since 1900 and only the third National Leaguer.

Mathewson First to Do It

Christy Mathewson, famed Giant hurler at the turn of the century, was the first National Leaguer to do it. Johnny Vander Meer, then with the Reds, did it years later and Johnny is still the only one to do it in successive starts. Vander Meer's last was also achieved at Ebbets Field, the occasion being the first game to be played under lights in Brooklyn on June 15, 1938.

American Leaguers who hurled two no-hitters in this century were Cy Young, who also tossed one before 1900; Bob Feller, who did it three times; Hub Leonard, Addie Joss, Allie Reynolds and Virgil Trucks.

This also marked the ninth no-hit performance by a Dodger hurler. In addition to Erskine's two, the others were by Nap Rucker, Dazzy Vance, Mal Eason, Tom Lovett, Tex Carleton, Ed Head and Rex Barney.

For the Giants, this was the sixth time they have been the victims of a no-hitter. Barney was the last one to hold the Giants hitless, before Erskine, in 1948.

Another noteworthy feature of Erskine's performance was that it marked the third complete game to be tossed by a Dodger pitcher against the Giants this season. Erskine did it the first time at the Polo Grounds on April 25 and Roger Craig made it Friday night at Ebbets Field.

In the 22 games with the Giants last year, the Brooklyn mound staff was able to account for only two route-going jobs. Erskine pitched one, and Billy Loes the other.

The Box Score

NEW YORK (N)	ab.	r.	h.	po.	a.
Lockman, rf.	4	0	0	2	0
Dark, ss.	3	0	0	1	0
Mays, cf.	2	0	0	7	1
Rhodes, lf.	3	0	0	1	1
Spencer, 2b.	3	0	0	0	1
White, 1b.	3	0	0	6	0
Cstleman, 3b.	2	0	0	1	0
aMueller	1	0	0	0	0
Thmpsn, 3b.	0	0	0	0	1
Katt, c.	3	0	0	6	0
Wrthngtn, p.	2	0	0	0	3
Grissom, p.	0	0	0	0	0
bWilson	1	0	0	0	0
Total	27	0	0	24	7

BROOKLYN (N)	ab.	r.	h.	po.	a.
Gilliam, 2b.	4	0	1	0	1
Reese, ss.	3	2	1	1	1
Snider, cf.	3	1	2	3	0
Campnlla, c.	4	0	1	3	2
Hodges, 1b.	3	0	1	3	1
Robinson, 3b.	2	0	0	2	2
Amoros, lf.	4	0	0	2	0
Furillo, rf.	2	0	0	2	0
Erskine, p.	4	0	1	1	3
Total	29	3	6	27	10

aLined out for Castleman in eighth.
bFouled out for Grissom in ninth.

New York .... 0 0 0 0 0 0 0 0 0—0
Brooklyn .... 0 0 1 0 0 0 2 0 .—3

Errors—None.
Runs batted in—Robinson, Snider, Campanella.
Two-base hits—Erskine, Snider. Left on bases—New York 2, Brooklyn 9. Bases on balls—Off Erskine 2, Worthington 7. Struck out—By Erskine 3, Worthington 4, Grissom 1. Hits—Off Worthington 6 in 6 1/3. Grissom 0 in 1 2/3. Runs and earned runs—Off Worthington 3 and 3. Winning pitcher—Erskine (2-2). Losing pitcher—Worthington (1-3). Umpires—Donatelli, Boggess, Gorman, Pinelli. Time—2:10. Attendance—24,588 (17,395 paid).

The New York Times (by Neal Boenzi)

PITCHED: Carl Erskine, in seventh inning of no-hit game

May 13, 1956

Hitless Till 10th, Braves Win in 11th

By The Associated Press.

MILWAUKEE, May 26—The Milwaukee Braves, who came within one out of winning a zany game in which they were held hitless by three Cincinnati hurlers for nine and two-thirds innings, pulled out a 2-1 decision in the bottom of the eleventh today to cling to the National League lead.

Frank Torre batted in both Milwaukee runs, and both were scored by Hank Aaron before 22,936 at County Stadium. Joe Black was the losing pitcher and Ray Crone, who shut out the Redlegs for eight and two-thirds innings, the winner.

Until the ninth, Milwaukee seemed to be on the way to a decision in the regulation distance, after taking advantage of Johnny Klippstein's wildness to score one run in the second without a hit.

In the eleventh, Aaron tripled, and after the bases were loaded on walks Torre singled him home.

In the Redlegs' half of the ninth, with only one out between them and a shutout loss of a no-hit game, Ted Kluszewski dropped a single in front of Billy Bruton in center field.

Then Wally Post slammed a double off the left-field fence scoring Jim Dyck, who ran for Big Ted, to tie the score. Post's double was the sixth hit off Milwaukee's Ray Crone, who had scattered four singles until the ninth in his bid for a shutout.

When Black put the Braves down again without a hit, after Hershell Freeman had done the same in the eighth, they and Klippstein manufactured a new niche in the major league record book—the first time three pitchers collaborated to give no hits over the regulation nine innings.

Jack Dittmer got the first Milwaukee hit in the bottom of the tenth, when he belted a double with two out.

The Braves took their lead in the second inning, when Aaron was hit by a pitched ball. Klippstein then walked Bobby Thomson and Billy Bruton to fill the

The Box Score

CINCINNATI (N.)	ab	r	h	po	a		MILWAUKEE (N.)	ab	r	h	po	a
Temple, 2b	2	0	0	2	1		O'Conn'l, 2b	3	0	0	1	2
dBailey	1	0	0	0	0		bCovington	1	0	0	0	0
Bridges, 2b	1	0	0	0	0		Dittmer, 2b	1	0	1	1	1
Robinson, lf	2	0	1	3	0		Logan, ss	4	0	2	3	
aCrowe	1	0	0	0	0		Mathews, 3b	5	0	0	0	0
Palys, lf	2	0	0	2	0		Aaron, rf	4	2	1	0	0
cThurman	1	0	0	0	0		Thomson, lf	2	0	4	0	
Black, p	2	0	0	0	0		gTanner	0	0	0	0	0
Bell, cf	5	0	1	3	0		Bruton, cf	2	0	0	6	0
Klus'ski, lf	4	1	1	5	1		Torre, 1b	4	0	1	14	1
bDyck, 1b	1	0	1	4	0		Crandall, c	2	0	0	5	1
Post, rf	3	0	1	3	0		Crone, p	2	0	0	0	2
Burgess, c	4	0	2	5	0							
McMill'n, ss	2	0	0	3	1		Total	30	2	3	33	10
Klipps'n, p	2	0	0	0	1							
Freeman, p	0	0	0	0	0							
cFrazier, lf	2	0	0	0	0							
Total	38	1	7	61	6							

*One out when winning run scored.
aFlied out for Robinson in third.
bStruck out for O'Connell in seventh.
cGrounded out for Klippstein in eighth.
dGrounded out for Temple in eighth.
eGrounded out for Freeman in ninth.
bRan for Kluszewski in ninth.
gWalked for Thomson in eleventh.
Cincinnati ....000 000 001 00—1
Milwaukee ....010 000 000 01—2
Error—Torre.
Runs batted in—Torre 2, Post.
Two base hits—Bell, Post, Dittmer. Three base hit—Aaron. Sacrifice—Crone, Bruton, McMillan. Sacrifice fly—Torre. Double play—O'Connell and Torre; Kluszewski and McMillan; O'Connell, Logan and Torre. Left on base—Cincinnati 9, Milwaukee 10. Bases on balls—Off Klippstein 7, Crone 4, Black 2. Struck out—By Klippstein 4, Crone 3. Hits—Off Klippstein 0 in 7 innings, Freeman 0 in 1, Black 3 in 3. Runs and earned runs—Off Klippstein 1 and 1, Black 1 and 1, Crone 1 and 1. Hit by pitcher—By Klippstein (Aaron). Winning pitcher—Crone (3-1). Losing pitcher—Black (2-2). Umpires—Secory, Landes, Goetz and Dascoli. Time of game—2:39. Attendance—22,936.

bases, and Torre hit a sacrifice fly. that Frank Robinson caught only after a spectacular run, to score Aaron.

Milwaukee theatened again in the seventh, when Klippstein's wildness filled the bases, but with the two out Wes Covington batted for Danny O'Connell and struck out.

Klippstein, who had a leg up on the dubious distinction of becoming the first pitcher in major league baseball to pitch and lose a no-hit game over the regulation nine innings, was lifted for a pinch hitter by Manager Birdie Tebbetts in the top of the eighth after muffling the Braves for seven innings. He wal!   en, struck out three and hit one batsman.

Six other pitchers have set down their opponents without a hit for nine innings, then lost in extra frames. The last to do this was Bobo Newsome with the St. Louis Browns, who held the Red Sox hitless for nine innings in 1934, then gave up a single in the tenth to lose, 2—1.

Klippstein, a 28-year-old right-hander, had a 10-10 lifetime record against the Braves going into today's contest.

May 27, 1956

Long Extends Homer Streak

FRIEND'S 2- HITTER TOPS BROOKS, 3-2

Pirates' Pitcher Helped in Posting No. 8 by Long's 8th Homer in 8 Games

By JOHN DREBINGER
Special to The New York Times.

PITTSBURGH, May 28—There was no stopping Dale Long or the Pirates tonight.

Responding to the roars of 32,221 fans, the Bucs' spectacular first sacker exploded another home run for his eighth four-bagger in eight consecutive games. The blow broke the record of seven homers in seven games set by Long in Philadelphia last Saturday.

And while he was about this, the rambunctious Pirates, behind the two-hit pitching of Bob Friend, brought down Carl Erskine and the Dodgers, 3 to 2, in the opener of a two-game series.

The outcome enabled the Pirates to retain their hold on third place and it dropped the stunned world champions deeper in the second division. Friend scored his eighth mound triumph of the year against two defeats. The Pittsburgh right-hander has won five in a row, the last four being complete games.

Homer for Snider

Jarred in the first inning by Duke Snider's 450-foot two-run homer, the Bucs fought heroically for this game. And they made it when two of Long's colleagues, Lee Walls and Hank Foiles, weighed in with triples, each productive of a tally.

Long hit his homer in the fourth and it was something more than ornamental. Leading off the inning, it tied the score at 2—all.

It was a well stroked ball that sailed into the lower right-field stands beyond the 375-foot marker. It was No. 14 for the six-foot four-inch, 30-year-old Long who, prior to last season, had spent most of his first eleven years in baseball in the minor leagues.

Fans were still streaming into the arena when Junior Gilliam, leading off for the Brooks in the first, drew a pass. After Pee Wee Reese, trying to bunt, had gone out on a pop foul, Snider sent a mighty drive down the center of the fairway. It cleared the wall just alongside the 436-foot marker. The homer was the Duke's seventh of the year.

Associated Press Wirephoto

HE CONTINUES TO HIT, but this time it's the jackpot for Dale Long of the Pirates. Using the back of General Manager Joe L. Brown, Long signs new contract for $16,500, a rise of $2,500, at Forbes Field. The increase was a reward for his record-setting homer-hitting streak. He has clouted eight home runs in the Pittsburgh team's last eight games.

Mantle Hits 19th and 20th Homers

BOMBERS RECORD 4-3, 12-5 VERDICTS

Mantle's First-Game Homer 18 Inches Short of Going Over Roof at Stadium

By JOSEPH M. SHEEHAN

Mickey Mantle clouted two homers, including one of colossal proportions, as the Yankees, with five four-baggers in all, downed the Washington Senators, 4—3, and 12—5, before a throng of 29,825 at the Stadium yesterday.

As a result of their double triumph, Casey Stengel's rampaging Bombers stretched to six games their lead over the second-place White Sox, who beat the Indians twice.

No more than eighteen inches of elevation kept the muscular Mantle from achieving the distinction of being the first player to hit a fair ball out of the Stadium.

Mantle Connects in Fifth

Mickey's nineteenth homer, hit off Pedro Ramos on a 2-2 count in the fifth inning of the opener, was a skyscraper wallop to right that hit just below the top of the roof cornice high above the third deck.

Even though Mantle did not quite get enough loft to clear everything, he reached previously unplumbed territory with his mighty drive. No one previously got close to hitting the roof facade at the home of champions.

A check of Stadium blueprints disclosed that the ball struck at a point about 370 feet from the plate some 117 feet above the ground. While it obviously was descending when it hit the cornice, it retained enough velocity to rebound on to the field.

"I've never seen anything like it before," the Yankees said between games.

Mickey allowed, "it was the best I ever hit a ball left-handed."

There was nothing modest, either, about the dimensions of Mantle's twentieth homer, which he clouted off Pascual in the fifth inning of the nightcap.

It carried halfway up into the right-field bleachers, just to the left of the bullpen.

16 Homers for Month

With sixteen homers in this merry month of May, Mickey is eleven games ahead of Babe Ruth's record sixty-homer pace of 1927. The Babe hit No. 20 in his fifty-second game on June 11, and had only fourteen on Memorial Day.

By way of demonstrating his versatility, Mantle also contributed a nifty third-strike drag bunt single, a right-handed line single, a stolen base and a rifle throw in the first game and drew a pass in the second game.

Excused after seven innings of the second game, Mantle ended the day leading the majors in six offensive departments: Runs (45), hits (65), total bases (135), homers (20), runs batted in (50) and batting average (.425).

Hank Bauer and Eddie Robinson joined Mantle as homer hitters in the second game, in which the Bombers pounded Camilo Pascual, Bunky Stewart and Truman Clevenger for thirteen hits. Hank hit two, No. 10 leading off in the first, and No. 11, inside-the-park, in the eighth. Eddie rapped his second leading off in the second.

Mantle's fifth-inning homer put the Bombers ahead to stay and they settled matters with a five-run outburst in the sixth, marked by Joe Collins' three-run double.

Bob Turley was the beneficiary of this assorted slugging. However, Bob became wild and needed help from Tom Sturdivant to bag the victory.

Besides being a conversation piece, Mantle's homer was the chief factor in the Yankee's opening-game victory. Mickey touched off his big blast with two mates aboard to erase a 1-0 lead Washington had taken on Johnny Kucks in the second.

The Bombers added a tally in the sixth on a single by Kucks and Hank Bauer's long double to center. However, Kucks apparently cooked himself scoring from first on Bauer's blow.

The Senators ripped into Johnny for three hits and two runs in the seventh. When Kucks got into further difficulties in the eighth, Casey Stengel called in Tom Morgan to preserve the youngster's sixth victory.

May 31, 1956

Five Dodgers Walk

However, after that blow Friend was to give up only one more hit, a single by Gilliam in the third. Five other Dodgers got to first on walks.

The Bucs scored their first tally in the second when Walls sent Snider chasing his long triple in left center. Walls scored on Gene Freese's sacrifice fly.

Then, after Long had sent the crowd wild by tying the score with his record shot in the fourth, Foiles tossed the gathering into another uproar in the fifth.

First up, the Pirate catcher hit a foul on an attempted bunt. Then he smacked the ball over Snider's head in deep center for another three-bagger. A pinch single by Bob Skinner sent Hank home and Friend made the run stand up to the end.

Long's homer was his only blow of the night. He grounded out the first time up and fanned on his last two tries. Clem Labine, who pitched the eighth for the Dodgers, got Dale for the second strike-out.

The defeat was Erskine's fourth against two victories. It also marked the third time the Hoosier right-hander had failed to go the distance after his no-hitter against the Giants on May 12.

BROOKLYN (N.)

	ab.	r.	h.	po.	a.
Gilliam, 2b.	3	1	1	1	1
Reese, ss.	3	0	0	3	4
Snider, cf.	3	1	1	3	1
C'mp'nella,c	4	0	0	5	0
Hodges, 1b.	3	0	0	9	2
Robinson,3b	3	0	0	1	1
Amoros, lf.	3	0	0	3	0
Furillo, rf.	3	0	0	1	0
Erskine, p.	2	0	0	1	3
bJackson	1	0	0	0	0
Labine, p.	0	0	0	0	1
Total	**26**	**2**	**2**	**24**	**16**

PITTSBURGH (N.)

	ab.	r.	h.	po.	a.
Virdon, cf.	4	0	1	3	0
Groat, ss.	4	0	0	1	7
Long, 1b.	4	1	1	14	0
Thomas, lf.	4	0	2	1	0
Walls, rf.	4	1	1	1	0
Freese, 3b.	3	0	0	0	3
Foiles, c.	2	1	1	5	1
J.O'Brien,2b	1	0	0	1	2
aSkinner	1	0	1	0	0
Roberts, p.	1	0	1	1	2
Friend, p.	2	0	0	0	1
Total	**30**	**3**	**8**	**27**	**16**

aSingled for J. O'Brien in fifth.
bGrounded out for Erskine in eighth.
cRan for Thomas in eighth.

Brooklyn .... 2 0 0 0 0 0 0 0 0—2
Pittsburgh .... 0 1 0 1 1 0 0 0.—3

Error—Gilliam.
Runs batted in—Snider 2, Freese, Long, Skinner.
Two-base hit—Roberts. Three-base hits—Walls, Foiles. Home runs—Snider, Long. Sacrifice—Friend. Sacrifice fly—Freese. Double plays—Erskine, Reese and Hodges; Groat, J. O'Brien and Long; Groat, Roberts and Long. Left on bases—Brooklyn 3, Pittsburgh 6. Bases on balls—Off Erskine 1, Friend 6. Struck out—By Erskine 1, Labine 1, Friend 3. Hits—Off Erskine 7 in 7 innings, Labine 1 in 1. Runs and earned runs—Off Erskine 3 and 3, Friend 2 and 2. Winning pitcher—Friend (8-2). Losing pitcher—Erskine (2-4). Umpires—Ballanfant, Gore, Jackowski and Crawford. Time of game—2:13. Attendance—32,221.

May 29, 1956

Yankees' Box Scores

FIRST GAME

WASHINGTON (A.)

	ab.	r.	h.	po.	a.
Yost, 3b.	4	0	0	1	1
Luttrell, ss.	4	0	2	5	5
Herzog, lf.	4	0	1	3	0
Sievers, 1b.	4	0	0	10	0
Lemon, rf.	2	0	0	2	0
K'brew, p.	2	0	0	0	3
Olson, cf.	4	1	3	1	0
Berberet, c.	2	0	1	0	1
Courtney, c	2	0	1	0	1
Ramos, p.	2	0	0	0	0
aRunnels	1	1	1	0	0
Stewart, p.	0	0	0	0	0
cPaula	1	0	0	0	0
Total	**33**	**3**	**8**	**24**	**8**

NEW YORK (A.)

	ab.	r.	h.	po.	a.
Bauer, rf.	4	1	1	1	0
McD'g'd, ss.	3	1	1	2	5
Mantle, cf.	4	1	3	3	0
Berra, c.	2	0	0	6	1
Collins, 1b.	3	0	0	2	1
bHoward	1	0	0	0	0
Rob'son, 1b.	3	0	0	6	0
Carey, 3b.	4	0	1	0	3
Kucks, p.	3	0	1	1	0
Morgan, p.	1	0	0	0	0
Total	**31**	**4**	**7**	**27**	**12**

aTripled for Ramos in seventh.
bGrounded out for Collins in seventh.
cFlied out for Stewart in ninth.

Washington ...... 0 1 0 0 0 0 2 0 0—3
New York .... 0 0 0 0 3 1 0 0.—4

Errors—Killebrew, Martin.
Runs batted in—Berberet, Runnels, Luttrell, Mantle 3, Bauer.
Two-base hits—Herzog, Runnels. Three-base hit—Herzog. Home run—Mantle. Stolen base—Mantle. Sacrifice—Herzog. Double play—Martin, McDougald and Robinson. Left on bases—Washington 7, New York 8. Bases on balls—Off Ramos 5, Kucks 3. Struck out—By Ramos 1, Kucks 7 in 7 1-3, Stewart 2 in 1 2, Morgan 1 in 1 2-3. Runs and earned runs—Off Ramos 4 and 4, Kucks 3 and 3. Winning pitcher—Kucks (6—2). Losing pitcher—Ramos (3—2). Umpires—Summers, McKinley, Flaherty and Rice. Time—2:36.

SECOND GAME

WASHINGTON (A.)

	ab.	r.	h.	po.	a.
Yost, 3b.	2	0	1	2	3
Luttrell, ss.	3	0	1	3	0
Herzog, lf.	3	0	1	4	0
Sievers, 1b.	4	0	0	5	0
Courtney, c.	3	2	1	7	0
Olson, cf.	5	0	1	3	0
Lemon, rf.	2	1	0	3	0
Kill'brew, 2b.	3	1	1	3	2
Pascual, p.	2	1	1	0	0
aPaula	1	0	0	0	0
Stewart, p.	0	0	0	0	0
bOravetz	1	0	0	0	0
Clev'nger, p.	0	0	0	0	1
Total	**30**	**5**	**8**	**24**	**7**

NEW YORK (A.)

	ab.	r.	h.	po.	a.
Bauer, rf.	6	3	3	2	0
Martin, 2b.	3	1	1	4	2
cJ.C'man, 3b	1	0	0	0	0
Mantle, cf.	4	1	1	0	0
Howard, lf.	4	1	1	0	0
Berra, c.	4	2	2	6	1
Col'ns, lf.rf.	4	1	1	2	1
Robi'son, 1b.	4	1	1	0	0
M'D'gald, ss.	3	1	1	0	4
Carey, 3b.	2	0	1	3	0
Turley, p.	4	0	2	1	2
Stur'vant, p.	1	0	0	0	0
Total	**37**	**12**	**13**	**27**	**13**

aFouled out for Pascual in seventh.
bWalked for Stewart in eighth.
cGrounded out for Martin in eighth.

Washington ...... 0 1 1 1 0 0 0 2 0—5
New York .... 1 2 0 0 1 5 0 3.—12

Errors—Sievers, Lemon.
Runs batted in—Baue 3, Lemon, Robinson 2, Mantle 2, Herzog, Killebrew, Collins 3, Turley, Oravetz, Yost, Carey.
Two-base hits—Yost, Berra, McDougald, Collins, Carey. Home runs—Bauer 2, Robinson, Killebrew, Mantle. Stolen bases—Carey 2. Sacrifice—Luttrell. Sacrifice fly—Lemon. Double plays—Berra and Martin; McDougald, Martin and Robinson. Left on bases—Washington 10, New York 12. Bases on balls—Off Turley 9, Pascual 1, Sturdivant 1, Clevenger 1. Struck out—By Turley 6, Pascual 6. Hits—Off Pascual 10 in 6 innings, Stewart 1 in 1, Clevenger 2 in 1, Turley 7 in 7 2-3, Sturdivant 1 in 1 1-3. Runs and earned runs—Off Pascual 9 and 7, Turley 5 and 5, Clevenger 3 and 3. Wild pitch—Turley. Winning pitcher—Turley (7—2). Losing pitcher—Pascual (2—6). Umpires—McKinley, Flaherty, Rice and Summers. Time of game—3:10. Attendance—29,825.

MUSIAL FIRST IN POLL

Cards' Star Named Player of Decade—DiMaggio Second

ST. LOUIS, July 7 (AP)—Stan Musial, St. Louis Cardinals' outfielder-First baseman who owns a hatful of National League records, today was named the player of the decade by the Sporting News.

The national baseball weekly reported Musial won the honor for the period 1946-55 in a poll of 260 players, club officials, umpires, writers and sportscasters.

Joe DiMaggio, former top-flight outfielder of the New York Yankees, was second in the balloting and Ted Williams, the Boston Red Sox slugging outfielder, was third.

Musial received 2,654 points, DiMaggio 2,433 and Williams 2,312 on the basis of fourteen points for a first-place vote, nine for second and running down to one for tenth.

Musial will receive the prize award, a grandfather's clock, at a luncheon of the Touchdown Club in Washington on Monday, the day before he appears in his thirteenth All-Star game.

July 8, 1956

National League Beats American as Mays and Musial Set Pace With Homers

EARLY DRIVE WINS FOR FRIEND, 7 TO 3

Pirates' Pitcher Victor, but Antonelli Also Excels for National League Stars

By JOHN DREBINGER
Special to The New York Times.

WASHINGTON, July 10—Combining a powerful offensive with a stout defense, the National League today continued its mastery over the American League and there just wasn't anything Casey Stengel could do about it.

The forces of the senior loop, directed by the Dodgers' Walter Alston, brought down Casey's American Leaguers, 7 to 3, before a gathering of 28,843 in the twenty-third annual All-Star game. Since the Capital is strictly an American League town, the majority doubtless were highly sympathetic toward the Yankee manager. But Casey needed more than sympathy on this summery afternoon.

Willie Mays and Ted Kluszewski, late starters for the Nationals, provided the highlights. The Giants' Mays, entering the struggle in the fourth, clouted a two-run homer. Cincinnati's Kluszewski, who at the outset had sat on the sidelines while five of his team-mates picked in the fan poll disported themselves on the field, weighed in with successive doubles in the sixth and seventh.

And in the sixth, Stan Musial of the Cards, engaging in his thirteenth All-Star encounter, drove a homer into the packed left-field bleachers to raise his own All-Star homer record to five.

Spahn Routed in Sixth

Against this the American Leaguers were able to offer only one brief flurry. In the sixth they routed Warren Spahn, the Braves' southpaw, when successive homers by Ted Williams and Mickey Mantle accounted for all three of the junior circuit's tallies.

But the Pirates' crack right-hander, Bob Friend, had held them tightly bottled up in the first three innings and after Spahn was put to rout with none out in the sixth, the Giants' Johnny Antonelli took over and blanked the American Leaguers the rest of the way.

Thus the Nationals gained their sixth All-Star victory in their last seven tries and though the American League still leads in the series, which started in 1933, the margin now stands at 13—10.

As for Stengel, the Yankee skipper had a dour day. Not only did he go down to his fifth defeat in six All-Star managerial performances, but his plan to check the National Leaguers with three left-handers didn't pan out.

The White Sox Billy Pierce went the first three innings and gave up only one run, but the Yanks' own Whitey Ford lasted only one round and was the victim of the Mays homer. By the time Casey got around to his third southpaw, Herb Score, in the eighth, the battle was pretty well lost.

Although under the rules, Friend was named the winner, Antonelli did an equally fine job. The giant lefty went four full innings in blanking the American Leaguers after relieving Spahn in the sixth. The rules forbid a pitcher from starting more than three innings unless the game goes into overtime, so Antonelli's tenure did not break the rules.

Boyer Stars in Field, At Bat

Not to be overlooked in the Nationals' triumph was the play of the Cardinals' youthful third sacker, Ken Boyer, who contributed three successive singles and as many dazzling plays in the field.

Nor was the defeat all that caused Stengel woe. In the sixth, his star catcher, Yogi Berra, who had singled his first two times up, went out of action with two bashed fingers, the result of a foul tip.

Mantle, playing with his injured right knee heavily braced and bandaged, nevertheless went all the way. But his homer was his only contribution to the American League cause. On three other trips to the plate, Mickey struck out.

Williams' homer also was Ted's only blow. In the eighth Ted almost put Musial out of commission. Finally trying to cross up the Nationals' overshift defense to the right, Williams popped one into short left on which Musial, in making the catch, collided with Boyer. Neither was hurt but Alston decided to withdraw Musial even though Stan was to lead off the National's ninth.

Since the game was dedicated to the late Clark Griffith, the pre-game ceremonies, which opened with a parade to the center field flagpole by the United States Air Force Band, concluded with Calvin Griffith II, a 15-year-old grandson of the

former owner of the Senators, throwing out the first ball.

Commissioner Ford C. Frick originally was to have attended to this little detail, but at his request the shift was made in deference to the Griffith family. The crowd, which had paid $105,982, cheered. Most everyone seemed confident of an American League victory.

Then the starting hurlers, Pierce and Bob Friend, took over. Pierce required just nine pitches to dispose of the first three National League batters. He fanned Johnny Temple and Frank Robinson. Then Musial grounded out on the first pitch.

As Friend took the mound in the lower half, there was no mistaking the Redlegs' five National League starters with their flaming red sleeves and vestlike uniforms. However, it was Boyer of St. Louis who displayed the game's first fielding gem as Harvey Kuenn, the Americans' lead-off batter, slashed a low drive that appeared headed for left field.

The ball never left the infield as Boyer dived headlong toward

his left and snared it in his glove. Later he took another hit away from Kuenn with a dive to the right.

Friend, sweeping through the first inning, erased Nellie Fox on an easy infield roller and fanned Williams.

The second round also went scoreless, although each hurler gave up a single. In the third, the Nationals broke the spell with a run. With Ed Bailey out of the way on a pop foul back of first, Roy McMillan drew a pass. The Cincinnati shortstop moved to second on Friend's sacrifice and scored on Temple's line single into center.

For a moment, as Friend finished his three-inning stint in the lower half of the inning, it looked as though the Americans would break into the scoring. For after Friend retired the first two, Kuenn and Fox hit successive singles into left.

But Williams, with the Nationals going into the familiar overshift to the right, disdained trying for a hit in the unprotected left side. He ended the threat by thumping a harmless

Box Score of All-Star Game

NATIONAL LEAGUE	AB	R	H	PO	A	E	AMERICAN LEAGUE	AB	R	H	PO	A	E
Temple, 2b	4	1	2	2	3	0	Kuenn, ss	5	0	1	2	3	0
Robinson, lf	2	0	0	1	0	0	Fox, 2b	4	1	2	1	0	0
dSnider, cf	3	0	0	1	0	0	Williams, lf	4	1	1	2	0	0
Musial, rf, lf	4	1	1	2	0	0	Mantle, cf	4	1	1	0	0	0
Aaron, lf	3	0	0	0	0	0	Berra, c	2	0	2	10	1	0
Boyer, 3b	5	1	3	3	1	0	gLollar, c	2	0	1	4	0	0
Bell, cf	1	0	0	2	0	0	Kaline, rf	3	0	1	0	0	0
bMays, cf, rf	3	2	1	2	0	0	Piersall, rf	1	0	0	1	0	0
Long, 1b	2	0	0	6	0	0	Vernon, 1b	2	0	0	4	0	0
fKluszewski, 1b	2	1	2	2	0	0	hPower, 1b	2	0	1	3	0	0
Bailey, c	3	0	0	3	1	0	Kell, 3b	4	0	1	0	1	0
Campanella, c	0	0	0	1	0	0	Pierce, p	0	0	0	0	1	0
McMillan, ss	3	1	2	1	5	0	aSimpson	1	0	0	0	0	0
Friend, p	0	0	0	0	0	0	Ford, p	0	0	0	0	0	0
cRepulski	1	0	0	0	0	0	Wilson, p	0	0	0	0	1	0
Spahn, p	1	0	0	0	0	0	eMartin	1	0	0	0	0	0
Antonelli, p	1	0	0	1	0	0	Brewer, p	0	0	0	0	0	0
							iBoone	1	0	0	0	0	0
Total	36	7	11	27	10	0	Score, p	0	0	0	0	0	0
							Wynn, p	0	0	0	0	0	0
							jSievers	1	0	0	0	0	0
							Total	37	3	11	27	7	0

aStruck out for Pierce in third.
bHit homer for Bell in fourth.
cFouled out for Friend in fourth.
dFlied out for Robinson in fifth.
eGrounded out for Wilson in fifth.
fDoubled out for Long in sixth.
gSingled for Berra in sixth.

hFlied out for Vernon in sixth.
iLined out for Brewer in seventh.
jPopped out for Wynn in ninth.

National League	0 0 1 2 1 1 2 0 0—7
American League	0 0 0 0 0 3 0 0 0—3

Runs batted in—Temple, Mays 2, Boyer, Williams 2, Mantle, Musial, Kluszewski.

Two-base hits—Kluszewski 2. Home runs—Mays, Williams, Mantle, Musial. Stolen Base—Temple. Sacrifice—Friend. Double play—McMillan, Temple and Kluszewski. Left on bases—National League 7, American League 7. Bases on balls—Off Pierce 1 (McMillan), Ford 1 (Bailey), Brewer 1 (Mays), Score 1 (Temple). Struck out—By Pierce 5 (Temple, Robinson 2, Bell, Long), Ford 2 (Musial, Long), Wilson 1 (Mays), Brewer 2 (Temple, Snider), Score 1 (Antonelli), Wynn 1 (Mays), Friend 3 (Williams, Mantle, Simpson), Spahn 1 (Mantle), Antonelli 1 (Mantle). Hits—Off Pierce 2 in 3 innings, Friend 3 in 3, Ford 3 in 1, Wilson 2 in 1, Spahn 4 in 2 (faced three batters in sixth), Brewer 4 in 2, Score 0 in 1, Wynn 0 in 1, Antonelli 4 in 4. Runs and earned runs—Off Pierce 1 and 1, Ford 2 and 2, Wilson 1 and 1, Spahn 3 and 3, Brewer 3 and 3. Wild pitches—Brewer 2. Winning pitcher—Friend. Losing pitcher—Pierce. Umpires—Berry (A.), Pinelli (N.), Hurley (A.), Gore (N.), Flaherty (A.), Jackowski (N.). Time of game—2:25. Attendance—28,843. Receipts (gross)—$105,982.50.

grounder down the first base line that the Pirates' Dale Long scooped up for the third out.

Ford Takes Mound

So the Nationals led, 1—0, as the first switch of pitchers went into effect in the fourth, with Ford opposing Spahn.

Ford's tenure was brief and unhappy. He slipped a third strike over on Musial, but Boyer singled to left for his second hit and then Alston made his first strategic move of the afternoon.

He called on Mays to bat for the Redlegs' Gus Bell, who had fanned in his one time up. The Giant star wasted no time grabbing the spotlight. The Say Hey Kid smacked the second pitch half way up the packed left field bleachers and the Nationals had two more runs.

The homer was Willie's first in All-Star play and Alston promptly decided to keep Mays in the game as an outfielder. Willie played center in the fourth and when Duke Snider entered the game in the fifth to take over center, Mays shifted to right and Musial, who had opened in right, moved to the left.

All this must have been a bit bewildering to Stengel who has a monopoly on this sort of two-platooning.

With the fifth, Casey decided his southpaw pitching strategy was not paying off. He fetched up the White Sox' right-hander, Jim Wilson. But that didn't work out so well either, as the Nationals made off with another tally.

Temple outgalloped a bunt, advanced on an out and scored on Boyer's third hit in a row, a single to center.

Stil another run followed for the Nationals in the sixth as Tom Brewer, the Red Sox' right-hander, went to the mound. Kluszewski, batting for Long, opened with a two-bagger that he sliced into left. Ted presently tallied on a wild pitch.

Meanwhile, Spahn blanked the Americans through the fourth and fifth and so enjoyed a 5-0 margin as the battle moved into the last of the sixth. The Americans, however, had a few bombs of their own and before Spahn had retired a man in the sixth, he was out of there.

Fox Opens With Single

Fox opened with a single and Williams sent a booming fly down the center of the fairway. The Nationals' two most gifted ball hawks, Snider and Mays, were off in hot pursuit and both got under it. However, neither could get to it, as the ball fell in the bullpen, 425 feet away.

It was Williams' fourth All-Star homer and his first since 1946, when he hit two in one game.

Mantle then followed with his second All-Star homer and it seemed that the American League was ready to roll.

When Mantle followed with his homer, Antonelli replaced his

Spahn. Though the Giant lefty got tagged for two more singles, he snuffed out the threat by getting George Kell to drill into a double play.

With the seventh, the Nationals put on more pressure as Musial regained his exclusive hold on the All-Star homer record. With Brewer still on the mound, Stan drove one into the left-field bleachers.

Before the round was over, the Nationals had still another marker. With two away, Mays walked and then, on a hit and run play, Willie scored from first as Kluszewski connected

for his second straight two-bagger, this one a lusty belt into right.

That just about finished the day for the American Leaguers. All too late Stengel was to see the left-handed Score blank the Nationals in the eighth while the Indians' right-hander, Early Wynn, held them scoreless in the ninth.

But Antonelli was giving the Americans no chance to retaliate. They did get two singles in the ninth with only one out, but the Giant lefty lost no time collecting those final two outs.

And so the Nationals tri-

umphed with perfect balance. The league-leading Redlegs and the fourth-place Cardinals might have dominated the action, but the tail-end Giants helped, too, in bringing another sad All-Star venture to a close for Charles Dillon Stengel.

July 11, 1956

Ted Williams Fined $5,000 in Outburst

Associated Press

Ted Williams

Special to The New York Times.

BOSTON, Aug. 7—Ted Williams, the Boston Red Sox' slugging outfielder, was fined $5,000 by the baseball club today for spitting at fans and newspaper men during a game with the New York Yankees.

Williams, who had put on similar exhibitions earlier in the season, showed his contempt at the end of the eleventh inning of the game, won by the Red Sox, 1 to 0. Williams first missed a fly ball and then made an outstanding catch for the third out on another drive. He started spitting as he neared the Red Sox dugout amid a mixture of cheers and jeers. An hour and a half after the game Joe Cronin, the Red Sox' general manager, announced the club was fining Williams "for his conduct on the field." Williams, whose annual salary is $100,000, was notified of the fine by phone in his hotel suite.

"We just can't condone that sort of thing," said Cronin. "It was a great game and a great crowd. After he muffed that ball he made a great catch on Yogi Berra to end the inning. It was too bad he had to spoil it.

"When I got him on the phone and told him of the fine, he said, 'I was sorry I did it a minute later. I just have no explanation as to why I did it'."

[The United Press reported Williams as saying, "I'm not a bit sorry for what I did. I'd spit again at the same fans who booed me today. If I had the money, I wouldn't be out there tomorrow."]

Williams gained the distinction of matching one Babe Ruth record, though in his spectacular career he has missed most of the others. In 1925 the Bambino was fined $5,000 by Miller Huggins, then the Yankee manager, for insubordination and breaking training rules. This remained baseball's highest player fine until equaled today by Williams.

Fined Twice Before

Temperamental Ted has been fined twice before by the Red Sox. Each previous fine was for $100, one for throwing a ball over the roof in an exhibition game in Atlanta in 1939, and the other in 1941 for rattling a hit off Fenway Park's left field wall, then walking in a pet to second base because Umpire Bill McGowan had irritated him.

This season his outburst of spitting has had Boston newspapermen as its principal target. Several times Williams has referred to Hub writers as being a "gutless" lot.

On one occasion Ted commented:

"Nobody's going to make me stop spitting. The newspaper guys in this town are bush. And some of those fans are the worst in the world."

Williams first spit this season as he crossed home plate following the 400th home run of his major league career.

Ted made another spitting gesture July 20, the night Cronin was honored for his election to baseball's Hall of Fame.

Cronin said Tom Yawkey, the club owner, "was listening to the game on the radio and was very upset by Ted's actions."

Umpire Ed Runge said that he would include in his official report a description of Williams' action of throwing his bat in the air after drawing the walk that decided the game. However, Runge did not say whether the spitting incident would be included in the report.

Will Harridge, the American League president, had talked to umpires after an earlier game marked by Williams' spitting and they reported "nothing to the incident."

"If there is anything at all to it, I presume it will be handled by the Boston club," Harridge said.

That is what the Red Sox did.

August 8, 1956

Mantle Heads Both Leagues in Homers, Runs Batted In and Batting Percentage

YANKEE FINISHES WITH .353 MARK

Mantle, in Pinch Role, Drives in Run as Bombers Lose to Red Sox in 10th, 7-4

By WILLIAM J. BRIORDY

Mickey Mantle yesterday became the fourth player to win the major league triple batting crown.

The switch-hitting centerfielder of the Yankees closed the 1956 season with a batting percentage of .353, fifty-two homers and 130 runs batted in. Mantle drove in one run as the American League's champion Yankees ended their regular campaign by bowing to the Boston Red Sox, 7 to 4, in ten innings at the Stadium.

Since the Cleveland Indians lost to the Detroit Tigers, the Bombers completed their 154-game schedule nine games in front of the pack.

The fact that the Red Sox pushed three runs over the plate in the top of the tenth to beat the Yankees was secondary. Mantle commanded the news as he became the first Yankee to perform the batting feat for both leagues since Lou Gehrig turned the trick in 1934.

The last player to take the three championships in the majors was Ted Williams of Boston. He headed both leagues in 1942. Williams also led the American League in the three divisions in 1947.

Rogers Hornsby, with the Cards in 1925, was the first to win honors in both leagues.

Mantle, who will be 25 on Oct. 20, had already clinched the laurels in the home run department. On Saturday he had virtually sewed up the batting honors in his fight with Williams.

Kaline Closest Rival

The only man who had a chance to beat the Oklahoman for the runs-batted-in title was Detroit's Al Kaline. Kaline batted two runs across yesterday to finish with 128.

Mantle had every intention to start yesterday's game, but Manager Casey Stengel saw it otherwise. Mickey, bothered by a pulled groin muscle, was kept on the bench until the ninth inning.

Stengel and the tenants of the Stadium press box had been receiving up-to-the-minute reports on Kaline's progress. The Ol' Perfessor said earlier in the day that in the event Mantle's runs-batted-in title was in jeopardy, he planned to send the Oklahoman in as a pinch-hitter.

Casey did just that. Mantle hit for Jim Coates, a rookie right-hander, in the ninth. With Jerry Lumpe stationed at third base, Mantle's grounder to third brought in the run that tied the score, at 4—4.

Tom Morgan, the fourth Yankee pitcher, was clubbed for three hits and three runs as nine Red Sox went to the plate in the top of the tenth.

Dave Sisler, Red Sox right-hander, pitched well in beating the Bombers for the second time this year. He yielded three runs and five of the Bombers' nine hits in the first two innings. Then he applied the clamps to gain his ninth victory against eight defeats.

The Yankees went ahead in the first when Yogi Berra smashed his thirtieth homer into the lower right field seats.

Berra, who matched his major league high for homers, connected behind Norm Siebern's double with two out.

BOSTON (A.)	ab.r.h.po.a.		NEW YORK (A.)	ab.r.h.po.a.
Bolling, 3b.	4 2 1 1 0		Bauer, rf.	3 0 1 1 0
Klaus, ss	4 0 1 4 3		Wilson, rf	2 0 0 0 0
Williams, lf.	0 0 0 0 0		Siebern, lf.	4 1 1 3 0
aSthps.lf.cf	5 0 1 5 0		cSlaughter	1 0 0 0 0
Zauchin, 1b.	3 1 0 8 0		Cerv, cf.	5 0 1 5 1
Thrnbry, rf.	5 1 2 2 0		Berra, c.	4 1 1 8 0
Piersall, cf.	1 0 0 0 0		Skowron, 1b.	3 0 1 2 0
Gernert, lf.	2 1 2 1 0 0		Noren, 1b.	2 0 0 4 1
Consolo, 2b.	..		McDougal, ss	3 0 0 1 1
Daley, c.	4 1 3 8 0		Hunter, ss.	1 0 0 0 1
Sisler, p.	3 0 0 1 1		Martin, 2b.	3 1 1 2 0
			Coleman, 2b.	1 0 0 3 3
Total	35 7 9 30 8		Carroll, 3b.	2 0 1 0 0
			Lumpe, 3b.	2 1 1 1 1
			Turley, p.	2 0 0 0 0
			McDrmt, p.	1 0 0 0 0
			Coates, p.	0 0 0 0 0
			bMantle	1 0 0 0 0
			Morgan, p.	0 0 0 0 2
			Total	40 4 9 30 10

aRan for Williams in first.
bGrounded out for Coates in ninth.
cFouled out for Siebern in tenth.

Boston .. .. 1 0 0 2 1 0 0 0 0 3—7
New York .. .. .. 2 1 0 0 0 0 0 0 1 0—4

Errors—Sisler, Stephens. Runs batted in—Zauchin, Berra 2, Bauer, Daley 4, Throneberry, Mantle, Klaus. Two-base hits—Siebern, Martin, Bauer, Daley. Home run—Berra. Sacrifices—Sisler 2, Gernert. Double play—Cerv and McDougal. Left on bases—Boston 11, New York 7. Bases on balls—Off Turley 5, Coates 2, Morgan 3, Sisler 1. Struck out—By Turley 6, McDermott 1, Sisler 7. Hits—Off Turley 5 in 5 innings, McDermott in 3, Coates 0 in 1, Morgan 3 in 1. Runs and earned runs—Off Turley 4 and 4, Morgan 3 and 3, Sisler 4 and 3. Wild pitch—Coates. Winning pitcher—Sisler (9—8). Losing pitcher—Morgan (6—7). Umpires—Paparella, Hurley, McKinley and Chylak. Time of game—2:30. Attendance—39,397.

October 1, 1956

Larsen Beats Dodgers in Perfect Game; Yanks Lead, 3-2, on First Series No-Hitter

Mantle's Home Run and Bauer's Single Send Maglie to 2-0 Loss

By JOHN DREBINGER

Don Larsen is a footloose fellow of whom Casey Stengel once said, "He can be one of baseball's great pitchers any time he puts his mind to it." Larsen had his mind on his work yesterday.

He pitched the first no-hit game in world series history. Not only that, but he also fired the first perfect game—no batter reaching first base—to be posted in the major leagues in thirty-four years.

This nerve-tingling performance, embellished with a Mickey Mantle home run, gained a 2-0 triumph for the Yankees over the Dodgers and Sal Maglie at the Stadium. It enabled Casey Stengel's Bombers to post their third straight victory for a 3-2 lead in the series. The Bombers are within one game of clinching the series as it moves back to Ebbets Field today.

Crowd Roars Tribute

With every fan in a gathering of 64,519 hanging breathlessly on every pitch, Larsen, a 27-year-old right-hander, slipped over a third strike on Dale Mitchell to end the game.

Dale, a pinch hitter, was the twenty-seventh batter to face Larsen. As he went down for the final out, the gathering set up a deafening roar, while jubilant Yankees fairly mobbed the big pitcher as he struggled to make his way to the dugout.

The unpredictable Larsen had triumphed at a time when the Bombers needed it most with one of the most spectacular achievements in diamond history. Last spring the tall, handsome Hoosier, who now makes his home in San Diego, Calif., had caused considerable to-do in the Yankees' St. Petersburg training camp. In an early dawn escapade, Don wrapped his automobile around a telephone pole. He later explained he had fallen asleep at the wheel.

Yesterday big Don remained wide-awake through every moment of the nine innings as he wrapped his long fingers around a baseball to make it do tricks never seen before in world series play.

He did it, too, with a most revolutionary delivery, which might account for his sudden rise to fame. Don takes no wind-up at all. Each pitch is served from a standing delivery that he adopted only a little over a month ago.

In the history of baseball this was only the seventh perfect game ever hurled in the major leagues and only the fifth in baseball's modern era, which dates back to the beginning of the present century. A perfect game is one in which a pitcher faces exactly twenty-seven men with not one reaching first base through a hit, base on balls, error or any other means.

The last perfect game in the majors was achieved by Charlie Robertson of the Chicago White Sox on April 30, 1922, when he vanquished the Detroit Tigers, 2—0.

No-hitters during the season, of course, have been common enough. In fact, Maglie, beaten yesterday despite a commendable five-hitter, tossed one earlier this year for the Dodgers.

In modern world series play, which started in 1903, three pitchers missed no-hitters by one blow. Ed Reulbach of the Cubs fired a one-hitter against the White Sox on Oct. 10, 1906. Jiggs Donohue, the White Sox first baseman, wrecked that no-hit bid.

Rudy York of the Tigers made the only hit off Claude Passeau of the Cubs on Oct. 5, 1945. In that game Passeau allowed only one other Tiger to reach first base, that one on a pass.

Bevens' Bid Fails

On Oct. 3, 1947, Floyd Bevens, a Yankee right-hander, got closest of all to the no-hit goal, when, against the Dodgers at Ebbets Field, he moved within one out of his objective. Then Cookie Lavagetto rattled a pinch two-bagger off the right-field wall that not only broke the no-hit spell but also defeated the Yankees.

So amazing was Larsen's feat that only four batted balls had a chance of being rated hits. One was a foul by inches. Three drives were converted into outs by miraculous Yankee fielding plays.

In the second inning, Jackie Robinson banged a vicious grounder off Andy Carey's glove at third base for what momentarily appeared a certain hit. But Gil McDougald, the alert Yankee shortstop, recovered the ball in time to fire it for the put-out on Jackie at first base.

In the fifth, minutes after Mantle had put the Yanks ahead, 1—0, with his blast into the right field stand, Gil Hodges tagged a ball that streaked into deep left center, seemingly headed for extra bases.

But Mantle, whose fielding in the series has at times been a trifle spotty, more than made amends. He tore across the turf to make an extraordinary glove-fanned seven.

On the next play, Sandy Amoros leaned into a pitch and rocketed a towering drive toward the right field stand. This drive promised to tie the score, but at the last moment the ball curved foul.

And then, in the eighth, Hodges once again was victimized by a thrilling Yankee fielding play. Gil drove a tricky, low liner to the left of Carey. The Yankee third sacker lunged for the ball and caught it inches off the ground.

For a moment it was hard to say whether he had caught the ball or scooped it up. Andy, just to make certain, fired the ball to first in time to make the putout doubly sure. Officially, it was scored as a caught ball.

So accurate was Larsen's control that of the twenty-seven batters to face him, only one managed to run the count to three balls. That was Pee Wee Reese, the doughty Dodger captain and shortstop, in the first inning. Pee Wee then took a third strike. In all, Larsen fanned six.

For Maglie, the performance by his youthful rival was a heartbreaker. The 39-year-old Barber, whose astounding comeback this year had reached its peak when he hurled the Dodgers to victory in the series opener last Wednesday, did a pretty good job of pitching, too.

For three and two-third innings the one-time Giant star right-hander matched Larsen batter for batter, turning back the first eleven Yankee batters.

The New York Times

NO HITS, NO RUNS, NO NOTHING: Scoreboard at Stadium after yesterday's game

The Box Score

FIFTH GAME
BROOKLYN DODGERS

	AB.	R.	H.	PO.	A.
Gilliam, 2b.	3	0	0	2	0
Reese, ss.	3	0	0	4	2
Snider, cf.	3	0	0	1	0
Robinson, 3b.	3	0	0	2	4
Hodges, 1b.	3	0	0	5	1
Amoros, lf.	3	0	0	3	0
Furillo, rf.	3	0	0	0	0
Campanella, c.	3	0	0	7	2
Maglie, p.	2	0	0	0	1
a-Mitchell	1	0	0	0	0
Total	27	0	0	24	10

NEW YORK YANKEES

	AB.	R.	H.	PO.	A.
Bauer, rf.	4	0	1	4	0
Collins, 1b.	4	0	1	7	0
Mantle, cf.	3	1	1	4	0
Berra, c.	3	0	0	7	0
Slaughter, lf.	2	0	1	0	0
Martin, 2b.	3	0	1	3	4
McDougald, ss.	2	0	0	0	2
Carey, 3b.	3	1	1	1	1
Larsen, p.	2	0	0	0	1
Total	26	2	5	27	8

a—Called out on strikes for Maglie in ninth.

Brooklyn .....0 0 0 0 0 0 0 0 0—0
New York .....0 0 0 1 0 1 0 0 .—2

Errors—None.
Runs batted in—Mantle, Bauer.
Home run—Mantle.
Sacrifice—Larsen.
Double plays—Reese and Hodges; Hodges, Campanella, Robinson, Campanella and Robinson.
Left on bases—Brooklyn 0, New York 3.
Bases on balls—Off Maglie 2 (Slaughter, McDougald).
Struck out—By Larsen 7 (Gilliam, Reese, Hodges, Campanella, Snider, Maglie, Mitchell); Maglie 5 (Martin, Collins 2, Larsen, Bauer).
Runs and earned runs—Off Maglie 2 and 2.
Winning pitcher—Larsen.
Losing pitcher—Maglie.
Umpires—Pinelli (N.), plate; Soar (A.), first base; Boggess (N.), second base; Napp (A.), third base; Gorman (N.), left field, and Runge (A.), right field.
Time of game—2:06.
Attendance—64,519 (paid).

But with two out in the fourth and the bases empty, Mantle blazed his homer into the lower right stand.

A moment later Yogi Berra appeared to have connected for another hit as he stroked a powerful low drive toward left center. However, Duke Snider tore over from center field and snared the ball with a headlong dive.

In the sixth, the Yanks tallied their second run when they ganged up on the Barber for three singles, although they needed only two of them to produce the tally. Larsen had a hand in the scoring.

Carey had opened the inning with a single over second for only the second blow off Maglie. Then Larsen, one of several accomplished batsmen Stengel lists among his pitchers, laid down a perfect bunt sacrifice.

That sent Carey to second. On the heels of the sacrifice, Hank Bauer drove another single to center to send Carey scampering over the plate. For a moment it looked as though the Yanks would pile up some more runs as Joe Collins followed with a single into right that swept Bauer around to third.

A rather freakish double play put a quick finish to this rally. Mantle crashed a sharp grounder down the first base line. Hodges scooped up the ball and stepped on the bag almost in the same instant to retire Mantle. Then, seeing Bauer heading for home, Hodges got the ball to the plate in time to head off Hank, who was tagged in a rundown between third and home.

Double Play Helps Maglie

Another double play had saved the Barber in the fifth. Enos Slaughter had opened with a pass only to be forced at second on Billy Martin's sacrifice attempt. Then McDougald followed with a drive that appeared headed for left center.

But the ball never cleared Reese, who leaped in the air, deflected the ball with his glove, then caught it. Martin, certain the drive was a hit, had gone too far off first to get back and was doubled off the bag.

With two out in the seventh, the irrepressible Martin singled to left and McDougald walked to receive the second and last pass given up by Maglie. But the Barber ended this threat by inducing Carey to slap into a force play at second.

Just to show he still had plenty left, the ancient Barber swept through the eighth by fanning three Yanks in a row. Maglie got Larsen, Bauer and Collins and as he walked off the mound toward the Dodger dugout he received a rousing ovation.

Nevertheless, the noise then was barely a whisper compared with the din set up minutes later when Larsen finished his perfect game.

One could have heard a dollar bill drop in the huge arena as Carl Furillo got up as the first Dodger batter in the ninth. Carl lifted a fly to Bauer in right and one roar went up. Roy

Associated Press

Yogi Berra jumps on Don Larsen after the last out of the perfect game.

Campanella slapped a grounder at Martin for out No. 2 and the second roar followed.

Then only Mitchell, batting for Maglie, remained between Larsen and everlasting diamond fame. The former American League outfielder, for years a sure-fire pinch hitter with the Cleveland Indians, ran the count to one ball and two strikes.

Mitchell fouled off the next pitch and as the following one zoomed over the plate Umpire Babe Pinelli called it strike three. At this point the Stadium was in an uproar.

Mitchell whirled around to protest the call and later he said it was a fast ball that was outside the strike zone. But Dale was in no spot to gain any listener. The Yanks were pummeling Larsen and the umpires were hustling off the field.

Doubtless for Pinelli, this, too, could have provided his greatest thrill in his long career as an arbiter. For after this series, Babe, as the dean of the National League staff of umpires, is to retire.

And so, with this most spectacular of all world series spectaculars, the pattern, in reverse

of last October's series between these two rivals continues to hold. Last fall the Dodgers blew the first two games at the Stadium, then swept the next three in Ebbets Field. Returning to the Stadium, they lost the sixth game to tie it at three-all, but then bagged the seventh to gain Brooklyn's first world championship.

This time the Yanks hold the 3-2 advantage. They need only one more victory to clinch it. But that victory will have to be gained either today or tomorrow in the lair of the Dodgers and the Yanks haven't won a world series game at Ebbets Field since Oct. 4, 1953.

Even Larsen, yesterday's no-hit hero, couldn't win there when he pitched the second game of the series last Friday. In fact, Don started that game, which wound up with the Yanks going down to a 13-8 defeat. He went out in the second inning after the Bombers had got him off to a 6-0 lead.

However, with two out, the Dodgers had scored only one run when Stengel removed Larsen with the bases filled. What followed was the doing of others and some experts had hinted Casey had been a bit hasty in hauling Don out so soon.

All's Well That Ends Well

Stengel later admitted this could have been the case. "However," added the philosophical skipper of the Bombers, "it might also help to get him really on his toes the next time he starts." And that it most certainly did yesterday.

At a late hour last night, Stengel was still undecided whether in today's encounter, which could win it all for him, he would start Johnny Kucks or Bob Turley.

Johnny, a 23-year-old sophomore right-hander and an eighteen-game winner the past season, also appeared briefly in that Friday rout in Flatbush. He followed Larsen and gave up the bases-filled single to Reese that drove in two runs. He then gave way to Tommy Byrne, who was tagged for Snider's three-run homer.

Turley is the right-hander who also joined the Yanks along with Larsen in the Baltimore eighteen-player deal.

Walter Alston of the Dodgers, now fighting desperately to remain alive in the series, will stake all on his prize relief specialist, Clem Labine. Clem has been used only sparingly as a starter this year, but in this trying hour Alston suddenly seems to have no other choice.

UNEARNED TALLIES SINK BOMBERS, 2-1

Indians' Late Drive Decides After Herb Score Suffers Broken Nose, Eye Injury

By LOUIS EFFRAT
Special to The New York Times.

CLEVELAND, May 7 — Of tremendously greater concern to the Indians than the 2-1 decision they took from the Yankees tonight was an accident that befell Herb Score, their million-dollar southpaw. Felled by a line drive from the bat of Gil McDougald in the first inning, Score, the sight in his right eye endangered and his nose fractured, was removed on a stretcher and taken to Lakeside Hospital.

Dr. C. W. Thomas, a local and prominent eye specialist, examined Score. The physician reported hemorrhaging in the eye so severe that it would be several days before the exact nature or the extent of the injury to the eye could be determined.

Nothing, including the seventh and eighth inning runs that the Tribe scored to beat Tom Sturdivant could make anyone forget what had happened in the first three minutes of the ball game. Even the Yankees, who were to see their six-game winning streak snapped by two unearned runs, were upset by the misfortune that befell Score.

The popular pitcher had disposed of Hank Bauer, the first Yankee he faced, on a grounder to Al Smith at third base. A moment later, McDougald, the second man, slashed a drive directly toward Score.

Smith Recovers Ball

Unable to get his glove up in time, Herb was hit squarely on the right eye. The ball caromed toward Smith, who threw out McDougald. Score, who had dropped as though hit by a bullet, lay on the mound.

Members of both teams rushed to Score's side. Ice packs were applied and a stretcher brought out. The public address announcer requested: "If there is a doctor in the stands, will he please report to the playing field." Within twenty seconds, six physicians, including Dr. Don Kelly, the club doctor, had sped to the middle of the diamond.

His eye closed, and bleeding from the nose and mouth, Score was carried off on the stretcher and taken to the hospital. Dr. Kelly's diagnosis disclosed that Score's nose was broken. The physician was more worried about the eye, though, and called for Dr. Thomas.

At no time did Score lose consciousness. In fact, while in the clubhouse, awaiting the ambu-

October 9, 1956

HERB SCORE IS INJURED: Indians' pitcher lying stunned on mound at Cleveland last night after being struck by a ball hit by Yanks' Gil McDougald. At the left is Jim Hegan.

captured twenty. His 245 strikeouts in 1955 and 263 in 1956 were the most by any hurler in either circuit. He had fanned thirty-nine in thirty-six innings this campaign before the accident.

Score had the sympathy of 18,386 spectators at Municipal Stadium. It will be recalled that the Boston Red Sox recently bid $1,000,000 for Score's services. The offer was rejected.

With Score injured, Bob Lemon warmed up hurriedly and he and Sturdivant engaged in a tense duel through six scoreless rounds. In the seventh, Elston Howard singled, advanced on Andy Carey's sacrifice and Sturdivant's infield out, then crossed the plate on a bad-hop single by Bauer.

That was a lucky run for the Yankees, but the Tribe of Kerby Farrell was luckier—twice. For the Indians capitalized on New York errors that led to the tying and the winning run.

NEW YORK (A.)						CLEVELAND (A.)					
	ab.r.h.po.a						ab.r.h.po.a				
Bauer, rf.	3 0 1 2 0					Strickl'nd,2b.	4 0 0 2 1				
McD'gald, ss.	4 0 0 0 0					Woodling, lf.	4 1 2 2 0				
Mantle, cf.	4 0 0 2 0					Smith, 3b.	4 0 0 2 2				
Berra, c.	4 0 1 10 0					Wertz, 1b.	3 1 2 9 1				
Skowron, 1b.	4 0 1 6 0					Raines, ss.	0 0 0 0 1				
Martin, 2b.	4 0 0 2 0					Maris, cf.	3 0 1 3 0				
Howard, lf.	3 1 1 1 0					Colavito, rf.	2 0 0 4 0				
cSlaughter	1 0 0 0 0					Carr'squl ss.	3 0 0 0 3				
Carey, 3b.	2 0 1 1 4					aAltobelli,1b.	1 0 0 1 0				
dCollins	1 0 0 0 0					Hegan, c.	2 0 0 2 0				
Sturdivant,p.	2 0 1 0 0					bWard	1 0 0 0 0				
						Nixon, c.	0 0 0 1 0				
Total	32 1 6 24 4					Score, p.	0 0 0 0 1				
						Lemon, p.	3 0 0 1 3				
						Total	30 2 5 27 12				

aFlied out for Carrasquel in seventh.
bStruck out for Hegan in seventh.
cFlied out for Howard in ninth.
dStruck out for Carey in ninth.

New York ....0 0 0 0 6 0 1 0 0—1
Cleveland ....0 0 0 0 0 0 1 1 .—2

Errors—Smith 2, Carey, Martin, Bauer. Runs batted in—Skowron, Colavito. Two-base hit—Skowron. Sacrifices—Sturdivant, Carey, Colavito. Double plays—Carrasquel, Strickland and Wertz; Berra and Martin. Left on bases—New York 7, Cleveland 8. Bases on balls—Off Sturdivant 2, Lemon 1. Struck out—By Sturdivant 9, Lemon 7. Hits—Off Score 0 in 2-3 inning, Lemon 6 in 8 1-3. Runs and earned runs—Off Sturdivant 2 and 0, Lemon 1 and 1. Hit by pitcher—By Sturdivant (Maris). Winning pitcher—Lemon (2—3). Losing pitcher—Sturdivant (1—2). Umpires—Rice, Rommel, Stevens and Napp. Time of game—2:29. Attendance—18,386.

May 8, 1957

lance, Herb joked: "I wonder if Gene Fullmer felt this way." He referred to the recent knockout Fullmer suffered in his title bout with Ray Robinson.

Rated Best in Majors

The 23-year-old Score, who was born in Rosedale, L. I., but now makes his home in Lake Worth, Fla., is rated by most experts the best pitcher in the majors. He was a ten-game winner in 1955, his first year in the big show, and last season he

Frick Sidetracks Three Redlegs After Avalanche of Ohio Votes

Commissioner Names Musial, Aaron and Mays to All-Star Posts—Cincinnati Still Has Five Starters on Team

By MICHAEL STRAUSS

Spurred to action by a late avalanche of votes from Cincinnati that threatened to make a farce of the All-Star Game balloting, Ford C. Frick, the Baseball Commissioner, untangled the situation yesterday.

Aware that the disproportionate voting from the Ohio city would place Redlegs in all eight National League fielding positions, Frick did some adjusting. When he was finished three members of the Cincinnati club had been sidetracked.

Assured of definite starting berths on the team, although only second in the official balloting for their respective positions, were Stan Musial, St. Louis (first base), Willie Mays, New York (center field), and Hank Aaron, Milwaukee (right field).

The trio joined five Redlegs who were either leading or challenging the leaders before the "deluge" from Cincinnati. The Cincinnati players "in" were Johnny Temple (second base), Don Hoak (third base), Roy McMillan (shortstop), Frank Robinson (left field) and Ed Bailey (catcher).

Trio Is Counted Out

Redleg players counted out of the starting picture by Frick's move were George Crowe (first base), Gus Bell (center field) and Wally Post (right field). Until the voting outburst from Cincinnati, Crowe had not been listed among the leaders, Bell had been third, behind Mays, with about 43,000 votes, while Post had been second behind Aaron, with about 50,000.

Frick's move was made in concurrence with Warren Giles, the president of the senior loop, and Will Harridge, the president of the American League, after 550,000 votes had been received from Cincinnati in the last week.

The Redleg votes turned over to Frick's tabulators at the last moment ranged from a total of 481,862 for Hoak to 220,836 for Crowe. Last year the most popular choice, Dale Long, then with the Pirates, polled only 179,744 votes.

Ordinarily, the names of the chosen players would not have been made known until Monday. But in view of the situation Frick decided an earlier announcement was necessary.

"I took this step," he said, "in an effort to be entirely fair to all fans and with no reflection on the sincerity or honesty of the Cincinnati poll. A re-study of the ballots had to be made on the percentage of ballots cast in all cities."

Frick explained that there was no such problem in the American League and that the roster for that loop would be made known on schedule Monday. The game will be played in St. Louis on

Tuesday, July 9. The balloting closed last Thursday.

"The rules as set up provide that the eight men receiving the largest number of ballots would constitute the starting line-up, and remain in the All-Star Game for three innings," said Frick. "The National League, while recognizing this rule, feels that the overbalance of Cincinnati ballots has resulted in the selection of a team which would not be typical of the league.

Five Already Ahead

"There is little doubt that the five members of the Cincinnati team who received All-Star positions were either leading or in contention for their places. About the three others, however, there was plenty of question.

"It may be," he continued, "that Musial will still beat Crowe out for first base. Stan possibly can win by a few thousand votes. But Aaron and Mays had no chance in view of this late rush from Cincinnati."

In Cincinnati, Manager Birdie Tebbetts of the Redlegs told The Associated Press last night that Bell, Post and Crowe at least should be named honorary members of the All-Star team. He added that they also should have the privilege of selecting a gift that goes to every All-Star player.

General Manager Gabe Paul of the Redlegs went a bit farther. He expressed the view that the three players sidetracked by Frick as starters should be included on the squad.

Giles proposed a new method of selection to prevent a recurrence. He said each major league city should receive an equal number of official ballots and then it should be up to that city to get out the vote.

New System Sought

It was recalled yesterday that last summer there was some grumbling when five Redleg regulars started in the All-Star Game and three more were picked for the team by the manager, Walt Alston of the Brooklyn Dodgers. There was a move shortly thereafter to devise a new way to pick players. Nothing developed.

The All-Star Game, important to players these days because from it comes revenue for their pension funds, was started in 1933. It began as a promotion by The Chicago Tribune in connection with Chicago's World Fair.

In its early years the game met opposition from owners as well as many of the selected players. To the owners it represented an unnecessary lapse in the league schedules. To the stars it presented the possibility of being injured in an exhibition game.

June 29, 1957

American League Staves Off Late Drive by National to Win St. Louis Game

BUNNING OF TIGERS GAINS 6-5 VERDICT

Retires Nine Batters in Row —National League's Rally Falls Short in Ninth

By JOHN DREBINGER
Special to The New York Times.

ST. LOUIS, July 9—The American League, which left this city four years ago, returned today to relive the days of its earlier midsummer triumphs. It tripped the National League, 6 to 5, in the twenty-fourth annual All-Star game before a gathering of 30,693.

The victory was only the second for the junior loop in the last seven interleague encounters and only the second for Casey Stengel in seven tries as manager of the American League forces. The triumph raised the American's lead in the contests to a 14-10 margin. It once stood at 12—4.

However, there were some tense moments near the end when it looked as if Casey wouldn't make it at all. For after doing some masterful player manipulating behind six innings of shutout pitching by the Tigers' Jim Bunning and the Orioles' Billy Loes, the Yankees' famed skipper almost came a cropper in the seventh and ninth.

Despite some pre-game caustic remarks that Stengel had directed toward his Cleveland rivals for using Early Wynn in a starting role last Sunday, Casey daringly called on the Indians' right-hander to pitch the seventh for the American Leaguers.

Bell Belts Double

Wynn faced only four batters. He was pounded for two runs, a two-bagger by Gus Bell driving in both. That shaved an early American League advantage to 3-2.

Then, in the ninth, directly after the Stengel cohorts had moved into another commanding lead by belting Walter Alston's Clem Labine for three runs, with the aid of a damaging Red Schoendienst error, the National Leaguers roared back in the lower half of the final round.

They routed the White Sox' crack southpaw, Billy Pierce. And also chased Cleveland's lefty, Don Mossi, as they rushed

three runs across the plate. A three-bagger by a limping Willie Mays was one of the key shots in this rally. A single by the Cubs' Ernie Banks drove in the third run.

But on this same hit, Bell, the hero of the Nationals' two-run seventh, gummed things up with some overzealous base-running. He was cut down at third for the second out as he tried to go around from first on the single into left field.

Minutes later, after Stengel had called on his own Bob Grim to become his third hurler of the inning and the sixth of the game, the struggle ended as Gil Hodges, in the role of pinch hitter, lined a drive into the waiting hands of Minnie Minoso in left. The Americans therefore wound up one run ahead after leading all the way.

They scored two runs in the second when they routed the Nationals' starter, Curt Simmons, before the Phils' southpaw could retire a man. Then, after Lew

Burdette had checked this splurge along with tossing three more scoreless rounds, the Phils' Jack Sanford took over and was clipped for a tally in the sixth.

In the ninth, Alston suffered his final crusher, when his own Dodger relief ace, Labine, yielded a closing cluster of three. The most damaging blow here was a double by Minoso, who had just entered the game as a replacement for Ted Williams.

Big Guns Misfire

Apart from scoring the first two American runs after being put on base by way of an infield hit and a pass, respectively, neither the Yanks' Mickey Mantle nor the Red Sox' redoubtable Williams distinguished himself. The closest Williams got to a long blow was in the eighth, when he rocketed a drive into left center. But Mays hauled this one down near the bleacher wall.

Both sides got off swimmingly in the first inning under a blaz-

Associated Press Wirephotos

UNEASY MOMENT: Roy McMillan of Nationals catches high pop fly by Mantle in third inning despite bumping by Frank Robinson, left. Willie Mays backs up the play.

FIRST HIT: Mickey Mantle of Americans, who eventually scored first run, arrives at first on infield hit in second inning. Stan Musial leaps for Don Hoak's throw from third.

ing Missouri sun. Simmons, chosen by Alston, after deep and careful thought, for his starting pitcher, snuffed out the first three American Leaguers. Bunning, a beanpole right-hander reminiscent of Ewell Blackwell and his whiplike sidearm delivery turned in a similar job on the top three National Leaguers.

But with the second, Simmons' grip on the situation vanished in almost no time at all. Mantle topped a dribbler down the third base line and before Don Hoak could get the ball over to first, Mickey had streaked over the bag for a hit. Hoak's throw was a bit high, but even had it been perfect it would have done no good.

Simmons' difficulties mounted rapidly. He walked Williams, after running up the count to three-and-two, and when Vic Wertz sliced a single into left field Mantle dashed home with the first tally.

Alston at this point doubtless did a lot of squirming, but he was still hopeful Simmons would right himself. But when the Phillie southpaw walked Yogi Berra on four pitches, filling the bases, the Dodger skipper waved in Burdette, the star Milwaukee right-hander.

Lew appeared to have the situation under control as he got George Kell to pop out to Stan Musial back of first and retired Bunning on an infield fly. But Burdette then pitched too cautiously to Harvey Kuenn.

He ran the count to three-and-two, then tossed an inside pitch that walked the Tiger shortstop and forced in Williams with the second run of the inning.

Nellie Fox flied out to left, ending the inning, but the Americans were in front, 2—0. With the third, there wasn't a semblance of a National League threat as Bunning retired three more in a row.

The Detroit sophomore ace, in finishing his three-inning stint, had gone right down the National League batting order, wiping out nine successive batters. Since the Americans never did relinquish the lead, Bunning subsequently was named

the winner and Simmons the loser.

As Stengel made his first pitching shift in the fourth, calling on Loes, he made three other quick shifts in his battlefront. He withdrew Kuenn at short, Wertz at first and Kell at third. Casey had not looked with favor on the selection of these three by the fans for his starting line-up and even though Wertz did drive in the first run for him, the Yankee skipper lost no time getting all three out of there.

As expected, he started the fourth with his own Gil McDougald at short, Bill Skowron at first and the Red Sox Frank Malzone on third.

Two innings later this switch was to help the American Leaguers to their third run as Skowron fired a two-bagger off the right field wall. The Phillies' Sanford, who had just entered the game in the sixth inning as the mound successor to Burdette, was the victim of that blow.

A wild pitch put Skowron on third and a moment later Bill

was over the plate as Berra poked a single into left. Incidentally, incredible as it may seem, that was the first run-batted-in for Yogi in nine All-Star games.

Meanwhile, the National Leaguers were getting nowhere against the rival circuit's pitching. As Loes opened his three-inning chore in the fourth, the Nationals launched their first serious threat when they put runners on second and third with only one out.

Temple Strikes Out

After Johnny Temple, one of five Redlegs in the senior loop's starting line-up, had taken a third strike, Hank Aaron pushed a single just beyond Fox' reach into right field.

The crowd, predominantly National League, then got its first chance to let out a wholehearted cheer. Musial slammed a double into right field and Aaron pulled up at third.

But Loes, a former Dodger right-hander now starring in the American League, rubbed out Mays on the end of an infield pop fly and then got Ed Bailey to end the inning with a grounder down the first base line. So that prospective rally got no further.

Frank Robinson opened the Nationals' fifth with a single to center only to have this wiped out with some base running scarcely of All-Star caliber. For as Eddie Mathews, batting for Hoak, cracked a sinking liner to right. Robinson, thinking the ball would be caught, headed back to first base after starting for second.

As the ball landed in front of Al Kaline, Al merely had to fire it to second for a force-out and Mathews lost credit for a base hit.

It therefore wasn't until the seventh, as Stengel made his ill-starred venture with Wynn, that the Nationals' finally bestirred themselves. With one out. Mays punched a single into left field and swept around to third as Bailey stroked one into right.

Here Bell, batting for Robinson, sliced a two-bagger down the left field line that drove in both Mays and Bailey and the Nationals trailed by only a single tally. But though they managed to push Bell as far as third, they couldn't make it the rest of the way. At least not in this inning.

Pierce Takes Mound

For Stengel wasted no time hustling Wynn off the mound and calling on Pierce. Billy retired Mathews on a roller down the first base line, Bell taking third on the play, and Ernie Banks struck out.

It was after the Cards' Larry Jackson had blanked the Americans in the seventh and eighth that Alston made his ill-starred move with Labine in the ninth.

Pierce got an infield hit. McDougald grounded to Red Schoendienst who, as he spun around to make a toss to second, dropped the ball. After Fox sac-

Box Score of All-Star Game

AMERICAN LEAGUE	AB	R	H	PO	A	E	NATIONAL LEAGUE	AB	R	H	PO	A	E
Kuenn, ss	2	0	0	0	1	0	Temple, 2b	2	0	0	3	0	0
McDougald, ss	2	1	0	1	0	0	eSchoend'nst, 2b	2	0	0	0	0	1
Fox, 2b	4	0	0	2	4	0	Aaron, rf	4	0	1	2	0	0
Kaline, rf	5	1	2	1	1	0	Musial, 1b	3	1	1	9	0	0
Mantle, cf	4	1	1	4	0	0	Mays, cf	4	2	2	2	0	0
Williams, lf	2	1	0	2	0	0	Bailey, c	3	1	1	2	0	0
Minoso, lf	1	0	1	1	1	0	hFoiles	1	1	1	0	0	0
Wertz, 1b	2	0	1	3	0	0	Robinson, lf	2	0	1	5	0	0
Skowron, 1b	3	1	2	5	1	0	bBell, lf	1	0	1	0	0	0
Berra, c	3	0	1	6	0	0	Hoak, 3b	1	0	0	1	0	0
Kell, 3b	2	0	0	0	1	0	bMathews, 3b	3	0	0	1	0	0
Malzone, 3b	2	0	0	1	1	0	McMillan, ss	1	0	0	2	0	0
Bunning, p	1	0	0	0	0	0	cBanks, ss	3	0	1	0	3	0
aMaxwell	1	0	1	0	0	0	Simmons, p	0	0	0	0	0	0
Loes, p	1	0	0	0	1	0	Burdette, p	1	0	0	0	0	0
Wynn, p	0	0	0	0	0	0	Sanford, p	0	0	0	0	0	0
Pierce, p	1	1	1	1	0	0	dMoon	1	0	0	0	0	0
Mossi, p	0	0	0	0	0	0	Jackson, p	0	0	0	0	1	0
Grim, p	0	0	0	0	0	0	gCimoli	1	0	0	0	0	0
							Labine, p	0	0	0	0	1	0
							iHodges	1	0	0	0	0	0
Total	37	6	10	27	11	0	Total	34	5	9	27	5	1

aSingled for Bunning in fourth. bHit into force play for Hoak in fifth. cHit into double play for McMillan in fifth. dGrounded out for Sanford in sixth.

eFlied out for Temple in sixth. fDoubled for Robinson in seventh. gCalled out on strikes for Jackson in eighth. hSingled for Bailey in ninth. iFlied out for Labine in ninth.

American League	0 2 0	0 0 1	0 0 3—6
National League	0 0 0	0 0 0	2 0 3—5

Runs batted in—Wertz, Kuenn, Berra, Bell 2, Kaline 2, Minoso, Mays, Banks.

Two-base hits—Musial, Skowron, Bell, Minoso. Three-base hit—Mays. Sacrifice—Fox. Double play—Malzone, Fox and Skowron. Left on bases—American 9, National 4. Bases on balls—Off Simmons 2 (Williams, Berra), Burdette 1 (Kuenn), Jackson 1 (Mantle), Pierce 2 (Musial, Bell). Struck out—By Bunning 1 (Mays), Loes 1 (Temple), Pierce 3 (Banks, Cimoli, Aaron), Labine 1 (Mantle), Mossi 1, (Mathews). Hits—Off Simmons 2 in 1 inning (faced four batters in second), Bunning 0 in 3, Burdette 2 in 4, Sanford 2 in 1, Loes 3 in 3, Wynn 3 in 1/3, Jackson 1 in 2, Labine 3 in 1, Pierce 2 in 1 2/3 (faced four batters in ninth), Mossi 1 in 2/3, Grim 0 in 1/3. Runs and earned runs—Off Simmons 2 and 2, Sanford 1 and 1, Wynn 2 and 2, Labine 3 and 1, Pierce 3 and 3. Wild pitches—Sanford, Pierce. Winning pitcher—Bunning. Losing pitcher—Simmons. Umpires—Dascoli (N.), Napp (A.), Dixon (N.), Stevens (A.), Landes (N.) and Chylak (A.). Time of game—2:43. Attendance—30,693. Receipts (net)—$104,349.62.

rificed, Kaline slashed a single to center scoring two runs.

Mantle went down swinging at a third strike, but Minoso followed with his two-base drive to right center. It fetched home Kaline and that was the run that eventually won it.

A pass to Musial started the Nationals' counter offensive against Pierce in the last of the ninth. Mays, still limping on the painfully bruised left instep he injured last week, blasted a triple down the right foul line to score Musial.

A moment later, as Pierce was delivering to a pinch hitter, Hank Foiles, Willie charged home on a wild pitch. Foiles then singled and when Bell drew a pass, Casey sent in the left-handed Mossi.

The Cleveland southpaw fanned Mathews, but Banks rifled a single through Malzone at third and that had the crowd in an

uproar. But on the blow that was to see Foiles score the third run of the inning, the rally ran up a siding.

Bell, with the play before him, rounded second and boldly headed for third. But Minoso's fine peg to Malzone nailed the speeding Redleg for the second out and that was to prove as close as the Nationals were to get to averting defeat.

Though Banks advanced to second on the throw, Stengel now waved in his relief star, Grim, who hadn't worked since July 4. Alston countered with his slugging first sacker, Hodges, but the tying tally remained marooned on second. Hodges lined one to left that Minoso collared and the struggle was over.

July 10, 1957

GIANTS WILL SHIFT TO SAN FRANCISCO FOR 1958 SEASON

Board of Directors Approves, by 8-1 Vote, Coast Offer of 35-Year Stadium Lease

TEAM HERE SINCE 1883

Move From Polo Grounds Is Independent of Any Action Planned by Dodgers

By BILL BECKER

They'll be the San Francisco Giants in 1958.

The board of directors of the National Exhibition Company, the corporation operating the New York Giants, voted yesterday, 8 to 1, to move the baseball franchise to San Francisco next spring. The Giants have been a New York institution for seventy-four years.

Horace C. Stoneham, the club president, said he planned to fly to San Francisco within the next week for the formal signing of the contract. Mayor George Christopher of the Coast city indicated the contract would be drawn up within a few days.

Mr. Stoneham announced the transfer at the Giants' executive offices, 100 West Forty-second Street.

"It's a tough wrench," he said. "We're very sorry we're leaving. I'm very sentimental about the Giants and New York City. But conditions were such we had to accept now or they might not be so favorable again."

12-Point Plan Offered

The twelve-point San Francisco plan includes construction of a stadium seating between 40,000 and 45,000. It will be rented to the Giants on a thirty-five-year lease. The rental was set by the city at 5 per cent of receipts after taxes and other deductions, with a minimum annual rental guarantee of $125,000 by the Giants.

Asked what forced the decision to move, Mr. Stoneham

said: "Lack of attendance. We're sorry to disappoint the kids of New York, but we didn't see many of their parents out there at the Polo Grounds in recent years."

He declined comment on the transfer of the Brooklyn Dodgers to Los Angeles, which has been hanging fire for months. But he did venture a prediction that both the National and American Leagues—and perhaps a third major league—would continue to expand westward.

Seals' Stadium Available

Warren C. Giles, the president of the National League, said that the Giants' move would in no way affect the Dodgers if the Brooklyn club decided to remain in New York.

"I have studied the language of the resolution concerning the moves (adopted by the league in May) and it was my understanding that either one or both could go," Mr. Giles said in Cincinnati. "While consent was given on a roll-call vote, that is the way I interpreted the language in my study of the resolution," he said.

Mayor Christopher, who has been the prime mover in promoting big league baseball for the West Coast, was on the phone to congratulate the Giants' directorate immediately after they had taken the action.

The Mayor said the contractors were hopeful that the new stadium could be completed by the opening of the 1958 season. But, he said, in the event it was not finished, the Giants could arrange the rental of the 22,000-seat Seals Stadium temporarily. The Mayor said the city had reached a tentative agreement with Paul Fagan, the owner of Seals Stadium, where the Pacific Coast League team has played for years.

Mr. Stoneham indicated that the club was willing to start the season in Seals Stadium and probably would move into its new Bayview Park home later in the year.

The director who voted against the move was M. Donald Grant, a partner in the Wall Street firm of Fahnestock & Co.

"It just tears my heart to see them go," said Mr. Grant. "I've been a Giant rooter all my life. Then, too, as a business man, I think they would do better staying here. I would rather have a National League franchise here than in any other city."

Mr. Grant said he couldn't see any sense in relinquishing New York to the Yankees, especially with four more years to go on the Polo Grounds lease. The Giants are obligated to pay $131,254.40 a year for rental and taxes there through 1961.

The directors voting for the transfer were Mr. Stoneham, his son, Charles H. (Petey) Stoneham, and his nephew, Charles S. (Chub) Feeney, vice presidents; Edgar P. Feeley, treasurer; Joseph J. Haggerty. Max Schneider, Dr. Anthony M. Palermo and Charles Aufderhar, Horace Stoneham's brother-in-law.

They undoubtedly were swayed by Mr. Stoneham's recent report to stockholders that he could assure an annual profit of $200,000 to $300,000 if the club moved to San Francisco. The Giants reportedly have lost money in all except two of the last eight years.

Proposal Is Outlined

Here is what San Francisco offered the Giants:

1. A new stadium seating from 40,000 to 45,000 in the Bayview Park area, south of San Francisco, to be constructed as to permit expansion if desired.

2. The city will operate and collect revenue from a parking area holding from 10,000 to 12,000 cars.

3. The Giants will operate and receive revenue from all concessions, including a club and restaurant similar to the Yankees' Stadium Club.

4. The Giants will have exclusive occupancy for roughly six months of the year, although the city may rent the stadium for special events when the team is on the road.

5. Rental shall be 5 per cent of gross receipts after deducting taxes, visiting clubs' and the National League's shares. The Giants are to guarantee a minimum of $125,000 against the rental.

6. The city shall equip the stadium with everything needed

for operation, including the lights for night games.

7. Office space will be provided for the Giant executives at the stadium.

8. The city will maintain the physical property, but the club is to pay for maintenance during the baseball season.

9. A thirty-five-year lease. Mayor Christopher said the city could not legally give an option now to renew this lease, but said he saw "no reason why a new lease cannot be negotiated" later.

10. Final plans for the stadium—to cost about $5,000,000—are subject to the Giants' approval. Other developments in the Bayview sector will cost at least another $5,000,000, the Mayor estimates.

11. The Giants will have exclusive advertising privileges on the stadium fences; the city will have the same under the stands.

12. The Mayor will appoint a Northern California Citizens Committee to promote the sale of season tickets before the 1958 season opens.

Damages Not Mentioned

The terms of San Francisco's offer were spelled out in a letter of intent signed by the Mayor and Francis McCarty, a member of the Board of Supervisors, which governs the City and County of San Francisco.

Mr. Stoneham had nothing to say about the amount of damages that the club and/or league will have to pay the Pacific Coast League for the invasion of its territory. It has been reported that this figure might be in the neighborhood of $1,000,000.

The Giants' president also declined comment on whether the club would indemnify the Boston Red Sox to move the San Francisco franchise, which the American League club owns. Some reports have stated that the Giants would pay $125,000 to have the Seals transferred, possibly to Salt Lake City. Other versions have the Giants trading their Minneapolis franchise to the Red Sox for full rights to San Francisco.

The promise of closed-circuit

television was a factor—"but not a big one," Mr. Stoneham said.

The Giants will play all day games in San Francisco, Mr. Stoneham said, with the exception of Tuesday and Friday nights. The spring and early summer nights are chill and damp in San Francisco—not to mention the traditional fog. A heating system will be installed in the stadium.

The club president also assured employes of the organization that they "will certainly be welcome" to accompany the team to San Francisco. He said he had not yet decided whether he and his family would move to the Coast.

Mr. Stoneham made it plain that the team—despite its 3,000-mile shift from the Harlem River—would still be called the Giants.

This probably afforded scant consolation to the faithful of Coogan's Bluff who have followed the team through its salad days—seventeen pennants, five world's championships—and its recent skim-milk diet.

Few teams in the history of baseball so captured the sports public's imagination as the Giants under the late John (Muggsy) McGraw. The team, first known as the Nationals, entered the National League in 1883, and has called the present Polo Grounds home since 1911.

Pennants were won in 1888, 1889, 1904, 1905, 1911, 1912, 1913, 1917, 1921, 1922, 1923, 1924, 1933, 1936, 1937, 1951, 1954. World series victories were recorded in 1905, 1921, 1922, 1933 and 1954.

Mr. McGraw managed the team from 1902 to 1932. Christy (Bix Six) Mathewson was the pitching nonpariel of the 1911-13 pennant winners. A decade later such stars as Frankie Frisch and Bill Terry were the mainstays of the team.

Mr. Terry succeeded Mr. McGraw and managed until 1941. Mel Ott, another Giant great, ran the team from 1941 to 1948. He was followed by Leo Durocher, who was the manager from 1948 to 1955. The incumbent, Bill Rigney, took over in 1955.

The transfer of the Giants will be the fourth—and farthest—move made by the major leagues in the last four years.

The Braves shifted from Boston to Milwaukee in 1953. The St. Louis Browns became the Baltimore Orioles in 1954 and the Athletics moved from Philadelphia to Kansas City in 1955.

All transfers have been successful financially, particularly in Milwaukee, which has set league attendance records.

San Francisco Giants

August 20, 1957

Spahn's 41st Shutout Sets Mark As Braves Subdue Cubs by 8-0

Milwaukee Hurler Tops Loop Record for Left-Handers— Aaron Belts No. 39

CHICAGO, Sept 3 (AP)—Warren Spahn pitched the pennant-bound Milwaukee Braves to a 8-0 victory over the Chicago Cubs today, registering the forty-first shutout of his career for a National League record for left-handers.

The 36-year-old hurler, rounding out thirteen years in the league, stifled the Cubs on six hits for his fourth blanking job of the season, his eighth straight decision and his eighteenth victory against eight defeats.

Spahn increased his shutout total over the previous record of forty, shared by Eppa Rixey and Larry French. The league record is ninety, set by a right-hander, Grover Cleveland Alexander.

The Braves were blanked for six innings by Dick Littlefield, who gave four hits and struck out seven in that span. However, he was blasted for five runs in the seventh inning, three of them unearned.

The Box Score

MILWAUKEE (N.)						CHICAGO (N.)					
	ab.	r.	h.	po.	a.		ab.	r.	h.	po.	a.
Schoen't,2b	3	1	1	4	4	Adams,3b	4	0	1	1	1
Jones,1b	4	2	3	8	1	Walls, lf	4	0	1	1	0
Mathews,3b	5	2	2	2	1	Moryn, rf	4	0	2	3	0
Aaron, cf	5	2	3	2	0	Banks, ss	4	0	1	0	6
Pafko, rf	4	0	0	1	0	Bolger, cf	4	0	0	2	0
Mantilla, ss	4	1	1	2	4	Long, 1b	3	0	0	7	0
Cov'ton, lf	4	0	1	1	0	Neeman, c	3	0	1	2	0
Crandall, c	5	1	0	6	1	Moryan, 2b	3	0	0	4	1
Spahn, p	5	0	0	1	0	Littlefield, p	3	0	0	0	2
						aKin ral	1	0	0	0	0
Total	39	8	11	27	11	Poholsky,p	0	0	0	0	1
						Total	32	0	6	27	4

aPopped out for Littlefield in eighth.

Milwaukee ....0 0 0 0 0 0 5 3 0—8
Chicago ....0 0 0 0 0 0 0 0 0—0

E—ror—Adams.
Runs batted in—Mathews. Aaron 4. Mantilla, Covington, Crandall.
Two-base hits—Schoendienst. Adams, Schoendienst and Jones. Left on bases—Milwaukee 10, Chicago 6. Bases on balls—Off Littlefield 6, Spahn 1. Struck out—By Littlefield 8, Spahn 5, Poholsky 1. Hits—Off Littlefield 11 in 8 innings, Poholsky 0 in 1. Runs and earned runs—Off Littlefield 8 and 5. Wild pitche—Littlefield. Winning pitcher—Spahn (18-8). Losing pitcher—Littlefield (5-2). Umpires—Delmore, Smith, Conlan and Donatelli. Time of game—2:31. Attendance—7,490.

In the eighth inning, Hank Aaron slammed his thirty-ninth homer of the year into the left-field seats with two on, to hike his runs-batted-in total to 118.

Spahn retired the first eleven men he faced and yielded the first Chicago hit, a blooper into short center by Walt Moryn, in the fourth.

September 4, 1957

DODGERS ACCEPT LOS ANGELES BID TO MOVE TO COAST

Team Will Play in California in '58 After Representing Brooklyn Since 1890

CITY TO SEEK NEW CLUB

Wagner Will Name Group to Get Replacement—Rights to Territory Uncertain

---

By EMANUEL PERLMUTTER

The Dodgers will play their baseball in Los Angeles next year.

The Brooklyn Baseball Club announced yesterday it was proceeding with the necessary steps to move to Los Angeles.

Warren C. Giles, president of the National League, hailed the Dodger move to the West Coast as proof of the league's "professional" nature. He said he and the league would miss New York, however.

Thus ended a colorful and often zany baseball era in Brooklyn. The Dodgers had represented Brooklyn in the National League since 1890. They had become world famous, first because of their erratic baseball and then because of their winning teams. In their flight to the Pacific, they join the New York Giants, who are moving to San Francisco.

Yankees Voice Regret

The Yankees, who will now have the New York baseball territory to themselves, issued a public statement of regret at the departure of the Dodgers.

"We are sorry to see the Dodgers go, and we wish them the best of luck in Los Angeles," Dan Topping, co-owner of the American League club, said. "Now that they have definitely gone, there are so many things to be considered that we will have no further comment until after the next American League and joint major league meetings in December."

Meanwhile, the Yankees have more pressing problems. They meet the Milwaukee Braves today at the Yankee Stadium in the sixth game of the world series. Bob Turley is scheduled to pitch for the Yankees and Bob Buhl for the National League club.

Club Sought Downtown Site

Upon learning of the Dodgers' decision to move, Mayor Wagner immediately announced at City Hall that he soon would appoint a committee of citizens to try to get another National League team for New York.

New York and Los Angeles had engaged in a tug-of-war for the Dodgers since early in the year. A plan by which the city hoped to condemn a slum area in downtown Brooklyn and build a stadium there collapsed when the cost of the over-all project was estimated at $30,-000,000. Offers by Nelson A. Rockefeller to help defray the costs also were fruitless.

The announcement of the Dodger move was cheered yesterday by residents of Los Angeles. Their City Council had approved an ordinance on Monday that embodies an agreement with the Brooklyn club.

The Los Angeles ordinance was officially signed last night by Mayor Norris Poulson, making it an official city statute. The signing took place in the Mayor's office, and was witnessed by the ten Councilmen who voted for it Monday. Four Councilmen had been opposed.

In Brooklyn, the news was received with mixed reaction. Business men in the vicinity of Ebbets Field, where the Dodgers had played since 1913, were hopeful that apartment houses would be built there and bring economic gain to the area. Fans interviewed generally felt the Dodger owners had bickered so long for a site that they had lost the esteem of Brooklyn rooters.

Cashmore Disappointed

Borough President John Cashmore expressed disappointment at the Dodgers' decision to leave. He said that he had worked hard to get the Dodgers to stay here and that he would "leave nothing undone" to get another team for Brooklyn.

Although both the Dodgers and the Giants are leaving because they assertedly feel the financial pickings are better in California, Brooklyn has been a profitable place for the Dodger owners.

The Dodgers have made more money in recent years than any other National League club. However, the Giants, who have finished poorly in the league standings, have suffered in gate receipts.

The end of New York as a National League baseball city was announced at 4 P. M. by

Team's Managers

Following is a list of Dodger managers since 1890:
1890—William McGunnigle
1891-92—John Montgomery Ward
1893-96—Dave Foutz
1897—William Barnie
1898—Barnie, Mike Griffin and C. H. Ebbets
1899-1905—Ned Hanlon
1906-8—Patsy Donovan
1909—Harry Lumley
1910-13—Bill Dahlen
1914-31—Wilbert Robinson
1932-33—Max Carey
1934-36—Casey Stengel
1937-38—Burleigh Grimes
1939-46—Leo Durocher
1947—Burt Shotton
1948—Durocher and Shotton
1949-50—Shotton
1951-53—Charlie Dressen
1954 to present—Walter Alston

---

publicity representatives for both the Dodgers and the league in the world series press room at the Waldorf-Astoria Hotel. Neither Mr. Giles, nor Walter F. O'Malley, the Dodger president, was present.

The Dodgers' statement was brief. It read:

"In view of the action of the Los Angeles City Council yesterday and in accordance with the resolution of the National League made Oct. 1, the stockholders and directors of the Brooklyn Baseball Club have today met and unanimously agreed that necessary steps be taken to draft the Los Angeles territory."

Mr. Giles issued the following statement:

"The National League has again demonstrated it is a professional organiaztion. The transfer of the Giants and the Dodgers means that two more great municipalities are to have major league baseball without depriving another city of that privilege.

"The National League, and I, personally, will miss New York, but it is only human nature to want to reach new horizons. We look forward to 1958, when National League baseball will be played on the West Coast."

A spokesman for Ford C. Frick, Commissioner of Baseball, announced that Mr. O'Malley had already filed with the commissioner his formal "notice of intent to acquire the Los Angeles territory for the purpose of operating a National League club therein."

"Following the rules of baseball, Mr. O'Malley's communication has been forwarded to the President of the Pacific Coast League, the president of the Los Angeles ball club, the president of the National Association of Professional Baseball Leagues and the president of the Ameri-

can League," Mr. Frick's statement concluded.

Before the Dodgers can start playing baseball in Los Angeles, they will have to iron out territorial rights to that area. At present, both Los Angeles and Hollywood have teams in the Pacific Coast League.

'58 Park Not Decided

Although the Dodgers own the Los Angeles team, they must reach an agreement with the minor league. Should they fail to reach an understanding, the matter will be settled by arbitration. The Giants must follow similar procedures in their move to San Francisco.

The question of which ball park the Dodgers will use next year is still undecided. Harold (Red) Patterson, assistant general manager and publicity man for the team, said it would be either Wrigley Field, the Los Angeles Coliseum, or both. The Dodgers own Wrigley Field, but its capacity is only 22,000.

Under terms of their agreement with Los Angeles, the Dodgers are to construct a $10,-000,000 stadium in Chavez Ravine, seating 50,000 persons. They will also give Wrigley Field to the city. However, the new stadium will not be ready next year.

The Dodger management said that the team would have spring training again next year at its Vero Beach, Fla., camp. However, the spring training schedule has not yet been worked out, the club added.

New York's official efforts to get a ball club to replace the Dodgers and the Giants may be impeded by the American League. Last week, the American League offered the National the borough of Queens as a future baseball site, reserving the other boroughs for itself. The matter is to be discussed at the December meeting of the two leagues in Colorado Springs.

Although Mayor Wagner has indicated that the city might be willing to build a stadium in Flushing Meadow Park, Queens, for use by a major league team, this might not prove as attractive as Manhattan, the Bronx or Brooklyn to an out-of-town prospect.

The Mayor was asked at his press conference yesterday whether he thought Mr. O'Malley had acted in good faith in his negotiations with the city.

"I can only say that in my conversations with him he said that he had no commitments, and I have to take the man's word," Mr. Wagner replied.

In another development, Gordon Gray, executive vice president and general manager of WOR-TV, which televised the Dodger games, announced that the station would return to its "regular programming schedule."

October 9, 1957

FANS ADDED ZEST TO LORE OF 'BUMS'

'Next Year,' the Watchword in Daffy Era, Came Often During Postwar Period

TEAM ENDED COLOR BAR

Rickey Brought First Negro Into Majors—Ebbets Built 'Dream' Field in 1913

By JOSEPH M. SHEEHAN

In deserting Brooklyn for Los Angeles, the Dodgers will leave an aching void in the Borough of Churches. Few baseball clubs have had greater identity with, and greater impact on, their communities than the Dodgers have had on Brooklyn.

A mention of New York seldom evokes a chain-of-idea response of "Giants" or "Yankees" such as Brooklyn does of "Dodgers."

Brooklyn basically has always been the city's dormitory and for sixty-odd years its major league ball club has been its principal claim to public attention.

Perhaps because of this situation, Brooklynites generally have raised louder hosannahs at Dodger successes and have taken Dodger failures harder than baseball fans in other cities.

It is peculiarly expressive of the Dodger fan's fierce devotion that he could scream from the Ebbets Field stands—and mean it—"Ya, bums, ya," without surrendering one iota of loyalty.

Bumblers Struck a Chord

Paradoxically, the Dodgers probably ranked highest in Brooklyn's native affections during the two decades of aimless floundering between their pennant victories of 1920 and 1941.

The zany antics of various lovable Dodger bumblers of this era struck a particularly responsive chord among Brooklyn's fanatical baseball followers. Brooklynites boasted about, rather than condemned, the Dodgers' hilarious basepath pile-ups and fielding blunders. And, at the end of each disappointing season, they would send out a defiant cry of "Wait till next year!"

There was a spontaneous enthusiasm to rooting for the Dodgers in those days that was not exceeded even in the club's golden era after World War II.

Dodgers Forsake Brooklyn for Los Angeles

Charles H. Ebbets

Ebbets Field, home grounds of the ball team, was built in 1913 by **Charles H. Ebbets,** who started with the club as an office boy and worked up to become president and owner.

Leo Durocher was beloved by the fans for his umpire-baiting. In 1941 he led team to its first pennant since 1920.

Team's emergence as front-runner began in 1938 under **Larry MacPhail,** left, and developed under **Branch Rickey's** aegis.

during which the Brooks captured six of twelve National League pennants and only twice sank as low as third place.

Brooklyn had obtained a National League franchise in 1890, after functioning for one season in the Interstate League and for six in the American Association.

That the team was nicknamed Dodgers was another expression of its identity with Brooklyn. The appellation derived from the fact that Brooklynites in general were jocularly called Trolley Dodgers because of the wide presence in the borough of the clanking streetcars.

First Season a Success

Such other team designations as Bridgegrooms, Superbas and Robins failed to survive and it is still as Dodgers that the team leaves its long-time home to join baseball's westward gold rush.

The Dodgers made a spectacular debut as a major league club. They won the National League pennant in their maiden season of 1890, under Bill McGunnigle. They also captured flags in 1899 and 1900, under Ned Haanlon, and in 1916 and 1920, under the beloved Wilbert Robinson.

But while later pickings were generally slim until Larry MacPhail and then Branch Rickey rehabilitated the franchise in the late Nineteen Thirties and early Forties, the Dodgers could never be charged with dullness.

In the worst Dodger years, the buoyant Brooklyn fans always had some rallying points for their loyalty—great stars who shone in adversity or amiable buffoons who won their hearts.

The team's first permanent home was the "new" Washington Park, between First and Third Streets and Third and Fourth Avenues in South Brooklyn. The Dodgers set up there after an unsuccessful 1893 venture into the fastnesses of East New York. This had followed their desertion of the original Washington Park, between Fourth and Fifth Avenues and Third and Fifth Streets.

An Ex-Office Boy's Dream

Dodger heroes of those early days included Willie Keeler, who "hit 'em where they ain't"; Hughie Jennings, Bill Dahlen, Fielder Jones, Joe McGinnity, Nap Rucker and Otto Miller.

In 1913, Charles H. Ebbets, who had started with the Dodgers as an office boy and worked his way up to club president and sole owner, realized a great dream. With financial help from the McKeevers—Steve and Ed—he built Ebbets Field.

The most glowing chapters in Brooklyn's baseball history were written in this now-outgrown park in upper Flatbush. This was the chief stamping ground of such Dodger immortals as Zack Wheat, Jake Daubert, Casey Stengel, Dazzy Vance, Burleigh Grimes, Babe Herman,

Season Records Since 1890

The following table shows how many games the Dodgers won and lost, the team's percentage and where it finished each year since it began competing in the National League:

	W.	L.	Pct.	Fin.		W.	L.	Pct.	Fin.
1890	86	43	.667	1	1926	71	82	.464	6
1891	61	76	.445	6	1927	65	88	.425	6
1892	95	59	.617	3	1928	77	76	.503	6
1893	65	63	.508	6	1929	70	83	.458	6
1894	70	61	.534	5	1930	86	68	.558	4
1895	71	60	.542	*5	1931	79	73	.520	4
1896	58	73	.443	*9	1932	81	73	.526	3
1897	61	71	.462	*6	1933	65	88	.425	6
1898	54	91	.372	10	1934	71	81	.467	6
1899	88	42	.677	1	1935	70	83	.458	5
1900	82	54	.603	1	1936	67	87	.435	7
1901	79	57	.581	3	1937	62	91	.405	6
1902	75	63	.543	2	1938	69	80	.463	7
1903	70	66	.515	5	1939	84	69	.549	3
1904	56	97	.366	6	1940	88	65	.575	2
1905	48	104	.316	8	1941	100	54	.649	1
1906	66	86	.434	5	1942	104	50	.675	2
1907	65	83	.439	5	1943	81	72	.529	3
1908	53	101	.344	7	1944	63	91	.409	7
1909	55	98	.359	6	1945	87	67	.565	3
1910	64	90	.416	6	1946	96	60	.615	†2
1911	64	86	.427	7	1947	94	60	.610	1
1912	58	95	.379	7	1948	84	70	.545	3
1913	65	84	.436	6	1949	97	57	.630	1
1914	75	79	.487	5	1950	89	65	.578	2
1915	80	72	.526	3	1951	97	60	.618	‡2
1916	94	60	.610	1	1952	96	57	.627	1
1917	70	81	.464	7	1953	105	49	.682	1
1918	57	69	.452	5	1954	92	62	.597	2
1919	69	71	.493	5	1955	98	55	.641	1
1920	93	61	.604	1	1956	93	61	.604	1
1921	77	75	.507	5	1957	84	70	.545	3
1922	76	78	.494	6					
1923	76	78	.494	6	*Tie for place.				
1924	92	62	.597	*2	†Lost first-place play-off to				
1925	68	85	.444	*6	St. Louis, 2 games to 0.				

‡Lost first-place play-off to New York, 2 games to 1.

Jacques Fournier, Lefty O'Doul and many others.

Here, Brooklyn fans suffered with Uncle Robbie, who had to make do with inferior player personnel after 1920. Here, too, they commiserated with Max Carey, Stengel and Grimes, who had no better managerial luck, with the club's meager financial resources largely tied up in estate settlements.

Then, in 1938, the ebullient MacPhail took charge as general manager. He introduced night baseball, initiated play-by-play radio broadcasting of Dodger games, hired Babe Ruth as a coach and bought new talent.

Leo Durocher became playing-manager the following season. Durocher's brawling, scrapping Dodgers, featuring such acquisitions as Dixie Walker, Dolph Camilli, Joe Medwick, Whit Wyatt, Kirby Higbe, Hugh Casey and Mickey Owen and bolstered by such young stars as Pete Reiser and Pee Wee Reese, fought their way up in the standings.

Finally, to great rejoicing in 1941, they brought Brooklyn its first pennant in twenty-one years.

During World War II, MacPhail left Brooklyn, never to return. Rickey succeeded him in front-office command and patiently filled the player pipelines with young talent that was to bring Brooklyn baseball riches that surpassed the fondest dreams of Flatbush.

9 Pennants Won

The following table shows how the Dodgers have fared in their nine world series. The winning team is listed first. The numbers in parentheses indicate the games won by each team:

1916—Boston A.L., 4....vs. Brooklyn N.L., 1
1920—Cleveland A.L., 5...vs. Brooklyn N.L., 2
1941—New York A.L., 4....vs. Brooklyn N.L., 1
1947—New York A.L., 4....vs. Brooklyn N.L., 3
1949—New York A.L., 4....vs. Brooklyn N.L., 1
1952—New York A.L., 4....vs. Brooklyn N.L., 3
1953—New York A.L., 4....vs. Brooklyn N.L., 2
1955—Brooklyn N.L., 4....vs. New York A.L., 3
1956—New York A.L., 4....vs. Brooklyn N.L., 3

The final catalytic agent in the Dodgers' postwar rise to National League dominance was Rickey's daring breach of the color line. He brought Jackie Robinson up to the Dodgers in 1947. Roy Campanella and Don Newcombe soon followed.

These outstanding Negro players, plus Reese and such Rickey farm-system products as Gil Hodges, Duke Snider, Carl Furillo, Carl Erskine and Clem Labine, provided a nucleus that made the Dodgers the scourge of the league.

This team won pennants for Durocher, for Burt Shotton, for Charley Dressen and for Walter Alston. In 1955, sixty-five years after becoming a major league team, the Dodgers defeated the Yankees in a seven-game series to bring home Brooklyn's first world championship.

October 9, 1957

Braves Beat Yanks, 5-0, to Win Series

Burdette Hurls 7-Hit Shutout in 7th Game for His 3d Victory

By JOHN DREBINGER

Milwaukee, which less than five years ago didn't even boast a major league club, bestrides the baseball universe today.

Manager Fred Haney's Braves, playing inspired ball behind another brilliant pitching effort by their tireless Lew Burdette, smothered the supposedly invincible Yankees, 5 to 0, in the seventh and deciding world series game at the Stadium yesterday.

The victory, generously cheered by a gathering of 61,-207 as Burdette gained his third mound triumph of the classic, gave the National Leaguers the series, 4 games to 3. It brought to Milwaukee a world championship in its first crack at the title.

Inversely, it wound up a damaging campaign for New York. In little more than a month Old Gotham had lost two ball clubs, the Dodgers and Giants. Yesterday it was shorn of the world series crown it had held, with one or another of its three entries, since 1949.

Takes It From Both Sides

One sharp, decisive four-run thrust in the third inning yesterday gave the Milwaukeans a stranglehold they never relinquished. There just wasn't a thing the inexhaustible baseball brain of Casey Stengel could do about it.

Haney, a one-time pint-sized infielder who was appearing in a world series for the first time, had Stengel licked from the start of the game.

A costly error by Tony Kubek, rookie star of the Bombers during the earlier stages of the series, opened the gates for the Braves in the third. Before the inning was over, Don Larsen, Casey's starting pitcher, had been put to rout.

The big fellow, hero of last year's epic perfect game against the Dodgers, had been carefully groomed for this one. But he couldn't weather the punishment he took from both sides.

Eddie Mathews unloaded a two-run two-bagger. Bobby Shantz replaced Larsen, but the Braves rolled on. Hank Aaron and Wes Covington singled. Before the little Yankee southpaw

Associated Press Wirephoto

Fans at home in Milwaukee show their appreciation for Burdette, the winning pitcher, and Mathews, who starred at bat and in the field.

could stem the tide, four runs were in and the American Leaguers were about out on their feet.

For good measure and by way of giving his team additional security, Del Crandall, Burdette's catcher, dropped a home run into the left-field stand in the eighth. But that shot was not needed.

For by then one Selva Lewis Burdette Jr., 30-year-old right-hander and one-time farm hand in the Yankee chain, was putting the finishing touches to one of the most astounding exhibitions of sustained pitching mastery in more than a half-century of world series competition.

Burdette vanquished the Yankees in the second game, 4 to 2, last Thursday in New York. Last Monday in Milwaukee he shut them out, 1 to 0, in the fifth game to put the Braves in front. Yesterday, with his second dazzling shutout after only two days of rest, he completed a stretch of twenty-four scoreless innings. In the twenty-seven innings of his three complete games he allowed only two runs.

Only one hurler, perhaps the greatest of all, topped this. In 1905, the immortal Christy Mathewson rolled up twenty-seven innings of scoreless hurling to win three shutouts for the Giants.

Seven 3-Game Winners

Burdette yesterday became the seventh pitcher to gain three victories in a world series. The last was Harry Brecheen in 1946. But the Cardinal southpaw gained one in a relief role.

Four, besides Burdette, posted three complete-game victories. They were Mathewson, Jack Coombs of the Philadelphia Athletics in 1910, Babe Adams of the Pittsburgh Pirates in 1909 and Stanley Coveleskie of the Cleveland Indians in 1920.

The only other pitcher to win three games was Urban Faber of the Chicago White Sox in 1917. But in one of his triumphs he was removed for a relief hurler.

For Milwaukee, of course, yesterday easily was the day of days. That metropolis, home of the brew, the Braves and the finest of cheeses, doubtless will remain in a daze for some time to come.

Milwaukee entered the National League officially on March 18, 1953, when Owner Lou Perini moved his Braves from Boston. It was the first franchise shift in the senior league in more than half a century.

The transfer started a chain of upheavals. The Athletics moved from Philadelphia to Kansas City, the Browns from

St. Louis to Baltimore, where they became the Orioles, and next year will see the New York Giants playing in San Francisco and the Brooklyn Dodgers in Los Angeles.

Four seasons of frustration followed the shift to Milwaukee. The Braves, despite a tremendous improvement from their sixth-place finish in Boston, were second in 1953, third in 1954, and second again the next two years. The 1956 season was the most bitter disappointment, for Haney's men let the pennant slip away in the last few days.

Sixth Yankee Setback

For New York, defeat perhaps was not too difficult to take. Seventeen times in the past have the Yankees brought the title here. This was only their sixth series setback.

For Stengel the defeat was only his second in his nine seasons as manager of the Bombers. He has been the winner six times.

He fought hard to save this one. In desperation he even returned Mickey Mantle to action in a surprise move. The Oklahoma slugger had gone to the sidelines with a shoulder injury after the fourth game and almost everyone thought he had made his last appearance save for a possible role as pinch-hitter.

But there he was, out in center field, playing the entire game. He singled for one of the seven hits permitted by Burdette.

Even Bill Skowron, out since the first game with a lame back, got into it in the closing innings.

The Braves, on the other hand, played without their wounded. Red Schoendienst, crippled in the fifth game with a groin injury, remained on the sidelines. Warren Spahn sat it out in the bullpen. The ace lefty was to have hurled this game but had to be sidetracked because of a mild influenza attack on Wednesday.

The incredible Burdette, however, needed no help once the Yankees let the game fall apart in the third inning.

Larsen had just retired his mound adversary, Burdette, on a foul back of third for the first out in the fateful inning when Bob Hazle, a rookie outfielder, stroked a "wrong field" single to left. Then came a play that doubtless will remain seared in Stengel's amazing memory through many a wintry night.

Peg to Second Wide

For the player who gummed it up had been the apple of Casey's eye all season—the brilliant and versatile Kubek. Tony had started the series last week at third, then switched to left field and center when Mantle went out of action. With Mantle back in center, Tony was on third again and that's where all the trouble started.

Johnny Logan slammed a grounder at Kubek. It looked like a sure-fire double play. But Tony's peg to second was wide. It pulled Jerry Coleman off the bag and there was no out there.

Desperately, Jerry fired the ball to first in an effort to get at least one man. But Logan beat the throw and the Braves, instead of having been retired, had two on with one out.

It reminded one of what Uncle Wilbert Robinson of early Brooklyn baseball vintage, once described as the "phantom double play."

A moment later Mathews lined a two-bagger down the right-field foul line. Before the ball could be brought back to the infield both Hazle and Logan had scored. That was all for the crestfallen Larsen. Shantz went in.

Aaron, one of the Braves' top hitters in the series, punched a single into center and Mathews scored. Covington singled to left, sending Hank to third. Then when the Yanks failed to complete a double play by way of second base on Frank Torre's grounder to Coleman, Aaron streaked home with the fourth tally.

After that nothing really mattered as Burdette kept firing his bewildering assortment of screwballs, sliders and sinkers.

So perfect was his control he walked only one batter, and that was intentional. It came after Hank Bauer had opened the Yankee first inning by belting Burdette's first pitch for a double.

This gave Hank the distinction of having connected in fourteen consecutive games for a world series record. Bauer had hit in each of the seven games in last October's classic.

He topped by one the former mark of thirteen games held jointly by Frank Schulte of the Cubs fifty years ago and Harry Hooper of the Red Sox of 1915, 1916 and 1918. To add luster to the performance was the fact that the Yanks' ex-Marine had compiled his mark in only two series.

However, nothing else came of this blow even though there was a slight mix-up by the Braves on the next play. Enos Slaughter grounded to Burdette. This hung up Bauer between second and third.

But the Brave inner defense didn't play well and Hank scrambled back to second. However, the situation still was saved for Milwaukee since by then Slaughter had ambled down to second and so was an easy out.

Mantle, taking his first turn at bat since the tenth inning of the fourth game, then went out on a grounder to the mound. Yogi Berra was intentionally passed and Gil McDougald ended the inning with an infield pop-up.

Following the four-run third, Art Ditmar and Tom Sturdivant held the Braves scoreless

for two innings apiece and Tommy Byrne did well enough in the last two.

But in the eighth, with two out and the bases empty, Byrne was guilty of one errant pitch. Crandall lifted it into the left-field seats, the ball just going beyond Slaughter's frantic reach.

After the Yanks' brief first-inning splurge, they didn't get a man on base until Coleman singled in the fifth.

In the sixth the Bombers made another bid, which didn't get started until two were out. Here Mantle singled and Mathews fumbled Berra's grounder. But McDougald then grounded to Mathews, who this time froze to the ball.

Game to the end, the Bombers made a despairing effort to break through Burdette in the last of the ninth. With one away, McDougald flied out. After Kubek flied out, Coleman out-galloped an infield tap for his second hit.

Byrne then smashed a hard grounder over second base. It threatened to ruin Burdette's shutout. But Felix Mantilla, again substituting at second for Schoendienst, threw himself headlong at the ball and blocked its path. It was a hit, but merely filled the bases. The Yanks still were looking for a run. Skowron banged a sharp one-hopper down the third-base line. Mathews scooped it up, stepped on third and the series was over.

A record attendance of 394,-712 was set for a seven-game series. This topped the former mark of 389,763 set by the Yankees and Dodgers in 1947. The total receipts, exclusive of revenues from radio and television, reached $2,475,978, also a record.

But perhaps its greatest record was the bringing of the first world championship to what could well develop into the most fanatic baseball center in the nation. At least it has given the newcomers, Los Angeles and San Francisco, something to shoot at.

On March 15, 1953, when the prospect of Milwaukee getting the Braves' franchise was still a rumor, a crowd of 15,000, unmindful of wind and snow, gathered at Milwaukee's Municipal Stadium. They undoubtedly dreamed of the day when perhaps they might win a pennant and world series. Last night in that sizzling midwestern metropolis that dream came true.

Back in 1914 another Braves' team made history. That was when the "Miracle Braves" came out of the National League cellar on July 4 to win the pennant and then down the then formidable Athletics four straight in the world series. But that was out of Boston. Thirty-nine years later Boston was to give up on the Braves.

Now Milwaukee rules the roost. It will be many a year before they'll forget the pitching of Lew Burdette.

SEVENTH GAME

MILWAUKEE BRAVES

	AB.	R.	H.	PO.	A.
Hazle, rf	4	1	2	3	0
dPafko, rf	1	0	0	0	0
Logan, ss	5	1	1	2	4
Mathews, 3b	4	1	1	3	4
Aaron, cf	5	1	2	3	0
Covington, lf	3	0	1	2	0
Torre, 1b	4	0	0	8	0
Mantilla, 2b	4	0	0	2	0
Crandall, c	4	1	2	4	0
Burdette, p	2	0	0	0	3
Total	34	5	9	27	11

NEW YORK YANKEES

	AB.	R.	H.	PO.	A.
Bauer, rf	4	0	1	2	0
Slaughter, lf	4	0	0	2	0
Mantle, cf	4	0	1	2	0
Berra, c	3	0	0	4	1
McDougald, ss	4	0	1	2	1
Kubek, 3b	4	0	1	3	4
Coleman, 2b	4	0	2	4	3
Collins, 1b	1	0	0	5	0
Sturdivant, p	0	0	0	0	0
cHoward	1	0	0	0	0
Byrne, p	1	0	1	0	0
Larsen, p	0	0	0	0	1
Shantz, p	0	0	0	0	0
aLumpe	1	0	0	0	0
Ditmar, p	0	0	0	0	0
bSkowron, 1b	3	0	0	3	2
Total	35	0	7	27	12

aStruck out for Shantz in third.
bHit into force out for Ditmar in fifth.
cStruck out for Sturdivant in seventh.
dFouled out for Hazle in eighth.

Milwaukee ......004 000 010—5
New York ......000 000 000—0

Errors—Kubek, McDougald, Berra, Mathews.

Runs batted in—Mathews 2, Aaron, Torre, Crandall.

Two-base hits—Bauer, Mathews.

Home run—Crandall.

Sacrifices — Covington, Burdette, Mathews.

Double play—McDougald, Coleman and Skowron.

Left on bases—Milwaukee 8, New York 9.

Bases on balls — Off Larsen 1 (Torre), Byrne 2 (Torre, Burdette), Burdette 1 (Berra).

Strike outs—By Larsen 2 (Hazle, Mathews), Ditmar 1 (Burdette), Sturdivant 1 (Aaron), Burdette 3 (Collins, Lumpe, Howard).

Hits—Off Larsen 3 in 2⅓ innings, Shantz 2 in ⅔, Ditmar 1 in 2, Sturdivant 2 in 2, Byrne 1 in 2.

Runs and earned runs—Off Larsen 3 and 2, Shantz 1 and 0, Byrne 1 and 1.

Losing pitcher—Larsen.

Umpires—McKinley (A), plate; Donatelli (N), first base; Paparella (A), second base; Conlan (N), third base; Secory (N), left field; Chylak (A), right field.

Time of game—2:34.

Attendance—61,207.

October 11, 1957

Dodgers, Behind Erskine, Beat Giants

STARTER CREDITED WITH 6-5 VICTORY

Labine Relieves Erskine in 9th as Dodgers Triumph—Sauer Poles 2 Homers

By LAWRENCE E. DAVIES
Special to The New York Times

LOS ANGELES, April 18—Carl Erskine waited nineteen months and traveled 3,000 miles from Ebbets Field to California for his revenge against the Giants. He got it today.

The dean of the Dodgers pitching corps led the Los Angeles National League baseball club, formerly the Brooks, to a 6-to-5 victory over the San Francisco Giants in dedicating the Los Angeles Coliseum to major league ball.

He was not in at the end, having been replaced by Clem

Labine at the start of the ninth inning, but he got credit for the victory in the Dodgers' first game in their adopted city.

Allan Worthington started for the Giants. He was replaced in the fifth by Mike McCormick, who gave way in the next inning to Johnny Antonelli. Marvin Grissom was sent to the mound in the eighth to finish the game. The defeat was charged to Worthington.

A crowd of 78,672 turned out under a smoggy sky, through which, however, the sun broke without much trouble.

Three home runs, two from the bat of Hank Sauer, Giant outfielder, crashed over or to the right of the forty-two-foot left-field screen 250 feet from home plate.

The Dodgers' third baseman, Dick Gray, accounted for the third.

The old Polo Grounders started out as if they were determined to win their third game of the season against their old rivals. The Giants took the opening series in their new home town, two games to one.

Davenport Hits Double

The Giants began the scoring

in the third. With two out. Davenport collected his sixth successive hit in two days, a single. Kirkland sent him to third with a double and Willie Mays walked, filling the bases. Daryl Spencer drew a pass from Erskine, letting Davenport score.

In their half of the third the Dodgers took a one-run lead. Jim Gilliam walked and went to second when Pee Wee Reese grounded out. With the crowd demanding action, Duke Snider singled to center. The clout went through Mays, against whom an error was recorded, and Gilliam scored while Snider went to second. The Duke tallied on a single by Charley Neal to right center.

The Giants tied it at 2 to 2 in the fourth inning hit by Sauer, but the Dodgers retaliated with three runs in the fifth.

Gil Hodges, who had struck out on his first two trips to the plate, flied out to right field. Neal, up next, walked and went to second on Gray's single. Gino Cimoli hit into right and Willie Kirkland rifled the ball to the plate, but Bob Schmidt. catching for the Giants, dropped the ball.

Neal and Gray scored before it was recovered. Cimoli added the inning's third score after a wild pitch. He had advanced to third base on a fielder's choice.

The Dodgers scored their final tally in the seventh on Gray's homer, a mighty blow to the right of the now famous left-field screen.

Schmidt Wallops Triple

The San Franciscans collected one each in the sixth, eighth and ninth innings. Schmidt tripled to center in the sixth and scored on a passed ball. In the eighth Sauer got his second home run, one that zoomed clear over the left field screen.

The Giants' ninth inning began with a double by Davenport to the le corner.

Manager Walter Alston of the Angelenos took out Erskine at that point and sent Labine to the slab. Kirkland hit almost to the 430-foot mark in dee, center, but Davenport, en route home, was called out for not touching third base. Kirkland scored on Mays' single and a bad throw.

This was the first time Erskine had faced the Giants since Sept. 7, 1956, when he lost a 6 to 2 engagement at Ebbets Field. Not since May 12 of that year had he beaten the former New Yorkers. That was a 3-to-0 no-hitter. He did not pitch against the Giants last season, when an ailing arm bothered him and he ended with a record of five victories and three defeats.

SAN FRANCISCO (N.)				LOS ANGELES (N.)			
	ab.	r.	h.	rbi			
Davenport, 3b..	5	1	3	0	Gilliam, lf.....3	1	0	0
Kirkland, rf ..	5	1	3	0	Reese, ss.....4	0	1	0
Mays, cf..	4	0	2	0	Snider, rf.....5	1	2	1
Spencer, ss. 2b.	4	0	0	1	Furillo, rf.....0	0	0	0
Cepeda, 1b...	4	0	0	0	Hodges, 1b....4	0	0	0
Sauer, lf	4	2	2	2	Neal, 2b.....3	1	2	1
Schmidt, c ...	3	1	2	0	Gray, 3b.....3	2	2	1
O'Connel, 2b	2	0	0	0	Cimoli, cf.....3	1	1	1
bKing	0	0	0	0	Roseboro, c....1	0	0	0
Bressoud, 2b	0	0	0	0	aJackson 1	0	0	0
eLockman ...	0	0	0	0	Pignatano, c....1	0	0	0
W'rthingt'n, p.	2	0	0	0	Erskine, p.....4	0	0	0
McCormick, p.	0	0	0	0				
cSpeake	1	0	0	0	Total 32	6	8	4
dGomez	0	0	0	0				
fJablonski ..	1	0	0	0				
Rogers, ss...	0	0	0	0				
Antonelli, p...	0	0	0	0				
Grissom, p ...	0	0	0	0				
Total	35	5	12	3				

aGrounded out for Roseboro in fifth.
bWalked for O'Connell in sixth.
cStruck out for McCormick in sixth.
dRan for King in sixth.
eSacrificed for Bressoud in eighth.
fStruck out for Antonelli in eighth.
San Francisco ......0 0 1 1 0 1 0 1 1—5
Los Angeles ....6 0 2 0 3 0 1 0 .—6
Errors—Mays, Gray, Schmidt, Reese. Assists—San Francisco 7, Los Angeles 9. Double plays—Erskine and Neal; Gray, Neal and Hodges. Left on bases—San Francisco 8, Los Angeles 9. Two-base hits—Kirkland, Davenport. Three-base hits—Schmidt, Kirkland. Home runs—Sauer 2, Gray. Stolen base—Neal. Sacrifice—Lockman.

	IP.	H.	R.	ER.	BB.	SO.
Worthington (L., 0—1)	4⅓	7	5	3	5	4
Erskine (W., 1—0) ...	8	10	4	4	4	6
McCormick	⅓	0	0	0	0	0
Antonelli	2	1	1	1	2	0
Grissom	1	0	0	0	0	0
Labine	1	2	1	1	0	0

Wild pitch—McCormick, Erskine. Umpires—Venson, Conlon, Secory and Dixon. Time of game—3:00. Attendance—78,672.

April 19, 1958

Haddix Hurls 12 Perfect Innings But Loses to Milwaukee in 13th

Pirate Southpaw Retires 36 in Row—Double by Adcock Wins for Braves, 2 to 0

By United Press International.

MILWAUKEE, May 26 — Harvey Haddix of the Pittsburgh Pirates pitched twelve perfect innings tonight but lost in the thirteenth. The first hit he yielded, to Joe Adcock, gave a 2-0 victory to the Milwaukee Braves.

Haddix, who retired thirty-six men in a row, became the first major league pitcher to carry a perfect performance past nine innings.

Seven major league pitchers have hurled, and won, nine-inning perfect games. Don Larsen of the Yankees did it most recently, in the 1956 world series against the Dodgers. The longest previous no-hitter, eleven innings, dated back to Oct. 4, 1884. It was pitched by Edward J. Kinber of Brooklyn against Toledo.

Felix Mantilla was the first man to face the slender, 33-year-old curveball specialist in the thirteenth. He hit a grounder to the Pirates' third baseman, Don Hoak, who threw into the dirt at the feet of the first baseman, Rocky Nelson.

Mantilla was safe on the throwing error. Haddix' perfect string was snapped but the no-hitter was intact.

Ed. Mathews, the next man up, sacrificed the fleet Mantilla to second. Hank Aaron, the major' leading batter, received an intentional base on balls.

Then Adcock connected. The hit barely cleared the right-center-field fence and the big first baseman hesitated a moment before starting around the bases. Then two boys crawled under the barricade and snatched the ball.

Adcock at first was credited with a home run, and the final score was announced as 3—0. But then he was declared out for passing Aaron between second and third base and his home run became a double. The jubilant Aaron, who had cut across the diamond without touching third, was sent back by his mates to touch third and then home.

Confusion developed immediately after Adcock's blow cleared the fence. The umpires stopped the action as players swarmed out on the field. Aaron and

Associated Press
Harvey Haddix

Mantilla were ordered to retrace their steps and cross the plate. It was not until some minutes after the game was over that Umpire Frank Dascoli handed down his ruling on the play.

The putout of Adcock was Skinner lined out to Adcock with men on first and third and third and two out.

The National League president. Warren Giles, said later in Cincinnati that he believed the final score of the game eventually would be changed by official ruling to 1—0.

Giles said he could make "no official ruling" until he studied reports on the game. but expressed the opinion that only the number of runs sufficient to win the game for Milwaukee should have been allowed to count by the umpires.

Until his downfall in the thirteenth Haddix had used a fast ball that was always on target and a curve that cleverly nipped the corners. The closest thing to a base hit during the regulation nine innings was Johnny Logan's line drive in the third that the shortstop, Dick Schofield, speared on a leaping catch. Haddix fanned eight men.

Virdon Hauls Down Drives

In the eleventh inning, both Wes Covington and Del Crandall sent towering drives to center field that the center center field that Bill Virdon hauled down at the fence.

Haddix' loss was his third this season and the toughest in baseball history.

Several pitchers have gone nine hitless innings and then lost the game in extra innings · among them Bobo Newsom of the old St. Louis Browns in 1934. Tom Hughes of the

Yankees in 1910, Leon Ames of the Giants in 1909 and Earl Moore of the Indians in 1901.

Fred Toney of the Reds and Jim Vaughn of the Cubs matched hitless pitching for nine innings on May 2, 1917. Toney won when the Reds pushed across a run in the tenth.

Lew Burdette went the route for the Braves. He won his eighth game of the season against two losses, allowing twelve hits, walking none, and striking out two batters.

The Pirates bunched three hits in the third inning, two of them infield singles, but failed to score. They got two hits in the ninth inning but again failed to push across a run. Bob Skinner lined out to the first baseman, Adcock, with men on first and third and two out.

Haddix, a native of Medway, Ohio, was obtained last winter by the Pirates in a deal with the Cincinnati Reds. He won eight games and lost seven with the Reds last season.

He broke in with the St. Louis Cardinals in 1952 and in 1953 had his best record in the majors—twenty victories and nine losses with a 3.06 earned-run average.

He had an 18-13 record the next year but slumped to 12-16 in 1955 and the Cardinals traded him to the Phillies on May 11, 1956. He had a 13-8 record that season, and was 10—13 with the Phillies in 1957.

The box scores:

PITTSBURGH (N.)					MILWAUKEE (N.)				
	ab.	r.	h.	rbi.		ab.	r.	h.	rbi.
Schofield, ss	.6	0	3	0	O'Brien, 2b	..3	0	0	0
Virdon, cf	..6	0	1	0	bRice	1	0	0	0
Burgess, c	..5	0	0	0	Mantilla, 2b	.1	0	0	0
Nelson, 1b	.5	0	2	0	Mathews, 3b	.4	0	0	0
Skinner, lf	..5	0	1	0	Aaron, rf	4	1	0	0
Mazeroski, 2b	.5	0	1	0	Adcock, 1b	..5	0	1	2
Hoak, 3b	...5	0	2	0	Covington, lf	.4	0	0	0
Mejias, rf	..3	0	1	0	Crandall, c	..4	0	0	0
aStuart	1	0	0	0	Pafko, lf	...4	0	0	0
Christopher, f	.1	0	0	0	Logan, ss	...4	0	0	0
Haddix, p	...5	0	1	0	Burdette, p	..4	0	0	0
Total	47	0	12	0	Total	...38	2	1	2

aFlied out for Mejias in 10th; bFlied out for O'Brien in 10th.

Pittsburgh .0 00 000 000 000 0—0
Milwaukee .0 00 000 000 000 2—2

Two out when winning runs scored.
E—Hoak. A—Pittsburgh 13, Milwaukee 21. DP—Logan and Adcock; Mathews, O'Brien, Adcock; Adcock, Logan. LOB—Pittsburgh 8, Milwaukee 0.
2B Hit—Adcock. Sacrifice—Mathews.

	IP.	H.	R.	ER.	BB.	SO.
Haddix (L, 3—3)	..12⅔	1	2	1	0	8
Burdette (W, 8—2)	..13	12	0	0	0	2

Umpires—Smith, Dascoli, Secory, Dixon.
Time—2:54. Attendance—19,194.

May 27, 1959

Indians' Colavito Hits 4 Homers Against Orioles

RECORD EQUALED IN 11-8 CONTEST

Colavito 8th Major Leaguer to Get 4 Homers in Game —Bell Indians' Victor

BALTIMORE, June 10 (AP) —Cleveland's Rocky Colavito tied a major league record of four home runs in a game as the Indians beat the Baltimore Orioles, 11—8, tonight.

The young outfielder now has eighteen homers for the season. He is the eighth major leaguer to hit four homers in a game and the sixth of the modern (post-1900) era. The last to do it was Joe Adcock of the Milwaukee Braves on July 31, 1954.

Only two other American Leaguers had done it — Lou Gehrig of the New York Yankees in 1932 and Pat Seerey of the Chicago White Sox in 1948. National Leaguers who have hit four homers in a game, in addition to Adcock, are Bobby Lowe of the Boston Nationals in 1894, Ed Delehanty of the Philadelphia Nationals in 1896, Chuck Klein of the Philadelphia Phillies in 1936 and Gil Hodges of the Brooklyn Dodgers in 1950. Only Lowe, Gehrig and Colavito hit the homers in consecutive times at bat.

Klaus Drives In 3

After walking in the first inning, Colavito hit homers in the third inning with a man on against Jerry Walker, in the fifth with none on and the sixth with one on against Arnie Portocarrero and in the ninth with none on against Ernie Johnson. Colavito drove in six runs.

By winning, the third-place Indians moved to within a half-game of the second-place Orioles. Gary Bell was the victor although he was driven out in the seventh. In that inning, trailing by 10—3, the Orioles scored four runs, three on Billy Klaus' double off Mike Garcia.

CLEVELAND (A.)					BALTIMORE (A.)				
	ab.	r.	h.	rbi.		ab.	r.	h.	rbi.
Held, ss	...5	1	1	0	Pearson, cf	..3	1	2	0
Power, 1b	...4	1	0	0	Pilarcik, rf	..5	1	1	2
Francona, cf	.5	2	2	1	Woodling, lf	.5	1	3	1
Colavito, rf	.4	5	4	6	Triandos, c	..2	0	1	0
Minoso, lf	...5	1	3	3	Ginsberg, c	..1	1	0	0
Jones, 3b	...3	0	0	0	Hale, 1b	...3	0	0	0
Strickland, 3b	.2	0	1	0	Zuverink, p	...0	0	0	0
Brown, c	...4	0	1	0	bBoyd	1	0	0	0
Martin, 2b	...3	1	1	1	Johnson, p	...0	0	0	0
aWebster, 2b	.1	0	0	0	cNieman	...1	1	1	0
Bell, p	3	0	0	0	Klaus, 3b	..5	0	2	4
Garcia, p	1	0	0	0	Carrasquel, ss	.5	0	0	0
					Garnder, 2b	..4	1	1	0
Total	. 40	11	13	11	Walker, p	...1	1	1	0
					Portocar'ro, p	.1	0	0	0
					Lockman, 1b	..1	1	0	0
					Total	...38	8	12	8

aPopped up for Martin in 7th; bFlied out for Zuverink in 7th; cDoubled for Johnson in 9th.

Cleveland ....3 1 2 013 001—11
Baltimore ....1 2 0 000 401— 8

E—None. A—Cleveland 6, Baltimore 9. LOB —Cleveland 5, Baltimore 8.
2B Hits—Brown, Held, Francona, Klaus, Nieman. HR—Minoso, Martin, Colavito 4. SB—Minoso. Sacrifice Fly—Triandos.

	IP.	H.	R.	ER.	BB.	SO.
Bell (W, 5—5)	....6⅓	8	7	7	4	3
Garcia	.........2⅔	4	1	1	0	0
Walker (L, 4—3)	..2⅓	4	6	6	1	4
Portocarrero	....3⅓	7	4	4	1	3
Zuverink	.........1⅓	0	0	0	0	0
Johnson	2	2	1	1	0	0

Umpires—Summers, McKinley, Soar, Chylak.
Time—2:54. Attendance—15,883.

June 11, 1959

National Leaguers Beat American on Mays' Triple in 8th of All-Star Game

ANTONELLI VICTOR IN 5-TO-4 CONTEST

Giants' Southpaw Wins for National Leaguers After Face Is Routed in 8th

By JOHN DREBINGER
Special to The New York Times.

PITTSBURGH, July 7—The National League settled an old score with Casey Stengel today.

Minutes after the Yankees' super-stategist had put on a bewildering display of masterminding that sent the American Leaguers ahead with a three-run splurge in the upper half of the eighth inning, Fred Haney's Nationals turned the tables on the Ol' Perfessor.

Willie Mays of the San Francisco Giants, who swings a powerful bat but doesn't do too much thinking, bounced a tremendous 436-foot triple off the center field wall of picturesque Forbes Field. The blow scored the second of two runs and with that tally the senior loop made off with the twenty-sixth annual All-Star game, 5 to 4.

It was, therefore, a jubilant afternoon for the majority in a crowd of 35,277, which included Vice President Richard M. Nixon and which enriched the players pension fund by $194,303.

Ford Losing Pitcher

For this is a National League town and by way of rubbing it in, Stengel's southpaw ace, Whitey Ford, freshly in the game as the American League's hurler, was tagged with the defeat.

A single by Ken Boyer, a sacrifice by Dick Groat and another single for Hank Aaron —his second of the day—had accounted for the first run off Ford. That tied the score at 4—all. A moment later Mays untied it with his three-bagger.

All too late Casey put in Kansas City's left-hander, Bud Daley, who collected the final two outs in the inning. But the mischief had been done.

Haney and the Nationals, who had bowed two years in a row to Stengel, finally brought Casey up short. They plastered him with his sixth All-Star defeat against only three victories.

It was a game of power pitching and power hitting, with the latter finally prevailing. For six innings the combined efforts of the White Sox's Early Wynn and the Yanks' Ryne Duren had held the Nationals to a lone tally, a first-inning homer by Eddie Mathews off Wynn.

In the same interval, the Dodgers' Don Drysdale and the Braves' Lew Burdette held the Americans to one run. A fourth-inning homer by Al Kaline had produced that marker off Burdette.

When Stengel called on the Tigers' Jim Bunning in the seventh, Bunning was stung for two runs, which put the Nationals ahead, 3—1. It was in the top of the eighth that Stengel, in desperation, went off the deep end in his deep thinking. He did momentarily gain the lead with three runs, but he wound up defeated despite having used twenty-two players.

Face Pounded Hard

Elroy Face, Pittsburgh's pitching pride and joy, with a record of twelve victories against no defeats, all in relief, was the victim of that American League uprising. With two out, Nellie Fox singled. Harvey Kuenn, who had replaced Kaline, walked and Vic Power, a late-inning replacement for Bill Skowron, singled. That sent in one run.

Here Ted Williams, the 40-year-old Red Sox slugger, appearing in his fifteenth mid-summer classic, got up as a pinch hitter for Rocky Colavito. Williams walked, filling the bases. Gus Triandos then came through with a two-bagger down the left field line. This scored two and the Americans were in front, 4 to 3.

The double finished Face and the Giants' star southpaw, Johnny Antonelli, went to the mound. Johnny faced only two batters, but he became the eventual winner. After walking Roy Sievers, a pinch hitter, he turned back still another pinch hitter, Sherm Lollar, and that ended the inning.

In the lower half of the eighth the Nationals again swept ahead and that was it. Haney had one more trump to play. Don Elston, a Cub right-hander and a last-minute replacement on the National League squad for the Cards' Wilmer Mizell, blanked the Americans in the top of the ninth.

There was one last anxious moment at the end when, with two out, Fox, who, with Minnie Minoso played the entire game for the American League, singled for his second hit. A wild pitch put Fox on second.

Kuenn Fouls Out

But there he remained as Kuenn fouled out back of third. Mickey Mantle, who had gone in as pinch runner for Triandos in the dizzy eighth, had remained in the game as the right fielder. But the Yanks' famed Switcher never got a chance at the plate.

The Nationals, who made this their eleventh victory against fifteen defeats in the All-Star series, wound up with six players playing from start to finish. Haney shifted only when he had to.

In a setting that provided an almost prefect day for baseball, Vice President Nixon started the show by tossing out the first ball. The Vice President, despite a rugged evening trying to decode Stengel's converational gyrations at last night's All-Star dinner, nevertheless was in fine form.

Coatless, the Vice President reared back and let fly with a high hard one that cleared the heads of the photographers and might even have headed for outer space had not Del Crandall, the National League's starting catcher, reached up and checked its flight.

However, the crowd was not too deeply interested in pitching, although what Drysdale turned in for his first three innings was just about perfection. The 22-year-old 6-foot 6-inch right-hander, making his first All - Star appearance, snuffed out nine batters in a row, four of them on strikes.

Mathews Connects in First

It was power hitting the folks wanted most to see and the Nationals did not keep the gathering long in suspense. Wynn, the American Leaguers' starting pitcher, had retired only one batter in the first inning when Mathews, who leads the National League in homers, with twenty-five, arched one over the high screening in front of the lower right field stand.

Oddly, this not only was the first All-Star homer for the Braves' slugging third sacker, but it also was his first hit in four of these games.

In the second, the Nationals threatened to pick up more runs when the Cubs' Ernie Banks smacked a double into left center to open that round. But Wynn adroitly pitched himself out of this spot by getting Orlando Cepeda on an infield pop-up, walking Wally Moon, then fanning Crandall and Drysdale.

Drysdale's superb hurling kept the Nationals in front until the fourth, when Burdette took over. Lew had just retired the top two batters, Minoso and Fox, when Kaline sent the ball sailing a good 400 feet, clearing the ivy-covered red brick wall in left field.

That squared it at 1-all, although for a moment it appeared the Americans would collect more when Skowron and Colavito followed with singles and Triandos weighed

DECISIVE: Willie Mays of San Francisco triples in the eighth inning to drive in winning run and give the National League a 5-4 victory in the All-Star game at Pittsburgh.

All-Star Box Score

AMERICAN LEAGUE

	AB.	R.	H.	RBI.	PO.	A.
Minoso, Cleve., lf	5	0	0	0	1	0
Fox, Chicago 2b	5	1	2	0	3	0
Kaline, Detroit, cf	3	1	1	1	1	0
Kuenn, Detroit, cf	1	1	0	0	1	0
Skowron, N. Y., 1b	3	0	2	0	3	0
Power, Kan. City, 1b	1	1	1	1	2	0
Colavito, Cleve., rf	3	0	1	0	1	0
bWilliams, Boston	0	0	0	0	0	0
cMcDougald, N. Y., ss	0	0	0	0	0	0
Triandos, Baltimore, c	4	0	1	2	8	0
fMantle, N. Y., rf	0	0	0	0	0	0
Killebrew, Wash., 3b	3	0	0	0	0	1
Bunning, Detroit, p	0	0	0	0	0	0
dRunnels, Boston	0	0	0	0	0	0
eSievers, Wash.	0	0	0	0	0	0
Ford, N. Y., p	0	0	0	0	0	1
Daley, Kan. City, p	0	0	0	0	0	0
Aparicio, Chicago, ss	3	0	0	0	4	2
gLollar, Chicago, c	1	0	0	0	1	0
Wynn, Chicago, p	1	0	0	0	1	0
Duren, N. Y., p	1	0	0	0	0	0
Malzone, Boston, 3b	2					
TOTALS	36	4	8	4	24	5

NATIONAL LEAGUE

	AB.	R.	H.	RBI.	PO.	A.
Temple, Cincinnati, 2b	2	0	0	0	1	3
aMusial, St. Louis,	1	0	0	0	0	0
Face, Pittsburgh, p	0	0	0	0	0	0
Antonelli, San Fran., p	0	0	0	0	0	0
hBoyer, St. Louis, 3b	1	1	1	0	1	0
Mathews, Milw., 3b	3	1	1	1	2	1
iGroat, Pittsburgh	0	0	0	0	0	0
Elston, Chi., p	0	0	0	0	0	0
Aaron, Milw., rf	4	1	2	1	2	0
Mays, San Fran., cf	4	0	1	1	2	0
Banks, Chicago, ss	3	1	2	0	1	2
Cepeda, San Fran., 1b	4	0	0	0	6	0
Moon, Los Ang., lf	2	0	0	0	1	0
Crandall, Milw., c	3	1	1	1	10	0
Drysdale, Los Ang., p	1	0	0	0	0	0
Burdette, Milw., p	1	0	0	0	0	0
Mazerowski, Pitts, 2b	1	0	1	1	1	0
TOTALS	30	5	9	5	27	6

a—Popped out for Temple in 6th; b—walked for Colavito in 8th; c—ran for Williams in 8th; d—announced as batter for Bunning in 8th; e—walked for Runnels in 8th; f—ran for Triandos in 8th; g—hit into force play for Aparicio in 8th; h—singled for Antonelli in 8th; i—sacrificed for Mathews in 8th.

American .... 0 0 0 1 0 0 0 3 0—4
National .... 1 0 0 0 0 0 2 2 .—5

Error—Mathews. Double play—Aparicio and Srowron. Left on base—American 8, National 4.

Two-base hits—Banks 2, Triandos. Three-base hits—Mays. Home run—Mathews, Kaline. Sacrifice—Groat.

	IP.	H.	R.	ER.
Drysdale	3	0	0	0
Burdette	3	4	1	1
Face	1 2/3	3	3	3
Antonelli (W.)	1/3	0	0	0
Elston	1	1	0	0
Wynn	3	2	1	1
Duren	3	1	0	0
Bunning	1	3	2	2
Ford (L.)	1/3	3	2	2
Daley	2/3	0	0	0

Base on balls—Off Face 2 (Kuenn, Williams), Antonelli 1 (Sievers), Wynn 1 (Moon), Duren 1 (Banks). Struck out—By Drysdale 4 (Fox, Kaline, Colavito, Wynn), Burdette 2 (Duren, Minoso), Face 2 (Killebrew, Aparicio), Elston 1 (Minoso), Wynn 3 (Aaron, Crandall, Drysdale), Duren 4 (Mays, Moon, Burdette, Mathews), Bunning 1 (Moon), Daley 1 (Banks). Wild pitch—Elston. Umpires—Barlick (N.), Runge (A.), Donatelli (N.), Paparella (A.), Crawford (N.) and Rice (A.). Time—2:33. Attendance—35,277.

in with a powerful drive into right center. But the Nationals had a powerful pair of outfielders converging on the ball in Mays and Hank Aaron and Hank made the catch for the third out.

This also ended the scoring off Burdette even though an error, ironically by his teammate, Mathews, plunged the Milwaukee hurler into a hole in the sixth.

Kaline Safe on Error

Burdette was just about to finish his three-inning stint, having retired the first two batters in the sixth, when a sharp grounder by Kaline went through Mathews' legs. On the heels of that Skowron got his second single, sending Kaline to third.

But Burdette turned back this threat by inducing Colavito to slap into a force play at second base.

Meanwhile, Duren was blinding the Nationals in his middle three innings with his blazing fast ball. Duren walked one batter, another, Aaron, singled in the sixth, and that was all. Four batters fanned.

Even Stan Musial, making perhaps his final all-star appearance, found the Yankee fireballer too much for him. Pinch hitting for Johnny Temple in the sixth, the Cardinal star, appearing in his sixteenth All-Star game, went out on an easy pop-up.

And so the one-all deadlocked endured until the last of the seventh when, with Bunning on the mound for the Americans, the Nationals erupted for two runs

Banks started the uprising with his second double of the afternoon. Bunning retired the next two, but Crandall singled, driving in Banks. After Crandall had taken second on a pointless throw-in, Bill Mazeroski singled the Braves' catcher home. This put the Nationals in front, 3—2.

The lead was shortlived. For then came the whirlwind eighth, which saw first the Americans, then finally the Nationals, move in front.

So Stengel has nothing more to look forward to than another crack at his rivals in Los Angeles, where the year's second All-Star game will be played on Aug. 3.

3D LEAGUE HURLS CURVE AT MAJORS

New Group Ready to Spend Large Sums to Join Baseball Industry

By HOWARD M. TUCKNER

After more than half a century as a two-league operation, big-time baseball this week was faced with the prospect of a third major league. Although it had been rumored for some time, the formation of the new league—called the Continental—caused considerable surprise among both fans and major league officials.

Since 1901, when the American League was formed — the National has been in business since 1876—there have been only two major leagues. The third league, with founding teams in New York, Houston, Denver, Toronto and the Twin Cities of Minneapolis-St. Paul, expects to begin operating as an eight, ten or even a twelve-team circuit by 1961.

Each franchise owner of the founding teams has deposited $50,000 in the league's treasury. Each owner is prepared to spend between $2,500,000 and $3,000,000, exclusive of stadium construction costs.

Some of the teams in the Continental League are planning to erect new stadiums, the construction of which will run into the millions. New York's stadium—a 52,000-seat ballpark that will cost $12,000,000—is to be erected at Flushing Meadow, Queens, the site of the old World's Fair grounds. Players whose salaries average $15,000

and can run to over $100,000 a year must be purchased from the existing major league teams.

Big Business

Baseball is a big business, although not always a profitable one.

Most major league teams operate at a subsistence level, and the "have-nots" in each league often end their seasons with a deficit. It is estimated that the sixteen major league clubs—eight in the National and eight in the American—have a total income not exceeding $50,000,-000. After operating expenses and taxes are paid, total profit is not more than $5,000,000.

While still below the post-war peaks of more than 20,000,000, major league attendance has made a modest comeback from its low of 14,400,000 in 1953, and has leveled off at around 16,500,000 a year.

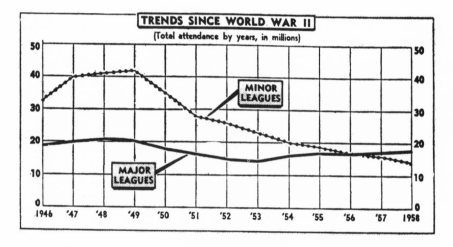

TRENDS SINCE WORLD WAR II
(Total attendance by years, in millions)

MINOR LEAGUES

MAJOR LEAGUES

1946 '47 '48 '49 '50 '51 '52 '53 '54 '55 '56 '57 1958

Unlike the minor leagues, which as a group lost $2,900,000 in 1956 and are still losing vast sums, the majors have been able to boost their take from radio and television rights to their games.

Senate Study

Aside from attendance worries and rising costs, professional baseball today is faced with other problems. The business is under Congressional investigation to decide just what kind of business it is. Last week the Senate's Antitrust and Monopoly subcommittee, headed by Estes Kefauver, Democrat from Tennessee, heard testimony in an attempt to clarify the status of professional baseball, football, basketball and hockey under the antitrust laws. On Friday Senator Kefauver, a strong advocate of the third major league, warned baseball executives that their attitudes toward the proposed new league would be watched closely.

What led to the formation of the third major league?

In December, 1957, a few months after the Giants and Dodgers transferred to California, Mayor Wagner selected a committee to study ways to bring another major league team to New York. William A. Shea, a New York corporation lawyer, was picked to head the committee. After almost a year's efforts to attract another team had failed, Mr. Shea last November went ahead with plans for a third league.

Owners Opposed

Most owners of big-league clubs are against the formation of a third league. Competition is the chief reason. Instead of bidding against fifteen teams for the services of potential stars, they would compete against twenty-three or even more clubs. The stadiums of some major league teams — such as Shibe Park in Philadelphia and Griffith Stadium in Washington — are run down and have poor parking facilities. What will be the reaction of Philadelphia and Washington fans, for example, when the Continental League begins building modern stadiums or spacious sites?

A meeting between the founders of the Continental League and a seven-man committee from the National and American League is set for Aug. 16.

For the Continental League to begin operations in 1961—or ever, for that matter—it must receive the blessings of the major league committee on Aug. 18. It is doubted that the majors will invite the Continental League into its camp at that meeting. If they do, though, the third league's problems — in such things as money raising, player acquisition, stadium building and revamping long-established traditions like the World Series—will be just beginning.

Giants' Jones Halts Cards in 7-Inning No-Hitter, 4-0

By JOSEPH M. SHEEHAN
Special to The New York Times.

ST. LOUIS, Sept. 26—Leave it to the Giants to do something spectacular. Against all the odds, San Francisco stayed in the three-team chase for the National League pennant tonight by defeating the Cardinals, 4—0, in a game called because of rain in the top of the eighth inning.

Sam Jones was pitching a no-hitter when a tempest that had St. Louisans scrambling into their storm cellars ended play and also washed out the second game of the scheduled double-header. That game will be part of a double-header tomorrow, weather permitting.

A well-heralded weather front that involved violent electrical discharges and scattered tornadoes hit Busch Stadium with a blast at 8:55 P. M., New York time.

Umpire Frank Dascoli, whose decision it was to wait or postpone, waited through one hour thirty-seven minutes of intermittently deluging showers, then called the game.

Day of Decision

"I just couldn't see fighting it any longer," said Dascoli. With ankle-deep puddles spotting the outfield and the rain still falling, no one was inclined to quarrel with his judgment.

Certainly not the Giants. The victory gave them a reprieve into the last day of this hectic pennant race and a chance, if only a slim one, to match the heroics of the 1951 New York Giants, who finished the regular season tied for first and beat the Brooklyn Dodgers in a pennant play-off.

One and a half games behind the Dodgers and Braves, who are tied for the lead, the Giants can tie for the pennant by winning their games tomorrow while both their rivals lose.

While there still is little hope in the situation, San Francisco at least remains alive as a contender, and after tonight's bizarre developments who's to say what may happen?

There was irony, as well as glory, in the magnificent pitching performance Jones gave to the San Francisco team he has carried on his broad shoulders for much of the season.

Earlier this season, on June 30, big Sam had pitched what everyone except the official scorer agreed was a not-hitter against the Dodgers.

The scorer gave a hit to Junior Gilliam on an eighth-inning bounder that was mishandled by Andre Rodgers.

Since this game didn't go the route, Jones won't get listing for another no-hitter to match the conventional nine-inning one he pitched for the Cubs against the Pirates on May 12, 1955.

However, there certainly could be no faulting of the job Sam did in turning in the twenty-first victory of the greatest season he has had in a checkered seven-year career in the major leagues.

All but one of the twenty-one outs he registered were easy. Don Blasingame came within a whisker of spoiling the no-hitter in the sixth with a bunt toward third that José Pagan just got to Willie McCovey in time.

The Cardinals protested that the throw hadn't beaten Blasingame. Manager Solly Hemus of the Redbirds charged onto the field to challenge Umpire Tom Gorman's decision at first base. It was wasted breath, of course.

Two bases on balls kept Jones from a perfect pitching performance. He walked Joe Cunningham with one out in the first and Alex Grammas, the first man to face him in the sixth. Grammas, who advanced on Blasingame's unsuccessful bid for a bunt hit, was the only Cardinal to reach second base.

The laconic, loose-jointed Jones, acquired from the Cardinals shortly before the start of the season in exchange for Bill White, has been a tower of pitching strength for the Giants all year.

Time after time, Manager Bill Rigney has called on him for relief duty between starts. "It was Sam's own idea," Rigney has said. "'Any time you want me, coach, I'm ready,' he told me way back in April. We wouldn't be in the race without him."

It took hitting as well as pitching to win the contest. Willie Mays and Willie McCovey were the chief providers of this other important commodity. Against Wilmer (Vinegar Bend) Mizell, Mays clouted his thirty-fourth homer with the bases empty in the first inning.

Against Ernie Broglio, the former Giant farmhand who succeeded Mizell at the start of the seventh inning, McCovey walloped his thirteenth homer high over the right-field roof with a runner aboard.

SAN FRANCISCO (N.)					ST. LOUIS (N.)				
	ab.	r.	h.	rbi		ab.	r.	h.	rbi
Pagan, 3b	4	0	1	0	Blasingame, 2b.	2	0	0	0
Alou, rf	4	0	0	0	Cun'ngham, rf.	2	0	0	0
Mays, cf	3	2	2	1	Musial, 1b	3	0	0	0
McCovey, 1b	3	2	2	2	Boyer, 3b	3	0	0	0
Cepeda, lf	2	0	1	1	Cimoli, lf	3	0	0	0
Spencer, 2b	4	0	0	0	H. Smith, c	3	0	0	0
Bressoud, ss	4	0	0	0	Flood, cf	2	0	0	0
Schmidt, c	3	0	3	0	Grammas, ss	1	0	0	0
S. Jones, p	2	0	0	0	Mizell, p	1	0	0	0
					aShannon	1	0	0	0
					Broglio, p	0	0	0	0
Total	29	4	9	4	Total	20	0	0	0

aStruck out for Mizell in 6th; *Awarded first base because of catcher's interference.

San Francisco ....1 0 1 0 0 0 2 0—4
St. Louis .... 0 0 0 0 0 0 0—0

E—Smith, Musial, Boyer. A—San Francisco 8, St. Louis 14. DP—Boyer, Blasingame, Musial; Boyer, Grammas, Musial. LOB—San Francisco 7, St. Louis 2.

2B Hits—Cepeda, Mays. HR—Mays, McCovey. Sacrifices—S. Jones, Blasingame.

	IP.	H.	R.	ER.	BB.	SO.
S. Jones ..(W, 21—15)	7	0	0	0	2	5
Mizell (L, 13—10)	6	8	2	2	2	0
Broglio	1⅔	1	2	0	0	3

HBP—By Mizell (Cepeda). Wild pitch—Mizell. Umpires—Gorman, Secory, Landes, Dascoli. Time—1:51. Attendance—8,000.

September 27, 1959

Dodgers Beat Braves in 12th, 6-5, To Win Pennant Play-Off Series

By JOHN DREBINGER
Special to The New York Times.

LOS ANGELES, Sept. 29— The Dodgers today brought a National League pennant to Los Angeles in the city's second year in major league baseball.

Before a roaring crowd of 36,528, Walter Alston's Angelenos made it a two-game sweep of the pennant play-off series as they conquered the Milwaukee Braves, 6 to 5, in a tense, dramatic, twelve-inning struggle. They will meet the White Sox in the first game of the world series in Chicago on Thursday.

Trailing by three runs in the last of the ninth, the Dodgers drew even in a frenzied spurt that had Fred Haney frantically throwing three of his hurlers into the fray.

And in the last of the twelfth, it was fittingly enough, 37-year-old Carl Furillo, a veteran of six Dodger pennant triumphs in the days when the club performed in Brooklyn, who helped break up today's torrid conflict.

It was an infield hit by Furillo, coupled with a wide throw to first base by Felix Mantilla, that enabled Gil Hodges to go tearing in from second base with the deciding run.

With two out and Bob Rush on the mound for the Braves, Hodges drew a pass. Joe Pignatano singled to left and the Dodgers had runners on first and second.

Rush had snuffed out a Dodger threat in the eleventh, going to the mound with the bases loaded and two out. But this time the Angelenos were not to be denied.

Furillo then drilled a sharp grounder over second. Mantilla, who had been forced to shift from second to short because of an injury to Johnny Logan earlier in the day, really made a brilliant stop. However, his desperate peg to first not only arrived too late, but also shot past Frank Torre, Milwaukee's first baseman.

That sent Hodges scooting over the plate and the encounter was over. The Dodgers, who had won the first play-off game by 3-2 in Milwaukee yesterday, thus bagged their thirteenth National League pennant.

In National League history, there have been only three play-offs and the Dodgers appeared in all of them. But not until today were they able to win one. They bowed to the Cardinals in 1946 and to the Giants in 1951.

But today, with the aid of a towering, 23-year-old right-hander, Stan Williams, they made it. Williams was the sixth pitcher to be used by Manager Alston. He entered the game in the tenth, reeled off three scoreless innings and received credit for the victory.

Williams had one tight squeeze in the eleventh when he walked three, but he fired his way out of that one.

And so the Dodgers capped a comeback that must be ranked as one of the most astounding in major league history. For the Dodgers, after their sad seventh-place finish in their first year in Los Angeles last season, were picked by few to finish in the first division, let alone win the title.

Yet, curiously enough, they never were far from the top, though they only occasionally held the lead. After the early April skirmishing—they were in first place on April 26—they never were, on top again until Sept. 20. On that day they swept a three-game series with the Giants in San Francisco.

The Giants, season-long frontrunners, thus dropped out of the lead and virtually out of contention. It then became touch and go between the Dodgers and Braves, with these two finally finishing in a tie on Sunday.

Mathews Belts Homer

The Braves, with the aid of Eddie Mathews' homer, which helped bring about the rout of Don Drysdale in the fifth, were holding a three-run lead and Lew Burdette appeared to have his twenty-second victory of the year all wrapped up when the Lodgers suddenly went on their frenzied spurt in the ninth.

Up to that moment only Charley Neal had been able to do anything with the Braves' starter. Neal accounted for the Dodgers' first two runs, the first with a triple, the second with a homer.

Wally Moon opened that last-ditch stand with a single to center. Duke Snider followed with another to the same sector and Hodges singled to left.

Don McMahon replaced Burdette, only to be slapped for a two-run single by Norm Larker. In came Warren Spahn, the Braves' stalwart southpaw.

But Spahn couldn't prevent a pinch hitter, Furillo, from lifting a sacrifice fly to right, which scored Hodges with the tying run. Then Maury Wills singled for the fifth hit of the inning, sending Pignatano, running for Larker, to second. Here Haney made another mound switch.

He called in Joey Jay, who got a pinch hitter, Ron Fairly, to ground into a force play at second. This moved Pignatano to third but Joe got no further. For Hank Aaron in right made a fine running catch of Jim Gilliam's bid for a hit that would have ended it.

The struggle then went into overtime, with Jay on the firing line for the Braves and Williams for the Dodgers.

Played under a cloudless sky and with the temperature in the sun-baked arena around 80, the game had scarcely begun when the Braves jumped into a two-run lead.

An Early Disagreement

With one out, Drysdale walked Mathews and Hank Aaron followed with a two-bagger to left center. Aaron slid into second just ahead of Duke Snider's throw, and Neal, the Dodger second sacker, did some loud squawking. But this in no way influenced Umpire Augie Donatelli and the Braves had runners on second and third.

A moment later both were over the plate on Torre's well-placed single through the hole between short and third. The inning ended with Lee Maye grounding into a double play.

The Dodgers got a run back

The Box Score

MILWAUKEE (N.)					LOS ANGELES (N.)				
	ab.	r.	h.	rbi.		ab.	r.	h.	rbi.
Bruton, cf	6	0	0	0	Gilliam, 3b	5	0	1	0
Mathews, 3b	4	2	2	1	Neal, 2b	6	2	2	1
Aaron, rf	4	1	2	0	Moon, rf, lf	6	1	3	1
Torre, 1b	3	0	1	2	Snider, cf	4	0	1	0
Maye, lf	4	0	0	0	eLillis	0	0	0	0
aPafko, lf	1	0	0	0	Williams, p	2	0	0	0
bSlaughter, lf	1	0	0	0	Hodges, lf	5	2	2	0
DeMerit, lf	0	0	0	0	Larker, rf	4	0	2	2
kSpangler, lf	0	0	0	0	fPignatano, c	1	0	1	0
Logan, ss	3	1	2	0	Roseboro, c	3	0	0	0
Schoend'st, 2b	1	0	0	0	gFurillo, rf	2	0	2	1
dVernon	1	0	0	0	Wills, ss	5	0	1	0
Cottier, 2b	0	0	0	0	Drysdale, p	1	0	0	0
lAdcock	1	0	0	0	Podres, p	1	0	0	0
Avila, 2b	1	0	0	0	Churn, p	0	0	0	0
Crandall, c	6	1	1	0	cDemeter	1	0	0	0
Mantilla,2b,ss	5	0	1	1	Koufax, p	0	0	0	0
Burdette, p	4	0	1	0	hEssegian	0	0	0	0
McMahon, p	0	0	0	0	Labine, p	0	0	0	0
Spahn, p	0	0	0	0	jFairly, cf	2	0	0	0
Jay, p	0	0	0	0					
Rush, p	1	0	0	0					
Total	**44**	**5**	**10**	**4**	**Total**	**48**	**6**	**15**	**5**

aFlied out for Maye in 5th; bPopped out for Pafko in 7th; cLined out for Churn in 8th; dStruck out for Schoendienst in 9th; eRan for Snider in 9th; fRan for Larker in 9th; gHit sacrifice fly for Roseboro in 9th; hAnnounced for Labine in 9th; jHit into forceout for Essegian in 9th; kWalked for DeMerit in 11th; lHit into forceout for Cottier in 11th.

```
Milwaukee ....210 010 010 000—5
Los Angeles ..100 100 003 001—6
```
Two out when winning run was scored.

E—Snider, Neal, Mantilla 2. DP—Wills, Neal, Hodges; Torre, Logan, Torre. LOB—Milwaukee 13, Los Angeles 11.

PO—Milwaukee 35: Bruton 4, Mathews 2, Aaron 3, Torre 10, Maye 2, DeMerit, Spangler 3, Logan 2, Avila, Crandall 6, Mantilla. Los Angeles 36: Gilliam 4, Neal 3, Moon 3, Snider, Hodges 11, Larker 2, Pignatano 2, Roseboro 5, Wills 2, Drysdale, Fairly. A—Milwaukee 13: Mathews 2, Torre 2, Logan 5, Crandall, Mantilla, Burdette 2. Los Angeles 14: Gilliam 3, Neal 2, Moon, Roseboro, Wills 5, Drysdale, Churn.

2B Hit—Aaron. 3B—Neal, Crandall. HR—Neal, Mathews. SF—Mantilla, Furillo.

	IP.	H.	R.	ER.	BB.	SO.
*Burdette	8	10	5	5	0	4
†McMahon	0	1	0	0	0	0
Spahn	1/3	1	0	0	0	0
Jay	2⅓	1	0	0	1	1
Rush (L, 5—6)	1	2	1	0	1	0
Drysdale	4⅓	6	4	3	2	3
Podres	2⅓	3	0	0	1	1
Churn	1⅓	1	1	1	0	0
Koufax	2⅓	0	0	0	3	1
Labine	1/3	0	0	0	0	1
Williams (W, 5—5)	3	0	0	0	3	3

*Faced 3 batters in 9th; †Faced 1 batter in 9th.

HBP—By Jay (Pignatano). Wild pitch—Podres. PB—Pignatano. Umpires—Barlick, Boggess, Donatelli, Conlan, Jackowski, Gorman. Time—4:06. Attendance—36,528.

in their half when Neal connected for his first extra-base blow of the game. It was a triple that sailed over Bill Bruton's head in center. The run followed when Wally Moon stroked a single into left.

Burdette then fanned Snider and retired six more Dodgers in a row through the second and third before the Angelenos scored their next tally. Neal delivered this one with a towering fly that sailed over the trick forty-foot barrier in left field. It was Charley's nineteenth of the year and thirteenth in the Coliseum.

That cut the Braves' margin to one run, but not for long. In the fifth Mathews hooked one of Drysdale's deliveries down the right-field foul line.

It skirted just inside the foul pole and into the stand.

The homer was Mathews' forty-sixth of the season, breaking his tie with Ernie Banks of

the Chicago Cubs for the major league leadership. The American League leaders were Rocky Colavito of the Cleveland Indians and Harmon Killebrew of the Washington Senators, with forty-two each.

When Drysdale walked Aaron, Alston decided to take no further chances with his erratic right-hander. He called on his southpaw, Johnny Podres, whom he had passed up as a starter yesterday in Milwaukee. The lefty quickly retired the side.

For a time Podres did all right, although it took a spectacular catch by Norm Larker to prevent Logan from getting a hit to left center in the sixth. But in the seventh Johnny appeared headed for trouble when Mathews and Aaron weighed in with singles.

However, a fine throw by Moon to Jim Gilliam nipped Mathews as he tried to reach third base on the Aaron blow and that helped. For Podres unfurled a wild pitch that put Aaron on third and he also walked Torre.

That had Alston bringing in his rookie right-hander, Clarence Nottingham Churn, called Chuck, who managed to ward off further trouble there. But in the eighth Chuck yielded a run. Del Crandall clubbed him for a triple and Mantilla fetched the Braves' catcher home with a sacrifice fly.

In the seventh the Braves ran into a bad scare when for a moment it looked as though their shortstop, Logan, had met with a serious mishap. After Larker had opened with a single, John Roseboro grounded to Torre, who fired the ball to second just as Larker came slamming into Logan, intending, of course, to break up a double play.

Logan Goes Sprawling

In this he failed, for Logan got the ball away in time to complete the twin killing on Roseboro at first. But the Brave shortstop had been knocked sprawling and every Milwaukee player rushed to Logan's side as he rolled on the ground, apparently in considerable pain.

However, after Logan had been carried off the field on a stretcher, it was disclosed that he had suffered nothing beyond having the wind knocked out of him. The Braves finished the inning with Mantilla shifting from second to short, while Red Schoendienst, recently returned to the active list after a siege of tuberculosis, went to his old position at second.

Meanwhile, Burdette seemed merely to be toying with the Dodgers. So it came as a jolt when the Dodgers suddenly routed the Brave right-hander with three successive singles that eventually were to plunge the struggle into overtime.

CLEVELAND LANDS BATTING CHAMPION

Indians Part With Powerful Colavito to Get Kuenn, a .353 Hitter in 1959

LAKELAND, Fla., April 17 (AP) — The Detroit Tigers today traded Harvey Kuenn to the Cleveland Indians for Rocky Colavito.

Kuenn was the American League batting champion last year with a .353 average. Colavito batted only .257 for the Indians, but shared the league home run title with Harmon Killebrew of Washington. Each had forty-two homers.

It was a straight player deal with no cash involved.

The trade was disclosed by Rick Ferrell, the vice president of the Tigers, in the press box at Henley Field during the Detroit-Kansas City exhibition game.

The deal was made in a telephone conversation between Bill DeWitt, the Tigers' president, who is in St. Louis, and Frank Lane, the general manager of the Indians.

Kuenn and Colavito will switch uniforms when the Tigers and Indians open the season in Cleveland Tuesday.

Kuenn, 29, had nine homers last year and drove in seventy-one runs. The 26-year-old Colavito drove in 111 runs.

Harvey Kuenn

September 30, 1959

National League Wins Again

Rocky Colavito

Colavito joined the Indians in 1955 and hit 129 home runs for them in five seasons.

Kuenn had been with the Tigers since 1952. His lifetime average is .314. Only once in his career, in 1957, has he failed to hit .300.

Hailed and Farewelled

"I have a high regard for Harvey Kuenn's ability as a player," DeWitt said. "But we felt we needed more power at the plate and we're hopeful this move will enable us to score more runs."

Kuenn stepped off the University of Wisconsin campus and played over sixty-three games in the minor leagues before establishing himself as one of the foremost Tigers. He spent five seasons as a shortstop and five times was named to the American League's All-Star team.

Detroit switched him to center field at the start of the 1958 season. Last season he moved to right field and led the league in fielding at that position.

Kuenn was the oldest of the Detroit players in point of service. His salary is about $47,500, nearly $10,000 more than his 1959 pay. He was a holdout this spring for several days.

Colavito gets approximately $35,000, an increase of $8,000 from last season.

April 18, 1960

MAYS STANDS OUT IN 6-TO-0 CONTEST

Has a Homer, 2 Singles and Stolen Base for Nationals, Who Use 26 Players

By JOHN DREBINGER

National League baseball returned briefly to New York yesterday and the fans got a glimpse of what they've been missing these past three seasons.

For it was almost no-contest at Yankee Stadium. The Nationals, riding high on four home runs, crushed the American Leaguers, 6 to 0, before 38,362 fans in the second and concluding all-star game of 1960.

Coming on top of Monday's 5-3 triumph in Kansas City, this gave the Nationals a sweep of the games. Walter Alston, the manager, called on six pitchers and they tossed the third shutout in all-star history.

Willie Mays, playing his first major league game here since the Giants hauled him away to San Francisco after the 1957 season, hit a homer leading off the third inning. He also hit two singles in addition to stealing a base.

For the two all-star games, Willie the Wonder had six hits in eight times at bat—a home run, a triple, a double and three singles.

Mathews Finds Range

In the second inning Eddie Mathews of the Braves poled a two-run homer. The Yankee southpaw, Whitey Ford, served up this one as well as the one to Mays.

But the mightiest cheers of the sweltering afternoon came in the seventh inning when 39-year-old Stan Musial, appearing as a pinch hitter, blasted one into the upper right-field deck. It was the Cardinal star's nineteenth all-star game and the homer was his sixth, tops for the competition.

Then another St. Louis star, Ken Boyer, drove a two-run homer in the ninth as a final crusher to Al Lopez' stunned American League cast. The homers accounted for all of the National runs.

In manipulating the shutout, Manager Alston used Vernon Law of the Pirates for the first two innings and followed with his Dodger hurlers, Johnny Podres and Stan Williams, for two rounds apiece.

Larry Jackson of the Cards, Bill Henry of the Reds and

All-Star Box Score

NATIONAL LEAGUE

	AB.	R.	H.	RBI.	PO.	A.
Mays, cf	4	1	3	1	5	0
Pinson, cf	0	0	0	0	0	0
Skinner, lf	3	0	1	0	2	0
Cepeda, lf	2	0	0	0	0	0
Aaron, rf	3	0	0	0	1	0
hClemente, rf	0	0	0	0	0	0
Banks, ss	3	0	1	0	2	3
iGroat, ss	1	0	0	0	0	1
Adcock, 1b	2	1	1	0	3	0
White, 1b	1	0	0	0	2	0
kLarker, 1b	0	1	0	0	3	0
Mathews, 3b	3	1	1	2	0	1
Boyer, 3b	1	1	1	2	1	0
Mazeroski, 2b	2	0	0	0	0	0
Neal, 2b	1	0	0	0	1	2
Taylor, 2b	1	0	1	0	2	1
Crandall, c	2	0	0	0	3	0
S. Williams, p	0	0	0	0	0	0
dMusial	1	1	1	1	0	0
Jackson, p	0	0	0	0	0	0
Bailey, c	1	0	0	0	0	0
Law, p	1	0	0	0	0	1
Podres, p	0	0	0	0	0	0
bBurgess, c	1	0	0	0	2	0
Henry, p	0	0	0	0	0	0
McDaniel, p	0	0	0	0	0	0
Total	34	6	10	6	27	10

AMERICAN LEAGUE

	AB.	R.	H.	RBI.	PO.	A.
Minoso, lf	2	0	0	0	1	0
eT. Williams	1	0	1	0	0	0
fRobinson, 3b	1	0	0	0	0	0
Runnels, 2b	2	0	0	0	0	1
Staley, p	0	0	0	0	1	1
gKaline, lf	1	0	1	0	3	0
Maris, rf	4	0	1	0	0	0
Mantle, cf	4	0	1	0	3	0
Skowron, 1b	1	0	0	0	6	0
Power, 1b	2	0	0	0	5	1
Berra, c	2	0	0	0	4	1
Lollar, c	2	0	1	0	0	0
Malzone, 3b	2	0	0	0	2	2
Lary, p	0	0	0	0	0	0
iSmith	1	0	0	0	0	0
Bell, p	0	0	0	0	0	1
Hansen, ss	4	0	2	0	2	4
Ford, p	0	0	0	0	0	0
aKienn	1	0	0	0	0	0
Wynn, p	0	0	0	0	0	0
cFox, 2b	3	0	1	0	0	1
Total	33	0	8	0	27	12

aFlied out for Ford in 3d; bStruck out for Podres in 5th; cSingled for Wynn in 5th; dHit homer for S. Williams in 7th; eSingled for Minoso in 7th; fRan for T. Williams in 7th; gWalked for Staley in 7th; hWalked for Aaron in 8th; iHit into double play for Banks in 8th; jPooped out for Lary in 8th; kWalked for White in 9th.

National	0 2 1	0 0 0	1 0 2—6		
American	0 0 0	0 0 0	0 0 0—0		

Errors—None. Double plays—Law, Banks, Adcock; Banks, Neal, White; Fox, Hansen, Power. Left on bases—National 5, American 12.

Two-base hit—Lollar. Home runs—Mathews, Mays, Musial, Boyer. Stolen base—Mays. Sacrifice—Henry.

	IP.	H.	R.	ER.
Ford (L)	3	5	3	3
Wynn	2	0	0	0
Staley	2	2	1	1
Lary	1	1	0	0
Bell	1	2	2	2
Law (W)	2	1	0	0
Podres	2	1	0	0
S. Williams	2	2	0	0
Jackson	1	1	0	0
Henry	1	2	0	0
McDaniel	1	1	0	0

Bases on balls—Off Lary 1 (Clemente), Bell 2 (Larker, Pinson), Podres 3 (Minoso, Runnels, Skowron), S. Williams (Maris), Jackson 2 (Malzone, Kaline). Struck out—By Ford 1 (Skinner), Wynn 2 (Adcock, Burgess), Law 1 (Minoso), Podres 1 (Berra), S. Williams 2 (Runnels, Mantle). Umpires—Chylack (A.), Boggess (N.), Honochick (A.), Gorman (N.), Stevenson (A.), Smith (N.). Time—2:42. Attendance—38,362.

Lindy McDaniel of the Cards finished with an inning each.

The losers got eight hits, including one by Ted Williams. The Red Sox slugger, six weeks

away from 42, cracked a pinch single in the seventh. Law was the official victor.

Alston backed up his superlative pitching with a parade of twenty-six players, a record for an all-star game. The American Leaguers had set the previous mark of twenty-five in striving to stave off Monday's defeat.

Plenty of Yankee Dolor

The Yankees had five players in the American starting lineup, but they cast a rather sorry picture. Their southpaw ace, Ford, started on the mound and was the loser because he was tagged for three tallies in his three innings.

Mickey Mantle and Roger Maris, the only American Leaguers who played the entire game, came up with one hit between them. This was an eighth-inning single by Mantle. Maris twice failed with the bases filled and two out.

Of the pitchers Lopez employed, only Early Wynn, of Al's own White Sox, and Frank Lary of the Tigers acquitted themselves in all-star fashion. Gerry Staley was the victim of Musial's homer and Gary Bell gave Boyer's homer.

Although it was steaming in high humidity, the temperature in the Stadium, at 88 degrees, was some twelve degrees cooler than it had been in Kansas City. But that was small comfort to the shirt-sleeved, sweltering fans who were thankful that the sun managed to break through the haze only occasionally.

For the introductory ceremonies, the Yankees' Bob Sheppard, master of English and professor of elocution, handled the public address system.

A Round of Cheers

Honors in the ovation sweepstakes were about evenly divided between those two venerable campaigners, Musial and Williams, the latter appearing in his eighteenth all-star game. Only slightly less in volume was the applause for Mays and Maris, while Mantle, as usual, drew his customary round of boos.

Then came the singing of the national anthem by Della Reese, accompanied by Guy Lombardo's Royal Canadians. After that, the struggle was on.

Mays stroked Ford's first pitch for a single to left. Willie moved to second on Bob Skinner's infield hit and then thrilled his one-time Polo Grounds following by stealing third.

However, after Hank Aaron and Ernie Banks had popped to the infield, Mays over-reached himself. With Ford pitching to Joe Adcock, Skinner bolted for second, but crafty Yogi Berra did not throw to that base. Instead he whipped the ball to third and Mays was trapped between third and home for the third out.

There was no checking the

Nationals in the second. Adcock opened with a single and Mathews followed with his homer into the right-field stand, giving a two-run lead to the Alston forces.

In the third Mays made certain he would fall into no more traps. He lined a pitch into the lower left-field stand and the Nationals led by three.

Meanwhile Law was picking up where he had left off in Kansas City. There, working in relief, he had erased the last two batters in the ninth. The Priates' crack right-hander, in his two innings here, faced only six batters.

Bill Skowron singled in the second, but his Yankee teammate, Berra, ended the inning by slapping into a double play.

With the third, Podres went to the mound and for a few minutes it looked as if the erratic Dodger southpaw would let the National advantage slip away. After Ron Hansen had singled between outs, Podres filled the bases by walking Minnie Minoso and Pete Runnels.

The tension increased as Podres, pitching to Maris, ran up a count of three balls and one strike. But Johnny then got in a second strike and the threat ended when Maris lifted a fly that Del Crandall, the catcher, grabbed a few feet in front of the plate.

Another Chance Missed

In the fifth, with Stan Wililams pitching, the Americans missed another scoring chance when Hansen opened with his second single and Nellie Fox outgalloped a pinch bunt for a hit. But the threat passed out in the murky haze when Minoso grounded into a double play and Runnels fanned.

Williams appeared to be inviting trouble again in the sixth when he walked Maris, the lead-off batter. But he curved over a third strike on Mantle. Vic Power then flied to Mays in center and Sherman Lollar grounded to Banks at short.

In the seventh the National League sympathizers got another chance to roar when Musial blasted his homer just inside the right-field foul pole. It was his nineteenth hit in all-star competition.

NATIONAL LEAGUE POWER: Willie Mays of the Giants swings for the fences in third inning of all-star game at Yankee Stadium. Willie collected a home run, a triple, a double and three singles for eight times at bat in this year's all-star contests.

In the last of the seventh the Americans organized another threat on a pass, Ted Williams' single and another pass. For the second time Maris had a chance to put his team back in the game.

But Jackson, the Cards' right-hander, snuffed out the American League's leading home run hitter with a fly to center that enabled Mays to treat his admirers to one of his familiar basket catches.

In the eighth came one last gasp from the Americans, Mantle opened with a single. With one out, Lollar doubled, but the runners remained on second and third while Al Smith and Hansen went out on infield pops.

With two down in the ninth, Kaline got an infield hit and that gave Maris a final chance to do something. But Roger ended it all with a roller down the first-base line.

So the American League, which once led this midsummer classic by a tremendous margin —it won twelve of the first sixteen games—now has only a 16-13 margin. The Nationals have won nine of the last thirteen games.

As for Alston, the Dodger tactitian has directed three all-star victories, while Lopez' managerial all-star record stands at three defeats and no victories. In fact, the gay señor's luck in all-star play has been all bad. As a player he was on the losing side twice and as a coach once.

The New York Times (by Ernest Sisto)

AND RESERVE: Stan Musial of St. Louis, playing in his nineteenth all-star game, hits pinch homer in 7th.

July 14, 1960

PIRATES WIN, 10-9, CAPTURING SERIES ON HOMER IN 9TH

By JOHN DREBINGER
Special to The New York Times.

PITTSBURGH, Oct. 13—The Pirates today brought Pittsburgh its first world series baseball championship in thirty-five years when Bill Mazeroski slammed a ninth-inning home run high over the left-field wall of historic Forbes Field.

With that shot, Danny Murtaugh's astounding Bucs brought down Casey Stengel's Yankees, 10 to 9, in a titanic struggle that gave the National League champions the series, four games to three.

Minutes later a crowd of 36,683 touched off a celebration that tonight is sweeping through the city like a vast conflagration. For with this stunning victory, which also had required a five-run Pirate eighth, the dauntless Bucs avenged the four-straight rout inflicted by another Yankee team in 1927.

First Title Since 1925

The Steel City thus had its first world title since 1925, when the Corsairs of Bill Mc-Kechnie conquered the Washington Senators.

As for the 70-year-old Stengel, if this is to be his exit—his retirement has been repeatedly rumored—the Ol' Professor scarcely could have desired a more fitting setting short of a victory.

For this was a terrific, nerve-tingling struggle that saw a dazzling parade of heroes who followed on the heels of one another in bewildering profusion.

It saw the Bucs dash off to a four-run lead in the first two innings as they clobbered Bob Turley and Bill Stafford. The first two runs scored in the first inning on a homer by Rocky Nelson.

Berra Hits 3-Run Homer

But in the sixth the Bombers suddenly opened fire on their two arch tormentors of the series, Vernon Law and the Bucs' ace reliever, ElRoy Face. Law, with the help of Face, was seeking his third victory over the Bombers, but the Yanks scored four times in this round, three riding in on a homer by the incomparable Yogi Berra.

These four tallies, along with one which they had picked up in the fifth on a Bill Skowron homer, had the Yanks in front, 5 to 4. When they added two off Face in the eighth for a 7-4 lead, Stengel appeared to have his eighth world series title wrapped up, along with the Bombers' nineteenth autumn triumph.

But in the eighth the Corsairs suddenly erupted for five runs, the final three scampering across on an electrifying homer by Hal Smith. That had the Bucs two in front, but still the conflict raged.

In the ninth the embattled Yanks counted twice as once again they routed Bob Friend. Then left-handed Harvey Haddix, winner of the pivotal fifth game, brought them to a halt.

In the last of the ninth it was the clout by Mazeroski, first up, that ended it. Ralph Terry, the fifth Yankee hurler, was the victim. It made him the losing pitcher and Haddix the winner.

So, instead of the Bombers winning the nineteenth title, they had to accept their seventh world series defeat. As for Stengel, he remains tied with Joe McCarthy, a former Yankee manager, with seven series triumphs. The setback was his third. McCarthy lost two, one with the Yanks and one with the Chicago Cubs.

Bobby Shantz, a diminutive left-hander, who had gone to the box in the third to do some brilliant relief hurling for five innings, was one victim of the Bucs' startling five-run eighth.

The assault opened with Gino Cimoli, hitting for Face, cracking a single to right. Bill Virdon followed with a vicious grounder to short that resulted in doubtless the crucial play of the entire series.

It looked like a double play until the ball took a freak hop and struck Tony Kubek in the larynx. Instead of a double play, Tony was stretched on the ground. Virdon was on first with a single and Cimoli was

The Box Score

SEVENTH GAME
NEW YORK YANKEES

	AB.	R.	H.	RBI.	PO.	A.
Richardson, b.	5	2	2	0	2	5
Kubek ss	3	1	0	0	3	2
DeMaestri, ss	0	0	0	0	0	0
dLong	1	0	1	0	0	0
eMcD'gald, 3b.	0	1	0	0	0	0
Maris, rf	5	0	0	0	2	0
Mantle, cf	5	1	3	2	0	0
Berra, lf	4	2	1	4	3	0
Skowron, 1b.	5	2	2	1	10	2
Blanchard, c.	4	0	1	1	1	1
Boyer, 3b, ss	4	0	1	1	0	3
Turley, p.	0	0	0	0	0	0
Stafford, p.	0	0	0	0	0	1
aLopez	1	0	1	0	0	0
Shantz, p.	3	0	1	0	3	1
Coates, p.	0	0	0	0	0	0
Terry, p.	0	0	0	0	0	0
Total	40	9	13	9	24	15

PITTSBURGH PIRATES

	AB.	R.	H.	RBI.	PO.	A.
Virdon, cf.	4	1	2	2	3	0
Groat, ss	4	1	1	1	3	2
Skinner, lf	2	1	0	0	1	0
Nelson, 1b.	3	1	1	2	7	0
Clemente, rf	4	1	1	1	4	0
Burgess, c	3	0	2	0	0	0
dChristopher	0	0	0	0	0	0
Smith, c.	1	1	1	3	1	0
Hoak, 3b.	3	1	0	0	3	2
Mazeroski, 2b.	4	2	2	1	5	0
Law, p.	2	0	0	0	0	1
Face, p.	0	0	0	0	0	1
cCimoli	1	1	1	0	0	0
Friend, p.	0	0	0	0	0	0
Haddix, p.	0	0	0	0	0	0
Total	31	10	11	10	27	6

aSingled for Stafford in third.
bRan for Burgess in seventh.
cSingled for Face in eighth.
dSingled for DeMaestri in ninth.
eRan for Long in ninth.

New York......000 014 022— 9
Pittsburgh ...220 000 051—10

None out when winning run was scored.

Error—Maris. Double plays—Stafford, Blanchard and Skowron; Richardson, Kubek and Skowron; Kubek, Richardson and Skowron. Left on bases—New York 6, Pittsburgh 1.

Two-base hit—Boyer. Home runs—Nelson, Skowrun, Berra, Smith, Mazeroski. Sacrifice—Skinner.

Associated Press Wirephoto

THE HERO COMES HOME: Gleeful Pittsburgh fans and a happy coach, Frank Oceak, greet Bill Mazeroski as he rounds third in ninth on series-winning homer against Yanks.

on second. Kubek had to leave the game and was rushed to a hospital.

Meanwhile the Pirate attack rolled on. Dick Groat followed with a single to left, scoring Cimoli. That was all for Shantz and Jim Coates, a lean right-hander, took the mound.

Bob Skinner, back in the Buc line-up despite a still swollen left thumb, sacrificed the runners to second and third. Nelson flied out, leaving the position unchanged, and then came another rough break for the Stengeleers.

Bob Clemente dribbled a grounder to the right of the mound. Skowron scooped up the ball and this should have been the third out of the inning had Coates covered first base. But the tall Virginian failed to get to the bag in time. Clemente thus got an infield hit that enabled Cimoli to score the second run of the inning.

Three more followed as Smith, a one-time Yankee prospect, belted the ball high over the left-field wall. The Bucs were in front, 9—7, and the fans were in a delirium.

They cooled perceptibly in the top of the ninth. Murtaugh called on Friend, twice knocked out earlier in the series, to protect that two-run lead. But Bobby Richardson singled, as did Dale Long, a pinch-hitter, and Murtaugh lost no time hustling in his fifth-game winner, Haddix.

The little lefty retired Roger Maris on the end of a foul back of the plate, but Mickey Mantle singled to right, scoring Richardson and sending Long to third.

Another bewildering play followed. Berra grounded sharply down the first-base line. Nelson grabbed the ball, stepped on the bag for one out, then made a lunge for Mantle who, seeing he had no chance to make second, darted back to first. Mickey made it with a headlong dive that sent him under Rocky's tag.

Meanwhile, Gil McDougald, in as a runner for Long, crossed the plate and the score was 9-all. Haddix, getting Skowron to ground to Groat, brought the round to a close. Minutes later the game was over.

Although the weather again was warm and summery, the sun for the first time had difficulty breaking through a haze which enveloped the park with something akin to a Los Angeles smog.

However, no one was paying much attention to the weather and once the game got on the way it could have snowed without anyone paying the slightest attention.

For this was Pittsburgh's first big chance to win a world championship in three and a half decades and the fans were out to make the most of it. Nor did the Bucks keep their cohorts long in suspense.

The cheers, following the setting down of the first three Yankees in the first inning by

Law, barely had subsided before they broke out afresh.

Turley, Stengel's starting choice over the youthful Stafford, got by the first two Pirates, but Skinner walked.

Next came Nelson. Before the series returned here, Murtaugh had been emphatic that, regardless of Yankee pitching, Dick Stuart would be his first baseman. Yet here was the 36-year-old Nelson in the starting line-up as the first baseman.

Rocky, a left-handed swinger who began his professional baseball career eighteen years ago and spent most of the intervening time trying to convince managers he was a major league ball player, waited for Turley to run up a count of two balls and one strike. Then he lifted one that had just enough carry to clear the thirty-foot screen in front of the lower right-field stand at a point about 350 feet from home plate.

The fans went wild with joy as Nelson rounded the bases behind Skinner. Rocky had appeared in one series before this one. That was as a Brooklyn Dodger in 1952, when he was up four times as a pinch-hitter, but got no hits.

In the second, the Bucs went to work on Turley again, but this time not for long. For after Smoky Burgess had opened with a single to right, Stengel called on Stafford, the 22-year-old right-hander who had pitched five scoreless innings in relief in a hopeless Yankee cause in the fifth game.

In fact, Stengel had to weather some rough second-guessing after that defeat because he didn't start the youngster in that game instead of Art Ditmar.

This time Stafford spared his manager further embarrassing moments so far as this game was concerned. He walked Don Hoak and allowed Mazeroski to outgallop a bunt for a hit that filled the bases.

Stafford momentarily did get a grip on the situation when he induced Law to slap a roller to the mound. Stafford converted this one into a double play via the plate.

However, the Bucs still had runners on second and third and a moment later Virdon drove both home with a single to right, to which Maris added a fumble to put Virdon on second. The error didn't matter, but the Bucs were four in front.

Meanwhile Law, making a heroic bid to pitch his third victory of the series, held the Yanks in a tight spot. Like Ford yesterday, Law was back with only three days' rest, but he certainly didn't show it in the first four innings.

A dazzling stop and throw by Hoak took a possible hit away from Berra in the second. Hector Lopez delivered a pinch single in the third and Mantle singled with two down in the fourth.

In the fifth inning, the first tinge of uneasiness swept

through the stands. Skowron stroked an outside pitch into the upper right deck. It was the Moose's second homer of the series and his sixth in series competition.

An inning later almost the entire arena was enveloped in a deep and profound silence. The Yanks ripped into both Law and Face for their cluster of four to take the lead.

Richardson, a thorn in the side of the Bucs throughout the series, opened the assault with a single. When Kubek drew a pass Murtaugh decided the moment had arrived for Face to do his usual flawless relief work.

He had done the rescue work in the three Pirate victories preceding this game, saving Law twice and Haddix in the fifth game.

This time he encountered trouble. He retired Maris on a foul back of third, but Mantle punched a single over second which a diving Groat just missed flagging down. The hit scored Richardson and sent Kubek to third.

Up stepped Berra, who again was in left field for the Bombers while a rookie, John Blanchard, worked behind the plate in place of the injured Elston Howard. The latter had gone out with a fractured hand when hit by a stray pitch in the sixth game.

Yogi fouled off one pitch. Then he unfurled a lofty shot that sailed into the upper right-field deck close to the foul pole, which at the base measures only 300 feet from the plate. Mantle and Kubek scored ahead of Berra.

It was Yogi's eleventh homer in world series competition, tying him for third place with the Dodgers' Duke Snider.

The Yanks were now a run in front and in the eighth they clubbed Face for two more tallies.

The trim right-handed reliever had the Yanks' two most formidable clouters, Maris and Mantle, out of the way, when Berra drew a pass. Skowron sent a bounder down the third-base line which Hoak fielded but couldn't play. It went for a single and Berra was on second.

Two sharp thrusts did the rest. Blanchard pulled a single into left, scoring Yogi. Cletis Boyer drove a two-bagger down the left-field line, sending in Skowron. Moose's single was his twelfth hit, thereby tying another world series record.

Meanwhile, with Shantz reeling off one scoreless inning after another, the game looked tucked away for the Bombers. For five innings the little lefty allowed only one hit, a single. But in the Pittsburgh eighth the real pyrotechnics began. They never stopped until Mazeroski, with a count of one ball and no strikes in the ninth, whacked the ball over the left-field brick wall directly over the 402-foot mark.

October 14, 1960

NATIONAL LEAGUE ADMITS NEW YORK, HOUSTON FOR 1962

Some Obstacles Remain, but 10-Team Baseball Circuit Appears a Certainty

NEW STADIUM IS LIKELY

New York Club Expected to Play in 55,000-Seat Park at Flushing Meadow

By LOUIS EFFRAT
Special to The New York Times.

CHICAGO, Oct. 17—New York and Houston received franchises in the National League today.

If all goes well, as baseball officials expect, the new clubs will start playing in the 1962 season. The league, organized in 1876, will have ten clubs under the new arrangement. The National League has had clubs in New York before but never in Texas.

The club owners, in special session at the Sheraton Blackstone Hotel, responded with "unanimous enthusiasm" to the proposal that both cities be accepted for membership. The action surprised no one.

The proposal was made by Walter F. O'Malley, the president of the Dodgers. Ironically, O'Malley was the man who, in October of 1957, took the Dodgers out of Brooklyn and moved them to Los Angeles.

O'Malley also convinced Horace Stoneham to take the New York Giants out of the Polo Grounds and into San Francisco at the same time. Stoneham was one of the eight who voted in favor of today's action.

Giles Discloses Move

Warren C. Giles, the president of the National League, disclosed the expansion move after the owners had taken a break for lunch.

He said the following resolution was approved by the National League in the morning:

"Resolved that the National League approve and adopt the recommendations of its expansion committee in the following respects:

"1—That the National League

expand effective with the 1962 season to add two clubs, each additional club to be a member club of the Continental League which meets the qualifications for membership in the National League.

"2—That within a period of four years, the National League shall reappraise the situation with a view to carrying out its policy of further expansion."

New York and Houston were members of the proposed Continental League, which aspired to be the third major league. It disbanded when the National and American Leagues agreed to admit four of its eight members.

Giles, in identifying the franchise winners, referred to New York as the "Payson group" and Houston as the "Cullinan group." Mrs. Charles Shipman Payson of New York and Manhasset, L. I., heads the New York club. Craig F. Cullinan Jr. is the leader of the Texas club.

The owners felt that both groups qualified for membership in every way and that certain obligations, including indemnification to minor-league clubs, would be met.

Other details are to be ironed out, including the amount of money—"They are going to have to have a lot of money," Giles said—the two groups must spend.

There may or may not be a membership fee. Each new club must deposit a still unspecified sum to gain equity in the league treasury. It is believed that the National League reserve fund holds $1,500,000.

The site and size of the stadium each city will call home, and the method of acquiring playing personnel were among items occupying the owners' attention this afternoon.

American League Has a Say

Perhaps the most important item, though, concerned New York. Formal approval for entry into the city, thereby infringing on the territorial rights of the Yankees, must be considered by the American League.

Whether the American League goes along with the proposition is not likely, however, to affect the situation. The National League is certain .t will have the support of Ford Frick, Commissioner of Baseball.

Baseball law dictates that the commissioner cast the deciding vote if the two major leagues cannot agree. The National League will propose at the joint meeting of the majors at St. Louis on Dec. 7 a change in Rule 1-C. This deals with territorial rights and calls for unanimous approval of all sixteen clubs before a second team may invade a city.

"It is possible the American League will vote along with us on this proposition," Giles said. "They have been very coopera-

tive. However, if they vote in the negative we are confident that the commissioner will decide in our favor. He has stated publicly as well as to me that he is in favor of New York being open territory."

No New Yorkers Present

New York was not represented by any active member of its group today. Mrs. Payson, M. Donald Grant, Dwight Davis Jr., G. H. Walker Jr. and William Simpson, identified by Giles as the "Payson group," remained in New York. This was done upon the advice of O'Malley.

"I talked with Grant, as well as with Bill Shea, the chairman of Mayor Wagner's Baseball Committee, in New York," O'Malley said. "We talked it over and I felt there would be no point in any of them coming here. I said I would represent them, and I guess I did a pretty fair job of representing them."

The "Cullinan group" is made up of Cullinan, Judge Roy Hofheinz, R. E. Smith, K. S. (Bud) Adams and George Kirksey. Adams was a founder of the American Football League, which began operations this season. Cullinan, Hofheinz and Kirksey were on hand, and Cullinan, an oil man and sportsman, said all were elated.

"This climaxes four years of hard work," he said. "Now we must really prove we're big league. We will work harder than even before."

Construction of a $14,500,000 stadium in Harris County in Houston will begin on Feb. 1. It will have 43,197 seats.

Where the New York club will play its home games is a matter for its owners to decide. "We feel that's their own problem and that they will solve it," Giles said.

The construction of a 55,-000-seat stadium at Flushing Meadow, Queens, has been assured by Mayor Wagner. Until then, the New York club could move into the Polo Grounds or share Yankee Stadium with the Yankees.

O'Malley and Stoneham were happy over today's developments.

"When we left New York," O'Malley said, "we tried to get a National League club to go in at that time. Now it has a fair chance of working out, if they come up with some fair players."

How that is to be accomplished is a matter for conjecture. Some feel the player limit for each club will be reduced from twenty-five to twenty-three for 1962. There is likely to be a plan offering three players from each present club to the new members. Houston already has acquired a dozen players from the Western Carolina League.

"I am happy that New York is back in the National League," Stoneham said. "I'm certain that in the near future they will have a fine, representative team. Mrs. Payson and the new people will do well by their franchise and for the fans of

New York. She was an avid Giant fan and I am happy for her sake, too."

The possibility of an American League club now moving into Los Angeles was mentioned to O'Malley.

"I don't think that would be very smart," the president of the Dodgers said. "I believe they will go to the Coast eventually. San Diego and Seattle are wonderful cities. Right now, the American League faces a realignment problem before expansion."

The National League has operated with six, eight and twelve clubs, but never with ten. Originally made up of eight teams, the circuit expelled New York and Philadelphia in 1877 because both clubs refused to make the last Western trip that season.

Numerous franchise shifts were made through 1900. From 1892 through 1899 there were twelve teams in the league. From 1900 through 1952 eight clubs played. They were Boston, Brooklyn, Chicago, Cincinnati, New York, Philadelphia, Pittsburgh and St. Louis.

The shift of Boston to Mil-

waukee by Lou Perimi, the Braves' principal owner, was the first break-through major league franchise shift of the century. After the 1957 season, Brooklyn became Los Angeles and New York became San Francisco. Until today's action, that was the way the National League lined up.

Excluding suburban areas, New York City has a population of 7,710,346 and Houston 932,680, according to preliminary figures from the 1960 Federal census.

New York ranks first among the nation's cities in population. Houston is sixth, following Chicago, Los Angeles, Philadelphia and Detroit. Los Angeles is the only city in the nation with a larger area than Houston.

The club representatives were Philip K. Wrigley and John Holland of Chicago, Gabe Paul of Cincinnati, O'Malley of Los Angeles. Perini, John McHale and Birdie Tebbetts of Milwaukee; Bob Carpenter of Philadelphia, John Galbreath and Joe L. Brown of Pittsburgh, August A. Busch Jr., Dick Meyer and Anthony Buford of St. Louis and Stoneham of San Francisco.

October 18, 1960

American League, in '61, to Add Minneapolis and Los Angeles

By JOHN DREBINGER

The American League, taking the most revolutionary step in its history, voted yesterday to become a ten-club circuit.

What is more, the league will begin the expanded operation in 1961, getting a jump of a year on the rival National League.

These lightning moves made the expansion possible:

¶Calvin Griffith, owner of the Washington Senators, received permission to move his franchise to Minneapolis - St. Paul.

¶A new club for Washington was approved, assuring the capital of continued major league baseball. The owners of the new franchise will be disclosed later.

¶Still another new franchise was approved for Los Angeles, also under owners to be identified later.

The announcement was made by the league president, Joe Cronin, after a day-long session of the top executives of the eight present clubs at the Savoy Hilton Hotel.

The news startled the baseball world. While there had

been endless speculation on the league's expansion plans, few had expected such speedy action.

But the American Leaguers apparently were determined to beat the National League to the punch. Last week the National League had announced it was expanding to ten clubs with the addition of New York and Houston. However, the new teams will not begin play until 1962.

Thus, for the first time since the American League was founded in 1900, the two leagues will present uneven alignments next year.

The American League will operate with New York, Boston, Washington, Baltimore and Cleveland in the East and Los Angeles, Minneapolis-St. Paul, Kansas City, Chicago and Detroit in the West. It will play a 162-game schedule.

Each club will play eighteen games against every other club. The eight clubs in the National League will adhere to the usual 154-game schedule, with twenty-two meetings between each club.

So swiftly did the American Leaguers move that not even Commissioner Ford C. Frick seemed prepared for it.

"I haven't seen anything officially yet," said the Commissioner at his office. "There are so many angles to be considered, such as ball parks and what to do regarding players, that I cannot make any comment until I have talked to the people involved officially."

However, the American Leaguers already appeared assured that ball parks would offer no problem even if the new ownerships in Washington and Los Angeles remained a secret for a few more weeks.

The Senators will move into Metropolitan Stadium in Minneapolis, which was built in 1956 and has a seating capacity of 22,000. However, the Twin Cities organization already has started increasing this to 40,000 for the 1961 football season. Some new seats should be ready for the baseball season.

Washington already has started work on a new stadium, a Federal project that will be completed by September, 1961. It will seat 40,000 persons and is near the National Guard Armory, only about five minutes by cab from the Capitol.

Until the new stadium is ready, the new Washington club will play at Griffith Stadium, which up to now has been the home of the Senators. Calvin Griffith, the Senators' owner, will retain ownership of the park for the present. He said he would rent it to the new club.

In Los Angeles the situation is less settled, although Cronin said everything would be worked out satisfactorily well before the opening of the 1961 season.

Los Angeles Prepared

It is presumed that the American League entry in Los Angeles will play in the Coliseum, now the home of the National League Dodgers. If this cannot be worked out, Wrigley Field is available, according to Del Webb, the chairman of the American League expansion committee.

Whether the new club eventually will move in with the Dodgers when the latter's Chavez Ravine stadium is completed cannot be answered at this time, said Webb.

Immediately after the meeting, the general managers of the eight clubs went into another session to draw plans that will help the Washington and Los Angeles clubs stock their rosters. The Minneapolis-St. Paul club will be manned by the Washington Senator players of 1960.

The player plans will be submitted for ratification at another league meeting on Nov. 17. It is possible that the league will make additional expansion announcements at that time.

Detroit Tigers
Hank Greenberg

For in disclosing the new ten-club set-up, Cronin called it "only the first step."

"The American League is considering other fine baseball cities," said Cronin, "for a possible future expansion to twelve clubs."

It was, in all, a bewildering day. Scrapped, apparently, and with no attempt made to explain why, was the so-called commitment made by the two leagues to the defunct Continental League last summer.

A joint expansion committee of the two leagues assured the Continental League then that each league would absorb two Continental cities if the Continental League dissolved.

However, none of the Continental League groups figured in yesterday's moves. Minneapolis-St. Paul does get a ball club, but it will be operated by Griffith's organization.

Out of the picture completely go Dallas-Fort Worth and Toronto, which had been optimistic about gaining entry to the American League. However, there seemed to be no hard feelings.

Eliminated but Elated

"We are elated over what has happened," said Wheelock Whitney of the Twin City Continental group. "Our major object has from the first been to get the Twin Cities into a major league. Now that that is assured, we are ready to do everything possible to help Griffith make a success of his new move."

Griffith had tried for many years to get into Minneapolis but the American league had always balked him. He said he wanted the shift for the "betterment of our corporation."

The Twin Cities organization, Griffith said, was guaranteeing him 1,000,000 attendance for each of the next five years. Revenues from radio and television also will be substantially higher than in Washington.

"In Washington," said Griffith, "our radio-TV brought us about $180,000. Our new contract in Minneapolis should bring us about $500,000 annually."

Although no vote totals were

disclosed, it was understood that the shift from Washington had been approved by 6 to 2, just enough to make it. The vote was unanimous on the franchise for Los Angeles and the new ownership for Washington.

The identity of the new owners will likely remain a mystery for at least two or three weeks. However, the Washington group will not include Hank Greenberg, who had frequently been mentioned as a possible buyer. Greenberg is the vice president of the Chicago White Sox.

Greenberg, who attended the meeting, declined to commit himself on whether he might be involved in the Los Angeles venture. Webb also has been mentioned frequently in connection with the Los Angeles club.

Though Webb is a Yankee co-owner, most of his other business interests are in the West. He said yesterday, however, that there was nothing to the reports that he was interested in a Los Angeles operation.

Although disappointed that for the present they had been sidetracked, the Dallas-Fort Worth group, headed by Amon Carter Jr. and Joseph A. W. Bateson, apparently took comfort in Cronin's statement that the American League wasn't stopping at ten clubs.

Another indication of how strikingly sure the American Leaguers were of themselves was the fact that they never even bothered to advise the National League in advance of their plans.

"We didn't feel it was necessary to discuss it with them," said Cronin. "They made their move last week, today we've made ours. We made our move into Los Angeles with the assurance from Commissioner Frick that he was declaring Los Angeles an open city just as he did New York."

In Cincinnati, Warren C. Giles, the National League president, appeared to show no resentment over the American League action.

"I still think it more practical to expand to ten clubs in 1962, as we've announced. However, they know what's best for their league," he said.

This marks the fifth time the American League has shifted its field, with this one the most drastic. Until now the league always has operated with eight clubs. The last franchise shift was in 1955, when the Philadelphia Athletics were moved to Kansas City.

October 27, 1960

Carey, Hamilton Gain Hall of Fame

Max Carey and the late Billy Hamilton, who rivaled Ty Cobb as base-stealers, were voted into baseball's Hall of Fame yesterday by the Baseball Writers Association of America.

Carey set the modern National League record for stolen bases (738) during a twenty-two-year career. Hamilton established major-league marks of 115 stolen bases in one season and 937 for his career. He had a batting average of .344.

For the final voting, the writers cut the original list of forty-five to twenty-nine and then made both Carey and Hamilton unanimous choices.

Carey, who will be 70 years old on Feb. 11, is a resident of Miami Beach. Hamilton was born on Feb. 16, 1868, in Newark, and died in 1940 at the age of 72.

Max Carey in 1939

Spahn Pitches No-Hitter for His 290th Victory

SOUTHPAW WINS BY 1-0, WALKS 2

Runners Erased by Double Plays as Spahn, 40, Gets 2d No-Hitter of Career

MILWAUKEE, April 28 (UPI) — Warren Spahn, the amazingly durable 40-year-old southpaw of the Milwaukee Braves, pitched the second no-hitter and the 290th victory of his major league career tonight when he defeated the San Francisco Giants, 1—0.

Spahn, who celebrated his fortieth birthday last Sunday, put the Giants down one, two, three in all but two innings. He permitted only two runners to reach base. He walked Chuck Hiller in the fourth and Willie McCovey in the fifth. Both runners were erased in double plays started by Spahn.

Hank Aaron won the game for Spahn in the first inning when he singled after two were out to score Frank Bolling from second. Bolling had singled and advanced on a passed ball, one of two during the game by Ed Bailey, the Giants' new catcher.

Shutout No 52

Spahn's fifty-second shutout—increasing his league record for left-handers—was the Braves' fifth victory in their last six games and moved them past the Giants into first place.

Spahn, who pitched his first no-hitter last Sept. 16 here against the Philadelphia Phillies, had only two close calls. In the sixth Jose Pagan drove a hot grounder to Roy McMillan's left. The shortstop bobbled the ball momentarily and threw out Pagan by a step.

In the eighth, McCovey popped a fly into short center that Aaron had to run hard to catch.

Sam Jones, the Giants' hard-throwing right-hander, allowed only five hits. He gave only two through the first five innings and struck out eight batters during that span. Milwaukee threatened in three other innings, but each time he was able to choke off the budding rally.

Bob Feller and Cy Young are the only "modern" major leaguers to pitch three no-hitters. Only eight others—Carl Erskine, Tom Hughes, Addie Joss, Dutch Leonard, Christy Mathewson, Allie Reynolds, Virgil Trucks and Johnny Van Der Meer—have pitched two.

With 290 victories, the curve-balling native of Buffalo needs only ten more to become the sixth modern pitcher to win 300 games in a career. Those who have reached the 300-mark are Walter Johnson, Mathewson, Grover Cleveland Alexander, Eddie Plank and Lefty Grove.

Spahn is also the second oldest pitcher ever to pitch a no-hitter in the majors. Young pitched his third at the age of 41 in 1908.

The small crowd of 8,518 was hushed as the ninth started. Bailey led off by striking out. Then Matty Alou was sent in to pinch-hit for Pagan. He rolled a grounder to Spahn, who picked it up halfway between first and the mound and tossed to the first baseman, Joe Adcock, for the second out.

Joe Amalfitano batted for Jones and grounded sharply to McMillan, who juggled the ball momentarily and then tossed out the runner by a step.

The entire Braves dugout, led by Manager Charlie Dressen, mobbed Spahn along with dozens of youngsters from the bleachers.

Spahn's no-hitter was the first of the major league season, the best previous effort being a one-hitter by Frank Lary of the Detroit Tigers against the Chicago White Sox on April 14.

Lew Burdette, a team-mate of Spahn, and Don Cardwell of the Chicago Cubs also pitched no-hitters last season. Spahn has achieved the last two no-hitters pitched in the major leagues.

Spahn, who believes he will reach the No. 300 in July or August, has won twenty games in eleven seasons, a major league record for left-handers.

He has won twenty games in each of the last five seasons. This marked his second straight triumph of the 1961 season following a 2-1 loss to the St. Louis Cardinals on opening day. He beat the Pirates last Sunday.

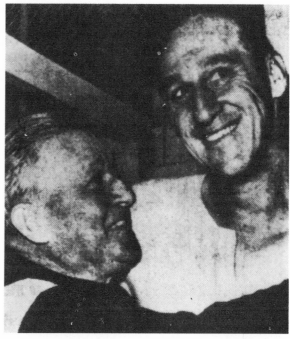

Associated Press Wirephoto

PITCHES NO-HITTER: Warren Spahn, right, Braves' southpaw, is congratulated by Charlie Dressen, his manager, following performance against Giants at Milwaukee.

SAN FRANCISCO (N.)	ab.r.h.rbi	MILWAUKEE (N.)	ab.r.h.rbi
Hiller, 2b	2 0 0 0	McMillan, ss	3 0 0 0
Kuenn, 3b	3 0 0 0	Bolling, 2b	3 1 2 0
Mays, cf	3 0 0 0	Mathews, 3b	3 0 0 0
McCovey, 1b	2 0 0 0	Aaron, cf	3 0 1 1
Cepeda, lf	3 0 0 0	Roach, lf	4 0 1 0
F. Alou, rf	3 0 0 0	Spangler, lf	9 0 0 0
Bailey, c	3 0 0 0	Adcock, 1b	3 0 1 0
Pagan, ss	2 0 0 0	Lau, c	2 0 0 0
aM. Alou	1 0 0 0	DeMerit, rf	4 0 0 0
S. Jones, p	2 0 0 0	Spahn, p	4 0 0 0
bAmalfitano	1 0 0 0		
	————	Total	29 1 5 1
Total	25 0 0 0		

aGrounded out for Pagan in 9th; bGrounded out for Jones in 9th.

San Francisco ..... .0 0 0 0 0 0 0 0 0—0
Milwaukee ... . .1 0 0 0 0 0 0 0.—1

E—McCovey. A—San Francisco 3, Milwaukee 11. DP—Spahn, McMillan, Adcock 2. LOB—San Francisco 5, Milwaukee 11.
Sacrifice—McMillan.

	IP.	H.	R.	ER.	BB.	SO.
Jones (L, 2—1)	8	5	1	0	5	9
Spahn (W, 2—1)	9	0	0	0	2	5

HBP—By Jones (Bolling). PB—Bailey 2. Umpires—Donatelli, Burkhardt, Pelekoudas, Forman, Conlan. Time of game—2:16. Attendance—8,518.

April 29, 1961

United Press International

Billy Hamilton in 1920's

Carey, born in Terre Haute, Ind., broke into the majors with Pittsburgh in 1910. He remained with the Pirates until the Brooklyn Dodgers claimed him on waivers in July of 1926. He finished his playing career with the Dodgers in 1929.

Hamilton began his career with Kansas City in 1888. With Philadelphia in 1891, he led the National League in batting with a .338 average. In that season, he amazed the baseball world by stealing 115 bases.

Both players were outfielders. Carey also did some managing. He directed the Dodgers in 1932 and 1933. The last time he was active in the game was in 1956 as manager of Louisville in the American Association.

The two will be formally installed into the hall of fame on July 24 in ceremonies at Cooperstown, N. Y. Hamilton probably will be represented there by his sister, Mrs. Robert Jones of Ojai, Calif.

January 30, 1961

Mays Wallops Four Home Runs

RECORD EQUALED IN 14-4 CONTEST

Mays, Ninth to Connect 4 Times in One Game, Paces 8-Homer Giant Offense

MILWAUKEE, April 30 (AP) —Willie Mays today became the ninth player in major league history to hit four home runs in one game as the San Francisco Giants routed the Milwaukee Braves, 14–4.

Mays, who drove in eight runs, connected in the first, third, sixth and eighth innings. In the ninth, with the crowd of 13,114 cheering for him to get another turn at bat, Willie advanced to the on-deck circle. But Jim Davenport, the Giant immediately preceding him in the batting order, ended the suspense by grounding out.

The effort by Mays contributed to the setting or tying of five home-run records. Hitting eight home runs in all, the Giants accomplished the following:

¶Set a National League record of thirteen home runs in two consecutive games. They had hit five yesterday.

¶Equaled the major league record for home runs in two consecutive games.

Willie Mays

New York Times

¶Equaled the major league record of eight homers in one game.

¶Equaled, with the help of Milwaukee's two homers, the National League record of ten four-baggers in one game by two teams.

Mays, who had hit only two homers previously this season, tied a mark shared by Lou Gehrig, among others.

Mays Put Out Once

The last major league player to hit four homers in one game had been Rocky Colavito, who belted four in a row for the Cleveland Indians on June 10, 1959. The last National Leaguer had been Joe Adcock of the Braves, who connected on July 31, 1954. Colavito is now with the Detroit Tigers.

Mays did not connect in succession. The string was broken in the fifth, when Moe Drabowsky retired him on a line drive to the center fielder.

Lew Burdette, who started for the Braves and pitched three innings, yielded the first two homers to Mays. The Giant center fielder hit his third off Seth Morehead and his fourth off Don McMahon.

Mays hit one homer with two men on base, two with one on and the other with the bases empty. His eight runs batted in fell four short of the one-game record.

Henry Aaron was the Braves' batting star, hitting both Milwaukee homers.

Pagan Hits 2 Homers

José Pagan hit two of the San Francisco home runs, the first of his major league career. He entered the game with a batting average of .056 and made four hits in five tries. Orlando Cepeda and Felipe Alou hit the other four-baggers.

The club's thirteen homers in two games broke the league record of twelve set by the Braves in a double-header at Pittsburgh on Aug. 30, 1953, and tied the major league high set by the New York Yankees in a double-header on June 28, 1939.

Other major leaguers who hit four homers in one game were Gil Hodges for the Brooklyn Dodgers; Pat Seerey, Chicago White Sox; Chuck Klein, Philadelphia Phillies; Ed Delahanty, Phillies, and Bob Lowe of the old Boston Braves. May 1, 1961

SAN FRANCISCO (N.)	ab.	r.	h.	rbi	MILWAUKEE (N.)	ab.	r.	h.	rbi
Hiller, 2b	6	2	3	1	McMillan, ss	4	1	1	0
Davenport, 3b	4	3	1	1	Bolling, 2b	4	1	2	0
Mays, cf	5	4	4	8	Mathews, 3b	4	0	1	0
McCovey, 1b	3	0	0	0	Aaron, cf	4	2	2	4
Marshall, 1b	0	0	0	0	Roach, f	4	0	1	0
Cepeda, lf	5	1	1	1	Adcock, 1b	4	0	0	0
M. Alou, lf	0	0	0	0	Lau, c	3	0	1	0
F. Alou, rf	4	1	1	1	McMahon, p	0	0	0	0
Bailey, c	4	0	0	0	Brunet, p	0	0	0	0
Pagan, ss	5	3	4	2	cMzye	0	0	0	0
Loes, p	3	0	0	0	DeMerit, rf	4	0	0	0
					Burdette, p	1	0	0	0
					Willey, p	0	0	0	0
					Drabowsky, p	0	0	0	0
					aMartin	1	0	0	0
					Morehead, p	0	0	0	0
					MacKenzie, p	0	0	0	0
					bLogan	1	0	0	0
					Taylor, c	0	0	0	0
Total	39	14	14	14	Total	34	4	8	4

aFlied out for Drabowski in 5th; bFanned for MacKenzie in 7th; cWalked for Brunet in 9th.

San Francisco		1 0 3	3 0 4	0 3 0—14
Milwaukee		3 0 0	0 0 1	0 0 0— 4

E—Mathews. A—San Francisco 9, Milwaukee 15. DP—Davenport, Hiller, Marshall; Burdette, McMillan, Adcock; Bolling, McMillan, Adcock. LOB—San Francisco 6, Milwaukee 4. 2B—Hits—Hiller 2. 3B—Davenport. HR—Mays 4, Pagan 2, Cepeda, F. Alou, Aaron 2. Sacrifices—Loes 2.

	IP.	H.	R.	ER.	BB.	SO.
Loes (W, 2–1)	9	8	4	4	1	3
*Burdette (L, 1–1)	.3	5	5	5	0	0
Willey	1	3	2	2	0	0
Drabowsky	1	0	0	0	1	0
Morehead	1	2	4	4	1	1
MacKenzie	.1	0	0	0	0	1
McMahon	1	3	3	3	2	0
Brunet	1	1	0	0	0	0

*Faced 1 batter in 4th.
WP—By Burdette (Davenport), by MacKenzie (Bailey). Umpires—Pelekoudas, Forman, Conlan, Donatelli, Burkhart. Time— 2:40. Attendance—13,114.

National League Triumphs in 10-Inning All-Star Game Marked by 7 Errors

HIT BY CLEMENTE ENDS 5-4 CONTEST

Pirate Player's Single Beats American League Team Before 44,115 on Coast

By JOHN DREBINGER
Special to The New York Times.

SAN FRANCISCO, July 11—In as loosely played a game as baseball's midsummer classic ever has known, the National League today defeated the American League in the first of 1961's two all-star games before a roaring crowd of 44,115 fans.

Seven errors were committed, five by the Nationals and two by the Americans. The total broke the all-star record of six set at Ebbets Fields in 1949.

The National Leaguers won it in the last of the tenth, 5 to 4. A two-bagger by the Giants' redoubtable Willie Mays drove in the first tally and a single by Bob Clemente sent Willie across the plate with the winning run.

But minutes before this, Danny Murtagh's Nationals all but had the victory blown out of their grasp as their players were caught in the swirling winds of San Francisco's Candlestick Park. They made four errors in the last two innings while the Americans tied the score with two runs in the ninth and then moved one ahead in the top of the tenth.

For eight innings, in the stillness of an unusually hot and almost windless afternoon, brilliant National League pitching, starting with Warren Spahn, had held the vaunted American League power to just one hit while the senior loop piled up a 3-1 lead.

Killebrew Finds Range

That on hit had been a homer by Harmon Killebrew as he entered in the sixth inning as a pinch-hitter. It was smacked off Mike McCormick of the Giants.

But by then the Nationals already had scored a run off Paul Richards' starter, Whitey Ford. Clemente of the Pirates drove this one home in the second with a triple. In the fourth the Nationals picked up their second tally with the help of an American League misplay. And in the eighth, George

Associated Press Wirephoto

THEY DIDN'T GET THIS ONE: Mickey Mantle, left, and Roger Maris, outfielders for the American League all-star team, can not catch up with ball hit by Roberto Clemente in second inning. Clemente wound up at third with a triple and later scored the game's first run.

Altman, a Cub outfielder, stroked a homer over the right-field barrier.

That had the Nationals two in front as the encounter moved into the ninth. With a spanking breeze already stirring up a lot of dust, local fans, knowing full well what was coming, were heading for the exits before being blown into the bay.

But within minutes, more than wind was swirling in the arena. Mickey Mantle, hitless in three tries at bat, was no longer in the American League line-up as the wind and everything else hit the stunned National Leaguers from all sides.

With one out and ElRoy Face, the Pirates' star reliever, all set to lock up the victory, Norm Cash started the Americans' ninth-inning drive with a two-bagger.

Kaline Gets Single

It was the second hit for the harried Richards forces. The third one followed immediately as Al Kaline, Mantle's replacement, singled to score the Detroit first baseman.

Now Manager Murtagh began reaching desperately into his bullpen. Out popped Sandy Koufax, a Dodger left-hander, only to be slapped for a single by Roger Maris. It scored Nellie Fox, who had gone in to run for Cash. That was all for Sandy and the Giants' Stu Miller took over.

It was now blowing in lively fashion and, if what followed seems an incredible performance for men considered the highest craftsmen in their profession, it nevertheless was excusable.

Miller, a diminutive right-

hander, immediately committed a balk that advanced Kaline and Maris to third and second, respectively. Rocky Colavito followed with a grounder that Ken Boyer, crack third baseman of the Cardinals, stumbled all over for an error.

Kaline scored the tying run while Maris held up at second. The scoring for the inning ended here, but not the errors, which continued to give Candlestick's record crowd a violent case of jitters.

Burgess Drops Foul

The catcher, Smoky Burgess, dropped a foul near the plate on Tony Kubek, who then struck out. Yogi Berra, appearing as a pinch-hitter, grounded to the second baseman, Don Zimmer, whose wide throw to first pulled Bill White off the bag. However, that merely filled the bases, and the gathering, which had tossed $250,230.81 into the players' pension pool, was still breathing, but with difficulty.

When Dick Howser followed with the third out, leaving the score tied, the sigh of relief from the fans almost matched the ever-increasing gale.

But the folks were still uneasy when Hoyt Wilhelm, the sixth and last of the American League hurlers Richards trotted out, held the Nationals scoreless in the last of the ninth.

In the tenth they nearly died. With one out, Miller walked Fox, who had remained in the game as the Americans' second baseman. Then Boyer followed with his second error, the most ghastly of the afternoon. The Cards' third baseman, scooping up Kaline's grounder, fired the ball into right field and Fox scored all the way from first.

That had the Americans in front for the first time, but the lead was brief. Hank Aaron, the noted Braves' slugger pinch-hitting for Miller, opened the Nationals' tenth with a single to center.

Berra, who had remained as a catcher in the ninth, only to give way immediately to Elston Howard because of Wilhelm's elusive knuckleball, now was to see his Yankee team-mate have his troubles. Howard let one of Wilhelm's flutter balls get away for a passed ball while Hoyt was pitching to Mays.

That put Aaron on second. When Willie the Wonder followed with his two-bagger. Aaron galloped home to tie the score again.

The wind was now even raising havoc with Wilhelm's knuckler. The Orioles' brilliant reliever hit Frank Robinson with a stray pitch.

A moment later. Clemente, who had driven in the Nationals' second tally of the afternoon with a sacrifice fly in the fourth, ended it all with a sharp single to right. Almost casually

Mays jogged in from second and that was it.

With this victory the onrushing Nationals have now whittled the American League lead in all-star competition to a 16-14 margin. It was the Nationals' fourth triumph in the last five games and tenth in the last fourteen.

The Americans, for all the flurry they made at the end, connected for only four hits. The National League pitchers fanned a total of twelve batters, which tied an all-star record.

Out-of-towners, who had been hearing tales of the frosty gales that in the twinkling of an eye convert Candlestick Park into an icy wind tunnel, were more than a mite mystified as they entered the picturesque, sun-drenched arena nestled under the lee of Morvey's Hill.

In no time at all, they were in their shirtsleeves and perspiring as profusely as if they were sitting under the lee of Coogan's Bluff watching a July 4 double-header between the Giants and Dodgers in the old Polo Grounds.

There was scarcely a breath of air stirring and the thermometer read 85 degrees. It could have been Kansas City or a place they rarely mention in these parts. On a map it's called Los Angeles. The wind was still to come.

It was, however, a gay and festive gathering and there were lusty cheers for all the stars as they were formally introduced in the pre-game ceremonies. But the noisiest ovation of all was saved for the National League's "grand old man," the 40-year-old Stan Musial, who was appearing in his twentieth all-star game.

And there were still some pre-game cheers left when Casey Stengel, as guest of Commissioner Ford C. Frick, reared back to toss out the first ball. It was a well-delivered, left-handed pitch by the one-time left-handed dental student who ranked as one of baseball's greatest managers.

As the game got on the way, it was even more difficult to grasp the idea that baseball is a young man's game. For no sooner had the opening salute to Musial died down than the fans began cheering another 40-year-old, Spahn of the Braves.

Last April 28, the Milwaukee southpaw hurled a no-hitter. He might well have repeated that performance today were it not for all-star rules that bar a pitcher from working more than three innings. Spahn's three innings were letter perfect. He faced nine batters and they went down like tenpins, three of them on strikes.

Meanwhile, Ford, the American League's sixteen-game winner, was still having trouble shedding his all-star jinx of long standing, although Whitey acquitted himself better than in most of his previous mid-summer appearances.

With one out in the second, Clemente drove a liner to the wire railing in right center. As Mantle and Maris converged on the ball, Maris reached first.

All-Star Score

AMERICAN LEAGUE

	AB.	R.	H.	RBI.	PO.	A.
Temple, 2b	3	0	0	0	1	2
fGentile, 1b	2	0	0	0	2	0
Cash, 1b	4	0	1	0	6	1
gFox, 2b	0	2	0	0	1	0
Mantle, cf	3	0	0	0	3	0
Kaline, cf	2	1	1	1	1	0
Maris, rf	4	0	1	0	3	0
Colavito, lf	4	0	0	1	1	0
Kubek, ss	4	0	0	0	1	2
Romano, c	3	0	0	0	7	0
hBerra, c	1	0	0	0	0	0
Hoawrd, c	0	0	0	0	0	0
B. Robinson, 3b	2	0	0	0	0	2
Bunning, p	0	0	0	0	1	0
dBrandt	0	0	0	0	0	0
Fornieles, p	0	0	0	0	0	0
Wilhelm, p	1	0	0	0	0	0
Ford, p	1	0	0	0	0	0
Lary, p	0	0	0	0	0	0
Donovan, p	0	0	0	0	0	0
cKillebrew, 3b	2	1	1	1	0	0
Howser, 3b	1	0	0	0	0	1
Total	38	4	4	3	27	8

NATIONAL LEAGUE

	AB.	R.	H.	RBI.	PO.	A.
Wills, ss	5	0	1	0	0	2
Mathews, 3b	2	0	0	0	0	0
Purkey, p	0	0	0	0	1	0
bMusial	1	0	0	0	0	0
McCormick, p	1	0	0	0	0	0
eAltman	1	1	1	1	0	0
Face, p	0	0	0	0	0	0
Koufax, p	0	0	0	0	0	0
Miller, p	0	0	0	0	0	0
iAaron	1	1	1	0	0	0
Mays, cf	5	2	2	1	3	0
Cepeda, lf	3	0	0	0	1	0
F. Robinson, lf	1	0	1	0	2	0
Clemente, rf	4	1	2	2	2	0
White, 1b	3	0	1	1	7	1
Bolling, 2b	3	0	0	1	3	3
Zimmer, 2b	1	0	0	0	0	0
Burgess, c	4	0	1	0	13	0
Spahn, p	0	0	0	0	0	0
aStuart	1	0	1	0	0	0
Boyer, 3b	2	0	0	0	0	1
Total	37	5	11	5	30	8

aDoubled for Soahn in 3d; bFlied out for Purkey in 5th; cHit home run for Donovan in 6th; dStruck out for Bunning in 8th; eHit home run for McCormick in 8th; fStruck out for Temple in 9th; gRan for Cash in 9th; hSafe on error for Romano in 9th; iSingled for Miller in 10th.

American	000 001 002 1—4
National	010 100 010 2—5

None out when winning run was scored.
Errors—Cepeda, Kubek, Boyer 2, Burgess, Zimmer, Gentile. Left on base—American 6, National 9.
Two-base hits—Stuart, Cash, Mays. Three-base hits—Clemente. Home runs—Killebrew, Altman. Stolen base—Robinson. Sacrifice flies—White, Clemente.

	IP.	H.	R.	ER.
Spahn	3	0	0	0
Purkey	2	0	0	0
McCormick	3	1	1	1
Face	1⅓	2	2	2
†Koufax	0	1	0	0
Miller (W)	1⅔	0	1	0
Ford	3	2	1	1
*Lary	0	0	0	0
Donovan	2	4	0	0
Bunning	2	0	0	0
Fornieles	⅓	2	1	1
‡Wilhelm (L)	1⅔	3	2	2

*Faced 1 batter in 4th. †Faced 1 batter in 9th. ‡Faced 3 batters in 10th.
Bases on balls—Off McCormick 1 (Maris); Miller 1 (Fox); Wilhelm 1 (Boyer). Struck out—By Spahn 3 (Cash, Mantle, Maris); Purkey 1 (Romano); McCormick 3 (Cash, Mantle, Brandt); Face 1 (Gentile); Miller 4 (Kubek, Wilhelm, Gentile, Maris); Ford 2 (Mays, Bolling); Donovan 1 (Boyer); Bunning 2 (White, Boyer); Wilhelm 1 (Clemente). Hit by pitched ball—By Robinson (F. Robinson).
Balk—Miller. Passed ball—By Howard. Umpires—Landes (N.), Umont (A.), Crawford (N.), Runge (A.), Vargo (N.), Drummond (A.). Time—2:53. Attendance—44,115. Receipts—$259,230.81.

For a moment it looked as if the Yankee right-fielder had made a backhand catch of the ball. But he couldn't hold it and before Mantle could recover the ball and get it to the infield, Clemente was on third with a triple. He scored on Bill White's sacrifice fly by Mantle in center.

Although stung for a two-bagger by a pinch-hitter, Dick Stuart, in the third, Ford finished his three-inning stint without further trouble.

But with the fourth, fresh annoyances cropped up for the American Leaguers. As Frank Lary, the Tigers' ace right-hander, stepped to the mound, Kubek, the Yanks' crack short-stop, made a two-base boot of Mays' sharp grounder on the first play.

At the same time Lary had to leave the game. The Detroit star, who had pitched a nine-inning, three-hit shutout against the Angels on Sunday, complained of an ailing right shoulder and the Senators' Dick Donovan was hastily called in from the bullpen. Later it was learned Lary was suffering from an inflamed tendon in his right shoulder.

Donovan couldn't prevent Mays from scoring. Willie advanced to third on Orlando Cepeda's infield out and galloped home, with cap flying off, on Clemente's sacrifice fly to Maris in right.

Incidentally, that tally enabled Mays to set an all-star record of most runs scored, with a total of twelve. He had been tied with Musial at eleven.

In the fifth Musial made his official bow and exit, as a pinch-hitter. With two on, he flied to left. Though Mays then singled, filling the bases, Donovan got out of this jam.

While this was going on, the Nationals continued to get two more innings of flawless pitching from the Reds' Bob Purkey, who had replaced Spahn after the third.

Even the fact that Cepeda opened the fourth by making a two-base muff of Johnny Temple's fly in left did not seem to disturb the Cincinnati right-hander. He snuffed out the next three batters to end the fourth and repeated the performance in the fifth.

With the sixth, however, the American League's power finally asserted itself long enough to crack the Nationals' two-run lead in half. With one out and the Giants' McCormick on the mound, Killebrew belted a towering fly toward left. It cleared the barrier just beyond Cepeda's reach.

According to local authorities, it was one of the highest flies ever to clear that sector of the park, where the prevailing wind blows from left to right. It had not started to blow yet. However, with the eighth, there was a spanking breeze blowing as Altman, a Cub outfielder, belted one over the 375-foot marker in right center and into the bleachers just beyond.

Mike Fornieles of the Red Sox, who had just replaced Jim Bunning in this inning, was the victim of that shot. It was made on Mike's first pitch. When Frank Robinson followed with a single, along with a stolen base, Richards brought in his own ace reliever, Wilhelm.

The latter made quick work of the next two batters and that is the way matters stood as the struggle moved into its windblown finale, the Nationals leading by two, but not for long.

July 12, 1961

Ruth's Record Can Be Broken Only in 154 Games, Frick Rules

Ford Frick threw a protective screen around Babe Ruth's season record of sixty home runs yesterday. The baseball commissioner ruled that no batter would be credited with breaking the record unless he did it in 154 games.

The ruling was prompted by the home run feats this season of Roger Maris and Mickey Mantle of the Yankees. Maris had hit thirty-five homers before last night's double-header with the Orioles and Mantle had clouted thirty-two.

Maris is nineteen games ahead of the pace Ruth set in 1927 when he established the mark with the Yankees. Mantle is eight games ahead of Ruth's schedule.

Ten Teams Play Now

The prospects of the record being broken are further enhanced by the expanded schedule in the American League. With ten teams in the league, the Americans are playing 162 games.

The National League will add Houston and New York next year and also will expand to 162 games.

However, Frick said that any player who hit more than sixty homers after the 154th game would get a distinctive mark in the record book to show it was compiled under a 162-game schedule.

It had been assumed that

Frick would require some formal distinction in if the record was set in more than 154 games, but he decided to make a formal ruling because of the unusual interest in the case.

He did not go into other records that might fall under the longer schedule.

Frick's ruling:

"Any player who may hit more than sixty home runs during his club's first 154 games would be recognized as having established a new record. However, if the player does not hit more than sixty until after his club has played 154 games, there would have to be some distinctive mark in the record books to show that Babe Ruth's record was set under a 154-game schedule and the total or more than sixty was compiled while a 162-game schedule was in effect.

"We also would apply the same reasoning if a player should equal Ruth's total of sixty in the first 154 games, he would be recognized as typing Ruth's record. If in more than 154 games, there would be a distinction in the record book."

July 18, 1961

Pitchers Tame Sluggers as Major League All-Stars Play to Their First Tie

GAME ENDS AT 1-1 AFTER 9TH INNING

Rain Halts Action at Boston —Colavito Homer, White Single Drive in Runs

By ROBERT L. TEAGUE
Special to The New York Times.

BOSTON, July 31—Baseball's finest pitchers won their psychological war with The Wall and their dangerous guessing contest with the sport's best batters in the major league all-star game at Fenway Park today.

Rain prevented further embarrassment for the sluggers, halting play after nine innings with the American and National Leagues deadlocked at 1—1. It was the first tie game in thirty-one all-star contests and it interrupted the Nationals winning streak at three.

If the Nationals want to claim statistical superiority, there are some excellent numerical arguments to support them. They collected five hits while the Americans made four. And they reached third base three times.

Rocky Colavito of the Detroit Tigers got the first hit of the day—a home run off Bob Purkey of the Cincinnati Reds in the first inning. The lofty drive cleared the left-field wall and struck the screen, 315 feet from the plate. No other American Leaguer got farther than second base.

A Low-Pressure Rally

The Nationals manufactured the tying run in the sixth, against Don Schwall of the Boston Red Sox, Bill White of

Associated Press Wirephoto

Luis Aparicio of the White Sox leaps to avoid spikes of Willie Mays as the Giants' star slides into second in eighth inning. Rain halted game after nine innings.

the St. Louis Cardinals drove it across with the second consecutive infield single of the inning.

A base on balls to Ed Mathews of the Milwaukee Braves and a hit batsman — Orlando Cepeda of the San Francisco Giants—had started this low-pressure uprising after one man had been retired.

An eleventh-hour comeback by the Americans seemed imminent when Al Kaline of the

Tigers opened the last of the ninth with a solid single to center and stole second base.

Stu Miller of the Giants was on the mound at the time. The San Francisco "junkman" did not allow the runner to budge again, striking out Mickey Mantle and Elston Howard of the Yankees and Roy Sievers of the Chicago White Sox in succession.

By then, the rain that had begun falling lightly in the

American half of the eighth was so heavy that the umpires ordered the field covered. About thirty minutes later, they called the game.

Miller's performance in the ninth against three reputable long-distance clouters was the most stirring of the day. However, it was rivaled by the six other hurlers who saw action on both teams.

Jim Bunning of Detroit, the American League starter, pitched three perfect innings. Only one ball was hit out of the infield off the right-hander. In this season's first all-star meeting, won by the Nationals on July 11, Bunning had hurled two perfect innings in relief.

Batters Missing Mark

Bunning was followed by Schwall and Camilo Pascual of the Minnesota Twins. Purkey's National League successors were Art Mahaffey of the Philadelphia Phillies, Sandy Koufax of the Los Angeles Dodgers and Miller. All of them stood out, as bats whipped up miniature cyclones around the batter's box. Seven National Leaguers and eight American Leaguers struck out.

No one can be sure whether the sluggers were concentrating too hard on that short left-field wall. It is certain, though, that they were under no orders to ignore it. Before the contest the rival managers said that, generally speaking, they would leave the hitters on their own.

Paul Richards, the sage from Baltimore, went further.

"Still generally speaking," he said, "if I had these guys on my regular ball club, I'd leave 'em on their own all year."

Colavito's homer was hit on his first at-bat against Purkey. The Tiger outfielder backed off from a pitch in close at the letters. Then he belted the next offering over the wall and the screen. The wall is thirty-seven feet high.

The Americans' second hit was a single to left by Brooks Robinson of the Orioles in leading off the fifth against Koufax. The Los Angeles left-hander immediately got into the clear as Schwall, attempting to sacrifice, bunted into a double play.

All-Star Score

NATIONAL LEAGUE

	AB.	R.	H.	RBI.	PO.	A.
Wills, ss..........	2	0	1	0	1	1
Aaron, rf.........	2	0	0	0	1	0
Miller, p..........	0	0	0	0	0	0
Mathews, 3b......	3	1	0	0	0	2
Mays, cf.........	3	0	1	0	1	0
Cepeda, lf........	3	0	0	0	0	0
Clemente, rf......	2	0	0	0	0	0
Kasko, ss.........	1	0	1	0	2	4
eBanks, ss.......	1	0	0	0	0	0
White, 1b........	4	0	2	1	11	1
Bolling, 2b.......	4	0	0	0	3	2
Burgess, c........	1	0	0	0	2	0
Roseboro, c.......	3	0	0	0	6	0
Purkey, p........	0	0	0	0	0	1
aStuart	1	0	0	0	0	0
Mahaffey, p......	0	0	0	0	0	0
cMusial	1	0	0	0	0	0
Koufax, p........	0	0	0	0	0	0
dAltman, rf......	1	0	0	0	0	0
Total 32	32	1	5	1	27	11

AMERICAN LEAGUE

	AB.	R.	H.	RBI.	PO.	A.
Cash, 1b.........	4	0	0	0	11	0
Colavito, lf......	4	1	1	1	3	0
Kaline, rf........	4	0	2	0	1	0
Mantle, cf.......	3	0	0	0	2	0
Romano, c.......	1	0	0	0	1	0
bMaris	1	0	0	0	0	0
Howard, c........	2	0	0	0	6	0
Aparicio, ss......	2	0	0	0	1	3
fSievers	1	0	0	0	0	0
Temple, 2b.......	2	0	0	0	2	3
B. Robinson, 3b..	3	0	1	0	0	3
Bunning, p.......	1	0	0	0	0	0
Schwall, p.......	1	0	0	0	0	0
Pascual, p.......	1	0	0	0	0	0
Total 30	30	1	4	1	27	9

aGrounded out for Purkey in third; bPopped out for Romano in fourth; cStruck out for Mahaffey in fifth; dFlied out for Koufax in seventh; eStruck out for Kasko in eighth; fStruck out for Aparicio in ninth.

	IP.	H.	R.	ER.
Bunning, Tigers.....	3	0	0	0
Schwall, Red Sox...	3	5	1	1
Pascual, Twins.....	3	0	0	0
Purkey, Reds........	2	1	1	1
Mahaffey, Phils.....	2	0	0	0
Koufax, Dodgers.....	2	2	0	0
Miller, Giants......	3	1	0	0

National ......000 001 000—1
American ......100 000 000—1

Called, rain.

Error—Bolling. Double plays—Bolling, Kasko, White; White. Kasko, Bolling. Left on bases—National 7, American 5.

Two-base hits—White. Home run—Colavito. Stolen base—Kaline.

Bases on balls—Off Schwall 1 (Mathews), Pascual 1 (Mays), Purkey 2 (Aparicio, Temple), Mahaffey 1 (Mantle). Struck out—By Bunning 1 (Burgess), Schwall 2 (Roseboro, Musial), Pascual 4 (Roseboro 2, Mathews, Banks), Purkey 2 (Cash, B. Robinson), Koufax 1 (Mantle), Miller 5 (Aparicio, Temple, Mantle, Howard, Sievers).

Hit by pitcher—By Schwall (Cepeda). Passed ball—Burgess. Umpires—Napp (A.), Secory (N.), Flaherty (A.), Sudol (N.), Smith (A.), Pelekoudas (N.). Time of game—2:27. Attendance—31,851. Net receipts—$172,298.19.

Meanwhile, the Nationals were having their troubles at the plate against Bunning and Schwall. In the fourth, Maury Wills of the Dodgers and Willie Mays of the Giants sandwiched singles around a putout. Schwall retired the next two batters on infield plays, however.

In the fifth the Red Sox rookie found himself in another hole when White led off with a line double to center. The Cardinal star advanced to third on an infield out. Then Schwall fanned Johnny Roseboro of the Dodgers and Stan Musial of the Cards to check the threat. This, incidentally, was Musial's twenty-first appearance in all-star competition.

Schwall walked Mathews with one down in the sixth. And after Mays had flied out, the pitcher hit Cepeda in the back. Ed Kasko of the Reds then rapped a slow bounder to deep short. Luis Aparicio of the White Sox fielded it cleanly, but had no play. That filled the bases.

Here, White drove a ball through Schwall's legs. Aparicio fielded this one behind second base, but again too late for a play. Mathews scored. The next man flied out.

Maris Hits 61st in Final Game

Yank First to Exceed 60 Home Runs in Major Leagues

By JOHN DREBINGER

Roger Maris yesterday became the first major league player in history to hit more than sixty home runs in a season.

The 27-year-old Yankee outfielder hit his sixty-first at the Stadium before a roaring crowd of 23,154 in the Bombers' final game of the regular campaign.

That surpassed by one the sixty that Babe Ruth hit in 1927. Ruth's mark has stood in the record book for thirty-four years.

Artistically enough, Maris' homer also produced the only run of the game as Ralph Houk's 1961 American League champions defeated the Red Sox, 1 to 0, in their final tune-up for the world series, which opens at the Stadium on Wednesday.

Maris hit his fourth-inning homer in his second time at bat. The victim of the blow was Tracy Stallard, a 24-year-old Boston rookie right-hander. Stallard's name, perhaps, will in time gain as much renown as that of Tom Zachary, who delivered the pitch that Ruth slammed into the Stadium's right-field bleachers for No. 60 on the next to the last day of the 1927 season.

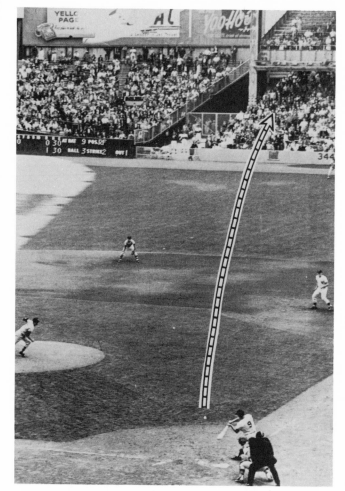

Associated Press

Roger Maris hitting his sixty-first home run of the season yesterday in the fourth inning at Yankee Stadium.

Along with Stallard, still another name was bandied about at the Stadium after Maris' drive. Sal Durante, a 19-year-old truck driver from Coney Island, was the fellow who caught the ball as it dropped into the lower right-field stand, some ten rows back and about ten feet to the right of the Yankee bull pen.

For this achievement the young man won a $5,000 award and a round trip to Sacramento, Calif., offered by a Sacramento restaurant proprietor, as well as a round trip to the 1962 World's Fair in Seattle.

Maris was fooled by Stallard on an outside pitch that he stroked to left field for an out in the first inning. He let two pitches go by when he came to bat in the fourth with one out and the bases empty. The first one was high and outside. The second one was low and appeared to be inside.

Waist-High Fast Ball

The crowd, interested in only one thing, a home run, greeted both pitches with a chorus of boos. Then came the moment for which fans from coast to coast had been waiting since last Tuesday night, when Maris hit his sixtieth.

Stallard's next pitch was a fast ball that appeared to be about waist high and right down the middle. In a flash, Roger's rhythmic swing, long the envy of left-handed pull hitters, connected with the ball.

Almost at once, the crowd sensed that this was it. An ear-splitting roar went up as Maris, standing spellbound for just an instant at the plate, started his triumphant jog around the bases. As he came down the third-base line, he shook hands joyously with a young fan who had rushed onto the field to congratulate him.

Crossing the plate and arriving at the Yankee dugout, he was met by a solid phalanx of team-mates. This time they made certain the modest country lad from Raytown, Mo., acknowledged the crowd's plaudits.

He had been reluctant to do so when he hit No. 60, but this time the Yankee players wouldn't let Roger come down the dugout steps. Smiling broadly, the usually unemotional player lifted his cap from his blond close-cropped thatch and waved it to the cheering fans. Not until he had taken four bows did his colleagues allow him to retire to the bench.

Ruth's record, of course, will not be erased. On July 17, Commissioner Ford C. Frick ruled that Ruth's record would stand unless bettered within a 154-game limit, since that was the schedule in 1927. Maris hit fifty-nine homers in the Yanks' first 154 games to a decision. He hit his sixtieth four games later.

Maris Homers Day by Day

HR NO.	GAME NO.	DATE APRIL	OPPOSING PITCHER AND CLUB.	WHERE MADE.
1.	10	26	Foytack, Detroit (R)	Detroit
		MAY		
2.	16	3	Ramos, Minnesota (R)	Bloomington
3.	19	6	Grba, Los Angeles (R)	Los Angeles
4.	28	17	Burnside, Washington (L)	New York
5.	29	19	Perry, Cleveland (R)	Cleveland
6.	30	20	Bell, Cleveland (R)	Cleveland
7.	31	21	Estrada, Baltimore (R)	New York
8.	34	24	Conley, Boston (R)	New York
9.	37	28	McLish, Chicago (R)	New York
10.	39	30	Conley, Boston (R)	Boston
11.	39	30	Fornieles, Boston (R)	Boston
12.	40	31	Muffett, Boston (R)	Boston
		JUNE		
13.	42	2	McLish, Chicago (R)	Chicago
14.	43	3	Shaw, Chicago (R)	Chicago
15.	44	4	Kemmerer, Chicago (R)	Chicago
16.	47	6	Palmquist, Minnesota (R)	New York
17.	48	7	Ramos, Minnesota (R)	New York
18.	51	9	Herbert, Kansas City (R)	New York
19.	54	11	Grba, Los Angeles (R)	New York
20.	54	11	James, Los Angeles (R)	New York
21.	56	13	Perry, Cleveland (R)	Cleveland
22.	57	14	Bell, Cleveland (R)	Cleveland
23.	60	17	Mossi, Detroit (L)	Detroit
24.	61	18	Casale, Detroit (R)	Detroit
25.	62	19	Archer, Kansas City (L)	Kansas City
26.	63	20	Nuxhall, Kansas City (L)	Kansas City
27.	65	22	Bass, Kansas City (R)	Kansas City
		JULY		
28.	73	1	Sisler, Washington (R)	New York
29.	74	2	Burnside, Washington (L)	New York
30.	74	2	Klippstein, Washington (R)	New York
31.	76	4	Lary, Detroit (R)	New York
32.	77	5	Funk, Cleveland (R)	New York
33.	81	9	Monbouquette, Boston (R)	Boston
34.	83	13	Wynn, Chicago (R)	Chicago
35.	85	15	Herbert, Chicago (R)	Chicago
36.	91	21	Monbouquette, Boston (R)	Boston
37.	94	25	Baumann, Chicago (L)	New York
38.	94	25	Larsen, Chicago (R)	New York
39.	95	25	Kemmerer, Chicago (R)	New York
40.	95	25	Hacker, Chicago (R)	New York
		AUG.		
41.	105	4	Pascual, Minnesota (R)	New York
42.	113	11	Burnside, Washington (L)	Washington
43.	114	12	Donovan, Washington (R)	Washington
44.	115	13	Daniels, Washington (R)	Washington
45.	116	13	Kutyna, Washington (R)	Washington
46.	117	15	Pizarro, Chicago (L)	New York
47.	118	16	Pierce, Chicago (L)	New York
48.	118	16	Pierce, Chicago (L)	New York
49.	123	20	Perry, Cleveland (R)	Cleveland
50.	124	22	McBride, Los Angeles (R)	Los Angeles
51.	128	26	Walker, Kansas City (R)	Kansas City
		SEPT.		
52.	134	2	Lary, Detroit (R)	New York
53.	134	2	Aguirre, Detroit (L)	New York
54.	139	6	Cheney, Washington (R)	New York
55.	140	7	Stigman, Cleveland (L)	New York
56.	142	9	Grant, Cleveland (R)	New York
57.	150	16	Lary, Detroit (R)	Detroit
58.	151	17	Fox, Detroit (R)	Detroit
59.	154	20	Pappas, Baltimore (R)	Baltimore
60.	158	26	Fisher, Baltimore (R)	Baltimore
		OCT.		
61.	162	1	Stallard, Boston (R)	New York

Recapitulation: 49 homers off right-handed pitchers; 12 off left-handed pitchers. (Maris bats left-handed, throws right-handed.)

Game numbers do not include a tie game played by the Yankees in 1961. It was the eighth game of the year, April 22, against Baltimore. Maris did not hit a homer in the game.

However, Maris will go into the record book as having hit the sixty-first in a 162-game schedule.

Maris finished the season with 590 official times at bat. Ruth, in 1927, had 540 official times at bat. Their total appearances at the plate, however, were nearly identical—698 for Maris and 692 for Ruth.

According to the official baseball rules, a batter is not charged with an official time at bat when "he hits a sacrifice bunt or sacrifice fly, is awarded first base on four called balls, is hit by a pitched ball or is awarded first base because of interference or obstruction."

Though it had taken 162 games (actually, 163, since the Yankees played one tie) a player finally had risen from the ranks to pass Ruth's majestic record. Maris himself missed only two of these games, although he sat out a third without coming to bat when, after playing the first inning in the field, he was bothered by something in his eye.

For thirty-four years the greatest sluggers in baseball had striven to match Ruth's mark. Mickey Mantle fought Maris heroically through most of the season, but in the closing weeks he fell victim to a virus attack and his total stopped at fifty-four.

The two who came closest in the past were Jimmy Foxx and Hank Greenberg. In 1932, Foxx hit fifty-eight. In 1938, Greenberg matched that figure. Indeed, Greenberg had the best chance of all to crack the record. When he hit No. 58, he still had five games to play in a 154-game schedule.

When Stallard came to bat in the fifth the fans, who earlier had booed him when it seemed he might walk Maris, now generously applauded the hurler.

In the sixth, Maris, coming up for the third time, tried mightily to oblige the crowd with another home run. This time, however, Stallard struck him out on a 3-and-2 pitch. With the Boston right-hander then stepping out for a pinch-hitter, Chet Nichols, an experienced 30-year-old left-hander, opposed Maris on his last turn at bat in the eighth. Roger ended the inning with a pop fly that the second baseman, Chuck Schilling, caught for the third out.

Apart from Maris, the Yankee hitters did not overly distinguish themselves, but Manager Ralph Houk saw enough to satisfy him. Superlative pitching made the biggest home run of 1961 stand up to the end.

Bill Stafford, who is to pitch the third game of the series against the Reds, hurled the first six innings and allowed only two hits, both by Russ Nixon. The first was a single, the second a triple. Hal Reniff then retired three Red Sox in the seventh and Luis Arroyo held them to one single in the last two innings.

Yanks' Score

BOSTON (A.)	ab.r.h.rbi	NEW YORK (A.)	ab.r.h.rbi
Schilling, 2b	4 0 1 0	Richards'n, 2b	4 0 0 0
Geiger, cf	4 0 0 0	Kubek, ss	4 0 2 0
Yast'mski, lf	4 0 0 0	Maris, rf	4 1 1 1
Malzone, 3b	4 0 0 0	Berra, lf	2 0 0 0
Clinton, rf	4 0 0 0	Lopez, lf, rf	1 0 0 0
Runnels, 1b	3 0 0 0	Blanchard,	
Gile, 1b	0 0 0 0	rf, c	3 0 0 0
Nixon, c	3 0 2 0	Howard, c	2 0 0 0
Green, ss	2 0 0 0	Reed, lf	1 0 1 0
Stallard, p	1 0 0 0	Skowron, 1b	2 0 0 0
bJensen	1 0 0 0	Hale, lf	1 0 1 0
Nichols, p	0 0 0 0	Boyer, 3b	2 0 0 0
		Stafford, p	2 0 0 0
Total	30 0 4 0	Reniff, p	1 0 0 0
		aTresh	1 0 0 0
		Arroyo, p	0 0 0 0
		Total	29 1 5 1

aPopped up for Reniff in 7th; bPopped up for Stallard in 8th.

Boston .... 0 0 0 0 0 0 0 0 0—0
New York .... 0 0 0 1 0 0 0 0 .—1

E—None. LOB—Boston 5, New York 5.

PO—Boston 24: Schilling 3, Geiger, Yastrzemski, Clinton 4, Runnels 7, Nixon 5, Stallard, Gile, Green. New York 27: Richardson, Kubek 3, Maris 3, Blanchard 3, Howard 7, Skowron 4, Boyer, Lopez 2, Reed, Hale 2. A—Boston 5: Schilling 2, Green 2, Stallard. New York 8: Richardson, Kubek 3, Boyer, Howard 2, Hale.

3B Hits—Nixon. HR—Maris. SB—Geiger. Sacrifice—Stallard.

	IP.	H.	R.	ER.	BB.	SO.
Stallard (L, 2–7)	7	5	1	1	1	5
Nichols	1	0	0	0	0	0
Stafford (W, 14–9)	6	3	0	0	0	7
Reniff	1	0	0	0	0	1
Arroyo	2	1	0	0	0	1

Wild pitch—Stallard. PB—Nixon. Umpires—Kinnamon, Flaherty, Honochick, Salerno. Time—1:57. Attendance—23,154.

YANKS BEAT REDS A THIRD TIME, 7-0; FORD SETS RECORD

Pitcher Raises Series Mark to 32 Scoreless Innings Before Injury in 6th

O'TOOLE LOSES AGAIN

New York Team One Game Away From Final Victory —Richardson Gets 3 Hits

By JOHN DREBINGER
Special to The New York Times.

CINCINNATI, Oct. 8 — The Yankees defeated the Cincinnati Reds, 7 to 0, today and moved within a game of winning the 1961 world series.

Babe Ruth's forty-three-year-old pitching record of twenty-nine and two-thirds scoreless innings fell along with the Reds. The record was broken by the skillful Whitey Ford.

Ford was able to pitch only five innings before leaving with a bruised toe. But he departed with a world series mark of thirty-two consecutive scoreless innings. Before today, he had pitched three successive series shutouts.

The victory gave Ralph Houk's American League champions a 3-to-1 lead in games. They need only one more in the four-of-seven-game struggle to end it.

Reds on the Brink

They can end it here tomorrow, when Cincinnati gets its last view of the show. Should the Reds escape another defeat, the series will return to New York for the sixth game on Wednesday.

But there were few who felt Freddy Hutchinson's National Leaguers could salvage the series.

Roger Maris, whose homer won yesterday's game, hit no homers today. In fact, he got no hits in three official times at bat. His last time up, he struck out. On two other appearances he was walked, once intentionally.

Mickey Mantle, playing with a painful right hip, had to retire in the top half of the

fourth, but not before he had delivered a damaging single. Mantle's hit paved the way for the Yanks' first run.

That run, and a run in the fifth, were scored off Jim O'Toole, the crack young left-hander who was beaten by Ford's two-hitter in New York last Wednesday and was opposing Whitey a second time.

Coates Wraps It Up

When Ford withdrew after facing one batter in the sixth, Jim Coates, a tall right-hander from Virginia, took over. He held the shutout to the end before a crowd that totaled 32,589 for the second successive day.

The frustrated Reds never knew from which side the next blow would fall.

After O'Toole had yielded the fifth-inning tally, Hutchinson gambled with a pinch-hitter who didn't hit. The relief pitcher who followed, Jim Brosnan, didn't pitch well either.

The Yanks cuffed Brosnan for six hits in the sixth and seventh innings, scoring twice in the sixth, three times in the seventh.

There were no Yankee homers, but there were eleven hits. Bobby Richardson, who somehow needs a world series to inspire him, came up with three hits, one a double. This brought his series total of hits to eight. Bill Skowron also connected for three hits.

Ford hit himself on the right foot with a foul tip in the sixth. When he retired in the bottom of the inning after Elio Chacon had opened with a single, Ford received a rousing round of applause from the fans.

With his five scoreless innings, Ford had erased a record cherished by Ruth. The Bambino always had been mighty proud of that mark, which he rolled up in the series of 1916 and 1918 for the Boston Red Sox before he became the Sultan of Swat.

Last October Ford had pitched nine-inning shutouts against the Pittsburgh Pirates in the third and sixth games of the world series. In the opener of this series last Wednesday, he tossed another shutout.

Since Ford received credit for today's victory, he increased to nine his own world series record of most pitching triumphs. However, because he did not complete the game, he did miss tying Christy Mathewson's record of four world series shutouts.

Mathewson, the former great right-hander of the Giants, pitched three of his shutouts against the Athletics in 1905 and the fourth against the Athletics in 1913.

Fans in Shirt Sleeves

This was another day right

The Box Score

FOURTH GAME
NEW YORK YANKEES

	AB.	R.	H.	RBI.	PO.	A.
Richardson, 2b.	5	1	3	0	4	4
Kubek, ss.	5	0	1	1	0	4
Maris, rf., cf.	3	2	0	0	3	0
Mantle, cf.	2	0	1	0	1	0
aLopez, rf.	3	1	1	2	3	0
Howard, c.	4	1	1	0	3	0
Berra, lf.	2	1	0	0	4	0
Skowron, 1b.	3	0	3	1	9	0
Boyer, 3b.	4	0	1	2	0	2
Ford, p.	2	1	0	0	0	0
Coates, p.	1	0	0	0	0	0
Total	34	7	11	6	27	10

CINCINNATI REDS

	AB.	R.	H.	RBI.	PO.	A.
Chacon, 2b.	4	0	1	0	4	4
Kasko, ss.	4	0	1	0	1	2
Pinson, cf.	4	0	0	0	4	1
Robinson, rf.	1	0	0	0	2	0
Post, lf.	4	0	1	0	1	0
Freese, 3b.	4	0	0	0	1	2
Coleman, 1b.	4	0	0	0	5	0
D. Johnson, c.	2	0	2	0	5	0
cBell	1	0	0	0	0	0
Zimmerman, c.	0	0	0	0	3	0
O'Toole, p.	1	0	0	0	1	0
bGernert	1	0	0	0	0	0
Brosnan, p.	0	0	0	0	0	0
dLynch	1	0	0	0	0	0
Henry, p.	0	0	0	0	0	0
Total	31	0	5	0	27	9

aRan for Mantle in fourth.
bHit into force play for O'Toole in fifth.
cGrounded out for D. Johnson in seventh.
dStruck out for Brosnan in eighth.

New York......000 112 300—7
Cincinnati......000 000 000—0

Error—Pinson. Double plays—Kasko, Chacon and Coleman; Kubek, Richardson and Skowron; Freese, Chacon and Coleman; Coleman (unassisted). Left on bases—New York 6, Cincinnati 7. Two-base hits—Richardson, Howard, Boyer.

	IP.	H.	R.	ER.
O'Toole (L)	5	5	2	2
Brosnan	3	6	5	5
Henry	1	0	0	0
*Ford (W)	5	4	0	0
Coates	4	1	0	0

*Faced one batter in sixth.
Bases on balls—Off O'Toole 3 (Skowron, Maris, Ford), Brosnan 3 (Berra 2, Maris), Coates 1 (Robinson). Struck out—By O'Toole 2 (Kubek, Howard), Brosnan 3 (Lopez, Howard, Coates), Henry 2 (Kubek, Maris), Ford 1 (Chacon), Coates 2 (Lynch, Freese). Hit by pitcher—By Ford (Robinson), by Coates (Robinson). Wild pitch—Brosnan.
Umpires—Donatelli (N), plate; Runge (A), first base; Conlan (N), second base; Umont (A), third base; Crawford (N), left field; Stewart (A), right field. Time of game—2:27. Attendance—32,589.

out of July, with not a cloud in the sky, the temperature around 80 and the fans sitting in their shirt sleeves in the sun-drenched right-field bleachers and lower left-field stand.

The Reds dug into the past for another notable figure to toss out the first ball. Yesterday it had been the oldest living former major league player, 99-year-old Dummy Hoy. Today it was Bill McKechnie, the popular Deacon, who managed the last Cincinnati pennant-winning teams in 1939 and 1940.

Ford passed Ruth's pitching record in the third inning. After retiring six Reds in a row in the first two innings,

Whitey had one away in the third when Darrell Johnson, who was back in the Cincinnati lineup as the catcher, caused a mild flurry. The former third-string receiver of the Bombers plunked a single into left.

However, the suspense didn't last for long. O'Toole forced Johnson at second and Chacon ended the inning with a grounder to Richardson.

In connection with Ruth's record, there has always been a question whether the two-thirds of an inning should have counted.

In the first game of the 1916 World Series between the Red Sox and the Dodgers Ruth was tagged for a first-inning homer with two out by Hi Myer.

He then held the Dodgers scoreless until the Sox won the game, 2—1, in fourteen innings. The Babe thus received credit for thirteen and one-third innings of scoreless pitching.

In the 1918 series against the Cubs, Ruth pitched a nine-inning shutout in the opener. In the fourth game blanked the Chicagoans for seven and one-third innings before they scored twice. Many contend that in a record of this sort fractions of an inning should not count.

O'Toole, as in the first game of the series, kept pace with Ford for three innings, then gave a tally in the fourth. It was Whitey's bosom pal, Mantle, who struck the decisive blow.

Skowron's Hit Wasted

Maris, who had fouled out in the first inning, drew a pass in opening the fourth. Mantle followed with a single to left center and Maris raced to third.

Mantle might have made it a double but he was limping badly as he ran to first. Houk immediately took him out of the game.

Hector Lopez was sent to run for Mickey, and when Elston Howard grounded into a double play, Maris scored.

In the fifth the Bombers picked up their second tally, although Skowron's inning-opening single was wiped out when Cletis Boyer slammed into a double play.

Ford drew a pass, however. Richardson and Tony Kubek weighed in with singles and Whitey scored. Richardson, one of the surprise hitting stars in last year's world series, also had hit a double in the third.

With O'Toole's departure for a pinch hitter in the fifth, Brosnan, the distinguished author and relief specialist, entered for the Reds in the sixth. He was promptly roughed up for two runs.

With one down, Howard doubled, Yogi Berra walked and Skowron outgalloped an infield hit. Then Boyer doubled to left, Howard and Berra scoring and Skowron stopping at third.

The inning ended on an odd note. Ford grounded out to the first baseman, Gordy Coleman, who tore across the diamond to track down Skowron between third and home. He completed the double play on the Moose single-handed.

Ford's Last Stand

It was also in this inning that Ford, just before grounding out, fouled off the ball that hit his toe.

The Reds had made only three hits in the first five innings, all singles. There wasn't much apprehension when Chacon opened the sixth with a single, except that for a moment it was feared that Berra, in making a diving stab for the ball, had hurt himself.

However, after receiving ministrations from Trainer Gus Mauch, Yogi found himself still in one piece and able to continue. He did have a slight cut over the right eye.

Meanwhile Houk had gone to the mound to confer with Ford and before anyone seemed aware a change was about to be made, Coates ambled up from the bull pen.

Apart from hitting Frank Robinson with a pitched ball, Coates had no difficulty making this a scoreless round, so that Ford's string of thirty-two scoreless innings remains intact. He can add more to it this year or in any future series.

Another Hit for Bobby

Finding Brosnan still around, the Yanks romped off with three more runs in the seventh while the home fans looked on in glum silence. Richardson's third hit began this assault. It was a single, with Bobby grabbing an extra base when Vada Pinson fumbled the ball.

Kubek flied out but Maris drew an intentional pass, and after a wild pitch had put the runners on second and third, Lopez scored both with a single to center.

Lopez took second on a futile throw to the plate. This, after Howard had fanned, induced Brosnan to give Berra an intentional pass. But that didn't help either.

Skowron's third straight single, a smash that rifled through the box and into center field, fetched home the third and final tally.

In suffering this second shutout of the series, the Reds collected only five hits, four off Ford, one off Coates. All were singles. Ford and Coates each hit one batter (Robinson both times) and Coates walked one (Robinson again). Only three Cincinnatians reached second base. None got to third.

October 9, 1961

National League Beats American

PINCH HIT LEADS TO 3-1 CONQUEST

Musial Helps Break 0-0 Tie in His 22d All-Star Game —Wills Excels on Bases

By JOHN DREBINGER
Special to The New York Times.

WASHINGTON, July 10 — The National League spiked the big guns of the American League today, turned on a bit of blinding speed in its own behalf and won the first of 1962's two all-star games. The score was 3—1.

A crowd of 45,480 that included President Kennedy and Vice President Johnson saw the action in Washington's new $24,000,000 District of Columbia Stadium. The turnout was the largest to attend a ball game there.

Maury Wills, a lithe, swift-moving bundle of nerves, paced Freddie Hutchinson's National Leaguers to two of their runs.

With the teams locked in a scoreless tie in the first of the sixth, the Cardinals' 41-year-old Stan Musial, appearing in his twenty-second all-star game, cracked a pinch-hit single to right. It was made off Camilo Pascual, the classy right-hander of the Minnesota Twins.

Amid thundering cheers, Musial stepped aside as Wills, the shortstop for the Los Angeles Dodgers, went in to run for him. A moment later Maury, who thus far this season has stolen forty-six bases, was on his way to second.

Battey Just Looks

So great was Wills' start that the American League catcher, Earl Battey, never even bothered to make the throw. Maury slid in at second for a clean steal. Dick Groat of the Pittsburgh Pirates, the batter, had further disconcerted Battey by swinging at the pitch.

Groat then singled and Wills scored the first run of the game. Another followed in the same inning. Groat advanced to second on Roberto Clemente's third hit of the game, a single to right. A long fly by Willie Mays sent Groat to third and an infield out by Orlando Cepeda fetched the Pirate infielder home.

Two innings later, after the Americans had cut the two-run deficit in half with a run in the sixth, Wills turned it on again.

Associated Press Wirephoto

DEFENSIVE GEM: Willie Mays leaps against fence in center field and turns long drive by Roger Maris into a long out. Rich Rollins, who was at third base, tagged up after catch and scored American League's only run.

This time, with Dick Donovan of Cleveland on the mound for the Americans, Maury opened the Nationals' eighth with a pop-fly single that dropped in short left.

Jim Davenport followed with another single. It was fielded by Rocky Colavito in left. Wills rounded second base in high gear, but with no chance to make third. Rocky, who possesses a powerful throwing arm, felt certain that the speedy Dodger had overreached himself.

Relay Arrives Late

He fired the ball to second. But Wills kept right on going for third and made it with a grand slide as the relay from second arrived too late.

Scarcely had the crowd recovered from this than Felipe Alou lifted a pop foul down the right-field line. It wasn't deep, but as Leon Wagner caught the ball, Wills again turned on an Olympian sprint that sent him sliding across the plate after the catch.

And that put the game beyond the reach of Ralph Houk's American Leaguers. The

losers made just four hits off the combined pitching of Don Drysdale, Juan Marichal, Bob Purkey and Bob Shaw.

Drysdale blanked them for the first three innings. Marichal, the eventual winner, shut them out for the next two. Purkey gave the run in the sixth and Shaw held the Americans scoreless in the last two.

The Yanks' famed M-boys contributed a sacrifice fly between them. Mickey Mantle, playing only four innings, struck out the first time up, walked the second and gave way to Colavito.

Maris, after fanning in the first inning, had the satisfaction of seeing Mays do a bit of stepping in the fourth before he caught his fly to deep center. And in the sixth, Roger came within inches of a three-run homer. On this drive, Willie the Wonder leaped high in the air alongside the 410-foot marker and speared the ball in his glove as he crashed against the railing.

That shot, however, did bring in the American run. The inning had opened with Rich Roll-

All-Star Score

NATIONAL LEAGUE

	AB.	R.	H.	RBI.	PO.	A.
Groat, ss	3	1	1	1	3	3
Davenport, 3b	1	0	1	0	0	1
Clemente, rf	3	0	3	0	2	0
F. Alou, rf	0	0	0	1	0	0
Mays, cf	3	0	0	0	3	0
Cepeda, 1b	3	0	1	2	2	2
Purkey, p	0	0	0	0	0	1
cCallison	1	0	1	0	0	0
Shaw, p	0	0	0	0	0	0
T. Davis, lf	4	0	0	0	2	0
Boyer, 3b	2	0	0	0	1	0
Banks, 1b	2	0	0	0	4	1
Crandall, c	4	0	0	0	5	0
Mazeroski, 2b	2	0	0	0	1	0
Bolling, 2b	2	0	0	0	1	3
Drysdale, p	1	0	0	0	1	0
Marichal, p	0	0	0	0	0	0
cMusial	1	0	1	0	0	0
dWills, ss	1	2	1	0	1	1
Total	33	3	8	3	27	12

AMERICAN LEAGUE

	AB.	R.	H.	RBI.	PO.	A.
Rollins, 3b	2	1	1	0	1	3
Robinson, 3b	0	0	0	0	0	1
Moran, 2b	3	0	1	0	0	0
Richardson, 2b	1	0	0	0	1	0
Maris, cf	2	0	0	1	2	0
Landis, cf	1	0	0	0	2	0
Mantle, rf	1	0	0	0	0	0
bColavito, lf	1	0	0	0	1	0
Gentile 1b	3	0	0	0	8	0
Wagner, lf, rf	4	0	0	0	4	1
Battey, c	2	0	0	0	1	0
Romano, c	2	0	1	0	1	0
Aparicio, ss	4	0	1	0	3	2
Bunning, p	0	0	0	0	0	0
aThomas	1	0	0	0	0	0
Pascual, p	1	0	0	0	0	0
Donovan, p	0	0	0	0	0	0
fSiebern	1	0	0	0	0	0
Pappas, p	0	0	0	0	0	0
Total	29	1	4	1	27	8

aPopped out for Bunning in 3rd; bRan for Mantle in 6th; cSing'ed for Marichal in 6th; dRan for Musial in 6th; eSingled for Purkey in 8th; fGrounded out for Donovan in 8th.

National .... 0 0 0 0 0 2 0 1 0—3
American .... 0 0 0 0 0 1 0 0 0—1

Errors—None. Double plays—Cepeda, Groat, Drysdale; Battey, Rollins.
Left on base—National 5, American 7. Two-base hit—Clemente. Three-base hit—Aparicio. Stolen bases—Mays, Wills. Sacrifice flies—Maris, F. Alou.

	IP.	H.	R.	ER.
Bunning	3	1	0	0
Pascual (L)	3	4	2	2
Donovan	2	3	1	1
Pappas	1	0	0	0
Drysdale	3	1	0	0
Marichal (W)	2	0	0	0
Purkey	2	2	1	1

Bases on balls—Off Pascual 1 (Mays), Drysdale 1 (Gentile), Marichal 1 (Mantle), Shaw 1 (Colavito). Struck out—By Bunning 2 (Boyer, Drysdale), Pascual 1 (Cepeda), Drysdale 3 (Maris, Mantle, Moran), Purkey 1 (Gentile), Shaw 1 (Landis). Hit by pitched ball—By Drysdale (Rollins), By Shaw (Robinson). Umpires—Hurley (A), Donatelli (N), Stewart (A), Venzon (N), Steiner (N), Schwarts (A). Time—2:23. Attendance—45,480.

KENNEDY NEARLY GETS A SOUVENIR: The President stands and removes his sun glasses as a fly ball from the bat of Bobby Richardson passes close at all-star game in Washington. At right is David Powers, the receptionist at the White House.

ins getting a single off Purkey and Billy Moran following with another that sent Rollins to third. When Mays turned Maris' home-run bid into a sacrifice fly, Rollins scored.

Bunning of Tigers Effective

Of the four pitchers that Houk sent to the mound, only the first and the last came up to expectations. The starter, Jim Bunning of Detroit, matched Drysdale's three scoreless innings. And Milt Pappas of the Orioles took over in the ninth and retired three Nationals in a row.

In the last of the ninth, Shaw put two on with a walk and a single by John Romano. But a sparkling catch by Tommy Davis of a foul down the left-field line broke the back of this scoring bid and the struggle

ended with Mays making one of his familiar basket catches in deep center.

Thus the American Leaguers' once overwhelming margin of superiority, built up in the golden era of Babe Ruth, Lou Gehrig, Jimmy Foxx and other titans of that day, has now dwindled to a sixteen-fifteen edge. In the last sixteen all-star games, the Nationals have won eleven, the Americans four and one ended in a tie.

As the sun beat down from out of a cloudless sky, there unfolded perhaps the most glittering spectacle yet offered by baseball in this day of multi-million-dollar stadiums. Every seat in the vast, picturesque arena was occupied as the players were introduced.

There was a surprisingly noisy demonstration for Casey Stengel. Casey, as first-base coach for the Nationals, was playing a strange role in this

game. His normal role had been as manager. It also marked his first appearance in Washington since 1960, his last year as manager of the Yankees. But the folks remembered him.

The greatest ovation of all went to Musial. Then came another great roar as President Kennedy and his retinue emerged from the American League dugout.

July 11, 1962

Cheney of Senators Fans Record 21 in 16 Innings

WASHINGTON STAR TOPS ORIOLES, 2-1

Cheney Sets Strikeout High in Overtime Game—Zipfel Homer in 16th Decides

BALTIMORE, Sept. 12 (UPI) —Tom Cheney, a baldish, much-traveled 27 - year - old right-hander, set a record of twenty-one strikeouts for a game of any duration in pitching the Washington Senators to a 2-1 victory in sixteen innings over the Baltimore Orioles tonight.

But Zippel won the game with one out in the sixteenth when he hit a home run off Dick Hall.

Cheney, who had only three complete games in his twenty previous starts this season, had thirteen strikeouts in the regulation nine innings. He added two in each of the tenth and eleventh innings.

He equaled the modern record of eighteen by fanning Marv Breeding for the second out in the fourteenth innning. He made Hall his nineteenth victim for the third out of the fourteenth and got No. 20 to surpass even pre-1900 marks when he fanned Russ Snyder for the second out of the fifteenth inning. He wound up the game by getting a pinch hitter, Dick Williams, on a called third strike.

Feller, Koufax Hold Mark

Bob Feller and Sandy Koufax share the mark of eighteen strikeouts for a nine-inning game. The record for extra innings in the modern era was also eighteen and was held by Jack Coombs, who did it twice, and Warren Spahn. A pre-1900 record of nineteen strikeouts in a nine-inning game was set by Charles Sweeney and one-armed Hugh Daley in 1884.

Cheney, who gave ten hits, in all, didn't allow a hit between Boog Powell's single with one out in the eighth and Dave Nicholsons single with one out in the sixteenth for a string of eight hitless innings.

Baltimore made the score 1—1 in the seventh when Breeding doubled and Charlie Lau, batting for the Oriole starter, Milt Pappas, singled him home.

The Senators had scored in the first when Ron Stillwell got an infield single, went to third on Chuck Hinton's double and scored on Zipfel's grounder.

Cheney, who broke into the major leagues with the St. Louis Cardinals in 1957, has had a checkered career. After failing to win a game for St. Louis he pitched in the Pittsburgh Pirate chain, appeared in the 1960 world series with the Pirates and was purchased by the Senators from Columbus of the International League on June 29, 1961.

Tonight's victory was only his ninth in the majors against thirteen losses. For the season he is 6—8.

The Washington manager, Mickey Vernon, has always maintained that Cheney had as much equipment as any other member of the Senators' staff.

WASHINGTON (A.)				BALTIMORE (A.)			
	ab.r.h.rbi				ab.r.h.rbi		
Kennedy, ss	6 0 1 0			Adair ss	6 0 2 0		
Stillwell, 2b	3 1 1 0			Snyder, rf	7 0 2 0		
bKing	1 0 1 0			Robinson, 3b	5 0 1 0		
Cottier, 2b	2 0 0 0			Gentile, 1b	7 0 1 0		
Hinton, rf	7 0 1 0			Powell, lf	6 0 1 0		
Zipfel, 1b	7 1 3 2			Nicholson, cf	7 0 1 0		
Retzer, c	7 0 0 0			Landrith, c	6 0 0 0		
cOsteen	0 0 0 0			eBrandt	1 0 0 0		
Schmidt, c	0 0 0 0			Breeding, 2b	6 1 1 0		
Hicks, cf	5 0 1 0			fWilliams	1 0 0 0		
dSchaive	1 0 0 0			Pappas, p	2 0 0 0		
Piersall, cf	0 0 0 0			aLau	1 0 1 1		
Lock, lf	7 0 1 0			Hall, p	3 0 0 0		
Brinkman, 3b	5 0 1 0			Hoeft, p	0 0 0 0		
Cheney, p	6 0 0 0			Stock, p	0 0 0 0		
Total	57 2 10 2			Total	58 1 10 1		

aSingled for Pappas in 7th; bSingled for Stillwell in 10th; cRan for Retzer in 16th; dFouled out for Hicks in 16th; eFlied out for Landrith in 16th; fStruck out for Breeding in 16th.

Washington . 1 0 0 0 0 0 0 0 0 0 0 0 0 0 0 1—2
Baltimore ... 1 0 0 0 0 0 1 0 0 0 0 0 0 0 0 0—1

E—Adair, Breeding. A—Washington 12, Baltimore 16. LOB—Washington 13, Baltimore 13. 2B Hits—Hinton, Snyder, Adair, Gentile, Hicks, Breeding. HR—Zipfel. SB—Adair. Sacrifice—Cheney.

	IP.	H.	R.	ER	BB	SO
Cheney (W, 6- 8)	16	10	1	1	4	21
Pappas	7	4	1	1	3	4
Hall (L, 6—6)	8⅓	5	1	1	1	4
Hoeft	⅓	1	0	0	0	0
Stock	⅓	0	0	0	0	0

Wild pitch—Cheney. Balk—Pappas. Umpires—McKinley, Chylak, Umont, Stewart. Time—3:59. Attendance—4,098.

September 13, 1962

Wills Sets Mark as Dodgers Lose

He Steals 96th and 97th Bases, but the Cards Win, 12-2

ST. LOUIS, Sept. 23 (UPI)—Maury Wills of the Los Angeles Dodgers stole two bases today to bring his total to 97 for 156 games, but the St. Louis Cardinals defeated the league leaders, 12—2.

Wills went one ahead of Ty Cobb's modern stolen base mark in the seventh inning. After reaching base on a single, he stole second easily. The throw, high over the bag, was not held.

He tied Cobb in the third after reaching base on a hit. With a crowd of 20,743 roaring its approval, Wills stole second as Carl Sawatski's throw bounced past Dal Maxvill.

Wills was retired when he tried to go to third base on a grounder to short. He received an ovation while he trotted off the field into the Dodger dugout where he was congratulated by waiting teammates.

When he went to the plate in the ninth, the game was stopped and the public address announcer presented a base to Wills, saying, "And you won't have to steal this one." After the game, Wills received the actual base that he had stolen to pass Cobb. Cobb had also amassed his total in 156 games.

The Cards had little trouble handing the stumbling Dodgers their fifth defeat in seven games. They collected 15 hits off five Dodger pitchers, putting together two three-run innings and one four-run inning.

Don Drysdale was pinned with his eighth loss, his third to the Cards, against his league high of 25 victories. He yielded three runs in the first and single runs in the third and fourth innings before leaving in the Cardinals' four-run fourth.

LOS ANGELES (N.)				ST. LOUIS (N.)			
	ab.r.h.rbi				ab.r.h.rbi		
Wills, ss	5 0 2 0			Javier, 2b	4 3 2 1		
Gilliam, 2b	4 1 3 0			Flood, cf	4 3 3 2		
Snider, lf	5 1 3 1			Musial, lf	3 1 2 3		
T. Davis, 3b	5 0 3 1			aShannon, lf	1 0 0 0		
Fairly, 1b	4 0 0 0			White, 1b	5 0 2 3		
Howard, rf	4 0 0 0			Boyer, 3b	5 0 3 1		
W. Davis, cf	3 0 1 0			Sawatski, c	4 0 0 1		
Roseboro, c	4 0 0 0			Kolb, rf	5 1 1 0		
Drysdale, p	2 0 0 0			Maxvill, ss	3 3 1 0		
Perranoski, p	0 0 0 0			Jackson, p	3 1 1 0		
J. Smith, p	0 0 0 0			Total	37 12 15 11		
Richert, p	0 0 0 0						
bHarkness	1 0 0 0						
Koufax, p	0 0 0 0						
cMoon	1 0 0 0						
Total	38 2 12 2						

aRan for Musial in 5th; bGrounded out for Richert in 7th; cStruck out for Koufax in 9th.

Los Angeles .... 2 0 0 0 0 0 0 0—2
St. Louis .... 3 0 1 4 3 0 1 0 .—12

E—T. Davis. A—Los Angeles 7, St. Louis 12. DP—Wills, Fairly. LOB—Los Angeles 11, St. Louis 9.
2B Hits—Gilliam, Snider, Flood, White, Boyer, Musial. SB—Wills 2. Sacrifice—Jackson. SF—Sawatski.

	IP.	H.	R.	ER	BB	SO
Drysdale (L, 25--8)	3⅓	6	8	6	2	2
Perranoski	1	5	3	3	0	1
J. Smith	1	1	0	0	0	0
Richert	1⅓	2	0	0	0	2
Koufax	2	1	1	1	3	2
Jackson (W, 15—11)	9	12	2	2	1	6

HBP—By Drysdale (Flood), by Jackson (W. Davis). Umpires—Donatelli, Secory, Venzon, Pryor. Time—2:52. Attendance—20,743.

September 24, 1962

The Mets' Long Season Ends With Their 120th Defeat, 5 to 1

By LOUIS EFFRAT
Special to The New York Times.

CHICAGO, Sept. 30—It mattered not that the New York Mets won or lost, or even how they played the game today before 3,960 fans at Wrigley Field. For the record, though, the season's final, for which Casey Stengel asked and obtained volunteers, went to the Cubs, 5—1.

It was the Mets 120th defeat in this, their initial campaign, and it left them in the National League cellar, 60 games from the top. The season was concluded as it had started—with a setback—after the Mets had been victimized by an eighth-inning triple play.

Had the season been fun?

"I would have to say no to that one," Stengel said. "It was a rough season for me. I had to get used to losing all over again. It was saddening and shocking — saddening because we won only 40 games and shocking because we didn't win at least 50, because there were at least 10 games we lost that we should have won.

"Imagine, 40 games! I won with this club what I used to lose." (That bit of Stengelese, which is slightly exaggerated, referred to Casey's long and successful managerial regime with the Yankees.)

"But we'll do better in 1963," the 72-year-old manager promised. "For one thing, we'll know more about each other. This year, everything was new, including the manager and coaches. We'll do better, all right, just wait and see. But the rest of the league is gonna have to help us through deals."

Today, the team with the most losses in modern baseball history fell behind Bob Buhl in the second inning when Bill Hunter yielded a single and three successive walks.

Nelson Mathews doubled home another Cub run in the third,

which minimized Frank Thomas's 34th homer of the year in the fourth.

Chicago's third run was wild-pitched home by Craig Anderson, who had succeeded Ray Daviault.

The triple play was the final embarrassment.

Sammy Drake and Richie Ashburn had put together singles at the start of the eighth. Then Joe Pignatano broke his bat while hitting what appeared to be a bloop single to the right of second base. At least, Ashburn and Drake thought it would be a single.

Ken Hubbs, the Cubs' second baseman, thought differently. He nonchalantly went out, caught the ball for one out and flipped it to Ernie Banks at first for the second. Banks relayed it to Andre Rogers for the third out.

NEW YORK (N.)				CHICAGO (N.)			
	ab.	r.	h.	rbi.			
Ashburn, 2b	4	0	1	0	Hubbs, 2b	4	0	1	0
MacKenzie, p	0	0	0	0	Santo, 3b	4	1	1	0
Coleman, c	3	0	0	0	Williams, lf	4	1	0	0
Pignatano, c	1	0	0	0	Banks, 1b	4	1	0	0
Christopher, rf	4	0	0	0	Altman, rf	3	2	3	1
Thomas, lf	3	1	2	1	Mathews, cf	2	0	2	2
Throneb'ry, 1b	2	0	0	0	Rodgers, ss	3	0	0	0
Kranepool, 1b	1	0	0	0	Barragan, c	3	0	0	1
Mantilla, 3b	4	0	1	0	Buhl, p	4	0	0	0
Hickman, cf	3	0	0	0					
Chacon, ss	2	0	0	0	Total	31	5	7	4
Hunter, p	0	0	0	0					
Daviault, p	0	0	0	0					
aTaylor	1	0	0	0					
C.Anderson, p	0	0	0	0					
bDrake, 2b	1	0	1	0					
Total	30	1	5	1					

aGrounded out for Daviault in 5th; bSingled for C. Anderson in 8th.

New York	0 0 0 1 0 0 0 0 0—1
Chicago	0 1 1 0 1 0 2 0 .—5

E—Christopher, Mantilla, Ashburn. A—New York 13, Chicago 12. DP—Ashburn, Throneberry. TP—Hubbs, Banks, Rodgers. LOB—New York 5, Chicago 8. 2B Hits—Mantilla, Mathews. HR—Thomas. SB—Santo, Altman.

	IP.	H.	R.	ER.	BB.	SO.
*Hunter (L 1-6)	1	1	1	1	4	0
Daviault	3	3	1	1	1	2
C. Anderson	3	3	3	0	1	1
MacKenzie	1	0	0	0	0	0
Buhl (W, 12-14)	9	5	1	1	3	6

*Faced 4 batters in 2d.
Wild pitch—C. Anderson. Umpires—Secory, Venzon, Pryor, Donatelli. Time—2:16. Attendance—3,960.

October 1, 1962

Chicago Cubs

Giants Win Playoff, 6-4, in 9th; Oppose Yanks in Series Today

By JOHN DREBINGER
Special to The New York Times.

LOS ANGELES, Oct. 3—One of the most dramatic and nerve-racking pennant races in years came to an astounding end today when the San Francisco Giants vanquished the Dodgers, 6 to 4, in the third and deciding game of the National League playoff.

Before an incredulous crowd of 45,693 the Dodgers, holding a 4-2 lead in the ninth inning, came apart. Al Dark's San Franciscans jammed four runs across the plate that inning on two singles, four walks and a Dodger error.

Thus the Giants, moving into their 17th National League pennant, will face the American League champion Yankees in the World Series, which will open in San Francisco tomorrow.

Game time will be noon (3 P.M., New York time) as the Giants and Yankees meet for the seventh time in a World Series.

Ironically, just 11 years ago the Giants brought the Dodgers down in the ninth inning of the deciding playoff game on the wings of Bobby Thomson's electrifying three-run homer.

Today, however, the Giants' triumph wasn't quite so dramatic. Rather, in the earlier stages of the game, Walter Alston's Dodgers supplied most of the thrills.

They wrenched one run from Marichal in the fourth. In the sixth came what almost everyone in the steaming arena believed to be the turning point. After the Giants had filled the bases on three hits with nobody out, Ed Roebuck went to Podres's rescue and stopped the Giants cold on four pitches.

In the last of the sixth the crowd went into a frenzy as the Dodgers swept ahead on a two-run homer by Tommy Davis. The mercurial Maury Wills added a run in the seventh.

Connecting for a single, his fourth hit of the day, Maury, who already had stolen a base, now stole second. He then stole third, and when a frustrated

throw by the catcher, Ed Bailey, sailed by that base, the fleet Dodger kept running and scored. Wills closed the season with 104 stolen bases, a modern major league record.

That seemed to wrap it up. The Dodgers were leading, 4—2, and with Roebuck moving serenely along with brilliant relief pitching, preparations already were under way for the opening of the World Series in Chavez Ravine.

But then came the Giants' decisive ninth. It opened with Matty Alou batting for Larsen and singling. He was forced by Harvey Kuenn for the first out.

Then Roebuck's control deserted him. He walked a pinch-hitter, Willie McCovey, who gave way to a pinch-runner, Ernie Bowman. Felipe Alou also walked, filling the bases.

Mays Singles In Run

Now Willie Mays, hitless up to here though he had drawn two walks, slammed a single that caromed off Roebuck. The ball remained in the infield, but Kuenn scored and the bases remained filled.

Roebuck gave way to Stan Williams, who saw Orlando Cepeda lift a sacrifice fly to right that scored Bowman with the tying run. The fly also advanced Felipe Alou to third.

When a wild pitch that rolled only a few feet from the plate sent Mays to second, Alston ordered an intentional walk to Bailey, again filling the bases.

But that also backfired, for Williams, never noted for his control, also walked Jim Davenport. This forced in the tie-breaking run.

Left-handed Ron Perranoski relieved Williams and appeared to have brought matters under control with the Dodgers still trailing by only one run. But Larry Burright, who had taken over as the Dodgers second baseman in a late-inning defensive maneuver, fumbled José Pagan's grounder behind second. Mays raced across the plate on the play, and the Giants had a 6-4 lead.

The Giants never needed that extra margin. Dark, recalling how his Giants had frittered away yesterday's second game after holding a 5—0 lead, was taking no chances this time.

Pierce Shuts the Door

To pitch the last of the ninth he called in his brilliant left-hander, Billy Pierce, who had blanked the Dodgers on three hits in the playoff opener on Monday. The stunned Dodgers were helpless again.

A grounder, two fly balls that Willie the Wonder caught in dead center, and to paraphrase the immortal words of Chuck

Box Score of 3d Playoff Game

SAN FRANCISCO (N.)						
	AB.	R.	H.	RBI.	PO.	A.
Kuenn, lf......	5	1	2	1	2	0
Hiller, 2b......	3	0	1	0	4	1
bMcCovey	0	0	0	0	0	0
cBowman, 2b..	0	1	0	0	0	0
F. Alou, rf....	4	1	1	0	4	0
Mays, cf......	3	1	1	1	3	0
Cepeda, 1b....	4	0	1	1	8	0
Bailey, c......	4	0	2	0	3	0
Davenport, 3b.	4	0	1	1	2	4
Pagan, ss.....	5	1	2	0	1	0
Marichal, p..	2	1	1	0	0	0
Larsen, p.....	0	0	0	0	0	1
aM. Alou	1	0	1	0	0	0
dNieman	1	0	0	0	0	0
Pierce, p......	0	0	0	0	0	0
Total	36	6	13	4	27	7

LOS ANGELES (N.)						
	AB.	R.	H.	RBI.	PO.	A.
Wills, ss......	5	1	4	0	3	0
Gilliam; 2b-3b..	5	0	0	0	3	1
Snider, lf......	3	2	2	0	2	0
Burright, 2b...	1	0	0	0	3	2
eWalls	1	0	0	0	0	0
T. Davis, 3b-lf.	3	1	2	2	1	1
Moon, 1b......	3	0	0	0	8	0
Fairly, 1b-rf..	0	0	0	0	2	0
Howard, rf....	4	0	0	1	0	0
Harkness, 1b..	0	0	0	0	0	0
Roseboro, c....	3	0	0	0	3	1
W. Davis, cf...	3	0	0	0	2	0
Podres, p......	2	0	0	0	0	2
Roebuck, p....	2	0	0	0	0	0
Williams, p....	0	0	0	0	0	0
Perranoski, p..	0	0	0	0	0	0
Total	35	4	8	3	27	14

aSingled for Larsen in 9th; bWalked for Hiller in 9th; cRan for McCovey in 9th; dStruck out for M. Alou in 9th; eLined out for Burright in 9th.

```
San Francisco Giants.............. 0 0 2   0 0 0   0 0 4—6
Los Angeles Dodgers.............. 0 0 0   1 0 2   1 0 0—4
```

Errors—Marichal, Podres, Roseboro, Gilliam, Pagan, Bailey, Burright. Double plays—Gilliam, Wills and Moon; Wills, Burright and Fairly. Left on bases—San Francisco 12, Los Angeles 8.

Two-base hits—Snider, Hiller. Home run—T. Davis. Stolen bases—Wills 3, T. Davis. Sacrifices—Hiller, Marichal, Fairly. Sacrifice fly—Cepeda.

	IP.	H.	R.	ER.	BB.	SO.	HBP.	WP.	Balks
*Marichal	7	3	4	3	1	2	0	1	0
Larsen (W, 5-4)	1	0	0	0	2	1	0	0	0
Pierce	1	0	0	0	0	0	0	0	0
†Podres	5	9	2	2	1	0	0	0	0
Roebuck (L, 10-2)	3⅓	4	4	3	3	0	0	0	0
Williams	½	0	0	0	2	0	0	0	0
Perranoski	⅓	0	0	0	1	1	0	0	0

*Faced one batter in 8th. †Faced three batters in 6th.

Bases on balls—Off Marichal 1 (T. Davis), Larsen 2 (Roseboro, W. Davis), Podres 1 (Mays), Roebuck 3 (Mays, McCovey, F. Alou), Williams 2 (Bailey, Davenport). Struck out—By Marichal 2 (Roseboro, Podres), Larsen 1 (Howard), Perranoski 1 (Nieman). Wild pitch—Williams. Umpires—Boggess (plate), Donatelli (first base), Conlan (second base), Barlick (third base). Time of game—3:00. Attendance—45,693.

Dressen, there was nothing to say but "The Dodgers is dead."

Podres was the third pitcher to go to the mound in this playoff with only two days of rest—Don Drysdale and Jack Sanford were the others. Podres got by well enough in the first two innings. But in the third, the Dodgers suddenly took to tossing the ball around in a manner that would have had the Mets green with envy.

Podres himself committed one of three errors. When the Giants added three hits to the mixture, the astonishing part was the Dodgers escaped with only two runs scored against them.

After Pagan had opened the third with a single, Marichal followed with a bunt that Podres fielded, then fired into center field in a bold attempt to force Pagan at second. That put Pagan on third and Marichal at first.

Kuenn then singled to left, scoring Pagan and moving Marichal to second. Then came another butter-fingered play. As Chuck Hiller missed a bunt attempt, Marichal appeared hopelessly trapped off second. But John Roseboro's throw sailed into center field and allowed Marichal to reach third.

A bizarre play followed. When Hiller flied to Duke Snider in short left, Marichal remained glued to third. But Kuenn broke for second and drew a throw to Jim Gilliam, who fired the ball to first in the hope of nailing the retreating Kuenn. But the ball cracked Harvey on the back of the head, and Marichal scored on this error.

Behind all this came a single by Felipe Alou that sent Kuenn to third. Felipe took second on the throw-in. But Podres finally got matters under control by intentionally walking Mays, then getting Cepeda to slap into a double play.

Those two runs had most of the crowd glum, but not for long. In the fourth the Dodgers got back one run after Snider, their old reliable, had opened with a double to right. Tommy Davis singled sharply to left,

but the Duke had to hold at third. He was still there after Wally Moon had lifted a fairly long fly to right.

However, when the Giant infield failed to convert Frank Howard's grounder into a double play by way of second, Snider finally crossed the plate.

In the sixth the Giants finished Podres, but before this inning was over it was the San Franciscans who were groaning. A big Giant killing appeared in the making as singles by Cepeda and Bailey and a beautifully executed bunt single by Davenport filled the bases with nobody out.

Roebuck emerged from the Dodger bull pen, and the Giant threat vanished with the smog. Pagan grounded to Wills for a force play at the plate. Marichal also grounded to Maury, who stepped on second, then whipped the ball to first for an inning-ending double play.

Minutes later, the sun really shone for the home folks as the Dodgers swept ahead on Tommy Davis' homer. Snider opened the Dodger sixth with a single to left, his second hit of the day. Then, with the count 3 and 1, Tommy drove the ball 400 feet into the bleachers in left center.

It was homer No. 27 for this Davis, who also wound up the season as the National League's leading batter.

The Dodgers fattened their lead to 4-2 on Wills's heroics in the seventh. But Maury's derring-do was forgotten as the Giants rallied in the ninth and made it good-by pennant race, hello World Series.

October 4, 1962

Mantle Wins Most-Valuable-Player Award Third Time

SELECTORS OMIT MARIS IN VOTING

Winner Last 2 Years Yields to Mantle, Yank Teammate —Killebrew Is Third

By JOHN DREBINGER

Mickey Mantle, beaten by narrow margins the last two years in controversial contests for the American League's annual most - valuable - player

award, yesterday won one that doubtless came as a surprise even to him.

The renowned 31-year-old slugger of the world champion Yankees, shackled for almost a third of the season with injuries, nevertheless scored a decisive victory for the league's 1962 award with a total of 234 points.

Bobby Richardson, the Yankees crack second baseman and generally regarded as a strong favorite for the prize, placed second with 152 points in the poll of the 20-man committee of the Baseball Writers Association of America.

Harmon Killebrew of the Minnesota Twins, who led the league in homers with 48 despite a .243 batting average,

finished third with 99 points. Leon Wagner, the distance-hitting outfielder of the Los Angeles Angels, was fourth with 85.

Roger Maris, who had defeated Mantle in the 1960 and 1961 photo finishes, finished nowhere at all, although he did hit 33 home runs. The Yankee outfielder, who last year had topped Babe Ruth's 60-home run record with 61, didn't get a point this year.

Third Yankee Triple

Points are scored on a basis of 14 for the first place, 9 for second, 8 for third and down to 1 for tenth.

For Mantle this marked the third most-valuable award. The Switcher won it in 1956 with a perfect 336 score and repeated

in 1957 with 233. Mickey thus joins two other Yanks—Joe DiMaggio and Yogi Berra—and Jimmy Foxx as the only three-time winners in the American League.

In 1960, Maris topped Mantle, 202 points to 198, although Mantle had nipped Maris for the home run title, 40 to 39. Many disagreed loudly with this result.

Last year the contest was even closer, despite Maris's record feat. The Roger won this one, 225 to 222, and again the result brought sharp criticism.

Mantle's tremendous value to the Yankees, of course, was never denied over the past season when he was physically fit to play. He batted .321, finishing second to Pete Runnels's league-leading .326, and he hit 30 home runs.

However, because of repeated injuries he was able to appear in only 123 of the Yankees' 162 games and in more than a dozen of these he appeared only as a part-time player or pinch-hitter. He also slumped badly in the World Series, although World Series play doesn't count in the most-valuable voting.

Richardson the Reliable

Richardson, on the other hand, was the solid man of the Yanks throughout the campaign. He missed only one game and in addition to his brilliant play at second base, batted .302. Most important of all, he compiled 209 hits, becoming the first Yankee to reach the 200-hit mark since Phil Rizzuto in 1950.

Discussing the outlook for the most-valuable vote during the World Series last month, Mantle conceded that he thought Richardson would win it. "I hope he gets it," said Mickey. "He certainly deserves it."

Manager Ralph Houk at the time seemed to share similar views.

"With our big sluggers not hitting the homers the way they did last year," said the skipper, "there is no denying that Bobby's steady hitting, especially with those timely two-baggers, played a tremendous role in putting us over the top." Bobby led the club in doubles with 38.

However, the home run still holds sway, and Mantle's 30, against only eight for Richardson, apparently carried the vote for Mickey.

Mantle was named on all 20 ballots, with 13 first-place votes, two seconds, three thirds and two sixths. Richardson had only five first-place votes and was named on 16 of the 20 ballots. He picked up three seconds, four thirds, two fourths, one fifth and one eighth.

A Yankee Habit

Nine Yankees have now won the most-valuable-player award. These nine have totaled seventeen such awards, which far surpasses the figure of any other club. This also marked the third straight year the Yanks had run one, two in the balloting.

However, apart from Mantle and Richardson, only three other Bombers are to be found among the thirty-three players who scored points this year. The Yankee rookie star, Tom Tresh, placed 12th with 30 points and one first-place ballot. Ralph Terry finished 14th with 79 and Whitey Ford was 28th with 6.

Dick Donovan of the Cleveland Indians led the pitchers with 64 points, placing fifth over all. Killebrew drew the only other first-place ballot.

MARICHAL NO-HITTER

Coast Right-Hander Faces 29 Colts in 1-to-0 Triumph

By United Press International

SAN FRANCISCO, June 15—Juan Marichal pitched a no-hit, no-run game against the Houston Colts today for a 1-0 victory that lifted the San Francisco Giants back into first place in the National League.

Marichal, who broke into the majors three years ago by pitching a one-hitter against the Philadelphia Phillies, allowed two walks and struck out five in posting his sixth straight victory and 10th of the season.

Ironically, Marichal's last defeat came on May 11 when Sandy Koufax of the Dodgers beat the Giants with a no-hitter in Los Angeles.

Willie McCovey kept Marichal's string going in the seventh inning when he reached over to his right and reached up high with both hands to snag a line smash by Carl Warwick with Bob Aspromonte on first base.

The right-hander from the Dominican Republic faced 29 batters.

It was the first no-hitter pitched by a Giant since May 8, 1929, when Carl Hubbell turned back the Pittsburgh Pirates for the New York Giants.

It was a tough defeat for Dick Drott, who didn't give a run until the eighth inning and held the Giants to three hits in going the distance.

Jim Davenport opened the eighth with a double to left field for the Giants' first hit since Willie Mays's infield single in the first. Drott retired the next two batters, but Chuck Hiller lined a double to right field that scored Davenport.

Drott's won-lost record now is 2—4. He has been beaten by the Giants 11 times in his 14 decisions with San Francisco.

Spangler Draws Walk

The only Colts to get on base were Al Spangler, who walked in the fifth, and Aspromonte, who walked in the seventh. Spangler was erased when Bob Lillis hit into a fielder's choice that ended the inning. Then McCovey caught Warwick's liner in the seventh and that inning ended as Rusty Staub flied to Mays in center.

A crowd of 18,869 was on its feet cheering when Marichal came out to open the ninth inning. First he retired a pinch-hitter, Johnny Temple, on a foul fly to the first baseman, Orlando Cepeda. Then Pete Runnels, twice the American League batting champion, stepped in to pinch-hit for Ernie Fazio and went down swinging. A rookie, Brock Davis, followed Runnels and looked at a called third strike, ending the game.

Marichal's no-hitter was the third in the majors this year. In addition to Koufax, Don Nottebart of the Colts pitched a no-hit victory over the Philadelphia Phillies May 17, although allowing one run.

Only 89 Pitches

Larry Jansen, the Giants' pitching coach, said that Marichal had thrown only 89 pitches.

"As far as I'm concerned," said Jansen, "that's about the minimum. I've been in baseball 20 years, and this is the first time there has ever been a no-hitter pitched on my club."

Marichal, now 10—3, said he wasn't nervous but he realized he had a possible no-hitter going the fifth or sixth inning.

"Then when they started popping out so fast," he said, "I

Juan Marichal

HOUSTON (N.)				SAN FRANCISCO (N.)			
	ab.r.h.rbi				ab.r.h.rbi		
Fazio, 2b	3 0 0 0			Hiller, 2b	3 0 1 0		
cRunnels	1 0 0 0			F. Alou, rf	4 0 0 0		
Davis, cf	4 0 0 0			Mays, cf	3 0 1 0		
Aspromonte, 3b	2 0 0 0			McCovey, lf	2 0 0 0		
Warwick, rf	3 0 0 0			Cepeda, 1b	3 0 0 0		
Staub, lb	3 0 0 0			Bailey, c	3 0 0 0		
Spangler, lf	3 0 0 0			Davenport, 3b	3 1 1 0		
Bateman, c	3 0 0 0			Pagan, ss	3 0 0 0		
Drott, p	2 0 0 0			aM. Alou	1 0 0 0		
bTemple	1 0 0 0			Bowman, p	0 0 0 0		
				Marichal, p	3 0 0 0		
Total	27 0 0 0			Total	24 1 3 1		

aStruck out for Pagan in 8th; bFouled out for Drott in 9th; cStruck out for Fazio in 9th.

Houston .... 0 0 0 0 0 0 0 0 0—0
San Francisco .... 0 0 0 0 0 0 0 0 1—1

E—None. A—Houston 5, San Francisco 6. DP—Bateman, Lillis. LOB—Houston 2, San Francisco 4.
2B Hits—Davenport, Hiller.

	IP.	H.	R.	ER.BB.SO.
Drott (L, 2-4)	8	3	1	1 3 6
Marichal (W, 10-3)	9	0	0	0 2 5

Umpires—Sudol, Forman, Gorman, Landes.
Time—1:41. Attendance—18,869.

June 16, 1963

WYNN REGISTERS HIS 300TH VICTORY

Right-Hander Goes 5 Innings in 7-4 Triumph After A's Set Back Indians, 6-5

By The Associated Press

KANSAS CITY, July 13—Early Wynn scored his 300th major league pitching victory today as the Cleveland Indians defeated the Kansas City Athletics, 7-4, in the second game of a double-header. The A's won the opener, 6-5.

Wynn, the 14th major league pitcher to win 300, lasted only five innings, the minimum distance a starter has to hurl to be credited with a victory.

The 43-year-old right-hander left after the fifth with the Indians ahead, 5-4, and Jerry Walker blanked the A's in the last four innings.

Warren Spahn of the Milwaukee Braves is the only other active major-leaguer in the 300-victory circle.

Wynn, who first pitched in the majors in 1939 with the Washington Senators, reached his goal in his eighth try. He made three attempts last year with the Chicago White Sox and five since he was signed as a free agent by Cleveland last month. He won No. 299 on Sept. 8 of last year.

Wynn, who yielded six hits and struck out three men, set another record when he walked three. His career total of bases on balls now is 1,765, one more than the previous record held by Bob Feller.

Wynn, five times a 20-game winner, has lost 243 games, one

just started pitching faster and faster. I had good control today but not really good stuff."

He said he had been more excited when the Giants beat Los Angeles for the National League pennant in the playoff last fall.

"That got us into the World Series," said Marichal, "and you can't get a bigger thrill than getting into your first World Series."

Manager Alvin Dark, asked if he had ever seen a game this well played, replied:

"You just can't beat this kind of pitching. We got only three hits off Drott who pitched a fine game, too. But Juan was wonderful."

June 16, 1963

this year. He was given a 5-1 lead on a four-run burst in the fifth but yielded three runs in the A's half before retiring.

FIRST GAME

CLEVELAND (A.)		KANSAS CITY (A.)	
	ab.r.h.rbi		ab.r.h.rbi
Francona, lf	5 1 2 0	Lumpe, 2b	4 1 1 1
Brown, 2b	4 0 1 0	Causey, ss	4 2 2 0
cRomano	1 0 0 0	Alusik, rf,lf	3 1 1 0
Kirkland, cf	5 0 2 0	Siebern, 1b	4 1 3 2
Alvis, 3b	4 1 2 0	Edwards, c	4 0 1 0
Whitfield, 1b	3 1 1 1	Charles, 3b	2 1 1 3
aAdcock, 1b	1 0 0 0	Essegian, lf	2 0 0 0
Luplow, rf	4 1 2 3	Del Greco, cf	0 0 0 0
Azcue, c	4 1 2 0	Tartabull, cf	3 0 1 0
Kindall, ss	3 0 0 0	Segui, p	2 0 0 0
Kralick, p	4 0 1 0	Bowsfield, p	0 0 0 0
Bell, p	0 0 0 0	bHarrelson	1 0 0 0
		Wyatt, p	0 0 0 0
Total	38 5 13 4	Total	30 6 10 6

aHit into doubleplay for Whitfield in 7th; bStruck out for Bowsfield in 7th; cLined out for Brown in 9th.

Cleveland .... 2 0 3 0 0 0 0 0 0—5
Kansas City ...... 0 0 0 0 0 0 0 0 2—6

E—Segui. A—Cleveland 14, Kansas City 13. DP—Causey, Siebern; Lumpe, Causey, Siebern; Causey, Lumpe, Siebern; Alvis, Brown, Whitfield; Alvis, Brown, Whitfield. LOB—Cleveland 6, Kansas City 4.
2B Hits—Alvis, Siebern, Azcue, Edwards. HR—Charles, Azcue, Lumpe, Alusik. SB—Francona. Sacrifices—Bowsfield, Alusik.

	IP.	H.	R.	ER.BB.SO.
Kralick (L, 8-3)	7⅓	9	4	4 1 4
Bell	⅔	0	0	0 1 0
Segui	3	8	5	2 0 2
Bowsfield	3	4	0	0 1 3
Wyatt (W, 2-2)	2	1	0	0 0 1

Umpires—Stevens, Napp, Kinnamon, Umont.
Time—2:17.

SECOND GAME

CLEVELAND (A.)		KANSAS CITY (A.)	
	ab.r.h.rbi		ab.r.h.rbi
Francona, lf	5 0 1 0	Tartabull, cf	5 1 1 0
Tasby, lf	0 0 0 0	Causey, ss	5 0 0 0
Howser, ss	5 1 2 0	Lumpe, 2b	4 0 1 3
Kirkland, cf	5 2 1 0	Alusik, rf	3 1 1 1
Alvis, 3b	4 1 0 0	Lau, c	3 0 1 0
Adcock, 1b	1 1 1 3	Charles, 3b	2 0 1 0
Adcock, 1b	4 1 1 3	Essegian, lf	4 0 0 0
Romano, c	3 2 1 0	Harrelson, 1b	3 1 2 0
Luplow, rf	2 0 2 0	Drabowsky, p	1 0 1 0
Brown, 2b	4 0 1 1	aCimoli	1 0 1 0
Wynn, p	2 1 1 0	bLaRussa	0 0 0 0
cHeld	1 0 1 0	Fischer, p	0 0 0 0
Walker, p	0 0 0 0	Lovrich, p	0 0 0 0
		eEdwards	1 0 0 0
Total	35 7 12 7	Total	38 4 9 4

aSingled for Willis in 5th; bRan for Cimoli in 5th; cDoubled for Fischer in 8th; dStruck out for Fischer in 6th; ePopped up for Lovrich in 9th.

Cleveland .... 0 1 0 0 4 0 1 0 1—7
Kansas City ...... 0 0 0 1 3 0 0 0 0—4

E—Harrelson. A—Cleveland 11, Kansas City 12. DP—Lumpe, Held, Harrelson. LOB—Cleveland 8, Kansas City 7.
2B Hits—Lumpe, Held, Lau. 3B—Kirkland. HR—Alusik. SB—Kirkland. Sac—Adcock.

	IP.	H.	R.	ER.BB.SO.
Wynn (W, 1-1)	5	6	4	4 3 3
Walker	4	3	0	0 2 2
Drabowsky (L, 0-6)	4⅔	6	5	5 5 5
Willis	⅓	2	1	1 0 0
Fischer	2	3	0	0 1 1
Lovrich	2	1	1	0 2 1

Umpires—Knapp, Kinnamon, Umont and Stevens. Time—2:43. Attendance—13,565.

July 14, 1963

Mets Top Cubs and End Craig's String

2-OUT SHOT IN 9TH WINS 7-3 CONTEST

Home Run on 3-2 Pitch Ends 18-Loss Streak—Thomas, 2 Cubs Also Connect

By WILL BRADBURY

The Ballad of Roger Craig, a woeful tale of one of the great right-handed tragic heroes of modern times, came to a glorious end last night as the New York Mets ended his losing streak by defeating the Chicago Cubs, 7-3, at the Polo Grounds.

As with all important ballads, the end of Craig's 18-game losing streak was accompanied by drama, individual heroism and high tension.

The greatest hero of all, of course, was Craig. He toiled valiantly through nine innings despite two Chicago home runs, two triples and four other hits.

As the game moved into the last of the ninth inning, however, Jim Hickman deftly lifted the hero's mantle from Craig's shoulders and ended the game in truly majestic fashion.

With two men out in the ninth, the score tied at 3—3 and the bases filled, the rangy third baseman hit a 3-and-2 pitch off the scoreboard in left field for a home run. It made Craig a winning pitcher for the first time since April 29.

Homer by Thomas Helps

Through eight innings against Paul Toth, the Cubs' starter, the Mets had performed with little more than their usual aggressiveness in support of Craig. A home run by Frank Thomas in the third and two unearned runs in the fifth was all that had kept them in the game.

Then, in the ninth, while the Met fans in the crowd of 12,116 roared encouragement and a red and white umbrella twirled along the first-base line, Casey Stengel's men came to life.

After Thomas had flied to left to open the inning, Joe Hicks singled to right.

Clarence (Choo Choo) Coleman followed Hicks to the plate and struck out for the second out, but Al Moran moved Hicks to third with a line double to the left-field corner. Lindy McDaniel relieved for the Cubs at this point and Stengel sent Tim Harkness up to hit for Craig.

McDaniel had trouble finding the plate against Harkness and

walked the slender first baseman with an intentional fourth ball.

Hickman then walked to the plate and waited as the tension mounted and the count ran out. Then he hit the home run that unleashed happy cries of "Break up the Mets" as the crowd headed for the exits.

3-Game Winning Streak

In addition to ending Craig's losing streak one defeat short of the major league record of 19, Hickman's blow gave the Mets their third three-game winning streak of the season.

The mark that Craig almost equaled was established by John Nabors of the Philadelphia Athletics in 1916.

Craig held the Cubs in check through the first four innings. Then Andre Rodgers and Lou Brock rapped him for home runs in the fifth. The Cubs' final run came in the eighth on a triple by Billy Williams and a sacrifice fly by Ron Santo.

Duke Snider almost gave the Cubs a run in the seventh when he made a three-base error on a line drive by Brock to right. Brock, on the other hand, turned a hit-and-run line drive by Ron Hunt into a double play in the eighth and made a superb catch of a long fly by Hicks in the fourth.

The Mets picked up their unearned runs in the fifth inning with the benefit of a throwing error by Santo, a walk and singles by Snider and Duke Carmel.

The victory, as every Met fan should know, was Craig's third against 20 losses. Toth, who became a father for the first time before the game, suffered his seventh defeat in 10 decisions.

CHICAGO (N.)		NEW YORK (N.)	
	ab.r.h.rbi		ab.r.h.rbi
Brock, rf	5 1 3 1	Hickman, 3b	5 2 1 4
Burton, cf	4 0 0 0	Carmel, 1b	3 0 1 1
Williams, lf	4 1 2 0	Hunt, 2b	4 0 0 0
Santo, 3b	3 0 1 1	Snider, rf	4 0 1 0
Ranew, 1b	4 0 0 0	Thomas, lf	4 1 2 1
Hubbs, 2b	3 0 1 0	Hicks, cf	4 1 2 0
Bertell, c	4 0 0 0	Coleman, c	4 0 0 0
Rodgers, ss	4 1 1 1	Moran, ss	3 2 1 0
Toth, p	2 0 0 0	Craig, p	2 0 0 0
McDaniel, p	0 0 0 0	aHarkness	0 1 0 0
Total	35 3 8 3	Total	33 7 9 7

aWalked for Craig in 9th.

Chicago .... 0 0 0 0 2 0 0 1 0—3
New York .... 0 0 0 1 2 0 0 0 4—7
Two out when winning run was scored.

E—Toth, Santo, Snider. A—Chicago 8, New York 16. DP—Hickman, Carmel; Brock, Ranew. LOB—Chicago 7, New York 4.
2B Hit—Moran. 3B—Brock, Williams. HR—Thomas, Rodgers, Brock, Hickman. SF—Santo.

	IP.	H.	R.	ER.BB.SO.
Toth (L, 3-7)	8⅔	8	5	3 2 6
*McDaniel	0	1	2	2 1 0
Craig (W, 3-20)	9	8	3	3 1 8
*Faced 2 batters in 9th.				

HBP—By Craig (Hubbs). PB—Bertell. Umpires—Forman, Gorman, Landes, Sudol. Time—2:31. Attendance—11,566.

August 10, 1963

Spahn Beats Phils for No. 20 And Ties Mathewson's Record

Braves' Left-Hander Becomes 20-Game Winner for 13th Time With 3-2 Victory

PHILADELPHIA, Sept. 8 (AP). — Warren Spahn, Milwaukee's 42-year-old pitching great, hurled the Braves to a 3-2 victory over the Philadelphia Phils today and became a 20-game winner for the 13th time. He tied Christy Mathewson for the most 20-victory seasons in National League history.

The major league record for 20-victory seasons is 16 held by Cy Young. He pitched for Cleveland and Boston in the American League and St. Louis in the National League, mostly before the turn of the century. Mathewson compiled his record with the New York Giants.

Gene Oliver produced the deciding blow with a two-run homer that broke a 1—1 tie in the top of the eighth.

Spahn, who recently took over seventh place among baseball's career winners, earned his 347th victory by scattering nine hits.

For six innings it appeared Spahn might hurl his 61st shutout. But in the seventh, Tony Gonzalez lined a ball to center that took a weird hop past Lee Maye for a triple. Gonzalez scored on a sacrifice fly by Roy Sievers.

Spahn, who has lost only five games this season, gave two singles following the run, but retired Bob Oldis and Bob Wine on infield outs to end the inning.

In the ninth, Don Demeter hit a homer to bring the Phillies within one run and Don Hoak followed with a double. But Spahn bore down and got Oldis on a grounder and Wes Covington on a fly to end it.

Milwaukee scored its first run in the first inning on a single by Maye, who took second on an overthrow by the Phillie pitcher, Dallas Green. Frank Bolling sacrificed Maye to third and he scored as Hank Aaron grounded out.

MILWAUKEE (N.)				PHILADELPHIA (N.)			
	ab.	r.	h.	rbi	ab.	r.	h.	rbi
Maye, cf, lf	5	1	2	0	Taylor, 2b	4	0	0	0
Bolling, 2b	4	0	0	0	Callison, rf	4	0	1	0
Aaron, rf	5	0	0	1	Gonzalez, lf	4	1	2	0
Mathews, lf	3	1	2	0	Sievers, 1b	3	0	1	1
Cline, cf	1	0	0	0	Demeter, cf	4	1	2	1
J. Torre, c	4	0	0	0	Hoak, 3b	4	0	3	0
Oliver, 1b	4	1	1	2	Oldis, c	4	0	0	0
Menke, 3b	4	0	3	0	Wine, ss	3	0	0	0
McMillan, ss	3	0	2	0	Short, p	0	0	0	0
Spahn, p	3	0	1	0	aCovington	1	0	0	0
					Green, p	2	0	0	0
Total	36	3	11	3	Amaro, ss	1	0	0	0
					Total	34	2	9	2

aFlied out for Short in 9th.

Milwaukee	1 0 0	0 0 0	0 2 0—3
Philadelphia	0 0 0	0 0 0	1 0 1—2

E—Green. A—Milwaukee 15, Philadelphia 14. DP—Menke, Bolling, Oliver. LOB—Milwaukee 10, Philadelphia 6.
2B Hit—Hoak. 3B—Mathews, Gonzalez. HR—Oliver, Demeter. SB—Menke. Sacrifice—Bolling. SF—Sievers.

	IP.	H.	R.	ER.	BB.	SO.
Spahn (W, 20—5)	9	9	2	2	0	0
Green (L, 5—4)	7⅔	11	3	3	3	1
Short	1⅓	0	0	0	0	2

Umpires—Walsh, Jackowski, Crawford, Burkhart. Time—2:22. Attendance—8,807.

September 9, 1963

Grimes, Huggins, Faber and Manush Gain Baseball Hall of Fame

KEEFE AND WARD ARE ALSO NAMED

2 Pre-1900 Stars Among 6 Selected by Old-Timers Hall of Fame Board

Six former stars were voted into baseball's Hall of Fame yesterday, raising the total enrollment in the Cooperstown (N. Y.) museum to 100. The additions came from the group of players retired for at least 20 years.

Enrolled were Burleigh Grimes and Urban (Red) Faber, two of the last spitball pitchers; the ex-New York Yankee manager and six-time pennant-winner, Miller Huggins; an outfielder, Heinie Manush, and two men from pre-1900 days—Tim Keefe and John Montgomery Ward.

270 Victories for Grimes

Of the six new members, only three are alive today. Grimes lives in Trenton, Mo., Faber in Chicago and Manush in Sarasota, Fla. They will be formally inducted July 27 before the annual Hall of Fame exhibition game in Cooperstown.

The Baseball Association's committee on old-timers was allowed to select up to six men this year to clear up the backlog in that category. Normally the selection is restricted to two a year.

Grimes, who is 70 years old, was the last of the legal spitball pitchers when he retired in 1934 with a record 270 games won and 212 lost in a career dating to 1916.

He pitched for Pittsburgh, Brooklyn, New York, Boston, St. Louis and Chicago in the National League and wound up with the New York Yankees in the American. He managed the Dodgers in 1937 and 1938 and has been a scout and minor league manager.

Faber, 75, also was a right-handed spitball pitcher. He spent his entire career from 1914 through 1933 with the Chicago White Sox, compiling a 253-211 won-lost record.

Informed of his election by telephone, Faber said, "I've got to call up Cracker." Cracker is Ray Schalk, his old catcher, who already is in the Hall of Fame.

Huggins managed the Yankees to six pennants in 12 seasons from 1918 until his death at the age of 50 in 1929. He also managed the St. Louis Cardinals for five years. He played second base for Cincinnati and St. Louis from 1904 to 1916, batting .265.

Manush, 62, was a powerful left-handed-hitting outfielder. He compiled a .330 average from 1923 through 1939, mostly in the American League with Detroit, St. Louis and Washington. He won the batting title with .378 at Detroit in 1926.

After his retirement, Manush managed in the minors, scouted for the Boston Braves and Pittsburgh and was a coach at Washington.

Keefe won 346 games and lost 225 from 1880 through 1893, pitching 42 victories for the New York Giants in 1886. Only six pitchers in baseball history have won more games.

In 1888, the right-hander, who was one of the first to throw a change-of-pace ball, won 19 straight. His feat later was tied by Rube Marquard, also of the Giants, in 1912. Keefe died in 1933.

Ward was a baseball pioneer, managing in both the Players League and the National League and also acting as attorney for the National League.

He pitched a perfect game for Providence in the National League in 1880, won 158 games in seven years as a pitcher and batted .283 from 1878 through 1894 as an outfielder, shortstop, second baseman and third baseman. He died in 1925.

February 3, 1964

Luke Appling, White Sox Shortstop for 21 Years, Named to Hall of Fame

SELECTION COMES ON SECOND BALLOT

Two-Time Batting Champion Who Once Hit .388 Tops Ruffing by 5 Votes

BOSTON, Feb. 17 (UPI)— Luke Appling, the old Chicago White Sox shortstop, today won the 101st niche in baseball's Hall of Fame after a special runoff election among the nation's baseball writers.

Appling, who topped the regular biennial election on Jan. 22 but was nine votes short of selection, topped the special ballot announced today by the Baseball Writers Association of America.

Appling—for 21 years a stellar member of the White Sox infield, mostly as the shortstop —scored a five-vote victory over a former New York Yankee pitcher, Charles (Red) Ruffing. The special election was ordered

HALL OF FAME VOTING

	Votes		Votes
Luke Appling.	189	Ernie Lombardi	9
Red Ruffing	184	George Kell	8
Roy Campanella	138	Bucky Walters	8
Joe Medwick	130	Allie Reynolds	6
Pee Wee Reese	47	Arky Vaughan	6
Lou Boudreau	43	Bobby Doerr	5
Al Lopez	34	Ralph Kiner	5
John Vander Meer	20	Pepper Martin	5
Chuck Klein	18	Bob Lemon	3
Marty Marion	17	Hal Newhouser	3
Mel Harder	14	Leo Durocher	2
Johnny Mize	12	Tommy Bridges	1
Lloyd Waner	12	Phil Cavarretta	1
Phil Rizzuto	11	Joe Gordon	1
Billy Herman	9	Bobo Newsom	1

when no one got the required number of votes on the regular ballot.

The 55-year-old Appling greeted news of his selection as "wonderful", but said he had been hoping for a call clarifying his coaching job with the Kansas City Athletics. He said he had been waiting to hear if the Athletics' spring training site and date would stand up through the controversy between the club owner, Charles O. Finley, and other American League owners.

Appling Is Happy

Appling, known as "Old Aches and Pains" for his oft-publicized physical ailments while taking turns at all four infield positions for the White Sox, said he didn't care about not having been chosen in the first election.

"I'm really proud. No. I don't care if I made it on the second third or 40th election or had to crawl to get in. It's a great honor and makes up for never having played on a pennant winner," he said.

The former White Sox shortstop polled 189 of a possible 225 votes—20 more than the 75 per cent needed for election to the Cooperstown, N. Y., baseball shrine. Ruffing also broke the 75 per cent barrier at 184 votes, but was not elected under the rule that only the top man on the runoff list would be chosen.

Campanella Is Third

Roy Campanella was third on the list at 138 votes, Joe Medwick finished fourth at 130 and Pee Wee Reese a distant fifth with 47. The top five plus Lou Boudreau and Al Lopez finished in exactly the same order on the earlier regular ballot.

Appling, a coach with Baltimore last season, won two batting championships during his career. He is only the fourth shortstop elected to the Hall of Fame by the baseball writers.

He played 2,422 games for the White Sox during a career that extended from 1930 through 1950. He had a .310 career batting average, reaching his peak with a .388 title-winning pace in 1936 and taking the batting crown again in 1943 with .328.

Appling's Career

YEARLY RECORDS

YEAR	G.	A.B.	H.	R.B.I.	AVG.
1930	6	26	8	2	.308
1931	96	297	69	28	.232
1932	139	489	134	63	.274
1933	151	612	197	85	.322
1934	118	452	137	61	.303
1935	153	525	161	71	.307
1936	138	526	204	128	.388
1937	154	574	182	77	.317
1938	81	294	89	44	.303
1939	148	516	162	56	.314
1940	150	566	197	79	.348
1941	154	592	186	57	.314
1942	142	543	142	53	.262
1943	155	585	192	80	.328
1944		In Military	Service		
1945	18	58	21	10	.362
1946	149	582	180	55	.309
1947	139	503	154	49	.306
1948	139	497	156	47	.314
1949	142	492	148	53	.301
1950	50	128	30	13	.234
	MAJOR	LEAGUE	TOTALS		
20 YRS.	2422	8857	2749	1116	.310

February 18, 1964

Giants Top Mets Twice as 7-Hour-23-Minute, 23-Inning 2d Game Sets Mark

NEW YORK DROPS 5-3, 8-6 CONTESTS

57,037, Season's Top Crowd in Majors, Attend Games— Mets Make Triple Play

By JOSEPH DURSO

Baseball's transcontinental archrivals—the New York Mets and San Francisco Giants— battled through 10 hours and 23 minutes of a titanic double-header at Shea Stadium yesterday that included the longest game on a time basis ever played in the major leagues.

Endurance records, attendance records and performance records fell through nine innings of the first game and 23 innings of the second before the largest crowd of the baseball season anywhere—57,037.

The huge throng saw the Giants square the spectacular holiday weekend series with the Mets by winning, 5-3 and 8-6. And the 8,000 to 10,000 still on hand when the action ended at 11:25 P.M. saw 41 players struggle for 7 hours and 23 minutes, a record, in the second game.

They saw baseball rarities like a two-man triple play executed in the 14th inning of the second game by Roy McMillan and Ed Kranepool, the second triple play in Met history.

Two Strike-Out Records

They saw 12 pitchers share in two strike-out records—36 in one game and 47 in one day.

They saw the Mets carry the second game into extra innings on Joe Christopher's three-run seventh-inning home run. Then, 16 innings later, they saw a pinch-hitter, Del Crandall, the 40th man in the game, break the tie with a double into the right-field corner.

Finally, they saw history repeat itself for two pitchers, Gaylord Perry of the Giants and Galen Cisco of the Mets. Tht pitched an entire game in relief—10 innings for Perry and nine for Cisco—in a duplicate of the 15-inning struggle in San Francisco two weeks ago. A home run by Willie Mays sent that game into extra innings before the Giants won, 6—4, with Perry the winner and Cisco the loser.

But most of the performance records pale alongside the monumental endurance records that the Giants and Mets set:

¶They played the longest game in time elapsed in major-league history: 7 hours 23 minutes. This was 23 minutes longer than the 22-inning struggle between the New York Yankees and Tigers at Detroit on June 24, 1962, won by the Yankees, 9—7.

¶They played the longest double-header in history: 9 hours 52 minutes on the field. Many fans sat for about 10½ hours, including the intermission, and many small boys who hate to miss batting practice doubtless sat for a dozen hours.

¶They played the most innings ever played by big-league teams in one day: 32. This surpassed the 29 innings that the Boston Red Sox and Philadelphia Athletics labored through in a double-header on July 4, 1905.

¶They played the fourth longest game in baseball history. Brooklyn and Boston hold the marathon record, 26 innings to a 1-1 tie on May 1, 1920. There were two 24-inning games in the American League and a 23-inning tie, again between Brooklyn and Boston.

So the Giants and Mets played the longest National League game to a decision when the Giants made the decisive moves with two out and nobody on base in the 23d inning.

By that time the lights had been on nearly four hours; Alvin Dark, the Giants' manager, had been ejected from the game, and Mays had gone back to center field after playing shortstop.

The first blow was struck by Jim Davenport, whose home run had ended the 15-inning game in San Francisco. This time he drove a long liner into the right-field corner for a triple. The Mets then gave Cap Petersen an intentional base on balls. The Giants countered by calling Crandall in from the bull pen to swing for Perry, their fifth pitcher.

Crandall responded with a whistler into the right-field corner that went for a ground-rule double, scoring Davenport and breaking a deadlock that had persisted for 16 innings.

For good measure on this day of incredible baseball, Jesus Alou outgalloped a topper to the right of the mound and Petersen scored, making it 8—6.

For the Mets, Chris Cannizzaro and John Stephenson struck out and Amado Samuel hit a fly to right field. The clock read 11:25 and the score board read Giants 8, Mets 6.

Before the end, both sides had performed wild feats of thwarting rallies as they toiled overtime.

San Francisco had started strong against Bill Wakefield, giving Bob Bolin, their first pitcher, a cushion of six runs.

The major power was displayed in the third inning when the Giants shook off a two-week batting slump during which they had hit .173, pushing across four runs. These were produced by singles by Alou, Orlando Cepeda, Tom Haller, Chuck Hiller, Jim Hart and Bolin.

The Mets nibbled away, however, narrowing the margin to 6—3 and finally, in the seventh, sending the game into extra innings on one tremendous drive.

McMillan and Frank Thomas were aboard with singles when the lightning struck with a count of 3 balls and no strikes. Bolin came in with a fast ball over the plate and Christopher powered it 400 feet over the fence in left-center beyond a mighty leap by Mays.

For the next 16 innings extraordinary defensive play

First Game Score

SAN FRANCISCO (N.)					NEW YORK (N.)				
	ab.	r.	h.	rbi.		ab.	r.	h.	rbi.
Kuenn, lf	5	0	3	1	Kanehl, 2b	4	0	1	0
cM. Alou, lf	0	0	0	0	McMillan, ss	4	0	0	0
Crandall, c	4	0	0	0	Gonder, c	4	0	0	0
Mays, cf	3	1	1	0	Thomas, lf	4	0	1	0
Hart, 3b	4	1	1	0	bR. Smith, lf	0	0	0	0
Cepeda, 1b	4	2	3	1	Christ'pher, rf	4	1	1	0
Davenport, 2b	3	0	1	1	Kranepool, 1b	4	1	1	0
J. Alou, rf	4	1	2	1	Hickman, cf	4	1	2	3
Garrido, ss	3	0	1	0	C. Smith, 3b	3	0	2	0
Marichal, p	4	0	0	0	Jackson, p	1	0	0	0
					aAltman	1	0	0	0
					Sturdivant, p	0	0	0	0
					Bearnarth, p	0	0	0	0
					dStephenson	1	0	0	0
Total	34	5	12	4					
					Total	34	3	8	3

aStruck out for Sturdivant in 7th; bRan for Thomas in 8th; cRan for Kuenn in 9th; dStruck out for Bearnarth in 9th.

San Francisco ......000 103 001—5
New York ....030 000 000—3

E—Hickman, Hart. A—San Francisco 10; New York 14. DP—Garrido, Davenport, Cepeda; McMillan, Kranepool. LOB—San Francisco 6, New York 6.

2 B Hits—Cepeda, C. Smith. HR—Hickman. SB—Cepeda. Sacrifices—Crandall, Jackson, Garrido. SF—Davenport.

	IP.	H.	R.	ER.	BB.	SO.
Marichal, (W, 8—1)...9		8	3	3	0	7
*Jackson (L, 3—7)...5		8	4	4	1	3
Sturdivant 2		2	0	0	0	0
Bearnarth 2		2	1	1	0	1

*Faced 3 batters in 6th.
HBP—By Marichal (C. Smith.) Umpires—Burkhart, Sudol, Pryor, Secory. Time—2:29.

Baseball's Longest Game

SAN FRANCISCO GIANTS (N.)					NEW YORK METS (N.)				
	ab.	r.	h.	rbi		ab.	r.	h.	rbi
Kuenn, lf	5	1	0	0	Kanehl, 2b	1	0	0	0
Perry, p	3	0	0	0	cGonder	1	0	0	0
jCrandall	1	0	1	1	Samuel, 2b	7	0	2	0
Hendley, p	0	0	0	0	McMillan, ss 10		1	2	0
J. Alou, rf 10		1	4	2	Thomas, lf 10		1	2	0
Mays, cf, ss..........9		1	1	1	Christopher, rf 10		2	4	3
Cepeda, 1b	9	1	3	0	Kranepool, 1b 10		1	3	1
Haller, c 10		1	4	1	Hickman, cf 10		1	2	0
Hiller, 2b	8	1	1	1	C. Smith, 3b	9	0	4	1
Hart, 3b	4	0	1	1	Cannizzaro, c	7	0	1	1
hM. Alou, cf, lf.....	6	0	0	0	Wakefield, p	0	0	0	0
Garrido, ss	3	0	0	0	aAltman	0	0	0	0
fMcCovey	1	0	0	0	bJackson	0	0	0	0
Davenport, ss, 3b..	4	1	1	1	Anderson, p	0	0	0	0
Bolin, p	2	0	1	0	Sturdivant, p	0	0	0	0
MacKenzie, p	0	0	0	0	dD. Smith	1	0	0	0
Shaw, p	0	0	0	0	Lary, p	0	0	0	0
gSnider	1	0	0	0	eTaylor	1	0	0	0
Herbel, p	0	0	0	0	Bearnarth, p	3	0	0	0
iPeterson, 3b	4	1	0	0	Cisco, p	2	0	0	0
					kStephenson	1	0	0	0
Total	81	8	17	8					
					Total	83	6	20	6

aWalked intentionally for Wakefield in 2d; bRan for Altman in 2d; cFlied out for Kanehl in 2d; dGrounded out for Sturdivant in 5th; eStruck out for Lary in 7th; fStruck out for Garrido in 8th; gGrounded out for Shaw in 9th; hGrounded out for Hart in 10th; iLined out for Herbel in 13th; jDoubled for Perry in 23d; kStruck out for Cisco in 23d.

San Francisco ....204 000 000 000 000 000 000 02—8
New York ....010 000 300 000 000 000 000 00—6

Errors—Garrido, Haller, Cepeda, Cisco. Putouts and assists—San Francisco 69-14, New York 69-31. Double plays—Perry, Davenport, Cepeda; Davenport, Cepeda; Christopher, Kranepool. Triple play—McMillan, Kranepool. Left on bases—San Francisco 16, New York 14.

Two-base hits—J. Alou, Kranepool, Cepeda, Crandall. Three-base hits—Kranepool, Haller, Davenport. Home run—Christopher. Sacrifices—Herbel, Hiller, C. Smith, Cisco.

	IP.	H.	R.	ER.	BB.	SO.
Bolin	6 2/3	8	6	5	2	7
*MacKenzie	0	1	0	0	0	0
Shaw	1 1/3	1	0	0	0	1
Herbel	4	3	0	0	0	3
Perry (W, 3—1)	10	7	0	0	1	9
Hendley	1	0	0	0	0	2
Wakefield	2	2	2	2	2	1
Anderson	1/3	4	4	4	0	0
Sturdivant	2 2/3	3	0	0	1	2
Lary	2	0	0	0	0	2
Bearnarth	7	3	0	0	2	4
Cisco (L, 2—5)	9	5	2	2	2	5

*Faced 1 batter in 7th.
*Hit by pitcher—By Shaw (Samuel); by Cisco (Cepeda). Passed ball—Cannizzaro. Umpires—Sudol, Pryor, Secory, Burkhart. Time—7:23. Attendance—57,037.

---

and relief pitching on both sides kept the score at 6-6.

McMillan supplied the most dramatic play in the 14th after Alou had singled and Mays walked. Cepeda then hit a liner behind second base that McMillan speared as Alou and Mays ran full speed ahead. McMillan stepped on second, doubling off Alou, who was halfway to third, and fired the ball to Kranepool to catch Mays.

It was the second triple play of the season, the Philadelphia Phillies having executed one against the Houston Colts. The Mets made their first on Memorial Day, 1962, when Elio Chacon, Charlie Neal and Gil Hodges collaborated.

Davenport Ends Threats

In the 15th and 17th innings, Davenport made dazzling tags at second base in starting double plays that held off the Mets. And among the relief pitchers Larry Bearnarth worked seven innings after going two in the first game, while Cisco added nine to seven he had pitched on Thursday.

The first game had had its moments, too, although they seemed remote by the time the day ended.

For one thing, the Mets broke one of their most frustrating streaks of the year—they had gone 37 innings without providing any runs for Al Jackson. Then, they provided three, but it was not enough.

The Mets scored their three runs off Juan Marichal in one cluster after Christopher and Kranepool, just back from Buffalo, had singled. Jim Hickman then lined his third home run of the season and his second of the weekend into the left field stand.

But in the sixth, the Giants, retaliated. Captain May walked, Jim Hart singled and Cepeda doubled to left. Tom Sturdivant relieved Jackson at this point. Davenport's long fly to center scored Hart with the tying run and sent Cepeda to third.

After one strike to Gil Garrido, Cepeda came thundering down the base line as Sturdivant threw a low, outside knuckleball. Cepeda slid across the plate to steal home before Jesse Gonder could make the tag. Ironically, Garrido then singled to left, but the Giants had a 4-3 lead they never relinquished.

The double victory for the Giants evened the four-game series with the Mets, but left the Mets one-up in nine games played for the year.

The crowd raised attendance for the three days this weekend to 150,571—a figure that is believed safe until next weekend, when the Los Angeles Dodgers come to town.

236

June 1, 1964

Bunning Pitches a Perfect Game; Mets Are Perfect Victims, 6 to 0

By GORDON S. WHITE Jr.

Jim Bunning of the Philadelphia Phillies pitched the first perfect game in the National League in 84 years yesterday when he retired all 27 New York Met batters.

The Phils won the contest, the first game of a double-header at Shea Stadium, by 6—0 before 32,904 fans who were screaming for Bunning during the last two innings.

The lanky right-hander became the eighth man in the 88-year history of major league baseball to pitch a perfect game. He is the first man to pitch one in the majors since Don Larsen of the New York Yankees did not permit a Brooklyn Dodger to reach base in the fifth game of the 1956 World Series. That was the only perfect game ever pitched in a World Series game.

Bunning also became the first pitcher in the modern era (since 1901) to hurl a no-hit game in each major league. The former Detroit Tiger pitcher held the Boston Red Sox hitless on July 20, 1958. That performance, during which he walked two batters and hit one, came in the first game of a Sunday double-header on a hot day at Fenway Park in Boston.

Yesterday's perfect pitching turned the usually loyal Met fans into Bunning fans in the late innings. From the seventh inning on, the 32,904 Bunning had the crowd virtually 100 per cent behind him as he toiled in the 91-degree heat.

When Bunning struck out a rookie, John Stephenson, the 27th and last Met hitter, he received a standing ovation that lasted for many minutes. He was mobbed by his teammates, and when he went to the dugout, the crowd began calling, "We want Bunning! We want Bunning!"

He returned to the field to be interviewed behind home plate by Ralph Kiner on a television show. The crowd, still standing, gave him one of the biggest ovations ever heard in the Mets' new stadium.

Ward Hurled Last One

The last National League pitcher to hurl perfect ball was John M. Ward for Providence against Buffalo on June 17, 1880. Five days before that, John Lee Richmond of Worcester hurled the first perfect game against Cleveland in the National League (The American League was established in 1901.)

Many rules have been changed since the achievements of Ward and Richmond. In 1880, the distance from the pitcher to batter was 45 feet. The distance now is 60 feet 6 inches. Also in 1880, it took nine balls to gain a base on balls and a batter was out if a foul ball was caught on the first bounce.

Met Scores

Perfect Game

PHILADELPHIA PHILS (N.)

	AB.	R.	H.	PO.	A.	Bi.
Briggs, cf	4	1	0	2	0	0
Herrnstein, 1b	4	0	0	7	0	0
Callison, rf	4	1	2	1	0	1
Allen, 3b	3	0	1	0	2	1
Covington, lf	2	0	0	1	0	0
aWine, ss	1	1	0	2	1	0
T. Taylor, 2b	3	2	1	0	3	0
Rojas, ss, lf	3	0	1	3	0	0
Triandos, c	4	1	2	11	1	2
Bunning, p	4	0	1	0	0	2
Totals	32	6	8	27	7	6

NEW YORK METS (N.)

	AB.	R.	H.	PO.	A.	Bi.
Hickman, cf	3	0	0	2	0	0
Hunt, 2b	3	0	0	3	2	0
Kranepool, 1b	3	0	0	8	0	0
Christopher, rf	3	0	0	4	0	0
Gonder, c	3	0	0	7	1	0
R. Taylor, lf	3	0	0	1	0	0
C. Smith, ss	3	0	0	1	1	0
Samuel, 3b	2	0	0	1	0	0
cAltman	1	0	0	0	0	0
Stallard, p	1	0	0	0	3	0
Wakefield, p	0	0	0	0	0	0
bKanehl	1	0	0	0	0	0
Sturdivant, p	0	0	0	0	1	0
dStephenson	1	0	0	0	0	0
Totals	27	0	0	27	8	0

a—Ran for Covington in 6th; b—Grounded out for Wakefield in 6th; c—struck out for Samuel in 9th; d—Struck out for Sturdivant in 9th.

Philadelphia ... 110 004 000—6
New York ..... 000 000 000—0

Errors—None. Left on Bases—Philadelphia 5, New York 0.

Two Base Hits—Triandos, Bunning. Home Run—Callison. Sacrifices—Herrnstein, Rojas.

	IP.	H.	R.	ER.	BB.	SO.
Bunni'g(W. 7-2)	9	0	0	0	0	10*
Stallard (L, 4-9)	5 2-3	7	6	6	4	3
Wakefield	1-3	0	0	0	0	0
Sturdivant	3	1	0	0	0	3

*Bunning struck out Hickman 3, C. Smith, Hunt, Kranepool, Christopher, R. Taylor, Altman, Stephenson.

Wild Pitch—Stallard. Time—2:19. Umpires— Sudol, Pryor, Secory, Burkhart. Attendance—32,026.

The New York Times (by Ernest Sisto)

Tony Taylor, second baseman of the Phillies, leaping to knock down a line drive hit by Jesse Gonder of Mets in the fifth inning. Taylor's play saved perfect game for Bunning.

SECOND GAME

PHILADELPHIA (N.)					NEW YORK (N.)				
	ab.	r.	h.	bi		ab.	r.	h.	bi
Briggs, cf	5	1	1	1	Hickman, cf	5	0	0	0
Herrnstein, 1b, rf	5	0	0	0	Hunt, 2b	5	0	0	0
	5	0	0	0	Kranepool, 1b	3	0	0	0
Callison, rf	3	1	1	1	Christopher, rf	5	0	1	1
Sievers, ph, 1b	2	0	1	0	Gonder, c	3	1	1	0
Allen, 3b	3	1	0	0	B. Taylor, lf	4	0	1	0
Amaro, 3b	1	0	1	0	C. Smith, ss	3	0	0	0
Covington, lf	3	1	2	0	Samuel, 3b	2	0	0	0
Wine, pr, ss	2	1	1	0	Altman, ph	1	0	0	0
T. Taylor, 2b	4	2	2	2	Stephenson, 3b	0	0	0	0
Rojas, ss, lf	2	1	1	1	Lary, p	0	1	0	0
Dalrymple, c	2	0	1	2	Kanehl, ph	1	0	0	0
Wise, p	2	0	0	1	Cannizzaro, ph	0	0	0	0
					D. Smith, ph	1	0	0	0
Totals	34	8	11	8	Totals	33	2	3	1

Philadelphia .... 3 0 1 1 3 0 0 0 0—8
New York .... 0 1 1 0 0 0 0 0 0—2

E—T. Taylor, Allen 2, Wine. DP—New York 1. LOB—Philadelphia 7, New York 11. 2B—Covington, T. Taylor. HR—Briggs (1), Callison (10). SF—Dalrymple, Wise.

	IP.	H.	R.	ER.	BB.	SO.
†Wise (W, 1—0)	6	3	2	0	2	0
Klippstein	3	0	0	0	3	2
*Lary (L, 0—2)	4	6	6	3	2	2
Sturdivant	1	1	2	2	0	0
Hunter	2	2	0	0	0	0
Wakefield	1	0	0	0	0	0
Cisco	1	1	0	0	0	0

*Faced 1 man in 5th; †Faced 1 man in 7th.

HBP—By Lary (Rojas), by Sturdivant (Rojas), by Klippstein (Kranepool, Stephenson). WP—Wise, Sturdivant, Hunter, Klippstein 2. PB—Gonder. Time—2:51. Attendance—32,026.

Since the turn of the century, five American League pitchers have recorded perfect games. Larsen's achievement was the first since Charlie Robertson of the Chicago White Sox pitched one against the Detroit Tigers on April 30, 1922. Thus Bun-

ning's was the first regular-season major league perfect game in 42 years.

Traded Last December

Bunning, who became disenchanted last season with the Detroit Tigers' manager Chuck Dressen, was traded with a catcher, Gus Triandos, to the Phillies for Don Demeter, an outfielder, and Jack Hamilton, a pitcher, last Dec. 4. Bunning has been a star this season in the Phillies' bid for their first pennant in 14 years. Triandos caught the perfect game yesterday.

. It was Bunning's seventh victory of the season against two defeats.

Bunning threw only 86 pitches with his customary three-quarter motion. The Mets were baffled by his fast curve, and by the slider he used now and then as he struck out 10. Only three Mets came close to getting a hit. One, Jesse Gonder, nearly broke up the perfect game with a hard shot toward right field in the fifth inning.

Gonder slammed one half way between Tony Taylor, the second baseman, and John Herrnstein, the first baseman. It was Taylor's play, and he made it.

With a diving stab at the hard-hit ball, Tony slapped it

to the ground. He quickly recovered it then easily tossed out Gonder. The ball was hit so hard that by the time Taylor had control of it, Gonder was only about a third of the way to first base.

In the third inning, Amado Samuel lined a ball over shortstop, but Cookie Rojas jumped about two or three feet and caught the liner for the out.

In the fourth, Ron Hunt, the Mets' leading hitter, popped a fly ball along the right-field line. The ball was out of the reach of Johnny Callison, who was playing toward right-center for the right-handed Hunt.

The ball landed a foot in foul territory, however, and the perfect game was saved. Hunt then struck out after getting the count to three balls and two strikes.

Bunning fanned Jim Hickman, the Mets' lead-off batter, three times.

Hawk Taylor, who was called out on strikes in the eighth, ran the count to 3 and 2, as did Hunt in the fourth. But after Taylor was called out by the plate umpire, Ed Sudol, Triandos dropped the ball. But Triandos jumped on the ball quickly and tossed to Herrnstein to put out Taylor.

The Phils who also won the second game, 8—2, had an easy

time in the opener against three pitchers, collecting eight hits, one a home run by Callison leading off the four-run sixth inning.

The Met pitching victim in the sixth was the starter, Tracy Stallard. Bunning's double drove in the last two runs and drove out Stallard. Bill Wakefield took the mound.

Tom Sturdivant pitched the last three innings without permitting a run. Stephenson was hitting for Sturdivant in the ninth when he fanned for the final out.

In the second game, the Mets were held to three hits by a rookie, Rick Wise, and John Klippstein. Frank Lary, who was traded from the Tigers to the Mets only three weeks ago, and was once a team-mate of Bunning's, was the Mets' starter and loser.

Johnny Briggs started Lary to defeat with a lead-off homer in the first inning. Callison also hit another homer with the bases empty.

The sweep of the twin bill increased the Phils league lead to two games.

June 22, 1964

National League Beats American, 7-4, on Homer in Ninth

CALLISON'S CLOUT DRIVES IN 3 RUNS

Radatz Yields Hit With Two Out as Nationals Square All-Star Game Series

By LEONARD KOPPETT

The ninth-inning heroics of Willie Mays, an all-star among all-stars, and John Callison, one of the rising young stars of the rising Philadelphia Phillies brought the National League a dramatic 7-4 victory yesterday over the American in the 35th All-Star Game before 50,850 spectators at Shea Stadium.

Mays, who led off the last half of the ninth with his team trailing, 4-3, scored the tying run almost single-handedly — or, more accurately, single-footedly.

Mays drew a walk, stole sec-

ond, moved to third when Orlando Cepeda's looping fly fell out of reach in short right center, and raced home when the precautionary throw to the plate took a bad bounce over the catcher's head.

A little later, with two out and two men on base, Callison ended the game with a home run off Dick Radatz. The huge relief specialist of the Boston Red Sox had the hero's role in his grasp until the ninth started.

This comeback, which evened the All-Star Game series at 17 victories for each league with one tie, constituted the most exciting last-ditch rally in these games since the 1941 contest. In that one Ted Williams hit a three-run homer with two out in the ninth to give the American League a 7-5 triumph at Detroit.

Equality Is Achieved

That was during the period of American League dominance of the All-Star Game. The American Leaguers forged a 12—4 lead in the series by 1949. Since then, the balance of baseball power has been swinging toward the National League. Equality was achieved as the

National League posted its sixth victory in the last seven decisions.

The triumph, registered during one of the most eventful innings of the 31-year-old competition, was sparked by a series of "little" incidents that don't show in the box score.

The American Leaguers had tied the score on Brooks Robinson's two-run triple in the sixth and had taken a 4—3 lead in the seventh. They got the go-ahead run when Elston Howard was hit by a pitch, Rocky Colavito doubled and Jim Fregosi flied to Mays in center. The drive was deep enough to let even the slow-footed Howard score from third ahead of an impressive throw by Mays.

Manager Al Lopez promptly sent Radatz into action to try to preserve the lead. For two innings, the 6-foot 5-inch, 235-pound right-hander did a perfect job.

He struck out four of the six men he faced in the seventh and eighth. When a fine play by Bobby Richardson provided the final out in the eighth and prevented Mays from going to bat with a man on base, the American League seemed in command.

Mays Fools Radatz

Radatz began the ninth with the same power and confidence. His first pitch to Mays was a strike; his second was fouled off. Then Willie fouled off five more pitches before he walked.

No one doubted that Mays would try to steal second when Cepeda went to bat. On the second pitch he beat Howard's throw to Richardson at second base by a comfortable margin.

"I thought I could keep him close to first, make him start back to the bag," Radatz said later, calmly and sadly. "On the first pitch, he did. I thought he did on the second : o—but he didn't."

Cepeda had swung at both pitches and missed. He swung at the next one also, hitting it with the handle of his bat on a high arc into short right center.

Colavito, the right fielder, was playing much too deep to reach the ball. Jimmy Hall, the center fielder, was playing toward left center and never figured in the play. Joe Pepitone, the first baseman, raced out, but couldn't get within 10 feet of the ball.

Box Score of All-Star Game

AMERICAN	ab.	r.	h.	rbi.	po.	a.	NATIONAL	ab.	r.	h.	rbi.	po.	a.
Fregosi, ss	4	1	1	4	1	1	Clemente, rf	4	1	1	0	1	0
Oliva, rf	4	0	0	0	0	0	Short, p	0	0	0	0	0	1
Radatz, p	1	0	0	0	0	0	Farrell, p	0	0	0	0	0	0
Mantle, cf	4	1	1	0	2	0	gWhite	1	0	0	0	0	0
Hall, cf	0	0	0	0	0	0	Marichal, p	0	0	0	0	0	0
Killebrew, lf	4	1	3	1	0	0	Groat, ss	3	0	1	1	0	0
Hinton, lf	0	0	0	0	0	0	dCardenas, ss	1	0	0	0	1	0
Allison, 1b	3	0	0	0	9	0	Williams, lf	4	1	1	1	1	0
fPepitone, 1b	0	0	0	0	1	0	Mays, cf	3	1	0	0	7	0
Robinson, 3b	4	0	2	1	2	2	Cepeda, 1b	4	0	1	0	6	0
Richardson, 2b	4	0	1	0	4	4	hFlood	0	1	0	0	0	0
Howard, c	3	1	0	0	9	0	Boyer, 3b	4	1	2	1	0	2
Chance, p	1	0	0	0	0	1	Torre, c	2	0	0	0	5	0
Wyatt, p	0	0	0	0	0	1	Edwards, c	1	0	0	0	5	0
bSiebern	1	0	0	0	0	0	Hunt, 2b	2	0	1	0	1	0
Pascual, p	0	0	0	0	0	1	jAaron	1	0	0	0	0	0
eColavito, rf	2	0	1	0	0	0	Drysdale, p	0	0	0	0	0	3
							aStargell	1	0	0	0	0	0
							Bunning, p	0	0	0	0	0	0
							cCallison, rf	3	1	1	3	0	0
Total	35	4	9	4	26	10	Total	34	7	8	6	27	6

aGrounded out for Drysdale in 3d; bFlied out for Wyatt in 5th;
cPopped out for Bunning in 5th; dRan for Groat in 5th; eDoubled
for Pascual in 7th; fRan for Allison in 8th; gStruck out for Farrell in
8th; hRan for Cepeda in 9th; jStruck out for Hunt in 9th.

American	1	0	0	0	0	2	1	0	0–4
National	0	0	0	2	1	0	0	0	4–7

Two out when winning run was scored.
Error—Pepitone. Left on bases—American 7, National 3.
Two-base hits—Groat, Colavito. Three-base hit—Robinson. Home
runs—Williams, Boyer, Callison. Stolen base—Mays. Sacrifice fly—
Fregosi.

	IP.	H.	R.	ER.	BB.	SO.	HBP.	WP.	Balks
Chance	3	2	0	0	2	2	0	0	0
Wyatt	1	2	2	2	0	0	0	0	0
Pascual	2	2	1	1	0	1	0	0	0
Radatz (L.)	2⅔	2	4	4	2	5	0	0	0
Drysdale	3	2	1	0	0	3	0	1	0
Bunning	2	2	0	0	4	0	0	0	0
Short	1	3	2	2	0	1	0	0	0
Farrell	1	2	1	1	1	1	1	0	0
Marichal (W.)	1	0	0	0	0	1	0	0	0

Bases on balls—Farrell 1 (Allison), Radatz 2 (Mays, Edwards).
Struck out—Drysdale 3 (Mantle, Allison, Howard), Chance 2 (Clem-
ente, Groat), Bunning 4 (Allison, Richardson, Howard, Fregosi),
Short 1 (Oliva), Pascual 1 (Boyer), Farrell 1 (Mantle), Radatz 5
(Edwards, Hunt, White, Cardenas, Aaron), Marichal 1 (Radatz).
Hit by pitcher—By Farrell 1 (Howard). Wild pitch—Drysdale. Passed
ball—Torre. Umpires—Sudol (N.), plate; Paparella (A.), first base;
Secory (N.), second base; Chylak (A.), third base; Harvey (N.), left
field; Salerno (A.), right field. Time—2:27. Attendance—50,850.

And neither could Richardson who was playing close to second base to keep Mays from getting too big a lead. Since the shortstop, Fregosi, was playing Cepeda to pull the ball, holding Mays close to the base became the second baseman's responsibility. Because Mays represented the tying run, he had to be kept close to the base so that he couldn't score on a single to left.

Pepitone Throws Wild

Richardson said later that from a normal fielding position, he probably could have caught Cepeda's hit. As it was, the ball fell safely and Mays, standing on second until he could see the ball touch the ground, ran to third. Pepitone picked up the ball with his back to the plate.

Mays stopped at third and took a step or two toward home. Pepitone, looking over the situation, threw home to keep Mays on third. The throw was true, but bounced 10 or more feet in front of Howard and took a high skip. Howard leaped, touched it with his glove, but barely deflected it.

Radatz, meanwhile, had been slow to leave the mound to back up the throw to the plate. At the same time he seemed undecided whether to back up a play toward third or home. When the ball bounced, Radatz was more to the third base side of the plate instead of directly behind Howard. The pitcher had to run toward the play, then stoop to try to scoop up the ball.

As for Mays, he took off for home as soon as the ball passed Howard. Willie made it easily. Cepeda, at the same time, moved to second.

Suddenly all the initiative was with the National League. The score was 4—4 and the potential winning run was on second with none out. Only an ordinary single was needed to send the run home.

Aaron Fans for Hunt

Ken Boyer, who had hit a home run in the fourth inning, was the next batter. Radatz made him pop up to Robinson not far from the plate.

John Edwards, the left-handed-hitting catcher from Cincinnati, went to bat next and he was walked intentionally creating a double-play possibility.

It was Ron Hunt's turn to bat next. But Manager Walt Alston had a pinch-hitter available for just this spot.

The pinch-hitter was Hank Aaron, whose qualifications couldn't be questioned even by the most rabid New Yorkers eager to see the only Met in the game get a crack at glory.

Radatz struck out Aaron with four pitches.

Callison then drove the next pitch into the upper right-field stand, close to the foul line and a few rows over the auxiliary scoreboard at the end of the grandstand.

As abruptly as that, it was all over.

The National League players jumped out of their dugout to greet Callison as he completed his run around the bases. They pounded his back and laughed and cheered.

Don Drysdale of the Dodgers and Dean Chance of the Angels, the two best right-handed pitchers in Los Angeles and rarely surpassed anywhere else, were the starters.

Drysdale was touched for an unearned run in the first inning. Fregosi led off with a ground single through third and shortstop and took second on a passed ball charged to Joe Torre. With two out, Fregosi scored on Harmon Killebrew's long single to left.

Drysdale allowed no one else to reach base in his three-inning turn.

Chance was even more impressive. He allowed only two singles, but they were separated and harmless. Of the 37 pitches he threw to 11 batters, only seven were called balls.

Jim Bunning relieved Drysdale and made history simply by appearing. He's the only man to pitch for both leagues in All-Star competition. He appeared in six games as an American Leaguer before the Detroit Tigers traded him to Philadelphia last fall.

Bunning Strikes Out 4

Now he was back on the mound where he had made much more significant history last month by pitching a perfect game against the Mets.

This time two men got on base, Killebrew with an infield single and Robinson with a line single to right in the fourth inning. In his two-inning turn, Bunning struck out four.

Meanwhile, John Wyatt had replaced Chance. The big reliever from Kansas City didn't have it. Billy Williams of the Cubs hit Wyatt's first pitch over the fence in right center.

Mays fouled out, but Cepeda lined the ball off Wyatt's shin, a drive Wyatt was able to recover and turn into an out. Then Boyer drove his second All-Star homer into the left field bull pen and the National League led, 2—1.

In the fifth, against Camilo

Pascual, the Nationals took a 3-1 lead. With two out, Roberto Clemente bounced a hit off second base. Dick Groat lined a double out of Killebrew's reach in left center and Clemente scored.

Short Yields Big Triple

Chris Short, another Philadelphia pitcher and the only left-hander to appear in the game, replaced Bunning and couldn't hold the lead. Short was suffering from a pulled

muscle in his side, but the injury was not serious enough for him to forgo his All-Star appearance.

He struck out Tony Oliva, but was tagged for singles by Mickey Mantle and Killebrew. Bob Allison flied to Mays, and Robinson sent a triple to the wall in right center.

The ball went beyond Mays, who tumbled in a desperate effort to reach the ball on the fly. Both runners tallied and the score was 3—3. But Richardson could not put his team ahead. He tapped back to short.

The lead run was scored in the seventh in unusual circumstances. Dick Farrell of Houston was the pitcher. He hit Howard on the left shoulder to start the inning. Then Colavito was sent to bat for Pascual.

Nine times of 10, the situation would call for a bunt, but that was not what Lopez intended by choosing Colavito. Even the National League defense ignored the possibility of a bunt, so Rocky smashed a double out of Mays's reach in left center. Fregosi's fly drove in Howard.

That was the situation Radatz inherited. Farrell had yielded a walk and single in the eighth, and Mays had saved at least another run with a brilliant running catch of Howard's drive to left center for the final out.

Juan Marichal retired three men in order in the ninth and became the winning pitcher by doing the least amount of work.

Callison, meanwhile, had entered the game as unobtrusively as he had made the squad. He did not finish first or second in the players' balloting for right fielders. Clemente and Aaron were chosen No. 1 and No. 2, respectively. Callison was one of three "extra" men named by Alston to round out the 25-man squad.

Mays Is Star of Stars

In the fifth, with one out and none on, Callison went into the game as a pinch-hitter for Bunning against Pascual and popped up. He stayed in to play right field and batted against Radatz with two out in seventh. He swung at the first pitch and flied deep to Mantle in center, almost 400 feet from the plate.

He was the only batter to swing twice against Radatz and each time he swung on the first pitch.

Mays, the Giants' star, went hitless. But his All-Star Game average is .392 for 15 games. His sixth stolen base and his 16th run scored constituted records, and his seven putouts in center tied a record.

It was Mays, with his stolen base and the ever-present threat of his speed and alertness who helped the National Leaguers gain their victory. That's why the All-Stars look upon Willie, now 33 years old, as the star of stars.

July 8, 1964

The Greatest Pitcher Of Them All

By LEONARD KOPPETT

FOR the last four years, the brilliant pitching feats of Sandy Koufax, Brooklyn's gift to Los Angeles and to contemporary American folklore, have given new life to an old diversion: choosing a designee for the title of "The Greatest Pitcher in the History of Baseball."

Not even the interruptions caused by two serious injuries—a damaged finger which kept him idle for two months in 1962, and an injured elbow which ended the current season for him seven weeks early—have altered Sandy's status as a prime stimulant for such discussion.

Last year, Koufax capped a sensational regular-season performance by striking out 15 New York Yankees in the first game of the World Series, and then beating them again four days later for a startling four-game sweep by his Los Angeles Dodgers. The World Series about to start is not likely to offer anything half as exciting.

This June, he pitched a no-hitter for the third straight year (an unprecedented feat) against the Philadelphia Phillies, who were well on their way to succeeding the Dodgers as National League champions. Before hurting his elbow in August, he had compiled an all-around record good enough to be called the best in baseball this year: 19 victories, 5 defeats, 223 strikeouts in exactly that many innings, and an earned-run average of 1.74. He breaks some sort of record almost every time he pitches.

Is Koufax, then, "the greatest pitcher?" Or is it someone from the distant, or not so distant, past— someone who is only a name to most present-day baseball fans — like Walter Johnson, Grover Cleveland Alexander, Christy Mathewson, Cy Young? Or someone who remains a vivid memory from a later era, like Lefty Grove or Bob Feller? Or even someone else pitching today?

ANY answer to such a question has to be intensely personal, which is probably why a proposition so basically unprovable remains so popular. As a rule, the younger generation takes for granted that today's "greatest" anything is automatically superior. Older people, or at least those

LEONARD KOPPETT is a reporter in the sports section of The New York Times.

with longer memories, frequently insist that the "really great" ones were the heroes of antiquity—a period which, among sports fans, invariably coincides with the adolescence and early adulthood of the speaker. With such a privately defined "golden age" embedded in each interested party, an objective evaluation is difficult and a thoroughly exhilarating, riproaring argument always possible.

My own choice is Johnson—a man I never saw pitch. The best I've ever seen are Feller and Koufax. But Sandy doesn't really qualify for reasons best explained by an exceptionally well-informed source: Sanford Koufax himself.

"To talk of me in such terms is ridiculous," he says, in a typically sincere, analytic speech. "I had a great year, and I'm proud of it. I hope to have many more. I don't feel any false modesty about my natural gifts, and I try to work hard at my job, which is winning games.

"But before you compare me with the great pitchers of all time, let me be around a while. Let me prove I can do some of these things over a long period of time. Don't put me in a class with pitchers like Warren Spahn and Whitey Ford until I've shown I can win games for 10 or 15 years. Spahn's been doing it for 20. That's what it takes to rate as a great ballplayer, not a couple of good years, but a whole career."

KOUFAX is 28 years old, and the opinion that he is the best pitcher working today is as close to unanimous as anything in baseball can be. Yet this is only his fourth season as an established regular and only his second as a superstar. He signed with the Dodgers in his native Brooklyn in 1955 for a modest bonus (about $14,000) during his freshman year at the University of Cincinnati. Because of rules covering bonus players at that time, he couldn't be sent to the minors to learn his trade. He spent three seasons, therefore, sitting around and pitching infrequently in over-matched situations. Only after the club moved to Los Angeles in 1958 did he begin to work regularly, and only in spring training of 1961 did he acquire the key to his present success.

Below, Sandy Koufax, a near-unanimous choice as the best pitcher working today, who in June pitched his third no-hitter and by August, when he was injured, had won 19 games and fanned 223, for an earned-run average of 1.74.

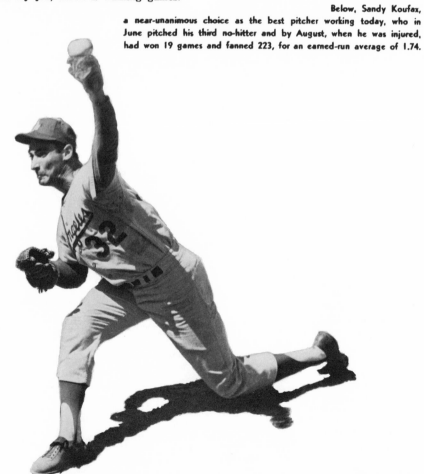

GREATS, PAST AND PRESENT—Above, Walter Johnson, "the Big Train," who in 20 years with the indifferent Washington Senators won 414 games—more than anyone else in the modern era—and also set records for shutouts (113), strikeouts (3,508), consecutive scoreless innings (56) and consecutive games won (16).

obstruction which gradually numbed the forefinger of his pitching hand. He couldn't pitch at all the second half of the season—and if the last of a series of modern medical treatments hadn't succeeded, amputation might have been necessary. This year's injury was more routine: an inflamed elbow.

LONGEVITY, then, is one of the fundamental standards in judging the "greatest." We are trying to single out one man among the thousands who have pitched in the major leagues over a period of many decades; however distinguished the achievements of any of them may be, only those who could maintain their superiority for the full span of career possibility—about 20 years—can be considered for the No. 1 ranking.

This immediately rules out some famous names whose moments of glory were every bit as bright as Koufax's and somewhat longer. Dizzy Dean, for instance, in 1933-37, was as commanding a figure as any pitcher could be (he won 30 games in 1934, something no one has done since). But in the 1937 All-Star game, a line drive broke his toe; when he tried to resume pitching too soon, he favored the leg and strained his arm, and he was never great again. Less celebrated, and certainly less remembered, is Addie Joss, who won 155 games for Cleveland in his first eight major-league seasons and pitched two no-hitters, one a perfect game. But Joss died of tuberculosis in 1911, at the age of 31.

A MORE recent example is Herb Score. Less than a decade ago, he was the magnet for all the superlatives now heaped on Koufax. After the 1956 season, the Boston Red Sox offered Cleveland $1,000,000 for his contract—and were turned down. But the very next year a line drive hit Score in the eye. His sight was saved, but he never could regain his pitching rhythm and soon developed a sore arm. He kept trying until last year, when he finally retired to become a play-by-play broadcaster for the Chicago White Sox—still only 31 years old.

All right, then; longevity narrows the field to those who lasted 20 years or so. What are the other standards of pitching greatness? There are

So Koufax may be, some day, a prime candidate for the title of "greatest"—if he is fortunate enough to retain good health. Pitchers' arms are notoriously fragile; the wear and tear is tremendous, and the risk of injury on a ball field is considerable. Sandy himself has had to face this uncertainty in a particularly vivid manner. Two years ago his career was almost destroyed by a freak accident.

IT was during the first half of the 1962 season, when he had reached his full development and was on his way to a carload of records and honors. One day he bruised his hand while batting. The result was a circulatory

four: stuff, control, craft and poise. At this point, some remarks on the art of pitching are in order.

In baseball language, "stuff" refers to the physical element of a pitcher's equipment: How hard can he throw? How much can he make a curve ball break? Basically, exceptional "stuff" is the product of strength and hair-trigger coordination. It seems to be an innate quality, subject perhaps to improvement by practice and technique, but not acquirable.

Control, of course, is exactly what it implies: the ability to throw the ball—with "stuff" on it—where the pitcher wants to with extraordinary accuracy.

CRAFT comprises the knowledge that comes with experience, analytic powers, meticulous observation and resourcefulness. Craft is what tells a pitcher where and how to apply the stuff he can control.

Poise includes the ability to apply one's craft under the most severe competitive conditions, to rise to an occasion, to produce best when the need is greatest.

Fundamentally, a pitcher is trying to keep the batter from hitting the ball squarely. The ball is round; it travels up to 90 miles an hour. The bat is round. Only a tiny area of these two round surfaces is the "right" area for hitting the ball. Anything the pitcher can do to prevent them from meeting is good pitching.

For this, the pitcher has two dimensions to work with: space and time. He can make the batter swing off balance (just a trifle is enough) by making the trajectory of the ball deceptive. Or he can change the speed of the delivery so that the batter's timing is disrupted. And, of course, he can combine the two weapons in a variety of proportions.

A PITCHER with a great fast ball can simply throw it past hitters, but this is never enough by itself to defeat major league hitters. A pitcher with exceptional "breaking stuff"—curves of various types or trick deliveries like knuckleballs—is better equipped provided his fast ball is fast enough to be a useful contrast. A pitcher with pinpoint control is best off, as long as his stuff is moderately good, because he can exploit

the weak spot that every batter has.

Naturally, the more stuff a pitcher has, the harder it is to control, and usually control is acquired at the sacrifice of some power. Furthermore, both the practice that produces control and the experience that produces knowledge and poise are time-consuming. In the process, age and the attrition of muscular strain take their toll. Usually, by the time a pitcher masters his craft, some degree of his physical gift has been lost.

It is very rare, therefore, to find a man who possesses the highest degree of stuff, control and craft simultaneously. It is so rare, in fact, that our list of eligibles for the "greatest pitcher" designation is immediately reduced to quite manageable terms.

Warren Spahn and Whitey Ford are the most distinguished pitchers active today. Spahn, finishing his 20th major league season at the age of 43, already holds the record for most victories by a left-handed pitcher. (He had 350 before this season began.) Ford, who has spent his 14-year career with the perpetually successful Yankees, has the best winning percentage in the history of the game.

BUT neither of them, outstanding as they are, ever had speed and power comparable to that possessed by Johnson, Feller or Koufax. The same was true of Carl Hubbell, Herb Pennock, Ted Lyons and a dozen others. They were artists, worthy of a place in Baseball's Hall of Fame, but not contenders for No. 1 ranking.

Others, like Dean, Lefty Gomez, Dazzy Vance and Rube Waddell, did have overpowering stuff, but they never perfected the craft. Untouchable for a while, they became merely very good pitchers when their exceptional speed was lost.

That narrows our list to Johnson, Alexander, Mathewson, Grove and Feller.

Cy Young must be mentioned. He won 511 games, more than any other pitcher on record. But his career began in 1890, when conditions of play were simply too different to make any comparison meaningful. Major-league baseball was stabilized in its familiar form in 1903, after the American League had shaken down. All those being considered pitched after that

(although Young did last until 1911, too).

Feller is next to be eliminated, partially by fate. To a blinding fast ball he added one of the biggest, most bewildering curve balls ever used. He joined Cleveland in 1936, at the age of 17, and started breaking strikeout records right away. In all, he won 266 games, pitched three no-hitters and 12 one-hitters, and set a record for strikeouts in one season (348 in 1946) which still stands.

BUT Feller was robbed of almost four full seasons, at the very height of his powers, by World War II. He was only 23 years old when he went into service, and took up where he left off when he returned at 27. Granted peaceful times, he might have posted 100 more victories and 1,000 more strikeouts. He might have made his claim to No. 1 undeniable. Even when his fast ball was long since gone, in 1951, he won 22 games. But the lost years eliminate him.

Grove, according to most testimony, was faster than Feller. "He was the fastest pitcher who ever lived," says Ford Frick, Commissioner of Baseball, who spent the 1920's and early 1930's as a baseball writer. Grove never had Feller's curve, but he kept his fast ball longer. In 17 American League seasons, he won exactly 300 games (losing only 140) and was still the league-leader in earned-run average at the age of 39 (in 1939).

BUT Grove did it all on power. Mathewson had power, too, and more finesse. He threw a famous "fadeaway," a pitch that today would be called a "right-handed screwball." His career with the New York Giants ran from 1900 to 1916. Of his 373 victories, 365 came in a 14-year span, which means an *average* of 26 per year.

Still, Mathewson was usually with a winning team. Alexander and Johnson were not.

"I would have to say," says Casey Stengel, who ought to know, "that Johnson was the most amazing pitcher in the American League and Alexander in the National. Alexander had to pitch in that little Philadelphia ball park, with the big tin fence in right field, and he pitched shutouts, which must mean he could do

it. He had a fast ball, a curve, a change of pace and perfect control. He was the best I

CHRISTY MATHEWSON—Of his 373 wins, 365 were in a 14-year span, which would come to 26 a year.

batted against in the National League."

Alexander was 24 years old when he joined the Phillies in 1911. As a right-hander, that 250-foot right-field barrier in Baker Bowl presented a special hazard, since left-handed hitters were the ones who had a crack at it. It's true, the lively ball was not yet in use but, by the same token, hitters who weren't swinging at the fences were much harder to strike out. In his first seven seasons with the Phillies, Alexander won 190 games.

He moved on to Chicago and St. Louis and in 1926, at the age of 39, was the World Series hero for the Cardinals as they defeated the Yankees in seven games.

Altogether, Alexander won 373 games. He pitched 90 shutouts, still the National League record, and this is a peculiarly significant statistic. "A good pitcher's main job," Sal Maglie, the Giant ace of the 1950's, once observed, "is not to give up the first run." If a pitcher holds the opposition scoreless, his team can't lose. Once his own team scores, the pitcher's job is to give the other side one less. A shutout is proof positive that the pitcher has done his team job to perfection.

Strikeouts are important in this respect, too. Base-runners can't advance on strikeouts. With a man on third, a winning run can be scored on a fly-out or a ground-out—but not on a strikeout. Alexander struck out 2,198 batters. (Grove, by the way,

GROVER CLEVELAND ALEXANDER—He pitched 696 games, won 373 (90 of them shutouts), fanned 2,198 and walked only 951.

fanned 2,266; Feller, 2,581; Mathewson, 2,505.) That's why "stuff" is so important. At the same time, control is even more important, and Alexander walked only 951 men — averaging about one walk for every six innings pitched, and he pitched in 696 games.

IF our accolade was to be for "the most complete pitcher of all time," Alexander would be it. But Johnson was greater still.

Walter Perry (Barney) Johnson was primarily a fast-ball pitcher, the fastest of all. He developed a fairly good curve after a while, but mostly he just leaned back and fired the fast ball with a three-quarter-arm motion, almost side-arm.

"You might know it was coming," says Stengel, "but you couldn't hit it. He had perfect control, too."

"When I batted against him, in 1921," says Fred Haney, now general manager of the Los Angeles Angels, but then a Detroit infielder, "he looked so fast I couldn't believe it. When I got back to the bench, they told me, 'You should have seen him 10 years ago; he was twice as fast then.' Heck, I was glad I didn't see him 10 years before; I didn't want to see him the way he was now."

"Johnson," says Frick, "always worried that his fast ball might kill someone if it hit him in the head. His control was so perfect, though, that he didn't even have to throw close to hitters. He just kept throwing it over the plate."

Johnson came out of Humboldt, Kan., in 1907 at the age of 19. He went straight to the Washington Senators and never pitched for any other team in organized baseball—except one inning for Newark in the International League in 1928, when he was the manager. The Senators then, as ever, were seldom successful. During his first 16 years with them, they finished in the second division 10 times. They were last or next-to-last seven

Babe Ruth as a pitcher for the Boston Red Sox in 1918.

times. He didn't get a chance to pitch in the World Series until 1924, when he was almost 37 years old. Then he lost two games to the Giants, but won the seventh and deciding game to give Washington its first and only world championship.

DESPITE this minimal support, Johnson won 414 games —more than anyone else in the modern era.

"He was, besides, a wonderful man," says Frick. "The scene that sticks in my memory is the end of the 1925 World Series. Johnson was at the end of his career, and

pitching in the seventh and deciding game at Pittsburgh. Roger Peckinpaugh, a great shortstop who was having a terrible series, made an error, and then KiKi Cuyler hit a bases-loaded double and Johnson was beaten.

"When the inning was over, he waited at the mound until Peckinpaugh came by on the way off the field—and he put his arm around Peckinpaugh's shoulders in a comforting and forgiving gesture. That was Johnson the man."

AND this was Johnson the pitcher: He pitched 113 shutouts, a record that stands by itself. He struck out 3,508 batters — about 1,000 more than anyone else. He once pitched 56 consecutive scoreless innings—still a record. He had a 16-game winning streak in 1912, setting an American League record that has been tied but not surpassed. He started, finished and appeared in more games than any other pitcher. From 1910 through 1919 he won 264 games, or more than one-third of all the games won by his team during those 10 years (the Senators won 755).

Statistics in themselves prove little, but Johnson's are beyond quibbling. Anyone might have another candidate for "the greatest pitcher of all," but no one can ever call Johnson an unreasonable choice.

October 4, 1964

Cards Set Back Mets, 11-5, Take Pennant

GIBSON WINS 19TH IN RELIEF EFFORT

Mets Lead, 3-2, in Fifth but Homers by White, Flood Assure Flag Victory

---

By JOSEPH DURSO
Special to The New York Times

ST. LOUIS, Oct. 4—The St. Louis Cardinals won the most savagely contested pennant in National League history today on the last day of the season by overpowering the New York Mets, 11—5, while the Philadelphia Phillies were knocking the Cincinnati Reds out of a first-place tie.

Before a roaring sellout throng of 30,146, the Cardinals finally defeated Casey Stengel's 10th-place tigers 48 hours after the Mets had cut the Cardinals' league lead from one game to half a game and 24 hours after they had wiped it out.

The tumult in Busch Stadium mounted with every run scored here and 350 miles away in Cincinnati, where the Phillies were overwhelming the Reds, 10—0. The Phillies, who led the league by 6½ games two weeks ago, thus enjoyed the supreme irony of the season's final hours by thwarting the Reds, who had wrenched first place from

them one week ago today only to lose it two days later to the Cardinals.

St. Louis rushed its No. 1 pitcher, Bob Gibson, into the game in relief of Curt Simmons to hold back the Mets and forestall a three-way tie threatened by the Phillies.

Now for the Series

Gibson pitched four solid innings. St. Louis finished first by one game. the Phils and Reds shared second place — and the Cardinals open the World Series here Wednesday against the New York Yankees.

There was jubilation in the Cardinals' dressing room after the game and August A. Busch Jr., the president and owner of the club and of Anheuser-Busch, Inc., a brewery, served champagne to Manager Johnny

Keane, and the players. "This is the happiest day of my life." Busch shouted hoarsely to Keane. "I just want to say hello to you and bring you this glass of champagne."

For almost six innings the outcome was in serious doubt as the Mets tied the Cardinals, 1—1, in the fourth, passed them in the fifth and drew near again in the sixth.

But St. Louis broke the game open with three runs in the fifth, three in the sixth and three in the eighth against half a dozen pitchers dispatched to the scene by Stengel.

Cards Take Lead

The Cards broke on top in the second inning, after Tim McCarver hit a liner into the left-field corner for a double. Mike Shannon drove a 2-and-2 pitch into left for a single, and St. Louis was ahead for the first time all weekend, 1—0.

With two out in the fourth, just as three runs were being hoisted on the scoreboard for the Phillies in Cincinnati, Charlie Smith tempered the joy by hitting a towering fly down the right-field line, just fair and onto the roof for his 20th home run.

In the bottom of the fourth, Dick Groat doubled into the right-field corner and, after the next two men had gone out, Dal Maxvill singled to center and the Cards were on top, 2—1.

But in the fifth the first signs of panic appeared when George Altman singled over second, Cisco advanced him with a bunt and Bobby Klaus and Roy McMillan doubled in succession. That put the Mets back in command, 3—2, and caused the Cardinals to call for Gibson, who had pitched eight innings and lost to the Mets Friday, 1—0.

After that Gibson (and Barney Schultz in the ninth) restrained the Mets with three hits and no more runs while the Cardinals exploded for nine runs in four innings. The victory was Gibson's 19th of the year.

In the fifth, Lou Brock walked on a 3-and-2 pitch, Bill White lined a single to right, Ken Boyer doubled into the left-field corner and the game was tied, 3—3, with the Cards finally rolling.

Bill Wakefield relieved Cisco,

Cardinals' Score

NEW YORK (N.)	ab.r.h.bi	ST. LOUIS (N.)	ab.r.h.bi
Klaus, 2b	4 1 2 1	Flood, cf	4 1 1 1
McMillan, ss	4 1 1 2	Brock, lf	4 2 2 0
Ch'topher, rf	4 0 1 0	White, 1b	5 2 2 2
Hickman, cf	4 0 0 0	Boyer, 3b	2 3 1 1
Smith, 3b	5 1 1 1	Groat, ss	5 2 2 1
Taylor, c	3 1 2 0	McCarver, c	4 1 3 3
Elliot, ph	1 0 0 0	Shannon, rf	5 0 1 1
Kanehl, ph	1 0 1 1	Maxvill, 2b	4 0 2 2
Kranepool, 1b	4 0 1 0	Simmons, p	1 0 0 0
Altman, rf	3 1 1 0	Gibson, p	2 0 0 0
Cisco, p	0 0 0 0		
Gonder, c	1 0 0 0		
Totals	34 5 10 5	Totals	36 11 14 11

New York .... 0 0 0 1 2 1 . 0 0 1 — 5
St. Louis .... 0 1 0 1 3 3 0 3 .—11

E—Hickman, Klaus. DP—New York 1, St. Louis 1. LOB—New York 11, St. Louis 8. 2B—McCarver 2, Groat 2, Boyer. Klaus. HR—Smith (20), White (21), Flood (5). S—Cisco 2.

	IP.	H.	R.	ER.BB.SO.
*Cisco (L, 6—19)	4	7	5	5 4 0
Wakefield	2⅔	0	0	0 0 1
Fisher	⅓	0	0	0 0 1
Hunter		3	3	3 1 1
Ribant	1⅔	2	3	3 1 2
Locke	⅓	0	0	0 1 0
Simmons	4⅓	7	3	3 1 0
Gibson (W, 19—12)	4	2	2	2 5 2
Schultz	⅔	1	0	0 0 1

*Faced 3 batters in 5th. HBP—By Gibson, Christopher. WP—Gibson. PB—McCarver 2. T—3:06. A—30,146.

but Groat scored White on a shot off Wakefield's glove, Maxvill lined a single to right with two out, Jack Fisher was in for the Mets and the Cards led. 5—3.

In the sixth, Brock doubled to right for his 200th hit of the year and White bombed one over the roof in right for his 21st home run. And in the eighth Curt Flood put one onto the roof in a three-run inning, and the weeks of suspense and upsets were over.

October 5, 1964

LEAGUE REFUSES TO ALLOW BRAVES TO MOVE TILL '66

Team to Stay in Milwaukee Next Season, but May Go to Atlanta Thereafter

By United Press International

PHOENIX, Ariz., Nov. 7— The National League ruled today that the Braves must remain in Milwaukee for the 1965 season but may move to Atlanta in 1966.

Warren Giles, the league president, said the league held a special meeting here to discuss the Milwaukee situation. The Milwaukee representatives were asked to leave the room, and in their absence, the other league representatives voted unanimously to instruct Milwaukee to remain in the Wisconsin city next year, Giles said. The league also ruled, he added, that "it was in the best future interests of baseball to have the club move to Atlanta in 1966."

The Braves stated on Oct. 21 that they hoped to move to Atlanta next season.

Ford Frick, the baseball commissioner, said after the final joint session of both leagues here this morning that it was the concensus of all attending that the regular baseball convention in Houston in December would take up the proposed adoption of a free-agent draft and an unrestricted draft that would include all players once every club had reached its limit of 40 players.

Centralization of Office

Frick said the baseball owners also agreed to the centralization of baseball headquarters, preferably in a two-league city, which would mean New York, Chicago or Los Angeles. However, he said no preference for a city was expressed.

Frick said the owners, who wound up a three-day closed-door meeting at the Arizona Biltmore, also agreed to restore the more sweeping authority of the Commissioner, which was taken away after the death of Commissioner Kenesaw Mountain Landis.

Frick said at a briefing after the session that the baseball owners had also expressed interest in developing and training umpires and in subsidizing four geographical leagues for college players in which talent could be developed without the players losing their amateur status.

The Milwaukee decision of the National League was the only official action taken at the meeting. Frick said any official decisions on the matters discussed would be made after the Houston baseball convention.

November 8, 1964

The Ex-National Sport Looks to Its Image

By LEONARD KOPPETT

MAJOR league baseball, a mass spectator sport still steeped in its 19th-century origins, is suffering today from that most modern of 20th-century maladies: "bad image."

The illness has occurred relatively recently. Until a decade ago few people bothered to challenge base-

LEONARD KOPPETT is a reporter in the sports department of The New York Times.

ball's right to a place alongside Mom, apple pie and freedom of assembly. There were those who didn't care, but not many who did failed to accept baseball as a peculiar, indigenous and vaguely defined "special" element in the fabric of American culture.

Today this favored position is not merely challenged—it has disappeared. While millions of people still feel a passionate interest in every sort of baseball news, fewer and fewer regard it as essentially different from other forms of entertainment. Even baseball's own hierarchy admits that the aura has gone, or is

going. Commissioner Ford C. Frick, in a top-secret report to the 20 major-league club owners last month in Phoenix, spelled out the "bad image" problem and blamed the owners for it. As with most top-secret stories in baseball, this one made headlines right away. At the regular winter meetings of the majors and minors, however, held in Houston two weeks ago, officials occupied themselves with other matters and gave Frick's "image" warning only passing notice.

The chances are that the issue will not escape the loquacious attention of the hot-stove leaguers this winter as they relive past seasons and speculate on those to come. What, indeed, has happened to bring about the change? What was the baseball of the "old days" like, before the "image" got tarnished? Well, a generation ago it would have sounded sacrilegious to identify the sport as "part of the *entertainment* industry."

(Today, of course, that very phrase is used to justify the purchase of the New York Yankees by the Columbia Broadcasting System.) A fan attended an event, not a performance. He had as little interest in — and awareness of—the commercial background of the goings-on on the field as the audience at a concert or opera has of the financial problems involved in a musical evening.

The supply of heroes seemed endless: Mathewson, Johnson, Cobb, Ruth. These, and a hundred others slightly less famous, were not merely great ball players; each had a distinct character in the eye of the fan. This character did not always coincide with the man in real life, but it was clear-cut, consistent, identifiable and human.

THE fan, a generation ago, believed that victory on the field was the most important thing in the world to all those concerned with baseball. And he was deeply loyal to locale. He knew that the players who wore, let's say, a Brooklyn uniform were recruited from all over the country, but as long as they wore it, they were part of Brooklyn.

To a great extent the prominent players did become a part of the community they played in. They settled in the residential neighborhoods that surrounded the ball parks built in the early years of the century; they frequented local restaurants, shops (yes, bars, too); they mingled with the fans entering and leaving the park.

Consider, for example, Ebbets Field. The structure was small, the stands close to the foul lines and the sense of intimacy very great. A fan yelling "Throw him a fish!" when Lonnie Frey booted a ball at shortstop could be heard clearly throughout the park. Players' shouts at one another could be heard, too.

When a man came to a game—a day game—he brought his children, who became converts. Older children could come by themselves — after school in spring and fall, or to doubleheaders in summer. Relatively few seats were boxes and almost any location in the park was available the day of a game.

In such surroundings, the Dodgers could, and did, become national as well as civic celebrities. Their "daffiness," their overpopulation of third base, their brushes with death from fly balls to the head were known to baseball fans everywhere. When they got into a fight (which Red Barber, their radio announcer, established once and for all as a "rhubarb"), no one could help taking sides.

A personal rivalry, like the one between John McGraw, supreme dictator of the New York Giants, and Uncle Wilbert Robinson, kindly but often bum-

bling manager of the Dodgers, helped divide Brooklyn from New York as sharply as Scotland from England. No mere political unity could erase the lines drawn.

An incident in the early life of Casey Stengel illustrates the communal atmosphere in which baseball players used to live. When Casey played for the Dodgers, he used to commute by trolley car to a boarding house. One day, after a game, he was riding the trolley when he saw one of his teammates on the sidewalk. The teammate, who had gone hitless that day, had caught one of his children swiping some fruit and was applying discipline and education with sharp smacks.

Stengel leaned out of the speeding trolley car, hanging on by one hand, and yelled: "When you go oh-for-four, you take it out on the kid, eh?"

The point is that everyone around knew who the players were and what they were talking about.

LATER, when the Dodgers had earned the affectionate title of "Bums," they started to win pennants. They became the epitome of the successful underdog. The love lavished on Pee Wee Reese, Jackie Robinson, Gil Hodges, Roy Campanella and the others of the postwar era was a beautiful thing.

In 1948, when Leo Durocher switched from managing the Dodgers to managing the Giants, the sense of shock was as real as if an Englishman had been suddenly elected Premier of France. When the lights were turned out at Ebbets Field and 30,000 fans lit matches to simulate a birthday cake for Pee Wee Reese, it was a press-agent-instigated idea, yes, but instigated by a press agent in tune with the populace.

When the Dodgers won the 1941 pennant, their first in 21 years, fans marched across Brooklyn Bridge and stood for hours on West 42d Street, booing the darkened offices of the Yankees, whom they would play in the World Series.

AND what is it like today? The Dodgers have ceased to exist, although there is a team by that name playing in a place called Los Angeles. At the new Dodger Stadium, almost half the seats are boxes. A man is more likely to bring a client than a son. (This is even more true at Yankee Stadium today.) The players, having become members of the

upper middle class, live in suburban communities 20 and 30 miles away; they are scattered, and the community life in which they take part is suburban, not local in the fans' sense of the term.

Inside the Los Angeles park, the customer can get dinner, plenty of liquor, souvenirs by the dozen, a host of special services—all far removed from the hot dogs and peanuts that used to represent the limit of ball park fare. This makes him more comfortable, and probably overweight, and it also drives home the point that his money is being sought at every turn.

Where have the fans' illusions that baseball was "something special" gone? How could they be maintained for half a century, then eroded in the last five years? The steps are easy to identify.

First, by yielding to the pressure (perhaps unavoidable) for unlimited night games, the majors gave up one of their distinctive characteristics. The difference between a night game and a day game may be hard to define, but its easy to feel: the one connotes sport, the other performance; one belongs to the young of all ages, the other to seekers of entertainment. A few night games were attractive galas, like extra Sundays or holidays; a steady diet undermined one psychological prop of the "something special" illusion.

Then, by jumping franchises in all directions for the avowed purpose of making more money, baseball destroyed the very stability, statistical validity and competitive integrity that made the game so attractive.

Between 1903, when the American League solidified and won major status, and 1953, when the Braves moved from Boston to Milwaukee, the major league structure stood as a monument to security in a frightening, changing world. The same 16 teams, located in only 11 cities with fairly compact travel connections, played a similar schedule pattern year after year, creating records that could be compared and discussed. What changes occurred were few, minor and easily understood.

The first few franchise shifts did not have an immediately disastrous effect. But then, in 1957, the point of no return was reached when, after months of rumors and denials, the Dodgers and Giants were moved to Los Angeles and San Francisco.

The moving of these teams to new towns tore the fabric of stability beyond repair. If Brooklyn could be deprived of its Dodgers, if the Giants of McGraw could leave Broadway, if all the accumulated tradition could be brushed aside, the fan could feel no more sure of his baseball than of anything else in a bewildering universe.

And again, details were disturbing. All sorts of regulations had to be rewritten to make the shifts legal, even in baseball terms. The Dodgers had to play (for four years, it turned out) in a football stadium with 90,000 seats but no suitable playing field. The Pacific Coast League, highest of the minor leagues, had its status summarily destroyed. Coast-to-coast travel was required of players with no essential change in schedule patterns. In other words, honorable business dealings and decent conditions for playing the games had to be sacrificed for potential profit.

THE next step was expansion. In the fall of 1960, the American League decided to go to 10 teams immediately; the National League would do so in 1962.

This was organized baseball's answer to a proposed third major league, to be called the Continental. After tossing up roadblocks of one sort and another, the majors finally decided to take in what appeared to be the strongest members of the developing league. This killed third-league talk. Only one of the Continental groups—the New York Mets—actually wound up with a franchise.

To stock the four new clubs, the existing teams supplied 100 of the least desirable players on their rosters for a total of about $8,000,000. In other words, the initiation fee for each newcomer was something over $2,000,000; the profit for each existing club was about $600,000. And, competitively speaking, the talent supplied, with few exceptions, was practically worthless.

All this, of course, received extensive press coverage, and its effect on baseball's image as a sport need not be belabored.

EXPANSION also meant 10-team leagues, playing 162-game schedules, with back-breaking travel. There were two serious drawbacks to this scheme. One is that a 10-team

245

league is bottom-heavy with also-rans; a contending team can play only two-ninths of its games with other contenders (that is, the top three teams in the standings at any given time).

The other is that all the records and statistics, so precious a part of baseball lore, were compromised, and events conspired to underline this point immediately. In 1961, Roger Maris of the Yankees hit 61 home runs, breaking Babe Ruth's record; but instead of being hailed as the most glamorous of all baseball feats, this only generated arguments about the validity of records made in 162-game schedules vs. 154-game schedules.

Meanwhile, the players themselves were doing their share to disillusion the fan. When they achieved a fabulous pension plan, financed by World Series television income, most fans identified with them and cheered; when they foisted a second all-star game on the public to increase pension funds, they revealed themselves in a mercenary light.

More and more, players complained of the hardships of travel and night ball—and the fans read their remarks. More and more, players made plain their concern with business connections, post-baseball careers, income from endorsements and personal appearances and other "I play baseball just for the money" attitudes. Whether or not expressing such feelings is an expression of honesty, it certainly dispels illusion.

Baseball's increasing dependence on radio and television income has also helped prevent the creation of illusion, especially in children. Messages selling beer and cigarettes, delivered 20 times per game day after day, may or may not be desirable from any of a dozen points of view; they definitely do not, however, instill an image of pure sport.

Radio had been a help to baseball, whetting the appetite of the true fan, keeping him informed and making new addicts. Television, however, was a short-term bonanza leading to long-term disaster which is only now beginning to be recognized.

THE trouble with television is that it exists. It creates a demand for the one big thing, seen now, by everybody, everywhere, and makes any sort of minor-league operation difficult. The major leagues, however, were not content to let attrition take its course, let alone develop a plan for combating it: they piped major league games into minor league territories and promptly killed off the minors then and there.

The main thing is that a baseball game on television remains a television show: it may make some baseball addicts, but it certainly makes more television addicts. Thus, one more distinguishing feature of baseball is removed and it becomes "just another entertainment."

Other problems, which the fan did not seek out, were thrown into his illusion-making machinery.

The Congressional hearings about whether or not baseball (and other sports) should be granted specific antitrust exemptions contributed a great deal of illusion-wrecking information and speculation. Congress still hasn't taken any action, but exactly how much business and how little sport there is in today's corporate-structure, tax-conscious, peripheral-income-oriented baseball "clubs" has been spelled out too often to be ignored.

And the unprecedented increase in shifting of players, stimulated by expansion, corroded much fan identification. By June, 1962, the turnover of personnel on all major league rosters in the preceding 12 months exceeded 50 per cent.

ALL these factors, then, bruised baseball's image and robbed it of its special status. The events of 1964 knocked the image flat on its back.

Chief among them was the purchase of the Yankees in August by C.B.S. for $14.2 million. There was talk of conflict of interest; antitrust action seemed possible; for weeks the papers were full of stories about why the deal might be a bad thing. Aside from anything else, it certainly tied baseball closer to the "entertainment industry"; in fact, both the Yankees and C.B.S. boasted of this.

In October, the Braves decided to move to Atlanta, having milked Milwaukee dry. (Attendance, after an average of 2,000,000 a year for seven years, had dropped to under 1,000,000 in the last three.) The avowed reason: Atlanta had a better TV-market area potential!

Milwaukee authorities went to court to make the Braves stay. The National League ordered them to stay, then approved the move for 1966, and a lease with Atlanta's new stadium was signed. Milwaukee citizens insist they'll find another big league team to come to Milwaukee by then. (It might be Cleveland, which after much consideration of Seattle, Oakland and Dallas, decided to stay in Cleveland "for one more year," and perhaps longer, if the citizens bestir themselves to buy enough tickets.)

It is no wonder, then, that in November even Frick, who had never before shown the slightest inclination to rock a boat, told the owners off, stating that "baseball people are unwilling to abide by the rules which they themselves make" and that "expediency is permitted to replace sound judgment." It was, in a sense, a farewell gesture. He will retire from his $65,000-a-year job next October after 14 years.

CAN anything be done? Not really. Public relations consultants may be called in (they have been called in before, without effect), and Frick's suggestion that the commissioner be given greater powers —like those possessed by the late Judge Kenesaw Mountain Landis, who ruled baseball with an iron hand until 1945—was adopted at the winter meetings. However, the effectiveness of any such change in powers will be wholly dependent on how strong a man the owners choose—in other words, want—as their next commissioner.

The only real change on the horizon is further expansion. Within a few years, the leagues will probably expand to 12 teams, playing in six-team subdivisions. Thus, six teams in the Western half of the National League may play one another 20 times each, and the six in the Eastern half nine times a year, with all games counting in the standings, but with two separate standings. This would mean a 154-game schedule, with two divisional pennant races and no team ever lower than sixth. The divisional winners would play off for the right to go into the World Series against the American League winner, determined the same way.

This particular case of expansion will help. It will cut travel, heighten fan interest in pennant races, remove the bottom layer of dead weight and improve statistics.

But it will not restore baseball to the unique position it once held. Nothing will. Times, as even the owners and Frick have finally admitted, change.

BASEBALL seems destined to remain a profitable, respected, important segment of the mass entertainment industry, a growing field. It will still command a certain number of fanatics. But it must share billing with pro football, and with television it simply cannot compete.

For the average fan, something has gone out of the game; or rather, come into it: a wariness that makes total emotional commitment difficult. Years ago, a columnist commented on the coldly efficient, perpetually victorious Yankees: "Rooting for the Yankees is like rooting for U. S. Steel." Now the joke has become a reality, and it's pretty hard to root for a business — especially a business that may move away when a better offer comes along.

The old fan's motto might have been: "My ball club, right or wrong, but right or wrong, my ball club still." Today's fan had better feel: "Eat, drink (beer), smoke (the right brand) and make merry — for tomorrow they may move the franchise." And if that be bad image, perhaps baseball had better make the most of it.

December 20, 1964

Pro Football's Growth Rivals Baseball

By LEONARD KOPPETT

Has professional football supplanted major league baseball as the country's No. 1 spectator sport?

This question, which in itself needs qualification, is the subject of increasing debate among fans and those concerned with the sports business in some way. Most of the discussion takes place in a factual vacuum. the sports business in some way. Plenty of isolated statistics are available to advocate some particular viewpoint, but comprehensive figures which would make comparison meaningful are virtually nonexistent.

The following figures are an attempt to bring some broad perspective to the picture, and to put various arguments into some sort of context. They lead to two very general conclusions: that football's phenomenal growth has put it into baseball's class economically, and that baseball's economic position remains extremely strong and probably No. 1.

2 Sports in Spotlight

First, though, the qualification is necessary. Why should the discussion be limited to pro football and major league baseball? Because these are the only two sports that command a day-in, day-out national spotlight focused on their compact group of teams and individuals.

Total basketball attendance is huge, but interest in specific teams is fundamentally fragmented and sectional at the high school and college level, and the professional league has limited stature. Hockey is unknown to most of the country. Horse racing and harness racing do immense business, but the primary attraction is legal betting. Major fights generate universal interests, but they take place infrequently at irregular intervals. College football, with few exceptions, is essentially regional in its appeal.

Professional football and major league baseball, therefore, are in a class by themselves, creating simultaneous, continuing interest. All baseball fans respond to news of Mickey Mantle, all football fans to an exploit by Y. A. Tittle or Jimmy Brown, apart from local considerations.

A Statistical Comparison

Here, then, are some basic facts and figures:

There are 20 major league baseball teams located in 17 cities with an aggregate metropolitan-area population of 54 million.

There are 22 major pro football teams (both leagues), in 21 cities with an aggregate population of 60 million.

During the 1964 regular season (excluding the World Series), baseball drew 21,280,-346 paying spectators. This can be expressed as 40 per cent of the area population.

In 1964, the two football leagues drew 5,950,000, or 10 per cent of the area population.

However, football is played once a week, baseball every day. There were only 154 football games but (allowing for double-headers) some 1,400 baseball playing dates.

In terms of maximum possible seating capacity, football sold 76 per cent of its seats and baseball 34 per cent.

However, the number of empty seats at mid-week baseball games is not really relevant. A better guide would be "attendance per team per week at home."

Concessions Aid Income

During football's 14-week season, the average attendance per team per week was 38,600 (for the National League alone, it was 46,000).

During baseball's 25-week season, the average was 85,100 per team per week.

What about money?

Football tickets, on the average, are about three times as expensive as baseball tickets. in gate receipts per team, therefore, there's not too much difference: baseball sells four times as many seats at one-third the price per seat.

In concessions, an important type of side income, baseball does better because it has more openings. One person going to 10 different games will spend more on scorecards, beer, hot dogs, and so forth, than 10 people at one game.

In television income, the totals are hard to compare, but baseball probably comes out ahead. The football leagues sell all their games as one league package; baseball teams make individual deals for local and regional radio-TV and also share in a national program. Next year, for instance, the two football leagues will collect about $22 million from two networks for all their games. Baseball's total income from all regular-season games is estimated to be "convatively, at least $20 million" by Tom Moore, the president of the American Broadcasting Company.

Those sums do not include World Series and playoff games. Baseball gets an additional $3.5 million for the World Series. The National Football League gets $1.8 million for its championship game and the American League will get something up to $1 million.

It should be noted also that in many cases baseball clubs get income from profootball as landlords and concessionaires, while no football team collects anything from baseball. On the other hand, football teams are usually free of basic maintenance expense that baseball clubs are responsible for. In general, all baseball's operating expenses (travel, player development, plant) are much higher than football's.

But both, it is clear, are pretty big business.

December 24, 1964

PART V

New Problems, New Records
1965-1974

Sandy Koufax in action.
The New York Times

Associated Press Wirephoto

IN A STATELY PLEASURE DOME: Yankees and the Houston Astros meet in first game in Houston's new stadium

Johnson Attends Opening of Houston's Astrodome

By ROBERT LIPSYTE

Special to The New York Times

HOUSTON, April 9—With President Johnson present, the Astrodome — the world's largest air-conditioned room —opened tonight with the first indoor major league baseball game.

The President, accompanied by Mrs. Johnson, arrived here from Washington before going on to Johnson City, Tex., for the weekend. A bomb threat, telephoned to a local radio station, was given as the reason for an unheralded entrance by the Presidential party into the ball park.

Few in the crowd of 47,876 knew the President was in the stadium until it was announced after the first inning of the exhibition game between the New York Yankees and the Houston Astros.

While the White House group was being slipped into Judge Roy M. Hofheinz's private elevator and up to the club president's private right-field box, Gov. John

Connally of Texas threw out the first ball and Mickey Mantle, the leadoff batter got the first base hit, a line single to center field.

Mr. Johnson's presence enhanced an opening that had been marred earlier by the discovery that the dome's Lucite skylights so diffused the hard Texas sunlight that fly balls were all but untrackable during daylight hours.

Experiments, begun today with orange baseballs, will continue tomorrow with cerise, yellow and red baseballs, specially tinted glasses and, perhaps, a new covering for the dome.

There was no problem tonight. Seated on an overstuffed yellow velvet swivel chair, the President saw Mantle hit the Astrodome's first home run. The sixth-inning smash caromed off a railing in the right center-field pavilion seats, about 400 feet away.

Somewhat ungenerously, the

Astrodome's two-acre scoreboard flashed T-I-L-T after Mantle's homer. Just before the President left after the eighth inning, however, the scoreboard ran through its celebrated Alamo-storming 45-second pyrotechnic display.

Usually reserved for an Astro homer, the display brought Mr. and Mrse. Johnson to their feet. They applauded, and the President began a series of double handshakes as they slowly moved back to the elevator.

Judge Hofheinz's box, about 380 feet from home plate, includes a half-kitchen, a gilded bathroom and a sumptuous living room as well as the viewing area. The judge, a former mayor of Houston, once served as campaign manager for Mr. Johnson, then running for the State Legislature.

Temperature Is 71

During the game, the temperature within the stadium was 71 degrees, the same as

outside, and humidity was a comfortable 50 per cent. The skies were clear.

Although there were many empty seats, the stadium had been sold out for the event. More than 3,000 standing-room tickets were sold.

The spectators — most of whom were dressed in business suits or colored dresses—came early, streaming into the officially named Harris County Domed Stadium (built on $31.6 million of public credit) out of the simmering flatland. The temperature was about 80 degrees outside when the doors opened at 4:30 P.M. and the ball park was a pleasure dome indeed.

"It's really cool," cried a white-gloved woman with gray curls, and her escort could only say, "Fabulous, really fabulous."

It was a frequent comment, from the sophisticated Yankee ballplayers, from visitors from some of the 38 states represented in the crowd and from people "down the road" who had "opened the major leagues" in Houston in 1962.

Colors leaped at them—red, orange, black, purple, yellow, old gold and, on the top rim, the royal blue of the 53 private boxes, each in front of a private room of Orientale or Moderne or Westerne gaud.

"When we Texans put things up." said a Santa Fe Railroad engineer, "we put them up right big."

The engineer and his wife and daughter had driven 650 miles from Amarillo for the opening. He could remember back 30 years when this area, seven miles south of downtown Houston. was grazing land.

Now his wife just beamed and said. "First ball game I ever been at where I enjoyed the seats."

The seats are all upholstered in this park, like theater seats. Even the 3,000 bleacher chairs (called pavilion seats and sold for $1.50) have seat cushions, with rounded wooden backs.

'No Warmth,' She Says

"Frankly," said a young women, "I think it's rather sterile. No warmth, no real humanity here."

She seemed alone in her feelings, as the crowds swept in, eating frankfurters (somewhat redder and spicier than most ball-park hot dogs), giggling and even looking at the $325 Lady Hamilton wristwatch in the Galaxie Gift Shop.

From the symbols to the original mosaics in the private boxes, victory or defeat belonged to Judge Roy M. Hofheinz, the broad, cigar-smoking 53-year-old former Houston Mayor. Pacing up and down his private box in right field in an open-necked white shirt, Judge Hofheinz restlessly surveyed the park as it began to fill.

Below him, flash bulbs popped as Houston mothers took pictures of their children, pictures of the dome, pictures of the eight orange space-suited, black combat-booted, white helmeted groundskeepers, called Earthmen.

"Old man has some imagination," said one of the Earthmen of Hofheinz, the club's president. "This here uniform's something else again, ain't it?"

The Earthman, Richard Sykes, allowed as how life would be easier here than in the club's previous stadium. which still stands, hot and mosquito-ridden, next door.

"No tarp to pull over the grass," he said, "come rain or anything, no tarp to pull."

"Beautiful, real purty," they cried as they flowed up the ramps, past the Domeskeller, a beer hall in the outfield; past the moderately priced Countdown cafeteria with Roman friezes, past spacettes in blue boots and gold lamé dresses.

For those who count their pleasures in primary statistics — economically, architecturally and historically — the Texas bubble is filled with grandiose numbers.

'Foreign' Money

The Greater Houston Convention and Visitors Bureau esti-mated that the weekend exhibition series would bring in at least $500,000 of fresh, out-of-town money, and perhaps as much as $1 million. All hotel and motel accommodations within a 10-mile radius of the Astrodome (which is seven miles from downtown Houston) were solidly booked through Saturday night. The major clubs (there are no open hard liquor bars in town) had near-capacity advance reservations.

Judge Hofheinz had stated earlier that 65 per cent of the tickets were bought by persons living outside Harris County, and 40 per cent by out-of-staters. More than 200,000 spectators were expected for the five games. The two games on Saturday and two on Sunday are all separate-admission contests.

The spectators were coming to see, among other things, the world's largest greenhouse (carpeted by 3½ acres of Tifway Bermuda grass imported from Georgia), the largest scoreboard (six acres), and the longest baseball dugouts (120 feet each). The length of the dugouts is a reflection of Judge Hofheinz's theory that people like to say they sat behind the dugout.

At its highest point, the dome rises 208 feet—higher than an 18-story building. Sitting up there, out in the heat, is a weather station that will control the air-conditioning, and a traffic spotter, who will radio warnings of potential tie-ups to police stations as far as five miles away.

The carpers in the crowd, however, were able to point to the 4,596 transparent Lucite rectangles in the dome and snicker. Black under the night sky, the skylights are blindingly bright in the afternoon. Yesterday, Astro outfielders stumbled and cringed under high fly balls, complaining that the baseball disappeared against the latticework rectangles of Lucite and concrete.

Although the Astros will play only 21 of their 81 home games during daylight hours, it is generally agreed that something will have to be done to dim the glare through the top, to create special sunglasses or special helmets, or a new color for the baseball.

Most subtle carpers, of course, need only say that there is nothing new under the sun, including the dome. After all. Emperor Vespasian had a domed stadium built in Rome about 1,895 years ago. The roof was a cloth awning that covered six acres of the Flavian amphitheater and stretched as high as 161 feet.

April 10, 1965

320 Are Picked in Baseball Draft

Selections Continue Today for Rights to Free Agents

By LEONARD KOPPETT

Baseball's first free-agent draft was conducted with unexpected efficiency at the Hotel Commodore yesterday, with all 20 major league clubs represented by top executives and busy staffs.

Robert James (Rick) Monday. a 19-year-old left-handed hitter at Arizona State at Tempe who is universally acknowledged to be the most desirable prospect available, was the No. 1 choice. He was picked, as expected, by the Kansas City Athletics.

A total of 320 players were selected in about seven hours before the officials adjourned the meeting until today, when the drafting will resume.

Under the regulations adopted last December, teams draft the exclusive right to negotiate with the player named. Choices are made in reverse order of last year's standings, so that the weaker teams get the earlier selections. The main motive is to eliminate competitive bidding that has led to huge bonus payments; the secondary purpose is to equalize player talent among the teams.

Such drafts will be held each June and January. In practice, each major league club could choose as many men as it wanted, but technically the first round was for major league rosters, the next two for Class AAA teams, the next four for Class AA and the rest for Class A. In all cases, the major league team did the choosing for its minor league affiliates.

Mets Draft Left-Hander

The No. 2 choice in the first round belonged to the New York Mets. They took Leslie Rohr, a 6-foot-5-inch left-handed pitcher from Billings, Mont. He is 19 years old.

The New York Yankees had the 19th turn in the first round. They selected William Burbach; a 17 - year - old right-handed pitcher from Dickeyville, Wis.

Each team had compiled a list of 200 to 500 prospects. Most lists overlapped, but there were plenty of differences among them. The total number of players listed was estimated at 1,500.

"I feel I've taken part in something historic," said Bing Devine, No. 2 in command of the Mets. "As you know, I've been in favor of giving this rule a chance, even though the official position of the club has been against it, and I was very impressed with how the first few rounds went."

George Weiss, the president of the Mets, is one of the baseball officials strongly against the draft. Also opposed are the Yankees and Los Angeles Dodgers.

Devine singled out another aspect of the draft that he considered progress.

"A team can concentrate its effort on evaluating players, and then on negotiating with the players chosen, instead of spending so much time in the frustrating chase of a few high-priced bonus players beyond limit."

Monday, a power hitter who is a sophomore at Arizona State at Tempe, is playing in the college baseball World Series. Kansas City officials said he would not be approached until that was over. His bonus may be $100,000 because he is so outstanding a prospect.

Devine, Bavasi and Houk all said they would have made Monday their first choice if they had the rights to him.

The teams have six months in which to negotiate with the prospects picked. If terms are not agreed to by then, the player goes into a pool for a special draft (from which the team he rejected is excluded) before the next free-agent draft in January. In any case, it is no longer possible for any player, once drafted, to choose freely which team to sign with.

Leading Draft Choices

By The Associated Press

1—KANSAS CITY ATHLETICS—Rick Monday, 19 year old, outfielder from Arizona State University (Tempe) and Santa Monica, Calif. 6 foot 3 inches, 195 pounds.

2—NEW YORK METS—Leslie Rohr, 19, left-handed pitcher from Billings (Mont.) High School, 6-5, 200.

3—WASHINGTON SENATORS—Joe Coleman Jr., 17, right-handed pitcher from Natick (Mass.) High School, 6-3, 165.

4—HOUSTON ASTROS—Alex Barrett, 18, right-handed shortstop from Atwater High School, Winton, Calif., 6-0, 175.

5—BOSTON RED SOX—Bill Conigliaro, 17, right-handed outfielder-pitcher from Swampscott (Mass.) High School, 6-0, 175.

6—CHICAGO CUBS—Richard James, 17, right-handed pitcher from Coffee High School, Florence, Ala., 6-0, 200.

251

7—CLEVELAND INDIANS—Raymond Fosse, 18, right-handed catcher from Marion (Ill.) High School, 6 3, 210.

8—LOS ANGELES DODGERS—John Scott Wyatt, 17, right-handed shortstop from Bakersfield (Calif.) High School, 6-2, 200.

9—MINNESOTA TWINS—Ed Leon, 18, right-handed shortstop from University of Arizona and Tucson, Ariz., 5-11, 165.

10—PITTSBURGH PIRATES—Douglas Dickerson, 17, outfielder from Ensley High School, Birmingham, Ala., 6-1, 188.

11.—LOS ANGELES ANGELS—James Spencer, 17, first baseman from Anderson High School, Glen Burnie, Md., 6-0, 190.

12—MILWAUKEE BRAVES—William Grant, 19, first baseman from Watertown High School, Swampscott, Mass. 6 4, 205.

13—DETROIT TIGERS—William Lamont, 18, catcher from Hiawatha High School, Kirkland, Il., 6 1, 180.

14—SAN FRANCISCO GIANTS—Alan Gallagher, 19, third baseman from Santa Clara University Daly City, Calif., 6-0, 182.

15 BALTIMORE ORIOLES—Scott McDonald, 18, right-handed pitcher from Marquette High School, Yakima, Wash. 6-1, 195.

16—CINCINNATI REDS—Bernardo Carbo, 17, third baseman from Livonia (Mich.) High and Garden City, Mich., 5-11, 170.

17—CHICAGO WHITE SOX—Kenneth Plesha, 19, catcher from Notre Dame University and McCook, Ill., 5-11, 185.

18—PHILADELPHIA PHILLIES—John Michael Adamson, 18, right-handed pitcher from Point Loma High School, San Diego, 6-2, 185.

19—NEW YORK YANKEES—William Burbach, 17, right-handed pitcher from Wahlert High School, Dubuque, Iowa and Dickeyville, W s., 6-4, 195

20. ST LOUIS CARDINALS—Joe Di Fabrio, 21, right-handed pitcher from Delta State College and Cranford, N. J., 5-11, 195.

NEW YORK AREA CHOICES

CLASS AAA—Frank Pepedino, Wingate H. S., Brooklyn, by Baltimore Orioles (for Rochester).

CLASS AA—George Mercado, Bishop Dubois H. S., New York, by Los Angeles Dodgers (for Albuquerque); Doug Brittelle, Massapequa H. S., L. I., by New York Mets (for Williamsport); Fred Kamp, Shore Regional H. S., Monmouth Beach, N. J., by Cleveland Indians (for Reading); Robert Chlupsa, Manhattan College, New York, by Philadelphia Phils (for Chattanooga); John Hurley, Port Richmond H. S., Staten Island, by New York Yankees (for Columbus, Ga.).

CLASS A—Thomas Capowski, Fordham, by Phils (for Huron); Jeffrey Albies, Long Island University, Glendale, Queens, by Milwaukee Braves (for Yakima); Donald Conk, L. I. U., Massapequa, L. I., by Phils (for Eugene); George Lauzerique, New York, by Kansas City Athletics (for Burlington); John Dunn, Woodside, Queens, by Athletics (for Leesburg); Bob Crosby, the Bronx, by Los Angeles Angels (for San Jose); Henry Kniffel, Franklin Square, L. I., by Chicago Cubs (for Duluth); Gil Torres , New York, by Washington Senators (for Geneva); Paul Giglio, White-

New York Mets

Nolan Ryan

stone, Queens, by Pittsburgh Pirates (for Kingston); Will Beauchemin, Point Pleasant, N. J., by Orioles (for Appleton).

OTHER CHOICES

YANKEES—Class AAA: Danny Thompson, shorstop, Capron, Okla., and Dennis Baldridge, outfielder, Finn Rock, Ore. Class AA Stanley Bahnsen, right-handed pitcher, Council Bluffs, Iowa; Leslie Howell, catcher, Louisville, Ky.; John Hurley, right-handed pitcher, Staten Island, and Darcy Fast, first baseman, Olympia, Wash. Class A: Scott Lund, pitcher, Davenport, Iowa; Gary Girouard, pitcher, Woburn, Mass.; Fred Dawson, outfielder, Bernico, La.; James Alvey, first baseman, Leitchfield, Ky.; Donald Alley, catcher, Denver; Robert Hall, third baseman, Villanova U.; Dwain Davidson, third baseman, Mountain Hope, Ark.; Steve Mezich, catcher, Seattle; Morton Zenor, first baseman, Lawton, Iowa.

METS—Class AAA: Randolph Caldwell Kohn, catcher, Greenville, S. C., and Joe Moock, infielder, Baton Rouge. Class AA: Ken Boswell, Infielder, Austin, Tex.; Douglas Brittelle, right-handed pitcher, Massapequa, L. I.; Harold Roberson, right-handed pitcher, Alma, Mich., and Mike McClure, infielder, Poth, Tex. Class A: McClure, infielder, Poth, Tex. Class A: Roger Harrington, pitcher, Sunnyvale, Calif.; Louis Williams, catcher, Baltimore; Roger Stevens, outfielder, Pasadena, Calif.; James McAndrew, pitcher, Iowa City; Nolan Ryan, pitcher, Alvin, Tex.

June 9, 1965

Mays vs. Mantle: A Comparison

Injuries to Yankee Over Years Give Edge to Giant

By LEONARD KOPPETT

FOURTEEN years ago, after the 1951 baseball season, the most popular topic in hot-stove - or - cold - drink circles was: Who's going to be better, Willie Mays or Mickey Mantle?

Today, fate has pretty well resolved the question in favor of Mays, strictly in terms of physical well-being. Willie has gone through a career in good health, with only minor ailments from time to time, and this season won the National League Most Valuable Player Award at the age of 34. Mantle, who is five months younger, was crippled more than half the time in 1965 and went through the least productive season of his life. Mickey had osteomyelitis, a bone disease, in one leg even before he reached the major leagues, and his Yankee career has been blighted by serious injuries to both knees and one shoulder, a broken foot and countless severe muscle tears.

No one knows, therefore, what Mantle might have been if reasonably healthy. But what can be known, in considerable detail, is how Mantle's and Mays' statistical accomplishments compare. Seymour Siwoff, the man in charge of the Elias Sports Bureau (which is the country's largest independent sports

About Baseball

United Press International
Willie Mays

Associated Press
Mickey Mantle

statistical service) made such a comparison as a labor of love recently.

The result was an amazing over-all similarity. In most of the basic departments of hitting, Mantle and Mays have produced nearly identical figures. In more specialized departments, where one has a decided edge, the other has an equally distinct edge in some other respect.

Mantle's career has embraced more consistent conditions. He started the 1951 season with the Yankees, was sent back to the minors for a few weeks, came back in August and ever since has been playing with Yankee Stadium as his home field.

Mays came up in May of 1951, spent most of 1952 and

1953 in the Army, returned to the Polo Grounds as a home base from 1954 through 1957, and moved to San Francisco with the Giants in 1958.

For the first two years on the Coast, the Giants' home park was little Seals Stadium, a home-run heaven for right-handed hitters. Since 1960, it has been Candlestick Park, a fairly difficult home-run park.

In terms of team success, Mantle has been far more fortunate. In 15 seasons he has played on 12 pennant winners. Mays has been on only three. Consequently, Mantle holds all sorts of World Series records and May doesn't—but Willie has been in a class by himself as the star-of-stars in All-Star Games, in which Mantle has done poorly.

Careers at a Glance

Category	Mays	Mntl
Games played	2.005	2.005
At Bats	7.594	6.894
Walks	949	1.464
Hit by Pitch	27	11
Sacrifice Flies	63	36
Sacrifice Bunts	4	13
Total Times at Bat	8,637	8.417
Ttl Tms reached base	3,357	3,583
"On base" Average	.389	.426
Runs scored	1,497	1,517
Runs batted in	1.402	1.344
Hits	2,381	2.108
Batting average	.314	.306
Singles	1,381	1,264
Doubles	375	301
Triples	118	70
Home runs	505	473
Total Bases	4,507	3,968
Slugging average	.593	.576
Stolen Bases	276	145
Caught Stealing	86	34
"Stealing" average	.762	.810
Struck Out	893	1,424
Grounded into DP	174	86
Intentional Walks	140	107
Games in outfield	1.987	1.922
Putouts	5.216	4,266
Assists	160	115
Errors	98	82
Double Plays	51	27
Fielding Average	.952	.982

●

Mantle has won three most-valuable-player awards, Mays two. Each has won a batting title once, and each has led his league in homers four times.

The differences in their records are revealing. Mantle has struck out much more often—and walked almost exactly as much more often. Therefore, although Mays has a somewhat higher batting average. Mantle has a somewhat higher "reached-base" average. Mays has stolen twice as many bases—but has hit into twice as many double plays. (And Mantle's percentage of success in base-stealing is higher than Willie's).

In one respect, however, Mays is clearly ahead and it reflects a true superiority defensively: although they have identical fielding averages, Willie has made nearly 1,000 more putouts than Mickey.

June 12, 1965

National League Wins All-Star Game, 6-5

MAYS AND TORRE CONNECT IN FIRST

American League Ties Game After Trailing by 5-0— Infield Hit Decides

By JOSEPH DURSO
Special to The New York Times

BLOOMINGTON, Minn., July 13.—The National League overpowered the American League, 6-5, in a free-swinging All-Star Game today and took its first lead in the series since Babe Ruth won the opening game with a home run 32 years ago.

Five home runs were struck, to the delight of a sellout crowd of 46,706 persons who watched in bright sunshine at Metropolitan Stadium, the home of the Minnesota Twins in the farmlands south of Minneapolis.

The Nationals got off to a rousing five-run start in this pastoral setting. They did it on three home runs in the first two innings by Willie Mays, Joe Torre and Willie Stargell. With Juan Marichal pitching three shutout innings, the team rated as one of the weakest ever to take the field for the American League appeared as dead as the smart money had predicted.

But the underdogs — with no New York Yankees in the starting line-up for the first time—staged one of the great revivals in All-Star history.

They rocked Jim Maloney for one run in the fourth inning and four in the fifth on home runs by Dick McAuliffe and Harmon Killebrew.

So, 32 years and five innings after they first started, the major league All-Stars were deadlocked at 17 victories, one tie and five runs apiece.

Mays Scores Decisive Run

When the decisive run scored two innings later it was an anticlimax. Mays raced home with the winning run in the seventh on Ron Santo's high bounder behind second base that hopped past Bobby Richardson before it was finally tracked down by Zoilo Versalles.

When Bob Gibson threw a fast ball past Joe Pepitone in the ninth inning for the final out, the Nationals had their third straight victory, their 14th in the last 19 games and a lead of 18 to 17 in the rivalry.

Al Lopez of the Chicago White Sox suffered his fifth straight defeat as the American League's manager. For Gene Mauch of the Philadelphia Phillies, it was his first victory in his first shot at the controls.

Sam McDowell of the Cleveland Indians had the misfortune to be pitching when Santo bounced the winning hit over the mound. And Sandy Koufax of the Los Angeles Dodgers gained his first victory in an All-Star Game—after pitching one long, shaky inning.

All of these little victories and defeats and ironies were watched by a noisy crowd in shirtsleeves, many wearing green or red coolie hats on a sunny, hot day after an all-night rain.

Every Corner Jammed

They jammed every corner of the Twins' green - and - white stadium and filled the upper deck of the left-field bleachers that were completed only four days ago. They stood to sing the National Anthem before the game and they roared for the six Minnesota players who represented the home town in the game.

Nobody had to wait long for action.

Mays led off for the National League against Milt Pappas of the Baltimore Orioles—a spot ordained by Mauch because he wanted Willie "to hit more often, maybe five times." That is exactly what Willie did.

Mays was returning to the city he had left in 1951 with a .477 batting average and a ticket to New York to play for the Giants.

Today he hit Pappas's first pitch foul. But the second was hit fair. 400 feet fair to deep left-center, where Vic Davalillo of the Cleveland Indians backed against the fence, waited, then watched helplessly as the towering drive dropped into the bleacher seats.

It was Willie's third home run in an All-Star Game, his 21st hit (breaking a record he had shared with Stan Musial), and his 17th run scored (also a record). It also gave Marichal, his San Francisco teammate, a 1-0 led that was about to grow.

After Henry Aaron had flied out to left, Stargell lined a single to center. Richie Allen then popped to shortstop, but Torre hit a tremendously high fly down the left-field line that struck the foul pole for a two-run homer.

In the second inning, Jim Grant of the Twins replaced Pappas, but the National League attack continued unabated.

A Homer for Stargell

Marichal singled over second base. Mays walked on four pitches and Aaron hit into a double play. Then Stargell, with 21 home runs for the Pittsburgh Pirates this season, bombed a 400-foot drive into the right-field bull pen—where plenty of warming up was going on.

That made it 5-0, and at that point the 7-5 odds favoring the National League looked conservative, to say the least.

The American League finally got a hit in the third—a single through the middle by Davalillo. And it finally got a run in the fourth.

McAuliffe, the Detroit Tigers' shortstop whose election to the team had raised some eyebrows around the league, greeted Maloney with a single to center. Brooks Robinson struck out, but Killebrew walked. Both runners moved up on a wild pitch and Rocky Colavito of the Indians then cracked a single to left-center that made the score 5-1.

The National League's trouble began for real in the fifth after the first two hitters had gone out.

Maloney started it himself by walking Jimmie Hall of the Twins, a pinch-hitter for Pete Richert after two solid innings of relief pitching by the Washington Senators' left-hander.

Then McAuliffe got into the act again, this time in a large way. He drove Maloney's 1-and-1 pitch 410 feet to right-center for a two-run home run. Mays nearly climbed the fence trying to retrieve it, but not even Willie could get that far back.

Robinson kept the rally going with a hard shot down the third-base line that Ron Santo backhanded but couldn't handle. And then Killebrew—who had beaten the Yankees Sunday with a two-out, two-run homer in the ninth—came to bat.

Box Score of All-Star Game

NATIONAL	AB.	R.	H.	RBI.	PO.	A.		AMERICAN	AB.	R.	H.	RBI.	PO.	A.
Mays, cf	3	2	1	1	4	0		McAuliffe, s	3	2	2	2	3	0
Aaron, rf	5	0	1	0	0	0		McDowell, p	0	0	0	0	0	1
Stargell, lf	3	2	2	2	1	0		fOliva, rf	1	0	1	0	0	0
eClemente, lf	2	0	0	0	0	0		B. Robinson, 3b	4	1	1	0	1	2
Allen, 3b	3	0	1	0	0	1		Alvis, 3b	1	0	0	0	0	0
Santo, 3b	2	0	1	1	2	0		Killebrew, 1b	3	1	1	2	7	1
Torre, c	4	1	1	2	5	1		Colavito, rf	4	0	1	1	1	0
Banks, 1b	4	0	2	0	10	0		Fisher, p	0	0	0	0	1	1
Rose, 2b	2	0	0	0	2	4		hPepitone	1	0	0	0	0	0
Wills, ss	2	0	1	0	2	0		Horton, lf	2	0	0	0	2	0
Cardenas, ss	0	0	0	0	0	0		Mantilla, 2b	2	0	0	0	1	1
Marichal, p	1	1	1	0	0	0		Richardson, 2b	2	0	0	0	1	1
bRojas	1	0	0	0	0	0		Davalillo, cf	2	0	1	0	1	0
Maloney, p	0	0	0	0	0	0		Versalles, ss	1	0	0	0	2	1
Drysdale, p	0	0	0	0	0	0		Battey, c	2	0	0	0	4	1
dF. Robinson	1	0	0	0	0	0		Freehan, c	1	0	1	0	4	0
Koufax, p	1	0	0	0	0	0		Pappas, p	0	0	0	0	0	1
Farrell, p	0	0	0	0	0	0		Grant, p	0	0	0	0	0	0
gWilliams	1	0	0	0	0	0		aKaline	1	0	0	0	0	0
Gibson, p	0	0	0	0	0	1		Richert, p	0	0	0	0	0	0
								cHall, cf	2	1	0	0	0	0
Total	36	6	11	6	27	9		Total		5	8	5	27	11

aGrounded out for Grant in 3d; bFlied out for Marichal in 4th; cWalked for Richert in 5th; dStruck out for Drysdale in 6th; eHit into force play for Stargell in 7th; fGrounded out for McDowell in 7th; gGrounded out for Farrell in 8th; hStruck out for Fisher in 9th.

National	3	2	0	0	0	0	1	0	0	6
American	0	0	0	1	4	0	0	0	0	5

Errors—None. Double plays—B. Robinson, Mantilla and Killebrew; Wills, Rose and Banks; McDowell, Richardson and Killebrew. Left on bases—National 7, American 8.

Two-base hit—Oliva. Home runs—Mays, Torre, Stargell, McAuliffe, Killebrew. Sacrifice—Rose.

	IP.	H.	R.	ER.	BB.	SO.	HBP.	WP.	Balks
Marichal	3	1	0	0	0	0	0	0	0
Maloney	1⅔	5	5	5	2	1	0	1	0
Drysdale	⅓	0	0	0	0	0	0	0	0
Koufax (W)	1	1	0	0	2	1	0	0	0
Farrell	1	0	0	0	0	0	0	0	0
Gibson	2	2	0	0	1	3	0	0	0
Pappas	1	4	3	3	1	0	0	0	0
Grant	2	2	2	2	1	3	0	0	0
Richert	2	1	0	0	2	0	0	0	0
McDowell (L)	2	3	1	1	1	2	0	0	0
Fisher	1	0	0	0	0	1	0	0	0

Bases on balls—Off Maloney 2 (Killebrew, Hall), Koufax 2 (Horton, Freehan), Farrell 1 (Killebrew), Pappas 1 (Rose), Grant 1 (Mays), McDowell 1 (Mays). Struck out—By Maloney 1 (B. Robinson), Koufax 1 (Hall), Gibson 3 (Horton, Killebrew, Pepitone), Grant 3 (Allen, Banks, Rose), Richert 2 (Mays, Stargell), McDowell 2 (Rose, Robinson).

Umpires—Stevens (N.), plate; Meyer (N.), first base; Dimuro (A.), second base; Williams (N.), third base; Valentine (A.) and Kibler (N.), foul lines. Time of game—2:45. Attendance—46,706.

The count went to two balls and two strikes. When Maloney tried to slip a fast ball over for a third strike. Killebrew slugged it high and far. 410 feet into the bleachers in left-center. It gave the American League a four-run inning and a 5-5 tie.

The momentum appeared to have swung toward the American League, especially when Koufax entered the game in the sixth and threw four balls to Horton and three more to Richardson. However. Koufax then straightened out a bit, got Richardson on a fly to Mays and Versalles on a pop-up to Maury Wills. He walked Bill Freehan, but slipped a third strike past Hall.

Now came the winning run, almost unobstrusively after the earlier cannonading.

McDowell was pitching for the American League when May opened the seventh by walking. Aaron then punched a single to right and Willie galloped all the way to third, braving the rifle arm of Colavito.

Mays had to wait on third while Robinson fielded Roberto Clemente's grounder and forced Aaron at second, but he didn't have to wait long. Santo, the next batter, hit his high hopper over the mound and behind second base, where Versalles finally flagged it down. Santo beat Versalles's throw to first for a single while Mays raced home with the winning run.

The National League now had a 6-5 lead and also had Gibson to protect it. The Cardinals' World Series hero did just that. but with one precarious moment. That came in the eighth. when the American League again stirred with two outs.

Versalles walked and Freehan hit the first pitch to center for a single, taking second on the throw to third. Then Hall rammed a 380-foot drive to deep center.

Mays misjudged the ball. started to backpedal, slipped on the soft grass, got up, drifted back and finally made a one-handed catch as he fell back toward the fence.

In the ninth, Tony Oliva of the Twins doubled to left-center, raising memories of last year's ninth-inning victory by the Nationals in Shea Stadium. But Gibson himself caught Max Alvis's pop-up bunt, then struck out Killebrew on a 1-and-2 fast ball.

That's where Pepitone pinch-hit for Eddie Fisher, went to three balls and two strikes, and struck out swinging.

"If that line-up can't handle it." Mauch had said before the game, "there's not much I can do."

It was that close, but they handled it.

July 14, 1965

Marichal Hits Roseboro With Bat and Starts Brawl as Giants Top Dodgers

CATCHER SUFFERS 2-INCH HEAD CUT

Marichal Ejected and Faces Possible Suspension — Giants Triumph by 4-3

By LEONARD KOPPETT
Special to The New York Times

SAN FRANCISCO, Aug. 22 —In a burst of uncontrollable temper under circumstances still unclear, Juan Marichal of the San Francisco Giants attacked John Roseboro of the Los Angeles Dodgers today with a baseball bat.

Marichal's bat hit Roseboro on the top of the head at least twice and opened a two-inch cut that bled profusely. The injury was apparently no more serious than that, but as Roseboro accompanied his teammates on a flight to New York this evening, he was being observed for symptoms of brain concussion.

It happened before 42,807 spectators, the largest Candlestick Park crowd of the year, and many television viewers in the Los Angeles area. It occurred in the third inning of the fourth and final game of a series in which the Dodgers and Giants have been battling for the National League lead.

The Giants went on to win. 4-3, but the eventual effect of the incident on the pennant race could be profound. Marichal was ejected from the game and a lengthy suspension is a distinct possibility once the league president, Warren Giles, gets his report from the chief umpire, Shag Crawford.

Scuffling Lasts 15 Minutes

The flare-up precipitated free-for-all scuffling that interrupted the game for 15 minutes. Both teams were left emotionally shaken.

Fights that erupt under pennant pressure are not unusual, but they are always fist fights. Players, coaches and managers of both teams here could not recall ever seeing an attack with a bat.

Fights usually break out after an exchange of "bean balls," pitches thrown close to batters' heads to "keep them loose." There had been such an exchange in this game—but everyone concerned seemed to agree it was not the thing that angered Marichal.

The two directly concerned, Roseboro and Marichal, left the park long before the game ended. Their accounts could not be obtained anyway, since a dozen policemen had barred the dressing rooms to reporters until the end of the game.

As pieced together, the story seemed to be that Marichal believed that Roseboro, in throw-

United Press International Telephoto

Marichal holds bat over head of Roseboro as Tito Fuentes, San Francisco teammate, rushes in with his own bat to join the fray. Shag Crawford, umpire, Charlie Fox, Giants' coach, and Koufax attempt to break up the fight, which almost turned into a riot.

ing the ball back to the pitcher, tried to hit Marichal in the back of the head. Marichal turned and went after Roseboro with his bat.

Actions Speak Loudest

Not a word was spoken, according to Crawford, who was the umpire at home plate and was two feet from the action.

The next three men to arrive on the scene were Sandy Koufax, the Dodger pitcher who had just taken the return throw from Roseboro; Charlie Fox, the Giants' coach at third base, and Tito Fuentes, rookie Giants' shortstop who had been in the on-deck circle.

Fuentes also was brandishing a bat, but he did not appear to be using it as a weapon. All three and Crawford seemed intent on separating Marichal and Roseboro.

In the melee that followed within a few seconds, peace-making seemed desperately urgent, and there didn't seem to be the usual taking of sides. Everyone seemed horrified by the nature of the attack and by the sight of blood streaming down Roseboro's face.

Further antagonism, then, was carried on by those who seemed to be reacting to the mode of attack rather than to whatever real or imagined injustice had set it off.

Ozark Joins the Fray

When some degree of order had been restored, Danny Ozark, one of the Dodger coaches, had to be restrained from going after Marichal again. But this altercation was quickly quelled, too.

In Candlestick Park, both teams use the same passageway to the dressing rooms. The police ran to be on hand as Marichal, having been expelled, and Roseboro, going for treatment, started for the dressing rooms.

However, not only was there no further trouble, but the rest of the game had a subdued air.

As play was resumed, Willie Mays, who was most conspicuous in the frantic efforts to prevent a real riot, promptly hit a three-run homer that settled the issue.

Mays had remarkable success in attempting to calm Dodgers as well as Giants. Most of those present remembered an incident in Pittsburgh in 1958, when Orlando Cepeda went into battle waving a bat and Willie tackled him before any contact could be made.

The game had begun in an entirely different atmosphere. Here was the first face-to-face meeting of the season between baseball's two most glamorous pitchers, Koufax and Marichal. Koufax had a 21-4 won-lost record, Marichal 19-9, and the Dodgers were trying to cling to a narrowing league lead.

Maury Wills bunted Marichal's opening pitch and got a hit. With two out, a double by Ron Fairly into the left-field corner gave Koufax a 1-0 lead. Sandy struck out three Giants in the home half.

In the second, a double by Wes Parker and single by Rose-

boro made it 2-0, and Wills went up with two out. Marichal

Giants' Box

LOS ANGELES (N.)	ab	r	h	bi	SAN FRANCISCO (N.)	ab	r	h	bi
Wills, ss	5	1	1	0	Fuentes, ss	4	0	0	0
Gilliam, 3b	4	0	0	0	Davenport, 3b	2	1	0	0
W. Davis, cf	4	0	1	0	McCovey, 1b	3	1	0	0
Fairly, rf	4	0	1	1	Mays, cf	3	1	2	3
Lefebvre, 2b	4	0	0	0	Hart, lf	3	0	0	0
John, p, f	4	0	2	0	Peterson, rf	3	1	1	1
Parker, 1b	3	2	1	0	M. Alou, rf	1	0	0	0
Roseboro, c	3	0	1	1	Lanier, 2b	3	0	1	0
Torborg, c	3	0	1	0	Berteli, p	3	0	0	0
Koufax, p	3	0	0	0	Marichal, p	0	0	0	0
LeJohn, ph	1	0	0	1	Schroder, ph	1	0	0	0
					Herbel, p	2	0	0	0
Totals	36	3	8	3	Totals	28	4	4	4

Los Angeles .... 1 1 0 0 0 0 0 0 1—3
San Francisco .... 0 1 3 0 0 0 0 0 x—4

E—Gilliam 2, Lanier. DP—Los Angeles 1. LOB—Los Angeles 5, San Francisco 5. 2B—Fairly, Parker. HR—Peterson (3), Mays (38). S—Davenport.

	IP.	H.	R.	ER.	BB.	SO.
Koufax (L, 21-5)	8	4	4	4	4	8
Marichal	3	4	2	2	0	4
Herbel (W, 8-6)	6	4	1	1	1	2
Murakami	0	0	0	0	1	

HBP—By Herbel (Parker). WP—Koufax. T—2:18. A—42,807.

promptly flattened him with a classic high-and-tight pitch, presumably in retaliation for the bunt.

Mays was the first Giant batter in the second, and Koufax made the token retaliation with his first pitch. He threw it over Mays's head, a sign that if a head-throwing contest was to start, he would do his part. But Sandy, whose control was off all day, threw it so high that it went back to the screen.

With two out in that inning, Cap Peterson hit a home run, cutting the Dodger lead to 2-1.

Marichal Leads Off

It was Marichal's turn to lead off the third. The first pitch was a strike, the next a curve ball low and inside. Suddenly the fight was on. If Koufax had thrown at Marichal, the cause of anger would have been clear. But he hadn't.

The cause was deeper than that, according to several Giants and Dodgers, all of whom said they got their information second or third hand.

They said that Wills, earlier in the series, had reached back and hit Tom Haller, the Giants catcher, with his bat and earned first base by having the umpire call catcher's interference; that Matty Alou had tried the same trick a day later, and that Roseboro had resented it and uttered threats; that Marichal, as Roseboro threw the ball back to Koufax, thought Roseboro was trying to hit him with it.

At any rate, Marichal was ejected.

"Nobody would have been ejected," said Crawford, "but he used a bat."

When the game was resumed, Bob Schroder finished Marichal's turn at bat and struck out, and Fuentes flied deep to left. But now Koufax lost control. He walked Jim Davenport and Willie McCovey in succession and made one pitch to Mays, who hit it about 450 feet against the bleachers in left center for his 38th homer and a 4-2 lead.

"It was a high fast ball, over the middle of the plate," said

Koufax ruefully afterward, "the last place in the world I wanted to throw the ball. But my control was poor the whole game—and the game before, too."

Control or no, Koufax allowed only one more single in his remaining five innings of pitching, but it was too late.

Ron Herbel took Marichal's place and emerged as the Giant hero. He shut out the Dodgers on three singles for the next five innings. But when he nicked Wes Parker on the foot with a pitch with one out in the ninth and Jeff Torborg singled, Herbel needed help.

Masanori Murakami provided it. He made Don LeJohn, a pinch-hitter, hit a perfect double-play ball back to the mound—only to have Hal Lanier drop the throw at second. Now it was 4-3, with two men on. But Murakami made Wills pop up and got a called third strike past Jim Gilliam, ending the game.

The Dodgers remained in first place, because Milwaukee also lost. But now the Giants are second by a percentage point, half a game behind Los Angeles.

August 23, 1965

Latest Giants-Dodgers Brawl Brings a Few Others to Mind

By GERALD ESKENAZI

The bat-swinging incident in San Francisco yesterday involving Juan Marichal of the Giants and John Roseboro of the Dodgers was only the latest flare-up between the teams, who have the most famed and intense rivalry in baseball.

A well-remembered fight that occurred before the teams left New York was between the Dodgers' quick-tempered right fielder, Carl Furillo, and the Giants' manager, Leo Durocher, a graduate of the St. Louis Cardinals' Gashouse Gang.

Furillo went after the Giants' manager after he had been hit on the wrist by a ball pitched by Ruben Gomez. In the scuffle that followed, someone stepped on Furillo's hand and the outfielder, who was in contention for the league batting title, was out of commission for 10 days with a broken bone in his left hand.

Gomez became a more active participant in a later episode. In 1955 he had a fist fight with Willie Mays before a Winter League game in San Juan, P. R. Mays dropped Gomez with a right-hand punch.

Also in 1955, at Ebbets Field, with the hated Sal Maglie pitching for the Giants, Jackie Robinson became involved twice in one game in incidents that could have reached riot proportions.

Maglie had brushed back Robinson with a tight pitch. Hoping to retaliate, Robinson pushed a bunt down the first-base line, expecting Maglie would field it. But Maglie stayed out of harm's way and Robinson bowled into Davey Williams, knocking Williams to the ground. The next inning, Al Dark crashed into Robinson, playing third. Robinson lost the ball and his composure. The battling pair had to be separated.

The next year Gomez put on one of the fastest sprinting exhibitions seen in baseball. It happened in a game at Milwaukee. He nicked Joe Adcock, the Braves' huge first baseman, on the wrist. Adcock walked to first, then suddenly veered toward Gomez. Gomez picked up the ball and threw it at Adcock. Then Gomez ran, with Adcock in pursuit. Gomez made the dugout first, where he remained until he was given a police escort back to his hotel room.

Rarely have players used a bat, however. Earlier this season, Frank Thomas did and his team, the Philadelphia Phils, released him almost immediately. Thomas swung the bat in a pregame bout with a teammate, Richie Allen.

One of the more rollicking melees occurred in a 1933 game between the Washington Senators and New York Yankees.

Buddy Myer of the Senators started things off with a kick that caught Ben Chapman in the back. A riot followed and Chapman and Myer were ejected. On his way out, Chapman passed the Senators' bench and lingered long enough to hear a few words from Earl Whitehill. Another riot was on, finally broken up by the police.

What should have been one of the happier days in Ebbets Field—Joe Medwick's first appearance as a Dodger, in 1940—turned into a riot. Medwick went to bat against his former Cardinal teammate, Bob Bowman. Bowman immediately hit Medwick in the head with a pitch. As Medwick slumped to the ground unconscious, players streamed out on the field, some with bats in their hands. After order was restored, Bowman needed a police escort to get out of the ball park.

August 23, 1965

STENGEL IS RATED HIGH AS MANAGER

Ability to Evaluate Players, Tactical Skills Assessed

By LEONARD KOPPETT

How good a manager was Casey Stengel? A genius? A fraud? He has been called both. Upon retirement, he deserves an attempt at objective evaluation.

The idea that any manager can be a "genius" is hard to justify. Baseball just isn't that complicated a game and no matter what decision a manager makes the result comes from the physical action of some player. A manager's functions can be put into two categories: "handling" personnel, and tactical decisions.

Handling personnel involves several factors: evaluating a man's abilities, point by point; understanding the man's personality and finding ways to make him do his best; and communicating your desires to the men who must carry them out.

On the first point, Stengel was an outstanding manager in his Yankee and Met period. He knew every player's capabilities thoroughly and was ingenious in making maximum use of them. He found ways to keep players out of situations unfavorable to them as well as times to play them when they had the edge.

Bias for Aggressive Type

Since few players—or other human beings—have a firm, objective grasp of their own shortcomings, most players didn't like it when Stengel did this. Nevertheless, in countless instances, his judgment of their abilities was proved correct, and as years went by, many former players came to admit this.

On the second point, Stengel wasn't as strong as on the first, but still pretty good. He had a bias for the aggressive type of man, and considering the nature of his business—professional competitive athletics—it was a pretty reasonable bias. He believed that a man could be driven by abuse or other means, into a quiet rage that made him a more effective player.

However, in recent years, Stengel's life-long psychology became somewhat out-dated—not because he himself was old, but because the young people who came along were so different in their reactions from the young people of even the preceding decade. The one thing Stengel never did adjust to completely was the demand for perpetual pampering that today's young players demand.

This was the factor that made it more difficult for Stengel to communicate with players in the nineteen-sixties than in the nineteen-fifties. The older players may have resented Stengel's criticisms, but they didn't curl up around their wounded feelings as a result; many of today's players do.

More to the point, however, is the fact that most of Stengel's criticisms were always well-founded and constructive. And that's where his tactical skill came in.

The Record Speaks

Tactics, for a manager, include: making a batting order, changing pitchers, making instantaneous decisions about hitting or taking a pitch, ordering a bunt or a hit-and-run, shifting fields. These have meaning only in the context of particular players with particular abilities in particular situations.

Two elements go into such decisions: memory (what happened in similar circumstances before) and powers of observation (noting any significant slight difference in pattern, position, performance).

A report card on Stengel as a manager, therefore, would read like this:

In 1934-1943, managing the Brooklyn Dodgers and Boston Braves: always in the second division, never enough material to expect much else, perfecting his craft.

In 1944-48, managing in the minors; secure in his methods and ideas, fluctuating talent and fluctuating results.

In 1949-60, managing the Yankees: in complete command of his managerial skills with material to make them work, resulting in almost perpetual success.

In 1962-65, managing the Mets: always last, with hopelessly inadequate material, his skills unimpaired, but his advantages decreased—because, after his Yankee success, much of what was originality on Casey's part in 1950 has become standard procedure for everyone in 1965.

Summary: by any set of standards, certainly not perfect, but one of the best managers baseball has ever had.

August 31, 1965

Stengel: 'You Could Look It Up'

RECORD AS PLAYER
REGULAR SEASON

Year	Club	G.	HR.	RBI.	BA
1910	Kankakee....(League disbanded in July)				
1910	Maysville	69	2	—	.223
1911	Aurora	121	4	—	.352
1912	Montgomery	136	—	—	.290
1912	Brooklyn	17	1	12	.316
1913	Brooklyn	124	7	44	.272
1914	Brooklyn	126	4	56	.316
1915	Brooklyn	132	3	43	.237
1916	Brooklyn	127	8	53	.279
1917	Brooklyn	150	6	69	.257
1918	Pittsburgh	39	1	13	.246
1919	Pittsburgh	89	4	40	.293
1920	Phila., NL	129	9	50	.292
1921	Phila., N.Y.	42	0	6	.284
1922	New York NL	84	7	48	.368
1923	New York NL	75	5	43	.339
1924	Boston NL	131	5	39	.280
1925	Boston NL	12	0	2	.077
1925	Worcester	100	10	—	.320
1926	Toledo	88	0	27	.328
1927	Toledo	18	1	3	.176
1928	Toledo	26	0	12	.438
1929	Toledo	20	0	9	.226
1931	Toledo	2	0	0	.375

Maj. League Totals 1,277 60 518 .284

WORLD SERIES

Year	Club	G.	HR.	RBI.	BA
1916	Brooklyn	4	0	0	.364
1922	New York	2	0	0	.400
1923	New York	6	2	4	.417
	Totals	12	2	4	.393

RECORD AS MANAGER
YEAR BY YEAR

Year	Club	League	Pos.	W.	L.
1925	Worcester	East	3	70	55
1926	Toledo	A.A.	4	87	77
1927	Toledo	A.A.	1	101	67
1928	Toledo	A.A.	6	79	88
1929	Toledo	A.A.	8	67	100
1930	Toledo	A.A.	3	88	66
1931	Toledo	A.A.	8	68	100
1934	Brooklyn	Nat.	6	71	81
1935	Brooklyn	Nat.	5	70	83
1936	Brooklyn	Nat.	7	67	87
1938	Boston	Nat.	5	77	75
1939	Boston	Nat.	7	63	88
1940	Boston	Nat.	7	65	87
1941	Boston	Nat.	7	62	92
1942	Boston	Nat.	7	59	89
1943	Boston	Nat.	6	68	85
1944	Milwaukee	A.A.	1	91	49
1945	Kansas City	A.A.	7	65	84
1946	Oakland	P.C.	2	111	72
1947	Oakland	P.C.	4	96	90
1948	Oakland	P.C.	1	114	74
1949	New York	Amer.	1	97	57
1950	New York	Amer.	1	98	56
1951	New York	Amer.	1	98	56
1952	New York	Amer.	1	95	59
1953	New York	Amer.	1	99	52
1954	New York	Amer.	2	103	51
1955	New York	Amer.	1	96	58
1956	New York	Amer.	1	97	57
1957	New York	Amer.	1	98	56
1958	New York	Amer.	1	92	62
1959	New York	Amer.	3	79	75
1960	New York	Amer.	1	97	57
1962	New York	Nat.	10	40	120
1963	New York	Nat.	10	51	111
1964	New York	Nat.	10	53	109
*1965	New York	Nat.	10	31	64

*Games through July 24

MAJOR LEAGUE SUMMARY

	Club.	W.	L.	T.	Total
Brooklyn	Nat.	208	251	4	463
Boston	Nat.	394	516	6	916
New York	Nat.	144	340	2	486
New York	Amer.	1,149	696	6	1,851

Totals 1,895 1,803 18 3,716

WORLD SERIES SUMMARY

	Club	W.	L.	T.	Total
New York	Amer.	37	26	0	63

ALL-STAR SUMMARY

Club.	W.	L.	T.	Tot.
American League	4	6	0	10

Koufax of Dodgers Hurls Perfect Game

By The Associated Press

LOS ANGELES, Sept. 9— Sandy Koufax of the Los Angeles Dodgers pitched a perfect game tonight in a 1-0 victory over the Chicago Cubs and became the first pitcher in baseball history to pitch four no-hitters in his career.

Outpitching Bob Hendley in a brilliant duel between left-handers, Koufax hurled his fourth no-hitter in four years and surpassed the record for multiple no-hitters held by Bob Feller, Cy Young and Larry Corcoran.

Hendley, who allowed only one hit, yielded a run in the fifth inning when the Dodgers scored without a hit. Lou Johnson walked to open the inning, was sacrificed to second, stole third and raced home when Chris Krug, the catcher, threw wild.

That was enough for the Dodgers, who remained half a game behind San Francisco in the National League pennant race.

The only hit off Hendley — and the only hit of the game— was Johnson's bloop double to right field with two out in the seventh inning.

Koufax, 29 years old, whose career was in jeopardy three years ago because of a circula-

Associated Press

HE DID IT AGAIN: Sandy Koufax pitched perfect game against the Cubs. It was his fourth no-hitter.

.tory ailment in his pitching hand, retired 27 Cubs in order.

Koufax Strikes Out 14

Koufax struck out 14, lifting his major-league-leading total to 332, as he posted the first perfect game in his 11-year career, the eighth in modern baseball history and only the third in National League annals. Jim Bunning of Philadelphia accomplished the feat last year.

Feller, the long-time Cleveland ace, pitched no-hitters in 1940, 1946 and 1951. Corcoran pitched three pre-1900 no-hitters for the Cubs in 1880, 1882 and 1884. Young pitched his first no-hitter for Cleveland, which was then in the National League, in 1897, and pitched no-hitters for Boston of the American League in 1904 and 1908.

Koufax, bringing his won-lost record to 22-7, was overpowering with his assortment of fast balls and breaking stuff. He struck out the last six batters he faced and seven of the last nine.

In the eighth he faced two of the Cubs' hardest-hitting players, Ron Santo and Ernie Banks. He struck out both, then ended the inning by fanning Byron Browne, a rookie left fielder.

Tension Mounts

In the ninth as the tension mounted in the crowd of 29,139, Koufax fired a third strike past the young Cubs' catcher, Krug. A pinch-hitter, Joey Amalfitano, also went down swinging—on three pitches. Then it was up to another pinch-hitter, Harvey Kuenn, the former American League batting champion.

Kuenn also went down swinging—and Koufax had his first perfect game.

He also closed in on another of baseball's most spectacular achievements. Feller's strikeout record of 348 in one season. Koufax now is 16 shy of matching that feat.

There were no tough chances for the Dodger fielders as only seven batters hit the ball well enough to get it to the outfield.

In the second inning, Browne lofted one to center field. In the third, Krug flied to center and Don Kessinger flied to right. In the fourth, Glenn Beckert flied to right field, and in the fifth Santo flied to left. In the seventh, Beckert flied to right field and Williams to left.

The perfect game with no runner getting to first base—was the first since Bunning accomplished the feat against the New York Mets on June 21 last year. The only other perfect game in modern National

The Box Score

CHICAGO (N.)					LOS ANGELES (N.)				
	ab	r	h	bi		ab	r	h	bi
Young, cf	3	0	0	0	Wills, ss	3	0	0	0
Beckert, 2b	3	0	0	0	Gilliam, 3b	3	0	0	0
Williams, rf	3	0	0	0	Kennedy, 3b	0	0	0	0
Santo, 3b	3	0	0	0	Davis, cf	3	0	0	0
Banks, 1b	3	0	0	0	Johnson, lf	2	1	1	0
Browne, lf	3	0	0	0	Fairly, rf	3	0	0	0
Krug, c	3	0	0	0	Lefebvre, 2b	3	0	0	0
Kessinger, ss	2	0	0	0	Tracewski, 2b	0	0	0	0
Amalfitano, ph	1	0	0	0	Parker, 1b	3	0	0	0
Hendley, p	2	0	0	0	Torborg, c	3	0	0	0
Kuenn, ph	1	0	0	0	Koufax, p	2	0	0	0
Totals	27	0	0	0	Totals	24	1	1	0

Chicago   000 000 000—0
Los Angeles   000 010 00x—1
E—Krug. LOB—Chicago 0, Los Angeles 1. 2B Johnson. SB—Johnson. S—Fairly.

	IP.	H.	R.	ER.	BB.	SO.
Hendley (L, 2-3)	8	1	1	0	1	3
Koufax (W, 22-7)	9	0	0	0	0	14

T—1.43. A—29,139.

League history was by Harvey Haddix.

Haddix, then with Pittsburgh, pitched 12 innings of perfect ball against Milwaukee in 1959. However, he gave up a hit in the 13th and eventually was the loser.

Other perfect games were pitched by Young in 1904, Addie Joss of Cleveland in 1908, Ernie Shore of Boston in 1917, Charles Robertson of Chicago in 1922 and Don Larsen of the New York Yankees in 1956. Larsen pitched his perfect game in the World Series.

Koufax, who won the Cy Young award as the best pitcher in the majors in 1963 when he posted a 25-5 record, pitched his first no-hitter against the New York Mets, June 30, 1962, winning 5-0. His second came May 11, 1963, against San Francisco, with the Dodgers winning 8-0. Koufax made it three no-hitters last year, June 4, against Philadelphia, winning 3-0.

The no-hitter was the third in the majors this season. Cincinnati's Jim Maloney pitched two, winning one and losing another. In Maloney's losing no-hitter he gave up a hit in the 10th inning.

Koufax, whose career was threatened following the 1962 season, also was presented with another chilling possibility when it developed this spring that he was suffering from arthritis in the elbow of his pitching arm.

Doctors at first feared that Koufax would be a once-a-week hurler, but the ace left-hander has managed to take his turn every four days. However, he packs his arm in ice after each game to guard against any serious injury.

His no-hitter was the first pitched by a Dodger since Sal Maglie pitched one against Philadelphia, Sept. 25, 1956.

Hendley also had a perfect game going until Johnson walked in the fifth, and became the game's first base runner.

September 10, 1965

Ashford First Negro Umpire Hired by American League

BOSTON, Sept. 15 (AP)— The American League hired its first Negro umpire today with the purchase of Emmett L. Ashford from the Pacific Coast League.

Joe Cronin, the league president, said that Ashford would join a staff of 23 umpires at spring training next year.

Ashford, who will be 47 years old on Nov. 23, has been in the Pacific Coast League for 12 years, the last three as umpire-in-chief. He began his professional umpiring career in the Southwest International League in 1951. He spent seasons in the Arizona-Texas and Western International Leagues before moving up to the Pacific Coast League.

September 16, 1965

DODGERS TRIUMPH OVER TWINS, 2-0, AND TAKE SERIES

Koufax Fans 10 and Yields 3 Hits in Gaining His 2d Shutout in 4 Days

KAAT IS ROUTED IN 4TH

Johnson's Homer and Hits by Fairly and Parker Decide 7th Game

By LEONARD KOPPETT
Special to The New York Times

BLOOMINGTON, Minn., Oct. 14—Sandy Koufax completed a season of incredible personal accomplishment by pitching the Los Angeles Dodgers to a 2-0 victory over the Minnesota Twins today in the seventh and deciding game of the World Series.

Less than seven months ago, the 29-year-old left-hander from Brooklyn was afraid that his brilliant career was prematurely finished. He had discovered that he had a chronic arthritic condition in his left elbow, which was swollen and bent, and one week before the baseball season was to begin no one could tell whether Koufax would ever be able to pitch again.

Only 2 Days Rest

Today, pitching with only two days of rest, or one fewer than the ordinary healthy pitcher usually needs, he overpowered the Twins after a shaky beginning. He allowed only three hits, walked three men and struck

out 10. He retired 14 of the last 15 batters he faced.

It was Koufax's second victory and second shutout of this series, and it put the ultimate embellishment on his year's work. During the regular season, he never missed a starting turn, won 26 games, set a season strike-out record, pitched a perfect game and did his best work during a stretch drive that enabled the Dodgers to win the pennant.

Including the World Series, Koufax pitched 360 innings and struck out 411 batters with an arm that needed constant medication.

His performance today, therefore, involved determination and response to pressure as much as sheer talent and skill. When it was over, he seemed too tired to show elation and even his teammates avoided the usual Series-ending ritual of mob congratulations.

End of Long Season

As Bob Allison swung and missed for the final out, Sandy walked wearily toward the dugout while the crowd of 50,596

a record here at Metropolitan Stadium—seemed silent and depressed. It wasn't until he was across the third-base foul line that Koufax was joined by his fellow victors, and even then there was little leaping and back-pounding.

The most excited escort was Lou Johnson, who arrived late from his position in left field. It was his home run off Jim Kaat in the fourth inning that had provided the indispensable run.

A minor-leaguer most of his career, the 32-year-old Johnson went to the Dodgers last May only because Tommy Davis broke an ankle. He frequently powered the limited Dodger offense throughout the tight pennant race. Today, he made the most important hit of all—and he is not the type of man to hide his emotions.

257

The second Dodger run came immediately after the homer, which hit the left-field foul-pole screen. It was produced by three other often unappreciated Dodgers: Ron Fairly Wes Parker and Manager Walt Alston.

Fairly followed Johnson's drive with one just fair into the other corner of the field for a double. This was with nobody out in the fourth inning, so it was natural to expect the Dodgers to sacrifice Fairly to third, from where he could score on an out.

The Twins set their infield defense for this eventuality, but Alston, speaking to Parker before he went to the plate, told him to swing and try to hit the ball past the charging infield. Parker did exactly that. He bounced a single over the head of Don Mincher, the onrushing first baseman, and Fairly scored.

Thus the Dodgers became champions of the baseball world for the second time in three years, and for the fourth time in five chances under Alston's regime.

Alston became manager of the Dodgers when they were still in Brooklyn, and still had a star-studded line-up, in 1954. The next year, Brooklyn had its first and only world championship, thanks to a 2-0 victory in the seventh game at Yankee Stadium. The man who pitched that one — Johnny Podres — sat in the Dodger bull pen all day today, no longer needed.

In 1956, the Dodgers again battled the Yankees through seven games, but lost the last one. After the 1957 season, they moved to Los Angeles, and in 1959 won the pennant in a post-season playoff with Milwaukee. They then defeated the Chicago White Sox in the World Series. 4 games to 2.

In 1962, with fundamentally the same personnel now playing, the Dodgers lost a pennant playoff to the San Francisco Giants. But in 1963, they won the pennant handily and swept the Yankees, 4-0, with Koufax pitching two outstanding games. Last year, however, the Los Angeles club couldn't even win half its games and finished in a tie for sixth.

Koufax, Don Drysdale and Claude Osteen, plus Ron Perranoski and Bob Miller as relievers, gave the Dodgers superb pitching this year. And the bunt-run-steal-scamper attack led by Maury Wills produced enough runs.

That was the pattern used in this Series. In the first two games here, the attack didn't function, Drysdale and Koufax were not sharp, and the Twins won easily.

In the next three games in Los Angeles, Osteen pitched a shutout, Drysdale a five-hitter and Koufax a shutout — and the Dodger offense ran wild. Yesterday here, the offense died again and when Osteen made one bad pitch (which Allison hit for a two-run homer) the Series was all even.

Box Score of 7th Series Game

LOS ANGELES (N.)	AB.	R.	H.	RBI.	PO.	A.
Wills, ss	4	0	0	0	2	1
Gilliam, 3b	5	0	2	0	2	1
Kennedy, 3b	0	0	0	0	0	0
W. Davis, cf	2	0	0	0	1	0
Johnson, lf	4	1	1	1	3	0
Fairly, rf	4	1	1	0	0	0
Parker, 1b	4	0	2	1	6	0
Tracewski, 2b	4	0	0	0	1	0
Roseboro, c	2	0	1	0	12	1
Koufax, p	3	0	0	0	0	0
Total	32	2	7	2	27	7

MINNESOTA (A.)	AB.	R.	H.	RBI.	PO.	A.
Versalles, ss	4	0	1	0	0	2
Nossek, cf	4	0	0	0	4	0
Oliva, rf	3	0	0	0	0	0
Killebrew, 3b	3	0	0	0	4	0
Battey, c	4	0	0	0	8	1
Allison, lf	4	0	0	0	1	0
Mincher, 1b	3	0	0	0	10	0
Quilici, 2b	3	0	1	0	1	3
Kaat, p	1	0	0	0	0	1
Worthington, p	0	0	0	0	1	1
aRollins	0	0	0	0	0	0
Klippstein, p	0	0	0	0	0	0
Merritt, p	0	0	0	0	0	0
bValdespino	1	0	0	0	0	0
Perry, p	0	0	0	0	0	0
Total	30	0	3	0	27	10

aWalked for Worthington in 5th.
bFouled out for Merritt in 8th.

Los Angeles Dodgers	0	0	0	2	0	0	0	0	0—2
Minnesota Twins	0	0	0	0	0	0	0	0	0—0

Error—Oliva. Left on bases—Los Angeles 9. Minnesota 6.
Two-base hits—Roseboro, Fairly, Quilici. Three-base hit—Parker. Home run—Johnson. Sacrifice—W. Davis.

	IP.	H.	R.	ER.	BB.	SO.	HBP.	WP.	Balks
Koufax (W)	9	3	0	0	3	10	0	0	0
Kaat (L)	3	5	2	2	1	2	0	0	0
Worthington	2	0	0	0	1	1	0	0	0
Klippstein	1⅔	2	0	0	1	2	1	0	0
Merritt	1⅓	0	0	0	1	1	0	0	0
Perry	1	0	0	0	1	0	0	0	0

*Faced 3 batters in 4th.
Bases on balls—Off Koufax 3 (Oliva, Killebrew, Rollins), Kaat 1 (Koufax), Worthington 1 (Roseboro), Klippstein 1 (Roseboro), Perry 1 (Wills). Struck out—By Koufax 10 (Versalles, Battey 2, Allison 2, Mincher, Kaat, Oliva 2, Quilici), Kaat 2 (Wills, Tracewski), Klippstein 2 (Tracewski, Koufax), Merritt 1 (Roseboro), Perry 1 (Koufax). Hit by pitcher—By Klippstein (W. Davis).
Umpires—Hurley (A.), plate; Venson (N.), first base; Flaherty (A.), second base; Sudol (N.), third base; Stewart (A.), left field; Vargo (N.), right field. Time of game—2:27. Attendance—50,596.

It was, therefore, up to Koufax today. Drysdale was ready, however, to take over at any time. And three times in the first five innings it appeared that he would be needed.

Koufax almost had a run to work with at the start. Jim Gilliam singled with one out in the first and was bunted to second by Willie Davis. He was on his way home when Tony Oliva raced in and made a tumbling catch of Johnson's looper to right.

Control was Sandy's problem in the first. He was consistently high as he struck out Zoilo Versalles and retired Joe Nossek on a grounder. He walked Oliva on a full count and Harmon Killebrew on four pitches. Then he fired a third strike past Earl Battey and was out of the inning.

In the third, the Dodgers failed to score even though John Roseboro led off with a double and Koufax walked. Kaat made Wills bounce out, advancing the runners, and forced Gilliam to fly out to right field, too short for any attempt to score. Then he got Davis to foul out.

In the home half of the inning, Koufax had his second crisis, and he got a break. Versalles singled with one out and was trying to steal second when Nossek swung at a 1-1 pitch. In doing so Nossek clearly interfered with Roseboro's unsuccessful throw to second, so Umpire Ed Hurley declared Nossek out and sent Versalles back to first.

After getting his 2-0 lead, Koufax retired the Twins in order in the fourth, but had to struggle again in the fifth.

Frank Quilici lined a two-base hit off the fence in left-center with one out and Rich Rollins, a pinch-hitter for the pitcher, worked a full-count walk. The tying runs were on with one out and the top of the batting order was up.

Here Koufax got fielding support. Versalles smashed a sharp grounder down the third-base line. Gilliam, with a lunge, smothered it back-handed, scrambled to his feet and got over to the base in time for a forceout. Nossek's grounder to Wills then proved a third-out force at second.

From that point on, Koufax

seemed to have much better control. Battey hit a line drive at Wills in the sixth and Versalles flied deep to left in the eighth, but no one got on base until Killebrew lined a single to left with one out in the ninth.

That meant a home run could tie the game and Koufax had to "reach back" for whatever strength he had left in his 360th inning.

He fired two strikes past Battey and hit the outside corner for a called strike three. Allison fouled the first pitch to him and took two balls, both high. Then he swung and missed for strike two. Finally Sandy reached back for the last time and threw strike three as Allison swung and missed.

It might have been an easier task for Koufax, but the Dodgers wasted three scoring opportunities after they had their runs.

In the fourth, Parker's single knocked out Kaat and Parker took second when Oliva bobbled the ball. Al Worthington relieved and made a fine catch on Dick Tracewski's pop bunt along the third-base line. Worthington walked Roseboro semi-intentionally, fielded Koufax's soft tap to the mound while the runners advanced, and made Wills foul out to Killebrew.

Parker tripled off Johnny Klippstein with one out in the sixth, but Tracewski bunted foul for the third strike on an attempted squeeze play. An intentional pass to Roseboro and a strike-out of Koufax ended the inning.

With one out in the seventh, Gilliam singled and Davis was hit on the foot by a pitch. Johnson's slow bounder to third left men on second and third with two out.

At that point Manager Sam Mele called Jim Merritt, a lefthander, in from the bull pen to face Fairly. It was an excellent decision because Fairly, who had been murdering Minnesota's right-handed pitchers, flied meekly to right field.

In the final analysis, then, the old baseball adage was proved true once more: The arm is mightier than the bat.

October 15, 1965

Baltimore Orioles

Retired General Replaces Frick As the Commissioner of Baseball

By United Press International

CHICAGO, Nov. 17—William D. Eckert, a 56-year-old retired lieutenant general of the United States Air Force, was named commissioner of baseball today in a surprise move by the major league club owners.

General Eckert's selection was approved unanimously by representatives of the owners of the 20 major league teams. He will succeed Ford C. Frick, who is retiring. The general accepted a seven-year contract at $65,000 a year, the same salary Commissioner Frick received.

Lee MacPhail, the president and general manager of the Baltimore Orioles, who was reported to be among those being considered for the commissioner's job, was named administrator of the commissioner's office, and thus will become General Eckert's executive assistant. Mr. MacPhail received a three-year contract at $40,000 a year.

Joe Cronin, who was also among those considered for the commissioner's job, accepted a new contract extending his term as president of the American League for seven years.

Although General Eckert was one of 150 candidates originally suggested as Frick's successor, his name was not among those recently mentioned publicly in speculation for the job.

General Eckert said he had had "a few weeks" to consider whether he would accept the job after he was first approached about it by John Galbreath of the Pittsburgh Pirates and John Fetzer of the Detroit Tigers, members of the screening committee assigned by the owners to nominate the commissioner.

'Pleased and Honored'

General Eckert said he was not surprised but "pleased and honored" to be elected. "After 35 years in the Air Force," he said, "I don't think I'm the type to be surprised."

"I'm going to call the signals as I see them in all fairness and equity in the interests of the public, the players and the franchises," he said. "I agree that I have full authority to step in and do the job that needs to be done."

The general said he would rely on Mr. Frick and the commissioner's staff to help him become oriented to baseball and that he would ask Mr. Frick to "assist, advise and officiate at the coming meeting" of baseball club owners in Miami, Dec. 1.

"I'm ready to go to work now," he said, "and I plan to get in touch with Frick's staff immediately. I want to encourage clean sports and honest competition, but I'll be better prepared in three months to say how I'll handle the job as commissioner of baseball."

The general was asked his opinion of the transfer of the Milwaukee Braves to Atlanta, but before he could answer Mr. Frick intervened and said "let's give the man a chance. It's unfair to ask the new commissioner questions like that."

The new commissioner, however, said he would not evade the question and would attempt to answer all questions to the best of his ability at any time.

"I hope the Milwaukee problem will be worked out to the satisfaction of the communities concerned," he said. "However, I am not familiar with the legalities of the situation."

Thin Baseball Background

General Eckert, who retired from the Air Force in 1961, said he did not believe he was hired by the club owners because of his baseball background. His only competition was in Madison (Ind.) High School.

"I don't think they hired me to put me out on the field," he said.

Instead he said he believed his business background with the Air Force, in procurement, research and personnel, was a major factor in determining his qualifications for the job. Since his retirement the general has been a member of numerous industry and defense advisory boards, but he said he planned to resign from most of them.

General Eckert graduated from West Point in 1930 and later was a fighter plane pilot. While he served in the Army he received a Master's Degree in Business Administration at Harvard.

During World War II he was a bomb group commander in Europe, and later chief of maintenance and supply for the 9th Air Force Service Command. He later was assigned to Air Force Headquarters and in February, 1960, became Comptroller of the Air Force.

November 18, 1965

Orioles Acquire Robinson From Reds

SLUGGER IS KEY IN 4-PLAYER DEAL

Baltimore Gets Long-Ball Hitter for Two Pitchers and Rookie Outfielder

BALTIMORE, Dec. 9, (UPI) Frank Robinson, one of the National League's best outfielders, was traded to the Baltimore Orioles today in a four-player deal that sent Milt Pappas and Jack Baldschun, pitchers, to the Cincinnati Reds.

The interleague swap was the biggest of the offseason and capped a long-time effort by the Orioles to obtain a top-drawer, long-ball-hitting outfielder.

Along with Pappas and Baldschun, the Reds received Dick Simpson, a rookie outfielder. Simpson batted .301 for Seattle of the Pacific Coast League last season and .222 with the Cali-

fornia Angels when they brought him up near the end of the year.

The key player in the four-man package was the 30-year-old Robinson, who had been offered to a number of clubs recently after driving in 113 runs, hitting 33 homers and batting .296 for the Reds last season.

"This is the guy we've been looking for," said Hank Bauer, Baltimore's delighted manager. "I think he's a helluva ballplayer. At least he has been for 10 years. He drives in 100 runs a year and from the reports I have he's a good man to have on the club, a team leader. I know we gave up a lot to get him, but any deal is a gamble."

Bill DeWitt, the Cincinnati owner who negotiated the trade with Baltimore's new general manager, Harry Dalton, called it "a million-dollar deal."

He said that the 26-year-old, right-handed Pappas would strengthen the Reds' starting staff; the 29-year-old Baldschun their bull-pen corps and the 22-year-old Simpson their outfield reserves.

Pappas, one of the Orioles' most consistent pitchers last season, had a 13-9 won-lost record with a 2.61 earned-run

average. Baldschun was 5-8 with the Phillies in relief and had a 3.82 earned-run average in 65 contests.

Neither Baldschun nor Simpson has worn a Baltimore uniform. Baldschun came to the Orioles last Monday in a deal for Jackie Brandt, an outfielder, while Simpson was acquired by Baltimore from the Angels during the baseball meetings in Florida last week in exchange for Norm Siebern, a first baseman.

Several other clubs had a crack at Robinson during the last few weeks, including the Houston Astros and New York Yankees, but backed off, claiming the Reds' asking price was too high.

Even the Orioles lost interest at Miami Beach last week when the Reds asked for Pappas and Curt Blefary, an outfielder, for Robinson and Joey Jay, a pitcher.

Talks Were Resumed

That line of conversation broke off at one point and later was resumed when the Orioles obtained Baldschun from the Phillies. The Reds had been after the screwball specialist for a couple of years.

With the addition of Robinson, Bauer said, the Orioles would have "four good hitters."

He listed them as Brooks Robinson, a third baseman, John (Boog) Powell, a first baseman, Blefary and Frank Robinson, who will be the club's right-fielder.

Bauer said he was sorry to lose Pappas, a 16-game winner in 1964, but it couldn't be helped.

"At least this gives us a chance to try one of our young pitchers as a starter to make up for the loss of Pappas," said the Baltimore manager. "We've got Jim Palmer, John Miller and Frank Bertaina and one of them ought to win at least seven or eight games and we ought to pick up the rest somewhere else."

Pappas's departure leaves Steve Barber, a left-hander, as the only surviving Baltimore member of what once was known as the "Kiddie Korps." That group of pitchers was composed of Barber, Pappas, Chuck Estrada and Jack Fisher.

December 10, 1965

Koufax and Drysdale Agree to One-Year Contracts Totaling Over $210,000

SOUTHPAW'S PAY BELIEVED $120,000

But Dodger Stars Have No Comment on Original Plan to Share Settlement

By BILL BECKER
Special to The New York Times

LOS ANGELES, March 30 — Sandy Koufax and Don Drysdale ended their holdout against the Los Angeles Dodgers today and became the two highest-paid players ever to perform on the same baseball team.

Both agreed to sign one-year contracts calling for a combined total of "more than $210,000" for the 1966 season, E. J. (Buzzy) Bavasi, the Dodgers' general manager, announced at a hastily called news conference.

Koufax and Drysdale were beaming participants at the conference, and with good reason. It was believed that Koufax would receive $120,000 and Drysdale $105,000.

That was far short of the $500,000 apiece over three years they had sought when they began their holdout in February. Koufax indicated the one-year package was for at least $225,000.

Koufax and Drysdale earned about $70,000 each last season.

Stand Next to Mays

Koufax and Drysdale now rank behind Willie Mays of the San Francisco Giants, who is to draw close to $130,000 this year.

Earlier, the players had said they planned to divide their total package evenly if they signed separately, but they would not confirm this today. Drysdale agreed to terms first.

During the holdout, Bavasi had remained steadfast in offering Drysdale $15,000 less than Koufax.

Yesterday the players had spurned Bavasi's $210,000 offer —$112,500 to Sandy and $97,500 to Don. The Dodgers' first offer had been $100,000 for Koufax, $85,000 for Drysdale.

"They met us pretty close to the middle," Sandy said at today's conference. By the middle he meant the halfway point between the $333,333 the players wanted per year and the $185,000 with which the club

opened. That point would be $260,000, but a Dodger source said that total was too high.

Movie Contract Canceled

The players immediately were released from a motion picture commitment. They said they planned to join the club in Phoenix, Ariz., on Friday.

"I hope to pitch a couple of innings this weekend," said Drysdale. The Dodgers play the Giants Saturday and Sunday in Arizona. The big right-hander has been working out at a local junior college field for a week.

He and the left-handed Koufax, last year's Cy Young Award winner, said they hoped to be ready to pitch in the first week of the season.

"Not the opener," said Sandy, "but with luck, the first or second series. But I'll leave that up to Manager Walter Alston."

The season opens on Tuesday, April 12.

Koufax, at 196 pounds, said he was seven pounds under his normal pitching weight, even though he had done no pitching and very little running in the off season.

"I just watch my diet and don't eat as much when I'm not active," Sandy said.

Drysdale Weighs 215

Drysdale said he weighed 215, about five pounds over his playing norm.

New York Times

Sandy Koufax and Don Drysdale

Bavasi was ebullient. When Koufax told reporters that "Don and I are both happy" and was asked, "Who's happier?" Bavasi interjected, "I am."

Without the pair, the world champion Dodgers would be hard-pressed to finish in the National League's first division. Koufax won 26 games and lost eight in 1965 and set a strike-out record of 382. Drysdale won 23 and lost 12.

The holdout of the 30-year-old, Brooklyn-born Koufax, and Drysdale, a 29-year-old Californian, with all its Hollywood overtones, had been the most persistent and publicized since the days of Babe Ruth.

Income Tax Bite Big

The Babe's top salary was $80,000, when the take-home was about 95 per cent. Koufax and Drysdale will have to pay income taxes of about 60 per cent, tax experts have reckoned.

The players received notification from Howard W. Koch, the president of Paramount Studios, that he would release them from their contracts in "Warning Shot," which was scheduled to start next week. The boys began rehearsal Monday, but their heart didn't seem to be in it.

J. William Hayes, the lawyer who represented the pitchers in their negotiations with the Dodgers, was not present at today's conference because of the death of his father-in-law. But Koufax said the deal had Hayes's approval.

Koufax stressed that Hayes was not his agent, but his lawyer, and would not get any specific cut of the pay increase.

"He has been my lawyer for three years," said Sandy.

To which Bavasi added, with a grin: "I think he's going to be mine for the next 10."

March 31, 1966

Artificial Grass Installed On Astrodome Outfield

HOUSTON, July 9 (AP) — Workmen installed artificial grass in the outfield area of the Astrodome this week.

The infield area was previously covered with the synthetic grass called Astroturf.

An Astro spokesman said the final slice of grass and turf removed from the outfield would be shipped to Leo Durocher, the Chicago Cubs manager, who has been a bitter critic of the artificial grass.

July 10, 1966

Journey Back To Bushville

By ELIOT ASINOF

IN the years before World War II, every town in America had a ball club to glorify its name. On summer Sunday afternoons, excitement packed thousands of ball parks across the country. Baseball, the national pastime, was loved by Americans in a way no other game could match, and every kid who ever shagged a fly ball nursed dreams of growing up to be a Major Leaguer. Organized baseball was in its heyday, with over 500 minor-league teams bringing professionalism to those communities enterprising enough to win a franchise. They were a magnet for all young aspirants; to them it meant playing for money seven days a week in a circuit that could lead to the top.

I was one of those dedicated dreamers. To satisfy my craving, I spent a few undistinguished seasons in the bush leagues until Pearl Harbor put an end to such folly. Now, 25 years later, I wanted to see what the minor leagues were like today. Beside the grim statistics of decline (there are fewer than 120 teams functioning today), what else had changed? Was life much different for the players? What were they like? Were they as good as we were?

Since none of the clubs I played with are still in operation, I decided to visit Batavia, N. Y. It is a typical small American town, nestled in a patchwork of rolling farms, with a Main Street shopping center a few blocks long. The ball park looked familiar—a decrepit structure sorely in need of paint and repair, the light poles topped with too few reflectors, the small, tacky dressing rooms under the stands smelling of sweaty playing togs and bad plumbing.

At first glance, everything seems very much the same.

THEN the picture begins to change. A spanking new Chevrolet Impala swings into the gravel parking area driven by a tall, well-dressed young man. His attractive wife and infant daughter kiss him good-by and

ELIOT ASINOF is a writer and former professional ballplayer with the Phillies farm system (1939-41). He wrote "Man on Spikes" and "Eight Men Out: The Black Sox and the 1919 World Series."

he steps out looking like a young suburban executive arriving at his country club. This is Richard Noe, college graduate from Newton, Pa., a pitcher for the Batavia Trojans, Class A club in the N.Y.P. (New York-Pennsylvania) League. His affluence is derived from a substantial five-figure bonus from the Baltimore Orioles.

Exceptional? Not at all. Noe is one of the many clean-cut bonus babies who now dominate the baseball world in the same way as the tough, tobacco-chewing, no-bonus rubes did in my day. Several more new cars (and wives) pull in to confirm this. Eighteen-year-old high-school ballplayers regularly pick up from $2,500 to $25,000 or more just for signing their names. Nobody, it seems, plays ball for the love of it any more (and no one would admit it if he did). It is a far cry from Babe Ruth's famous remark in his rookie year: "What, they're gonna pay me to play ball?!!!"

Twenty-seven years ago, I left New York City on a three-day bus ride to a minor-league town like this one, having signed with the Phillies for no bonus money and a monthly salary of $80 (that, too, was not exceptional). Today, salaries average over $500 a month, and it is a strange thing to hear teen-agers tell you they made a mistake in signing for only $10,000.

Not that they are especially greedy for money; the size of the bonus is mostly a mark of their status in the eyes of their mentors. "The more they give you, the quicker you're going to go up." Pitcher Noe, who is proud of his bundle, explains: "It's the way the 'Biggie' scouts think of you that matters."

THIS is the new breed of big-league dreamer. Though he is usually from a small town (baseball was never a big-city game and is even less so today), our TV/mass-communications culture has brought him close to the mainstream. He talks, dresses and thinks much like everyone else. There are no rubes or hayseeds any more, no illiterates or itinerant bums in baseball. They all wear tight pants, on and off the diamond.

Even these boys at the bottom of the baseball ladder look and act like middle-class respectables; it is as if their way of life was as much a part of big-league preparation as their performance on spikes. Shop talk is less about the science of the game than endless speculation about who is going to make it or how well some recent teammate is doing after being moved up. One can picture their wives, equally involved, having the same conversation up in the grandstand.

Their manager, however, is of a different breed. Though I was looking forward to meeting this ex-big-league star, it was unsettling to find Max Lanier in a dirty little cubicle just off the dressing rooms, surrounded by a clutter of socks and jocks and broken bats. He is not in the least embittered, however. In fact, he is pleased to have one of the few managerial jobs left in an ever-dwindling market overloaded with ex-major-leaguers who want to stay in baseball. His former greatness is almost irrelevant; to the players, he is just another skipper who turns in weekly reports on how they are doing. They know little about the brilliance and turbulence of his pitching career: 14 years in the majors, almost all of them with the pennant-winning St. Louis Cardinals, with an impressive 108-82 won-lost record — a career interrupted by his disastrous jump to the ill-fated Mexican League in 1946 that all but knocked him out of baseball.

At 5 feet 9, Max Lanier was an average-sized ballplayer; beside these boys, he is a shrimp. "Look how big they are!" he says proudly. "There are at least a dozen of them over 6 feet, all 200-pounders. And most of them can run 100 yards in 10 seconds."

True enough, I could see. But were they really any good?

"They're good, all right . . . but they're lazy." He gropes for a proper qualifying remark. "Trouble is, they just don't have enough desire."

THERE'S a plaintive bewilderment in his soft Southern drawl as he says this. How can a talented American boy with an opportunity like this not give it everything he has? Why doesn't he think only of playing ball, night and day? Why doesn't he drive himself as if his whole life depended on it?

This, after all, is the key to Lanier's own background. The men he played with were all desperate competitors. Baseball was their one good shot at success, and they scratched and clawed to make the best of it. But for the modern ballplayer an affluent America offers too many lucrative alternatives and a lot more security. As one ballplayer told me: "At first they offered me a lousy $500 a month to come here. Why, a guy could make that much digging ditches!"

He will give baseball a try, yes—but primarily on his own terms. If he's having a good

season, he is apt to call the front office (collect) to complain about the deal he is getting, openly threatening to quit unless they promise to send him up the ladder with a raise in pay—and all this in the presence of his manager!

A Negro slugger from San Antonio, Tex., named Clarence Gaston, a big five-figure bonus baby leading the league in home runs, had a different beef: "I can't get an apartment so as to bring my wife. It gets me down, and just can't play my best. I let them know in the front office . . ." The implication was that he'd be moving out shortly.

AT the time those words were spoken, Max Lanier himself was unable to get a suitable apartment for his family, but he would never ask for a change of assignment. At 51, he is a quiet, gentle man, his dark, round face showing the lines of age and troubles, his once-rugged body taking on weight around the middle.

After his retirement in 1953 he worked at various jobs before opening a supper club in his home town of St. Petersburg, Fla. He lost his wife in an automobile accident, raised a son named Hal and finally returned to baseball in 1961 in what he humorously refers to as a "package deal"; the San Francisco Giants paid $50,000 for Hal and sent Max to manage in the West Carolina League. This is his first season in Batavia, a deal arranged through the Baltimore Orioles, whose players dominate the Trojan roster. Like his players he ponders his prospects, wondering where he will be sent next.

He can still snap off a decent curve as he takes his turn pitching batting practice. He works hard with his pitchers, who, ironically, are the weakest part of his hard-hitting third-place team. He cares deeply about winning ("Show me a good loser and I'll show you a loser!"), for winning is the mark of his talent as a manager. (His players have a tendency to be more casual. One of them confessed to me: "If I have a good night out there and rap out a few, I don't give much of a damn *who* wins!")

At a bad decision, Lanier will get on an umpire with a ferocity that seems alien to his gentle nature, and he will never let up. "It's tough enough to beat nine men, let alone 11!" he says (there are usually only two umpires in the minors as against four in the

majors). He lets his boys know he is in the ball game all the way. Occasionally, he runs morning practice sessions to rectify the mistakes of the previous night and to keep them all sharp when he feels they are dogging it.

Then, when the others have showered and left to eat, he will grab a shovel, rake and wheelbarrow to work on the pitcher's mound, because no one else around can do it correctly. In the otherwise empty ball park, one sees a dedicated man who loves baseball, and I, too, remember the feeling. As a teen-ager, I would go to bed pounding the pocket of a new glove.

BATAVIA'S population has remained around 19,000 for as long as anyone there remembers, generally prospering from rich muck land, dairy farming and such thriving industries as Sylvania Electronics and the Trojan Division (tractors) of Eaton, Yale & Towne, Inc. (for which the ball club was named in exchange for the price of new uniforms).

Since 1939, when the W.P.A. built the ball park for the town, which patriotically named it MacArthur Stadium, Batavia has had a minor-league ball team. That there is still minor-league ball there is primarily due to one man, known affectionately in the area as "Mister Baseball"—Ed Dwyer, successful shoe merchant for 30 years, ex-semi-pro ballplayer and long-time president of the Genesee County Baseball Club (the Batavia Trojans), a strictly nonprofit organization.

For Ed Dwyer it is more than a hobby; it is a passion. He comes to every home game and is usually too busy to sit in his private box with his wife. During the season he solicits ads, organizes special fund-raising projects such as lotteries, bat nights, merchant nights—all in hopes of keeping the club a few dollars in the black. Every spring he travels to the Florida training camps, where he hobnobs with big-league potentates and pleads his cause, making the best deal he can for a manager, players and big-league working relationships. This year he got Lanier from the Giants, seven players from the Orioles and 14 others from a total of 12 clubs, each of which pays the salaries of its particular farmhands. This diffusion of control is barely workable. All other N.Y.P. teams are solidly entrenched with a single major-league organiza-

tion which supports the farm club with money and players.

One of Dwyer's ambitions is to arrange such an agreement for Batavia. Another is to see the N.Y.P. League expanded from six to eight teams. As it stands now, the schedule is divided into two separate races of 65 games, the winner of each competing for the pennant in a September playoff. If one team should win both (as is likely to happen), there is no playoff and a normally lucrative week is sacrificed.

"Most of all, I would like to win that pennant," Dwyer says with a twinkle, and you know he means it as much as the kids playing for him mean to get out of his bush-league town.

THE truth is, to these Class A ballplayers, this is strictly a Class D setup. There are seldom as many as 500 fans in the rickety stands, with their 3,600 capacity. The playing field itself is laid out disastrously: at game time, 7:30 P.M., the sun begins to set behind the left-center-field fence at an angle that blinds the hitters, especially when facing a right-hander.

The lighting is a sad hangover from prewar construction, with each of the eight short wooden poles showing at least two reflectors out of order. There is always a derisive titter when the lights are turned on.

On the day I arrived the infield grass had not been cut in over a week and was embarrassingly high. Business manager Jon Patterson, a sociology student at Buffalo University during the winter, is also in charge of grounds-keeping, and had tried to borrow a power mower from one of the club vice presidents, who, unfortunately, was out playing golf; it wasn't until game time that a mower was delivered.

Under the stands the tiny Trojan dressing room has only two shower stalls for the 20 players and manager. The visitors' room is so small, with only one stall, that incoming clubs prefer to dress at home, though it means a two- or three-hour bus ride back in sweaty uniforms. This is barely tolerable, I remembered, only if you have had a good night.

ALL this was not dissimilar to my own experience, for there are few minor-league towns with elaborate facilities. A major difference, however, was the complete failure of the Batavia sporting crowd to support the Trojans.

There is hardly a store window poster on Main Street to boost the club. There is less newspaper coverage of the Trojans' games in The Batavia Daily News than of those of the local high school (the chief sports reporter is also principal of the high school) and almost no press promotion. The radio station cannot get a sponsor to broadcast the games, and potential fans receive little news of the team's makeup or progress. Just beyond the outfield fence the Little League Stadium runs its games side by side with the Trojans and sometimes actually outdraws them! Six weeks after opening day the P.A. announcer at the park was still mispronouncing players' names.

And there are no more rewards like steak dinners for home runs or a new pair of slacks for a shutout. The outfield fence has one sign that sums it up: "Hit a grand-slam homer and win a pair of sunglasses!" When one kid homered with only one man on, he showed up the next day sporting a pair of sunglasses with only one lens.

The wife of another ballplayer, wanting to establish credit at a local grocery, was amazed to find that the grocer did not even know there was still a ball club in town.

As Dick Noe puts it: "On the road into Batavia there's a sign that reads 'BUSHVILLE, N. Y.' That's where we are, all right!"

In my day, every town I ever played in gave us full support. A ballplayer, however mediocre, was a prince; we wore our team jackets along Main Street as proudly as marine war heroes. We were feted during the season by fraternal organizations and invited to dinner at the best homes. When we were racing down the home stretch for the pennant, dozens of people would wish us luck at every turn, from the local pool parlor to the mayor's office. They all cared. They came to the games, and let you know they were there. They even *sang* "The Star-Spangled Banner" before the game.

"It's true, those days are gone," President Ed Dwyer has to admit. "Even the Trojan boosters would rather play golf or sit home watching TV."

The sad truth is, all over America, baseball has lost its appeal in the minors. The same cultural changes that have made those small-town 19-year-old bonus kids so sophisticated have also educated the small-town fan to other pas-

times. The minors have shrunk from over 50 leagues in 1941 to under 20 at present. And for years now none of the surviving circuits has been self-supporting. Batavia takes in less from gate receipts than from its hot-dog concession and outfield fence ads. The entire season's income from attendance would barely pay club salaries for a single month.

As a result, the minors are strictly a big-league sponsorship, operating almost solely for big-league benefit. A top player seldom remains with a club for a full season, thus limiting the fans' identification with the local team. And there are no home-towners playing any more. The whole operation has become cold and impersonal.

There is no room even for ex-big-leaguers on their way down. In my day every minor-league club had an old-timer who had been up to the top if only for that proverbial "cup of coffee," and he lent class to the team with his extra know-how. In 1941, in Wausau, Wis. (Northern League, Class C), I played with Wally Gilbert, ex-third baseman for the Brooklyn Dodgers under Wilbert Robinson. There was seldom a game when he wasn't able to pull some great trick out of his bottomless bag. He would slap a bunt past a charging third baseman, pick a runner off base by faking a throw to one base and throwing to another, pull a delayed steal when a rookie catcher threw lazily back to an unwary young pitcher. He was growing beefy and slow from too much booze and too many frustrations, but when he put on spikes he was anything but dead.

Today such men are gone from the scene; the minors are run exclusively for kids on the way up, and a steady stream of top baseball scouts in the stands is evidence of the only remaining importance of these leagues (every ballplayer can spot them the moment they walk in).

IN the face of this decline, it is ironic that these young ballplayers are infinitely better than I remember my contemporaries to have been. Their speed and power are nothing short of awesome. Defensively, they move around the infield like young colts in their huge new gloves, defying a hitter to drive one through them. Tall, rangy pitchers rear back and throw jumping fast balls that seem like peas, and equally defiant giants with the wood in their hands smash

400-foot shots caroming off the fences.

How many will make "the Biggies" is up to the gods to decide. The percentages are against each of them, and everyone has his own ideas of the best route to the top. A sad cynicism predominates. "It's who you know that counts! . . . You just gotta be lucky, that's all. . . . Somebody has to put the right word in the right guy's ear at the right moment!" And it's true the best ballplayer doesn't always make it, any more than the best man is always elected President of the United States.

They all accept this as a fact of life, and are constantly hungry for significant gossip. The word of any slump or injury from above gets to them through a quick and mysterious grapevine that sends them running to the phone with a long-distance reminder to the front office of how well they are doing.

MEANWHILE, they go through the long season, often a thousand miles from home, never knowing how long they will remain. If there is no practice or traveling, their days are spent mainly in bed, sleeping away the hours before game time. ("Man, there's just nothing else to do in this town!") Some of the unmarrieds sack in as many as 12 hours out of every 24. For the sleepless, there is always the local pool hall on Main Street and several have tried to make use of the Y.M.C.A., but they were made to feel unwelcome. One of the Main Street eateries offers them meals at discount prices, however, and remains open late at night so that they can eat well after games, serving as another gathering place.

Most of them live in upstairs rooms in old Batavia homes for which they pay $30 to $50 a month, but they remain transient without privileges in the kitchen or living rooms. Their romantic experiences are also limited by their lack of status among local girls, a trend that struck me as sadly significant. "Every decent-looking girl has a local boy friend," one young ballplayer told me. "All we get are the leftovers!" There are a few nightspots and discothèques on the outskirts of town where they go for a few beers, but a strict curfew prevents them from staying out after 1 A.M.

Though the average age is only 20.6, half the Trojans are

already married. The fortunate ones have found three-room apartments ($100 a month) where their wives cook meals and there is a semblance of family life, their babies crowded in with them. At night the women gather in the grandstand behind home plate for girl talk, but spend most of their energy keeping the infants pacified.

Occasionally, families will gather for an afternoon picnic, or, if they can swing it, a pool party. Then the action will be spirited and youthful, but inevitably the talk will drift back to the prospects of life in the Biggies.

FOR all of them, life is focused on the nightly three hours of baseball. Every one of them firmly believes he is good enough to go up, and many of them are right. They will devote at least three years to this effort, by which time they will either be well on their way to the top or know that it just isn't in the cards. In the winter they supplement their incomes with odd jobs in their home towns as gas station attendants, store clerks, construction workers, substitute teachers or athletic coaches or continue with their education.

They are warm and friendly with each other, desperately needing companionship to support their mutual insecurities. Negro and white mix smoothly together without conflict — or even a suggestion of conflict— and that, too, is part of the new sophisticated urbanity. They are aware of their bargaining power and will use it whenever possible, but they never forget they are bucking a system that will defeat most of them. They are all young Don Quixotes with a trace of cynicism—a bunch of nice kids bewildered by a world that sooner or later will put another kind of uniform on them. But if you scratch their cool facades, you can sense the sheer pleasure they get from playing this still most marvelous of all games.

And *that*, I would bet, will never change.

Ruth! Gehrig! DiMaggio! Mantle! Etc.!

A Yankee Dynasty Can Never Come Back

By LEONARD KOPPETT

HOW quickly can the Yankees come back? The answer is: Never. Not to what they were. Not to the level that symbolized perpetual success, power and wealth. Not to that monopoly of victory which brought them five pennants in a row twice, four in a row two other times, and three straight three times. Not to levels where they could win the World Series five times in succession, and account for 66 per cent of all American League pennants—29 out of 44—from 1921 through 1964.

Not the Yankees—nor anyone else. It is no longer possible for any baseball team to achieve such superiority, and it never will be again. Too much has changed, and the conditions that made the Yankee dynasty possible just don't exist any more. The fact that the Columbia Broadcasting System now owns the ball club really has very little to do with these changes—although they could have been partially foreseen and thus better understood. To see why this is so, we must look back at how Yankee supremacy was created and how it was maintained so long and renewed so often.

THERE is no mystery or uncertainty about how Yankee success began: it was bought.

On Jan. 5, 1920, the Yankees purchased Babe Ruth from the Boston Red Sox. He was an outstanding left-handed pitcher who was such a good hitter that he also played the outfield. In 1919, Ruth had broken all records by hitting 29 home runs. When the Yankees announced that they had paid $100,000 for his contract, it was a major event, the biggest deal till then in baseball history. Ruth revolutionized the game—both the way it was played and in the scale of its appeal for the public.

But it wasn't only Ruth. In the

LEONARD KOPPETT is a sports reporter for The Times who regularly covers the Yankees.

space of three years, the Yankees bought 14 other outstanding players, all from the Red Sox.

And there was a story behind the story.

Immediately before, and during, World War I, the Red Sox were the strongest team of the time. They won pennants in 1912, 1915, 1916 and 1918, and defeated four different National League champions in the World Series. But in 1917 they had been acquired by Harry Frazee, a theatrical producer whose need for money periodically became acute. One recognizable method of raising money was selling players.

The Yankees, meanwhile, had never won anything. The American League had established itself as a second major league in 1901, but the Yankees had not been created until 1903. The team originally belonged to Frank Farrell, well known as the operator of a big gambling house, and Bill Devery, who had been New York's chief of police. They paid $18,000 for the Baltimore franchise, which was transferred to New York.

In 1915, they sold the club — for $460,000 — to Jacob Ruppert, the brewer, and Tillinghast L'Hommedieu Huston, an engineer who had made his fortune building public works in Cuba, where he had remained after fighting in the Spanish-American War.

Two years later, when Huston was back at war in France, Ruppert hired a new manager for the Yankees— Miller Huggins, who had been managing the St. Louis Cardinals. Huston was enraged. He had wanted Wilbert Robinson, the Brooklyn manager. There was an angry exchange of cables, and the breach between the two owners was never healed. From that point on, Ruppert was in command of the Yankees.

UNLIKE most other American League owners, Ruppert had plenty of money and a burning desire to spend it on creating a winning team.

And Frazee of the Red Sox was eager to sell; if his outstanding players were going to be converted into cash, they would have to go to the richest, and most willing, fellow owner.

At the end of the 1918 season the Yankees picked up Ernie Shore and Hub Leonard, pitchers, and Duffy Lewis, a great outfielder, for $50,000, giving three lesser players in return. And during the 1919 season they got Carl Mays, a still better pitcher, for another $50,000. That year the Yankees climbed to third place and the Red Sox fell to sixth.

But Frazee still needed money. In 1919, he asked Ruppert for a $500,000 loan. Ruppert, instead, offered to buy Ruth. So Frazee sold Ruth for $100,000, and took a $350,000 loan.

Then, in a succession of one-sided trades with Frazee from 1920 to 1923, the Yankees acquired Waite Hoyt, Wally Schang, Joe Bush, Sam Jones, Herb Pennock, Joe Dugan, Deacon Scott, George Pipgras, Mike McNally and Harry Harper.

They were in business — and the Red Sox fell to last place. (Today, such a loan would not be permitted, on ethical grounds. When C.B.S. acquired the Yankees two years ago, the biggest objection raised was the possibility of conflict of interest, since some C.B.S. stock was held by other American League owners. They got rid of it.)

In 1920, with Ruth hitting an incredible total of 54 home runs (15 per cent of all home runs hit in the league), the Yankees ran third in a close race. In 1921, when Ruth hit 59 home runs, the Yankees won their first pennant. But they lost the World Series to the Giants.

Ruppert wasn't satisfied. He had brought in Ed Barrow, who had been field manager of the Red Sox, as business manager, a position that rarely existed in those days. The Giants, who recognized the advantage Ruth and victory were giving the Yankees in the battle for patronage, decided early in 1922 to push the Yankees out of the Polo Grounds, which both teams shared. Ruppert's reaction was to begin building Yankee Stadium across the Harlem River. Huston again disagreed and sold out, leaving Ruppert sole owner.

Both the Yankees and Giants won pennants again in 1922, and again the Giants won the Series. But in 1923, the Yankees opened the season in their own huge stadium. Ruth hit a home run. The Yankees won another pennant and drew more than 1,000,000 customers—almost 200,000 more than the Giants. This time, the Yankees won the World Series, too.

The dynasty had been established.

FOR the next decade, it was maintained by judicious purchases. In those days, minor-league clubs were

1936 On Sept. 9 the Yanks clinched the pennant. Their final standing—19½ games ahead of Detroit—set an American League record.

FINAL STANDING OF CLUBS

	New York.	Detroit.	Chicago.	Wash'gton.	Cleveland.	Boston.	St. Louis.	Phila'phia.	Won.	Lost.	Percentage
New York.		14	14	13	16	15	14	16	102	51	.667
Detroit......	8	—	14	11	13	9	11	17	83	71	.539
Chicago.....	7	8	—	16	12	10	13	15	81	70	.536
Wash'gton.	9	11	5	—	8	14	19	16	82	71	.536
Cleveland..	6	9	10	14	—	18	15	13	80	74	.519
Boston......	7	18	12	8	9	—	12	13	74	80	.481
St. Louis...	8	11	8	3	7	10	—	10	57	95	.375
Phila'phia.	6	5	7	6	9	9	11	—	53	100	.346
Games lost	51	71	70	71	74	80	95	100	—	—	

1966 On Sept. 9 the erstwhile Bombers were inhabiting the cellar (below). The team hasn't ended a season last since 1912.

Standing of the Clubs

	W.	L	Pc.	G.B.
Baltimore ..	89	51	.636	---
Detroit	79	62	.560	10½
Minnesota ..	77	65	.542	13
Chicago	73	70	.510	17½
Cleveland ..	72	71	.503	18½
California ..	70	70	.500	19
Washington	64	81	.441	27½
Kansas City.	63	80	.441	27½
Boston	64	82	.438	28
New York .	62	81	.434	28½

independently owned, and sold their best players each year to the highest bidders. In such a market, the Yankees had three big advantages. Barrow, an experienced baseball man, had complete business authority in evaluating talent; Ruppert, insatiable in his desire for winners, was willing to spend any amount of money; and the club, with Ruth and the new Stadium, was taking in more money at the gate than any other club. The Connie Macks and the Clark Griffiths, who owned teams and had as much baseball experience as Barrow, didn't have the money. The owners who had more money didn't have a Barrow in charge.

That was the secret of the first stage of Yankee power: money to spend, and a good baseball brain to spend it.

By the end of the nineteen-twenties, though, a superior team was developed by Connie Mack in Philadelphia. The Yankees won pennants in 1926-27-28, but the Athletics beat them out in 1929-30-31. It was still possible to compete with them.

But now the Depression had begun. The Athletics became "White Elephants," and Mack had to sell off his stars. Meanwhile, Sam Breadon and Branch Rickey, operating the St. Louis Cardinals, had developed the farm system idea. Since a farm system meant that the major-league team would take responsibility for supplying players and financing minor-league teams, it was an obvious solution to many minor-league problems during the Depression, as local owners failed right and left.

Barrow could see that a farm system was a fine way to develop future talent. Ruppert, whatever the general economic conditions were, still had plenty of money to spend. Barrow started pouring Yankee money into a farm operation, hiring scouts, acquiring teams, signing large numbers of young prospects.

And one of the men Ruppert and Barrow hired to run the farm system was George Weiss, who had been a successful minor-league operator in New Haven and Baltimore. Weiss, it developed, was a tireless and immensely effective executive.

In the late twenties and early thirties, the Yankees had been replenished by such purchases in the minors as Tony Lazzeri, Mark Koenig, Earle Combs, Frank Crosetti, Bob Muesel, Lefty Gomez, Bill Dickey. Lou Gehrig had been found right on the nearby Columbia campus. In 1930 they got Red Ruffing from the Red Sox.

And the last important minor-league purchase the Yankees made was the best. In 1933, an 18-year-old kid burned up the Pacific Coast League so impressively that his owner wouldn't sell him, holding out for a better price than those that had been bid. In 1934, the kid badly injured his knee, and all the prospective buyers shied off — except the high-quality Yankee scouts Barrow had hired. For $25,000, and five players to be delivered subsequently, the Yankees took an option on the convalescing player and let him play the 1935 season at San Francisco. He hit .398. His name was Joe DiMaggio, and in 1936 he started a new sequence of Yankee supremacy.

Meanwhile, the farm system had been established, and here again the Yankee wealth produced a unique advantage. The Yankees could keep the candidates who were clearly the best prospects; they could let more questionable, but still promising, cases mature; and they still had plenty of surplus to trade for an older player when an older player was needed to plug a particular gap in a pennant-contending situation.

Between 1928 and 1936 the Yankees won only one pennant, in 1932, but they finished second five times and third once. In 1936, with DiMaggio added, they had one of the most powerful teams ever assembled, comparable to the 1927 team for which Ruth had hit 60 home runs as it won 110 games.

The 1936 Yankees won the pennant by a 19½-game margin. And they won it in 1937, and 1938, and 1939— plus the World Series as well each time.

Now the cry, "Break up the Yankees," first heard in 1927, acquired a desperate timbre. The flow of material from the farms seemed overwhelming: Joe Gordon, Charlie Keller, Red Rolfe, Spud Chandler and a dozen others. And so, in 1940, a rule was passed aimed specifically at the Yankees: No team would be allowed to trade with the team that had won the pennant the previous year. But the Yankees did not win in 1940. Crippled by injuries, and perhaps victims of the law of averages, they ran third in an extremely close race. And the no-trading rule was promptly repealed.

But they did win again in 1941 (by 17 games), and in 1942 and 1943. Phil Rizzuto, Gerald Priddy, Marius Russo, Billy Johnson, Tiny Bonham, Atley Donald, Buddy Rosar — the stream from the farm system was a flood.

WORLD WAR II, it seemed, was what finally stopped the Yankees in 1944 and 1945, when all baseball was a disordered scramble. However, a totally new chapter was in the making. Ruppert had died in 1939, and Barrow had remained in charge as president. In 1945, Ruppert's heirs decided to sell. A three-man syndicate bought the club for $2,800,000. The three were Dan Topping, heir to a tin-and-banking fortune and well-known as a man-about-town and sports promoter; Del Webb, a self-made contractor who had prospered during the war years; and Larry MacPhail, the man who had introduced night baseball to the major leagues (in Cincinnati in 1935) and had brought the Brooklyn Dodgers out of the second division to the promised land of a National League pennant in 1941.

In 1946, the year the stars were all back from service, the Yankees finished a disappointing third. But in 1947 they won the pennant again, by 12 games—and a tumultuous seven-game World Series from the Dodgers. The victory party was even more tumultuous. MacPhail had a fight with his partners. They bought him out. Topping became president of the club, and Weiss moved in as general manager. In 1948, the Yankees finished third, missing the pennant by two games, and manager Bucky Harris was fired. Weiss made his own choice (backed by Webb) of a successor: Casey Stengel.

And so it happened that under Stengel came the greatest success of all: 10 pennants in 12 years, most of them in dramatic last-gasp races. The farm system was never better: Mantle, Ford, Howard, Berra, Vic Raschi, Gil McDougald, Hank Bauer, Bobby Brown, Jerry Coleman, Johnny Lindell—and later Bill Skowron, Tony Kubek, Bobby Richardson, Tom Tresh, Joe Pepitone, Mel Stottlemyre. When a veteran was needed, a whole group of young players could be traded for him (Johnny Sain, Maris, Bob Turley, Don Larsen, Bobby Shantz became Yankees in this way).

In 1960, Topping decided he could dispense with Stengel and Weiss, on grounds of finding "new blood." Houk, a coach under Stengel, had won the complete confidence of Topping and the Yankee players. He was a firm choice as Stengel's successor. He had had other offers, and if he weren't promoted now, Topping would lose him. So the 70-year-old Stengel would be "retired," and so would the 66-year-old Weiss. Roy Hamey, an experienced but not particularly forceful baseball man, with no great history of success, would replace

Weiss, and Topping himself would be more active.

Actually, Topping's thoughts boiled down to the idea that the machine was running so smoothly that nothing could upset it. And it certainly seemed that way for the next three years. Under Houk, for a while, at least, the team seemed stronger than ever, and 1961 was a banner year—attendance up, a decisive victory over Detroit in a race that stayed close until September, a home run spree by Maris that surpassed Ruth's record of 60 and an easy victory in the World Series.

But 1961 was also the year the league expanded to 10 teams. Some of the Yankee surplus strength was drawn off in stocking the new teams. And in 1962 the league was so weak that the Angels, one of the expansion teams, finished third. The Yankees won again, but attendance fell. In 1963, they won again, and so easily that an uncharacteristic idea was honored: Hamey, who hadn't been well, could retire; Houk, who had no front-office experience, could become general manager; and Yogi Berra, always popular with Yankee fans, could become manager, boosting the gate.

WHY was the idea uncharacteristic? Because it broke Yankee patterns in several significant ways. The front office had always been in the hands of an immensely experienced and strong executive—Barrow, MacPhail, Weiss. Even Hamey had held every conceivable baseball job, from league president down, before stepping in as head of the Yankee organization. And the field manager had also always been a man of tremendous experience in that peculiar profession—Huggins, McCarthy, Harris, Stengel. Houk, as Yankee manager, came especially well prepared for the specific team, having managed many of the key players in the farm system, and having served as a coach under Stengel.

But now the team on the field was to be put into the hands of a man whose playing career hadn't quite ended, and who had never managed anywhere; and into the front office went Houk, who had nothing whatever in his background to qualify for such a position beyond his native strong will, ambition and alertness.

It was a concept based on the arrogance that came with decades of supremacy. Anything we want to do, we can do, the Yankees seemed to say. So the peak was reached in 1961 —and extended, in a way, through 1963. Another pennant was going to

In 1936 DiMaggio (right, with Yankee owner Jacob Ruppert before a minor-league exhibition game) started a new cycle of Yank supremacy.

be won in 1964, but just barely. The underlying deterioration was well under way.

THERE were (and are) four main reasons for the decline.

First, the rules governing operation of the farm system were revised after World War II—at least partly in an attempt to counteract the overpowering success of teams like the Yankees. In the old days a major-league team could control hundreds of farm players, shuffling them from one minor league team to another, letting them develop slowly, stockpiling here, moving in for a man they wanted there, at just the right time.

Under today's regulations, no team can really control more than 40 players. The stockpiling of talent is not possible, however brilliant or hard-working a club's staff may be. If a team loads up its 40-man roster with promising youngsters, it gives up the veterans it needs to win in the majors. If it keeps the best older players, its minor league prospects will be picked off by weaker clubs. Thus, the traditional Yankee technique of rebuilding simply doesn't exist any more.

Other rules that had similar effects dealt with bonus players. By 1950, untried high school prospects were getting $100,000 just to sign a contract, as 16 major-league teams bid for the best ones. At first, limits were placed on the size of such payments, but these rules were widely ignored. Then it became compulsory to keep a "bonus player"—one who received more than a nominal amount—on the parent club for two years before he could be farmed out. Then first-year players, if not kept on the major club, could be drafted the next year for a nominal fee. Finally, in 1965, the "free-agent draft" went into effect. Now teams don't compete for prospects at all; they "draft" the right to negotiate—one team opting for one particular player, each time around—choosing in reverse order of the previous year's standings.

Second, an equalization of the power of money has occurred. There are no "poor" clubs in the major leagues today. While some may have greater resources than others, even the weakest have sufficient capital to operate effectively without selling talent to make ends meet. The expansion of radio and the development of television have greatly increased the revenues available to major-league clubs (at the expense of the minors, incidentally). Marketing methods—for tickets, concessions, etc.—have been modernized. The growth of suburban areas has broadened the base for customers wherever sufficient parking facilities exist.

Third, the talent pool of promising young players has, in general, been greatly diluted. As recently as a generation ago a career with one of the

16 major-league clubs was still the only realistic opportunity for wealth and fame as an athlete (except for boxing). Today young athletes can and do concentrate on football, basketball and golf—as tickets to college and as careers in themselves. The minor leagues in baseball no longer pay a competitive living wage. And the talent that is left is now spread among 20 teams—and in a few years will be spread among 24.

Fourth, along with more money have come know-how and aggressiveness in the front offices of most big-league teams. Where these qualities were once exceptional, they are now universal. Yankee victims learned from Yankee methods. The new owners—Ruppert-type owners—are men with vast resources in other businesses, interested in baseball for the prestige and fun of it and able to generate tremendous financial leverage under the tax laws that would have been impossible 30 or 40 years ago.

When the Yankees made it five pennants in a row in 1964, they still seemed unstoppable, but it was not so. Even under Weiss, in the late nineteen-fifties, they had started losing ground. As the new regulations piled up, they were increasingly facing what amounted to a stacked deck. By the nature of the game, only a couple of teams each year could be strong contenders, while five or six had to be also-rans. Whenever "socialistic"—or "equalizing"—legislation came up, the have-nots would be in the majority. Eventually, the have-nots prevailed.

With such rules in the offing, the Yankees needed front-office leadership of the highest calibre: first, to oppose such rules effectively; second, to devise totally new ways of operating under them. In the inexperienced Houk, and the less interested Topping, the Yankees didn't have them.

For Topping had become less interested. For personal and financial reasons, he had decided to sell the club (and Webb went along). He had passed 50; he had been married six times and had many children. Tax considerations and family obligations made him seek a buyer. C.B.S. became the buyer in August, 1964, paying $11.2 million for an 80-per-cent share of the club. Topping and Webb each kept 10 per cent.

UNDER Berra, the Yankees were floundering, but staying alive. C.B.S. made it clear that, for the time being, Topping and Houk would remain in charge. But both had become disenchanted with Yogi, and had decided to replace him.

By now, the Yankee team was essentially the same as it had been for three seasons. The usual rate of replacement wasn't working. The farm system was producing isolated bright spots, but not a steady flow. Nevertheless, the Yankees of 1964 made a

great drive in September and won the pennant on the next-to-last day. From one direction, they looked great, because they had just made it five championships in a row; but from another, it could be seen that they were essentially no better than the teams that finished second and third (Chicago and Baltimore). They had come back to the pack.

Houk and Topping, along with most baseball fans and experts, took the rosy view. They proceeded with the firing of Berra, and Keane was brought in (he had just resigned from the Cardinals after beating Berra in the World Series); a new era of invincibility was supposed to start in 1965.

It didn't. Injuries contributed to the debacle, but it was much more than that. Overnight, the 1965 Yankees were just another club. They finished sixth, out of the race for the first time in 40 years.

All last winter Yankee management tried to shrug off 1965 as a peculiar misfortune. But as soon as the new season began things looked just as bad. The team lost 16 of its first 20 games — and Keane was dropped. Houk returned to the dugout, leaving the front office, in effect, unoccupied. The team picked up momentarily, but Maris, Mantle and Ford got hurt again, and that was that.

And so, as the season wore on, the Yankees sank to the bottom. What promising young players there were were kept in the minors. (There are potential stars among them, but in nothing like the quantity of dynastic days.)

DID C.B.S. make a mistake? That depends on what it expects from the deal. One way or another, the Yankees will always do well enough to show a profit, although the size may fluctuate. Did Topping shrewdly "unload" a deteriorating property? Probably not, because if he had really recognized deterioration it might not have come so fast. Forces of the times were pulling the Yankees down to a common level, but the fall right through to the bottom, in two years, took everyone by surprise—including Topping. Two weeks ago, with the team locked in the cellar, he got out entirely, selling his 10 per cent interest (Webb had sold his in 1965) to C.B.S. and leaving the corporation in sole charge of the team.

The original deal had been based on Topping's friendship with William S. Paley, head of C.B.S., and came about partly because it made sense financially (the books showed sizable Yankee profits for a period of many years) and partly because C.B.S. thought to gain prestige by acquiring the elite of an "entertainment field."

The prestige aspect has blown up, once and for all. Yankee teams may win pennants again—may, in fact, win one fairly quickly—but for the forseeable future they will be "just another team," win or lose.

And the financial picture has one overriding blemish: Yankee Stadium itself. So magnificent when built, it is now obsolete structurally, hemmed in by what many consider a declining neighborhood, choked for parking space, less accessible through deteriorating public transportation and not as attractive as the city-built Shea Stadium that the Mets occupy. How much money should, or will, C.B.S. invest? Will the corporation build a new park, rebuild this one, or try to share Shea Stadium with the Mets? These are questions only the highest echelons of C.B.S. can answer.

Along with the collapse has come the evaporation of the Yankee *mystique*. Opponents no longer feel the awe, and the Yankee players themselves no longer feel the magic power. Nor do the Yankee fans, who rode so high for so long. Today, considering the uncertainties of the future, all concerned must take comfort from one thought: it sure was some dynasty while it lasted.

October 2, 1966

Frank Robinson of Orioles Named American League's Most Valuable Player

BALTIMORE TAKES THREE TOP PLACES

Brooks Robinson Is Second and Powell Third—Winner First to Pace 2 Leagues

By JOSEPH DURSO

Frank Robinson of the Baltimore Orioles was unanimously elected the most valuable player in the American League yesterday, and thereby became the first man in baseball history to win such an award in both major leagues.

The 31-year-old outfielder, who was traded to Baltimore by the Cincinnati Reds 11 months ago, finished far ahead of two teammates — Brooks Robinson and Boog Powell — giving the world champions the second one, two, three sweep since the voting began in 1931.

But the Orioles' joy was diminished when Robinson disclosed by telephone from his home in Los Angeles that he was facing an operation on his right knee.

"In May," he said, "I stretched the tendons in the knee and played the rest of the season in some pain. The doctors told me to rest for six weeks after the World Series. The six weeks are just about up now, and it still hurts.

"I'm a little skeptical about an operation, but I'm almost willing to be persuaded. We'll know in a few days. I'd be in the hospital 10 days and on crutches two or three weeks, and then I'd have to exercise it for two or three months."

He Played in 155 Games

Even with his stretched tendons, Robinson played in 155 games for the Orioles last season—after 11 years as a ranking star in the National League.

He paced the Orioles to their first pennant and a four-game sweep over the Los Angeles Dodgers in the series. And he won the triple crown by leading the league with 49 home runs, 122 runs batted in and a batting average of .316.

The general feeling was that the Orioles had achieved one of the great coups in sports trading—by acquiring Robinson from Cincinnati for Milt Pappas, Jack Baldschun and Dick Simpson.

Robinson was paid $70,000 for his labors this year, and the only cloud on the Baltimore horizon seemed to involve the amount he would demand next year.

However, the ultimate cost of Robinson's surgery to the club immediately pre-empted all concern about the cost of Robinson's services to the club.

Meanwhile, the right-handed slugger completed one of baseball's most remarkable success stories. He had been named most valuable player in the National League in 1961, but had slipped to 18th place in the voting last year just before being traded.

Ballots for the award are cast by two baseball writers in each league city, and the voting this season produced these unusual results:

¶The Orioles duplicated the sweep of Nelson Fox, Luis Aparicio and Early Wynn of the 1959 Chicago White Sox.

¶Robinson became the third player in 35 years to win all the first-place votes. The others were Al Rosen of the 1953 Cleveland Indians and Mickey Mantle of the 1956 New York Yankees.

¶The Yankees placed no one in the top 10 this year—for the first time in their history.

November 9, 1966

Baltimore Orioles

The 1966 Balloting

	Pts.
Frank Robinson, Baltimore	280
Brooks Robinson, Baltimore	153
Boog Powell, Baltimore	122
Harmon Killebrew, Minnesota	96
Jim Kaat, Minnesota	84
Tony Oliva, Minnesota	78
Al Kaline, Detroit	66
Tommy Agee, Chicago	63
Luis Aparicio, Baltimore	51
Bert Campaneris, Kan. City	36
Stu Miller, Baltimore	25
Norm Cash, Detroit	23
Jack Aker, Kansas City	22
Bobby Knoop, California	14
Earl Wilson, Detroit	13
Bill Freehan, Detroit	9

Andy Etchebarren, Baltimore	7
Mickey Mantle, New York	5
Tom Tresh, New York	5
Jack Sanford, California	4
Rick Reichardt, California	4
Fred Valentine, Washington	4
Willie Horton, Detroit	4
Leon Wagner, Cleveland	4
Joe Pepitone, New York	2
Tony Conigliaro, Boston	1
Pete Richert, Washington	1
Sonny Siebert, Cleveland	1
Carl Yastrzemski, Boston	1
Jim Fregosi, California	1

A first-place vote is worth 14 points, a second-place vote 9 points, third-place 8, fourth-place 7 and so on down to 1 point for a 10th-place vote.

Rickey and Lloyd Waner Elected

EXECUTIVE SET UP FIRST FARM CLUBS

He Also Broke Color Line—Waner Holds Singles Mark and Hit .316 for 19 Years

The late Branch Rickey, who broke baseball's color line, and Lloyd (Little Poison) Waner, half of one of the sport's greatest brother acts with the Pittsburgh Pirates, were elected yesterday to the Hall of Fame. Their selection was made unanimously by the 10-man Veterans' Committee of the Baseball Writers' Association of America.

Rickey, who died last year at the age of 84, signed Jackie Robinson, who became the first Negro player in the major leagues. Rickey also developed the farm system, and established baseball dynasties with the St. Louis Cardinals and Brooklyn Dodgers and laid the groundwork for the Pittsburgh Pirates' championship team in 1960.

The last baseball venture of Rickey, known as the "Mahatma," ended in failure when he tried to establish the Continental League as a third major league. His efforts paid off to some extent by forcing the American and National Leagues to expand from eight to 10 clubs, however.

Famous as Singles Hitter

Waner, who spent 19 years in the majors, joins his late brother, Paul, who was nicknamed "Big Poison," in the Hall of Fame. Lloyd, 61, now lives in Oklahoma City. He became famous for his ability to punch out singles during his career, posting a career batting average of .316 in 1,993 games and collecting 2,459 hits. He led the National League in singles four times and established a modern record with 198 singles in 1927.

Waner played 15 seasons with Pittsburgh before he was traded to Boston and then to Cincinnati in 1941. In 1942, he was unconditionally released by Cincinnati and signed by the Philadelphia Phillies, who later traded him to the Brooklyn Dodgers. He temporarily retired in 1943 after going to Brooklyn, but came out of retirement in 1944 to play for the Dodgers again.

He Began as a Catcher

A bushy-browed ex-farm boy, Rickey started his major-league career as a catcher with Cincinnati in 1904 and played for the St. Louis Browns and New York Yankees. During his colorful 57-year career, he managed the St. Louis Browns and Cardinals and took over the Brooklyn Dodgers in 1942. He also served as general manager of the Pirates.

The Cardinals were turned into title teams by Rickey in the nineteen-twenties, thirties and early forties, and he also met with success with the Dodgers during the late forties and early fifties. He then went to Pittsburgh, but was dismissed before the club won the world championship.

When Rickey took over the Cardinals, he was forced to develop a farm system since his club didn't have enough cash or talent to deal for better players on the other teams. In 1946, Robinson was signed by Rickey to play for Montreal of the International League, and Rickey's judgment proved successful again when Robinson developed into a star.

In St. Louis, Rickey's widow, Mrs. Jane Rickey, was "just delighted" at the selection of her late husband for organized baseball's highest honor.

Mrs. Rickey said that despite the joy she knew her husband would have felt at being named, he actually had derived more pleasure out of being a member of the Hall of Fame's nominating committee.

"He felt very much that rather than being voted into the Hall of Fame himself, he would prefer to be on the nominating committee and being allowed to put in the names of the people he knew so many years and ones he felt should be in the Hall of Fame."

January 30, 1967

Ruffing Is Named to Hall of Fame

EX-YANK PITCHER DEFEATS MEDWICK

Ruffing Selected on 260 of 306 Votes by Writers—Campanella Is Third

By DAVE ANDERSON

Charles Herbert (Red) Ruffing, who acknowledged that he had become "a little bitter" at not being elected to the Baseball Hall of Fame in recent years, mellowed somewhat yesterday.

Ruffing, the winner of 273 major-league games as a right-handed pitcher (231 for the New York Yankees), was voted into the red-brick shrine at Cooperstown, N. Y. on a special run-off ballot conducted by the Baseball Writers' Association of America.

The 61-year-old Ruffing was named on 260 of 306 votes counted yesterday by Jack Lang, the secretary of the writers' group, at the office of the Commissioner of Baseball, William D. Eckert.

Joe Medwick, a slugging outfielder with the St. Louis Cardinals three decades ago, was second with 248 votes. Medwick also received more than 75 per cent of the vote necessary for election. Ruffing had 87 per cent, Medwick 81 per cent. But under the rules of a run-off ballot, only the top vote-getter is selected unless there is a tie.

The run-off ballot had developed when no former player earned 75 per cent of the vote in the original ballot last month.

170 Name Campanella

In that vote Ruffing and Medwick had tied, each with 212 votes of a possible 292. Roy Campanella, a hard-hitting catcher for the Dodgers when they represented Brooklyn, was third in the original ballot with 204 votes. In the run-off, Campy's name was on 170 ballots.

Two others, Luke Appling in 1964 and Charlie Gehringer in 1959, had qualified on similar run-off ballots.

Ruffing will be enshrined at Cooperstown on July 24, along with Lloyd Warner and the late Branch Rickey. Waner, who had teamed with his brother Paul in the outfield for the Pittsburgh Pirates, and Rickey, a front-office genius with the Dodgers and Cardinals, were named on Jan. 29 by the Old Timers Committee.

Had Ruffing been snubbed this year, he would have come under the jurisdiction of the Old-Timers Committee. For Medwick next year's ballot will be his last chance with the writers.

"I hope to God that Joe makes it." Ruffing said over a telephonic loudspeaker from his home in Beachwood, Ohio. "I was a little leery that he'd beat me out this time. When it comes to a choice between a pitcher and an outfielder or infielder who plays every day, they kind of lean toward them a little."

Delay Annoys Ruffing

Ruffing, the pitching coach of the New York Mets in 1961 but now out of baseball, sounded annoyed at the delay in his election and also at his unemployment.

"I was a little bitter," he said. "If they put men in for their record, I think I should have been in before. I was wondering if it was a popularity contest or if they were going on a man's record. I think if a man plays 20 years in the major leagues he should be in automatically."

Ruffing, a 6-feet-1-inch 210 pounder, toiled 22 seasons with the Boston Red Sox, Yankees and Chicago White Sox despite the loss of four toes in his left foot in a coal mine accident in Nokomis, Ill.

February 17, 1967

Two Oriole Pitchers Hold Tigers Hitless, but Lose, 2-1

BARBER IN CHARGE FOR 8⅔ INNINGS

Tigers Get 2 Runs on Wild Pitch and Error in 9th —Win 2d Game, 6-4

BALTIMORE, April 30 (AP) —Steve Barber, pitching 8-2/3 innings, and Stu Miller held Detroit hitless today, but the Tigers still won the opener of a doubleheader, 2-1, from the Baltimore Orioles. Detroit scored two ninth-inning runs on a wild pitch and an error. The Tigers also took the second game, 6-4, and moved into first place by half a game.

The performance by Barber and Miller was the first time in baseball history that two pitchers combined for a no-hitter and lost in nine innings. Ken Johnson, then with the Houston Astros, is the only one

FIRST GAME

DETROIT (A.)	ab.r.h.bi	BALTIMORE (A.)	ab.r.h.bi
McAuliffe, 2b	3 0 0 0	Aparicio, ss	3 0 0 1
Horton, ph	1 0 0 0	Snyder, cf	4 0 0 0
Lumpe, 2b	0 0 0 0	F. Rob'son, rf	4 0 1 0
Stanley, cf	2 0 0 0	B. Rob'son, 3b	3 0 0 0
Wert, 3b	3 0 0 0	Epstein, 1o	4 0 0 0
Kaline, rf	3 0 0 0	Blefary, lf	2 1 0 0
Northrup, lf	4 0 0 0	Held, 2b	2 0 0 0
Freehan, c	1 0 0 0	Haney, c	0 0 0 0
Cash, 1b	1 0 0 0	Etcheb'rren, c	2 0 1 0
Tracewski, ss	0 1 0 0	Lau, ph	1 0 0 0
Oyler, ss	2 0 0 0	Belanger, 2b	0 0 0 0
Wood, 1b	0 1 0 0	Barber, p	1 0 0 0
Wilson, p	3 0 0 0	S. Miller, p	0 0 0 0
Gladding, p	0 0 0 0		
Total	24 2 0 0	Total	25 1 2 1

Detroit .... 0 0 0 0 0 0 0 0 2—2
Baltimore .... 0 0 0 0 0 0 0 1 x—1

E—Kaline, Barber, Belanger. DP—Detroit 1, Baltimore 1. LOB—Detroit 11, Baltimore 4. S—Cash, Oyler, Wert, Wilson, Barber, Held. SF—Aparicio. SB—Freehan, F. Robinson.

	IP.	H.	R.	ER.BB.SO.
Wilson (W, 2-2)	8	2	1	1 4 4
Gladding	1	0	0	0 0 1
Barber (L, 2-1)	8⅔	0	2	1 10 3
S. Miller	⅓	0	0	0 0 0

HBP—By Barber (McAuliffe, Freehan). Wild pitch—Barber.
T—2:38.

to pitch a no-hitter and lose in nine innings. He was beaten by the Cincinnati Reds, 1-0, April 23, 1964.

Barber, who had a no-hit bid against the California Angels ruined by Jim Fregosi's one-out double in the ninth in his first start this year, came within one out of a 1-0 no-hit victory.

But the 28-year-old left-hander, who walked seven and hit a batter over the first eight

SECOND GAME

DETROIT (A.)	ab.r.h.bi	BALTIMORE (A.)	ab.r.h.bi
McAuliffe, 2b	4 1 1 0	Aparicio, ss	5 0 2 0
Wert, 3b	5 1 1 1	Snyder, cf	0 0 0 0
Brown, lf	4 1 1 1	Blair, cf	3 1 2 2
Stanley, cf	0 0 0 0	F. Rob'son, rf	4 0 1 1
Kaline, rf	4 1 1 2	B. Rob'son, 3b	4 0 0 0
Northrup, cf	4 0 1 0	Blefary, lf	4 1 2 1
Cash, 1b	3 1 3 2	Epstein, 1b	4 0 1 0
Freehan, c	4 0 0 0	Held, 2b	3 0 0 0
Oyler, 2b	3 1 0 0	Haney, c	4 1 1 0
Sparma, p	2 0 0 0	Palmer, p	1 0 0 0
Wick'sham, p	1 0 0 0	Wyatt, p	0 0 0 0
		B. Johns'n, ph	1 0 0 0
		Watt, p	0 0 0 0
		Bowens, ph	1 1 1 0
		Fisher, p	0 0 0 0
		Lau, ph	1 0 0 0
Total	33 6 8 6	Total	35 4 10 4

Detroit .... 0 0 0 0 6 0 0 0 0—6
Baltimore .... 0 0 1 0 0 1 2 0 0—4

E—Aparicio. DP—Detroit 2. LOB—Detroit 5, Baltimore 7. 2B—Northrup, Kaline, F. Robinson, 3B—McAuliffe. HRS—Cash (2), Blefary (5). S—Sparma.

	IP.	H.	R.	ER.BB.SO.
Sparma (W, 2-0)	6	7	4	4 3 3
Wickersham	3	3	0	0 0 2
Palmer (L, 1-1)	5	6	6	6 4 3
Watt	2	0	0	0 0 2
Fisher	2	2	0	0 0 0

T—2:30. A—26,884.

innings, issued successive walks to Norm Cash and Ray Oyler at the start of the ninth.

Earl Wilson sacrificed the runners to second and third and, after Willie Horton fouled out to the catcher, Larry Haney, Barber threw a wild pitch and a pinch runner, Dick Tracewski, scored the tying run.

Barber then walked Mickey Stanley and was replaced by Miller.

Don Wert lashed a grounder up the middle. Luis Aparicio raced to his left and came up with the ball, but the second baseman, Mark Belanger, dropped Aparicio's throw on the attempted forceout for an error as Wood scored the winning run.

Wilson, who had allowed only two hits through eight innings, gave way to Fred Gladding in the ninth and the reliever retired the Orioles in order.

The Orioles had scored a run in the eighth without a hit to take a 1-0 lead. Wilson walked Curt Blefary and Woodie Held sacrificed. Charlie Lau drew an intentional walk, but Wilson also walked Barber, filling the bases. Aparicio then delivered the run with a sacrifice fly to left.

In 1956, three Cincinnati pitchers—John Klippstein, Hershell Freeman and Joe Black—combined for nine hitless innings against Milwaukee, but the Braves got to Black for a hit in the 10th and then won the game in the 11th inning, 2-1.

Other pitchers have gone past nine innings with a no-hitter, but Johnson is the only pitcher to lose in a regulation nine-inning game.

May 1, 1967

National League Wins Longest All-Star Game, 2-1

AMERICAN LEAGUE LOSES 5TH IN ROW

Allen and Brooks Robinson Also Clout Homers — 30 Strike-Outs Set Record

By JOSEPH DURSO
Special to The New York Times

ANAHEIM, Calif., July 11—The National League won baseball's 38th and longest All-Star Game today by defeating the American League, 2-1, on a 15th-inning home run by Tony Perez of the Cincinnati Reds.

It was the fifth straight victory for the National Leaguers and their 16th in the last 21

games. And it required 3¾ hours of overpowering pitching on both sides, plus four records, before a decision was reached.

A crowd of 46,309 sat in hot, sunny weather in the $20-million home of Gene Autry's California Angels in suburban Los Angeles as the pitching parade passed by.

Richie Allen of Philadelphia hit a home run off Dean Chance of Minnesota in the second inning. Brooks Robinson of Baltimore hit one off Ferguson Jenkins of Chicago in the sixth inning. And then nobody else scored until Perez went to bat in the 15th in his first All-Star Game and hit a 375-foot home run to left-center field off Jim (Catfish) Hunter of Kansas City.

Seaver Protects Lead

Then, in the last half of the 15th, a kind of footnote to All-Star history was written when Manager Walter Alston of Los

Angeles turned his team's one run lead over to the only man in California wearing a New York Mets uniform.

He called in Tom Seaver, the Mets' 22-year-old rookie, to replace Don Drysdale and protect the National League's margin.

Seaver, who is used to living dangerously, walked one batter, Carl Yastrzemski, but he struck out Ken Berry of Chicago for the final out and for the 30th strike-out of baseball's longest All-Star show.

The following records were set in deciding the issue here in the citrus-and-neon groves of Orange County, the shrine of Mickey Mouse, Donald Duck and other Walt Disney heroes —and today the center of baseball:

¶Length of the game—15 innings, surpassing the previous marathon of 14 innings, which the National League won in

1950 on a home run by Red Schoendienst.

¶Total number of strike-outs —30, demolishing the former record of 20, set in 12 innings in 1955. Today's mark was divided as follows: 17 American Leaguers and 13 National Leaguers fanned. Along the way, they also broke the record for strike-outs in nine innings, which had been a mere 18.

¶Strike-outs by one pitcher—six, by Jenkins, the Canadian prodigy of the Chicago Cubs. He followed Juan Marichal, pitched the three normally middle innings and equaled the six strike-outs of Carl Hubbell in 1934, Johnny Vander Meer in 1943 and Larry Jansen in 1950.

¶Strike-outs by one batter—four, by Roberto Clemente of Pittsburgh. In its way, this was the most astonishing. Clemente, the winner of two batting titles, arrived in the West with an average of .352. But after beat-

Box Score of All-Star Game

NATIONAL	AB.	R.	H.	BI.	PO.	A.
Brock, lf......	2	0	0	0	2	0
cMays, ph, cf..	4	0	0	0	3	0
Clemente, rf...	6	0	1	0	6	0
Aaron, cf, lf...	6	0	1	0	2	0
Cepeda, 1b.....	6	0	0	0	6	0
Allen, 3b......	4	1	1	1	0	2
Perez, 3b......	2	1	1	1	0	3
Torre, c.......	2	0	0	4	1	
Haller, c.......	1	0	0	0	7	0
gBanks, ph.....	1	0	1	0	0	0
McCarver, c....	2	0	2	0	7	1
Mazeroski, 2b..	4	0	0	0	7	1
Drysdale, p....	0	0	0	0	0	0
kHelms, ph.....	1	0	0	0	0	0
Seaver, p......	0	0	0	0	0	0
Alley, ss......	5	0	0	0	1	3
Marichal, p....	1	0	0	0	0	0
Jenkins, p.....	1	0	0	0	0	0
Gibson, p......	0	0	0	0	0	1
tWynn, ph......	1	0	1	0	0	0
Short, p.......	0	0	0	0	0	1
iStaub, ph.....	1	0	1	0	0	0
Cuellar, p.....	0	0	0	0	0	0
jRose, ph, 2b..	1	0	0	0	0	0
Total 51	2	9	2	45	13	

AMERICAN	AB.	R.	H.	BI.	PO.	A.
B. Robi'son, 3b	6	1	1	1	0	6
Carew, 2b ..	3	0	0	0	2	2
McAuliffe, 2b..	3	0	0	0	3	2
Oliva, cf..	6	0	2	0	4	0
Killebrew, 1b..	6	0	0	0	15	1
Conigliaro, rf..	6	0	0	0	4	0
Yastrzemski, lf..	4	0	3	0	2	0
Freehan, c....	5	0	0	0	13	0
Petrocelli, ss...	1	0	0	0	0	1
McGlothlin, p...	0	0	0	0	0	0
bMantle, ph...	1	0	0	0	0	0
Peters, p....	0	0	0	0	0	1
dMincher, ph...	1	0	1	0	0	0
eAgee, pr ...	0	0	0	0	0	0
Downing, p....	0	0	0	0	0	0
hAlvis, ph....	1	0	0	0	0	0
Hunter, p.....	1	0	0	0	0	0
iBerry, ph....	1	0	0	0	0	0
Chance, p	0	0	0	0	0	0
jFregosi, ph, ss	4	0	1	0	2	3
Total 49	1	8	1	45	16	

a Singled for Chance in 3d; b Struck out for McGlothlin in 5th; c Struck out for Brock in 6th; d Singled for Peters in 8th; e Ran for Mincher in 8th; f Singled for Gibson in 9th; g Singled for Haller in 10th; h Grounded into fielders' choice for Downing in 10th; i Singled for Short in 11th; i Flied out for Cuellar in 13th; k Grounded into double play for Drysdale in 15th; l Struck out for Hunter in 15th.

```
National .............. 0 1 0  0 0 0  0 0 0  0 0 0  0 0 1—2
American .............. 0 0 0  0 0 1  0 0 0  0 0 0  0 0 0—1
```

Double play—Robinson, Carew and Killebrew; McAuliffe and Killebrew. Left on bases—National 5, American 7. Two-base hit—Yastrzemski, McCarver. Three-base hit—None. Home runs—Allen, B. Robinson, Perez. Stolen base—Aaron. Sacrifice—Freehan, Mazeroski. Sacrifice fly—None.

	I.P.	H.	R.	E.R.	B.B.	S.O.	H.B.P.	W.P.	Blk.
Chance	1		1	0	1	0	0	0	0
McGlothlin	2	1	0	0	2	1	0	0	0
Peters	2	1	0	0	0	4	0	0	0
Downing	2	2	0	0	0	2	0	0	0
Hunter (L.)	5	2	1	0	0	4	0	0	0
Marichal	3	1	0	0	0	3	0	0	0
Jenkins	3	3	1	1	0	6	0	0	0
Gibson	2	2	0	0	0	2	0	0	0
Short	2	0	0	0	1	1	0	0	0
Cuellar	2	0	0	0	0	2	0	0	0
Drysdale (W.)	2	1	0	0	0	2	0	0	0
Seaver	1	0	0	0	1	1	0	0	0

Bases on balls—Off Short (Yastrzemski), off Seaver (Yastrzemski). Struck out—By Marichal 3 (Oliva, Yastrzemski, Freehan), Jenkins 6 (Killebrew, Conigliaro, Mantle, Fregosi, Carew, Oliva), Gibson 2 (Conigliaro, Freehan), Short 1 (Fregosi), Cuellar 2 (B. Robinson, Oliva), Drysdale 2 (Hunter, Killebrew), Seaver 1 (Berry), Chance 1 (Clemente), McGlothlin 2 (Allen, Alley), Peters 4 (Mays, Clemente, Cepeda, Allen), Downing 2 (Clemente, Allen), Hunter 4 (Alley 2, Clemente, Perez).

Umpires—Runge (A.), plate; Secory (N.), first base; Dimuro (A.), second base; Burkhart (N.), third base; Ashford (A.) and Pelekoudas (N.), foul lines. Time of game—3:41. Attendance—46,309.

ing out a minihit in the first inning, he struck out four times in a row.

Marichal Allows One Hit

A record for courage was probably set, too, by the home-plate umpire, Ed Runge. He was officiating when the most poignant moments of the game were reached within a matter of minutes. First, Mickey Mantle pinch-hit for the American League in the fifth inning to a roaring, standing ovation; a few minutes later, Willie Mays pinch-hit for the National League to a similar roaring, standing ovation.

Both had come into the big leagues in 1951 and both had hit more than 500 home runs. Both were bypassed in the voting by the players, and both were named to the All-Star teams by the managers. Runge called both out on strikes.

All these wondrous things were seen for the first time by a "prime time" television audience in the East. The game started at 4:25 P.M., Pacific Daylight Time, putting it on home screens along the Atlantic Seaboard at 7:15 P.M. And the novel arrangement cast a long shadow toward the time when All-Star Games and even World Series would be played (and televised) at night.

The long day's journey into night began with Dean Chance of Minnesota pitching against Marichal, the impresario of San Francisco, a man with one of the fanciest records in All-Star history. In five previous games,

the 28-year-old Dominican had allowed only six hits and one run.

For three innings today he showed the American League what has tormented the National for half a dozen years. He retired eight straight batters before Jim Fregosi singled. But then he got Brooks Robinson on a grounder (for the second time), and turned the pitching over to Jenkins, Bob Gibson, Chris Short, Mike Cuellar, Drysdale and Seaver.

Chance, meanwhile, was faring almost as well. Clemente chopped a pitch to the right side in the first and beat it out. Henry Aaron, who forced Clemente, stole second base. But otherwise Chance's only bad moment came in the top of the second inning when Allen led off.

The Philadelphia slugger dorve Chance's third pitch deep in the temporary bleachers in right-center past the 393-foot marker, and the Nationals had a one-run lead.

Chance was succeeded in the fourth by Jim McGlothlin, the 23-year-old redhead who pitches for California. The young right-hander was nicked for a single by the first batter, Aaron, but he got both Aaron and Orlando Cepeda on a double-play grounder and then struck out Allen.

The American League tried to break through Jenkins's service in the fourth when Tony Oliva singled over second base with one down. But he was caught stealing and Harmon Killebrew of Minnesota looked at a third strike.

McGlothlin, throwing a giant-sized dropping curve, retired

Joe Torre, Bill Mazeroski and Gene Alley in order in the fifth. And then the Americans stirred again.

After Tony Conigliaro had struck out, Yastrzemski hit a low line drive to center field. Aaron, normally a right-fielder, appeared to lose the ball in the haze as he ran in, then got his glove on it briefly before it squirted away for a double.

However, Jenkins retired Bill Freehan of Detroit on a pop fly to shortstop and then caught Mantle looking at a fast ball for a third strike.

Robinson Hit Ties Score

In the bottom of the sixth, the Nationals suddenly lost their lead. Robinson, playing in his 11th straight All-Star Game at third base, lined Jenkins's second pitch into the left-field bull pen for his first home run in the series.

That tied the score, and the score stayed tied for the next eight innings.

McGlothlin was followed by Gary Peters, Al Downing and Hunter, and except for the home-run hitters nobody got past second base until the 13th. At one stretch, between the fourth and ninth innings, McGlothlin and Peters retired 15 batters in a row.

The American Leaguers might have capitalized on this air-tight pitching several times. Yastrzemski, for example, got on base five straight times on three hits and two walks, but four times in extra innings, the American Leaguers ended their time at bat with strike-outs.

Hunter Victim of Perez's Hit

Then, in the bottom of the 15th, just as the teams set the record for endurance, the end came fast.

Hunter was pitching his fifth inning by then, which was a distinction in itself. He was the first man to pitch more than four innings since Johnny Antonelli in the 1956 game. He is so talented that, at 21 years of age, he already has been on two All-Star teams. But when he tired today, it proved fatal.

Hunter's peak had come two innings earlier when Tim McCarver doubled into the left-field corner with nobody out and was bunted to third. But Catfish struck out Alley and retired Pete Rose on a fly to center.

In the 15th, though, Cepeda opened with a fly to deep right. Conigliaro, who had made the catch of the day in the 10th on Cepeda, got this one, too. Then up came Perez.

The 25-year-old right-handed infielder was born in Cuba, lives in Puerto Rico and works in Cincinnati. He had been filling in for Allen at third base since the 10th inning. He took a strike from Hunter, then drilled the ball 375 feet into the seats in left-center. And after the Mets' Mr. Seaver had held the fort in the bottom of the 15th, the longest All-Star game in history was over.

July 12, 1967

Chance Hurls No-Hitter

PITCHER TRIUMPHS OVER INDIANS, 2-1

Strikes Out 8, Walks 5—Twins Take Opener, 6-5 —Lead by Half-Game

CLEVELAND, Aug. 25 (AP)—Dean Chance of Minnesota pitched a no-hit game against the Cleveland Indians tonight and the Twins moved into first place with a 2-1 victory in the second game of a twilight-night double-header.

The Twins won the first game, 6-5, in 10 innings. The Twins now lead the second-place Chicago White Sox by a half-game. The Boston Red Sox are third, also a half-game out of first but a percentage point behind Chicago.

Just 19 days ago, Chance pitched five perfect innings, defeating Boston, 2-0, in a rain-shortened game. Although he was credited with a complete game for that performance, organized baseball records list only no-hitters of nine or more innings.

Chance Walks Five

Chance struck out eight but was wild, walking five batters, including the first two he faced.

He allowed a run without a hit in the first inning when Lee Maye and Vic Davalillo opened with walks. An error by Cesar Tovar loaded the bases for the Indians, and then Chance's wild pitch allowed Maye to score.

But Chance escaped the jam by striking out Max Alvis and getting Joe Azcue on a fly ball.

The Twins' 26-year-old right-hander walked the leadoff man in two other innings, passing Maye again in the third and Vern Fuller in the fifth. He also walked Chuck Hinton in the sixth.

The Twins got their first run against Sonny Siebert in the second inning when Tony Oliva opened with a single and raced all the way home on Harmon Killebrew's single.

Killebrew Snaps Tie

It was Oliva's single and Killebrew's triple that broke a 4-4 tie and gave the Twins their victory in the opener.

With one out in the sixth of the second game Cesar Tovar singled and raced to third on Oliva's hit. Then Siebert balked Tovar across.

After that, Chance was in complete control. He walked Hinton in the sixth, but a double play bailed him out of the inning and then he set down the last nine batters.

In the ninth, Chance got a swinging strike on Vic Davalillo before retiring him on a bouncer to Rod Carew.

Then Carew, the Twins' second baseman, made a brilliant play to save the no-hitter. Hinton tapped a slow roller past Chance, who fell down trying to field the ball. But Carew dashed in, scooped up the ball and threw Hinton out.

Tony Horton then bounced the next pitch to Tovar at third, and Chance had his masterpiece.

FIRST GAME

MINNESOTA (A.)	ab.	r.	h.	bi	CLEVELAND (A.)	ab.	r.	h.	bi
Carew, 2b	5	0	0	0	Hinton, rf	5	2	3	1
Uhlaender, cf	5	3	2	2	Davalillo, cf	5	1	2	0
Tovar, 3b	4	0	1	0	Wagner, lf	4	0	1	1
Oliva, rf	4	1	2	1	Horton, 1b	5	0	0	0
Killebrew, 1b	4	1	3	2	Alvis, 3b	5	1	2	1
Valdespino, lf	4	0	1	1	Sims, c	4	0	2	0
Izquierdo, c	3	0	0	0	Salmon, pr	0	0	0	0
Reese, ph	1	0	0	0	Azcue, c	1	1	1	1
Versalles, ss	5	0	0	0	Fuller, 2b	5	0	0	0
Hernandez, ss	3	0	1	0	Brown, ss	5	0	0	0
Allison, ph	1	0	0	0	Williams, p	1	0	0	0
Zimmerman, c	1	0	1	0	King, ph	1	0	0	0
Grant, p	2	1	2	0	Allen, p	0	0	0	0
Roland, p	0	0	0	0	Maye, ph	0	0	0	0
Perry, p	0	0	0	0	Demeter, ph	1	0	1	1
Kline, p	2	0	0	0	Pena, p	0	0	0	0
					Whitfield, ph	1	0	0	0
Total	40	6	13	6	O'Donoghue, p	0	0	0	0
					Total	43	5	13	5

Minnesota .... 1 0 1 2 0 0 0 0 2—6
Cleveland .... 1 0 0 1 1 0 0 0 1—5
E—Brown, Hernandez. LOB—Minnesota 9, Cleveland 9. 2B—Demeter. 3B—Killebrew. HR—Hinton (8), Uhlaender (6), Azcue (9). S—Tovar, Grant. SF—Oliva, Valdespino.

	IP.	H.	R.	ER.	BB.	SO.
Grant	5⅓	9	4	4	0	3
Roland	0	1	0	0	0	0
Perry	⅓	0	0	0	0	0
Kline (W, 6-0)	4	3	1	1	1	2
Williams	5	8	4	3	1	4
R. Allen	1	1	0	0	0	2
Pena	3	1	0	0	0	2
O'Donoghue (L, 7-7)	1	3	2	2	0	2

Balk—H. Allen.
T—3:10.

SECOND GAME

MINNESOTA (A.)	ab.	r.	h.	bi	CLEVELAND (A.)	ab.	r.	h.	bi
Carew, 2b	5	0	1	0	Maye, lf	2	1	0	0
Uhlaender, cf	4	0	1	0	Davalillo, cf	3	0	0	0
Tovar, 3b	4	1	1	0	Hinton, rf	3	0	0	0
Oliva, rf	3	1	2	0	Horton, 1b	4	0	0	0
Killebrew, 1b	3	0	2	1	Alvis, 3b	3	0	0	0
Valdespino, lf	4	0	0	0	Azcue, c	3	0	0	0
Zimmerman, c	3	0	0	0	Whitfield, 2b	1	0	0	0
Versalles, ss	3	0	0	0	Fuller, 2b	1	0	0	0
Hernandez, ss	3	0	0	0	Gonzalez, 2b	0	0	0	0
Reese, ph	1	0	0	0	Brown, ss	3	0	0	0
Chance, p	3	0	0	0	Siebert, p	2	0	0	0
					Wagner, ph	1	0	0	0
Total	33	2	7	1	Culver, p	0	0	0	0
					Total	26	1	0	0

Minnesota .... 0 1 0 0 0 1 0 0 0—2
Cleveland .... 1 0 0 0 0 0 0 0 0—1
E—Tovar. DP—Minnesota 2, Cleveland 1. LOB—Minnesota 8, Cleveland 3. 2B—Carew.

	IP.	H.	R.	ER.	BB.	SO.
Chance (W, 17-9)	9	0	1	1	5	8
Siebert (L, 6-1)	8	7	2	2	2	7
Culver	1	0	0	0	2	1

HBP—By Siebert (Chance). Wild pitches—Chance, Culver. Balk—Siebert.
T—2:46; A—10,519.

August 26, 1967

Red Sox Win Pennant

BOSTON RALLY LED BY YASTRZEMSKI

Star Bats Across 2 Tallies in 5-Run 6th and Gets 4 Hits—Lonborg Wins 22d

By JOSEPH DURSO
Special to The New York Times

BOSTON, Oct. 1—The Boston Red Sox completed one of baseball's great rags-to-riches stories today by defeating the Minnesota Twins, 5-3, and winning the tightest American League pennant race in history.

They won it before a roaring crowd of 35,770 persons in the 162d and final game of the season, one year after they had finished ninth in the league and 21 years after they had won their last pennant.

They also won it in a dramatic tale of two baseball cities with help from the California Angels, the final hurdle standing between the Detroit Tigers and a possible playoff.

But when the Tigers lost to the Angels, 8-5, in the second game of their double-header in Detroit—and in the last game of their season—the three-team free-for-all was finally ended. The Tigers and Twins finished in a tie for second, one game behind.

Series Starts Wednesday

As a result, the Red Sox—a second-division team for nine years — will open the 64th World Series on Wednesday against the St. Louis Cardinals.

They will open it in Fenway Park, where the Red Sox won their second straight game over Minnesota today behind the seven-hit pitching of Jim Lonborg and four straight hits by Carl Yastrzemski.

Yastrzemski, with three singles and a double, batted across two runs for the Red Sox. They were both scored in the sixth inning of a gripping struggle, when the Red Sox rallied for five runs and overcame a 2-0 lead that Minnesota had built for Dean Chance.

Two innings later, Yastrzemski made a key throw from left field to second base killing a counter-rally staged by Minnesota and ending two days of heroic performance that carried the Red Sox to the top.

For 5½ innings this afternoon, though, the gloom thickened in Fenway Park as the Red Sox and Twins fought it out under their rookie managers, Dick Williams and Cal Ermer.

Lonborg, gunning for his 22d victory, retired the first two batters, then walked Harmon Killebrew. Then came the first of two errors that put Minnesota ahead. Tony Oliva banked a line drive off the left-field fence just over Yastrzemski's head and the ball bounced toward center field.

Reggie Smith, in pursuit, picked it up and fired a good throw toward home plate. But George Scott, the first baseman, cut off the throw 25 feet in front of the plate and flung it high and wide to the screen as Killebrew scored.

In the third, trouble brewed for Boston again with two out. This time Lonborg walked Cesar Tovar, and Killebrew lined a single to left. Tovar normally would have stopped at second base, but when the ball skipped past Yastrzemski to the wall, he scored and it was 2-0, Minnesota.

And that's the way things stood until the sixth. Yastrzemski had singled in the first, Rico Petrocelli had singled in the second, Lonberg had singled in the third and Yastrzemski had doubled in the fourth—but still Chance had protected his 2-0 lead.

A Lucky Chance

The closest call for Minnesota developed in the fourth, when Yastrzemski led off with a lone drive off the left-field wall, just missing a home run. Ken Harrelson flied out to Oliva, but Scott ripped a vicious liner toward center field. However, Chance instinctively reached up, clutched the ball in the netting of his glove, whirled and threw to second base to double up Yastrzemski.

Two innings later, the Red Sox abruptly broke through with a spectacular thrust that may rank with the Brink's robbery as one of the stunning events of Boston history. They sent 10 batters to the plate, four hit safely, one walked, one reached base on a fielder's choice, four advanced on a pair of wild pitches—and five scored.

Lonborg, who was pitching but losing a two-hitter at that point, started it all by curling a perfect bunt down the third-base line for a single. Jerry Adair hit the next pitch past the diving Rod Carew into center for a single. Dalton Jones, after fouling off the first pitch while trying to bunt, lined a single past third and the bases were loaded with nobody out.

The batter was Yastrzemski, who was leading the league in most offensive departments and who had hit two singles and a home run the day before.

Surrounded by deafening noise, he took a ball inside and then lined a single into center as Lonborg and Adair scored to tie the game and Fenway Park went wild.

The hit was the third straight of the game for Yastrzemski and his fifth in a row in the series. Before the game was over, he was to single again and run his streak to six hits in a row and seven for eight during the climactic weekend series. He also wound up with 121 runs batted in, and the feeling in Boston was

unanimous that Nos. 120 and 121 were his most important.

Versalles Throws Home

While paper and streamers were still swirling through the air, Harrelson followed by chopping a high bouncer over the mound to the left of second base, where Zoilo Versalles grabbed it. He had a play at first but fired the ball instead to home plate, too late to intercept Jones, who was scoring the third run.

Chance, foiled in his bid for his 21st victory, was relieved by Al Worthington while José Tartabull went in as a pinch-runner for Harrelson, who had joined the Red Sox a month ago from the embroiled Kansas City Athletics.

There were still no outs and, when Scott squared away to bunt on the first pitch, Worthington pitched hard on the outside and off his catcher's glove. The runners each moved up a base.

Two pitches later, Worthington delivered another wild pitch into the dirt and, as it bounced into the front row boxes near the Boston dugout, Yastrzemski scored and Tartabull took third. Scott finally struck out.

Minnesota's hour of despair was not over, though. Rico Petrocelli walked, and Reggie Smith cracked a hard grounder off Killebrew's glove at first base. As the ball bounced into foul territory, Tartabull scored the fifth and final run of the inning.

MINNESOTA (A.)	ab	r	h	bi		BOSTON (A.)	ab	r	h	bi
Versalles, ss	3	0	0	0		Adair, 2b	4	1	2	0
Reese, lf	1	0	1	0		Andrews, 2b	0	0	0	0
Tovar, 3b	3	1	0	0		Jones, 3b	4	1	2	0
Killebrew, 1b	2	2	2	0		Yastrzemski, lf	4	1	4	2
Oliva, rf	3	0	2	0		Harrelson, rf	3	0	0	1
Allison, lf	4	0	1	1		Tartabull, rf	1	1	0	0
Hernandez, ss	0	0	0	0		Scott, 1b	4	0	0	0
Uhlaender, cf	4	0	1	0		Petrocelli, ss	3	0	1	0
Carew, 2b	4	0	0	0		Smith, cf	4	0	0	1
Zimmerman, c	2	0	0	0		Gibson, c	2	0	0	0
Nixon, c	1	0	0	0		Siebern, ph	1	0	0	0
Rollins, ph	1	0	0	0		Howard, c	1	0	1	0
Chance, p	2	0	0	0		Lonborg, p	4	1	2	0
Worthington,p	0	0	0	0						
Kosco, ph	1	0	0							
Roland, p	0	0	0	0						
Grant, p	0	0	0	0						
Total	31	3	7	1		Total	35	5	12	4

Minnesota .... 1 0 1 0 0 0 0 1 0—3
Boston .... 0 0 0 0 0 5 0 0 x—5
E—Scott, Yastrzemski, Killebrew. DP—Minnesota 3, Boston 2. LOB—Minnesota 5, Boston 7. 2B—Oliva, Yastrzemski

	IP.	H.	R.	ER.	BB	SO
Chance (L. 20-14)	5	8	5	5	0	2
Worthington	0	3	0	0	0	0
Roland	0	1	0	0	1	0
Grant	2	1	0	0	1	5
Lonborg (W. 22-9)	9	7	3	3	1	4	5

T 2.25 A 35,770.

October 2, 1967

American League Approves Shift of Athletics to Oakland

LOOP OF 12 TEAMS SLATED BY 1971

New Franchises Will Be Situated at Kansas City and Possibly Seattle

By LEONARD KOPPETT
Special to The New York Times

CHICAGO, Oct. 18 — The American League voted tonight to allow Charles O. Finley to move his Kansas City Athletics to Oakland, and to expand the league to 12 teams, "as soon as practicable, but not later than the 1971 season," with the new franchises to be situated in Kansas City and Seattle.

This compromise solution was arrived at after more than 11 hours of hearings and deliberations at the Continental Plaza hotel here. There were a few conditional aspects to the final decision. Seattle's franchise is contingent on the provision of suitable stadium facilities; a bond issue for this purpose will be voted on in Seattle in February.

Also, the entire arrangement is "subject to suitable baseball rules and procedures." Details must be worked out, including the coordination of the expansion plans with the commissioner of baseball and with the National League.

Dallas People Invited

Throughout the day the American League owners and their staffs heard presentations from Finley, Kansas City officials, Oakland officials, the Seattle delegation and two representatives from Dallas (Lamar Hunt and Dick Butler). The Dallas people were invited to attend only yesterday and were, in Hunt's words "surprised to be here."

Underlying the entire decision process was a rivalry between the American and National League. Both wanted Seattle, the last major marketing area in the country untouched by major league baseball.

American Leaguers felt strongly that the National League beat them in prior moves in California, Houston and Atlanta and were determined not to lose Seattle. That is why they made the commitment to Seattle now although no physical facility exists for fielding a team.

The bond issue will concern a multi-purposed domed stadium and must be carried by a 60 per cent vote. But even if it is beaten there exist possibilities of private development. The Seattle representatives, Johnny O'Brien (well-known former athlete) and David Cohn expressed "delight" at the situation.

Blow to Kansas

From Kansas City's point of view, the granting of a deferred expansion franchise was a bitter disappointment. The Kansas City people, whose delegation included Stuart Symington of Missouri and Mayo Ilus Davis, had stressed of their desire for "uninterrupted baseball."

The Dallas maneuver was widely interpreted as a courtesy move to people who had shown some interest in the past, but did not seem terribly eager or prepared for immediate expansion.

Within the American League, the big battle was between those who advocated immediate expansion for 1968 and those who wanted a more cautious and slower approach. The compromise, then, consisted of a time-table that may extend to 1971 but with an immediate identification of the expansion cities involved.

October 19, 1967

Cepeda of Cards Elected Most Valuable Player in National League

SLUGGER IS GIVEN UNANIMOUS VOTE

Star First in League to Get All Ballots—McCarver Is 2d and Clemente 3d

By JOSEPH DURSO

Orlando Cepeda, the "Baby Bull" of the St. Louis Cardinals, was unanimously elected the most valuable player in the National League yesterday.

The 30-year-old first baseman from Puerto Rico received all 20 first-place votes cast by a committee of the nation's baseball writers, and thereby became the first player in the league's history to corner the market.

He was followed in the balloting by his teammate on the world champion Cardinals, Tim McCarver, and by last year's most valuable player, Roberto Clemente of the Pittsburgh Pirates.

Cepeda scored his sweep of first-place votes a year and a half after undergoing a knee operation that threatened to end his career. He was injured in

1965 while playing for the San Francisco Giants, appeared in only 33 games that season, then was traded to St. Louis the following May.

In a dramatic comeback this year, he hit .325 with 25 home runs and 111 runs batted in as the clean-up hitter on a team of formidable sluggers. He

United Press International
Orlando Cepeda

ranked sixth in the league in hitting and first in runs batted in.

He became the 10th Cardinal to win the award since it was established 37 years ago, and the only first baseman in the National League to win it in 21 years.

The voting is conducted like this: 20 ballots are cast, two for each city in the league. First place on a ballot is worth 14 points, second place 9 points, third place 8 points and so on down to 10th place.

Cepeda, with 20 first-place votes, came up with a perfect score of 280 points. Four players in the American League have been unanimous choices — Hank Greenberg of Detroit in 1935, Al Rosen of Cleveland in 1953, Mickey Mantle of New York in 1956 and Frank Robinson of Baltimore last year.

But the closest anybody came in the National League was Carl Hubbell of the New York Giants in 1936. The league consisted of eight teams then, and eight ballots normally were cast. Somehow two writers failed to vote and, although Hubbell received all six of the remaining first-place votes, his election was rated just short of unanimous.

In yesterday's balloting, McCarver got eight votes for second place and finished with a total of 136 points. He hit .295 last season with 14 home runs and 69 runs batted in, and was the Cardinals' regular catcher and No. 1 hitter in the clutch.

In third place was Clemente, with seven of the second-place votes and a grand total of 129 points. He won the major league batting title with .357, was second in his league to Cepeda in runs batted in (110) and hit 23 home runs. He was the only player besides Cepeda who was mentioned somewhere on all 20 ballots. However, Pittsburgh finished a disappointing sixth in the league, 20½ games behind St. Louis.

After the top three came Ron Santo of Chicago, Henry Aaron of Atlanta (who led the league with 39 home runs), Mike McCormick of San Francisco (who won the Cy Young Award last week as the league's best pitcher), Lou Brock of St. Louis, Tony Perez of Cincinnati, Julian Javier of St. Louis and Pete Rose of Cincinnati.

Nobody on the Los Angeles Dodgers was mentioned on the ballots. The Dodgers have been next to the Cardinals with eight most-valuable-player awards over the years. But last season, after winning three of the last four pennants, they tumbled from Olympus.

The Mets, who have lived in the foothills of Olympus all their lives, placed two men on the list. Tom Seaver, the rookie pitcher who won 16 games, was ranked 25th in the balloting with 5 points. Tommy Davis was 26th, with 3.

November 8, 1967

Yastrzemski Named Most Valuable in American League

19 OF 20 VOTES GO TO RED SOX STAR

Tovar of Twins Gets Other First-Place Ballot—Yanks Shut Out for First Time

By JOSEPH DURSO

Carl Yastrzemski of the Boston Red Sox was voted the most

valuable player in the American League yesterday in an election that marked the end of a baseball era: For the first time in the 37-year history of the award, no member of the New York Yankees was mentioned on any ballot.

Yastrzemski, by contrast, was mentioned on all 20 ballots cast by a committee of baseball writers and he received 19 of the 20 votes for first place.

Cesar Tovar, the jack-of-all-trades infielder for the Minnesota Twins, got the other first-place vote. And that prevented the hero of New Eng-

land — who won the triple crown of batting and everything else in sight—from making it unanimous.

The voting, like the chaotic four-team race for the pennant, was dominated by the Red Sox, the Minnesota Twins, the Detroit Tigers and the Chicago White Sox.

Following Yastrzemski came Harmon Killebrew of the Twins, who were dislodged from first place by Boston on the final day of the season. Then came Bill Freehan of the Tigers, who were eliminated two hours later in the second

game of a double-header on the same fateful day.

Horlen in 4th Place

In fourth place was Joe Horlen of the White Sox, who lost their grip in the last four days. Then came Al Kaline of Detroit, Jim Lonborg of Boston (who won the Cy Young Award as the league's best pitcher), Tovar and Jim Fregosi of California in a tie for seventh place, Gary Peters of Chicago and George Scott of Boston.

They were the top 10 players of the 24 who received votes. No. 11 was Frank Robinson, who won the award plus the triple crown last year before the great decline set in for the Baltimore Orioles.

The Yankees, whose great decline set in even earlier, disappeared from the balloting after monopolizing it since 1931.

THE COMPLETE VOTE

	1 2 3 4 5 6 7 8 9 10	Pts.
Yastrzemski, Bos.	19 1 0 0 0 0 0 0 0 0	275
Killebrew, Minn.	0 11 5 1 1 1 1 0 0 0	161
Freehan, Det.	0 4 7 3 1 2 2 0 0 0	137
Horlen, Chi.	0 2 0 4 3 4 1 0 1 1	91
Kaline, Det.	0 1 4 3 0 2 0 5 0 1	85
Lonborg, Bos.	0 1 2 1 5 3 0 1 1	82
Tovar, Minn.	0 1 1 2 2 1 3 3 0	70
Fregosi, Calif.	0 0 1 4 2 0 1 4 2 2	70
Peters, Chi.	0 0 0 1 1 2 2 0 4	37
Scott, Bos.	0 0 0 0 1 0 5 2 0 1	33
F. Robinson, Balt.	0 0 0 0 1 2 1 2 2 1	31
Wilson, Det.	0 0 0 1 0 1 1 0 1 2	22
Chance, Minn.	0 0 0 0 0 1 1 2 2 0	19
Hansen, Chi.	0 0 0 1 1 0 0 0 0 0	13
Adair, Bos.	0 0 0 0 1 1 0 0 0 0	11
Blair, Balt.	0 0 0 0 1 0 0 1 0 0	9
Petrocelli, Bos.	0 0 0 0 0 0 0 1 2 0	7
Howard, Bos.	0 0 0 0 0 0 0 0 3 1	7
Oliva, Minn.	0 0 0 0 0 1 0 0 0 0	6
Kaat, Minn.	0 0 0 0 0 0 1 0 0 0	4
Casanova, Wash.	0 0 0 0 0 0 0 1 1 1	3
Mincher, Calif.	0 0 0 0 0 0 0 0 0 3	3
Lolich, Det.	0 0 0 0 0 0 0 0 1 0	2
Rojas, Calif.	0 0 0 0 0 0 0 0 0 1	1

They won it 16 times, and even last year, when they dropped into last place, **Mickey Mantle** ranked 18th in the poll, with **Tom Tresh** and **Joe Pepitone** close behind. But this year— the year of the Yaz—the Yankees were shut out.

Yastrzemski's credentials for the award were unassailable, as were those of Orlando Cepeda of the St. Louis Cardinals, who was unanimously named the most valuable player in the National League last week.

Led the Great Revival

The 28-year-old outfielder from Southampton, L. I., led the Red Sox from ninth place in 1966 to first place in 1967 in one of baseball's great revivals. He hit .326, with 44 home runs and 121 runs batted in, and he made 10 hits in his last 13 times at bat as Boston swept to the pennant.

He received 275 points of a possible 280 in the voting, which is conducted this way: 14 points for first place, 9 points for second, 8 for third and so on.

Only he and Killebrew were named on all 20 ballots, with Killebrew getting 11 votes for second place and enough other votes for a total of 161 points. The only other player with more than 100 points was Freehan, the Tigers' catcher, with 137.

But the most remarkable development in the voting was the rise of the Red Sox and the fall of the Yankees. Last year Yastrzemski and Tony Conigliaro got one vote each — for 10th place.

November 16, 1967

Medwick Elected to Baseball Hall of Fame

EX-CARD SLUGGER GETS 240 BALLOTS

Campanella Falls Short by 8 Votes of 213 Needed for Election to Shrine

By JOSEPH DURSO

Joe Medwick, the rough-and-tumble outfielder of St. Louis's Gashouse Gang of a generation ago, was elected to baseball's Hall of Fame yesterday.

He was the only one of 48 candidates to survive the annual election, and he will be enshrined alongside 107 other baseball heroes at Cooperstown, N. Y., on July 22.

Medwick, now a 56-year-old insurance man in St. Louis, was named on 240 of the 283 ballots cast by the nation's baseball writers. He needed 75 per cent of the votes (or 213) and got about 85 per cent.

He outscored Roy Campanella, the former catcher for the Brooklyn Dodgers, whose career was ended 10 years ago this month by an automobile accident on Long Island. Campanella was mentioned on 205 ballots (which have spaces for 10 names), and was just 8 short of election.

Mize, Reynolds Trail

Far behind the two leaders came Lou Boudreau, with 146 votes; Enos Slaughter (129) and Ralph Kiner (118). The top 10 was rounded out by Johnny Mize (103), Allie Reynolds (95), Marty Marion (89), Arky Vaughan (82) and Pee Wee Reese (81).

Under the rules, a player is not eligible until five years after he has retired. Then he must be elected within the next 15 years or be transferred to a special "old-timers" category, where the memories are dimmer and the competition is keener.

For Medwick, this year's election was peculiarly dramatic. He retired in 1948, and this was his last chance under the regular rules. Besides, he had tied Red Ruffing for first place last year, only to lose in a run-off.

"It was like a 20-year slump," he said during a tele-

United Press International

Medwick in playing days. He was a top hitter and scorer.

phone interview at his insurance office in St. Louis.

Barracuda on Field

Medwick, who had the temperament of a barracuda as a ballplayer, conceded that he had spent a sleepless night awaiting the election results. He had long campaigned for his election, arguing that the voters should "do their homework and check the record books."

The record books show that he was born in Carteret, N. J., and played 17 seasons in the major leagues after breaking in with the Cardinals in 1932. He hit .300 or higher in 14 seasons and finished with a career average of .324 and 205 home runs. His best year was 1937: an average of .374 with 31 home runs and 154 runs batted in.

He was flamboyant and tough, and in 1934 became the first player to be expelled from a World Series game. He achieved this in Detroit after the following sequence: He hit a triple (his 11th hit of the Series), took a hard tag at third base from Marvin Owen of the Tigers, barreled into Owen and set off a barrage of fruit and vegetables from the Detroit fans.

Medwick, who was known as Ducky Medwick most of his career, was traded from St. Louis to Brooklyn in 1940.

Medwick's Career Record

Year	Club	G.	H.	HR.	RBI.	BA.
1932	St. Louis	26	37	2	12	.349
1933	St. Louis	148	182	18	98	.306
1934	St. Louis	149	198	18	106	.319
1935	St. Louis	154	224	23	126	.353
1936	St. Louis	155	223	18	138	.351
1937	St. Louis	156	237	31	154	.374
1938	St. Louis	146	190	21	122	.322
1939	St. Louis	150	201	14	117	.332
1940	St. L.-Bklyn.	143	175	17	86	.301
1941	Brooklyn	133	171	18	88	.318
1942	Brooklyn	142	166	4	96	.300
1943	Bklyn.-N.Y.	126	138	5	70	.278
1944	New York	128	165	7	85	.337
1945	N.Y.-Boston	92	90	3	37	.290
1946	Brooklyn	41	24	2	18	.312
1947	St. Louis	75	46	4	28	.307
1948	St. Louis	20	4	0	2	.211
Totals		1,984	2,471	205	1,383	.324

WORLD SERIES RECORD

		G.	H.	HR.	RBI.	BA.
1934	St. Louis	7	11	1	5	.379
1941	Brooklyn	5	4	0	0	.235
Totals		12	15	1	5	.326

a week later, he was struck in the head by a ball pitched by Bob Bowman of the Cardinals, and his power began to wane. He later played for the New York Giants and Boston Braves. Recently, he signed as a batting instructor with his old club, the Cardinals.

Campanella, who was third in the voting last year, accepted his near-miss philosophically this year.

"Well, that's too bad," he said when told he had missed by 8 votes. "But there's always next year."

January 24, 1968

Goslin, Cuyler Named to Hall of Fame

VOTE IS UNANIMOUS FOR FORMER STARS

Both Outfielders Entered Major Leagues in 1921 —110 Now in Shrine

Leon (Goose) Goslin and Hazen (Kiki) Cuyler were voted into baseball's Hall of Fame yesterday by a unanimous vote of the Committee on Veterans.

Ford Frick, chairman of the committee that considers play-

ers who have been retired 20 years or longer, said the two former outfielders were chosen by each member of the 12-man board. Cuyler was elected posthumously.

Joe (Ducky) Medwick was elected to the Hall of Fame by a vote of the Baseball Writers' Association of America last week. The addition of these three members brings the number of those enshrined at Cooperstown, N. Y., to 110.

Goslin, born Oct. 16, 1900, in Salem, N.J., broke into the major leagues with the Washington Senators in 1921 and remained with them until 1930, when he was traded to the St. Louis Browns. He also played for the Detroit Tigers and returned twice to the

Senators, in 1933 and for his final year in 1938.

A left-handed batter who threw right-handed, Goslin was known as a superior hitter, but not quite so good a fielder. He received his nickname because he resembled a bird in the manner he carried his arms while chasing a fly ball.

Goslin Proud of Honor

Speaking by telephone from his home in Bridgeton, N. J., Goslin said, "You're always proud to accomplish something like this. I didn't have a college education, and this honor makes me very proud. I'm so happy I probably won't sleep tonight."

Goslin compiled a career batting average of .316 during his 18 big-league seasons. He batted

.300 or more in 11 of them and his best mark was .379 in 1928.

Goslin was scouted personally by the Washington owner, Clark Griffith, while he was with Columbia (S.C.) of the Sally League. The day Griffith appeared, Goslin hit three home runs, but he was almost beaned a few times by fly balls.

Cuyler was a stocky, curly-haired speedster who hit with er. Oddly, his major-league career paralleled Goslin's. He started with the Pittsburgh Pirates in 1921 and completed his time with the Brooklyn Dodgers in 1938. He also saw service with the Chicago Cubs and Cincinnati Reds.

Cuyler's career average was .321, with a high of .360 in 1929 for the Cubs. He died Feb. 11, 1950.

January 29, 1968

Hunter of A's Pitches Baseball's 10th Perfect Game

OAKLAND HURLER DRIVES IN 3 RUNS

Only 6 Balls Hit to Outfield as Hunter Strikes Out 11, Killebrew Three Times

OAKLAND, Calif., May 8 (AP)—Jim (Catfish) Hunter pitched the American League's first perfect game in regular season play since 1922 tonight and drove in three runs as the Oakland Athletics routed the Minnesota Twins. 4-0.

Hunter, a 22-year-old right-hander in his fourth major league season, set down 27 of the hard-hitting Twins in becoming the 10th man to pitch

a perfect game in baseball history.

The 6-foot-5-inch, 195-pound Hunter struck out 11 and needed the help of just one outstanding defensive play—Sal Bando's stab of a fifth inning grounder to third base by Bob Allison. Harmon Killebrew, the Minnesota slugger was a strike-out victim three times.

The last perfect game was pitched by Sandy Koufax of the Los Angeles Dodgers three years ago against the Chicago Cubs.

The last American Leaguer to pitch one was Don Larsen of the New York Yankees, who did it in the 1956 World Series against the Brooklyn Dodgers.

But Charlie Robertson of the Chicago White Sox, in 1922, was the last to pitch one in a regular season contest. He did it against Detroit.

Hunter completed his feat by getting a pinch-hitter, John Roseboro, to ground out in the ninth, then striking out Bruce Look and Rich Reese. The latter

Associated Press
DOWN TO THE LAST MAN: Jim (Catfish) Hunter of Oakland pitching to Minnesota's Rich Reese in the ninth inning of his perfect game last night. He struck out Reese, who had fouled off five straight pitches, to win the game, 4 to 0.

had fouled off five straight pitches. Only five balls were hit out of the infield against Hunter.

Delivers Bunt Single

Hunter delivered a run-scoring bunt single in the seventh and a two-run single in the eighth.

Hunter, who signed with the Athletics for a $75,000 bonus in 1964, had a 13-17 won-lost record last year. He has a 2-2 mark this season.

The Athletics, who moved to C ...d this year from Kansas City, had not had a no-hitter since Bill McCahan threw one against Washington on Sept. 3, 1947, when the club was in Philadelphia.

Hunter's no-hitter, witnessed by 6,298 spectators, the second smallest turnout this season at Oakland Coliseum, was the second of the season. Tom Phoebus of the Baltimore Orioles pitched a 6-0, no-hit victory against the Boston Red Sox on April 27.

Dave Boswell pitched six scoreless innings for Minnesota. In the A's seventh Rick Monday doubled, took third on Boswell's second wild pitch, then scored when Hunter beat out a bunt.

With the bases filled in the eighth, Ron Perranoski replaced Boswell and walked Danny Cater, forcing a run. Hunter followed with his two-run single.

Hunter went to a 3-2 count on only six batters. He had a count of 3-0 on Tony Oliva in the second inning, then struck out the dangerous two-time league hitting champion.

"I just tried to throw strikes to everybody; control is the name of the game," Hunter said.

MINNESOTA (A.)					OAKLAND (A.)				
	ab.	r.	h.	bi		ab.	r.	h.	bi
Tovar, 3b	3	0	0	0	Campaneris, ss	4	0	2	0
Carew, 2b	3	0	0	0	Jackson, rf	4	0	0	0
Killebrew, 1b	3	0	0	0	Bando, 3b	3	0	1	0
Oliva, rf	3	0	0	0	Webster, 1b	4	1	2	0
Uhlaender, cf	3	0	0	0	Donaldson, 2b	3	0	0	0
Allison, lf	3	0	0	0	Pagliaroni, c	3	1	0	0
Hernandez, ss	2	0	0	0	Monday, cf	3	2	2	0
Roseboro, ph	1	0	0	0	Rudi, lf	3	0	2	0
Look, c	3	0	0	0	F. Robinson, p	0	0	0	0
Boswell, p	2	0	0	0	Cater, rf	0	0	0	1
Perranoski, p	0	0	0	0	Hunter, p	4	0	3	3
Reese, ph	1	0	0	0					
Total	27	0	0	0	Total	31	4	10	4

Minnesota .... 0 0 0 0 0 0 0 0 0—0
Oakland .... 0 0 0 0 0 0 1 3 x—4

E—Boswell. DP—Minnesota 2. LOB—Oakland 9. 2B—Hunter, Monday. SB—Campaneris.

	IP.	H.	R.	ER.	BB.	SO.
Boswell (L, 3-3)	7⅓	9	4	4	4	6
Perranoski	⅔	1	0	0	1	0
Hunter (W, 3-2)	9	0	0	0	0	11

HBP—By Boswell (Donaldson). Wild pitches—Boswell 2.
T—2:28. A—6,298.

May 9, 1968

National League Adds Montreal and San Diego

EXPANSION MOVE EFFECTIVE IN 1969

Shift to Canada for 12th Team Is Surprise—Price Is $10-Million Apiece

By JOSEPH DURSO
Special to The New York Times

CHICAGO, May 27 — Major league baseball crossed its first international frontier tonight when Montreal was voted into the National League along with San Diego.

The vote came on the 16th secret ballot after 10 hours of discussion and argument, and was unanimous. It will bring big league baseball to Canada next April, when the league expands from 10 teams to 12.

Montreal and San Diego beat out three other cities that had campaigned aggressively for franchises. They were Buffalo, Milwaukee and Dallas - Fort Worth, and all expressed "shock" and disappointment tonight when the vote was announced after an all-day closed meeting of the league's club owners.

Conditions Are Suitable

The selection of San Diego was no upset. Though close to Los Angeles and Anaheim, which already have big-league teams, San Diego has a new stadium that seats 45,000 persons. It also has an ideally mild climate and a successful team in the American Football League.

Montreal, though, had been given only an outside chance of surviving the battle of the cities. It is a shrine of ice hockey, but has had no high-level baseball since the Montreal Royals, a one-time International League farm team of the old Brooklyn Dodgers, were disbanded in 1960.

However, Montreal made a strong pitch for admission by promising that a domed stadium—the second in baseball—would be built by 1971 with a capacity of 55,000. Until then, the new team will play in the Expo Stadium, which will be enlarged to seat 45,000 persons.

The cost of passing a baseball milestone will be high for both cities. They will pay $10-million apiece for the privilege. It will cost them $6-million each for 30 players, who will be bought from the 10 other National League clubs plus $4-million for initiation and a split of television revenue.

Follow the Leader

The decision tonight guarantees that the National League will expand precisely on schedule with the American, which voted last October to add two clubs. They are Seattle and Kansas City, which also will field teams in 1969.

The Nationals had been reluctant to be "stampeded" into expansion. They felt there were insuperable conflicts of geography and scheduling and feared that the available baseball talent would be diluted.

But the resistance to expansion broke down tonight under the threat that the rival league would cross the bridge to the talent first and would siphon off the best.

No decision was reached by the National League on whether to divide the 12 teams into two conferences of six teams each. The American League has already drawn such a blueprint and will wind up with two pennant winners each September

with a playoff determining who gets into the World Series.

However, both leagues will meet here tomorrow with the commissioner of baseball, William D. Eckert, and a symmetry probably will be established. If not, a lopsided pattern would result, with one league holding a championship playoff, while the other awarded the pennant to the number one team of all 12 at the end of the season.

What Went Wrong?

The losers in the balloting were disconsolate with strong overtones that cities in the United States had been bypassed for a Canadian city.

"It's unthinkable," said Judge Robert Cannon of the Milwaukee delegation, "that baseball would do this to cities in the United States — which made baseball what it is."

"It's a shock," said J. Frederick Schoelkopf 4th of the Buffalo group. "Erie County has already voted money for a domed stadium and we can't understand what went wrong."

Milwaukee had been fighting to return to the major leagues, which abandoned the city in 1966, when the Braves decamped to Atlanta.

The Dallas group, led by oil millionaires such as Lamar Hunt, had made a strong appeal despite the fact that Houston, with its roofed Astrodome, was only 200 miles away.

Buffalo had campaigned as the "eighth largest television market in North America," with a radius that would include parts of Canada surrounding Toronto.

The Montreal team will be operated by a syndicate of seven men headed by Jean-Louis Levesque, a financier. However, the principal ball-carrier was Jerry Snyder, the vice mayor, and the chief momentum came from Expo '67.

The San Diego group will include E. J. (Buzzie) Bavasi, executive vice president and general manager of the Los Angeles Dodgers.

ROYALS

May 28, 1968

Drysdale Sets Scoreless Record

DODGERS WIN, 5-3

Drysdale Hurls 58 2/3 Innings Without Allowing Run

By The Associated Press

LOS ANGELES, June 8—Don Drysdale set a major-league record by pitching 58⅔ consecutive scoreless innings before being driven from the mound tonight in the Los Angeles Dodgers' 5-3 victory over the Philadelphia Phils.

Drysdale broke Walter Johnson's major-league record of 56 consecutive scoreless innings when he retired Roberto Pena on a grounder opening the third inning. A capacity crowd of 50,060 gave the 31-year-old right-hander a standing ovation.

But the string ended at 58 2/3 when Howie Bedell, a pinchhitter, delivered a sacrifice fly with two out in the fifth, scoring Tony Taylor from third base. Singles by Taylor and Clay Dalrymple set up the run.

Drysdale Departs in 7th

Drysdale allowed a sixth-inning homer to Bill White and was knocked from the box when Cookie Rojas singled home the seventh-inning run that narrowed the Los Angeles lead to 4-3.

The Dodgers got their winning margin with four runs in the first four innings against Larry Jackson.

Ken Boyer singled home a first-inning run. The Dodgers then scored three in the fourth after Tom Haller had doubled and taken third on Boyer's single.

Haller scored on a fielder's choice. Boyer scored on an error by Pena and Zoilo Versalles ended the rally with a run-scoring fly.

Parker Hits Home Run

Wes Parker hit a seventh-inning homer for the Dodgers.

The victory was the Dodgers' sixth straight and their ninth in their last 10 games.

After Drysdale broke the scoreless inning record in the third, the plate umpire, Augie Donatelli, examined the pitcher's hair, apparently looking for excess grease. He again checked Drysdale before the fourth inning, but took no action on either occasion.

PHILA. (N.)					LOS ANGELES (N.)				
	ab	r	h	bi		ab	r	h	bi
Rojas, 2b	5	0	2	1	Parker, 1b	4	1	2	1
Briggs, cf	2	0	0	0	Davis, cf	4	1	0	0
Sutherland, ph	1	0	0	0	Gabrielson, lf	4	0	1	0
Farrell, p	0	0	0	0	Fairey, lf	0	0	0	0
Gonzalez, lf	4	0	0	0	Haller, c	3	1	3	0
Callison, rf	3	0	0	0	Boyer, 3b	4	1	2	1
White, 1b	4	1	1	1	Fairly, rf	4	1	1	1
Taylor, 3b	4	1	1	0	Popovich, 2b	4	0	1	0
Dalrymple, c	2	1	1	0	Versalles, ss	3	0	0	1
Allen, ph	1	0	0	0	Drysdale, p	2	0	0	0
Ryan, c	0	0	0	0	Aguirre, p	1	0	0	0
Pena, ss	4	0	0	0	Total	33	5	10	4
L. Jackson, p	1	0	1	0					
Bedell, ph	0	0	0	1					
G. Jackson, p	0	0	0	0					
Lock, cf	2	0	0	0					
Total	33	3	6	3					

Philadelphia ..... 0 0 0 0 1 1 1 0 0—3
Los Angeles ..... 1 0 0 3 0 0 1 0 x—5

E—Pena, Versalles, Fairly. DP—Philadelphia 1. LOB—Philadelphia 7, Los Angeles 6. 2B—Haller. HR—White (6), Parker (3). SB—Davis. SF—Versalles, Bedell.

	IP.	H.	R.	ER.	BB.	SO.
L. Jackson (L, 6-6)	4	5	4	3	1	1
G. Jackson	2	1	0	0	0	2
Farrell	2	4	1	1	0	1
Drysdale (W, 8-3)	6⅔	6	3	2	2	5
Aguirre	2⅓	0	0	0	1	2

T—2:29. A—50,060.

June 9, 1968

M'LAIN DEFEATS ATHLETICS FOR 30TH VICTORY

RALLY IN 9TH WINS

Tigers' Pitcher First to Achieve Feat Since Dean in 1934

By LEONARD KOPPETT
Special to The New York Times

DETROIT, Sept. 14—What no major league pitcher had been able to do since 1934 and what only two had accomplished in the last 48 years was achieved by Dennis Dale McLain of the Detroit Tigers today when he posted his 30th victory of the season.

The 24-year-old right-handed extrovert won it sitting on the bench, because he had been removed for a pinch-hitter in the home half of the ninth inning.

The pinch-hitter, Al Kaline, walked and set off a two-run rally that gave the Tigers a 5-4 victory over the Oakland Athletics.

Grove Did It in '31

But the dramatic finish, typical of a Tiger team that has moved within four victories of clinching the American League pennant, in no way minimized McLain's triumph. He had pitched a strong game, hurt only by two home runs by Reggie Jackson, Oakland's budding star, and by the only walk he issued, which was turned into a run. McLain struck out 10 men and pitched his 27th complete game in 38 starts.

All the significance was packed into the "30." A 20-game winner is a member of baseball's elite. Only a handful of pitchers have won 30. The last had been Dizzy Dean, who hurled the St. Louis Cardinals to the 1934 National League pennant with a 30-7 record. Bob (Lefty) Grove of the Philadelphia Athletics was the last in the American League with a 31-4 season in 1931. No one else had won 30 since 1920.

When Willie Horton's drive over the left fielder's head

Tigers' Box Score

OAKLAND (A.)					DETROIT (A.)				
	ab	r	h	bi		ab	r	h	bi
Campaneris, ss	4	0	1	1	McAuliffe, 2b	5	0	1	0
Monday, cf	4	0	1	0	Stanley, cf	5	1	2	0
Cater, 1b	4	1	2	0	Northrup, rf	4	1	0	0
Bando, 3b	3	0	0	0	Horton, lf	5	1	2	1
Jackson, rf	4	2	2	3	Cash, 1b	4	1	2	3
Green, 2b	4	0	0	0	Freehan, c	3	0	1	0
Keough, lf	3	0	0	0	Matchick, ss	4	0	1	0
Duncan, c	2	1	0	0	Wert, 3b	2	0	0	0
Dobson, p	1	0	0	0	Brown, ph	1	0	0	0
Aker, p	0	0	0	0	Tracewski, 3b	0	0	0	0
Lindblad, p	0	0	0	0	McLain, p	1	0	0	0
Donaldson, ph	1	0	0	0	Kaline, ph	0	0	0	0
Segui, p	1	0	0	0	Total	34	5	9	4
Total	30	4	6	4					

Oakland .... 0 0 0 2 1 1 0 0 0—4
Detroit .... 0 0 0 3 0 0 0 0 2—5

E—Matchick, Bando, Cater. DP—Detroit 1. LOB—Oakland 2, Detroit 10. HR—Jackson 2 (28), Cash (21). S—McLain, Bando, Donaldson.

	IP.	H.	R.	ER.	BB.	SO.
Dobson	3⅓	4	3	3	2	4
Aker	0	0	0	1	0	0
Lindblad	⅓	0	0	0	0	0
Segui (L, 5-5)	*4⅓	5	2	1	2	1
McLain (W, 30-5)	9	6	4	4	1	10

*One out when winning run was scored.
Wild pitch—Aker.
T—3:00. A—33,688.

United Press International

WHOOPING JOY: Denny McLain, right, and Al Kaline celebrate as the winning run driven in by Willie Horton, crosses the plate. The run gave McLain his 30th victory this season.

ended the game by knocking in the tie-breaking run with one out, a wild scene erupted. It was an appropriate climax to an event carried by the National Broadcasting Company to millions of home television screens, and no set of script-writers could have surpassed what reality had provided.

In the stands were 44,087 people, 33,688 of them paying customers and the rest children admitted in groups, and they became part of the show.

His Mates Mob Him

As Horton's hit fell safe, McLain raced out of the dug-

out to embrace the teammates who had brought him his prize after it had passed out of his own power to gain. They, in turn, surrounded and lifted him, precariously, in a march to the dugout. Photographers, television crews and fans started to converge on the scene and there was a terrific crush near the third-base dugout.

Finally, McLain was able to say a few words on camera with Dean, who was present for the occasion, and with Sandy Koufax, who retired two years ago and removed himself from the glory McLain had attained.

On a personal level, there is the record itself, the argument for a $100,000 contract next year and the limitless possibilities for outside income for McLain and his organ-playing career.

But on a team basis, his superb season made possible the pennant the Tigers failed to win last year only on the last day, so the jubilation did not stem merely from statistics.

'We Want Denny!'

When McLain finally disappeared into the clubhouse, the crowd remained, chanting, "We want Denny!" When he heard about it, he insisted on going out again to wave, acknowledge the cheers and pose for more pictures. Half an hour later he was still gleefully answering questions inside while the clubhouse door was besieged by admirers.

The game, which lasted 3 hours 3 minutes, formed a perfect build-up. Jackson's first homer, with a man on, had put Oakland ahead, 2-0, in the

fourth inning. But Norm Cash hit one with two on in the Tigers' half, and McLain had a 3-2 lead.

He lost it in the fifth to a leadoff walk, a sacrifice and a single by Bert Campaneris, and with two out in the sixth, Jackson hit another homer, the 28th of his first full major league campaign.

Now it was up to Diego Segui, Oakland's fourth pitcher, to hold off the Tigers, and he did for three innings.

With two out in the eighth, a walk and an infield single, on which Segui had failed to cover first, gave Detroit two men on with two out. Gates Brown, the Tigers' best pinch-hitter, bounced out on the first pitch. Had he walked, McLain would have had to be removed for a hitter right then, with unknown results.

Kaline Draws a Walk

As it happened, though, McLain breezed through the ninth and Kaline led off for him in the home half. Fouling off two 3-2 pitches, Kaline drew a hard-earned walk. Dick McAuliffe, after fouling back two bunt attempts, popped out on a foul, but Mickey Stanley grounded the next pitch through the box into center for a single and Kaline hustled into third.

Bob Kennedy, the Oakland manager who had checked Detroit's fourth-inning rally by using two reliefers to pitch to one man each, now went out to discuss matters with Segui. Jim Northrup, a left-handed pull-hitter, was up, and a home run was a real danger. But Kennedy left Segui in and, from a pitching point of view, events did not prove him wrong.

But with the infield drawn in to try to cut down the tying run at the plate, Northrup bounced to Danny Cater, the first baseman. There was plenty of time to get Kaline, but Cater's throw was high and wild, and while Kaline scored Stanley raced around to third.

In the dugout McLain, who had been watching quietly most of the inning, leaped up and shouted. He thought Stanley, too, might score on the overthrow.

"Calm down, calm down," drawled Manager Mayo Smith.

McLain laughed and calmed down.

Now it was up to Horton. Only the man on third counted, and both the infield and outfield played close, since a long fly-out would be as decisive as a home run. Segui put up quite a battle, until Horton smacked a 2-2 pitch beyond Jim Gosger's reach.

September 15, 1968

Slider Is the Pitch That Put Falling Batting Averages on the Skids

By JOSEPH DURSO

Satchel Paige, a 60-year-old pitcher for the Atlanta Braves, says his best pitch these days is a slider.

Denny McLain, who is young enough to be Satchel's grandson, won over 30 games this year for the Detroit Tigers. His pitching coach, Johnny Sain, reports McLain is throwing an improved slider.

Rocky Colavito, an outfielder who hit 372 home runs in 1,796 games, caused a sensation last month by pitching for the New York Yankees — and announced that his best pitch was a slider.

Baseball has seen the fastball, curveball, slowball, sinkerball, spitball, fadeaway, spinner, screwball, forkball, and even something called the emery ball. But now, in this year of the domineering pitcher and the disappearing hitter, the most talked-about tool of the trade is the slider.

Pitch Denied to Koosman

It has been derided as "a 5-cent curveball," scorned as a junkball, lionized as the greatest "out" pitch of this generation. It has been banned by the Mets from the repertory of Jerry Koosman, because its captivating quality might cause him to neglect his curveball. Steve Hamilton of the Yankees calls it "a nonexistent pitch." Sain says some pitchers throw it 40 times a game.

Whatever the slider is, it has become the favorite weapon of the strong-armed men who are making pitching the black art of a game that once belonged to the hitters.

To them, it is a ball that approaches home plate like a fastball but that suddenly veers—or slides—a few inches to one side and perhaps even down. It does not "drop off the table" like Sandy Koufax's big curve. It does not "tail away" like Bob Gibson's fastball. It slides—like a fast 5-cent curveball.

Nobody knows for sure who invented the slider or whether it was just there all the time waiting to be harnessed, like electricity.

Frank Crosetti, who joined the Yankees 34 years ago, remembers that old-time pitchers such as George Blaeholder and Johnny Babich threw natural mini-curves.

Sailing Fastball Renamed

Jim Turner, the pitching coach for the Yankees, recalls that a "sailing fastball" or "any short curve" before World War II became known as a slider. Phil Rizzuto thinks that it may have evolved from the "slip pitch" taught by Paul Richards, a smart catcher who now runs the Atlanta Braves.

"When I came up in 1941," Rizzuto said, "Al Milnar of Cleveland was the only pitcher who threw a slider regularly. Then after the war, the young pitchers like Mel Parnell came along and everybody started to throw breaking pitches that we now call sliders."

"I spent four years in the lowest minor leagues, the 'D' leagues," Sain said, "and I never had over-powering speed. So I kept practicing my breaking stuff, big curves and short ones. I started in 1936, and by the time I came up to the big leagues with Boston in 1942 I was throwing sliders."

"When I came up in 1951," Mickey Mantle recalled, "you'd get ahead of the pitcher and you could expect a fastball. If the pitcher was a hard thrower like Virgil Trucks, it was 90 to 1 that you'd get a fastball. But now they nibble you to death with breaking pitches, sliders, curves, even knuckleballs."

"I didn't throw a slider until 1961," said Whitey Ford, who became a Yankee in 1950. "Then I began losing my speed and had to develop new pitches. Johnny Sain joined the club that year as a coach and taught me the slider. I used it all the time. It broke over and down, and the batters would even chase it into the dirt.

"Ted Williams told me this summer that he had only two pitches to worry about when he started—fastball and curveball. And the pitchers knew he could hit fastballs, so his guessing was narrowed to curveballs. Later they started throwing sliders, Ted said, and really had him guessing. It's got to be one of the reasons for lower batting averages these days."

The big difference between a curve and a slider, Ford says, is this:

The curve is thrown with maximum spin, preferably down. It starts high, then about

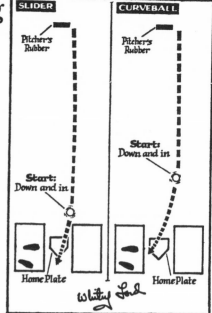

This is how a slider and curve ball break over the plate. The diagram is for left-handed pitcher throwing to right-handed batter. Whitey Ford of Yankees provided diagram and modeled grips in pictures.

Grip for fastball   Grip for a curve   Grip for a slider

15 feet from the plate starts to break down and away.

Easy Pitch for Hurler

The slider is thrown more like a fastball, but with the wrist turned to the side. It looks like a fastball until it gets three or four feet from the batter, then breaks just enough to throw him off stride or to miss the fast part of his bat.

Everybody agrees that the slider has grown popular for two reasons: it's relatively easy for the pitcher to throw. But it's relatively hard for the batter to "read" or recognize.

It has the potential danger of not breaking far enough away from the batter, the way a curve should. But it is such an all-purpose pitch that the Mets' coach, Rube Walker, told Koosman not to use it this year for fear he would stop developing his curveball. Koosman has abstained, with success, but he is an exception.

"Ford learned it one day and used it immediately," Sain said. "If you can throw it, you usually can control it. And if you're in the business of fooling people, you throw it."

September 22, 1968

ST. LOUIS WINS, 4-0, IN SERIES OPENER; GIBSON SETS MARK

Cardinal Hurler Strikes Out 17 Tigers to Break Record of 15 Held by Koufax

M'LAIN LEAVES IN SIXTH

Winners Score Three Runs in Fourth — Brock Clouts a Home Run in Seventh

By JOSEPH DURSO
Special to The New York Times

ST. LOUIS, Oct. 2 — Bob Gibson outpitched Denny McLain, overpowered the rest of the Detroit Tigers and struck out 17 batters today as the St. Louis Cardinals won the opening game of the World Series, 4-0.

The 32-year-old Nebraskan broke the Series strike-out record of 15, set by Sandy Koufax of the Los Angeles Dodgers against the New York Yankees in 1963. He allowed five hits and resolved baseball's "pitching duel of the century" before the game was half over.

He was the man of the hour on this summery afternoon as 54,692 persons in Busch Memorial Stadium and a national television audience watched. He left no questions unanswered as he conquered McLain, the first man to win 31 games in the major leagues in 37 years.

By winning his sixth straight game in three Series in five years, he tied the record set by Lefty Gomez and Red Ruffing of the Yankees between 1932 and 1942.

Another Record Falls

By working his sixth straight complete game in Series competition, he broke the record set by Ruffing for pitchers who finish what they start when the money is on the table.

Gibson, who started life in the slums of Omaha and now earns $90,000 a year, pitched to only 32 Detroit hitters. He also became the National League's No. 1 World Series

Handshake for Great Performance

Associated Press

Bob Gibson, Cardinals' pitcher, being congratulated by Tim McCarver after striking out 17 in St. Louis yesterday.

winner. Other pitchers have won more games — Whitey Ford leads everybody with 10 victories during the Yankee era — but nobody has won more for the senior league than Gibson in 65 World Series.

He got all the runs needed for all this statistical success during one inning. It was the fourth, an inning marked by a fatal loss of control by McLain, who had walked only 63 batters in 336 innings this season.

This time the fresh-faced extrovert and organist walked two batters on the minimum total of eight pitches. Then Mike Shannon and Julian Javier singled and Gibson suddenly was staked to a three-run lead.

The other run was produced in the seventh inning by Lou Brock, who was Gibson's chief ally in the Cardinals' victory last fall against the Boston Red Sox. He bombed a 3-and-2 pitch into the center-field bleachers off Pat Dobson for a 400-foot home run.

But the essence of the day

was Gibson's overwhelming fast ball and his surprisingly sharp curve.

He had won 22 games and lost nine this year, with 15 victories in a row, 13 shutouts and a league record for efficiency — allowing only 1.12 earned runs a game. He also had won three games in the World Series last year, including the final one. So today he was back at the old stand.

He walked one man and gave up four singles and one double. He struck out Dick McAuliffe to open the game, then added Al Kaline. He fanned Norm Cash, Willie Horton and Jim Northrup in the second inning, then got Bill Freehan and McLain in the third. So he struck out seven of the first nine men, including five in a row.

He struck out everybody in the Detroit line-up and he took care of the renowned Kaline three times and the power-hitting left-hander, Norm Cash, three times.

By the ninth inning, he had 14 strike-outs and needed one more to tie Koufax's memorable performance in Yankee Stadium five years ago.

Stanley Delays Inevitable

There was a pause while

Mickey Stanley singled to center field, raising some faint thoughts about the Tigers' talent for raising a rumpus late in ball games. Thirty times this year they had won games in their final turn at bat. But not today.

Kaline, playing in his first series in a 16-year career, then swiped at a 1-and-2 pitch and missed for strike-out No. 15. Gibson seemed serenely unaware of the milestone he had reached, but many persons in the crowd knew, especially those with transistor radios.

They rose and gave him a standing ovation. A bit startled, Gibson peered over his shoulder just in time to see the news flashed on the right-field scoreboard.

Then he struck out Cash on a 2-and-2 pitch and got another standing ovation. And finally, for good measure, he threw a curveball past Horton for his 17th strike-out and the final out of the day.

While all this was going on, what of McLain, the 24-year-old man-child of Detroit, the musician and self-styled mercenary soldier, the prime mover in Detroit's first American League title in 23 years?

He had approached his confrontation with Gibson without losing his flair. He was not unduly upset by reports that he had top billing on the Cardinals' clubhouse bulletin board for his remark: "I want to humiliate the Cardinals."

On the eve of battle, he even packed the lobby of a downtown hotel by sitting down at an organ in a lounge and giving an impromptu recital. He played appropriate mood music like "Stardust," then soared into ad-lib rock tempos. Then this afternoon he met Gibson.

The result: McLain pitched five innings before leaving for a pinch-hitter. He allowed three hits and three walks, struck out three Cardinals and saw three runs cross the plate. His "thing" with the number 3 included errors — the Tigers committed three behind him.

He almost jumped off to a fast start when Stanley singled solidly to left field with one down in the first inning.

This was the young Stanley, the best center fielder in the league, who had been switched to shortstop in order to make room for more bats in the Tiger line-up. Playing with a borrowed infielder's mitt, he behaved professionally at shortstop and got two of the five hits off Gibson.

However, Stanley tried to steal second base on the next pitch after his single and was thrown out by Tim McCarver. Then Gibson struck out Kaline, and so much for McLain's fast start.

McLain, meanwhile, retired

the first four Cardinals. Then, with one down in the second, McCarver lined the first pitch into the alley in right-center. He gambled that he could beat the relay and he did when McAuliffe's throw to third base went wide and McCarver wound up with a triple. But McLain struck out Mike Shannon and Javier to end the threat.

However, that turned out to be McLain's finest hour. In the third, he flirted with trouble by walking Dal Maxvill. Then Gibson bunted Maxvill to first. Brock followed with a grounder to McLain, who turned and stalked Maxvill between second and third, finally throwing him out with Stanley covering second.

Brock, who had been safe during this maneuvering, promptly stole second base for his eighth steal in eight Series games over the last two years. When Freehan's throw skipped into right field, Brock made it to third. But he was still there when Curt Flood popped up to Stanley.

The inning proved indecisive, though it may haunt the Cardinals before the Series ends. Brock jammed his right shoulder while sliding into second base and required some deep-freeze spray to ease the pain.

Then came the fourth inning and big trouble for the man-child. McLain opened the inning by throwing four straight balls to Roger Maris, who will retire

Box Score of First Series Game

DETROIT (A.)

	AB.	R.	H.	RBI.	PO.	A.
McAuliffe, 2b.	4	0	1	0	3	0
Stanley, ss	4	0	2	0	3	2
Kaline, rf	4	0	1	0	2	0
Cash, 1b	4	0	0	0	7	1
Horton, lf	4	0	0	0	2	0
Northrup, cf.	3	0	0	0	2	0
Freehan, c.	2	0	0	0	4	1
Wert, 3b	2	0	1	0	0	1
bMathews, ph.	1	0	0	0	0	0
Tracewski, 3b.	0	0	0	0	0	0
McLain, p.	1	0	0	0	0	2
aMatchick, ph.	1	0	0	0	0	0
Dobson, p	0	0	0	0	0	0
cBrown, ph	1	0	0	0	0	0
McMahon, p.	0	0	0	0	1	0
Total	31	0	5	0	24	7

ST. LOUIS (N.)

	AB.	R.	H.	RBI.	PO.	A.
Brock, lf	4	1	1	1	2	0
Flood, cf	4	0	1	0	1	0
Maris, rf	3	1	0	0	1	0
Cepeda, 1b	4	0	0	0	11	1
McCarver, c.	3	1	1	0	17	1
Shannon, 3b.	4	1	2	1	0	0
Javier, 2b.	3	0	1	2	2	0
Maxvill, ss.	2	0	0	0	2	0
Gibson, p.	2	0	0	0	1	0
Total	29	4	6	4	27	2

aGrounded out for McLain in 6th.
bStruck out for Wert in 8th.
cFlied out for Dobson in 8th.

Detroit (A.) ....0 0 0 0 0 0 0 0 0—0
St. Louis (N.) ....0 0 0 3 0 0 1 0 x—4

Errors—Freehan, Horton, Cash. Left on bases—Detroit 5, St. Louis 6. Two-base hit—Kaline. Three-base hit—McCarver. Home run—Brock. Stolen bases—Brock, Javier, Flood. Sacrifice—Gibson.

	IP.	H.	R.	ER.	BB.	SO.	HBP.	WP.	Bks.
McLain—L	5	3	3	3	3	3	0	0	0
Dobson	2	2	1	1	1	0	0	0	0
McMahon	1	0	0	0	0	0	0	0	0
Gibson—W	9	5	0	0	1	17	0	0	0

Bases on balls off McLain 3 (Maxvill, Maris, McCarver), Dobson 1 (Javier), McMahon (none), Gibson 1 (Freehan). Struck out by McLain 3 (Shannon, Javier, Gibson), Dobson (none), McMahon (none), Gibson 17 (McAuliffe, Kaline 3, Cash 3, Horton 2, Northrup 2, Freehan 2, McLain, Wert, Stanley, Mathews).

Umpires—Gorman (N.) plate; Honochick (A.) first base; Landes (N.) second base; Kinnamon (A.) third base; Harvey (N.) left field; Haller (A.) right field. Time of game—2:29. Attendance—54,692.

after the Series and become a beer distributor in Florida. Then McLain threw two balls to

Orlando Cepeda and immediately had company on the mound—Manager Mayo Smith.

Smith returned to the dugout and Cepeda fouled out. But McLain threw four straight balls to McCarver, Shannon lined a 2-and-2 pitch to left for one run and, when Horton bobbled the ball, McCarver took third base and Shannon second.

On the next pitch, Javier grounded a single into right field and both runners scored. That made it 3-0 and then McLain got Maxvill on a fly to left and Gibson on a strike-out.

Denny was followed by Pat Dobson of Depew, N. Y., who worked the next two innings, and by Don McMahon of Brooklyn, who worked the last two. They kept order except for the seventh-inning home run by Brock, who hit .414 in the Series last year with 12 hits, including a home run.

When it was all over—at least until Gibson and McLain meet again on Sunday—Gibson said he had relied chiefly on his fastball.

"But I had a good breaking ball," he said. "I think I was more of a surprise to them than anything else."

McLain conceded he had hurt himself with eye-high pitches that were called balls.

"That bad inning was typical of me," he said, not quite speechless. "A couple of walks, then the whole thing comes undone."

October 3, 1968

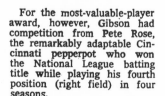

GIBSON IS VOTED MOST VALUABLE

Gets National League Player Award—Rose Is 2d

The selection of Bob Gibson of the St. Louis Cardinals as the most valuable player in the National League yesterday put an official stamp of the Year of the Pitcher on the 1968 baseball season.

Dennis McLain, the 24-year-old right-hander who won 31 games while pitching the Detroit Tigers into the World Series, took both top American League awards—the most valuable player and the Cy Young Award for the outstanding pitcher. Gibson, who is 33, took the National League's Cy Young Award by an equally wide margin.

For the most-valuable-player award, however, Gibson had competition from Pete Rose, the remarkably adaptable Cincinnati pepperpot who won the National League batting title while playing his fourth position (right field) in four seasons.

McCovey Places Third

Gibson received 14 of the 20 first-place votes cast by a committee of the Baseball Writers Association of America composed of two voters in each league city. Rose got the 6 others.

On a point basis (14 for first, 9 for second and so on through 10th), Gibson got 242 points, Rose 205 and Willie McCovey, who placed third, 135. Gibson and Rose were named on every ballot, Rose no lower than fourth, Gibson as far down as seventh on one.

This is the first time pitchers

have swept all four top awards. The Cy Young, set up in 1956, was not split between the leagues until last year.

A Cy Young-most valuable double was scored in 1956 by Don Newcombe of the Brooklyn Dodgers and in 1963 by Sandy Koufax of the Los Angeles Dodgers. But in both years, the American League's most valuable award did not go to a pitcher.

Last year, when there were two Cy Young awards, the most valuable players were Orlando Cepeda of the Cardinals and Carl Yastrzemski of the Boston Red Sox.

Controversial Point

There is always controversy when a pitcher wins the most-valuable award, since many baseball people feel that everyday players should not be compared with pitchers, who work

every fourth day at best. Only the most exceptional performance by a pitcher, combined with the absence of an overwhelming performance by a regular player, results in a most-valuable award for the pitcher.

Gibson's credentials rested as much on what he had meant to the winning of a pennant by the Cardinals as on his statistical accomplishments. His 1.12 earned-run average was a National League record, breaking a mark set by Grover Cleveland Alexander in 1915, and 13 of his 22 victories were shutouts. He had a 15-game winning streak, pitched 28 complete games in 34 starts and at one stage yielded only two runs in nearly 100 innings.

November 14, 1968

Baseball Rules Committee Makes 3 Decisions to Produce More Hits and Runs

MOUND IS DROPPED TO 10-INCH LEVEL

Strike Zone Is Reduced and Vigilance Against Illegal Pitches Will Be Kept

By GEORGE VECSEY
Special to The New York Times

SAN FRANCISCO, Dec. 3—The baseball rules committee made three decisions tonight in the hope of producing more hits and more runs next season. The committee, which has the authority to make changes without further consultations with owners or general managers, voted to lower the pitching mound, to shrink the strike zone and to enforce the current rule about illegal pitches.

The action was taken at the suggestion of the baseball commissioner, William D. Eckert, and following several proposals from a meeting of managers and general managers yesterday. Eckert said today the rules changes were a "good step forward" to producing "more action" in games next year. Last season seemed to be a blur of 1-0 games because of the superiority of the pitchers.

To counteract the dominance of the pitchers, the rules committee voted to drop the mound from 15 inches to 10 instead of the original suggestion of eight inches. Also, all mounds must be sloped gradually so that pitchers will not look as if they are firing from a steep cliff to the batters down below.

Vigilance Is Extended

The second change involved the strike zone, which has been considered anything between the shoulders and the knees. The strike zone next year will be from the tops of the knees to the armpits.

Rather than make the umpires, batters and pitchers adjust to the shift on their own, the committee will have sketches made of hitters in their normal stance. Presumably arrows will note where armpits and tops of knees are situated, so that all men will be prepared when the moment of truth occurs. After all, matadors must learn the anatomy of the bull before entering the ring, so there is a precedent for this move.

The third decision was to keep the vigilance against illegal pitches, or, as Jim Gallagher of the Commissioner's office put it, "those naughty things." It is still illegal to put spit, Vaseline, emery or most any foreign substance on a baseball. If a pitcher throws a ball with a foreign substance on it, the umpire may eject him from the game.

This was the rule last year, and the committee voted to enforce it next year. Also, if a pitcher puts his hands to his mouth while inside the mound area, the umpire shall call an automatic ball, even if the pitcher does not throw the pitch. This is the same rule from last year, and will be enforced.

The committee made two other changes. Next year, a tied, extra-inning game that is stopped for curfew or any other reason will be resumed from that point as soon as possible. Previously, the game was considered a tie and was replayed from the start.

Also, the new type of stud-spike, which Maury Wills was forbidden to wear in league games, has been legalized for next year. The committee realized there was nothing objectionable about the thicker, golf-type spike, and it took them only a year of Maury Wills's life.

The committee also said it had not considered strengthening the 20-second limit for pitchers, or the long-discussed "wild-card pinch-hitter for pitchers."

Finally, the committee appointed a group to study synthetic fields. Bing Devine of St. Louis, Clark Griffith of Minnesota and Dick O'Connell of Boston will work with Spec Richardson of Houston.

Richardson has inside knowledge of synthetic fields since baseballs have been taking unpredictable bounces on the wiggly carpet ever since the Astrodome was opened in 1965. Many baseball executives are interested in synthetic fields so they can do away with mud and maintenance problems, even if they incur a few bad bounces.

December 4, 1968

Bowie Kuhn, Wall St. Lawyer, Named Commissioner

$100,000 CONTRACT TO RUN FOR A YEAR

Choice of National League Lawyer Ends Deadlock Over Burke and Feeney

By LEONARD KOPPETT
Special to The New York Times

BAL HARBOUR, Fla., Feb. 4—Bowie Kuhn, a 42-year-old Wall Street lawyer who has been intimately involved with various baseball problems for more than a decade, was named Commissioner Pro Tem today for a one-year term at a salary of $100,000.

He was selected unanimously on one ballot by the 24 major league clubs as the answer to the deadlock that had arisen with the American League supporting Michael Burke, president of the New York Yankees, and the National League supporting Charles S. (Chub) Feeney, vice president of the San Francisco Giants. No vote was taken on their candidacies.

Instead, Feeney and Burke were added to the planning committee, whose task it is to restructure baseball administration. Jerry Hoffberger of Baltimore is chairman of that committee and Dick Meyer of St. Louis and John Holland of the Chicago Cubs are the other members.

Kuhn's task was defined as providing the leadership for this committee, which went into session immediately after the announcement of Kuhn's election at 5:40 P.M. at the Americana Hotel here. He will also assume all the traditional duties of the commissionership, but the first priority is to carry out a thorough re-examination and reshaping of baseball's structure.

Last Act for Eckert

This ended William D. Eckert's two-month interval of lame duck administration. Eckert, a retired Air Force general with no previous baseball connection, had been given a seven-year contract at $65,000 a year in November, 1965. He was forced to resign last Dec. 6, and will collect the remaining four years' pay due him. But when the clubowners failed to choose between Burke and Feeney on Dec. 20, Eckert's continuance in office led to increasing instability.

Today, therefore, the owners found themselves still unable to unite behind either Burke or Feeney, and they knew it going into the meeting. It was promptly suggested that restructuring should get first consideration, and a seven-man committee went off to recommend means.

The committee was composed of Gabe Paul, of Cleveland, leader of the Burke faction; Walter O'Malley of Los Angeles, leader of the Feeney support; Meyer, Lee MacPhail, vice president of the Yankees; John Galbreath of Pittsburgh, Arthur Allyn of the Chicago White Sox and Frank Dale of Cincinnati.

This group came up with Kuhn's name. When it proposed it to the entire meeting, the reaction was "Why, of course, yes," and Kuhn was elected immediately.

Raised in Washington

Although unknown to the public, Kuhn is not only a known quantity, but an immensely respected figure within the baseball community.

He is a member of Willkie, Farr and Gallagher, a general corporate legal firm that has handled the National League since 1936. He became active in baseball affairs around 1950, on joining the firm out of the University of Virginia Law School, and took over more and more of the load on general baseball business, as well as National League matters, in recent years. He has been involved in franchise shifts (no-

New York Times

Bowie Kuhn

tably the Milwaukee-Atlanta case), pension plans, Player Association negotiations, Congressional hearings, etc.

He comes from Tacoma Park, Md., a suburb of Washington, D. C. He grew up in Washington and attended Theodore Roosevelt High School there before going on to Princeton (Class of '48). He served in the Navy during World War II. His home now is Ridgewood, N. J., and he and his wife Louisa have four children—George, 16; Paul, 12; Alexandra, 9, and Stephen, 7.

"I was always a baseball fan, and sports fan in general," he said, when asked to tell about himself, "and back in 1939 or 1940, I worked inside the scoreboard at Griffith Stadium, where the Senators played. My salary was $1 a day," he added, his eyes twinkling, "and I've been waiting for years to make that public."

The $100,000 he will receive for a one-year term will represent a considerable decrease from his normal income.

"I'll try to terminate my partnership with the firm in some fashion," he explained, "and I will disassociate myself as counsel to the Players Relations Committee. [This is the committee negotiating with the players now.] The Commissioner does have functions as an arbitrator, but I will excuse myself from all pending cases between players and clubs. I will not enter into any of the negotiations now going on with the players."

Breakthrough Seen

Dale, acting as spokesman for the owners, hailed today's action as "a major breakthrough in baseball history."

"This may be the last time we meet as separate leagues, having separate caucuses," he said. "We arrived at this in a combined way, among 24 clubs, and the main job now is to restructure as quickly as possible."

Kuhn struck the same note.

"We are major league baseball," he said, "not the major leagues of baseball. A phenomenon is emerging here, a unified operation which is essential today."

In an unusual display of unity and cooperation, all the owners remained seated at their tables while Kuhn conducted his first news conference. Afterward, all who were questioned expressed great satisfaction with the result, and spoke highly of Kuhn's special qualifications. They seemed to feel that a great dividing line had been crossed in solving the Burke - Feeney dilemma, and that with Kuhn's leadership the planning committee could really modernize and strengthen their business.

February 5, 1969

Maloney of Reds Pitches No-Hitter

CINCINNATI STAR FANS 13 BATTERS

Maloney's No-Hitter Is 2d of Career—Chaney Saves It With Great Catch

CINCINNATI, April 30 (AP)—Jim Maloney of the Cincinnati Reds pitched the second no-hitter of his career tonight, overpowering the Houston Astros, 10-0, with a 13-strike-out performance.

Maloney yielded five walks in becoming the second National Leaguer to hurl hitless ball this year.

Montreal's Bill Stoneman pitched a no-hitter against the Phillies 13 days ago.

Darrel Chaney, the Reds' shortstop, raced into short left field and made an over-the-shoulder catch of Johnny Edwards's looping fly ball in the sixth inning. That preserved the no-hitter.

Edwards, a former Red, had caught both of the previous games in which Maloney pitched no-hit ball for nine or more innings.

Maloney pitched nine innings of no-hit ball, but lost, 1-0, on a 10th-inning homer by Johnny Lewis of the Mets on June 14, 1965. Then he pitched a 10-inning no-hitter to beat the Chicago Cubs, 1-0, on Aug. 19 of the same year.

The 28-year-old right-hander struck out 18 in the first game, equaling the National League record, and 12 in the second game.

Sandy Koufax leads the list of no-hit pitchers with four.

Bob Feller, Cy Young and Larry Corcoran each pitched three.

Maloney, who has 125 career victories, has pitched four one-hitters and eight two-hitters since entering the National League in 1960. He holds the Reds' club record for strikeouts, the 265 he achieved in 1963 when he won 23 games and lost seven.

The Reds, after picking up an unearned run in the first inning, chased the Astro starter, Wade Blasingame, in the fourth inning when they sent 11 batters to the plate while piling up seven runs.

Maloney said he had pitched harder earlier this year, but tonight he "just had better stuff on the ball . . . and they weren't hitting."

It was his third victory this year. He has lost none.

He refused to comment on problems of arm tightening that have plagued him through the season.

"I don't even want to think about it," he said.

The no-hitter was hardly any different from his others, he said.

"You just walk out there and if you've got a no-hitter you've got one."

HOUSTON (N.)	ab	r	h	b	CINCINNATI (N.)	ab	r	h	b
Morgan, 2b	3	0	0	0	Rose, cf	4	2	0	0
August, lf	4	0	0	0	Tolan, rf	5	0	3	4
Wynn, rf	2	0	0	0	Johnson, lf	3	1	1	0
Rader, 3b	3	0	0	0	Savage, lf	0	0	0	0
Mil cr, rf	3	0	0	0	Perez, 3b	4	0	1	0
Menke, ss	2	0	0	0	Bench, c	3	1	1	0
Blefary, 1b	3	0	0	0	May, 1b	3	1	0	1
Edwards, c	3	0	0	0	Helms, 2b	4	2	1	0
Blasingame, p	1	0	0	0	Chaney, ss	4	1	1	2
Ray, p	0	0	0	0	Maloney, p	3	2	1	1
Geronimo, ph	1	0	0	0					
Guinn, p	0	0	0	0	Total	33	10	9	8
Geiger, ph	1	0	0	0					
Coombs, p	0	0	0	0					
Total	26	0	0	0					

Houston .... 000 000 000—0
Cincinnati .... 100 700 02x—10

E—Menke, Blefary. DP—Houston 1, Cincinnati 1. LOB—Houston 4, Cincinnati 6. 2B—Maloney. 3B—Tolan.

	IP	H	R	ER	BB	SO
Blasingame (L. 0-5)..	3⅓	2	7	6	3	2
Ray	1⅓	3	1	1	1	1
Guinn	2	2	0	0	0	3
Coombs	1	3	2	2	0	1
Maloney (W, 3-0)	9	0	0	0	5	13

HBP—By Blasingame (Johnson), (May). Coombs (Johnson). Wild pitch—Blasingame, Ray.
T—2:28. A—3,898.

May 1, 1969

Wilson Hurls No-Hitter

2D CLASSIC IN ROW PITCHED AT PARK

Wilson Fans 13, Duplicating Maloney Feat—Astros End 8-Game Loss Streak

CINCINNATI, May 1 (UPI)—Twenty-four-year-old Don Wilson pitched the second no-hitter of his brief major league career last night as the Houston Astros scored a 4-0 victory over the Cincinnati Reds. Jim Maloney of the Reds held the Astros hitless last night at Crosley Field in a 10-0 victory.

Wilson, who pitched a no-hitter against the Atlanta Braves on June 18, 1967, struck out 13 and walked six before 4,042 fans. Maloney also struck out 13 last night.

Last Sept. 17 and 18 Gaylord Perry of the San Francisco Giants and Ray Washburn of the St. Louis Cardinals traded

no-hitters in Candlestick Park, the only other time no hitters were pitched in consecutive days in the same park.

Wilson, who allowed only one ground ball, struck out Tony Perez on a 3-2 pitch to open the ninth inning. Johnny Bench then flied to center on a 3-1 pitch. After walking Fred Whitfield on a 3-1 pitch, he got Tommy Helms on the first pitch to foul out to Doug Rader at first base to end the game.

It was the third no-hitter of the young season, all in the National League. Bill Stoneman of the Montreal Expos pitched one 14 days ago against the Philadelphia Phillies.

Astros End Famine

Houston had lost 13 straight road games this season and had lost its last eight in a row.

The last no-hitter against the Reds was turned in by Ken Johnson of the Astros in 1964, but he lost the game. The last time the Reds were beaten in a no-hitter was in 1941 when Lon Warneke of the Cards beat them 2-0.

Wilson, picking up his second victory against three losses this season, was beaten, 14-0, by the Reds April 22 when he was knocked out in the sixth inning.

Wilson had most of his problems in the eighth inning. He walked Jim Stewart. a pinch-hitter, on a 3-2 pitch. Harry Walker, the Astro manager, visited Wilson on the mound after the big right-hander threw two balls to the next batter. Jim Beauchamp, another pinch-hitter. Beauchamp, after working the count to 3-2, went down swinging.

The count was also 3-2 on Pete Rose when Don Bryant, the Astro catcher, dropped a foul pop. Rose then walked after fouling off two more pitches.

Wilson weathered the threat by retiring Bob Tolan on a fly to Norm Miller in right field and then getting Alex Johnson on a fly ball to Jimmy Wynn in center.

Noted for Strike-Outs

The native of Monroe, La., who signed with Houston as a free agent, is noted for his strike-outs. He tied two major league records against Cincinnati on July 14, 1968, when he fanned 18. The 18 strike-outs tied the record. and a string of eight in a row during the game tied another mark. He also struck out 16 in another game against the Reds last season.

Wilson struck out 159 batters in 184 innings in 1967 while posting a 10-9 won-lost mark and struck out 175 last season in 209 innings while recording a 13-16 mark.

Jim Merritt, the Reds' starter, blanked the Astros without a hit for the first three innings. but was tagged for a leadoff homer by Rader in the fourth.

The Astros added two runs in the fifth on a walk to Joe Morgan, a single by Wynn and a double by Denis Menke. Curt Blefary tripled in the eighth and scored on Wilson's sacrifice fly to center.

HOUSTON (N.)					CINCINNATI (N.)				
	ab	r	h	bi		ab	r	h	bi
Morgan, 2b	3	1	1	0	Rose, cf	2	0	0	0
J Alou, lf	5	0	0	0	Tolan, rf	4	0	0	0
Wynn, cf	4	1	1	0	A. Johnson, lf	4	0	0	0
Rader, 3b	4	1	1	1	Perez, 3b	4	0	0	0
Menke, ss	4	0	2	2	Bench, c	3	0	0	0
Miller, rf	4	0	0	0	Whitfield, 1b	2	0	0	0
Blefary, 1b	3	1	2	0	Helms, 2b	4	0	0	0
Bryant, c	4	0	2	0	Chaney, ss	4	0	0	0
Wilson, p	2	0	0	1	Carroll, p	0	0	0	0
					Stewart, ss	0	0	0	0
Total	34	4	9	4	Merritt, p	1	0	0	0
					Rist. 1b	1	0	0	0
					Beauchamp, ph	1	0	0	0
					Nottebart, p	0	0	0	0
					Total	27	0	0	0

Houston .... 0 0 0 1 2 0 0 1 0—4
Cincinnati ..... 0 0 0 0 0 0 0 0 0—0

E—Helms, Tolan, Bryant. DP—Cincinnati 1. LOB—Houston 10, Cincinnati 7. 2B—Menke. 3B—Blefary. HR—Rader (2). SB—Bench. S—Morgan. SF—Wilson.

	IP	H	R	ER	BB	SO
Wilson (W. 2-3)	9	0	0	0	6	13
Merritt (L. 1-2)	5	6	3	3	3	4
Carroll	2⅓	3	1	1	1	1
Nottebart	1	0	0	0	1	1

HBP—By Merritt (Wilson), Wilson (Bench). T—2:32. A—4,042.

May 2, 1969

National League Routs American, 9-3 as McCovey Wallops 2 Home Runs

5 CLOUTS ARE HIT IN ALL-STAR GAME

Nationals Gain 7th Straight Triumph, Scoring 5 Runs Off Odom in 3d Inning

By JOSEPH DURSO
Special to The New York Times

WASHINGTON, July 23 — Denny McLain, the flying pitcher, kept his dental appointment in Detroit today and then flew back to Washington just in time to watch the American League lose its seventh straight All-Star Game to the National League.

The score was 9-3 and, if any persons in the crowd of 45,259 were as late as McLain, they missed some of the early fireworks, too. The Nationals scored one run in the first inning off Mel Stottlemyre—who started in place of the tardy Detroit Tiger—and then two in the second, five in the third and one in the fourth.

By then, McLain was watching the bombardment from the pitcher's mound, where he had an exceptional view of the fifth and final home run.

Two were hit for the National League by Willie McCovey of San Francisco and one by John Bench of Cincinnati, while Frank Howard of Washington and Bill Freehan of Detroit connected for the American.

National's 22d Victory

It all added up to the most free swinging game in the series since 1962, and when it

was over the National League had increased its lead to 22 victories as against 17 defeats and one tie.

McLain, the business conglomerate and 31-game winner for the world champion Tigers, was not the only celebrity missing when the home runs began to fly around the Robert F. Kennedy Memorial Stadium. The game was originally scheduled for last night but, because of a three-hour downpour, was postponed until this afternoon —the first rainout since the series started in 1933.

That meant that President Nixon had to forgo his performance of throwing out the first ball. Instead, he headed west on the first leg of his world tour and Vice President Spiro T. Agnew delivered the executive pitch.

At about the same time, McLain was headed west, too, in

his twin-engined turboprop. He had a long-standing appointment with his dentist in Detroit, which he kept at 7 o'clock this morning. It lasted three hours, then Denny flew the one hour back to the capital.

He arrived in the second inning, and by then Stottlemyre was delivering the early pitches for him and they were being swatted around the ball park.

In fact, the first pitch that Stottlemyre threw was looped into short left field by Matty Alou for a single. Alou took second when Don Kessinger bounced a grounder wide of first base and was thrown out, Boog Powell to Stottlemyre. Then Alou took third on a wild pitch and scored when Henry Aaron lifted a high fly into short left field.

Aaron's fly looked like an easy out for Howard, the hometown hero of the Senators who

Willie McCovey   San Francisco Giants

Box Score of All-Star Game

NATIONAL	AB.	R.	H.	BI.	PO.	A.
M. Alou, cf	4	1	2	0	5	0
Kessinger, ss	3	0	0	0	0	0
gMenke, ss	1	0	0	0	1	0
fMays, ph	1	0	0	0	0	0
H. Aaron, rf	4	1	1	0	0	0
Singer, p	0	0	0	0	0	0
pBeckert, 2b	1	0	0	0	0	0
McCovey, 1b	4	2	2	3	2	0
kMay, 1b	1	0	0	0	3	0
Santo, 3b	3	0	0	0	2	1
lT. Perez, ph	1	0	0	0	1	1
C. Jones, lf	4	2	2	0	3	0
rRose, lf	1	0	0	0	2	0
Bench, c	3	2	2	2	4	0
mHundley, c	1	0	0	3	0	0
Millan, 2b	4	1	1	2	1	1
Koosman, p	0	0	0	0	0	0
Dierker, p	0	0	0	0	0	0
P. Niekro, p	0	0	0	0	0	0
Carlton, p	2	0	1	1	0	1
Gibson, p	0	0	0	0	0	0
dBanks, ph	1	0	0	0	0	0
hClemente, rf	1	0	0	0	0	0
Total	40	9	11	8	27	4

AMERICAN	AB.	R.	H.	BI.	PO.	A.
Carew, 2b	3	0	0	0	0	2
jAndrews, 2b	1	0	0	0	0	0
Jackson, rf	2	0	0	0	2	0
iYastrzemski, lf	1	0	0	0	1	0
F. Robinson, rf	2	0	0	0	0	0
eBlair, cf	3	0	0	0	2	0
Powell, 1b	4	0	1	0	9	1
Howard, lf	1	1	1	1	0	0
bR. Smith, lf	1	1	0	0	0	0
Bando, 3b	3	0	1	0	0	1
McDowell, p	0	0	0	0	0	0
Culp, p	0	0	0	0	0	0
sWhite, ph	1	0	0	0	0	0
Petrocelli, ss	3	0	1	1	1	3
qFregosi, ss	1	0	0	0	0	0
Freehan, c	2	1	2	1	4	0
nRoseboro, c	1	0	0	0	6	0
tC. May, ph	1	0	0	0	0	0
Stottlemyre, p	0	0	0	0	1	0
Odom, p	0	0	0	0	0	0
Knowles, p	0	0	0	0	0	0
aKillebrew, ph	1	0	0	0	0	0
McLain, p	0	0	0	0	0	0
cMincher, ph	1	0	0	0	0	0
McNally, p	0	0	0	0	0	0
oB. Robinson, 3b	1	0	0	0	1	1
Total	33	3	6	3	27	8

aFlied out for Knowles in 3d. bRan for Howard in 4th. cStruck out for McLain in 4th. dLined out for Gibson in 5th. eReplaced F. Robinson in 5th. fFlied out for Kessinger in 5th. gReplaced Kessinger in 5th. hReplaced H. Aaron in 5th. iReplaced Jackson in 6th. jReplaced Carew in 6th. kReplaced McCovey in 6th. lReplaced Santo in 6th. mReplaced Bench in 6th. nReplaced Freehan in 7th. oReplaced Bando in 7th. pReplaced Millan in 7th. qReplaced Petrocelli in 8th. rReplaced Jones in 8th. sStruck out for Culp in 9th. tStruck out for Roseboro in 9th.

National	1 2 5	1 0 0	0 0 0	—9
American	0 . 1	1 0 0	0 0 0	—3

Errors—Petrocelli, F. Howard. Two-base hits—Petrocelli, Millan, Carlton. Home runs—Howard, Freehan, McCovey 2, Bench. Left on base—National 7, American 5.

	IP.	H.	R.	ER.	BB.	SO.	H.B.P.	WP.	Bk.
Carlton (W)	3	2	2	2	1	2	0	0	0
Gibson	1	2	1	1	1	2	0	0	0
Singer	2	0	0	0	0	0	0	0	0
Koosman	1 2/3	1	0	0	1	0	0	0	0
Dierker	1/3	1	0	0	0	0	0	0	0
Niekro	1	0	0	0	2	0	0	0	0
Stottlemyre (L)	2	4	3	2	0	1	0	1	0
Odom	1/3	5	5	4	0	0	0	0	0
Knowles	2/3	0	0	0	0	0	0	0	0
McLain	1	1	1	1	2	2	0	0	0
McNally	2	1	0	0	1	1	0	0	0
McDowell	2	0	0	0	0	3	0	0	0
Culp	1	0	0	0	0	2	0	0	0

Bases on Balls—Off Carlton (Jackson), Gibson (Howard), McLain 2 (Santo, Bench), McNally (Alou).
Struck out—by Carlton 2 (F. Robinson, Petrocelli), Gibson 2 (Powell, Mincher), Koosman (B. Robinson), Niekro 2 (White, May), Stottlemyre (Carlton), McLain 2 (H. Aaron, Millan), McNally (McCovey), McDowell 3 (M. Alou, Menke, L. May), Culp 2 (Perez, Hundley).
Umpires—Flaherty (A.), plate; Donatelli (N.), first base; Stewart (A.), second base; Gorman (N.), third base; Springstead (A.), left field; Venzon (N.), right field.
Time of game—2:38. Attendance—45,259.

had just been introduced to a standing ovation. But the 6-foot-7-inch outfielder looked uncertainly into the misty sky, then looked uncertainly at the shortstop, Rico Petrocelli, and finally he lunged while the ball plopped off his glove for an error.

Stottlemyre, who has won 14 games for the New York Yankees, got the side out after that. But he began to suffer again in the second when Cleon Jones of the Mets singled on the first pitch, with Petrocelli making a diving stop near second base.

That brought up Bench, the Cincinnati catcher. He has been taking two weeks of Army re-

serve training in Virginia but received permission to appear in the game. When it was postponed last night, he telephoned his base and got an extension.

So he was in the game literally on a pass. Bench promptly bounced a two-strike pitch off the box seats in the mezzanine for a two-run homer.

McLain arrived in the dugout during this outburst and watched with nine new dental caps and a sheepish look. The strain was eased momentarily

in the bottom of the inning when Howard atoned for his error with a tremendous home run. It was hit on a 1-and-1 pitch thrown by Steve Carlton of St. Louis, and it traveled 440 feet to the center-field mezzanine.

That made the score 3-1, and gave the American League its first run in the rivalry in two years. But the third inning was at hand and with it came the real deluge.

2 Runs on 4 Pitches

The new pitcher for the American League was John

(Blue Moon) Odom of Oakland, who also had been moved higher in the rotation because of McClain's aerial excursion.

On his first pitch, Aaron singled. On his fourth pitch, McCovey lined a 400-foot home run off the center-field scoreboard. One out later, Petrocelli booted Jones's grounder and Bench singled.

Felix Millan followed by bouncing a single over Sal Bando's head down the left-field line, and two more runs scored. Then Carlton, up for the second time in three innings, doubled into the alley in left-center and

Millan scored the fifth run.

Mayo Smith of Detroit, the American League manager, got the message and rescued Odom, who had tied a record by allowing five hits in one inning. The Nationals also tied their record of five runs in one time at bat (1954 at Cleveland, when they lost, 11—9). But they ended the inning one run short of the American League's six-run binge at the Polo Grounds in 1934.

The score was now 8-1 and, if the pitchers were still dominating baseball, few people were noticing. Even the American League had the range. In the bottom of the inning, Freehan hit Carlton's third pitch off the left-field mezzanine for a homer, the fourth in three innings.

Then it was the fourth inning and McLain finally made the scene. Disdaining a ride in the bull-pen go-cart, the pitching pilot walked in and struck out Aaron. But McCovey lined his third pitch to him over the right-field fence for his second homer in consecutive innings.

That made McCovey the fourth man in 40 All-Star games to hit two the same day. The others were Arky Vaughan, Ted Williams and Al Rosen. But the two-team total of five homers fell one short of the record of six, set in 1951 and matched in 1954.

Before McLain finished his one inning of work, he also walked Ron Santo and Bench. Then he disappeared, with the National League firmly in command.

Before both teams subsided over the last five innings, the American League scored its final run off Bob Gibson in the fourth. It came on a walk to Howard, plus singles by Bando and Freehan.

After that, order was maintained by Bill Singer, Jerry Koosman, Larry Dierker and Phil Niekro for the Nationals and by Dave McNally, Sam McDowell and Ray Culp for the Americans.

There were two high spots down the homestretch. In the fifth, the Nationals failed to score for the first time but distinguished themselves by producing two uncommon pinch-hitters — Willie Mays and Ernie Banks, who have hit

1,085 homers in their combined total of 36 seasons.

Mays, appearing in his 20th All-Star Game, was greeted with a standing ovation, then flied out to right field. Banks hit a line drive to the shortstop.

In the sixth, the best defensive play was made by Carl Yastrzemski. He went back to the seven-foot-high left-field fence, leaped, reached over it and hauled back Bench's bid for a second homer.

When it was all over, the Nationals still had a six-run margin, seven straight victories and Juan Marichal and Tom Seaver ready in the bull pen. By any definition in professional baseball's 100 years, they were in control of the situation.

July 24, 1969

Mets Top Cards, 4-3, Despite Carlton's Record 19 Strike-Outs

SWOBODA CLOUTS PAIR FOR ALL RUNS

His Second Homer in 8th Brings Victory and Widens Lead to 4½ Games

By JOSEPH DURSO
Special to The New York Times

ST. LOUIS, Sept. 15—Steve Carlton of the St. Louis Cardinals set a major league record tonight by striking out 19 New York Mets. But the Mets still won the game, 4-3, on a pair of two-run home runs by Ron Swoboda and extended their lead to 4½ games with 15 to play.

Carlton, a 24-year-old left-hander, struck out the side in four of the nine innings as he surpassed the record of 18 strike-outs set by Sandy Koufax, Bob Feller and Don Wilson. He even fanned Swoboda twice—on his first and third times at bat.

But on his second and fourth trips to the plate, the Maryland muscleman drove home runs into the left-field seats—both

times with a man on base, both times with the Mets trailing by one run.

Cubs in a Tailspin

As a result, the Mets swung even higher on their high-flying trapeze with two and a half weeks to play. They put 4½ games between themselves and the Chicago Cubs, who lost to the Montreal Expos and continued one of the stunning tailspins of the baseball season.

The Mets' victory — despite Carlton's virtuoso performance —was No. 27 in their last 34 games. They trailed Chicago by 9½ games on Aug. 13, but since then have soared to the top of the Eastern Division of the National League, and tonight marked the 20th straight game in which their pitchers did did not allow an enemy home run.

Carlton, though, suffered a bittersweet evening precisely because he threw the home-run pitch twice to the right-handed Swoboda—who had won Saturday's game with a grand-slam home run in Pittsburgh.

The 6-foot-4-inch 200-pounder from Miami pitched his way into the baseball record books by striking out half of the 38 batters he faced. He got 27 outs—19 on third strikes—but allowed nine hits and two walks, and took his 10th defeat against 16 victories.

Three to Go in Ninth

Going into the ninth inning tonight, Carlton had 16 strike-

Mets' Box Score

NEW YORK (N.)					ST. LOUIS (N.)				
	ab.	r.	h.	bi		ab.	r.	h.	bi
Harrelson, ss	4	0	1	0	Brock, lf	4	1	2	0
Otis, lf	5	0	0	0	Flood, cf	5	2	2	1
Agee, cf	4	1	1	0	Pinson, rf	4	0	3	1
Clendenon, 1b	3	1	1	0	Torre, 1b	4	0	1	1
Swoboda, rf	4	2	2	4	McCarver, c	4	0	0	0
Charles, 3b	4	0	0	0	Shannon, 3b	4	0	0	0
Grote, c	4	0	2	0	Javier, 2b	4	0	0	0
Weis, 2b	4	0	1	0	Maxvill, ss	3	0	0	0
Gentry, p	2	0	0	0	Browne, ph	1	0	0	0
Pfeil, ph	1	0	1	0	Carlton, p	3	0	0	0
Gosger, pr	0	0	0	0	Gagliano, ph	1	0	0	0
McGraw, p	1	0	0	0	Nossek, pr	0	0	0	0
Total	36	4	9	4	Total	37	3	8	3

New York .... 0 0 0 2 0 0 0 2 0—4
St. Louis .... 0 0 1 0 2 0 0 0 0—3
E—Javier, Charles 2, Clendenon, Harrelson. DP—New York 1. LOB— New York 7, St. Louis 9. HR—Swoboda 2 (9). SB—Pinson, Brock.

	IP.	H.	R.	ER.	BB.	SO.
Gentry	6	7	3	3	1	3
McGraw (W., 8-3)	3	1	0	0	1	3
Carlton (L, 16-10)	9	9	4	4	2	19

Wild pitch—Carlton.
T—2:23. A—13,806.

outs, meaning he had to fan the side to establish the record. He had already struck out three Mets in the first, second and fourth innings. He had struck out Amos Otis three times and four other Mets twice apiece.

Then in the final inning, he struck out Tug McGraw, who had relieved Gary Gentry in the seventh inning of a game that had been delayed twice by rain for a total of 81 minutes. That was No. 17.

Next came Bud Harrelson, and he looked at strike three for No. 18. And finally, Otis—just recalled from the minor leagues—swung and missed a third strike for No. 19 and the record.

"It was the best stuff I ever had," said Carlton, like a sculptor who has just created a masterpiece and then accidentally chipped it. "When I had nine strike-outs, I decided to go all the way. But it cost me the game because I started to challenge every batter."

Before he began challenging Swoboda, though, the Cardinals provided a one-run lead in the third on a walk to Lou Brock and singles by Curt Flood and Vada Pinson. They might have scored more, but Brock was thrown out at the plate by Tommie Agee when he tried to score from first on a single that slowed to a stop on the wet outfield grass.

In the fourth, though, Donn Clendenon walked and Swoboda lined the two-strike pitch into the left-field mezzanine for his eighth home run of the season.

Carlton then fanned the side, but he now was behind, 2-1.

However, the Cardinals put him ahead again in the fifth with four straight singles off Gentry with two down. The singles were hit by Brock, Flood, Pinson and Joe Torre, and now Carlton was ahead again, 3-2.

But in the eighth, Agee singled to center, Clendenon struck out and up came Swoboda. Carlton challenged him again, but on the 2-and-2 pitch Swoboda lined another home run into the same section for the deciding run.

September 16, 1969

Mets Win, 5-3, Take the Series

By JOSEPH DURSO

The Mets entered the promised land yesterday after seven years of wandering through the wilderness of baseball.

In a tumultuous game before a record crowd of 57,397 in Shea Stadium, they defeated the Baltimore Orioles, 5-3, for their fourth straight victory of the 66th World Series and captured the championship of a sport that had long ranked them as comical losers.

They did it with a full and final dose of the magic that had spiced their unthinkable climb from ninth place in the National League — 100 - to - 1 shots who scraped and scrounged their way to the pinacle as the waifs of the major leagues.

At 3:17 o'clock on a cool and often sunny afternoon, their impossible dream came true when Cleon Jones caught a fly ball hit by Dave Johnson to left field. And they immediately touched off one of the great, riotous scenes in sports history, as thousands of persons swarmed from their seats and tore up the patch of ground where the Mets had made history.

Lovable Winners Now

It was 10 days after they had won the National League pennant in a three-game sweep of the Atlanta Braves. It was 22 days after they had won the Eastern title of the league over the Chicago Cubs. It was eight years after they had started business under Casey Stengel as the lovable losers of all sports.

They reached the top, moreover, in the best and most farfetched manner of Met baseball.

They spotted the Orioles three runs in the third inning when Dave McNally and Frank Robinson hit home runs off Jerry Koosman.

But then they stormed back with two runs in the sixth inning on a home run by Donn Clendenon, another in the seventh on a home run by Al Weis and two more in the eighth on two doubles and two errors.

The deciding run was batted home by Ron Swoboda, who joined the Met mystique in 1965 when the team was losing 112

games and was finishing last for the fourth straight time.

But, like most of the Mets' victories in their year to remember, the decision was a collective achievement by the youngest team in baseball, under Manager Gil Hodges—who had suffered a heart attack a year ago after the Mets "surged" into ninth place.

The wild, final chapter in the story was written against the desperate efforts of the Orioles, who had swept to the American League pennant by 19 games as one of the most powerful teams in modern times.

Orioles' Wings Clipped

The Orioles had not won since the opening game last Saturday in Baltimore and needed three straight victories to survive. In the third inning, they lashed out at Koosman with three runs and erased the memory of the six no-hit innings he had pitched against them Sunday.

Mark Belanger led off with a looping single over first base. He was nearly caught off the base by Jerry Grote, the New York catcher, who was backing up the play. But in a brief shoving contest, Belanger was called safe as he scrambled back to the base, where Grote took a throw from Swoboda.

On the next pitch, McNally hit a home run into the Baltimore bull pen in left field and the Orioles led, 2-0.

McNally, who had lost the second game to Koosman, is a 27-year-old left-hander who

can hit as well as pitch. He didn't lose a game this season until Aug. 3, then finished with 20 victories. He also hit three home runs last year, including a grand slam, and another this year.

His drive off Koosman was the first extra-base hit for Baltimore in 35 innings and it cast a pall over the fans who had come to see the Mets reach the stars. Two outs later, Frank Robinson bombed Koosman's first pitch over the center-field fence, Baltimore led by 3-0 and the Mets' magic suddenly seemed remote.

But Koosman settled down after that and checkmated the Orioles on one single for the final six innings. He retired 19 of the last 21 batters, closed with a five-hitter and even swung a mean bat when the Mets began to do their "thing."

They almost revived in the third when Koosman doubled past third base. Nothing came of it because McNally knocked off the next three batters, but it was an omen: Koosman had made only four hits in 84 times at bat all season.

Then, in the sixth, another omen appeared. Each team argued in turn that a batter had been hit by a pitched ball. The Orioles, though, lost their argument; the Mets won theirs. And the game veered inexorably toward the "team of destiny."

Motion Is Denied

The Orioles pleaded their case first. With one out in the top

of the sixth, an inside fastball plunked Frank Robinson on his right thigh. The home-plate umpire, Lou DiMuro, ruled that it had glanced off the bat first for strike two. Baltimore's volatile manager, Earl Weaver, who had been banished from Wednesday's game argued that it had simply struck Robinson, who already had started for first base.

When the Orioles were overruled, Robinson disappeared into the runway behind the dugout for five minutes while the trainer sprayed his thigh with a freezing medication and while everybody in the stadium waited. Then he returned, was greeted by a sea of waving handkerchiefs and struck out.

In the bottom of the sixth, it was the Mets' turn to plead an identical case and, in the amazing spirit of their new fortune, they won it on an appeal.

Jones was the leadoff batter and he was struck on the right instep by a dropping curveball. The umpire called it a ball; Jones insisted he had been hit. Hodges, the old hero of Ebbets Field, retrieved the ball from the Mets' dugout, where it had bounced, and executed the old "look-at-the-ball-trick."

DiMuro duly looked at the ball, detected a swatch of shoe polish on its cover, reversed himself and waved Jones to first base. Now Weaver shot out of the dugout to voice his indignation, but lost his point and soon his ball game.

The next batter, Clendenon, went to a count of two balls and two strikes, then whacked a home run off the auxiliary scoreboard on the facing of the left-field loge seats.

It was his third home run in three games (he had hit 16 during the regular schedule) and it punctuated a remarkable season for the 34-year-old ex-student of law.

His homer yesterday, which put him one short of the Series record of four shared by Babe Ruth, Lou Gehrig, Hank Bauer and Duke Snider, put the Mets back in business. In the next inning, Al Weis brought them even on McNally's second pitch.

Weis, the silent supersub, drove the pitch over the 371-foot sign in left-center as the crowd rocked the stadium, and the game was tied, 3-3. It marked another achievement for the right-handed platoon that Hodges deploys against left-handed pitching and it was no mean achievement for Weis.

Box Score of Fifth Series Game

BALTIMORE (A.)	AB.	R.	H.	RBI.	NEW YORK (N.)	AB.	R.	H.	RBI.
Buford, lf	4	0	0	0	Agee, cf	3	0	1	0
Blair, cf	4	0	0	0	Harrelson, ss	4	0	0	0
F. Robinson, rf	3	1	1	1	Jones, lf	3	2	1	0
Powell, 1b	4	0	1	0	Clendenon, 1b	3	1	1	2
Salmon, pr	0	0	0	0	Swoboda, rf	4	1	2	1
B. Robinson, 3b	4	0	0	0	Charles, 3b	4	0	0	0
Johnson, 2b	4	0	1	0	Grote, c	4	0	0	0
Belanger, ss	3	1	1	0	Weis, 2b	4	1	1	1
Etchebarren, c	3	0	0	0	Koosman, p	3	0	1	0
McNally, p	2	1	1	2					
Motton, ph	1	0	0	0	Total	32	5	7	4
Watt, p	0	0	0	0					
Total	32	3	5	3					

Baltimore (A.) ....0 0 3   0 0 0   0 0 0—3
New York (N.) ....0 0 0   0 0 2   1 2 ..—5

Errors—Powell, Watt. Left on base—Baltimore 3, New York 6. Doubles—Koosman, Jones, Swoboda. Home runs—McNally (1), F. Robinson (1), Clendenon (3), Weis (1). Stolen base—Agee.

	IP.	H.	R.	ER.	BB.	SO.
McNally	7	5	3	3	2	6
Watt (L, 0—1)	1	2	2	1	0	1
Koosman (W, 2—0)	9	5	3	3	1	5

Hit by pitch—by McNally (Jones).
Time of game—2:14. Attendance—57,397.

During Weis's two seasons with the Mets, 212 home runs had been hit in Shea Stadium—none by Al. He had hit only two all year, both in Chicago in July. But in the World Series, the quiet little infielder turned tiger with four walks, four singles and one historic home run.

Finally, the stage was set for the last full measure of Met magic.

In the eighth, with Eddie Watt pitching for Baltimore, Jones looked at three straight balls and then a strike. Then he lined the 3-and-1 pitch off the center-field fence for a double.

Clendenon, who was voted the outstanding player in the Series, fouled off two attempts to bunt. Then he lined a long fly into the right-field corner, just foul, then bounced out to Brooks Robinson, with Jones holding second base.

The next batter was Swoboda and, with first base open, the Orioles might have walked him intentionally. But they elected to challenge him and Swoboda drilled the second pitch down the left-field line, where Don Buford almost made a brilliant backhand catch off the grass. But the ball dropped in for a double as Jones streaked for home to put the Mets in front, 4-3, and tumult broke out across Flushing Meadow.

Ed Charles lifted a fly to Buford for the second out. But Grote followed with a low line drive toward John Powell and the 250-pound first baseman booted it for an error. He

chased the ball, though, to his right and lobbed it to Watt, who was rusing over from the mound to cover first base.

By this time, Grote was flashing across the bag and, when Watt juggled the throw and dropped it, Swoboda was flashing across the plate with the second run of the inning.

That made it 5-3 and the Mets were three outs from fantasy. There was a brief delay when Frank Robinson opened the ninth with a walk. But then Powell forced him at second base, Brooks Robinson flied out to Swoboda in right and—at 3:17 P.M.—Johnson lifted a fly to Jones in left-center.

Jones made the catch with a flourish, then he and his old high-school mate from Mobile, Tommie Agee, turned and streaked across the outfield to

the Mets' bull pen in right.

The beat the avalanche by a split second and, as they ducked into the safety of the stadium's caverns, the crowd let go. Children, housewives, mature men, all swarmed onto the field where the Mets had marched. They tore up home plate, captured the bases, ripped gaping holes from the turf, set off orange flares and firecrackers and chalked the wooden outfield fence with the signs of success.

The Mets were the champions of the world on Oct. 16, 1969.

"I never saw anything like it," said Joe DiMaggio, the old Yankee, who had thrown out the first ball.

October 17, 1969

Killebrew, Twins' Slugger, Named Most Valuable Player in American League

ORIOLES' POWELL SECOND IN VOTING

Killebrew First by 67 Points With 294—Frank Robinson of Baltimore 3d at 162

By LEONARD KOPPETT

Harmon Killebrew of the Minnesota Twins, leading slugger in the major leagues last season, has beeen named the American League's Most Valuable Player for 1969, it was announced yesterday by the Baseball Writers Association of America, which conducts the balloting.

Killebrew won by a decisive margin over John (Boog) Powell and Frank Robinson, of the Baltimore Orioles. Baltimore swept the Twins in three straight games in the playoff for the American League pennant, but the vote is conducted strictly on the basis of regular-season play and the ballots were filed before the playoffs began.

A 24-man committee, two from each league city, gave Killebrew 16 first-place votes, Powell 6 and Robinson 2. Each ballot lists 10 names, with 14 points for first, 9 points for second and so forth. Killebrew was named on every ballot (seven seconds and one third) and totaled 294 points, while Powell, who was also mentioned by every voter, had 227 points. Robinson, placing third with 162 points, was not named at all by three experts.

Led Majors in Homers

In all, 37 players were mentioned. Last year's unanimous winner, Denny McLain of the Detroit Tigers, placed sixth with 85 points, the highest ranking attained by any pitcher. Above him, after the top three, were Frank Howard of Washington and Reggie Jackson of Oakland, also home-run hitters.

Killebrew led the majors with 49 home runs and 140 runs batted in. He is one of the game's authentic "all-time class" long-range blasters: at the age of 33, he has 446 home runs to his credit and already ranks 13th in baseball history. A stocky (5 feet 11 inches, 210 pounds) right-handed slugger who established himself only in his middle 20's, Killebrew's home-run rate (per time at bat)

United Press International

HONORED: Harmon Killebrew of the Minnesota Twins was voted the American League's Most Valuable Player of the year yesterday. He led league in homers and runs batted in.

for his 11-year career is among the top five ever.

His triumph was especially gratifying because he tore his left hamstring muscle so badly in the 1968 All-Star Game at Houston that it was feared his career might be over. Instead, he bounced back to one of his finest years, winning (or sharing) the American League home run championship for the sixth time. His batting average was .276.

"Since I consider this the biggest award, I'm honored to get it," he said yesterday from his home in Ontario, Ore. "I really just hoped I'd be able to play a lot this year, after the injury. Next year I just hope I can play as well."

Killebrew will leave soon for Japan, where he will demonstrate a batting instruction device his firm is marketing.

Only two New York Yankee players received votes. Mel Stottlemyre, the pitcher, got a fifth-place vote and a ninth-place vote for 8 points; and Roy White, the outfielder, got a ninth-place vote worth 2 points. Two teams, Cleveland and Chicago, got no representation at all.

November 13, 1969

Reserve Clause Breeds Bitterness

By LEONARD KOPPETT

BITTER feelings about baseball's reserve clause, and bitter feelings towards those who challenge it, are nothing new.

The whole subject, in fact, reached explosive proportions just 80 years ago, and the effects of what was known as the "Brotherhood War" linger on within the baseball community today. In many cases subliminal, in others an explicit view of history, the attitudes formed by that early baseball experience color the views of most baseball men.

About Baseball

More important even than what actually happened in 1890, when major league players formed a union, rebelled, started their own league and broke almost everyone concerned, is what baseball people believe happened. The stories of that time have been handed down from one generation of owners and players to another, and the assumptions have persisted among those who neither know nor care about the historical events.

A review of the Brotherhood War, therefore, sheds some light on the intensity of emotion in today's struggle, which centers on Curt Flood's antitrust suit. The hardest thing to understand, for most outsiders, is the apparent obtuseness of the baseball establishment in resisting any and all change. Even a few famous, high-priced players defend the status quo (although no minor-leaguer has yet leaped to its defense). After all, it sounds silly for supposedly responsible business men to hint at "total destruction" of their affairs if so much as a comma is changed.

But everything has origins, even unreason. It's easy enough for mid-Twentieth Century lawyers to say "devise a less restrictive substitute." Driven into the baseball consciousness, however, is the idea that the present system, which did evolve gradually, has worked profitably; that alternatives tried in the past—even if it was the dim past—did fail; and "alternatives" presented in theory can lead to numerous booby traps in reality.

In this light, the reluctance of the establishment to confront change is more comprehensible, if not necessarily more justified. Perhaps the real criticism of today's baseball brass should be on other grounds. Its rigid stance implies timidity, a self-confessed lack of confidence in its ability to act imaginatively, constructively and with goodwill, to devise improvements.

At any rate, this is what happened almost a century ago:

The first group that approximated a major league was formed in 1871. It was called the National Association of Professional Baseball Players, and it failed after five years because there was no way to keep players from jumping from team to team.

In 1876, the National League of Baseball Clubs was formed, putting all authority in the hands of club owners rather than players. This did provide stability—in financing, in team identity, in rooting interest. But players still could, and did, move around freely between seasons.

By 1879, the practice of putting several of a team's best players "on reserve" was adopted. This meant that the other clubs in the league agreed not to sign the five players designated by any one club as "on reserve" for the following season. Quickly, the number on reserve grew to nine to 11 to 15. (Today, automatically, all players are "on reserve" with some club, with insignificant exceptions.)

But by 1882, there was a second "major" league in operation, the American Association, and in 1884 a third league took the field, the Union Association. Competition for experienced players was keen, and salaries were high. But the Union Association folded after one year, and the other two leagues arranged to observe each other's reserve lists, and a true reserve clause came into being in 1885.

Competitively, at the gate, and in public esteem, baseball thrived at that point. But the club owners also used the reserve clause to drive salaries down, and imposed a salary ceiling (at a level of about half what the top stars were already making).

Led by John Montgomery Ward, captain and star infielder of the New York Giants and a law school graduate, the players formed a union, called the Brotherhood of Professional Baseball Players. Through the union, they negotiated with the club owners to have the salary ceiling and some other restrictions removed. (It was Ward who first referred to the reserve clause as "slavery," at a time when men who had fought in the Civil War were still less than 50 years old.)

After the 1888 season, the owners agreed to Ward's proposals—and Ward went on a round-the-world baseball tour promoted by Albert Spalding. While he was out of the country, the owners reneged on their agreement. Ward returned to New York in March, 1889, on the eve of a new baseball season, and found his Brotherhood members ready to strike.

He persuaded them, instead, to play out 1889 under the oppressive contracts but to use the time to find investors so that they could form their own league.

They did. In 1890, the Players' League contained most of the established big leaguers from the National and the A.A.—Ward, Buck Ewing, King Kelly, Tim Keefe, Charles Comiskey and so forth. They purposely put teams into seven of the eight National League cities, and scheduled games at the same time, and they concentrated their fire on the New York franchise.

●

The total attendance for baseball reached a peak — but the burden for every individual club was intolerable. The National League owners persuaded the backers of the Players League that there was no future in such a competition. (Most of the Players League teams had their players as shareholders). Some backers quit, some bought into the National League—and in 1891, almost all the big leaguers were back in the National, burned by their excursion into free enterprise.

The National then proceeded to wipe out the A.A. and to operate as a 12-team monopoly—which failed badly. In 1901, the American League set itself up as a rival major league, raided the National for players, and won a peace treaty in 1902. The present system has been essentially unchanged since.

Was the Brotherhood War a valid test? Was it abandoned too quickly? Is it relevant to today? The probable answers are no, yes, no—but that's in the realm of opinion, and the men who built the present system (between 1900 and 1930) were men who had lived through that experience. Their ideas have been handed down to today's baseball leaders, and perhaps the time has come to re-examine them.

January 25, 1970

Pilots' Move to Milwaukee Is Cleared by Court Decision

REFEREE REJECTS DISMISSAL PLEA

Action in Bankruptcy Case Paves Way for Transfer of Seattle Franchise

SEATTLE, March 31 (UPI)—A Federal bankruptcy court referee granted owners of the financially-plagued Seattle Pilots permission tonight to sell their one-year-old American League baseball franchise to Milwaukee interests.

Sidney C. Volinn, the bankruptcy court referee to whom the Pilots turned for help, ruled a $10.8-million offer for the purchase of the club by the Milwaukee Brewers was in order.

Since the American League had voted approval for transfer of the club from Seattle to Milwaukee in a telephone conference call yesterday, the Pilots became the Milwaukee Brewers upon Volinn's consent. The Brewers had signed a purchase agreement for the Pilots on March 8 and the agreement was to expire tomorrow morning.

Thus, Milwaukee, without a big league club since the Braves moved to Atlanta four years ago, rejoined baseball's select group, only this time as a member of the American League.

Short-Lived Franchise

For Seattle, it marked one of the shortest-lived franchises in the history of baseball. One has to go all the way back to the turn of the century to find another city that held a big league franchise for so short a time. The Pilots reportedly lost $1-million in their one and only season in Seattle and stood to lose another $1.5-million if they remained there this year.

Milwaukee, a charter member of the American League in 1900 became the St. Louis Browns in 1902.

Volinn's ruling came after a last-ditch effort for dismissal of the case from bankruptcy court by William Dwyer, special Washington State Assistant Attorney General, was turned down.

Volinn listened to testimony in a steamy court room before calling a halt late in the afternoon.

He had set the next hearing for tomorrow morning but was reminded that he ran the risk of voiding the contract entered into by the Pilots and Brewers. It was then that he said he would reach a decision sooner.

Left standing is an antitrust suit filed by the City of Seattle and the State of Washington seeking $82-million in damages from the American League and the ire of Seattle baseball fans. Among them are two United States Senators Warren Magnuson and Henry Jackson. The two have said they would move for enactment of a bill that would do away with baseball's immunity from the antitrust laws, which the sport has enjoyed since a 1922 Supreme Court ruling.

The American League came out of the case with some embarrassment and William Daley and Dewey and Max Soriano, principal Pilot owners, with a $1-million profit for holding the franchise only one year.

Volinn said he pondered long and hard over his decision and came to the conclusion that he had only one way to go.

"This is a problem of major magnitude because of the time element," Volinn said. "It might be a burden on all parties under the circumstance, and because of the imminence of the baseball season, an emergency does exist.

"This matter presents a posture in which the debtor is without funds and the only alternative would be deficit financing by the American League, perhaps upwards of $10-million.

"It's obvious that the club cannot pay its debts and may well be insolvent.

"The unique character of a major league baseball team has been considered, and its importance to the community has been considered, but it's obvious the debtors (Pilots) are incapable of carrying on. That is beyond question."

Volin's concern, too, was the long line of creditors the Pilots have picked up. Under Chapter II of the Bankruptcy Act he is obliged to take their interests under consideration as well as the interests of those who came to him for help.

April 1, 1970

Seaver Strikes Out 19, Including Record 10 in a Row

GAME TOTAL TIES BIG-LEAGUE MARK

Victory Is His 13th in a Row —Padres Get Only 2 Hits, One a Homer by Ferrara

By JOSEPH DURSO

Tom Seaver pitched the New York Mets to a 2-1 victory over the San Diego Padres yesterday and pitched himself into the baseball records by striking out 19 batters—10 in a row.

Along the way, the cover boy of the Mets pitched a two-hitter, retired the last 16 men, scored his 13th straight victory in regular-season play and broke the club record of 15 strike-outs — which had been set only last Saturday by Nolan Ryan.

In fact, Seaver did everything but bat home the winning run and his roommate, Bud Harrelson, took care of that with a triple in the third inning. Otherwise, the 25-year-old Californian staged a one-man show for 14,197 fans on a clear and cool afternoon and these were the highlights:

¶He struck out 19, tying the major league record set by Steve Carlton of the St. Louis Cardinals last Sept. 15 against the Mets. Carlton lost that game, 4-3, when Ron Swoboda reached him for a pair of two-run home runs.

¶Moreover, since Carlton pitched his strange game at night, Seaver broke the record for strike-outs in an old-fashioned daytime game. The previous high was 18, shared by Bob Feller of Cleveland, Sandy Koufax of Los Angeles and Don Wilson of Houston.

¶By knocking off the last 10 batters, he also broke the major league record of eight consecutive strike-outs. That was shared by four men in modern times, all National Leaguers — Max Surkont of Milwaukee, Johnny Podres of Los Angeles, Jim Maloney of Cincinnati and Wilson.

Seaver did all this on 136 pitches, 65 of which were fastball strikes. He threw another fastball strike, but Al Ferrara hit that one over the left-field fence in the second inning. The only other man who hit Seaver safely was Dave Campbell, who singled off Joe Foy's glove at third base in the fourth.

Ferrara Concerto No. 2

The only other man who reached base was Ferrara, who walked in the fourth — giving Ferrara his most memorable day since he played a piano solo in Carnegie Hall as a child.

Seaver showed a fine sense of history by his performance, too. Just before the game, he accepted the Cy Young Award as the outstanding pitcher in the National League in 1969— when he won 25 games, including a nearly perfect one-hitter against the Chicago Cubs on July 9.

He started the business side of the afternoon a little slowly, though. The Mets scored in the first inning when Harrelson singled and Ken Boswell doubled. An inning later, Ferrara hit his home run for San Diego. But in the third, Tommie Agee singled, Harrelson tripled into the right-field corner and Seaver had a 2-1 lead with six innings to go.

"Actually, he wasn't that strong in the early innings," said Jerry Grote, his catcher. "He just kept building up as the game went on. The cool weather helped and by the end of the game he was stronger than ever."

With two out in the sixth, the game was still up for grabs and Seaver had struck out

The Box Score

SAN DIEGO (N.)						METS					
	ab.	r.	h.	bi			ab.	r.	h.	bi	
Arcia, ss	4	0	0	0		Agee, cf	3	1	1	0	
Roberts, p	0	0	0	0		Harrelson, ss	3	1	2	1	
Kelly, 3b	4	0	0	0		Boswell, 2b	4	0	1	1	
Gaston, cf	4	0	0	0		Jones, lf	4	0	0	0	
Ferrara, lf	3	1	1	1		Shamsky, rf	2	0	0	0	
Colbert, 1b	3	0	0	0		Swoboda, rf	1	0	0	0	
Campbell, 2b	3	0	1	0		Foy, 3b	2	0	0	0	
Morales, rf	3	0	0	0		Kranepool, 1b	2	0	0	0	
Barton, c	2	0	0	0		Grote, c	3	0	0	0	
Corkins, p	2	0	0	0		Seaver, p	3	0	0	0	
Webster, ph	1	0	0	0							
Slocum, ss	0	0	0	0		Total	27	2	4	2	
Total	29	1	2	1							

San Diego .... 0 1 0   0 0 0   0 0 0—1
Mets .... 1 0 1   0 0 0   0 0 x—2

LOB—San Diego 3, Mets 6. 2B—Boswell. 3B—Harrelson. HR—Ferrara (1). SB—Agee.

	IP.	H.	R.	ER.	BB.	SO.
Corkins (L, 0-2)	7	4	2	2	5	5
Roberts	1	0	0	0	0	2
Seaver (W, 3-0)	9	2	1	1	2	19

T—2:14. A—14,197.

nine. Then he threw a third strike past Ferrara and began to run out his remarkable string of 10.

Seaver working against San Diego during the ninth inning

He struck out the side in the seventh and again in the eighth, when he broke Ryan's club record of 15. He broke it, more-over, by fanning Ivan Murell—who pinch-hit for Jose Arcia, the only man in the San Diego line-up who had not struck out.

"Everybody congratulated me when I got No. 16 in the eighth inning," Seaver said later, studying the day's pitching chart, which had been kept by Jerry Koosman. "I just told them, let's get some more runs. All I could think of was that Carlton had struck out 19 of us and still lost."

In the ninth, though, he threw three fastballs past Van Kelly for No. 17 (and No. 8 in a row). Then he caught Clarence Gaston looking at a fastball over the plate for No. 18. And finally, he threw two sliders and two fastballs to Ferrara for No. 19 and No. 10 in a row.

Strikes While Iron's Hot

"I was still worried I'd make a mistake and Ferrara might hit it out," Seaver said. "But when I got two strikes on him, I thought I might never get this close again so I might as well go for it."

He went for it and got it and restored the Mets' poise after two weeks of indifferent play. He outpitched Mike Corkins, a rookie right-hander who allowed the Mets only four hits in seven innings. And Seaver did it with mainly hard stuff —81 fastballs, 34 sliders, 19 curves and two change-ups.

In fact, most of the time the man-child of the Mets seemed to be playing catch with Grote—who also set a record for catchers. Thanks to the strike-outs and one foul pop fly, Grote made 20 putouts, breaking the record of 19 that had been shared by John Roseboro of Los Angeles and Bill Freehan of Detroit.

April 23, 1970

Books of The Times

Not All Peanuts and Cracker Jack, Exactly

By CHRISTOPHER LEHMANN-HAUPT

BALL FOUR. My Life and Hard Times Throwing the Knuckleball in the Big Leagues. By Jim Bouton. Edited by Leonard Shecter. Illustrated. 400 pages. World. $6.95.

How about that! as the Yankee baseball announcer Mel Allen used to say in those long-ago pubescent days when I thought Mel Allen was the grooviest—Jim Bouton has actually gotten me interested in baseball again, and I didn't think that was possible. So there, Commissioner Bowie Kuhn! So much for your notion that Bouton's book is all bad for the game.

For those of you who aren't baseball fans (and you may as well keep reading, because "Ball Four" is a people book, not just a baseball book): Jim Bouton (pro-

nounced BOW-ton) was a fireball pitcher in the last glory years of the New York Yankees—1963 and 1964—when he won a total of 39 regular-season and two World Series games. He threw so hard that his cap would fly off on almost every pitch, revealing a burr of blond hair and a warm, intelligent face. He was also what is known in the trade as a flake, a kook, or a clubhouse lawyer, which is to say, he thought for himself, said what he thought, and said it with wit and vocabulary. He did not particularly fit into the image of the Yankee team, which was supposed to be 25 highly polished ingots all in a row and just as expressionless. But he was good, so they kept him.

Let Air Currents Do It

Then in 1965 the gods of baseball zapped Bouton in his right arm and took his fastball away, and when it became clear that it was not going to come back the gods of the Yankees sent his body away—to the Seattle Pilots, an "expansion" team, composed of cast-offs and expendables. Because Bouton really loved playing baseball, loved it in the corniest way imaginable, he decided to stick with it and build from scratch. He decided to develop his knuckle-ball, which is a pitch thrown off the fingertips with no spin at all so that the air currents between the pitcher's mound and home plate will make the ball dance like a butterfly in a gale—a pitch that requires so little effort that pot-bellied men in their middle 40's can make a living off it. Bouton also decided to keep a tape-record diary of his comeback year of 1969. "Ball Four" is the droll result.

Mr. Bouton leaves very little for you to imagine. He tells you things you never dreamed of when your father took you out to the old ballgame and bought you some peanuts and Cracker Jack. You've probably guessed that ball players bend an elbow now and then, but did you know that a lot of them keep their pizzazz up with "greenies" (scientifically known as dextroamphetamine sulfate)? You may have thought baseball was their favorite sport, but actually it's "beaver-shooting"—which is done with an awl, a hotel-room door, and the off chance that there's a young airline stewardess on the other side, "or better yet, a young airline stewardess and friend." You may think that the major leagues are integrated, but did it ever occur to you, as it did to Jim Bouton, that in 1968, while 19 of the 30 top hitters were black, the ratio of all blacks to whites was hardly 2 to 3, which means you have to be extra good to be black and a major leaguer?

He tells you gossip you wouldn't even hear about your fellow workers around the water cooler. How ballplayers think about sex about 27 hours a day. How they while away their few sexless hours playing mindless, but often very funny, practical jokes and games. How Joe Pepitone maintains two hairpieces. How Carl Yastrzemski loafs. How general managers lie in their teeth. How umpires get even with players they don't like and snigger at Emmett Ashford, the only black man among them. How no one in particular works very hard to create an ideal for American youth to live up to. How baseball people are petty and mean and hidebound, generous, funny, and occasionally intelligent—but mostly human.

The Way It Really Is

Bad Jim Bouton. Disloyal Jim Bouton, you say. Bowie Kuhn, commissioner of baseball, was right to slap his wrists for splattering the national pastime's noble image, you think. Not a bit of it. Because no intelligent person can seriously believe that all players love each other all year round, or that playing a game and traveling with a couple of dozen other men for eight months of the year wouldn't drive

anyone a little around the bend, or the idiotic notion that professional baseball should be a packaged product—a washday miracle that gets your whites whiter and your colors brighter.

Besides, Bouton has done it all so charmingly. His prose is smart and witty. His sense of timing is perfect. And he is candid about himself, too, and paints us a highly engaging portrait of a sensitive young man in love with a silly game and living through a year of crisis.

How did he do, by the way? Like his knuckleball when it was working, he went down and up and out and in. He was shipped to the minor leagues early in the season, but pitched his way back to the "biggies" again. Then he languished with a very mediocre Seattle team because his pitching coach, the great Sal the Barber Maglie, remained convinced that he couldn't get by on one pitch. Then hallelujah! He was traded to the Houston Astros and into the thick of a pennant fight. They didn't win, but near the end of the season, one of Bouton's children "turned his big eyes up at" him and said shyly, "Hey Dad, you're Jim Bouton, aren't you."

June 19, 1970

UMPIRES PICKET PITTSBURGH PARK

Substitutes, 6 From Minors, Work Playoff Game There and One in Minnesota

By MURRAY CHASS
Special to The New York Times

PITTSBURGH, Oct. 3—Major league umpires struck for the first time in baseball history today. They picketed outside Three Rivers Stadium while four minor league umpires worked the opener of the National League playoff between Cincinnati and Pittsburgh.

At Bloomington, Minn., where the Twins faced the Baltimore Orioles in the American League playoff, there was no picketing, but an improvised umpire crew was on the job.

The strike developed over a dispute on the pay scale for the playoffs and World Series. The Major League Umpires Association asked an increase from $2,500 to $5,000 for the

playoffs and $6,500 to $10,000 for the Series. The leagues offered $3,000 and $7,000.

Harry Wendelstedt, among the six umpires who had been scheduled to work the Reds-Pirates series, stood outside an entrance to the stadium carrying a sign that said, "Major League Umpires on Strike for Wages."

"We're not here to put on a demonstration," said Wendelstedt, wearing his blue umpire's uniform. "We came here to work. We're here in good faith. If they're ready to talk money with us, we're ready to go to work this minute."

"They've led people to believe we pulled this at the last minute, but we've been negotiating since July. All they've come up with in that time is $500."

"We don't want to do anything harmful to baseball. We love the game. We want people to see it. We just want fair compensation. All of us are sick that we're not working because we came here to work."

Standing next to him was Nick Colosi, another umpire originally assigned to the playoff. The four other members of the crew—Stan Landes, Bob Engel, Paul Pryor and Doug Harvey — picketed other stadium entrances.

Inside, meanwhile, four minor league recruits worked for $3,000-$2,500 in salary and

$500 for "reporting"—plus $40 a day expenses. John Grimsley, 37 years old of Wilson, N. C., umpired behind the plate; Fred Blandford, 35, of Elmira, N. Y., was at first; Hank Morgenweck, 38, of Teaneck, N. J., at second and George Grygiel, 29, of South Bend, Ind., at third.

All worked in the Triple A level of the minors this season, Grimsley and Blandford in the American Association and Morgenweck and Grygiel in the International League.

On arriving at the stadium at 10:45 A.M., 45 minutes after the six National League umpires had removed their equipment from the umpires' locker room, the rookies talked briefly with newsmen, then toured the playing field before dressing for their major league debut.

They said they were asked last Tuesday about working and considered the situation. They also said there had been no discussion of special inducements, such as the promise of major league jobs in the future.

"I feel I had to come," said Grimsley, who has worked in the minors for 11 years, after the game. "I wanted to do what was good for baseball. Baseball is the primary object. I feel if they were going to put on this game. I was the best qualified to work it outside the major league umpires.

"Nobody in the union of 48 umpires has reached me to talk

this thing over. I think I'm one of the veteran umpires in baseball and they should go to myself or Mr. Blandford. We probably would like to be in a union—all minor league umpires—but no one has approached us.

"I'm an individual. I have to talk contract for myself. No one talks for me or for any of the minor league umpires. We all have to talk contract individually."

Besides Grimsley, who called balls and strikes, Blandford was the busiest of the rookies, getting several close plays at first. None of the calls resulted in an argument.

"I felt relaxed and confident," Blandford said. "I wouldn't have come here if I thought I would make a spectacle of myself. When I got the call, I figured it was a chance to prove to myself after 14 years in the minors that I could do the job at the major league level.

"I would like to think the regular umpires would accept what I did as something I had to do. It's strange, but last night I bumped into Paul Pryor on the street. I hadn't seen him in two years. I told him I believed I owed it to my family and myself to be here."

Blandford declined to say what Pryor had told him, saying it was Pryor's place to disclose his part of the conversation.

293

Grygiel, the youngest of the working umpires, guessed that their action would incur the wrath of the strikers.

"There probably will be a lot of umpires not happy with us for accepting this assignment," he said, "but we are victims of circumstances. We are controlled by the minor leagues, and if they ask us to work and we turn them down, we might as well forget about umpiring."

There were few instances where the Reds or Pirates questioned decisions. One instance was in the first inning when Roberto Clemente asked Grimsley about a called third strike.

"He asked me if the pitch was high enough, and I said yes," Grimsley related. "He's a real pro, and he was checking on my strike zone. The way I answered him probably convinced him I was right."

The major league umpires gained official recognition as a collective bargaining unit last year in a case stemming from the dismissal of two American League umpires, Bill Valentine and Al Salerno.

Wendelstedt said the association was 100 per cent behind the strike, and added he knew of several Triple A umpires who had rejected a request to work.

"In a way I feel rather sad about the umpires who agreed to work," he said. "The minor leagues are not organized, so there's nothing we can do except appeal to their common sense. We feel whatever we gain will be to their benefit because they want to be major league umpires."

Neither the managers nor players seemed concerned about the game being handled by minor leaguers. But Marvin Miller, executive director of the Players Association, expressed doubt about the move.

"For a series this important," he said, "to have umpires less than major league caliber is disastrous. It's a mistake."

Miller believed the umpires had a point in seeking higher pay.

"For many, many years," he said, "they were unorganized and, like many unorganized people, they were vastly underpaid. I think a problem like this should've been resolved long ago. Owners don't realize a problem until it hits them in the face."

As for the substitute umpires, Miller declared, "Scabs are scabs."

Danny Murtaugh, the Pirate manager, didn't think of the situation in such labor terms.

"We're just going to play the game the way we've played it all year," he said.

The 20,000 empty seats did not appear to be an indication of the effect of the picketing. More likely, fans in the Pittsburgh area, not one of the most affluential in the country, had preferred to remain at home and watch on television.

At Bloomington, the American League umpires were: home plate, John Stevens; first, Bill Deegan; second, Donald Stachell, and third, Charlie Berry. There were no foul-line umpires.

Stevens and Berry were retired American League umpires, still working for the league in supervisory capacities. Stevens, as a swing man, worked about 65 games this season. He is 57 years old and was forced to retire two years ago because of a mandatory retirement rule.

Berry, who is 66, retired six or seven years ago, but has worked this season in the college world series and Mexican clinics. He scouts umpires for the league.

Deegan is 35 and has worked the last four years in the Southern League. Stachell, 34, has been in the International League the last two seasons and in the lower minors before that. Both have worked as instructors in the umpiring school supported by the Commissioner's office in Florida.

Neither Stevens nor Berry is a member of the Umpires Association, which was formed after their active careers. The newcomers do not belong to a union either.

Joe Cronin, American League president, said he wasn't sure yet whether they would shift positions for subsequent games, but they would remain throughout the playoff. The World Series is the Commissioner's problem.

Negotiations between both leagues and the regular umpires had been in progress for weeks. A key meeting was held in mid-September, which made the break obvious. However, the umpires did not take a strike vote until yesterday, and some baseball executives had expected them to vote against striking.

There are 12 umpires in the playoffs and six in the Series, so the pay issue comes to a difference of $24,000 plus $18,-000 of a gross income of more than $4-million just from gate receipts, not counting radio and television.

October 4, 1970

Bench Is Most Valuable Player

By JOSEPH DURSO

Johnny Bench, the 22-year-old catcher for the Cincinnati Reds, became the youngest man in baseball history yesterday to win the Most Valuable Player Award.

He was elected No. 1 in the National League for 1970 in a landslide vote by a committee of 24 baseball writers, receiving 22 votes for first place and two for second. Billy Williams of the Chicago Cubs got the two other first-place votes and finished second, with Tony Perez of Cincinnati third.

Bench was paid $40,000 by the Reds last season, his third in the big leagues, and returned the favor by leading the majors with 45 home runs and 148 runs batted in, while hitting .293.

The Reds won the National League's West and the pennant but lost the World Series in five games to the Baltimore Orioles, whose Boog Powell was named most valuable in the American League last week.

"I set goals and surpassed them," Bench said yesterday, "but I never expected to have such a season. I wanted to hit 30 homers, drive in 100 runs and bat about .285.

"Things have happened to me in the last five years that most people don't realize in a lifetime. I get a funny feeling when I remember that it was just a few years ago that I was just another wide-eyed youngster watching every move Mickey Mantle used to make."

Bench became only the second player in the 40-year history of the balloting to win at the age of 22. Stan Musial of the St. Louis Cardinals was 22 when he was named in 1943, but he turned 23 that year on Nov. 21. Bench will not be 23 until Dec. 7. Musial, however, took the award in his second season in the big leagues, the earliest that any player has made it.

Bench also became the first catcher to win the award in the National League since Roy Campanella of the 1955 Brooklyn Dodgers, and the first Redleg since Frank Robinson in 1961.

Five members of the Cincinnati team received votes this year—Bench, Perez, Pete

The Balloting
First-place votes in parentheses

	Pts.
John Bench, Cincinnati (22)	.326
Billy Williams, Chicago (2)	.218
Tony Perez, Cincinnati	149
Bob Gibson, St. Louis	110
Wes Parker, Los Angeles	91
Dave Giusti, Pittsburgh	72
Pete Rose, Cincinnati	54
Jim Hickman, Chicago	52
Willie McCovey, San Fran.	37
Rico Carty, Atlanta	43
Manny Sanguillen, Pittsburgh	36
Roberto Clemente, Pittsburgh	33
Don Clendenon, New York	26
Gaylord Perry, San Fran.	24
Willie Stargell, Pittsburgh	20
Bob Tolan, Cincinnati	17
Henry Aaron, Atlanta	16
Joe Torre, St. Louis	15
Tommie Agee, New York	13
Bud Harrelson, New York	10
Ferguson Jenkins, Chicago	8
Jim Merritt, Cincinnati	8
Don Kessinger, Chicago	6
Clarence Gaston, San Diego	5
Deron Johnson, Philadelphia	4
Luke Walker, Pittsburgh	4
Carl Morton, Montreal	3
Tom Seaver, New York	2
Bob Robertson, Pittsburgh	1

Cincinnati Reds

Rose (seventh place), Bob Tolan (16th) and Jim Merritt (22d). The Pittsburgh Pirates, the Eastern Division champions, placed only Dave Giusti in the top 10, though four others were among the 29 players who received votes. The Houston Astros were the only team shut out.

The highest-ranking member of the New York Mets, last year's world champions, was Donn Clendenon in 13th place. Then came Tommie Agee in 19th, Bud Harrelson in 20th and Tom Seaver, 28th.

The results were announced by Jack Lang, secretary-treasurer of the Baseball Writers Association of America. The committee consists of two writers from each city in the league, with first place counting 14 points, second place 9, third place 8 and so on. In the point totals, Bench scored a runaway 326, and Williams had 218, with two votes for first place, and 17 for second.

November 19, 1970

Josh Gibson Was The Equal of Babe Ruth, But...

By ROBERT PETERSON

To give recognition to diamond greats who, in an earlier day, were barred from the big leagues, organized baseball's Hall of Fame now has a special niche for the likes of Satchel Paige and, eventually, Josh—"the other half of what was probably the greatest battery ever."

SATCHEL PAIGE, pitcher, raconteur, hemispheric traveler and an authentic American legend, is in baseball's Hall of Fame. Approximately. When he is formally inducted Aug. 9 in ceremonies at the National Baseball Hall of Fame and Museum in Cooperstown, N. Y., his plaque will be hung in a special corner of the museum to be reserved for stars of Negro baseball. Those of seven old-time white major leaguers—none of whom made the impact on the sporting scene that Paige did—will be placed in the austere Hall of Fame gallery alongside Babe Ruth, Ty Cobb, Honus Wagner and Walter Johnson.

Baseball Commissioner Bowie Kuhn, in announcing Paige as the first of a one-a-year trickle into Cooperstown of black men who played behind baseball's color line during the first half of the century, noted that "technically" they would not be in the Hall of Fame because they had not played at least 10 years in the major leagues as required by the rules for election. In fact, nearly all of the players mentioned prominently as probable choices to follow Paige into the shrine (Negro baseball division) never played in the big leagues at all.

But Commissioner Kuhn described the Hall of Fame as "a state of mind," not merely a particular room in a particular place, and said that in his view Satchel and his successors will be Hall of Famers. Paige himself seemed bewildered by sportswriters' questions about his attitude toward the separate but presumably equal accommodations for black baseball's greats. "I'm proud to be in wherever they put me in the Hall of Fame," Satch said.

HE could hardly have been surprised by his niche apart from base-

ball's holy-of-holies. Satch had been there before. He spent nearly his whole career of 32 years pitching in the separate and very much unequal world of Negro baseball—2,500 games in metropolis and hamlet in every corner of the nation, in Puerto Rico, Mexico and other points.

It was another time and another place. When he started in baseball, the term "civil rights" rolled strangely off the tongue, black panther was lower case, and baseball's major leagues (and the organized minor leagues) had been lily white for a generation.

Today, when more than a quarter of the major leaguers and a majority of the superstars are black, it takes an effort of the imagination to remember that only 25 years ago there was not a single Negro in organized baseball—and had not been since 1898. It was on April 18, 1946, that Jackie Robinson breached the color line with the Montreal Royals of the International League. A year later he moved to the old Brooklyn Dodgers as the first of a long line of black players who have dominated the big leagues now for nearly two decades. In 1962, Robinson achieved another first when he was selected for the authentic, nontechnical Hall of Fame in the annual election of the Baseball Writers' Association. A second black star, Dodger catcher Roy Campanella, joined him there in 1969.

Satchel Paige made it to the majors in 1948 as a venerable rookie of 42, give or take a couple of years. He helped the Cleveland Indians to win the American League pennant with

six victories and one defeat, and in the process he established attendance records in Cleveland and Chicago. But in five years in the big leagues, Satch won only 28 and lost 31, hardly Hall of Fame performance.

NO, it is as the best-known symbol of the nether world of Negro baseball that Satchel Paige is joining his peers at Cooperstown, if only, once more, by the back door. His arrival will be the end of a long, meandering road that began in 1926. Satch was two years out of an Alabama reform school, in which he had spent five years for the theft of a handful of toy rings from a store, when he joined the Chattanooga Black Lookouts. He was about 20 years old, a 6-foot, 3½-inch, 140-pound scarecrow with a fastball that hissed as it passed the batter and exploded in the catcher's mitt. His salary was $50 a month.

The Black Lookouts were about as far from the Hall of Fame as it is possible to get. They were members of the Negro Southern League, a minor circuit in the loose configuration of Negro baseball. The parks were often rickety, rundown and rock-filled, the players sometimes came up empty-handed on payday because there was nothing in the till, and occasionally, after riding through the night to the next town, they slept in the bleachers at the ball park because there was no money for even a fifth-rate hotel.

But Satchel endured and even prospered, reaching the phenomenal salary level of $275 a month after

ROBERT PETERSON is the author of "Only the Ball Was White," a history of Negro baseball.

serving five clubs during his first five years. Then in 1931 he joined the Pittsburgh Crawfords, a team he would later call the best in baseball history, black or white. The claim may be taken with several grains of salt, since there is by no means unanimity among old black ballplayers that it was even the best in Negro baseball history. Old-timers will cite the 1910 Leland Giants of Chicago, who won 123 and lost six, or the Lincoln Giants of New York in the pre-World War I era, the Chicago American Giants of 1921, the Kansas City Monarchs of the twenties and thirties, or the Homestead, Pa., Grays of 1939.

NEVERTHELESS, there is no denying that the Crawfords were a great team that could, and did, do better than hold its own against major leaguers. From 1932 to 1934, the roster listed, besides Paige, four men who are likely candidates for the Negro players' room at Cooperstown: catcher Josh Gibson, probably the pre-eminent power hitter in history, not excepting Babe Ruth; outfielder James (Cool Papa) Bell, said by Satchel Paige to be so fast that he could flip the light switch and jump into bed before the light went out; the manager, Oscar Charleston, a first baseman then but in his younger days an outfielder with whom, in the judgment of those who can remember, Willie Mays suffers by comparison; and third baseman Judy Johnson.

In addition, the Crawfords had such stars of only slightly lesser magnitude as pitchers Sam Streeter, a veteran lefthander, and a hard-throwing rookie named LeRoy Matlock; outfielders Jimmie Crutchfield and Ted Page, both defensive standouts and left-handed line-drive hitters; Chester Williams, a very quick, flashy infielder, and versatile W. G. Perkins, who could catch or play the outfield brilliantly. The word stars is used here in a qualitative sense; most of these men were unknown outside the ghettos of the Negro major-league cities and a few nearby small towns, but they were the Willie Mayses, Henry Aarons, Bob Gibsons and Curt Floods of their time.

EXCEPT that the Crawfords were somewhat more solvent than most clubs, the story of their rise and decline is fairly representative of Negro baseball at the top level.

Pre-eminent power hitter Gibson on the attack. There are no record books for black baseball, but it is thought likely that his career total of home runs exceeded Ruth's 714.

Like most Negro clubs, the Crawfords were the brainchild and pet of one man. In this case he was W. A. (Gus) Greenlee, a tavern owner and the numbers king in Pittsburgh's black Hill District who, in 1935, also entered boxing as manager of John Henry Lewis, the light heavyweight champion. Greenlee took over a Pittsburgh semipro team called the Crawford Colored Giants in the summer of 1931 and began adding some certified pros. Among his early acquisitions were Paige and his catcher, W. G. Perkins, who came to Pittsburgh after their club, the Cleveland Cubs, disbanded—a casualty of the great Depression.

Other players, attracted by the promise of regular paydays with Greenlee, simply jumped their contracts with other teams (if they had contracts) to join the Crawfords. Outfielder Jimmie Crutchfield recalls that he was playing without a contract for the Indianapolis ABC's that year. "And we weren't being paid," Crutchfield said. "That would go on for maybe two months, till we had a good gate. Then perhaps you'd get some of your back pay." When the ABC's got to Pittsburgh for games in that area, Crutchfield said, he was recommended to Greenlee by Satchel, Perkins and Streeter, his teammates on the Birmingham Black Barons in 1930. "So Greenlee gave me $25 or $50 —more than I'd gotten all year — so I stayed," Crutchfield remembers. "They said they were going to have a good ball club, but just to be with Satchel was enough."

Crutchfield, who had gotten $90 a month from Birmingham, was signed by the Crawfords for $150, an average salary on a top black club in the early thirties and about one-fifth of what a young white player of his talents commanded in the major leagues of that era. "If you asked the manager about a raise," he said, "you'd hear, 'Well, we're paying you more than we're paying so-and-so.' To be honest with you, I imagine they could have cut half the boys on the team and they still would have played baseball because, after all, in 1931 and '32, if you didn't play baseball, what were you going to do?"

AS befitted a man who was fast becoming Negro baseball's biggest drawing card, Satchel Paige was the highest paid member of the Crawfords at $250 a month, augmented by frequent bonuses of $100 to $500 for pitching for area semipro teams on loan from Greenlee.

With such windfalls coming his way, Paige would sometimes be away from the club for a week at a time. Crutchfield remembers: "Satchel would pitch for us on Sunday —he'd shut out some team in Yankee Stadium, and we wouldn't see him maybe until the following Sunday. Maybe we'd be playing in Cleveland or some other big city. We'd leave the hotel, go to the ball park—no Satchel. Fifteen minutes before game time, somebody would say, 'Hey, Satchel just came in the dressing room.' He was always full of life. You'd forgive him for anything because he was like a great big boy. He could walk in the room and have you in stitches in 10 minutes' time. He'd warm up by playing third base or clowning with somebody and then he'd go out and pitch a shutout. How could you get mad at a guy like that?"

Paige's talent for showmanship was not confined to pre-game antics. Sometimes, when a game was safely in hand, he would call in his outfielders and pitch with only his infielders behind him. Just the sight of him, tall and languorous and his face expressing the serene confidence that is the mark of the supreme artist, was enough to cow most batters.

If the look was not enough,

Paige made them believers by delivering Long Tom, his *fast* fastball, as distinguished from Little Tom, a pitch that merely hummed by the batter. Long Tom was once described by Biz Mackey, a Negro baseball veteran, in tones of awe. "Satchel's fastball," Mackey said, "tends to disappear. Yes, disappear. I've heard about Satchel throwing pitches that wasn't hit but that never showed up in the catcher's mitt nevertheless. They say the catcher, the umpire and the bat boys looked all over for the ball but it was gone. Now how do you account for that?"

THE question borders on the occult, and in 1931 Gus Greenlee realized that a man with such powers deserved his own showcase. So the following year, at a time when nearly all black clubs rented or leased parks, many of them from teams in white organized baseball, Greenlee built a ball park on Bedford Avenue in the Pittsburgh Hill District for Paige and Company.

It cost $75,000, a lavish sum to invest in Negro baseball during the Depression. Its brick grandstand and bleachers along the foul lines seated 7,000 for baseball and 10,000 for boxing. Greenlee Field was also the home field of the Crawfords' neighbors and arch rivals, the Homestead Grays, for several years until, with the growing popularity of Negro baseball in the late thirties, both clubs abandoned it in favor of the Pirates' Forbes Field.

Like most black teams, the Crawfords traveled by bus, a six-cylinder, 79-horsepower Mack which was, The Pittsburgh Courier, a Negro weekly, noted, "capable of 60 miles an hour"—presumably on the down grade. By midseason 1932, the new bus already had logged 17,000 miles for the Crawfords, who, like every other black club, were on the road a great deal of the time.

The bus became a second home for the players. "We'd come home to Pittsburgh once in a while and get clean clothes and ride right out," Judy Johnson remembers.

Their destination might be New York, Chicago or Cleveland, or it might be Steubenville, Canton or Warren in Ohio, Butler or Altoona in Pennsylvania, or a coal-mining town in West Virginia. Although during most of their years the Crawfords were members of the Negro National League, two-thirds of their 150 to 200 games a season were played against the white semipro teams that flourished all over the country until the early nineteen-fifties.

As a rule they played two or three league games a week. They might, for example, play the Philadelphia Stars a doubleheader in Philadelphia or New York on Sunday and go to Baltimore for a game with the Black Sox Tuesday night. During the rest of the week, they would play each evening against white semipro clubs within driving distance of those two cities. At home, they followed the same pattern, playing Negro league clubs two or three games in Pittsburgh and filling out the rest of the week's schedule with area semipro teams.

Until Negro baseball's boom period during and immediately after World War II, crowds for Negro league games were predominantly black, with only a speckling of white faces. For games with semipros, most of which were played in small towns, the crowds naturally were largely white.

Gate receipts for league games were split on a percentage basis, with the home club taking the lion's share, but for independent games, owners of black clubs had some latitude for shrewd negotiations. An old player explains their course: "When a white ball club wrote and asked us for a game, they might offer a $500 guarantee. Well, if they offered a guarantee, you won't accept that; you want a percentage. But if they say they will give you 60 per cent of the gate, *then* you ask for a guarantee. Simple as that! Because when they want to give you a big guarantee, they *know* they're going to make it. And when they're not sure they're going to make it, they want you to

take a percentage, so you want a guarantee."

Because they played in a different town almost every day on the road — and sometimes in two or three towns on the same day — black teams were constantly on the move, some even more often and farther than the Crawfords. By common consent, the Homestead Grays were the most inveterate tourists, often riding 200 miles out of Pittsburgh, playing a ball game or two, and then riding 200 miles back home that night.

Bill Yancey, a shortstop who played for several black clubs from 1923 to 1936, recalls that when he reached the plateau of excellence demanded by Cumberland W. (Cum) Posey, who had built the Grays into a Negro baseball power, he rejected the idea of playing for them, "because those guys would play one of their 'home' games in New Orleans and the next night they were liable to be in Buffalo, man, ridin' over those mountains!" (Yancey signed instead with the Lincoln Giants, who rarely had to venture far from the New York metropolitan area to find a game.)

YANCEY exaggerates for effect, but not by much, for the memories of men who played on the Grays and nearly every other black club abound with tales of marathon trips. Negro baseball lived and died before the age of superhighways, and 35 to 40 miles an hour was a good average over the narrow, often tortuous roads that webbed the nation. The black barnstormers, packed nine men in a car or jouncing interminably in a bus as the Crawfords did, were itinerants because they had to be. In Negro baseball, barnstorming meant survival.

Judy Johnson, who, like Yancey, is now a scout for the Philadelphia Phillies, recalls a not-unusual, 800-mile endurance test the Crawfords had in 1935 after playing a night game in Chicago: "Right after the game we had a meal, and then we started out for Philadelphia. We had our bus all packed before the

game. And we rode all the way to Philadelphia without sleeping, except for naps on the bus. The only thing we had to eat was sandwiches and pop. And when we got to Philadelphia, my ankles were swollen 10 inches wide. We got in Tuesday morning and played a doubleheader that afternoon."

The necessity for speed to make schedules was the main reason for such nonstop journeys, but it was not the only one. Another was the fact that black travelers could not be sure of getting restaurant service or lodging along the way except in cities with large black populations. Jack Marshall, an infielder for the Chicago American Giants during the thirties, remembers: "When we left Chicago to go to St. Louis and play, there was no place where we could stop and eat — not unless we stopped in a place where they had a colored settlement. From St. Louis to Kansas City, same thing. So many times we would ride all night and not have anything to eat because they wouldn't feed you. Going from Chicago to Cleveland, same thing. So the boys used to take sardines and a can of beans and pour them into a jar. They'd take some crackers, too, and that was their food. They'd eat out of that jar. That's the way we had to do it."

ENDURING as they did such traveling and living conditions, it is hard to believe that the top black clubs could play on even terms with major leaguers, but the evidence shows that they did. In 1932, for example, the Crawfords won five out of seven in a post-season series with a team of major leaguers headed by the Chicago Cubs' Hack Wilson, who still holds the National League home-run record of 56 for one season. In other years, Satchel and his mates won a majority of their tests against barnstorming major-leaguers, including such stars as Joe Di-Maggio, Charlie Gehringer, Dizzy Dean (who called Paige the greatest pitcher he ever saw), Lefty Grove, Bill Dickey, Heinie Manush,

Rogers Hornsby and Babe Herman.

Because statistics were kept casually, if at all, in Negro baseball — both for teams and individual players (and not much better for Negro league standings), it is impossible to measure objectively the quality of the Crawfords.

There is general agreement among black baseball veterans that the top clubs were not of major-league caliber day in and day out, chiefly because their rosters had little depth. Most teams carried from 14 to 18 players, and if a regular was injured, the lineup was considerably weakened. Only during the twilight years of Negro baseball in the middle forties did the rosters go up to 22 men, still three short of the major-league limit.

But, says Bill Yancey, "if we could have selected the best of the colored leagues and gone into the major leagues, I'd say we could have won the championship. We could have selected maybe five clubs out of all the colored teams that would have held their own in the major leagues."

Buck Leonard, a slugging first baseman for the Homestead Grays, who played Gehrig to Josh Gibson's Ruth from 1938 until Gibson's death in 1947, remembers, "We didn't have star men at every position. We didn't have — as the majors did — two good catchers and six or seven good pitchers and good infielders and outfielders. We had pitchers that we would pitch in league games and mediocre pitchers that we just used against white semipro teams. Sockamayocks, we used to call 'em."

When the sockamayocks were on the bench and the regular lineup was intact, however, the first-line black clubs were a match for anybody. And when black all-star teams were formed during the winter to barnstorm on the Pacific Coast or play in Latin American leagues, the available records indicate that Yancey is right in believing a Negro league all-star team could have been world's

champions. In three winters during the middle thirties, for instance, the Paige Stars compiled a 128-23 record on the Coast, with at least 40 of their victories coming at the expense of major-league barnstormers.

BASEBALL in retrospect can exist on two levels: in the mind's eye and ear and in the cold numbers of the record book. An old fan easily can call up the vision of Babe Ruth trotting toward first with dainty, mincing steps and hear the deep-throated, rising roar from the crowd as the ball soars toward the fence. He can see again Joe DiMaggio, feet spread wide, bat cocked, waiting, waiting, and then the fluid swing and the crack of bat against ball. Or gangling Marty Marion moving to his left with balletlike grace, scooping up the hard grounder on the short hop and throwing almost disdainfully to nip the runner at first.

For these men, the fan can also consult the record book for Ruth's 60-home-run season, DiMaggio's 56-game hitting streak, and Marion's fielding averages. His intuitive certainty of their greatness is reinforced by the printed word.

But for Negro baseball's stars, no such reinforcement is possible. The old fan can bring to mind Josh Gibson standing loose and easy in the righthand batter's box at Yankee Stadium during a Negro league doubleheader in 1934 and almost effortlessly propelling the ball over the third tier next to the left field bull pen, the only fair ball ever hit out of the Stadium. He cannot go to a record book and find Gibson's career home-run total, which in his 17 years in black baseball probably surpassed Ruth's 714. He cannot even be certain about the top figure for a single year, which was reported to be 89.

And so the legends have grown, fed, in the absence of reliable statistics, by the stop-time visions of men who remember. Gibson's picture swing, the sharp retort of the bat, and the ball a white blur

rising toward the distant horizon. Cool Papa Bell, his flying feet seeming barely to touch the ground as he goes from first to second in seven steps and a slide. Or center-fielder Oscar Charleston, stationing himself almost within spitting distance of second base, and then, just before bat meets ball, turning to race back to the distant reaches of the outfield, the ball appearing to hang overhead until he catches up with it.

There is truth in such visions, more truth perhaps than in statistics, but they can be shaky guides to team strength, too. For despite Satchel Paige's assertion that the Crawfords of the early thirties were the best team in history, the fact is that they won a clear-cut victory in the Negro National League pennant races only once in the four years they were in the league before they were wrecked by whole-sale desertions in 1937.

GUS GREENLEE organized the second Negro National League in 1933 (the first had operated in the Midwest during the twenties) and entered his Crawfords. They finished one game behind the Chicago American Giants in the first half of the split-season schedule. The league broke up during the second half and, not unnaturally, the American Giants claimed the championship.

In the spring of 1934, Greenlee, as league president, awarded the 1933 pennant to his own club. The Chicago management protested, but without unseemly vigor, because the pennant carried with it no financial reward; the clubs merely split gate receipts for their games and there was no special incentive for placing high in the standings except the honor of it and the fact that for the following season the pennant winners could legitimately advertise themselves as "colored world's champions."

In 1934, the Crawfords finished second and third in the split-season schedule, despite Satchel Paige's record that season of 31-4. The following year, after Paige jumped the club in a salary dispute with

Greenlee and went to Bismarck, N. D., to pitch for a white semipro team, the Crawfords finally won the N. N. L. pennant. In 1936, with an unrepentant Paige back in the fold, they won the second half, but no play-off was held with the Washington Elite Giants, first-half winners.

Greenlee's dream of a baseball dynasty was souring that year, and toward the end of the season, Josh Gibson, the other half of what probably was the greatest battery ever, jumped the Crawfords to return to his first club, the Homestead Grays. Gibson was listed on the spring roster of the Crawfords in 1937 but was described as a holdout, and subsequently his contract was traded to the Grays for two journeymen players.

MEANWHILE, the foot-loose Paige was making ready to jump again. While at spring training with the Crawfords in New Orleans, he heard the rustle of money — $30,000 if he would recruit eight other Negro league stars and go to the Dominican Republic to play under the banner of President Rafael L. Trujillo Molina.

Unaccountably the dictator was being opposed for re-election, and his opponent had imported a ball club called Estrellas de Oriente that was capturing the attention of the volatile, baseball-mad Dominicans by drubbing every other club on the island. There was only one thing to do — assemble a club that could beat the Estrellas. Trujillo's lieutenants naturally went to the top — Satchel Paige.

Cool Papa Bell, a star for 30 years and now a guard at the St. Louis City Hall, recalls what happened:

"They got guys from Cuba, Panama and guys out of the Negro leagues — they had a lot of boys from the States— but they wanted Satchel. He was down in New Orleans training with the Crawfords, and he didn't want to go. So they trailed Satchel to a hotel in New Orleans. Someone told them Satchel was in there. So two of them went in to look for him, and Satchel slipped out the side door and jumped into his car and tried to get away from them, but they blocked the street and stopped him.

"Now Satchel was the type of guy that if you showed him money — or a car — you could lead him anywhere. He was that type of fella. He did a lot of wrong things in baseball, but he was easily led. So these fellas said they wanted him to go down to Santo Domingo, and he said, 'I don't wanna go.' He didn't really want to jump again, that's why he was ducking those people. But when they offered him a big salary, then he jumped and went down there.

"In that year, Gus Greenlee, who was in the numbers racket, had lost a lot of money. He had a little boy working for him, sweeping around where they counted the numbers money, and he was tipping off the detectives whenever they was counting the money. Gus didn't know just why, but every time they would move, the detectives would be there.

"Gus Greenlee had lost so much money he was giving the ball players a tough way to go. So a lot of the boys on the Crawfords were ready to get out. Some of the boys got jobs in Pittsburgh in a mill where they had a team, and I had an application in there. I was going to quit as soon as I had a job. Some of the boys were jumping the league, too — it was going bad again.

"So then Satchel called from down in Santo Domingo and got in touch with LeRoy Matlock, Harry Williams and Sam Bankhead."

THAT phone call had an ominous ring for the Pittsburgh Crawfords because eight men from the club, including Bell, jumped to join Satchel. Paige and his Trujillo Stars won the tournament in Santo Domingo under very close chaperonage. They lived under armed guard in a private club, and the games were played under the watchful eyes of a large part of Trujillo's army, with the sun glinting off long knives and bayonets. Satchel and his mates could not get out of Trujillo land fast enough after that series.

He and a few of the other refugees from Latin America returned to the Crawfords for 1938, paying a nominal fine of one week's salary for jumping, but the season had not begun before Satchel was on the run, this time to Mexico.

Paige never again appeared in a Crawfords uniform and their glory days were over for good. Greenlee Field was dismantled to make way for a housing development, and the Crawfords, bereft of both Paige and Gibson, the two top attractions in Negro baseball, moved on to other cities. In 1939 they played out of Toledo, and in 1940 they were in Indianapolis. For several years thereafter, they barnstormed in the Northwest, far from the pallid limelight of the Negro leagues.

In 1945, Greenlee, by now a pariah to Negro league owners, challenged them by forming the United States Baseball League, with franchises in several major cities, including one for his Pittsburgh Crawfords. The United States League did not become a threat to the two established Negro major leagues operating that year and barely managed to stumble through the season. But it qualified for a footnote in baseball history because the league included the Brooklyn Brown Dodgers, a club which Branch Rickey, president of the Brooklyn Dodgers, used as a screen to scout Negro players without upsetting his major-league brethren. That October, Rickey shocked the sports world and heralded the end of segregated baseball by signing Jackie Robinson to play for Montreal, the Dodgers' top farm club, in 1946.

THE Pittsburgh Crawfords, one of the brighter lights in the shadow world of Negro baseball, are only a vivid memory now in the minds of a dwindling band of men who once discerned greatness on a baseball field far from the magnificence of the big leagues. So, too, the Homestead Grays, Kansas City Monarchs, Hilldale Club of Darby, Pa., the Lincoln Giants, Baltimore Elite Giants, St. Louis Stars and Chicago American Giants — all once proud names in the black back streets of baseball. Their uniforms were worn with distinction by men named Rube Foster, John Henry Lloyd, Smoky Joe Williams, John Donaldson, Cannonball Dick Redding, Bullet Rogan, Bingo DeMoss, Willie Wells and Martin Dihigo, men who were lucky to make $1,000 a season at a time when apprentice major leaguers were earning three to four times as much.

They played for love of the game on the only teams open to them.

Jimmie Crutchfield, now a postal worker in Chicago, thoughtfully closes his scrapbook of yellowing clippings about the Crawfords and says, "I have no ill feeling about never having had the opportunity to play in the big leagues. There have been times — you know, they used to call me the black Lloyd Waner. I used to think about that a lot. He was on the other side of town in Pittsburgh making $12,000 a year, and I didn't have enough money to come home on. I had to borrow money to come home.

"It seemed like there was something wrong there. But that was yesterday. There's no use in me having bitterness in my heart this late in life about what's gone by. That's just the way I feel about it. Once in a while I get a kick out of thinking that my name was mentioned as one of the stars of the East-West Game (the Negro all-star game) and little things like that. I don't know whether I'd feel better if I had a million dollars.

"I can say I contributed something." ■

April 11, 1971

Baseball's Front Door Opens to Satchel Paige

Satchel Paige was given full membership yesterday in the Baseball Hall of Fame instead of being honored in a separate niche reserved for players of the old Negro leagues.

Earlier this year, it had been announced that a separate wing of the baseball museum was being set aside for players in the Negro leagues, which flourished before black players were admitted to the major leagues, and Paige was chosen as the first player to be honored.

However, in response to severe criticism of this "separate-but-equal" treatment, Baseball Commissioner Bowie Kuhn and Paul Kirk, president of the Hall of Fame and museum at Cooperstown, N. Y., said Paige and future Negro league inductees would be given full membership.

July 8, 1971

Holtzman Beats Reds on 2d No-Hitter

CINCINNATI, June 3 (AP)—Ken Holtzman, the Chicago Cubs' 25-year-old left-hander, pitched the first no-hitter of the season tonight, beating the Cincinnati Reds, 1-0.

Holtzman, who pitched a no-hitter for the Cubs on Aug. 19, 1969, against the Atlanta Braves, struck out six, walked four and kept Cincinnati's Big Red Machine pounding the ball to Cubs' infielders.

In the Reds' ninth inning, Hal McRae flied out to John Callison on a 1-0 pitch. Then Tommy Helms struck out on a 1-2 pitch.

That brought up Lee May, who ran the count to two balls and two strikes before striking out to end the game.

Pitcher Tallies, Too

Holtzman scored the game's run in the third when he led off and reached on Tony Perez's throwing error. The pitcher moved up on Don Kessinger's infield out and scored on Glenn Beckert's single to right-center.

Holtzman got into his toughest jam in the bottom of the third when he walked Buddy Bradford leading off. Bradford moved up on a wild pitch and went to third as Dave Concepcion grounded out.

That brought up Gary Nolan, the losing pitcher, who bounced in front of the plate. Danny Breeden, the catcher, pounced on the ball and tagged Nolan, Bradford remaining at third. Holtzman then retired McRae on a fly to center.

Beckert Snuffs Bid

The Reds' closest bid for a base hit came in the seventh when Beckert, the second baseman, threw out Perez on a ground ball to the right of second.

Johnny Bench surprised Holtzman with a bunt leading off the seventh, but the ball rolled foul by inches.

Holtzman, who retired the last 11 Reds in order, dropped six of his first eight decisions this season. He took an earned-

Associated Press
Ken Holtzman of Chicago after pitching no-hitter.

run average of 5.40 for 73 1-3 innings into the game.

A 17-game winner in each of the last two seasons, he is in his sixth year with the Cubs.

CHICAGO (N.)					CINCINNATI (N.)				
	ab.	r.	h.	bi		ab.	r.	h.	bi
Kessinger, ss	4	0	1	0	McRae, lf	3	0	0	0
Beckert, 2b	4	0	2	1	Helms, 2b	4	0	0	0
Williams, lf	4	0	1	0	May, 1b	3	0	0	0
Santo, 3b	4	0	0	0	Bench, c	3	0	0	0
Pepitone, 1b	4	0	1	0	Perez, 3b	3	0	0	0
Davis, cf	4	0	0	0	Foster, cf	3	0	0	0
Callison, rf	3	0	1	0	Bradford, rf	1	0	0	0
Breeden, c	3	0	0	0	Concepcn, ss	3	0	0	0
Holtzman, p	3	1	0	0	Nolan, p	2	0	0	0
					Ferrara, ph	1	0	0	0
Total	33	1	6	1	Gibbon, p	0	0	0	0
					Total	26	0	0	0

Chicago .... 0 0 1 0 0 0 0 0 0—1
Cincinnati .... 0 0 0 0 0 0 0 0 0—0
E—Perez. DP—Chicago 1. LOB—Chicago 5, Cincinnati 3. SB—Kessinger, McRae.

	IP.	H.	R.	ER.	BB.	SO.
Holtzman (W, 3-6)	9	0	0	0	4	6
Nolan (L, 3-6)	8	5	1	0	0	3
Gibbon	1	1	0	0	0	0

Wild pitch—Holtzman. T—1:55. A—11,751.

June 4, 1971

American League Stars Win, 6-4

By JOSEPH DURSO
Special to The New York Times

DETROIT, July 13—Vida Blue gave up two home runs in three innings tonight, but his American League teammates recovered from that shock to defeat the National League, 6-4, and break an eight-game losing streak in baseball's 42d All-Star Game.

It was the first time since 1962 that the American Leaguers had won, and only the second time in the last 14 games in the series. They had to match homers with their celebrated rivals to do it.

Six home runs were hit in the game before 53,559 persons in Tiger Stadium, three by each side accounting for all the scoring, and most of them were awesome shots. For the National League, they were hit by John Bench of Cincinnati and Hank Aaron of Atlanta, both off the 17-game winner, Blue; and Roberto Clemente of Pittsburgh off Mickey Lolich of Detroit.

Homers Are Countered

But they were countered by three two-run homers for the American League — by Reggie Jackson of Oakland, as a pinch-hitter, and Frank Robinson of Baltimore, both off Dock Ellis of Pittsburgh in the third inning; and by Harmon Killebrew of Minnesota off Ferguson Jenkins of Chicago.

The half-dozen homers tied a record for All-Star games that had been set in Tiger Stadium in 1951 and matched in Cleveland's Municipal Stadium in 1954. But tonight's game, in the "hitter's park" that is the home of the Detroit Tigers, was less a statistical event than a showcase for the ranking personalities in baseball.

They were led by Blue, the 21-year-old left-hander for the Oakland Athletics, who, in his first regular season in the American League, already had pitched 17 victories against three defeats with more than one strike-out an inning. And confronting him were the patriarchs of the National League, led by the 40-year-old Willie Mays and the 37-year-old Aaron, the only living players with more than 600 homers.

The confrontation, for one inning at least, veered sharply toward Blue as he snuffed out

three hitters on seven blazing pitches. Four were strikes, and three were hit for easy outs—by Mays, the leadoff batter, on a grounder to shortstop; by Aaron on a grounder to third base, and by Joe Torre on a pop fly to second base.

So far, so good, for the bright southpaw, from Louisiana in the green and white Oakland uniform—an impressive pitcher whipping the ball toward Mays, in his 22d All-Star appearance, and Aaron in his 20th. But, after Ellis had retired the American League in the bottom of the first, Blue suddenly encountered the realities of life in the second.

He started it by hitting Willie Stargell of Pittsburgh with a pitch in the back. Then he struck out Willie McCovey of San Francisco, but Bench followed by driving the 0-and-1 pitch over the 415-foot sign into the second deck in right-center. That made it 2-0, National League, and gave Bench two home runs in three games in the series—and he was a doubtful starter because of a bruised left wrist until game time.

One inning later, Blue faced Aaron again and learned something that National Leaguers had known for a long time—that nobody fools Bad Henry all the time. On the 1-and-2 pitch, Aaron slugged a home run upstairs in right-center, and now it was 3-0.

The home runs were the only hits off Blue in his three innings of work, and they were unusual hits for him. In 184 innings this season in the American League, he had allowed only six homers—about one every 31 innings. But on this clear and windy evening, he was throwing to some uncommon hitters in an uncommon park with gusts to 31 miles an hour, and his fastball carried down-range.

In three innings, he delivered 35 pitches. Seven were called balls, six were hit for outs, 20 were strikes and two went upstairs.

But help was at hand in the bottom of the third inning, and it got Blue off the hook just as quickly. Luis Aparicio of Boston led with a single off Ellis and then Jackson pinch-hit for Blue, rocking the 1-and-2 pitch high over the second deck in

Box Score of All-Star Game

NATIONAL LEAGUE	AB.	R.	H.	BI.
Mays, cf	2	0	0	0
Clemente, rf	2	1	1	1
Millan, 2b	0	0	0	0
Aaron, rf	2	1	1	1
May, 1b	1	0	0	0
Torre, 3b	3	0	0	0
Santo, 3b	1	0	0	0
Stargell, lf	2	1	0	0
Brock, ph	1	0	0	0
McCovey, 1b	2	0	0	0
Marichal, p	0	0	0	0
Kessinger, ss	2	0	0	0
Bench, c	4	1	2	2
Beckert, 2b	3	0	0	0
Rose, rf	0	0	0	0
Harrelson, ss	2	0	0	0
Jenkins, p	0	0	0	0
Colbert, ph	1	0	0	0
Wilson, p	0	0	0	0
Ellis, p	1	0	0	0
Davis, cf	1	0	1	0
Bonds, cf	1	0	0	0
Total	**31**	**4**	**5**	**4**

AMERICAN LEAGUE	AB.	R.	H.	BI.
Carew, 2b	1	1	0	0
Rojas, 2b	1	0	0	0
Murcer, cf	3	0	1	0
Cuellar, p	0	0	0	0
Buford, ph	1	0	0	0
Lolich, p	0	0	0	0
Yastrzemski, lf	3	0	0	0
F. Robinson, rf	2	1	1	2
Kaline, rf	2	1	1	0
Cash, 1b	2	0	0	0
Killebrew, 1b	2	1	1	2
B. Robinson, 3b	3	0	1	0
Freehan, c	3	0	0	0
Munson, c	0	0	0	0
Aparicio, ss	3	1	1	0
Blue, p	0	0	0	0
Jackson, ph	1	1	1	2
Palmer, p	0	0	0	0
Howard, ph	1	0	0	0
Otis, cf	1	0	0	0
Total	**29**	**6**	**7**	**6**

National League	0	2	1	0	0	0	0	1	0—4
American League	0	0	4	0	0	2	0	0	x—6

Double plays—National League 2, American League 1. Left on base—National League 2, American League 2. Home runs—Bench, Aaron, Jackson, F. Robinson, Killebrew, Clemente.

	IP	H	R	ER	BB	SO	HBP	WP	Balk
Ellis (L)	3	4	4	4	1	2	0	0	0
Marichal	2	0	0	0	1	1	0	0	0
Jenkins	1	3	2	2	0	0	0	0	0
Wilson	2	0	0	0	1	1	0	0	0
Blue (W)	3	2	3	3	0	3	1	0	0
Palmer	2	1	0	0	0	2	0	0	0
Cuellar	2	1	0	0	1	2	0	0	0
Lolich	2	1	1	1	0	1	0	0	0

Umpires—Umont (A.L.), plate; Pryor (N.L.), 1b; O'Donnell (A.L.), 2b; Harvey (N.L.), 3b; Denkinger (A.L.), rf line; Colosi (N.L.), lf line. Save—Lolich. Hit by pitch—by Blue (Stargell). Time of game—2:05. Attendance—53,559.

right-center, more than 100 feet above the ground. The ball would have left the stadium, but bounced off a little shed at the base of a light tower for one of the longest home runs since the All-Star games began in 1933.

Two outs later, after a walk to Rod Carew of Minnesota, it was Frank Robinson's turn. The hero of the Baltimore Orioles socked Ellis's 1-and-2 pitch on a curving line drive into the lower right-field seats, and the American League took the lead.

One of a Kind

Robinson, the only player in baseball history who has been elected the most valuable player in both leagues, thereby became the only player in All-Star Game history to hit a home run for both leagues. He did it for Cincinnati in 1959, was traded to the Orioles in 1966 and was in the midst of an 0-for-10 slump in the midsummer classic when he unloaded.

The score held at 4-3 until the sixth, with Juan Marichal

pitching two scoreless innings for the Nationals and Jim Palmer of Baltimore following Blue for the Americans. Then Jenkins took up the pitching in the sixth, Al Kaline of Detroit singled to center and Killebrew hit a two-run homer into the lower left-field seats for a 6-3 lead.

The National League had one shot left, and it was fired in the top of the eighth inning, with Lolich pitching and Clemente swinging. The ball wound up in the upper deck in right field, making the score 6-4, and that's where it stayed.

When it was over, the National League had survived its first meeting with the great Blue, who, according to Bud Harrelson of the Mets, "is no Nolan Ryan on sheer speed."

But the American League finally had broken its eight-year plague, had narrowed the series standing to 23-18 (and one tie) in favor of the Nationals and had helped to restore the two-party system to baseball's summertime show.

July 14, 1971

Shifting of Senators to Texas Approved by American League

Vote Is 10 to 2 For Conditional Move in 1972

BOSTON, Sept. 21 (UPI) — American League owners voted tonight to shift the franchise of the financially ailing Washington Senators to Arlington, Tex., between Dallas and Fort Worth, for next season.

Joe Cronin, the league president, said the owners had approved the shift on a 10-2 vote with conditions relating to the number of seats and a lease for Turnpike Stadium in Arlington. The stadium now seats 21,000

and, it was said, could be expanded to 50,000.

The owner of the Senators, Robert Short, conceded that he had "failed in Washington to field a team successfully." He has said the Senators lost $3-million over the last three years.

Apologizes to Fans

"I was not able to do in Washington what I did my best to do," said Short. He thanked those who had "helped me try to find a solution," and apologized to Senator fans for shifting the club.

Short said he would continue as owner, indicating that he would not sell part of the franchise in making the move to Texas.

Baseball Commissioner Bowie Kuhn described the decison as "a sad day for Washington," but said the Texas area had

"long deserved major league baseball."

Officials would not disclose the exact financial terms of the lease, but Short said they gave him "a more favorable position than any major league operator that I know of."

Mayor Thomas Vandergriff of Arlington said he was "most proud and pleased" to obtain the franchise and predicted it would be one of the most successful in baseball. He said Short would be charged a basic rental of $1 a year until at least a million in attendance had been reached.

Orioles, White Sox Dissent

Cronin said the league had received "a last offer" from a Washington food magnate, Joseph Danzansky, during the more than 12 hours of discus-

sion. The Baltimore Orioles and the Chicago White Sox filed the two dissenting votes, he said.

Danzansky was both disappointed and puzzled. He said he and two other men originally offered $7-million for 80 per cent of the franchise stock months ago and later increased the offer to $7.5-million for 90 per cent of the stock.

Cronin said he had felt the Washington group was "thinly capitalized."

While there was discussion about President Nixon's suggestion of playing some Oriole games in Washington next season, he said, "we haven't had time to make a decision of any kind."

In Washington, the City Council chairman, Gilbert Hahn, expressed "bitter disappointment" at the development. He said there was no chance any team would play in the capital next season.

"The baseball hierarchy discouraged any overtures to any other clubs while the Senators were here," Hahn said. But he insisted that the city would be interested in making offers to the San Diego Padres and San Francisco Giants.

Hahn also suggested that each major league club could play one game at Robert F. Kennedy Stadium next season.

"Considering the nature of Washington, which is made up of transients an dlarge numbers of people who are from other cities, it might be the best solution," he said.

President Nixon said earlier this week it would be disappointing to lose the Senators.

September 22, 1971

Blue Wins American League's Cy Young Award

By JOSEPH DURSO

Vida Blue was named the winner of the Cy Young Award yesterday as the best pitcher in the American League and became the youngest player in baseball history to be elected.

The 22-year-old left-hander for the Oakland Athletics outscored Mickey Lolich of the Detroit Tigers and Wilbur Wood of the Chicago White Sox in the voting by the Baseball Writers Association of America.

He did not acheive a clean sweep, getting 14 of the 24 first-place votes cast by the writers' committee while Lolich got nine and Wood one. But he was the only pitcher named on all the ballots and he accumulated enough votes for second and third place to finish with 98 points to 85 for Lolich.

Wood, a knuckleball pitcher, was third with 23 points and then came Dave McNally of the Baltimore Orioles, Dick Drago of the Kansas City Royals and Andy Messersmith of the California Angels.

For Blue, the award was the first of many he will probably receive this winter as the sensation of the baseball season. It was his first full summer in the major leagues after two spells of September pitching in the two previous years, and he started it with a stunning series of performances.

Associated Press
Vida Blue

By mid-July, ne had built a record of 17 victories and only three defeats with six shutouts and the honor of starting the All-Star game for the American League. He was pitching every fourth day, though, and tired after that with a 7-5 won-lost record over the final two months.

By the end of the season, the Oakland team had run away with the league's Western championship and the hard-throwing youngster from Mansfield, La., had compiled this record: 24 victories, 8 defeats,

8 shutouts, 24 complete games, 301 strikeouts and an earned-run average of 1.82.

Meanwhile, the 31-year-old Lolich went into the second half with a 14-6 mark and then came on strong down the stretch. He finished with 25 victories, the most in the majors; 14 defeats, 29 complete games, 308 strikeouts and an earned-run average of 2.92.

They had two things in common: Both are left-handers and both are workhorses. Blue started 39 of Oakland's 162 games, Lolich 45 of Detroit's. The No. 3 man in the poll, Wood, is a former relief pitcher who won 22 games, lost 13 and was second to Blue with seven shutouts and a 1.91 earned-run average.

The youngest man to win the award before Blue was Dean Chance of the Angels in 1964 at the age of 23.

The committee consists of two writers from each of the 12 cities in the league. A similar award for the National League will be announced next week.

The votes are cast before the playoffs and World Series, and the handwriting may have been on the wall.

October 27, 1971

Baseball Strike Is Settled; Season to Open Tomorrow

By JOSEPH DURSO

The first general strike in baseball history ended in its 13th day yesterday when the players and owners agreed to start the season tomorrow without making up any of the 86 missed games.

The settlement was reached in Chicago, where the owners of the 24 major league teams gathered yesterday, and in New York, where the player representatives had been meeting for three days.

The original issue—an in-

crease in the players' pensions, which are financed by television money — already had been solved by a compromise raise of $500,000. The final issue— whether to pay the players for games rescheduled because of the strike — was settled by the bobtailed season.

As a result, some teams like the Houston Astros and San Diego Padres will play nine games less than a full season of 162, all teams will miss at least six games and division

championships will be decided on a straight percentage basis. They customarily are decided that way, but most clubs usually manage to complete full seasons, despite bad weather, by scheduling double-headers.

For the 600 players, whose salaries will begin tomorrow instead of a week ago yesterday, the cost will be nine days' pay. For those at the minimum level of $13,500, the loss will total $675; for those at the big league average of $32,500, it will be $1,600; for Henry Aaron of the Atlanta Braves, who is bearing down on Babe Ruth's home-run record at nearly

$200,000 a season, just over $9,880.

Victory for Nobody

Despite the bitterness of the two-week strike, neither side made extravagant claims of victory after the settlement was announced at 4:15 P.M.

"Everybody recognizes that nobody won," said Donald Grant, chairman of the board of directors of the New York Mets.

"I think it's fair to say nobody ever wins in a strike situation," said Marvin Miller, the onetime steel-union economist who now directs the Players'

Association. "This one is no exception. We're not going to claim victory even though our objectives were achieved."

"I really feel good that it's over," said Joe Torre of the St. Louis Cardinals, the ranking hitter in baseball last season, "but there will probably be some catcalls from the stands when we start to play ball."

"It's inevitable that there will be hard feelings," said Bowie Kuhn, the commissioner of baseball. "My job is to hold them to a minimum. Who won? Nobody. The players suffered. The clubs suffered. Baseball suffered."

In New York, the Yankees and Mets found their original timetables reversed by the strike. The Yankees, who had been scheduled to open the season at home April 6, now will open in Baltimore tomorrow after working out at Yankee Stadium this afternoon. The Mets, who would have started in Pittsburgh, now will open against the Pirates at home after working out in Shea Stadium this morning.

Some clubs, though, jumped the gun because the strike obviously was moving toward a close as the owners and players convened separately yesterday. In San Francisco, the Giants worked out for three hours in Candlestick Park before the settlement and Manager Charlie Fox said they were ready for the opener in Houston tomorrow. Across the Bay, the Oakland Athletics mustered about half their men and exercised, while Sal Bando, the team captain, observed:

"I don't know how we'll do at the start. When you lose two weeks at this time of year, you are almost in the position of having to go to spring training all over again."

Some early-birds, though, ruffled the feathers of their owner of the Kansas City Royals, said he would protest to the American League president any games his club had to play this weekend against the Chicago White Sox. His reason: the White Sox had "disregarded" a league stipulation that no players be allowed to work out in major league stadiums during the strike.

"I've talked on the telephone with most of our players and with all of our pitchers," said Ralph Houk, the manager of the New York Yankees and a career optimist. "And although we'll be more cautious for a time, I don't think there'll be any danger from the two-week layoff. The pitchers may be ahead of the hitters for a few days. We had three pitchers

ready to go nine innings when we left Florida, and I don't think they lost anything."

As for the strike settlement, both sides went into the home stretch yesterday with a handshake agreement on the players' benefits fund, which had been financed by a $5.45-million allotment each year from national TV receipts from the World Series.

The players asked that their share this year be raised to cover the cost of living, and calculated the pension increase at 17 per cent, or $1-million. The owners eventually offered to add $490,000 to that part of the plan that covers medical benefits but insisted on no raise in pensions.

By last Tuesday, the 11th day of the strike, the players had lowered their demand to $600,000 for pensions and the owners had raised their offer from zero to $400,000. By then, they were talking not about new money—but about the wisdom of diverting surplus money that had accumulated within the pension fund from investments.

They decided to split the difference at $500,000. But the question remained: Would the ball games that had been postponed be made up and, if so, would the players be paid for them? For the last 48 hours, that was the only issue left, but it delayed the season two more days.

The owners themselves were divided as they gathered in Chicago—the American League generally favoring a shorter season anyway, the National preferring the full 162 games. However, the National League did not make a fight of it and a formula was reached that was telephoned to New York, where Miller and the players were waiting.

The owners thereupon dispatched a task force to New York to translate the agreement into a memorandum, which must be signed by midnight tonight. They will be represented by Charles Feeney, president of the National League; Joe Cronin, president of the American, and John J. Gaherin, their labor-relations adviser, who bore the brunt of the negotiating with Miller.

By midnight, though, everybody expected players to be back with their clubs or en route from the West Coast and Caribbean, with 12 games scheduled tomorrow to pick up the pieces.

April 14, 1972

Baseball's Exempt Status Upheld by Supreme Court

By LEONARD KOPPETT
Special to The New York Times

WASHINGTON, June 19—Baseball, and only baseball, remains exempt from the antitrust laws, the Supreme Court ruled today by a 5-3 margin. But the Court again urged Congress to resolve the problem.

The decision ended the Curt Flood case in defeat for the player who challenged baseball's reserve system, a set of arrangements that ties a player to one club indefinitely.

Flood, then a 32-year-old outfielder earning $90,000 a year, objected to being traded from St. Louis to Philadelphia after the 1969 season. He sued for $3-million in damages, claiming that reserve rules had prevented him from playing for any other club. The Major League Players Association supported his suit financially and former Justice Arthur Goldberg represented him.

A trial in May, 1970, resulted in a lower court decision that the merits of the case need not be considered because baseball was made exempt from antitrust laws by Supreme Court decisions in 1922 and 1953.

Today's decision, delivered by Justice Harry A. Blackmun, also bypassed the merits of the reserve system and stressed the Court's refusal to overturn previous rulings. It acknowledged that baseball's special status was an "aberration" and an "anomaly," but re-affirmed the position taken in several prior cases that it was up to Con-

gress to remedy the situation with legislation.

Voting with the majority were Chief Justice Warren E. Burger, who expressed "reservations," and Justices Byron R. White, Potter Stewart and William E. Rehnquist.

Justices William O. Douglas and Thurgood Marshall filed dissenting opinions, in which Justice William J. Brennan Jr. joined. Justice Lewis F. Powell Jr. did not participate.

The 1922 ruling, referred to as Federal Baseball, stated that baseball was not the sort of business that the antitrust laws were intended to cover.

In 1953, in a case called Toolson vs. New York, the Court ruled, 7-2, that the exemption should be continued, even though legal philosophy had changed, because the industry had been allowed to develop for 30 years on the assumption of its immunity. Justice Blackmun stressed this point.

"We continue to loathe, 50 years after Federal Baseball and almost two decades after Toolson, to overturn those cases judicially when Congress, by its positive inaction, has allowed those decisions to stand for so long," he wrote.

During the last 20 years, many bills have been introduced to grant uniform antitrust exemptions to all major professional sports, but none has passed both houses of Congress in the same session.

Even as the Supreme Court was issuing today's ruling, a Senate hearing was in progress on a proposed Federal sports commission that would have jurisdiction over professional

Curt Flood with his attorney, former Associate Justice Arthur J. Goldberg, during outfielder's trial in 1970.

team sports, and the House Judiciary Committee was scheduling hearings starting July 24 on the general topic of sports and antitrust regulations.

Justice Douglas, in a footnote to his dissent, declared: "While I joined the Court's opinion in Toolson, I have lived to regret it, and I would now correct what I believe to be its fundamental error."

He argued that the inaction of Congress could be seen two ways.

"If Congressional inaction is our guide, we should rely upon the fact that Congress has refused to enact bills broadly exempting professional sports from antitrust regulation. . . . There can be no doubt that were we considering the question of

baseball for the first time upon a clean slate, we would hold it to be subject to Federal antitrust regulation. The unbroken silence of Congress should not prevent us from correcting our own mistakes."

But Chief Justice Burger, in his brief concurring opinion, said:

"Like Mr. Justice Douglas, I have grave reservations as to the correctness of Toolson; as he notes in his dissent, he joined in that holding but has 'lived to regret it.' The error, if such it be, is one on which the affairs of a great many people have rested for a long time. Courts are not the forum in which this tangled web ought to be unsnarled.

"I agree with Mr. Justice

Douglas that Congressional inaction is not a solid base, but the least undesirable course now is to let the matter rest with Congress; it is time the Congress acted to solve this problem."

Justice Marshall, in his dissent, stressed the importance of upholding antitrust laws in the general interest. "They are as important to baseball players as they are to football players, lawyers, doctors, or members of any other class of workers."

He pointed out, however, that overruling Federal Baseball and Toolson would not necessarily mean that Flood won. "I would remand this case to the District Court for consideration whether . . . there has been an antitrust violation."

The prevailing view, however, was Justice Blackmun's. He found that Federal laws took precedence over state antitrust suits, and that there was no need to consider the argument that the reserve system was a matter for labor negotiation and therefore exempt from antitrust.

"If there is any inconsistency of illogic in all this, it is an inconsistency and illogic of long standing that is to be remedied by the Congress and not by this Court," he wrote.

"Under these circumstances, there is merit in consistency even though some might claim that beneath that consistency is a layer of inconsistency."

June 20, 1972

National League All-Stars Win on Morgan's Single in 10th, 4-3

McGraw Victor —Aaron Hits Home Run

By JOSEPH DURSO
Special to The New York Times

ATLANTA, July 25 — The largest baseball crowd in Atlanta's 125-year history watched the National League defeat the American League, 4-3, in 10 innings tonight in the 43d All-Star Game.

The Nationals did it with theatrical flair, too, tying the game with one run in the bottom of the ninth and winning it in the 10th on a single by Joe Morgan of the Cincinnati Reds.

It was the seventh extra-inning game in the series and the seventh won by the Nationals, who thereby increased their lead to 24 victories against 18 defeats with one tie. It also was their ninth triumph in the last 10 years, a decade of dominance that was interrupted only last summer in Detroit.

The Nationals stayed in command the hard way tonight though. They fell one run behind in the third inning, then went ahead in the sixth on a two-run home run by Henry Aaron—who called it "the most dramatic" of his 19-year career.

Rojas Gets 2-Run Clout

But they watched in wonder

two innings later when Aaron, the hometown hero, was upstaged by Cookie Rojas of Kansas City, who got the lead back for the American League by pinch-hitting a two-run home run.

Still, three outs from an ironic loss, they rallied in the ninth for a 3-3 tie. Then they took it in the 10th against Dave McNally of the Baltimore Orioles on a walk to Nate Colbert, a sacrifice bunt and a line single to right-center by Morgan, one of four men in the game who played the full game.

Morgan, who was voted the most valuable player on the field, also made a winner of Tug McGraw of the New York Mets, who pitched two scoreless innings with four strikeouts.

The 53,107 fans paid up to $12 apiece to watch the 56 ranking players perform in the home stadium of the Atlanta Braves in the first All-Star game ever held in the Southeast. Not only that, but the Braves returned 18,000 ticket orders they couldn't handle.

The chief interest — except for a flurry of bickering and second-guessing among the players themselves — centered on the old issue of interleague rivalry. The National League clubs have spurted ahead in recent years in new parks, attendance and celebrity players.

Most of the skirmishing involved pitching assignments and second - team selections

Box Score of All-Star Game

AMERICAN LEAGUE					NATIONAL LEAGUE				
	AB	R.	H.	BI.		AB	R.	H.	BI.
Carew, 2b	2	0	1	1	J. Morgan, 2b	4	0	1	1
Rojas, 2b	1	1	1	2	Mays, cf	2	0	0	0
Murcer, cf	3	0	0	0	Cedeno, cf	2	1	1	0
Scheinblum, rf	1	0	0	0	H. Aaron, rf	3	1	1	2
R. Jackson, rf	4	0	2	0	A. Oliver, rf	1	0	0	0
D. Allen, 1b	3	0	0	0	Stargell, lf	1	0	0	0
Cash, 1b	1	0	0	0	B. Williams, lf	2	1	1	0
Yastrzemski, lf	3	0	0	0	Bench, c	2	0	1	0
Rudi, lf	1	0	1	0	Sanguillen, c	2	0	1	0
Grich, ss	4	0	0	0	L. May 1b	4	0	1	1
B.Robinson, 3b	2	0	0	0	Torre, 3b	3	0	1	0
Bando, 3b	2	0	0	0	Santo, 3b	1	0	0	0
Freehan, c	1	1	0	0	Kessinger, ss	2	0	0	0
Fisk, c	2	1	1	0	Carlton, p	0	0	0	0
Palmer, p	0	0	0	0	Stoneman, p	1	0	0	0
Lolich, p	1	0	0	0	McGraw, p	0	0	0	0
G. Perry, p	0	0	0	0	Colbert, ph	0	1	0	0
R. Smith ph	1	0	0	0	Gibson, p	0	0	0	0
Wood, p	0	0	0	0	Blass, p	0	0	0	0
Piniella, ph	1	0	0	0	Beckert, ph	1	0	0	0
McNally, p	0	0	0	0	Sutton, p	0	0	0	0
					Speier, ss	2	0	0	0
Total	33	3	6	3	Total	33	4	8	4

American .... 0 0 1   0 0 0   0 2 0 — 3
National .... 0 0 0   0 0 2   0 0 1   1 — 4

DP—American 2, National 2. LOB—American 3, National 5. 2B—R. Jackson, Rudi. HRS—H. Aaron (1), Rojas (1). SB——. Morgan. S—Palmer, Speier.

	IP.	H.	R.	ER.	BB.	SO.	HBP.	WP.	BLK.
Palmer	3	1	0	0	0	0	0	0	0
Lolich	2	1	0	0	0	1	0	0	0
G. Perry	2	3	2	2	0	1	0	0	0
Wood	2	2	1	1	1	1	0	0	0
McNally (L. 0-1)	*⅓	1	1	1	1	0	0	0	0
Gibson	2	1	0	0	0	0	0	0	0
Blass	1	1	1	1	1	0	0	0	0
Sutton	2	1	0	0	0	2	0	0	0
Carlton	1	0	0	0	1	0	0	0	0
Stoneman	2	2	2	2	0	2	0	0	0
McGraw (W. 1-0)	2	1	0	0	0	4	0	0	0

T—2:26. A—53,107.
*One out when winning run was scored.

made by Earl Weaver of the Baltimore Orioles, the American League manager. His rival manager was Danny Murtaugh, retired boss of last year's world champion Pittsburgh Pirates. The starting line-ups were picked from the 3,171,556 votes cast by the public.

Pitchers Start Well

In a park renowned for long-range hitting, the players kept the crowd waiting before finding the range. In fact, they kept them waiting before doing much of anything while Bob Gibson of St. Louis and Jim Palmer of Baltimore pitched easily through two scoreless innings.

Then, in the top of the third, Steve Blass of Pittsburgh relieved Gibson and dug a little hole by walking the first batter he faced, Bill Freehan of Detroit. A sacrifice bunt by Palmer advanced Freehan to second and then Rod Carew of Minnesota lined a single through the middle for his first hit six All-Star games and a 1-0 lead.

It was a lead that stood up during another inning of pitching by Palmer and two by Mickey Lolich of Detroit, whose 17 victories for the first half of the season lead both leagues and who was thereby irritated when passed over for tonight's starting assignment.

The Nationals, meanwhile, also were getting stout pitching from Don Sutton and Steve Carlton in the middle innings, and so the one-run lead was still good as they went to the bottom of the sixth.

The new pitcher for the American League was Gaylord Perry, a 16-game winner. Perry had pitched in two previous games for the National League while with the San Francisco Giants, who traded him last winter to the Cleveland Indians.

Now he got two fast outs and then gave up a single to left field by Cesar Cedeno of Houston, who had just replaced Willie Mays in center. That brought up Aaron, the hometown hero, who already had received two standing ovations.

With 659 home runs in his career, Aaron stood only 55 short of Babe Ruth's record of 714, but he had hit only one in 20 previous All-Star games —and had batted only .183 besides. But this time he ripped Perry's first pitch high to left field and just over the fence at the 375-foot marker.

The ball dropped into the yard behind, not far from a sign noting that Aaron had hit the 600th home run of his career there a year ago April — off Gaylord Perry.

"The ball I hit was a spitter," Aaron said later, bringing up an old issue about Perry's famous wet one. "But not one of his best spitters."

To which Perry replied clinically, "Fastball inside."

Whatever it was, the script now was tailored to hometown perfection: Aaron hits home run in the sixth to win it for the Nationals, 2-1. But enter Octavio Rivas Rojas of Havana and Miami.

There were two down in the top of the eighth when Rojas got the nod from hometown Manager Weaver, who had said to him earlier, "If I don't use you, will you be terribly disappointed?" And Rojas, a career understudy, had answered, "You're the boss."

But now in the eighth Weaver learned that Carew had strained the muscles in his rib cage again, so he sent Rojas up to pinch-hit even though he was a right-handed batter swinging against a right-handed pitcher, Bill Stoneman of Montreal.

Williams's Run Ties It

Carlton Fisk of Boston was on first base after a single and the count on Rojas went to one ball, two strikes. Then he lifted an inside slider high to left field. It backed Billy Williams of the Chicago Cubs against the wire fence about 15 yards inside the foul pole and dropped beyond as Williams leaped and lunged, almost making a dramatic catch over the top strands.

That made it 3-2 and gave Rojas the distinction of having trumped Aaron's ace in Atlanta. But, as the hitters on both side came to life late, Rojas soon was upstaged by other people.

Williams opened the bottom of the ninth for the Nationals with a single to center off Wilbur Wood, the left-handed knuckleball ace of the Chicago White Sox. He made third on a single through the middle by Manny Sanguillen of Pittsburgh and scored the tying run while Bobby Grich of Baltimore was making a fancy play on Lee May's bouncing ball to the shortstop's right.

The Nationals had a pretty good shot at winning the game right there. But they were checked when Sal Bando smothered a slam by Ron Santo and started the double play that sent them into overtime at 3-3.

Hank Aaron

Atlanta Braves

July 26, 1972

305

A's Conquer Tigers, 5 to 0, For 2-0 Playoff Margin

Campaneris, Hit by Pitch, Fires Bat at Hurler

By MURRAY CHASS
Special to The New York Times

OAKLAND, Oct. 8 — John (Blue Moon) Odom threw a three-hitter at the Detroit Tigers today, but it was a bat that Bert Campaneris threw at Lerrin LaGrow that ignited one of the most inflammatory incidents of the 1972 baseball season.

Odom's three-hitter and Campaneris's three hits sparked the Oakland A's to a 5-0 victory and a commanding two-game lead in the American League pennant playoff.

However, Campaneris may not be around when the three-of-five-game series resumes in Detroit Tuesday because he may learn tomorrow that he has been suspended.

Joe Cronin, the league president, conferred with the umpires following the game but withheld disclosure of any possible action he may take. Cronin explained that he never announces any action without first informing the player by telegram.

Fryman Knocked Out

The outcome of the game, realistically, was resolved by the time the Campaneris-LaGrow incident popped up in the seventh inning. The A's had ripped into Woodie Fryman and two Tiger relief pitchers for five runs, four in the fifth, and Odom was on his way to retiring the last 16 batters he faced.

Campaneris, who singled in the first and scored on Joe Rudi's single and then singled again in the third and fifth, led off the seventh and was hit on the outside of his left ankle by LaGrow's first pitch, the latest of several pitches that had come close to him during the game.

The 30-year-old Cuban, who is 5 feet 10 inches and weighs 160 pounds, fell to the ground, then got up and flung the bat at LaGrow, a 6-5, 220-pound right-hander. LaGrow ducked as the bat sailed over his head and players from both dugouts raced onto the field.

Billy Martin, the Detroit manager, who grew up in nearby Berkeley in a neighborhood where fighting was a way of life, led the Tiger charge and had to be restrained by Larry Barnett, the third-base umpire. Campaneris, meanwhile, had been pushed back by Nestor Chylak, the plate umpire.

By the time the teams returned to their benches, both Campaneris and LaGrow had been ejected from the game. The reason for Campaneris's ejection was obvious but not so for LaGrow's.

"There's no place in the world for a player to throw a bat at another player," Chylak said. "I didn't say LaGrow was throwing at Campaneris. I got him out just to keep peace, so I wouldn't have any further incidents. I didn't know what might happen later."

Martin knew what would have happened if he had been able to get to Campaneris.

"You bet I was going after Campaneris," the manager said, still fuming over the incident. "Anytime a guy throws a bat at my pitcher, I'd be no manager if I didn't try to protect my pitcher.

"I won't do anything further when we play them again, but if we ever get in a fight, I'll go after the gutless guy. I just hope we have the opportunity to knock him out to left field about 15 rows up.

"He's got to be suspended.

I've never seen a guy throw a bat at anyone. I have no respect for a guy who uses a bat as a weapon. I've never seen anything as dirty in my life. I woulda respected him if he had gone out to the mound to fight, but that was gutless. If a mosquito bit him, he'd be

Associated Press

A's Box Score

DETROIT (A.)	ab.	r.	h.	bi.		OAKLAND (A.)	ab.	r.	h.	bi.
McAuliffe, ss	4	0	0	0		Campan's, ss	3	2	3	0
Kaline, rf	4	0	1	0		Maxvill, ss	0	0	0	0
Sims, c	3	0	0	0		Alou, rf	4	1	1	1
Cash, 1b	3	0	1	0		Rudi, lf	3	1	2	1
Horton, lf	3	0	0	0		Jackson, cf	4	0	1	2
Northrup, cf	3	0	1	0		Bandc, 3b	4	0	0	0
Taylor, 2b	3	0	0	0		Epste n, 1b	3	0	0	0
Podriguez, 3b	3	0	0	0		Hegar, 1b	0	0	0	0
Fryman, p	1	0	0	0		Tenace, c	3	0	0	0
Zachary, p	0	0	0	0		Green, 2b	1	0	0	0
Scherman, p	0	0	0	0		Henrick, ph	1	1	1	0
Haller, ph	1	0	0	0		Kubiak, 2b	1	0	0	0
LaGrow, p	0	0	0	0		Odom, p	2	0	0	0
Hiller, p	0	0	0	0						
G. Brown, ph	1	0	0	0						
Total	29	0	3	0		Total	29	5	8	4

Detroit .... 0 0 0   0 0 0   0 0 0—0
Oakland .... 1 0 0   0 4 0   0 0 x—5
E—McAuliffe. DP—Detroit 1. LOB—Detroit 2, Oakland 4. 2B—Rudi, Jackson. SB—Campaneris 2. S—Odom.

	IP.	H.	R.	ER.	BB.	SO.
Fryman (L, 0-1)	4⅓	7	4	4	1	5
Zachary	0	1	1	1	1	0
Scherman	⅔	1	0	0	0	1
LaGrow	1	0	0	0	0	1
Hiller	2	0	0	0	0	1
Odom (W, 1-0)	9	3	0	0	0	2

HBP—by LaGrow (Campaneris). Wild pitch—Zachary 2. T—2:37. A—31,088.

Oakland's Bert Campaneris winding up to throw his bat at Lerrin LaGrow, Tigers' pitcher, after being hit by a pitch in the seventh LaGrow ducked as the bat flew, both dugouts emptied, and both players were ejected.

out. That's how much guts he has."

Campaneris wasn't around after the game to give his version of the incident. The A's said he had dressed and gone to Merritt Hospital for X-rays of his ankle, which were negative. He then joined the team on the chartered plane for the flight to Detroit.

Campaneris obviously felt La-Grow was throwing at him, but both the pitcher and the manager denied it.

"The pitch was low and inside; it just got away from me," said LaGrow, a rookie who appeared in 16 games for Detroit this season. "That's the way I always pitch to him. After he got up, I saw him draw back, so I thought he might throw the bat and I had time to react. It was a little off to my left side but it was level with my head."

Martin added that if he ever ordered a pitcher to throw at a batter, he'd instruct him to hit the batter in the ribs. "I wouldn't tell him to hit the guy in the foot," Martin said, "and I never would tell a pitcher to throw at a guy's head."

Campaneris, Joe Rudi and Reggie Jackson perpetrated the most damage to Detroit's sinking World Series hopes.

In the first inning, Campaneris led off with a single, stole second and third and scored as Rudi lined a single between Aurelio Rodriguez at third and Dick McAuliffe at short, who were playing in.

Campaneris singled again in the third but was forced at second by Matty Alou, who then was picked off by Fryman before Rudi doubled.

If the Tigers thought they could come back and overcome the one-run deficit, the A's quashed that idea with a four-run explosion in the fifth.

George Hendrick started the outburst with a single as a pinch-hitter for Dick Green, the first second baseman in Manager Dick Williams' shuttle system. Odom sacrificed Hendrick to second, who then went to third on Campaneris"s third single.

Alou followed with another single, increasing Oakland's lead to 2-0 and knocking Fryman out of the game. Chris Zachary relieved Fryman and he made a brief but costly appearance, throwing two consecutive wild pitches. The first permitted Campaneris to score and the second was ball four to Rudi.

Fred Scherman then replaced Zachary, and Jackson brought in two more runs with a double to left-center.

October 9, 1972

Reds Take Flag on Wild Pitch

Pirates Are Beaten, 4-3; Bench's Clout Ties Score

By JOSEPH DURSO
Special to The New York Times

CINCINNATI, Oct. 11—The Cincinnati Reds won the National League pennant on a wild pitch today when they rallied for two runs in the last half of the ninth inning to defeat the Pittsburgh Pirates, 4-3.

It was a chaotic finish to a playoff that went the five-game limit and to a game that also went the limit, with the Pirates leading all the way in the defense of their world title —until the last inning.

Then Johnny Bench hammered a home run into the empty football seats beyond the right-field fence against Dave Giusti, and the Reds—the champions of the Western Division—were finally even. Two outs and two singles later, Bob Moose bounced his 1-and-1 pitch into the dirt past the pinch-hitting Hal McRae and the pennant bounced with it to Cincinnati.

13-10 Playoff Underdogs

For the Big Red Machine, the pitch that Moose uncorked into the dirt to the right of home plate marked the end of a long road back. Two years ago, the Reds won the West and swept the playoff against the Pirates. Last year, they subsided to fourth place while the Pirates won the pennant. And this year, they revived in the West while the Pirates dominated the East.

But in the playoff, which they entered as 13-10 underdogs, the Reds were always one day late. They dropped the opener, then tied the series the next day. Then they dropped behind again and were one defeat from extinction. But they survived with a 7-1 victory yesterday and then struggled today while Pittsburgh took leads of 2-0 in the second inning, 3-1 in the fourth and 3-2 in the fifth.

Going into their final turn at bat, they were still losing by 3-2 and had scrounged only four hits off Steve Blass, though one of the four was a homer by Cesar Geronimo that

Reds' Box Score

PITTSBURGH (N.)	ab	r	h	bi	CINCINNATI (N.)	ab	r	h	bi
Stennett, lf	4	0	1	0	Rose, lf	3	0	1	1
Oliver, cf	3	0	0	0	Morgan, 2b	4	0	0	0
Clemente, rf	3	1	1	0	Tolan, cf	4	0	0	0
Stargell, 1b	4	0	0	0	Bench, c	4	1	2	1
Robertson, 1b	0	0	0	0	Perez, 1b	4	0	1	0
Sanguillen, c	4	2	2	0	Foster, pr	0	1	0	0
Hebner, 3b	4	1	2	0	Menke, 3b	3	0	1	0
Cash, 2b	3	0	0	0	Geronimo, rf	4	1	1	1
Alley, ss	4	0	0	0	Chaney, ss	4	1	1	0
Blass, p	3	0	0	0	Gullett, p	0	0	0	0
R. Hernandez, p	0	0	0	0	Borbon, p	0	0	0	0
Giusti, p	0	0	0	0	Uhlaender, ph	1	0	0	0
Moose, p	0	0	0	0	Hall, p	0	0	0	0
					Hague, ph	0	0	0	0
					Concepcion, pr	0	0	0	0
					Carroll, p	0	0	0	0
					McRae, ph	0	0	0	0
Total	33	3	7	2	Total	31	4	7	3

Pittsburgh .... 0 2 0 1 0 0 0 0 0—3
Cincinnati .... 0 0 1 0 1 0 0 0 2—4

E—Chaney. DP—Cincinnati 1. LOB—Pittsburgh 5, Cincinnati 7. 2B—Hebner, Rose. HRs—Geronimo (1), Bench (1). S—Gullett, Oliver, Rose.

	IP.	H.	R.	ER.	BB.	SO.
Blass	7⅓	4	2	2	2	4
R. Hernandez	0	0	0	0	0	0
Giusti (L, 0-1)	0	3	2	2	0	0
Moose	0	0	0	0	0	0
Gullett	3	6	3	3	0	2
Borbon	2	1	0	0	0	0
Hall	3	1	0	0	1	4
Carroll (W, 1-1)	1	0	0	0	0	0

*Two outs when winning run was scored.
Wild pitch—Gullett, Moose.
T—2:19. A—41,887.

kept them within striking distance. And, with three outs to go, they struck.

For those final three outs, the Pirates switched to their longtime relief ace, Giusti, a 32-year-old right-hander who had pitched 54 times this summer with an earned-run average of only 1.92. But it was a calculated risk, because Giusti was replacing Ramon Hernandez, a 31-year-old left-hander who had pitched 53 times with an even better earned-run average, 1.67.

The risk was taken because Cincinnati's three hitters in the ninth were all right-handers. But it promptly backfired on Giusti's fourth pitch, which Bench pounded over the 375-foot marker in right field for his 41st homer of 1972.

Now the Reds were back in business, at 3-all, and business even picked up when Tony Perez hit the next pitch through the middle for a single. He was replaced by a pinch-runner, George Foster, who then raced to second when Denis Menke punched a single through the left side of the infield.

The crowd of 41,887 was up and howling just as it had been two hours earlier while the dramatic play-by-play from Detroit was being flashed on the electric scoreboard. And the noise grew louder when Giusti, trying to foil a bunt by Geronimo, threw two high pitches.

For Giusti, who had got nobody out, that was it. He was replaced by Moose, who had got nobody out in the first inning of the second game. But Moose was one of Pittsburgh's regular starters, a right-hander who had pitched 31 times this year, though only once in relief.

He did nobly, too, until the one disastrous pitch that cost the Pirates the pennant. But first he got Geronimo to foul off two pitches, one bunting and one swinging, and then Geronimo lifted a 370-foot fly to Roberto Clemente at the base of the right-field wall. Foster tagged up and flew to third.

When Darrel Chaney popped a high fly into short left field, Gene Alley ran back from shortstop and Rennie Stennett ran in from left, with Alley making the catch as they collided. But that made two outs, and now the Pirates stood one out from sending the game into extra innings.

They never got the out, though. With Foster leading off third and Menke off first, McRae pinch-hit for Clay Carroll. The count rose to one ball, one strike. Then, 159 games after the season had begun, Moose heaved the next pitch on the bounce past Manny Sanguillen. And, as the ball skipped to the box-seat railing behind home plate, Foster scored the run that brought—and cost—the pennant.

It was a long time coming for the Reds, longer even than scheduled, because the game was delayed 1 hour 28 minutes by rain and didn't start until 4:30. The canvas covering the artificial turf was removed several times, and Don Gullett and Blass warmed up twice.

Gullett, in fact was ready to pitch from the mound when things were delayed the first time.

Pirates Score Twice

When he finally got his chance an hour and a half later, he looked off-target and Blass looked sharp, which is the way they looked in the opener last Saturday. Then, in the second inning, Sanguillen singled to left and Richie Hebner pulled a double down the right-field line. Sanguillen stopped at third, but when the relay got away from Chaney at second base he scored. And when Dave Cash singled to center, Hebner scored and it was 2-0, Pittsburgh.

One inning later, the Reds mounted their first comeback. Chaney singled to right and Gullett bunted him to second. Pete Rose, who made nine hits in the five games, followed with a shot behind first base that took a high hop off Willie Stargell's glove for a double and a run.

But in the fourth, Sanguillen and Hebner led with singles and Gullett immediately was replaced by Pedro Borbón. That didn't work, either, because Cash singled again on Borbón's second pitch and it was 3-1, Pirates.

The Reds narrowed the margin an inning after that when Gerónimo, who had only one hit in 17 times at bat in the playoff, pulled his homer over the fence in ight, making it 3-2. Then they bided their time while Borbón, Tom Hall and Carroll shut out the Pirates on one single over the last five innings.

Hall, the lithe left-hander who won the second game in long relief, did the fanciest work: three innings, one single by Stennett, one intentional walk, four strike-outs. His biggest strike-out was delivered against Stargell with two runners on base in the eighth. It was the 15th straight time the Reds had retired Stargell in the playoff, which proved to be one of the critical things that kept them close to the hardest-hitting team in baseball.

That brought them to the ninth, with Pittsburgh's "dynasty" three outs from another pennant. But the Pirates saw it slip away as McRae leaned over the plate and Moose let fly his historic slider.

October 12, 1972

American League to Let Pitcher Have a Pinch-Hitter and Stay In

By JOSEPH DURSO

The owners of the 24 major league baseball teams took a radical step yesterday to put more punch into the game. They voted to allow the American League to use a "designated pinch-hitter," who may bat for the pitcher without forcing him from the game.

The plan will be tried experimentally for the next three seasons by the American League, which has been hurt financially in recent years and has been searching for ways to energize baseball. But it will not be used in the National League, which has resisted the change, or in the World Series, the All-Star Game between the two leagues or interleague exhibition games.

The action was voted at a joint meeting of the major leagues in Chicago yesterday, with Commissioner Bowie Kuhn breaking an impasse between the leagues. As a result, for the first time since the American League was organized in 1901, the two big leagues will play under differing rules.

Another proposal to dramatize baseball — regular games between teams from the rival leagues—was turned over to study committee, with expectations that it might be approved for 1974. And, in a further development, the owners got word of some easing of their labor-relations stalemate with the players.

The chief change in the bargaining talks reportedly was a proposal by the players that the crucial "reserve-clause" issue be separated from the others. If so, the two sides would bypass the gravest danger of a strike when the season opens in April.

But the historic action of the seven-hour meeting of the owners concerned the "designated pinch-hitter," who would become the 10th man in the team's line-up but whose only function would be to bat for the pitcher.

By approving the experiment, which was tried in the high minor leagues three years ago, the club executives made the most basic change in the rules since 1903. That was when foul balls were ruled strikes. Since then, the spitball was banned in 1920, the "lively" ball was introduced in 1930, the strike zone was enlarged in 1962 and reduced again in 1969 and the pitcher's mound was lowered the same year.

But none of those changes revolutionized the rules that were essentially followed since the days of the old New York Knickerbockers baseball club a century and a quarter ago.

Pitcher Can Stay in Game

The rules called for nine men on a side with the stipulation that if a pinch-hitter went to bat for one of the nine, then that player had to leave the game. The most frequently replaced players were the pitchers because they were usually the weakest hitters.

Under the change forced yesterday by the American League, eight of whose 12 teams lost money last season, the manager would follow this procedure if he wished:

¶He would give the umpires a line-up card before the game with the nine regular players listed by position and the 10th player listed as the "designated pinch-hitter." His only job would be that. When it came time for the pitcher to bat, the designated man would swing for him. The pitcher, though, would stay in the game and the pinch-hitter would go back to the bench until the next time round.

¶If the starting pitcher was replaced later by a relief pitcher, the designated pinch-hitter would bat for him.

¶If the manager decided to replace the designated pinch-hitter with another pinch-hitter, he could do that at any time. But the second man then could be used only for that purpose and could not play in the field, while the first pinch-hitter would be out of the game.

¶Except for the "designated" man, all the other players customarily used as pinch-hitters would follow the old rules. They could bat for a player, then stay in the game at any position the manager wished.

Games Are Shorter

When the experiment was tried in the International League in 1969, several things happened: Batting averages rose 10 per cent, the number of runs scored rose 6 per cent and games took six minutes less time to play on the average. The reason for that was no surprise to the fan or television viewer: Changing pitchers is the most time-consuming maneuver in baseball.

"I hope it works," Commissioner Kuhn said after casting the vote that broke the stalemate between the two leagues. "I would have preferred that both leagues did it. But if it's successful in one, then I hope the National follows suit."

"We are happy that the American League got the experimental ruling," said Charles S. Feeney, president of the National. "We can get a real test on it. If it does work out, we wouldn't be hesitant to adopt it."

"I don't think it will necessarily cause more scoring," observed Chuck Tanner, manager of the Chicago White Sox. "In fact, it may cut down scoring on one side if the other team leaves a pitcher like Nolan Ryan in the game."

Tanner, though, foreshadowed the strategic stampede that is bound to follow. He said that he would immediately "put in a call to Orlando Cepeda"—the 35-year-old first baseman recently dropped by the Oakland A's. Cepeda, after knee surgery, can no longer run, but he can still hit his home runs.

Another result was expected to be a cut in the number of pitchers carried on the 25-man squads. Most teams now carry 10 or 11 pitchers; they probably can get by with seven or eight now that the manager can use a pinch-hitter without losing his pitcher.

The National League's opposition to the change was bluntly expressed by Feeney: "We like the game the way it is."

But the American League, under heavy financial pressure, kept campaigning for innovations. Only three teams in the American League passed the million mark in attendance last season; only three teams in the National did not. The American League plays mostly in old stadiums, the National mostly in new ones with artificial turf.

At the baseball business meetings in Honolulu last month, the American League voted unanimously for the pinch-hit change. The National voted against it. The American League then forced a new vote yesterday, and it will be certified in the next week by the Playing Rules Committee of both leagues.

While the owners were mulling the impact of the change, they showed some signs of relief over a report by their labor-relations committee. The chief negotiator, John J. Gaherin, would not comment on the talks, but he said: "I like what happened here today."

He presumably was alluding to the players' offer to study the reserve clause for a year without forcing a decision now.

January 12, 1973

Irvin Named to Hall of Fame In Special Vote for Blacks

Ex-Giants' Star Bemoans Late Call to Majors

By JOSEPH DURSO

Monte Irvin was elected to baseball's Hall of Fame yesterday with the reflection that "I wasted my best years in the Negro leagues" before the sport was integrated.

The former star of the New York Giants was the only person chosen by the Special Committee on the Negro Leagues. He also became the fourth player selected since the committee was created in 1971 to open the 35-year-old museum to the one-time heroes of black baseball.

The others were Satchel Paige, Josh Gibson and Buck Leonard, and Irvin will be enshrined alongside them and 134 other players at Cooperstown, N.Y., on Aug. 6. Another plaque will be unveiled to honor Warren Spahn of the Boston-Milwaukee Braves, who was named in the regular election last month.

And another will probably honor Roberto Clemente of the Pittsburgh Pirates, who was killed in a plane crash New Year's Eve and who is now being considered in a special poll.

Robinson Paved Way

Irvin, now an assistant to Baseball Commissioner Bowie Kuhn, was one of the many black athletes barred from the major leagues until Jackie Robinson joined the Brooklyn Dodgers in 1947.

Two years later, Irvin joined the Giants from the Newark Eagles of the Negro National League and he played both the outfield and infield in the majors for the next seven seasons.

"I'm philosophical about it," he said yesterday at a ceremony in the Americana Hotel. "There's no point in being bitter. You're not happy with the way things happen, but why make yourself sick inside? There were many guys who could really play who never got a chance at all."

When he finally made it Irvin was 30 years old, he had spent a decade riding the rickety buses across the Negro leagues and he had served three years in the Army Engineers.

"I was way past my peak then," he said. "My only regret is that I didn't get a shot at 19, when I was a real ballplayer.

A Spark of Hope

"After the war, things started to change. There were black factory workers and secretaries and the social structure started changing, and then I thought there was a chance.

We guys in the Negro leagues kept asking ourselves why we were being denied a chance when we could run, throw and hit as well as anybody.

"When Jackie Robinson finally broke the color line, it gave those of us under 30 the hope that we might go up soon. Even the old veterans hoped for a year or two in the big time."

For Irvin, born to a sharecropper's family in Alabama in 1919, the "chance" covered seven seasons. He already had established himself as a remarkable athlete at Orange High School in New Jersey, where he won 16 letters and all-state ranking in football, baseball, basketball and track.

But he was too poor to accept a football scholarship to the University of Michigan and, after studying history at Lincoln University in Pennsylvania, he joined the Newark Eagles in 1939.

He batted as high as .422, hit as many as 41 home runs in a season, played in the Cuban League and Mexican League. moved to the Jersey City Giants of the International League and finally made New York.

His best season was 1951, when he hit .312 with 121 runs batted in while the Giants raced through September to their dramatic playoff pennant victory over the Dodgers.

"He could do everything," Roy Campanella recalled yes-

Associated Press
Monte Irvin as a player with Giants in 1950.

terday in the New York University Medical Center, where he was undergoing treatment for his long series of ailments. "Willie Mays was there, too, but Preacher Roe would say in those days that he'd take his chances with Willie — it was Irvin he couldn't get out with men on base."

Sid Gordon and Willard Marshall of the old Giants attended the ceremony yesterday with Larry Doby, the first black player in the American League. To make it, Irvin needed six of the eight votes on the committee and he got six.

Three votes were cast for Judy Johnson and Jim (Cool Papa) Bell; two for Martin DiHigo and one each for Ray Dandridge and Willie Foster.

February 8, 1973

Clemente Is in Hall of Fame

By JOSEPH DURSO

Special to The New York Times

ST. PETERSBURG, Fla., March 20—Eleven weeks after he was killed on a mercy mission, Roberto Clemente was voted into baseball's Hall of Fame today in an extraordinary special election.

The longtime outfielder for the Pittsburgh Pirates and folk hero in Puerto Rico thereby became the first Latin-American player picked for the museum at Cooperstown, N. Y. He also became the first player in baseball history to be elected in a special mail poll without the normal five-year wait, though Lou Gehrig of the New York Yankees was chosen by accla-

mation in 1939 when fatally ill.

Clemente made it by receiving 93 per cent of the 424 ballots cast by 10-year members of the Baseball Writers Association of America. They were asked to decide on his immediate election with these results: 393 voted yes, two abstained and 29 voted no — most of them explaining that they simply opposed waiving the five-year rule.

The results were announced at a brief and solemn ceremony here in the heart of baseball's spring training area on the West Coast of Florida. It was one year after Clemente had opened his 18th season in the major leagues and 79 days

after he was lost in a plane crash into the sea off San Juan while taking relief supplies from Puerto Rico to victims of Nicaragua's earthquake.

Acknowledging the vote were the baseball commissioner, Bowie Kuhn; officials of the Pirates, led by General Manager Joe L. Brown, and Vera Clemente, whom Roberto married in 1964 after a chance meeting in her father's drugstore.

Mrs. Clemente, fighting back tears, said only, "Thank you for everything." But later, in an interview, she noted that it was the first time since the accident on New Year's Eve that she had left her three sons: Roberto, who is 8 years

United Press International
Roberto Clemente

309

old; Luis, 7, and Enrique, 4.

"They are not old enough yet to understand any of this," she said in a sad whisper. "I don't know exactly how much they understand—the oldest, maybe. I explained to the boys where I was going, not the details, just that I would be gone two days. The oldest said, 'I want to go with you,' but I said, 'No, you must go to school.'

"My youngest, Ricky, still picks up the telephone every day and dials numbers as though he was talking to his father. Now I have promised to take the boys to Pittsburgh for the opening game of the season next month, even though it will be so hard for me and the children."

Beyond her family, Vera Clemente added, there are still daily reminders in San Juan of her husband's stature as a national hero.

"I do not go back to the beach any more," she said. "Once I went back and there were 50 boats of people throwing flowers into the water. For two months every day I would receive a big package of mail from all over the world. I started to answer the letters myself but can't do it. I still get 10 or 12 a day.

"I knew from traveling with him that everybody loved him, but when I received all that mail, I knew how far it went. Some people even sent poems, beautiful things about him. People I don't know still come and stand in front of our house. The Puerto Rican people are proud of Roberto.

"He didn't like to talk baseball with me. But he told me that when he finally quit baseball, he wanted to stay home

with the people. He was tired of traveling but said he would play a few more years."

Mrs. Clemente said she would stop tomorrow in Bradentown, about 30 miles south of here, to visit the wives of other Pirate players in the Pittsburgh camp. Then, home to her sons and to the memorials building up for her husband — including the fund for the Youth City complex he supported, which now has passed $500,000 in gifts, half from baseball fans.

Another memorial was dedicated to Clemente today: the trophy given by the commissioner each year to a ballplayer of high reputation was named the Roberto Clemente Award. It was given tonight at the annual Governor's Dinner to Al Kaline, 38-year-old outfielder for the Detroit Tigers. Johnny Bench of the Cincinnati Reds was second in the voting.

Clemente's plaque at Cooperstown will be unveiled Aug. 6 when five other baseball figures enter the Hall of Fame in the annual induction. They are Warren Spahn, the pitcher; Monte Irvin, who was elected by the special committee on the old Negro leagues, and Billy Evans, George Kelly and Mickey Welch, voted in by the Veterans Committee.

During 18 seasons with Pittsburgh, Clemente became one of the great defensive stars of the game and batted .317 with 240 home runs and 3,000 hits. The last hit, a double off Jon Matlack of the Mets on Sept. 30, made him the 11th player in history to reach 3,000. He was 38 years old when he said good-by to his wife at the airport on New Year's Eve and took off with a plane-load of relief supplies for Nicaragua.

March 21, 1973

Ryan Hurls His 2d No-Hitter of Year

DETROIT, July 15 (AP) — Nolan Ryan of the California Angels hurled a no-hitter and struck out 17 in beating the Detroit Tigers, 6-0, today, becoming the fourth pitcher in baseball history to hurl two no-hitters in one season.

Rudy Meoli saved the no-hitter when the Angel shortstop made a leaping catch of Gates Brown's liner with one out in the ninth. The ball was the hardest hit by the Tigers all game. For the 12th time this season and 43d time in Ryan's career he fanned at least 10 in a game. The 26-year-old right-hander allowed four baserunners, all on walks.

Ryan, a 6-foot-2-inch, 195-pound native of Alvin, Tex., pitched his first no-hitter against the Kansas City Royals on May 15, exactly two months ago, walking three and fanning 12.

The only other pitchers to throw two no-hitters in the same year were Johnny Vander Meer of the Cincinnati Reds in 1938, Allie Reynolds of the New York Yankees in 1951 and Detroit's Virgil Trucks in 1952. Vander Meer is the only man to pitch consecutive no-hitters.

Jim Maloney of the Reds nearly gained the select group in 1965. He pitched 10 hit-

less innings against the Mets, only to lose on two hits in the 11th. He then won a 10-inning no-hitter later that season.

The Detroit baserunners who walked were Brown with two out in the first inning, Mickey Stanley leading off the fourth, Dick Sharon with one out in the fifth and Brown again with two out in the sixth. None got past first base. Ryan retired the last 10 Detroit batters.

Only 10 Tigers hit the ball against Ryan as he evened his won-lost record at 11-11 and increased his strike-out total to 220 in 189 innings. Other than Brown's ninth-inning line drive to short, only Jim Northrup's fly ball to the center fielder, Ken Berry, leading off the sixth, was hit hard, but it was still a routine catch.

The Angels got the first run against Jim Perry in the third on one-out singles by Art Kusnyer and Sandy Alomar and Vada Pinson's sacrifice fly. They added five in the eighth against Perry and three relievers on a two-run pinch single by Winston Llenas, a run-scoring single by Bob Oliver and a two-run single by Alan Gallagher.

The crowd of 41,411 was rather complacent, despite

Nolan Ryan working against Tigers yesterday in Detroit

Ryan's brilliant pitching, until the ninth, when they cheered him on.

The hard-throwing hurler, who was traded to the Angels by the Mets on Dec. 10, 1971, faced Stanley, Brown and Norm Cash, the second, third and fourth-place hitters in the Detroit line-up, in the ninth inning.

Stanley grounded to short on a one-strike pitch, Brown lined to short and Cash popped to Meoli.

Ryan tied his career high of 17 strikeouts with one out in the eighth when he fanned Eddie Brinkman. But he fell one short of the American League nine-inning record of 18 set by Cleveland's Bob Feller in 1938.

The modern major-league record of 19 is shared by Steve Carlton, then a St. Louis Cardinal who set it in 1969, and Tom Seaver of the Mets, who matched it in 1970.

Ryan struck out the side in the second, fourth and seventh innings. He fanned Duke Sims and Dick Mc-Auliffe three times apiece. At one point, he fanned five in a row—Cash to end the first; Sims, McAuliffe and Sharon in the second, and Aurelio Rodriguez to open the third.

In addition to Ryan's two no-hitters Kansas City's Steve Busby held the Tigers hitless on April 27 for the only other major league no-hitter this season.

Ryan led the major leagues last season with 329 strike-outs, fourth best total in history. His other 17-strike-out game came against Minnesota last Sept. 30 and tied the A.L. mark for strike-outs in a nine-inning night game.

```
CALIFORNIA (A.)          DETROIT (A.)
        ab.r.h.bi                ab.r.h.bi
Alomar, 2b  5 0 2 0   Northrup, lf  4 0 0 0
Pinson, rf  4 0 0 1   Stanley, cf   3 0 0 0
McCraw, cf  2 0 0 0   G. Brown, dh  2 0 0 0
Llenas, ph  1 0 1 2   Cash, 1b      4 0 0 0
Stanton, lf 0 0 0 0   Sims, c       3 0 0 0
Epstein, 1b 3 1 1 0   McAuliffe, 2b 3 0 0 0
Oglivie, cf 3 1 1 1   Sharon, rf    2 0 0 0
Berry, c    3 0 0 0   Rodriquez, 3b 3 0 0 0
Gallagher,3b 4 0 1 2  Brinkman, ss  3 0 0 0
Meoli, ss   4 1 1 0   Perry, p      0 0 0 0
Kusnyer, c  3 2 1 0   Scherman, p   0 0 0 0
Ryan, p     0 0 0 0   Miller, p     0 0 0 0
                      Farmer, p     0 0 0 0
Total      32 6 9 6   Total        32 0 0 0
California   0 0 1 0 0 0  0 5 0—6
Detroit      0 0 0 0 0 0  0 0 0—0
DP—Detroit 2. LOB—California 5, Detroit
4. 2B—Epstein. SF—Pinson.
            IP. H. R. ER.BB.SO.
Ryan (W, 11-11)... 9   0  0  0  4  17
Perry (L, 9-9) .... 7⅓  5  3  3  3  2
Scherman ......... ⅓  0  0  0  0  0
Miller ........... 0  3  3  1  0  0
Farmer ........... 1⅓  2  0  0  1  0
  T—2:21. A—41,411.
```

July 16, 1973

ANAHEIM, Calif., Sept. 28 (UPI) — Nolan Ryan of the California Angels broke Sandy Koufax's season strike-out record of 382 tonight by fanning Rich Reese of the Minnesota Twins in the 11th inning.

The Angels won the game for Ryan, 5-4, in the 11th. Ryan wound up with 16 strike-outs, 383 for the year and his 21st victory.

Ryan went into game needing 15 strike-outs to equal the record set by Koufax for the Los Angeles Dodgers in 1965. He tied the mark by getting Steve Brye in the eighth.

The 26-year-old right-hander from Alvin, Tex., also broke Koufax's two-season strike-out mark of 699 set in 1965-66 when he fanned Rod Carew in the second inning.

September 28, 1973

Mets Win East Title

By JOSEPH DURSO
Special to The New York Times

CHICAGO, Oct. 1 — The New York Mets completed their rousing dash from last place and finally won the most complicated race in baseball history today when they defeated the Chicago Cubs, 6-4, to capture the Eastern Division title in the National League.

They thereby eliminated the St. Louis Cardinals and Pittsburgh Pirates from the free-for-all one day after it was supposed to have ended and one day after the Montreal Expos and Cubs also had been eliminated.

The victory was the 23d in the last 32 games for the Mets, who spent two months in last place during waves of injuries this summer and were still last on Aug. 30.

But then they charged past the five other teams in the division, reached the top 10 days ago and clinched the title in a drizzle this afternoon before only 1,913 fans in Wrigley Field.

2d Game Called Off

The four umpires supervising the series, which had been twice delayed by rain, showed a neat regard for history by calling off the second game of today's double-header. The official reason was wet grounds. The practical reason was that the game had become moot and the net result was that the Mets were able to celebrate their dramatic comeback with full-flowing spirits.

Tug McGraw, who stopped the Cubs cold over the final three innings after Tom Seaver had been knocked out of the box, led the cheers in a victory scene reminiscent of the Met "miracle" of 1969.

Only 11 players whooping it up in the vibrating little clubhouse were with the team four years ago, when it unexpectedly won the division title, the league pennant and the World Series.

The Mets still had a formidable course to follow before history could repeat, however. They will open the three-of-five-game playoff for the pennant Saturday in Cincinnati against the Reds, the best in the West. The winner will enter the World Series on Saturday, Oct. 13, against the Baltimore Orioles or the Oakland A's of the American League.

For a few hours this afternoon, the dangers of the future were drowned out by the noise of the present. While McGraw stood on an equipment trunk chanting, "You got to believe!" Manager Yogi Berra stood besieged in his tiny office, reflecting on a season that had almost cost him his job as successor to the late Gil Hodges.

"It's been a long year," Yogi said. "I was on 14 Yankee teams that won, but this has to be a big thrill because we had to jump over five clubs to do it. We were 12 games back and hurt.

"I told the guys here Friday, I'm proud of you whether you win or lose the next four. Just give me 100 per cent for the next few days."

The Mets responded by losing the first game of a double-header yesterday, 1-0. But they won the second, 9-2, assuring a tie for the top, although Pittsburgh and St. Louis still had mathematical shots.

Today, in a game that began at 11:20 A.M., after a short rain delay, they rushed to a 5-0 lead in 4½ innings.

The hitting heroes were Cleon Jones, who drove a home run into the bleachers in right-center field in the second, and Jerry Grote,

who singled home two runs in the fourth.

Seaver, meanwhile, was struggling along, and for the third time in his last four starts, was unable to go the distance. He has been in a late-season slump, caused partly by a tender right shoulder.

Jones supplied his early margin, though, by hitting the 1-and-0 pitch from Burt Hooton above the ivy-covered brick wall. It was his 11th home run of the season, but his sixth in the final 10 games after he had suffered assorted injuries.

Two innings later the Mets loaded the bases with nobody out when Rusty Staub singled and John Milner and Jones walked. Then Grote lined his single to center and suddenly they led by three.

They wasted the chance for more runs then, but atoned in the next inning with two more. Wayne Garrett led that charge with a double down the right-field line, Felix Millan singled and, with Mike Paul now pitching, Staub singled to right to make it 4-0. And when Milner followed with a sacrifice fly to center, it became 5-0.

In the bottom of the inning the Cubs rattled Seaver with two runs, starting with a leadoff single by Ken Rudolph. Then, after a fly to center, they bunched singles by Rick Monday, Don Kessinger and Billy Williams.

Now the score was 5-2 and, with three innings to go in a bizarre season, the Mets managed a final run in the seventh off Jack Aker. It came on a single by Staub, his third in a row; a one-out walk to Jones and a two-out grounder that was booted by Ron Santo.

Cubs Narrow Gap

In the home half of the inning the Cubs narrowed the gap to 6-4 on a single by Dave Rosello and a home run by Monday, who had struck out five times yesterday. It was the 11th hit off Seaver

Mets' Box Score

METS (N.)	ab.r.h.bi	CHICAGO (N.)	ab.r.h.bi
Garrett, 3b	4 1 2 0	Monday, cf	4 2 3 2
Millan, 2b	5 1 2 0	Beckert, ph	1 0 0 0
Staub, rf	5 2 4 1	Kessinger, ss	4 0 1 1
Milner, 1b	3 1 0 1	Williams, lf	4 0 1 1
Jones, lf	3 1 1 1	Santo, 3b	4 0 0 0
Grote, c	4 0 2 2	Cardenal, rf	4 0 1 0
Hahn, cf	5 0 0 0	Marquez, 1b	3 0 2 0
Harrelson, ss	3 0 1 0	Fanzone, 1b	1 0 0 0
Seaver, p	3 0 1 0	Popovich, 2b	2 0 0 0
McGraw, p	0 0 0 0	Paul, p	0 0 0 0
		LaCock, ph	1 0 0 0
		Aker, p	0 0 0 0
		Hickman, ph	1 0 0 0
		Locker, p	0 0 0 0
		Rudolph, c	4 1 3 2
		Hooton, p	1 0 0 0
		Rosello, 2b	3 1 1 0
Total	37 6 13 5	Total	37 4 12 4

Mets . . . . 010 220 100—6
Chicago . . . . 000 020 200—4

E—Santo. DP—Mets 2, Chicago 2. LOB—
Mets 11, Chicago 6. 2B—Garrett, Harrelson.
HRs—Jones (11), Monday (26). S—Garrett.
SF—Milner.

	IP.	H.	R.	ER.	BB.	SO.
Seaver (W, 19-10)	6	11	4	4	0	2
McGraw	3	1	0	0	0	0
Hooton (L, 14-17)	4	7	5	5	2	1
Paul	2	3	0	0	1	0
Aker	2	3	1	0	1	0
Locker	1	0	0	0	3	1

Save—McGraw (25). HBP—by Aker (Mc-
Graw). T—2:28. A—1,913.

and Berra promptly called for McGraw to hold off the Cubs.

McGraw responded by getting the final nine outs with only one ball hit out of the infield—a ground single by Rudolph in the ninth. The left-hander, pitching for the 60th time this year, struck out Rosello after Rudolph's hit, and when Glenn Beckert pinch-hit a looping fly behind first, Milner grabbed it and stepped on the bag to double off Rudolph and close out the Perils of Pauline.

For McGraw, the season's turnaround had been no less stunning than for the whole club. He didn't win a game until August, then won four and saved 12 during 17 appearances while the Mets rose implausibly through the ranks.

As they headed back to New York tonight, the Mets stood 1½ games ahead of St. Louis, 2½ in front of Pittsburgh, 3½ over Montreal and five over Chicago. They finished with the lowest winning percentage of any first-place team ever: 82 victories, 79 defeats for .509.

Since their melodramatic sweep in 1969, they had finished third three years in a row and had won 83 games in each of those years. This time, with one less victory, they took the big prize.

For the players, the aches and pains will be soothed by cash. For winning the division title each man is guaranteed $5,000. If they eventually win the World Series, the booty will total $20,000 apiece.

"I'm the eternal optimist," Seaver said while the locker room jumped and champagne flowed, "but this summer strained even my eternal optimism."

October 2, 1973

METS WIN, 9 TO 2, AS FIGHT ERUPTS; LEAD PLAYOFF, 2-1

Fans Hurl Debris, Forcing Reds to Evacuate Field —Staub Hits 2 Homers

By JOSEPH DURSO

Fists, cups, beer cans, assorted debris and even whisky bottles filled the clamorous afternoon air at Shea Stadium yesterday as the Mets and their public fought the Cincinnati Reds in one of baseball's memorably riotous games.

The game was won by the Mets, 9-2, which brought them within one victory of completing a five-week march from last place to the National League pennant. But they had to fight their way to that milestone before 53,967 roaring, cheering

and booing fans in a series of skirmishes and two fistfights.

Pete Rose of the Reds and Bud Harrelson of the Mets fought the main event after Rose had barreled into second base trying to break up a double play in the fifth inning. Pedro Borbon of the Reds and Buzz Capra threw punches while 50 players rolled and milled around.

Warned of Forfeit

The fans pelted Rose with flying objects, the Reds evacuated the field and New York was warned that it would forfeit the game unless order was restored.

Then, while Mayor Lindsay and the rest of the crowd watched in amazement, Yogi Berra led a peace delegation across the outfield lawn to quiet the fans—Tom Seaver, Cleon Jones, Rusty Staub and 42-year-old Willie Mays.

They stood in the no man's land in left field, where Rose had just ducked a whisky bottle and where the Cincinnati outfielder had pegged junk back at the box-seat customers.

With his arms outstretched, Mays made his first appearance since announcing his retirement two weeks ago, and appealed with feeling for calm. Then the mission marched back to the dugout 100 yards away, nine attendants cleared the debris and the game continued.

He Rips a Cap

Before it was over, though, the president of the National League left his box to intervene; the umpires suggested Rose be switched to center field; Borbon found that he somehow was wearing a Met cap, bit it and ripped it in half, and the crowd stood and roared for the embattled home team.

"I'll be honest, I was trying to knock him into left field," the 200-pound Rose said later. "I play to win. In 1970, all I did was try to score a run in the All-Star game by running through the catcher, and I've been criticized for three years."

The 146-pound Harrelson said:

"They've been coming in hard all year. I thought he came in hard and I didn't like it. I said something, he turned and asked, 'What?' and it sud-

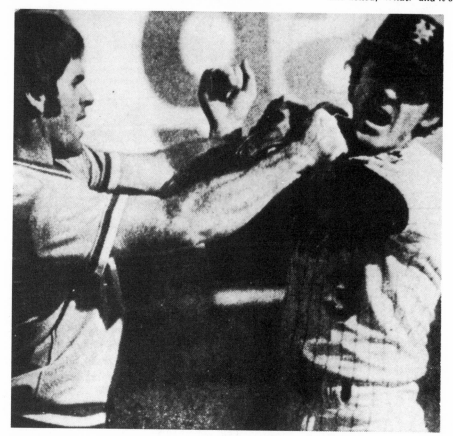

Pete Rose of the Reds, left, and Bud Harrelson of the Mets in a fracas at second base following a double play in the top of the fifth inning at Shea Stadium.

Associated Press

denly became a shoving match."

Said Sparky Anderson, manager of the Reds: "It's awful dangerous to throw a whisky bottle at a player. I can't believe that in America today a man would do that. Pete came in and told me, 'Spark, they just threw a whisky bottle out,' and I said, 'That's enough for today.' Then an umpire said we better get this straightened out, and I replied, 'Let me know when you do.'"

Charles (Chub) Feeney, president of the league, said: "I went into the dugout and asked Yogi and Willie Mays to come out and talk to the fans. They'll recognize Willie, but if I went out there, they'd probably throw things at me."

For Berra, whose team stood last in the Eastern Division on Aug. 30, the immediate issue was urgent: quiet the crowd or forfeit a 9-2 lead in the fifth inning.

To Johnny Bench, the Cincinnati catcher, the issue was urgent, too — the Reds were dropping their second game in a row to the underdog Mets and were in danger of dropping the playoff for the pennant in one more afternoon.

"Here we are," he said in the stunned locker room. "It was a small battle, but we're losing the war."

They began losing the war Sunday in Cincinnati, when the Mets bounced back from a 2-1 defeat in the opening game Saturday and scored a 5-0 victory to square the series.

Then, in the first inning yesterday, Staub drove Ross Grimsley's 2-and-2 pitch over the right-field fence with two down and the war started slipping away from the Reds again.

This was the Mets' first appearance in postseason play at Shea Stadium since Oct. 16, 1969, when they dramatically won the World Series from the Baltimore Orioles. Since then, they had spent three seasons in third place and most of this summer in last place.

Their pitcher yesterday was Jerry Koosman, who also pitched that October game four years ago. This time the left-hander from the Minnesota farm country got plenty of early support before the fighting broke out.

The Mets batted around in the second inning on four hits and two walks, and cashed five more runs.

They opened with a walk to Jerry Grote and a single to right by Don Hahn, one of the hottest October bats. Harrelson flied out, but Koosman curled a bunt toward the mound and, when Grimsley slipped and fell on the grass, everybody was safe with the bases loaded.

Wayne Garrett followed with a fly to center for one run and Felix Millan singled to right for another. Then Anderson rescued Grimsley and called for his slender left-handed relief pitcher Tom Hall, who had faced seven batters in two days and got only one out.

Hall threw one strike to Staub before lightning struck again. Staub, who played with two damaged hands this season, pulled a high home run off the facing of the loge seats down the right-field line, his second in two innings and third in two days, and three more runs crossed.

Half an inning later, the Reds finally got stirring when

Mets' Box Score

CINCINNATI (N.)	ab	r	h	bi
Rose, lf	4	0	2	0
Morgan, 2b	4	0	1	1
Perez, 1b	4	0	0	0
Bench, c	4	0	1	0
Kosco, rf	4	0	0	0
Armbr'ster, cf	4	0	1	0
Menke, 3b	4	1	1	1
Chaney, ss	3	0	0	0
Gagliano, ph	1	0	0	0
Grimsley, p	0	0	0	0
Hall, p	0	0	0	0
Stahl, ph	1	1	1	0
Tomlin, p	0	0	0	0
Nelson, p	1	0	0	0
King, ph	1	0	1	0
Borbon, p	0	0	0	0
Total	35	2	8	2

METS (N.)	ab	r	h	bi
Garrett, 3b	4	0	0	1
Millan, 2b	3	2	1	1
Staub, rf	5	2	2	4
Jones, lf	3	1	2	0
Milner, 1b	4	0	1	1
Grote, c	3	2	1	0
Hahn, cf	4	1	2	0
Harrelson, ss	4	0	0	0
Koosman, p	4	1	2	1
Total	34	9	11	8

Cincinnati	002	000	000	—2
Mets	151	200	00x	—9

E—Kosco, Garrett. DP—Mets 1. LOB—Cincinnati 6, Mets 6. 2B—Jones, Bench. HRs—Staub 2, (3), Menke (1). SF—Garrett.

	IP.	H.	R.	ER.	BB.	SO.
Grimsley (L, 0-1)	1⅔	5	5	5	1	2
Hall	⅓	1	1	1	1	1
Tomlin	1⅔	5	3	3	1	1
Nelson	2⅓	0	0	0	1	0
Borbon	2	0	0	0	0	2
Koosman (W, 1-0)	9	8	2	2	0	9

T—2:46. A—53,967

Denis Menke hit a home run into the left-field bull pen. Then Larry Stahl pinch-hit a single, Rose added a single to left and Joe Morgan singled to right, making it 6-2.

But the Mets were high as kites for this one, and they retaliated with another run in the bottom of the third and two more in the fourth.

They made it 7-2 in the third on singles by Grote and Koosman, then completed the job in the fourth on a walk, a double by Jones, an outfield error and singles by John Milner and Hahn.

Then the teams were in the fifth and, with one down, the irrepressible Rose singled through the middle for his second hit. Morgan, who had been hitless the first two games, bounced one wide of first, where Milner fielded the ball and started a photo-finish double play by way of Harrelson at second.

That was when Rose slid into the bag, coming up hands-high as Harrelson fired back to Milner for the second out.

By the time order had finally been restored, most of the fight seemed to have been drained out of the teams. The Reds made only two hits off Koosman over the last four innings and the Mets made none off the fourth and fifth Cincinnati pitchers.

Nobody was thrown out of the game by the officials, and the crowd kept a noisy sort of order the rest of the afternoon. The police, though, packed the left-field foul line and left-field grandstand porch to prevent new outbreaks. And when the Reds left the stadium by chartered bus, they had a police escort for their trip back to Manhattan while several hundred fans booed and shouted.

The melee on the field was wilder than last year's in Oakland, when Bert Campaneris of the A's threw a bat at Lerrin Lagrow of Detroit in the American League playoff. And it resembled, in some tempestuous ways, the garbage-throwing blast aimed at Joe Medwick of the St. Louis Cardinals in the 1934 World Series.

The playoff continues at 2 o'clock this afternoon, with Fred Norman pitching for Cincinnati and George Stone for New York. Both sides said they would try to behave better in their fight for the pennant.

October 9, 1973

Jackson Unanimously Most Valuable

By MICHAEL STRAUSS

Reggie Jackson of the Oakland A's was voted unanimously yesterday the American League's most valuable player of 1973 by the Baseball Writers Association of America.

"I'm not necessarily surprised at the award," the slugger said modestly in Oakland, "but I'm astonished I was named first on all of the ballots. I didn't think anyone could be that valuable."

In receiving 24 first-place votes (two writers from each of the 12 league cities voted), Jackson became only the sixth player in the 52 years of the award to make the sweep. The others were Hank Greenberg (1935), Al Rosen (1953), Mickey Mantle (1956), Frank Robinson (1966) and Dennis McLain (1968).

Jackson, who batted .293 during the regular season and led the league in home runs and runs batted in with 32 and 117, respectively, emerged with a one-sided total of 336 points. The closest to him was Jim Palmer, who last week was picked as the Cy Young Award winner. The Baltimore pitcher received 172 points.

Third in the voting, in which 35 players were named, was Amos Otis. The Kansas City outfielder had 112 points. Then came Rod Carew, Minnesota second baseman (83); John Hiller, Detroit reliever, and Sal Bando, Oakland third baseman, each with 83.

Outvoted by a huge margin, but not forgotten, was Dick Allen, the Chicago White Sox slugger, last year's winner. This time he barely got into the picture, receiving only one 10th-place vote. He missed more than half the season because of a broken leg.

"It's a culmination of things that makes this my most exciting moment," said Jackson, who plays the outfield. "It's icing on the cake—to be on the team that wins the world championship two years in a row, to be named the most valuable player in the World Series and then to have this happen.

"After all, I have not hit .300 yet. I have not hit more than 50 home runs a season and I have not stolen 40 bases. There are lots of things I can do in the game that I haven't done. Until I do them, I will be shortchanging myself, the fans, the owners, the team and everyone else. I would like to be the best."

Jackson missed the 1972

World Series after injuring his leg stealing home with the decisive run in the final playoff game. Just before this year's playoffs, he received a death threat, which caused him to acquire a bodyguard. Nevertheless, he played.

The 27-year-old, left-handed hitter showed no hesitancy in disclosing his feelings about his worth to the A's. He said that he and Jim (Catfish) Hunter, the ace, pitcher, should become Oakland's first players to make $100,000.

He hinted he would like a one-year contract in the area of $150,000, which was believed to be double the figure

he and Hunter commanded during the recent season.

"Reaching the $100,000 plateau is like the sun coming up," he said. "Eventually, I'm going to make that salary, and I figure on going on right past that."

Jackson took time out to praise Manager Dick Williams. He was reminded that he had complained to Williams in midseason about the club's coaching staff.

"He never got his feathers ruffled," said Jackson. "I don't know if that incident was responsible for my good year. But I did say to one of our players, subsequently, that I would have to play ball hard from now on."

November 14, 1973

Ron Santo

Santo First to Veto Trade by His Club

By JOSEPH DURSO
Special to The New York Times

HOUSTON, Dec. 4—Baseball's winter trading market started to boom today when the Pittsburgh Pirates sent Nelson Briles to the Kansas City Royals and the Cincinnati Reds got Merv Rettenmund from the Baltimore Orioles for Ross Grimsley.

But the big news of the sport's business convention was made by a star player who refused to be traded: Ron Santo of the Chicago Cubs. He became the first major leaguer to invoke the new rule that allows a 10-year man to veto any deal, and he did it as the Cubs appeared on the verge of exchanging him for frontline pitching.

Santo, 34 years old, has been Chicago's third baseman for 14 seasons and has grown into a $110,000-a-year slugger with high value in the talent market. He hit 20 homers last season and was being hotly pursued by three or four clubs when he exercised his veto by telephone from his home in Chicago.

Santo conceded that he had been receiving vibrations that he was on the trading block, and he wasted no time refusing all offers. He acted under the "bill of rights" that the players won from the owners a year ago, specifically under a section that allows a man a choice if he has been in the

majors 10 years, five with the same team.

"I got a call from John Holland today," Santo said in a telephone interview, referring to the Cubs' general manager. 'He didn't mention any clubs, but he did say that several were interested. I replied that I elected not to leave Chicago, for personal reasons."

It was learned that Holland also took the precaution of calling another senior slugger on the team, Billy Williams, the 36-year-old, **$125,000 a-year left fielder.** He raised the same question: How would Williams react to a trade. And he got almost the same answer: Williams doubted that he would leave, but would think it over.

"He didn't say yes and he didn't say no," Holland acknowledged later.

The veto cast by Santo could be the first of many under the players' new privilege. In the National League, there are 16 men with enough service to qualify as "untouchables," ranging from Henry Aaron to Ed Kranepool. In the American, there are 11. But four veterans have recently acquiesced in trades: Willie McCovey, Jim Kaat, Jim Perry and Dick McAuliffe.

The Cubs' problems with the player veto provided the week's second bizarre situ-

ation. In the first, the New York Yankees were still trying to locate their missing manager — whether he was Ralph Houk, who abdicated to the Detroit Tigers, or Dick Williams, who tried to abdicate from the Oakland A's.

The solution to that tangle rested with the controversial owner of the world champion Oakland team, Charles O. Finley. He arrived here tonight and was scheduled to air his case tomorrow in a meeting with the Yankees and the president of the American League, Joe Cronin. But for now the Yankees were still in the unusual position of trying to acquire a shortstop or second baseman who would play for a manager-to-be-named-later.

To add insult to injury, the Yankees also lost one of their coaches, Jim Hegan, who agreed today to join Houk in Detroit. Hegan, the father of the Yankee first baseman, Mike Hegan, had been a Yankee coach for 13 years.

The overt action of the day, meanwhile, shifted to managers who were not legally embroiled and to players who were not exercising the veto.

The Mets lost one chance to land a center fielder when Baltimore traded Rettenmund to Cincinnati. The deal meant that the Orioles now would keep Paul Blair, whom the Mets had been pursuing for their glaring vacancy in center.

"Yes, it forecloses a deal for Blair," said Frank Cashen, general manager of the Orioles. "We need him in our outfield now with Rich Coggins, Don Baylor and our other guys. Bob Scheffing's an honest man, painfully honest, and he said he just couldn't afford to give up Tom Seaver, Jon Matlack or Jerry Koosman. So we had to look someplace else for pitching."

The someplace else was Cincinnati, and the somebody else was Grimsley, the 23-year-old left-hander who has won 37 games in his three seasons with the Reds. He now will join Baltimore's pitching staff while Rettenmund joins the Reds as either the center-field replacement for Bob Tolan, recently traded to San Diego, or the regular right fielder.

Rettenmund is a 30-year-old right-hander hitter who batted .262 with nine home runs last summer, mainly against left-handed pitching. He once was voted "minor league player of the year" and twice led Baltimore in hitting, but he has slipped from his peak level the last two years. He will be accompanied to Cincinnati by two minor league players: Junior Kennedy, a shortstop, and Bill Wood, a catcher.

The Pirates, who have been the Mets' chief rival in the National League's East for the last four seasons, kept realigning their club in the trade with Kansas City, their third since the World Series.

Briles, an aspiring entertainer who sang the National Anthem at the Series in Shea Stadium in October, went to the Royals with Fernando Gonzalez, a minor league shortstop. In return, Pittsburgh got Ed Kirkpatrick, an outfielder who also catches and plays first base (but doesn't sing); Kurt Bevacqua, an infielder; and Winston Cole, a 19-year-old sprinter who plays first base.

Briles, who is 30, pitched in the World Series with St. Louis in 1964 and 1967 and again with Pittsburgh in 1971. He also led the Pirates' staff this year with 14 victories and a 2.84 earned-run average. But the Pirates recently obtained Jerry Reuss from Houston and felt they could afford to surrender a regular starter.

"The trade would not have been made if Cole hadn't been in it," said Joe Brown, the team's general manager.

"We had to give up a lot," agreed Danny Murtaugh, the manager. "But Cole can become as good at first base as Gil Hodges, and we wanted him."

December 5, 1973

Dave Anderson

An Honor, Not a Thrill, for Cool Papa

Most people assume "cool" is a mod word that didn't exist until recently. But it was part of the black vocabulary at least 50 years ago. That's when Cool Papa Bell got his nickname.

"I was only 19 and they thought I'd be afraid of big crowds," he recalled. "I took it so cool, they began to call me Cool. But that wasn't enough, so they added Papa to it."

That philosopher of the ages, Satchel Paige, liked to say that Cool Papa Bell was "so fast he could turn out the light and jump in bed before the room got dark." Cool Papa could run. He claims he once was timed circling the bases in 12 seconds. And he remembers stealing 175 bases one season. Cool Papa could hit, too.

Sports of The Times

In 27 seasons as a slender 6-foot, 145-pound center fielder, his lowest average was .308; his highest was .411 when he was 43 years old. But his speed is what they still talk about. The only thing he couldn't outrun was the color line that existed in the major leagues when he was in his prime. He traveled with such teams as the St. Louis Stars and the Homestead Grays and the Kansas City Monarchs of the black leagues. But yesterday, in baseball's annual examination of conscience, James (Cool Papa) Bell was announced as a member of the Hall of Fame by its special committee on black baseball. He's 70 years old now, but he hasn't changed. He took it cool.

'I Helped Jackie a Little'

"I'm grateful for it," he was saying, "but I don't get excited. I don't stand up and holler and call all my friends. They'll find out about it."

He was wearing a bow tie, a new charcoal gray suit and his best cool. Even when he found out last week that he had joined Paige, Josh Gibson, Buck Leonard and Monte Irvin at Cooperstown for their accomplishments in the black leagues, he didn't get excited. Joe Reichler of Commissioner Bowie Kuhn's office had phoned him.

"You're in," Reichler said.

"Yeah, that's O.K." Cool Papa replied.

"You don't understand."

"Yes, I do," Cool Papa said. "I knew it was going to come eventually."

"Is this your biggest thrill?"

"No, it's my biggest honor. My biggest thrill was when they opened the door in the majors for the black players."

But that player was Jackie Robinson, not him.

"I helped Jackie a little," Cool Papa was saying now. "Jackie was a good young ballplayer, but he was a shortstop then. We heard he was going up, but we knew he couldn't make it at shortstop. He didn't have enough range. I could hit a ball where I wanted to nine times out of 10, so to give Jackie a message, the first two times up I hit the ball to his right. He got to them but he had to take two steps to throw. By that time I'd beaten them out. He got the message. He played second base in the majors. Jackie Robinson was a good ballplayer, but . . ."

He turned toward Monte Irvin, now an aide in the commissioner's office.

"That's the man we wanted to be first," he said. "He could do everything."

He didn't sound bitter that he never had had an opportunity in the majors.

"Life was that way then," he said "I lived in that time. When we went to major league games, we couldn't always sit in the stands. We had to sit in the bleachers. But even so, I didn't feel any difficulty. It was that way when I was born in Starkeville, Mississippi; it was that way when I worked in the packinghouse in St. Louis before I played baseball. People lived that life before I did."

His Talks With Wills

He's retired now. When baseball ended for him, he was a nightwatchman at the city hall in St. Louis, where he lives.

"I don't go to the Cardinal games much anymore, not since they moved into the new ball park," he said. "The old ball park was near my home. I used to sit out in the pavilion with men I used to work in the packinghouse with. I'd see players sometimes. The year Maury Wills stole 104 bases, their catcher, John Roseboro, phoned me. Some of the Dodgers wanted me to talk to Wills, and I told him: 'You could steal even more bases. Sometimes you've got a base stolen but the hitter fouls the ball off. Junior Gilliam waits on you, but the others don't. Give 'em a signal that you're running.' He told me, 'I hadn't thought of that.' I had to see him after the game. Roseboro told me he left a ticket for me, but at the ticket window they wouldn't give me the pass, they said I wasn't Bell."

Maybe the Cardinals will recognize him now. But his Hall of Fame honor hasn't changed the world around him.

"My wife, Clarabelle, had to stay home," he said. "In our neighborhood, if some guys know you're out of the house, they break in. They did that to us twice."

The New York Times/Don Hogan Charles

James (Cool Papa) Bell with Commissioner Bowie Kuhn

February 14, 1974

Aaron Hits 715th, Passes *Babe Ruth*

By JOSEPH DURSO
Special to The New York Times

ATLANTA, April 8—Henry Aaron ended the great chase tonight and passed Babe Ruth as the leading home-run hitter in baseball history when he hit No. 715 before a national television audience and 53,775 persons in Atlanta Stadium.

The 40-year-old outfielder for the Atlanta Braves broke the record on his second time at bat, but on his first swing of a clamorous evening. It was a soaring drive in the fourth inning off Al Downing of the Los Angeles Dodgers, and it cleared the fence in left-center field, 385 feet from home plate.

Skyrockets arched over the jammed stadium in the rain as the man from Mobile trotted around the bases for the 715th time in a career that began a quarter of a century ago with the Indianapolis Clowns in the old Negro leagues.

It was 9:07 o'clock, 39 years after Ruth had hit his 714th and four days after Aaron had hit his 714th on his first swing of the bat in the opening game of the season.

The history-making home run carried into the Atlanta bull pen, where a relief pitcher named Tom House made a dazzling one-handed catch against the auxiliary scoreboard. He clutched it against the boards, far below the grandstand seats, where the customers in "Home-Run Alley" were massed, waiting to retrieve a cowhide ball that in recent days had been valued as high as $25,000 on the auction market.

So Aaron not only ended the great home-run derby, but also ended the controversy that had surrounded it. His employers had wanted him to hit No. 715 in Atlanta, and had even benched him on alien soil in Cincinnati.

The commissioner of baseball, Bowie Kuhn, ordered the Braves to start their star yesterday or face "serious penalties." And tonight the dispute and the marathon finally came home to Atlanta in a razzle-dazzle setting.

The stadium was packed with its largest crowd since the Braves left Milwaukee and brought major league baseball to the Deep South

United Press International
Aaron during presentation ceremony after record-breaker

nine years ago. Pearl Bailey sang the national anthem; the Jonesboro High School band marched; balloons and fireworks filled the overcast sky before the game; Aaron's life was dramatized on a huge color map of the United States painted across the outfield grass, and Bad Henry was serenaded by the Atlanta Boy Choir, which now includes girls.

The commissioner was missing, pleading that a "previous commitment" required his presence tomorrow in Cleveland, and his emissary was roundly booed when he mentioned Kuhn's name. But Gov. Jimmy Carter was there, along with Mayor Maynard Jackson, Sammy Davis Jr. and broadcasters and writers from as far away as Japan, South America and Britain.

To many Atlantans, it was like the city's festive premiére of "Gone With the Wind" during the 1930's when Babe Ruth was still the hero of the New York Yankees and the titan of professional sports. All that was needed to complete the evening was home run No. 715, and Aaron supplied that.

The first time he batted, leading off the second inning, Aaron never got the bat off his shoulder. Downing, a one-time pitcher for the Yankees, wearing No. 44, threw a ball and a called strike and then three more balls. Aaron, wearing his own No. 44, watched them all and then took first base while the crowd hooted and booed because their home town hero had been walked.

A few moments later, Henry scored on a double by Dusty Baker and an error in left field, and even made a little history doing that.

It was the 2,063d time he had crossed home plate in his 21-year career in the majors, breaking the National League record held by Willie Mays and placing Aaron behind Ty Cobb and Ruth, both American Leaguers.

Then came the fourth inning, with the Dodgers leading by 3-1 and the rain falling, with colored umbrellas raised in the stands and the crowd roaring every time Aaron appeared. Darrell Evans led off for Atlanta with a grounder behind sec-

ond base that the shortstop, Bill Russell, juggled long enough for an error. And up came Henry for the eighth time this season and the second this evening.

Downing pitched ball one inside, and Aaron watched impassively. Then came the second pitch, and this time Henry took his first cut of the night. The ball rose high toward left-center as the crowd came to its feet shouting, and as it dropped over the inside fence separating the outfield from the bull pen area, the skyrockets were fired and the scoreboard lights flashed in six-foot numerals: "715."

Aaron, head slightly bowed and elbows turned out, slowly circled the bases as the uproar grew. At second base he received a handshake from Dave Lopes of the Dodgers, and between second and third from Russell.

By now two young men from the seats had joined Aaron, but did not interfere with his 360-foot trip around the bases into the record books.

As he neared home plate, the rest of the Atlanta team had already massed beyond it as a welcoming delegation. But Aaron's 65-year-old father, Herbert Aaron Sr., had jumped out of the family's special field-level box and outraced everybody to the man who had broken Babe Ruth's record.

By then the entire Atlanta bull pen corps had started to race in to join the fun, with House leading them, the ball gripped tightly in his hand. He delivered it to Aaron,

Braves' Box Score

LOS ANGELES (N.)	ab.	r.	h.	bi.	ATLANTA (N.)	ab.	r.	h.	bi.
Lopes, 2b	2	1	0	0	Garr, rf	3	0	0	1
Lacy, 2b	1	0	0	0	Lum, 1b	5	0	0	1
Buckner, lf	3	0	1	0	Evans.....				
Wynn, cf	4	0	1	2	Evans, 3b	4	1	0	0
Ferguson, c	4	0	0	0	Aaron, lf	3	2	1	2
Crawford, rf	4	1	1	0	Office, cf	0	0	0	0
Cey, 3b	4	0	1	1	Baker, cf	2	1	1	0
Garvey, 1b	4	0	1	0	Johnson, 2b	3	1	1	0
Russell, ss	4	0	1	0	Foster, 2b	0	0	0	0
Downing, p	1	1	1	1	Correll, c	1	0	0	0
Marshall, p	1	0	0	0	Robinson, ss	0	0	0	0
Joshua, ph	1	0	0	0	Tepedino, ph	1	0	0	0
Hough, p	0	0	0	0	Perez, ss	2	1	1	0
Mota, ph	1	0	0	0	Reed, p	2	0	0	0
					Oates, ph	1	0	0	1
Total	34	4	7	4	Capra, p	0	0	0	0
					Total	29	7	4	6

Los Angeles ....003 001 000—4
Atlanta ....010 402 00x—7

E—Buckner, Cey, Russell 2, Lopes, Ferguson. LOB—Los Angeles 5, Atlanta 7. 2B—Baker, Russell, Wynn. HR—Aaron (2). S—Garr. SF—Garr.

	IP.	H.	R.	ER.	BB.	SO.
Downing, (L, 0-1) ...	3	2	5	2	4	2
Marshall	3	2	2	1	1	1
Hough	2	0	0	0	2	1
Reed (W, 1-0)	6	7	4	4	1	4
Capra	3	0	0	0	1	6

Save—Capra (1). Wild pitch—Reed. PB—Ferguson. T—2:27. A—53,775.

Henry Aaron of the Atlanta Braves smashing the 715th home run of his 21-year career

Associated Press

who was besieged on the grass about 20 feet in front of the field boxes near the Braves' dugout.

Besides the ball, Henry received a plaque from the owner of the team, Bill Bartholomay; congratulations from Monte Irvin, the emissary from Commissioner Kuhn, and a howling, standing ovation from the crowd.

The game was interrupted for 11 minutes during all the commotion, after which the Braves got back to work and went on to win their second straight, this time by 7-4. The Dodgers, apparently shaken by history, made six errors and lost their first game after three straight victories.

"It was a fastball, right down the middle of the upper part of the plate," Downing said later. "I was trying to get it down to him, but I didn't and he hit it good—as he would."

"When he first hit it, I didn't think it might be going. But like a great hitter, when he picks his pitch, chances are he's going to hit it pretty good."

Afterward the Braves locked their clubhouse for a time so that they could toast Aaron in champagne. Then the new home-run king reflected on his feat and on some intimations that he had not been "trying" to break the record in Cincinnati.

"I have never gone out on a ball field and given less than my level best," he said. "When I hit it tonight, all I thought about was that I wanted to touch all the bases."

April 9, 1974

Ryan Equals Record By Fanning 19 in Game

ANAHEIM, Calif., Aug. 12 (UPI)—Nolan Ryan, who came within two outs of a no-hitter in his last start, equaled the major league single-game strike-out mark by fanning 19 tonight while pitching the California Angels to a 4-2 triumph over the Boston Red Sox.

Ryan, who increased his major league leading strike-out total to 260, notched his 15th victory while tying the major league record for most strikeouts in a single game established by Steve Carlton of the Philadelphia Phils in 1969 and Tom Seaver of the New York Mets in 1970. He broke Bob Feller's 36-year-old American League of 18 strikeouts.

Ryan also tied the major league record for most strikeouts in two consecutive games with 32. Luis Tiant of the Red Sox previously set the record.

August 13, 1974

Ryan's Fastball Clocked at 100.9 M.P.H.

ANAHEIM, Calif., Sept. 8 (AP)—Nolan Ryan almost matched his unpublicized record of 100.9 miles an hour for a pitched baseball last night and said he didn't care for the scientific scrutiny of his pitches. "I don't like to do it because it takes too much away from my concentration," the California Angel strike-out king said after beating the Chicago White Sox, 3-1. His fastest pitch recorded by infra-red radar was 100.8 m.p.h., a ninth-inning fastball to Bee Bee Richard, who wound up walking.

But it was disclosed before the game that Ryan actually broke Bob Feller's 28-year-old record of 98.6 m.p.h. last Aug. 20 when he struck out 19 Detroit Tigers in an 11-inning defeat. He threw 100.9 twice in that game, the first time against the Tigers' first batter, Ron LeFlore. The Angels said they did not reveal Ryan's Aug. 20 test because they had wanted to hold the contest last night where more than 6,000 fans guessed the speed. A crowd of 13,510 paid to see Ryan win his 18th game against 15 defeats. He gave up six hits, striking out nine and throwing 159 pitches.

September 9, 1974

Brock Breaks Record

ST. LOUIS, Sept. 10 (AP)—Lou Brock stole second base in the seventh inning of the Cardinals' game against the Philadelphia Phillies tonight and set a major league record of 105 stolen bases for one season.

Brock's theft, his second of the game, came during the Cards' 142d game and his 134th. It eclipsed the previous record of 104 set by the Los Angeles Dodgers' Maury Wills in 1962.

His first steal came in the opening inning following a single to left before an enthusiastic Busch Stadium crowd of 27,285.

Brock led off the seventh with a single to left. Following the steal, Brock's teammates and photographers poured onto the field and Brock was presented with the historic base that he stole.

The game was stopped and Brock, who addressed the crowd, embraced the Cards' second baseman, Ted Sizemore, an injured player who usually bats behind him.

In a salute to his throng of admirers, the 35-year-old outfielder said, "The left-field fans probably knew I was going to steal 105 before I did. They were behind me all the way."

One of the dark moments for the crowd, however, was that the Cardinals lost, 8-2, and fell 3½ games behind Pittsburgh in the National League's Eastern Division. Mike Schmidt drove in four runs for the Phillies with a homer and two doubles, and Brock, trying for his 106th steal, was thrown out in the last inning.

Brock, who had vowed to set the record before a home crowd, remained at first base for only one pitch before each steal.

Lou Brock of the Cardinals breaking the stolen-bases record at St. Louis last night as Larry Bowa of the Phillies waited for the late throw in the seventh inning.

He broke rapidly in the first inning as Philadelphia's right-hander, Dick Ruthven, fired to the plate and reached second base well ahead of the throw.

In the seventh, Brock waited until the count was 0-1 and streaked to second, once again well ahead of the catcher's wide throw to the bag.

The thefts by Brock, who has been thrown out 29 times, also lifted him to 740 for his career, eclipsing the previous record of 738 set by Max Carey of the Pittsburgh Pirates in 1929, his final season in the majors.

Only Ty Cobb, who has 892, and Eddie Collins, who had 743, stole more bases during their careers.

Brock, who has stolen 14 bases in 15 games this season against the Phillies, broke Carey's mark in the first inning after singling.

Ruthven, after yielding the hit to Brock, threw a called strike to the Cardinals' Ron Hunt and tried one pickoff throw to first base before Brock took off on the second pitch.

His chase to the bag easily beat a throw into the dirt by the Philadelphia catcher, Bob Boone, and Brock continued on to third as the ball bounced into center field.

PHILADELPHIA (N.)					ST. LOUIS (N.)				
	ab.	r.	h.	bi.		ab.	r.	h.	bi.
Cash, 2b	5	1	1	0	Brock, lf	5	1	2	0
Bowa, ss	4	3	2	0	Hunt, 2b	5	0	0	0
Schmidt, 3b	4	2	3	4	Smith, rf	4	1	2	1
Montanez, 1b	5	0	1	2	Simmons, c	4	0	1	1
Luzinski, lf	3	0	0	0	McBride, cf	3	0	1	0
Anderson, rf	0	0	0	0	Torre, 1b	4	0	0	0
Johnstone, lf	4	1	3	0	Reitz, 3b	4	0	1	0
Unser, cf	3	1	0	0	Tyson, ss	2	0	1	0
Boone, c	3	0	1	1	Hernandez, ph	0	0	0	0
Ruthven, p	4	0	1	1	Mumphrey, pr	0	0	0	0
					Siebert, p	0	0	0	0
					Cruz, ph	1	0	1	0
					Osteen, p	0	0	0	0
					Foster, p	2	0	0	0
					Folkers, p	0	0	0	0
					Dwyer, ph	1	0	0	0
					Heidemann, ss	1	0	0	0
Total	35	8	12	8	Total	36	2	9	2

Philadelphia ..... 2 0 1 0 3 0 0 2 0—8
St. Louis ..... 2 0 0 0 0 0 0 0 0—2

E—Boone, Ruthven, Bowa. DP—St. Louis 1. LOB—Philadelphia 5, St. Louis 10. 2B—Smith, Reitz, Johnstone, Schmidt 2. 3B—Bowa, Cash. HR—Schmidt (35). SB—Brock 2, Bowa, Johnstone, McBride.

	IP.	H.	R.	ER	BB	SO.
Ruthven (W. 9-11)	9	9	2	2	3	8
Foster (L. 7-10)	4	7	4	4	1	0
Folkers	2	2	2	2	1	0
Siebert	2	3	2	2	3	1
Osteen	1	0	0	0	0	0

T—2:43. A—27,285.

September 11, 1974

Baseball's Longest Night Ends 3½ Hours Before Sunrise

By JOSEPH DURSO

For all those anxious wives and mothers who telephoned Shea Stadium in the early morning hours yesterday, asking if there was a curfew on a baseball game, the answer—as they probably know by now—is no. At least, not for the team that Casey Stengel used to call "my amazing Mets."

If there were a curfew, then the Mets and St. Louis Cardinals would not have played 25 innings, starting shortly after 8 o'clock Wednesday night and ending at 3:13—a marathon that involved 50 players, 12 records, 15 dozen baseballs, five sweepings of the infield and many phone calls

from worried relatives of the thousand or so diehard fans left from the original crowd of 13,460.

It was not the longest game in major league history, since it fell one inning short of the record of 26, played to a 1-1 tie in 1920 by the Brooklyn Dodgers and Boston Braves. Nor was it the longest in elapsed time: though it lasted 7 hours 4 minutes, it stopped 19 minutes shy of the record set by the Mets and San Francisco Giants on May 31, 1964. But it was the longest at night by any measure and even exceeded the previous longevity for the

Mets, who went 24 innings in a night game at Houston in 1968.

But, apart from the fact that they lost all three of those never-ending games, the Mets did their bit to keep alive New York's reputation for late hours. And in that effort, they received support Wednesday night from the Yankees, who were playing, and also losing, in Baltimore in 17 innings and taking 4 hours 12 minutes to do it.

The Yankees started 2½ hours before the Mets because they were playing a double-header against the Orioles. But they still managed to go 17 innings in the first game and nine in the second before the

American League's week-night curfew of 1 A.M. By then, the Mets were still grinding along back in Shea Stadium, wondering what would have happended if Ken Reitz of the Cardinals had not hit a two-run homer with two outs in the ninth and sent their game into five hours of extra innings.

Almanacs may someday note that the Mets finally lost the game, 4-3, and that the sun rose about three hours later at 6:34 A.M. Most of the players on both sides didn't get to bed until dawn, while a small army of 60 sweepers with brooms was cleaning out the debris until 9:30 in the morning when most of the city's commuters were already reaching their offices.

"I knew we were getting close to history," reflected Rusty Staub, the Mets' right-fielder. "I played all 24 innings in that game in Houston—against the Mets."

"Why does it always happen to me?" moaned Ed Sudol, the umpire at home plate, who called every pitch thrown to the record total of 202 batters.

It "always" happens to Sudol because he happens to be in the wrong place at the wrong time: around the Mets. He also was the umpire behind the plate when they went 23 innings in 1964 and when route to his personal record they went 24 in 1968. En of 25 innings this time, he got hit four times by baseballs and ejected Manager Yogi Berra from the game at 1:30 A.M. during a raging argument. So Yogi retreated to his office beneath the stands and watched glumly on his television set.

"I finally got home at 4:20," Berra reported when he arrived back at the stadium at 3:30 yesterday afternoon. "My wife and son Larry were with me, and one of the neighbors who came to see the game.

"How does it feel? It feels bad. If you play 25 innings and win, you feel a lot better than when you play 25 and lose."

"I don't know," joked Joe Torre of the Cardinals, who saved the game with a diving catch in the 23d. "That was the fastest 25-inning game I ever played."

"It takes six to eight hours to sweep out the place after a game. They usually start at midnight because we don't sweep with people still in the seats. This time, they started at 3:30 in the morning and kept going till 9:30. Everybody sort of worked a double day. We had 85 special guards on duty from 6 P.M. They usually work six hours. This time, they stayed until 4 in the morning.

"On electricity, it might cost us $1,700 to $2,000 alone. We pay a flat amount each month whether we turn the lights on or not, say $12,000. Then, when you do turn them on, there's what they call an energy charge, and that's where it cost us last night."

At 1:30 A.M., about the time Yogi Berra was getting the judicial heave-ho, a woman who had been listening to the game on the radio in Manhattan made a decision: She was so entranced that she drove out to the stadium in Flushing and bought two gift certificates for tickets to future games. She was able to buy them at that hour because the advanced-ticket window always stays open until the game ends—and this time it was open until 3:13 A.M.

The gift certificates were sold to her by Joe Millan, who was manning the office and who was impressed. But he was distracted by a personal problem: He is also a student at Brooklyn College and he had an 8 A.M. class.

Emma Fuchs, chief telephone operator for the Mets, may have set a staff record during the marathon. She went to work at 9 o'clock Wednesday morning as usual, wondered why her relief operator didn't show up at 5:30 as usual, then ran the switchboard herself until 3:30 Thursday morning, completing an 18½-hour day.

Ralph Kiner, who never played 25 innings in one game as a home-run hitter, had his own endurance test as one of the Mets' broadcasters. He left the TV booth in the eighth to go below the stands to the studio where he conducts "Kiner's Corner" after the game. "I sat around for five hours working like mad," he said. "Every inning we had to change the film strips for the show. We kept getting new heroes."

Other endurance feats were performed by the nine players who went the full distance, three of the four umpires who never left the field; Commissioner Bowie Kuhn and his wife, who came out to see Lou Brock and who wound up seeing seven hours of baseball; Brock, who got one hit in nine times at bat but who was thrown out trying to steal base No. 106 of the season; Claude Osteen, who pitched 9 1-3 scoreless innings for St. Louis without getting the victory; Duffy Dyer, who caught 23 innings for the Mets without setting a record (though a woman telephoned the Mets to complain that his uniform was dirty) and McBride, who sprinted from first base all the way home on the fateful pickoff throw.

The crowning irony of it all was that Bob Engel, the umpire at first base, called a balk on Webb's wild throw to first base in the 25th. Not many persons realized it and nothing was changed by it. But Engel said later, "before they revised the rule a few years ago, the runner would have been stopped at second base."

"Under that rule," he said, with a shudder, "McBride might not have scored and they could still be playing the game."

Nobody knows how much of the television audience stayed awake to the finish, but the Mets estimated that about a thousand hardy souls were still in the park when Bake McBride scored the deciding run on a wild pickoff throw by the pitcher, Hank Webb, and a fumbled throw home by the catcher, Ron Hodges.

The hot-dog venders had left the aisles in the ninth inning (around 10:20 P.M.), as they customarily do, but half the refreshment stands—and the Diamond Club upstairs—stayed in business to the bitter end.

"It was a good crowd," said James K. Thomson, vice president of the Mets, who has run stadiums for the Yankees, Dodgers and Mets. "One guy was even dancing in the aisles every inning in right field. It amazes me that the people stay that late. At 3 in the morning, you had a chant of 'Let's Go, Mets.' You didn't have it by many people, but you had it.

WEDNESDAY NIGHT

ST. LOUIS (N.)	ab.r.h.bi	METS (N.)	ab.r.h.bi
Brock	9 0 1 0	Harrelson, ss	7 0 0 0
Godby, lf	2 0 0 0	Boswell, 3b	4 0 0 0
Sizemore, 2b	10 1 1 0	Millan, 2b	10 1 4 0
Smith, rf	8 0 1 0	Jones, lf	9 2 3 2
Torre, 1b	*9 0 2 1	Webb, p	0 0 0 0
Simmons, c	3 0 1 0	Pemberton, ph	1 0 1 0
Herndon, pr	0 1 0 0	Milner, 1b	10 0 2 1
Hills, c	1 0 0 0	Garrett, ss	10 0 0 0
Scheinblm, ph	1 0 0 0	Schneck, cf	11 0 2 0
Billings, c	5 0 1 0	Ayala, rf	2 0 1 0
McBride, cf	10 1 4 0	Hahn, cf	6 0 0 0
Reitz, 3b	10 1 4 2	Gosger, lf	0 0 0 0
Tyson, ss	2 0 0 0	Dyer, c	9 0 2 0
Hernandez, ph	1 0 0 0	Boisclair, ph	0 0 0 0
Folkers, p	0 0 0 0	Hodges, c	0 0 0 0
Cruz, ph	1 0 0 0	Koosman, p	2 0 0 0
Bare, p	0 0 0 0	Martinez, ph	1 0 0 0
Osteen, p	4 0 0 0	Parker, p	0 0 0 0
Siebert, p	1 0 0 0	Kranepool, ph	1 0 0 0
Forsch, p	1 0 0 0	Miller, p	0 0 0 0
Melendez, ph	1 0 0 0	Theodore, ph	1 0 0 0
Garman, p	0 0 0 0	Apodaca, p	1 0 0 0
Hunt, ph	1 0 0 0	Cram, p	3 0 1 0
Hrabosky, p	0 0 0 0	Staub, rf	1 0 0 0
Dwyer, ph	0 0 0 0		
Heidemann, ss	6 0 3 0		
Total	86 4 18 3	Total	89 3 16 3

*Awarded first base on obstruction by catcher.

St. Louis ..100 000 002 000 000 000 000 000 1—4
Mets .....100 020 000 000 000 000 000 000 0—3

E—Tyson, Schneck, Dyer, Osteen, Webb, Hodges. DP—St. Louis 1, Mets 2. LOB—St. Louis 20, Mets 25. 2B—Milner, Schneck 2. HRs—Jones (13), Reitz (6). SB—McBride. S—Koosman, Forsch, Millan, McBride, Jones.

	IP.	H.	R.	ER.	BB.	SO.
Forsch	6	5	3	2	4	3
Garman	2	0	0	0	0	2
Hrabosky	3	2	0	0	0	3
Folkers	2	3	0	0	1	2
Bare	⅓	0	0	0	1	0
Osteen	9⅓	4	0	0	2	5
Siebert (W, 8-8)	2⅓	2	0	0	3	1
Koosman	9	5	3	3	4	5
Parker	3	2	0	0	0	0
Miller	1	1	0	0	1	1
Apodaca	3	2	0	0	1	1
Cram	8	7	0	0	2	4
Webb (L, 0-1)	1	1	1	0	0	1

HBP—by Koosman (Tyson), Parker (Dwyer). Wild pitch—Forsch, Koosman, Cram. PB—Simmons. T—7:04. A—13,460.

September 13, 1974

Ryan Pitches Third No-Hitter

By United Press International

ANAHEIM, Calif., Sept. 28—Nolan Ryan pitched the third no-hitter of his career tonight, striking out 15 Minnesota batters and winning his 22d game of the season in a 4-0 victory for the California Angels over the Twins.

Ryan, traded by the New York Mets three seasons ago at age 24, became the sixth pitcher in major league history to throw three no-hitters. He joined Sandy Koufax, the only man to pitch four; Bob Feller, Jim Maloney, Larry Corcoran and Cy Young.

The Angels' right-hander, who already this year has become the first pitcher to surpass 300 strikeouts for three seasons in a row, has 367 new to go with his major-league record 383 in 1973 and 329 in 1972.

He pitched no-hitters last season against the Kansas City Royals and Detroit Tigers and has thrown three one-hitters.

* * * * *

MINNESOTA (A.)	ab.r.h.bi.	CALIFORNIA (A.)	ab.r.h.bi.
Brye, cf	2 0 0 0	Nettles, rf	4 1 2 3
Carew, 2b	2 0 0 0	Doyle, 2b	4 0 1 0
Braun, 3b	3 0 0 0	Bochte, 1b	3 0 0 1
Darwin, rf	4 0 0 0	Lahoud, dh	4 0 1 0
Oliva, dh	3 0 0 0	Stanton, rf	4 0 1 0
Histle, lf	3 0 0 0	Chalk, 3b	2 1 0 0
Bourque, 1b	3 0 0 0	Balaz, lf	2 1 1 0
Killebrew, ph	0 0 0 0	Meoli, ss	2 1 1 0
Terrell, pr	0 0 0 0	Egan, c	2 0 0 0
Gomez, ss	2 0 0 0	Ryan, p	0 0 0 0
Soderholm, ss	2 0 0 0		
Borgman, c	3 0 0 0		
Decker, p	0 0 0 0		
Butler, p	0 0 0 0		
Total	27 0 0 0	Total	27 4 7 4

Minnesota ....0 0 0 0 0 0 0 0 0—0
California ....0 0 2 2 0 0 0 0 x—4

E—Braun. LOB—Minnesota 8, California 4. 2B—Meoli, Balaz. SB—Nettles. S—Egan. SF—Bochte.

	IP.	H.	R.	ER.	BB.	SO.
Decker (L. 16-14	2⅔	4	2	1	0	1
Butler	5⅓	3	2	2	3	8
Ryan (W, 22-16)	9	0	0	0	8	15

T—2:22. A—10,872.

September 29, 1974

Frank Robinson Is First Black Manager

By DAVE ANDERSON
Special to The New York Times

CLEVELAND, Oct. 3—With the poise that has characterized his career as a slugger of 574 home runs and as a clubhouse leader, Frank Robinson was named today by the Cleveland Indians as major league baseball's first black manager. He received a one-year contract.

At a crowded news conference in Cleveland Stadium, a congratulatory telegram from President Ford was read by Phil Seghi, the Indians' general manager, who chose the 39-year-old Robinson to succeed Ken Aspromonte as the American League team's 28th manager and ninth player-manager, the most of any major league team.

President Ford described Robinson's selection as "welcome news for baseball fans across the nation" and a "tribute to you personally, to your athletic skills and to your unsurpassed leadership." Attending the news conference were Bowie Kuhn, the Commissioner of Baseball, and Lee MacPhail, the president of the American League.

"We got something done," Kuhn commented, "that we should have done before."

Wearing a black and white plaid suit with a vest, Robinson attempted to reduce his sociological burden.

"The only reason I'm the first black manager is that I was born black," he said calmly. "That's the color I am. I'm not a superman, I'm not a miracle worker. Your ballplayers determine how good a team you have. I might influence the ballplayers to some extent, but if we have a good team, they deserve the credit. If a ball club fails, I think the manager should be held responsible. I want to be judged by the play on the field."

Asked if he foresaw any additional pressure on him to succeed as a black manager, he replied:

"I don't see any pressure. I don't see any goals I have to achieve as the first black manager. The pressure from within is not there."

He was hired nearly three decades after the late Jackie Robinson was the major league's first black player in 1947.

"I thank the Lord that Jackie Robinson was the man he was in that position," the Indians' new manager said. "If he wasn't it would have set back the whole idea of signing more black players. The one wish I could have is that Jackie Robinson could be here today to see this happen."

Asked if he believed a similar reponsibility to succeed as a manager now was on him, Robinson replied:

"No, this is a different ball game altogether. Different society. I just hope baseball people don't say, 'All right, Frank Robinson is the first black manager, we have one, that's it.' In my heart, I don't think I was hired because I was black. I hope not. I think I've been hired because of my ability."

"Frank Robinson sits before you," Seghi said, "because I think he has the qualities that I was searching for in a manager, not because he was black or white. He has all the leadership qualities necessary to lead a major league ball club. You know what he did at Cincinnati, you know what he did in Baltimore; he's a true leader."

Robinson helped the Baltimore Orioles represent the American League in four World Series in his six seasons there. He had led the Reds to one National League pennant. He is the only major leaguer selected the most valuable player in both leagues. Through 19 seasons he has a career .295 average with 2,900 hits and 1,778 runs batted in.

Now a designated hitter, Robinson will be the major league's first playing manager since Solly Hemus of the St. Louis Cardinals in 1959. Eddie Joost, with the Philadelphia Athletics in 1954, was the American League's last playing manager.

His salary of $175,000 next season was agreed upon shortly after the Indians acquired him on Sept. 12 from the California Angels for the $20,000 waiver price. When the managerial position later developed, he sought a two-year contract through 1976, but accepted the one-year offer in return for the opportunity to fulfill his ambition to be a manager.

As a playing manager, Robinson will receive the same $175,000 plus the fringe benefits accorded managers such as a hotel suite on road trips and an expense account. Unlike other managers, he also will receive living expenses in Cleveland next year and the use of an automobile here. His contract was negotiated by Ed Keating of International Management, Inc.

In listing Robinson's credentials, Seghi also mentioned his five seasons managing Santurce in the Puerto Rican winter league.

In five seasons there, Robinson's teams finished first twice, third twice and fourth once. When he joined Santurce for the 1968-69 season, he was the first American black to manage an integrated team of white, black and Latin players.

During nearly two hours of questions and answers, Robinson spoke easily and articulately, more so than many major league managers. At the formal news conference in the stadium club, he was flanked by Seghi; Nick Mileti, the Indians' president, and Ted Bonda, the Indians' executive vice president. Later, in the press room, he sat with his wife, Barbara Ann, and Seghi while continuing to discuss his managerial philosophies:

¶On discipline: "I can't say I've never missed a curfew, but I've never been caught. I believe men are men. I'm not going to set a time limit on when they have to be in the hotel. I'm not going to be a baby-sitter. I'm not going to sit in the lobby to see who's late. I'll need my sleep because I'll be playing myself. But if I walk into a cocktail lounge and see a couple of players, I won't expect them to run out. I might even buy them a drink now that I've got an expense account."

¶On arguing with umpires: "I don't think I've had trouble with umpires. I've been thrown out of about 15 games in Puerto Rico in five seasons. But only twice last year. I select my words better now. Any manager that goes through a season without being thrown out isn't doing his job. You've got to show your players you're backing them up. And you've got to show the umpires that you're not going to let them run over you."

¶On his coaches: "I haven't had time to sit down and select my staff. I have a few people in mind, but I haven't talked to them yet. I'll say this, if I select two black coaches and one white coach, I don't want people reading anything into that. And if I select two white coaches and one black coach, I don't want people reading anything into that either. I'll pick my coaches on ability, people I think can do the job."

¶On himself as a player: "I'm counting on Frank Robinson the manager to talk to Frank Robinson the player. I'll be the first one not to write Frank Robinson's name in the line-up."

¶On the Indians, who finished fourth in the American League East with a 77-85 won-lost record: "In the years I was in Baltimore, we always figured we could win three out of four with the Indians and maybe all four. But this year the Indians became a team to be reckoned with. I think the strong part of the ball club is offense. Every team needs more pitching. But in my heart, I don't think there's a team in the American League with the youth and experience we have."

¶On the demand of Gaylord Perry, the Indians' ace pitcher, for $1 more in salary than Robinson's $175,000 contract: "I don't negotiate salaries. Mr. Seghi handles that. I don't think Gaylord and I are incompatible. Gaylord's a real competitor and a real professional. So am I, and if he's satisfied, I'm sure we'll get along."

With a one-year contract, the Indians' new manager obviously is on trial, but he commented:

"I hope that in September next year I will have justified the Indians' confidence in me and that I'll be rehired. If not, I don't foresee any problem in firing me or any black manager if he's not doing the job. If the Indians aren't satisfied with the job I'm doing, fire me. There won't be any repercussions.

"The public is pretty smart. That guy up in the stands knows if you're doing a good job or not."

October 4, 1974

Appendix

AMERICAN LEAGUE PENNANT WINNERS

1903	Boston	1921	New York	1939	New York	1957	New York
1904	Boston	1922	New York	1940	Detroit	1958	New York
1905	Philadelphia	1923	New York	1941	New York	1959	Chicago
1906	Chicago	1924	Washington	1942	New York	1960	New York
1907	Detroit	1925	Washington	1943	New York	1961	New York
1908	Detroit	1926	New York	1944	St. Louis	1962	New York
1909	Detroit	1927	New York	1945	Detroit	1963	New York
1910	Philadelphia	1928	New York	1946	Boston	1964	New York
1911	Philadelphia	1929	Philadelphia	1947	New York	1965	Minnesota
1912	Boston	1930	Philadelphia	1948	Cleveland	1966	Baltimore
1913	Philadelphia	1931	Philadelphia	1949	New York	1967	Boston
1914	Philadelphia	1932	New York	1950	New York	1968	Detroit
1915	Boston	1933	Washington	1951	New York	1969	Baltimore
1916	Boston	1934	Detroit	1952	New York	1970	Baltimore
1917	Chicago	1935	Detroit	1953	New York	1971	Baltimore
1918	Boston	1936	New York	1954	Cleveland	1972	Oakland
1919	Chicago	1937	New York	1955	New York	1973	Oakland
1920	Cleveland	1938	New York	1956	New York	1974	Oakland

NATIONAL LEAGUE PENNANT WINNERS

1903	Pittsburgh	1921	New York	1939	Cincinnati	1957	Milwaukee
1904	New York	1922	New York	1940	Cincinnati	1958	Milwaukee
1905	New York	1923	New York	1941	Brooklyn	1959	Los Angeles
1906	Chicago	1924	New York	1942	St. Louis	1960	Pittsburgh
1907	Chicago	1925	Pittsburgh	1943	St. Louis	1961	Cincinnati
1908	Chicago	1926	St. Louis	1944	St. Louis	1962	San Francisco
1909	Pittsburgh	1927	Pittsburgh	1945	Chicago	1963	Los Angeles
1910	Chicago	1928	St. Louis	1946	St. Louis	1964	St. Louis
1911	New York	1929	Chicago	1947	Brooklyn	1965	Los Angeles
1912	New York	1930	St. Louis	1948	Boston	1966	Los Angeles
1913	New York	1931	St. Louis	1949	Brooklyn	1967	St. Louis
1914	Boston	1932	Chicago	1950	Philadelphia	1968	St. Louis
1915	Philadelphia	1933	New York	1951	New York	1969	New York
1916	Brooklyn	1934	St. Louis	1952	Brooklyn	1970	Cincinnati
1917	New York	1935	Chicago	1953	Brooklyn	1971	Pittsburgh
1918	Chicago	1936	New York	1954	New York	1972	Cincinnati
1919	Cincinnati	1937	New York	1955	Brooklyn	1973	New York
1920	Brooklyn	1938	Chicago	1956	Brooklyn	1974	Los Angeles

WORLD SERIES WINNERS

1903	Boston (A)	1921	New York (N)	1939	New York (A)	1957	Milwaukee (N)
1904	*not played*	1922	New York (N)	1940	Cincinnati (N)	1958	New York (A)
1905	New York (N)	1923	New York (A)	1941	New York (A)	1959	Los Angeles (N)
1906	Chicago (A)	1924	Washington (A)	1942	St. Louis (N)	1960	Pittsburgh (N)
1907	Chicago (N)	1925	Pittsburgh (N)	1943	New York (A)	1961	New York (A)
1908	Chicago (N)	1926	St. Louis (N)	1944	St. Louis (N)	1962	New York (A)
1909	Pittsburgh (N)	1927	New York (A)	1945	Detroit (A)	1963	Los Angeles (N)
1910	Philadelphia (A)	1928	New York (A)	1946	St. Louis (N)	1964	St. Louis (N)
1911	Philadelphia (A)	1929	Philadelphia (A)	1947	New York (A)	1965	Los Angeles (N)
1912	Boston (A)	1930	Philadelphia (A)	1948	Cleveland (A)	1966	Baltimore (A)
1913	Philadelphia (A)	1931	St. Louis (N)	1949	New York (A)	1967	St. Louis (N)
1914	Boston (N)	1932	New York (A)	1950	New York (A)	1968	Detroit (A)
1915	Boston (A)	1933	New York (N)	1951	New York (A)	1969	New York (N)
1916	Boston (A)	1934	St. Louis (N)	1952	New York (A)	1970	Baltimore (A)
1917	Chicago (A)	1935	Detroit (A)	1953	New York (A)	1971	Pittsburgh (N)
1918	Boston (A)	1936	New York (A)	1954	New York (N)	1972	Oakland (A)
1919	Cincinnati (N)	1937	New York (A)	1955	Brooklyn (N)	1973	Oakland (A)
1920	Cleveland (A)	1938	New York (A)	1956	New York (A)	1974	Oakland (A)

MOST VALUABLE PLAYER AWARDS

AMERICAN LEAGUE

1931	Lefty Grove (Phi.)
1932	Jimmie Foxx (Phi.)
1933	Jimmie Foxx (Phi.)
1934	Mickey Cochrane (Det.)
1935	Hank Greenberg (Det.)
1936	Lou Gehrig (N.Y.)
1937	Charlie Gehringer (Det.)
1938	Jimmie Foxx (Bos.)
1939	Joe DiMaggio (N.Y.)
1940	Hank Greenberg (Det.)
1941	Joe DiMaggio (N.Y.)
1942	Joe Gordon (N.Y.)
1943	Spud Chandler (N.Y.)
1944	Hal Newhouser (Det.)
1945	Hal Newhouser (Det.)
1946	Ted Williams (Bos.)
1947	Joe DiMaggio (N.Y.)
1948	Lou Boudreau (Cle.)
1949	Ted Williams (Bos.)
1950	Phil Rizzuto (N.Y.)
1951	Yogi Berra (N.Y.)
1952	Bobby Shantz (Phi.)
1953	Al Rosen (Cle.)
1954	Yogi Berra (N.Y.)
1955	Yogi Berra (N.Y.)
1956	Mickey Mantle (N.Y.)
1957	Mickey Mantle (N.Y.)
1958	Jackie Jensen (Bos.)
1959	Nellie Fox (Chi.)
1960	Roger Maris (N.Y.)
1961	Roger Maris (N.Y.)
1962	Mickey Mantle (N.Y.)
1963	Ellie Howard (N.Y.)
1964	Brooks Robinson (Bal.)
1965	Zoilo Versales (Min.)
1966	Frank Robinson (Bal.)
1967	Carl Yastrzemski (Bos.)
1968	Denny McLain (Det.)
1969	Harmon Killebrew (Min.)
1970	Boog Powell (Bal.)
1971	Vida Blue (Oak.)
1972	Dick Allen (Chi.)
1973	Reggie Jackson (Oak.)
1974	Jeff Burroughs (Tex.)

NATIONAL LEAGUE

1931	Frankie Frisch (St. L.)
1932	Chuck Klein (Phi.)
1933	Carl Hubbell (N.Y.)
1934	Dizzy Dean (St. L.)
1935	Gabby Hartnett (Chi.)
1936	Carl Hubbell (N.Y.)
1937	Joe Medwick (St.L.)
1938	Ernie Lombardi (Cin.)
1939	Bucky Walters (Cin.)
1940	Frank McCormick (Cin.)
1941	Dolph Camilli (Bkn.)
1942	Mort Cooper (St.L.)
1943	Stan Musial (St.L.)
1944	Marty Marion (St.L.)
1945	Phil Cavarretta (Chi.)
1946	Stan Musial (St.L.)
1947	Bob Elliott (Bos.)
1948	Stan Musial (St.L.)
1949	Jackie Robinson (Bkn.)
1950	Jim Konstanty (Phi.)
1951	Roy Campanella (Bkn.)
1952	Hank Sauer (Chi.)
1953	Roy Campanella (Bkn.)
1954	Willie Mays (N.Y.)
1955	Roy Campanella (Bkn.)
1956	Don Newcombe (Bkn.)
1957	Hank Aaron (Mil.)
1958	Ernie Banks (Chi.)
1959	Ernie Banks (Chi.)
1960	Dick Groat (Pit.)
1961	Frank Robinson (Cin.)
1962	Maury Wills (L.A.)
1963	Sandy Koufax (L.A.)
1964	Ken Boyer (St. L.)
1965	Willie Mays (S.F.)
1966	Roberto Clemente (Pit.)
1967	Orlando Cepeda (St.L.)
1968	Bob Gibson (St.L.)
1969	Willie McCovey (S.F.)
1970	Johnny Bench (Cin.)
1971	Joe Torre (St.L.)
1972	Johnny Bench (Cin.)
1973	Pete Rose (Cin.)
1974	Steve Garvey (L.A.)

Index